DATE DUE

HANDBOOK OF

PUBLIC

RELATIONS

HANDBOOK OF
PUBLIC
RELATIONS

ROBERT L. HEATH
EDITOR

GABRIEL VASQUEZ
CONTRIBUTING EDITOR

Sage Publications, Inc.
International Educational and Professional Publisher
Thousand Oaks ▪ London ▪ New Delhi

For information:

Sage Publications, Inc.
2455 Teller Road
Thousand Oaks, California 91320
E-mail: order@sagepub.com

Sage Publications Ltd.
6 Bonhill Street
London EC2A 4PU
United Kingdom

Sage Publications India Pvt. Ltd.
M-32 Market
Greater Kailash I
New Delhi 110 048 India

Printed in the United States of America

Library of Congress Cataloging-in-Publication Data

Main entry under title:

Handbook of public relations / edited by Robert L. Heath.
    p. cm.
  Includes bibliographical references and index.
  ISBN 0-7619-1286-X (cloth : alk. paper)
  1. Public relations. I. Heath, Robert L. (Robert Lawrence),
1941-
  HD59 .H267 2000
  659.2—dc21   00-008736

01 02 03 04 05 06 7 6 5 4 3 2 1

Acquiring Editor:	Margaret H. Seawell
Editorial Assistant:	Heidi van Middlesworth
Production Editor:	Astrid Virding
Editorial Assistant:	Nevair Kabakian
Copy Editor:	D. J. Peck
Typesetter/Designer:	Marion Warren
Indexer:	Cristina Haley
Cover Designer:	Ravi Balasuriya

CONTENTS

▪ SECTION 2: Defining the Practice

DYNAMICS OF CHANGE

■ SECTION 3: In Search of Best Practices

▪ SECTION 5: Globalizing Public Relations

PREFACE

█ This project, for me, began as one of several topics I had discussed with Margaret Seawell of Sage Publications over several glasses of iced tea on a lovely day on the terrace at the University of Houston Hilton Center. At that time, the thought of drawing together some of the best thinkers on public relations was a delightful challenge. I relished the prospect. This handbook began to sail with bright sun and favorable winds.

After the launch, it did not go steady to the wind. It has taken longer than any of us would have wanted and has caused frustrations that were nightmarish. I thank those chapter authors who labored to get their manuscripts to me and to make their needed changes in a timely fashion. The goodwill and work ethics of these authors is wonderful.

I also appreciate the creativity of the authors. From the beginning, I dreamed of a comprehensive treatment of theory that could define the field and advance the practice. I hoped to be able to address the best practices of all the subfunctions of public relations. I wanted to see advances into new territories, especially those in technology and international challenges.

I also wanted chapters that never materialized. I hoped for contributions from certain authors who did not wish to participate. I wanted the development of certain perspectives that were not developed. But in all, I think this handbook is a solid statement by leaders in the academic approach to public relations. I am more pleased than I can tell you that we have contributors from programs and practices around the world. This handbook celebrates globalization in practice.

I believe that this handbook, short of being perfect or comprehensive, distinguishes itself by what it says. Even the casual reader can sense a revolution, or an evolution, in thought. Relationship, community, symmetry, shared meaning, growth in pedagogy, refinements in best practices, ethics, daunting efforts to meet the challenges of technology that changes daily and of globalization that resists full understanding—these themes are clearly marked and prudently discussed.

The handbook is not a finished product in an academic sense. This is not a definitive statement. Indeed, it is a step in a long pathway that eventually will lead to an even stronger era in public relations scholarship and pedagogy.

I am pleased to see the wholesome marriage of many disciplinary origins that bring their individual strengths to support our understanding of public relations. Some of us who labor for the "cause" believe that public relations is a distinct and valued academic and professional discipline that is founded in multidisciplinary underpinnings. Slowly, the multidisciplinary nature will meld into a clearer definition of what constitutes the unique core of public relations. The discipline has come a long way, as this handbook testifies. But it has a long way to go. Even when that point is not made explicitly by chapter contributors, those of us who read this book carefully will recognize the underdeveloped and less well-stated arguments and conclusions that need to be addressed.

Some years down the line, we should do this again. It could be our class reunion. We could look back and find themes that had died or prospered in ways that we could not have imagined. We could revisit old conversations that had endured. We could marvel at accomplishments that had been unseen at the time when we cast our chapters.

If that time comes, I believe that we will be pleased that we did good work.

To the authors of the chapters, I say thanks to you collectively. To the Sage personnel who hoped for and labored to produce this spoiled child, I say thanks as well. Thanks to Astrid Virding, production editor, and Marion Warren, typesetter, for their meticulous work.

ROBERT L. HEATH
University of Houston

DEFINING THE DISCIPLINE

Shifting Foundations

Public Relations as Relationship Building

ROBERT L. HEATH

Section 1 of the handbook addresses the very broad question: What is public relations—how *do* we define the discipline? Academics delight in using that question to initiate the first class session of an academic semester. It is asked during job interviews and appears on internship and scholarship applications. Although some definitions persist, even a casual review of the professional and academic literature of public relations suggests that answers to the question change over time.

Authors who have contributed to this section of the handbook were not specifically charged with the task of answering that question. Nevertheless, the themes they addressed are sufficiently basic that their answers to the question are implied in their contributions to this section. The section is intended to press each reader to rethink his or her definition of the field. Reading this section might lead each of us to come away believing that our definition—the answer to the question—has become more blurred than clarified. Each chapter raises issues ignored and slighted in the previous chapters. Like a good mystery, just as we think we have the clues sorted out, a new one is revealed in each chapter in this section.

Worth noting is the fact that very little discussion in this section addresses the use of public relations to promote and protect the image or reputation of an organization relevant to product or service publicity or promotion. This section focuses more on the rationale for using public relations to reduce the cost of conflict than for increasing awareness of an organization's products or services or for motivating buyers to purchase them, donors to contribute to nonprofit projects, or lawmakers to fund governmental projects. Academic discussions tend to address public policy issues relevant to advancing harmony between organizations and publics, whereas practitioners spend the bulk of their time dealing with other dynamics of the marketplace. Most professionals base their practice on attracting buyers, protecting or promoting image, promoting donations, and/or attracting tax funding to various governmental agencies and projects. An evening spent at an awards banquet of the Public Relations Society of America or the International Association of Business Communicators gives a much different view of the field than is reflected in this section.

Scholars are more interested in conflict reduction as the rationale for public relations than in the ability of public relations to help organizations generate market share and income—revenue, donations, or funding. Scholars who have contributed to this section might defend this bias by offering a *cost* reduction paradigm as the foundation for a *revenue generation* paradigm. Proponents of this line of reasoning might suggest that people (markets, audiences, publics, stakeholders, stakeseekers, and constituents) like to do "business" with organizations (for-profit, nonprofit, and governmental) that meet (do not violate) their expectations and that also create and maintain harmonious, mutually beneficial relationships. Therefore, a relationship development rationale for public relations can justify a revenue enhancement paradigm, but probably more indirectly than is assumed by many practitioners who devote attention to media relations, publicity, and promotion.

Concerns and intellectual or professional choices force us to think about the rationale for public relations—the definition of the discipline. How do practitioners justify their staff and line functions in organizations? What roles do they play in society? Do they add material value to organizations while, or perhaps because of, adding value to society? Are they more than flack masters and spin doctors?

To address those questions, many considerations must be made. One consideration centers on where we have come from and where we are going. In the simplest sense, we have come from mass communication (often limited to journalism) origins and are becoming something much more than that, both in terms of communication tools and in terms of the intellectual rationale for the discipline.

The mass media rationale can limit the vision of the discipline to an interest in message design and dissemination to achieve awareness (publicity and promotion at their best), to inform, and to persuade—even manipulate. Carried to its extreme, that mass communication view embraces the engineering of consent and other narrowly self-interested utilitarian, functional outcomes as the underpinning principles of the discipline. Indeed, a case can be made that each of the chapters in this section reacts to and rejects that rationale of public relations. One underpinning assumption in this section is that corporations tend to be bad and engage in public relations either to mask that evil nature or to be responsive to community expectations of a better vision of corporate performance.

If the chapters in this section indicate future directions that the discipline should and will take, then one can conclude that engineering of consent is the past, probably in practice as well as in theory. Shifting foundations for the discipline suggest that a new set of terms is the heart and soul of current intellectual ferment. The emerging vocabulary of the new definition of the discipline includes the following: relationships, shared control, trust, social capital, shared meaning, argumentativeness, listening, openness, mutually beneficial relationships, multiple publics (stakeholders and stakeseekers), epistemological issues of fact, axiological issues of value, ontological issues of choice-based actions, chaos in place in linearity, cognitive involvement, legitimacy gap, problem recognition, constraint, power, and collaborative decision making. The heart of the new view of the practice of public relations is the mutually beneficial relationships that an organization needs to enjoy a license to operate. Instead of engineering acceptance of a product or service, the new view of public relations assumes that markets are attracted to and kept by organizations that can create mutually beneficial relationships. Likewise, activists are less likely, as is government, to punish organizations that establish mutually beneficial relationships with them.

For this reason, no term is more important to understanding relationships than is *community.* Many of the chapters in this section stress the role that community plays as independent and dependent variables in the practice, theory, and research of public relations. Despite its positive implications, we know that "community" can become a hegemonic tool that an advocate uses to claim a privileged definition of community (e.g., "You cannot seek to protect owls because this community needs the jobs provided by the timber industry," "You cannot attack tobacco because this community needs its revenue").

And so, we turn our attention to themes that feature relationships. J. Grunig (Chapter 1) recaps and expands his interest in the ethical practice of public relations. Centering attention on publics as the basis for stakeholder relations, his analysis relies on principles of systems theory to offer solutions to the problems that organizations—primarily commercial ones—create for their publics. Grunig has searched for an approach that is capable of recognizing, or even empowering, the publics who are seeking to influence the actions, statements, and policies of organizations.

The key to creating and maintaining beneficial and harmonious relationships, Grunig reasons, is high-quality communication processes—more symmetrical than asymmetrical. So long as some part of a system is out of balance with another of its parts, corrective forces are going to be at work. Thus, public relations needs to be one, if not the major, corrective force. In the latest advance of this perspective on public relations, Grunig opts for mixed-motive responses by organizations to their publics. The quality of these responses should constitute the rationale for the practice and pedagogy of public relations by excellent organizations. An excellent organization exhibits characteristics that make it a more positive part of its larger system.

Thus, to achieve harmony, the organization might constantly adapt itself to the ethical preferences of its publics. Awareness that critics doubt the wisdom of asking organizations to sacrifice their interests for those of their publics has led Grunig to modify his theoretical perspective to champion a mixed-motive approach to reconciling interests in conflict. This advance in theory recognizes the reality that public relations practitioners are expected to advance the interests of their organizations rather than easily abandon them in deference to the interests of its publics. In this sense, public relations is a professional practice that helps organizations and publics to understand each other's interests. Once these interests are understood, efforts can be made to blend them or at least reduce the conflict by helping the publics and the organizations to be less antagonistic toward each other. We have the predicate that the win-win approach to conflict resolution is preferred. Thus, a systems approach supplies a process rationale for public relations, but it does not explain the roles that ideas and words play in ethical harmony-building activities.

To establish a more embracing rationale for public relations, Heath (Chapter 2) draws on the rhetorical heritage, which in Western thought reaches back to the golden age of Greece and the Roman Empire to draw on the works of Plato, Aristotle, and other thinkers who followed their leadership. These rhetorical theorists pondered how being a good and articulate spokesperson is essential to society—the community. In that way, a rhetorical perspective strengthens or even replaces some aspects of the systems theory underpinnings of public relations. Rhetorical theory can explain and guide the actions and discourse tactics that key players use to strategically maneuver to be in harmony with one another. A rhetorical foundation for public relations can explain how statements count in the dialogue by which individual and collective ideas are formed. By this logic, we can explain the constructive roles that facts, values, and policies play in the marketplace and public policy arena.

A rhetorical approach to public relations justifies the proposition that organizations build effective relationships when they adhere to the best values—those most admired by the community of interest—as a first step toward being effective communicators. Once they meet ethical standards—defined through dialogue with other members of their community—organizations can more effectively advocate their interests, which never are separate from or indifferent to the interests of their markets, audiences, and publics. A rhetorical rationale for public relations reasons that the limit of one ethical perspective is the presence of a more compelling one. The limits of the accuracy of one set of facts is the presence of a more compelling set. The limits of commercial and public policy is the presence of a more compelling policy. Thus, rhetoric is dialogic. Ideas and ethical positions are not privileged. Manipulation cannot sustain itself because others will disclose and vilify the manipulator. Selfish interests cannot prevail because advocates will persuasively advance their countervailing interests.

Rhetoric is the rationale of suasive discourse. It presumes that ideas are better for having been debated. Interests are clarified and protected through advocacy. Such advocacy is the stuff of public policy discourse, but once we find a rationale for this process by connecting the rhetorical heritage and enactment theory, we have an even stronger underpinning for the need for public relations as well as the rationale for its practice. Rhetorical enactment theory reasons that all of what an organization does and says is a statement. It is a statement that is interpreted idiosyncratically by each market, audience, and public. Whether in public or merely in the privacy of personal thought, individuals and collective publics can agree with, respond to, reject, or even ignore the statement enacted by the organization. Thus, public relations can draw on the claim that each organization makes statements that can build better relationships when they are agreeable to those markets, audiences, and publics whose interests are at stake because of the actions and statements of the organization. This theoretical perspective views rhetoric not as hollow talk or the strategy of merely telling people what they want to hear—either of which is manipulative. The rhetorical enactment approach to public relations reminds us that ideas count epistemologically, axiologically, and ontologically. By helping to discover and bring to bear the best facts, values, and policies, public relations can help to build mutually beneficial relationships that foster the well-being of community through the creation of social capital.

This rationale for using public relations to build community is advanced by Starck and Kruckeberg (Chapter 3). Their attention focuses on the constructive or destructive roles that corporations play in domestic and international communities. This line of reasoning, Starck and Kruckeberg contend, is even more important as the new century gives us reason to reflect on the extent to which the actions and policies of corporations narrowly advance their own interests or more fully add value to the communities in which they operate. Do corporations seek to work cooperatively with communities, or do they dominate those communities? How that question is answered defines the quality of the communities in which they operate and challenges public relations practitioners to defend the quality of communities. Setting high standards for the ethical operation of businesses and the responsible practice of public relations, Starck and Kruckeberg end their chapter with a challenge: "Corporations must recognize that the greatest stakeholder—the ultimate environmental constituency—is society itself, to which such corporations are ultimately and irrefutably answerable" (p. 59). Public relations practitioners are charged with learning how to communicate *with,* rather than *to,* their publics. Organizations operate by consent of communities, their ultimate stakeholders.

To better respond to community interests, practitioners need to know what those interests are. They need to be able to hear society—to understand and appreciate the opinions that are on the minds of people whose goodwill is vital for the mandates of their organizations. These principles grow out of rhetoric, systems, and community. To address issues central to these concerns, Leichty and Warner (Chapter 4) reason that the thoughts of society break into cultural topoi. Topoi is a concept that was used by classical rhetoricians to express the collective and embracing thoughts that lead people to draw one set of conclusions as opposed to another. People arrive at different conclusions because they subscribe to different cultural topoi.

To adjust organizations to society and to adjust society to organizations require an understanding of how the substance of both agrees or is in conflict. Cultural topoi are zones of meaning. Some are shared, and others are in conflict—or at least appear to be. One of the daunting challenges of public relations practitioners is to find points of agreement and to work toward consensus by increasing agreement and reducing disagreement. Understanding these topoi can help practitioners to understand where the opinions of organizations can be adjusted to society and where society can be adjusted to organizations. Thus, practitioners are prudent to take perspectives—to see their organizations' statements, policies, and actions from the perspectives of the cultural topoi held dear by their publics. Careful examination and prudent strategic use of cultural topoi can help practitioners to build agreement and reduce disagreement. This approach to public relations features the reality that organizations are in dialogue with their publics. This dialogue consists of a complex set of arguments that people—individually or collectively—use to achieve social capital. Social capital increases when organizations and people work to add value to society rather than expecting society to conform to their narrow self-interests.

This line of analysis is advanced by McKie (Chapter 5), who asks scholars and practitioners to abandon a linear, "old scientific" approach to the study and practice of public relations. A linear, old scientific approach is narrowly self-interested, and for that reason, it decenters society and destroys the quality of relationships. McKie calls for practitioners and scholars to become interested in the "new science," which he believes enriches thought and strategic choices because it acknowledges the diversity of complexity and the nonlinearity of chaos. The weakness of the old linear science of public relations, McKie contends, is a false sense that the skilled practitioner can understand and control the process. That approach to public relations was epitomized by Edward Bernays' belief that practitioners could and should engineer consent. Such incentives are driven by the dysfunctional desire to control rather than adjust to opinions, a desire that is frustrated by the complexity of diverse opinions, values, and interests.

The inherently weak linear approach assumes that opinions and actions of key publics can be known and controlled. Instead of taking that dysfunctional approach, practitioners and scholars need to embrace "continuous adaptation to unexpected changes in circumstances and timetables" (p. 90)—the principles of complexity and chaos.

Instead of seeking to control publics, the paradigm of the discipline has come to feature strategies that foster trust and build community. As R. Leeper (Chapter 6) demonstrates, society is stronger when individual interests are melded into community interests. Used manipulatively, community can stifle individualism through prescriptions of the following type: Do this or do not do this in the "name of community." Community can be a tyranny manipulated to the interests of some through language. The ideology of sound collectivism, communitarianism, reasons that society becomes stronger when individuals and organizations shoulder the responsibility of blending their visions with other visions to define the ends of society. Individual responsibilities and rights are made real and whole by blending into community. "Community is seen as necessary to the development of the individual" (p. 97), reasons Leeper. Thus, public relations is challenged to define itself as a professional practice that stresses "commitment to and the quality of relationships, a sense of social cohesion, the importance of core values and beliefs, balancing rights and responsibilities, citizen empowerment, and a broadening of perspective so as to reduce social fragmentation" (p. 99). If such a challenge is valuable for the practice of public relations in any community (including the community of each country), then it is even more important as we seek to forge a global community. Communitarianism is a challenge not for organizations to expect communities to accept them or for communities to demand unreasonable contributions by organizations. The challenge of public relations is to use rights and responsibilities to balance interests and resolve conflicts so that communities become better places for the individuals—human or corporate.

Adding his voice to those advocating a relationship approach to public relations, Coombs (Chapter 7) challenges scholars and practitioners to search for variables that define the quality of relationships and also can predict qualitative changes in such relationships. Coombs wants scholars and practitioners to look beyond the principles of mass communication as the rationale for defining the discipline. Rather than relying on the mass dissemination of information and influence, building relationships stresses the virtue of harmony and the blending of stakes and stakeholders into mutually beneficial arrangements. Coombs reasons that "excellence suggests that communication helps the organization not only to understand but also to negotiate expectations" (p. 112). Thus, the dominant model of public relations based on interpersonal communication theory sees the practice as chat, conversation, and accommodation to build mutual benefit between the engaged parties. This paradigm moves us beyond a linear mass communication approach. Dialogue replaces monologue in the advancement of public relations theory and practice.

At times, scholars and practitioners might err by thinking that the practice is defined by dialogue between one organization and one public. Some leading research and theory might even make that mistake. Addressing the need for a multipublic approach to public relations, Springston and Keyton (Chapter 8) draw on the literature of group dynamics. A group is a composite of individuals, each of whom has ideas, facts, values, and policy preferences that may agree or disagree with those of others in the group. Recognizing this dynamic principle of groups, theorists have worked to explain how groups can achieve consensus despite these types of differences. That line of research and analysis is vital to the practice of public relations. The organization using public relations often is confronted by the prospect that two or more publics vital to its future do not agree with each other and might agree or disagree with the organization on key points.

The call for community as the dominant paradigm of public relations must acknowledge that community exists through the comanagement of agreement and disagreement of multiple complementary and competing perspectives. Springston and Keyton discuss how such agreement and disagreement can be identified and used to work toward mutually beneficial outcomes. The authors demonstrate how field dynamics theory complements and refines other theories to better understand a contingency-based negotiation perspective of public relations. Calling for community is easy. Understanding how to achieve it is more difficult. Positions need to be blended and compromised. Stakes need to be exchanged. Interests need to be advanced, as well as sacrificed, in a steady march toward the forging of mutually beneficial relationships.

Such relationships result from dialogue between organizations and publics. This is a well-established theme in the definition of the discipline. What is less well understood is the nature of publics and the dynamics of their relationships with key organizations. According to Leitch and Neilson (Chapter 9), publics demonstrate unique (relatively minor to dramatically different) lifeworlds, and they accomplish different amounts of internal and external network positioning. For this reason, publics seek to define who they are, what they believe, and the role they play in the dynamic process of policy formation in society. Leitch and Neilson reason that researchers make mistakes if they assume that publics are defined only by the organizations that are responding to them. Prudent public relations practice and theory acknowledge the unique defining efforts of publics to advocate important lifeworld perspectives and to play power roles in public policy formation.

Publics influence the practice of public relations. They support or criticize organizations on their own terms and with their own power dynamics. Consequently, they must be enjoined in dialogue based on who they are rather than merely on who the organizations (which are under attack) define them to be. In this way, Leitch and Neilson advocate that theory and practice of the discipline can be enriched by developing a public-centered view of the practice rather than looking essentially at organizations (which are under attack) and taking an organization-centered view of the practice. The interests of the organization and of community may be advanced if the practitioner can prudently understand, appreciate, and champion the perspectives and interests being asserted by each public. The interests of the organization and community at large can be enhanced if each public is embraced and its structure is incorporated into the larger power and decision-making structure of the community. Public relations is most constructive when practitioners approach each public from its unique point of view rather than from that of the organization or the community at large. Public relations is a means for fostering dialogue so that the players come into meaningful contact to resolve differences and advance individual and collective interests.

Joining the discussion of publics, Vasquez and Taylor (Chapter 10) review the origins of that concept as the foundation for better understanding what publics are and the role that they play in the rhetorical dialogue of society. A rhetorical rationale for public relations is supported by the view that a public is a "rhetorical community that develops a group consciousness around a problematic situation" (p. 151). In this process, members of the public function as "homo narrans"—people who share a narrative view of life and who enact that view in concert (conflict and cooperation) with others who enact similar or competing narratives. Thus, the substance of each public—what it believes and says—reflects its narrative view of reality that it creates through discussions that help members recognize that they have had similar experiences and so share narratives and the opinions that make those narratives unique. Whereas Leichty and Warner (Chapter 4) focus on cultural topoi, Vasquez and Taylor use homo narrans theory to explain how individuals use communication to "first become and then function as a public" (p. 146). The rhetoric of public relations is a dynamic clash of narratives that can require that negotiation occurs to resolve differences and achieve mutually beneficial outcomes.

As McKie (Chapter 5) suggests, the dynamics of public relations can occur in a chaotic environment fraught with complexity. Chaos and complexity are key concepts that help us to understand the dynamics of crises. Practitioners who are responsible for making comments during a crisis are wise to understand and attempt to accommodate to the chaos and complexity that they cannot manage but might be able to mitigate. Seeger, Sellnow, and Ulmer (Chapter 11) set themselves to the task of defining the discipline from a crisis response mode. Crises can occur. They can be poorly managed and thereby become issues. Issues can be poorly managed and, consequently, become crises. Thus, public relations seeks orderly responses to a disorderly environment. Rather than embracing a manipulative information and opinion control model of crisis response, Seeger et al. suggest that an organization experiencing a crisis is prudent to make open, timely, informed, and consistent responses. Public relations needs to help the community interested in the crisis to form a narrative—homo narrans—that allows interested parties to understand the crisis and to foretell its happy conclusion—". . . all lived happily ever after."

The positions taken in this section dramatically change the paradigm of public relations. The underpinning assumption is that public relations is a relationship-building professional activity that adds value to organizations because it increases the willingness of markets, audiences, and publics to support them rather than to oppose their efforts. Will this view of public relations sustain itself and live up to its promise? In one sense, only time will tell. Scholarship and practice grow as individuals put their minds to the task of improving the discipline. To assess how well the practice is going, the editors of the handbook invited Cheney and Christiansen (Chapter 12) to reflect on the chapters that were devoted to defining the discipline. This gives our diagnosis and prescription the benefit of a "second opinion." Just as patients are prudent to request a second opinion, scholars also can benefit from independent review of the evidence. So, we ask of Cheney and Christiansen: Are we healthy, and what prescriptions are necessary for recovery and good health?

This section of the handbook is devoted to defining the field of public relations. Cheney and Christiansen believe that this section largely accomplishes that goal but also falls short in several key ways. Their diagnosis and prescriptions are likely to help jar academics and leading practitioners to continue to refine their thinking on several key challenges. Thus, they argue that public relations theory and research need to address, rather than gloss over or dismiss, issues of power and influence that is exerted by and against corporations. This body of literature also needs to differentiate more clearly the roles and responsibilities of marketing, advertising, and public relations. The discussion would be enriched by close analysis of the role of public relations in the struggle for democracy in cultures that are dominated by, or at least largely biased toward, corporatism. The authors caution against limiting public relations definitions to principles that feature a Western rationalist set of assumptions. Can we take a nonmanagerial approach to public relations and thereby discover a research agenda that features public relations as a discipline that helps to liberate and foster the human spirit and identity? That is a daunting challenge. It might shape the agenda of the next generation of scholarly output.

CHAPTER 1

Two-Way Symmetrical Public Relations

Past, Present, and Future

JAMES E. GRUNIG

Before the 1970s, public relations scholars seldom, if ever, tried to explain the behavior of public relations practitioners. Until that time, scholars typically accepted the behavior of practitioners as given and looked for ways in which to describe, evaluate, and improve whatever practitioners did in the name of public relations. In J. Grunig (1992b), I described the previous research in this way:

> Until about 1970, research on public relations in the United States consisted mostly of biographies of leading practitioners, case studies of public relations practice, and some highly applied studies—such as research on the factors leading to the acceptance of news releases or the proportion of content in the news media that comes from public relations sources. In addition, public relations educators and practitioners considered much of communication research to be relevant to their problems—although they did little of this research themselves. Relevant research was that on public opinion, attitudes and persuasion, effects of the mass media, effects of information campaigns, and—to a lesser extent—interpersonal and organizational communication. (p. 107)

In J. Grunig (1976), I published the first of a large number of studies that began to look at public relations as a dependent variable to be explained rather than as an independent variable whose effects were to be described. In that study, I identified two patterns of public relations practice that I described as synchronic and diachronic public relations, using Thayer's (1968) concepts of two types of communication. I extended these two types of public relations into the concept of four models of public relations and developed an instrument to measure them in an article published in 1984 (J. Grunig, 1984).[1]

I then used the models throughout our 1984 textbook, *Managing Public Relations* (J. Grunig & Hunt, 1984). In that book, we used the four models both to describe the historical development of public relations in the United States and as a set of ideal types that described typical ways in which contemporary public relations is practiced. These four models were called press agentry/publicity, public information, two-way symmetrical, and two-way asymmetrical. Press agentry/publicity and public information both are one-way models. Practitioners of press agentry seek attention for their organizations in almost any way possible, whereas public information practitioners are journalists-in-residence who disseminate accurate, but usually only favorable, information about their organizations. With the two-way asymmetrical model, practitioners conduct scientific research to determine how to persuade publics to behave in the ways their client organizations wish. With the two-way symmetrical model, practitioners use research and dialogue to bring about symbiotic changes in the ideas, attitudes, and behaviors of both their organizations and publics.

In *Managing Public Relations* (J. Grunig & Hunt, 1984), we speculated that a contingency theory would explain when and why organizations practice these models; that is, each of the different models of public relations could be effective, depending on the structure of the organization and the nature of its environment. In later work (J. Grunig, 1989e; J. Grunig & L. Grunig, 1989, 1992), however, we dropped this contingency approach. Both research and conceptual development of the theory suggested that organizations could practice each of the models under certain contingent conditions and contribute to organizational effectiveness. We also suggested, however, that using the two-way symmetrical model or a combination of the two-way symmetrical and two-way asymmetrical models (called the mixed-motive model) almost always could increase the contribution of public relations to organizational effectiveness.

Murphy (1991) developed the idea of a mixed-motive model, based on concepts from game theory. She equated the symmetrical model with games of pure cooperation in which one side always tries to accommodate the interests of the other side. In a mixed-motive model, by contrast, organizations try to satisfy their own interests while simultaneously trying to help publics satisfy their interests. In actuality, I never viewed the two-way symmetrical model as one of pure cooperation or of total accommodation of a public's interests. Therefore, Murphy's mixed-motive model accurately described the two-way symmetrical model as we originally conceptualized it (J. Grunig & L. Grunig, 1992, pp. 309-312).

CRITICAL REACTIONS TO THE MODELS AND SYMMETRICAL THEORY

For many reasons, the models of public relations and the two-way symmetrical model, in particular, have become popular theories and topics of research in public relations. In 1992, J. Grunig and L. Grunig reviewed many of the studies published by that date. In addition, the models have been the focus of numerous other studies, theses, and dissertations throughout the world. The models have stimulated many studies of public relations in both developed and developing countries of the world.

This research generally has confirmed that the models do describe the practice of public relations in many cultures and political systems, but it also has suggested variations in the models, in particular, patterns of practice that can be described as personal influence and cultural interpretation models (J. Grunig, L. Grunig, Sriramesh, Huang, & Lyra, 1995). Research also has suggested that practitioners in countries such as Korea are most likely to practice the craft models of press agentry and public information, although they aspire to practice the two-way symmetrical and asymmetrical models (Kim & Hon, 1998).

Many scholars have embraced the models because they seem to fit well with reality and to describe the experience of many practitioners. At the same time, the models have been useful teaching tools for distinguishing between the typical practice of public relations and more advanced practices. The models also have become a useful research tool for analyzing public relations practice in numerous settings and for explaining why public relations is practiced in these different ways.

Whenever a theory becomes as ubiquitous as the models of public relations have become, it also becomes the target of criticism by scholars who want to defend or develop competing theories. Therefore, it is not surprising that the models have become the target of several critics. Most of these critics have focused on J. Grunig's

(1989e) and J. Grunig and L. Grunig's (1992) suggestion that the two-way symmetrical model provides the normative ideal for public relations in most situations.

I have distinguished between a positive and a normative theory many times in describing the models of public relations (e.g., J. Grunig & L. Grunig, 1992, pp. 290-292). A positive model is a theory that describes and explains how public relations *is* practiced. A normative model explains how public relations *should be* practiced. A normative theory often is practiced positively, which adds support to the idea that it *can be* practiced.

Some scholars have reacted negatively to the suggestion that the symmetrical model is normatively superior to the others because they believe that one or more of the other models represent acceptable public relations practice. Critical scholars have asserted that the symmetrical model misrepresents the reality of what they consider to be an evil practice. Other theorists accept public relations as a legitimate profession but have maintained that symmetrical public relations is a utopian ideal that cannot be practiced in reality.

DEFENSES OF ASYMMETRICAL AND CONTINGENCY THEORIES

Some theorists, such as Miller (1989), have reacted defensively to the symmetrical model because it appears to challenge the dominant role that theories of persuasion have played in communication science. Like Miller, they believe that public relations and persuasion are "two Ps in a pod" (pp. 45-48) and that public relations is asymmetrical by nature. Van der Meiden (1993), for example, defended an asymmetrical approach to public relations by arguing that the symmetrical model means that organizations would have to abandon their self-interests, something he considered to be unrealistic as well as ill advised.

By contrast, we have stated consistently that the symmetrical model actually serves the self-interest of the organization better than an asym-

metrical model because "organizations get more of what they want when they give up some of what they want" (J. Grunig & White, 1992, p. 39). In addition, as early as in J. Grunig and Hunt (1984), we wrote that persuasion still is a relevant concept in the symmetrical model. The difference is that the public relations professional sometimes must persuade management and at other times must persuade a public: "If persuasion occurs, the public should be just as likely to persuade the organization's management to change attitudes or behavior as the organization is likely to change the public's attitudes or behavior" (p. 23).

Leichty and Springston (1993) were among the first to point out that most organizations practice a combination of the four models. They also maintained that our original contingency approach to the models is more realistic than our more recent recommendation that the symmetrical model is the best normative approach to public relations under most situations. Leichty (1997) added that there are limits to collaboration, especially when crises caused by activist opposition require a confrontational response or when opponents are unreasonable or unwilling to collaborate.

Murphy and Dee (1992) described such a case in a conflict between DuPont and Greenpeace that they concluded would continue despite some agreement between the two on solutions to the issue. Murphy and Dee used multiple regression analysis to set up decision profiles that both DuPont and Greenpeace used to evaluate issues. They also asked each group to estimate the profiles of the other group. Although the actual profiles of both groups were closer than the profiles they projected for each other, the researchers could not get the two groups to agree on a compromise solution they had constructed to represent the interests of both parties:

> Both corporate public relations practitioners and environmental activists doubtless want to enhance public awareness of their position on environmental issues. In taking its case to the public, DuPont could rightly emphasize the similarities between its position and those of environmental activists. However, Greenpeace would surely pre-

fer to emphasize the differences rather than the similarities between its position and DuPont's. If DuPont aligns itself with environmental activism, Greenpeace loses the use of DuPont, an evil other, as a rallying point. (pp. 30-31)

Murphy and Dee's (1992) study did not call the value of the symmetrical model into question. I never have believed, or said, that the symmetrical model always would be successful. Indeed, Leichty (1997) was correct when he pointed out that there are limits to collaboration. We acknowledged similar limits when we listed several reasons, identified by Gray (1989), why organizations often refuse to collaborate:

institutional disincentives (such as environmental groups that do not want to dilute their advocacy of a cause), historical and ideological barriers, disparities in power, societal dynamics (such as individualism in the United States), differing perceptions of risk, technical complexity, and political and institutional cultures. (J. Grunig & L. Grunig, 1992, p. 319)

Then, in support of the idea that symmetrical public relations is not inevitably successful, we quoted Gray (1989), who said,

Clearly the record of collaborations to date is a checkered one. Many experiences contain aspects of both success and failure. While the evidence is not 100 percent favorable, it is heartening. For example, even when parties do not reach agreement, they frequently applaud the process. Moreover, the numbers of disputes and problems for which collaboration is a possible alternative is growing. Finally, as we learn more about what works and what does not, the number of successes should increase. (p. 260, quoted in J. Grunig & L. Grunig, p. 319)

Susskind and Field's (1996) book, *Dealing With an Angry Public,* is, in essence, a manual on how to practice the two-way symmetrical model in conflict situations. In their chapter on conflicts based on differences in values, however, Susskind and Field acknowledged that such conflicts (e.g., the abortion conflict) are particularly

difficult to resolve "because basic notions of self-worth are at stake" (p. 155). They explained,

Debates involving values are not only about what we want, but also [about] who we think we are and who we think "they" are in relation to us. Debates involving values upset our view of the world and ourselves. In value-laden debates, to compromise or to accommodate neither advances one's self-interest nor increases joint gains. Compromise, in its most pejorative sense, means abandoning deeply held beliefs, values, or ideas. To negotiate away values is to risk giving up one's identity. Thus, such conflicts are intense. (p. 155)

Nevertheless, Susskind and Field (1996) suggested a number of incremental steps that can be taken to at least defuse the conflict, get the parties to talk with one another, and achieve small areas of agreement. "First-level" changes can be accomplished, they said. "The disputants may agree on peripheral changes that do not eliminate the ongoing hostilities but alleviate specific problems" (p. 158). For example, after employees were killed at a Planned Parenthood clinic, the Catholic Church called for a moratorium on sidewalk demonstrations and asked protesters to move their vigils inside churches. "Second-level changes alter some aspects of the ongoing relationship, but fundamental values are not challenged or transformed, at least in the short run" (p. 159). For example, groups opposing each other on abortion

agreed to meet to discuss adoption, foster care, and abstinence for teenagers. Surprisingly, these groups agreed to support legislation to pay for the treatment of pregnant drug addicts. They also established an ongoing dialogue that transformed the way they dealt with each other. For instance, they began to meet individually, on a personal basis, to work on problems they had in common. (p. 159)

Susskind and Field (1996) added that "third-level change is far more difficult" because it requires change "in the way people view themselves" (p. 159). They explained that, for individuals, such change requires extensive therapy. As a result, they said, "In the practical world of day-to-day management, we do not think it is likely that any one institution, be it a corporation or a government agency, can bring changes at the third level" (p. 159).

In short, the two-way symmetrical model sometimes will be less effective than it will at other times. The major question, then, is whether an asymmetrical approach will be more successful when a symmetrical approach is not completely effective. That question has been the major focus of a program of research by Cameron and his associates (Cameron, 1997; Cancel, Cameron, Sallot, & Mitrook, 1997; Cancel, Mitrook, & Cameron, 1999; Yarbrough, Cameron, Sallot, & McWilliams, 1998).

Like others cited previously, Cameron and his colleagues took issue with our conclusion that the symmetrical model is the most effective normative model in most situations. In the first article in the series, Cancel et al. (1997) equated the symmetrical model with accommodation and equated the asymmetrical model with advocacy. In its place, they developed a contingency theory defining 87 conditions that might explain why public relations professionals decide whether to accommodate publics or to engage in advocacy only for their organizations.

I believe that equating the symmetrical model with accommodation is a misrepresentation of the model. I never have defined the symmetrical model as the accommodation of a public's interests at the expense of the organization's self-interest. In fact, the concept of symmetry directly implies a balance of the organization's and the public's interests. Total accommodation of the public's interests would be as asymmetrical as unbridled advocacy of the organization's interests.

In later publications, Cameron's research team has softened its criticism of the symmetrical model. For example, Yarbrough et al. (1998) said in a parenthetical statement, "The authors believe that some degree of accommodation or openness to accommodation is at the crux of two-way symmetrical communication" (p. 40). Obviously, this is the case. Public relations could not be symmetrical without accommodation, but the essence of the symmetrical model is that

the organization and a public each must be willing to accommodate the interests of the other.

Cameron and his colleagues have stated in each of their articles that they believe that public relations professionals are least likely to practice symmetrical public relations when an organization considers the stance of a public to be morally repugnant. In such cases, they challenge our claim (J. Grunig & L. Grunig, 1996; J. Grunig & White, 1992) that the symmetrical model is inherently ethical: " For some issues, taking a moral stand means *not* engaging in two-way symmetrical communication because to do so would place communication process above ethical principle" (Cancel et al., 1999, p. 173, italics in original). In short, they believe that accommodating a morally repugnant public ("the Hitlers of the world" [Yarbrough et al., 1998, p. 40]) is morally wrong.

Again, however, the symmetrical model is not about accommodation alone. It might be unethical to accommodate a repugnant public; it is not unethical to talk with its representatives. And as Susskind and Field (1996) have shown, there are examples in which competing parties have improved their relationship with groups that they previously considered morally repugnant. In addition, I believe that organizations far too often believe that publics with which they are in conflict are morally repugnant and that the organizations' stances are morally superior. The same also is true of activist groups, such as Greenpeace, that believe that they have a moral duty to oppose "evil" corporations (as exemplified in Murphy & Dee, 1992).

Yarbrough et al. (1998) acknowledged the problem of believing that one's position is morally superior to that of the opposition when they said, "Organizations necessarily weather charges of paternalism when members of the organization are convinced that they know more about the situation and are acting in the best interests of all parties or for a greater good" (pp. 40-41). In J. Grunig (1989e), I provided some examples of the dangers of such paternalism:

> Although the asymmetrical perspective may sound like a reasonable position, keep in mind that organizations often expect publics to accept strange things as a result of "cooperation": pollu-

tion, toxic waste, drinking, smoking, guns, over-throw of governments, dangerous products, low-ered salary and benefits, discrimination against women and minorities, job layoffs, dangerous manufacturing plants, risky transportation of products, higher prices, monopoly power, poor product quality, political favoritism, insider trad-ing, use of poisonous chemicals, exposure to car-cinogens, nuclear weapons, and even warfare. The list could go on and on. (p. 32)

In short, there obviously are situations in which an organization or a public has a more rea-sonable or moral position than the other. How-ever, the point of the symmetrical model is that neither side can really know the morality or rea-sonableness of the other side's interests without talking with its representatives. If, after dialogue, one side finds that it cannot accommodate the other side, then the symmetrical approach sug-gests that advocacy of its interests or withdrawal from the dialogue is ethically reasonable.

Cancel et al. (1999) added two additional scenarios when collaboration is difficult or im-possible: (a) when antitrust law prohibits collu-sion among competitors and (b) when "an orga-nization faces two publics locked in intractable moral conflict" (p. 173) such as a corporation that must deal with both Planned Parenthood and an anti-abortion group. The first situation is not really a public relations situation; it describes organization-to-organization communication, not organization-to-public communication. The second example is well known in the conflict resolution literature and has been recognized by Vercic (1997) in the public relations literature. Multiparty conflicts do not call the efficacy of the symmetrical model into question; instead, they require more sophisticated means of symmetri-cal communication and conflict resolution, methods that research is only beginning to iden-tify.

In spite of these criticisms, however, the con-tingency theory proposed by Cameron and his colleagues does not really challenge the symmet-rical model. Rather, I see the theory as an elabo-ration of the symmetrical model. Symmetry in public relations really is about balancing the in-terests of organizations and publics, of balancing

advocacy and accommodation. As their research shows, the management of an organization is not always willing to accommodate a public. In some situations, it is willing to accommodate; in oth-ers, it is not. In addition, their case studies illus-trate well the interactions among public rela-tions professionals, top management, and publics that characterize real-life application of the symmetrical model.

CRITICISM OF SYMMETRICAL PUBLIC RELATIONS AS IDEALISM

Although scholars of persuasion generally seem to believe that persuasion is ethical and part of a "wrangle in the marketplace" (Heath, 1992b, p. 17), critical scholars such as Gandy (1982), Kersten (1994), and L'Etang (1996a) typically have viewed public relations as "necessarily par-tisan and intrinsically undemocratic" (L'Etang, 1996a, p. 105). Thus, to them, the symmetrical model represents a utopian attempt to make an inherently evil practice look good:

There is, however, a problem in the attempt which some make to maintain the ideal of "symmetry" alongside the role of public relations as advocate. Surely, symmetry and advocacy are in opposition. The only way around this tension is to argue that public relations ensures that all views are held, i.e., that the playing field is level. Whether this sort of pandering to the liberal conscience is justifiable is a matter for debate: a debate which has yet to take place with public relations. (pp. 96-97)

Pieczka (1996) also objected to the use of the symmetrical model as a normative theory of how public relations should be practiced as well as a descriptive theory of how public relations is practiced. She said that using the symmetrical model as a normative ideal is a closed-minded attempt to impose a single point of view on oth-ers: "This is rather reminiscent of Victorian mis-sionaries explaining savages' habits of walking about naked or praying to rain by their lack of civilization. It is not a bad explanation; but it is a good one only from a particular point of view" (p. 154).

What Pieczka ignored in using this analogy is the research evidence accumulated in support of the claim that the symmetrical model is the most effective model in practice as well as in theory (see, e.g., Dozier, L. Grunig, & J. Grunig, 1995; J. Grunig & L. Grunig, 1992) and the numerous revisions of the theory we have made over the years as a result of research. I believe that the purpose of public relations research is to construct new and better ways of practicing the profession. Surely, it is not Victorian paternalism to recommend that public relations be practiced in the way research shows it can be practiced most effectively.

By contrast, Pieczka (1996a) expressed more interest in criticizing the symmetrical theory than in constructing a replacement: "The author here is more interested in critiquing frameworks than in building them" (p. 126). In a professional field such as public relations, I believe, scholars must go beyond criticizing theories; they also have the obligation to replace theories with something better—an obligation that many critical scholars do not fulfill.

The view that the symmetrical model is utopian also can be found in critiques such as those of Kunczik (1994), L'Etang (1995), and Pieczka (1995), all of whom argued that the symmetrical model is overly idealistic and is based on assumptions that seldom exist in reality. Their specific criticism, however, seems to have been more of Habermas's (1984) ideal communication situation or of Pearson's (1989a) application of Habermas's theory to the symmetrical theory than of our formulation of the theory. In addition, these critics typically have ascribed theoretical assumptions to the symmetrical theory that are different from our presuppositions about the theory. In particular, they have argued that the theory assumes liberal pluralism (Dozier & Lauzen, 1998), functionalism (Pieczka, 1996a), or a shared desire for equilibrium and harmony in society (Pieczka, 1996a; Vasquez, 1996).

If all of these theoretical presuppositions were accurate, then the theory of two-way symmetrical communication would envision public relations as a force that allows competing groups

in a pluralist society equal access to decision makers, maintains functional equilibrium in a society, and produces goodwill and harmony. In addition, all competing organizations, groups, and publics would enter into dialogue with the intent of achieving consensus. For example, Vasquez (1996) described the two-way symmetrical model in this way: "Namely, the two-way symmetrical model conceptualizes public relations as a negotiation situation in which parties hold or perceive they hold compatible, rather than incompatible, goals. Simply put, the compatible goal is a shared mission of social progress" (p. 65). To this perceived assumption of "a shared mission of social progress," Pieczka (1996b) added the equally naive assumption, which we already have discussed, that public relations always is successful:

> The view of society that seems to be assumed is that in which various interest groups (and publics) are unavoidably pitched one against another but where conflict can always be resolved by the process of negotiation, which breeds at least as much mutual understanding as is necessary for compromise. (p. 64)

Finally, L'Etang (1996a) finished this naive construction of the symmetrical theory by stating that the theory assumes that all public relations is practiced in a utopian fashion: "What these arguments do is present public relations as being intrinsically moral in its peace-keeping function as well as in its promotion and support of democracy" (p. 96).

Moloney (1997) wrote that this naive utopian portrayal of the two-way symmetrical model has been adopted by public relations educators in the United Kingdom, particularly as a way of justifying the teaching of public relations when the popular perception of public relations is one of opprobrium:

> For university teachers seeking to found their work on an academically respectable basis, his [J. Grunig's] and Hunt's work were welcome to staff competing on campuses for resources against teachers of older and more established disciplines. The Grunigian paradigm gave them aca-

demic status. More emotionally, it met internal-ized needs of U.K. public relations teachers who had to convince themselves that they were worth a place on higher education campuses. Whatever the explanations, the outcome in the lecture thea-tre has too often been: "Public relations is a good thing called symmetrical communications" rather than "Maybe it should be that, but the data seem not to fit." (p. 140)

Moloney went on to distinguish between posi-tive and normative models. He added to this dis-cussion, however, by pointing out that it is a mis-take to believe that a normative theory describes all positive practice:

> Now the distortion by disciples enters in. Teachers (as well as trainers and articulate public relations professionals) do not adequately express this im-balance of types between majority "bad" practice and minority "good" practice. They over-empha-size the latter, forgetting its feeble grip on actual public relations behaviour in the U.K., at least as witnessed by the public. In doing so, they laud the normative but minority practice so much so that the distinction between practice and norm is blurred to the point of erasure by frequent repeti-tion. The normative aspect of symmetrical com-munication has, so to speak, been over-stamped on its minority existence. (p. 140)

Both the disciples of the symmetrical theory and critical scholars who debunk it seem to have reconstructed the theory inaccurately in their minds—to the extent that the theory appears to be ridiculous. In my conceptualization, by con-trast, symmetrical public relations does not take place in an ideal situation where competing in-terests come together with goodwill to resolve their differences because they share a goal of so-cial equilibrium and harmony. Rather, it takes place in situations where groups come together to protect and enhance their self-interests. Argu-mentation, debate, and persuasion take place. But dialogue, listening, understanding, and rela-tionship building also occur because they are more effective in resolving conflict than are one-way attempts at compliance gaining.

Public relations people who use a symmetri-cal approach can facilitate collaborative pro-cesses because they are educated professionals who have expertise in working with others to fa-cilitate dialogic communication and relation-ship building. To be successful, however, they must be able to convince their client organiza-tions and publics that a symmetrical approach will enhance their self-interests more than will an asymmetrical approach and, at the same time, that it will enhance their reputations as ethical, socially responsible organizations and publics.

Even though they might understand the symmetrical theory as just described, however, there still are critical scholars who argue that or-ganizations generally have greater power than their publics and have no reason to engage in symmetrical communication. They argue that organizations can enhance their self-interests more easily by dominating their publics through asymmetrical communication (Dozier & Lauzen, 1998; Kersten, 1994). In L'Etang's (1996b) words, the symmetrical theory does not "explore the social or political contexts which al-low certain interests an enhanced position in which they have more choice in the nature and type of communicative acts they carry out" (p. 122).

These critical scholars seem to ignore the countervailing power that publics have when they organize into activist groups and use tactics such as media advocacy (Wallack, Dorfman, Jernigan, & Themba, 1993), litigation, legisla-tion, and regulation (Mintzberg, 1983) to ac-complish their goals. Indeed, many public rela-tions practitioners believe their organizations have lost control to activist groups.

It is ironic that activist groups often use pub-lic relations to enhance their power vis-à-vis cor-porations and government agencies. One criti-cal scholar, Karlberg (1996), even advocated that activist groups use the symmetrical model to better enhance their interests. Karlberg critiqued our program of research on symmetrical public relations as "two-way symmetrical theory...be-ing applied within an asymmetrical research agenda" (p. 271). Research on the symmetri-cal model, he said, has been done from the per-spective of "already privileged organizations"

(p. 273). "Symmetry," he explained, "assumes that all segments of the population have the communication skills and resources to represent themselves in public discourse" (p. 273). Using the conventional language of critical researchers, Karlberg described our program of research as *instrumental* (in service of powerful corporations and the state) rather than *critical* (in service of citizens and the less powerful).

Nevertheless, Karlberg (1996) deviated from most critical theorists by arguing that public relations scholars should do research to help activist groups, as well as corporations and the government, do public relations. To illustrate the point, he rewrote a quote of J. Grunig's (1993b) that described the power of activist groups to limit the ability of organizations to accomplish their goals to suggest a more symmetrical research agenda:

> Active publics are important *initiators of* (rather than targets for) public relations programs because they are most likely to be aware of and concerned with what *organizations are doing.* In addition, if *citizen groups* do not communicate with organizations and attempt to manage conflict, *those organizations can limit the ability of citizens* to create the kind of communities in which they would like to live. (Karlberg, 1996, p. 272, italics in original)

J. Grunig and L. Grunig (1997) responded to Karlberg's (1996) challenge to make public relations theory relevant for activist groups, as well as for corporations and government, by developing a working theory that combines symmetrical and asymmetrical strategies. Our theoretical understanding of how activist groups should practice public relations is only beginning to emerge. At this point, however, we can answer Karlberg's question of how "excluded members of the population" should practice public relations as follows:

1. Use the logic of the situational theory of publics (J. Grunig, 1997) to identify potential publics that share problems. Organize those publics, usually using interpersonal communication given that

members of these unempowered publics seldom pay attention to mass-mediated messages. If constraint recognition limits the likelihood that these publics will organize, then emphasize the potential of collective action to reduce the effect of constraints on individual behavior.

2. If the organized public lacks power, then use strategic public relations planning and coalition building to identify other complementary activists, thus enlarging and empowering the original activist group.

3. When the public or coalition has been organized, make an attempt to communicate symmetrically with the organization causing the problem or having the potential to solve the problem. If the organization responds symmetrically, then use principles of conflict resolution to negotiate with the organization. This symmetrical initiative makes subsequent asymmetrical techniques more ethical.[2]

4. If the organization does not respond to the symmetrical initiative, then use asymmetrical techniques to force the organization to consider the public's problem also to be its problem. Media advocacy, government lobbying, and litigation are the most common methods used to create this problem for the organization (although research might identify other ethical means of asymmetrical communication). These asymmetrical techniques will be ethical if the activist group discloses its persuasive intent at all times.

5. Once media pressure, governmental intervention, or the courts have forced the organization to consider the public's problem also to be its problem, return to symmetrical communication and conflict resolution to search for a win-win solution and to build a long-term relationship between the organization and the activist group.

These five steps represent a relatively undeveloped normative theory of public relations for activist organizations, but the developing theory already has received empirical support in dissertations by Kovacs (1998) on activist relations with the British Broadcasting Corporation and by Sha (1999) on the public relations strategies of the Democratic Progressive Party on Taiwan.

In short, the symmetrical theory has proven to be remarkably resilient to its critics. In many instances, their criticism can be resolved by correcting inaccurate conceptions of the theory. In other instances, the criticisms have stimulated revisions that have improved the theory.

TOWARD AN ELABORATED SYMMETRICAL MODEL

When J. Grunig first developed the models of public relations, they were little more than what Shapere (1977) called an "initial vague idea" (p. 553, n. 4)—a useful but undeveloped concept that stimulates additional research. Thus, much of the criticism already discussed has been based on some of my earliest writings on the symmetrical model or on misunderstanding of the initial vague idea. Vasquez's (1996) article on public relations and negotiation provides an example of this misunderstanding of science as described by Shapere. Vasquez said, "My critique differs from previous efforts in that it examines the two-way symmetrical model's view of public relations as negotiation. Generally, I take the position that the two-way symmetrical model is underdeveloped as a form of communication and negotiation" (p. 65). Compare this conclusion with the following introduction to a brief review of theories of conflict resolution in J. Grunig and L. Grunig (1992):

> If this reconceptualized model of symmetrical public relations is a major characteristic of excellence in public relations, a logical next step for public relations theorists is to develop the model further as a normative theory to guide the practice of public relations. *To begin this process,* we review theories of dispute resolution, negotiation, mediation, and conflict management in this final section because of the similarities in the presup-

positions of these theories and those of the symmetrical model. (p. 313, italics added)

We wrote the preceding passage as an introduction to a brief review of theories related to collaboration and conflict management to suggest that other scholars follow our lead in using these theories to develop the symmetrical model from a vague general idea to a more elaborated theory. Good theories always provide more questions than answers.[3] Thus, in contrast to Vasquez's (1996) critique, the symmetrical theory is strong, not weak, because it suggests where research is needed to elaborate the theory—something Vasquez went on to do as he reviewed communication theories of conflict resolution that help to elaborate the symmetrical theory.

Nevertheless, the criticisms of the models of public relations and, in particular, of the two-way symmetrical model have identified conceptual ambiguities in the theory that need to be addressed as well as fruitful ideas for reformulating and improving it. The multiyear study of *Excellence in Public Relations and Communication Management* (Dozier et al., 1995; J. Grunig, 1992c) has provided evidence that helps to improve the conceptualization of the models and the conditions under which they are most appropriate.

THE MODELS IN THE INTERNATIONAL ASSOCIATION OF BUSINESS COMMUNICATORS *EXCELLENCE* STUDY

In 1985, a research team I headed that included Larissa Grunig (University of Maryland), David Dozier (San Diego State University), Jon White (City University of London), William Ehling (Syracuse University), and Fred Repper (Gulf States Utilities of Texas) began what probably is the most extensive study ever undertaken of the public relations profession. The study was funded through a $400,000 grant from the International Association of Business Communicators (IABC) Research Foundation. The study sought answers to two fundamental research questions:

1. How, why, and to what extent does public relations make an organization more effective, and how much is that contribution worth in a monetary sense?
2. What characteristics of the public relations function increase the contribution that communication management makes to organizational effectiveness?

The research team began the project with a thorough review of literature that would shed light on the first question (the *effectiveness* question) and of literature on each of 14 characteristics of what the team called *excellent* public relations departments. The use of the two-way symmetrical or mixed-motive model appeared in 4 of those 14 characteristics of excellence. The results of the literature review and conceptualization were published in *Excellence in Public Relations and Communication Management* (J. Grunig, 1992c). The team concluded that public relations increases organizational effectiveness when it builds long-term relationships of trust and understanding with strategic publics of the organization—those that affect or are affected by the organization as it identifies and pursues its mission. The team also reasoned that the use of the two-way symmetrical model, either alone or in combination with the two-way asymmetrical model (the mixed-motive model), would be more likely to result in such relationships than would the other models.

The research team then operationalized the 14 characteristics of excellence as well as three effects of communication excellence on relationships—meeting communication objectives; reducing the costs of litigation, regulation, and activist pressure; and maintaining employee job satisfaction—in the form of three questionnaires. The questionnaires, which contained about 1,700 items of information before they were combined into indexes, were administered to the senior public relations manager, to one of the senior executives (the chief executive officer [CEO], when possible), and to an average of 12 employees in each organization. All three questionnaires were completed by 270 organizations, although 321 organizations participated in the survey by completing at least one of the three questionnaires. Of these 321 organizations, 226 were in the United States, 58 were in Canada, and 37 were in the United Kingdom. The organizations represented 148 corporations, 71 government agencies, 58 not-for-profit organizations, and 44 trade or professional associations.

The four models of public relations were measured in four ways: (a) by the extent to which the senior communicator estimated that each model was applied to communication programs for each of what he or she considered to be the three most important publics of the organization (the most frequent publics named were media, employees, community, customers, members of associations, government, and investors), (b) by the extent to which the senior executive interviewed believed that the dominant coalition (the most powerful members) of the organization preferred each model, (c) by the extent to which the senior communicator believed that the dominant coalition preferred each model, and (d) by the senior communicator's estimate of the extent to which the public relations department possessed several items of knowledge that were indicators of each model. In addition, indexes were constructed to measure the extent to which the system of internal communication in the organization was symmetrical or asymmetrical.

Factor analysis or analysis of the reliability of indexes, or both, were conducted to measure the models in each of these forms as well as the other concepts identified as characteristics of excellent public relations. A final factor analysis of all the variables associated with excellence in public relations then was conducted to determine whether all of them were correlated highly enough to produce a single index of excellence. The results of the factor analysis, which are shown in Table 1.1, did establish the presence of a single excellence factor. A complete explanation of these results and the measures that went into them is available in an *Initial Data Report and Practical Guide* (J. Grunig et al., 1991a) and in the

TABLE 1.1

Factor Analysis to Produce a Single Scale of Excellence in Public Relations

Variable	Communality	Excellence Factor
Senior executive variables		
Public relations in strategic planning	.08	.28
Support for public relations by dominant coalition	.17	.41
Value of public relations department	.11	.32
Importance of communication with external groups	.11	.34
Preference for two-way asymmetrical model	.15	.39
Preference for two-way symmetrical model	.11	.33
Preference for managerial role	.13	.36
Preference for communication liaison role	.12	.35
Senior public relations manager variables		
Public relations in strategic planning	.31	.56
Perceived support for public relations by dominant coalition	.32	.57
Estimate of the value that dominant coalition would assign to public relations	.33	.57
Estimate of preference for the two-way asymmetrical model by the dominant coalition	.23	.48
Estimate of preference for the two-way symmetrical model by the dominant coalition	.31	.55
Public relations head in manager role	.31	.56
Public relations head in communication liaison role	.24	.49
Knowledge of two-way asymmetrical model in public relations department	.41	.64
Knowledge of two-way symmetrical model in public relations department	.44	.67
Knowledge of managerial role in public relations department	.52	.72
Formal education in public relations	.02	.14
Characteristics of organizational excellence		
Participative culture	.06	.24
Symmetrical system of internal communication	.01	.19
Organic structure	.01	.12
Individual job satisfaction	.03	.16
Organizational job satisfaction	.04	.19
Treatment of women—employees	.05	.23
Treatment of women—senior executives	.10	.32
Treatment of women—senior public relations managers	.25	.50

NOTE: Percentage of variance explained = 19%. The factor analysis was performed using the principal axis method.

team's second book, *Manager's Guide to Excellence in Public Relations and Communication Management* (Dozier et al., 1995). In addition, the three authors of the second book are at work on a third and final book in this excellence series (L. Grunig, J. Grunig, & Dozier, in preparation) that will provide complete results of the study.

The factor loadings in Table 1.1 show that all of the measures of both the two-way symmetrical and two-way asymmetrical models had high loadings on the excellence factor (loadings are correlations with the overall factor). The measures of the extent to which the models were applied to individual communication programs were not included in this initial factor analysis because not all organizations named the same publics, and including these measures would have limited sample size. In fact, along with several measures of the managerial role of the senior communication manager, the knowledge of these three models and the estimates by the senior executive and senior communication manager of the dominant coalition's preference for them were the strongest indicators of excellence in public relations.

The measure of symmetrical internal communication did load positively on the excellence factor, although the loading was not as high as for the other indicators of the symmetrical model. When a two-factor solution was allowed, the employee variables produced a separate factor, and all of the indicators of excellence loaded highly (as predicted): .86 for symmetrical internal communication, .63 for organic structure, .62 for individual job satisfaction, .73 for organizational job satisfaction, and .69 for participative culture. At the same time, asymmetrical internal communication had a loading of −.48, mechanical structure had a loading of −.55, and authoritarian culture had a loading of −.46 on this factor.

These contextual variables might not have loaded so highly on a single factor because they were measured from the employee questionnaire, and few of the variables measured with data from employees loaded as highly on the excellence factor as did measures from the senior public relations manager and senior executive questionnaires. Note, for example, the lower loading of the index for treatment of women from the employee sample compared to the loadings from the senior executive and senior public relations manager.

In spite of these measurement difficulties, however, the variables related to the organizational context did not seem to explain the variables of public relations excellence as well as did

the other variables loading on the excellence factor. Organizational culture was the best predictor among the contextual variables, but it was the weakest of variables retained in the final index of excellence. Sriramesh, J. Grunig, and Dozier (1996) explored these relationships in depth and concluded that culture had a strong relationship only to the internal variables. Similarly, Deatherage and Hazleton (1998) constructed indexes of symmetrical and asymmetrical organizational worldviews and found only weak correlations with the practice of the models of public relations. However, their worldview scales consisted mostly of a number of items taken from our indexes of culture, structure, and internal communication. As a result, the measures of worldview seemed to be largely a composite of our contextual variables; therefore, their results were consistent with ours.

Those results follow the pattern identified by J. Grunig and L. Grunig (1992) when they reviewed a number of studies that attempted to explain which models organizations would practice based on contextual variables such as structure, size, technology, environment, culture, and power (what the dominant coalition chooses). Generally, these variables could not explain why organizations practice the models of public relations that they do, although culture and power seemed most promising. Dozier et al. (1995) concluded that the knowledge of the practitioners (which models they know how to practice) and shared understanding with senior management (agreement on which models to practice) were the two strongest predictors of models practiced. Culture provided a context for excellent public relations, but without a knowledgeable senior practitioner and supportive top management, culture could not produce an excellent model of public relations.

After the preliminary analysis of variables, the indexes of the press agentry and public information models did not correlate highly enough with the other indicators of excellence to be included in the final excellence factor. However, it is important to note that when these models were included in a preliminary factor analysis with three factors, they did not have high negative loadings on the excellence factor. The dominant coalition's preference for the press agentry model as indicated by the senior executive had a nonsignificant loading of .10 on a factor similar to the final excellence factor, and that preference as indicated by the senior communication manager was .12. The same loadings for the public information model were −.11 and .03, respectively.

Importantly, however, the knowledge needed to perform the press agentry and public information models loaded about as highly on the preliminary excellence factor (.63 and .71, respectively) as did the knowledge needed to perform the two-way symmetrical and asymmetrical models. In other words, excellent public relations departments seem to center their practice on the two-way symmetrical and asymmetrical models, but they also have the knowledge to perform the two one-way models. They do not seem to exclude those models from their practice. These results suggest that excellent public relations departments might engage in some form of two-way communication with publics, most likely by doing research, before using the mediated informational activities that are common in the press agentry and public information models.

For the final quantitative analysis of the four models, we correlated the indexes of the four models, measured in the questionnaire for the senior public relations manager, for communication programs intended for the seven most common publics of organizations. The results again showed a moderate to high correlation of both the two-way symmetrical and two-way asymmetrical models with the excellence factor as well as a nonsignificant correlation with the press agentry and public information models (Table 1.2).

The correlations of the two-way models with the excellence factor were lowest for the governmental public. We think that this is because government relations, especially lobbying, tends to be managed by lawyers or the CEO directly and because lobbyists and other public affairs specialists typically rely more on their contacts in government than on their knowledge of communication principles. Thus, governmental relations programs may be relatively autonomous from the rest of the public relations function and

"may march to a different drum than do other communication programs" (Dozier et al., 1995, p. 205).

We can summarize these quantitative results by saying that excellent public relations departments do indeed practice the two-way symmetrical model. Therefore, it is a positive model that actually is practiced rather than only a normative theoretical model. However, excellent departments are just as likely to practice the two-way asymmetrical model. Excellent public relations, in other words, seems to be based on the mixed-motive model. At the same time, excellent public relations departments do not exclude the press agentry and public information models from their repertoires of public relations activity. The best explanation is that their one-way communication activities often are preceded by research, that is, research that might be indirectly linked (in the minds of our respondents) to the informational activities. In fact, however, the typical activities of the press agentry and public information models may have a two-way and symmetrical base.

After completing the quantitative portion of the *Excellence* study, the research team conducted qualitative research to probe in greater depth 24 of the 321 organizations surveyed during the initial phase. The qualitative phase of the research was designed to help determine the economic value of excellent public relations departments to their organizations. A smaller number of less-than-excellent organizations were studied as well in an attempt to measure the cost of not having effective public relations. At the same time, the team members tried to fill in gaps of understanding left by the survey research. For the purposes of this chapter, the case studies provided additional evidence of the practice of a mixed-motive model of public relations.

Like the quantitative results, the results of the qualitative research firmly established that the two-way symmetrical approach to public relations is a positive or descriptive model as well as the normative or the ideal. One additional pattern that emerged from the 24 case studies was that the most excellent departments engaged in all four models more than did the less excellent departments. In other words, more excellent

TABLE 1.2

Correlations of the Excellence Factor With Models of Public Relations Used
in Specialized Communication Programs

Public for Communication Program	Percentage With Program	Model of Public Relations			
		Press Agentry	Public Information	Two-Way Asymmetrical	Two-Way Symmetrical
Media	93	−.12	−.11	.40	.35
Employees	67	.07	.02	.51	.48
Community	52	.03	−.08	.39	.34
Customers	36	−.01	−.02	.55	.45
Association members	21	−.10	−.08	.43	.47
Government	19	−.14	−.03	.23	.29
Investors	19	.10	.09	.55	.47

public relations programs seem to practice public relations more extensively than do less excellent programs, and extensive practice seems to combine all four models. It is not possible to provide complete evidence of these generalizations in this chapter, but complete details can be found in the *Phase 2* report of the study published by the IABC Research Foundation (L. Grunig, Dozier, & J. Grunig, 1994).

A NEW MODEL OF EXCELLENT TWO-WAY PUBLIC RELATIONS

Both the quantitative and qualitative results of the *Excellence* study suggested a new contingency model that includes both symmetrical and asymmetrical elements. Rather than placing the two-way asymmetrical model at one end of a continuum and the two-way symmetrical model at the other end, as J. Grunig and L. Grunig (1992) did, Dozer et al. (1995) introduced the model in Figure 1.1, which depicts either end of the continuum as asymmetrical. A public relations strategy at either end would favor the interests of either the organization or the public to the exclusion of the other. The middle of the contin-

uum contains a symmetrical win-win zone where organizations and publics can engage in mixed-motive communication.

With this new model of combined two-way public relations, the difference between the mixed-motive and two-way symmetrical models disappears. In fact, describing the symmetrical model as a mixed-motive game resolves the criticism that the symmetrical model forces the organization to sacrifice its interests for those of the public. Dozier et al. (1995) described the new model in this way (with comments inserted to relate to literature discussed in the present chapter):

In the model, organizations and publics are viewed as having separate and sometimes conflicting interests. Nevertheless, negotiation and collaboration make it possible for organizations and publics to find common ground, the win-win zone. The model suggests that a number of outcomes are possible within the win-win zone. Unsatisfactory and unstable relationships exist on either side of the win-win zone, with one party exploiting the other. To the left of the win-win zone, the organization's position dominates to the public's disadvantage. To the right, the public's position dominates to the organization's disadvantage.

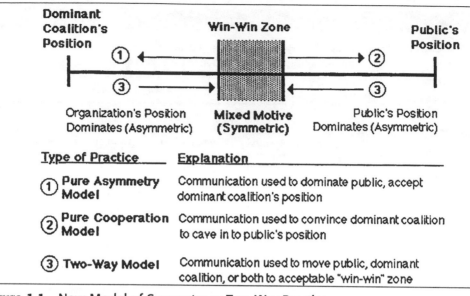

Figure 1.1. New Model of Symmetry as Two-Way Practices
SOURCE: Dozier, L. Grunig, and J. Grunig (1995).

Communication can be used to manipulate or persuade publics to accept the dominant coalition's position. This is indicated by Arrow 1 in Figure [1.1]. Instead of negotiating for a relationship in the win-win zone, communicators try to take advantage of publics. Such practices are the zero-sum or win-lose game played by communicators practicing pure two-way asymmetrical communication.

Communication can be used by publics to persuade the organization's dominant coalition to accept the public's position outside the win-win zone. When communicators in the organization try to help publics to do so, they use the pure cooperation model [which Murphy (1991) and Cancel et al. (1997) directly, and Van der Meiden (1993), indirectly, equated with the two-way symmetrical model]. This practice is indicated by Arrow 2 in Figure [1.1]. [As Van der Meiden (1993) pointed out,] dominant coalitions are unlikely to appreciate public relations practitioners who persuade the organization they work for to accept clearly undesirable positions that benefit publics at the expense of organizations. (pp. 48-49)

Dozier et al. (1995) concluded that Arrow 3 in Figure 1.1 represents the two-way symmetri-

cal model better. That is, communicators negotiate with both publics and dominant coalitions to reach an outcome or relationship in the win-win zone. In communicating with publics, public relations practitioners try to persuade publics to move toward their organizations' position. In communicating with dominant coalitions, they try to persuade dominant coalitions to move toward their publics' position. This new contingency model is an excellent two-way model of public relations that subsumes the former two-way symmetrical and asymmetrical models of public relations. Depending on the situation, asymmetrical tactics sometimes may be used to gain the best position for organizations within the win-win zone. Because such practices are bounded by a symmetrical worldview that respects the integrity of long-term relationships, the two-way model is essentially symmetrical.[4] Practically speaking, the two-way model also means treating dominant coalitions as another public influenced by communication programs.

This new model of excellent two-way public relations seems now to provide an ideal combination of a positive and a normative theory. Positively (descriptively), it provides a model of how excellent public relations departments balance the divided loyalties they encounter as they try to serve the interests of their client organizations and the interests of the publics to which they have a social responsibility. Normatively, the new model specifies the ideal public relations situation in which organizations strive to reach the win-win zone as they build relationships with their publics. The characteristics of a relationship in the win-win zone also can provide a criterion for evaluating the success of public relations. Also, the model provides suggestions for strategies that public relations practitioners can use when they find the relationship tipped toward one or the other end of the continuum.

We need to know much more about strategies that practitioners can and do use at different points on this continuum. Plowman (1995, 1998) searched the literature on conflict resolution looking for strategies that could be applied in public relations. Then, he conducted case studies of 10 organizations, 6 of which also were participants in the qualitative portion of the *Excellence* study. Plowman found that all of the organizations used one or more strategies of resolving conflict that he identified in the literature or from an analysis of his results.

At the organizational-asymmetrical end of the continuum in Figure 1.1, Plowman (1995, 1998) found that public relations practitioners used the strategies of *contending* and *avoiding*. At the public-asymmetrical end of the continuum, practitioners used strategies of *accommodating* and *compromising*. Within the normatively ideal win-win zone, organizations used the strategies of *cooperating, being unconditionally constructive* (Fisher & Brown, 1988), and *win-win or no deal* (Covey, 1989). Plowman (1995) summarized the results of his study as follows:

> Note the absence of the terms asymmetrical and symmetrical. That is because the definition of mixed motives is a combination of asymmetric and symmetric communications. This model deals with degrees of each over the entire spectrum of asymmetric and symmetric communication. The only way to represent two ends on either side of the model would be to represent the one-way models of press agentry and public information. The two-way models would not quite extend

to the one-way model ends. Two-way symmetrical communication is not entirely win-win. It can include elements of compromise, accommodation, and even avoidance since part of avoidance is unconditionally constructive or win-win or no deal. Likewise, two-way asymmetrical is not entirely contending but can include elements of all the other negotiation tactics. Remember, mixed motives still looks after the best interests of the organization itself. It is an enlightened self-interest stating that what is best for itself is best for its public, too. (p. 260)

FUTURE RESEARCH ON PUBLIC RELATIONS STRATEGIES

It's All in the Name

My purpose in writing this chapter has been to provide an update to the previous reviews of research on the models of public relations (J. Grunig & L. Grunig, 1989, 1992) and also to address the numerous criticisms and misinterpretations of the models and of the symmetrical theory of public relations that have appeared in the literature. In retrospect, much of the criticism of the symmetrical theory seems to have arisen from the name itself. To many, the term *symmetrical* has suggested concepts such as equilibrium (not *partial equilibrium* and *moving equilibrium,* the terms I used in J. Grunig, 1989), social harmony, equality, mutual goodwill, and/or ideal communication situations. Obviously, these concepts suggest a utopian society and an overly idealistic vision for public relations.

The essence of a theory is the idea—the meaning—in the mind of the theorist. The successful theorist, however, must be able to explain his or her idea in a way that allows others to reconstruct a similar idea in their own minds. The misinterpretations of my idea cited in this chapter suggest that I have not always been successful in conveying the idea behind the term *symmetry.* As I said at the beginning of this chapter, my original choice of a name for the model of public relations was *diachronic,* but when I learned that that term related more to time than to process, I dropped it in favor of the term *symmetry.* The basic idea was that public relations should go beyond the advocacy of self-interest without concern for the impact of an organization's behavior on others to a *balance* between self-interest and concern for the interests of others.

What I failed to convey in choosing *symmetry* and *balance* as descriptors was that symmetrical public relations refers more to a process than to an outcome. That is why I used the term *moving equilibrium* in J. Grunig (1989a) rather than *equilibrium, social harmony,* or *consensus.* Spicer (1997) explained the difference well when he said that the symmetrical model is "often discussed in terms of consensus. My reading and thinking, though, have moved me beyond the relative notion of consensus as an end-product to the more process-oriented experience of collaboration" (p. 202).

Balancing self-interest with the interests of others is a give-and-take process that can waver between advocacy and collaboration or what Spicer (1997) called *collaborative advocacy* and Raiffa (1982) called *cooperative antagonism* (see our application of this term in Dozier et al., 1995, p. 97). Heath (1998b) described the process in this way: "Enactment assumes that symmetry and asymmetry are more a matter of the dynamics between parties than something that either thinks, does, or says independent of the other" (p. 17).

Therefore, symmetry might not have been the best choice of name for the model of public relations I had in mind, but unfortunately, it probably is too late to change the name. Mixed motives, collaborative advocacy, and cooperative antagonism all have the same meaning as does symmetry. Symmetry means that communicators keep their eyes on a broader professional perspective of balancing private and public interests. Their job consists of more than argumentation or "a wrangle in the marketplace." They must listen as well as argue. This does not mean, however, that they do not argue or attempt to persuade. Rather, they must consistently remind themselves and management that they might not be right and, indeed, that their organizations might be better off if they listen to others.

Recently, my research has moved toward the development and maintenance of relationships as the central goal of public relations (J. Grunig & Huang, 2000). The literature on interpersonal relationships has been enormously helpful in conceptualizing the characteristics of a good relationship as well as the strategies that are most effective in maintaining these relationships (e.g., Canary & Stafford, 1994). Therefore, instead of placing public relations strategies into one of the "four boxes" (Cancel et al., 1997, p. 32) described by the models of public relations, we can begin to think of dimensions or strategies that underlie the models.

The relationship literature suggests what might be the best term to describe what I have long had in mind when I talked of symmetrical public relations. Baxter (1994) applied the theory of dialogism developed by the Russian scholar Bakhtin, who "produced the majority of his work during the 1920s and 1930s in the Soviet Union" (p. 234).

According to Baxter (1994),

> The "dialogue" is the centerpiece of dialogism. To Bakhtin, the essential quality of a dialogue was its simultaneous fusion or unity of multiple voices at the same time that each voice retained its differentiated uniqueness. This dynamic tension between fusion-with and differentiation-from the Other served for Bakhtin (1981, p. 272) as a general metaphor for all social processes. (pp. 234-235)

Simultaneous fusion with the Other while retaining the uniqueness of one's self-interest seems to describe well the challenge of symmetrical public relations—or, perhaps we should begin to say, dialogical public relations.

From Models to Dimensions of Public Relations Behavior

The four models of public relations began as a vague general idea that has stimulated a great deal of attention and positive descriptive research on how public relations is practiced in many types of organizations and in many countries. The two-way symmetrical model also has focused attention on ideas of how to build a normative model of ethical and socially responsible public relations. As a result, the models have served a valuable function for the public relations discipline.

Now, however, it is time to move on from the four (or more) models of public relations to develop a comprehensive theory that goes beyond the typology represented by the four models. Typologies are a useful way in which to begin the development of a theory, but for science and scholarship to progress, we need to move beyond typologies to theories composed of continuous rather than discrete variables.

I believe that my colleagues and I moved toward such a theory in developing the new two-way model of excellent, or dialogical, public relations. To further develop this model, we have isolated four underlying variables that define the models. We can call these variables maintenance strategies used in public relations practice. The first set of these variables is *symmetry* and *asymmetry* or the extent to which collaboration and advocacy describe public relations strategy or behavior.

The second set of variables includes the extent to which public relations is *one-way* or *two-way.* These variables were part of my original conceptualization of the models (J. Grunig, 1984). In addition, results from the *Excellence* study suggested that direction of communication should be measured separately from symmetry and asymmetry. Three of the four indicators of the two-way asymmetrical model measured the extent to which organizations used asymmetrical forms of research in their public relations practice. These research-based variables were the most reliable of the four indicators. The fourth indicator, which simply stated that the purpose of public relations was to persuade publics to behave as the organization wanted them to behave, did not correlate as highly with the index as did the other variables.

Therefore, those results suggested that the strong showing of the asymmetrical model in the excellence factor might have resulted more from use of the research activities measured by the index than from the asymmetrical nature of that research. In other words, respondents might not have been able to distinguish asymmetrical research from symmetrical research or research in general.

The third set of variables is the use of *mediated and interpersonal forms of communication.* This dimension also was suggested by the results of the *Excellence* study, which showed that excellent public relations departments do not seem to avoid the press agentry or public information models and, in fact, that the most excellent communication functions seem to practice all forms of public relations more extensively than do the less excellent functions.

In addition, J. Grunig et al. (1995) identified what they described as a personal influence model of public relations in India, Taiwan, and the United States. This model is common in lobbying and in media relations where public relations practitioners use interpersonal relationships and connections to facilitate communication. In their research, J. Grunig et al. found that these interpersonal connections usually were asymmetrical and manipulative, but they concluded that these personal relationships could be symmetrical just as easily as they could be asymmetrical. Thus, the discovery of the new model of personal influence also can be interpreted as the realization that an essential element underlying the original four models was the distinction between interpersonal and mediated forms of communication.

The fourth dimension is the extent to which public relations practice is *ethical.* We generally have said that the symmetrical model is inherently ethical and that the other models can be ethical, depending on the rules used to ensure ethical practice (J. Grunig & White, 1992; J. Grunig & L. Grunig, 1996).

Three students at the University of Maryland already have used these four dimensions of public relations behavior in dissertation and thesis research. Huang (1997) developed measures of the four dimensions and used them in a study of the relationships between public relations practitioners in the executive branch of the Taiwanese government and elected members of the legislative branch and their staff members. Huang found that, of the four dimensions, symmetrical communication and ethical communication (which actually came out together on one factor in a factor analysis) correlated most strongly with the relationship indicators of control mutuality and trust.

Sha (1999) used the four dimensions to study the public relations behaviors of an activist group, the Democratic Progressive Party, on Taiwan. She found that the organization "engaged in behaviors that were ethical, two-way, symmetrical, mediated, and interpersonal" (p. 266). However, when it communicated internally with members of the party,

> the organization was less ethical and symmetrical, and it used more one-way communication than it did when communicating with the average citizen—[resulting] from the needs of the party to attract electoral votes [from average citizens] and to maintain internal discipline [among party members]. (pp. 266-267)

Finally, Rhee (1999) replicated major portions of the *Excellence* study in Korea, using the measures of these four dimensions rather than the original measures of the four models. An index of excellence produced in Rhee's study was identical to the index from the original study with the new dimensions added. Excellent public relations was both symmetrical and asymmetrical, two-way, ethical, and both mediated and interpersonal. The one-way and two-way variables fit into a single scale—a single continuum. Symmetrical and asymmetrical practices did not fit into a single scale, however, showing that they are not mutually exclusive.

The latter finding again supports the notion that asymmetry and symmetry (or advocacy and collaboration) work in tandem in excellent public relations. Therefore, we now seem to have a much better developed theory of symmetrical (dialogic, collaborative advocacy) public relations that should serve well as a model for research, teaching, and practice of public relations during the 21st century.

NOTES

1. Some explanation is necessary here to clarify my use of the terms *theory* and *model* throughout this chapter. I use *model* to mean a simplified representation of reality (J. Grunig & L. Grunig, 1992, p. 286), in this case to refer to simplified representations of how practitioners think about and practice public relations. I use *theory* in accord with the semantic conception of theories (Suppe, 1977, pp. 221-230). The semantic conception of theories means that a theory is the abstract meaning, or the idea, in a scientist's mind. The scientist can express this theory only through different types of representations such as through words, diagrams, mathematical equations, and other types of models. Therefore, the models of public relations are representations that I use as part of an underlying public relations theory that links the models to other variables such as organizational structure, environments, culture, and power. As the underlying theory (my thinking) has developed, however, I have begun to see the symmetrical model in broader terms. It has become a theory that goes beyond the description of one type of practice to a broader normative theory of how public relations should be practiced.

2. For a discussion of the ethics of symmetrical and asymmetrical approaches, see J. Grunig and L. Grunig (1996).

3. As Suppe (1977) put it, a good theory always is underdetermined by data: "Examination of successful, illuminating products of science throughout its history reveals one pervasive characteristic—the most impressive achievements of science are the ones which are underdetermined by the available data. Characteristic of science is the acceptance and rejection of comprehensive theories on the basis of available data which, in principle, are insufficient to establish either the truth or falsity of these theories" (pp. 17-18).

4. See also J. Grunig (1994) for a discussion of evidence that an asymmetrical worldview has pervaded the thinking of public relations practitioners throughout history.

CHAPTER 2

A Rhetorical Enactment Rationale for Public Relations

The Good Organization Communicating Well

ROBERT L. HEATH

This handbook exemplifies the rhetorical heritage—the rationale for suasive discourse. In these pages, many rhetors have their say on theory, research, and practice to shape the future of public relations. Each statement is a counterstatement to another position. Each advocate realizes that he or she can suffer the pains of defending against or accepting counterstatements.

This book champions humans' commitment to rhetorical dialogue as the process for forging conclusions and influencing actions. The process is a two-way one. Through statement and counterstatement, people test each other's views of reality, value, and choices relevant to products, services, and public policies. Not absolute, but rather relative, knowledge constitutes the concurrence that people need to coordinate their activities.

Public relations research and theory search for sound epistemological, axiological, and ontological foundations with which to inform, critique, and guide the practice. Such theory focuses attention on knowledge-generating and value-laden communication processes as well as on the shared meaning that results from them.

Shared meaning, a vital outcome of public relations, results when each market, audience, or public that has a stake in some matter co-creates meaning through dialogue. By refining its theory, public relations can serve society by adding to organizations' bottom lines while fostering the lives of persons who have mutually beneficial interests at stake.

This chapter reasons that rhetorical enactment theory can meet epistemological, axiological, and ontological requirements needed to demonstrate how public relations should operate to add value to clients as well as to society. A rhetorical enactment rationale fits comfortably with social scientific methods and assumptions that are used to explain the processes of communication and community building. A rhetorical approach to the discipline gives insights into the social importance of the meaning that public relations practitioners help to shape in their efforts to assist the building of society—of community.

The term *rhetoric* arouses pejorative connotations such as vacuousness, manipulativeness, pandering, and "mere." Critics who are ignorant of the rhetorical tradition suggest that they have discovered these flaws, not realizing that those issues extend back at least to the 5th century B.C., the era of Plato, who voiced complaints against rhetoric. Rhetoric can be vacuous but may express ideas that shape society and address human interests. Rhetoric can manipulate until other voices uncover this manipulation and turn minds against it. Rhetoric can pander by telling people what they want to hear. On the other hand, it can challenge pandering and forewarn persons to watch for that manipulative technique. For these reasons, rhetoric never is "mere."

Unlike systems theory, rhetoric does not assume a benign view of how people interpret data and make product, service, or public policy decisions. It recognizes that advocacy is a necessary part of the process of co-creating meaning. It deals with process and content (meaning). It gives voice to participants who have self-interested and altruistic reasons to engage in dialogue about facts (epistemology); evaluations (axiology); and policy, product, and service choices (ontology). It realizes that choices are contestable.

This rationale for public relations adds depth to the issue of symmetry, which in social scientific terms tends to be limited to listening respectfully to others' views and concerns. Rhetoric recognizes that symmetry ultimately is a matter of the strength of each idea contested in public. A rhetorical enactment view of public relations acknowledges that all of what each organization—as well as all of what each market, audience, and public—does and says becomes meaningful because of interpretations that people place on those actions and statements. Rhetoric views thoughtful dialogue, rather than the transfer or transmission of information, as the essence of symmetry.

The rhetorical tradition champions the cognitive role of propositions and, with the assistance of Burke (1966, 1969a), realizes that words have propositional value. The tradition assumes that propositions clash in ways that help to inform judgments and actions, clarify and order the evaluative (value) dimensions of thought and choice, and justify or deny the expedient wisdom of competing policies. Defending that process, Lentz (1996) reasoned, "Truth should prevail in a market-like struggle where superior ideas vanquish their inferiors and achieve audience acceptance" (p. 1). Rhetoric is ethical because it empowers participants to engage in dialogue (private or public).

Some scholars accept the humanistic side of rhetoric while dismissing or vilifying persuasion—especially what can be called scientific persuasion. Rhetoric is the art of persuasion—suasive discourse (see also L'Etang, 1996b). The art is committed to knowing which propositions an audience should and will accept and reject. It acknowledges—a crucial point—that, individually and collectively, people respond mentally and publicly to the propositions asserted by other voices.

Statement and counterstatement—dialogue—constitute the process and shape the content of rhetoric. It is a means for seeking truth, knowledge, good reasons, sound choices, and wise policies. It is ethical because individuals use dialogue to define and advance their interests within the limits of others' opinions about those matters.

Rhetoric cannot sustain itself with hollow words spoken or written by persons who have no commitment to truth and no desire to help key publics to make informed and ethical decisions. Organizations (especially companies with ostensible "deep pockets") that attempt to use rhetoric to control and manipulate the opinions of key stakeholders and stakeseekers suffer public exposure of their tactics as well as the flaws in the content they espouse. L'Etang (1996b) noted that persuaders suffer the knowledge that their arguments might have weaknesses.

The First Amendment to the U.S. Constitution springs from the rhetorical tradition. It affirms the right of individuals to not have their freedom of speech abridged or their right to assemble to petition government to redress their grievances. This amendment places faith in people to be able to make thoughtful judgments and draw sound conclusions from what they hear, see, and read. It privileges people and organizations to speak because people—markets, audiences, and publics—have the right to receive and consider information and arguments. Humans do not live by information acquisition and transfer alone; they use contentious, interpretive, judgmental, and opinion-forming discourse to critically judge the information available to them.

Exploring these themes, this chapter reviews classic and contemporary works on rhetoric, a tradition devoted to understanding how society is helped through open and vigorous contest of ideas. The review features classical Greek and Roman thinkers as well as Kenneth Burke, who raised awareness of the power of words and the meanings they have for the events in our lives (Heath, 1986). This legacy substantiates the belief that society is made better when articulate persons (individual or corporate) espouse opinions and supply evidence for others to examine. Opinion and actions, in the long run, fail if they are not well expressed by persons (individual or corporate) who exhibit high ethical standards.

This chapter features a rhetorical enactment view of public relations that draws on epistemological issues of relativism, axiological issues of corporate responsibility, and the ontology of choice. It explains how public relations helps to establish marketplace and public policy zones of meaning. The analysis evaluates the rhetorical perspective to see whether it squares with molar concepts and meets ethical criteria vital to the practice of public relations. Rhetoric helps us to understand how ideas pose rhetorical exigencies that require responses by public relations practitioners who strive to create meanings that justify norms and build relationships vital to society.

RHETORICAL CONTEXT FOR PUBLIC RELATIONS

This section explores rhetorical aspects of the context that gives rise to the practice of public relations that is normatively preferred as two-way symmetrical communication. Public relations is called to action when an organization's routine activities fail to produce the desired results. One need is the co-creation of ideas through public contest. Society and organizations need shared meaning to operate. Large organizations (governmental, for-profit, and nonprofit) play a vital role in the formation of opinion in society. Individual and collective voices respond to those of organizations. This dialogue forms the rationale for public relations discourse along with the ethical problems associated with the potential dominance of corporate voices.

Market and public policy forces give individuals and corporate entities an incentive to communicate. Sometimes these forces clash; often they join in complex ways to solve individual and societal problems. Public relations helps organizations to obtain and prudently manage financial and human resources. It helps them to strategically adapt to market and public policy positions by solving problems that frustrate the development of mutually beneficial relationships.

Building such relationships is fraught with rhetorical problems. Rhetorical problems arise from needs or problems that can be solved by strategically meaningful actions and discourse (Bitzer, 1968). Each of the following needs constitutes a typical rhetorical problem for public relations.

- Need to increase or decrease awareness of an organization, a problem, an issue, a product, a service, an issue advocate, an action, a fact (information), a value, a policy, and so forth
- Need for understanding or agreement on the part of an organization, stakeholders, or stakeseekers regarding a fact (information), a value premise, or a policy position
- Need to build, repair, or maintain mutually beneficial and satisfying relationships
- Need to create, sustain, repair, or apply identification
- Need to create, repair, and maintain a clear and coherent persona (voice) for the organization

■ Need to understand and implement appropriate standards of social responsibility

■ Need to accept stewardship by taking issue stands

These needs can be conceptualized in coorientational terms—understanding (agreement), accuracy, and satisfaction (Broom, 1977; Broom & Dozier, 1990). Needs can be conceptualized as resulting from perspectives that also are counterperspectives (Heath, 1992b). Perspectives center on choices that yield to rhetorical dialogue, the dispute or contest of preferable choices.

Needs become focal points for relationship building. Marketplace relationships foster the exchange of stakes of financial value. Public policy relationships foster the exchange of stakes of policy value. Community relationships foster the exchange of stakes of mutual support, regard and welcome for each entity that adds value (financial and moral) to a community.

Strategic responses required by these needs might not be satisfied if we limit the definition of public relations to the management of communication. According to systems theory, one entity—public relations personnel—manages the flow of information between it and one or more publics. That definition appears to privilege the organization that empowers itself to define its publics and the conditions under which it interacts with them (Leitch & Neilson, 1997).

A systems approach to the management of communication says nothing about the co-definition of that information or the purpose to which its management is aimed. As Motion (1997) argued, the information management orientation might ignore the centrality of discourse. She preferred to feature public relations "as primarily concerned with the creation and maintenance of relationships and the production, exchange, and negotiation of meanings" (p. 2).

Motion (1997) and others move beyond the minimalism of information flow to address the content, process, and purpose of meaning formation. Leitch and Neilson (1997), for example, suggested that public relations is concerned

about different forms of communication as well as "power, strategy, objectives, and the manifold ways each articulates and overdetermines, constructs and deconstructs, organises and disorganises, the other" (p. 26). Thus, we might at least feature public relations as the co-management of meaning and, by extrapolation, as the co-management of cultures. A rhetorical enactment perspective offers principles and theoretical connections to supply the foundation for co-management, co-definition, and co-creation.

Communication is inherently two-way interaction (Heath & Bryant, 1992, esp. chap. 2). Since its dawning in the age of ancient Greece, the rhetorical perspective has acknowledged that discourse is a two-way process. Statement and counterstatement assume at least two participants: advocate and counteradvocate. Reactions to any statement—concurrence or rejection—occur whether it is voiced or not. Simply put, publics, markets, and audiences interact with any communicator even if they do nothing more than ignore or reject its message.

Symmetry can be viewed as a normative challenge (J. Grunig, 1992a). A rhetorical enactment explanation of public relations offers powerful insight into the normative challenge of symmetry. Symmetry can become distorted if an ethical balance is imposed onto the process rather than emerging from the relative strength of positions that are contested. Thus, one approach to symmetry can be that "outsiders" define it by focusing on the quality of communication process. A rhetorical enactment perspective assumes that symmetry is a dynamic of each situation contested by the participants and predicated on the quality of discourse, the ideas that are contested, and the ability of participants to achieve mutually satisfactory outcomes.

A rhetorical perspective views symmetry as the heart of the process as well as its outcome based on epistemological, axiological, and ontological assumptions. First, a rhetorical perspective presumes that some ideas, and therefore some advocates, are superior to others by being more veridical (epistemic) (Scott, 1976). Second, some ideas champion or reflect a superior evaluative perspective (axiology) than do their counterparts (Wallace, 1963; Weaver, 1953, 1970). Third, some ideas recommend a superior set of action choices (ontology), a preferred set of identifications and attitudes (choices regarding the purchase of products, support of candidates, or public policy preferences) (Burke, 1969b). Rhetorical symmetry assumes that advocates are equal until their ideas are tested. Then, superior ideas defeat bad ones (Lentz, 1996).

A rhetorical view presumes that, in terms of their right to speak, all parties are symmetrical. Ostensibly powerful organizations might attempt to use their deep pockets to marginalize their opponents. They might even take the rhetorical stance that their opponents' arguments fail to advance the best interests of the community. Such use of the hegemony of community predisposes the rhetorical clash over its definition, which can play to the advantage of one side or another (Brummett, 1995). For example, in the tobacco wars, anti-smoking advocates had been substantially less privileged— marginalized—until the past few years. Tobacco companies argued that the spirit of community should restrain anti-smoking advocates. Tobacco advocates contended that critics should not oppose the sale of tobacco because it supports millions of people such as farmers, manufacturers, laborers, advertisers, distributors, and even public relations professionals. Those advocates challenged any attack as being contrary to the good of the community. They reasoned that smokers should not be denied access to legal products and that persons who smoke are adults, well warned of any hazards of their actions, and so are responsible for their choices. To infringe on such liberty and the economic good of the community is damaging, they reasoned.

That dialogue moved to new levels when anti-smoking advocates privileged their arguments in the name of community. Anti-smoking advocates couched their arguments in the community interests, interpreted as health, safety, honesty, truth, and economic policy of reduced medical costs. They seem to have prevailed by generating data that are interpreted in terms of smoking-related health consequences (episte-

mology). If a product is bad for health (axiology), then it is subject to regulatory and legislative constraints regarding preferred actions (ontology).

Through dialogue, participants co-create or co-define meaning by the rhetorical processes of statement and counterstatement. One side wins because its arguments are more compelling. This view of symmetry assumes an equality of right to speak but does not presume that all points of view are equal in rhetorical potency. Through persuasion and counterpersuasion, some ideas win and others lose even when parties eventually achieve mutually satisfying decisions.

Activism is a fight for rhetorical symmetry because some publics (individuals or groups) feel alienation (Cheney, 1992), strains (Smelser, 1963; Toch, 1965), and other incentives to resist a hegemony of community that denies the virtue of partisan statements (Brummett, 1995). Motivated by these feelings, "they may offer defensive responses to system encroachment or the colonization of the lifeworld," or they may take actions against the organization (Leitch & Neilson, 1997, p. 24). If no differences exist, then one has less reason to employ public relations. Rhetoric is useful insofar as there are needs and disputes. The best evidence of this is the absence of any discussion of rhetoric in More's (1965) "Utopia." In a utopia, people have what they need and have no reason for dispute—rhetoric or public relations.

Thus, public relations, as a discipline, seeks to advance marketplace and public policy discourse by pursuing relational excellence in actions (organizational responsibility) and discourse that lead to the co-creation, co-management, or co-definition of meaning (zones of meaning) that reconcile strains and alienation and foster mutually beneficial relationships (Heath, 1994, 1997). Public relations and issues management professionals can advance this process through publicity, promotion, public debate, and collaborative decision making. These techniques include thoughtful listening and well-formulated propositions founded on facts and good reasons. Discourse must withstand high standards of knowledge, value, and expedience because wise advocates know that they will be tested by the dialogue in the marketplace and public policy arena.

To extend this point of view, the next subsection examines various definitions of public relations.

Defining Public Relations: A Rhetorical Challenge

Definitions of public relations focus on the form, privilege, and product of discourse. According to the Public Relations Society of America's (1997/1998) "Official Statement on Public Relations,"

> Public relations helps our complex, pluralistic society to reach decisions and function more effectively by contributing to mutual understanding among groups and institutions. It serves to bring private and public policies into harmony.... To achieve their goals, these institutions must develop effective relationships with many different audiences or publics such as employees, members, customers, local communities, shareholders, and other institutions, and with society at large. (p. 2)

This statement proposes that public relations can co-manage meaning and culture to build mutual understanding and harmonious relationships.

Relevant to this view, Cutlip, Center, and Broom (1994) defined public relations as "the management function that establishes and maintains mutually beneficial relationships between an organization and publics on whom its success or failure depends" (p. 6). Public policy discourse leads to these ends. Thus, Cutlip (1994) observed, "Only through the expertise of public relations can causes, industries, individuals, and institutions make their voice heard in the public forum where thousands of shrill, competing voices daily re-create the Tower of Babel" (p. ix). Through dialogue, individuals and groups co-create and negotiate identity, interest, and meaning (Mead, 1934). As a management

function, public relations includes planning, research, collaborative decision making, public communication, promotion, and publicity to foster an organization's ability to strategically listen to, appreciate, and respond to those persons and groups whose mutually beneficial relationships it needs to achieve its mission and vision.

A partner to public relations, issues management entails the management of organizational and community resources through the public policy process to advance organizational interests and rights by striking a mutual balance with those of stakeholders and stakeseekers. It supports strategic business planning and management by understanding public policy and communicates to foster understanding, accuracy, and satisfaction as well as to minimize conflict. It adapts products, services, or operations to public policy and seeks to change policy to support products, services, or operations. It recommends strategic planning options that may change operations, products, or services as well as communicate to establish mutual interests and achieve harmony with stakeholders. It scans, identifies, tracks, monitors, and analyzes issues to determine which strategic planning, ethical, and communication options meet the challenges facing the organization. It keeps the firm ethically attuned to its community and positioned to exploit, mitigate, and foster public policy changes as they relate to the corporate mission (Heath, 1997).

Viewed in this way, public relations is the management function that rhetorically adapts organizations to people's interests and people's interests to organizations by co-creating meaning and co-managing cultures to achieve mutually beneficial relationships.

The Rhetorical Tradition: The Good Persons Speaking Well

To add depth to the rationale for public relations, this subsection draws on the rhetorical tradition. Given its 2,400-year heritage, some consider rhetoric to be the queen (or lady or dame

[Brummett, 1995; L'Etang, 1996b]) of communication studies. Campbell (1996) championed rhetoric as "the study of what is persuasive. The issues it examines are social truths, addressed to others, justified by reasons that reflect cultural values. It is a humanistic study that examines all the symbolic means by which influence occurs" (p. 8). The perplexing heritage of rhetoric was eloquently posed in a rhetorical question by Burke (1946): "How can a world with rhetoric stay decent, how can a world without it exist at all?" The heritage of rhetoric was framed by Kennedy (1963): "In its origin and intention, rhetoric was natural and good; it produced clarity, vigor, and beauty, and it rose logically from the conditions and qualities of the classical mind" (p. 3).

The fear of those who oppose or hold reservations about a rhetorical rationale for public relations is that rhetoric is manipulative or vacuous or both. The heritage of rhetoric has struggled with that paradox. The paradox focuses attention on the fact that humans disagree. When they do, they engage in discourse to persuade one another to agree and cooperate.

That discourse is subject to public scrutiny, at least by those who are its target. Only those propositions that are justifiable and ethical can sustain themselves against the scrutiny of counter-rhetoric. On this point, Quintilian (1951), a scholar of rhetoric in ancient Rome, was firm: "My ideal orator, then, is the true philosopher, sound in morals and with full knowledge of speaking, always striving for the highest" (p. 20). He continued, "If a case is based on injustice, neither a good man [or woman] nor rhetoric has any place in it" (p. 106).

The rationale of rhetoric is to seek the highest standards in the form, substance, privilege, and product of discourse. It must excel to guide people's efforts to gain adherence for views and actions through disputed analysis of ideas, facts, value perspectives, and policies. Especially relevant to the use of rhetoric to support public relations, Heath (1992b) warned,

> If irresponsible and empty communication becomes the norm, audiences become skeptical. They come to doubt the value of using words to solve problems and to create a reasonable society. Slick and facile discourse cannot displace insightful, well-informed statements without harming a society that assumes that thoughts and policies should be shaped through informed discussion. (p. 33)

Rather than a flaw in society, rhetoric is necessary for individuals' attempts to reconcile differences and to create compatible and complementary zones of meaning that suffice their need for coordinated actions. It explains how individuals come to know and understand one another as well as how they refine and shape their thoughts and preferences.

Despite Kennedy's (1963) sense of ancient Greeks' love for public discourse logically crafted and eloquently presented, Plato (1952) cautioned that "rhetoric is not an art at all, but the habit of a bold and ready wit, which knows how to manage mankind; this habit I sum up under the word 'flattery'" (p. 262). This assessment of rhetoric, which also is voiced today, extends to public relations if it is vacuous, manipulative spin doctoring. To support socially responsible ends, public relations must put into play the best information evaluated by the most ethical observations in support of mutually beneficial choices.

Responding to Plato's (1952) challenge, Aristotle (1952b) defended rhetoric as "the counterpart of dialectic" (p. 593). Dialectic was devoted to the discovery of sound ideas. Rhetoric was used to form, assert, and dispute ideas in public forums to achieve socially relevant ends. As Aristotle viewed this relationship between the discovery and exposition of ideas, he concluded that rhetoric is "the faculty of observing in any given case the available means of persuasion" (p. 595). The essence of persuasion is demonstration given that "we are most fully persuaded when we consider a thing to have been demonstrated" (p. 594).

With rhetoric, people make collective decisions and form policy for the public good. In the opinion of Aristotle (1952a), "If all communities aim at some good, the state or political community, which is the highest of all and which embraces all the rest, aims at good in a greater degree than [do] any others, and at the highest good" (p. 445). Thus, rhetoric is judged by the quality of the process and its outcomes: "A man [or woman] can confer the greatest of benefits by a right use of these [techniques] and inflict the greatest of injuries by using them wrongly" (Aristotle, 1952b, p. 594).

Classical thinkers knew that rhetoric can be used unethically. For that reason, they called for stewardship—acting responsibly in the public interest. The public interest is the foundation of social power. Power grows from community standards that privilege choices in discourse form, content, and outcome (Barnes, 1988).

Power originates from definitions of privilege that empower some groups and marginalize others. As Leitch and Neilson (1997) observed, public relations theorists tend to think of publics from the vantage point of each organization. In this sense, a public is something that the organization recognizes and to which it responds largely on its own terms. A truly symmetrical approach presumes that publics develop personae that they enact. "Thus publics are made up of intersecting, overlapping, and changing sets of individuals" (p. 22). Each public shares an identity and social reality—a zone of meaning. Through dialogue, publics and the views they espouse are "constructed and reconstructed through an ongoing process of discursive struggle" (p. 24).

Because it intersects other choices, power calls for stewardship in mutual benefit of those who have an interest in the resolving differences and making important choices. Like Aristotle, Isocrates (1929) observed that rhetoric was the responsibility of each citizen

> because there has been implanted in us the power to persuade each other and to make clear to each other whatever we desire, not only have we escaped the life of wild beasts, but we have come together and founded cities and made laws and invented arts; and generally speaking, there is no institution devised by man which the power of speech has not helped us to establish. For this it is which has laid down laws concerning things just

and unjust, and things honourable and base; and if it were not for these ordinances, we should not be able to live with one another. It is by this also that we confute the bad and extol the good. (p. 327)

The key to discourse is not its nature alone but also its role in society. Sham and deceit may occur in the substance and strategies used by rhetors, but time will reveal those devices (Isocrates, 1929). Quintilian (1951) considered social values to be an implicit or explicit part of each statement: "If a case is based on injustice, neither a good man nor rhetoric has any place in it" (p. 106). The quality of discourse is inseparable from the character of the person who chooses the side of an issue as well as the form and substance with which to address it. For the ancients, rhetoric took vitality not from what could be said to win some point of view but rather from how public dialogue could make society better by assisting the people to make sound choices.

In modern times, the rhetor is likely to be a spokesperson for an organization, but the rationale of rhetoric is the same. As Cheney and Dionisopolous (1989) observed, "Corporate communication (in practice and in theory) is fundamentally rhetorical and symbolic in responding to and in exercising power (in public discourse) and in shaping various identities (corporate and individual)" (p. 140). Such discourse can shape the symbolic boundaries of the organization, help define its image, and inject its views into public dialogue.

What, according to Aristotle (1952b), is the source of persuasiveness? "A statement is persuasive and credible either because it is directly self-evident or because it appears to be proved from other statements that are so" (p. 596). Aristotle believed that "persuasion is achieved by the speaker's personal character when the speech is so spoken as to make us think him [or her] credible. We believe good men [and women] more fully and more readily than other[s]" (p. 595).

Whether a person or an organization, character is central to the rhetorical process because outcomes have consequences. For Aristotle (1952b), rhetoric served to give counsel "on matters about which people deliberate; matters, namely, that ultimately depend on ourselves and which we have it in our power to set going" (p. 599). What do people rely on as they draw conclusions of that sort? According to Aristotle, "good sense, good moral character, and goodwill" (p. 623). Like other rhetoricians, Aristotle thought that bad character undoes persuasion:

> False statements and bad advice are due to one or more of the following three causes. Men [or women] either form a false opinion through want of good sense; or they form a true opinion but because of their moral badness do not say what they really think; or finally, they are both sensible and upright but not well disposed to their hearers, and [they] may fail in consequence to recommend what they know to be the best course. (p. 623)

To what ends are statements designed? Booth (1981) asked even more of Aristotle, believing that his rhetoric

> does not itself teach us what ends it should serve; it is still an art without essential restraints other than those provided by the counter rhetoric created by other warriors or competitors. The world it builds, left on its own, is a world of a free market of atomized persons and ideas, each privately seeking victory and hoping that in the melee a public good will be produced by some invisible hand. (pp. 32-33)

In a sense, this challenge returns us to the charge leveled by Plato. Does a world of knowledge and sound choice exist independent of the rhetorical process? Is the rhetorical process—dialogue—engaged by ethical people the best means for discovering truth and making sound judgment?

Addressing this problem, Aristotle believed that the ends of discourse were social good. This problem cuts to the crux of the tug of war between absolute truth and relative truth. Disputants and audiences are the judges of harm or good, independent of any a priori absolute view of truth or knowledge. Ethics arises from the process. The end is not predetermined but rather

forged through the process. If an a priori conclusion exists, then rhetoric is not needed; it operates in the realm of the contingent—of decision making. When a rhetor recommends a conclusion or an action, he or she does so "on the ground[s] that it will do good; if he [or she] urges its rejection, he [or she] does so on the ground[s] that it will do harm" (Aristotle, 1952b, p. 598). People and societies are evaluated by the ends to which they aspire (p. 608).

Aristotle knew that the role of rhetoric was neither to espouse absolute truth or knowledge nor to confirm predetermined conclusions. It was used to explore ways of achieving happiness by making choices that will do good and avoid harm. He observed, "When we know a thing and have decided about it, there is no further use in speaking about it" (Aristotle, 1952b, p. 639). On this point, J. Grunig (1992a) seemed to agree with Aristotle. In the *Excellence* project, Grunig reasoned that a good organization is best equipped to engage in two-way symmetrical communication.

If we adopt the logic of Quintilian, then the paradigm for public relations is the good organization communicating well. Each organization should strive to be moral and to communicate to satisfy the interests of key markets, audiences, and publics that strive to manage personal and public resources, make personal and sociopolitical decisions, and form strong and mutually beneficial relationships.

CONTEMPORARY RHETORICAL RATIONALE: IDENTIFICATION AND TRANSFORMATION

This section extends the classical tradition by adding other modes of rhetorical appeal and emphasizing the role of dialectic or dialogue. Inherently two-way, rhetoric assumes many voices engaged in dialogue, not monologue. As Burke (1969b) noted, society is a marketplace of ideas, facts, values, and policies: "the Scramble, the Wrangle of the Marketplace, the flurries and flare-ups of the Human Barnyard, Give and Take, the wavering line of pressure and counter pressure, the Logomachy, the onus of ownership, the War of Nerves, the War" (p. 23).

This reasoning justifies highlighting the concept of public in public relations. Openness assumed in rhetoric is driven by the wills of persons who articulate an interest in marketplace and public policy choices. Wrangles occur when information is examined to determine whether it is true and to put it to the task of creating sound decisions. Openness features public inquiry, public debate, publication, public record, public scrutiny, and key publics. Groups of individuals who have a stake in the outcome of issues participate as well as witness public dialogue. As any savvy public relations person knows, every fact, action, choice, and preference has a way of becoming public—of being visible—subject to public scrutiny.

As Burke (1973a) said, democracy institutionalizes "the dialectic process by setting up a political structure that gives full opportunity for the use of competition to a cooperative end" (p. 444). "Rhetoric is thus made from fragments of dialectic" (Burke, 1969b, p. 207). Dialectic, the cooperative use of competition, progresses from division, to merger, to identification.

> A rhetorician, I take it, is like one voice in a dialogue. Put several such voices together, with each voicing its own special assertion, let them act upon one another in cooperative competition, and you get a dialectic that, properly developed, can lead to views transcending the limitations of each. (Burke, 1951, p. 203)

Competition is essential to the forging of sound ideas, Burke (1983) reasoned, because knowledge evolves dialectically in that "(a) one acts; (b) in acting, one encounters the resistance to one's purpose; (c) one learns by suffering the punishment dealt by such resistance" (pp. 22, 26). "Beginning with the particulars of the world, and with whatever principle of meaning they are already felt to possess," dialectic "proceeds by stages until some level of generalization is reached that one did not originally envisage, whereupon the particulars of the world itself

look different, as seen in terms of this 'higher vision' " (Burke, 1969a, p. 306).

Pursuing this theme, Burke (1969b), although impressed by Aristotle, wanted to move beyond the tendency of classical rhetoric to stress "the element of explicit design in rhetoric enterprise" (p. 35). To do this, Burke stressed the power that words, especially idioms, have to create identification (p. xiv). For Burke, "Identification is affirmed with earnestness precisely because there is division. Identification is compensatory to division" (p. 208). Identification is possible because people use terms to define and name themselves. Identification, shared views of reality and identity, results from the human tendency to engage in merger and division.

Rhetoric "involves the use of verbal symbols for purposes of appeal" (Burke, 1969b, p. 271). Through naming and the identifications that result from it, "persuasion ranges from the bluntest quest of advantage, as a sales promotion or propaganda, through courtship, social etiquette, education, and the sermon, to a 'pure' form that delights in the process of appeal for itself alone, without ulterior purpose" (p. xiv). It is in this sense "the use of language as a symbolic means of inducing cooperation in beings that by nature respond to symbols" (p. 43). Cooperation results from merger and identification.

Rhetoric is courtship, a call to join in identification with others. For example, as environmentalists call for others to join in opposition to polluters, industrial complexes attempt to counter those appeals by reasoning that such actions are unjustified. Through this exchange, combatants move toward common ground on which they join and with which they identify. Thus, rhetoric operates in "the region of the Scramble, of insult and injury, bickering, squabbling, malice and the lie, cloaked malice and the subsidized lie" (Burke, 1969b, p. 19). Despite its rough edges, the process is a beauty of exchanged and contested ideas.

Rhetoric deals with "the ways in which the symbols of appeal are stolen back and forth by rival camps" (Burke, 1937, p. 365). Burke (1965) cautioned, "Let the system of cooperation become impaired, and the communicative equipment is correspondingly impaired, while this impairment of the communicative medium in turn threatens the structure of rationality itself" (p. 163). The dialectic goes like this. Environmentalists argue that green (including green products) is good to create that identification. Extending that logic, manufacturers of consumer products appeal for identification based on claims that their products are green and environmentally sound.

Rhetoric occurs because language is evaluative. With language, people form preferences that guide their actions: "When one talks of the will, one is necessarily in the field of the moral; and the field of the moral is, by definition, the field of action" (Burke, 1969a, p. 136). Action entails choices that are eternally focused on achieving perfection (Burke, 1966). Perfection is achieved through transcendence. Transcendence is an inherent quality of language. If environmentalism, then perfect environmentalism. If corporate responsiveness, then perfect responsiveness. By the same token, we can have the opposite. If corporate deception, then perfect deception.

The desires for identification, transcendence, and perfection, according to Burke, are universal motives for rhetoric and the choices that it addresses. Through rhetoric, ideas clash. "The role of opposition is by no means negligible in the shaping of society. The victory of one 'principle' in history is usually not the vanquishing, but the partial incorporation, of another" (Burke, 1968, p. 71). Harmony is possible because words allow us to reconcile opposites that, when viewed from "another point of view . . ., cease to be opposites" (Burke, 1961, p. 336).

This dialectic progression demands "a third term that will serve as the ground or medium of communication between opposing terms. And whatever logical problems such a third term may give rise to, we are being logical in feeling the need for it" (Burke, 1969a, p. 405). Rhetoric, linguistic transformation, grows through act and counteract. In public relations, an organization or a spokesperson suffers opposition based on what it or he/she does or says: "The dialectical (agonistic) approach to knowledge is through the act of assertion, whereby one 'suffers' the kind of knowledge that is the reciprocal of this act" (pp. 39-40).

Burke's theory supplies a rhetorical rationale for public relations. The organization or an activist group, for example, acts. Bill Gates and Microsoft created a product that is challenged as monopolistic. A similar business arrangement led to similar complaints against John D. Rockefeller. The tobacco industry developed nicotine delivery systems that were successfully criticized. Thus, act invites counteract; statement invites counterstatement. Through the dialectic of cooperative competition, merger solves division. Identification replaces division. Transcendent rationale for cooperation results from the dialectical fragments of rhetoric. Relationships forged through rhetoric are achieved by the discovery of transcendent principles.

Enactment Rationale: A Good Organization Doing and Saying Well

This subsection makes explicit the rhetorical impact of doing and saying. The ontological challenge is to blend action and statement into a coherent rhetorical rationale for the practice of public relations. This can be done by noting that people experience one another and organizations in society by what they do and say. This interpretive experience is communicative and offers a rhetorical enactment rationale for public relations. Enactment is meaningful as co-created narrative.

The analysis builds on Mead's (1934) view of the dialectical formation of mind, self, and society:

> Our society is built up out of our social interests. Our social relations go to constitute the self. But when the immediate interests come in conflict with others we had not recognized, we tend to ignore the others and take into account only those which are immediate. The difficulty is to make ourselves recognize the other and wider interests, and then to bring them into some sort of rational relationship with the more immediate ones. (pp. 388-389)

A society—people and organizations— learns from mistakes. As a profession, public relations can serve society by solving these mistakes. Public relations can serve organizations by making them good as a prerequisite for their being articulate. Thus, public relations can assist organizations' narrative enactments (Heath, 1994; Weick, 1987) as undirected plays (Pearce & Cronen, 1980).

Characterizing people as "homo narrans," Fisher (1987) reasoned that we live life as narrative—an ongoing story. What Fisher (1985, 1987, 1989) called the narrative paradigm assumes that "there is no genre, including technical communication, that is not an episode in the story of life (a part of the 'conversation') and is not itself constituted by logos and mythos" (Fisher, 1985, p. 347). Seeing people as storytellers and co-authors, Fisher (1987) reasoned, "A narrative perspective focuses on existing institutions as providing 'plots' that are always in the process of re-creation rather than existing as settled scripts" (p. 18). For this reason, "all forms of human communication need to be seen fundamentally as stories—symbolic interpretations of aspects of the world occurring in time and shaped by history, culture, and character" (p. xi). Fisher concluded that knowledge "is ultimately configured narratively, as a component in a larger story implying the being of a certain kind of person, a person with a particular worldview, with a specific self-concept, and with characteristic ways of relating to others" (p. 17). Narrative is not devoid of rational or ethical content. The substance of narrative is good reasons, "values or value-laden warrants for believing or acting in certain ways" (p. xi).

Narratively, rhetoric must meet the criteria of probability and fidelity, standards "for judging the merits of stories, whether one's own or another's" (Fisher, 1985, p. 349). The standard of narrative probability requires that each story hold together and be free from internal contradiction, whereas fidelity focuses on the weight of values, good reasons, consideration of fact, consequence, consistency, and the degree to which a story has a bearing on relevant issues.

Narrative gives people the knowledge they need to coordinate actions and contest points of view at three interdependent levels. Narration$_1$ is individuated forms, narration$_2$ is generic forms, and narration$_3$ is "a conceptual framework, like dramatism, for understanding human decision, discourse, and action" (Fisher, 1989, p. 55). This hierarchy occurs in companies and throughout society because each story is an example of its type (narration$_1$), generic stories abound (narration$_2$), and all judgments and enactments in an organization are meaningful because they can be interpreted through encompassing terministic screens (narration$_3$). Each enactment is part of a larger enactment that gives it meaning and against which it is judged.

Through co-authored narratives, each public achieves collective opinions, judgments, and actions that govern its behavior and public policy preferences. Organizations can adopt or seek to influence the narratives of society by what they say and do. Co-created meaning leads to a sense of community through shared narratives that supply people with knowable ways in which to act toward organizations and one another. Narratives voice expectations regarding how organizations should act toward one another and the people of society.

Applying dramatistic insights to augment this point, Burke (1966) reasoned,

> A character cannot "be himself" [or herself] unless many others among the dramatic personae contribute to this end, so that the very essence of a character's nature is in a large measure defined, or determined, by the other characters who variously assist or oppose him [or her]. (p. 84)

Morgan (1997) echoed this view by emphasizing how paradoxes and tensions "are created whenever elements of a system try to push in a particular direction. Each phase of development sets up conditions leading to its own transformation" (p. 299).

Actions by one character in an enacted drama come to life through enactments by other characters. Weick (1987) viewed enactment as a trap that organizations fall into when they base their operations on their view of themselves as a part of society. The limit to enactment is each counterenactment. Enactment exists as one entity acts and another entity reacts to what it does and says. What is said and done is interpreted according to the narratives that each party uses to frame and understand the enactment. Interpretation is governed by perceptions of how each enactment fits into the "voice" of society. This voice—co-created meaning—is the product of what others say in response to one another (Heath, 1994).

Bringing divergent interpretations together is the rhetorical rationale for public relations, bridging division with merger. Meaning is created by interpretations of what an organization is thought to do and say. Enactment entails all that is said and done by organizations that strategically operate to achieve mutually beneficial relationships with their markets, audiences, and publics.

Relativism and Dialogue: Forging Agreement

Absent consensus based on absolute knowledge, rhetoric wrestles with relative and expedient knowledge in search of concurrence. Addressing this point, this subsection features the epistemological rationale for the efforts of public relations to forge agreement in the face of relativism.

Does public relations—or any discipline—have means for knowing absolute truth? The answer to this epistemic question probably is *no* (Rorty, 1979; see also Bernstein, 1983, and Cherwitz & Hikins, 1986, who contended that "all ways of knowing are inherently rhetorical" [p. 92]). Even scientific studies advance knowledge rhetorically by examining premises supported by evidence, evaluative opinions, and degrees of certainty calculated as probabilities. Are we stuck with an expedient relativism? If so, can it satisfy the persons who join in making any particular set of mutually satisfying decisions?

Through rhetoric, people share and analyze evidence (facts and information) and reason from it to draw conclusions. These conclusions serve their needs and are framed in the interests of society. Campbell (1996) compared scientists for whom "the most important concern is the discovery and testing of certain kinds of truths," whereas "rhetoricians (who study rhetoric and take a rhetorical perspective) would say, 'Truths cannot walk on their own legs. They must be carried by people to other people. They must be ex-

plained, defended, and spread through language, argument, and appeal' " (p. 3). From this foundation, Campbell reasoned, rhetoricians take the position that "unacknowledged and unaccepted truths are of no use at all" (p. 3).

This observation is particularly relevant for the consideration of the viability of theories of public relations that rest on systems theory. Systems theorists treat information as static (self-revealing) rather than dynamic (contestable). A rhetorical perspective realizes that people interpret information by advocating contestable propositions regarding its accuracy, sufficiency, and relevance. As advocates for various interpretations of the data, participants in symmetrical communication seek to advance their views as being accurate and supportable. They use what they believe to be relevant value premises to interpret the data. They defend and attack conclusions and recommendations based on the data available to each dialogue. For this reason, data are meaningless until interpreted. Interpretation requires advocacy. Advocacy implies persuasion and counterpersuasion. This rhetorical perspective offers an epistemic rationale for public relations.

Rhetoric "has always been seen as a way of managing contingent human affairs through symbols. Rhetoric is a way of manipulating meanings so as to secure cooperation" (Brummett, 1990, pp. 89-90). Brummett (1990) advised that we accept the tug-of-war between rhetoric and relativism; relative knowledge is the bailiwick of rhetoric. The unknown is contestable. Rhetoric is a tool that public relations can use to test ideas and forge opinions in terms of the certain, the probable, the possible, and the plausible. It presumes that publics are passionate participants in the development of conclusions about factual information, an epistemological concern.

Rhetoric can be monologue or dialogue. Championing dialogue, Buber (1965) featured the preposition *between*. Derived from the Greek word *dialogos,* dialogue blends *logos* (word) and *dia* (through or across). Taken this way, dialogue is

> both a quality of relationship that arises, however briefly, between two or more people and a way of

thinking about human affairs that highlights their dialogic qualities. Dialogue can identify the attitudes with which participants approach each other, the ways they talk and act, the consequences of their meeting, and the context within which they meet. (Cissna & Anderson, 1998, p. 64)

The standard of dialogue set by Buber (1965) depends on whether the participants have "in mind the other or others in their present and particular being and turn to them with the intention of establishing a living mutual relation between [themselves and the others]" (p. 19).

Championing public relations as dialogue, Pearson (1989b) concluded,

The goal of public relations is to manage these communication systems such that they come as close as possible to the standards deduced from the idea of dialogue. This is the core ethical responsibility of public relations from which all other obligations follow. (p. 128)

Dialogue consists of exchange and challenge. Rhetoric, according to Pearson, is "the use of symbols to achieve agreement, to persuade, or to induce cooperation" (p. 113). Rhetoric is needed because collective, socially relevant decisions are predicated on probabilities instead of on certainties. It is a means for achieving prudent choices in the face of ambiguity and alternatives not reducible to absolutes.

Dialogue highlights the communal character of society. This view of human rationality assumes that ideas grow in one's mind as well as through social interaction because of the ability of any idea to survive in contest with other ideas. Developing this analysis, Fairclough (1995b) challenged us to consider two approaches to discourse. One views discourse as "social action and interaction, people interacting together in real social situations" (p. 18). The other view, which Fairclough suggested is more vital, sees "discourse as a social construction of reality, a form of knowledge" (p. 18). The second approach treats it as "the ideational function of language" (p. 18).

Denying objectivism as unattainable and total relativism as unacceptable, Pearson (1989b) reasoned, "It takes two minds to make truth, whether scientific or moral. Likewise, the public policy approach [to corporate responsibility] says business cannot act unilaterally but must consult and communicate with others through public policy mechanisms" (p. 121). A balance between two extreme views forms the crux of public relations:

One approach involves an organization with implicit objectivist views. This organization believes it "knows best" and seeks to educate publics. The other approach involves an organization with relativist views. This organization practices a sophistical public relations; given the lack of standards on which to base its actions, it would be inclined to base them on self-interest. (p. 122)

Neither objectivism nor extreme relativity is adequate in organizations' efforts to build mutually beneficial relationships with their stakeholders and stakeseekers. Through dialogue, an expedient relativism can be forged as sides concur and co-create a mutually acceptable view of reality.

This dialogue assumes the following risk: (a) a genuine clash of ideas, (b) shared control by the parties in dialogue, and (c) willingness by each participant to risk his or her point of view by submitting it for scrutiny. That challenge, for Pearson (1989b), informs the strategic planning and ethical justification for public relations. Through dialogue, participants achieve sufficiently compelling and expedient agreement in regard to public policy, organizational image, and the quality of an organization's products, services, and community relationships.

Thus, Pearson (1989b) concluded that dialogic exchanges produce an intersubjectivity that blends shared and opposing views on key issues. Although consensus might not result on every issue, sufficient agreement—concurrence— allows parties to continue dialogue in cooperative competition. Disagreement gives motive and rationale for such exchange to test which zone of meaning achieves coordinated and mutually rewarding behavior.

Rhetoric can locate and build on agreement in its effort to eliminate or lessen disagreement. Each party learns the power of its advocacy by examining the extent to which it influences the judgment of others. Rhetoric forces the relational balance between domains of interest. Seeing this contest of relationships, Leitch and Neilson (1997) suggested that good definitions of publics will assist our efforts "to come to terms with the power differentials between discourse participants" (p. 17).

Dialogue demands resolution because differences of opinion strain the patience and challenge society's desire for consensus or concurrence. As Burke (1969b) reasoned, "A persuasive communication between kinds (that is, persuasion by identification) is the abstract paradigm of courtship" (p. 177). Courtship acknowledges differences and works for merger, shared reasons, and identification. Rhetoric allows humans to look for sufficient agreement—zones of meaning—that supports collective actions. Each rhetorical situation is a battleground on which people contest the encompassment of the personal pronoun *we* (Burke, 1973b, p. 271).

Dialogue begins with assertion—action or statement—and suffers counterstatement. As Heath (1994) reasoned, "The dialectic of act and counteract characterizes relationships between companies [and other organizations] and their stakeholders" (p. 235). Viewed in this way, a rhetorical enactment rationale for public relations fits comfortably with social scientific methods and assumptions that are used to explain the processes of communication and community building. A rhetorical approach to public relations gives insights into the social importance of the meaning that practitioners help to shape so as to build shared meaning that supports the operation of society.

This rhetorical approach to public relations has epistemic implications; it explains how people come to know and form opinions. It has ontological implications because the act and counteract of rhetoric are real, forming opinion in public. The axiological challenge is to achieve shared values that bring the society together as people seek rewards and minimize losses from their societal relationships. These conditions are the rationale for rhetoric by which people work individually and collectively to forge functional zones of meaning.

Rhetoric is the sense-making function of language, the cognitive processes of definition—thinking about reality and preferences—and the expression of preferences in ways that lead others to adopt and use them to coordinate their efforts. This view of rhetoric privileges evidence—what can be said empirically about reality and the preferences and value-laden choices that can be made. If evidence and reasoning exist, then there must be value premises against which conclusions are judged.

CORPORATE RESPONSIBILITY: FORGING AGREEMENT WITHOUT WHICH SOCIETY FAILS

The previous section dealt with epistemological problems of rhetorically forging concurrence to co-create versions of reality. This section centers on problems of concurrence associated with evaluative principles, axiological issues of preference and expectation. Rhetoric is a means by which people define, examine, and wrestle with hierarchies of values.

Organizations need to know and enact prevailing standards of corporate responsibility. Stakeholders and stakeseekers expect each organization to act in ways that foster and do not offend their self-interests. Disagreement and contest of those standards occur because self-interests are value laden. Capturing this spirit, J. Grunig (1992a) advised organizational managements to keep "an eye on the effects of their decisions on society as well as on the organizations" (p. 17).

To foster the good of society, Isocrates (1929) challenged communicators to realize that character is essential to effective communication. Rhetoric is a means by which people publicly assert and challenge one another's ideas, evidence, values, and reasoning, thereby holding one another to high standards of thought and character. Rhetorical discourse can lead society to achieve a better version of itself and to form conclusions that solve problems rather than ignore or trivialize them (see esp. Wallace, 1963; Weaver, 1953, 1970).

Forming ethical standards, whether to guide communication or to evaluate its outcome, is an axiological problem. What constitutes the good is a question that is contested rhetorically. As Campbell (1996) cautioned, "When we have looked at the data and examined the logic of the conclusions drawn from them, we still must make decisions that go beyond the facts and make commitments that go beyond sheer logic" (p. 5). What value-laden truth is rhetoric designed to serve? Campbell answered,

> Because rhetoric is addressed to others, it gives reasons; and because it is social and public, it uses as reasons the values accepted and affirmed by a subculture or culture. In this way, rhetoric is tied to social values, and rhetoricians' statements will reflect the social norms of particular groups, times, and places. (p. 7)

Corporate actions are evaluated by key publics. For this reason, corporate responsibility is value-informed choice making (Heath, 1997). Ascertaining appropriate ethical responses is a rhetorical problem vital to strategic planning used by excellent organizations that aspire to build and maintain mutually beneficial relationships.

Public relations persons enjoy an ideal position to counsel executives on which values fit best with the interests of their markets, audiences, and publics. To help solve this problem, practitioners can recognize that the limit of any value perspective is the counterstatement voiced by key publics. A rhetorical perspective forces us to look closely at the value-laden expectations and power bases—public policy or market resource management—that occur as one organization or public enlists concurrence from other organizations and publics.

Organizational policies are enacted value behaviors that make public managements' decisions regarding which values are appropriate. Organizations enact their self-interests. In dialogue, customers assert their self-interested expectations as they select one product or service over others and as they think favorably or unfavorably about the value-laden enactments of organizations. From either side of the dialogue, this rhetorical enactment can attract supporters to create a coherent and useful zone of meaning regarding the standards of corporate responsibility.

The values that organizational executives enact are constrained by each public's opinions and preferences. What each organization or individual does and says is the product of its will in counterstatement to the limits and privileges imposed or allowed by individuals and other organizations that have self-interests in its opinions, policies, and actions. Through this dialectic, boundaries of actions and opinions achieve concurrence and become shared value premises. Based on these premises, standards of corporate responsibility allow persons to coordinate their efforts as executives realize that their interests cannot be obtained without yielding to stances advocated by others (Brummett, 1995). Knowledge of rhetoric helps executives to make strategic adjustments to fit their organizations to people as well as to invite people to adapt to organizations.

Given the sense-making and value-establishing power of rhetoric, public relations can help executives and other people to understand, critique, and employ value-laden choices. The rationale of rhetoric is its ability to give voice to the social and political needs of people who must enact value perspectives that support collective interests. People need to know what they expect of one another. This dialogue weighs the values by which people coordinate society. This dialogic progression serves as the rationale for shaping the mind, self, and society (Mead, 1934).

Zones of Meaning and Publics: A Search for Coordination and Community

Choices lead to actions, by organizations and individuals, that enact social narratives. Opinions are incipient actions; actions objectify value-laden choices, an ontological issue. This subsection discusses the reality that public relations would lack much of its rationale if people did not hold important opinions that differ and if those differences did not lead to conflicting choices.

An organization may communicate strategically to bring matters of importance to the attention of key markets, audiences, and publics; engage in collaborative decision making with them; and demonstrate its identification with their interests, opinions, and values. As the organization makes such choices, it enacts the values it believes to be best, as do its markets, audiences, and publics. Such choices serve as evidence of the values that the organization, market, audience, or public holds dear.

A multipublic, multimarket, and multiaudience view of society presumes that groups struggle to form, agree on, and collectively apply premises in their judgments about what is, what ought to be, and what ought to be done. Reasoning from evidence through evaluative premises leads individuals to know and test each other's analysis of reality and preferred expedient modes of action. Each stage in this progression is open to contest. Rhetors challenge one another and compete for adherents. Evidence is contestable according to accepted standards that are used to judge the accuracy of empirical observation. Premises are challenged to be worthy of use in drawing value-laden conclusions and prescribing actions that satisfy the needs and interests of each community. In this sense, expedient relativity is predicated on the best available judgments that are sensitive to the constraints of knowledge and preference that exist in each domain of opinion.

Publics are definable in many ways. One characteristic of a public is its idiosyncratic opinions and the corresponding choices that they prescribe. Values and opinions that lead to choices are made evident through the actions that the public takes. Each segment of society expresses its self-interests as well as its altruistic interests by what it says and does. Differences between publics arise over ontological choices regarding public policy issue positions; product or service choices; and attitudes about a person, a group, or an organization that constitute their images.

Those differences account for various outcomes that are valued. Differences that yield to rhetorical scrutiny lay the foundations for choosing preferred actions. A public policy position may be valued because it is ethical. Markets exist because persons have tastes, wants, and needs that shape their choices. Choices are value laden.

Public relations cannot exist only as image without substance. What forces the substance of public relations are the choices made by markets, audiences, and publics as well as the organization's choices in regard to them. To be a constructive and strategic force in society, the organization must attract favorable attention; justify one policy position in preference to another; and focus attention on product, service, and organization attributes that are favored and capable of being demonstrated through evidence, reasoning, and performance. To make the organization worthy of public trust, public relations needs to serve as a rhetorical force in an organization internally as well as externally. It adds value to the organization when it reduces conflict and increases the extent to which it is an approved part of individuals' lives.

In this way, rhetoric is self-reflexive as well as externally directed. People and organizations persuade themselves as they strive to persuade others; they enact a sense of which zones of meaning are best and most fruitful for their efforts. They are audiences for their own statements (Heath, 1991). If their ideas are not accepted by others, then those statements must be considered in their thinking about any other positions they advocate. This rhetorical perspective of public relations assumes, at a minimum, the constructive need to adjust people to ideas and to adjust ideas to people (Bryant, 1953) through the blending of relevant zones of meaning.

The means by which this can be done are rhetorical. Motion (1997), for example, posed three rhetorical alternatives that she called *technologies:*

1. "Positioning is a subjectifying process of locating and being located within discourse sites or spaces. . . . Discursive positioning involves the struggle to create what may be known and how it may be known" (p. 7).
2. Commodification results from positioning. Commodification is "the discourse practice in which the market discourse of production, distribution, and consumption dominates" (p. 11).

3. Aesthetics is the third alternative. "A public relations function is to assist the subject to aesthetically commodify and promote the self, to cultivate, fashion, and style the self" (p. 12).

The identity of something (e.g., organization, product, service, public self, issue position) is the result of reactions to its use of these technologies. This analysis underpins rhetorical enactment; the organization uses various technologies in its strategic enactment so as to be interpreted in a particular way by relevant markets, audiences, and publics.

Ontological choice is driven by societal preferences that are refined through discourse. Preferred actions are codified, as in the following examples. Drive at a speed no greater than X. Stop at red lights. Do not take others' property. These value-laden choices are expressed as laws on behalf of the community. Because these norms exhibit a narrative quality, they are knowable and predictable. They define and prescribe the approved actions of a society. Brummett (1995) championed the power of narrative as he characterized public relations as "the practice of telling and managing stories that are told about people, institutions, and groups" (p. 24). He believed that "every group has a story to tell, even if every group cannot, does not, or will not use expositional argument or statistical proofs" (p. 24).

Through discourse, people reflect on their experiences and interests as well as on those of others—persons and organizations as value-laden actions that are framed by social narratives. Meaning is co-created through the actions that individuals and organizations take as they advance their self-interests in contest, concurrence, or conjunction with others. The meaning of community is the product of these actions. Through action, people and organizations become meaningful to one another. Actions take on meaning as they are interpretable in terms of narratives that operate in each community. This is the rationale for socially responsible public relations, enacted narratively through choices that it makes as well as those it invites on the part of markets, audiences, and publics.

Molar Theories: Rationale for Public Relations as Enacted Discourse

Normatively, public relations enacts discourse to assist individuals and corporate entities in making enlightened choices. This subsection explores several theories that justify this conclusion.

Public relations can help people to reduce uncertainty. Uncertainty reduction can explain the human incentive, within limits, to seek information (Berger & Calabrese, 1975). People are open to receive information because uncertainty is uncomfortable. Such information is interpreted rhetorically. The amount of meaning in a message is its impact on the interpreters' uncertainty.

Subjective expected utilities features individual and collective efforts to balance rewards and punishments. People, individually and collectively, make evaluative choices that are intended to lead them to preferable states that are subject to rhetorical decision making.

Social exchange underpins the processes by which persons and corporate entities take moves and countermoves to achieve balanced relationships. Social exchange theory reasons that "an exchange can be thought of as a transference of something from one entity to another in return for something else" (Roloff, 1981, p. 14). As Prior-Miller (1989) observed,

> Organizational conflict will occur when inputs and outputs are not in balance and one organization or the other refuses to act to restore that balance. Organizational change will result from continually negotiating inputs and outputs. Organizational management will be both reactive and proactive in such negotiations. (p. 72)

Because of its stress on resource management, social exchange theory gives a rationale for the rhetorical processes through which people contest and define the norms of reciprocity required to build and maintain mutually beneficial relationships.

Theory of reasoned discourse (Ajzen & Fishbein, 1980) and information integration theory (Fishbein & Ajzen, 1975) reason that attitudes are a product of evaluations coupled to beliefs—subjective probabilities that traits are associated with objects, situations, persuasions, behaviors, and choices. Discourse leads people to make choices based on estimates of which one achieves the best possible outcome under the circumstances, an issue of subjective expected utilities. Coupled to this choice is each person's sense of what important others think that person should do.

Cognitive involvement theory explains why individuals seek and receive information and are thoughtful about it when it is thought to lead to important attitudes worthy of their cognitive efforts. Individuals prefer messages that are more likely to supply information and evaluation that they need to form useful opinions (Petty & Cacioppo, 1986).

Of related interest to these theories are the concepts of trust and control, which are vital to forming mutually beneficial decisions that support the development and maintenance of relationships.

Standards of Excellence for a Rhetorical Enactment Approach to Public Relations

This subsection examines key criteria for the effective practice of public relations and considers whether a rhetorical enactment view of public relations meets those standards. J. Grunig (1992a) reasoned that organizations are most likely to practice successful public relations when they are committed to human resources that support personal growth, organic structures that eliminate bureaucracy and empower people, intrapreneurship, symmetrical communication systems, leadership, participative cultures, strategic planning, social responsibility, opportunities for women and minorities, quality, effective operational systems, and a collaborative societal culture.

A rhetorical rationale for public relations meets these criteria of excellence. Rhetoric is organic; it assumes that policy and preference are forged through assertion and counterassertion. Rhetoric is symmetrical because each idea placed in the marketplace or public policy arena stands on its own merit. No idea is privileged even if it has an advocate with deep pockets. Rhetoric empowers policy discussants to seek adherents and to have their say in circumstances that affect them even if they only privately reject the points being made by corporate or other organizational rhetors. Rhetoric is used by leaders who seek followers and adherents to take advantage of opportunities and respond appropriately to threats. It is participative; the limit of one opinion is the substantiated assertion of another opinion. This criterion couples with quality because people who realize that ideas are tested in public are more attuned to the quality of those arguments as well as the persona of the organization—the good organization communicating well.

Rhetoric is strategic; it requires planning in response to a rhetorical problem. Planning considers which responses are needed, which responses are available, and which responses are likely to resolve the differences and achieve coherent and compatible zones of meaning. Rhetoric is predicated on the superiority of some ideas, evidence, policy positions, and product/service preferences that are improved through the contest of alternatives. Rhetoric assumes that collaboration entails open contest of preferences whereby some emerge to serve as expedient truth and policy with which participants concur. The counseling function of public relations is vital to intrapreneurship, a means by which organizations are helped to see the need for innovation by accepting the rhetorical limits to what they want to do and say as well as being willing to exploit opportunities. Through collaboration, interested parties work through differences to achieve mutually beneficial outcomes. Through rhetoric, women and minorities are privileged to compete for access to all aspects of society; sound argument is gender and race free, although each culture's language can be hegemonic—a shackle and a challenge to opinions changed through rhetoric. Rhetoric as a social force and process is a dialectic, the ultimate social process by which people learn how to enact society and through which narrative that enactment transpires.

All of these criteria are basic to the full functioning of a community. Building community is a goal for the practice, pedagogy, conceptualization, and research relevant to public relations. The concept of community, however, can be used as an incentive and as a rhetorical hegemony by one entity that defines community to privilege its point of view. Kruckeberg and Starck (1988) opted for a theory and practice of public relations "as the active attempt to restore and maintain a sense of community" (p. xi). How does this view square with the rhetorical tradition? Rhetoric is called for by Kruckeberg and Starck's challenge that "those responsible for public relations should approach communication as a complex, multiflow process having the potential to help create a sense of community" (p. xiii). To do so, rhetoric is an essential vehicle for ascertaining which information is most accurate, which values are highest, and which actions foster and affirm the sense of community.

Rhetoric presupposes the multidirectional flow of information, evaluation, and opinion. It privileges all players to assert their ideas, offer value-laden propositions, and propose and interpret recommendations. This dialectic goes beyond the processes of information exchange basic to systems theory that postulates that the rationale of systems and subsystems is to obtain and transfer information. The rhetorical process is enacted through expressions of preferences of opinions and behaviors that have consequences for the self-interests of organizations, individuals, and society as a whole.

As Kruckeberg and Starck (1988) noted,

A community is achieved when people are aware of and interested in common ends and regulate their activity in view of those ends. Communication plays a vital role as people try to regulate their own activities and to participate in efforts to reach common ends. (p. 53)

Viewed in this way, community is the product and instantiation of the democratic ideal that consists of "functionally interdependent and integrated individuals" (p. 53). "Communication is instrumental as it liberates us from the otherwise overwhelming pressure of events and enables us to live in a world of things that have meaning" (p. 59). What is sought is an approach to communication as a process that fosters "social involvement and participation" (p. 63). Rhetorical enactment meets that requirement. It is the "communal" or "communitarian" aspect of discourse (p. 62). Through communication, people form communities that liberate individuals through mutually beneficial interests and shared meaning.

CONCLUSION

Rhetoric is the voice of community. It is dialogue, statement, and counterstatement. It is the self-correcting and self-maintaining process by which people in each community derive the expedient truth and policy that they need to achieve concurrence and to coordinate their activities. In this way, community is created and maintained as the dynamic expression of self-interested participants. It offers a theoretical, practical, and critical rationale for the study, teaching, and practice of public relations.

This approach to public relations is epistemological, axiological, and ontological. Public relations is epistemic—the analysis of what is. It is axiological—the analysis of what is best. It is ontological—the meaning of what is done and said. This view of public relations downplays a transfer of information or a manipulation approach to communication that privileges the source and assumes the potential of absolute agreement and understanding. As rhetoric, public relations enables various entities to become meaningful to and influential for one another. That is the rationale for a socially responsible view of public relations.

CHAPTER 3

Public Relations and Community

A Reconstructed Theory Revisited

KENNETH STARCK

DEAN KRUCKEBERG

*Few trends could so thoroughly undermine the very foundations
of our free society as the acceptance by corporate officials
of a social responsibility other than to make as much
money for their stockholders as possible.*

—Milton Friedman (1982, p. 133)

*There are plenty of socially conscious managers. The problem is a
predatory system that makes it difficult for them to survive.*

—David Korten (1995, p. 212)

■ A dozen years ago, Kruckeberg and Starck (1988) argued that public relations is best defined and practiced as the active attempt to restore and maintain a sense of community that had been lost because of the development of modern means of communication/transportation. We defended our thesis thusly:

Our suggestions are radical only in the sense that they advocate a refocusing of efforts, that is, more conscientious and sustained attempts on the part of public relations practitioners to help their organizations and their communities restore and

maintain desirable elements from an earlier social life.

. . . The suggestions grow out of an idealism that we hope many public relations practitioners share. The suggestions we offer tend to be abstract, but the theory in which they are rooted is more intelligible and defensible than are most of the theories espoused in today's public relations literature. (pp. 118-119)

We argued that enlightened public relations practitioners who philosophically subscribe to and possess a theoretical understanding of community building can exploit modern means of communication to build and enhance a desirable sense of community. Thus, these practitioners can help to reduce humankind's sense of anomie that the authors maintained is the root cause of many organizations' public relations problems.

However, skepticism must accompany any consideration of recommendations made more than a decade ago. Immense societal changes have resulted during recent years from the escalating development of three phenomena that promise incalculable continuing effects on humankind:

1. Communication/
   transportation technology
2. Multiculturalism
3. Globalism

These inextricably linked phenomena have created ironic paradoxes. Through communication/transportation technology, new communities can and are being formed, yet anomie and societal fragmentation exist perhaps as never before. Social relationships are being rapidly changed in ways that are not fully understood. Traditional paradigms are being challenged and discredited, yet new values have not evolved to fill the resulting void, creating what Etzioni (1993) called "rampant moral confusion and social anarchy" (p. 24). Educational goals remain uncertain as teachers, government, and parents ponder what knowledge and skills students will need to live in a future world that is impossible to predict and thus difficult to prepare for. Some examples include the following:

- Previously homogeneous small towns in America's hinterlands are becoming rapidly diverse as multiculturalism invades even the most insular U.S. communities, but requisite corresponding harmony, tolerance, and cultural literacy remain elusive.
- The most professionalized of occupations, medicine, is seeing its private practices being absorbed into corporations that reduce professional autonomy. Physicians whose practices were inviolate are being evaluated through corporate marketing research that gauges patient (consumer) satisfaction but might not ensure good health care.
- The very definition of "work" is changing as technology replaces not only human labor but also skills and knowledge in roboticized, "workerless" factories, while the remaining human workers embrace keyboards and mice.
- "Merger mania" is creating international linkages. Grim corresponding realities are "downsized" employee numbers and "outsourced" work to countries offering the cheapest labor, with products marketed elsewhere globally where people can afford them.
- Amorphous and fragmentized global power differentials in the post-cold war era are resulting in unpredictable (and perhaps untrustworthy) political alliances.
- A technological global society can retain very few secrets, just as there were no secrets in the American villages of the 1800s.
- Cultural norms and values are being challenged as some traditional institutions become obsolete and/or impotent.
- Although technology is becoming available to increasing numbers of people, only the technologically elite are fully availing themselves.
- The world's legacy of cruelty and exploitation is appearing to remain the same.

DEMOCRACY

The future well-being of democracy would seem assured given that communication technology provides unprecedented avenues for self-government. Yet, despite cold war victories, democracy and democratic principles will be challenged as never before. Past overt ideological confrontations have been replaced by more nebulous, and potentially more insidious, technological and economic challenges. These will have a direct impact on the concept of democracy and on contemporary forms of government. Sclove (1995) contended,

> If citizens ought to be empowered to participate in determining their society's basic structure, and technologies are an important species of social structure, it follows that technological design and practice should be democratized. . . . We can see that this involves two components: Substantively, technologies must become compatible with our fundamental interest in strong democracy itself. Procedurally, we require expanded opportunities for people from all walks of life to participate in shaping their technological order. (pp. 91-92)

Furthermore, although democracy has proven to be ideologically victorious, ironically, democracy will become increasingly threatened by one outcome of its cold war victory—increased power and influence of global transnational corporations that can challenge the power of nation-states including those that are democratically governed. Such corporations also become the primary beneficiaries of communication/transportation technology, according to Schiller (1995):

> [Transnational corporations] constitute the driving force for the creation of a global marketplace, for a deregulated world arena, and for global production sites selected for profitability and convenience. . . .
>
> The launching of the global information superhighway project comes at a time when most of the preconditions for a corporate global "order" are in place. There is, first and foremost, the actual existence of a global economy, organized and directed by a relatively tiny number of transnational corporations. (p. 20)

Schiller called this "world corporate order" a major force in greatly reducing the influence of nation-states whose governments are relinquishing important duties to increasingly powerful corporations that are making fundamental decisions affecting huge numbers of people. However, these corporations report to no one except their own executives and major shareholders (p. 21).

Indeed, it is unlikely that corporate constitutions and policies can be depended on to preserve and safeguard human and civil rights or to embrace democracy and democratic principles. Left unaccountable, these behemoth organizations will not likely foster tomorrow's "communities" or become transnational corporate "tribes" that will protect *all* of their stakeholders including society at large.

Bellah, Madsen, Sullivan, Swidler, and Tipton (1992) argued that there are problems with how corporations are institutionalized in American society. The authors proclaimed that these problems cannot be resolved without reforming the institution itself (p. 11). Perhaps the new millennium becomes a judicious time to advocate this reform, not because of the millennium's numerical significance but rather because it symbolizes the immediate urgency that forces reconsideration of basic precepts of democracy and capitalism. The role of the corporation, specifically the transnational corporation that transcends national borders, must be reexamined in light of changes that have come about because of communication/transportation technology, multiculturalism, and globalism—as well as increasing global democratization.

We must begin with the recognition that corporations are neither inherently good nor inherently evil. They serve an important societal, as well as economic, function and undoubtedly are necessary in some form in modern society. Neither should the assumption be made that regulation and containment are desirable means to ensure corporate responsibility and accountability.

Rather, the relationship of these increasingly powerful transnational institutions must be examined in light of their power and influence and their effect on society as well as their potential threat to democracy. This relationship must be examined particularly from the perspective of public relations, whose practitioners are perhaps best qualified intellectually and professionally to address questions related to corporations' relationships with their stakeholders.

Ultimately, the greatest stakeholder of any corporation remains society itself. That is, not only do corporations carry out a societal role, but that role represents their greatest responsibility. The truth of the matter is that corporations do not possess an inherent right, even in a democracy, to exist as institutions.

In this spirit, and in a reaffirmation (even in the global multicultural arena) of what has become known as the Kruckeberg and Starck "community-building theory" of public relations, we make these recommendations to corporations—particularly transnational corporations—that we believe should form a basic public relations philosophy and set of operating principles of all organizations. We ask these corporations to ponder their organizational missions and goals and to consider larger questions that deal with society and, ultimately, with life itself and the values that give life meaning for each of us.

CORPORATIONS AND PUBLIC INTEREST

Arguably, the most distinguishing characteristic of the modern age is the need to be actively engaged in constant learning. Without the ability and willingness to learn, individuals—as well as institutions—flounder in a sea of change. This does not mean that we must embrace every new idea or technology when it comes along. We should cling strongly to those traditions and ethical practices that have served us well in the past. But it does mean that we must be responsive to changes taking place in our environment and, in fact, keep the proverbial ear to the ground and the moist finger in the air to detect signs that can warn of impending hazards or emerging opportunities.

For corporations, this means taking the initiative in interacting with all segments of what we might call their *environmental constituencies*. Only in this way will an organization be able to

build relationships that will result in establishing and maintaining the sense of community that we are talking about.

In examining corporate citizenship, it might be prudent to begin at the beginning. Why and how did corporations come about in the first place? A number of writers (Bellah et al., 1992; Estes, 1996) remind us that government granted charters to corporations to carry out particular functions with the public interest in mind.

Note that phrase—public interest. During colonial times, *corporations* (a term borrowed from English law [Bellah et al., 1992, p. 71]) came to include organizations such as municipalities, churches, and colleges. Most of us would agree that such corporations serve a public interest. Indeed, in exchange for this special standing, corporations were deemed to have a special obligation to act in the public's interest. But this changed during the 19th century. State legislatures began to charter business corporations. The corporations paid fees, had to comply with certain regulations, and came to be regarded "at law as having the natural rights of persons . . . free to enter into contracts, including labor contracts, on whatever terms the market allowed" (Bellah et al., 1992, p. 71).

Thus, although it might come as a surprise to many, today's corporations have their roots firmly embedded in the concept of public interest. The idea, sometimes referred to as *stakeholder capitalism,* asserts that "prosperous business owes society something" (Badaracco, 1998, p. 267). The question, then, becomes one of how well the public interest is being served.

Estes (1996), in a scathing indictment of today's corporations (which he claimed are ruled by the *bottom line*), framed the question this way: "We should ask how well and in what ways the corporation has served, and how it has harmed, the public interest—because there is no other reason for us to charter corporations and to grant them special business privileges" (p. 31).

What is at issue is the nature of the contract between corporations and society. This suggests that more than a little social responsibility rests with corporations. Often, the relationship between corporations and society—or at least the reasoning that defines that relationship—revolves around "us versus them," that is, corporate interests versus community interests. What has emerged, according to Korten (1995), is a corporate libertarianism that has become the dominant philosophy of political culture (pp. 147-148). The result has been a corporate mind-set that pays more attention to immediate instrumental interests than to the future well-being of the corporations themselves and the environment in which they operate and that is vital to continuing corporate survival.

Korten (1995) went further. He argued that the world is moving toward market tyranny. Changes in ideology, politics, and technology, in turn, are driving "a process of economic globalization that is shifting power away from governments responsible for the public good and toward a handful of corporations and financial institutions driven by a single imperative—the quest for short-term financial gain" (p. 12). Likewise, in Korten's estimation, globalization has made many of the political roles of government obsolete (p. 127). Corporations on a global scale may wield more power than some nations.

If this is the case—if transnational business organizations possess such economic and political clout—then social responsibility must be assigned even greater weight in our consideration of environmental constituencies.

CORPORATIONS AND ACCOUNTABILITY

Next, we turn our attention to how corporations discharge social responsibility. Essentially, we are talking about accountability. To whom? For what? Implemented how?

At one level, we can say that market forces determine accountability. That is, if a product or service does not attract sufficient clientele to survive, then the issue of accountability is moot. But just because a business survives or even thrives is no assurance that the organization is fulfilling a socially responsible role, let alone full and complete accountability. Required is an assessment of accountability that takes into account the en-

vironmental constituencies, not merely the obvious identifiable publics such as employees, customers, stockholders, and relevant geographic communities. A different and broader accountability method is in order, one that takes into account as much as possible all entities among the environmental constituencies that are potentially affected by the corporation.

This approach to accountability involves two major steps. One calls for a different way of thinking about the traditional profit/loss statement. The second step, closely linked to the first, asks for an accounting of corporate information that goes well beyond the financial. Predicated on the idea that a corporation's very existence depends on official public authorization, should society not expect an accounting that considers all public consequences—the good as well as the bad?

Estes (1996), whose résumé includes serving as chief financial officer of a company, a senior accountant at a "Big Six" accounting firm, an expert court witness on economic costs of corporate wrongdoing, and a professor of business administration, encapsulated this new accountability in this way:

> For accountability, we need a new scorecard, one that will measure corporate success in terms of the corporation's public purpose. It must show the effects on, the returns to, all stakeholders and not just the returns to stockholders. Management—and corporate—performance will be tallied up in terms of the effects on all stakeholders; with adequate information, stakeholders, acting in their own best interests, will reward responsible corporations and penalize irresponsible ones. (p. 16)

What is meant when we consider accountability in terms of *stock*holders and *stake*holders? The differentiation might be obvious. For both groups, we are looking at statements of net profit/loss. The old accountability, however, concerns itself primarily with profit/loss to stockholders. The new accountability takes into account the public nature of what we somewhat mistakenly call *private* business and examines profit/loss on behalf of all stakeholders. For starters, stakeholders include employees, customers, stockholders, suppliers, lenders, neighboring communities, and society at large (Estes, 1996, p. 29). Such an accounting would call for disclosure of corporate information that far exceeds today's requirements.

Is such an approach desirable—or even workable? Given mind-sets of the past, probably not. But the great changes engulfing the world today require new thinking about corporate accountability. Given the growing gulf between "have" and "have-not" nations, an approach to accountability that looks beyond the bottom line for stockholders is simply the morally right thing to do.

But can a corporation be both moral and profitable at the same time? The best answer is another question: Why not? Studies have been done on this very question. Although the findings are not conclusive, indications are that companies that "treat customers, employees, communities, and the environment in a responsible and reciprocal manner do somewhat better on financial dimensions over the long run" (Estes, 1996, p. 238).

An important dimension of accountability, as we have argued, involves the concept of "community." Community encompasses what we also refer to as *environmental constituents,* that is, all those groups that affect or are affected by an organization. To put this in communication terms, environmental constituents consist of partners in communication between an organization and all those groups with which it interacts. It is the dimensions of those interactions to which we now turn our attention.

CORPORATIONS AND GLOBALIZATION

The topic of globalization merits our attention because of the economic and technological changes that have bound the world together in a web of interdependency. Communication technology has forced us to rearrange our perception of time. National economies have become so intertwined that a disturbance here or there can produce ripples anywhere in the world.

We can resist change or debate the value of these changes, as many scholars have done (see, e.g., Brook & Boal, 1995), but the bottom line is the inevitability of some change and the challenge of responding sensibly and responsibly. Corporations, and all organizations for that matter, have an unusual opportunity to respond to change in a way that can mutually benefit both the organizations and society. But there must be a reconceptualization of how corporations communicate with—rather than communicate *to*—their environmental constituents. The vision must go beyond the traditional bottom line of profit/loss and creation of a bottom line of accountability to all environmental constituents.

Communicating with all environmental constituents equates with building relationships vital to creating a sense of community. Community can be seen as a form of *social bonding.* Korten (1995) pointed out how certain species depend on social bonding for their very survival, arguing that we need a similar approach in coping with today's disintegration of society (p. 278). Rather than *disintegration,* we would prefer to say *globalization,* an appellation with which we think Korten would agree. He wrote, "It is a fundamental, though often neglected, fact that social bonding is as essential to the healthy functioning of a modern society as it was to more traditional or tribal societies" (p. 278).

An economic perspective that strives to build a civil society on the basis of communication also can simply be good business. Korten (1995) cited Putnam's research in Italy in which it was found that healthy networks of nonmarket relationships built a generalized sense of trust and reciprocity that increased the efficiency of human relationships (p. 278).

Let us take a closer look at the popularly used, yet infrequently defined, concept of globalization. *Globalization* refers generally to the economic and cultural ways in which nations' activities have become increasingly interlinked. Or, according to a dictionary of communication terms published in the mid-1990s, "the term refers to that whole complex of flows and processes which have increasingly transcended national boundaries in the last twenty years" (O'Sullivan, Hartley, Saunders, Montgomery, & Fiske, 1994, p. 130).

Our intent is not to offer a critique of globalization. Instead, we want to clarify our use of the concept. We do not agree with those who maintain that globalization necessarily portends harmonious relations among nations or that it represents a new form of colonialism—namely cultural imperialism—or, for that matter, that the whole discussion amounts to "globaloney" (see, e.g., Featherstone, 1990; Giddens, 1990; Mattelart, 1994; Schiller, 1969; Tomlinson, 1991). We endorse the proposition that national interactivity is inevitable and that, instead of being obliterated ("McDonaldized" or "Coca-Colanized"), local cultures will learn and adapt to changing circumstances. The basis of these intercultural relationships, whether business or culturally oriented, will be communication.

Thus, and now we return to our original thesis, what and how we perceive communication emerges as paramount in our view of public relations in an increasingly globalized, diversified, multicultured world. Communication builds relationships. If relationships are to be built and maintained, then communication becomes an indispensable component.

Furthermore, communication must be practiced in its ritualistic sense, as contrasted with a transmission view of communication. The latter has the communicator doing something (persuading? advocating?) to someone. Ritualistic communication, on the other hand, has the communicator doing something *with* someone. The theoretical implications of the two approaches are enormous, as we pointed out in our original argument more than a decade ago and to which we added, "Just as great are the implications in the realm of the practical" (Kruckeberg & Starck, 1988, p. 62).

This means predicating communication on the mutual respect found in the two-way symmetrical model (Dozier, L. Grunig, & J. Grunig, 1995). The realization is that results will be mutually affective. The slogan "Think globally, act locally" transforms to "glocalization" (Featherstone, Lash, & Robertson, 1995; Robertson, 1992; Wang, 1997; Wilson & Dissanayake, 1996). That

is, through communication, societies influence and, in turn, are influenced by one another.

Some refer to the outcome as "hybridization" or "blending" (Willnat, He, & Xiaoming, 1997). Regardless of terminology, the theoretical linchpin of our argument remains the same: Public relations ought to be perceived and practiced as communication that contributes to restoring and maintaining community. How this might be done is explored in the next section.

PUBLIC RELATIONS AND THE NEW COMMUNITY

In a world where communication technology has become a dynamic force and national economies have become inextricably intertwined, it is clear that a new global community is emerging. For public relations practitioners and scholars, this represents a number of challenges. But perhaps the most pressing—and problematic—will be the ability to understand what is taking place and to develop a frame of mind that will be receptive not only to change but also to new ways of doing things. Assuming that the new global community will be built on principles of democracy and equality, public relations professionals, while remaining strong advocates of their own points of view, must approach other cultural perspectives with open minds.

At one level, the challenge can be seen as daunting if not hopeless. As has been implied, structural (including legal) changes might have to precede anything that public relations practitioners can do. Recall our reference to Estes's (1996) approach to accountability in terms of stockholders and stakeholders. It would seem to make sense to conduct and account for business in a way that is inclusive of stakeholders. As a reviewer of Estes's book wrote,

> Nothing could be more obvious: The bottom line of a financial statement does not measure the total effect of a corporation's activities on everybody. The bottom line may look good, but employees may be trading their health for their jobs.

Customers may be buying products that will cause an early death. (Sharpe, 1996, p. 60)

Sharpe (1996) went on to cite other dreary consequences that generally extract a heavy social cost in the name of private interests:

Mr. Estes asks in his subtitle why corporations make good people do bad things. Possibly because they gain by it and then interpret the bad things as good things. Mr. Estes, do you really believe that people who are making a fortune using the present accounting system will change it because yours is self-evidently better? It would be nice to hang a bell around the cat's neck, but which mouse is going to approach the cat and hang the bell? (p. 60)

What to do? To begin with, we must not lose faith in a democratic system that espouses life, liberty, and the pursuit of happiness. Such goals represent an ideal, and as we know, ideals are to be sought after despite never being fully realized. Next, we must recognize that the way of the United States is not necessarily the way of other nations. Each nation has its own distinctive set of historical and cultural circumstances and must discover its own path. In addition, from our positions of influence as public relations educators, we should encourage corporations to provide complete and accurate information to the public including all environmental constituents.

Finally, a major contribution that public relations educators can make is to help students become interculturally literate, for the sine qua non of this newly emerging global community is intercultural communication. One of our major goals should be to promote intercultural literacy among present and future public relations practitioners.

Even though this is easier said than done, at least we ought to be clear about direction. O. L. Taylor (1989) pointed the way a few years ago in an address to a group of mass media educators. Although focusing primarily on journalism, he argued that interculturally literate communicators must understand that (a) most, if not all, truths are perceptions of truth viewed through the prism of culture; (b) a communicator's effec-

tiveness, verbal as well as nonverbal, is enhanced through intercultural competence; (c) the perception of what constitutes relevant information, as well as gauging its importance, is culturally determined; and (d) interpretations and perceptions of those engaged in communication are culture bound, meaning that errors of interpretation and perception are inevitable without sensitivity to and knowledge about cultural differences.

As we struggle toward a better society and a more hospitable world, the questions—let alone the answers—might not always be clear. But there must be a realization that, to some extent, we are not pawns at the mercy of change but instead have a voice in the outcomes. As Boal (1995) commented in his essay on technology and modernism, "We make our selves as we make the world" (p. 13).

CONCLUSION

More than a decade ago, Kruckeberg and Starck (1988) argued that public relations is best defined and practiced as the active attempt to restore and maintain a sense of community that had been lost because of the development of modern means of communication/transportation. Now, in the new millennium and in light of massive societal changes that have evolved, to a great extent, because of escalating development of communication/transportation technology, multiculturalism, and globalism, we reaffirm our belief in our original thesis. And we reattest our conviction of the importance of community in contemporary society. However, we do so with more urgency in our voices.

We believe that corporations are neither inherently good nor inherently evil, and we do not advocate abolition of corporations. Nor are we calling for increased regulation or attempts at containment of the size of corporations, although we ask the reader to ponder the immense scope of the transnational corporations.

We are suspicious, however, of the increasing power of corporations, particularly that of transnational corporations that can effectively circumvent accountability because, as organizations, they answer to no one government or to people. Left unaccountable, they can be a threat to governments including to democratic governments that, ironically, have fostered their growth and prosperity.

We believe that such corporations ultimately operate by consent of society, which remains in fact the ultimate stakeholder of such corporations to which these organizations are answerable. Society has the right—indeed the obligation—to examine these corporations in light of their power and influence as well as their effect on society. And threats to democracy must be substantively removed.

All of this is best accomplished, however, not by societal restriction but rather by proactive efforts on the part of corporations to be accountable to society and answerable to all governments and peoples where they operate as well as to the inherent democratic principles of such nations.

There is much that corporations can do proactively, and we would argue that most important is the active attempt to restore and maintain the sense of community that was lost. Nothing is obsolete in our original treatise in *Public Relations and Community: A Reconstructed Theory* (Kruckeberg & Starck, 1988). Community building can be proactively encouraged and nurtured by corporations with the guidance and primary leadership of these organizations' public relations practitioners. These practitioners must consider, in their community-building efforts, their environmental constituencies, that is, all entities potentially affected by the corporations. This new approach to accountability is predicated on the idea that the very existence of corporations depends on public authorization.

Corporations must recognize that the greatest stakeholder—the ultimate environmental constituency—is society itself, to which such corporations are ultimately and irrefutably answerable.

CHAPTER 4

Cultural Topoi

Implications for Public Relations

GREG LEICHTY

EDE WARNER

■ If one starts with a definition of public relations as "the art of adjusting organizations to environments and environments to organizations" (Crable & Vibbert, 1986, p. 413), then one is left with the question of what is being adjusted. This chapter proposes that culture is the essence of what is being adjusted. Public relations is first and foremost concerned with meaning. Meaning and interpretation are the central processes of all public relations activities. Organizational environments are dynamic cultural processes constituted by symbols, beliefs, rituals, and cultural norms. Organizations manipulate and deploy evocative symbols to attain legitimacy and thereby gain and retain societal support (Suchman, 1995). Consent is not so much engineered as it is an ongoing social process of open-ended negotiation (Vasquez, 1996). Agreements are provisional and are open to revision. Relating is unfinished business. This chapter introduces an approach for describing how public relations is conditioned by cultural discourse and how public relations contributes to the same discourse system. The chapter seeks to extend rhetorical approaches to public relations (Heath, 1993), by explicating the warrant structures that are repeatedly used in value debates.

Public relations practice has a strategic or organizational bias. The organization usually is considered to be the central actor in sociocultural environment. There is relatively little focus on how social institutions constrain public relations practice. Most accounts of publics, for example, implicitly assume that publics are reactive entities that arise in response to organizational actions. In fact, publics often exist prior to and independent of the organization. Publics may have their own goals and internal dynamics (Botan & Soto, 1998). Moreover, public relations theory does not have developed perspectives of social institutions that constrain organizations. Within organizational theory, institutional perspectives emphasize sector-wide dynamics that generate broad cultural processes that are beyond the control of any single organization's issue management capabilities (Suchman, 1995).

Whereas organizational theory has a robust institutional perspective (e.g., Powell & DiMaggio, 1991), public relations theory is only beginning to inquire how societal culture influences public relations practices (Sriramesh & White, 1992).

We believe that a rhetorical theory offers a good opportunity to develop a robust account of the interpenetration of public relations and culture. Rhetorical approaches to public relations begin with the axiom that meaning constrains the prerogatives of both individuals and organizations (Heath, 1993). Public relations itself is an institutional feature of rhetoric in contemporary society. Rhetoric has become increasingly organizational, and organizations have become increasingly rhetorical (Cheney, 1991). Democracy is a means "for institutionalizing the dialectic process by setting up a political structure that gives full opportunity for use of competition toward a cooperative end" (Heath, 1992b, p. 20). Public relations is an essential part of how voices compete toward cooperative ends in contemporary democratic societies. This chapter was written to extend the rhetorical paradigm of public relations (Botan & Soto, 1998; Heath, 1992b, 1993) and to raise questions about the goals and methods of public relations.

THE CULTURAL TOPOI PROJECT

Heath (1992a) noted that arguments can establish warrants or use established ones. However, the most striking thing about value debates is how predictable they are. Rhetors use established warrants over and over again. Hirschman (1991) showed that three basic warrants against proposed social changes were repeatedly recycled in British social policy debates for more than 200 years. Far from being highly creative, the arguments of the contending parties often become so predictable that one can readily anticipate what each side will say. Although rhetoric might help to constitute social reality, it does so within recognizable parameters (Douglas, 1996).

Our ability to anticipate such discourse suggests that values and beliefs come in just a few

packages (Thompson, Ellis, & Wildavsky, 1990). When disagreements about justice emerge, the ideological justifications almost invariably crystallize into a very small number of ideological alternatives (Fiske & Tetlock, 1997). These packages or cultural biases enable people to interpret social events in ways that support their preferred patterns of social relations (Douglas, 1982).

This chapter describes five cultural biases and their related topoi (i.e., topics or premises). It outlines how they influence message encoding and message interpretation and thereby how they influence the work of public relations. As a working hypothesis, we propose that five cultural biases and related topoi generate and organize a large proportion of value discussions in human societies. A topos or topic structure consists of general themes that can be broadly used in persuasion. A topos can be used to support propositions on a wide variety of topics (Kennedy, 1991). A cultural topos is a systematic line of assumptions and arguments that reinforces a preferred pattern of social relationships. A cultural topos emerges out of a core rhetorical vision of the way in which the universe is. It involves epistemological, ontological, and moral commitments. Each cultural topos represents an argument structure that sprouts from a cultural bias or paradigm view. Each cultural topos exhibits distinctive logic or rationality. We propose that understanding and using cultural topoi is central to what public relations practitioners do.

A cultural topoi framework would model the multiple rationalities that are used to produce and interpret messages. It would identify the general lines of argument that can be adopted on values or value-related debates. The framework also would enable one to anticipate how different audiences will interpret the same message (audience by message interactions). To understand how a message will be interpreted, one need not understand the intricacies of cognitive dynamics so much as understand the cultural bias that the message interpreter buys into. It also would flesh out how enthymemes are constructed—how people make connections and inferences beyond what is said. Enthymemes are cultural constructions. One's cultural bias applied to an action or a message enables the individual to fill in unstated premises and develop a coherent interpretation.

This chapter integrates two lines of work in anthropology: Mary Douglas's and Aaron Wildavsky's development of cultural theory (Douglas, 1996; Douglas & Wildavsky, 1982; Schwartz & Thompson, 1990; Thompson et al., 1990) and Alan Fiske's theory of elementary structures of social relationships (Fiske, 1991; Fiske & Tetlock, 1997). Cultural theory has been applied to issues as varied as risk perception (Schwartz & Thompson, 1990), traffic safety engineering (Adams, 1995), and shopping and fashion (Douglas, 1996). Fiske's theory has primarily been applied to social perception and ideological discourse (Cvetkovich & Earle, 1994; Fiske & Tetlock, 1997).

THEORETICAL OVERVIEW

Cultural theory proposes that *culture* is an ecosystem inhabited by a finite number of ways of life. A *way of life* consists of a preferred pattern of *social relations* and a *cultural bias* or set of shared values and beliefs about human society and the natural world (Thompson et al., 1990). Both cultural bias (cultural beliefs) and social relations (social structure) are considered to be "reciprocal, interacting, and reinforcing. Adherence to a certain pattern of social relationships generates a distinctive way of looking at the world; adherence to a certain worldview legitimizes a corresponding type of social relations" (Thompson et al., 1990, p. 1). A way of life is viable only so long as its cultural bias and patterned social relationships are compatible and mutually reinforcing.

Cultural theory's more audacious claim is that there are only five viable ways of life that have enough internal consistency and coherence to survive. Only five types of social relations and cultural bias—fatalism, egalitarianism, hierarchy, autonomy, and individualism—meet the rigorous compatibility requirements (Thompson et al., 1990). Each way of life competes with the other ways of life for adherents. Each has a history of successes and failures in predicting and managing events and in debating its cultural competitors.

The cultural ecosystem has an inherent requisite variety because each way of life is defined by its competitors. Thompson et al. (1990) noted, "Each way of life needs each of its rivals, either to make up for its deficiencies, or to exploit, or to define itself against. To destroy the other (way of life) is to murder the self" (p. 4). Each way of life defines itself relative to its competitors, but each also has its miseries. Egalitarians get sentimental about community, but the very concept makes competitive individualists shudder. Competitive individualists are enamored with the efficiency of competition and markets, but egalitarians see conspicuous consumption that is wasteful and vindictive.

The competition among the ways of life constitutes a culture's form. Each society or group probably has a unique mix of the basic ways of life. A single way of life may dominate the scene at a particular time, or two ways of life may form a dominant coalition. The remaining ways of life may be marginalized, be driven underground, or simply be ignored. Representative democracy can be regarded as a coalition of cultures in which each way of life has a voice in the differentiated institutions of society (Thompson et al., 1990).

Fiske (1991) hypothesized that social relationships are based on a small number of fundamental relational structures. These structures are posited to be a fundamental part of the human cognitive endowment. Fiske argued that there are only four such structures: communal sharing, authority ranking, equality matching, and market pricing. These relationship types serve as templates for constructing larger social institutions. Each relational structure can be found to varying degrees in every culture. However, one or two relational structures and their associated social ideologies usually predominate in a given social group. In Fiske's view, all cultures are built out of the same building blocks, but groups differ in how they combine and implement the relational models.

Groups of people often generalize from a single relational structure to create broad social and political ideologies (Fiske & Tetlock, 1997). On the contemporary scene, communal sharing logic is evidenced in the egalitarian agendas of the socialists and greens, authority ranking in the hierarchical conservatism of the religious right, market pricing in libertarianism, fatalism in low voter turnout, and equality matching in the increasing trend toward independent voting. When combined with cultural theory's ways of life, this perspective provides a more powerful mechanism for describing cultural discourse than does the conservative to liberal continuum (Wildavsky, 1987). For example, one can anticipate when *conservatives* are likely to support social and political changes and when *liberals* or *progressives* are likely to be staunch supporters of the status quo (Wildavsky, 1987). One can describe up to 20 types of cultural transition.

Fiske's most innovative claim was that each relational structure has a distinct level of measurement for calculating social rights and responsibilities. Communal sharing uses categorical measurement to determine group memberships, authority ranking uses an ordinal scale to determine one's relative status in the hierarchy, equality matching uses interval-level measurement to maintain equality in relationship exchange, and market pricing uses ratio-level measurement to negotiate and monitor contracts. Thus, the ways of life can be ordered in terms of how much mindfulness or calculation they require to sustain the preferred social relationship. (From simple to complex, the order is as follows: egalitarianism, hierarchy, autonomous individualism, competitive individualism.)

Fiske's theory of relational structures supplemented cultural theory by elaborating our understanding of fatalism and autonomous individualism. Fatalist culture is curious because it is so apathetic and inactive. This might be because fatalism does not have a corresponding relational structure in Fiske's system. Fiske did discuss asocial or null relationships in which the relationship is treated as a means to an end rather than as an end in itself. Such relationships are dominated by short-term exploitative concerns and by pervasive distrust. Thus, fatalism appears as a way of life with a large proportion of asocial or null relationships. The fatalist way of life is ap-

athetic because it lacks a generative relational structure.

The autonomous individualist way of life also can be elaborated using Fiske's theory. Cultural theory portrays autonomy as so rare as to be "off the cultural map." The autonomous way of life seeks to avoid coercing others and being coerced by others. Cultural theory gives little insight into what type of sociality and exchange could sustain this way of life. Fiske's (1991) equality matching relational structure showed how exchange and interdependence can be structured to maintain equality and keep the relationship from becoming burdensome. Equality matching structures exchange so that one never becomes a long-term borrower or lender. Long-term dependence and power relations are minimized; thus, autonomy can be maximized.

Fiske's theory also modeled some of the competitive dynamics among cultural ideologies. Fiske and Tetlock (1997) noted that groups often must make difficult trade-offs between entities reflecting different relational models. When this occurs, people are offended by the trade-offs (e.g., how much car manufacturers should be required to invest per life to be saved by a design feature). When people face explicit choices between incompatible models, they experience anxiety, discomfort, and ambivalence. If they feel that others have arbitrarily made trade-offs between the relational models, then they are likely to experience moral outrage. Fiske and Tetlock (1997) added that the degree of moral discomfort or outrage will be a function of the distance and direction of the trade-offs between the two models (i.e., the levels of measurement embedded in the two relational models). The further the distance between the relational models being compared, the greater the moral outrage at the taboo trade-off between relational models, with the moral outrage generated by the less complex model against the higher order model. Fiske's theory helps to explain why egalitarians and competitive individualists fiercely oppose each other; they are furthest from each other in their underlying metrics. It also explains why egalitarian topoi often gain rhetorical advantage against better organized opposition; egalitarians have the topoi of moral outrage.

This chapter proposes that cultural topoi drive message production and message interpretation. The credibility of a message depends on how closely it matches with the receiver's cultural bias. When a message contains premises consistent with the receiver's cultural bias, enthymetic inference is facilitated. When it contains premises at odds with the receiver's cultural bias, the message probably will generate a corresponding resistance (Earle & Cvetkovich, 1995). The remaining sections of the chapter describe the cultural biases and topoi of each way of life and the implications that cultural topoi pose for public relations.

THE CULTURAL COMPETITORS

This section briefly highlights the cultural topoi that accompany the five competing ways of life. The foundational beliefs and cultural topoi of each way of life are summarized in Table 4.1. The section briefly compares the cultural topoi on their fundamental organizing beliefs and argument principles.

The value imperative of each way of life proposes a value to be maximized in human association. The value imperative is a rhetorical claim about how human relationships ought to be structured. Each value imperative is supported by beliefs about nature and human nature. The views of nature and human nature provide the bedrock topoi for each way of life. In response to the question of why, each responds, "Because this is how the world is" (Douglas, 1996). Based on these foundational premises, each cultural bias also has a justice principle, a preferred decision-making procedure, an activity principle regarding how one should pursue and experience activity, a preferred strategy to match resources to human desire, and a motive structure that each cultural bias promotes among its adherents. The five cultural topoi are summarized in Table 4.1. In the table, the cultural topoi are sequenced by the measurement complexity of the underlying relational model (Fiske, 1991).

The fatalist cultural bias sees both nature and human nature as capricious and unpredictable. In such a social world, self-exertion ends only in disappointment or calamity (Banfield, 1958). Fate decides everything, so the best that one can do is roll with the punches. Social distrust is so pervasive in this corner of the cultural map that appeals for cooperative social action are viewed with suspicion. They are seen as efforts to gain private advantage under the guise of public spiritedness.

The egalitarian cultural bias sees nature as fragile and under duress (Douglas, 1996). Nature's equilibrium is precarious and can be easily disrupted by thoughtless human interference. Likewise, human nature is good, but it is easily distorted and corrupted by social institutions that perpetuate inequality. Egalitarians seek to maximize equality so as to minimize these distortions. Ever suspicious of the corruptions of power and division, they cultivate intimacy in the form of group solidarity and make decisions by consensus. Because nature's equilibrium is precarious, egalitarians prefer to reduce human desire to a level that can be sustained within nature's resources. Spontaneity is prized in human relations and activity because it reflects natural and pure motivation. One should approach activities such as work and leisure for the intrinsic joys that they inspire. Egalitarians would rely on love to inspire both accomplishment and justice.

The hierarchical paradigm holds that both nature and human nature need structure. Hierarchical disciples seek to cultivate order in the world. Every garden needs a gardener, and human nature needs tending as well. It is bent and needs to be straightened through the discipline of carefully developed habits. Society must be organized to maximize the common good, and someone needs to be in charge of the effort. It is essential that everyone respects and obeys legitimately executed authority. Legitimate authority decides, and the chain of command implements. Human activity, whether work or leisure, requires diligent effort and the careful cultivation of good habits. By acquiring knowledge and planning carefully, the hierarchy culture believes that it can increase resources to meet human need and still manage the perils that cause egali-

TABLE 4.1	
Cultural Topoi Compared	

Fatalist topoi

Value imperative	Do not exert yourself
Human nature	Human nature is capricious and unpredictable
Nature	Nature is capricious and unpredictable
Decision principle	Let fate decide
Activity principle	Take it as it comes
Justice principle	Luck decides
Resources versus desires	Survive by coping
Motive cultivated	Social distrust
Measurement metric	None

Egalitarian topoi

Value imperative	Seek equality
Human nature	Human nature is good but has been corrupted by evil social structures
Nature	Nature is good, but its equilibrium is precarious
Decision principle	Seek consensus
Activity principle	Do it for love
Justice principle	From each according to ability, to each according to need
Resources versus desires	Reduce wants to match resources
Motive cultivated	Intimacy
Measurement metric	Nominal level

Hierarchical topoi

Value imperative	Seek order
Human nature	Human nature is bent, but hierarchy can straighten it
View of nature	Nature needs structure
Decision principle	Legitimate authority decides; the chain of command implements

tarians anxiety. However, hierarchalists fear that the social order might deteriorate, resulting in eventual anarchy and chaos—the nightmare of fatalism. Hence, they persecute those who signify counterhierarchical values.

Autonomous individualist culture is the refuge of the hermit. Nature is benevolent, and human nature can be enlightened. Autonomous individualists seek to avoid all coercive relationships and entanglements, especially the coercive demands for the correct way of thinking by groups. These distort experience and interfere with enlightenment. Human relationships and groups need to be structured to leave the exits clear; they must be structured in such a way as to enable individuals to withdraw at any time if the association becomes oppressive (Thompson, 1982). It is important to maintain equality in human relationships so that the norm of reciprocity is followed religiously. Each person receives an equal portion from group efforts, and each person has an equal say in any collective decisions.

Competitive-individualist culture holds that nature is bountiful and resilient. Human nature is self-seeking, but if this nature is challenged by competition, then it will be productively channeled. For the full potential of nature to be ex-

TABLE 4.1	
Continued	
Activity principle	Practice until you are good at it
Justice principle	Give and receive according to rank
Resources versus desires	Increase resources
Motive cultivated	Power
Measurement metric	Ordinal level

Autonomous individualist topoi

Value imperative	Avoid coercive entanglements
Human nature	Human nature is ignorant, but it can be enlightened
View of nature	Nature is benevolent if you match yourself to it
Decision principle	One person, one vote
Activity principle	If you do it, do not get attached to it
Justice principle	To each an equal portion
Resources versus desires	Fit needs within resources
Motive cultivated	Undistorted experience
Measurement metric	Interval level

Competitive individualist topoi

Value imperative	Seek liberty
Human nature	Human nature is self-seeking, but competition channels it productively
Nature	Nature is bountiful and resilient
Decision principle	Let the market decide
Activity principle	Do what you are best at
Justice principle	To each in proportion to his or her contribution
Resources versus desires	Increase both resources and appetites to the limit of your skill
Motive cultivated	Achievement
Measurement metric	Ratio level

ploited and for human potential to be fully developed, individual liberty must be maximized. Individuals are challenged to increase both appetites and resources to the limits that their skills permit. As many decisions as possible should be removed from groups and given over to freely transacting individuals; let the market decide. Life is seen as a competition in which justice demands that individual choices be rewarded and punished according to their merit. For group tasks, each individual should receive in proportion to his or her contribution. Because of the predominance of competition, it is important for people to engage in activities in which they excel and for which there are the greatest returns. Competitive individualist culture cultivates achievement motivation—the desire to be recognized for one's genuine accomplishments.

These brief sketches are primarily for illustrative purposes so that the reader can identify the component parts of a worldview or cultural bias. The cultural topoi displayed in Table 4.1 reflect qualitatively different beliefs about the nature of reality and about the values and ideals that can be pursued realistically. These assertions serve as basic warrants in daily persuasion as people advise, criticize, and account for their actions to one another (Douglas, 1982). Each cultural topos represents a comprehensive argument structure for advising people on how to make choices, for criticizing the choices that they actually make, and for justifying one's choices to others.

CULTURAL DYNAMICS

After our describing the competing ways of life, the reader might ask, "Now what? If I accept the description of the ways of life and their associated topoi, then how does this aid the search for common ground? Do we simply have a list of differences that are impossible to transcend? How are the adherents of the rival cultures able to understand each other, interact with each other, and even persuade each other?"

The problems of intercultural communication and understanding often are overstated (Thompson et al., 1990). In the first place, each person has a basic understanding of each position based on his or her experience with the relationship model that is a generative structure for each way of life (Fiske, 1991; Fiske & Tetlock, 1997). Moreover, communication routinely crosses cultural boundaries. Because there are only five ways of life, "individuals encounter the same arguments over and over. Repeated contact with the rationales and beliefs of rival ways of life helps individuals to make sense of much of what is said within these rival ways" (Thompson et al., 1990, p. 269). The semiotic relation among the ways of life also facilitates understanding at a deep level. If each way of life is defined in opposition to its competitors—by what it is against as much as what it is for (Douglas, 1996)—then one cannot fully comprehend one's selected way of life until he or she also understands the other ways of life. The adherents of the different ways of life often understand each other well enough; they just find it difficult to agree with one another.

Each cultural bias provides its adherent with a sense of relevance for detecting problems.

When it comes to risk perception, one's cultural bias tells one what to fear. The different ways of life are afraid of different things. One's cultural bias alerts one to some dangers and blinds him or her to others (Douglas & Wildavsky, 1982). Those who fear ozone depletion are not more fearful individuals than are others. In summary, an issue perceived to threaten one's way of life will arouse the individual. Egalitarians will be on the lookout for problems of inequality and the taboo trade-offs, hierarchical advocates will search for problems of deviancy and disorder, autonomous culture advocates will see threats to autonomy, and competitive individualists will detect threats to liberty via interference from well-meaning "bleeding hearts" and regulating groups. Because fatalists expect calamity, they might be aware of problems that frighten or enrage the other ways of life, but they will process this information quite passively and haphazardly (Dozier & Ehling, 1992).

Fatalist culture recognizes constraints on individual and collective action at every turn. Egalitarians recognize constraints on individual action but hope that righteous collective action will overcome them. Hierarchical culture recognizes constraints of disorder—things that will impede mobilizing and organizing collective action (e.g., lack of team spirit, selfish individualism). Competitive individualist culture will tend to perceive constraints related to bleeding hearts and bumbling authorities.

A cultural topoi perspective also enables one to anticipate how each way of life will be assailed by its competitors. The egalitarian way of life is routinely assailed as promoting equality of outcomes and thereby undermining discipline and the motivation to excel. The hierarchalists accuse egalitarians of undermining authority and discipline in social institutions. Competitive individualists rail against egalitarians for undermining achievement motivation. Competitive individualists see egalitarians as losers who are motivated by envy (e.g., "If you're so smart, then why aren't you rich?"). To this accusation, egalitarians understandably react with bewilderment because the ruckus is about illegitimate power, not envy.

A cultural topoi perspective also identifies the blind spots of each way of life. Competitive individualism is inattentive to the distorting influences of power that egalitarians see very clearly. In a similar vein, egalitarians hide the opportunity costs and trade-offs associated with their recommendations to decrease social inequalities. Competitive individualists see these hidden opportunity costs at every turn. They gleefully articulate how a policy weights most heavily on the poor and thereby increases the very inequality that egalitarians want to avoid such as when the recent settlement between the tobacco companies and the states was portrayed as a regressive tax grab by state governments (Samuelson, 1998).

Egalitarians attack hierarchy for being cruel and capricious. Hierarchy is seen to favor the strong and powerful over the weak. It is accused of using cruel and unjust methods on its adversaries. Competitive individualists often see hierarchy as capricious, but they primarily attribute this to its stupidity. They try to show that markets do better than authorities. If the government raises the minimum wage, then this will have the effect of raising the unemployment rate of people who have few skills. The road to hell is paved with good intentions because hierarchalists think that they can predict and control things that they cannot.

Competitive individualism is routinely attacked by both egalitarians and hierarchalists. Egalitarians condemn it for exacerbating social inequality, and hierarchalists attack it for promoting social breakdown and disintegration. Both of these ways of life create rhetorical constructions of children to assail competitive individualism. Competitive individualism assumes that individuals should bear the responsibility for their own welfare. The competing cultures try to show that the individualist ethos harms children who are not "competent competitive individuals." Egalitarians see corrupt forces exploiting and deceiving innocent youths in their search for profits (e.g., putting greed above the interests of children by inducing them to smoke an addictive drug). Hierarchalists desire to protect children from exposure to evil that under-

mines moral discipline (e.g., gambling, pornography, the gay lifestyle). Children need to be protected until they have internalized a systematic moral order that enables them to resist the allure of vice. When competitive individualist culture gains the upper hand, egalitarians and hierarchalists use children as their preferred rhetorical weapon.

Egalitarians construct fatalists to be quiet but heroic resisters against oppression (Ellis, 1998). Hierarchalists persecute fatalists because they see the latter as threats to a disciplined and ordered society. Competitive individualists see fatalists as losers who got their just desserts for making foolish choices. If one begins to protect people from their stupidity, then all of society will be afflicted by the greater stupidity of well-intentioned kindness. Fatalists shrug off the attacks against them and manage as best they can.

The ways of life also cooperate with each other. In some cases, they share values; in others, they share interests. Cultural theory illuminates the possibilities for cooperation and coalition among the ways of life (Thompson et al., 1990). Different ways of life may support a proposition for very different reasons. Each cultural group has some bases for cooperation with the other points on the map. Sometimes, these coalitions can create the illusion of great stability of culture over time, but coalition shifts also can create seemingly swift cultural changes (Lockhart, 1997).

Both individualism and egalitarianism may cooperate in fighting against hierarchy's perceived heavy hand (e.g., regulating speech on the Internet). Individualism and hierarchy have a shared interest in enforcing contracts and in defending social stratification. Indeed, this composite cultural bias tends to be quite prevalent and stable, with up to 37% of the samples in some communities belonging to cultural hybrids (Dake, 1992; Ellis & Thompson, 1997; Grenstad & Selle, 1997). Because they share a concern for group boundaries, egalitarians and hierarchalists often cooperate to preserve the health of the collective. Thus, we can understand the political alliance between the Patrick Buchanan social conservatives and the liberal democrats in opposing the North American Free Trade Agreement. Social conservatives worry about the erosion of national sovereignty and immigration, and egalitarians worry that the increasing openness of national boundaries will increase social inequality through job losses and increased environmental despoliation.

Fatalists usually just want to be left alone, but despite this alienation, they occasionally will be receptive to appeals by the more active ways of life. Fatalists might respond to individualist messages to avoid sacrificing for the group. Fatalists also are prone to support strong authoritarian regimes that will keep their neighbors in check (Banfield, 1958; Fukuyama, 1995; Grenstad & Selle, 1997; Putnam, 1993). Egalitarians and fatalists might unite to oppose hierarchalists when the latter want to impose regulations on people who are in the fatalist quadrant of the map (e.g., opposing zoning laws on the grounds that it will make affordable housing more expensive).

Egalitarian culture's construction of fatalist culture deserves special comment. Egalitarians look at the poor and dispossessed and see heroism (Ellis, 1998). Egalitarians are self-appointed defenders of the oppressed. They advocate on behalf of the fatalists, try to mobilize and organize them, and try to convert them to egalitarianism. Their efforts usually are frustrated and confounded by fatalists' apathy and external locus of control. Fatalists might readily recognize environmental dangers but believe that there is little recourse other than to live with the dangers (Dozier & Ehling, 1992; Grenstad & Selle, 1997). Egalitarians face the difficult task of convincing fatalists that collective effort can make a difference.

Autonomous individualist culture declines to participate in the push and pull of contending for converts. It politely declines the egoistic alienation of fatalism, the merging of selves of egalitarianism, the rigid disciplines of hierarchy, and the frenetic activity of competitive individualism. Autonomy is difficult to sustain because equality matching is difficult to sustain, but its austere requirements can be attractive for those who have had an earful of rhetorical din of the competing cultures. For some individuals, it is a

permanent aspiration; for others, it is a temporary retreat.

PUBLIC RELATIONS IMPLICATIONS AND APPLICATIONS

A cultural topoi perspective extends and elaborates a rhetorical paradigm for public relations. Some important implications for public relations theory and practice probably will become apparent as the perspective develops. This section identifies several applications that appear promising at the outset.

A paramount advantage of the cultural topoi perspective is that it parsimoniously describes an important body of tacit knowledge that astute practitioners possess. It is an accepted truism that public relations practitioners must have a "breadth of perspective" if they are to be effective in their roles (Culbertson, 1989b) and assist in the mutual adjustment between organizations and publics (Sriramesh & White, 1992). White (1988) wondered what vantage point the public relations manager could attain to gain the needed perspective. Working with a hierarchical metaphor, he noted that practitioners operate at a level below that of senior management yet claim to offer a higher perspective. White questioned how a practitioner tied to an organizational level, role, and language structure could understand both the organization and its publics. White concluded, "Theoretically, it is questionable that practitioners can develop the perspective they have claimed to offer" (p. 11).

The cultural topoi perspective shows that perspective taking is manageable from the standpoint of information processing. Perspective taking does not require superhuman abilities of discernment because the number of basic worldviews is quite finite. Because the relational models are a part of our intrinsic social knowledge (Fiske, 1991), perspective taking is not something that requires an omniscient vantage point so much as it requires clear memory. The task of perspective taking is really about avoiding blindness—unquestioning acceptance of a given cultural bias.

The real test of public relations managers and other boundary spanners is to resist the centripetal forces of organization culture that so easily turn them into lapdogs (Suchman, 1995). Effective public relations managers must develop the optimal degrees of detachment and courage—detachment to shift cultural topoi as needed and courage to articulate the resulting discoveries to management. This is difficult because public relations managers need to demonstrate enough loyalty to inspire management's confidence while retaining the necessary degrees of distance and independence.

This degree of detachment will best be accomplished in organizations where other cultural voices are tolerated or even cultivated and institutionalized (Sriramesh & White, 1992). Public relations managers ought to promote norms, procedures, and roles that enable alternative perspectives to be recognized and articulated in organizational discourse (e.g., ethics codes, devil's advocate role, ombudsman). These institutions and practices should enable them to practice a more enlightened type of public relations. Existing research suggests that public relations managers seldom play key roles in developing these institutional practices (cf. Fitzpatrick, 1996b).

A cultural topoi perspective also will enable public relations practitioners to accurately identify and describe their preferred cultural biases. The enthymemes of one's preferred bias appear to be the quite natural ones that a rational person ought to accept. However, the cultural topoi perspective serves notice that each type of rationality has its own strengths and weaknesses. Managers and technical people often think that more information will solve problems of disagreement on complex problems such as risk perception (Douglas, 1996). This fallacious belief (i.e., "If you knew what I know, then you would agree with me") assumes that once understanding is achieved, agreement will follow. A cultural topoi position forces the recognition that there are several plausible and sturdy ways of interpreting social life. Public relations practitioners must figure out how to generate the needed levels of

mutual respect among the antagonists to keep the dialogue engaged. Recognizing that each cultural bias and its accompanying topoi play a necessary part in maintaining the requisite variety of the social ecology should encourage a grudging respect for the opposition in cultural contests. The object is not to muffle the noise of cultural debates but rather to dampen personal animosities and motivate parties to seek provisional cultural agreements.

A cultural topoi perspective also adds depth to understanding how publics are constituted and maintained. Botan and Soto (1998) recently criticized the predominant definitions of publics for their organizational bias (i.e., portraying publics as reactive entities brought into action by organizational actions). Working from a semiotic perspective, they defined a public as "an ongoing process of agreement upon an interpretation" (p. 21) and proposed that publics have their own goals, processes, and dynamics that are internally generated. From the cultural topoi perspective, publics are interpretive communities organized by their common commitment to a way of life. Situating active publics in the cultural field serves to remind scholars that public relations sometimes must be improvisational. Organizations sometimes must react to publics. Moreover, publics sometimes have powerful incentives to be unreasonable; they engage the organization in a dramatic form that validates their preferred worldview and way of life (Leichty, 1997). The cultural topoi perspective would serve as a useful counterweight to organizational bias in public relations theory by giving publics greater respect; publics are part of the cultural environment of organizations.

A cultural topoi framework also should provide powerful tools for rhetorical analysis and planning. The topoi of the five cultural biases should be broadly applicable across time and context. A fully developed set of cultural topoi would enable scholars and practitioners to analyze and predict message by cultural bias interactions. Past public relations research has relied on cognitive models to describe how publics form and process information (e.g., J. Grunig, 1989c). A cultural topoi perspective suggests a more direct route to the same end—identifying the cultural beliefs that a person buys into and then predicting which issues he or she will find important and pay attention to.

The cultural topoi perspective should be particularly helpful for investigating issues management because the topoi of cultural content complement process models of issue development. Some news items generate a great deal of attention because they involve taboo trade-offs or reflect conflicts among ways of life as to which model should be applied. These issues have symbolic value that far exceeds their practical impact or significance. They are likely to be seized on as icons of injustice or stupidity. The recent decision of the Massachusetts Youth Soccer Association to sponsor "non-results-oriented" tournament competition for children under 10 years of age elicited the following derision:

> Marxism may be discredited worldwide but not on Massachusetts soccer fields. Win, lose, or draw, every team gets the same reward. Namely, no reward. Good players equal bad players, hard workers equal lazy slugs. Why put any effort into improving your game if all you get in the end is nothing? (Jacoby, 1998, p. A11)

The cultural topoi perspective also can illuminate the processes by which heroes and villains are made. Each way of life expresses somewhat unique criteria for "icons" of *good* and *evil.* Egalitarians search for powerful and wealthy villains who ruthlessly use their power to increase inequality and deprive innocent victims of their rights. This explains the interest in a 1998 *20/20* television program in which Donald Trump was accused of throwing an aged widow out of her home in Atlantic City, New Jersey. Trump convinced the Casino Reinvestment Development Authority in Atlantic City to use its power of eminent domain to acquire her property. The reporter, John Stossel, set up the villain intoning: "In Atlantic City, many people feel something's wrong." Local citizens then expressed their outrage at the transaction. One said, "That's not God's-made law, it's thieves-made law" (ABC News, 1998).

The cultural topoi perspective also would help to identify examples in which strategies are likely to fail because they combine incompatible cultural elements. Johnson Controls was unsuccessful in defending its policy of not allowing women of childbearing age to work in high-exposure lead areas. Johnson Controls' policy defense was unable to insulate the moral appeal to fundamental values (i.e., the safety of unborn children) from messages about upholding its fiduciary responsibility to stockholders. The acknowledgment of economic motivations for the decision undermined the potency of the argument that protecting unborn children from exposure to lead poisoning was the right thing to do (Hearit, 1997). Stated another way, when egalitarian and competitive individualist topoi are mixed, the latter undermine the potency of the former. Such analyses would not guarantee winning arguments, but they could identify arguments that are sure to lose because they are internally incoherent.

The cultural topoi perspective could aid the astute practitioner in identifying unintended consequences for an organization's actions. The plight of the tobacco industry can partially be attributed to the Joe Camel character. The success of this advertising campaign with children and young adolescents provided the opening for anti-smoking advocates to undermine the topos of individual choice and responsibility. This competitive individualist topos had been successfully used by the tobacco industry to defend against lawsuits by smokers. The egalitarian trope of children being seduced and exploited for the profit of cigarette companies was substituted in its place. When the issue changed from adult smoking to children smoking, the tobacco companies quickly lost ground. Tobacco executives were stunned at how quickly the tables turned against them (Goldberg, 1998).

A fully developed system of cultural topoi also would help practitioners to locate possible points of compromise and collaboration among the competing ways of life. Collaboration among three ways of life is infrequent, and many cooperative agreements are temporary in nature (Thompson et al., 1990). Even though competing cultures might support a given measure for different reasons, negotiating complex agreements and trade-offs is a necessary part of any collective (Fiske & Tetlock, 1997). A comprehensive set of cultural topoi might provide us with a means of identifying the possibilities for collaboration in a given instance. In any particular cultural moment, we might be able to negotiate provisional agreements that will have at least modest durability.

FUTURE DIRECTIONS

This chapter can only suggest some of the applications that might emerge from a cultural topoi perspective. In particular, research will be needed to address the role that public relations plays in producing, maintaining, and changing culture. A cultural topoi perspective on public relations should not only describe how cultural topoi function in public relations practice but also show how public relations can help to maintain and improve democratic institutions. Recent economic and political theory has reasserted the importance of culture in economic, social, and political development (Fukuyama, 1995; Putnam, 1993). Putnam (1993) argued that democracy and economics work best in societies that have large stocks of social capital. Social capital consists of the features of social organization such as dense social networks, norms, and trust that facilitate coordination and cooperation for mutual benefit. Moreover, Putnam's historical data showed that economic development is a consequence of civic engagement rather than the other way around. Putnam argued that civic associations teach the personal virtues and skills that are essential for democracy—listening, taking responsibility for one's views, and holding others accountable for their behaviors. Moreover, civic association enables people to converse and discover shared values.

The work on social capital drives home the point that healthy community life upholds healthy economic and political life. What is good for the community as a whole also is in the best interests of business. The work on social capital vindicates Kruckeberg and Starck's (1988) challenge that public relations should promote civic engagement. This raises a number of questions regarding the civic impact of public relations.

What Kruckeberg and Starck advocated often seems very far from what public relations actually does. Putnam (1995) was particularly concerned that the United States might be living on borrowed social capital. Many indicators of civic participation and social trust have declined (e.g., voting in elections, membership in bowling leagues, trust in authorities).

This raises empirical questions about how public relations practices affect the creation, maintenance, and destruction of social capital. Public relations practices also can be critiqued on the basis of how they affect social capital. How do specific public relations practices affect social capital? What would be the consequences for communication if everyone engaged in a particular practice? If a public relations routine depletes social capital and degrades the quality of societal communications, then the long-term practice of public relations becomes unsustainable. Where fatalist attitudes predominate, totalitarian politics usually follows close behind.

The sustainability of public relations practice should be an important criterion for critiquing specific public relations practices. Practices that deplete or degrade social capital should be identified and criticized. Likewise, public relations practices that maintain or increase social capital should be identified and encouraged. In particular, research should focus on how public relations can be used to establish connections across the familiar community divisions of age, education, race, and class (Earle & Cvetkovich, 1995). If these standards of critique were developed, they might ultimately become widely accepted and incorporated into public relations practice (Heath, 1992a).

The cultural topoi perspective suggests that a democratic society functions best when communication forums are accessible to multiple cultural voices. Cultural theory identifies many dangers that emerge when a single cultural bias achieves hegemony. The drive to universalize a cultural bias or worldview eventually confronts the reality that no relational structure or cultural ideology can be applied universally (Fiske, 1991). Each way of life has some relationships and niches for which it is best adapted. If this were not the case, then a way of life soon would perish. Pushing a cultural bias to its logical limits leads to cultural distortion and mobilizes the opposition. When cultural dialectics are suppressed, a single way of life collapses under the weight of its own internal contradictions.

This suggests that unilateral communication control is neither a feasible goal nor a respectable goal for public relations practice. Fear and distrust drive the desire for unilateral control. By comparison, an ethic of engagement entails a willingness to embrace uncertainty and to take reasonable risks in cross-cultural encounters (Earle & Cvetkovich, 1995). In a rhetorical exchange, it is not *manipulative* to make strong arguments in favor of one's position or even to desire to win the arguments. However, refusing to listen to the other party's arguments or refusing to be open to persuasion subverts the rhetorical encounter. Refusing to be open to *good reasons* is the ultimate type of communication asymmetry. Of the curses that inhabit the world, the desire for certainty probably is the worst. In the end, public relations should be about wooing, not dominating.

CHAPTER 5

Updating Public Relations

"New Science," Research Paradigms, and Uneven Developments

DAVID McKIE

During the late 1980s, the Public Relations Society of America (PRSA) commissioned a task force of educators and practitioners to set out the body of knowledge that defines the field. Commenting on the product of the commission's work, known as the PRSA *Body of Knowledge,* McElreath and Blamphin (1994) observed "a significant shift in research paradigms" and concluded that, with "few exceptions, public relations scholars and practitioners have yet to come to grips with this shift" (p. 76). This chapter confirms the accuracy of their observations. It also argues that these slow engagements, notably in relation to the discipline-spanning impact of "new science," reduce the field's conceptual resources, reinforce a low academic and intellectual status, and restrict responsiveness to changing conditions.

In postulating reasons for the field's insularity and late development, the chapter deploys new science—the "concepts, categories, images, and metaphors found in twentieth-century science" (Zohar, 1997, p. xvi)—as a way in which to extend the discipline's conceptual bases. In particular, it uses chaos, which (after quantum physics and relativity) probably is the most widely circulated of post-1950s scientific ideas, and complexity, which is chaos's most visible successor, to indicate how public relations might engage with that new science. However, before the chapter returns to the potential in public relations-science interactions, the first section examines how the traffic in ideas between public relations and other areas of knowledge is also restricted.

AUTHOR'S NOTE: I gratefully acknowledge Roslyn Petelin, editor of the *Australian Journal of Communication,* for permission to draw from material previously published in that journal; Marie Louise Hunt, co-researcher and co-writer on Australasian banking, for permission to use that research (and for inspiring it); colleagues, distinguished visitors, and students at Waikato Management School for ongoing stimulation; and the handbook editor for valuable feedback.

ISOLATING MATTERS I: DISCIPLINES, IDEAS, AND INTELLECTUALS

The restricted traffic between, and sometimes the isolation from, other disciplines has been perceived in fields close to the core business of public relations. Fleisher and Blair (1998) observed that, although public relations and public affairs "are essentially concerned with the same issues," the two fields "fail to take into account parallel literature" and "are framed by different academic and professional disciplines and practice." In this case, as well as in others (e.g., organization studies), the isolation involves relevant bodies of knowledge, scholar networks, and professional associations. The insularity increases when there is less overt overlap in methods and personnel than with public affairs (where many practitioners move between the fields or simply change job titles). In fact, if a field is not already part of the public relations canon of accepted feeder disciplines (e.g., management and decision theory, marketing, communication theory), then it has difficulty in gaining recognition regardless of its appropriateness or logical relevance. No one, for example, has taken up L'Etang's (1996c) proposal for considering public relations "in tandem with international relations" despite her persuasive argument that both link "to fundamental positions about the way individuals organize themselves into collectivities (whether publics or nations), form identities, and relate to other collectivities" (p. 34).

The failure to exchange ideas with disciplines close to the core activities and competencies of public relations expands, almost exponentially, with thinkers in less closely aligned fields. Theorists prominent enough to participate in a large number of disciplines do not seem to travel across, or be welcomed over, the discipline boundaries of public relations. To take just one example, the field's literature cites very few intellectuals named in *Fifty Key Contemporary Thinkers* (Lechte, 1994) and *The A to Z Guide to Modern Literary and Cultural Theorists* (Sim, 1995), and those who are cited appear very infrequently. Taking its cue from the limited circula-

tion of theorists from those collections, one recent paper titled "Postwar Public Relations Theory: An A to Z of Virtual Absences" (McKie, 1998) surveyed a gamut of notable absences from public relations of work published since 1945. The survey covered the lack of contributions from anthropology to zoology as well as from individual intellectuals ranging from academics and artists to scientists. The gaps were extensive enough to allow a nearly complete alphabet of absences, with most letters having multiple entries, from the A of cultural anthropologist and Asianist (both also neglected areas) Arjun Appadurai, to the Q of queer theory, to the Z of scientist and business consultant Danah Zohar.

Through the sheer range of missing thinkers and ideas, and their currency in other disciplines, McKie's (1998) survey confirmed the relative isolation of public relations theory. A similar pattern of neglect characterizes the field's attitude toward major idea clusters in contemporary knowledge. One obvious example is deconstruction, which has informed diverse fields from literature (Norris, 1982), to law (Cornell, 1991), to nursing (Ramprogus, 1995). Similarly, despite substantial and sophisticated work on rhetoric (Toth & Heath, 1992), especially in relation to the North American and classical tradition, the so-called discursive, or linguistic, turn in knowledge remains underexplored in public relations, with some notable exceptions (e.g., Motion & Leitch, 1996), compared to work from language (Fairclough, 1989) to psychology (Harré & Gillett, 1994).

ISOLATING MATTERS II: *EXCELLENCE* DECONSTRUCTION AND POSTMODERN ABSENCES

Why does the isolation matter? One answer turns on the usefulness of deconstructing some of the field's most pervasive vocabulary such as the notion of *excellence*. How, after all, can anyone rationally oppose being excellent? But what exactly does excellence mean in practice? If an agency is representing a tobacco firm to the extent of increasing the cultural acceptance of smoking and the sales of cigarettes, then to what degree are its public relations excellent? These are not merely academic questions, as accounts of the Hill & Knowlton public relations firm's involvement with Philip Morris suggest. Similar questions arise in relation to "strategic planning" (J. Grunig, 1992a, p. 17), one of the two key characteristics of excellent public relations identified by the *Excellence* study. Whose strategy is being planned? Is it the strategy of the board of directors, the chief executive officer, the key stakeholders, or the customers? And the question of the level of participation in the production of strategy arises as well. In the case of tobacco firms, for example, if the planning targets Third World consumers as major expanding markets, then differences in policy might be ones of life and death (on a large scale) and the level of strategic involvement might involve differing degrees of culpability for planners. In that context, it is worth following *strategy* back to its roots in the Greek *strategia,* meaning generalship. That continuing military connotation of something done out of sight of the enemy, rather than measures taken in front of the enemy, points to ongoing assumptions—at odds with professions of two-way symmetry—about the adversarial nature of communication with publics.

Such distinctions are, of course, necessarily context and action specific, and as theorists in fields such as critical discourse analysis and semiotics have shown, that cannot be communicated so easily. Meaning does not simply depend on the capacity of language to represent language or on the ability of speakers and writers to express what they think clearly. Abstract values such as excellence cannot be derived unambiguously from actions. Instead, meaning is embedded in context and is capable of multiple interpretations. This can easily be verified by anyone who has tried and failed to distribute press releases or leaflets. What, to a practitioner, might be an important statement of a firm's services carefully crafted onto a visually attractive promotional handout can, to busy journalists or shoppers, merely be a nuisance piece of paper to be quickly discarded. Similar problems surround

the *Excellence* project's selection of "the practice of symmetrical communication' (J. Grunig, 1992a, p. 17) as the second key characteristic of excellent public relations. The many subsequent theorists who have been interpreting what that characteristic means in different contexts ever since include several who doubt the possibility of symmetry in relations of unbalanced power: "When corporations engage in public communication, it is monologue" (German, 1995, p. 293).

The absence of productive dialogue with deconstruction is a pattern repeated with respect to widespread interest in the postmodern. Rose (1991b) tracked the growing history of postmodernism from pre-1920s poetry, to 1950s science, to contemporary architecture and geography (see also Soja, 1989); Rosenau (1992) followed up with an assessment of its impact right across the social sciences; Jagtenberg and McKie (1997) examined the condition of postmodernity in relation to communication and cultural studies; and Verschaffel and Verminck (1993) wrote *Zoology on (Post)Modern Animals.* Despite this burgeoning literature of substantial cross-disciplinary recognition, the public relations field, with isolated exceptions (e.g., Elwood, 1995), continues to resist engagement with postmodern ideas and theorists.

SIGNS OF THE TIMES: CHAOS AND POSTMODERN CONTEXTS

Corporations, industry, and other business academics are not so out of touch. BMW, the German car manufacturer, applied postmodern theory to its South Carolina factory. One visible result is the sign above the employee entrance: "Welcome to BMW . . . an information-processing and communications company that, as a happy by-product, shares in the building of fine automobiles for world markets" (cited in Eisenberg & Goodall, 1997, p. 174). That sign sets up certain attitudes in internal relations and also challenges the perception of many external publics. Postmodern theory and public relations converge in such a site, but discussions of it take place outside the field altogether in organization communication. Now, the BMW sign is not the whole story. In that particular factory, the sign was combined with a less hierarchical architecture, the practicalities of working with a multicultural workforce, and an associated commitment to more participative communication. In conjunction, these suggest a substantial shift away from the scientific managerialism associated with modernity. BMW's move toward postmodern practices also displays, as its sign demonstrates, increasing awareness of the reflexive elements of language. Undoubtedly, this growth has helped to put postmodern issues onto the agenda across nearly all boundaries. One of its key themes, reflexivity (as knowledge turning back on itself—or knowledge about knowledge), has made a whole era more aware of the central role played by language and metaphor. Concepts such as excellence no longer can be seen as simply reflecting an external world. Notions such as strategic planning cannot be, and elsewhere are not (see Whipp's [1996] creative deconstruction of the term *strategy* in organization studies), simply taken as transparent carriers of ideas.

Changes outside science, as well as inside science, may develop unevenly but emerge from the common cultural conditions and intellectual force fields of their time. Perhaps significantly, in terms of their joint neglect within public relations and their wide circulation outside of it, writers have identified the postmodern in culture as interlinked with chaos in science. Hayles (1990) positioned chaos as new in the sense of "having only recently coalesced sufficiently to articulate a vision" that "has deep affinities with other articulations that have emerged from the postmodern context" (p. 5). Zimmerman (1994) similarly positioned nonscientific postmodern thought as coterminous with, and logically akin to, the thinking that "guides chaos theory" (p. 346). The relevance of such affinities and articulations marks a transition from the scientific management of modernity to a postmodern period when "the *modus operandi* . . . may be 'business as *unusual*' " (Firat & Shultz, 1997, p. 183, italics in original).

Other areas of business and management already are exploring these affinities and articulations. Marketing has full-length book studies on postmodern marketing (Brown, 1995, 1998) and journal articles (e.g., Firat, 1992) devoted to the same subject and to "chaos science" (Diamond, 1993; McQuitty, 1992). Strategists have dipped into equivalent pools of theory for "Postmodern Culture and Management Development" (Fox & Moult, 1990) and "Business Intelligence in the Postmodern Era" (Soderlund, 1990). Discussions on complexity's importance, as well as on its potential applications, feature prominently in the pages of the journal *Long Range Planning,* as Johnson (1996) asserted that it "is the area where the strategic thinking of the 21st century is coming from" (p. 410), and Sanchez (1997) postulated that "incorporating systems and complexity concepts" might lead to "a major redefinition and expansion of the conceptual base" (p. 940).

Management itself has progressed from Berg's (1989) question mark at the end of "Postmodern Management?" to the unequivocally titled *Managing in the Postmodern World* (Boje & Dennehy, 1994). Organization theory has had more than a decade of diverse responses from Cooper and Burrell's (1988) pioneering introduction, to Clegg's (1990) book, to Hassard and Parker's (1993) edited *Postmodernism and Organizations.* By the time of its publication 3 years later, the introduction to *Postmodern Management and Organization Theory* (Boje, Gephart, & Thatchenkery, 1996b) could justifiably refer to the "first wave of postmodern intrusions," which "involved reflective essays on the potential of postmodernist thought for reconceptualizing management theory" (Boje, Gephart, & Thatchenkery, 1996a, p. 8), in the past tense. As a consequence, the editors could situate their collection as distinctive in advancing the field by actually applying "these postmodern concepts and ideas to the emerging managerial and organization issues that characterize the postmodern era" (Boje et al., 1996a, p. 8). Rather than a "first wave" of postmodern considerations, public relations can offer about one article each on postmodernism (Mickey, 1997), chaos (Murphy, 1996), and complexity (McKie, 1997). This slow breaking of ideas moves in tandem with the slow shifting of public relations research paradigms.

MISSING TRENDS: POSTMODERN FRAMES AND POSTCOLONIAL DIVERSITY

Postmodern trends also already frame research paradigms in other disciplines. In their introduction to the *Handbook of Organization Studies* (Clegg, Hardy, & Nord, 1996), for example, two of the editors usefully set out what they see as the new characteristics in their field:

> As the status of the subject is challenged, so too is that of the researcher . . . [who] is forced to re-examine, in a reflexive mode, his or her relation to the research process and the "knowledge" it produces. No longer a disinterested observer, acutely aware of the social and historical positioning of all subjects and the particular intellectual frameworks through which they are rendered visible, the researcher can only produce knowledge already embedded in the power of those very frameworks. No privileged position exists from which analysis might arbitrate. (Clegg & Hardy, 1996, p. 3)

During the same decade as the PRSA's *Body of Knowledge* work, Olasky (1989) raised the question of reflexive modes and power by reviving "the basic debate about public relations purpose [that] was aborted some 25 years ago because public relations practitioners had developed a comfortable paradigm and did not want to give it up" (p. 94). He concluded that a "trade was made: acceptance of a low status for public relations in return for acceptance of fat paychecks," and that without "multiple doses of research on the actual effects of manipulative attempts . . ., practitioners could continue whistling in the dark, at least all the way to the bank" (p. 94). Despite the provocative nature of Olasky's intervention, both the debate and research into the nature of *negative* manipulation have stayed mainly in the stillborn category.

In the absence of such published research, the gap has been partially filled in the public arena by books that take a strong anti-public relations slant. The most prominent example, Stauber and Rampton's (1995) *Toxic Sludge Is Good for You! Lies, Damn Lies, and the Public Relations Industry* topped the public relations section of business best-sellers in the highly visible Internet location of Amazon.com books for at least 2 years. Until the discipline's research takes up Olasky's (1989) challenge to reopen the debate and shift toward a less "comfortable paradigm," the profession is vulnerable to public exposure of bad practices and institutional complicity with unethical firms. Without robust self-criticism and self-questioning of its frameworks of power, public relations will deserve to retain its bad name.

Moreover, without a greater openness to other bodies of knowledge, the field's poor reputation is likely to be cemented in expanding areas such as diversity management. Despite increasing recognition of the importance of global and multicultural issues, public relations has no published work referring to subaltern studies and only one article (Roth, Hunt, Stavropoulos, & Babik, 1996) with brief references (referring to a total of two texts) from the vast postcolonial literature. More critical reflections, on ethnocentric tendencies in public relations, have barely begun. Noting that the concept of requisite variety has been imported into the field, Munshi (1999b) deconstructed its genealogy as a "metaphor borrowed from the realm of photography" (p. 39), albeit via organizational psychology, and described its adaptation to questions of diversity in public relations. He further noted that "just as photography is as much about the construction of reality as it is about the reflection of reality," requisite variety in public relations "is as much about controlling diversity as it is about acknowledging the importance of diversity in the internal and external publics of an organisation" (p. 39).

Such "contextual framing," for Munshi (1999b), tends to "consolidate control in the hands of a Western cultural elite" and, in fact, "impedes the progress of multiculturalism in public relations" (p. 39). In another paper, he proposed ways in which to adjust "the Western lens of public relations" to better reflect non-Western perspectives and adapted the idea of "subaltern counterpublics" from multiculturalist theory to help "decolonise" public relations (Munshi, 1998). These calls for greater reflexivity challenge public relations to address, with an awareness of complicity, the expectations fueled by demographic changes, global interdependency, and Asian megatrends—"if, that is, the West is willing to join in a new world where collaboration replaces domination, where diversity and convergence are far more attractive alternatives to homogeneity" (Naisbitt, 1997, p. 251).

UNEVEN DEVELOPMENTS I: BACK TO THE OLD SCIENTIFIC FUTURE

What drives the theoretical lateness of public relations? The rest of this chapter tracks back through some wider historical influences and attributes the delays to three of the field's ongoing attachments. The first is to outmoded ideas of science (especially reductionism), the second is to an associated quantitative methodology, and the third is to scientific management. The first two are basic assumptions underpinning what I term the "old science," which sometimes is called Newtonian or Cartesian (or combinations such as Cartesian-Newtonian) because these two thinkers are seen to have formulated its main characteristics. New science and contemporaneous new social movements (e.g., environmentalism, feminism) have, especially since the 1950s, increasingly called into question foundational aspects of old science and its knowledge assumptions.

Old science is associated with the reductionism of pre-quantum physics. Two elements of that type of reductionism remain relevant here. The first is constitutive reductionism, which is the idea that things can be comprehended by dismantling them into their component parts. That has been successfully challenged by the belief that the dynamics of any complex system cannot be comprehended by understanding the properties of its individual parts. So, in physics, rather than searching for the ultimate "god" particle at the base of everything, postquantum scientists might seek the nature of reality in relationships between different parts of the atom. The second element, theoretical reductionism, is an "attitude toward nature itself" and "nothing more or less than the perception that scientific principles are the way they are because of deeper scientific principles" and that "all these principles can be traced to one simple connected set of laws" (Weinberg, 1994, p. 41). The immense power attributed to quantitative methodology stems in part from that Cartesian-inspired belief—still held by physicists who believe in GUTs (grand universal theories) and TOEs (theories of everything)—in a scientific knowledge and methodology that ultimately can achieve a complete and definitive understanding of reality.

These dreams of final laws, ultimately reducible to mathematical equations, have substance because of the immense success that science has had in quantifying reality through numbers. Scientists have shown how cause and effect can be related proportionately and predicted accurately, sometimes in direct linear fashion (e.g., planetary motions). That success in turn fueled the massive industrialization program of modernity that used these scientific methods to try to predict and control the physical environment and later (especially through scientific management) the human environment. Remnants of the reductive belief still linger in areas of management science, and they maintain a disproportionate influence on a people-centered and unpredictable field such as public relations. Criticism of an overreliance on quantitative measures such as media coverage counts has come from many practitioners including Barbara Burns, managing director of Consultants in Public Relations: "Getting images on television doesn't necessarily mean getting people to act. . . . Public relations is designed to persuade people to action" (cited in Biagi, 1998, p. 238). The lingering residue of positivist beliefs also tends to cut theory off from existing practice where experience shows that behavior often transcends theoretical laws and cannot easily be decomposed into measurable components such as the number of media images.

Some of the slowness of public relations to take up recent research paradigm shifts can, therefore, be attributed to the ongoing influence of reductionist conceptions of science more appropriate to the 1950s than to the 1990s and the new millennium. Continuing to retard the field, this influence is observable in the associated deployment of numerical data and mathematical formulas imported from the scientific management associated with Frederick Taylor. As early as the 1880s, Taylor studied the movements of immigrant workers loading iron at a steel mill. His systematic approach involved clocking nearly all the movements of workers in the belief that "the rigorous, formulaic approach of the 'numbers' would yield boundless miracles in the 'scientific management of people'" (Kleiner, 1996, p. 10).

Despite impressive productivity gains in the short term, pure "Taylorism" did not continue to provide an efficient workplace over a longer time span. Instead, it led to resentment, stunted creativity, and "the propensity to sabotage" (Kleiner, 1996, p. 66). Back in the early 1980s, Hayles (1982) published a critique of outmoded scientific assumptions and the continuation of the Taylorist trend, which meant that "managers" had to "measure" (p. 121) by identifying a further crucial feature, the reduction or, where possible, the removal of human factors. With people "taken out of the loop," instruments "do the measuring," "produce numerically coded outputs," (p. 121), and increase managerial control. For public relations, one residual danger can be seen in the field's very narrow notion of efficiency, especially when combined with mathematical analysis. More than 60 years ago, Mannheim (1936) identified dangers in the trend whereby "the carrying over of the methods of the natural sciences" led to "attempts only to deal with those complexes of facts which are measurable according to a certain already existing method" (p. 261).

UNEVEN DEVELOPMENTS II: SHIFTING MANAGEMENT PARADIGMS, RATS, AND STATS

Leahigh's (1985-1986) article title, "If You Can't Count It, Does It Count?," signals the theory underpinning the retention of these influences in public relations. Indeed, for him, as well as for many of his successors in public relations research, the question remains rhetorical—in contrast to, for example, psychology and management literature since at least the early 1980s. Many 1950s psychological experiments with rats and statistics subsequently have been discredited along with the behaviorist school's reduction of all human activity to the equivalent of Newtonian mechanical dynamics. In more recent psychological literature, further specific problems with numerically driven studies, accompanied by analyses of statistical data, have come to a head. Jacob Cohen's work has exposed psychological research's continuing use of dubious statistical proofs without adequate hypotheses. In one article, "The Earth Is Round ($p < .05$)," Cohen (1994) proposed renaming "null hypothesis significance testing," or the acronym NHST, as "statistical hypothesis inference testing" (p. 997) to create an acronym suggestive of its value. Reviewing the work of Cohen and critical statistics, Hazleton and Kruckeberg (1998) usefully set out some of the implications for public relations and suggested that "researchers should distinguish between 'significant differences' in the statistical sense and 'meaningful differences' in the theoretical sense."

Although appearing only relatively recently, such quantitative concerns predate the nonlinear sciences of chaos and complexity and their implications. Corroborating Hayles's (1990) theory that common assumptions underpin knowledge shifts in different disciplines in the same time frame, chaos theory entered public discourse during the same decade as management values underwent a parallel public paradigm shift away from scientific management. The runaway business best-seller of the 1980s,

Peters and Waterman's (1982) *In Search of Excellence,* sold more than 5 million copies with a direct attack on scientific management's "numerative rationalist approach" (p. 29) and on its fundamental assumption that if one can read the bottom line, then one can manage anything. Far from excluding people from the loop, Peters and Waterman restored humans to the forefront of the balance sheets of successful companies: "Treating people, not money machines, as the natural resource may be the key to it all" (p. 39).

Six years later, Peters (1988), in the interestingly titled *Thriving on Chaos,* confirmed a trend still current in the management literature. That trend, in continuing to depart from command and control management, has gathered fresh impetus from new science ideas. In charting differences between traditional management thinking and the new management thinking, writers navigate by sets of binary oppositions such as the former's foundation in Newtonian science and the latter's foundation in post-Newtonian science. Aligned with that foundation opposition, other frequent binary pairs include understanding by dissection into parts versus a more holistic approach, growth as linear versus growth as organic and chaotic, and defining management as control and predictability against management as insight and participation (Allee, 1997). Other mainstream leadership thinkers endorse similar trends away from control. Zand (1997), in a manner extremely relevant to public relations and the new science alike, acknowledged that "progress" in knowledge work is "nonlinear" and "difficult to measure" (p. 21). He continued that, whereas leaders "with a traditional production, marketing, or accounting orientation find this notion difficult to comprehend and accept," it "is meaningless to demand that the quality of a decision made by a group of seven people be seven times as good as a decision made by one person" (p. 21).

In postulating that too much public relations literature overemphasizes the quantitative, especially an inadequately hypothesized quantitative, I acknowledge two fronts that require the retention of an appropriate numeric dimension. The first is "metaresearch" (e.g., J. Grunig, L. Grunig, Sriramesh, Huang, & Lyra, 1995), which, in synthesizing from diverse results, does make allowances for possible flaws and incompatibilities in statistical studies. The second is the need for practitioners to demonstrate measurable goals within businesses with leaders from Zand's (1997) "traditional production, marketing, or accounting orientation" (p. 21). Quite simply, public relations writing and practice must, and does (Lindenmann, 1997), address these industry demands for measurable outcomes. That necessity is consistently supported by the high ranking that such demands received in Delphi research into public relations priorities in North America (McElreath, 1980).

UNEVEN DEVELOPMENTS III: FIGURING CONTEXTS AND JOURNAL REFLECTIONS

After all those factors are acknowledged, however, writers on the sciences of complexity urge a useful caution: "Unnatural faith in the power of mathematics may say less about its actual potential" and "more about the common scientific faith" in what they term the "dogma of reductionism" (Coveney & Highfield, 1995, p. 25). Support for their caution, and an update of McElreath and Blamphin's (1994) article, can be found in the journal that originally published it. The *Journal of Public Relations Research* is one of the discipline's two leading international periodicals, and its issues over the 5-year period from 1994 to 1998 provide a guide to the state of the art of academic public relations research. The journal's output during those years, as I interpret it, demonstrates the continuing power of the quantitative in public relations and one major source of challenges to it but no conceptual traces of new science perspectives. During those 5 years, the journal produced four issues annually for a total of 60 articles. Of that total, only 16 articles (27%) contained no mathematical equations or tables. These proportions suggest that statistical significance, or at least the significance of statistical approaches, retained methodological preeminence in the *Journal of Public Relations Research*.

Among the journal's scarce nonmathematical pieces, one article stands out. At 62 pages, in a journal whose usual number of pages per issue is less than 72, Hon's (1995b) "Towards a Feminist Theory of Public Relations" was uncharacteristically long but was significant in more than its length. Distinguishing her perspective from 1950s-style quantitative science, Hon built on more up-to-date theories connecting feminism, science, and methodology (Harding, 1986, 1987) to construct an explicitly feminist, and markedly nonmathematical, approach. In the process, she abjured traditional scientific techniques in favor of methodologies taken from streams within science influenced by writings from the women's movement. Other qualitative pieces from feminist-influenced research, such as "The Language of Leadership for Female Public Relations Professionals" (Aldoory, 1998a), have followed. None of these qualitative articles, however, contains a single reference to the new science literature at a time when "metaphors drawn from complexity science" and "related to change and process" are being introduced to respond to "the world of continuous change, such as the biotech and Internet industries" (Lissack, 1997, p. 294) and leadership challenges (Blank, 1995). Now, as my own use of content counting indicates, I do not see the use of quantitative methods in themselves as of concern, and I emphasize that my arguments do not preclude the use of statistics—when decoupled from reductionist conceptualization—as a helpful multipurpose tool.

Apart from Hon's (1995b) brief invocation of Harding's decade-old feminist questioning of traditional science, the *Journal of Public Relations Research* has not published anything challenging old science assumptions. In book-length literature as well, in addition to adhering to numerical discourse and reductionist dogma, public relations writers show symptoms of the type of physics envy common to disciplines seeking status through the aura of common kinship with traditional science. On the verge of the 1990s, the text-book *Public Relations Research* (Brody & Stone, 1989) still stated unproblematically that "scientific method—the same basic process the natural sciences use in discovering answers to physical, chemical, and biological problems—provides the best starting point for public relations research" (p. 121). This statement is typical in registering no awareness that some processes of natural sciences have changed significantly and that, because the contemporary study of complex systems differs "so greatly from the simple systems that science has studied up to now," it "represents an entirely new chapter in the pursuit of scientific knowledge" (Casti, 1997, p. x).

BRIDGING TEMPORAL GAPS: BUSINESS LESSONS AND NEW SCIENCE

Instead of learning from the new chapter, prominent leaders in the public relations field still turn back the pages and routinely reiterate older versions of scientific method: "Our attempt to generalize from empirical data to higher levels of abstraction . . . is an essential activity for any scientific field" (J. Grunig et al., 1995, p. 167). The massive *Excellence* study (J. Grunig, 1992c) exemplifies the neglect of the new science. In nearly 700 pages, it barely—three index entries to a total of 3 pages—addressed science at all. The pages themselves point only briefly in the general direction of paradigm changes. Despite the "obvious benefits" of the scientific method, J. Grunig and White (1992) observed "many myths about it" including "the belief that science can be totally objective, that it can be kept neutral of values, and that it can discover 'truth' " (pp. 31-32).

After these brief reservations, J. Grunig and White (1992) drew two familiar conclusions. The first was that "scientific research and the theory it produces can help to bring order to the chaos of public relations" (p. 32). This simple equation, of chaos with anarchy, overlooks the contemporary use of chaos by mathematicians, meteorologists, and scientists. In that use, chaos is far from meaning the absence of laws in the physical world. Instead, it points out that, although the laws are of such complexity that they are virtually impossible for us to forecast accurately, their apparently random behavior can turn out to have parameters of predictability. Accordingly, by using more up-to-date science than J. Grunig and White's simple binary opposition between ordered science and anarchic human practices, public relations research would focus on the order in its turbulence rather than on the need to import an outmoded system. J. Grunig and White's (1992) second main conclusion was that "science is a very human undertaking and that humans impose their fundamental beliefs about the world on their thinking and observing" (p. 32). These two conclusions form an inadequate basis on which to engage with the shift to new science and do not match up to Eckersley's (1992) challenge that "the credibility of any Western philosophical worldview is seriously compromised if it is not at least cognizant of, and broadly consistent with, current scientific knowledge" (p. 50). To earn that type of credibility, public relations will need to tackle more complex translations from more recent science.

So, what might public relations as a discipline learn from undertaking that task? For the postreductive, post-Newtonian tendency, I quote at length from Margaret Wheatley, a respected former management professor and consultant. Arguing for a shift in business akin to the one that I am proposing for public relations, Wheatley (1994) rejected reductionist underpinnings as inappropriate for contemporary conditions:

> Each of us lives and works in organizations designed from Newtonian images of the universe. We manage by separating things into parts, we believe that influence occurs as a direct result of force exerted from one person to another, we engage in complex planning for a world that we keep expecting to be predictable, and we search continually for better methods of objectively perceiving the world. These assumptions . . . come to us from seventeenth-century physics, from Newtonian mechanics. . . . Intentionally or not, we work from a worldview that has been derived from the natural sciences. . . . If we are to continue to draw from the sciences to create and manage organizations, to design research, and to formulate hypotheses about organizational design, planning, economics, human nature, and change processes (the list can be much longer), then we need to at least ground our work in the science of our times. (p. 6)

PUBLIC RELATIONS AFTER REDUCTIONISM: REVIEWING CHAOS AND CRISES

The simple move beyond Newtonian principles, "a direct result of force exerted from one person to another" or from one group to another, acknowledges the complexity of existing public relations interactions. It also points beyond the simplicity of two-way symmetrical models toward the consideration of complex force fields of multiple competing powers in the real world of presidential impeachments. At this point, I acknowledge the positive role of the field's other leading international journal, *Public Relations Review*, in publishing the only two articles to date on public relations and chaos theory. Although the first *Public Relations Review* article (Cottone, 1993) was less than two pages long, it was followed 3 years later by a substantial piece, "Chaos Theory as a Model for Managing Issues and Crises" (Murphy, 1996).

In her article, Murphy (1996) pointed out that organizations practicing "symmetrical communication attempt to adjust their own behavior to accommodate the beliefs and concerns of their publics" (p. 110). For Murphy, the "price paid" by such practices is that "the organization accommodates whatever outcome may evolve over time," and so it becomes "somewhat problematical to talk about public relations objectives and goals which imply control" (p. 110). Murphy's "price paid" usefully points to a danger in linking public relations too closely to specific goals in fluctuating circumstances and also usefully points to the limits of control and reductive approaches. However, if she had focused more on chaos's transition phases (as she did elsewhere in her article), especially the concentration on discontinuous transition to another stable state or stable pathway of change (e.g., melting ice and stock market movements), she might have seen positive possibilities.

Although not explicitly drawing from new science, leading writers on crises and crisis management often chart similar types of patterns "including yielding to external forces or seeking to influence them as means for seeking harmony" (Heath, 1990, p. 43). Retrospective research into the ebb and flow of control and accommodation in crisis case studies might chart further transition phases of this interplay. It would offer opportunities to refine optimal pathway plans for certain emerging conditions (especially the Internet) as well as general guidelines. In the famous Intel case, for example, the company learned its nonlinear lessons—that alterations in an initial state can produce disproportional alterations in subsequent states—the hard way. By ignoring early Internet postings on tiny calculation errors in its computer chips, Intel needlessly lost credibility with key publics, generated negative publicity, and sustained financial losses.

In addition to illustrating the butterfly effect of large consequences from small changes at that early stage, Intel's subsequent recovery tends to conform to chaos theory's allied discovery that similar agents and circumstances can generate periods of relative stability with parameters of probability. In effect, although complex systems exhibit chaotic (in the ordinary sense) behaviors, the same elements can produce "quasi-stable" patterns that can, through "self-organizing" processes, set up times of " 'near-order' in otherwise chaotic phenomena" (Sanchez, 1997, p. 940). Organizations change continuously in easy, routine, and responsive ways, but that change cannot be arbitrarily controlled and, in many cases, exhibits self-organizing processes that transcend individual leaders or sections. Chaos and complexity can, in theory (and in practice in other disciplines), engage comfortably with move-

ments that alternate between control and accommodation. Such situations, on the edge of order and chaos, are common to current competitive environments when "agents" do not have "control" (Stacey, 1996b, p. 183) as currencies, markets, and stock markets fluctuate alarmingly all over the globe.

In such turbulence, chaos highlights the sensitive dependence on initial conditions in a manner at least as applicable to a firm's environmental behavior and public reputation as to meteorological forecasting. To a far greater extent than the fabled solitary butterfly flapping in Brazil contributes to setting off an imaginary tornado in Texas, a firm's public perception can be altered with elements of seemingly small significance. Australian corporate giant BHP, for example, was slow to see the value of commissioning a short film to present its Papua New Guinea operations in a more positive light. As a result, by the time the film was ready, it came too late in the media crisis to counter negative images aired by television program footage critical of BHP's OkTedi project. In retrospect, BHP management perceived the relatively small delay, in a minor part of its overall public relations management, as a significant contributing factor to the virtual tornado of adverse media coverage that erupted over the company's conduct in Papua New Guinea (Laver, 1996). Most observations on chaos dwell almost exclusively on that type of "butterfly effect" whereby "very small events can have massive outcomes in complex systems" (Turnbull, 1996, p. 159).

PUBLIC RELATIONS FUTURES I: STRUCTURING AND EVOLVING RELATIONSHIPS

Despite the importance of butterfly effects, and the support that they give to traditional practitioner wisdom of attending to small details with extreme care, there is more for public relations to learn from chaos than butterfly effects. In fact, according to Goerner (1995), chaos's "most important finding relates to one thing—structuring" or the "realization" that "interdependence produces such things as patterns, coherence, coordination, networks, and synchronization" (p. 4). Because that realization already has unlocked the secret of structures in the natural world and is increasingly providing points of entry to social structures, it merits exploration right across public relations. Chaos theory's emphasis on "structuring," along with a greater interest in the evolutionary structures of biology, has been extended by the sciences of complexity.

In offering "a new way of thinking about the *collective* behavior of many basic but interacting units" (Coveney & Highfield, 1995, p. 7, italics in original), complexity provides a common conceptual framework. The framework can be shared with different fields and can be applied to the majority of real-world problems that, like most public relations problems, cannot be easily compartmentalized. For Coveney and Highfield (1995), because "a human being is an emergent property of huge numbers of cells" and "a company is more than the sum of its pens, papers, real estate, and personnel" (p. 330), a different perspective is needed to make sense of emerging behaviors. The authors concluded that although perhaps not "able to precisely forecast the long-term behavior of a complex system, nonlinear dynamics shows that we can gain some insights into its global behavior" (pp. 330-331). Studies indicating the value of research along those lines do exist in public relations. One project has extended McElreath's Delphi work on U.S. public relations priorities approach to a 13-nation study including African, Asian, and Australian participants. The study generated insights into the extent to which the global (in the senses of both covering the planet and being universal) pattern of capitalist economic development overrode cultural, political, and regional differences (Synnott & McKie, 1997). Although only a small-scale research project, its results support the hypothesis of a global pattern transcending individual geocultural variations.

On a larger scale, chaos and complexity sharpen knowledge of change transitions in general as more predictable and manageable and so offer huge potential to add value. This is especially true at a time when technologies are introducing seemingly random levels of unpredictability. The Internet in particular—and there is some truth, however self-serving, in Andrew Grove's claim that the "world now runs on Internet time" (cited in Downes & Mui, 1998, p. 13)—enmeshes markets with new strategic publics. These are publics that public relations still is seeking to address effectively; they are publics that can be exposed to, and can respond widely to, ideas flashing across an interconnected globe in less time than it takes to write a press release (S. Alexander, 1996).

At this point in technological history, when Moore's Law (i.e., the processing power of the central processing units of computers doubles every 18 months) combines with Metcalfe's Law (i.e., network values increase dramatically with each new node), companies are increasingly seeking out digital strategies for market dominance (Downes & Mui, 1998). Central to their searches are how to manage key transition phases. These transitions range from relatively predictable change such as Moore's Law to discontinuous leaps when, for example, that law's cheaper, faster, and smaller (through the ongoing miniaturization of chips) central processing units combine with Metcalfe's network growth to expand the power of interlinked participants exponentially. The Amazon.com Internet bookstore has been estimated to hold 10 times the number of titles than the largest book superstore. However, it presents a picture of the future more "because the books it sells may be the least valuable service it provides" (Baskin, 1998, p. 49) as customers seek relationships rather than features. The relationships that Amazon.com creates with its virtual publics are forging future relations at a key site for all concerned with new technologies. Despite the fact that Amazon.com has yet, at the time of this writing, to register any significant profit, investors have backed the firm's judgment heavily. For public relations, Amazon.com's success encourages a new theorizing of cyberservices. Evolving relationships as technology evolves, Amazon.com's strategy has made it a market leader and exemplar during chaos-style transition phases of continuous change punctuated with discontinuous leaps.

PUBLIC RELATIONS FUTURES II: BANKING, MARKETING, AND TECHNOLOGICAL TRANSITIONS

Similar transition possibilities might help in the perennial public relations problem of distinguishing itself from marketing. Recent Australasian research in the banking sector examines how, since the 1980s, marketing has taken, at the expense of public relations, an increasing share of the sector's jobs, philosophy, and power (Hunt & McKie, 1998). Along with downsizing and increasing profitability, marketing's increased influence has been accompanied by reduced services and/or rising costs for many of the least powerful customers. If the idea of a new emerging order is adopted from chaos and complexity, then questions arise as to what extent and for how long downsizing and disrespect for the public in general, and for specific vulnerable publics in particular, can produce high returns. Future predictions further amplify the risks inherent in these tendencies. In advocating what business will have to do to gain "the millennium edge," Turnbull (1996) forecasted that there will be a new generation of customers in the 21st century. He argued that this group will demand that business demonstrate that it is motivated by community interest as well as self-interest. By collating consumer surveys and relating them with corporate actions, Turnbull (1996) concluded that "altruistic companies are the companies that balance the interest of all their stakeholders and see profit as a result of a company's total goals rather than as an end in itself" (p. 138).

The contrast with current banking practices is stark. One 1998 cover of *New Zealand Management* carried the heading, "Brickless Banks: Virtual Finance Gets Real," to draw attention to the establishment of a New Zealand-based Internet bank called BankDirect. Positioning BankDirect

as the technobank of the future, the inside story detailed the transfer into cyberspace—without any different ethical elements—of the current profit-driven marketing philosophy. The story's three subheadings neatly summed up the bank's aims: "The Race for e-Cash," "Building the Branchless Bank," and "Target Market" (Tapsell, 1998, pp. 38, 40). The conclusion on "what BankDirect is all about" confirmed the traditional marketing emphasis: "It's another product of the ASB Bank, which needs to grow its market share of the banking market" (p. 40). BankDirect further stresses the bottom line and self-interest on its Web site. No care is given to visuals, and the screen simply presents simple outlines of houses shaded in black with space in the center to contain, and emphasize, the following text:

- ❑ We don't pay rent
- ❑ Which means we can keep our lending rates low
- ❑ So you can buy a house and not pay rent either. (BankDirect, 1998)

BankDirect's Internet presence makes interesting distinctions between "them" (traditional brick building bankers) and "us" (virtual bankers) in relation to customers but remains firmly founded on the assumption of a common core in profit alone. In this climate, the banks are making profits, but they are not making friends, especially in public relations terms (defined by the Public Relations Institute of Australia as "the deliberate, planned, and sustained effort to establish and maintain understanding between an organisation and its publics" [cited in Tymson & Sherman, 1996b, p. 3]). A significant percentage of the Australian community increasingly regards bank managers and banks very negatively. Whereas 66% of the public "rated bank managers as the most honest and ethical individuals in the workforce" in 1976, that percentage "slipped to 60% in 1986, to 49% in 1990, and to 32% in 1997" (Milne, 1997, p. 17).

Consumer dissatisfaction should be registering strong danger signs in the sector because, for most customers, the list of alternatives to the banks is growing. Credit unions, building societies, mortgage originators, and community banks are not the end of the story. The banks themselves are virtually training the public to do without them by making bank transactions through automated teller machines, electronic funds transfer point of sale, and telephones. As the use of "smartcards" and Internet banking increases, the public will become accustomed to not dealing with people as representatives of their banks. That raises the question of whether or not it will matter to them whether the recorded voice at the end of a telephone, or the icon on the Web page, is a local bank, an overseas bank, or a virtual bank. All of this makes a single-minded reliance on economic drivers risky and, if the trends develop as predicted, will raise the potential value of the community-building activities of public relations. Amid banks' seemingly continuous run of recent profits, this points to the possibility of a discontinuous leap. By banking on its traditional relationship strengths (to its own and the public's advantage), public relations can align with the type of change phase routinely theorized by chaoticians.

PUBLIC RELATIONS FUTURES III: CONCEPTUAL ADVANTAGES, HYPERCOMPETITION, AND DEENGINEERING

The future for public relations outside the banking sector also might depend on how well and how soon it is able to evolve in a high-tech age so fast that one pair of analysts termed it "blur" (Davis & Meyer, 1998). This period of unprecedented transition also has been characterized as "hypercompetition" (D'Aveni & Gunther, 1994). In the present hypercompetitive climate of high-tech transformation, one leading British manager argued that what "businesspeople need to understand about twentieth-century science" is not "technical" but rather "conceptual" (Stone, 1997, p. xiii). Conceptually, one key lesson is that postreductive science is "holistic" and can cross all disciplines including the divide between "physical and biological" sciences (Zohar, 1997, p. 11).

Recognizing the centrality of technological transitions, theorists in other business disciplines already exploit conceptual advantages by crossing boundaries. Organizational strategists Brown and Eisenhardt (1998) extended their original research on the highly competitive computing industry to accommodate a "confluence of complexity and evolution theory" (p. ix). In the book that resulted, *Competing on the Edge,* they illustrated how ideas such as the "edge of chaos" and self-organization "play out in real firms" (p. x). They argued that such developments offer the best strategy for the current business environment because any "neat match of businesses with markets is all too fleeting in a world where opportunities come and go, collide and divide, and merge and morph" (p. 247). They concluded that although competing on this edge is "complicated and demanding," it also is "an approach to strategy that works" at this particular time "when the name of the game is change" (p. 247).

Strategic shifts to play the change game effectively involve conceptual shifts in paradigms as well as mathematics. For public relations, they point away from the field's "overwhelmingly instrumental" (Karlberg, 1996, p. 263) tradition of academic research. Drawing heavily from engineering sources such as Shannon and Weaver's (1949) classic *Mathematical Theory of Communication,* this tradition, much like its 1950s science contemporary, continues to be relayed into the 1990s. Edward Bernays had a propensity to call his version of instrumentalism the "engineering of consent," which he used as the title of two articles and a collection of essays. His commitment to the control end of the management spectrum can be seen consistently during different periods of his writings through book and article titles. He even published one ad with the headline "Watch Out, Industry; Human Problems Ahead" that asserted in the body of the text that "the social sciences can serve industry's human relationships in the same way that physical sciences serve industry's technological progress" (cited in Cutlip, 1994, p. 180).

Interviewed late in his life, Bernays stayed attached to command and control management. Responses in a 1984 interview revealed either no knowledge about or no sympathy with possible changes in the managerial heavens, particularly those symbolized by the more pluralistic and playful *Gods of Management* of Handy's (1985) almost contemporaneous book. Bernays clung unrepentantly to ideas of rule by the invisible hands of the powerful as supreme beings, and when he did use chaos, he associated it with the mess of democracy and kept to the traditional negative sense of disorder:

> We cannot have chaos. . . . Public relations counselors can prove their effectiveness by making the public believe that human gods are watching us for our own benefit. . . . People need sacred dances. Public relations counsel should be trained to call the tunes. (cited in Olasky, 1987, p. 81)

Bernays' association of chaos with unacceptable disorder, his manipulative intent, and his methodological approach survive remarkably intact in current public relations textbooks. In 1935, he set out an eight-step method of how to "engineer public consent":

1. Define goals and objectives.
2. Research public to find out whether goals are realistic, attainable, and how.
3. Modify goals if research finds them unrealistic.
4. Determine strategy to reach goals.
5. Plan action, themes, and appeals to public.
6. Plan organization to meet goals.
7. Time and plan tactics to meet goals.
8. Set up budget for out-of-pocket expenses for the program. (cited in Cutlip, 1994, pp. 186-187)

As late as the third edition of *The New Australian and New Zealand Public Relations Handbook,* Tymson and Sherman (1996b) provided two derivative step diagrams (p. 29). One was a 4-step diagram (set objectives, plan and budget, implement program, and evaluate), and the other was an 11-step diagram (management sets general objectives, target audiences defined, current opinions established, specific objectives agreed, media selected, budget prepared, plan and budget reviewed, final plan implemented, results evaluated, results reported, and program reviewed by board/management). Neither varies

much from Bernays' model from more than 30 years ago. The writers also perpetuated early transmission and message models by replicating an old Shannon and Weaver (1949)-type model diagram complete with original engineering terms of *noise* and *feedback* (Tymson & Sherman, 1996b, p. 11). At least some of this continued attachment to mechanistic models must reside in their assumed potential for manipulation and their association, however dubious, with the mathematical aspirations of scientific management. The residual influence of old engineering ideas also restricts participation in the "informational revolution" that will "form the basis for so-called normal science in the coming century" (Casti, 1997, p. xi).

PUBLIC RELATIONS FUTURES IV: INTEGRATING BIOLOGY, COMPLEXITY, AND SIMPLICITY

Part of that informational revolution is powered by a move toward simplicity through the integration of different fields. Not all interdisciplinary complexity research leads in the direction of complexity. It also searches for simple principles of organization to identify islands of relative stability in the middle of otherwise disordered environments. In their search for common islands amid disciplinary-divided seas, the Santa Fe Complexity Institute set up a program bringing together prominent biologists, economists, and physicists. Some of the participants subsequently produced a book whose very title, *The Economy as an Evolving Complex System* (Arrow, Anderson, & Pines, 1988), combined the ideas of evolution with economics. In this way, complexity theorists fostered a climate in which unusual commonality can be sought and found beneath obvious surface differences.

For public relations, rather than replicating the concentration of specialists in the *Excellence* study, future large-scale research might be better served with a collected assembly along the lines of Santa Fe's complexity work or the Manhattan Project (without its destructive focus). Both gathered together leading thinkers from distinctly different disciplines. In addition to crossing boundaries, Complexity has sought diversity by simulating real-world complications through direct imitations of the problem-solving capabilities of already existing biological systems, notably the human brain. Imprints of that attempt remain in the strongly biological metaphors and the implicit, and sometimes explicit, confrontations with the reductionist agenda. Reductionism in economics, for example, would try to understand things by breaking them down into the component parts of "rational economic people" and a linear world tending toward equilibrium through market forces. By direct contrast, complexity economists engage with nonlinear worlds of people and markets where, in both cases, uncertainty and fluctuating patterns are the norm.

Implications for public relations in these studies would include testing Chris Galloway's hypothesis, in a 1998 D.Phil. proposal to the University of Waikato Management School, that the linear assumptions guiding much industry practice "contribute to the equivocal view of the profession." In his view, they constrain effective performance in what clients know to be constantly changing, and largely unpredictable, environments. Indeed, the one area where nearly all current perceptions—by business writers, market forecasters, and futurologists alike—converge is on the idea of rapid and ongoing change: "In the decade of the 1990s, we are moving from managing control to leadership of accelerated change" (Naisbitt & Aburdene, 1990, p. 217). In such an environment, public relations objective setting and communication plans based on linear approaches to knowledge are increasingly likely to lack credibility with stakeholders whose activities form part of economic and social systems that are clearly observable as dynamic, fluid, and far from equilibrium.

Accordingly, complexity theorists reverse the textbook public relations approaches and move "away from the rigid step-by-step approach of systematic programming, through renewed emphasis on how nature solves problems" (Coveney & Highfield, 1995, p. 87). By similarly avoiding "deterministic" approaches, computer scientists have emulated features of evolution to tackle

seemingly "intractable problems" (p. 87). The widely promulgated point-by-point public relations planning model suggests itself as an obvious candidate for comparable treatment. By making the conceptual move to think of "organizations as living things coevolving with market ecologies" (Baskin, 1998, p. 155), public relations practitioners and firms would operate and plan less mechanically and more as living learning systems. Imitating other "organically modeled organizations," they could "use life's design principles" to "search for new and better ways to meet the changing needs of their markets" and "coevolve through self-organization" (p. 155). Although such moves would foster continuous adaptation to unexpected changes in circumstances and timetables, little public research currently is investigating possible parallels with other evolutions.

REALIGNING CONCLUSIONS

Before concluding, I reemphasize that public relations disinterest in the potential of new science for revolutionizing "human thinking" (Zohar, 1997, p. xvi) is not the case elsewhere in management. Zohar's (1997) book, *Rewiring the Corporate Brain: Using the New Science to Rethink How We Structure and Lead Organizations,* takes its place in a series of annual increments of managerial books based around new science paradigms. During the 1990s, these included Baskin's (1998) *Corporate DNA: Learning From Life,* Bergquist's (1993) linkage of chaos theory with *The Postmodern Organization,* Blank's (1995) "Quantum Leadership Paradigm" (p. 26) in *The 9 Natural Laws of Leadership,* Stacey's (1996a) *Complexity and Creativity in Organizations,* and Wheatley's (1994) *Leadership and the New Science.* All six books offer distinct but aligned sets of recommendations on how new science can improve on Newtonian models in business. All have yet to be taken up in the public relations field. In a final irony, given the arguments of this chapter, one environmentalist nominated public relations as "the paradigm science of the modern age"

(Athanasiou, 1996, p. 228). From the rest of his book, Athanasiou (1998) clearly saw this in terms of public relations practice rather than theory. He attacked public relations as anti-democratic and held it accountable in large measure for impending environmental and social catastrophes. This is the type of discontinuous future change that contemporary management has learned to theorize from new science, and it is one that public relations should be better prepared to consider.

In the face of such attacks and catastrophic scenarios, public relations theory cannot stick with the traditional "value-free and neutral scientific observations" (McElreath & Blamphin, 1994, p. 76) of old research paradigms and respond effectively to the environmental challenge and environmental challengers. A better model emerged at the Santa Fe Complexity Institute, where the Nobel Prize-winning physicist, Murray Gell-Mann, launched a Global Sustainability project despite deep scientific suspicion that the project might elude the "predictive role" of science and turn into "some kind of global environmental activism" (Gell-Mann, 1994, p. 375). Without catching up on comparable research paradigm shifts, public relations is unlikely to find answers for either academic or activist critics. By updating public relations with new science supplemented by its cultural and management interpreters, theorists in the field would extend the existing body of knowledge and, during an age of expanding interdisciplinarity, would usefully shed elements of debilitating insularity. Such moves also would foster a culture of intellectual flexibility and research diversity better suited to emerging business, environmental, social, and technological challenges.

CHAPTER 6

In Search of a Metatheory for Public Relations

An Argument for Communitarianism

ROY LEEPER

■ For some time, the field of public relations has been in search of a unifying theory. Kruckeberg and Starck (1988) made the argument that practitioners as well as scholars in the field are confused as to the nature of the discipline and that the multiplicity of definitions in the literature is a sign of "vagueness and disagreement and confusion" (p. 16). J. Grunig (1989e) argued that many theories apply to public relations but that there is no public relations theory. Because of a widespread recognition of the desirability of such a theory, there is an ongoing discussion among scholars as to which possible paradigm would be most valuable as a unifying theory (Ferguson, Sintay, & Botan, 1996; Hallahan, 1996a; Heath, 1993; Heath & Vasquez, 1996; Toth, 1992; Vasquez, 1993).

Littlejohn (1992) wrote that there are three levels of theory: metatheoretic (basic assumptions), hypothetical (picture of reality/framework for knowledge), and descriptive (operations and findings). Littlejohn recognized that the three levels cannot be separated in operation but argued that the separation is useful for analytical purposes. Within each of the levels, according to Littlejohn, there are four types of questions: epistemological, ontological, perspectival, and axiological. Metatheory encompasses "assumptions about the fundamental nature of the phenomena of interest. These assumptions are frequently unrecognized and influence choices of theory as well as method. Recognition of metatheoretic assumptions is necessary before other alternatives may be considered by theorists and researchers" (Hazleton & Botan, 1989, p. 7; see also J. Grunig, 1989e, and J. Grunig & White, 1992).

Although the concept of public relations is difficult to define (Kruckeberg & Starck, 1988), definitions provide a common ground for discussion. The concept of public relations that is used in this chapter is that advanced by the Public Relations Society of America (PRSA) and echoed by others. The "Official Statement on Public Relations" adopted in 1982 (PRSA, 1998-1999) identified the goal of public relations as being to help "our complex pluralistic society to reach decisions and function more effectively by contributing to mutual understanding among groups and institutions. It serves to bring private and public policies into harmony" (p. ii). Similarly, Seitel (1995) wrote that the "goal of effective public relations . . . is to harmonize internal and external relationships so that an organization can enjoy not only the goodwill of all the publics but also stability and long life" (p. 8). Among the functions or processes for achieving this goal, according to Seitel, are honest communication, openness and consistency, fairness, two-way communication, and research and evaluation of actions (p. 7).

This search for harmony, as used here, does not *always* necessitate agreement between an organization and its publics; genuine differences of interests and goals sometimes can exist. The harmony sought is at the base level of community cohesion and values that hopefully will lead to harmony on specific issues. While an organization seeks to influence and change its environment, the quest for harmony "should also foster open communication and mutual understanding with the idea that an organization also changes its attitudes and behaviors in the process—not just the target audience" (Wilcox, Ault, & Agee, 1998, p. 4). Such an approach to public relations aids in strengthening the community context within which organizations operate.

Using Littlejohn's (1992) approach to theory classification as a starting point, this chapter argues that communitarianism satisfies the call for a metatheoretical basis for the field of public relations. First, the chapter provides an introduction to communitarianism. Then, it explores the metatheoretical bases of the theory. Finally, it argues that using communitarianism as a basis for the field strengthens the quest for the goal of harmony by providing a sound foundation for the field in the areas of public relations models, the concept of publics, corporate social responsibility, and ethics.

INTRODUCTION TO COMMUNITARIANISM

This introduction to communitarianism places the recent interest in communitarian theory into a social context and then looks at the people and themes in the communitarian movement.

Context

In Western society, there are two basic metatheoretical approaches that have been competing for dominance: liberalism and communitarianism. (This chapter is concerned only with these approaches as basic theories, not with any specific social/political agendas that may be claimed as arising from the approaches. There are politically *liberal* communitarians just as there are politically *conservative* people who ascribe to the worldview of liberalism.) The history of communitarian thought goes back at least as far as Aristotle and Cicero (Avineri & de-Shalit, 1992). Although liberalism has been the dominant paradigm in American society (Walzer, 1995), there has been a significant resurgence in communitarian thought (Hallahan, 1996a; K. Leeper, 1996). The context for the renewed interest in communitarianism is one of a loss of trust in society and a concomitant loss of a sense of community. This loss of a sense of trust and of a sense of community, which seem to be tied together in a dependent relationship, has been written about by a large number of scholars including some in the public relations field (Bellah, 1985; Fukuyama, 1995; Kemmis, 1990; Kruckeberg & Starck, 1988; Putnam, 1995; Sullivan, 1986). Some trace the beginnings of this loss of community in the United States to around the turn of the 20th century or shortly thereafter (Kruckeberg & Starck, 1988; Sandel, 1996; Sullivan, 1986). Others see it as a more recent phenomenon of 50 years or less (Dionne, 1991; Fukuyama, 1995).

Reasons given for the decline of communitarian spirit vary from scholar to scholar. Among the primary causes that have been advocated are the rise of new communication and transportation methods that led to the development of mass society (Kruckeberg & Starck, 1988); changing economic conditions (Sullivan, 1986); the rights revolution of the 1950s and 1960s (Fukuyama, 1995); and, similar to the rights revolution, the cultural war of the 1960s (Dionne, 1991). Polling data often are used to document the declining sense of trust and community (Fukuyama, 1995).

This loss of trust in others and loss of a sense of community means that there is a loss of shared meaning that, in turn, affects cultural standards, moral standards, and political participation (Schlesinger, 1992; Wolfe, 1989). Kruckeberg and Starck (1988) argued that it was this loss of shared meaning that gave rise to the field of public relations, a profession whose purpose, they argued, is to "restore and maintain a sense of community" (p. xi). And it is the loss of a sense of trust and community that has led to an increased interest in communitarian thought.

People

An editorial in *The Economist* ("Freedom and Community," 1994) suggested that the recent communitarian movement could be divided into two groups: *high* communitarians who offer a theoretical challenge to liberalism and *low* communitarians who do not challenge liberalism at the theoretical level but question some of its priority choices. The latter group is represented by Amatai Etzioni and is responsible for publishing the journal *The Responsive Community: Rights and Responsibilities* (K. Leeper, 1996). This group is largely concerned with a political/social agenda that is outside the scope of the present chapter.

Unfortunately, there is no single body of writings that can be pointed to as definitive of the theoretical position of the high communitarians (Boswell, 1990). The consensus among the commentators about the movement is that the following individuals are its major theorists: Alasdair MacIntyre, Michael Sandel, Charles

Taylor, and Michael Walzer (Avineri & de-Shalit, 1992; Beiner, 1992; Mulhall & Swift, 1992). Although common themes unite these writers (Mulhall & Swift, 1992; Neal & Paris, 1990), there also are significant differences and some dispute over whether or not certain individuals should be classified as being within the movement (Beiner, 1992).

Themes

It is important to note that, with the exception of MacIntyre, the communitarian movement seems to be one of reformation, not rejection, of interest group liberalism (Mulhall & Swift, 1992). Although there certainly is a contrast between the ideal forms of liberalism and communitarianism (Spragens, 1995), the relationship between them has been variously described as one in need of a rebalancing between individualism and community (Fukuyama, 1995), as existing in "mutual tension" (Hewitt, 1989, p. 17), as presenting different faces of the same position while critiquing from within (Rosenbloom, 1989), as a "deep reconstructing of liberal theories and policies" (Selznick, 1992, p. 16), and as "an effort of reformation and recovery" (Spragens, 1995, p. 46).

Although differences exist among the four communitarian theorists listed earlier, Mulhall and Swift (1992) argued that "all four . . . are united around a conception of human beings as integrally related to the communities of culture and language that they create, maintain, and inhabit" (p. 162). Specifically, the common themes among the four theorists are that liberalism is excessively individualist and insufficiently historically based, that the liberal position that the state should be neutral in regard to ends misunderstands what community is all about, that state neutrality in regard to ends is itself a value choice, and that liberalism sees rights as transcendent rather than as historically contingent (Neal & Paris, 1990).

In a major recent work on trust, Fukuyama (1995) argued that America has factually been a land of strong communities and of high trust, although the myth of America has been one of extreme individualism. He made the case that for the past 50 or so years, while making some necessary corrections of societal injustice, that myth has started to become reality that is, on balance, not positive for the future of our society. As a result of this extreme individualism, rights, viewed as absolute, have become stressed over responsibilities to the community (Glendon, 1991; Norton, 1991; Selznick, 1992). A stress on rights viewed as absolute separates people from one another rather than leading to compromise and negotiation, which are necessary for common causes (Glendon, 1991). A focus on individual rights diverts attention from the goals of a society or group (Beiner, 1992). A return to a focus on responsibilities involves the development of a shared vision of the ends of society (Frohnen, 1996).

COMMUNITARIANISM AS METATHEORY

J. Grunig (1989e), among others, has argued that "if we are to improve both the ethical quality of public relations and its chance for success in resolving practical public relations situations," then we need to start at the metatheoretic level (p. 17). This entails examining the basic presuppositions that we make about the world. As already noted, in Western society, the two basic worldviews are liberalism and communitarianism. This section explores communitarianism and its critique of liberalism from the metatheoretical framework suggested by Littlejohn (1992).

Epistemology

Littlejohn (1992) wrote that there are two basic approaches, or worldviews, in epistemology. One view is "based on empiricist and rationalist ideas" and "is often called the *received view*" (p. 32, italics in original). The second worldview is

constructivist in approach and holds that knowledge "arises not out of discovery but from interaction between knower and known" (p. 32). The communitarian approach definitely is within the constructivist approach.

Taylor (1985b) argued that one of the appeals of the approach to ethics taken by groups such as Kantians, utilitarians, and Cartesians is the seeming reliance on *hard evidence* and a supposed ability to calculate costs of decisions. Taylor found such an appeal to be misplaced. He suggested that we should not assume, as the preceding approaches have assumed, that the study of human society is like the *hard* sciences in which practitioners can be persuaded by *hard evidence* that there is only one correct approach. Taylor argued that in the absence of such hard evidence, there can be no self-evident, discoverable, universal principles when approaching the study of humanity. MacIntyre (1984) agreed with Taylor and wrote that not only are there no necessary human principles, but the belief that there are has led to the loss of a belief that humans have an essence that needs to be recognized when studying society. The search for universal principles also has blinded us to the desirability of studying humans from within their traditions (MacIntyre, 1988). Both MacIntyre (1994) and C. Taylor (1989b) stressed the importance of context and history as opposed to the search for universal principles, when studying society.

The importance of history, tradition, and context is reemphasized when MacIntyre (1994) and Taylor (1992) discussed how knowledge is derived and passed on to others. Both argued for the position that learning is a shared experience—that the learning process is dialogical in nature. Taylor (1994) stressed the importance of stories in the development of a society and its values, and MacIntyre (1984) defined humans as storytelling animals. C. Taylor (1989b) argued that the notion of one's self cannot develop without language and stressed the importance of narrative to the development of one's identity over time. Both Taylor and MacIntyre contrasted this approach to epistemology with that taken by the major philosophers of the liberal tradition. C. Taylor (1989b) wrote that the major figures in the liberal tradition are monological in approach. Kant's ethical individual decided as a solitary figure what actions he or she can will to be a universal rule; the ethical utilitarian calculated an individual pleasure/pain quotient; and Descartes thought, therefore, that he was. What is lost in the liberal tradition is the notion of a *common* approach to values and society that can come only from a dialogical approach to knowledge.

Ontology

Littlejohn (1992) approached the ontological part of metatheory by looking at issues such as the extent to which humans make real choices, the extent to which experience is viewed as social or individual, the extent to which humans are viewed as states or as traits, and the extent to which communication is contextualized. As with epistemology, he saw two basic approaches to ontological questions: actional theory, which "assumes that individuals create meanings, have intentions, and make real choices"; and nonactional theory, which "assumes that behavior basically is determined by and is responsive to biology and environment" (pp. 32-33). These questions seem to be at the heart of the communitarian critique of liberal theory.

C. Taylor (1989a) wrote that two issues have tended to be confused in the liberal-communitarian debate: ontology and advocacy (or programmatic choices). Ontological issues are at the heart of the debate but often have been seen as advocacy issues. This results in a downplaying and misunderstanding of the more basic ontological questions. Ontology seems to be the basic focus of the writings of Taylor, MacIntyre, and Sandel. MacIntyre (1988) wrote that in liberalism, the ultimate data are individual preferences. Similarly, Taylor (1985a) wrote that in liberalism, choice is the basic data of analysis. For choice to be the basic data, the individual has to be seen as self-sufficient. Given this ontological approach of the priority of the individual and individual choice, liberalism sees the issue of justice and individual rights as prior to the issue of

what is a good life or the goal of society (Taylor, 1994). This results in the quest for universal principles and the denial of diversity as an acceptable approach (MacIntyre, 1984, 1988; Sandel, 1984).

Communitarians reject this ontological choice and see human community as the basic unit of analysis (MacIntyre, 1984; Sandel, 1982; Sullivan, 1986; C. Taylor, 1989b; Young, 1990). For communitarians, although the individual may be prior to association (Young, 1990), the individual is not prior to community; community is seen as necessary to the development of the individual (MacIntyre, 1984; C. Taylor, 1989b, 1992). As a result of the diversity among communities, there are no a priori universally valid principles; history and tradition become the best guides for the analysis of humanity (MacIntyre, 1984). Liberalism is, in fact, one of those traditions, and the liberal ontology is the result of that *particular* tradition and is unique to Western civilization (Taylor, 1985a; Walzer, 1995).

C. Taylor (1989a) saw the ultimate ontological issue as the conflict between an atomistic approach and a holistic approach to the study of humanity. The holistic approach sees the individual as situated in a particular community or tradition with that community as being necessary to the development of the individual. This is within the actional theory discussed by Littlejohn (1992). On the other hand, liberal theory stresses the nonsituated individual as the basic unit of study. Sandel (1984) argued that liberal ontology is inconsistent in that the effort to derive universal principles from atomistic individuals presupposes a prior moral tie that would unite the individuals. This prior moral tie could only come from some sort of community. Communitarians argue that the theory of the atomistic individual needs to be replaced with a theory of the situated self.

Perspective

Littlejohn (1992) saw the perspectival aspect of metatheory as definitional in nature. The field of public relations is struggling over definitional questions. For example, there is some controversy as to whether or not public relations is, or should be, two-way symmetrical (J. Grunig & L. Grunig, 1992, 1996). There also are questions about the social roles that public relations can and should play (J. Grunig & White, 1992) and issues of how to differentiate public relations from other disciplines (Hazleton & Botan, 1989). Kruckeberg and Starck (1988), after going through a series of definitions found in the public relations literature, wrote that there is "vagueness and disagreement and confusion" about the nature of the field (p. 16). Rakow (1989b) wrote that public relations texts tend to be inconsistent as to definitional and functional issues. Agreement on a theoretical perspective might help to eliminate some of the definitional confusion.

As with the definition of public relations, there are a number of different approaches to the definition of community. But there also seems to be considerable underlying agreement as to fundamental issues. Common definitional themes in the communitarian literature seem to be some element of fraternity, association, and participation (Norton, 1991; Spragens, 1995); the notion of some type of public sphere tied up with the idea of participation (Bellah, 1985; Taylor, 1992, 1995); that community is on a continuum between the individual and the centralized state (Boswell, 1990; Hallahan, 1996a; Taylor, 1995); that community involves shared values/ends (Kruckeberg & Starck, 1988; MacIntyre, 1984; Taylor, 1994, 1995); that community involves a covenant as opposed to the contract notion of liberalism (Sullivan, 1986; Young, 1990); and the importance of symbolic interaction (Hallahan, 1996a; Taylor, 1985a).

Ultimately, for theorists such as MacIntyre and Taylor, the definitional issue is the notion of the situated self versus the liberal notion of the atomistic self. The situating of the self entails participatory interaction within a public arena that produces common ends and agreed-on basic values. Heath (1992b) and Heath and Vasquez (1996) argued that such rhetorical participation is necessary for social responsibility and a sense of community. Hallahan (1996a) wrote that this concept could be compared to the idea of a public but that it is a "broader and richer concept" (p. 2).

Axiology

Littlejohn (1992) discussed the axiological portion of metatheory in terms of whether or not theory can be value free, the influence of the inquiry on the subject, and to what extent scholarship should attempt to achieve social change.

Communitarian theorists are quite clear in their position that theory is not value free, and they consciously attempt social change. MacIntyre (1984) was adamant in his claim that the current state of morality is one of disorder and that we have lost the ability to vindicate our moral positions. This feeling of disorder is reflected in the literature on public relations ethics (Kruckeberg, 1993a). It has led to a search for necessary universal moral principles by modern scholars such as Jurgen Habermas (R. Leeper, 1996). Communitarians argue that such a search is futile—there are no such principles to be found—and that moral reasoning is comparative rather than objective (MacIntyre, 1984; C. Taylor, 1989b). Taylor (1994) argued that the fact/value split, one of the cornerstones of the search for necessary universal principles, makes sense only within certain ethical frameworks or traditions. MacIntyre (1988) argued that practical ethical reasoning depends on examples and that how we interpret those examples depends on the ethical theory we embrace. If this is the case, then the modernist search for necessary universal principles is not itself value free but rather is a value choice (Sandel, 1996).

The search for universal principles has led to a liberal concern with justice being prior to virtue, with a stress on procedural correctness versus a stress on virtue, and with rights being viewed as more important than responsibilities (MacIntyre, 1988; Sandel, 1996; C. Taylor, 1985a, 1989a, 1989b, 1994). This has a number of implications that communitarians view as negative. First, this approach results in a stress of form over substance, which impoverishes social discourse (Sandel, 1996; C. Taylor, 1989b) and makes lawyers and judges our clergy (MacIntyre, 1988). Second, the stress on procedure leads to an ethics based on rules, rather than character development. Because no rules approach can cover all contingencies, it is argued that the rules approach is counterproductive. When unexpected situations arise, it is character that is needed for proper choice selection (MacIntyre, 1984; Taylor, 1994). Third, agreement on procedures often masks disagreement on substantive issues, thereby frustrating the search for the commonality necessary for community (C. Taylor, 1989b). Sandel (1982) argued that if the right is prior to the good, then what separates us is more important than what unifies us. Fourth, Taylor (1985a) suggested that an individual is confronted with a moral dilemma if he or she asserts a right at the expense of the community that gave the individual the capacity for asserting that right.

The liberal position in regard to the atomistic individual being primary to the community leads to a loss of accountability. An unsituated individual does not have the sense of continuing identity that MacIntyre (1990) argued is necessary for a sense of responsibility. Instead, there is a stress on rights at the expense of others and of the larger community. Because of the priority of the individual and different individual choices and preferences, liberals hold that the state/community should remain neutral with regard to promoting a particular view of virtue or the good life. Communitarians take the position that virtue and society can and should be tied together. The argument is that morality is learned within particular communities (MacIntyre, 1984), that self-governing communities need common goods and civic virtues to effectively survive, and that these can be developed only within a community that consciously promotes such virtues (Sandel, 1996; C. Taylor, 1989b). A major part of the programmatic communitarian agenda is to increase discussion of substantive value positions, to shift the balance from extreme individualism to more of a community orientation, and to enhance the ability

of the community to promote civic virtue. This is a rejection of the value-neutral approach to axiological issues.

IMPLICATIONS OF COMMUNITARIANISM AS A METATHEORY FOR PUBLIC RELATIONS

There are a number of implications involved in accepting communitarianism as a metatheoretical approach to the field of public relations. Culbertson and Chen (1997a) explored the usefulness of the theory as a foundation for communication symmetry. The assumptions of communitarianism that they found to be of value included the stress on commitment to and quality of relationships, a sense of social cohesion, the importance of core values and beliefs, balancing rights and responsibilities, citizen empowerment, and a broadening of perspective so as to reduce social fragmentation. In addition to public relations models and the question of communication symmetry, the present chapter explores the implications of communitarianism for the concept of publics, corporate social responsibility, and ethics.

Public Relations Models

The approach to public relations models most written about is the J. Grunig four-model approach, with the models classified as to whether they are one-way or two-way models and whether they are of a symmetrical or asymmetrical nature. J. Grunig (1989e) argued that these four models can be collapsed into two worldviews, with the asymmetrical models being instrumental and the symmetrical models being reciprocal in nature. J. Grunig called for setting out the basic presuppositions of these approaches or worldviews. Similarly, Dozier and Ehling (1992) advocated a coorientation model of public relations, which is symmetrical in approach and involves a very different worldview from that of the asymmetrical models. The symmetrical approach can be contrasted with an approach recently advocated by Rhody (1996):

> *Creating buy-in is what public relations is all about. Which is why the tool is so important. . . .* Unfortunately, the label this function carries confuses users as to its purpose. It isn't about relating with the public or communicating corporately. It is about getting the organization from where it is to where it wants to be with maximum support and minimum interference. It is about getting people to do something, not do something or letting you do something. It is about affecting behavior. (p. 231, italics in original)

As noted earlier, in Western society, there are two basic approaches to worldviews: liberalism and communitarianism. There are strong parallels between the communitarian worldview and the symmetrical models as well as between the liberal worldview and the asymmetrical models of public relations. The symmetrical models, like communitarianism, are based on an interactive epistemology, are based on actional theory as the correct ontological approach, define the public relations world as an interactive place, hold that theory is not value free, and hold that a function of theory is idealistic and change oriented (J. Grunig, 1989e; J. Grunig & L. Grunig, 1996).

One area in which the symmetrical models do not fit within the communitarian approach is their stress on procedural or system correctness. J. Grunig (1989e) listed the presuppositions of the symmetrical theories of communication as follows: Communication leads to understanding, holism (the whole is greater than the sum of the parts), interdependence, open systems, moving equilibrium ("cooperative and mutual adjustment" with other systems), equality, autonomy, innovation, decentralization of management, and interest group liberalism that "views the political system as a mechanism for open competition among interest or issue groups" (pp. 38-39; see also Heath, 1997, p. 37). These presuppositions are focused on procedures and seem to imply that if these procedures are satis-

fied, then the system is acceptable regardless of the substantive outcomes that are produced. C. Taylor (1989a) argued that there has to be a minimum threshold level of community values in place before a system of procedural correctness can be agreed on and be effective. It is this threshold of community values that communitarians see as eroding.

Among the assumptions of communitarianism are a need for social cohesion, agreement on core values, and citizen empowerment (Culbertson & Chen, 1997a). If the goal of public relations is harmony, then fostering these values is important. Without them, the result is apt to be confrontation, with publics focusing on self-interest or public alienation. Either attitude is negative for a public relations effort.

There are a number of directions that future research might take in regard to communitarianism and models of public relations. Some obvious questions include the following. Is the goal of public relations understanding (J. Grunig's first presupposition) or harmony? If the goal is harmony, then to what extent is it necessary to develop and communicate basic community values, and what model of public relations best brings the organization and community to that agreement? What is, or should be, the role of public relations in the fostering/restoring of threshold community values? In a public relations campaign, is it more effective to appeal to the fairness/correctness of the procedures used or to the outcomes desired?

Publics

If communitarianism, or some variation of it, is accepted as the metatheoretical base for the symmetrical models of public relations, then the notion of "public" as a basic unit of theory needs to be examined more closely. J. Grunig and Repper (1992) wrote, "Strategically managed public relations, therefore, is designed to build relationships with the most important stakeholders of an organization" (p. 123). Publics are defined as "stakeholders who are or become more aware and active" (p. 125). The authors viewed segmentation of publics as desirable so as to facilitate organizational adaptation.

There is some question as to whether or not the practice of segmenting publics to better tailor a message is consistent with the idea of symmetricality. Rakow (1989b) made the argument that such a practice still is in the "talking to" mode rather than in a "talking with" mode. The position is that public relations needs to see the general "public at the center of activity, *directing* the actions of institutions, which become its object and not the other way around" (p. 178). It is only through this power reversal that true symmetricality and "genuine democracy," or community, can be attained (pp. 180-181, italics in original). At least a hint toward this power reversal is found in the symmetricality literature (Culbertson & Chen, 1997a; J. Grunig & L. Grunig, 1996).

From a communitarian perspective, this notion of segmented publics raises several issues. First, there is a concern, recognized not only by communitarians but also by established public relations practitioners, about how fragmented our society has become (Alvarez, 1995). A question then arises as to the desirability of tailoring socially significant messages in such a focused way. Second, the concept of public has been critiqued from a communitarian perspective as being too narrow in that much public relations is practiced without publics being aware of it, that publics are not the only organizations involved with issues, that public relations can begin only after there has been public formation and recognition, and that the notion of publics does not lead to insights on the nature of communicating with groups (Hallahan, 1996a).

These concerns about the concept of publics lead to several questions for future research. Among such questions are the following: Are public relations appeals to overarching community values more or less successful than appeals to segmented publics? Does segmentation of publics lead to an erosion of agreement on more general community values? There are three dimensions of community building: involvement, nurturing, and organizing (Hallahan, 1996a). What is, and what should be, the role of organi-

zations and their public relations offices in such community-building efforts?

Corporate Social Responsibility

Improving the welfare of society is part of the communitarian agenda. Community provides the context for organizations, and problems within the community affect organizations. Social stability and trust among members of the community are important elements for business success (Fukuyama, 1995). Trust is an important public good (Bok, 1995; Kemmis, 1990). Public relations efforts tend to increase when trust is in decline (Gandy, 1992; L. Grunig, J. Grunig & Ehling, 1992; Kruckeberg & Starck, 1988). Social problems threaten not only society but also organizational productivity and profits.

The evidence is becoming increasingly compelling that a community's perception of corporate social responsibility has a positive influence on profits (Makower, 1994; Paluszek, 1996). There also is evidence that a perception of corporate social responsibility decreases community resistance to controversial organizational initiatives within the community (Kearns & West, 1996; Lowengard, 1989; Paluszek, 1996; Sandman, 1986). As a result, organizational reputation will be of increasing importance (Makower, 1994). Another way in which developing strong community ties helps organizations is that, when groups are upset with an organization and do not feel that they are getting satisfaction from the organization, the groups are likely to appeal to the government for regulatory help with their problem (Holcomb, 1996). It is in the organization's best interests to have a relationship with its community such that the community will try to work out the problem with the organization. In fact, it has been suggested that the best shield against big government and its regulatory powers is strong communities capable of taking care of their own problems (Fukuyama, 1995; Sullivan, 1986; Taylor, 1995; Wolfe, 1989).

Development of strong communities and community ties has been described as a "cardinal" business virtue (Norton, 1991; Novak,

1996). A number of examples can be provided as to the *why* and *how* of such development. Perhaps the best-known organization that promotes corporate social responsibility is a group called Business for Social Responsibility, whose membership has rapidly increased since its founding in 1992 (Makower, 1994). An example less written about is the development, in New York City, of business improvement districts that are engaged in revitalizing their communities out of a "sense of enlightened self-interest" (Traub, 1996, p. 31).

Such efforts often will go beyond even the most enlightened public relations theory based on symmetrical communication and reciprocity. They often will entail the organization *planning* with the community, not just discussing the organization's plan with the community, and encouraging employees to become active in their environment (Wuddock & Boyle, 1994). Such efforts might involve the organization providing the community with information, not just so that the community members can engage in a meaningful dialogue with the organization but also so that the community is capable of making its own independent decision on issues affecting the organization (Ferguson et al., 1996). Citizen empowerment decreases the dependency that leads to asymmetrical relationships (Culbertson & Chen, 1997a). This approach means that the organization does more than ask the community to trust it. The approach means helping the community to develop resources and institutions so that it can rely on itself, not on the organization, and it means provisional planning and resultant consultation, not strategic manipulation (Sandman, 1986).

J. Grunig and White (1992) wrote that public relations should play an idealistic role in society by serving the public interest, increasing mutual understanding, and encouraging debate and dialogue. Recognizing community as the context within which organizations operate, and recognizing the importance to organizations of establishing strong communities and organizational ties with those communities, is a good backdrop for realizing the idealistic role of public relations. Mau and Dennis (1994) wrote that there is

a pervasive sense in the United States today that so many things are wrong. As Americans have become more and more disenchanted with the capacity of government at all levels to address social problems such as declining schools, crumbling infrastructures, crime, and rising health costs, they have increasingly looked to business, not just for money but for ideas about how to set things right.... Responding to these core constituencies and the public's calls for help has become part of a company's core responsibilities. (p. 10)

Directions for future research might include questions such as the following. Can Business for Social Responsibility organizations continue to do well in an increasingly competitive environment? If so, then does their concern for social responsibility contribute to that success? What is or should be the role of public relations in meeting that social responsibility? Is it in the best interests of an organization to help enable the community to make independent decisions as to the interrelationship of the community and the organization?

Ethics

There seems to be a widespread concern that we are in an ethical decline, if not a crisis. The 1996 PRSA national conference theme was "Telling the Truth: Building Credibility in an Incredible World." A number of presentations, including a report on a new Roper Starch Worldwide report on honesty in the workplace, provided evidence of reason for concern. One of the headliners at the conference was Francis Fukuyama, who had just published a book on the subject of trust. Toward the end of his book, Fukuyama (1995) wrote that "communities of shared values, whose members are willing to subordinate their private interests for the sake of larger goals of the community as such, have become rarer. And it is these moral communities alone that can generate the kind of social trust that is critical to organizational efficiency" (p. 309). Trust has been labeled the "prime constituent for the social atmosphere" (Bok, 1995, p. 22).

However there is evidence that we are living off of an accumulated stock of public goods, such as trust, and have not found a way in which to replenish the supply of such goods (Fukuyama, 1995; Putnam, 1995). An analysis as to why there has been a decline in communal spirit and a call to repair the sources of that spirit is a basis of the communitarian movement (Culbertson & Chen, 1997a).

The approach to ethics in public relations tends to be from the liberal perspective as opposed to the communitarian perspective. Public relations practitioners, when confronted with an ethical issue, tend to approach the issue legalistically by turning to the Code of the PRSA, to codes of other professional organizations, or to in-house codes (Seib & Fitzpatrick, 1995). The author of a book on public relations ethics wrote that "ethics in public relations finds full flower when institutions and their PR [public relations] communicators express their intentions for ethical conduct through codes of ethics or standards" (Baker, 1993, p. 264). Codes are representative of the liberal/legalistic/rules approach to ethics. The emphasis in such an approach is on what is just and on individual rights. Kohlberg's stages of ethical growth model is reflective of this approach.

In discussing Kohlberg, J. Grunig and White (1992) wrote that what is needed is to recognize another stage in the development of ethics, a stage involving

> interactive competence or the ability to engage in dialogue. At that stage, people base morality on responsibility rather than on rights and develop a greater sense of interdependence and relationship. In short, the more ethically developed an individual is—and also an organization—the more he or she uses the concepts of reciprocity and symmetry to decide what is moral. (p. 60)

The communitarian critique of liberalism in the area of axiology forms a basis for the rejection of an excessive reliance on the rights approach and provides a foundation for a relational/responsibilities approach (Culbertson & Chen, 1997a). Communitarianism theorizes

that a constructivist basis for ethics is possible as opposed to reliance on consequential calculation (utilitarianism) or on universal reason (Kant and rule ethics). The basis for this constructivist approach is found in the reciprocity and symmetry that are necessary for the development of community, common values, and trust (for a minimalist approach to such a project, see Bok, 1995). The establishment of a public sphere(s) necessary for dialogue fits in with the Aristotelian notion that ethical fitness is like physical fitness in that it needs to be developed and trained (Beiner, 1992; MacIntyre, 1984). The dialogue process, as opposed to pointing to a rule, provides a training mechanism for the development of a moral sense. The notion of a public sphere as a basis for ethical decision making, as opposed to the solitary calculation or principle derivation of utilitarianism or Kantianism, also allows for a recognition of responsibility as a focal point in ethical decision making.

Directions for future research might include questions such as the following. Does character education provide a better basis for sound ethical decision making than training about specific codes of behavior? Does dialogue based on underlying values provide a better ethical decision process than a stress on rights and code provisions? Does communitarianism and its stress on relationships and tradition provide an adequate explanation of, or basis for, an alternative ethical system to that of Kohlberg?

CONCLUSION

A public relations theory needs to be not only positive but also normative (J. Grunig & L. Grunig, 1992). The normative function serves as a guide—as an ideal to strive for and as a measuring standard for success. There are two major worldviews, or metatheories, in Western society: the prevailing theory of liberalism and the competing theory of communitarianism. The differences between them are significant. In the area of epistemology, the liberal position is that there are universal truths that can be discovered. Communitarians hold to a constructive/interactive view of truth and stress the importance of history and context in the evaluation of truth. In terms of ontology, the basic unit of reality for liberals is the unsituated atomistic individual. Communitarians believe that the basic unit of reality is community that encompasses individuals situated within specific contexts. From a perspective standpoint, shared values, a public sphere for the development of those values, and symbolic interaction are of greater consequence for communitarians than for liberals. Finally, at the axiological level, communitarians reject the liberal quest for universal ethical rules and hold that ethical values have to be evaluated within the context of the community and its history and traditions.

From these differences between the two worldviews, Culbertson and Chen (1997a) drew out "some communitarian tenets" involving the importance of relationships, social cohesion, shared core values, acceptance of responsibility, citizen empowerment, and a broadening of perspective with a resultant decrease of societal fragmentation. Acceptance of and adherence to these tenets and communitarian metatheory, as opposed to the liberal metatheory, have significant implications for public relations from a normative standpoint. For communitarianism, a two-way symmetrical model for the practice of public relations would have to be the dominant model. If truth is constructed rather than discovered, and if the basic unit of analysis is not the atomistic individual but rather the community, then two-way symmetrical communication is necessary for that construction and for the development and analysis of community. One-way and asymmetrical communication models lend themselves to a monological discovery of truth and then its dissemination. Dialogue and the quest for truth construction are undervalued. Communitarianism, with its stress on social cohesion and shared core values, also would seem to question the increasing segmentation of pub-

lics. The ultimate segmentation of publics would lead to the liberal atomistic individual. At what point does this segmentation for message adaptation purposes decrease social cohesion and negatively affect shared core values? Some communitarians argue that we have now reached a danger level.

If social cohesion, citizen empowerment, and acceptance of responsibility are key values for the communitarian worldview, then the implications for corporate social responsibility are different from those if the world is seen as an arena for competing individuals who act in their own self-interest as liberalism believes. Involving the community in the organizational decision process and being willing to, on occasion, sacrifice what seems to be in the best interest of the organization to the good of the community is part of the communitarian worldview. Similarly, communitarianism affects the approach that is taken to ethical decision making. The liberal rights approach points to universal rules as the justification for a decision. This stresses procedures over substantive choices. There also is a problem if a rule does not cover a novel situation. Communitarians are more concerned with character development and individual virtue. This position involves substantive issues, and character is relied on to answer ethical questions. What is ethical is determined not by a monologue involving a rule but rather by dialogue. This has significant implications both for the evaluation of ethics in public relations practice and for public relations education.

Public relations, as the quest for harmony, fits comfortably within communitarian metatheory. Harmony between an organization and its surrounding community can best be furthered by a constructivist/interactive approach. Liberal metatheory, with its individualist epistemology and ontology, provides a less inviting home for the field of public relations. As a metatheory, communitarianism serves as a guide for public relations practice and education.

CHAPTER 7

Interpersonal Communication and Public Relations

W. TIMOTHY COOMBS

This book is testimony to the continuing quest of public relations to expand its body of knowledge by exploring new theories and perspectives on the practice. We must keep asking ourselves *how* and *why* if public relations is to grow as a discipline and as a profession. We must not only ask the questions but also systematically test our ideas about how and why. Public relations has long felt a need to move beyond intuition or "seat-of-the-pants" notions to reasoned action based on theory. Theories do not advance without conceptualization and research designed to test whether their propositions truly capture how things work (Botan, 1987). Public relations needs the continued conceptualization and application of theory to advance the field and professional practices.

Historically, public relations has turned to mass communication for its theories. Mass communication initially was a good fit because early public relations practitioners were trained in journalism and the practice emphasized media relations (J. Grunig, 1990; Sallot, 1997). However, as public relations matures and evolves, mass communication theory no longer is a singular influence because it is less of a good fit.

J. Grunig (1990) noted that "only the unsophisticated public relations practitioner would try to communicate with active publics through the mass media" (p. 19). So, where else can public relations turn for theories designed to energize and enlighten its research? This chapter offers interpersonal communication as one valuable source for public relations theory.

The idea of applying interpersonal communication theory to public relations is neither new nor radical, but it is an idea whose time has arrived. Calls to link public relations with interpersonal communication, as well as attempts to do so, are scattered throughout the history of public relations research. Broom's (1977) work on the application of coorientation to public relations marked an early attempt to apply interpersonal communication theory, whereas Ferguson (1984) and Toth (1995) both argued the value of interpersonal communication theory for public relations. A confluence of recent developments is making interpersonal communication even more relevant to public relations.

This chapter develops an argument for interpersonal communication as an important defining aspect of the public relations field. My position begins with definitions of terms to clarify the discussion. Next, past uses of interpersonal communication are organized and reviewed. This is followed by a discussion of recent trends that favor the increased use of interpersonal communication theory in public relations. Finally, a tentative research agenda is tendered.

DEFINITIONS OF KEY TERMS

Public relations, interpersonal communication, and *theory* are ambiguous terms that must be defined for this chapter to be clear. Cappella (1987) cautioned that "attempts to define whole domains of inquiry are usually doomed to be inaccurate or incomplete" (p. 185). Public relations and interpersonal communication both are domains of inquiry. Still working definitions are required for the sake of clarity.

Public relations is defined as the use of communication to manage the relationships between an organization and its stakeholders. The definition captures three essential features of public relations: communication, management, and relationships. The relationship between an organization and its stakeholders is widely recognized as a dominant concern for practitioners (Broom, Casey, & Ritchey, 1997). There also is a growing sense that public relations is a management function; it involves planning and problem solving (J. Grunig, 1992a). A critical aspect of the management function is managing the organization-stakeholder relationship. Communication includes both the words (spoken and written) and the actions of an organization (Coombs, 1995). Communication is essential to managing the organization-stakeholder relationship because it provides the two sides with a means of sharing information and engaging in a dialogue (J. Grunig & L. Grunig, 1992).

Much like public relations, *interpersonal communication* has myriad definitions. Cappella (1987) reduced interpersonal communication to its essential feature—influencing one another's behaviors beyond what can be attributed to

"normal baselines of action" (p. 228). When Person A communicates with Person B, each message may cause Person B to behave differently from how he or she would have acted otherwise. Interpersonal communication is defined by mutual influence. The idea of interpersonal communication is difficult to separate from the idea of relationship. In fact, many definitions of interpersonal communication actually are definitions of relationship (Cappella, 1987).

Relationship refers to the interdependence between two or more people (O'Hair, Friedrich, Wiemann, & Wiemann, 1995). People are involved in a relationship when they become linked in some fashion. The link could be moral, economic, social, emotional, geographic, or cultural, to name just a few types. The link serves to breed interdependence and facilitate interaction between the two parties; they need or want each other for some reason. Furthermore, relationship implies mutual interaction over time. There must be a *long-lasting* connection involving *mutual* exchanges between parties. Meeting someone once is not a relationship, nor is only one party sending messages to another party (Trenholm & Jensen, 1996).

The term *theory* does not suffer from an excessive number of definitions, but its different uses are problematic. It is important to state what one means by a theory instead of assuming that everyone uses the term in same fashion. Theories begin with conceptualization based on observation. Conceptualization identifies, defines, and establishes the relationships between the variables used in a theory. Conceptualization organizes the information that has been observed. A theory begins by describing the phenomenon it hopes to explain. Often, a taxonomy—a list of variables that describe the phenomenon—is created. For example, apologia provides a list of strategies a person might use to repair his or her damaged public image (Ware & Linkugel, 1973). Models go a step further by specifying the connections between the variables. But a good theory goes beyond description to prediction; it is able to predict outcomes and effects. To do so, a theory must explain the interrelationships between variables and how the variables affect one another. This chapter uses theory in the fuller sense of both description and prediction.

PAST USES OF INTERPERSONAL COMMUNICATION

A selective analysis of past public relations research that used interpersonal communication concepts provides a foundation for understanding the vitality of the fusion. The past interpersonal applications are divided into four categories. The categories roughly correspond to the process of theory building. Category 1 is simply observation, recognizing the relevance of interpersonal communication to public relations. Category 2 isolates specific interpersonal-based variables that have been applied to public relations. Category 3 reviews the interpersonal taxonomies and models that have been used to explain public relations phenomena. Category 4 examines the interpersonal theories that have been used to predict public relations phenomena.

Category 1: Recognizing the Importance of Interpersonal Communication

The earliest appearance of interpersonal communication in public relations writings is found in the public campaign literature. More than a half century ago, Cartwright (1949) suggested that the interpersonal communication channel was important to creating behavior change with campaigns. The interpersonal channel in public campaigns is an extension of the early reliance on mass communication theory. The initial campaign researchers were studying the effects of mass communication in campaigns. Along the way, these researchers found the interpersonal channel to be essential to the media mix (O'Keefe & Reid, 1990). Chaffee (1981), a mass communication researcher, illustrated the mass communication link. His idea of parallel sources of information posits that mass media and interpersonal communication work together in producing change from a campaign.

Later public relations-oriented campaign research affirmed the importance of the interpersonal communication channel (J. Grunig & Ipes, 1983; Ledingham, 1993). However, the recognition category is rather crude. Interpersonal communication is merely a channel or medium that helps to produce behavior change in a campaign. No detailed study of interpersonal communication as a channel is provided; it is only identified as a channel. Recognition is the first step toward integrating interpersonal communication into public relations. If we know that interpersonal communication can be important to public relations, then there is motivation for further exploration of the fusion.

Category 2: Interpersonal Communication Variables

Category 2 involves the use of variables from interpersonal communication to help explain public relations phenomena. The variables typically are psychological factors that influence the encoding (creating of) and decoding (interpretation of) messages. The variables research is exemplified by J. Grunig's (1989b) use of individual differences as the basis for the first nest in his nested approach to audience segmentation. The list of public relations studies using interpersonal variables is too long to cite here. Sallot's (1997) inventory of public relations research guided by interpersonal communication is an excellent resource. A few examples are used to illustrate the application of interpersonal variables.

Involvement, an individual's personal interest in an issue or a topic, is the most widely used interpersonal variable in public relations research. Involvement has been used in the discussion of public relations topics such as audience segmentation, issues management, and risk communication. Involvement is one of the three variables that form J. Grunig's situational theory and is one of the factors used to segment publics into active and passive communicators. The degree of active or passive communication helps public relations practitioners to understand each public's use of information seeking and information processing (J. Grunig & Hunt, 1984).

Heath used involvement in his work on policy issues and risk communication (Heath & Douglas, 1990, 1991; Heath, Liao, & Douglas, 1995). His issues management application involved the analysis of people's reactions to policy issues. Involvement was the link to Petty and Cacioppo's (1986) Elaboration Likelihood Model, which explains how people process information. High-involvement people focus more on the content than on the source of the message (the central processing route), whereas low-involvement people concentrate more on the source than on the content of the message (the peripheral route). High-involvement people know more arguments about a policy issue and are more actively seeking information about policy issues (Heath & Douglas, 1990, 1991). Knowing about a public's policy involvement can help public relations practitioners in their efforts to manage issues.

Variable application is an initial step for integrating interpersonal communication theory into public relations. Pieces of theories (the variables) are used to help explain public relations phenomena. In the case of situational theory, the variables become a part of a public relations theory. However, most variable applications use interpersonal concepts as small pieces in some larger puzzle; interpersonal variables provide partial insight due to their limited application.

Category 3: Interpersonal Communication Taxonomies and Models

Once variables are specified, a theorist places them into taxonomies and/or models. The taxonomies are lists of similar variables, whereas models identify the relationships between variables. Public relations moves closer to the full integration of interpersonal communication theory with the application of taxonomies and models from interpersonal communication. Four major applications capture the moves to taxonomies and/or models: game theory, field

theory, impression management, and relationship development.

Murphy has established a line of research that brings game theory to public relations (Murphy, 1987, 1991; Murphy & Dee, 1992). Game theory provides a means of conceptualizing and modeling interactions involving conflict and choice. It allows people to uncover the patterns in the interactions (Murphy, 1991). Hence, game theory is more a model than a true theory. A conflict-cooperation continuum is at the heart of game theory; relationships are classified according to their degree of conflict and/or cooperation. Zero-sum games represent pure conflict strategies, coordination games represent pure cooperation strategies, and mixed-motive games mix conflict and cooperation strategies (Murphy, 1991). Game theory is linked to public relations through the four models of public relations: press agentry, public information, two-way asymmetrical, and two-way symmetrical. Game theory is one way in which to explore what models are being used by an organization (Murphy, 1991).

But game theory can go beyond the models of public relations. Game theory provides a framework for analyzing a conflict relationship to (a) determine what went wrong and (b) help to explain why it went wrong. For example, Murphy and Dee (1992) examined the DuPont-Greenpeace conflict using game theory. *What* went wrong was the use of incompatible approaches for conflict resolution. *Why* the relationship went wrong was due to the demands from their constituencies that promoted the escalation of conflict. Thus, game theory provides one perspective from which to analyze the organization-stakeholder relationship.

Field dynamics is offered as a way of modeling and measuring the multiple publics/stakeholders that an organization must cope with simultaneously. Field dynamics is a general term to describe efforts to measure and represent the multiple perspectives from the parties involved in a group field (a particular setting, issue, or dispute). The organization's relationship to its various stakeholders constitutes a form of group field, hence the relevance of field theory to public relations. Springston, Keyton, Leichty, and

Metzger (1992) used the System for the Multiple-Level Observation of Groups (SYMLOG) to measure and model a group field composed of an organization and its publics for a specific issue. Both the theory and methods have roots in interpersonal as well as intergroup relationships. SYMLOG produces a multidimensional graph for modeling a relationship and tracking its development over time (Springston et al., 1992).

The SYMLOG application demonstrates how *theories* often must be adapted as one moves from the interpersonal to the public relations context. In its original form, SYMLOG has three dimensions: (a) dominance-submissiveness (level of overt and assertive interactions), (b) friendly-unfriendly (level of equality and disagreement) and (c) task controlled-emotionally expressive (mood of the interaction). When applied to public relations, the task controlled-emotionally expressive dimension is reconceptualized as self-orientation and group orientation. The reconceptualization of the third dimension reflects J. Grunig and L. Grunig's (1990) symmetrical-asymmetrical public relations continuum and grounds SYMLOG to public relations concepts (Springston et al., 1992). Field theory offers a means of modeling and measuring an organization's simultaneous relationships with its various stakeholders.

Impression management argues that people strategically use communication to create desired impressions of themselves. A person uses interpersonal communication to manage other people's impressions of himself or herself (Goffman, 1959). The process also is known as face management (Cupach & Metts, 1994). Researchers believe that organizations engage in impression management as well (e.g., Marcus & Goodman, 1991). In public relations, we typically refer to impression management as image or reputation management. Two complementary lines of research have emerged that examine organizational impression management relative to crises. Both Benoit (1995a) and Allen and Caillouet (1994) studied the impression management literature to reveal and explain the strategies that organizations employ to repair an image tarnished by a crisis.

A crisis involves a threat to an organization's reputation (Coombs, 1998a, 1999). The crisis is a mistake or miscue that reflects badly on an organization. When people make mistakes, they offer accounts—messages designed to explain the event and influence perceptions of themselves (Cupach & Metts, 1994). For example, an individual is an hour late in picking up a friend at the airport. The person's account not only explains why he or she is late but also tries to lessen the anger felt by the friend. Offending behavior warrants an account from the offending person. Similarly, a crisis event demands an account by the offending organization. Benoit (1995a) and Allen and Caillouet (1994) drew on the interpersonal communication taxonomies of impression management and account giving to develop taxonomies of crisis response strategies—strategies that an organization uses to manage impressions of a crisis and the organization in the crisis (Coombs, 1998a). Benoit (1995a) created a list of 14 "image restoration" strategies, and Allen and Caillouet (1994) produced a list of 16 "impression management" strategies. Each taxonomy has been used to analyze and evaluate crisis responses (Benoit, 1995a; Caillouet & Allen, 1996), thereby offering insights into the crisis management process.

Ledingham and Bruning have seized on the importance of *relationship* in public relations by advocating a relationship management perspective for public relations (Bruning & Ledingham, 2000; Ledingham & Bruning, 1998b). They have begun to apply an interpersonal taxonomy of relationship dimensions and a model of relationship development to organization-stakeholder relationships, with promising results.

An essential step in understanding relationships is to reveal the dimensions of specific relationships. Interpersonal researchers have articulated the dimensions to various relationships such as marriage and parent-child (Fitzpatrick, 1988; Fitzpatrick & Badinski, 1994). Ledingham and Bruning (1998b) identified 17 possible relationship dimensions for the organizational-consumer relationship. Given the nature of the relationship, the dimensions were drawn from interpersonal communication, marketing, and public relations. The relevance of the 17 dimensions then was examined. In the end, 5 relevant dimensions emerged: trust, openness, involvement, investment (time and effort), and commitment (decision to stay in the relationship).

Another step in understanding relationships is to identify and define the phases of a relationship. We cannot improve, maintain, or restore a relationship if we do not understand the phases of relationship development. Knapp's five-stage model of coming together and five-stage model of coming apart were adapted for the organization-stakeholder relationships (Knapp & Vangelisti, 1996). Participant expectations, communication patterns, and behaviors were specified for each phase. It is erroneous to assume interpersonal and organization-stakeholder relationships, although similar, are identical. The different qualities of the relationship context result in different defining qualities of a relationship stage because the interpersonal concepts must be modified for the public relations context.

Bruning and Ledingham's (2000) phases of the organization-stakeholder relationship development provide a method for evaluating the status of a relationship. Public relations practitioners need to look for specific relationship markers such as communication patterns. By knowing the phase of a relationship, the public relations practitioner can determine what actions are needed. For example, the practitioner can decide whether the relationship should be maintained as is, restored to some previous phase, moved to a "closer" and more advanced phase, or moved back a phase. The relationship dimensions and models provide tools for evaluating organization-stakeholder relationships and guiding future actions designed to alter the relationship.

Category 4: Interpersonal Theory

A true theory moves beyond description to prediction—how changes in one variable affect other variables. Knowing how their actions should and will affect stakeholders makes theory a valuable commodity when planning public re-

lations actions. The theory provides the reasoned action that replaces intuition and guesswork. A very limited number of studies apply interpersonal communication theory to public relations. Self-efficacy theory and attribution theory provide two examples of theory application.

Anderson (1995) used self-efficacy theory to explain and predict the effect of message design in health campaigns. Self-efficacy deals with one's ability to cope with threatening situations and is derived from one's perceived capabilities of coping successfully with a threatening situation. Information about one's ability to cope can alter perceptions of self-efficacy. The level of self-efficacy, in turn, affects the amount of effort used to manage a threatening situation. Anderson predicted that campaign messages designed to bolster self-efficacy would lead to stronger perceptions of efficacy and enhanced persistence of effort. Both predictions were proven to be correct. Those messages with self-efficacy components produced greater self-efficacy and stronger persistence than did those messages lacking a self-efficacy component. Self-efficacy theory helped to predict certain outcomes from a public relations health campaign.

Coombs (1995, 1998a) used attribution theory to explain and predict people's perceptions of crises and the impact of crises on an organization's reputation. Attribution theory asserts that people search for the causes of events, especially when an event is unexpected. People will attribute the event either to a person/group or to the situation (Weiner, Perry, & Magnusson, 1988). Assume that a baseball team loses a game that it should have won. The loss can be attributed to poor play by the team (the individual/group) or to rainy weather (the situation). Interpersonal communication researchers have long used attribution theory as a theoretical guide (e.g., Wilson, Cruz, Marshall & Rao, 1993).

Three causal dimensions affect the development of attributions: stability, external control, and personal control/locus. Stability indicates whether an event happens frequently (stable) or infrequently (unstable). The more stable the event, the stronger the attributions of the individual's responsibility for an event; the event is part of a pattern of the person's behavior. External control constitutes the extent to which an event is controlled by some outside agent. Stronger external control promotes attributions that the situation is responsible for the event. Personal control/locus reflects intentionality and a person's ability to control the event. Increased perceptions of personal control/locus promotes attributions of the individual's responsibility for an event (Russell, 1982; Wilson et al., 1993).

Coombs argued that crises are unexpected and, therefore, are logical situations for triggering an attributional search. The principles of attribution theory then were translated into language appropriate for crises and organizations. Attributions of organizational responsibility were claimed and proven to have a negative relationship with organizational reputation. A system of categorizing crises by external control and personal control/locus was tested and validated (Coombs, 1998a; Coombs & Holladay, 1996). Increased stability (a history of similar crises) and stronger perceptions of personal control/locus were predicted to increase perceptions of organizational responsibility for a crisis and to have a negative effect on organizational reputation. Support was found for these predictions. Stronger attributions of external control were predicted to lessen perceptions of organizational responsibility for the crisis and to have a positive affect on organizational reputation. No support was found for this prediction, and external control was dropped as a variable in this line of research (Coombs, 1998a). Attribution theory proved to be useful in predicting the effect of specific crisis types (based on personal control/locus) and crisis stability on perceptions of organizational responsibility for a crisis and the impact of the crisis on the organizational reputation.

Literature Analysis Summary

Although space limitations prevent a complete discussion of all interpersonal applications to public relations, the literature analysis provides insight into how interpersonal application can help to define the field. Variables from interpersonal communication were shown to provide the raw materials for public relations theory construction as well as to offer glimmers of insight into public relations phenomena. The glimmers expand into greater insight as the application is expanded to taxonomies, models, and actual theories. Interpersonal taxonomies and models have proven to be useful in mapping and analyzing relationships as well as effects of public relations actions on those relationships. Mapping and analyzing are essential to the planning and evaluation stages of public relations efforts. Taxonomies and models facilitate postmortems of campaigns by offering tools to dissect the actions and provide frameworks for analyzing the actions (Gibson, 1991-1992). Interpersonal theories have proven to be useful in predicting the impact of organizational and stakeholder actions on their relationship. Theories also provide useful tools for planning and evaluation. Theory increases the effectiveness of planning by reducing mistakes—reasoned action versus guesswork—and aids evaluation by providing guidelines to which the public relations action can be compared.

CONTINUING PUSH TOWARD RELATIONSHIPS

The literature analysis reflects the growing emphasis on relationships in public relations (Broom et al., 1997). The emphasis on public relations excellence (two-way symmetrical model) and recent social and technical developments undergird the shift.

Public Relations Excellence

Public relations excellence is rooted in stakeholder theory, the belief that an organization's success is dependent on the skill with which it manages the often conflicting demands of its numerous stakeholders—how well it manages its relationships (Mitchell, Agle, & Wood, 1997; Rowley, 1997). Public relations excellence helps to explain how the relationships are managed. Excellence is based in two-way symmetrical communication. Through this model of public relations, J. Grunig (1990) advocated the management of interdependence. Essentially, he advanced the need to focus on the relationship, a point he continued in later writings (e.g., L. Grunig, J. Grunig, & Ehling, 1992). The organization-stakeholder relationship becomes central in public relations because it is a key to success. By nature, an organization's environment is populated with various stakeholders. Moreover, the organization must have relationships with these stakeholders to survive. Building relationship permits greater freedom. Bad relationships can limit freedom by leading stakeholders to withhold needed resources or even by attacking the organization (e.g., boycotts, protests). The organization's success depends on how well it satisfies the demands of its stakeholders (L. Grunig et al., 1992). J. Grunig's call for relationships in public relations reflects the concerns and premises of stakeholder theory.

Communication is fundamental to J. Grunig's view of public relations excellence. Two-way symmetrical communication is based on a dialogue—the give-and-take between two parties. Thus, a relationship is built on interactive communication between the organization and the stakeholders. Both parties are involved in sharing ideas and shaping the nature of the relationship (J. Grunig, 1990; J. Grunig & L. Grunig, 1992). Excellence suggests that communication helps the organization not only to understand but also to negotiate expectations. Interaction implies that the relation continues over time. A relationship emphasizes long-term commitments instead of isolated incidents of communication. Although an organization might go 3 or 4 months without communicating to a stakeholder, the organization's current message still is embedded within the history of all its past interactions with that stakeholder. The idea of public relations excellence is a vital factor in the new focus on relationships in public relations.

Key Social and Technical Developments

The 1990s have seen an increase in the probability of stakeholders contacting an organization and/or taking a concern public. In a sense, stakeholders are becoming more active—more willing to communicate a concern or take action against an organization (Coombs, 1998b; Irvine & Millar, 1996). For example, consumers and shareholders have a heightened sense of awareness about their issues and are willing to speak out (Bradsher, 1996; Maynard, 1993). Stakeholders want and expect more dialogue/interaction with organizations. Stakeholders seem to conceive of their connection to the organization as a relationship involving communication to and from both parties. When the stakeholder-organization relationship is viewed as positive, it is premised on mutual benefit (Heath, 1994, 1997). Organizations have rightly encouraged stakeholder communication, knowing that it is essential to maintaining effective organization-stakeholder relationships (J. Grunig & L. Grunig, 1992).

Technology is facilitating stakeholder communication with the organization as well. Three elements of the Internet have the potential to promote two-way symmetrical communication/interactions: e-mail, discussion groups, and chat forums. E-mail provides stakeholders with an easy means for sending messages to an organization, especially if the organization's Web site provides an easy-to-use e-mail mailbox. A discussion group or newsgroup is an electronic bulletin board devoted to one topic. Users post messages, and readers can reply in private or post replies to the entire newsgroup. A thread is a chain of postings on the same subject that emerge from one posting. Most newsgroups have a command that allows a user to follow a thread from message to message. An organization can sponsor discussion groups on its Web site and thereby encourage stakeholder discussions and expressions of opinions; for example, Shell Oil has various discussion groups on its Web site.

Another option is for an organization to sponsor a chat forum, a special forum or conference that allows two or more users on-line to engage in conversation simultaneously by taking turns typing messages (Bobbitt, 1995). The chat forum should include organizational members and stakeholders. The chat forum allows a *direct* connection between the stakeholders and people in the organization. Each Internet element allows the stakeholders some control over the content of messages and the structure of the exchange because they decide the nature of the questions and comments. The interaction is mutual because each side has some element of control over the interaction. Heath (1998a) illustrated the mutual interaction in his analysis of the Brent Spar debate. Through their Web sites, Shell Oil and Greenpeace were able to create a "town meeting"-type forum for dialogue. Technology is making two-way symmetrical communication easier to realize.

CONCLUSION AND TENTATIVE RESEARCH AGENDA

Given current thinking, social, and technological trends, relationships will remain center stage in public relations. Interpersonal communication is an excellent resource for understanding and coping with the organization-stakeholder relationship. Public relations theorists and practitioners have just begun to mine the valuable resource of interpersonal communication theory. I would like to offer a limited research agenda that highlights some relevant topics and areas of study in need of further research. The agenda indicates the new focus that interpersonal communication brings to the field. The agenda is divided into variables, taxonomies and models, and theories.

Many interpersonal communication variables involve types of traits. Although many people talk about the skills needed by public relations practitioners, few address specific traits that should affect the practitioner's ability to function effectively. The traits or individual differences of practitioners should affect their ability to manage relationships. Argumentativeness and cognitive complexity are two promising traits. Argumentativeness is a positive personal-

ity trait in which people present and defend their positions on issues while attacking the positions of other people (Infante, Anderson, Martin, Herington, & Kim, 1993). Dialogues involve negotiation, and negotiation involves argument (Vasquez, 1996). A willingness and an ability to engage in argument (argumentativeness) facilitates the negotiation process. Hence, sufficient levels of argumentativeness among public relations people and stakeholders should facilitate the exchange of ideas central to dialogue. Public relations practitioners with low argumentativeness might avoid dialogues because they are afraid of arguments. This possibility is worth further consideration.

Cognitive complexity is a stable individual difference that is derived from individual development experiences. Those with higher cognitive complexity are better able to incorporate multiple perspectives to situations and to pursue multiple goals in communication (Bartunek, Gordon, & Weathersby, 1983). Given the complex nature of multiple stakeholder demands in most situations and the need to understand these various perspectives, greater cognitive complexity should affect the effectiveness of public relations practitioners. Some evidence exists to support the value of greater cognitive complexity for managers in general. It is possible that similar benefits accrue to public relations practitioners. Once more, these ideas have merit but are, as of yet, untested.

The previous applications of taxonomies and models are beginning to paint a picture of the phases of relationship development and the dimensions relevant to the organization-stakeholder relationship. This research must be extended. First, the important relationship dimensions of each major category of stakeholder should be identified. So far, we know only the dimension for consumers. Different stakeholders have different demands that could result in distinct dimensions for each stakeholder group. Further research will tell us what dimensions might be stable across stakeholders and what dimensions are stakeholder specific.

Second, organization-stakeholder relationships must be examined over time to reveal common interaction patterns. By analyzing interaction patterns, we can understand how organization and stakeholder words and actions affect the development of their relationship. Taxonomies for interaction analysis for interpersonal communication, such as the one developed by Millar and Rogers (1987), should prove to be useful in initiating research that analyzes the interactions between stakeholders and organizations.

Third, we must appreciate the fact that organizations have to manage multiple relationships simultaneously. Working from models such as SYMLOG, we can begin to gain insight into the process of balancing stakeholder relationships and demands. Changes in one organization-stakeholder relationship can spill over into another relationship. The challenge is to manage a constellation of stakeholder relationships. We have just begun to understand the organization-stakeholder relationship, and the taxonomies and models from interpersonal communication have much to offer the continuation of this understanding.

The concern for the relationship takes center stage in the application of interpersonal theories. Of particular concern to practitioners is how specific interventions can be used to alter the relationship in a desired fashion. Social penetration theory could be useful because it explains the effects of interventions on relationship development. The theory considers relationship development and the interpersonal behaviors involved in relationship development. Social penetration theory uses a four-stage approach to relationships. Three elements are important to the development of the four stages. Self-disclosure, reciprocity of disclosure, and intimacy of disclosure help to determine the relationship stage (Taylor & Altman, 1987). The stages and variables could be converted into analogous terms for public relations and used to better understand the organization-stakeholder relationship and factors affecting its development.

As public relations matures, it continues to outgrow its old conceptual and theoretical boundaries. The early dependence on mass communication theory has proven to be too limiting as relationships become a dominant focus in public relations thinking and practice. Interpersonal communication theory is beginning to establish its usefulness in the past and holds great promise for future applications to public relations. As public relations moves into the 21st century, interpersonal communication theory will provide important insights into the analysis and practice of public relations and will shape how we define the field.

CHAPTER 8

Public Relations Field Dynamics

JEFFREY K. SPRINGSTON

JOANN KEYTON

In 1987, Eli Lilly Corporation introduced Prozac, a drug heralded as a breakthrough treatment for depression. The drug, which was without many of the side effects of older alternatives, quickly became the best-selling antidepressant in history. In spite of widespread support from the medical community, Prozac and Eli Lilly came under attack from a group called the Citizens Commission on Human Rights, which later was discovered to be a nonprofit group established by the Church of Scientology. The church is known for its stance against using drugs for the treatment of psychiatric illness. This group was able to garner enough media attention to raise concerns among a number of publics about the alleged dangers of the drug including a purported tendency to induce violence or suicide in its users. Pressure became so strong that the Food and Drug Administration temporarily withdrew approval of the drug. However, Eli Lilly was joined by groups such as the American Medical Association and the American Psychological Association to redeem the image of the company and the drug. Eventually, Prozac was allowed back on the market, and Eli Lilly has won a spate of lawsuits affirming the safety of Prozac. This case demonstrates that organizations can, and usually do, operate in complex multipublic environments. Although Eli Lilly and the Church of Scientology were direct antagonists in this particular case, a variety of other actors in the field were salient. To effectively manage the public relations environment, Eli Lilly needed to deal with each of these publics in a unique manner.

The Eli Lilly case is typical of many public relations environments in that multiple publics were involved. However, as Leichty and Springston (1993) pointed out, most public relations models skirt the issues of multipublic environments or ignore the concept altogether in favor of a one-way or two-way conceptualization. A one-way or two-way model cannot capture the complexity of how an organization's interaction with one public affects its relationship with other publics. Yet, how the organization adapts to, negotiates with, collaborates with, challenges, acquiesces to, advocates against, and agrees with each public can have implications for its relationships with other publics.

Leichty and Springston (1993) also argued that normative theories prescribing a "one best" or ideal approach to public relations threaten to limit our understanding of public relations environments. Instead, they argued in favor of contingency approaches that place communication at the heart of the process. The focus of any model should be on the relationship level rather than on the organizational level. From this perspective, analysis of any public relations environment recognizes that an organization has a relationship history with each of its key publics, and these publics in turn often have relationships with one another, frequently independent of the organization. The direct perceptions of each public would better predict an organization's public relations orientation in a particular instance than would global assessments of the organization's environment. This perspective also portrays an organization's public relations behavior as an emergent property of the communication exchange between an organization and its publics.

Cancel, Cameron, Sallot, and Mitrook (1997) agreed with criticisms of prescriptive one best models and instead proposed a contingency theory of accommodation in public relations. Based on a continuum from pure accommodation to pure advocacy, they posited that antecedent, mediating, and moderating variables lead to greater or lesser accommodation by public relations practitioners. Such an approach is more reflective of the complexity of most public relations environments and follows the path of other subjects of inquiry. For example, leadership and conflict studies long ago abandoned normative theory for a contingency approach. Vasquez (1996) proposed a theoretical approach that is conducive to the contingency theory of accommodation. He argued that public relations is best conceptualized as negotiation within an issue development perspective. A negotiation metaphor puts communication squarely in the center of the process and is broad enough to usefully accommodate a wide range of relevant public relations scenarios including issues management, risk communication, and crisis management.

A contingency-negotiation approach holds much promise in furthering our understanding of public relations. The key will be in using a theoretical and practical approach flexible enough to capture the complexity of a multipublic negotiation environment. Group communication theory offers promise for such an approach. Group dynamics, as a field, has been studied by social psychologists and management and communication scholars for more than 50 years. The group literature spread across these disciplines advocates that groups are complex, fluid, and adaptive systems. From that point of view, groups resemble manifest publics, which are defined as groups of people who share a common interest, need, concern, or issue position. What can group literature offer the study of public relations?

BORROWING FROM GROUP THEORY

The contingency negotiation view of public relations requires that practitioners analyze the internal dynamics of publics to better understand the relationships among publics. The group literature can be helpful in two ways. First, it offers theoretically rich understandings of how groups form and are maintained or change over time. These principles may be instructive in understanding the formation and life cycles of publics. Some theorists (Tuckman, 1965; Tuckman & Jensen, 1977; Wheelan & Hochberger, 1996; Wheelan & Kaeser, 1997) have advocated that groups have a life cycle complete with a beginning, a middle, and an end and that groups develop through five stages or phases: forming, storming, norming, performing, and terminating. It is probable that many of the principles of small group development and evolution translate to the macro arena of organizational publics. Second, the group literature also can offer public relations practitioners a foundation for understanding the power dynamics within a public's membership. Because power translates to interpersonal influence over other group members, being able to identify the base of power exhibited in a public should help practitioners to strengthen or weaken its pull (French & Raven, 1968).

PUBLIC RELATIONS
FIELD DYNAMICS

What is needed is a method by which the dynamics of multipublic formation, evolution, and interaction can be measured and tracked over time. The objective of this chapter is to present public relations field dynamics (PRFD), a theoretical perspective based on group dynamics that has the capacity to capture the complexity of a multipublic environment. Complementing issue negotiation, PRFD provides a theoretical and coherent framework for understanding as well as a method for measuring an entire organizational field.

Three characteristics distinguish PRFD from previous theoretical frameworks. First, although other authors have noted and described the need for delivering strategic messages concurrently to multiple publics, a theoretically grounded methodology for assessing and analyzing messages sent to multiple publics has not been offered. PRFD provides a methodology to analyze the potential effects of messages before they are sent. Second, publics might be bound together in ways that are independent of the relationship with the organization, and often these relationships can have an impact on the organization. Without addressing this phenomenon, public relations practitioners might fail to fully recognize the importance of actors in the field and might develop strategies as if the organization were in a dyadic mode independently with each public. A better approach is to develop an analytical system that allows an organization, first, to identify the relationships among its various publics and, second, to separate potentially effective rhetoric from ineffective rhetoric based on its unique message points and the relationships with and among its publics. Finally, PRFD can be used as a framework to complement other theoretical perspectives that are viable in public relations research

and practice. A later section of this chapter details several possible complementary theoretical positions.

What Is PRFD?

PRFD methodology is adapted from the study of small group communication (Springston, Keyton, Leichty, & Metzger, 1992) and derived from Bales and Cohen's (1979) System for the Multiple-Level Observation of Groups (SYMLOG). At the center of PRFD is the notion of a fluid field encompassing all relevant actors. These actors, or an organization and its publics, can be measured at one point in time or across the development of a controversial issue. As a field theory like SYMLOG, PRFD "takes effective account of the fact that every act of behavior takes place in a larger context that is part of an interactive 'field' of influences" (Bales, 1988, p. 320).

From this position, it is impossible to clearly and thoroughly understand the behavior or actions of any one actor (organization or public) or the interactions between organization and public (or public and public) without considering the entirety of the field. The implication of the importation of field theory is that any strategy directed to one public must be selected while keeping in mind the potential impact on other publics in the field. Field theory takes into account that an organization and its publics are not isolated but rather react to and interact with others in an integrated environment. Field theory recognizes that an organization's and/or a public's behavior is determined by how others behave toward it and one another as well as by the situation or environment in which the interaction or relationship takes place.

Dimensions of the Public Relations Field

The original SYMLOG dimensions used to assess individual and group interaction are (a) dominance versus submissiveness, (b) friendliness versus unfriendliness, and (c) controlled versus emotionally expressive behavior (Bales & Cohen, 1979). Based on the analysis of a broad range of communication, psychological, and social psychological theories, Bales and Cohen (1979) argued that these orthogonal dimensions are the core dimensions by which humans assess and attribute interactions on an interpersonal level.

Springston (1997b) adapted SYMLOG to macro-level applications vital to public relations. The dimensions in the PRFD system reflect (a) low-influence versus high-influence capability, (b) self-orientation versus community orientation, and a (c) friendly versus unfriendly relationship. The first dimension measures respondents' perceptions about the degree to which a particular actor wields influence in a given situation. The second dimension measures the degree to which a respondent believes that a particular actor (individual or organization) is self-motivated and primarily interested in that actor's personal career or organizational advantage rather than primarily concerned with the community of actors in a given situation, irrespective of self-interest. Finally, the third dimension focuses on the perception of how friendly or unfriendly each relevant actor is in a situation.

Actors can be visually displayed on the three-dimensional field. In PRFD, the friendly versus unfriendly dimension is displayed by an anchor point on the horizontal axis. To the right of the field's center point, a public would be friendly; to the left of center, the public would be unfriendly. The location of a public on the self-orientation versus community orientation dimension is identified by an anchor point on the vertical axis. Above the neutral center point, a public would be community-oriented; below the center, the public would be self-oriented. A public's position on the third dimension, low influence versus high influence, is shown by the size of the circle encompassing the anchor points on the other two dimensions.

For example, a study by Springston et al. (1992) illustrated how key actors in a given situation can have differing perceptions along the three PRFD dimensions. As an abbreviated recap of the situation, during the late 19th century, the Ojibwa nation signed a treaty with the U.S. gov-

ernment that preserved the Ojibwa's rights to hunt and fish using traditional methods and did not confine them to the seasonal restrictions imposed on the rest of the citizens of Wisconsin. This treaty later was validated in a 1983 court case (*Lac Courte Oreilles Band v. Voight*, 1983). This court case sparked anger among a number of European Americans, who formed an active public known as Protect American Rights and Resources (PARR). The conflict between the Ojibwa and PARR became extremely contentious and, at times, violent.

A number of Ojibwa tribal elders and members of the PARR leadership agreed to participate in a survey using the PRFD instrument. The results displayed in Figure 8.1 demonstrate that the two groups not only viewed each other differently but also perceived others in the situation differently. Each perceived the other as being very unfriendly and self-oriented and as having high influence in the situation. However, perceptions of the Wisconsin Department of Natural Resources (DNR) differed. The Ojibwa viewed the DNR as friendlier and more community-oriented than did PARR. In addition, the Ojibwa perceived the existence of a European American pro-treaty public, whereas PARR did not. These differing perceptions among the primary actors confirm that attributional biases based on relational history or expectation of future interactions are not similar among all actors in the field.

These three dimensions are essential to the study of public relations. The *low-influence versus high-influence dimension* can help to determine which groups will be most attentive and involved in a public relations situation. For example, if a group perceives an organization to have a large influence on the group, then the group probably will be more attentive to the organization than to groups perceived to have little influence. Knowledge of how influential a public sees itself to be in relation to the organization provides insight into how likely that public is to exhibit active behavior. This information is useful in helping practitioners to determine communication strategy.

The *self-orientation versus community orientation dimension* reflects perceptions of how motivated an organization is to achieve either an in-

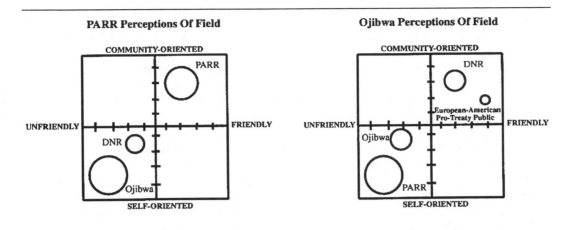

Figure 8.1. The Dimensions of Public Relations Field Dynamics
SOURCE: Adapted from Springston, Keyton, Leichty, and Metzger (1992).
NOTE: Perceived influence is demonstrated by circle size; the larger the circle, the more influential that particular actor is perceived to be. PARR = Protect American Rights and Resources; DNR = Wisconsin Department of Natural Resources.

tegrative or a distributive outcome in a given situation, something very conducive to Cancel et al.'s (1997) contingency theory of accommodation. This ties directly into perceptions of trust. Members of the media typically are skeptical of an organization's community orientation. In general, the more an organization can demonstrate to the media and other publics that it has a genuine community orientation, the more successful the organization will be in negotiating its position.

Finally, perceptions of friendly versus unfriendly behavior are relevant at all levels of interaction. The *friendly versus unfriendly dimension* taps fundamental notions of friend or foe. PRFD allows organizations to identify allies, antagonists, and potential mediators. Combined, the three dimensions provide a powerful framework to map the entire field or public relations environment.

Situating the three behavioral dimensions with field theory provides several advantages. First, the three dimensions are viewed as mutually exclusive. Thus, for any one interaction, behavior may be described as high influence or as low influence but not as both. Second, the dimensions are orthogonal. Placement on one dimension does not predict placement on other dimensions. Third, any specific placement on a dimension is not seen as inherently good or bad. Rather, the evaluation of behavior depends on other interaction in the public relations field. Fourth, PRFD allows behavior and perceptions to be tracked over time within a comparative framework. This is particularly useful to the study of issue negotiation because it allows organizations to test alternative public relations strategies as issues develop and change over time. Fifth, PRFD is a system for viewing the impact of a public's or an organization's internal dynamics on the larger interdependent field.

Another key strength of this system is its ability to map the relative degree of polarization and unification among the salient parties within a given environmental field. Parties that are a great distance apart along one or multiple dimensions are polarized, whereas parties that appear close to one another are unified. Polarization is the degree to which constituents are dissimilar in their opinions and perceptions; unification is the degree to which constituents are similar:

When a field of images is unified, the images tend to be perceived as similar in important respects . . .

and their differences may be minimized. When a field of images is polarized, the images tend to be divided into [at least] two subgroups . . . very different from each other—in fact, opposed to each other. (Bales & Cohen, 1979, pp. 32-33)

Polarization and unification can occur on a single dimension, on two dimensions, or on all three dimensions. The more dimensions apparent in the polarization, the more difficulty publics will have in communicating with each other in ways that make "sense" to the other publics. For example, an organization that views itself as community-oriented probably would use inclusive rhetoric. Yet, to a self-oriented organization, such rhetoric might appear to presuppose inclusion in a community in which the self-oriented organization might not want to belong. Likewise, an organization that perceives itself as having high influence probably would use dominating rhetoric in an attempt to defeat a less influential organization. Such an attempt probably would be seen as confirmation that the dominant organization is not willing to listen to the voices of others. The more dimensions on which parties are polarized creates additional opportunity for public relations rhetoric to be outside the scope that can be understood or tolerated by other publics.

Knowing the degree of unification-polarization could be very useful when devising issue negotiation strategy. For example, in Figure 8.1, the field diagrams of PARR and the Ojibwa reveal that a high degree of polarization existed between the two groups. Each group viewed the other as very negative, self-oriented, and influential. By contrast, each group perceived itself as more community-oriented and friendlier (especially the PARR group). Until some level of trust is developed between the parties, productive direct dialogue would be difficult. In the minds of each party, the other party was the enemy. One potential avenue for developing trust in this situation would be to communicate through a mediator respected by both PARR and the Ojibwa.

One key component of the system is its ability to identify potential mediators in a given situation. As in any type of negotiation, an organization attempting to negotiate public relations issues with publics or other organizations often is confronted with environments in which some key publics are too polarized from the organization to enter into meaningful dialogue. In such cases, the most useful strategy might be to work with a mediator to establish productive contact. Almost any actor in a relational field can be a mediator, but those actors who are most likely to be acceptable to disparate parties are ones who are more friendly than unfriendly, who are more community-oriented than self-oriented, and who have greater influence in the relational landscape. A mediator acts to make sure that the polarization does not amplify or continue too long (Bales & Cohen, 1979). Because a mediator is likely to be in a more neutral position than the extreme positions held by other actors, the mediator can translate or interpret from one position to another. Because both parties have greater trust in the mediator, he or she is in a better position to clarify positions and issues and to make suggestions to both parties. Best done in steps over time, this communication responsibility brings polarized parties closer to understanding others' positions and provides a bridge among differing perspectives.

For example, the field diagrams in Figure 8.1 reveal that the DNR could potentially serve as a mediator. The DNR is seen as community-oriented and friendly by the Ojibwa and probably would be accepted as a mediator by this group. PARR perceives the DNR as somewhat unfriendly and self-oriented, but these perceptions are not extreme. With some work on the part of the DNR to build trust, it is conceivable that PARR might begin to see the DNR in a more neutral or perhaps even friendly and community-oriented light.

Instrument Development

Consistent with the original SYMLOG instrument, the first iteration of the PRFD instrument included 26 Likert-type items that represented all possible combinations of the three orthogonal dimensions. Respondents were required to complete 26 items for each public, organization, or individual being rated. In the event that respondents were being asked to rate six actors in a given situation, they would have to complete 156 items. It quickly became apparent that although the instrument was useful for measuring perceptions in a laboratory setting, it was too labor intensive to be practical in most field study situations. As a result, Springston (1997b) developed and tested two abbreviated versions of the original instrument: a 12-item Likert-type instrument and a 3-item semantic differential instrument that was articulated on a 10-point scale.

These two new versions were compared to each other and to the original 26-item instrument for both convergent and predictive validity. Study results revealed that all three instruments were highly correlated with one another, indicating convergent validity. In addition, although all three instruments yielded significant positive correlations with the criterion variable, the three-item semantic differential instrument correlated most strongly, indicating predictive validity. Finally, 95% of respondents in the study preferred filling out the semantic differential instrument to filling out the other two instruments. Thus, the three-item PRFD instrument displayed in Figure 8.2 proved to be both valid and practical for public relations field research.

USING PRFD TO EXTEND THEORY AND PRACTICE

PRFD has been used in a variety of contexts including a statewide confrontation in Wisconsin involving Native American treaty rights (Metzger & Springston, 1992; Springston et al., 1992); a cancer screening promotion project (Springston, 1997b); an educational fund-raising study (Springston, 1997a); a risk communication study involving media personnel and members of the Michigan Emergency Management Response System (Springston & Brown, 1998); and a crisis communication study in Indianapolis, Indiana, involving a confrontation with city police officers, the mayor's office, and

an activist group in the city's African American community (Springston & Keyton, 1996).

These studies detail the theoretical promise and methodological development of PRFD. Reflecting on these studies, it also is possible to see how PRFD can extend theoretical development by using it in combination with a variety of complementary concepts and theories including coorientation (Broom, 1977), conflict and negotiation theories (Putnam & Roloff, 1992), situational identification of public theory (J. Grunig & Hunt, 1984), and fantasy theme analysis (Bormann, 1996). By using examples from some of the previously cited studies, we describe in the following subsections how each of these theories can be usefully melded with PRFD to extend the theory and practice of public relations.

Coorientation

Broom (1977) referred to the mutual attempts of two or more parties to orient to each other and the common aspects of their environments. This involves the congruence, accuracy, understanding, and agreement that each party has to the other and to the issue confronting them. PRFD provides a versatile methodology for assessing degrees and types of coorientation between actors in any given situation. PRFD can reveal a public's perception of the current states of affairs, desired states of affairs, or perceived states of affairs to be avoided. Bales and Cohen (1979) referred to these categories of behavior perception as actual, wished for, and rejected (or worst case) behaviors. For example, an organization might perceive itself as being friendly and customer service oriented, whereas the customer public might perceive the organization as neutral or even unfriendly and more self-oriented than customer oriented. A PRFD analysis would reveal the lack of accuracy that the organization has with regard to its understanding of customers' perceptions and would provide an avenue by which to compare its perceptions of desirable and undesirable states of affairs to those of the customers.

Culbertson (1989a) pointed to the need for public relations professionals to be able to recog-

First, please indicate your view of how much potential influence each person, group, or organization identified below has on the community by circling the appropriate number:
(1 = low influence, 10 = high influence, NI = no impression)

Actor A:

| 1 | 2 | 3 | 4 | 5 | 6 | 7 | 8 | 9 | 10 | NI |

Actor B:

| 1 | 2 | 3 | 4 | 5 | 6 | 7 | 8 | 9 | 10 | NI |

Actor X:

| 1 | 2 | 3 | 4 | 5 | 6 | 7 | 8 | 9 | 10 | NI |

Second, please indicate how friendly or unfriendly you feel that each person, group, or organization identified below is toward you by circling the appropriate number:
(1 = unfriendly, 10 = friendly, NI = no impression)

Actor A:

| 1 | 2 | 3 | 4 | 5 | 6 | 7 | 8 | 9 | 10 | NI |

Actor B:

| 1 | 2 | 3 | 4 | 5 | 6 | 7 | 8 | 9 | 10 | NI |

Actor X:

| 1 | 2 | 3 | 4 | 5 | 6 | 7 | 8 | 9 | 10 | NI |

Finally, please indicate your perceptions of persons, groups, or organizations with regard to how self-oriented or community-oriented they are. For example, do you believe that they are motivated more to advance or protect their personal careers and/or their agencies or organizations, or conversely, are they more motivated to provide service to the community?
(1 = self-oriented, 10 = community-oriented, NI = no impression)

Actor A:

| 1 | 2 | 3 | 4 | 5 | 6 | 7 | 8 | 9 | 10 | NI |

Actor B:

| 1 | 2 | 3 | 4 | 5 | 6 | 7 | 8 | 9 | 10 | NI |

Actor X:

| 1 | 2 | 3 | 4 | 5 | 6 | 7 | 8 | 9 | 10 | NI |

Figure 8.2.   Public Relations Field Dynamics Instrument

nize that other perspectives differ from their own. They also need to recognize the contents of these perspectives and take them into account in communication. PRFD offers a mechanism for discovering these perceptions. In addition, because the public field can be displayed in a visual format, it provides a versatile mechanism for educating others with regard to the various perceptions of the public field. The utility of theory and PRFD can be illustrated in several earlier studies.

Using PRFD to reveal coorientation helps to identify which publics are potentially open for collaboration and which are not. In addition, PRFD can be used to determine the views of other publics on the issue central to the situation to determine who might be able to serve as a mediator. As such, PRFD has a great deal to offer with regard to viewing the public relations process as conflict management and negotiation.

Conflict and Negotiation Theories

Vasquez (1996) argued for the conceptualization of public relations as negotiation within an issues development perspective. Putnam and Roloff (1992) identified four essential characteristics of negotiation communication: incompatible goals, interdependent parties, social interaction, and the exchange of offers and counteroffers. Vasquez (1996) noted that public relations functions as an important sentry to detect present or potential incompatibilities with other independent actors in the environment. It also is the function of public relations to interact with these groups or individuals and to exchange offers and counteroffers in attempting to manage issues in a manner advantageous to the organization and, if possible, to other actors in the environment. This process is characterized by a process of naming, blaming, and claiming between parties (Felstiner, Abel, & Sarat, 1981; Putnam & Holmer, 1992).

Putnam (1990) noted that issue negotiation merges integrative and distributive processes. Integration involves interaction that exhibits flexibility in position and an increased potential to attain joint mutual benefits between parties. Distributive processes are those that point negotiation in the direction of rigidity, conflict, polarization, and win-lose or lose-lose outcomes. PRFD offers a useful way in which to begin mapping the perceptions of the integrative and distributive posture of key actors. The self-orientation versus community orientation dimension captures perceptions of integration and distribution within the overall field, and the friendly versus unfriendly dimension helps to define perceptions of friend or foe that each actor has toward all other actors in the situation. The low influence versus high influence dimension provides insight into how much credibility each actor has with regard to the perceived level of influence that actor can exert in a given situation.

In addition, PRFD is a particularly useful method within an issues negotiation perspective because it provides a way in which to concurrently account for multiple actors. Few public relations environments involve only two actors. Group theory identifies the importance of other secondary actors in any conflict situation. For example, in his exploration of mediation techniques, Polley (1988) noted that when it is impossible to simultaneously satisfy the needs of opposing subgroups, the next best strategy is to introduce the presence of a mediator. He stated, "Interestingly, the group members need not change their own behaviors in order for the polarization to be reduced. The mere presence of the mediator figure tends to lessen the perceived severity of the polarization" (p. 74).

The presence of potential mediators is key in many conflict situations. In the treaty rights case discussed earlier, PRFD revealed the obvious polarization between the Ojibwa and PARR. This polarization made it unlikely that these two groups would be able to constructively interact with each other directly. However, PRFD did reveal that the DNR was in a position to serve as a mediator from the Ojibwa's perspective. Given PARR's somewhat negative perception of the DNR, a trust-building strategy would be necessary for PARR to accept the DNR in a mediator role. The DNR might begin to employ what Osgood (1972) termed a "graduated reduction in tensions" (GRIT) approach. The GRIT conflict resolution theory assumes that, in cases of extreme polarization, reconciliation has to progress in gradual stages. The assumption is that the critical element of mutual trust is fragile and must be built over time. Agreement on simple minor points must occur to build trust before the major points of disagreement can be tackled. Once PARR would begin to perceive the DNR as more community-oriented (i.e., integrative) and friendlier, the DNR could help the Ojibwa and PARR to productively negotiate a resolution to the dispute. In such situations, PRFD is an excellent tool for monitoring perceptions and mapping the evolution of groups and their relationships to one another over time. It could provide invaluable insight for choosing the best conflict and negotiation strategies in a given situation.

Situational Theory of Publics

PRFD also shows promise in extending our understanding of public relations environments when coupled with the situational theory of publics (J. Grunig & Hunt, 1984). In essence, situational theory offers a mechanism for classifying individuals in relation to the awareness and level of concern about a particular problem. Situational theory posits that a public's perceptions of a situation can be used to predict the extent to which members of that public will seek and process information about that particular situation. Three independent variables are used to make these predictions: problem recognition, constraint recognition, and level of involvement. PRFD does not directly measure these three variables, nor does it directly classify latent, aware, and active publics. Rather, it offers a way in which to identify the perceived behavior between key actors in a given situation. The two approaches can complement each other in that the model of situational publics can classify the type of publics involved, and PRFD can elaborate on the perceived relationships between those publics.

To illustrate, we draw on a study investigating the utility of using both approaches to promote the use of mammography screening (Springston, 1997b). Problem recognition refers to the perception that something is problematic or less than ideal. In the case of mammography screening, problem recognition refers to the degree to

which women perceived breast cancer as a serious and threatening disease. Constraint recognition refers to the perception of any obstacles that impede doing anything about the situation; for example, women might feel a sense of fatalism about getting the disease as well as a sense of powerlessness about the amount and quality of information they receive on the issue. Finally, the level of involvement refers to the extent to which people connect themselves to the issue; for example, does a woman feel susceptible to breast cancer, and does she feel that information about the disease is important to her?

Springston (1997b) surveyed 106 female staff employees at a large midwestern university regarding their perceptions of breast cancer and breast cancer screening. The women were asked to complete a 12-item situational theory instrument that addressed the perceived likelihood of getting breast cancer and perceptions about information available from health providers, the media, and the scientific community. These women also were asked to complete the PRFD instrument in which they rated doctors, nurses, mammography technicians, and health reporters along the three PRFD dimensions. (In this study, the self-orientation vs. community orientation dimension was defined in terms of a self-centered vs. patient-centered orientation.)

As predicted, women scoring higher on each of the three situational theory subscales were more likely to have received information about breast cancer screening and from a wider array of media. These women also were more knowledgeable about breast cancer screening and less fearful of the disease. With regard to the three PRFD dimensions, women perceived greater benefits from mammography when physicians were viewed as being more patient centered. Women perceived fewer barriers to screening when they viewed nurses and technicians to be friendlier and more patient centered. An association between situational theory and PRFD also was discovered. Situational involvement was found to be significantly related to the perceived impact of nurses and health reporters. The more involved a woman was, the more she perceived nurses and health reporters to have an impact on her. In addition, the more involved a woman was, the friendlier she perceived mammography technicians to be. Finally, the more involved a woman was, the more she perceived nurses to be patient centered.

Bormann's Fantasy Theme Analysis

Bormann's (1972, 1982, 1985, 1986, 1996) fantasy theme analysis, also known as symbolic convergence theory, is derived from Bales's (1970) premise that tension within groups promotes the development of stories or fantasy themes. Symbolic convergence occurs when group members create fantasies—interpretations of events that meet a group's emotional, psychological, or rhetorical needs. When group members' interpretations converge, a shared group consciousness is realized and a new reality is created. Bormann (1972) argued, "When group members respond emotionally to the dramatic situation, they publicly proclaim some commitment to an attitude" (p. 397).

The extent to which fantasies are shared and symbolic convergence occurs is a powerful indicator of the relational status of a group. A group in which members achieve convergence is more likely to have well-established relationships as well as similar accounts of events facing the group. Thus, symbolic convergence provides a consensual point for members of a public and also helps to define one public's stance in relationship to another public. When members of a public converge, they share enough symbolic ground to negotiate the shared reality among themselves. These common sentiments or emotional involvements become translated into a "story" about the issue or other publics.

The benefits of integrating fantasy theme analysis with PRFD can be illustrated with examples from Springston and Keyton (1996). A citywide crisis erupted in Indianapolis when 17 off-duty police officers became involved in a physical confrontation with 2 civilians. According to eyewitnesses, the European American officers shouted racial and homophobic slurs and made lewd suggestions to women while they walked down the street. When an African American male intervened on behalf of the women, a fight broke out. Leaders of the African American community sharply criticized the European American mayor for his handling of the discipline of the officers. The European American police chief resigned, and the African American deputy police chief assumed leadership of the police department.

Members of the African American community called for the suspension of all officers present during the brawl, but the mayor rejected this demand. Instead, the mayor and the deputy police chief stalled by calling for an internal police investigation. In response to the incident, a group of African American church pastors formed a group they called the Concerned Clergy, whose members were vocal in their opposition to what they viewed as a slow and tepid response by the mayor and deputy police chief. Eventually, the mayor agreed to forming a Civilian Oversight Task Force to review police department procedures for internal investigations and disciplinary action.

Thus, the four publics—the mayor, the deputy police chief, the Concerned Clergy, and the Civilian Oversight Task Force—were actively reported about in the media. As such, each public obtained and processed information about other publics with whom they interacted. Springston and Keyton (1996) collected PRFD data from Indianapolis citizens about their perceptions of these four publics. Not surprisingly, distinct perceptual differences were found on all three dimensions based on participants' race. A complement to this analysis would be a fantasy theme analysis of the stories that each public developed about the other publics with which they were interdependent. It is likely that perceptual differences could be accounted for by different versions of stories or fantasies that these publics believed about themselves and created for others.

CONCLUDING REMARKS

This chapter has introduced the application of field dynamics theory to public relations. Theory and methodology must be robust enough to account for the complexities inherent in the multipublic environments in which organizations find themselves. To this end, we applaud the efforts of Cancel et al. (1997), Vasquez (1996), and other scholars to move public relations scholarship toward a contingency-based negotiation perspective. Such an approach places communication at the center of study and promises to add to the theoretical and practical development of the field. PRFD provides a method for collecting and analyzing data that can be used to more effectively structure an organization's rhetoric. If field positions of salient publics are known, then public relations strategy can be targeted to achieve a more effective end through more efficient means (e.g., satisfying two disparate publics with one message or source, using a more neutral message or source for entry into the public debate). Most important, PRFD can be used to assess trial messages for their impact on various publics before their release. PRFD also can be a means of collecting and interpreting reactions to an organization's public relations practices. Rather than relying on the often few but loud voices that normally respond, practitioners can use PRFD in a proactive manner to gauge reaction to organizational rhetoric much like spinmasters track reaction to politicians' speeches and behavior.

This chapter has demonstrated that PRFD theory and methodology are robust enough to account for multiple publics and work in a complementary fashion within an issue negotiation perspective. By coupling PRFD with theories such as coorientation, conflict theory, situational theory of publics, and symbolic convergence theory, our understanding of public relations as issues negotiation can be extended. Future research also should begin to couple PRFD with other useful theories such as attribution theory, game theory, and the theory of image restoration strategies.

CHAPTER 9

Bringing Publics Into Public Relations

New Theoretical Frameworks for Practice

SHIRLEY LEITCH

DAVID NEILSON

The needs of the public relations profession have, to a large extent, driven the development of public relations as an academic discipline. Academics do no service to practice, however, if they confine their activities to serving the needs of the present as opposed to providing leadership for the future. During recent years, public relations scholarship has attempted to provide such leadership by forging links with new relevant bodies of social and cultural theory. This chapter contributes to that process by deconstructing the core public relations concepts of "publics," "relations," and "organizations" in the light of some of these new theoretical developments. A revised version of these core concepts is then offered as a framework for the reconstruction of public relations theory. The purpose of the chapter is to offer scholars and practitioners new ways of thinking about public relations.

There is little doubt that of the three core concepts considered in this chapter, publics has been the most seriously inadequate for the purposes of research and practice. As Karlberg (1996) and Moffitt (1994a) contended, the organizational perspective has tended to overwhelm and marginalize publics within public relations theory. That is, publics have been viewed solely from the perspective of the organization and not from that of the publics themselves. As a result, public relations theory has been unable to come to terms with the power relationships between discourse participants or with ethical issues relating to power differentials. It is with the concept of publics, then, that our analysis begins.

AUTHORS' NOTE: An earlier version of this chapter was published in the *Australian Journal of Communication*, 24(2), 17-32.

PUBLICS

The primary tension within and between the various definitions of publics to be found in widely used public relations textbooks arises between strategic and dialogic approaches (Baskin & Aronoff, 1992; Cutlip, Center, & Broom, 1994; J. Grunig, 1992c; J. Grunig & Hunt, 1984; McElreath, 1993; Seitel, 1995). The strategic approaches that dominate the field (Gandy, 1992) portray publics as consumers of targeted organizational messages. The dialogic approaches portray publics as active and equal participants in a dialogue with the organization. Both approaches emphasize the organizational perspective. Both focus on the nature of the relations that organizations have or should have with their publics rather than on the publics themselves. In the second approach in particular, publics are presented as organizational artifacts or constructs. That is, publics appear to come into existence only when an organization identifies them as publics. On a semantic level this might be true, but the semantic level surely is the most trivial level at which to seek an understanding of this core public relations concept. Moreover, for both the dialogic and strategic approaches, the organization always is the "subject position" from which publics are understood. Publics, as conceptualized in this literature, appear not to be actively involved in the ongoing construction of their own identities, strategies, or goals. This gap in public relations theory can lead to serious conceptual flaws. In practice, it can make practitioners blind to the presence of important publics.

Public relations theory does distinguish between latent and active publics (J. Grunig & Hunt, 1984). Latent publics literally refers to "paper classes" (Bourdieu, 1987) constructed by the organization out of social data suggesting that they have some potential to exist. Active publics are described as groups that have come into existence and see themselves as having a relationship of some type with an organization. However, even active publics are understood only from the position of the organization. This strategic perspective is somewhat mystified within public relations theory because publics and organizations generally are treated as interchangeable and equivalent entities. They are treated as interchangeable because, from the subject position of an organization, another organization is a public. They are treated as equivalent because they are interchangeable and because, in the dialogic approach in particular, publics and organizations are treated as if they are equal participants in a dialogue. This apparent equality, between equivalent and interchangeable entities, is reinforced by the complete absence of the concept of power in mainstream public relations theory (Coombs, 1993).

Publics From the Organizational Perspective

The current dominance of the organizational perspective within public relations theory undoubtedly stems from the highly influential, although much critiqued, work of J. Grunig and Hunt (1984). Working from a systems perspective, they developed four models that, they claimed, reflected both the historical evolution of public relations practice and the different approaches still used by practitioners. The four models, in terms of their evolutionary progress, were labeled the press agent/publicity model, the public information model, the two-way asymmetric model, and the two-way symmetric model (J. Grunig & Hunt, 1984, p. 13). They argued that the two-way symmetrical or dialogic model represented the most effective and most ethical way of conducting public relations work. Based in a version of systems theory, the model assumed that it was possible for an organization to meet its publics on equal terms and to rationally determine mutually beneficial outcomes.

The primary distinction that J. Grunig and Hunt (1984) drew between the two-way asymmetric and two-way symmetric models hinged on the nature of their relations with the environment. Practitioners working within the asymmetrical model would attempt to control the environment so that it met their organizational needs, whereas those working within the symmetrical model would attempt to adapt the organization to the environment rather than control it. The ethical superiority of symmetrical public relations was, then, rooted in the *attitude* of the organization and its openness to change. As J. Grunig and Hunt stated,

> The two-way symmetric model . . . consists more of a dialogue than a monologue. If persuasion occurs, the public should be just as likely to persuade the organization's management to change attitudes or behaviors as the organization is likely to change the public's attitudes or behaviors. Ideally, both management and publics will change somewhat after a public relations effort. (p. 23)

In their extensive study of public relations practice within organizations, J. Grunig and L. Grunig (1989) were, however, unable to find many instances of symmetrical public relations. Thus, despite their efforts to create a descriptive theory, J. Grunig and L. Grunig reluctantly acknowledged that the symmetrical model was primarily a normative theory.

The primary reason why J. Grunig and L. Grunig (1989) were unable to find much evidence of the symmetrical public relations in practice was that the model itself is flawed in several key respects. The concept of power, for example, appears in the model only as an absence (Coombs, 1993). Yet, power is a key element in the analysis of social relations in nearly all other disciplines (e.g., political science, psychology, media studies) and in social theory generally. According to Fairclough (1995a), within discourse theory, "Power is conceptualized both in terms of asymmetries between participants in discourse events and in terms of unequal capacity to control how texts are produced, distributed, and consumed (and hence the shapes of texts) in particular sociocultural contexts" (pp. 1-2). Thus, discourse symmetry is more than an organizational attitude. A willingness to listen to publics and to adapt one's behavior as a consequence of this interaction does not address the asymmetries inherent in discourse practices weighted in favor of one of the discourse participants and against the others. It is simply absurd to suggest that an interaction between, for example, a

transnational corporation and a public consisting of unskilled workers in a developing country can be symmetrical just because the interaction is symmetrical in form. It is even more absurd to suggest the reverse—that the interaction between this worker public and the corporation can be symmetrical if the workers adopt the correct attitude and are willing to compromise. In practice, in cases where access to resources is so unequal, attempting to practice symmetrical public relations might constitute a self-destructive discourse strategy for the least powerful participant.

That organizations may rightly perceive there to be no advantage in adapting to the environment through compromises with their publics is one reason why the symmetrical approach might not be adopted. Indeed, J. Grunig and Hunt (1984) acknowledged that model selection might be more of an indication of the nature of the organization, the nature of the public relations issue, and the organizational power of the practitioner than of the practitioner's expertise or ethics. Implicitly, then, J. Grunig and Hunt argued that all four models, including the symmetrical model, were strategic choices appropriate in different circumstances. This argument later was made explicit by J. Grunig and Repper (1992) when they stated, "We define *strategic* symmetrically rather than asymmetrically" (p. 123, italics in original). This definition creates problems for the earlier view that the symmetrical model is inherently more ethical than the other three models. Moreover, J. Grunig and L. Grunig's (1992, 1996) adaptation of the original model, which attempts to lend ethical respectability to some versions of asymmetrical public relations, serves only to further undermine the model's dialogic basis for assessing communication ethics. That the J. Grunig and Hunt (1984) model does not adequately distinguish between publics and organizations is a primary reason why symmetrical communication and communication ethics have been so tightly linked within the terms of the model.

The organization-centered view of publics was taken to the extreme by J. Grunig and Repper (1992) when they described publics as organizational artifacts: "A public, a market, or any other segment of a population exists only because a . . . [public relations] practitioner uses a theoretical concept to identify it" (p. 129). The act of theoretical construction does not, however, always (or simply) bring a group into being. Moreover, J. Grunig and Repper's definition implies that organizations cannot be publics. Within public relations theory generally, however, organizations are explicitly identified as potential publics. The difference between organizations and publics then becomes purely one of perspective. A theory that conceptualizes organizations and publics as interchangeable falls into the trap of abstractly representing organizations and publics as equivalent entities. If public relations is about the relations between organizations and their publics, then it would seem obvious to more clearly distinguish rather than conflate them. In the next subsection, we sketch out the basis for a more developed theory of publics before turning our attention to the second of our key concepts, organizations.

Importing the Public Into Public Relations

The notion that there is a need to import the public into public relations theory arises out of the gulf that exists between public relations and other areas that have engaged with this concept. It is as though some public relations scholars have felt the need to invent theory from the ground up even when well-developed appropriate theory already has existed in other disciplines. Whatever the reasons underlying this relative isolation, public relations theory has been the poorer for it. In this subsection, we seek to enrich the field by supplementing dominant public relations perspectives with social theories of the public sphere (Calhoun, 1992, 1995; Cohen & Arato, 1992; Habermas, 1962/1991), Habermas's (1987) distinction between system and lifeworld, and Fairclough's (1992, 1995a) discourse theory. These theorists now will be drawn on to enable us to identify different types of organizations and publics as well as different types of relations between them.

In Habermas (1962/1991), the concept of publics is related to the concepts of "the public"

and the "public sphere." The public is made up of all the citizens of a nation. The public sphere, as distinct from the private sphere, is the ensemble of public spaces available for debate between citizens. A town meeting can be a site for the public sphere, as can a discussion held in an Internet chat room. Democratic debate by the public within the many sites of the public sphere occurs in relation to, but distinct from, the "system." The system includes both "political subsystems" (state) and "economic subsystems" (economy). Thus, in its ideal form, the public sphere provides space for the discussion of important political and economic issues free from the interference of either state or economic forces. The public sphere is one element of the lifeworld that encompasses the lived experiences and habitus of individuals (Habermas, 1962/1991, 1987). Cohen and Arato (1992), drawing principally on the work of Habermas, offered a useful model (Figure 9.1) for integrating Habermas's major concepts. The private sphere of the lifeworld interacts with the system via the public sphere. In its ideal form, the public sphere provides the site in which public opinion can form. Through the democratic structures of society, public opinion places limits on and leads to reforms within the system. In practice, of course, public opinion might not be the unitary or easily interpreted concept that this simple formulation suggests. Moreover, public policy might not embody public opinion(s) at all but instead might reflect system-level goals.

Whatever its limitations might be in practice, a public sphere in which multiple competing voices may be heard is central to the functioning of democracy (Calhoun, 1988, 1992). Similarly, the notion of the public, understood as all private citizens who may participate in the public sphere, is a core component of democracy. Within mainstream public relations literature, however, there has been no acknowledgment of the role of the public sphere and a near universal abandonment of the notion of the public in favor of multiple publics. Cutlip et al. (1994), for example, declared that "there is simply no such thing" (p. 360) as the general public. Public relations scholars might not have intended to turn their backs on democracy, but this has been one

	Public	Private
System	Political subsystem or "state"	Economic subsystem
Lifeworld	Public sphere	Private sphere

Figure 9.1. Integrating Social Concepts

effect of the way in which many have theorized the discipline. It is, however, both unhelpful and unnecessary to abandon the public and its associated macrofocus at the level of the nation-state to validate the microfocus on organizational relations. Rather, the concept of the public can be retained as representing one possible configuration of individuals within a framework where multiple configurations are possible.

Conceptualized in this way, publics may be seen as groups of individuals who develop their own identities, and perhaps representations of their collective interests, in relation to the system. In Heath's (1994) terms, the members of a public may come to share a zone of meaning in relation to an issue, an event, or an organization. Individuals are not, of course, members of single publics but instead participate in the multiple sites of the public sphere as members of diverse publics. They may simultaneously hold a number of different subject positions within these sites and publics (Foucault, 1969/1972; Laclau & Mouffe, 1985; Moffitt, 1994a; Motion, 1996; Motion & Leitch, 1996). For example, the same individual may speak as a citizen in one forum, as a parent in another forum, and as an environmentalist in a third forum. These multiple subject positions may overlap, intersect, or conflict and always will be in a state of flux. Taken together, they provide the context within which individuals must negotiate their own public identities. Once the notion of multiplicity is accepted, it becomes clear that the zones of meaning associated with a particular public cannot be viewed in isolation. Instead, they constitute a series of threads that are woven together to form the fabric of public opinion (R. Heath, personal communication, June 30, 1998).

ORGANIZATIONS

Having reframed the concept of publics within the context of the system-lifeworld distinction, we now turn to organizations and the nature of their relations with publics. Before looking at organizations in more detail, however, it is necessary to distinguish among the different types of relations within current public relations practice. Three distinct types of organization-centered public relations can be identified:

1. Intersystem organization relations
2. Intraorganizational relations
3. Organization-public relations

Each of these sets of relations involves quite different public relations practices. Therefore, each ought to form part of the strategic planning framework or schema for any public relations practitioner. *Intersystem organization relations* refers to the public relations practiced between the organizations of state and economy. The relationship between a corporation and a government department would fall into this category. *Intraorganizational relations* refers to an organization's own internal public relations. *Organization-public relations* refers to relations between organizations and publics that are defined as internal to neither the organization nor other system organizations. It is this third type of public relations practice that is the focus of this chapter. This focus stems from our definition of publics as groups of individuals participating in the public sphere and our concern here with addressing the nature of relations between organizations and publics. The other two areas of public relations work are no less important but lie outside the scope of this chapter.

There are numerous competing definitions of the nature of organizations, ranging from the classical to the postmodern. The debates inherent within these competing theories are beyond the scope of this chapter. It must be noted, however, that stronger links need to be developed between the areas of organizational communication and public relations. For the purposes of this chapter, organizations are broadly conceptualized as frameworks of action that are defined by their own rules and goals but are limited by broader social frameworks. Organizations generally have been understood as system-based entities. According to Habermas, the system functions according to the logic of strategic or instrumental rationality, whereas the lifeworld is associated with communicative action. Instrumental rationality is goal driven, whereas communicative action is rooted in "negotiated intersubjectivity and normative thinking" (Dahlgren, 1995, p. 99). Thus, a strategic approach to public relations, for example, would use organizational objectives as a starting point, whereas a communicative approach would assume that objectives would be formed, intersubjectively, as part of the communication process. Habermas (1987) stated,

> In communicative action, participants pursue their plans cooperatively on the basis of a shared definition of the situation. If a shared definition of the situation is first to be negotiated, or if efforts to come to some agreement within the framework of shared situation definitions fail, the attainment of consensus, which is normally a condition for pursuing goals, can itself become an end. (p. 126)

There are obvious parallels between J. Grunig and Hunt's (1984) two-way asymmetrical model and Habermas's (1987) theory of instrumental rationality as well as between J. Grunig and Hunt's two-way symmetrical model and Habermas's theory of communicative action (J. Grunig & L. Grunig, 1996). However, a major point of departure between the two lies in J. Grunig and Hunt's attempt to attribute communicative action to system organizations, whereas Habermas's communicative action is a characteristic of the lifeworld alone. By 1992, Grunig and Repper (1992) were, moreover, writing of strategic symmetry that, in addition to creating major problems for the J. Grunig and Hunt models, is clearly at odds with Habermasian theory.

Within Habermas's work on the public sphere, the emphasis is placed on communication between individuals, the focus of which is the actions or policies of system organizations. It is possible, however, for publics that come to share zones of meaning (Heath, 1994) to develop their own organizations. Cohen and Arato's (1992) major work on contemporary civil society noted the increasingly institutionalized character of the public sphere. Therefore, a distinction needs to be made in public relations theory between the lifeworld organizations of the public sphere and the system organizations of state and economy. One might argue that as social movements develop professional organizational bases, they become part of the system. More exactly, however, they become part of the system only to the extent that they are incorporated into the decision-making centers of the system. The institutionalization and incorporation of the trade union movement into the normal functioning of the system is the classic example of this process.

A lifeworld organization may be distinguished from a system organization to the extent that, in the former, organization develops as an artifact of the communicative interaction of a public. That is, lifeworld organizations grow out of the debates that take place within the public sphere. System organizations, by contrast, embody the strategic rationality of the systems of state and economy. A simple typology from this basis can distinguish three different types of organizations:

1. System organizations
2. Lifeworld organizations
3. Organizations that have some characteristics of both

A motorway developer and the regulatory agency responsible for planning a motorway would constitute the first type of organizations. A public that came together to oppose the construction of a motorway through a suburban neighborhood would constitute an example of the second type of organization. An established environmental organization that received some state funding and representation in official forums, and that assisted the anti-motorway public by negotiating with the system organizations, might constitute a third type of organization.

Note that only the second type of organizations also are defined as publics in the sense that we outlined earlier. Thus, lifeworld organizations can be said to constitute a subset of lifeworld publics. At the point where lifeworld organizations come to embody strategic rationality or other characteristics of the system, their positioning as part of the lifeworld becomes highly problematic within the terms of the Habermasian model. It might be, however, that this also is the point where they start to become most effective in terms of achieving lifeworld goals.

There are some obvious differences in the relations that different types of organizations will have with publics. We now briefly sketch out the core elements of these different relationships before moving on to consider our final key concept of relations.

Publics in Relation to System Organizations

When publics relate to system organizations, they may offer defensive responses to system encroachment or what Habermas termed the "colonization of the lifeworld." For example, a local citizens group opposed to a new motorway acts to defend an existing habitus or lifeworld. Publics may, however, also adopt strategies and goals that are offensive in character (Cohen & Arato, 1992, p. 531). That is, in addition to opposing colonization by the system, they may pursue their own goals. Thus, the anti-motorway group might embark on a campaign to promote objectives such as clean air, safe places for children to play, and public transport in response to system initiatives to facilitate the continuing dominance of the motor car. Second-wave feminisms have this dual character. At one level, they are a defensive response to the patriarchal form of capitalist modernization. That is, they seek to defend the interests of women within a system constructed around a set of male-centered norms. However, at least one feminist response goes beyond a defense of a preexisting lifeworld pattern toward the system adoption of new institutions, norms, and values that recognize gender equality and/or difference (Habermas, 1987, p.

393). This second type of feminism seeks not only to further the interests of women within the existing system but also to challenge and change the system itself.

Publics in Relation to Lifeworld Organizations

Understanding the nature of the relations between publics and lifeworld organizations requires, first, that the two can be distinguished. This delineation has not always been clear within social theory. Habermas (1987), for example, used the term "new social movements" to encompass the activity of publics around particular issues or issue complexes. This term is problematic, however, because it suggests a unity of purpose or action that might not exist (Melucci, 1988). For example, the feminist movement encompasses a wide range of individuals and lifeworld organizations that have a variety of often conflicting agendas. The problem here is akin to that encountered earlier in the tendency of public relations theory to conflate organizations and publics. Here, there is a tendency to conflate lifeworld organizations and the publics out of which they emerge and with which they engage. For our purposes, it also is important to recognize that the distinction between publics and lifeworld organizations develops over time and is an ongoing process.

Social movements, seen here as publics, engage in defensive or offensive direct action in relation to the system. As they develop a sense of identity through shared sets of meanings, publics may invent their own organizational structures that give permanence to the goals of the movement and may cement in place formal membership and leadership structures. Thus, a lifeworld organization emerges out of a public as part of the process of debate and action occurring within that public. A social movement becomes a social actor at the point where such an organization takes form. It is possible, however, that a public will give form to more than one lifeworld organization, and these organizations might not necessarily share the same goals or values. The large number of competing environmental organizations provide one example of this multiplicity of social actors within a single social movement.

There also is a global dimension to social movements and their associated lifeworld organizations. For example, Greenpeace engages with system organizations at the local, national, and international levels and promotes global lifeworld solidarity between publics. The possibility of global publics arises out of the growth of communication technologies including satellites and the Internet and of international forums including the United Nations and the World Court. The necessity of creating such global publics and of using global public spheres arises for two reasons. First, the issues that lifeworld organizations combat often cross national boundaries. Environmental, labor, and feminist concerns offer obvious examples. Second, the system organizations with which the lifeworld organizations engage are increasingly transnational in their operations. For both of these reasons, system organizations might increasingly find themselves faced with globally based publics in the form of lifeworld organizations.

Publics in Relation to Mixed Organizations

This category of organizations shares characteristics with the previous two in terms of relations with publics. It generally comprises mature lifeworld organizations whose operations have become intertwined with those of the system, particularly those of the state (Offe, 1990). In becoming intertwined, they may exchange their offensive and defensive roles for amelioration roles. That is, rather than oppose the system, they work with the system to reduce the negative effects of system operations on the lifeworld. Charity and labor organizations might fit into this category, although mixed organizations retain their association with the causes of the lifeworld, their operation might in fact assist system colonization. That is, although such organizations might have been created as defensive responses to system encroachment, their operations actually might assist the introduction of

the logics of the system into the lifeworld. Relations between publics and mixed organizations will, therefore, often be of an ambivalent nature and will occur on the "seam" between the system and lifeworld that is the territory occupied by mixed organizations. It should be noted that many lifeworld organizations are acutely aware of the potential pitfalls of partial incorporation by the system. Greenpeace, for example, explicitly refuses to accept funding from either governments or corporations. In this way, Greenpeace seeks to defend its meaning and its identity both as a lifeworld organization and as independent of the system.

RELATIONS

Having defined publics and distinguished between organizations and publics as well as among different types of organizations, we now turn to the concept of relations. As noted earlier, there has been a tendency within public relations theory to accept, as the J. Grunig and Hunt (1984) models suggest, a focus on the form rather than on the purpose of public relations strategy. That is, the focus has been on the surface characteristics of the relationship rather than on its underlying structure or goals viewed from within a broader sociocultural context. This reductionist approach has led to the neglect of other arguably more important aspects of relations. At one level, public relations might be concerned with the different forms of communication between publics and organizations, but at a deeper level, it also is concerned with power, strategy, objectives, and the manifold ways in which each articulates and overdetermines, constructs and deconstructs, and organizes and disorganizes the other. Public relations is about the many ways in which different types of publics interact with different types of organizations, and vice versa, on a strategic terrain of competing discourses and unequal access to power and resources. Public relations is, then, a lot more complex in practice than a focus on form would allow. Moreover, a public relations theory based on discourse form is not adequate at a purely descriptive level, much less as a tool for practice or a framework for education. Our aim here is to examine different types of relations in terms of strategy, objectives, and power and resource differentials.

The overriding objective of system public relations is strategic in the Habermasian sense—to maximize the support of publics and to minimize or neutralize opposition so as to achieve organizational objectives (J. Grunig & L. Grunig, 1989). Thus, genuine dialogue is a problematic concept for system public relations because it has the potential to produce unpredictable and dangerous outcomes. To reduce both uncertainty and the potential for damage, system organizations may attempt to determine in advance the terms of any public debate in which they engage. As Cheney and Dionisopoulos (1989) stated, "In essence, corporate discourse seeks to establish public frames of reference for interpreting information concerning issues deemed important by corporate America" (p. 144). These "public frames of reference" are intended to influence what Heath (1994) termed "zones of meaning": "When favorable zones exist, companies attempt to show how their products and actions conform to them. When unfavorable zones exist, companies attempt to change them or disassociate from them" (p. 240). If the organization succeeds in establishing a particular frame of reference for its publics, then it also may create favorable zones of meaning between itself and these publics. The result probably will be an environment in which it is far easier for the organization to achieve its objectives. However, it also is possible that publics will create zones of meaning to which they challenge organizations to adapt or respond.

The extent to which the system organization can achieve its objectives and minimize opposition by, if not gain the support of, publics for these objectives is related to a host of factors. One starting point for gauging the type of public relations strategies that an organization will need to deploy, as well as the form of relations to be adopted, obviously is the extent to which the organization invades or destroys the lifeworld or conflicts with the more offensive (as opposed to

defensive) goals of lifeworld movements. The more the organization's goals are seen as neutral to or even as enhancing the lifeworld, the easier to achieve them. The nature of the system organization's objectives and actions will, then, at least partly determine the depth of outrage or support expressed by publics.

It might, however, be difficult for organizations to create the frames of reference that enable publics to view a particular issue in the way in which the organization wishes them to view the issue. The difficulty arises because creating frames of reference involves linking the norms and values of the individuals who make up the various publics with the objectives and requirements of the organization (Motion & Leitch, 1996). The stated objectives of the organization themselves might function as impediments to such linkages. In such cases, concession in terms of some objectives so as to achieve other objectives is one possible public relations strategy for ensuring the continuing survival and success of the organization. This process looks remarkably like the symmetrical model of public relations described earlier. Viewed from this angle, however, symmetrical public relations is revealed as one possible strategic choice among a number of strategic choices and, therefore, loses much of its force as a model for ethical practice.

Support for or opposition to system organizations by publics is a product of the relations between publics and the organization. Perceptions of the system organization's objectives and actions always are negotiated by the discourse participants rather than simply imposed by one of the participants. That is, the meanings that publics attribute to organizational objectives and goals are not purely organizational constructs, nor are they purely constructs of the publics themselves. They arise out of the interactions between publics and organizations that occur in a variety of sites. These sites might include the public sphere as well as the everyday experiences of individuals in their homes and communities.

System organizations, then, deploy different forms of public relations depending on the nature of their objectives and the initial positions of publics in relation to these objectives. Their task is to facilitate the creation of frames of reference that support particular interpretations of and responses to their objectives. The ability to produce and carry out the most effective strategies will, however, also depend on the discourse resources available to the organization. These resources include the ability to enlist the support of other system organizations. Furthermore, outcomes also will depend on the abilities, resources, and will of the publics themselves. Here, we can distinguish between unorganized and organized publics. Publics that lack an institutional structure, legitimated spokespeople, a clearly articulated agenda, and/or significant discourse resources will not relate to system organizations from a position of power. Their lack of organization might, however, be an obstacle to system organizations and, therefore, a source of strength to the extent that it is very resource intensive and difficult to communicate with such publics. It also is not possible to co-opt or compromise a public that has no leaders, nor is it easy to position such a public within constructs such as zones of meaning (Heath, 1994).

The relations between a system organization and its publics are not, however, only about communicating to achieve objectives. They also are about altering or constructing, to varying degrees, the nature and composition of the publics themselves. This process may occur through the subject positions offered by organizational public relations to individuals within publics (Motion, 1996). When public relations practitioners create campaigns or communicate in some way with their publics, they generally are offering individuals within these publics the subject positions that are most likely to articulate or link with the interests of the organization (Hall, 1986; Moffitt, 1994a; Motion & Leitch, 1996; Slack, 1996). Whether individuals are positioned as citizens or as consumers, for example, has consequences for their ability to participate, as well as for the nature of their participation, in important debates (Fairclough, 1992, 1995a). The construction of subject positions within publics can, therefore, be seen as a potential site of ongoing contestation between organizations and publics.

At a more fundamental level, however, the organization may attempt to create publics that have no existence outside of the public relations discourse (J. Grunig & Repper, 1992, p. 129). Members might have experienced no sense of shared identity or solidarity prior to becoming the object of public relations attention. When members of such publics do relate with the organization, it is (at least initially) only within the frame of reference established by the organization itself. It is likely that public relations conducted in this context would be substantially weighted in favor of the organization. It also is likely that the public has been constructed only because its existence serves the needs of the organization. For example, a piece of legislation might require an organization to consult with and gain the consent of local residents over environmental issues. The organization will, then, construct a public consisting of local residents solely to meet the regulatory mandate, and it will construct and relate to this public in ways that are most likely to meet organizational objectives.

Up to this point, the focus in this section has been on the characteristics of the relations that system organizations have with their publics. Lifeworld organizations obviously will share some of these characteristics. There are, however, at least two unique features of lifeworld public relations that we need to consider. The first feature is the relations between lifeworld organizations and the publics from which they have developed. The second is the relations between lifeworld organizations and system organizations. In the first instance, the publics construct the organizations. That is, the aims and goals of the movements, and even the forms of leadership, can be understood as the outcomes of the activities of publics. However, once organizational nuclei are established and become permanent, the dynamic may change. The relations between the lifeworld organizations and their publics of origin will begin to take on a more reflexive construction. For example, the organizations might employ public relations practitioners to increase membership, to mold and develop the membership's consciousness, and to neutralize or win over opponents. At this point, relations between the lifeworld organizations and their publics of origin will take on many of the characteristics of orthodox public relations practice associated with intraorganization relations.

In terms of the second feature, lifeworld organizations, as organized publics, engage in strategic "wars of position" with system organizations. Here, public relations becomes not only about organizations relating to publics but also about how publics can strategically interact with system organizations. The form of interaction can vary considerably and may involve a range of popular actions, texts, images, public spectacles, collective actions, and the like. It should be noted here that the form of relations is unlikely to be symmetrical in J. Grunig and Hunt's (1984) terms, nor is it likely to fulfill Habermas's (1987) criteria for communicative action. The goal is to maximize public sentiment and consciousness so as to put pressure on the system to concede some of the demands and goals of the lifeworld organizations. At some point, however, system concessions might mean incorporating the principles of the lifeworld organizations into the systems themselves, thereby modifying the systems but also potentially undermining the popular bases of the lifeworld organizations themselves. The lifeworld organizations may then become mixed organizations with characteristics of, as well as allegiances to, both the system and the lifeworld.

Lifeworld organizations have the potential to equal system organizations in terms of access to resources including public relations expertise. As Heath (1997) stated, "Major environmental groups raise money, buy land, commission research, and have extensive grassroots lobbying efforts" (p. 156). Rather than simply participating in discourses that center on system organizations, they might draw the system organizations into their own domains. Or, they might engage with the organizations in domains such as those of official or government discourse and via the public sphere of media discourse. Although the J. Grunig and Hunt (1984) models assume that the form of public relations adopted is defined by organizations, it is clear that publics, particularly if they develop their own organizational bases, may themselves make strategic choices about the approaches to and forms of communication. This notion is antithetical to much public relations theory in which publics are portrayed as more or less passive groups whose members are waiting for organizations to communicate with them. The quality of the public relations effort is assessed on the basis of whether or not practitioners have adhered to standard industry practices. Standard practices might, however, be of little use in the face of lifeworld publics with objectives of their own. As Heath (1997) noted, "Activism has become institutionalized" (p. 156) and is neither readily controlled nor easily manipulated.

FUTURE DIRECTIONS

The preceding discussion has purposely raised more questions than it has answered. Our intention has been to deconstruct the concepts that have formed the building blocks of public relations so as to provide a framework for a more robust body of theory. Publics and organizations, which are conflated in dominant public relations approaches, were more clearly distinguished. A framework then was constructed for identifying different types of organizations, different types of publics, and different types of relations between the various organizations and publics. This framework has provided the beginnings of a new approach to public relations theory. Such an approach not only provides organizations with a more strategic knowledge of publics but also provides the basis for a public-centered approach to public relations. A more developed framework, however, would need to draw more fully on scholarship in the areas of organization communication and social theory. In our concluding statements, we would like to sketch out some specific issues for theory development raised within this new framework in the hope that it will stimulate debate and further research.

In terms of publics, some of the major issues we have identified as requiring further development stem from the notion of multiplicity—of multiple subject positions occupied by individuals within multiple publics within the multiple sites of the public sphere. Multiplicity cannot be accommodated within the simple strategy models commonly taught to public relations students (Cutlip et al., 1994; Tymson & Sherman, 1996a). Such models imply a unidimensional world in which both publics and the opinions they hold can be readily identified through simple research techniques. The task for public relations practitioners, then, would appear to be to design the tools most likely to influence these publics and then to recalibrate these tools on the basis of a further stage of feedback research. However, publics are not fixed categories waiting to be identified but rather are constructed and reconstructed through the discourses in which they participate. Publics have their own views of themselves and their own views of the organizations with or about which they communicate. Although organizations may orchestrate the development of publics to serve organizational objectives, there is no guarantee that such publics will be content with their status as organizational artifacts or will accept the meanings that organizations have imposed on them. Moreover, if publics develop their own identities, then they will begin to pursue their own objectives and might even develop into lifeworld organizations.

Multiplicity also is a major issue for both the theory and practice of opinion research. The opinions that publics hold are not objects waiting to be discovered and recorded by public relations research. Instead, opinions are negotiated by discourse participants during any communicative event. The notion that the responses that individuals give to questions can be strongly influenced by the way in which questions are worded is a well-accepted but less well-understood point. Even more fundamental for public relations research, however, is the fact that the act of asking the questions might in itself create the opinions. Such opinions are organizational artifacts that might have no existence outside of the research process. To further complicate matters, it has become increasingly clear that individuals are quite capable of living with ambiguity. As Moffitt (1994a) demonstrated, individuals can simultaneously hold a range of apparently contradictory opinions about an issue, event, or or-

ganization. Few of the complexities discussed here are apparent in the research sections to be found within standard public relations textbooks. There is some evidence to suggest, however, that practice is ahead of the textbooks in this area and is only too conscious of the problems inherent in standard opinion research methods.

The concept of multiplicity also must be considered during the most basic of public relations exercises such as the writing of news releases or brochures. The meaning of such texts never is simply defined by the sender of the message. That is, the creator of a message has no way of determining how it will be received. Moreover, the same message may be received in a wide variety of ways by different publics and by different individuals within the same public. Individuals also may take multiple meanings from the same text either at one time or over a period of time. The whole process of interpretation becomes even more complex when communication becomes two-way rather than unidirectional. During any communicative exchange, meaning is created intersubjectively even when those involved attempt to impose it. In the face of the complexities and subtleties inherent in the concept of multiplicity, the dominant public relations models are revealed as inadequate frameworks for public relations practice.

Further development of the conceptual framework of public relations also is required before we can begin to develop links with appropriate theory on communicative ethics. The notion that public relations ethics is rooted in textual form has gained dominance precisely because of the inadequacy of existing theory. Surface characteristics are easy to identify, quantify, and assess. Measuring such characteristics allows us to avoid difficult questions about power inequalities between discourse participants. Such inequalities are, however, barely visible when viewed from the perspective of organization-centered public relations theory. The development of a truly public-centered public relations, in both theory and practice, is a challenge that still confronts us as we enter the 21st century.

CHAPTER 10

Research Perspectives on "the Public"

GABRIEL M. VASQUEZ

MAUREEN TAYLOR

Professionals in the field of public relations seek to build relationships between their organizations and key publics. Yet, for all the importance placed on the creation, maintenance, and adaptation of organization-public relationships, the term *public* is one of the most ambiguous concepts in the field's vocabulary. Public relations is not alone in its confusion about the term. Fields including political science, psychology, marketing, and advertising also have struggled to better define and apply this term. As Price (1992) noted, no other concept has resulted in such broad social concern, academic interest, or intellectual discussion. The ambiguity of terms used in public relations needs to be clarified because "definitions play crucial roles both in societal processes and in the minds of those who study and practice public relations" (Gordon, 1997, p. 58). For public relations to gain the respect that it desires, there must be consistency in professional terms.

An understanding of the concept of public also is an important foundation for the research agendas of a variety of other fields. Democratic theorists, social critics, sociologists, social psychologists, and empirical studies in mass media effects, marketing, and public relations all have contributed to the conceptualization, refinement, extension, and reconceptualization of a public (Allport, 1924, 1937; Bentham, 1838/1962; Bonoma & Shapiro, 1983; Bryce, 1888; Gordon, 1997; J. Grunig & Hunt, 1984; Lazarsfeld, Berelson, & Gaudett, 1944; Lippmann, 1922, 1925; Lowell, 1913; McDougal, 1920; Rosseau, 1762/1968; Tarde, 1890/1903).

Given the importance of organization-public relationships in the field of public relations, the concept of public should be receiving constant attention and be the subject of considerable research. Unfortunately, as Karlberg (1996) noted, many studies have focused on public relations as "a commercial management function—a means of influencing consumer value and behavior, of cultivating markets, of corporate image control, and of issue management" (p. 266). Although Gordon (1997) noted that the term *public* is "common to all definitions" of the practice of public relations, the public often is understood as a means to an organization's end goal. Publics are, however, an integral part of public relations practice, and as a communicatively constructed social phenomenon, they deserve serious attention.

This chapter provides a conceptual analysis of research on publics. The chapter complements the conceptual foundation created by Broom, Casey, and Ritchey (1997) as they explored the concept of "relationships" in the public relations literature. However, this chapter extends their work and focuses on the other part of the public relations dyad—the public. The following three basic questions about the relationship between public relations with publics underlie this examination. Where have we come from? Where are we now? Where are we going? These questions generally seek insight to the road map of understanding and knowledge with which researchers have traveled in their attempt to theorize on a public. This chapter charts the major conceptual pathways and bridges that link research on a public across diverse disciplines. It serves as the initial effort for development of a communication-based approach to a theory of a public. The chapter is comprised of three main sections: (a) a review of the major perspectives for research on a public, (b) a critique of the major perspectives, and (c) a concluding discussion of theory and research on a public.

PERSPECTIVES ON A PUBLIC

Price (1992) identified the term *public* as originating with the Latin phrase *poplicus* or *populus,* meaning "the people." Today the term generally refers to common access or matters of common interest and concern, especially in matters of office and state. For example, in the fields of political science (e.g., voting behavior, public opinion), history, and democratic philosophy, the concept of a public refers to a mass population of individuals involved in civic affairs under all circumstances. However, in the fields of social psychology, marketing, and public relations, the term *public* generally refers to a situational collection of individuals who emerge and organize

in response to a problem (Blumer, 1946a, 1948; Dewey, 1927; J. Grunig & Hunt, 1984). Public relations professionals traditionally "occupy the middle ground between journalists and the public" and, therefore, must serve both the public's and the organization's needs (Wyatt, Smith, & Andsager, 1996, p. 132).

There are several perspectives for theory and research on a public. Researchers, although sometimes not directly investigating a public, contribute to a conceptual understanding of a public. Perspectives for research on a public range from mass and situational views to more recent approaches such as the agenda-building and "homo narrans" views. The mass perspective regarded a public as a single population of aggregate individuals with enduring characteristics. This perspective draws primarily from the works of Allport (1937), Blumer (1948), Bryce (1888), Dewey (1927), Herbst (1993), Key (1961), Lippmann (1922, 1925), and Price (1992).

The situational perspective viewed a public as a single collection of individuals that emerges in response to some problematic situation. The situational perspective is deduced from the works of Bennett (1980); Blumer (1946a, 1948); Bonoma and Shapiro (1983); Dewey (1927); J. Grunig (1978, 1982, 1983b, 1983c); J. Grunig and Childers (1988); J. Grunig and Hunt (1984); J. Grunig, Nelson, Richburg, and White (1988); Herbst (1993); Lippmann (1925); Park (1904/1972); and Price (1992).

The agenda-building perspective represented a more modern democratic theory of political participation in the United States (Cobb & Elder, 1972, 1983). In this perspective, a public is conceived as an enduring state of political involvement. Agenda building, however, relies on reinterpretation of existing case studies to advance its perspective. Nonetheless, agenda building is included in this analysis because it represents a significant attempt to reconcile theories of public participation with practical reality.

Finally, the homo narrans perspective defined a public as "individuals that develop a group consciousness around a problematic situation and act to solve the problematic situation"

(Vasquez, 1993, p. 209). This perspective focused on the dynamic and communicative nature of a public and uses existing research in an attempt to advance theory building (Vasquez, 1993, 1994).

These perspectives often are taken for granted and accepted by scholars, if not by society as a whole. Consequently, little (if any) research has been conducted to examine the implicit assumptions underlying these perspectives. J. Grunig (1989b) argued that for the field of public relations to advance, it needs more examination of the implicit assumptions that guide theory and practice. This section provides an analysis of the major perspectives underlying theory building and driving research on a public. Each perspective is reviewed through an examination of its theoretical origins and state type (or generalized form that a public is assumed to exist as), and a research illustration is provided. Perspectives are presented in order of development from the early democratic view to the more recent communication-based view.

The Mass Perspective

Origins

The mass perspective has its origin in classical notions of democracy. The democratic philosophy of self-governance views a public as the entity of all citizens who have the civic duty to participate in all civic matters. Public participation involves the self-informed expression of well-articulated judgments about political matters. A public is responsible for identifying civic concerns, gathering information from events and debates, and articulating its judgment to governmental officials by some method of expression. In this manner, a public participates in the process of governance and is engaged in self-rule.

State Type

Classical democracy views a public as the sum of individuals who can respond to civic matters. Implicit within democratic philosophy

is the idea that a public is analogous to a permanent state of mind or collective consciousness. As a state of consciousness, a public is assumed to exist as a consistent, collective-level entity with a fairly stable pattern of characteristics. Sociological concepts of mass behavior also influenced a state-of-consciousness view of a public.

Scholarly interest in collective behavior led to the social-scientific extension of the state-of-consciousness view. Sociological concepts of mass behavior influenced a view of a public as a state of consciousness. This line of research eventually led to the development of the situational perspective and is reviewed in the next segment. For now, discussion centers on the influences of research on collective behavior within the mass perspective. Social scientists focused on the social-psychological characteristics of mass and crowd behavior. Researchers began to examine select groups within the total population (e.g., sectors of the population, groups that actively participate in public debate, the electorate, the population as a whole), not only for enduring characteristics and composition but also for their social-psychological nature. This focus extended notions of the state-of-consciousness perspective to include multiple states of consciousness; metaphorically, researchers began to examine the whole for its constituent parts. The inclusion of social-psychological attributes, therefore, served to extend scholarly discussion over the nature of the enduring consciousness, characteristics, and composition of a public.

Research Illustrations

A brief review of research on voting behavior exemplifies the mass perspective. Many political scholars generate research questions from results of the National Election Survey at the University of Michigan. Researchers have attempted to identify enduring characteristics that compose the voting public and affect its state of mind. Voting behavior is explained through a variety of collective-level concepts and operational definitions. For example, researchers have described a public as sophisticated (Key, 1961) and unsophisticated (E. Smith, 1993), influenced by the economy (Markus, 1993) or foreign policy (Aldrich, Sullivan, & Borgida, 1993), rational and irrational (Verba & Nie, 1993), and stable and unstable across party identification (Miller, 1991; Niemi & Weisberg, 1993).

Other researchers have used schematic models to examine how people organize and explain their political world. Conover and Feldman (1984) used Q-methodology to aggregate and quantify political views by voters. Iyengar (1987) argued that citizens' explanations of national affairs are influenced by how television news frames political information. Miller, Wattenberg, and Malanchuk (1986) concluded that voters have enduring dimensions through which to assess candidates.

Still other researchers have attempted to identify problems of a public. Lippmann (1922) believed that democratic philosophy asked too much of ordinary citizens and that citizens, for the most part, were incompetent to attend to all civic concerns. Dewey (1927) identified the problem not as incompetence but rather as insufficient methods for public communication—"the physical and external means of collecting information" (p. 180). Allen (1975), de Tocqueville (1835/1945), Noelle-Neumann (1984), and White (1961) warned of the dangers to minority viewpoints from majority opinion and pressure to conform. Edelman (1964), Kornhauser (1959), and Lippmann (1925) were concerned about the persuasive susceptibility of a public and the use of propaganda. Finally, Ginsburg (1986), Habermas (1962/1989), and Mills (1956) provided examples of researchers concerned with public domination by elites.

Summary

The mass perspective is "demo-centric." Firmly grounded in democratic philosophy, a public is a permanent, personified state of consciousness motivated to action by a concern for all civic matters. Theory and research on a public are limited to investigation of the enduring characteristics and composition of the aggregate individuals that participate in the process of governance and self-rule. Public participation in civic matters is explained through discovery of domi-

nant variables associated with a particular civic concern. Furthermore, a public is plagued with problems related to competency, communication, persuasion, and the expression of minority viewpoints. The mass perspective also has influenced and been influenced by social-psychological concepts of collective behavior. Moreover, these concepts provided a pathway to link and extend research across a variety of social science disciplines. This extension led to the development of a second perspective for research.

The Situational Perspective

Origins

The situational perspective has its origin in social-psychological concepts such as the mass, the crowd, and the public. At the turn of the 20th century, spontaneous crowds, strikes, mass demonstrations, and riots typified human social and psychological behavior (Herbst, 1993; Price, 1992). With an interest in mass and crowd behavior, scholars began to view a public as part of a larger social-psychological process. Interest focused on understanding a public considering broader sociological concerns for human relations and societal change. Scholars posited that human relations were adapted and that societal change occurred through public discussion and debate over issues.

State Type

Implicit within the social-psychological view is the belief that a public is analogous to a situational state of socio-/psycho-consciousness. As interests, issues, problems, states of arousal, and states of consciousness change from situation to situation, the characteristics and composition of a public also change. Differences are attributed to prevailing individual and social-psychological conditions. Therefore, a public is viewed as a situationally developing social entity that emerges through spontaneous argument, discussion, and collective opposition to some issue or problematic situation.

Social scientists focused on explicating the social-psychological nature of a public. Park (1904/1972) first explained a public as an emerging social entity characterized by (a) opposition and rational discourse, (b) organization in response to an issue, and (c) the ability to think and reason with others. Dewey (1927) defined a public as a group of people who (a) face a similar problem, (b) recognize that the problem exists, and (c) organize to do something about the problem. Blumer (1946a) extended Parks's analysis and refined the term *public* to "refer to a group of people who (a) are confronted by an issue, (b) are divided in their ideas how to meet the issue, and (c) engage in discussion over the issue" (p. 189).

Contributions to the social-psychological view of a public also were made by scholars from other social-scientific fields. Researchers in marketing, public relations, and advertising were interested in identifying the social-psychological characteristics and composition of a public as the public emerged in response to an issue. Identification and segmentation of the emergent social-psychological characteristics aided researchers and organizations in designing messages that respond to public concern. Today, segmentation of a public involves "differential response"—general differences in behavioral responses as identified through variables that attempt to predict such a response (e.g., attitudes, demographics, geographic location).

Differential responses to social-psychological variables allowed for the identification, segmentation, and targeting of publics. Researchers identify two types of variables used to segment the public: inferred and objective variables (Frank, Massy, & Wind, 1972; Kotler & Anderson, 1987; Massy & Weitz, 1977). Inferred variables are developed through direct interaction with a targeted group of people. Variables such as perceptions, cognitions, and attitudes are believed to provide for the prediction of desired behaviors and effects (Kotler & Anderson, 1987; Massy & Weitz, 1977). Objective variables refer to the use of secondary sources to identify and segment a public. Variables such as demographics, media use, and geographic location identify publics but are less effective in making predic-

tions of behaviors and effects (Frank et al., 1972; Kotler & Anderson, 1987; Massy & Weitz, 1977).

Research Illustrations

A review of variables used in public segmentation provides an example of research from the situational perspective. Most researchers and practitioners in the fields of marketing, advertising, and public relations use social-psychological situational variables to identify and segment a public. For example, researchers in marketing have used personal values to identify consumer behavior in marketing campaigns (Boote, 1981; Kahle, 1986; Kahle, Beaty, & Homer, 1986; Reynolds & Jolly, 1980; Vinson, Scott, & Lamont, 1977), whereas scholars in public relations have attempted to explain the application of psychographics and geodemographics to public relations research (Rice, 1988; Riche, 1990; Scott & O'Hair, 1989; Zotti, 1985).

In the most systematic investigation of social-psychological concepts for segmentation of a public, J. Grunig, a researcher at the University of Maryland, developed a situational theory of publics (STP). J. Grunig (1975, 1978, 1982, 1983b, 1983c, 1987, 1989b) extended the ideas of Parks, Blumer, and Dewey to develop, test, and validate an STP.

Situational theory results in eight publics that indicate when communication should be directed to a public based on the publics' information-processing and information-seeking behaviors. Situational theory provides for the precise identification and segmentation of a public based on a pattern of similar behaviors defined through independent and dependent variables. Problem recognition, constraint recognition, and level of involvement constitute the independent variables, whereas information seeking and information processing comprise the dependent variables.

Overall, J. Grunig's research has identified four generally enduring types of publics (J. Grunig, 1989b; J. Grunig & Hunt, 1984). An all-issue public is active on all issues. An apathetic public is inattentive to all issues. A single-issue public is active on one or a small set of issues that concern a portion of the population (e.g., saving the whales). A hot-issue public is active on those issues that involve nearly everyone (e.g., drunk driving, toxic waste).

J. Grunig (1989b) extended his own works and incorporated the efforts of Bonoma and Shapiro (1983) to develop a "nested" approach to social-psychological concepts that identify and segment a public. The innermost nest contained variables that segment and target individual communication behaviors and effects. Segmentation concepts, then, progress outwardly from individual to more general variables (e.g., communities, psychographics and lifestyles, geodemographics, demographics) that define but do not isolate individual communication behaviors and effects.

Summary

The situational perspective is "socio-/psycho-centric." The concern for mass and crowd behavior fused a democratic philosophical-political view with a social-psychological view. Building from but rejecting the mass perspective's state of consciousness, the situational perspective adopts a situational state-of-socio-/psycho-consciousness view. A public no longer is viewed as a permanent collection of individuals with enduring characteristics; rather, it is viewed as a collection of individuals, identified by social-psychological variables, that emerges in response to a problem. Theory and research attempt to identify (a) salient social-psychological variables that depict the characteristics and composition of individuals responding to a problem, (b) the larger state of social-psychological conditions and human relations affecting a public, or (c) the state of societal change. Public participation is explained through the discovered social-psychological variables, which also may be used to identify, segment, and target a public for communication.

Although researchers from the mass and situational perspectives have adopted, to some extent, the normative assumption that individuals participate in civic affairs, some political scientists have argued for a view of public participation from the "ways in which groups articulate grievances and transform them into viable issues that require decision-makers to provide some type of ameliorative response" (Cobb & Elder, 1971, p. 905). This line of reasoning has led to a third perspective for research on a public.

The Agenda-Building Perspective

Origins

Agenda building, a modern democratic theory for understanding participation in American politics, rejects the mass and situational views. Instead, it examines public participation through the ways in which different subgroups in a population become aware of and take part in political conflicts (Cobb & Elder, 1971, 1972, 1983; Cobb, Ross, & Ross, 1976). "The process by which demands of various groups in the population are translated into items vying for the serious attention of public officials can appropriately be called agenda-building" (Cobb et al., 1976, p. 126).

Agenda building explains public participation through an examination of how issues get on the agenda. The term *agenda* refers to "a general set of political controversies that will be viewed as falling within the range of legitimate concerns meriting the attention of the polity" (Cobb & Elder, 1971, p. 905). Two types of agendas are identified: public and formal. The public agenda consists of issues that are (a) the subject of widespread attention or awareness, (b) perceived as requiring action, and (c) the appropriate concern of some governmental unit. The formal agenda refers to the set of issues that decision makers have formally accepted for serious consideration. Therefore, any item that comes before any governmental body will constitute a portion of the formal agenda. The goal of agenda-building research, then, is to identify models and propositions that account for the various ways in which publics get issues on the agenda.

The agenda-building perspective is an issues-centered approach to a public and public participation. That is, a public is defined in light of issues. Public participation is specifically explained through an examination of issues. Research emphasizes the degree and direction of a public's effort to expand an issue. A description of the agenda-building perspective, therefore, provides insight to the functioning of publics.

State Type

Implicit within the agenda-building perspective is the belief that a public is a state of involvement with issues. Cobb and Elder (1983) identified four types of publics based on general characteristics that describe the ways in which groups participate in political conflicts. A specific public-identification group alludes to people who have a persistent sympathy with the generic interests of a specific group. These people participate in political conflicts out of concern for the group and can be made aware of the possible consequences of actions taken for or against the group (pp. 105-106). A specific public-attention group refers to people interested in and informed only about certain issues (p. 106). People in such a public participate in political conflict in response to an issue, not out of concern for a specific group. A mass public-attentive group identifies a "generally informed and interested stratum of the population" (p. 107). People that comprise this public generally are more educated, are of higher income, and tend to participate as opinion leaders to less active and less interested segments of the population. Finally, a mass public-general public captures "that part of the population that is less active, less interested, and less informed" (pp. 107-108) about political conflicts.

Research Illustrations

Theoretically, agenda building is concerned with how publics enlarge the conflict over issues to receive the attention and action of governmental decision makers. At a methodological level, scholars identify issues and seek to examine the process of conflict enlargement to explain why certain issues receive governmental attention and other issues of seemingly equal merit are bypassed. Little formal research has been conducted using an agenda-building perspective. Rather, Cobb and Elder (1972, 1983) analyzed several case studies by first reviewing major events and then reinterpreting them in terms of how publics enlarged the issues to receive formal agenda consideration. Rather than summarizing the results of these case studies, we identify their key concepts and models.

An agenda-building analysis assumes the existence of a public and provides insight into the functioning of a public by focusing on the origination of an issue and the degree and direction of a public's efforts to expand the issue. Moreover, this perspective advances its own set of definitions and models for scholarly investigation. According to agenda-building research, a public is most likely to expand an issue based on (a) the more ambiguous an issue is defined, (b) the social significance of an issue, (c) the temporal relevance of an issue, (d) the nontechnical nature of issue definition, and (e) the lack of a clear precedent for issue settlement.

Agenda-building research posits three different models to explain how publics receive the attention and action of decision makers (Cobb et al., 1976). The first, the outside initiative model, accounts for the process through which issues arise in nongovernmental groups and are then expanded sufficiently to reach, first, the public agenda and, finally, the formal agenda. The second, the mobilization model, considers issues that are initiated inside government and consequently receive formal agenda status almost automatically. The third, the inside initiative model, describes issues that arise within the governmental sphere and whose supporters do not try to expand them to the mass public. Instead, these supporters base their hopes of success on their own ability to apply pressure to ensure formal agenda status, a favorable decision, and successful implementation (pp. 127-128).

Collectively, the three models describe the process in which a public influences the structure of the political agenda (Cobb et al., 1976). Furthermore, the models are hypothesized to exist in any society with variations based on the individual political system and different rates of success at achieving agenda status.

Summary

The agenda-building perspective is "agenda-centric." Theoretically, agenda building is a modern philosophical response to the failure of (a) traditional democratic theory to explain mass participation in civic matters and (b) systems theory to explain limited participation in political matters. Research seeks to explain the functioning of modern democracy through the identification of models and propositions that explain how issues make it on the agenda. Within this perspective, a public is analogous to a state of involvement. Four types of publics consist of people who participate in issues to receive the attention and action of decision makers. Public participation is explained through an examination of how issues expand to get on the agenda of decision makers. Issues expand to larger publics based on their concreteness, social significance, temporal relevance, complexity, and technical nature. Furthermore, three models of agenda building have been proposed: the outside initiative, mobilization, and the inside initiative. Agenda-building research is limited to reinterpretation of existing case studies.

Sharing the general belief of group participation in issues of concern, speech communication scholars have entered the domain of theory and research on a public and offer a fourth perspective. Researchers focus on the communication processes and dynamics that account for the emergence of a public. Two camps exist: the homo narrans and semiotics views. The homo narrans view provides a paradigmatic explanation for the role of communication in how individuals first become and then function as a public. The semiotics view builds on advances from the homo narrans view and argues that publics exist through their own communicative constructions (Botan & Soto, 1998). This analysis acknowledges the semiotics view as a communication-centered approach to research on a public but emphasizes the homo narrans view due to the recency of the semiotics view, its extension from homo narrans, and the primacy of homo narrans in advancing a communication-based approach.

The Homo Narrans Perspective

Origins

A homo narrans perspective offers a communication-centered view of a public. As a communication phenomenon, a public has its origin in (a) the situational perspective's underlying logic for communication as central to the emergence of a public and (b) Vasquez's (1993, 1994) conceptualization and operationalization of a public as a rhetorical community. The underlying logic of the situational perspective is grounded in the assumption that a public emerges through spontaneous debate, discussion, and argument over time. The situational perspective, however, focuses on social-psychological variables, not on communicative aspects, to identify participants engaged in the discussion. Vasquez (1993, 1994) argued for a homo narrans paradigm for public relations by combining Bormann's symbolic convergence theory (SCT) and J. Grunig's STP. This paradigm represented an initial effort to understand how individuals first become and then function as a public, thereby providing a communication-based explanation for the emergence of a public.

Vasquez (1993) argued that the Blumer-Dewey-Grunig conceptualization of a public is analogous to Bormann's SCT view of a rhetorical community. A rhetorical community is an aggregation of individuals who have developed a group consciousness around an issue such that they are shaped into "a symbolic system that portrays a broad and consistent view of much or a portion of their social and material reality" (Bormann, 1983, p. 75). Symbolic reality is created, raised, and sustained through the exchange of shared and competing fantasy themes ("fantasy theme" is an SCT term that refers to shared interpretations of events [Bormann, 1972, 1983; Cragan & Shields, 1992]). "In SCT terminology, a public represents individuals who have created, raised, and sustained a group consciousness around a problematic situation" (Vasquez, 1993, p. 209).

Extending the works of Bormann, Cragan, and Shields, Vasquez (1994) explained the communicative process whereby individuals create, raise, and sustain a group consciousness around a problematic situation and become known as a public. SCT assumes that group consciousness is created through the sharing and eventual chaining out of group fantasy themes. *Chaining out* is a technical term used in SCT to describe the human communication activity of participation in a group's symbolic reality (Bormann, 1972, 1983; Cragan & Shields, 1981, 1990, 1992). The process of fantasy theme chaining occurs as people initiate, configure, reconfigure, and evolve an explanation of an event or issue (Cragan & Shields, 1995). The process of configuring and reconfiguring provides for the symbolic convergence of meaning about the event or issue. As people evolve and build a shared view of the event or issue, they symbolically order the world around them; they create a symbolic reality. Thus, from an SCT perspective, a public represents individuals who, through the process of configuring, reconfiguring, and evolving an explanation of a problematic event, have created, raised, and sustained a group consciousness around the problematic event or issue. The public's view of the event represents the public's symbolic reality. Results from an actual public relations campaign indicated support for the homo narrans paradigm of public relations. A homo narrans perspective, then, reformulates existing assumptions to provide a communication framework for theory building and research on a public (Vasquez, 1995).

State Type

Rather than generalizing the form or condition of a public, the homo narrans perspective provides insight to the communicative nature of a public. Namely, SCT-based master analogs provide a dramatistic explanation for individual participation in the symbolic reality of a problematic situation. Master analogs serve the same function as do state types discussed in the mass, situational, and agenda-building perspectives and are, therefore, included in this analysis.

Bormann, Cragan, and Shields (1992) identified at least three master analogs that compete as alternative explanations for symbolic reality. Master analogs are based on James's (1890) principles of psychology about the self. Cragan and Shields (1990) reconceptualized James's personae as righteous, social, and pragmatic analogs. A righteous persona is concerned with the right way of doing things without regard for personal friendships or financial costs. The social persona is keyed to interpersonal relations, trust, and friendship. A pragmatic persona stresses efficiency and practicality. Master analogs, in essence, provide insight to collective meaning, emotion, and motivation as individuals engage in a dramatistic communication process to make sense of events in their world.

Research Illustrations

A homo narrans view of a public is a recent effort undertaken to present a communication framework for advancing theory and research on a public. A homo narrans view contributes to a new understanding of a public by providing an alternative focus, definition, and analog. Vasquez (1994) tested the homo narrans view in an actual public relations campaign. Results of this investigation confirmed major aspects of the model, but refinements also were indicated. A homo narrans perspective generally accounted for (a) theory-segmented publics; (b) aggregation and composite profiles of publics using master analogs, demographics, psychographics, and sociographics; and (c) theory-based message content for theory-segmented publics.

Summary

The homo narrans perspective is "rhetocentric." Using a communication framework for theory building and research, this perspective views a public as a rhetorical community that emerges over time through communication interaction such that a group consciousness is developed around an issue of concern. Theory and research seek to explicate the communicative nature and process by which individuals first become and then function as a public. SCT's master analogs account for the dramatistic communication dynamics of a public. Major aspects of this perspective have been supported, but additional research is necessary.

This portion of the analysis has reviewed the major perspectives for advancing theory and research on a public. Four perspectives were identified and examined for their conceptual origins, state types, and research illustrations. The next section examines the major critiques of the four perspectives.

CRITIQUE

There are four main indictments against the mass, situational, and homo narrans perspectives on a public: (a) the state of consciousness fallacy, (b) the conceptualization of the individual, (c) the conceptualization of the public, and (d) the nature and role of communication. These indictments were developed inductively through review of the literature and provide a more intensive examination of theory and research on a public. Lacking a primary study, the agenda-building perspective is not included in this critique.

The State-of-Consciousness Fallacy

The major obstacle to a more flexible theory of a public is the view of a public as a permanent state of mind or collective consciousness (Bennett, 1980). When a public is regarded as an enduring entity or a set of social-psychological variables to be discovered and analyzed, efforts to research and theorize about a public has resulted in overgeneralized and contradictory results. For example, researchers in the mass and situational perspectives that focused on enduring collective characteristics have depicted a public as ignorant and uninformed versus rational and informed and as stable and unchanging versus enduring over time. Researchers have yet to identify and agree on the enduring characteristics and composition of a public as guided by

their conceptualization. Instead, mass and situational perspective researchers have advanced conflicting generalizations about a general concept. More important, a public as an enduring or situational state of consciousness lacks insight to processes and dynamics underlying public behavior.

By contrast, SCT-based assumptions of the homo narrans perspective provide a metatheoretical foundation that moves away from the state-of-consciousness fallacy. Master analogs displace the state-of-consciousness fallacy to provide a deep structure dramatistic explanation for the communication dynamics of public behavior. Several studies have verified the master analogs as a set of useful concepts for understanding small group and mass communication behavior (Cragan & Shields, 1977, 1981, 1990; Endres, 1989; McFarland, 1985; Vasquez, 1993, 1994).

The Conceptualization of the Individual

The mass and situational perspectives provide a limited view of an individual. The mass perspective is suspect due to its idealistic view of an individual as a citizen in democratic society. Democratic theory requires an individual citizen to be informed of and active in all civic matters. Bryce (1888) was the first to question the civic participation of citizens: "Public questions come in the third or fourth rank among the interests of life" (p. 8). Lippmann (1922) criticized democratic theory for asking too much of ordinary citizens. Lippmann believed that the political world is "out of reach, out of sight, out of mind" (p. 29) of the ordinary citizen. Price (1992) noted,

> Fifty years of survey research has pretty much overwhelmingly confirmed the early suspicions of Bryce (1888) and Lippmann (1922) that the bulk of the general population is both uninterested and uninformed on most matters that could be construed as public affairs. (p. 37)

Thus, the mass perspective's basic conceptualization of an individual is simply inaccurate.

The situational perspective views a public as an emergent aggregation of social-psychological variables generally concerned with problems of social change and harmonious human relations. Individuals are assumed to be rational reasoning entities who can be identified and described by dominant social-psychological conditions motivating action. Little (if any) consideration is given, for example, to meaning, emotion, or alternative sources of motivation. In addition, for both perspectives, the conceptualization of an individual directly affects the conceptualization of a public. This point is discussed about the following indictment.

A homo narrans perspective, however, expands a view of an individual. In this perspective, a public is comprised of individuals with emotions and motivations engaged in a symbolic communication process to make sense of their world. The conceptualization of an individual no longer is based on Platonic views of a citizen or as an aggregation of social-psychological variables. Rather, attention is given to individual communication behaviors and effects as well as individual participation in the symbolic reality of a problematic situation. Moreover, this view of the individual may contribute to a fuller understanding of a public.

The Conceptualization of a Public

In the mass and situational perspectives, the conceptualization of an individual directly influences the conceptualization of a public. The mass perspective generalizes individuals as an enduring state of consciousness. The situational perspective generalizes individuals as situational state-of-social/psychological variables. Both perspectives personify a public as an individual with composite characteristics. It is granted from the outset that an aggregation of characteristics and variables is pertinent and relevant to the investigation of a public. When individuals are generalized to reflect a state of consciousness or an aggregation of variables, research is confined to description of current conditions and identification of dominant variables that affect the characteristics and composition of a public. In other

words, conceptualization of individual and public is tautological; one is used to define and generalize the other. The effect of this circular nature may render the term *public* pejorative for the purpose of theory and research.

Implicit within the personification of a public is the overlooked reality that a public is composed of individuals. A public is not some super individual being consumed with civic matters or social problems. The public is a metaphor for a collection of individuals (Allport, 1937; Bennett, 1980). Because the public is personified as an individual, little research is undertaken to examine the dynamics of how individuals become a public, the internal workings of a public, how individuals cease to participate as a public, or individual behaviors and effects.

A homo narrans perspective accounts for the dynamic and communicative nature of the public. A homo narrans perspective views a public as a multi-individual situation in which individuals participate in the communication process of creating, raising, and sustaining a public consciousness around a problematic situation. Public behavior is captured through the aggregation of communication behaviors and effects as well as through dramatistic participation in a symbolic reality of the problematic situation. The aggregation and composite profile of individuals as a multi-individual situation is possible without overgeneralizing or creating a tautological conceptualization of individual and public. This conceptualization of a public further allows for the microsegmentation of individual communication behaviors and effects through the examination of individual participation in the symbolic reality of a problematic situation (Vasquez, 1994). A composite profile of the microsegmented public can be constructed using master analogs, demographics, psychographics, and sociographics as well as theory-based message content for strategic communication with the microsegmented public (Vasquez, 1994).

The Role of Communication

Mass and situational perspectives have marginalized the role of communication process and dynamics due to their demo-centric and socio-/psycho-centric conceptualization of a public. Both perspectives are outdated and lacking in correspondence validity as they attempt to account for the nature and role of communication in public dynamics. Correspondence validity is the question of whether or not concepts and relations specified can be seen in the observations of everyday life (Littlejohn, 1989).

The mass perspective represents a view of communication that is between 65 and 100 years old. Original democratic philosophy did not explicate the philosophical nature and role of communication as an external or internal dynamic to a public. Dewey (1927) was the first to identify communication as a problem of a public. Dewey's arguments centered on the external means for collecting information to make informed decisions about civic matters. However, advancements in mass communication technologies and television news programs, as well as the development of cable news networks (e.g., C-SPAN, CNN), have resulted in a diverse array of media outlets for obtaining civic information.

The situational perspective identifies communication as central to the emergence of a public but uses social-psychological variables to investigate a public. Only after the characteristics and composition of a public have been identified does communication become important as an outcome effect. Yet, the underlying "logic" of the situational perspective is grounded in the assumption of communication—public discussion, debate, and argument. The difference in conceptualization and operationalization is a source of tension for the situational perspective that has the effect of orienting the researcher to a socio-/psycho-centric view of a public. Neither the mass perspective nor the situational perspective reflects the contemporary communicative nature of a public. Thus, when a public is conceptualized as a state of consciousness or as a sum of aggregate variables, the nature, role, and influence of communication are overlooked completely or, at a minimum, are taken for granted.

In a homo narrans perspective, the general nature and role of communication is epistemic. Symbolic reality and individual knowledge of a problematic situation are created, raised, and sustained through the symbolic convergence (configuring and reconfiguring) of messages. Individuals participating in the evolved interpretation of a problematic situation gain knowledge of, and order their world as a result of participation in, the chaining out process of communication. In this sense, communication is reality and knowledge producing.

Much of the criticism of the two perspectives, then, is explicitly or implicitly related to the state-of-consciousness fallacy. The view of a public as a permanent state of mind or as a collective consciousness has resulted in (a) conflicting generalizations and contradictory results, (b) conceptual duplication of findings, (c) the negation of the individual, (d) the tautological conceptualization of individual and public, and (e) a view of communication that is outdated or out of touch with actual observations. Although the homo narrans perspective provides a strong foundation for viewing the public as a communication phenomenon, the perspective is not without need of some refinements. The homo narrans view combines a symbolic and a cognitive approach to communication behaviors and, to a degree, subsumes the cognitive approach instrumentally. One could question whether or not STP information-processing and information-seeking behaviors are appropriate variables of concern for explicating the communicative nature of a public. A single coherent approach is needed. Research is needed to refine and reconceptualize theoretical terms and linkages between the two theories, or the symbolic approach should be further conceptualized to negate the need for the cognitive approach, given that the benefits from the perspective result from the use of SCT. A further understanding of the communicative nature of the public is needed to refine and extend the homo narrans perspective.

DISCUSSION

This analysis has reviewed and critiqued the primary perspectives for research on a public. This section provides a concluding discussion of where we have come from, where we are now, and where we are going with theory and research on a public.

Where Have We Come From?

Theory and research on a public have evolved from normative models to communication-based process models of participation in democratic politics. Classical democratic philosophy first theorized the mass nature of a public as an enduring group of citizens with a duty to be active in all civic matters (mass perspective). Social scientists, with an interest in the prevailing individual and social-psychological conditions, contributed a situational understanding of a public as a developing social entity that emerges through spontaneous argument and discussion to address the state of human social relations (situational perspective). Attempting to understand the actual functioning of public participation, political scientists advanced a view of a public as a state of involvement with issues to receive the attention and action of decision makers (agenda-building perspective). Speech communication scholars argued for a public as a rhetorical community that develops a group consciousness around a problematic situation. The communication process of configuring, reconfiguring, and evolving an explanation for an issue accounts for how individuals first become and then function as a public (homo narrans perspective).

Table 10.1 provides a comparison of the mass, situational, agenda-building, and homo narrans perspectives to a public. Six categories—origins, underlying assumptions, state type, locus of analysis, nature of public participation, and nature of communication—are used to capture the theoretical and research nature of each perspective. For example, the state type category compares the way in which each perspective generalizes the form of a public. The mass perspective generalizes a public as a state of consciousness. The situational perspective generalizes a public as a situational state of socio-/psycho-consciousness. The agenda-building perspective

generalizes a public as a state of involvement with issues. The homo narrans perspective generalizes a public as three competing righteous, social, and pragmatic master analogs. Each perspective can be examined within and across the six categories to gain an understanding of the major perspectives to theory and research on a public.

Where Are We Now?

Theory and research on a public, when viewed as a whole, have expanded by extension and intension. Theory development is a constant process of testing and formulating sets of concepts believed to explain how things operate (Littlejohn, 1989). Theories grow by extension, "piece-by-piece, moving from an understanding of one bit of reality to an adjoining bit by adding new concepts to the old" (p. 28), or by intension, "the process of developing an increasingly precise understanding of individual concepts" (p. 28). Theory and research on a public generally have attempted to investigate the nature of a public and public participation in political events. The mass and situational perspectives have struggled with the fundamental issue of whether a public is a simple aggregation of individual views or a single, collective-level, emergent phenomenon. The agenda-building perspective accepts aspects of both the mass and situational views but takes a group conflict orientation to explain the nature of a public and public participation. The homo narrans perspective embraces aspects of the situational perspective and argues that communication processes are central to how individuals first become and then function as a public.

Equally important, arguments can be made regarding the duplication of findings. Researchers from different perspectives have conceptualized similar types of publics. In the agenda-building perspective, Cobb and Elder (1983) identified four types of publics. In the situational perspective, J. Grunig (1983b) found four types of publics. In the mass perspective, Price (1992), with a concern for voting behavior, detected five types of publics. Table 10.2 com-

TABLE 10.1

Comparisons of the Mass, Situational, Agenda-Building, and Homo Narrans Perspectives of a Public

Category	Mass	Situational	Agenda Building	Homo Narrans
Origins	"Demo-centric": demoocratic philosophy and theory	"Socio-/psycho-centric": social-psychological concern for mass behavior	"Agenda-centric": actual participation in political issues	"Rheto-centric": rhetorical and communication theory
Underlying assumption of a public	Single collection of aggregate individuals	Single collection of emergent individuals in response to a problem	Group participation to receive the attention and action of decision makers	Group consciousness that develops around a problematic situation
State type	Enduring mass state of consciousness	Situational state of socio-/psycho-consciousness	State of involvement with issues	Symbolic convergence theory-based righteous, social, and pragmatic master analogs
Locus of analysis	Enduring variables or schemata	Graphics (demo/socio), values, and lifestyles	Models and propositions that explain agenda building	New or preexisting fantasy themes that chain out
Nature of public participation	Normative: Attempts to explain how participation should occur in a democratic society	Situational: attempts to explain prevailing social-psychological conditions	Positive: attempts to explain the way in which groups actually participate in political matters	Communicative: attempts to explain communication processes
Nature of communication	Expression of political judgments	Arguments or discussion on the merits of an issue	Enlargements of conflict to receive attention and action	A process to evolve a shared understanding for an issue

pares the types of public by research perspective. Type of public refers to the conceptual definition given a public by researchers representing the agenda-building, situational, and mass perspectives.

For example, a public conceptually defined as active on all issues corresponds to Cobb and Elder's (1983) specific public-identification group, J. Grunig's (1989b) all-issue public, and Price's (1992) active public. The types of public remain comparable in spite of the difference in labels assigned by the researchers. In essence, researchers have arrived at similar conclusions from different conceptual starting points (i.e., the agenda-building, situational, and mass perspectives). The result, however, is a conceptual dead end. Implicitly, then, when a public is assumed to exist as a mass, situational, or agenda-building entity, theory building in public relations and other fields will be constrained.

Where Are We Going?

Theory and research on a public is in a developmental state characterized by two general directions. In one direction, scholars will continue to seek an understanding of a public from the mass and situational perspectives. These two perspectives are so accepted and seemingly taken for granted that some researchers have yet to question the basic set of assumptions used to

TABLE 10.2			

Type of Public by Research Perspective

Type of Public	Agenda-Building Perspective	Situational Perspective	Mass Perspective
	(Cobb & Elder, 1983)	(J. Grunig, 1983b)	(Price, 1992)
Publics active on all issues	Specific public-identification group	All-issue public	Active public
Publics inattentive on all issues	Mass public-general public	Apathetic public	General public
Publics active on a single or small set of issues that concern one part of the population	Attentive public	Single-issue public	Mass-issue public
Publics active on issues that involve nearly everyone	Mass public-attentive public (can contain all-issue or hot-issue public)	Hot-issue public	Attentive public

NOTE: The table provides the labels given to the publics by their respective researchers.

generate knowledge. When scholars have questioned the underlying assumptions, heated discussions have ensued (Dahl, 1956, 1961; Key, 1961, 1966; Lipset, 1960, 1967; Milbrath, 1965; Schumpeter, 1942). A public, as an enduring and situational state of response to an issue or a problem, will continue to be examined for its characteristics, composition, and social-psychological nature.

In another direction, some researchers have quietly sought alternative explanations for the nature of a public and public participation. Emphasis has been placed on bringing theory into a closer correspondence with observed reality. One such explanation is the agenda-building perspective. Through a focus on how issues receive the attention and action of decision makers, agenda building offered an alternative view of a public and public participation. That is, the angle of description and definition shifted to explain the ways in which groups articulate grievances and transform them into viable issues. Existing concepts, such as a public, an issue, and issue expansion, were redefined to develop agenda-building models. This perspective, how-ever, is hindered by its small body of research. The current practice of reinterpretation of existing case studies does not necessarily advance theory. Researchers have yet to initiate and advance a primary investigation. The agenda-building perspective, consequently, remains more a philosophical and descriptive theory.

An additional explanation is advanced by the homo narrans perspective. Speech communication scholars varied the locus of description and definition to emphasize communication processes and dramatistic dynamics to explain how individuals first become and then function as a public. Homo narrans is based in the existing works of communication and rhetorical theorists—Fisher, Bormann, Cragan, and Shields—and reflects Vasquez's attempt to theorize on the nature of public relations. This perspective, although promising, is limited by its recent conceptualization and operationalization. Further research is needed to examine the communicative nature of a public including the following questions. What are the underlying assumptions for a communication theory of a public? What constitutes a public fact? What action constitutes public/political behavior? What motivates a public? How should a researcher investigate public behavior? What constitutes a unit of analysis? And, finally, what is the role of communication in a theory of a public? The homo narrans perspective, therefore, offers heuristic potential for generating theory and research.

CONCLUSION

The implicit assumptions that have guided scholar and practitioner understandings of a public have been thoroughly examined in this chapter. The goal of this analysis was to advance the body of public relations knowledge by reviewing the major conceptual pathways for theory and research on a public. The mass, situational, agenda-building, and homo narrans perspectives were explained considering their origins, state types, and characteristic research activities. Historically, theoretical approaches have evolved from normative-oriented models to communication-based process models, and research has expanded by extension and intension. In fact, research still is in a state of development and change as more recent perspec-

tives have questioned existing assumptions. Scholars from the mass and situational perspectives will continue to conduct investigations of the social-psychological composition and characteristics of a public's response to issues. The agenda-building and homo narrans perspectives are constrained by their status as recent advances but have heuristic potential. Communication-type activities and processes have been found to be essential components of any perspective on a public, yet only the homo narrans perspective specifically operationalizes the communication process by which individuals first become and then function as a public.

In any event, the concept of a public will continue to endure and be a source of power in societies that move toward participatory government and consumer rights. Publics are a dynamic, communicatively constructed phenomenon, and more research, attention, and provocative thought are needed for the field to truly tap into the potential of successful organization-public relationships. The challenge for public relations scholars and professionals is twofold: to demystify the ambiguity of a public and to link theory with practice for more effective relationships with publics. These two tasks not only will serve the field's interests but also will serve the public's interest.

CHAPTER 11

Public Relations and Crisis Communication

Organizing and Chaos

MATTHEW W. SEEGER

TIMOTHY L. SELLNOW

ROBERT R. ULMER

■ Among other functions, public relations is a fundamental process to mitigating harm, responding to stakeholder needs, and repairing image following an organizational crisis. Traditionally, public relations research into crisis communication has detailed specific guidelines drawn largely from practitioner experiences (Katz, 1987; Lukaszewski, 1987; Newsom, Turk, & Kruckeberg, 1996). Contemporary research, however, has developed in two additional ways. First, theoretically grounded models have emerged from research on apologia and impression management (Allen & Caillouet, 1994; Benoit, 1995a; Coombs, 1995; Hearit, 1995b). This research seeks to delineate the range of image restoration strategies available to organizations during postcrisis situations. Second, crisis management has begun to move beyond postcrisis communication. Much current re-

search takes a comprehensive approach that includes understanding the role of issue management and risk communication in crisis incubation, developing crisis management plans, and understanding the constituent elements of effective postcrisis communication. This chapter examines the large and dynamic body of crisis and public relations literature and directs researchers toward chaos theory and Weick's theory of organizing as potential models for future inquiry (Murphy, 1996; Seeger, Sellnow, & Ulmer, 1998; Weick, 1988).

This review of the large and dynamic body of crisis communication and public relations literature incorporates both traditional and contemporary perspectives. It explores the relationship of issue management and risk communication to crisis communication, examines crisis planning and postcrisis communication, and articulates a set of guidelines for practice. Chaos theory and Weick's theory of organizing are offered as models for future inquiry.

NATURE OF ORGANIZATIONAL CRISIS

Organizational crises are rich with significance, drama, stress, and intensity. They have been defined as "specific, unexpected, and nonroutine events or series of events that create high levels of uncertainty and threaten or are perceived to threaten an organization's high priority goals" (Seeger et al., 1998, p. 233). Traditional views of crisis generally take a narrow perspective focusing on the specific event, during a limited time frame, as a source of threat and surprise and requiring a rapid response to control and limit damage. Threat, usually framed as an external force, includes potential damage to products, markets, reputation, facilities, profits, relationships, and organizational image. Public relations practitioners, according to this narrow view, have obligations primarily in terms of postcrisis information dissemination and strategies for image restoration.

More current work argues that crisis is a natural phase of an organization's development (Murphy, 1996; Pauchant & Mitroff, 1992b; Seeger et al., 1998; Weick, 1988). Crisis observers point to phases or stages of crisis including a precrisis or incubation stage before the crisis onslaught; an acute or crisis stage, which follows a dramatic trigger event; and a postcrisis or postmortem stage, when questions of cause, responsibility, and new precautions arise (Fink, 1986; Seeger et al., 1998; Turner, 1976). This more holistic view of crisis suggests that crisis and "business as usual," chaos and organization, and disruption and renewal are fundamental to an organization's life cycle (Seeger et al., 1998). Crisis management, then, can be viewed as either an opportunity for development or a threat to organizational well-being. From this comprehensive perspective, public relations professionals are expected to participate in crisis and issue moni-

toring, risk assessment and communication, and crisis planning as well as in postcrisis information dissemination, management, and image restoration.

CRISIS AND ISSUES MANAGEMENT

Issues management is a dominant paradigm of research and practice in public relations. It includes "the identification, monitoring, and analysis of trends in key publics' opinions that can mature into public policy and regulative or legislative constraint" (Heath, 1997, p. 6). Issues management argues that organizations should adopt an external focus and enact their environment by attending to relevant issues (Crable & Vibbert, 1985; Gaunt & Ollenburger, 1995; Heath & Nelson, 1986; Jones & Chase, 1979).

Issues management typically is concerned with identifying and communicating about and influencing an incubating set of organizationally relevant public perceptions and attitudes. These public policy issues represent contestable claims about facts, values, or policy. Organizations concerned with preventing potential crises are advised to monitor this environment for potential threats including those arising from developing public policy issues. By investigating issues with the potential for crisis, public relations specialists are better able to diffuse some crises before they erupt through dramatic trigger events. Public policy issues, and the impact that they portend, also may become crises. The public policy issue associated with the ethical treatment of animals, for example, often has escalated to a crisis for many of those organizations that use animals in their processes. Thus, issues management may be considered a proactive approach to organizational crises (Gaunt & Ollenburger, 1995; Heath, 1997, p. 298). Heath (1997) argued that effective issues management, along with an appropriate sense of corporate responsibility, may lessen crisis conditions (p. 290). Similarly, a crisis may organize the initial interest necessary to create or reinvigorate a public policy issue (p. 289). The Exxon Valdez oil spill, with its accompanying dramatic footage of oil-coated otters, birds, and beaches, helped to move the issue of environmentalism back onto the public policy agenda. In this case, the crisis helped to create the issue.

An issue is a contestable claim about a matter of fact, policy, or value. Although the fundamental facts of a crisis (e.g., the presence of an explosion, the occurrence of a crash) rarely are in dispute, questions of cause, responsibility, blame, relative harm, and remedial action almost always are disputed following a crisis (Seeger et al., 1998). Elements of issue management, therefore, almost always are part of an organization's postcrisis communication imperative. For public relations professionals, then, issue management and crisis communication are closely related activities at both the pre- and postcrisis stages.

RISK COMMUNICATION

Risk communication also is an important and dynamic area in public relations research and practice (Covello, 1992; Heath, 1995; Heath & Abel, 1996a, 1996b). This research suggests that organizations should encourage "exchange of information among interested parties about the nature, significance, or control of a risk" (Covello, 1992, p. 359). Organizations that fail in this function inhibit their constituents from making rational choices about how organizational activities can affect them. A basic tenet of risk management suggests that public relations practitioners should reduce the uncertainty surrounding organizational products or technologies that have the potential to affect others. This reflects an "information exchange and shared knowledge model" grounded in disseminating messages regarding the relative magnitude of risk, precautionary norms, and risk reduction strategies (Heath, 1995, p. 257). Risk communication is closely associated with the precrisis stages, where perceptions of risk contribute to the development of precautionary norms; the crisis stage, where timely information about risk may mitigate harm; and postcrisis, where new perceptions of risk are institutionalized in new precautionary norms and practices.

Risk communication has emerged as the development of "high-risk" technologies have come into contact with informed and activist stakeholders. Essentially, stakeholders claim a freedom of information-based right to know about the potential harms associated with products, services, manufacturing facilities, technology, transportation, and many other organizationally constituted processes and outcomes. The information exchange and shared knowledge model, then, has important implications for what and to whom an organization communicates.

Stakeholders face an almost endless list of possible risks, many of which represent very legitimate concerns. Other perceived risks, however, are media induced, are the consequence of rumor, or derive from poor and incomplete understanding. Heath (1997) pointed to the public's "chemophobia" as one such example. Public relations professionals often are charged with communicating reasonable information regarding risk and precautions so that appropriate and rational perceptions of risk result.

This form of communication, however, is complicated by the very nature of risk itself. Heath (1997) argued that uncertainty is endemic to risk, so that communication with certainty about risk is simply not possible. Rather, risk communication always must be grounded in the probable and potential harms weighed against benefits (p. 325). Nonetheless, risk communication has important implications for crisis management in establishing appropriate precrisis perceptions and understandings, inculcating precautionary norms, and creating positive stakeholder relations. Two examples illustrate the complex relationship between risk communication and crisis.

The long simmering issue of tobacco risk has been particularly influential in the ways in which public perceptions and understandings regarding risk communication have developed. The tobacco industry, long resistant to claims about the risk of its products, finally responded to public and political pressure and included health warnings on its products. The inclusion of these warnings subsequently has provided powerful legal defenses for the industry, which now claims that consumers have sufficient information to understand potential health harms and to accept the risk by freely choosing to smoke. Thus, communicating risk to stakeholders may reduce the legal threats of a potential crisis.

Risk communication also can be instrumental in the development of precautionary norms among stakeholders, affecting both the potential for crisis and the magnitude of potential harm. In the Bhopal incident, for example, Union Carbide had downplayed the risks associated with its manufacture of insecticides. When the explosion occurred, members of the community, unaware of precautionary norms, increased their exposure to the harmful chemicals. By contrast, the efforts to communicate the risks associated with unprotected sex have been largely successful in creating a new set of precautionary norms regarding AIDS, substantively reducing its spread.

Finally, appropriate risk communication can help to create positive stakeholder relations that later may translate into crisis resolution capacity. Heath (1997), in his analysis of the chemical industry in Texas, pointed to innovative practices such as "developing community advisory councils for soliciting and responding to community sentiments" and "encouraging open door policies" (p. 258). These practices, part of what Heath described as a communication infrastructure model of risk communication, features multiple constituencies with incompatible interests, differential understandings, and varying risk tolerances (Heath, 1995, p. 257). The community infrastructure model, then, focuses on building structures, relationships, understanding, and support systems across these multiple constituencies and understanding. Such structures may help in quick crisis resolution. Malden Mill's fire and subsequent rapid recovery is an example of how a mutually supportive community infrastructure, laid down during precrisis stages, may facilitate rapid crisis recovery.

Risk communication is closely related to perceptions of crisis and the precrisis creation of appropriate precautionary norms and plans. Inadequate precrisis communication increases the probability that a crisis event will be surprising,

that precautions will be inadequate, and that serious harm will occur. By contrast, precrisis communication of the type that Heath (1995) described as community based and leading to communication infrastructure may help constituencies to understand the risks of crisis and to prepare appropriately. Those public relations practitioners who embark on a carefully crafted program of risk communication are well positioned both to avoid many crises and, when such crises cannot be avoided, to manage their effects.

CRISIS MANAGEMENT PLANS

Preparation for crisis is an important tenet of effective crisis communication and management (Fink, 1986; Guth, 1995; Newsom et al., 1996; Pauchant & Mitroff, 1992b). This view suggests that those organizations able to imagine potential crisis situations are better able to prepare, create contingencies, and put into place preformulated responses. This approach is grounded in an assumption that organizational crisis occurs with some level of predictability. This predictability can be used to formulate plans for the basic structure of crisis management, freeing decision makers to focus on unanticipated elements and dynamic developments during the crisis. In general, activities and resources that may reduce uncertainty during the crisis itself are explored during crisis planning. This crisis planning approach generally involves three related activities: development of a crisis management team, development of preset responses and checklists, and maintenance of a crisis response and mitigation capability.

The establishment of crisis management teams is strongly advocated as a first step in crisis planning. These teams are coordinating structures designed to bring together various crisis management and response expertise (Seeger et al., 1997). Typically, such teams include public relations, legal affairs, operations, security, top management, a designated crisis spokesperson, and others with appropriate skills and resources. Such teams meet regularly to review and update plans, practice contingent responses, and consider new threats so that team members can become familiar with one another. Crisis teams also should be trained in effective group decision making, with particular emphasis on being open to information during the chaos and stress of crisis. The designated spokesperson, usually the chief executive officer (CEO), may undergo additional training in media relations and responding to a potentially hostile press. The crisis management team accomplishes three important goals: creating a designated group responsible for crisis planning and management; reducing crisis-induced stress and uncertainty; and separating the crisis management function from other operations so that, following a crisis trigger event, the rest of the organization can concentrate on returning to routine operations as quickly as possible.

During planning, crisis scenarios also are used to formulate checklists, decision guides, mitigation procedures, and prepackaged responses and press releases featuring important crisis information and contacts (Dyer, 1995; Lukaszewski, 1987). Checklists may include contacts for state and local regulatory and emergency agencies, outlines of relevant laws and regulations, medical facilities, internal and external resources for crisis response and remediation, supplier and customer contacts, media outlets and contacts, information about experts, and lists of any other relevant contingencies and resources. Preprepared responses may include generic press releases explaining that the company has incomplete knowledge of specific crisis details; some positive background information on products or other materials that have a bearing on the crisis; background on crisis response capability; and information from safety records, audits, and previous crisis events that may be used to bolster the organization's image. These checklists and preset responses serve to reduce uncertainty and to increase the organization's ability to respond quickly and provide at least some postcrisis response (Stocker, 1997).

A final step in crisis planning involves maintaining the crisis response capability. A number of celebrated organizational crises, including the Exxon Valdez oil spill, the Challenger disaster,

and the Bhopal-Union Carbide episode, were characterized by extreme decay in a crisis response capability. In these instances, well thought-out crisis response plans and capabilities had decayed over time to the point where they no longer were effective. In the Challenger shuttle disaster, risk belief systems and precautionary norms had become routinized because the shuttle had flown several times without incident. In these cases, the inadequacy of the risk norms and initial crisis responses resulted in significant accelerations of crisis-induced harm. Plans should be assessed, updated, revised, and practiced regularly. A crisis plan and response capability that has decayed might be a greater limitation on an organization than no crisis plan at all.

Similarly, crisis management teams must be sensitive to the need for flexibility and provisionalism. Crises, by definition, are dynamic unanticipated events characterized by high levels of uncertainty. Real crises rarely follow planning scenarios. Remaining open to new information, perspectives, contingencies, interpretations, and alternatives is particularly critical to effective crisis management.

Although the public relations literature almost universally advocates development of crisis plans, research suggests that such plans are not universal. Fink (1986), for example, found that only about 50% of the Fortune 500 firms he examined had such plans in place. Guth (1995) found a similar lack of adequate crisis planning, particularly among smaller firms and those that did not view public relations as a management function. Given the potential threat that most crises hold for organizations, the type of planning described heretofore would appear to be a very modest investment.

POSTCRISIS COMMUNICATION

A primary concern of traditional public relations research is determining effectiveness of postcrisis responses. This research has developed in two ways. First, case study research has delineated a number of important standards for crisis communication (Benson, 1988; Hearit, 1995b, 1996; Small, 1991). Among the lessons learned from prior crises, these cases suggest that a crisis-stricken organization should use a single spokesperson; provide open, prompt, and accurate communication to constituents; and maintain open communication with external sources. The irony surrounding this postcrisis communication, then, is that despite the fact that crises produce tremendous surprise and uncertainty, the media and other stakeholders demand an immediate, thorough, and unqualified response from the organizations. Anything less might be seen as stonewalling. Furthermore, the media often draw intense public attention to crises by framing them as compelling dramas (Hearit, 1996). This often extends the time that a crisis will remain part of the media agenda. Consequently, organizations must respond quickly to highly ambiguous situations. Despite the constraints posed by crises, previous research has identified an assortment of postcrisis communication strategies that may evoke a favorable response from an organization's multiple audiences. Existing research views these strategies from the perspectives of rhetoric and public relations. Strategies from each of these perspectives are described in the following two sections.

RHETORICAL STRATEGIES

Rhetorical approaches to analyzing postcrisis communication are rooted in apologia, beginning with the work on speeches of self-defense. Schultz and Seeger (1991) contended that apologia "may be expanded" from its typical focus on single-speaker situations to be applied to "rhetoric which is corporate rather than individual centered" (p. 51). They suggested, however, that the critic must be sensitive to how the characteristics of corporate rhetoric differ from those of individual rhetoric. For example, they stated, "While single speakers face multiple audiences, the modern corporation is unique in the degree of audience diversity and nature of their [audi-

ence members'] interests" (p. 51). Moreover, individual speakers often seek to absolve themselves of responsibility by attributing responsibility to corporations. Conversely, Cheney (1991) explained that matters of authorship, attribution, and responsibility for messages from organizations are difficult to ascertain. Cheney explained that corporate messages tend to "decenter" the individual (p. 5). This tendency to decenter can be seen in the conventions typical of corporate messages such as the use of passive voice, personification, and "synecdoche" (i.e., attributing messages to the organization).

Several authors have developed or contributed to typologies of apologia strategies that are fitting for exploring postcrisis corporate rhetoric. Benoit (1995a) expanded the typologies of self-defense to create a detailed typology of image restoration strategies for organizations. His typology consists of five general image restoration strategies: denial, evasion of responsibility, reduction of the offensiveness of event, corrective action, and mortification. A discussion of these strategies and how they have been extended by subsequent research follows.

When expressing denial, the accused either "repudiates the accusation or shifts elsewhere" (Benoit & Brinson, 1994, p. 77). Denial may take two forms. First, an organization may simply "deny that the act occurred, that the firm performed the act, or that the act was harmful to anyone" (Benoit, 1997, p. 179). Second, an organization may shift the blame for an act to another person or organization. Evasion of responsibility occurs when "the accused does not deny committing the offense but rather claims a lack of responsibility because the misdeed was a result of someone else's actions (provocation), a lack of information (defeasibility), an accident, or committed with good intentions" (Benoit & Brinson, 1994, p. 77).

Corporate advocates reduce the perceived offensiveness of the act with six variants. Three of these variants—bolstering, differentiation, and transcendence—come from earlier work. To these, Benoit and Brinson (1994) added "[minimizing] the offensiveness of the unpleasant act," "attacking the accuser to lessen the impact of the accusation," and "offering to compensate the injured party" (p. 77). Corrective action "can take the form of restoring the state of affairs existing before the offensive action and/or promising to prevent the recurrence of the offensive act" (Benoit, 1997, p. 181). Mortification differs from the previous options in that this strategy "requires the accused to admit the wrongful act and ask forgiveness" (Benoit & Brinson, 1994, p. 77).

The strategy of corrective action is particularly relevant to postcrisis communication. Hearit (1995b) explained that if an organization wishes to demonstrate "organizational adherence to the values that the critics have charged it to have transgressed," then it must enact the positive strategies of corrective action and reaffirmation (p. 10). Corrective action involves correcting the immediate problem and instituting "controls to ensure that it will not happen again" (p. 10). This form of long-term correction is essential in the relegitimation process because routine solutions, such as blaming and firing responsible individuals, might salvage an organization's reputation but do little to avert fears that similar crises will occur in the future. Conversely, original solutions that signal change within an organization often can enhance a perception of preventive long-term changes and can promote organizational legitimacy. Hearit (1995b) suggested that these corrective actions should be followed by "a form of epideictic, value-oriented discourse" in which the organization reaffirms its allegiance to the same values it is accused of violating (p. 11). Hearit cautioned that reaffirmation requires a sustained effort if relegitimation is to occur. Sellnow, Ulmer, and Snider (1998) argued that such corrective efforts do not necessarily imply guilt on the part of an organization. Rather, they claimed that an organization can offer extensive corrective action while engaging in image restoration strategies such as denial, bolstering, and evading responsibility. If an organization is viewed as legitimate prior to a crisis, then corrective actions may be viewed simply as ongoing efforts by the organization to maintain its social legitimacy whether or not the organization eventually is held liable for the crisis.

Hearit (1996), building on Benoit's work, offered "kategoria," or counttercharge, as an additional postcrisis strategy available to an organi-

zation. This strategy involves the organization taking the role of victim rather than defendant. For example, NBC's *Dateline* aired a story about General Motors trucks exploding on impact. The story threatened the corporation's legitimacy. When General Motors discovered that the video included in the story involved the use of incendiary devices to blow up the trucks, the corporation launched a powerful counttercharge of unethical journalism against NBC. As a result, NBC aired a public apology. Hearit (1996) explained that "by taking the role of victim, the apologist wrests definition hegemony from the accuser and, consequently, forces the accuser to the defensive" (p. 236). If successful, the organization then has the ability to "shape the communicative agenda" (p. 236). Naturally, organizations that have positive relations with the media prior to the crisis are less likely to have their claims of victimization treated with cynicism, portrayed as disingenuous, or ignored altogether by the press.

PUBLIC RELATIONS STRATEGIES

Whereas rhetorical strategies for postcrisis communication focus mainly on the content of external communication, public relations strategies focus more on timing, feedback, flexibility, and making contact with all stakeholders. Calloway (1991) argued that, in postcrisis communication, survival might depend on who can communicate the fastest. She suggested that organizations should "think of communications infrastructure in the same way that one thinks of fire and foam trucks at Kennedy Airport" (p. 91). Small (1991) advised organizations to ensure that the leadership is quickly and completely informed about a crisis so that appropriate responses can occur immediately. A decentralized structure generally is ineffective following a crisis and might compound the harm. Moreover, Small suggested that external communication, such as advertising and handouts, can enable an organization to quickly counter negative reactions from the public and the press.

Williams and Olaniran (1994) agreed with the fundamental tenet that an organization's postcrisis communication must be fast and efficient. However, they suggested that organizations, in making postcrisis decisions, are best served by an adaptive strategy of vigilance. Vigilant organizations select the best responses available by considering the needs of their multiple audiences. Organizations tend to fail when they do not solicit and remain open to feedback and adapt accordingly. Problems arise in postcrisis communication when organizations insist that no action is needed despite evidence to the contrary, when they stonewall or deny blame, when they seek to inappropriately shift blame, when they fail to show appropriate and credible remorse for the harm, or when they claim that whatever strategies they adopted initially are sufficient. Williams and Olaniran also argued that organizations are likely to fail if they "avoid cues that stimulate anxiety or other painful feelings" (p. 9). Conversely, they admonished organizations not to overreact to feedback by rushing to adopt the first available solution and then quickly abandoning it "for another seemingly plausible solution" (p. 9). Guth (1995) contended that, to select the best crisis response strategy, it is crucial for organizational leaders to have access to postcrisis feedback. To do so, he advocated making the organization's public relations specialists key figures throughout the postcrisis communication efforts. He argued that public relations experts have skills and knowledge that make them best able to conduct research and gather public feedback following a crisis.

Sen and Egelhoff (1991) saw flexibility as vital in postcrisis communication because no single approach will work for all crises. They argued that managers must be quick learners who are capable of changing strategies with little notice. For example, Sen and Egelhoff explained that an organization can accept responsibility for a crisis without accepting blame if the primary cause of the crisis is human error, technological faults, societal reasons, or a natural disaster. However, they insisted that blame cannot be shifted if the crisis is caused by managerial factors.

In crisis situations, organizations also are expected to communicate honestly with a potentially heterogeneous group of stakeholders. Sen and Egelhoff (1991) explained that, in crises caused by managerial or technological factors, stakeholders expect "to be constantly kept informed and involved in the crisis management process" (p. 80). Small (1991) agreed that accurate information should be shared with all stakeholders following a crisis. He argued that candor and repentance constitute the "only sensible policy" for postcrisis communication (p. 22). Small suggested that such candor should continue when, due to the inevitable uncertainty of crisis situations, the organization makes mistakes while responding to the crisis. He recommended that organizations keep programs in place that allow them to monitor media coverage. Tracing media coverage serves as an ideal means of gauging the effectiveness of postcrisis communication. Soliciting ideas from relevant special interest groups that are concerned about the crisis also can help to create positive rapport. Finally, Small suggested that establishing and nurturing positive relationships with politicians, regulatory agencies, and other potential critics should be an ongoing process. These relationships can be vital to the postcrisis image restoration process.

GUIDELINES FOR PRACTICE

When faced with a crisis, the organization's overall goal is to move beyond the crisis as quickly and thoroughly as possible while maintaining economic viability and social legitimacy. To some extent, the demands of each crisis are unique. Still, the existing rhetorical and public relations research points to several consistent principles for postcrisis communication. These are summarized in Table 11.1 and discussed in the following paragraphs. Although no guidelines can ensure success, postcrisis communication typically is more successful if the organiza-

TABLE 11.1

Crisis Management Guidelines

1. Communicate accurately and openly about the crisis, and maintain openness with stakeholders.
2. Communicate quickly to maintain a proactive response to the crisis.
3. Maintain flexibility consistent with the relative levels of uncertainty and ambiguity.
4. Closely monitor reactions in the media and from various stakeholder groups.
5. Maintain consistency of message with a credible designated spokesperson, usually the CEO.
6. Use a crisis management team to coordinate and assess the crisis response.
7. Engage in crisis planning to create and maintain a crisis response capability.
8. Work to establish positive stakeholder relations and corporate image prior to the crisis.

tion dedicates itself to making open, timely, informed, and consistent responses.

Previous research indicates that successful organizations are those that communicate openly and accurately to their multiple audiences immediately after crises occur. Withholding information or failing to be honest only exacerbates a crisis when, as usually is inevitable, the whole story eventually becomes known. The sooner an organization can share its message publicly, the better chance it has of avoiding negative publicity. As awareness of the crisis spreads, stakeholders demand to see or hear a response from the organization. This response may involve strategies ranging from complete denial to mortification and corrective action. Failure to provide this response typically leads to added scrutiny and criticism from consumers, the media, and regulatory agencies, among others. Thus, if an organization falls behind in its postcrisis communication, then it relinquishes the opportunity to be proactive. The most effective means for an organization to meet the imperative for a rapid response is to have a crisis management plan in place. A crisis management plan enables an organization to avoid inefficiency by predetermining some crises responses, identifying crisis management resources, assigning roles in advance, and generally reducing some of the crisis-induced stress and uncertainty.

Although a candid and expeditious response is needed, organizations also must account for the fact that crisis situations are fraught with ambiguity. For example, the decentered nature of organizations makes ascertaining responsibility for a crisis difficult (Seeger et al., 1998). Hence, organizations cannot always provide immediate responses to questions concerning cause and blame. Moreover, crises are, by their very nature, surprises. The shock of crises can leave organizations uncertain and all but paralyzed as to methods of resolution. As Weick (1995) noted, organizations cannot be certain that they are making the best responses until they enact strategies and evaluate their results. Because of this ambiguity, successful organizations are flexible in their crisis responses. They constantly monitor their environment to determine the degree to which their crisis responses are addressing the needs of their multiple audiences. If postcrisis strategies do not produce favorable reactions, then the organizations must be prepared to revise their approaches.

Monitoring reactions from the press is particularly crucial for organizations. The press tends to emphasize the most dramatic aspects of crises. Hearit (1996) contended that reporters often make attributions of guilt and innocence in their crisis coverage, which "is the antithesis of an objective story" (p. 237). Successful organizations follow media coverage closely so as to defend themselves against any false information that is reported. Furthermore, organizations can purchase advertising, fliers, and direct mailing to emphasize facts that are not included in the media's coverage of crises. Without remaining informed of media coverage and reacting to it, organizations risk being victimized by the press.

Despite the rushed and confused nature of crises, successful organizations produce consistent messages to the public. To meet this demand, internal organizational communication tends to be centralized to crisis management teams capable of making informed decisions quickly and consistently. When possible, organizations should communicate to their multiple audiences with a single unified voice. Typically, this role is best served by the organizations' CEOs. Consistency, however, should not begin with crises. Rather, organizations should make ongoing efforts to develop positive relationships with their potential critics prior to crisis events. For example, organizations that have developed ongoing relationships with special interest groups and stakeholders can use these relationships to monitor reactions, to solicit advice, and as a source of support during crises.

Organizations often can avoid contentious relationships with the media and other stakeholders if they communicate in an open, timely, informed, and consistent manner in both pre- and postcrisis phases. Organizations that fail to do so often are forced to endure close media scrutiny, contentious stakeholder relations, more criticism, and longer recovery periods. Organizations with records of poor public relations that historically have ignored stakeholders and communicated incomplete and inconsistent messages are much more vulnerable to crises. At worst, these organizations risk an extended and contentious postcrisis stage, long-term image damage, and threats to their basic social legitimacy.

FUTURE DIRECTIONS

Two contemporary theories well suited to describing the ambiguity, uncertainty, and disorder of crisis communication are chaos theory and Weick's theory of organizational enactment (Murphy, 1996; Seeger et al., 1998; Weick, 1988).

Chaos theory affords a representative model of crisis situations and provides a more comprehensive and expansive understanding of how these systems operate. For example, small issues seen as only tangentially related to the organization during precrisis often have the ability to iterate into full-blown crises. Research on the development of these types of issues could contribute to understanding the importance of unanticipated or poorly understood linkages, nonlinear cause-effect relationships, and unconventional patterns in the development of crisis. Implications for issues management and postcrisis responses also arise from chaos theory (Murphy, 1996). In particular, chaos theory suggests more sensitive and sophisticated pre- and postcrisis communication due to complex and interactive patterns in the relationships among public issues, stakeholders, and crisis development and between organizational responses and crisis resolution. Finally, chaos theory also holds promise for generating a richer view of crisis, one that positions uncertainty, change, plurality, and loss of control as central to organized systems. Crisis creates unanticipated outcomes that may be both emancipatory and threatening (Murphy, 1996, p. 101). Future research should concentrate on the effects of organizational crisis as bifurcation points, the role of stakeholder relationships in crisis development and management, and the role of deep structures or attractors in public relations responses. From this view, practitioners should be cognizant of the relationships between routine stakeholder interactions and the nonroutine exigencies of organizational crisis.

Weick's enactment-based model of organizing also is well matched to crisis research. Weick (1988) explained that sensemaking often is affected by public commitments, organizational members' capacity to perceive, and their expectations. These three factors have important implications for public relations professionals. First, public relations responses often form public commitments and public records that are difficult to deny or undo. Both precrisis commitments and postcrisis responses, therefore, are critical and have the potential to minimize or augment crisis effects. Organizations, then, should take the long view regarding the role of positive public and stakeholder relations. Second, capacity to perceive has direct implications for issues management and crisis planning. Public relations professionals should work to enhance the ability of their organizations to perceive issues with crisis potential. Weick (1988) suggested that one organizational factor related to the ability to enact a diverse environment is the requisite variety of managerial background and perspective. Finally, Weick explained that expectations often serve as self-fulfilling prophecies. Communication specialists should work to regularly challenge expectations, to consider the implications of what might be seen as unlikely, to examine the ramifications of public commitments, and to focus on determining how narrow frames of reference might reduce foresight and ultimately contribute to crisis.

CONCLUSION

Research on public relations and crisis is a dynamic and eclectic field. The increasing frequency of organizational crises has contributed to the growth of this field. Much of the research seeks to limit the frequency of crisis through careful environmental monitoring and issue management and to mitigate the effects of crisis by planning postcrisis responses. This chapter has suggested that research on risk communication and issues management, as well as on the practices of effective public relations (both pre- and postcrisis), is fundamentally related to these goals. The role of public relations practitioners in crisis communication, therefore, is expanding to match this broadened notion of crisis. Public relations, from this perspective, is a crisis and risk management function responsible for understanding the role of communication in crisis incubation, the development and maintenance of crisis management plans and response capacities, and the contingent elements of effective postcrisis communication. In an environment of increased crisis frequency, public relations practitioners must have a broad understanding of crisis—its causes, consequences, and strategies for mitigation—if they are to do more than merely respond to crisis events in reactive and defensive ways.

CHAPTER 12

Public Relations as Contested Terrain

A Critical Response

GEORGE CHENEY

LARS THØGER CHRISTENSEN

■ This handbook offers a broad overview of public relations and articulates multiple visions of what public relations is and ought to be. Like a number of the writers in this theoretical section of the volume, we see public relations as a contested disciplinary and interdisciplinary terrain. Of course, this fact or observation in itself does not distinguish public relations from other disciplines, especially at a time of so much ferment in the social sciences, humanities, and so-called hard sciences. But like its cousins of advertising and marketing, public relations grew out of a highly practical context and subsequently developed a theoretical apparatus to support the analysis and legitimation of its professional activity.

Theoretical development in public relations certainly has been following developments in the profession as well as broader social-political trends that surround them. Witness, for example, the rise of what has come to be called "corporate issue advocacy" during the mid-1970s and the provocative analyses of issue management by

Heath (1980), Sethi (1977), and others (e.g., Bostdorff & Vibbert, 1994; Cheney & McMillan, 1990; Crable & Vibbert, 1983) that came a bit later. The lag time between practice and theory is no cause for castigation, however, because the same observation could be made about many other areas of social inquiry, even those areas not so closely tied to a professional activity or title.

Still, it is important that a discipline's theoretical agenda not simply be beholden to trends already present or incipient in the larger society. Otherwise, a discipline can fail to exercise its own capacity for leadership on both practical and moral grounds. (The same often is said of the critical distance that a university ought to have with respect to its society [Readings, 1996].) A vibrant discipline, we believe, needs to pursue a vision—or visions—of what it ought to be. Without suggesting that a discipline must be united by a single set of values or require strict adherence to an ideological code, we contend that theoretical-practical reflection can and should be directed toward evocation, provocation, enlightenment, and social betterment (broadly construed).

Now is indeed a good time to reflect on the intellectual, practical, and moral roles of public relations in society given that we have behind us about 120 years of formal public relations practice in the industrialized world. (Here we trace the origins of public relations back to the organized attempts, on the part of the railroads and oil companies during the 1880s, to respond to criticisms of their practices by U.S. governmental agencies, muckraking journalists and novelists, and the general public.) There is no single, coherent, or unbroken narrative to be told about public relations, however, despite the typical presentation of itself in introductory textbooks in terms of a progressive development from reactive strategies of defending the corporation or agency against (unjust) attacks toward a more proactive and ultimately interactive means of crossing the boundary between organization and society. Again, public relations is not at all unique, or especially deserving of criticism, for offering such a positive and seamless self-presentation. Every discipline has its raison d'être and its *mythos;* in Frye's (1957) terms, every discipline has its own story and its own ideology. In fact, this must be so, not only for a discipline to announce to the world its justification for existence but also for a discipline to talk to itself and solidify its own identity (Cheney & Christensen, 2001). Furthermore, in today's competitive academic environment, it is rhetorically incumbent on every discipline, including public relations, to assert its importance loudly and even at the risk of hyperbole. This trend has come to be called the "marketization" of academic disciplines and careers (Fairclough, 1993).

There is no question that public relations lacks general respect in the academy. (But again, it is not alone here.) To some scholars, public relations is only a professional activity without theoretical import. Some scholars and critics would go even further to call public relations a shamelessly narrow, uninspired, and ultimately deceptive activity. The fact that public relations often is equated with the term *spin,* in both pop-

ular and academic writings, is telling. Ewen's (1996) *PR! A Social History of Spin* argued that public relations has had an elitist, strictly managerial, and even antidemocratic agenda from its inception. He claimed that Edward Bernays linked public relations and persuasion studies with propaganda studies to further such an agenda.

In a sense, public relations, and to some extent advertising, has inherited the roles of the ancient Athenian Sophists in the eyes of many observers. By this, we do not mean that either Isocrates or contemporary public relations practitioners are without moral commitment or a consistent sense of purpose; rather, we mean that both have been argumentatively *positioned* as lacking a moral compass, as being fickle, and as serving only very specific private or institutional interests. In fact, the first author recalls reading a paper on Aristotle's defense of advertising some years ago; the essay was aimed at rescuing advertising from academic disregard by suggesting that advertising theory and practice could well be analyzed and supported through appeals to *The Rhetoric* and *The Nichomachean Ethics* as frameworks. That paper, which we cannot now locate in print or out of print, clearly addressed the rhetorical exigency of the association of advertising with the narrowest conceptions of rhetorical exercise and device. This could just as well have been said about public relations. Marketing, on the other hand, has successfully dodged some of this criticism by cloaking itself in a democratic ethos—finding out and then giving people what they want. But even in its case, analyses of the narrow rhetorical constructions and goals of survey-response programs for testing public opinion have rightly called attention to the circularity and self-absorption of many marketing practices (Christensen, 1995, 1997; Laufer & Paradeise, 1990).

Looking at the 11 preceding chapters in this section of the handbook as a set, we see that the authors are struggling with some of these very issues. At base, they are posing questions such as the following. What is public relations? What is the position of public relations among academic disciplines? What is the intellectual and practical range of public relations? How can public relations pursue and perhaps realize some sort of moral agenda in today's society? What types of transformations in public relations and in the surrounding society might we expect during the coming years?

These are important and timely questions that demonstrate a sincere interest in moving the discipline beyond its traditional boundaries. Still, we must be aware of the irony that it is possible to pose and engage such questions in highly circumscribed ways. Again speaking of a discipline's communication with itself, it is possible for these questions to be engaged in ways that simply allow a discipline to confirm its own importance, conform to its own well-established narrative, and thereby evade intellectual and practical challenge. For example, how many state-of-the-art reviews in various disciplines simply help the scholars and practitioners to feel good about what they already are doing, that is, to leave the discussions with the comforting knowledge that they have something and that their fields of study are legitimate? In fact, communication studies, as a broad disciplinary and interdisciplinary arena, can perhaps be criticized for producing too many such reviews, and too often during recent years, in a determined effort to establish itself in its own eyes and in the eyes of its detractors in other fields. Sometimes, these reviews are not much more than meta-reviews, or reviews of reviews, because so few major studies have been published during the interim.

We are pleased to say that the set of chapters in this section of the handbook do not succumb to such a self-absorbed form of auto-communication. Rather than taking their discipline and associated professional activities for granted, in fact, these authors question both deeply and try to push their boundaries. For this reason, these chapters serve more to further the *conversation* about the scope, roles, and goals of public relations than to provide closure on any part of the history of public relations. This is exactly as the contributions should be for a volume like this. Therefore, we imagine that the chapters will help to make it a living and polyphonous volume rather than an overly orchestrated, univocal, and

closed book. This is not to say, however, that we place all of these chapters on an equal level in terms of their contributions to the theoretical (and practical) knowledge of public relations. But we do find important merits in each chapter's attempt to question fairly deeply the place and purpose of public relations in the world.

The remainder of our chapter is divided by topics rather than by proceeding chapter by chapter through our discussion. We have deliberately articulated broad categories for analysis because we consider them suitable for the wide-ranging chapters in this section of the handbook. Under each category, we have tried to make a few points by way of referencing what we see as the key contributions and limitations (*growth opportunities* in contemporary, colloquial, psychotherapeutic terms) of each chapter. Because of the sheer number of our subpoints, we are brief in each section. However, we hope to provide a useful "map" of the presently contested territory of public relations and its future directions.

LOCATING PUBLIC RELATIONS AS A FIELD OF INQUIRY: INTELLECTUAL RESOURCES AND DISCIPLINARY AGENDAS IN PUBLIC RELATIONS RESEARCH/PRACTICE

Public Relations vis-à-vis Marketing and Advertising

Although little addressed in this theoretical section of the handbook, the battle for supremacy among advertising, marketing, and public relations is ongoing. Although we could easily dismiss this conflict as being mere academic "turf" skirmishes, we find value in examining the points of contention in the debate as well as the reality of the blurring of distinctions among these three ostensibly external forms of organizational communication. Each of these disciplines and corresponding professions has brought to light certain aspects of the communication process and not only in terms of mass-mediated communication. For example, crucial to understanding contemporary public relations practice is the notion that effective public relations involves the building of interpersonal relationships and bonds of trust within the larger context of interorganizational and institutional relations with various publics. In fact, Coombs (Chapter 7) argues that insights from interpersonal communication ought to be seen as central to our full understandings of public relations theory and practice. Whereas a similar idea is shaping much marketing thought today (Grönroos, 1990), marketing is especially known for having infused all the activities and departments of the modern organization by professing to be the managerial function and outlook most attuned to the market and the consumer (Kotler, 1991). As such, marketing conceives of itself as an essentially responsive form of communication. As for advertising, we see today how this discipline has expanded from a rather narrowly circumscribed set of activities into the broad field of social (cause) marketing. A brief look at some of the most sophisticated advertisements, as judged by the annual advertising festival in Cannes, France, will convince us that advertising today is not limited to the furthering of brands and lifestyles; it also includes promoting, for example, the protection of children, human rights, and the preservation of the rain forests. Occasionally, we even find examples of "anti-ads" questioning consumption practices and ever rising expectations for material standards of living (see various issues of the magazine *Adbusters;* see also Holbrook, 1987).

Although there are practical reasons why public relations, like marketing and advertising, would try to assert its supremacy among the various institutionalized forms of external organizational communication, clear distinctions among these disciplines are becoming difficult to uphold. Just as marketing and advertising no longer are solely concerned about products and services, so is public relations no longer framed exclusively as specific responses to attacks on corporations. Like marketing and advertising, public relations today is heavily involved with the shaping of organizational identity and image. In fact, it might be argued (as we do else-

where [Cheney & Christensen, 2001]) that the identity theme has become so dominant in the organizational landscape of today that the boundary between public relations, on the one hand, and marketing and advertising, on the other, in many cases has become almost indistinguishable. This certainly is true of the now commonplace genre of communications by major oil corporations touting their myriad environmental achievements on land and under the sea. Moreover, as these disciplines have begun to conceive of their communications with their surroundings as proactive dialogues involving a growing number of publics and stakeholders, traditional boundaries between these activities are no longer meaningful.

Public Relations vis-à-vis Organizational Communication and Political Communication

Oddly, public relations has not been much considered with respect to the field of organizational communication. To be sure, both arenas are to blame for this lack of interaction, networking, and cross-fertilization of ideas. As has been pointed out from a variety of theoretical standpoints, the field of organizational communication has, until recently, tended to treat the organization as a container inside which communication "happens" (cf. Carlone & Taylor, 1998; Cheney & Christensen, 2001; Fairhurst & Putnam, 1999; R. Smith, 1993; Taylor & Cooren, 1997). Public relations generally has been dismissed by organizational communication scholars as being either beyond the province of their concern or too closely tied with a particular profession. Conversely, public relations scholars have tended to avoid contact with organizational communication, at conferences as well as in the pages of communication journals, preferring instead to maintain a rather closed network (Fleischer, 1998). Moreover, most public relations scholars have treated the organization itself (and this applies especially to the corporation) as either a taken-for-granted social actor or a black box whose internal affairs are held constant (for exceptions, see recent works by Botan, 1996, and

Heath, 1994). Clearly, these stances by public relations and organizational communication scholars have obstructed the potentially valuable sharing of ideas and the building of joint projects.

Fortunately, the barrier is beginning to come down. Two chapters in this section of the handbook reveal, albeit in very different ways, the merits of placing organizational communication and public relations in conversation with one another. Seeger, Sellnow, and Ulmer (Chapter 11) offer an interesting perspective on crisis management, reconsidering the traditional role of the defensive posture of public relations. The authors integrate a number of insights from rhetorical studies with some from organizational communication to explore, on both a theoretical and a practical level, actions that can be taken by an organization in crisis or in a situation of high risk. Seeger et al. rightly point out that certain organizational policies cannot be neatly defined as "reactive" or "proactive." Their observation that regulation of the tobacco industry, and specifically warnings on its products, has helped the industry to justify its activities is an interesting example. Moreover, the authors observe well how an organization helps to create much of the communication environment to which it inevitably responds.

Regrettably, these points, especially those following Weick's (1979) model of organizing, come very close to the end of the chapter and remain severely underdeveloped. It is exactly at this point that crisis and risk communication can come to be fully cognizant of contemporary issues in the epistemological and practical implications of "organizing." For example, when more and more organizations seek to "respond" proactively to issues before these issues unfold into crises, we need to develop our understanding of how proactivity potentially enacts and precipitates the very situations that organizations seek to escape (see, e.g., Cheney & Christensen, 2001). In a similar vein, recent works by Taylor and his colleagues (see, e.g., Taylor, Cooren, Giroux, & Robichaud, 1996) can help public relations scholars to appreciate the pragmatic points at which authority over a crisis situation is seen to emerge, as various organiza-

tional and "unorganized" actors vie for defining and controlling the situation.

Adopting a different perspective toward reconceptualizing public relations, Leitch and Neilson (Chapter 9) build on some recent developments in political and social theory (especially Cohen & Arato, 1992) to "decenter" the organization in public relations study and practice. Taking the term *publics* seriously, they explore what it would really mean to bring publics (organized and unorganized) into view of the public relations scholar and practitioner. In this way, Leitch and Neilson reposition both public relations and organizational communication by reframing them in terms of politics. Thus, the authors begin with questions about democratic practice and then approach public relations to see what it might have to offer if it were to be reconfigured as a genuinely democratic institution. While carrying some of the same idealism as Habermas's (1979a) perspective on dialogue and the "ideal speech situation," both Cohen and Arato (1979) and Leitch and Neilson offer a more postmodern appreciation for the fragmentation of power and the multiplicity of rationalities.

Perhaps the single greatest contribution of Leitch and Neilson's chapter lies in the authors' nuanced rejection of a univocal view of organizational-public relationships. They both recognize and call for a more in-depth consideration of the multiplicity of identities (or subject positions) on the part of individuals and, likewise, of the multiplicity of voices speaking for or on behalf of organizations.

The weakness of Leitch and Neilson's chapter is its rather uncritical reproduction of Habermas's notions of "system" and "lifeworld." These heavily value-laden terms are used here in a way that promotes overly simplified notions of organizations and publics. For example, whereas strategic rationality is described as belonging exclusively to the system, opposition is presented as an integral dimension of the lifeworld. Based on such definitions, the authors will have difficulties in understanding the many complex, and sometimes conflicting, roles played by the growing number of stakeholders in today's society. The rather naive description of Greenpeace as a "lifeworld organization" that is independent of the system testifies to this point.

As Leitch and Neilson themselves admit, their chapter raises more questions than it provides answers. It certainly would be useful to consider, in very practical terms, what advice the authors would give to public relations practitioners who would try to represent such a multiplicity of publics.

Public Relations vis-à-vis Rhetorical Studies

For some time, public relations research and theory have shown an affinity for the study of rhetoric (Crable & Vibbert, 1985; see also Heath's chapter in this volume [Chapter 2]). This linkage has become more important at the same time as rhetoric has expanded its own boundaries to consider organizational and institutional forms of persuasion (see review by Cheney & McMillan, 1990; see also Conrad, in press). This connection makes sense, whether we remain with a neoclassical conceptualization of rhetoric in terms of persuasive intention and design (Aristotle, 1954) or we widen the scope of rhetoric to include phenomena such as self-persuasion and various forms of identification (Burke, 1969b). By the early 1980s, for example, a number of public relations scholars had discovered rhetoric, whereas a number of rhetorical scholars had discovered public relations. Both groups recognized the benefits of such an intellectual marriage, even though within neither group could one find a unified conception of what rhetoric is. (But that is nothing new, and we do not necessarily see this lack of consistent usage as a problem.)

The study of rhetoric is not the mysterious or quaint approach to human relations and public discourse that many social scientists presume it to be. Rhetoric is centrally concerned with the ways in which discourse functions in various social contexts. In this way, it can be seen as an area allied with the contemporary studies of discourse analysis, conversation analysis, and sociolinguistics, even though reviews in the latter areas seldom reference rhetorical theory and criticism. The traditional concern of rhetoric with an individual speaker delivering a discrete message to a well-defined and fairly homogeneous audience brought to the forefront of human thought concerns about how language and other symbolic dimensions of human behavior are not only products of but also, to a great extent, constitutive of what is termed *reality*. Even Aristotle's (1954) *Rhetoric,* with its recipe-like approach to effective speechmaking, displays rather deep awareness of the ways in which human discourse functions to create "worlds" that then become contexts for future messages and occasions for persuasion.

Rhetoric's epistemological and moral dimensions have been debated since Plato critiqued the Sophists. Importantly, those disputes remain with us. Of great importance here is the way in which rhetoric itself is framed—alternatively, as decoration of discourse, as rational design by a communicator, as a monologic but escapable approach to communication, or as a suasive dimension of all human discourse including that which would present itself as neutral information or as nonadversarial dialogue. As with debates over the contested term of power in social theory (Lukes, 1978), debates over the nature and role of rhetoric are useful in reminding us of important differences between basic assumptions about communication. In fact, the juxtaposing of the terms *persuasion* and *power* themselves provides for a valuable heuristic exercise in how we perceive areas of intersection and nonintersection between the two domains (Cheney, Garvin-Doxas, & Torrens, 1999). Importantly, recent developments in rhetorical theory and criticism have gravitated more and more toward featuring power alongside persuasion, as a central term, aided by the importation of ideas from critical theory, poststructuralism, and postmodernism (Foss, Foss, & Trapp, 1991).

Public relations has been principally concerned with an intention-based, strategy-centered form of rhetoric, yet it has reflected very little on power. It is perhaps excessive concern for strategy that has helped to foster the negative general image of public relations that we alluded to earlier. During recent years, however, public relations scholars have brought systematic attention to the diverse rhetorical functions of the modern institution of public relations including unintended consequences and the ways in which public relations activities fulfill rhetorical roles not easily seen at a glance. Crable and Vibbert (1983), for example, helped to revive the study of rhetoric known as "epideictic" by showing how modern corporations have developed a value-based discourse that positions them as central *cultural* institutions (cf. Cheney & Vibbert, 1987). Moreover, attention to multiple forms of rhetoric, such as messages that affirm certain values or seek to construct certain identities, moves the study of public relations well beyond a linear analysis of distinct case studies of organized persuasion toward a deep appreciation of the interactions of various institutional forces in contemporary (post)industrial society.

Several of the chapters in this section of the handbook offer explicit consideration of rhetoric as it informs public relations study. Seeger et al. (Chapter 11) reevaluate the traditional reactive practices of public relations in terms of the rhetorical genre of *apologia*. This is valuable because of the rich tradition of the study of messages of defense and justification and the fact that organized rhetoric shows important parallels to forms of defense by individual speakers (rhetors) even as it has vastly more creative resources at its disposal. In the corporate landscape of today, we see the rhetoric of apologia take many different forms that are not all equally powerful or accepted. Following Seeger et al.'s analysis, it would be interesting to study why certain strategies of apologia are more persuasive than others. Why, for example, does the strategy of issuing a letter of apology to customers have less credibility today than it used to have? Why is it that more action-based strategies, such as closing a burger outlet for a few days as a response to illness among customers, have a stronger appeal? To suggest that this is simply because customers have become wiser or more critical is to miss the point that the latter action also is rhetorical in nature.

Leichty and Warner (Chapter 4) invoke the Aristotelian notion of cultural *topoi,* or key culturally situated arguments, to consider various resources for persuasion by organizations in designing public relations and other communication campaigns. J. Grunig's essay (Chapter 1), like several of the previous writings of Grunig and his colleagues, features a conception of rhetoric as being largely one-way, strategic, and noninteractive. Thus, Grunig uses rhetoric as a foil against which a more two-way, understanding-based, and dialogic model (the two-way symmetrical ideal) can be assessed. Finally, Heath (Chapter 2) offers a broad rhetorical "translation" of public relations in which he considers its axiological, epistemological, and ontological statuses.

Of these chapters that treat rhetoric explicitly, Heath's offers the most expansive consideration of rhetoric. This is not surprising given that Heath, unlike the other authors, begins with that objective. Thus, he incorporates concepts from both classical and modern rhetorical theories, as well as key ideas from social-scientific research on persuasion, to explain the utility of a rhetorical perspective on public relations. In this way, Heath's chapter is more about rhetoric than about public relations, but this is understandable given the only passing attention devoted to the explanation of rhetorical concepts in most writings on organizations that work from a rhetorical point of view. Especially important for Heath is to dispel notions of rhetoric as *necessarily* unidirectional, strategic, and unrelated to truth. Heath sees rhetoric more as the "ground" for than the "figure" of communication; he treats rhetoric as the communicative context (predicament) for all messages. Still, in Heath's grand effort to give rhetoric status in terms of values, knowledge, and reality, we are left wondering whether he goes both too far and not far enough. It might be that Heath leaves too little outside of the domain of rhetoric (to invoke an image of Venn diagrams). At the same time, we believe that Heath does not sufficiently explain the ontological and axiological dimensions of rhetoric. With regard to the former, Heath seems to relegate no role for material existence. With regard to the latter, Heath seems to move from perspectivism toward relativism.

Public Relations vis-à-vis Cultural Studies and Broad Societal Trends

Two of the chapters in this section of the handbook are especially concerned with placing public relations in the broadest possible context—global systems. These two essays are very different, however, in their approaches and conclusions. Starck and Kruckeberg (Chapter 3) characterize the globalization of symbolic and material systems as inevitable, arguing that such developments are neither good nor bad— they just are. These authors rightly call attention to the array of socioeconomic contexts for and influences on public relations today. They implicitly charge that the field and practice of public relations have been far too parochial. Globalization is seen in terms of far-flung economic interdependencies, rapid transportation and rampant mobility, and intensified and instantaneous information flow. All such developments, positioned against a somewhat glorified and more desirable past, have important implications for the reconfiguring of public relations, according to the authors.

Against the somewhat alienating effects of certain globalizing tendencies, Starck and Kruckeberg offer "community building" as an integrative concept for public relations. The authors' version of community is grounded in an appreciation for diverse types of relationships. At the same time, however, it tends to take the existing extent of corporate power for granted. In a way, the authors place all relationships on an equal footing, seeing possibilities for their coming together in some sort of larger community. However, while appealing to some recent sociological research on community (notably Bellah, Madsen, Sullivan, Swidler, & Tipton, 1985), Starck and Kruckeberg do not present a vision of community that coheres theoretically or practically. In the end, it is difficult to tell exactly what they are promoting except to grant their blessing to connections of all types among institutions and between organizations and individuals. Per-

haps their position of moral neutrality and descriptive taken-for-grantedness in accounting for forces of globalization (cf. Castells, 1996) leads them to adopt a political and moral perspective on community that could best be described as benign pluralism. In any case, the authors need to go further than they do in their chapter to articulate their vision of community building, lest it remain simply a slogan. After all, the metaphor of *community,* by definition, is a value-laden concept.

McKie (Chapter 5) takes a different tack on relocating public relations in broader contexts. His chapter considers certain insights from the "new science," postmodernism, and New Age philosophy to shake up the foundations of public relations. McKie is critical of both typical concepts and methods in public relations research. Like Starck and Kruckeberg, he finds public relations to be intellectually insular. Among the specific targets of the author's critique are reductionistic approaches to theoretical conceptualization, linear approaches to public relations planning, and excessive reliance on enumeration and statistical analysis. McKie does not offer a lot of specific illustrations of these disdained practices, however, perhaps because of a desire to maintain the critique at a more global rather than personal level.

McKie's chapter takes a path through diverse readings in contemporary philosophy, science, social theory, and management, promoting certain heuristics (e.g., from chaos theory) for introduction into public relations research. McKie's discussion relies heavily on Wheatley's (1994) *Leadership and the New Science* to explain how many organizational and administrative practices can be framed toward ideas of inclusion, multiplicity of rationalities, and the nonlinearity of social change. McKie especially takes an open-ended perspective on the further development of capitalism and the modern organization, seeing possibilities for their unfolding (or undoing or transformation) in a variety of ways. Still, it seems that McKie might have left the conclusion of his essay a bit too open-ended because the reader is not presented with a clear or detailed exemplar of the transformed/reformed public relations research and practice that the author advocates. The chapter would have been more powerful, in the end, with such a sustained case exploration, however hypothetical. This is especially true with the student readership in mind.

Public Relations as Condemned versus Public Relations as Celebrated

We already have commented on the range of attitudes toward public relations, its checkered history, and the fervent desire on the part of many public relations scholars and practitioners to elevate its moral and practical status in society. In a way, all 11 chapters in this section of the handbook share an interest in the "reconstruction" of public relations. That makes them a bit self-serving, of course, but necessarily so. More important, we should observe the specific principles and practices recommended by the various authors for enhancing the external credibility and internal integrity of public relations.

Leeper's essay (Chapter 6) offers both the metaphor of community and the contemporary practical philosophy of communitarianism as routes to the recovery of the dignity and moral coherence of public relations. Interestingly, however, he situates communitarianism at the level of metatheory, seeing it as a broad organizing principle for public relations that would include within its domain concerns of epistemology and axiology. Leeper's agenda for a communitarian revival of public relations is, therefore, very ambitious, for he also sees this move as extending to practical arenas and movements such as corporate social responsibility. At the broadest theoretical level, Leeper posits human community as a primordial and foundational unit of analysis. He relies on a host of contemporary writers, notably MacIntyre (1994) and Taylor (1992), to offer a pragmatic and socially situated outline for the reconstruction of moral philosophy in light of the undermining of various forms of institutional authority.

Leeper's quest for an organizing metaphor for public relations is noble and worthy of pursuit, even though his presentation of the community metaphor is, alternately, undefined or monolithic. The author does not fully explain what type of community his project entails, nor does he come to terms with the question of "Whose community?" as a poststructuralist theorist such as Foucault (1984) would query. More specifically, Leeper's version of community seems a bit idealistic in its soft-pedaling of conflict. Therefore, it succumbs to the temptation of an unreflective consensus bias. That is, in the author's effort to praise certain ideals of community and community building, he perhaps does not heed his own poststructuralist acknowledgment of social fragmentation, division, and dissensus—notions present in the texts of the very philosophers that Leeper cites. This has been perhaps the most important critique advanced against the communitarian movement (Sennett, 1998; cf. Coser, 1956). Thus, Leeper would do well to incorporate more of the full senses of the contemporary philosophical positions that he cites so as to present a model of community that is itself multivocal and subject to revision while being unified around certain basic commitments.

RELEVANT PUBLIC RELATIONS ACTIVITIES: DEFINING THE PRACTICAL DOMAINS OF PUBLIC RELATIONS

For us, as relative outsiders to the public relations network of scholars, a persistent and nagging question concerns the range of activities that count as public relations. To focus on some of the chapters in this section of the handbook, we find public relations defined in fairly traditional terms—with respect to organizations' attempts to manage their communicative environments in the face of threats, risks, and uncertainties. Other chapters, however, proceed from a broader conception of the scope and mission of public relations in society that does not take for granted the current institutionalized forms of public relations. Although we would be among the last scholars to insist on legislating territories and boundaries for academic and practical disciplines, we do find it useful to consider the functions of public relations on three important levels: intraorganizational, interorganizational, and societal.

Intraorganizational: Management Communication

This level of activity and analysis is growing in importance in the practical world of public relations, but one probably would not conclude that from reading these 11 chapters as a set. Of these chapters, only Coombs' (Chapter 7) and Leitch and Neilson's (Chapter 9) essays give explicit and sustained attention to the intraorganizational domain of public relations. Of course, mass communication research has long acknowledged the importance of the two-step flow of information, suggesting the interaction between mass-mediated messages and interpersonal relations, but this intermedia relationship always has proven to be difficult to examine in practice (see, e.g., Andersen & Guerrero, 1998; Planalp, 1999). Coombs makes important points about appeals to the body of research typically called interpersonal communication because of its emphasis on close, chiefly dyadic, and largely face-to-face communication. However at the same time, he is talking more generally about communication theory (which, until fairly recently, was bonded to interpersonal communication research), at least within the speech communication tradition. Coombs rightly identifies programs of research in attribution theory, impression management, and others as providing fertile ground for the enrichment of public relations research. However, his categories and references have a strongly cognitivist bias that do not leave room for recent insights in interpersonal communication in terms of the study of emotion. This often neglected dimension of interpersonal communication (and of human experience in general) can provide crucial insights into the ways in which people make apparently nonrational or even irrational decisions about consumer choices, organizational images, and risk assessment. Another problem in Coombs'

perspective, as we see it, is his implicit assumption that interpersonal communication theory is suitable to study the types of relationships we come across in the practice of public relations. As Coombs points out, both mass media and interpersonal communication are involved when organizations seek to influence their environments or set up systems of communication to be influenced by them. Clearly, the abilities of organizational actors to enter dialogues, master argumentation, and negotiate at high levels of complexity are important traits that facilitate the accomplishment of mutually satisfactory goals in the communication between organizations and their stakeholders. It is highly questionable, however, whether organizations can approach and understand meaningfully such stakeholders as individual persons. Although organizations occasionally interact and negotiate with people as individuals, their most significant and powerful stakeholders present themselves as organizations, behave as organizations, and make sense accordingly. Among such stakeholder organizations we find environmental groups, the media, the political system, and the like. Although this point is not to downplay the importance of interpersonal communication skills when interacting with stakeholders, we argue that the reception of various public relations efforts among individual constituencies is most often shaped and structured by the organizations to which these constituencies belong. Perhaps even involvement and the use and processing of information need to be understood in this light. As a consequence, we believe that theories within the fields of social psychology, sociology, and rhetorics are more suitable to understand the essence of the relationships between organizations and their surroundings.

Leitch and Neilson's concern is for audience involvement, and their perspective may be termed an activist radical version of stakeholder theory. We use the term *radical* here in the sense that Leitch and Neilson are deeply questioning the traditional role of "publics" in public relations as having no real agency. Within the range of the authors' visions are the roles and practical possibilities for various stakeholding groups including employees. Thus, they turn quite naturally to a consideration of the internal communication process of the organization. Acknowledging the fact that internal audiences typically are more involved in what organizations have to say than the external world normally can be expected to be (Christensen, 1997; Christensen & Cheney, 2001), we would urge the authors to consider, in more specific terms, the capacities for social agency and "voice" held by employees, as compared to other stakeholders "outside" the organization.

We assert that the activities of internal organizational communication are important to public relations scholars and practitioners for at least three reasons:

- The boundaries between internal and external forms of organizational communication are becoming increasingly blurred because of the emergence of critical (or so-called "political") consumers and employees, technological advances, geographic mobility and dispersion, and a "hyper-" and self-referential communication environment (Cheney & Christensen, 2001; cf. Baudrillard, 1983).
- Major corporations and other large organizations are coming to consolidate various communicative functions (e.g., marketing, human resource management), recognizing the multiple functions of messages, the overlap in audiences or stakeholding groups, and the permeability of organizational boundaries (Berg, 1986; Christensen, 1997; Hatch & Schultz, 1997).
- Organizations must confront the practical and ethical issue of integration (i.e., coordination and consistency) versus decentralization and multiplicity with regard to their communication campaigns (Cheney, 1992; Leitch & Motion, 1999).

All of these developments point to the need for public relations theory to engage the workings of the organization more directly and more completely. For example, interactive case studies of how presumably external messages are understood by employees would be valuable. How do employees "read" their employing organizations' value and mission statements as they appear in public communication campaigns (cf. Christensen, 1994)? How do employees see themselves with respect to their employing organizations' community images, especially during times of scandal or crisis? (cf. Dutton & Dukerich, 1991). How do employees' interactions with outside constituencies reinforce, contradict, or have no connection to formal unified public relations efforts by their employing organizations? These are just a few examples.

Interorganizational: Sets of Organizations as Strategic Alliances, Flexible Networks, Co-Producers of Markets, and the Like

A decade ago, Powell (1990) examined new forms of organization arising to challenge traditional conceptions of what an organization is. Although focusing on the private sector, Powell's observations about arrangements such as strategic alliances and flexible manufacturing networks also apply to the public and third sectors. In fact, the distinctions among those sectors in general are becoming more difficult to maintain as all sorts of joint ventures and partnerships are appearing. Today, we find new forms of organization encouraged by the pressures of competition and adaptation, just as these developments are enabled by computer-mediated communication.

New "supra-organizations," including many instances in which the parameters and boundaries of a set of organizations are quite fluid, confront traditional ideas of public relations as being essentially a relationship between a distinct organizational entity and its relevant publics. It might be useful to import concepts such as coalition development from political science, as well as to consider the social construction of authority in emergent networks, to understand more fully public relations campaigns by sets of organizations (Monge & Contractor, 2001). The latter focus also would imply considering the co-construction in interorganizational networks of standards for, say, environmental management and openness toward the media.

It is not that such activities are entirely new, of course. Coordinated public relations and advertising campaigns over the course of the 20th century have included massive efforts by the U.S. Chamber of Commerce, the National Association of Manufacturers, and the Conference Board to influence public policy (Carey, 1995). Today, however, the blurring of boundaries between domains of discourse means that the array of possibilities for corporate expression and influence has widened. Consider as one example the widespread use of "advertorials," which combine traditional advertising cues with statements of social values and public policy. A dramatic contemporary example is the recent creation of a global consortium of manufacturing and financial organizations dedicated to publicly combating the global warming thesis. The efforts of this association are aimed at enhancing the images of member institutions while undermining the potential for international accords to reduce industrial emissions.

Several trends are evident today in the arena of interorganizational relations that deserve the careful attention of public relations scholars:

- Private sector corporations are forming nets of relationships with other organizations, including competitors, to expand their capital bases, reduce the effects of competition, and control their environments. Ironically, in a world where "free trade" is touted, corporations actually are seeking to limit open possibilities for commerce and to diminish the factor of risk (Harrison, 1994).
- Coordinated campaigns by private sector corporations to influence public policy frequently involve the presumption of public interest. That is, many private organizations are presenting themselves as representing the public interest more effectively (and more efficiently) than the public sector and as putting the latter consistently on the defensive (Schiller, 1989).
- Private sector corporations are negotiating and striking deals with some of the most prominent environmental advocacy groups in an effort to contain certain issues. For example, McDonald's and the Environmental Defense Fund recently concluded an agreement in an effort to improve the fast-food enterprise's packaging policy. Simultaneously, however, this collaboration was used by the corporation and the environmental group effectively to close off opportunities for further discussion and debate (Livesey, 1999). Such accords often foster the impression that a problem has been fully resolved and that there is no need for any type of adversarial debate.
- Some corporations even create their own auxiliary grassroots organizations designed to help them lobby for ideas and causes that the corporations prefer not to further directly themselves. For example, when medical giant Glaxo Welcome realized that an existing group formed by migraine patients would not promote its medicine, the firm constructed its own grassroots organization to further its interests with respect to migraine and headache medicine.

These and related trends call for attention by public relations scholars. Public relations research ought to probe into the social dimensions of market construction and performance by which corporations coordinate strategy (per the preceding discussion), imitate one another (in terms of positioning and identity management), and ritualize certain symbolic activities (e.g., as seen in various forms of auto-communication) (cf. Berg & Gagliardi, 1985; Christensen, 1995, 1997; Meyer & Rowan, 1977; White, 1981). Thus, the treatments of the market in the chapters by Starck and Kruckeberg (Chapter 3) and McKie (Chapter 5) in this volume ought to be extended with detailed empirical and critical investigations.

SOCIETAL: IN TERMS OF MULTIPLE "PUBLICS"/STAKEHOLDERS/ AUDIENCES

At the broadest level, public relations concerns the status, roles, and potential for various segments of the citizenry. At this societal level, public relations must come to terms with widely disparate notions of "the public." In a manner parallel to the way in which public relations has tried to hold the internal affairs of the organization constant, public relations has tended not to penetrate its own assumptions about the public and public opinion.

Fortunately, a number of the chapters in this section of the handbook do reflect on the very concepts of publics and public opinion. As already mentioned, Leitch and Neilson (Chapter 9) call for a revitalized view of publics that would grant them real agency. Springston and Keyton (Chapter 8) consider multiple dimensions for assessing publics and their relations to the focal organization. Adapting the idea of "field dynamics" from small group research, these authors consider multiple dimensions on which different publics can be assessed empirically (in terms of their salience as well as their stances). Interestingly, they advocate a multimethod approach that would incorporate insights from both social-scientific and humanistic approaches to communication within and between groups. For example, they combine organizational perceptions of publics on quantitative measures with the analysis of key themes in the different groups' rhetoric. Further development and refinement of such techniques offers real promise for a more interactive treatment of organizations' relations with publics so long as the authors do not succumb to a view of publics that is inappropriately stable or unified (and thereby creates methodological artifacts or freezes relationships that actually are in flux).

One chapter in this section of the handbook is completely devoted to a consideration of publics. Vasquez and Taylor (Chapter 10) investigate the ambiguous and elusive notion of "the public" by examining the concept within the contexts of fields such as psychology, political science, and marketing. Although their stated purpose—to move public relations toward consistency in terminological use—seems misguided and impractical, Vasquez and Taylor offer a broad-ranging consideration of the polysemous and important point of reference—the public. The authors consider in depth what they term *situational, agenda-building,* and *narrative* perspectives on the public. The contrasts and comparisons they draw are very useful. The critical section of their chapter offers four indictments against all three perspectives involving problematic conceptions of consciousness, the individual, the public, and communication itself. However, Vasquez and Taylor do not incorporate insights about the political use of "the public" from recent critical-historical accounts, especially in the field of rhetoric (see, e.g., Hauser, 1998; McGee, 1975). Such research challenges even more deeply the notion of a public by reframing it in terms of the perception and power of the term's user (whether that be a head of state, a chief executive officer, or a public relations officer). Also, radical marketing research, such as the book *Marketing Democracy* (Laufer & Paradeise, 1990), calls into question the most sacred of modern techniques for knowing a public—the opinion poll.

INSTITUTIONALIZED BIAS IN PUBLIC RELATIONS ACTIVITY AND RESEARCH

By now, it should be clear to the reader that we see most traditional and contemporary formulations of public relations as parochial, utilitarian, and insufficiently self-reflective. At the same time, we applaud the authors of the set of chapters in this section of the handbook for pushing the boundaries of public relations, both intellectually and practically, through making connections with other fields of inquiry and for questioning the guiding concepts and principles of public relations. In our view, however, public relations ought to become even more intellectually expansive, more critically reflective, and more cognizant of the diverse forms of organizational activity in today's world. At the same time, public relations would do well to drop imperialistic pretensions (and the same may be said about marketing). We summarize and extend our critique of public relations research here by mentioning three biases: the illusion of symmetrical dialogue, explicit and implicit corporatism, and Western managerial rationalism.

As we have seen, public relations lays claim to a relational orientation—a stress on negotiations between groups or organizations. Public relations, at least in theory, is about two-way relationships. Thus, it is understandable and praiseworthy that Grunig and his colleagues (see citations in Grunig's chapter in this volume [Chapter 1]) have, for many years, tried to elevate public relations through the articulation and application of a two-way symmetrical model of practice. Their much discussed model features notions of a cooperative spirit, a genuine openness on the part of the organization toward its relevant publics, and something of a process of negotiation. The model is interactive and, to the extent possible, egalitarian, seeking to reduce the typical power relations that characterize corporations' and agencies' domination of the airwaves and public fora.

As the discussions in several chapters in this volume indicate, the field of public relations is deeply indebted to the writings of Grunig and his colleagues. For that reason, it seems only natural that several authors in this section of the handbook chose to present their own ideas as, more or less, explicit critiques of the two-way symmetrical model of public relations. For example, whereas Leitch and Neilson (Chapter 9) question the model's presumed balance of power between two parties (pointing out that access to resources most typically is unequal), Leeper (Chapter 6) addresses the fact that the "procedural correctness" promoted by the model does not in itself ensure that the public relations process is legitimate and acceptable. Adding to and expanding on these points of critique, we hope in what follows to demonstrate that the question of symmetry is far more complex than is suggested by the

largely idealized models of Grunig and his colleagues.

Evidence within the broad field of public relations has demonstrated that organizations of today need friends as much as they need customers (cf. Berg, 1989). As a consequence, many contemporary organizations find themselves involved in activities aimed at forging long-term mutual relationships with internal and external audiences. In a society where the notions of dialogue, symmetry, and responsiveness have become almost sacred terms (cf. Burke's [1966] notion of "god terms") in their capacity and power to inform, guide, and prescribe organizational discourse and behavior, it should be no surprise to find these notions often used and represented by decision makers in their descriptions of organizational practices. For this reason, we need to be very cautious not to take managerial accounts and self-reports, such as the ones presented in Grunig's chapter, at face value. Exactly because symmetrical practices, as Grunig points out, reflect important values about how organizations ought to behave in society, we cannot deduce all practice from official words. Managers are well aware of the significance of dialogue, symmetry, and responsiveness in today's society, and their frequent use of these and related terms probably has more in common with the "regurgitation" of answers to survey questions that Laufer and Paradeise (1990, pp. 87 ff.) find in many opinion polls than with the pragmatic use of such data in public relations practice. Answers and opinions often are, as Leitch and Neilson (Chapter 9) point out, organizational artifacts constructed through the very act of asking (see also Christensen & Cheney, 2001). The fact that Grunig heard a great deal about symmetry in communication during the *Excellence* study interviews does not necessarily indicate, as he concludes in his essay (Chapter 1), that the two-way symmetrical approach is more than a normative model. Interviews conducted during medieval times would, no doubt, have featured many references to God and religion without necessarily reflecting the practical level of piety in society.

However, because the two-way symmetrical model has been so influential within the field, our critique needs to move beyond these methodological observations. Following Leitch and Neilson's (Chapter 9) objection, we find it necessary to point out that the complex issues of power and influence tend to be toned down under the pleasing notion of two-way symmetry. Besides the obvious asymmetries between organizations and certain publics discussed by Leitch and Neilson, we would like to direct attention to a power imbalance that often exists in the shadow of so-called two-way symmetrical dialogues. Some organizations do take great pains to implement mutual and well-balanced systems of communication with their stakeholders, but they typically organize these communication efforts around specific publics seen as strategically important to the organizations and their goals (see, e.g., J. Grunig & Repper, 1992). Although this approach seems logical and necessary in a complex and turbulent environment, it not only calls into question the idea of "symmetricality" (see Leeper's chapter in this volume [Chapter 6]) but also narrows down the notions of dialogue, symmetry, and responsiveness to specifically circumscribed and manageable encounters between the organization and select publics. Within these encounters, we might well find mutuality and equality. But without open access to other, and perhaps less powerfully organized, publics, these encounters might obstruct symmetry and equality at a higher level (Cheney & Christensen, 2001). The fear, as mentioned by one interviewee of Grunig and his colleagues, that 14 protesters might look like 1,400 when presented by the media, and that 4 persons yelling might sound like 4,000, understandably propels many organizations to focus on relatively few strategic and powerful stakeholders. But we see in that approach a tendency for public relations to establish closed communication fora around the interests and goals of a narrow group of actors. To the extent that the decisions and compromises established in these fora have an impact on public policy and society in general, these fora can be described as corporatist constructions (see, e.g., Cawson, 1986).

Corporatism is an old phenomenon in Western politics, typically implying that major issues are being "cleared" between decision makers and powerful strategic stakeholders before they are presented to the public. We need to be aware of the potential corporatist, and therefore anti-democratic, tendencies in the communication systems that we choose to promote under the label of two-way symmetry. Unfortunately, Grunig and his colleagues are so preoccupied with symmetry as an organizational procedure or modus (see Leeper's chapter in this volume [Chapter 6]) that they ignore the larger picture. Just as the current value of democracy at the workplace no longer can be conceived of as a bounded practice without regard to interests outside of the organization, public relations scholars and practitioners no longer can pretend that dialogue, symmetry, and responsiveness are values and practices that concern only the actors involved in the resolution of specific corporate issues. Not only do we need to ask, on an ongoing basis, who is representing whose interests, we also need to look at the broader implications for conflict resolutions between organizations and their stakeholders, not the least when these resolutions are produced in so-called two-way symmetrical systems.

As we contemplate both the utility and the further development of the two-way symmetrical model, we must take a more realistic view of power and adopt a full appreciation of the postmodernist challenges to the idea of rational dialogue. The full extent of corporate power in the world today needs to be acknowledged. For example, how is it today that relatively unorganized and resource-poor groups or individuals enter into even two-way symmetrical discussions? Also, the ironies and strange twists to communication campaigns need to be included within any communication-centered dialogic model for public relations. After all, such value-laden concepts of dialogue can easily be distorted in terms that do not at all conform to the intentions and plans of their promoters. Dialogue is promoted as an ideal, but seldom are the structural and ideological limitations to open debate and discussion really considered. Furthermore, the political uses of terms such as *dialogue, negotiation, teamwork,* and *collaboration* have been little considered by public relations scholars. Here they would do well to examine, for example, recent labor-oriented critiques of the rhetoric of collaboration ("teamwork") in industry (Parker & Slaughter, 1988).

Having problematized prevailing notions of dialogue and symmetry within the field of public relations, it seems natural to devote the remaining space to a more general speculation about what we term a Western managerial and rationalist bias in public relations research. Specifically, and related to our previous points about circumscribed dialogues, we find that public relations as an institution has been more concerned with minimizing diversity of expression than with promoting it. This can be seen both historically, in terms of the parallel development of public relations with propaganda studies between the world wars, and with regard to its avowed interest in controlling public opinion (Sproule, 1990). There is no question that public relations has been dominated by a Western technical rationalism, viewing publics chiefly as objects to be assessed and then manipulated by managers and administrators (cf. Jacques, 1996).

Of course, the rationalist presumptions by organizations to control their environments do not mean that "the environment" always or even frequently conforms to these expectations. But such a perspective still does motivate an array of contemporary organizational functions—from production, to marketing, to personnel or human resource management—to a degree that would be favorably received by Frederick Taylor and his followers. Nor are we suggesting that organizations, any more than individuals, should cease to have "projects" or quit viewing the world

in terms of possible avenues for influence and the advancement of their own specific agendas. What we are saying is that public relations, like other modern management functions, often has been so absorbed in its own "design logic" that it has failed to appreciate possible alternative conceptions of its practices and ways in which it might learn from "alternative" publics.

In much the same way as the emerging area of "diversity management" has sequestered and then sought to control the variable of ethnic and other forms of organizational diversity, public relations can perhaps be accused of trying to maintain discussions within relatively limited Western corporate arenas. Not only has such a bias limited the possibilities of public relations within its own institutional borders, it also has left almost entirely out of view the question of how the diverse audiences of public relations might, in fact, teach the profession important lessons about the limitations of its conceptions (Munshi, 1999a).

Thus, we should ask the question: What would a non-Western, nonmanagerial, and nonrationalist form of public relations look like? In this section of the handbook, Leichty and Warner (Chapter 4) explain that we can analyze and predict message by cultural bias interactions. Why do we not treat public relations itself as the message and expose its fundamental cultural and ideological assumptions? What if we simultaneously decentered the role of the organization, seriously modified our ideas about technical rationality, and gave up on some of our objectives to bring diverse audiences in line with a dominant view of the organization? Could public relations live with such a contingent form of control over its environment?

DEFINING THE PRACTICE

The Dynamics of Change in Public Relations Practice

ROBERT L. HEATH

▊ The practice of public relations is a work in progress. Its growth and change are the products of thoughtful and strategic responses to dynamics that are occurring in marketplaces and public policy arenas. Some of these forces of change are external to the practitioners and academics who will shape the practice; these forces require careful analysis and strategic adjustments to develop new theories and strategies to bring public relations up to date so that its influence can be felt. Other forces of change result directly from innovations that are due to careful consideration of what public relations is and what it could do better to serve organizational and societal interests.

Section 2 of the handbook addresses many of the forces that are shaping the practice of public relations. The practice is affected by many internal and external forces to the profession. How well the practice adapts to change will determine its future—the role it can and will play in support of specific organizations and society at large.

To accommodate the range of key contributions and discussions that are occurring, this section is divided into four parts: the forces of change, the challenge of organizational legitimacy, the education of practitioners, and advances in ethical practices.

The part that addresses the forces of change begins by exploring the evolutions and entanglements that occur as practitioners and academics strain to define the practice.

Cropp and Pincus (Chapter 13) review the evolving and changing set of definitions that have been used to capture the essence of the practice and discipline of public relations. Rather than seeing this as an orderly and progressive trend, these authors suggest that the effort is a struggle on the part of practitioners and academics to find the center of public relations. Thus, the authors see this as a search—the unraveling of a mystery. The clues, they suggest, are in understanding its role, terminology, education/training, and reputation as a discipline that is a work in progress.

One of the identity challenges facing public relations is to define and defend its relationship with marketing. Some academics oppose a close relationship with marketing. Others see the survival of public relations as giving service to the marketing departments of large organizations. Others suggest that the relationship is well defined so that the integrated marketing communication movement is old hat. Still others argue that support for marketing is only one of many functions that are fulfilled by skilled practitioners. Hutton (Chapter 14) examines some of the intellectual and identity impediments that prevent public relations from creating a harmonious relationship with marketing. Narrowness, failure to partner and lend support to other disciplines, fear of encroachment that ultimately leads to encroachment, inflexibility, and other factors are central to Hutton's list of challenges to public relations. Its destiny, he believes, is in its hands. The game is its to win or lose.

Whether public relations practitioners play a major role in the guidance of organizations depends on the extent to which they are involved in organizational strategic planning. If practitioners are not in planning sessions, then they typically serve more of the technician roles. They often find themselves in more reactive than proactive stances in regard to what they can do to assist their organizations to be successful. Wilson (Chapter 15) works to help explain the dynamics and system of strategic planning. She offers a systematic approach to planning that can help public relations practitioners to know the steps to translate the organization's mission into the type of detailed communication plan that helps it to build effective relationships with its key markets and publics.

The choices made during strategic planning, at the management and communication function levels, are likely to have substantial implications for the success—even survival—of organizations. Wilson reasons that public relations becomes less useful when it is not part of the organization's strategic planning and when it fails to engage in its own strategic planning. Wilson worries that public relations practitioners focus too much on tactical planning and too little on strategic planning coupled with the organization's mission. In this way, practitioners fail to provide full value to the organization's need to establish its legitimacy, which becomes part of its identity. An organization needs an identity. If its identity is perceived to be positive, then it has legitimacy.

Part of the identity battle is the dynamic change in the sense of professionalism that is occurring. Pieckza and L'Etang (Chapter 16) believe that the professionalism that has occurred in public relations is a natural historical evolution. The profession grows and changes, but without some guiding principles. To achieve its full potential as a profession, it needs a clearly defined set of principles to use for guiding its growth and maturation. In its efforts to define its professionalism, the profession must address the issue of how it adds value to organizations and to society at large.

Gender is one of those forces of change, as Toth (Chapter 17) suggests and as she and her colleagues on many studies have suggested. Women are gravitating to the practice in increasing numbers. That trend has implications for the pay and status of the profession. Toth reasons that one of the dynamic changes is a trend toward discrimination that must be opposed. She advocates that the identity of students and practitioners is a vital part of the effort to defend the practice. In addition, corporate and public policies need to recognize and be brought to bear to support the rights and interests of women. First, this is the case because it is right. Second, it is important because women bring skills and perspectives to public relations that can advance its professionalism.

Another part of that growth toward professionalism depends on the profession's relationship with legal counsel that often influences corporate, activist, and governmental policy in areas that perhaps are the domain of public relations. Stressing that point, Parkinson, Ekachai, and Hetherington (Chapter 18) offer some interpretations of legal principles to help public relations practitioners to better understand the legal circumstances in which they operate. Public relations is expected to operate within the limits of the law, but it also has options that can be better explored strategically if it understands the law. Thus, the legal environment is one of many dynamic forces influencing the practice.

A discipline that does not set forth the measures of its impact is likely to find itself exerting less influence in the boardroom and in other strategic planning arenas. One of the forces of change is the accounting (revenue generation and cost reduction) paradigm that drives corporate policy. Watson (Chapter 19) centers his attention on the need for skilled and accurate measures of the impact of public relations. His exploration of the current models of evaluation leaves him with the perspective that public relations needs to be able to measure what it accomplishes in both the short term and the long term. Effective measurement grows out of a careful integration of public relations and strategic planning that can benefit mutually by a close and well-defined relationship.

Public relations has been, and might continue to be, a mass media-driven discipline. For that reason, media effects is not only a practical or pragmatic issue but also an ethical issue. We ask the question: To what extent do the media have a dominant effect on public and marketplace opinions, and is that effect positive or negative? The impact of any mediated message is likely to depend on the extent to which it encounters audiences with well-formed and dearly held opinions. Olson (Chapter 20) demonstrates that principle as she examines some instances of public relations success is creating at least short-term interest and commitment to specific products. News formats are highly influential outlets for messages that can have substantial impacts, hence the likelihood that public relations will have a media relations focus. Ultimately, however, the real answer to impact depends on the nature of the audience as well as on the message and the medium.

Because of the potential for placing messages that have impact, public relations has to confront a variety of ethical issues. That topic is explored in depth later in Section 2. Here, one of the dynamics of change is the trend, or at least the need for a trend, toward a commitment to stewardship. Kelly (Chapter 21) argues that stewardship is the fifth step in the public relations process. The practice is defined by its responsible practice and practitioners. To the standard ROPE (research-objectives-programming-evaluation) model, Kelly adds stewardship that is a challenge to practitioners to meet the dynamics of change. These dynamics include the need for reciprocity, responsibility, reporting, and relationship nurturing.

The state of the practice is heavily influenced by the dynamics of change forged by activism. One of the byproducts of the turbulent 1960s and 1970s has been the emergence of a myriad of activist groups. Some of these groups, especially civil rights, are older than the U.S. government. Many are as new as the past two decades. These collectivities allow individuals to have corporate influence over governmental and business policy. Addressing these forces of change, Smith and Ferguson (Chapter 22) recognize and explain that activists not only exert influence but also shape the content or meaning of society—the premises that underpin personal and societal decisions. With this meaning, individuals forge opinions that ultimately guide policies. Public relations can adapt to this dynamic change by looking for means to foster the development of mutually beneficial relationships between organizations and their activist critics.

One response to the development of these relationships is the ability of the organization and its activist critics to engage in conflict resolution. To help practitioners adapt to these forces of change, Plowman, Briggs, and Huang (Chapter 23) offer intellectual rationale and applicable models for engaging in and resolving conflict. Through such processes, the organization and its critics can define, advance, and balance their mutual interests.

Regardless of how we define public relations, it is useful only to the extent that it helps organizations, regardless of their type, to achieve and maintain legitimacy. As artificial persons created at the will of society, organizations exist only to the extent that they can garner support. Public relations can help them to achieve the support they need to exist and prosper. It can do so by helping organizations to position themselves to serve the needs of their communities. One might aspire to assist organizations in their efforts to achieve the high standard of creating mutually beneficial relationships between organizations and the people they are to serve.

This is a theme advanced by Everett (Chapter 24), who takes an organizational management and organizational communications perspective to discuss the topic of organizational legitimacy, the second part of Section 2. Drawing rationale from a systems perspective, he argues that public relations needs to help organizations adapt to and position themselves to be in harmony with their environment—an ecological approach to public relations. He encourages academics and practitioners to see the value of this perspective and to embrace it in practice, pedagogy, and performance measures.

Whereas Everett uses a systems perspective to explore organizational ecology, Metzler (Chapter 25) explores the same theme but does so from a rhetorical perspective. Her approach to organizational legitimacy features a messaging process whereby organizations persuade individuals and other organizations to adopt meaning that justifies—legitimizes—them. Through the process of co-definition, people and organizational managers create messages and form shared meaning. In this way, legitimacy can be achieved as individuals identify with organizations. Disputes that arise between organizations and key publics can be resolved through the co-management of meaning.

Offering an instance of these adjustment efforts gone bad, Pratt (Chapter 26) applies an issues management perspective to better understand why the tobacco industry has had such a collision with public policy and the value-driven interests of key publics. The author concludes that the industry opted for a confrontational approach to issues management rather than using dialogue. This asymmetrical approach became less likely to succeed once it was adopted as the essence of the industry's strategic planning.

Advancing these themes, Moffitt (Chapter 27) centers her attention on one of the problematic concepts in public relations—image. She draws on cognitive psychology to explain the cognitive processes that are relevant to the formation and maintenance of image. She believes that image is a vital part of the creation and maintenance of relationships. People respond to organizations based on their images of those organizations. If an image is bad, then the relationship is bad. Perhaps a bad relationship creates a bad image. The opposite circumstances are preferred. People see what they expect, and their perceptual frameworks prompt them to see some features instead of others. In this way, organizational legitimacy is tied to image creation and maintenance—the forming of shared zones of meaning.

The forces of change and the need to establish the legitimacy of organizations are going to affect the classroom—what we teach and how we teach it to future practitioners. Pohl and Vandeventer (Chapter 28) report on the tactical and strategic skills as well as on the knowledge that practitioners need to be successful. These skills and knowledge mature in response to the dynamics of change. Toward the ends of improving the quality of public relations education, accreditation has had, and will continue to have, an uncertain impact. Although accreditation can standardize and improve education, it can stifle the growth of a field if it adopts and seeks to implement the wrong standards. Thus, as Neff (Chapter 29) suggests, the education of practitioners can be assisted by accreditation, but the standards and application of that process need to be sophisticated and not provincial. Accreditation can respond to the dynamics of change only when it is apolitical, based on joint agreement between academics and practitioners, and current with the practice.

How we educate students to the practice will determine how they serve the profession. That premise is vital to the understanding of responses to the dynamics of change. This assumption is investigated by Pauly and Hutchison (Chapter 30), who are concerned that the selection of case studies skews students' understanding of the practice. Case studies are one of the essential tools with which students are educated and by which the industry measures itself. Pauly and Hutchison caution against being overly confident in the use of cases, which often is more naive and less insightful than is needed to serve the industry through the preparation of students.

In addition to preparing students to be thoughtful and skilled practitioners, academics and practitioners want them to be ethical. As is reflected throughout the handbook but is given special focus in the final part of Section II, knowing and educating students to ethical standards is easily championed but is much more difficult to achieve in the detail.

Part of the problem of developing meaningful ethical guidelines is the poorly understood and often blurred distinction between public relations ethics and standards of corporate responsibility. Public relations practitioners have difficulty in being ethical if asked to serve an organization that does not exhibit the highest standards of corporate responsibility. Should we adopt the paradigm that public relations is best when built on the rhetorical heritage of the good organization communicating well? That theme permeates the handbook. Thus, Daugherty (Chapter 31) suggests that public relations not only needs to be ethical in its practice but also should labor to raise the organization's standards of corporate responsibility.

Reflecting on the claims by critics of the practice, Day, Dong, and Robins (Chapter 32) argue that ethics needs to be built on a core concept (e.g., community) and translated into strategic practice (e.g., the use of dialogue). For these reasons, the search is for universal principles and normative selection of the tactics of the practice. One factor that frustrates the development of norms and principles is the variation in definitions of what public relations is. Definitions mature and vary, in part, due to dynamic forces of change. Thus, as Curtin and Boynton (Chapter 33) explain, ethics is a work in progress that responds to an understanding of the nature and value of organizations as they are understood by and allowed to operate in communities of interested publics.

Thinking through some of the thorny issues of ethics, Haas (Chapter 34) suggests that the struggle is between the philosophical issues coupled to deontology and utilitarianism. Deontology features the ethics of intention. Utilitarianism focuses attention on functional outcomes. One solution is to think of ethics as a balance between universality and particularity. The ethical challenge is to balance individual and collective interests. Such levels of generalization often are tantalizing but not universally applicable to the practice or to the education of students. To remedy that shortcoming, K. Leeper (Chapter 35) explores the opportunities and difficulties in measuring ethics.

As is the case for ethics, other elements of the practice currently are undergoing scrutiny. The objective is to improve the quality of the practice and of practitioners. To define the practice, academics and practitioners need to understand and respond to the forces of change. Their analysis must embrace issues related to organizational legitimacy, the education of practitioners, and challenges of ethical practice.

CHAPTER 13

■ DYNAMICS OF CHANGE

The Mystery of Public Relations

Unraveling Its Past, Unmasking Its Future

FRITZ CROPP

J. DAVID PINCUS

■ Since its inception, the notion of public relations has been a sort of Sherlock Holmes mystery to outsiders (those who rely on or fear its power and who reap its benefits or decry its harm) as well as insiders (practitioners and scholars alike who labor within the field's fuzzy and continually gerrymandered boundaries). Infinite attempts to define public relations and determine its exact role in the organizations it serves have yielded mixed results at best. Such attempts have just as often added to the confusion as the clarification of what this "thing" called public relations really is and what it is supposed to do.

Indeed, therein rests one of the most perplexing and persistent dilemmas of public relations: It is not one thing but rather many things, a fact that is both beneficial and detrimental to a field still evolving and searching for its true identity. All the many and varied definitions and categorizations of public relations proposed over the years are, in some ways, similar to one another yet different as well. Like a chameleon, public relations changes its colors with fluctuating organizational, situational, and market conditions. Ironically, its strongest and most durable asset—its malleability and adaptability as a concept and practice—also is its most debilitating liability, posing a potent threat to its ongoing evolution and maturation as a legitimate recognized profession and academic discipline.

This troubling paradox undoubtedly had something to do with Brody's (1992) observation that "public identification with 'public relations'...is progressively becoming more a liability than an asset" (p. 44). *What, then, are the implications for a field exploding with troubling confusion and limitless potential?* Disturbing, perhaps. Harmful to the growth, acceptance, and reputation of public relations, maybe. But cause for optimism, definitely.

AUTHORS' NOTE: The authors thank Kellye Crockett, Bryan H. Reber, Kathy Sharp, and Heather Wiebe for their assistance in preparing this chapter.

The common effort by past generations of public relations aficionados, in business and academia, has been aimed at bringing a preciseness of understanding to a field that is, by its very nature and history, imprecise. At the same time, some have argued that public relations' remarkable track record of expansion, adaptability, and resilience is a direct outgrowth of its schizophrenic nature, which is why public relations can so easily play a multiplicity of roles from one moment to the next (e.g., employee communication, public affairs, issues management, investor relations).

THE OBJECTIVE IS CLARITY

When the current state of affairs is viewed objectively, the field/discipline of public relations has been consistently hurt by two distinct yet interlocking factors: *increasing ambiguity of the central role of public relations* and *proliferating jargon that aggravates understanding of its role*. The ongoing proliferation of public relations specialties, accompanied by an array of seemingly interchangeable nomenclature, has spurred the field's recent emergence and expansion while simultaneously abrading understanding of its basic role and appropriate applications. Unfortunately, the upshot of being perceived as a mixed bag has been the emergence of a field suffering from a cloudy identity. A lack of exactness has prompted a steady erosion of the public relations' reputation as a profession and scholarly discipline (Pritchitt, 1992) and threatens to stunt its continuing advance as a crucial strategic organizational function. What is needed now, as never before, is to slow the erosion in understanding of the role of public relations and to bring clarity to the field/discipline.

The Guiding Questions

The questions we address in this chapter are no different from those asked by our predeces-

sors throughout the past century—questions without simple black-and-white answers:

- ◗ What should be public relations' central role for the clients and organizational managements it serves?
- ◗ Is there a universally appropriate and acceptable definition of public relations?
- ◗ Should public relations be called *public relations* or one of the many other tags often associated with it?
- ◗ What sets of skills, competencies, and knowledge will future professionals ideally need to be effective?

Like any good mystery, however, just when one thinks that he or she has it figured out, new clues pop up to keep one off-guard and pressing forward to uncover new data. Throughout this chapter, we analyze the questions just outlined, guided by our critical review of literature that covers a host of peripheral disciplines (e.g., management, human resources, psychology, sociology, communication). In addition, we not only consider the past and present but also train a watchful eye on the future needs of the field, hoping to take a giant step toward clarifying the perpetually misunderstood role and meaning of public relations.

We begin by exploring the causes of confusion over the role of public relations and gradually work our way toward suggestions for enhancing understanding of the profession's increasingly expanding, and therefore nebulous, role. Finally, in recognizing that public relations is continuing to mature and expand, we focus on issues that can perpetuate acceleration of the evolution toward a more strategic way of thinking about and practicing public relations.

A CHRONIC STATE OF CONFUSION

At the heart of the decades-long confusion over the nature and applications of public relations is a deteriorating clarity of its transcending purpose. *What, exactly, is public relations supposed to do for the organizations and clients it supports? Has this fuzzy role changed much over the years? If so, then how and why? Does the role tend to differ from industry to industry, from organization to organization, and from individual to individual?*

Not surprisingly, we found no pat answers. The confusion has been exacerbated by the myriad definitions and terminology applied to the various specialties, activities, and literature falling under the rubric of *public relations.* The central culprit, based on our analysis, is the absence of a universally accepted and functionally accurate understanding of the essential role of public relations.

To decipher the "true" role of public relations, we must review some of the more popular contemporary definitions of the field/discipline/ practice known as public relations. A working list of the universe of such definitions would fill pages. Authors of the many public relations textbooks (e.g., Cutlip, Center, & Broom, 1994; Seitel, 1998; Wilcox, Ault, & Agee, 1998) have offered readers "their" unifying definitions. To illustrate, Table 13.1 contains a small cross-sectional sample of some of the most frequently cited definitions.

The effort to bring clarity to the fuzzy concept of public relations has by no means been the private domain of academicians. Professionals, too, have at times attempted to reduce the vagueness. More than two decades ago, for example, Harlow (1976) compiled hundreds of varied attempts to define the term, an exercise repeated more recently by *The Ragan Report,* a trade newsletter, among a cross section of professionals and academics that yielded 20 or so variations ("Defining Public Relations," 1992). No universal definition or conclusion emerged, only confirmation of continuing proliferation of different ways in which to describe public relations. Definitions developed by members of the field's leading professional associations (e.g., Public Relations Society of America [PRSA], International Association of Business Communicators [IABC], International Public Relations Associa-

tion [IPRA]) differ in the aspects of the practice that they emphasize or highlight. Articles in trade publications (e.g., Blewett, 1993; Booth, 1985) and academic publications (e.g., Fiur, 1988) are replete with independent attempts to profile public relations professionals and what they do.

Definitions, like beauty, rest in the eyes of the beholders. Given an organization's or a practitioner's core interests or preferences, the working notion of public relations selectively emphasizes only *certain* facets of the practice or particular constituencies, processes, activities, or applications (J. Grunig & Hunt, 1984). This suggests that many public relations professionals and academics, depending on the situation and agenda, might be concerned with or exposed to only a portion of what is a vast and variable field. Thus, their views of overarching issues such as role, definition, and terminology are apt to be narrow and limited and skewed accordingly. Over time, such differences in experience and outlook, although occasionally opening new vistas for growth and learning, tend to widen the chasm in misunderstanding of public relations itself as well as between scholars and professionals and between insiders and outsiders, whose perspectives are necessarily divergent.

By contrast, there are some "across-the-board" approaches that seem preferred for any number of reasons. A case in point is Marston's (1963) research-action-communication-evaluation (RACE) model/process, which describes public relations as a universal multistep, systematic *activity* but which discloses little about the larger role and purpose of public relations. Such broad descriptive processes, when considered in conjunction with the flourishing array of formal definitions, are notable for, among other things, the particular *functional* aspects of public relations (e.g., roles, outcomes, tactics) stressed. Although perhaps appropriate and logical from certain points of view, such variations often are the lightning rod for disagreements and misunderstandings that heighten confusion among the cadre of parties inside and outside the field of public relations.

TABLE 13.1 Sample Definitions of Public Relations	
Denny Griswold, founder, *PR News* (cited in J. Grunig & Hunt, 1984, p. 8):	"Public relations is the management function which evaluates public attitudes, identifies the policies and procedures of an individual or an organization with the public interest, and plans and executes a program of action to earn public understanding and acceptance."
Public Relations Society of America (1999):	"Public relations helps an organization and its publics adapt mutually to each other."
Statement of Mexico, 1978, First World Assembly of Public Relations Associations (cited in Black, 1980, p. xi):	"Public relations practice is the art and social science of analyzing trends, predicting their consequences, counseling organizational leaders, and implementing planned programs of action which will serve both the organization's and public interest."
Merton Fiur, *Precision Public Relations* (Fiur, 1988, p. 339):	"Public relations is the management function primarily responsible for shaping and implementing policies of mediation among social, political, and economic interests capable of influencing the growth and/or survival of an organization's basic franchise. To this end, the public relations function has responsibility also for identifying the forces and effects of change in the organization's environment so as to anticipate potential new needs for mediation and to inform all other anticipatory activity within the organization."
Rex F. Harlow, "Building a Public Relations Definition," *Public Relations Review* (Harlow, 1976, p. 36):	"Public relations is the distinctive management function which helps establish and maintain mutual lines of communication, understanding, acceptance, and cooperation between an organization and its publics; involves the management of problems or issues; helps management to keep informed on and responsive to public opinion; defines and emphasizes the responsibility of management to serve the public interest; helps management [to] keep abreast of and effectively utilize change, serving as an early warning system to help anticipate trends; and uses research and sound and ethical communication as its principal tools."
Scott Cutlip, Allen Center, and Glen Broom, *Effective Public Relations* (Cutlip, Center, & Broom, 1994, p. 1):	"Public relations is the management function that establishes and maintains mutually beneficial relationships between an organization and the publics on whom its success or failure depends."
Don E. Schultz and Beth E. Barnes, *Strategic Advertising Campaigns* (Schultz & Barnes, 1995, p. 241):	"The public relations function is one of the most diverse areas in marketing communications. Public relations, broadly defined, concerns an organization's communications with its various publics. Those publics can include the company's suppliers, its employees, its stockholders, its products' consumers, and the community at large."

NOTE: Definitions of public relations continue to proliferate, with the common thread appearing to be that no one perspective or description is identical to another. This table represents a small sample.

AN EVER STRETCHING FIELD

This problem of misunderstanding is far more complex than simply the lack of a universally acceptable definition. As noted earlier, the root cause of the confusion points back to variations in one's perspective of public relations' eclipsing *objective*—its overarching end-point *function*. Just as the plethora of definitions is the residue of countless applications and processes as well as an ever burgeoning vocabulary and terminology, so too are the variations in fundamental beliefs as to the core *role* of public relations. Generally speaking, one's preferred definition stems from experience and philosophical perspective. A marketing communications professional, for example, is likely to define public relations substantially differently from how a lobbyist does, just as an agency executive's version is apt to differ radically from that of an academic.

Contrasting and clashing interpretations stretch across a number of sister disciplines, and each such effort sheds new light on our collective understanding of the depth and scope of public relations. Marketing professionals and academics have, as an illustration, frequently and consistently cited the essential role that public relations plays in marketing campaigns (Eisenhart, 1989; Levins, 1993; Marken, 1997; Trudel, 1991). As the two functions have become increasingly intertwined, rivalry for political control has spawned warnings of an encroaching "marketing imperialism" that, critics claim, threatens the integrity—indeed, the *role*—of public relations as allied to and independent of marketing (Lauzen, 1991). The struggle to determine the position of public relations vis-à-vis complementary fields, most notably "integrated communications" or "integrated marketing communications" ("Caywood Advocates," 1997; Gonring, 1994; Rose & Miller, 1994; Stanton, 1991)—terms seemingly facing their own set of definition problems—as well as advertising, especially image and issue advertising (Howard, 1994; Sorrell, 1998) and branding (Chandler & Drucker, 1993), might hold compelling insight into the discipline's capriciously evolving nature.

The upshot of all these views of public relations by other disciplines is to bring some additional, albeit limited, clarity to its function and role. However, we must remember that such perspectives are developed with little or no regard for diminishing confusion over the "true" niche and purpose of public relations.

THEORIES AND MODELS: HELP OR HINDRANCE?

In the ongoing effort to better explain the essence of the many facets of public relations, scholars have generated an assortment of theories and models that, when taken together, show public relations as a field comprised of a constellation of separate and linked subfields, perspectives, roles, and purposes. As such, one method of illustrating the interrelatedness of the discipline's multiplicity of components is to position them along a continuum.

Various continua depicting forms of public relations abound in the literature, each emphasizing a distinct set of variables and interrelationships. One increasingly cited view was developed by J. Grunig and Hunt (1984), who posed four distinct models of public relations to represent the public relations field/discipline: the press agentry or publicity, public information, two-way asymmetric, and two-way symmetric models. J. Grunig and L. Grunig (1992) later argued that whereas the two-way symmetrical model represents normative theory, *excellent* or ideal public relations consists of some combination of the symmetrical and asymmetrical models.

Attempting to clarify J. Grunig and Hunt's (1984) models, Hellweg (1989) argued that the notions of symmetrical (two-way) and asymmetrical (one-way) depend heavily on one's perspective, suggesting that such varying perspectives might better be contrasted if placed on a continuum. Using a game theory variation, Murphy (1991) suggested viewing this quartet of models along a continuum ranging from conflict to cooperation. This mixed-motive view forced a reconceptualization of the two-way symmetrical and asymmetrical models (J. Grunig, L. Grunig, & Dozier, 1996) and prompted Cancel, Cameron, Sallot, and Mitrook (1997) to develop the contingency theory of accommodation in public relations. This view maintained that "the practice of public relations is too complex, too fluid and impinged by far too many variables for the academy to force it into four boxes" (p. 32). It also argued that an advocacy to accommodation continuum more accurately depicted the practice. The complexity and wide-ranging variability of this seemingly simple field is exemplified by Cancel et al.'s finding that their contingency theory requires 87 variables that influence the nature of the practice.

The search for more creative and meaningful ways in which to study, view, and evaluate the diverse nature of public relations does not appear to be slowing. Indeed, the opposite appears to be true, another reminder of how much and how little we seem to know about the phenomenon— and how infrequently we can agree on what makes it tick. Gordon (1997), for example, called for a symbolic interactionism-based approach whereby practitioners are viewed as "participants in the ongoing societal construction of meaning" (p. 64). Employing a wholly different perspective, Botan (1993b) suggested the emergence of two distinct branches of public relations: applied (practical) and theoretical (scholarship).

As a concept, public relations is amoebic in its ease at changing shape to functionally conform to shifting situations and circumstances. As a result, and as the preceding examples illustrate, the public relations literature is increasingly dotted with varying ways in which to analyze the roles, practices, and effects of public relations. Some of the common analytical dichotomies confronted today by both scholars and professionals are broken down in Figure 13.1.

Ironically, although the divisions contained in Figure 1 were conceived to provide additional clarification, they appear to have had other impacts on the field as well. For one, the various axes, many of which are fairly recent developments, indicate the field's explosive expansion over recent decades. Unfortunately, they also ap-

pear to contribute to the field's willy-nilly fragmentation, its worsening public image, and confusion about its role and definition. For example, differences in role perspective (e.g., behavioral vs. situational [J. Grunig, 1993a], strategic vs. tactical [Pincus, 1997a])—which influences pivotal issues such as control, purpose, decision making, and resources—between the academic and professional branches of the field (Botan, 1993b) and between public relations and non-public relations functions/departments (e.g., marketing ["Caywood Advocates," 1997]) has resulted in countless reputation-damaging turf battles (Harris, 1991b; Lauzen, 1991) that merely exacerbate the thickening confusion and stall progress toward a consensus of understanding.

FRACTURED TERMINOLOGY FURTHER CONFOUNDS

Public Relations

The term itself seems to burst with meaning and synonyms, depending on one's viewpoint and background. However it is intended or applied, the term *public relations* has become so ingrained—not to mention overused and misused—in the popular language of society that it has evolved into an often misunderstood and misleading notion among all public relations key constituent groups. Certainly, the sheer weight of the jargon attached to public relations (Weiner, 1996, compiled a list of thousands of public relations-connected terms) has compounded the already confused state of affairs while fanning the flames of conflict between concerned parties.

Examples abound of how blurry public relations-related jargon has weakened efforts to communicate with key constituencies. A lack of verbal identity has negatively affected international organizations' internal communications programs (Freivalds, 1993), communicating benefits to employees (Katz, 1994), and U.S. government agencies' communication with citizens (Kogan, 1996).

Various Perspectives Across Public Relations

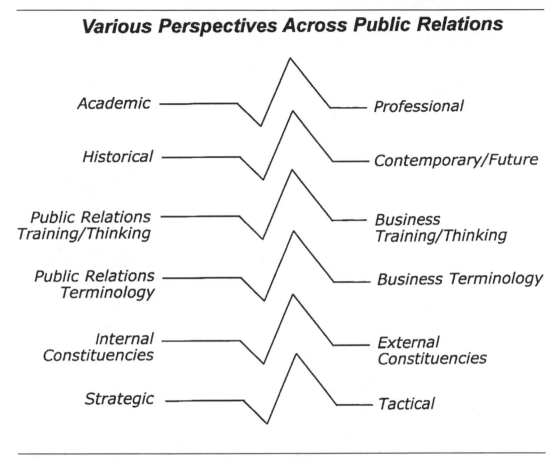

Figure 13.1. Various Perspectives Across Public Relations

NOTE: This matrix represents some of the divisions in the field of public relations today. Fueled by shifts in thinking about its role, the increasing number of subspecialties and peripheral fields, and a more complex business environment, there now is a nearly infinite number of ways in which to view public relations.

Lutz (1996) pointed out that language has increasingly been misused or abused to obscure truth or to hide meaning—a common offense, according to Swift (1997)—by "the perhaps selfish perspective of public relations and other professional communicators" (Swift, 1997, p. 4). Communication theorists have long maintained that for communication to be successful, the sender and receiver must be in sync. As public relations has increased in scope and sophistication, a growing realization is that communicating with different constituents requires adapting messages to the common language of the listener. But according to Pincus (1997a), public relations practitioners often have failed to realign their "insider" terminology with that used and understood by the business leaders whose backing they seek—arguably one of their most crucial publics.

The common terminology of a field reflects the deeper meaning of the overlapping concepts comprising it, a sort of shorthand for establishing understanding among divergent parties. The importance of language containing "instant common meaning" cannot be overstated. Where language confuses rather than clarifies, it can defeat the purpose that it is supposed to serve. When that happens, particularly within a field whose lifeblood is its proficiency and creativity with language, something must be done either to establish concrete meanings to which all interested parties can commit or to develop a new vocabulary.

THE ROLE EVOLVES: FROM PRESS AGENTS TO ORGANIZATIONAL POSITIONERS

To bring clarity to the contemporary nature of the role of public relations, a useful starting point is to look to the future instead of the past and to project how the core role of public relations is likely to differ a decade or two into the 21st century compared to what it is today.

Most attempts to define or categorize the nascent transcendent role of public relations have emanated from various historical, conceptual, and practical interpretations of a still evolving field/discipline. It is precisely our understanding, or lack of understanding, of that role and its derivation that determines nearly everything else important that we do as professionals and scholars. Any complex role does not materialize out of thin air, whim, or preference; the evolving nature of public relations emerges from top management's determination of how organizations must change to adapt to shifting marketplace and workplace forces. Figure 13.2 visually exhibits the fundamental interconnectedness among environment, organization, and public relations. Just as an organization must constantly reposition itself within an ever changing marketplace, so too must public relations adapt its role to undulating organizational needs.

Like Cancel et al. (1997), Hellweg (1989), and Murphy (1991), we see the fluid and enterprising nature of public relations best captured—and graphically depicted—as part of a continuum (Figure 13.3).

The "Evolving Role" Continuum

In developing this continuum, we considered many of the complex forces that have influenced the maturation of public relations including its history, objectives/purposes, activities, management thinking and business needs, and evolutionary nature. As is true with any continuum, the purpose is to graphically display in digestible terms the range of, and interrelationships among, a multiplicity of overlapping factors. It seeks to paint a general picture, not provide data or explain concepts in detail. The reader must call on his or her own knowledge, imagination, and open-mindedness in placing a case or example along the continuum. For example, at one extreme sits public relations' distant past, when press agentry dominated, and at the opposite end rests our vision of public relations' future central role as organizational positioner, that is, determining an organization's strategic and competitive *position*. Sandwiched between those two extremes spans a time line marking the evolutionary progression of public relations' dominant roles to date—what we have arbitrarily labeled publicity, information sharing, and relationship management. As depicted by the intersecting ovals in Figure 13.3, we see these role categorizations as loosely overlapping without fixed boundaries, each shaped by "big picture" trends that are refashioning a field in continuous transition. In addition, we have included generic reference points, purposefully aligned, of the growing sophistication of public relations as a practice and discipline (tactical to strategic) and as a contributing force within top management's inner circle (business ignorant to business savvy). The continuum is designed to capture what we know (and what we think we know) while adding new perspective and precision to the discipline's view of itself.

A DIFFERENT WAY OF "SEEING" THE ROLES OF PUBLIC RELATIONS

Press Agentry, to Publicity, to Information Sharing

By the turn of the 20th century, businesses had recognized the importance of publicity and

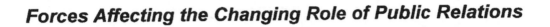

Forces Affecting the Changing Role of Public Relations

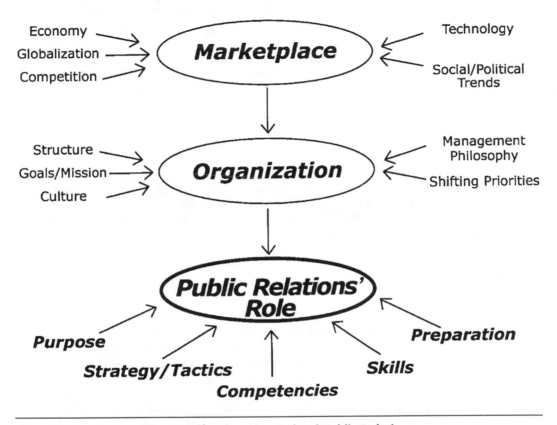

Figure 13.2. Forces Affecting the Changing Role of Public Relations

NOTE: As it evolves toward its role as organizational positioner, public relations grows in complexity and sophistication. At one extreme is public relations' distant past, when press agentry was its dominant role, and at the other extreme is our future vision of public relations' role as helping to determine an organization's strategic and competitive position in the marketplace. Included in this evolutionary depiction are references to gradual shifts in the field's emphasis from tactics to strategy, from "business-ignorant" to "business-savvy" practitioners, and from a functional position outside to one inside the top management circle. As with any continuum, only so much can be incorporated; thus, imagination and flexibility should be used in placing any case at a spot along the continuum.

media relations as an adjunct of advertising in promoting the sale of goods (Cutlip, 1994). By midcentury, as the business community was under increasing challenge by stakeholder groups to respond to their needs, the role of public relations began transforming into an information-dissemination function and, in time, an information-sharing (two-way) function expected to create understanding between organizations and

their most influential publics in hopes of avoiding or overcoming potentially destructive or embarrassing problems (Pasqua, Buckalew, Rayfield, & Tankard, 1990). In this role, public relations served as a conduit between organizational management and external constituencies, taking a significant hand in the shaping and delivery of information but having little say in its content.

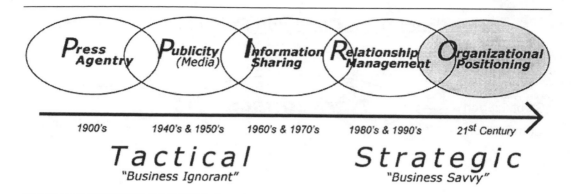

Figure 13.3. The Evolving Role(s) of Public Relations

NOTE: The role of public relations, however precisely defined, is shaped by fundamental forces of change in the business environment that prompt reactionary changes in how organizations operate. From an understanding of the meaning of those changes emerges the ever evolving essence of public relations. In all cases, the key question is, "What is needed?" As the role of public relations adapts to its changing environment, so too must practitioners' purpose, activities, skills, competencies, and preparation change.

Information Sharing to Relationship Management

Where the continuum moves into the modern-day period of the 1980s and 1990s, it is at that point where we see public relations beginning the shift from a largely tactics-driven function to one with strategic responsibilities. Indeed, this has been a time when top managements of every conceivable type of business have faced wrenching challenges to remain financially competitive while maintaining links with core stakeholders. In that effort, public relations is being given widening opportunities to assist in greater and more sophisticated ways. "The aftereffects of streamlining, downsizing, and other business strategies that have eroded employee trust and loyalty present communicators with opportunities and challenges in media relations, employee communication, strategic communication planning, investor relations, marketing, community relations, and related areas" (Clemons, 1994, p. 43).

As part of this shifting, the core role of public relations began the transformation process from a largely information-driven and -dependent practice to one increasingly responsible for building and maintaining *relationships* with vital publics. This step represents, we believe, a giant

leap forward and a turning point in the field's development. It is an unfinished step that is likely to continue for some time—a step rich in meaning as public relations becomes increasingly tied to notions such as relationships and strategic thinking. The sometimes hidden, value-added potential of modern-day public relations will come not from its ability to highlight and promote but rather from its ability to understand and shape productive linkages with constituents deemed strategically invaluable to an organization's prospects.

The field has been moving in this direction for many years, although the road at times has been bumpy and meandering and, not surprisingly, littered with many forks. Yet, as we are able to view it now, it also has been enlightening. Some 20 years ago, Broom and Smith's (1979) groundbreaking research suggested that public relations consisted of four simple and discrete roles: expert prescriber, communication facilitator, problem-solving process facilitator, and communication technician. Later studies that uncovered a relationship between the four roles and gender led to a collapsing of the first three roles, leaving two: manager and tactician (Broom & Dozier, 1986; Reagan, Anderson, Sumner, & Hill, 1990), wherein it was assumed that the public relations manager represented a stretch into the strategic realm. Subsequently, Sweep, Cameron, and Weaver Lariscy (1994) found constraints on both roles: for practitioners playing the technician role, disclosure of information about the organization (e.g., by top management, culture); for managers, participation in decision making.

Consistent with prior findings and illustrative of the field's ongoing struggle to define and step up into its broadening role, Carrington's (1992) study of senior public relations professionals revealed a strong desire to shift from the technician to the manager (more strategic) role. But the more demanding manager/strategist role is one that many public relations professionals still are learning to understand and play, according to Lukaszewski (1998), who contended that the future of the profession hinges on the ability of practitioners to develop a strategist's mind-set—nonlinear, expansive, business focused, and creative about decision making and work issues.

The objective of relationship management has become embedded in both scholars' and practitioners' thinking during recent years (Brody, 1994; Ledingham & Bruning, 1998b), although formal definitions within the public relations literature tend not to reflect that trend (Broom, Casey, & Ritchey, 1997). As mentioned earlier, most definitions focus most intensely on the "things" or activities driving the practice rather than on its most essential role or larger organizational purpose.

J. Grunig (1993a) noted this accelerating shift from image to substance within a *relationship* context, arguing that the field must move beyond its overconcern with symbolic relationships and address both symbolic and behavioral relationships. He saw involvement in long-term behavioral relationships as advancing the perceived value of public relations:

> For public relations to be valued by the organizations it serves, practitioners must be able to demonstrate that their efforts contribute to the goals of these organizations by building long-term behavioral relationships with strategic publics—those that affect the ability of the organization[s] to accomplish [their] mission[s]. (p. 136)

Relationship Management to Organizational Positioning

The role of relationship management as a driver of the role of public relations still might be in its early stages of development. Evidence abounds in the public policy arena, where issues management, for example, supports strategic business planning and, therefore, "advance[s] organizational interests and rights by striking a mutual balance with those of stakeholders" (Heath, 1997, p. 9), which on a higher conceptual plane moves public relations closer to management. Yet, to fully embrace the relationship management role might require considerably more time, training, and experience, making it a goal as much as a reality. In that same vein, we attempted to peer beyond the relationship management role and into the uncertain future, and we found a somewhat elevated role that we have labeled organizational positioning.

Interestingly, in viewing the role of public relations in evolutionary terms, we do not see new roles replacing former ones; rather, we envision the overall role incorporating prior and new ones as it grows in scope and complexity. In other words, the organizational positioning role that we project coming to the forefront will not exclude, but rather will incorporate, elements of all subsidiary and prior roles. Thus, no role is ever really discarded, only reprioritized against current and future needs and opportunities. In the organizational positioning role, we foresee practitioners becoming bona fide legitimate members of upper management, fully representing the organization (instead of answering to those that do) in all matters pertaining to its internal and external position vis-à-vis its major constituents. As noted on the continuum, public relations will move from a primarily tactical function to an enhanced strategic function as practitioners, increasingly understanding of business operations, terminology, and concepts, move inside the circle of management.

"The reinvented communication function should be strategic, focused on solving business problems and integrated with business processes," according to Shaffer (1997, p. 20). With tactical public relations being increasingly fashioned as a commodity ("What Next," 1998), the future's "help wanted" signs will call for public relations professionals who also are strategic thinkers and doers, with a premium attached to those with the business training, knowledge, and acumen to position their organizations favorably among the people comprising the stakeholder groups whose loyalty the organizations cannot do without.

What to Do About It?

Our continuum, perhaps, assists us in seeing what we have been, what we are, and what we are hoping to become. At most, it gives us the big picture to conjure. But what to do to move from concept to reality is another matter entirely. Where, then, does this leave us? *Confused?* For sure, but who would not be confused given the field's meandering evolution and conflicting nomenclature. *Stagnant?* Not really; the field continues to expand and mature at a rapid rate, even if in intersecting rather than aligned directions. *Lost?* Far from it; we just need to clarify what we are and what we are not. *Hopeful?* You bet; this chapter is just one of a number of examples of profession/discipline-wide efforts attempting to crystallize the multifaceted business role of public relations. From here on, we focus on the pivotal issues that can determine *how* we, as a profession and discipline, can diminish the confusion over the role and definition of public relations.

CUTTING THROUGH THE TERMINOLOGY: WHAT SHOULD WE CALL OURSELVES?

To begin, there is the term itself—*public relations.* The umbrella tag, long perceived by many insiders and outsiders in unsavory terms, presents us with a labeling issue of considerable weight. Does the term itself, considering its historically negative connotation and generally popular but often misleading denotation, help or hurt the cause of enhancing understanding of the *true* role of public relations? If it hurts more than it helps, as some (including the second author) have argued, then what is the answer? Should the venerable term *public relations* be scrapped—banned from our professional vocabulary so as never to be misperceived or misunderstood again? Should we rally around an alternative term—one that more accurately reflects the contemporary and future role of public relations? Or, are we making much ado about nothing, and are we better advised not to stir the pot any further and just allow the myriad terms to sort themselves out naturally, over time, as suggested more than a decade ago by the PRSA's Special Committee on Terminology (Lesly, Budd, Cutlip, Lerbinger, & Pires, 1987)? There are options aplenty, but none on its face appears capable of offering an adequate or harmonious solution to an enterprising field already awash in a glut of clashing definitions and vocabulary.

Expunging the term, as radical a step as it might be, is by no means a new idea; the suggestion has, over the years, sparked strongly divergent opinions (Brody, 1992; Edelman, 1996; Sparks, 1993). Why consider eliminating it? The argument goes that the expression *public relations* carries with it so much negative baggage—misunderstood, misinterpreted, and misused by proponents and detractors alike—that removing the term altogether might actually add clarity. In addition, such a move might send a resounding message of the field's resolve to bring public relations' image and reality into alignment. Or, would such a move merely create an uproar or a backlash that would worsen the confusion and heighten feelings of alienation among kindred spirits? Past intrafield debates over terminology (e.g., mass media vs. other media) have sparked nasty interdisciplinary turf battles involving public relations, advertising, sales promotion, and marketing that are, noted Brody (1994), counterproductive to all fields. Of some note, however, should be the fact that more and more practitioners, increasingly upset by what they see as a case of poor labeling, are refusing to identify themselves as public relations practitioners (Brody, 1992).

What to call this thing we know as public relations—the field, the profession, the discipline—if not *public relations* is a prickly and controversial question that should be explored by its most knowledgeable and loyal guardians—the professionals and scholars who know it best. As noted earlier, public relations already goes by innumerable general and specific terms, synonymous or otherwise. No doubt, opinions on the best and worst terms abound, as exemplified by Budd (1995), who argued that equating the term *communications* with *public relations* merely diminishes the value of public relations.

To illustrate how arbitrary terminology can be, our choice of role terms depicted in our continuum (Figure 13.3) reflects our (and others') analysis, but who is to say that there are not more accurate, better, or more readily acceptable terms? Perhaps Drobis ("Drobis Provides New Terminology," 1998) would, suggesting instead one of the seven roles he uncovered during interviews among a sample of top-level professionals who were asked to describe their major roles—chief scout, navigator, firefighter, interpreter, advocate, evaluator, and educator. To select one or another existing term, or to coin a new one, to replace the long popular term of *public relations* would be presumptuous, in our view, without involving all key sectors comprising this multipersonality field.

PREPARING FOR THE FUTURE: TOWARD ORGANIZATIONAL POSITIONING

Aside from the dual issues of *precisely* defining and semantically expressing the notion of public relations is the issue of preparing professionals to handle its continually evolving and increasingly demanding role. In other words, as the role of public relations grows more complex and sophisticated, in what ways will professionals be expected to adapt and upgrade their capabilities

to effectively play the role? As our continuum suggests, as the role changes and expands into relationship management and organizational positioning, a future professional's skill sets, competencies, knowledge, and education/training will need to adapt accordingly. A starting point for refashioning the role might be to consider variations of the four characteristics outlined by Shaffer (1998) in profiling the future of employee communicators: "strategic and operational; strictly managed for value, focused on consulting and counseling work; fostering departmental integration and building alliances" (p. 13).

The "Business" Difference

Our vision of tomorrow's public relations professionals is of individuals integrally involved in managing stakeholder relationships and in strategically positioning their organizations' reputations with those stakeholder groups. To fulfill that role, practitioners will need the tactical skills that they always have needed (e.g., writing, graphics, media relations). But in addition, they will be expected to possess a "business" frame of reference and set of competencies not historically typical of all professionals. In essence, they will need to think, make decisions, and communicate as savvy and believable members of their organizations' management teams. Tomorrow's practitioners—and scholars, for that matter—must be able to understand not only public relations and communication strategies and tactics but also economic and organizational change strategies.

We believe that the key to preparing for this role is an altered approach to public relations education and training, an issue that has received far more lip service than action to date. For about a decade (Turk, 1989), some academics and professionals have been calling for a more management-oriented framework for educating practitioners. Yet, few university public relations curricula today *require* much more than token business-focused course work or experiential opportunities (Kruckeberg, 1998b). In fact, most require no business training whatsoever, as their grounding remains rooted in strictly communication and journalism precepts, perhaps because most such programs remain housed in communication or journalism schools. Some insiders have called for educators to dramatically reshape public relations curricula so as to design *business*-literate professionals who possess a specialized knowledge of, and skill sets in, public relations/communication *and* human and organizational behavior ("Personal Competency," 1998; Pincus, 1997b).

On the brighter side, within the public relations academy, some curricular reevaluation efforts are under way. For example, a reconstituted Commission on Public Relations Education currently is reviewing how educational institutions can best prepare tomorrow's professionals (Kruckeberg, 1998b). The emergence of allied areas, such as integrated marketing communication, has prompted some programs to address a changing environment that makes public relations, integrated communications, and marketing course work harder to differentiate (Griffin & Pasadeos, 1998). Unfortunately, such attempts to reexamine current educational directions are few and far between across this multifaceted discipline. More efforts, motivated by a rising sense of urgency, are sorely needed *today* if programs are to retool in time to ready the generations of would-be practitioners waiting in the wings.

Time to Organize and Galvanize

In a field as diffuse and diverse as public relations, achieving consensus on any issue, however significant, is problematic. That might be why, to date, little has been done across the field to address the future of the profession or to differentiate the confusing issues we have outlined here ("What Next," 1998). If ever a discipline needed to put aside its differences, close ranks, and galvanize its factions to address compelling common concerns—starting with role, definition, terminology, and education (all linked issues)—we believe that the time is *now*.

One obvious, yet politically challenging, opportunity to mobilize the field is the formation of a profession-wide exploration to explore the issues we are grappling with here under the joint auspices of some of the field's leading institutions, journals, and independent organizations (e.g., PRSA, IABC, Association for Education in Journalism and Mass Communication, International Communication Association, IPRA, Institute for Public Relations Research and Education, IABC and PRSA research foundations, *The Ragan Report*, Burson-Marsteller, William M. Mercer) (Pincus, 1997a). With the locking of arms of established influential entities, to which most individuals in the field are connected in some way, might rest our best hope for moving as a field to new ground. Regrettably, up to now, the professional and academic organizations "that are supposed to represent the best interests of their members prefer to be guardians of the status quo rather than advocates for the future" ("Personal Competency," 1998, p. 2).

If we, the proverbial mediators, cannot find common ground and build consensus, then who can? As our marketing friends tell us, "timing is everything." Perhaps, standing as a profession/discipline at the dawn of the 21st century, the timing finally is right to hear the call to arms—time to look within our collective soul to solve the mysteries that have haunted us for far too long.

More than a decade ago, the PRSA's Special Committee on Terminology concluded that an umbrella term that clarifies the field will likely emerge by default (Lesly et al., 1987). That has not yet happened. If anything, confusion has worsened, exacerbated by terminology that confuses and further splinters the field and complicates the development of meaningful research projects. It appears unlikely that a single unifying term will emerge on its own, certainly not until we understand and can agree on the primary role of public relations. Thus, we believe that future research is needed to explore the emerging role of public relations and perceptions of that role by the discipline's many and varied constituencies, which may vary substantially across industries, by organization size, by types of customers/

clients, and so on. Understanding such varia-tions in perspective should help to identify where commonalities lie, heretofore hidden by our own confusion.

We believe that future research, in conjunc-tion with a discipline-wide clarifying effort, pro-vides cause for optimism. Although the mys-tery surrounding public relations remains elusive even to a sleuth the likes of a Sherlock Holmes, its resolution seems, to us, elementary: Focus on clarifying the role—terminology, edu-cation and training, reputation—and the rest of the pieces of the puzzle will begin falling into place.

Defining the Relationship Between Public Relations and Marketing

Public Relations' Most Important Challenge

JAMES G. HUTTON

■ Confusion and conflict have emerged during recent years surrounding integrated marketing communications (IMC) and similar ideas. Some public relations educators and practitioners have cried foul, claiming that IMC represents a form of marketing imperialism insofar as it seeks to subordinate public relations under a marketing umbrella (Duncan, Caywood, & Newsom, 1993; Lauzen, 1991; Rose & Miller, 1994). For the most part, however, IMC is a false issue, driven principally by the advertising industry, that has served to mask an underlying issue that is much more important to the future of public relations—the fundamental nature of the relationship between marketing and public relations.

Historically, the debate generally was about whether marketing and public relations should be partners or rivals in competing for organizational attention and resources. Now, the issue is quite different. Under a variety of monikers, the marketing field is methodically reinventing itself as public relations.

The public relations field has been very slow to respond to the challenge, both from practical and intellectual perspectives. Indeed, the public relations field might well have created the vacuum that marketing is now filling. There remains a critical need for public relations to define its intellectual and practical domain, especially vis-à-vis marketing, to regain control of its own destiny.

MARKETING AND PUBLIC RELATIONS: INDEPENDENT FUNCTIONS?

A logical place to begin the discussion of the relationship between marketing and public relations is an analysis of the similarities and differences between the two fields.

Few would disagree that marketing and public relations share much in common. Within organizations, they are the two functions most focused on external constituencies. Both deal with communication, persuasion, and relationships. Both deal with messages and media. Both deal with public opinion and segmentation of audiences. Ideally, both are strategic management functions that are anchored in research.

On the other hand, the differences are substantial. In terms of the scope of operation, marketing also is concerned with product development, physical distribution, location analysis, retailing, pricing, and customer service, whereas public relations is more concerned with the media, various government entities, community relations, investor relations, and employee relations.

Marketing practitioners need to be better versed in break-even analysis, competitive analysis, package design, and queuing theory, whereas public relations practitioners must know the ins and outs of journalism, the legal and policy requirements of the Securities and Exchange Commission and stock markets, how best to manage their organizations' charitable contributions processes, how to write speeches, and how to develop and implement an issues management program.

Regarding attitude as well, there appear to be substantial differences. Marketing tends to demand a more aggressive, competitive, hyperbolic, selling mind-set, whereas public relations often demands a more conciliatory, peacemaking approach. So, although their research, process, and objectives often are similar, the knowledge base, audiences, and mind-sets of marketing and public relations frequently are quite different.

Throughout most of their histories, the differences between marketing and public relations outweighed the similarities, causing them to tread generally divergent paths. For the most part, marketing focused on market research, product development, pricing, distribution, selling, advertising, and sales promotion functions, whereas public relations devoted most of its attention to media relations, public opinion, publicity, internal communications, government relations, and investor relations.

Over time, however, the differences between marketing and public relations diminished somewhat, to the point where they began bumping into one another with greater frequency and competing more directly for organizational resources. Clearly, the two fields could not act entirely independently any longer without compromising organizational effectiveness and efficiency.

MARKETING AND PUBLIC RELATIONS: PARTNERS OR RIVALS?

Kotler and Mindak (1978) were among the first to directly address the increasingly important issue of the marketing-public relations interface by asking whether marketing and public relations should be partners or rivals. The authors laid out five possible relationships: marketing and public relations as independent functions, marketing and public relations as overlapping functions, marketing as a subset of public relations, public relations as a subset of marketing, and marketing and public relations as the same function.

Unfortunately, they did not really provide criteria for choosing from among the five relationships. A simple but generally effective scheme is outlined in Figure 14.1 (Hutton, 1996a). The scheme is based on two simple questions, "What proportion of the marketing tasks confronting the organization are communication related?" and, conversely, "What proportion of the organization's communication tasks are marketing related?"

For example, if communication issues are a relatively small part of marketing and vice versa, then an organization might wish to opt for the "separate but equal" model ("a" in Figure 14.1). A public utility generally would be well suited to this model given the importance that the utility places on community, government, and media relations as well as the fact that media representatives, community interest groups, and government agencies generally are more comfortable dealing with a separate corporate communications, public relations, or public affairs depart-

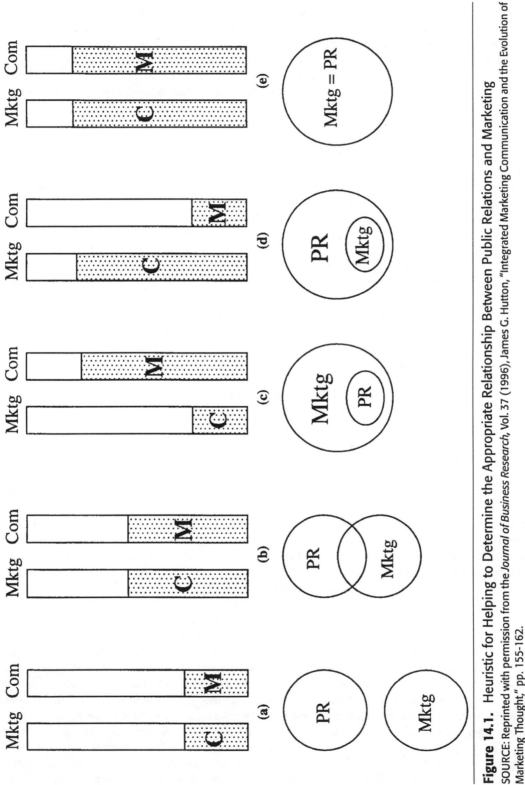

Figure 14.1. Heuristic for Helping to Determine the Appropriate Relationship Between Public Relations and Marketing

SOURCE: Reprinted with permission from the *Journal of Business Research*, Vol. 37 (1996), James G. Hutton, "Integrated Marketing Communication and the Evolution of Marketing Thought," pp. 155-162.

NOTE: Mktg or M = marketing; Com or C = communication; PR = public relations.

ment rather than a marketing department or a public relations department that reports to a marketing executive. Conversely, the noncommunication marketing functions of a public utility, especially physical distribution, capacity use, and new product development issues, constitute a high percentage of utilities' marketing efforts.

If a moderate proportion of the marketing issues confronting an organization are communication related and vice versa, then the "overlapping" model ("b" in Figure 14.1) probably is appropriate. Most large corporations likely fall into this category given the size, complexity, and frequent independence of the marketing and public relations issues confronting such organizations. Typically, day-to-day marketing activities such as product publicity, promotion, and sales force communications would be handled by the various line operations of the company. A corporate public relations or communications department, meanwhile, would handle financial communications, employee communications, the corporate identity program, the corporate advertising program, and other global communications because each of those functions touches many audiences (publics or stakeholders) besides prospects, customers, and other members of the marketing channel. Especially a company with a limited number of strong independent brands might wish to develop a strong "marketing public relations" function, as suggested by Harris (1991a). In any case, cooperation between the functions still is essential but is accomplished through staff meetings between the departments and at the highest level of the organization as well as through personal relationships and other informal means.

Of course, in many large complex organizations, there are multiple levels of some communication functions. For example, it is common to have corporate advertising and organization-wide employee communications emanate from the corporate level, whereas product advertising and local employee communications emanate from the division level.

The "marketing-dominant" model ("c" in Figure 14.1) probably is appropriate for a multibrand consumer products company whose brands are more visible to the public than is its corporate persona. In such cases, care must be taken not to slight other key audiences, but it might be appropriate to operate with a skeleton corporate communications staff and to let marketing supervise nearly all public relations activities as a line function because of the importance of product publicity, crisis communication (e.g., product recalls), sponsorships, special events, and other marketing-related public relations activities to developing and maintaining brand loyalty.

The "public relations-dominant" model ("d" in Figure 14.1) probably would be appropriate for most professional services, hospitals, universities, and assorted nonprofit organizations, which typically have fewer pricing and distribution channel issues than do consumer or industrial product manufacturers. The public relations-dominant model would be more appropriate for such organizations because, at least conceptually, it focuses on longer term issues of organizational culture, identity, and community outreach befitting the nature of those institutions. In addition, this model generally is more appropriate and effective for such organizations to engage in a subtler form of marketing, making greater use of softer sell tactics such as sponsorships and institutional advertising rather than harder sell techniques such as price-related advertising.

Finally, the "marketing = public relations" model ("e" in Figure 14.1) would be appropriate to most situations where a high percentage of marketing issues are communication related and vice versa, typical of a small business where there is great overlap between the two areas and neither is likely to be very sophisticated or highly developed.

In practice, of course, the choice among the five options often will be complicated by special circumstances, not to mention political and personnel considerations. Still, the scheme just described provides a general rationale and simple guidelines for the appropriate relationship between marketing and public relations in a given context. In both theoretical and practical terms, the choices first laid out by Kotler and Mindak (1978) suggested that no one model is best in all circumstances and that marketing and public relations should align themselves in whatever fashion is most conducive to accomplishing the organization's objectives. That commonsense approach to defining the marketing-public relations interface probably remains good advice but has been ignored by those who insist that there is one correct model (e.g., J. Grunig, 1992c) and who tend to dismiss or ignore a constructive partnership between marketing and public relations.

IMC: PUBLIC RELATIONS AS SUBORDINATE TO ADVERTISING?

During recent years, a wild card that has greatly complicated the marketing-public relations relationship has been advertising, mostly notable in the form of IMC.

Critics of IMC suggest that it is simply the latest in a line of attempts made by the advertising industry to expand its revenue base, at the expense of other communication disciplines, without a legitimate conceptual foundation. Ad industry veterans recall aborted variations on similar themes such as the "whole egg," "orchestration," and "new advertising" (Kalish, 1990), which sought to make advertising and related communications more consistent and coherent. The failure of such schemes (Levine, 1993) was largely the result of the unwillingness of the mainstream advertising business to let go of a system that, although antiquated, had been very lucrative to agency owners (Schultz, 1993b).

That self-contained system was (and sometimes still is) characterized by a media commission compensation structure that defied economic logic (Ogilvy, 1963), ego- and award-driven creativity, a "who stole whose client this week" trade press mentality, and a "let's put on a show" style of business in which agencies routinely subjected themselves to wasteful and often demeaning business pitches and competitive account reviews (Martin, 1994a).

The consensus among advertising executives (Duncan, 1993) seems to be that, this time, IMC will take hold because it is not simply about finding new sources of revenue and growth but also about survival of the advertising agency business. Fragmentation of the media, new communication technologies, new segmentation techniques, and the rise of databases have conspired to threaten major advertising agencies' dependence on traditional mass media advertising and traditional ways of viewing advertising.

Unfortunately, although many of the major advertising agencies have embraced IMC and trumpeted their role in integrating clients' marketing communications, there are serious questions about their sincerity. For example, major agencies generally have reduced or even eliminated their research functions (Ziff, 1992, p. 2) at precisely the time when one would presume that research would be emphasized as the foundation of a truly IMC program. Wolter (1993) reported that IMC practice suffered from "superficiality," "ambiguity," and "blurred focus." The binge of major advertising agency takeovers of the major public relations firms during the 1970s and 1980s has resulted in little real integration of those functions and often a great deal of turmoil (e.g., Hill & Knowlton's succession of embarrassing controversies following its acquisition [Roschwalb, 1994]).

So, although *integrated marketing communication* or IMC might be a necessary transitional term between *advertising* and *marketing communication*, an astute observer will recognize that the word *integrated* is superfluous, at best, and is little more than a confession that *non*integrated or *dis*integrated communications have been the norm in the past.

As suggested schematically in Figure 14.2, few would disagree, either from a conceptual or practical perspective, that all elements of marketing communications should work in unison and that organizations should use all appropriate means of marketing communication at their disposal. Clearly, there seldom would be a circumstance when marketing communications should *not* be integrated. In practice, the lack of integration generally is a function of poor communication or lack of cooperation rather than of any philosophical disagreement about whether marketing communications should or should not be integrated.

The more meaningful debate is about the relationship between what might be termed *inte-*

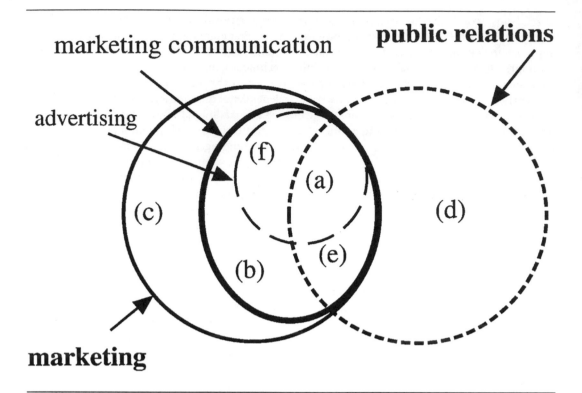

Figure 14.2. Relationships Among Marketing, Advertising, Marketing Communication, and Public Relations

SOURCE: Reprinted with permission from the *Journal of Business Research,* Vol. 37 (1996), James G. Hutton, "Integrated Marketing Communication and the Evolution of Marketing Thought," pp. 155-162.

NOTE: (a) = corporate advertising; (b) = sales force and marketing channel communications, trade shows, packaging, direct marketing, sales promotion, and the like; (c) = distribution, logistics, location analysis, pricing, new product development, and the like; (d) = investor relations, community relations, employee communications, public affairs/government relations, media relations, crisis communications, corporate identity, executive communications, charitable donations, and the like; (e) = product publicity, brochures and other collateral materials, part of media relations, part of crisis communications, part of corporate identity, sponsorships, and the like; (f) = traditional mass media advertising.

grated marketing (i.e., an organizational structure or authority in which all elements within the "marketing" circle in Figure 14.2 are united) and "integrated communications" (i.e., an organizational structure or authority in which all elements within the "public relations" circle are united). Theoretically, of course, it is highly desirable to have all functions of the firm "integrated." Realistically, however, in most situations marketing communications functions must be placed under the organizational authority of either marketing or communications.

MARKETING AND PUBLIC RELATIONS: THE SAME FUNCTION?

While the IMC debate rages on in many quarters, it often obscures a trend that is far more important to the future of public relations: Marketing (not just advertising) scholars and practitioners are methodically redefining the field of marketing as public relations. "Employee communications" is now "internal marketing" (Grönroos, 1981), "crisis communications" is now "crisis marketing" (Marconi, 1992), and virtually the whole of "public relations" is now "relationship marketing."

In a recent *Journal of Marketing* article, Duncan and Moriarty (1998) graphically depicted *marketing* as the replacement for *public relations* at the corporate staff level, relegating *public relations*—even as a line function—to a role as one of seven marketing communication "message sources" (along with personal sales, advertising, sales promotion, direct marketing, packaging, and events).

Many public relations practitioners and scholars are not even aware of the trend. Others see it as little more than a grab for power and turf by marketers.

From another perspective, however, it appears that marketing's interest in public relations is a natural stage of its evolution. To understand why, it is necessary to look a little deeper into the history of modern marketing thought (beginning roughly with the industrial revolution) from a marketing channels perspective (Hutton, 1996a).

From their origins in economics, marketing thinkers initially were concerned primarily with issues of economic efficiency, focusing on the production end of the channel and on questions surrounding economies of scale, pricing, and the relationship among mass production, mass distribution, and mass consumption. Within a few decades, the leading edge of marketing theory and practice had moved down the channel to distribution issues including extended discussions of the role of middlemen, ownership of goods in the channel, and power relationships in the channel.

As marketing theory and practice continued to progress down the marketing channel, the "selling concept" came to the fore, with its focus on sales management and selling techniques, followed by the rise of the "marketing concept," with its focus on (a) product branding and positioning and (b) customer wants and needs as the engine of the marketing process and the basis of the entire organization's philosophy.

Having reached the end of the channel (the consumer), the natural progression for the most forward-thinking marketers was to explore two new frontiers: (a) the application of the so-called marketing concept to nonbusiness organizations and activities and (b) a focus on the *context* of the entire marketing channel, which most marketing texts (e.g., McCarthy, 1975) previously had regarded as fixed or uncontrollable.

Explorations of the first frontier are documented in the debates about "broadening the concept of marketing" (Kotler & Levy, 1969), whereas exploration of the second frontier is perhaps best illustrated by Kotler's (1986) concept of "megamarketing," which added two more P's—politics and public relations—to marketing's traditional four P's (product, place, price, and promotion). Interestingly, in both cases the focus of marketing thought shifted from the channel itself to a range of external issues dealing with societal issues and relationships with noncustomer publics or stakeholders such as governments, activist groups, employees, and investors—the traditional domain of public relations.

The critical point is that marketing thought is evolving toward a public relations perspective to such an extent that marketing is essentially redefining itself as public relations. Duncan (1993), for example, defined IMC as "the process of strategically developing and controlling or influencing all messages used to build and nourish *relationships* with customers and other *stakeholders*" (emphases added). Plummer (1993) described advertising's job as "controlling the message," public relations' job as "managing the dialogue" (including crisis management and what Plummer called "positive communications"), and relationship marketing's job as "interacting with publics."

Kotler, perhaps marketing's most visionary thinker over the past 25 years, wrote about public relations extensively during that period, but under a variety of different names—"total" marketing (Kotler, 1992), "megamarketing" (Kotler, 1986), "generic" marketing (Kotler, 1972). In his generic marketing article, written more than 25 years ago, Kotler (1972) outlined three levels of marketing "consciousness." In Consciousness 1, he defined marketing as a business subject concerned with buyers, sellers, and economic products in which the core concept was market transactions. In Consciousness 2, marketing was distinguished by organization-client transactions not necessarily requiring payment, and it was practiced by museums, universities, churches, and the like, as well as by businesses. Finally, in Consciousness 3, marketing was applied to an organization's attempts to relate to all of its publics, not just its consuming public.

Thus, Kotler's definition of (generic) marketing, Plummer's definition of relationship marketing, and Duncan's definition of IMC are nearly identical, and all are simply definitions of public relations as it has been practiced by more enlightened organizations for decades.

THE CONTINUING IDENTITY CRISIS OF PUBLIC RELATIONS

Marketing and advertising's lack of acknowledgment or even recognition of their reinvention of public relations is due largely to the general lack of understanding of what public relations is and does. Marketing and advertising textbooks and "how to" business books (e.g., Hotchkiss, 1940; McCarthy, 1975; Wasson, 1983) traditionally have mistaken publicity- or marketing-related public relations as the whole of public relations, often portraying public relations as an afterthought to an advertising campaign, designed to garner whatever "free advertising" can be generated to complement the basic ad campaign. Top executives, typically trained in business schools, tend to perpetuate such misconceptions in practice.

Before public relations practitioners and scholars accuse marketing of imperialism, however, it would be prudent to examine a number of factors that have actually encouraged marketers to fill a large void created by public relations practitioners and scholars. Among the most important issues are the following:

1. *The ineffectiveness of public relations in educating businesspeople and business schools about public relations.* Pincus and others have looked at this issue extensively (e.g., Pincus, Ohl, & Rayfield, 1994). Ironically, many of the topics that are coming to the forefront of business school research and curricula, such as corporate culture, corporate identity, corporate equity (Hutton, 1996c), and "humanistic" approaches to relationships (Hutton, 1996b), are topics about which public relations practitioners have a wealth of knowledge and experience.

2. *Public relations' frequent lack of understanding of marketing and business in general.* Despite incessantly describing itself as a *management* function, public relations continues to suffer from a general lack of respect and a frequent lack of success in meeting organizational goals because so few of its practitioners and scholars exhibit a clear understanding of business subjects. For example, Ehling, White, and J. Grunig (1992), in describing the relationship between marketing and public relations, made a number of claims that would be considered nonsense by sophisticated marketing practitioners:

- "In contrast to public relations, marketing communication is characterized by unilateral design, unidirectional message flow, and one-stage operation" (p. 389). (The entire industry of database marketing is *based* on the notion of two-way message flow and continuous feedback.)
- "Marketing rationale and techniques are not . . . even useful to nonbusiness organizations such as educational institutions, not-for-profit hospitals, and public welfare agencies" (p. 359). (It would be difficult to find a major nonprofit organization that does not effectively use marketing techniques to at least some degree. Many such organizations are more sophisticated marketers than the average for-profit organization.)
- "The resolution of conflict and the mediation of disputes is essentially a public relations function and not a concern of marketing" (p. 369). (During the late 1950s and early 1960s, one of the most im-

portant areas of marketing research concerned conflict management and conflict resolution in the context of marketing channels. It remains a very important and active research topic.)

3. *The failure of public relations to define itself and to develop sophisticated and progressive theory.* In not developing a widely accepted definition and a central organizing principle or paradigm, the field of public relations has left itself vulnerable (a) to marketing and other fields that are making inroads into the traditional domain of public relations and (b) to critics who are filling in their own (typically very derogatory) definitions of public relations (for a broader discussion of the nature and scope of public relations, see Hutton, 1998).

Olasky (1984) described the problem as the "aborted debate within public relations" about what should be the fundamental purpose or nature of public relations. According to Olasky, the public relations profession chose not to challenge Edward Bernays' paradigm developed during the 1920s (including advocacy of the client's position and concurrent lack of concern for objectivity) because it was too lucrative for its practitioners: "The public relations occupation was too profitable for its beneficiaries to accept the reformation and reconstruction that paradigm changes require. . . . The trade was made: acceptance of a low status for public relations in return for acceptance of fat paychecks" (p. 94).

Others (e.g., Dover, 1995; Hutton, 1994; Ragan, 1994) have suggested that the problem is more related to factors such as closed-mindedness, arrogance, inbreeding, and the fear of new theories and new theorists rather than to financial gain. In any case, Olasky's (1984) basic observation about the lack of theory development in public relations appears to be correct and still applicable more than 15 years later.

4. *The inflexibility of public relations theorists.* As suggested earlier, the idea that there is one "best" structural relationship between marketing and public relations, regardless of context, probably is false and not in keeping with a true management orientation, which would argue that form should vary according to situation and objectives.

5. *The failure of public relations to develop its central tenet or core concept.* For example, Pavlik (1987, p. 122) and Broom, Casey, and Ritchey (1997) reported that although relationships often are discussed in public relations as a central theme—or as *the* central theme—in the field, (a) the term *relationship* seldom is even defined and (b) there is essentially no substantive research in the field of public relations regarding the measurement of relationships, the theoretical constructs of relationships, or relationships as the unit of analysis. Broom et al. "found the same paucity of useful definitions in the literature of other fields in which the concept of relationships is central" (p. 83) including interpersonal communication, psychotherapy, interorganizational relationships, and systems theory.

Surprisingly, however, Broom et al. (1997) overlooked a wealth of information from marketing. The omission of marketing as a domain of relationship theory is particularly puzzling given that some of the relationship marketing theory deals with precisely the issues that the authors were attempting to explain, such as the antecedents and consequences of relationships.

For example, one of the marketing theories directly relevant to public relations was titled the "commitment/trust" theory of relationship marketing (Morgan & Hunt, 1994). In their model, Morgan and Hunt (1994) posited trust and commitment as the core of relationships in a marketing context. The antecedents included shared values ("corporate culture" in public relations parlance), communication, and the costs of exiting the relationship. The desired outcomes (or consequences) of trust and commitment included acquiescence, (reduction in) uncertainty, cooperation, and functional (vs. dysfunctional) conflict. Although it still was under development, the authors made a compelling case for their theory, including an empirical pilot test of their trust/commitment model with a competing model using higher order statistical techniques.

6. *Implicit overreliance on "communications" or "communication" as the central tenet of public re-*

lations. Although public relations has not formally identified or developed its core concept, there is little doubt that a large majority of both public relations scholars and public relations practitioners were trained in communication(s) of one sort or another and tend to operate with that bias. To whatever extent Morgan and Hunt (1994) are correct in their hypothesis that trust and commitment are the foundation of strong relationships and that communication is just one antecedent (and probably not the most important one), public relations might need to go back to the drawing board and reassess its dominant focus on communication as the field's implicit foundation. Even more important, it must question whether it is going even further astray by moving toward concepts and terminology such as *image* and *reputation* management.

7. *The continuing disintegration of public relations.* A major consequence of the semantic confusion surrounding public relations is that, contrary to much talk about integrated communications, the public relations field generally is *dis*integrating. Particularly the higher end functions (i.e., those that are best paid, most influential, and closest to top management), such as investor relations and government relations, are being lost to other functional areas within organizations. For example, the National Investor Relations Institute reported that the percentage of investor relations managers reporting to chief financial officers or treasurers (rather than chief public relations officers) rose from 44% to 56% in just the 4-year span from 1988 to 1992 (Sweeney, 1994).

Similarly, many corporate public relations departments have lost responsibility for crisis communications to management consulting firms and marketing departments, some have lost responsibility for corporate identity programs to marketing departments, some have lost government relations to legal departments, and some have lost internal/employee communications to human resources departments. The extreme of this phenomenon was illustrated by Burger King a few years ago when it "integrated" its communications function into the organization by disbanding the public relations department. Its media relations (the only communications function that could not halfway logically be assigned to another functional area within the organization) was given to the "diversity" department.

CONCLUSION

The relationship between public relations and marketing is increasingly being defined by the marketing side. The reasons, however, have less to do with marketing imperialism than with (a) marketing's natural progression toward relationships and noncustomer publics and (b) the void that public relations has created, inviting marketing and other fields to assume responsibility for traditional public relations functions.

The result, one might argue, probably will not be good for either field. Marketing has more than enough to worry about in tending to customer demands, product development, pricing, advertising, sales promotion, sales management, market research, and other core marketing issues, and it might well be spreading itself too thin in attempting to manage relationships with a host of noncustomer publics. Public relations, on the other hand, almost certainly will suffer as both a practice and an intellectual discipline if it is subordinated or assimilated by marketing.

To stem the tide, public relations needs to systematically address the issues that have led to its frequent marginalization in the marketing-public relations relationship. If public relations fails to meet the challenge, then its future will be uncertain and largely in the hands of others. If public relations succeeds, then its future will be in its own hands and very bright indeed.

CHAPTER 15

Extending Strategic Planning to Communication Tactics

LAURIE J. WILSON

■ One of the prevalent buzzwords in business and communications today is *strategic*. Public relations firms boast of strategic planning, strategic communication, and strategic response. A concept drawn from the traditional bottom-line approach of American business management (Peters & Austin, 1986; Peters & Waterman, 1984; Wilson, 1996), the strategic management approach to public relations makes sense within a prevailing corporate mood of controlling the environment and organization influences to maintain or increase profits—the ultimate organizational goal (J. Grunig, 1993b; J. Grunig & Hunt, 1984; J. Grunig & Repper, 1992).

Indeed, *strategic* efforts or functions within an organization seemingly are given that designation because of their direct links to enhancing the bottom line. That measurement seems to have become the very definition of a strategic function. For example, the movement to combine public relations and advertising functions into integrated marketing communications (IMC) has "measurability and accountability [as its] cornerstones" (Schultz, 1993a, p. 5). Ultimately, that measurability and accountability uses a "return-on-investment formula . . . [to] demonstrate to clients how the IMC's synthesis of approaches not only communicates but also contributes to the bottom line" (Griffin & Pasadeos, 1998, p. 5).

Unquestionably, implicit in the definition of a strategic function is that it contributes to the overall organizational mission and goals. Hon (1998) asserted that determining effectiveness in public relations measures cost-effective achievement of communication goals that have been derived from organizational goals and objectives. So, the strategic function of public relations occurs when the efforts contribute to the overall success of the organization. Whether "overall success" is defined solely as profits or more broadly in terms of the organization's contribution to its community and diverse publics (Estes, 1996; Etzioni, 1998; Wilson, 1996), public relations, to be strategic, must support the organization's achievement of its mission and goals.

THE STRATEGIC VALUE OF PUBLIC RELATIONS

The highly competitive business environment of today requires the accountability of all organizational entities to the achievement of organizational goals. This accountability is assessed by measurement, usually quantitative. In a recent study on public relations evaluation, Hon (1998) observed that most practitioners "acknowledged [that] their companies' process for setting public relations goals and objectives has become more formalized as the demand for measurable results has increased" (p. 106). She also commented that "the systemization of public relations planning is a necessary precursor to meaningful public relations evaluation" (p. 106). In other words, public relations cannot be evaluated as strategic—contributing to the accomplishment of organizational mission and goals—if it is not systematically planned with that mission and those goals in mind.

Nevertheless, being strategic in public relations today seems to be as much a matter of transition as anything else. Most practitioners know the four-step process—research, planning, implementation, and evaluation—and usually can identify the strategic importance of each step. Most are familiar with methodologies to complete each step. Where our effectiveness falters is in the transition, or linkage, from one step to the next. In other words, today's public relations practitioners can do research, they can plan, they can produce communication tactics, and they can evaluate.

What practitioners might have difficulty doing is (a) devising an organizationally strategic plan that responds to and incorporates information from research and (b) creating tactics that actually succeed in accomplishing what the plan identifies needs to be done to support the organization's mission and goals. We know the steps, but we do not always know how to get from one step to the next so that they become an interactive process.

A case in point is the experience of the Salt Lake City Olympic bid committee in its bid for the 1998 (and subsequently the 2002) Winter Olympic Games (Wilson, 1997). The organizers decided to float a public referendum to demonstrate more effectively what opinion polls had shown as overwhelming public support of the effort. Although the opinion research of the bid committee showed overall strong support (upward of 80%), it identified weak support and even opposition among senior citizens and very conservative elements of the public. In an off-year election (when this referendum occurred), those public segments were the most likely to vote. The committee knew that its task—its strategic objective—was to get out the supportive vote.

The tactic was a series of

clever, creative, and visually appealing television spots which gave people a good feeling about the Olympic games in Utah. At the end of the spots, they showed a box with a check mark in it to indicate a vote supportive of the Olympic bid. But the ads were essentially still seeking public approval of the games because they never asked people *to get out of their chairs and go vote.* (p. 63, italics in original)

Nevertheless, the task of the bid committee was not to make people feel good about the Olympics in Utah; rather, its strategic task was to motivate those public segments that approved of the bid to get to the polls and vote. The message conveyed by the bid committee's tactic never requested that action. In the midst of overwhelming public approval, the referendum was passed by a very slim majority, and the bid committee was plagued for several years of the bid process with having to explain the low margin of recorded public support.

Even when research is done competently and exhaustively, including analysis, it often is not used as a resource base for decision making in the planning process. Similarly, once we have completed strategic planning, the plan often fails to guide the specific content and construction of individual tactics. We have a solid plan but end up with communication tactics that do not reach our publics with the messages needed to motivate them to accomplish our purpose. We see examples every day of messages that appear to have no target public and no recognizable appeal. They might be creative, but they are useless if they are not delivering a specific message to a target public so that the public will act to help us meet our objectives and accomplish our organizations' missions.

What is needed, then, is a methodology to bridge the gulf between research and planning and between planning and implementation. Bridging the first gulf, between research and planning, is relatively easy with a number of proven planning methods. Planning is a logical analytical function. It requires the same logical analytical processes as does research. But the second bridge, between the logical analytical process of planning and the creative state of tactic design and implementation, is more problematic. To be successful in developing tactics that get messages noticed in the deluge of information encountered every day by our key publics takes great innovation and creativity. The problem ensues in flowing the logical mind's strategic planning into the creative mind's tactical brainstorming.

The need, then, is to develop a strategic planning methodology that also can provide a bridge between the logical planning mind and the creative mind without stifling the creative energy and limiting the flow of ideas. The strategic planning methodology must contain a tool to channel the creative flow into the framework of a specific public, purpose and message, establishing a structure to guide the tactical development process before the creative process is unleashed. Just such a methodology and tool exists as the strategic program planning matrix and its associated copy outlines for development of communication tactics (Hainsworth & Wilson, 1992; Wilson, 1997).

STRATEGIC PROGRAM PLANNING

As mentioned previously, a strategic program is one that truly contributes to the accomplishment of organizational goals. Planning programs to solve specific problems and to accomplish specific goals requires step-by-step accomplishment of the tasks that comprise each step of the four-step public relations process. The public relations faculty at Brigham Young University have developed the strategic program planning matrix to aid in the development of strategic programs (Figure 15.1). It was designed to direct problem solving analytically, using research to make decisions in each step of campaign development. The matrix is used to solve public relations problems and to double check solutions to make sure that the implementation is based on the information (research) available. It helps practitioners to translate information into sound practice.

The Matrix Approach to Research

For some time, public relations professionals have acknowledged that the basis of effective public relations problem solving is good research. It provides the information necessary to define the problem, identify and understand key publics, and develop the best strategies and tactics to send messages to those publics. Cutlip, Center, and Broom (1985) identified the primary purpose of research in public relations as "reduc[ing] uncertainty in decision making" (p. 202).

The strategic program planning matrix divides the preliminary research step into four parts: background, situation analysis, central core of difficulty, and preliminary identification of publics and resources. Organizing research in this way helps to narrow the focus of what is known into a solution to the problem. It funnels research so that the practitioner can evaluate what is known and can identify how that will assist in the selection of publics and resources to solve the problem.

The first part of the research synopsis is the *background*. Once the client identifies a problem, the background provides a synthesis of information that lays the foundation for defining the problem. It is an integration of both primary and secondary research on the client's industry and

Research	1. Background	Synthesis of primary and secondary research providing background information on the industry and client, the product or program, market situation, and current trends in opinion and attitudes
	2. Situation analysis	A one-paragraph statement of the current situation and refinement of problem definition based on research; a second paragraph identifies potential difficulties and related problems to be considered
	3. Central core of difficulty	A one-sentence statement of the heart of the problem and potential harm to client if not resolved
	4. Preliminary identification of publics and resources	The first part identifies and profiles all potential publics that may be affected by the problem or need to be motivated to aid in its resolution; the second part identifies intervening publics and other resources (tangible and intangible) that can be drawn on for the campaign
	5. Campaign goal(s)	The end to be achieved to resolve the central core of difficulty
Planning	6. Objectives	Specific, measurable, attainable, and time-bound results that will facilitate achievement of the campaign goal(s)
	7. Key publics	Those audiences necessary to achieve the campaign objective and goals(s); identifies self-interests to aid in the development of messages that will motivate them; assesses current relationships with each public and identifies its strategic cooperative community to assist in identifying influentials
	8. Message design	Identifies the primary and secondary messages for each key public, taking care to incorporate each public's self-interest
	9. Strategies	Identifies specific strategies for each public designed to reach that public with its specially designed messages
	10. Tactics	Specifies tactics or media tools to support each strategy for each specific public; each strategy will need to be supported with a number of tactics designed to convey the message to that public through the channel designated by the strategy
	11. Calendar	A time-task matrix such as a Gantt chart to integrate implementation of the strategic plan; the calendar should be organized by public and strategy, scheduling each tactic
	12. Budget	Organized by public and strategy, the budget should project the cost of each tactic in very specific terms; it also should indicate where cost will be offset by donation or sponsorship
Communication	13. Communication confirmation	The communication confirmation table converts the plan devised for each public into short words in tabular form; the strategies and tactics for each public are reviewed to ensure that they are appropriate to send the messages; the message should be confirmed against the public's self-interests; the table provides verification of the analytical process to make sure that the plan will reach the publics with the messages that will motivate them to action such that the campaign goal(s) is accomplished
Evaluation	14. Evaluation criteria	Identifies specific criteria to measure success based on the campaign goals and objectives
	15. Evaluation tools	Specific evaluation tools appropriate to measure each of the evaluation criteria including those in the calendar and budget

Communication confirmation table (within item 13):

Key Public	Self-interests	Influentials	Strategy	Tactics/Tools	Message
1.					
2.					
3.					

Figure 15.1. Public Relations Strategic Program Planning Matrix

SOURCE: Laurie J. Wilson, *Strategic Program Planning for Effective Public Relations Campaigns* (2nd ed., 1997). Reprinted with permission of Kendall/Hunt Publishing Company.

issues related to the problem to be solved. It includes information about the client, the product or program, the current and potential market, and the competition. The background also examines current or previous communication and marketing activities as well as current trends in opinions and attitudes toward the client and the product or program.

Once practitioners have gathered and synthesized information about the client and the product or program, they are in a position to assess the client's definition of the problem and to define the present situation. This part of the research synopsis is known as the *situation analysis*. It states, in a couple of short paragraphs, a summary of the problem and the situation or environment within which the problem occurs. The situation analysis is followed by the *central core of difficulty* that, in one sentence, strips away the symptoms and ramifications of the problem to get to the heart of the difficulty to be solved.

The rest of the research is synthesized into the final part of the research section of the strategic program planning matrix, the *preliminary identification of publics and resources*. Here, the research on the publics is presented to segment and extensively profile probable and possible target publics. The public profiles should include psychographic (values, attitudes, and lifestyles) as well as demographic information. This part of the research section also identifies resources, including facilities and intervening publics, that might be useful in conducting a public relations campaign.

The Matrix Approach to Planning

The planning process spelled out by the program planning matrix is strategic because it ties communication planning to goals and objectives that support the organization's mission. It becomes intuitive for good planners. At the heart of the planning matrix is a simple formula determining the following:

◻ what needs to be accomplished to solve the problem (goals and objectives);

◻ who needs to be reached and motivated to support the accomplishment of those objectives;

◻ what needs to be communicated (messages) to gain the cooperation of the publics; and

◻ how to best send those messages (strategies and tactics) so that they reach those publics and move them to action that supports the accomplishment of the objectives. (Wilson, 1997, pp. 79-80)

The first step in matrix planning is to set the *goal*. The next step is to create specific measurable *objectives* to accomplish the goal. In these two critical steps, the goal and objectives must be created to support the organization's mission and goals.

After deciding what must be done to solve the problem or accomplish the organization's mission and goals, the *key publics* whose actions are necessary to achieve the goal and objectives are identified. *Messages* are designed for each key public that incorporates its self-interest. *Strategies and tactics* to send those messages to key publics are the next step in the matrix planning process. The final steps are the creation of a *calendar* or campaign timetable and of a complete public-by-public *budget* for the entire effort.

The Matrix Approach to Communication and Evaluation

The final two sections of the matrix address the implementation of communication tactics and campaign evaluation. Implementation on the matrix consists of the *communication confirmation table*, that simply charts the logic of the communication tactics to ensure that, while tactics are designed with creativity and imagination, they still meet the standards established by the analytical planning process. Each public is charted with its self-interests, influentials (or opinion leaders), and specially tailored messages to ensure that the creative tactics are following the research-based decisions on how to best communicate with and motivate each key public.

The evaluation section of the matrix identifies, prior to implementation of the plan, the

Specific targeted public(s):

    Secondary publics (if any):

Intervening public(s) (if any):

    Specific tactics to target intervening public(s):

Action desired from public(s):

    How that action ties into public's self-interest:

Main message to be conveyed:

    Secondary message or objectives:

Proposed headline for this news release:

Proposed lead for this news release:

Copy points (as many points and as much specific information as you need to communicate to your public to support your message):

1.

2.

3.

4. .

5.

(Use all copy points necessary to *completely* detail the information.)

Specific media to receive release:

Delivery method and follow-up activities with media (if needed):

Figure 15.2. Copy Outline for a News Release

SOURCE: Laurie J. Wilson, *Strategic Program Planning for Effective Public Relations Campaigns* (2nd ed., 1997). Reprinted with permission of Kendall/Hunt Publishing Company.

evaluation criteria for assessing success and the methods or *evaluation tools* for making those assessments. It emphasizes the necessity of planning for evaluation so that it will be benchmarked and ongoing throughout the process. Evaluation done without prior planning too often falls short of measuring the strategic contribution of public relations efforts.

A TOOL FOR DEVELOPING COMMUNICATION TACTICS

Once the planning process is completed and the appropriate tactics have been determined, we en-ter the more creative phase of the program—the design of the communication tools that carry the message to key publics. It also is possibly the most difficult point of transition because we move from the logical analytical mind into the creative mind. It is imperative that the planning methodology—the strategic program planning matrix—provides a tool to convert the logical structure of the plan to a framework or parameters that channel creativity in the development of each communication tactic. The copy outline is just such a tool.

The secret of the success of the copy outline in establishing the parameters for the creative process is its point-by-point relationship to the strategic plan (Figure 15.2). Each communication tactic is *planned* before it is *created*. The copy outline requires for each communication tactic the identification of the key public, the desired action by that public to contribute to the accomplishment of the plan's objectives, and the message to be sent to that public to motivate its action. Each of these elements of the copy outline draws the information as it is specified in the strategic plan.

The copy outline also delineates the copy points or the specific information to be communicated to support the message and enable the public to accomplish the desired action. Because it is comprehensive, the completed copy outline actually becomes the first draft of the communication tactic. It ensures that we identify all the pertinent information for the creative tactic to be strategic for it to motivate the public to act as needed to accomplish the objectives of the plan that support the mission of the organization. Finally, the copy outline specifies which media receive the tactic, how it is delivered, and what follow-up actions (if any) are appropriate.

Although the copy outline in Figure 15.2 is designed specifically for a news release, it is a simple matter to adjust the outline to apply to any type of communication tactic. The central structure of a copy outline for any communication tactic is to identify the key public, the action needed to accomplish objectives, and the message (including copy points) to motivate that action. Those elements are drawn from the strategic program planning matrix for the effort at hand. Also relatively universal is the identification of media, delivery process, and necessary follow-up actions. Where copy outlines for different communication tactics might differ is in any product-specific elements such as proposed headlines for news releases, art for feature stories and brochures, design elements for Web pages and newsletters, locations and settings for staged events and speeches, and links to related sites for Web pages.

It is a simple matter to analyze the elements of design and unique characteristics of specific tactics (e.g., news releases, brochures, newsletters, speeches, staged events) and include them as part of the planning framework of the copy outline. In this way, copy outlines can be tailored for

the type of product to be designed. Once the analytical parameters to channel the creative process are determined, the form can be used repeatedly to design that particular type of product.[1]

Although some might think that the structure limits creativity, the copy outline simply has the effect of channeling the creative process. Brainstorming still plays a role in the development of strategies and the determination of tactics, and creative license still is encouraged in writing, art, design, and distribution. The copy outline channels creativity to reach a particular public with a particular message for a particular purpose as identified in a strategic plan. It helps to avoid the creation of clever and unique tactics that do not reach the public, that do not send the appropriate message, or that do not accomplish the communication and organizational objectives. At the very least, it provides a benchmark against which to measure the final product to make sure that it meets the specifications of the strategic plan.

TOWARD SHAPING STRATEGIC PUBLIC RELATIONS PRACTICE

The strategic program planning matrix is a planning methodology to ensure that public relations efforts are strategic in that they truly contribute to the accomplishment of the organization's mission and goals. The copy outline extends the planning into an analytical tool that frames creative products to follow strategic planning and stay on target with public, purpose, and message. It contains the detail necessary to inform, persuade, and motivate a key public to act to support the accomplishment of organizational objectives. It makes the transition from the analytical planning process to the creative process of product design without losing the direction of the strategic plan designed to solve the problem or reach the communication objectives.

A good copy outline becomes the first draft of a product and actually will shorten the overall time expended on the production of a particular communication tactic. The result of using copy outlines to develop communication tactics typically is higher quality, more effective products in a shorter amount of time. It is a tool and a process that works.

In our highly competitive marketplace, in an environment where all organizational entities must show contributions to achieving the organization's mission and goals, and in the midst of publics that are bombarded with thousands of messages a day, the strategic planning methodology represented by the strategic program planning matrix and its ancillary copy outlines helps to generate communication tactics that cut through the clutter and cause publics to act in such a way that our public relations efforts contribute to organizational success. This proven methodology enables practitioners to use research as the basis for sound strategic planning and to bridge the gap between strategic planning and the development of creative communication tactics that result in the accomplishment of communication and organizational objectives. Using this methodology will help practitioners to join the ranks of those whose efforts make strategic contributions to the organization.

NOTE

1. Practitioners should learn to construct copy outline formats for the communications tactics they most frequently use. Although it would be almost impossible to maintain a sourcebook of copy outlines for every conceivable communication tactic, Wilson (1997) contained copy outlines for a number of frequently employed tactics.

16

Public Relations and the Question of Professionalism

MAGDA PIECZKA

JACQUIE L'ETANG

■ This chapter is about professionalism in public relations. We feel that, given the strong interest in professionalism on the part of educators, researchers, and practitioners, some critical reflection is needed to understand how this concept has been used. The chapter aims to bring a number of new concepts and empirical material into the field. A brief literature review of the sociology of the professions is presented, followed by a review of selected public relations literature in light of the sociological debates over the concepts of profession and professionalism. The resulting insights are contextualized by a brief review of the development of public relations in Britain so as to explore alternative interpretations of history and public relations.

UNDERSTANDING THE STUDY OF PROFESSIONALISM

Professions as a subject of study can be traced back to the late 19th century and the work of so-

ciologists such as Herbert Spencer, Emile Durkheim, and Max Weber but also of economists such as Cairnes (1887). A more systematic study developed during the 1920s and 1930s, the important early landmarks of this interest being Carr-Saunders and Wilson's (1933) study of 27 occupational groups and Parsons' (1939) article on professions and the social structure.

Like any field of inquiry, the sociology of the professions has been developing through a combination of empirical and theoretically driven research. Reviewing developments, one notices more or less consistent lines of research effort that sometimes run in parallel and sometimes in succession, one or two clear changes of direction, and a continuous chipping away at the problem from many bases while debating the merits of the various efforts. Underlying this diversity, however, the works of Durkheim (1933), Parsons (1939), and Weber construct the basic conceptual skeleton that has supported study of the professions from its early days. The profession is anchored in the social division of labor, instrumental rationality, and the institutional structures through which they are articulated. Thus, it is inextricably linked with the rise of the modern industrial society.

The history of this field normally is charted around the fissure of the paradigm shift that occurred sometime during the late 1960s. On the one side lies the *trait approach* allied with functionalist sociology; on the other lies the *power approach* and its extensions, indebted to the insights offered by interactionism but also to the revived interest in Marxism (for a detailed discussion, see Abbott, 1988; Burrage, 1990; Dingwall, 1983; Freidson, 1986, 1994; Macdonald, 1995). The following discussion is organized by the main concepts used by these different approaches before an analysis of the current situation is attempted.

The early writers and researchers agreed about—in fact, they took for granted—the important stabilizing role that professions play in the social structure (Durkheim, 1933, pp. 24-31; see also Macdonald, 1995, p. 2). This position was expressed in the following way by Carr-Saunders and Wilson (1933): "Professional organisations are stable elements in society. . . . They engender modes of life, habits of thought, and standards of judgement which render them centres of resistance to crude forces which threaten steady and peaceful evolution" (p. 497). As a result, researchers' efforts up to the 1960s were focused on cataloging the traits that set professions apart from other groups in society and accounted for their prominent role. Thus, a profession was defined by its foundation on a body of "complex formal knowledge and skill along with an ethical approach to . . . work" (Freidson, 1986, p. 29). In fact, as Millerson's (1964) comparison of numerous definitions showed, a more detailed set of characteristics had been developed and well established in the field:

> The list covers familiar ground—a specialised skill and service, an intellectual and practical training, a high degree of professional autonomy, a fiduciary relationship with the client, a sense of collective responsibility for the profession as a whole, an embargo on some methods of attracting business, and an occupational organisation testing competence, regulating standards, and maintaining discipline. (Elliott, 1972, p. 5)

A corollary of the efforts to build an "ideal-type" definition of the phenomenon under study was the realization that a method also had to be found to account for the differences not only among the accepted professions but also between professions and occupations (for a discussion of definitions, see Freidson, 1986, pp. 21-33). Terms such as *semi-professions* (Etzioni, 1969), *paraprofessions* (Freidson, 1970b), and *status* and *occupational professions* (Elliott, 1972) were introduced to deal with the differences in autonomy or status that different occupational groups possessed.

There emerged a clear difference between the straightforward and descriptive nature of the trait approach (which viewed professions as a static phenomenon) and the process approach (which focused, as the name suggests, on the nature of the process by which occupations attain professional status) (see, e.g., Vollmer & Mills, 1966). The process, called *professionalization*, was proposed as a historical model of the development of professionalism. This so-called "natural history of professionalism," developed in the works of Caplow (1954) and Wilensky (1964), consisted of five stages: "(1) the emergence of the full-time occupation; (2) the establishment of a training school; (3) the founding of a professional association; (4) political agitation directed towards the protection of the association by law; [and] (5) the adoption of a formal code" (Johnson, 1972, p. 28).

Professionalization rendered itself to operationalization and, therefore, was used in empirical work dealing with structuration such as Hickson and Thomas's (1969) study in which they established a hierarchy of professions in Britain (for critical discussions of traits and professionalization, see Abbott, 1988; Johnson, 1972; Rueschemeyer, 1964; Spangler & Lehman, 1982).

But presenting the first few decades of the study of the professions as driven purely by the trait approach and by functionalism is too crude. An alternative approach developed within the Chicago school by Everett C. Hughes was present from the 1930s and became particularly prominent with the publication of his *Men and Their Work* (Hughes, 1958) and later his *The Sociologi-*

cal Eye (Hughes, 1971) as well as the publication of his students' work—a classic ethnographic study, *Boys in White* (Becker, Greer, Hughes, & Strauss, 1961), and *Medical Dominance* and *Profession of Medicine* (Freidson, 1970a, 1970b).

In theoretical terms, the difference between these two approaches is the work of normative character linked to the concepts of the social structure and function as starting points as well as the work supported by the concepts of action and social interaction. The ethnographic approach used by the interactionist studies revealed aspects of professional practice and training that evaded other researchers, for example, the fact that young doctors developed cynicism rather than altruism in the course of their professional instruction. Thus, the term *profession* came to be seen as a symbolic label or ideology used by an occupational group:

> Ideal-typical constructions do not tell us what a profession is, only what it pretends to be. . . . Everett C. Hughes and his followers are the principal critics of the "trait" approach and ask instead what professions actually do in everyday life to negotiate and maintain their special position. (Larson, 1977, pp. xii, xiv, quoted in Macdonald, 1995, pp. 7-8)

If one reads the early history of the sociology of the professions in the way presented heretofore and puts it in the context of theoretical and methodological changes within the social sciences beginning during the late 1960s (Denzin & Lincoln, 1994) and perhaps even broader social and political trends of that time, then one cannot avoid the impression of doors closing on certain ways of thinking and opening on others:

> The mood shifted from one of approval to one of disapproval, from one that emphasized virtue over failings to one that emphasized failings over virtues. . . . This shift in evaluation and emphasis was reflected in a shift in conceptualization. The academic sociologists of the 1940s and 1950s were prone to emphasize as the central characteristics of the professions their especially complex formal knowledge and skill along with an ethical approach to their work. . . . Writers from the late

1960s on, however, emphasized instead the unusually effective monopolistic institutions of professions and their high status as the critical factor. (Freidson, 1986, pp. 28-29)

This new way of looking at professions came to be termed the *power approach*, whereby power is understood, broadly speaking, as ways in which professions win social approval to define and control their work and their relationships with other actors such as clients (Macdonald, 1995, p. 5). There is an influential body of published work that either is directly focused on various manifestations of professional power or can be regarded as a development of such interests (Abbott, 1988; Freidson, 1970a, 1970b, 1986; Johnson, 1972; Larson, 1977). Although there sometimes are big differences among these authors, for the purposes of this review, it is more important to see them as advancing a broadly similar approach that has firmly shaped the conceptual map of the field.

The fundamental area of convergence among these authors has to be located in the theoretical sources from which they drew or, perhaps even more important, in their preoccupation with theorizing itself. The trait approach was *a*theoretical, and Parsons' conceptualization (which explains the place of professions in the social structure as defined by the special nature of the social functions they fulfill and by their "collectivity orientation") came under attack. The theoretical inspiration for this renewed interest in professions came in the form of a number of concepts borrowed from Hughes's interactionism, Weberian ideas, and Marxist modes of explanation.

Hughes contributed *licence* and *mandate*, that is, the idea that the profession depends on social approval to carry out certain activities in exchange for money and "to define, for themselves and others, proper conduct in relations to work" (Dingwall, 1983, p. 5). Weber's concept of "social closure" was introduced by Parkin (1974) and subsequently used by others. Another of Weber's ideas borrowed by the sociologists of the professions was the view that a profession represented an "interest group" whose actions are oriented toward common economic and social interests. Finally, Marxist influence raised questions about the profession's relations to the state and the position of professionals in the class system. It also produced a stream of work tracking the traces of proletarianization of the professions (Braverman, 1974; Derber, 1982, Murphy, 1990), that is, their alleged loss of autonomy to bureaucratic systems that increasingly controlled the performance of professional work (Freidson, 1994, pp. 130-140).

The theorizing effort was further enriched by the study of professions outside the Anglo-American system, particularly studies of the French and German professions (Burrage, 1990, pp. 12-18). This Continental intervention highlighted the culture-specific nature of the concept by revealing a different model of the state's engagement with professions (Geison, 1984; Jarausch, 1990; Kocka, 1990). The differences begin with semantics (both French and German lack an exact equivalent of the term *profession* itself[1]) but go deeper into the definition of the concept, showing its inextricable links to political culture:

> In the meritocratic ideology of "classless" America, the professions have come to be seen as the most obviously "legitimate" way to claim, attain, or retain elite status. In French (and German) political culture, the social standing of noncapitalist elites has had a less distinct connection with their occupational role, and the "liberal professions" in particular have generally been perceived as a much less important social and political force. (Geison, 1984, p. 5)

Thus, *profession* emerges recast from a new mold. First, it comes to be seen as a special case of a more general type of *occupation*. The old traits are reworked into a dynamic model that places a profession in relation to the state, political culture, and social groups, be they elites, other professions, or clients. Knowledge in this model can be reinterpreted as an instrument in the profession's competitive positioning. It also becomes clear that the study of professions, or of any profession for that matter, has to extend over three levels of analysis: "the level of general social change, the level of occupational organisation,

and the level of individual life-cycle" (Elliott, 1972, p. 5).

Two such comprehensive models have been constructed and applied, known as the "professional project" (Larson, 1977) and the "system of professions" (Abbott, 1988) (for a discussion of both, see Macdonald, 1995, pp. 8-35). Larson's (1977) work was inspired by the Hughesian approach, but at the same time it rests firmly on the idea of the market as the focus around which economy, society, and professions are organized:

> Professionalization is . . . an attempt to translate one order of scarce resources—specialist knowledge and skills—into another—social and economic rewards. . . . The structure of the professionalization process binds together two elements . . .: a body of abstract knowledge, susceptible [to] practical application, and a market—the structure of which is determined by economic and social development and also by the dominant ideological climate. (pp. xvii, 40)

Thus, the professional project unfolds along two dimensions: market control and social mobility. Its ultimate goal is complete social closure or elite status. Larson (1977) reused the old idea of professionalization, but in her account it is the combination of economics and the ideological mechanisms rather than social function that supplies the explanation. Professions no longer are neutral or detached from the class structure; rather, they very clearly are lodged in it by their "proximity to power" (p. xv).

There are two other features of Larson's (1977) model that are important to our analysis: her understanding of the operations that are performed on knowledge in the process of professionalization and her understanding of the role that professional training plays. The first is captured by the opposition of *codification* versus *indeterminacy* (p. 41). The first of the pair refers to the part of the cognitive base of the profession that can be standardized and mastered as rules; the second describes areas that escape codification and may be covered by explanations such as *talent*. Freidson (1970b), who had used the idea of indeterminacy before in the context of medicine, explained it as the "firsthand experience" of the clinician as opposed to "book knowledge" or science (p. 169). High indeterminacy helps in the exclusion of competitors from the field and, therefore, can be expected to play an important part in professionalization. The second important point is Larson's (1977) treatment of training, which she saw as "the cooperative activity of instructors and students—[which] appears indeed as the production of a marketable commodity, namely the special skill of the professional producer" (p. 211).

Abbott's (1988) work is founded on two points: (a) that "the evolution of professions . . . results from their interrelations" (p. 8) and (b) that professional work is constituted by tasks that the profession has successfully claimed for itself. The hold that a profession establishes over a set of tasks is known as *jurisdiction.* Jurisdictions are maintained, extended, and redefined on the basis of "a knowledge system governed by abstractions [because only abstraction] can redefine [the system's] problems and tasks, defend them from interlopers, and seize new problems"(p. 9). The new element is the concept of the system of professions as the level of generalization above that of a single profession. Thus, a change in one profession's jurisdiction affects jurisdictional changes in other professions. At the same time, Abbott's model includes the intraprofessional differentiation (by status, client, organization of work, and career pattern) and a sensitivity to broader environmental factors that he considered under the rubrics of social and cultural environments. To understand a profession, therefore, one needs to pay attention to its jurisdictional competitors. In the case of public relations, these might be journalists or marketing specialists. One also should see diversity beyond the homogeneity implied by the labels of *lawyer, doctor,* and *public relations specialist.*

It seems appropriate to finish this historical review of the sociology of the professions with Freidson, who occupies a special position in the field. Freidson has been publishing on the sociology of medicine since 1960, and since his *Profession of Medicine* (Freidson, 1970b) he has developed a strong theoretical position in the sociology of the professions that has influenced writers such as Larson and Abbott. What is par-

ticularly valuable in Freidson's approach is both the reworked definition of the profession "as an occupation which has assumed a dominant position in the division of labor so that it gains control over the determination and substance of its own work" (Freidson, 1970b, p. xvii) and a more fundamental redefinition of the subject as the study of work based on application of knowledge to a variety of problems. The new element here is the retreat from the notion of objective knowledge to the notion of knowledge as a social construct (which for Freidson was not synonymous with extreme relativism):

> The profession claims to be the most reliable authority on the reality it deals with. . . . In developing its own "professional" approach, the profession changes the definition and shape of problems as experienced and interpreted by the layman. The layman's problem is re-created as it is managed—a new social reality is created by the profession. (p. xvii)

This leads logically to what Freidson (1970b) viewed as major questions that underpin the study of the profession: "First, one must understand how the profession's self-direction or autonomy is developed, organized, and maintained. Second, one must understand the relation of the profession's knowledge and procedures to professional organization as such and the lay world" (pp. xvii-xviii).

Freidson's (1970b) line of thought brought him to the following understanding of the current problems in the field. First, the trait approach—and he saw power as ultimately a version of the trait approach—cannot produce a theoretical basis for an explanation applicable to all manners of professions in all manners of countries (i.e., beyond its Anglo-American origins). Second, to build such a theoretical base, one must start with a comprehensive theory of occupations. Professions are to be treated only as special cases in which the claim made by the use of the title—Freidson called it "avowal" or "promise" (p. xvii)—has been successful. If the theory of occupations is to be general and abstract, then the theory of the professions should aim at explaining individual cases:

The future of profession lies in embracing the concept as an intrinsically ambiguous, multifaceted folk concept of which no single definition and no attempt at isolating its essence will ever be generally persuasive.... Profession is treated as an empirical entity about which there is little ground for generalizing as a homogeneous class or a logically exclusive conceptual category. (Freidson, 1994, p. 25)

Thus, *profession* should be understood as a "socio-political artifact" and as a study of the "role of the title in the aspirations and fortunes of those occupations claiming it" (p. 26).

This brief summary of the development of profession shows how the concept has moved from the macro level of analysis to that of specific social and political location as well as how it has been problematized and changed from a sociological tool to a conscious occupational strategy. It is this changed understanding of the concept that frames our analysis and reflection in the sections that follow.

PROFESSIONALISM IN PUBLIC RELATIONS

Looking into public relations from the vantage point offered by the sociology of the professions, we are struck by two observations. First, the way in which profession is understood in our field reflects the view largely abandoned by the theorists of the professions since the late 1970s. Second, some of the interests observed in the field of the sociology of work and occupations also are present in public relations, notably gender and work itself. Finally, the comparison reveals a number of themes not present in public relations research.

The use of professionalism normally is linked in our field with the expression of a need to improve the occupational standing. The familiar troika—body of knowledge, ethics, and certification—are understood as the defining characteristics of a profession (Cutlip, Center, &

Broom, 1994, pp. 129-163; J. Grunig & Hunt, 1984, pp. 66-69; Wylie, 1994), and there has been a consistent effort expounded by public relations professional associations and educators to develop these characteristics. American public relations, which seems to have the most developed institutional base for public relations with its big numbers of university courses, big numbers of practitioners associated with the Public Relations Society of America (PRSA), and its public relations journals, is the best example of this effort. In collaborative efforts, American academics and practitioners since 1973 have striven to develop and implement common standards for public relations education through a number of Association of Education in Journalism and Mass Communication commissions (Ehling, 1992). Since 1987, there has been work conducted under the auspices of the PRSA to define and develop the necessary body of knowledge (PRSA, 1990). The International Association of Business Communicators committed itself to funding the *Excellence* project, which subsequently has produced at least two major publications (Dozier, L. Grunig, & J. Grunig, 1995; J. Grunig, 1992c) and seemed to have worked as a focus for a lot of basic and applied research. Perhaps the most obvious symbol of these efforts is in the name of what was described as one of the "milestones on the road toward professionalism," that is, the Symposium on Demonstrating Professionalism (Ehling, 1992, pp. 442-443).

Thus, professionalism has become a loudly articulated group goal for public relations practitioners, guiding their efforts in developing public relations expertise but also inspiring a fair amount of introspective research (for a discussion, see J. Grunig & Hunt, 1984). Inspired by Wilensky (1964) and Vollmer and Mills (1966), J. Grunig's (1976) own research produced a scale operationalizing professionalism in public relations. Other researchers also have conducted studies based on measures of professionalism (McKee, Nayman, & Lattimore, 1975; Sallot, Cameron, & Lariscy, 1997; Wright, 1976).

Apart from research operationalizing professionalism, the occupational interests have been pursued in research dealing with gender (L.

Grunig, 1995; Sereni, Toth, Wright, & Emig, 1997; Tam, Dozier, Lauzen, & Real, 1995), public relations roles, and other topics, extending in a more or less direct manner ideas best labeled as "public relations excellence" (Dozier, L. Grunig, & J. Grunig, 1995).

So far, the most extensive engagement within the field of public relations with practitioners' work has come from research built around the concept of role (Broom & Dozier, 1986; Broom & Smith, 1979; Creedon, 1991; Dozier, 1992; Dozier & Broom, 1995). Theoretically, this stream of research uses one of the fundamental sociological concepts. Empirically, it has been advanced through surveys of American practitioners and the use of factor analysis at the analytical stage.

Up to this point, public relations has engaged selectively with the range of issues found in the sociology of occupations. For example, gender is a prominent issue, as it is in the field of sociology of work and occupations, where we have located the study of the profession. Yet, the relations between groups of people identified by other criteria, such as the amount of power they wield in an organization, have not generated the same level of analysis. This lack of interest in how people at work really relate and communicate might perhaps be explained by the strong normative drive present in public relations theorizing that focuses on proving that dialogue is the best way in which to enact work relations or even all relations. This situation can be explained convincingly as resulting from professionalization efforts that necessarily rely on an idealistic understanding of the profession.

If research interest has been expounded on the study of public relations at the level of career and role (i.e., linking individual and institutional levels), then the larger scale interests (i.e., looking at public relations in terms of its engagement with the state and the big social structures of society), has remained a fairly marginal interest. Typically, this has meant that when we engage with knowledge and discourse (rhetoric) in public relations, we link them to improved effectiveness of public relations or, more critically, to the issue of image and presentation. We have not,

however, been very bold in looking at the type of "social reality" that professional communication experts construct in their efforts to communicate more effectively.

PUBLIC RELATIONS IN BRITAIN AND PROFESSIONALISM

In presenting a culturally specific take on the development of public relations, we are following Freidson's approach to professionalization, which recognizes the importance of unique sets of historical circumstances in particular cases. In adopting such an approach, we are clearly abandoning the American progressivist model of the development of public relations, which we see as reflecting the ideological and cultural context of the United States.

Existing narratives of the origins and development of the public relations occupation are dominated by the experience of the United States (see the British civil servant and cultural critic, Pimlott, 1951, as well as the more recent and better known Americans: Cutlip, 1994; Ewen, 1996; J. Grunig & Hunt, 1984; Olasky, 1987; Pearson, 1992; Tedlow, 1979). One interpretation has come to dominate mainstream public relations literature—the historical model developed by J. Grunig and Hunt (1984), which suggests that public relations historically has passed through four developmental stages: publicity, public information, two-way asymmetry, and symmetry. The model is also used to classify types of current practice and often is the basis for deductive applied research, which dominates the discipline. This interpretation has become the most widely known not only because it offers a clear framework for analysis but also because it has been used to underpin ideas about the role and ethics of public relations practice.

Much literature emanating from the United States promotes the idea that this evolutionary model is universally applicable both as a historical explanation and as a typology that satisfactorily explains professional practice. The difficulty with this sort of approach is that it can fail to take account of significant cultural and political factors in non-U.S. settings.

In this chapter, we present a brief summary of the evolution of public relations in Britain, which clearly shows a different pattern of development from that in the United States and, therefore, implies that the developmental model is not rigidly applicable. A fuller account of developments up to the formation of the Institute of Public Relations (IPR) in 1948 is detailed in L'Etang (1998c), but here we endeavor to illustrate the interplay between specific cultural, political, and economic experiences and development of the practice.

Origins of British Public Relations

The most significant feature of British developments was the large role played by local and central government and the relatively small contribution of the private sector (largely confined to advertising agencies and a few key organizations discussed in L'Etang (1998c) and not reviewed here). Although central government in Britain determines overall legislation, locally elected bodies implement policy within the constraints of their local budgets (partly raised directly from the local populace in the form of a property tax) from which a wide range of services are provided to the local communities. Nineteenth-century social reforms that attempted to deal with the social problems caused by the industrial revolution resulted in a greater role for local government. At this time, the relationship and communications between government officials and the local populace became an issue. As a result, officials began to consider their public relations role as well as their professional status. In 1922, local and central government officials combined to form the Institute of Public Administration and, in 1923, established a journal, *Public Administration,* that published many articles on public relations, showing that by the 1930s there was a fairly sophisticated definition of public relations and a clear understanding of the importance of good public relations to facili-

tate smooth administration in a democratic context. It was argued that "intelligence" (in current terminology, this translates as issues management) was an intrinsic role of public relations (Wood, 1936, p. 46) and that internal public relations should facilitate information flow within and between an organization and its environment (Kent Wright, 1936; Wood, 1936). Government officials' awareness and conception of public relations were demonstrated in articles declaring the following: "The first essential . . . is to build up public understanding and appreciation of the services rendered to them [members of the public] and thus obtain their goodwill" (Whitehead, 1933, p. 272); "A public relations department exists . . . not indeed for making policy palatable but for making it understood" (Wood, 1936, p. 45), and, "If the taxes branch is to be successful as it has been in the past, it must derive its strength from the goodwill and local cooperation of the general body of taxpayers" (Kliman, 1936, p. 290).

Another important influence was central government peacetime propaganda. Although there was extensive debate about the appropriateness of propaganda in a supposedly democratic country during peacetime, the view that propaganda had a role to play in assisting effective democracy through educating and informing citizens and facilitating feedback to civil servants was influential and spawned a number of public and health communication campaigns. Likewise, the collaboration between Stephen Tallents, secretary of the Empire Marketing Board that aimed to make the Empire "live as a society for mutual help" (Lee, 1972, p. 51), and John Grierson, the acknowledged leader of the British film documentary movement, was crucial. Grierson was a Scot who studied at the University of Glasgow and then the University of Chicago, where his views of democracy were influenced by Lippmann and after which he turned to film as the mass medium that could help to break down the barriers to informed citizenship. There is evidence that his views influenced public relations discourse in Britain (L'Etang, 1999), and an illustration is given in the following quotation from Alan Campbell-Johnson (1956), IPR president during 1956-1957:

[There is] a growing gulf between the active and passive elements in our community—the leaders and the led, the experts and the laymen, the players and the spectators. To cope with this cleavage, intensified as it is by the industrial and technical revolution around us, is, I believe, the central function of public relations. (p. 52)

Tallents' (1932/1955) vision was laid out in *The Projection of England* in which he envisaged a "school for national projection" (p. 40), and this document formed much of the basis for the British Council established in 1934—"to make the life and thought of the British peoples known more widely abroad and to promote a mutual interchange of knowledge and ideas with other peoples" (White, 1965, p. 7). The relationship between Britain's colonial past and public relations is explored in more detail in the next subsection.

During both world wars, the British government made substantial propaganda efforts both at home and overseas—in allied, neutral, and enemy countries—using a range of media. Tactics included censorship and, particularly during World War II, the employment of "black propaganda" overseas involving the use of deception and subterfuge in disseminating misleading information. Some of those involved in such work (see L'Etang, 1998a, 1998c) became involved in public relations after the war, and the career paths of such individuals clearly suggests a difficulty in distinguishing between public relations and propaganda. It is evident that a background in propaganda was not seen as being problematic or in any way a barrier to public relations practice.

Politics, Economy, and the Postwar Development of Public Relations

In dramatic contrast to the United States, which after the war found itself the richest and most powerful nation, Britain ended the war the world's largest debtor nation, short of labor and food and with visible exports reduced to less than half of the prewar level. Yet, Britain still attempted to maintain an imperial role and during the 1940s and 1950s was paying up to 8% of gross domestic product on defense as the cold war escalated. The change to a Labour administration in 1945 brought about increased expenditure on social welfare, housing, and health. In this setting, there were several opportunities for public relations to become an established part of the socioeconomic framework: there was a large amount of new social legislation that needed to be explained to the public; goods had to be promoted, initially to export markets and then, with the increase of consumer durables, to the home market; and the new administration's interventionist economic policies required some explanation and triggered opposition from business in rhetorical campaigns that often appealed directly to the public.

The wartime experience had forced local government into a much closer relationship with the communities for which it was responsible. After the war, the 1942 Beveridge Report, which laid out the vision of the welfare state, was implemented by the new Labour government. The mass of new legislation that resulted had to be explained to citizens, as did the reorganization and repairs to the infrastructure of the country, particularly in urban centers that had been badly damaged by bombing. Consequently, local government began to appoint officials into newly created public relations posts, and in 1947 these officials came together to define public relations as

the deliberate, planned, and sustained effort to establish and maintain, by conveying information and by all other suitable means, mutual understanding and good relations between a firm, statutory authority, government, department, professional, or other body or group and the community at large. (Rogers, 1958, p.12)

This definition reflected the debates in *Public Administration* during the 1920s and the stated aims of both the Empire Marketing Board and the British Council (L'Etang, 1998c). Local government officials also were instrumental in contacting others in public relations roles in private and public sectors and in formulating the mission of the IPR in 1948. They had the administrative skills needed to set up the Institute and contributed a strong sense of the importance of serving the public and the role of communication in facilitating democracy. Thus, local government played a substantial role in the formation of the public relations occupation in Britain and its early steps toward professionalization.

In terms of domestic politics, the major policy shift was that of nationalization whereby government took ownership of core industries away from the private sector to safeguard the interests of citizens by achieving economies of scale and reducing costs for consumers through a central planning model. There were strong ideological aspects of nationalization (public ownership based on principles of fairness and equity) versus anti-nationalization (free enterprise based on principles of efficiency through competition). Although Britain traditionally has had less state ownership than have other European countries, wars in 1914 and 1939 required major economic transformation and, therefore, acted as a stimulus to state ownership and management.

On its election, Labour swiftly nationalized the Bank of England, railways, road haulage, electricity, and civil aviation. Subsequent nationalizations were to include gas and, more contentiously, iron and steel. The threat of nationalization roused response from private enterprises in the form of special organizations that could lobby on their behalf. One such organization was Aims of Industry, established in 1942 to protect free enterprise and oppose nationalization and "corporate socialism." According to Kisch (1964), Aims of Industry operated a covert strategy using Britain's "old boy network" (p. 29) and making high-level contacts in building support. In contrast to the United States, Britain evidently had much stronger social networks, and these offered opportunities for public relations because networks could be used in a campaign (Sampson, 1969, p. 640). The policy of nationalization drove industry to seek public relations staff to promote their interests in the face of what were regarded by some as "political assaults" (Miller, 1960, p. 37).

The example of nationalization illustrates two important points. First, it indicates that pub-

lic relations developed an interest in social elites apart from government and that public relations strategies entailed leveraging the power that social elites could offer. Second, it indicates the historical moment when public relations and business in Britain began to forge a closer alliance. Opposing views regarding the appropriate extent of government intervention and ownership as well as policies of nationalization and privatization (denationalization) from the postwar period to the present day have continued to have a substantial influence in creating opportunities for public relations practitioners to step in as advocates on behalf of business in response to government policy. Such policy is primarily explained on behalf of the politicians in power by technically neutral career civil servants in the Government Information Service, although since the 1980s government departments also have recruited public relations consultancies to help them explain their case (Miller & Dinan, 1998).

The postwar era threw up new challenges for the state, notably in its relationships with other countries, and the growth of public relations beyond Britain was, in some cases, stimulated by the process of decolonization. Again, such processes illustrate the difficulties in drawing clear boundaries between public relations, propaganda, intelligence, and psychological warfare operations, at least in the British context. For example, in Malaysia, there was a well-documented campaign to win over Malayan Chinese to the British government's side at the end of World War II. News management by the Malayan government sought to control information flow, to publicize the promise of independence in 1957, and to support counterinsurgency psychological warfare using a variety of tactics—leaflets, black propaganda newspapers, and "voice aircraft" (i.e., aircraft fitted with loudspeakers that either announce propaganda messages or play music or other distracting noises to intimidate local populations) (Carruthers, 1995, p. 91). The Department of Publicity and Printing in Malaysia was established in 1945 and remained an important element once Malaysia had achieved independence in developing information campaigns to support government policy initiatives, particularly in the field of development (Van Leuven, 1996, p. 209; Van Leuven & Pratt, 1996, pp. 95-97).

Decolonization affected not only the British government but also organizations operating in the colonies. As one practitioner working for a major international organization recalled,

> The board realized that in postwar black Africa, there was going to be a big resurgence of political agitation working for independence from the British Commonwealth. . . . [So, it was] proposed that we should practice public relations . . . solid, commonsensical, anticipating where African desires were going to lead and what sort of attitudes they were going to formulate with huge White imperialist companies that had been there for hundreds of years. We really learned by the seat of our pants. It was a question of impressing people with the idea that we were a good thing for them and their country. . . . We ran . . . a strip cartoon [in a newspaper] . . ., and through it the Africans . . . would learn what capital was, what profit was, what employment was . . . all those basic things which would help them understand the company. (Interview, March 26, 1997)

Thus, the company tried to look after its own interest in the postcolonial world by persuading the African community of the benefits of capitalism through an educational campaign. In this context, public relations seems to be a self-interested force for conservatism, developing personal relationships in the community in attempting to counteract the effects of any latent alienation or nationalism. Interestingly, the public relations effort is described both as "commonsensical" and as "seat of the pants"; on the one hand, it is obvious in that it is concerned with protecting the company's interests, yet on the other, the nature of the expertise cannot be described, perhaps because activities proceeded on a trial-and-error basis. In Britain, the inability to define specific expertise resulted in a jurisdictional struggle with journalists who thought that public relations practitioners were encroaching on their own domain (i.e., storytelling) as well as impeding the news-gathering process. The ten-

sions that resulted forced practitioners to try to justify themselves and establish a clear identity, both of which played a significant role in the public relations professional project discussed in the next subsection.

Legitimation, Education, and Professional Discourse

Professional status was sought in an effort to establish social legitimacy. The expansion of public relations required the occupation to negotiate social approval or the concepts identified earlier in this chapter as mandate and licence. Social respectability was the aim of many within the IPR, and proving the occupation's value to society and democracy in general was a strategy easily drawn from the local government public service ethos. Practitioners declared that "the correct intelligent practice of public relations is something without which modern society would be immeasurably improverished" (Hess, 1950, p. 5) and that "the philosophy of public relations is a policy of social responsibility" (Galitzine, 1960, p. 51). Thus, the route taken by public relations to legitimate itself was that of the public interest. However, there were competing legitimations within the practice, with some emphasizing truth telling and information (e.g., "The good public relations officer is one who is concerned with putting over facts which can be supported by the truth" [Paget-Cooke, quoted in "Eight Men," 1953, p. 20]) and others advocating persuasion and advocacy (e.g., "The public relations officer persuades. . . . I suggest we become realists and not visionaries" [Garnett, 1951, p. 16]).

Education was, and is, an instrument for the public relations occupation to achieve status by contributing to the legitimizing process of social acceptance and by helping to define public relations expertise and the scope of its operation. However, as L'Etang (1998b) showed, attempts to impose a system of entry to the professional institute based solely on qualifications failed during the 1960s because "experience" remained a tradable commodity. Qualifications (the first of which was established in 1957) were seen as a way in which to improve the image of public relations, but compliance constantly was deferred and delegated to the next generation. Following Larson's (1977) insight cited earlier, it appears to be the case that in British public relations practice, there has been and remains a gap between ideals/aspirations and practice. Although there remains a reluctance to identify the necessary abstract knowledge required to practice, specific personal skills and qualities are articulated consistently, and following Abbott (1988), it seems useful to begin to explore these in understanding the occupation. The selection of quotes displayed in Table 16.1 gives the views of practitioners of all ages about the necessary qualities required to be a successful operator. Practitioners do not identify specific knowledge but rather focus on personal qualities such as creativity, lateral thinking, flexibility, articulateness, persuasiveness, common sense, and integrity. Beyond that also is the implication that a practitioner must know how to behave with senior people and to possess appropriate cultural capital. Such qualities reveal something of the self-perception of practitioners and provide a link between legitimation processes and attempts to establish professional power. Although it is important to know how to deal with clients and to be credible in terms of convincing them that the public relations practitioner knows best, it is noticeable that there is no abstract knowledge claimed for the purposes of legitimation or definition of the expertise offered to employers and clients.

CONCLUSION

The main argument that we have pursued in this chapter is that professionalism has so far appeared in public relations discourse as merely an historical process but that it should in fact be regarded as a more or less consciously used mechanism that is to deliver specific occupational goals. First, we showed that the understanding of the term as it is used in public relations is strongly anchored in the more idealistic functionalist approach to professions. Then, taking our cue from more recent developments in the sociology of the professions, we presented public relations primarily as an occupational group pursuing its own interests in relation to the state and social elites as the source of cultural/ideological power. Therefore, our analysis should help practitioners to understand their own roles, not simply in terms of managerial/technical levels or organizational position but also in a much broader context in terms of the power of the occupational role in society. We suggest that further reflection on the nature of public relations expertise, particularly in view of its success in establishing itself as a distinct and commercially viable service, would be beneficial.

In advancing our argument, we chose to focus on a selected number of points relating to the prewar emergence and postwar development of public relations practice in Britain. Our starting point is the history of public relations, and the argument we put forward is that "history" is not just a dispassionate marshaling of facts but also a weapon in the struggle for improved status. A progressivist account of the development of the occupation tinged with claims of universal applicability could be seen as an ideological mechanism bestowing the status of universal truth on a particular account. In our view, a model drawn from one set of historical circumstances is likely to be of limited value in interpreting historical data elsewhere.

Our approach was to follow Freidson in seeing each case of public relations as explained by a unique configuration of "national" factors. In our case, this meant attending to the role played in the development of British public relations by a combination of institutional forces and the exigency of the state effort to manage national interests. Our analysis revealed a number of interwoven strands—the British documentary film movement, local bureaucracy, central government wartime and peacetime propaganda, decolonization, and economic theories. Tracking the interplay among these multiple elements offers a fuller historical understanding than does dividing them into apparently distinct phases of development that might imply continual progress and improvement.

TABLE 16.1

Practitioners' Views About the Qualities Required of a Successful Operator

"A lot of those people in those early days . . . were people of integrity . . . who could mix in so many areas . . . acceptable to leaders and . . . to people. . . . They were able to handle people, and in some ways that's ideal for public relations" (Interview, June 26, 1996).

"Great understanding, great forbearance, [and] a great spirit of attunement with one's fellow beings are essentials. . . . He must possess an exceptional breadth of mind. . . . A personal sensitivity . . . is infinitely more important than even the most methodical application of accepted techniques. There is no intellectual substitute for the human approach" (Hess, 1950, pp. 6-7).

"Personality [is important]. . . . You are flirting daily from one thing [or] another, so you need your wits about you" (Interview, June 28, 1998).

"One has to have lateral thinking like Edward de Bono" (Interview, August 22, 1995).

"Common sense [is important]. You need to be reasonably practical. Organization is very important. . . . You need to be able to communicate" (Interview, June 25, 1991).

"Critical ability [is important, as are] . . . [being] persuasive in writing and verbally . . ., integrity . . ., personal courage . . ., [and] a sense of humor. . . . It doesn't matter if they can write a press release" (Interview, June 25, 1991).

"[Practitioners should be] ideas men who . . . wish to change things, and that's what I mean by being creative" (Interview, July 25, 1996).

"People [who] speak up, who dress nicely, who've got something intelligent to say [can be successful]. . . . The old slap-dash approach is just not good enough. . . . Personality and good interpersonal skills [are important]" (Interview, March 13, 1997).

"Credibility [is important]. . . . People who can operate at a senior level on very sensitive topics [can be successful] . . ., so the ability to have those relationships is more important, in a way, than technical training. . . . There is a personality requirement. . . . Salesmanship is a crucial skill for the top people in consultancy. . . . In the noncommercial area, the key skill is persuasiveness" (Interview, March 17, 1997).

"More character than anything else [is important] . . ., getting along with clients . . ., being relatively intelligent, a streetwise intelligence . . . [and] a sense of humor. . . . [To be able to] come up with ideas and think at a bit of a tangent [is important]" (Interview, January 28, 1997).

NOTE

1. The term *public relations* presents a similar problem. It either appears in English, as happens in Poland, or is covered by terms such as *relations publiques* in French and *Offentlichkeitsarbeit* in German. The problem with the terminology may be seen as merely an expression of deeper cultural differences.

CHAPTER 17

How Feminist Theory Advanced the Practice of Public Relations

ELIZABETH L. TOTH

During the mid-1980s, public relations educators and researchers began reporting on the roles of women in public relations and on the increasing numbers of women entering the field of public relations. The initial roles research by Broom (1982) and Broom and Dozier (1986) not only established an indelible means of classifying public relations work as either managerial or technical but also established that women were more likely than men to perform the technician role. Public relations roles determined salary, and women made less money than men because they were disproportionately working in technician roles.

Reports on the increasing numbers of women entering public relations led to three first feminist theory publications. One was an entire special issue of the *Public Relations Review* on women that included a call for a feminist research agenda (L. Grunig, 1988) as well as the diverse voices of an African American practitioner and educator who became president of the Public Relations Society of America (PRSA) (Miller, 1988), a white male educator (Dozier, 1988a), and a white female corporate vice president (Stewart, 1988).

The other two publications represented first foundation-funded research reports on women in public relations: *The Velvet Ghetto: The Impact of the Increasing Percentage of Women in Public Relations and Business Communication* (Cline et al., 1986) and *Beyond the Velvet Ghetto* (Toth & Cline, 1989). These three publications provided benchmark information on the following four gender-related issues: threats to the status of the field, a clear pay gap, the "glass ceiling," and the "velvet ghetto" phenomenon (Toth, 1987).

In retrospect, the early research on public relations gender issues contained few theoretical perspectives, although there were some theoretical assumptions implied. For example, the research on salary surveys contained the assumptions of what we know today to be human capital theory. Human capital theory came from studies by economists who assumed that the investment in education and work experience was equally available to men and women. Human capital theorists assumed that factors such as job opportunities, job training, job tenure, and educational preparation were gender neutral. Another assumption of this theory was that the choices of individuals led to specific outcomes (Tolbert & Moen, 1998).

Human capital assumptions were evident in the annual salary surveys of the public relations field. For example, Jacobson and Tortorello (1991) reported that the gender gap had narrowed because the increase in median salary was higher for women than it was for men. The following year, Jacobson and Tortorello (1992) presented new salary survey data noting that the gender gap in pay had widened (p. 12). The subsequent year, Tortorello and Wilhelm (1993) predicted a trend toward male-female parity at lower executive levels (p. 12). These reports assumed that it was only time that stood in the way of men and women being paid equally for public relations work and that as women gained experience in public relations, they would be paid the same as men.

A special type of human capital theory, primarily the work of occupational sociologists Reskin and Roos (1990), identified factors that would stop the rational investment in education and work experience that led to salary increases. These factors included organizations having a preference for men over women in some jobs but preferring women in some cases because they were a "better buy" for the salaries or because women had preferred personality traits appropriate to the tasks. Public relations researchers sought other causes. For example, Tam, Dozier, Lauzen, and Real (1995) argued that women faced barriers in the workplace because of limited mentoring. Wright, L. Grunig, Springston, and Toth (1991) proposed that women were disadvantaged by inflexible work hours, sexual harassment, and lack of parental leave policies.

A third focus that provided useful theoretical assumptions was that organizational and societal cultures directed our beliefs about what men and women could do. For example, L. Grunig (1995), in a case study of women in the Foreign Service, posited that organizational culture, subcultures, and countercultures included specific values, language, and ways of doing things that explained how gender discrimination came about.

Today, in reviewing the research from the mid-1980s about women and public relations, there has developed over time a group of scholars providing a feminist theory paradigm for the practice of public relations. This feminist research, as with feminist research in other fields, is not monolithic or necessarily the work of researchers who agree on their feminist theory perspectives. These theorists, including Aldoory (1998a, 1998b), Creedon (1993a, 1993b), Dozier and Broom (1995), Toth and L. Grunig (1993), Hon (1995a, 1995b), and Toth, Serini, Wright, and Emig (1998), have provided feminist research that advanced our understanding of the practice of public relations. This chapter discusses their contributions to the advancement of public relations practice. It closes by suggesting that we act on what we have learned until we have provided the men and women of public relations with an occupation without bias.

FEMINIST RESEARCH IN PUBLIC RELATIONS

Although feminist public relations scholars have provided diverse voices on the meaning of gender in public relations, many have united in considering feminism to be the means to interpreting phenomena in a way that values the socially ascribed attributes and actions of women. Rakow (1989a) argued that feminism and its academic counterpart, feminist theory, are the lens through which we can see the gender issue in a different light by valuing the feminine and those characteristics traditionally relegated to women (p. 288). Toth et al. (1998) cautioned against those who would believe that women should be more like men when women's experiences needed to be given equal voice to those of men. Hon (1995b), citing Foss and Foss (1988), argued that for there to be a feminist theory of public relations, women must be treated as individuals whose perceptions, meanings, and experiences are appropriate and important data for analysis, rather than assuming that women are deficient as communicators and managers in some way (Hon, 1995b, p. 28). Dozier and Broom (1995) argued as follows regarding gender and roles: "Our presumption is that healthy humans and competent managers are highly androgynous, possessing attributes stereotypically associated with both men and women. We view with skepticism any scholarship that traffics in gender stereotypes" (p. 20).

Feminism is not just about women. It is about oppression through dominating beliefs, sometimes called the "white male model"—beliefs that favored "efficiency, rationality, individualism, and competition" (Rakow, 1989, p. 291) in ways of doing things. Foss, Foss, and Griffin (1999) expanded the term *feminism* to include respect for all voices devalued by the dominant culture "including but not limited to people of color, people with disabilities, people of different ages and socioeconomic classes, and lesbians and gay men" (p. 2). Van Zoonen (1994) defined feminism as "about gender and power" (p. 4) but with the challenge to theorize how multiple "relations of subordination, individual and collective identities such as gender and ethnicity, are being constituted" (p. 4).

How is this important to an understanding of public relations practice? Feminist theory asks us to look beyond the parsimonious observation. It asks us to consider more complicated scenarios of human behavior that include values and preferences of organizations based on gender, race, class, ethnicity, sexual orientation, disability, and the multiple meanings that we bring to these social groupings.

If we are to advance the practice of public relations, then we must have the insight to examine possible preference and bias in our own decisions. Public relations people deal in perceptions all the time from their positions as communicators. Also, they counsel managements about the diverse viewpoints of any number of constituent groups that have consequences for organizations. Feminist research gives public relations people further insights into organizational culture and its relationships with others so that they can communicate more responsibly to build relationships.

Aldoory and Toth (in press) listed six common criteria or characteristics suggested to define feminist scholarship:

1. explicit attention to inequitable power dimensions of gender relations;
2. including discussions of gender and other identities such as race and class;
3. sensitivity to participants' lives and ensuring diversity among participants;
4. critiquing and reconceptualizing androcentric methods and theory;
5. action-oriented research and findings linked to improving the status of women in their everyday lives; and
6. giving research participants roles in the research design as well as in the process.

Public relations feminist scholars have illustrated several goals for their research. Some scholars would be called "liberal" because they have called for solutions seeking only to correct the practices of discrimination and favoritism toward men currently carried out in public relations work. Others would be called "Socialist/Marxist" because they have urged changing institutional structures that have kept power in place and maintained power over those who differed in gender, race, class, sexual orientation, and disabilities. Few (e.g., Creedon, 1993a, 1993b) have provided radical public relations gender research, seeking not to transform social institutions. Many feminist scholars have been public relations practitioners and believe too passionately in the practice to find it devoid of any contribution to society. Despite these divisions in goals, feminist researchers of public relations have advanced the practice of public relations by increasing the dialogue about gender and, hopefully, dialogue about race, class, and other standpoints in the following ways.

A Women Majority in Public Relations: Threat or Contribution to Status?

Public relations feminist scholars have found that the growing number of women in public relations has opened up a professional area once considered to be a male-only occupation. However, as much as those in the field of public relations should be proud of making this opportunity available to women who do not have equal access to all professions, some public relations experts have seen only threats to the status of the field.

Women's share of the public relations workforce has continued to increase steadily since the 1970s (Dozier, L. Grunig, & J. Grunig, 1995, p. 153). During the early 1960s, women made up roughly 25% of the public relations labor force, according to U.S. Department of Labor statistics for the "public relations specialist" occupational category (p. 153). In 1982, women and men in public relations reached numerical parity (p. 153). More recent census statistics indicated that in 1997, women represented 65.7% of all U.S. public relations specialists (U.S. Department of Commerce, 1998, p. 417).

How was a female majority a threat to the field of public relations? Noted public relations practitioner Lesly (1988) wrote that the impact of a largely female field would have consequences such as creating the image of public relations as a soft, rather than a heavy-hitting, top management function; lowering professional aspirations because women wanted to do technical rather than managerial work; and lowering income levels because fields that became "female" experienced such losses. Lesly (1996) repeated his belief that women were detrimental when he cited them as a condition leading to the Balkanization of the field, noting "the unfortunate labeling of the field as a feminine one. Women are able and in some ways more skillful, but the image unfortunately has consequences" (p. 43).

Outside public relations, demographer Reskin (1989) wrote that a male-to-female resegregation involved two factors: "(1) a decline in the numbers of male workers because the occupation no longer attracts or retains men and (2) a large influx of female workers" (p. 259). Men left an occupation when the rewards of working in it were less attractive than those in other occupations. "For example, working conditions or job content may deteriorate; wages may fail to keep pace with those in other occupations requiring the same qualifications; advancement opportunities may disappear; more desirable jobs that demand similar qualifications may become available" (p. 259).

Reskin and Roos (1990) cited public relations as 1 of only 10 occupations since the 1970s to show a "disproportionate" increase in female workers. Reasons given by Donato (1990) for this gender switch were the sex-specific demand for women, women being a "better buy" than male employees, women being the new "consumer" public to whom women practitioners could communicate, public relations as a female-intensive industry appearing more receptive to women entering the labor force, affirmative action guidelines requiring that more women be hired and promoted into professional and managerial jobs, and a gender ideology of society that defined public relations as "women's work." Donato provided a framework by which to assess factors discriminating against women in public relations.

Donato's (1990) analysis did not include a feminist perspective. However, during the 1990s, three feminist studies on the increasing numbers of women in public relations did introduce feminist research in theorizing about the status issues of a female plurality.

Two of these studies, called the glass ceiling studies (published in the following articles: Serini, Toth, Wright, & Emig, 1997, 1998; Toth & L. Grunig, 1993; Toth et al., 1998; Wright et al., 1991), were conducted for the PRSA to audit its membership about gender issues. The third study was the *Excellence* study, the most comprehensive study of the 1990s of what constitutes excellence in public relations (Dozier et al., 1995; J. Grunig, 1992c).

The first glass ceiling study, published in 1991, provided a feminist theoretical framework for a quantitative study of more than 1,000 PRSA members. The authors concluded that women who worked in public relations often found themselves in a one-down position. After the 4th year, women earned less, even considering age, accreditation, and type of public relations practiced. Overall, women were less satisfied with their jobs than were men. Women perceived more gender-based inequities than did men (Wright et al., 1991, p. 32). The glass ceiling study authors (Wright et al., 1991, pp. 34-35) called on the PRSA to raise awareness that gender discrimination existed in public relations. The authors believed that educational institutions had a role in fostering women's attainment of career goals. Women were obligated to act to empower themselves. Finally, the authors believed that the solutions to gender discrimination must come from both men and women public relations practitioners.

In 1995, in a follow-up audit of PRSA members, the glass ceiling study authors found that, over time, the status of men and women had been influenced by the economic downturn of the 1990s (PRSA, 1997). Both men and women in this PRSA audit perceived less that women received lower salaries than men, compared to those in 1991. Men and women in this audit perceived less that men were promoted more quickly than women, compared to those in 1991. In the more recent PRSA audit, women perceived it as less difficult for women to reach the tops of their own organizations and throughout public relations. Both men and women perceived more significantly that it was important for public relations to permit flexible hours in the organization and that public relations be permitted to be carried out in flexible locations. Both men and women perceived the importance of parental leave. Although these differences in perception were interpreted as progress for women, they also could have been the result of men in top communicator positions having lost their jobs in the economic downturn or of a sample of PRSA membership that did not include as many top male communicators. In follow-up focus group research to the quantitative survey, Serini et al. (1997) found men to be "longing" for the past when there were perks to be had, whereas women spoke satisfactorily about increasing career opportunities.

The glass ceiling study authors (Toth et al., 1998) found, during the 5-year period between audits, that men and women were becoming more aware of institutional influences and their effect on both men and women. These authors concluded that roles in public relations were changing during economic circumstances that required practitioners—both men and women—to retool and reinvent themselves to respond and keep ahead of changes within their organizations.

The third feminist study examined how organizations achieved excellence in public relations and called for actions by practitioners to work for more diverse and equitable public relations practice. The authors of the *Excellence* study stated, "The role and status of communication in organizations is inexorably linked to the support and opportunities that organizations provide employees who are women" (Dozier et al., 1995, p. 152) because women were the future of public relations.

Dozier et al. (1995) hypothesized that organizations with excellent public relations also supported diversity in their workforces. The authors examined a wide range of policies and practices of organizations that helped hire, support, and encourage the advancement of women in public relations. They tested the hypothesis that when these items were in place, excellent public relations would be found.

The findings of the *Excellence* study, an examination of chief executive officers (CEOs), top communicators, and employees in about 300 U.S., Canadian, and British organizations, indicated that among the most excellent organizations, both CEOs and top communicators reported above average support for women. This support included three groups of items. The first group included nondiscrimination policies enacted to protect women employees such as "developing specific guidelines for handling sexual harassment problems and establishing effective policies to deal with sexual discrimination" (Dozier et al., 1995, p. 158). The second set of items provided a supportive work environment for women such as "fostering women's leadership abilities and paying men and women equally for equal or comparable work" (p. 158). The third set of items concerned mentoring and advancement programs established for women such as "enacting specific policies, procedures, or programs designed to promote an understanding of the concerns of female employees" (p. 158). These items represented some of the first action guidelines to be made available to organizations desiring to practice excellent public relations.

THE GENDER SALARY GAP

Public relations gender scholars have kept on the agenda the continuing salary gap between public relations women and men. Although they have not found the causes or solutions to this salary disparity, they have argued against the human capitalist assumptions that time is all that is needed for women's pay to catch up with men's (Toth, 1996).

Women in public relations have continued to make less money, on average, than men in the field. Why this is so has been the subject of many articles, conference presentations, and unpleasant debates. Reasons offered have included women having less experience and tending to be younger than men in the field, women clustering in the lower paying organizations, and women working in lower paying roles. Some researchers have argued that the salary statistics are wrong. Others have argued that the gap is narrowing.

The PRSA provided salary survey data of its membership based on representative samples between 1990 and 1993 (Jacobson & Tortorello, 1990, 1991, 1992; Tortorello & Wilhelm, 1993). All of these surveys reported that there was a gender gap in public relations salaries.

The most recent PRSA survey, based on representative samples of members and nonmembers, continued to report "disparities between the salaries of men and women. These exist across, age, experience, and job title. On average, men's salaries are 45% higher than women's ($59,460 vs. $41,110)" (PRSA, 1996b, p. 4).

Among the earlier feminist salary studies was a report by Toth and Cline (1991) that depicted the attitudes of 443 randomly selected public relations practitioners from two professional organizations: the International Association of Business Communicators and the PRSA. Their study found a salary disparity in public relations based on gender. Women faced special problems when attempting to advance into managerial positions. Women reported sexual bias. Also, respondents perceived differences in women's managerial motivation, willingness to sacrifice work over family demands, and ability to command top salary (p. 161). Although women perceived these career inequities, especially salaries, they still were choosing to work in public relations. Women seemed to have found options for life choices such as work, marriage, and family.

In 1991, feminist scholars Dozier and Broom (1995) repeated their longitudinal research on salary, roles, and gender. However, they were able to report on only 207 PRSA members, down from an original 1982 sample of 815 practitioners. They reported that roles still predicted salaries, with the managerial role being valued more than the technical role. However, they concluded that, based on their survey, "the relation between gender and salary is not statistically significant after controlling for the influences of professional experience, manager role enactment, and decision-making participation" (p. 17). This was a significant break in the previous research of these and other authors who had found a direct relationship between salary and gender. Dozier and Broom concluded that "the feminist movement in American society accounts for some of that change" (p. 17). They added, "We also believe that female practitioners who have struggled to break through the managerial 'glass ceiling' are seeing some of the fruits of their labor" (p. 19).

THE GLASS CEILING

The glass ceiling, according to Hymowitz and Schellhardt (1986), refers to an invisible barrier that blocks women from obtaining top jobs in corporations. Essentially, Hymowitz and Schellhardt made the argument that "brains and competence" as a means of achieving promotion worked only to a certain point. Then, CEOs promoted those with whom they felt comfortable working, people who have passed "invisible" tests such as getting along in the business world, having an "appropriate" temperament, having an acceptable "commitment," and having an acceptable "management style." The result of these invisible tests was the creation of an invisible glass ceiling on upper management jobs and, ultimately, "a caste system in corporate America of men at the top and women lower down" (p. D1).

The glass ceiling discussion in public relations came from the research done on public relations roles. Since 1979, researchers have chronicled what public relations people do, based primarily on a 1979 set of role categories that asked public relations practitioners to report on how frequently they perform specific activities (Broom & Smith, 1979).

In an initial quantitative study of 458 members of the PRSA who responded to 28 role items, Broom (1982) concluded that there were four roles: a communication technician role and a management role that included a combination of expert prescriber, communication facilitator, and problem-solving process facilitator (p. 18).

Broom (1982) found that men and women differed significantly on which roles they saw themselves performing: "About half of the women see themselves operating primarily in the communication technician role, while more than half of the men report the expert prescriber role as their dominant role" (p. 21). Broom reported that this difference could not be accounted for by differences in age or experience. Instead, he speculated a gender difference:

> It appears that even though both men and women are hired initially for their communication and journalistic skills, women tend to stay in the communication technician role to a greater extent than their male counterparts. Four out of five men in PRSA have expanded their roles to [those] of public relations experts and facilitators of communication and problem solving. On the other hand, only half of the women participate in these management-level public relations counseling and problem-solving functions as part of their primary roles. (p. 21)

Broom's (1982) study prompted a series of other studies that were reviewed by Dozier (1992). Most influential of the research that fo-

cused on the four-role typology was a longitudinal study by Broom and Dozier (1986). Broom and Dozier prefaced their conclusions by stating that "a practitioner plays all four roles in varying degrees" (p. 39). However, they chose to report on the dominant role of each respondent, the one role-played with greater frequency than any of the other roles. Based on this choice, Broom and Dozier reported that in the same group of PRSA members surveyed earlier, there was a continuing pattern of women still engaging in the technical activities with greater frequency than men (p. 49).

Dozier (1992) argued for a reduction of the four roles into two major roles, the "manager-technician" typology, based on a series of studies finding that these two roles were empirically and conceptually distinct, whereas the expert prescriber, communication liaison, and problem-solving process facilitator roles were not. He urged the use of the manager-technician typology because it provided "a parsimonious way to operationalize roles and test relations with antecedent and consequential constructs" (p. 334).

Although this argument for empirical parsimony helped to link public relations roles to excellent public relations practices, it disadvantaged thinking about the complexity of public relations practices and about how we viewed women and public relations. Ultimately, the Broom and Dozier studies established a worldview of a two-tier career ladder in public relations when public relations practitioners changed from technicians to managers. Their research contributed greatly to our discussion of gender and the glass ceiling because they concluded that "changing from the technician role to the predominantly managerial role is a transition biased in favor of male practitioners" (Broom & Dozier, 1986, p. 55).

Two feminist studies have countered the two-role perspective. The first, by Creedon (1991), argued that because the technical role had been linked to women, there was developing in the literature a devaluation of the technician role. She argued that the two-role mind-set reduced much more complex roles because of the search for statistical significance. She cited ample evidence of "technicians processing information but also managing the process" (p. 78).

Evidence of a much more complex description of roles also came from the first glass ceiling study (Wright et al., 1991). This might have been due, in part, to a different set of role categories from that used in the Broom and Dozier studies. Wright et al.'s analysis of a different set of 17 role activities, among 1,027 PRSA members, confirmed the existence of the same two dimensions—those of the manager and the technician—and that they were not mutually exclusive (p. 20). Wright et al. reported that gender predicted differences in roles on only 8 of the 17 role measures:

> Findings indicate that women are more likely than men to plan public relations programs; write, edit, and produce public relations messages; implement new programs; and carry out decisions made by others. Men are significantly more likely than women to be involved in counseling management and somewhat more likely to make communication policy decisions and to conduct and analyze research. (p. 24)

Wright et al. concluded, "Gender appears to be less significant in influencing a practitioner's occupational role. The number of years working in the field and whether or not a practitioner holds PRSA accreditation are more strongly associated with role than [is] gender" (p. 25).

In a follow-up study using the Wright et al. (1991) data set, Toth and L. Grunig (1993) argued that the exclusion of women from promotion was not simply based on gender but rather was based on differences in how women and men experience on-the-job public relations. Toth and L. Grunig reported that while women managers in public relations were performing management tasks, they still were performing technical tasks as well—in a sense, "doing it all" (p. 168).

Toth and L. Grunig (1993) based their conclusion on a factor analysis of Wright et al.'s (1991) 17 role activities but did not stop examining the dimensions at the higher factor loadings, as did the Dozier and Broom (1995) and Wright et al. (1991) studies. Because women in this study were doing significantly more activities under the managerial dimension, Toth and L. Grunig (1993) suggested that perhaps organizations were diminishing the importance that they placed on women performing managerial work by adding on to women's work the technical activities as well.

Alternatively, women might have been choosing to keep doing their entry-level tasks even when permitted to advance into managerial tasks because they lacked the confidence to leave these duties behind. In a sense, this was the "impostor syndrome" discussed in Wright et al. (1991). Women did not perceive themselves as fitting into the managerial role because it was defined by and for men. Women who became managers countered the stress of being outsiders by continuing to do the technical tasks that they felt more psychologically secure in doing.

In 1995, the glass ceiling study authors repeated their roles study of PRSA members (Toth et al., 1998). They found that the role profiles of men and women had changed, although women still seemed to be doing more activities than men and for less money. In 1995, there appeared to be three role profiles—managers, technicians, and agency profiles—instead of two. The manager role for men and women was reduced to midlevel public relations tasks such as planning and managing programs. The technician role for men and women was confined to disseminating messages and writing, editing, and producing messages. Little remained for men in providing a training ground to advance into management jobs. The agency role took away senior-level activities from the managers. The agency role was much more evident for men than for women. It included the activities of counseling; conducting research; making programming decisions; communicating with clients, peers, and subordinates; and handling correspondence and phone calls.

From the glass ceiling studies, the role concept appeared to be less stable than previous research had established. Roles for the sample of PRSA members had changed dramatically. Women's experiences on the job were not the same as men's. There was not a simple glass ceiling scenario.

THE VELVET GHETTO PHENOMENON

Public relations feminist theorists have examined women's potential for public relations—their willingness to work collaboratively with publics, their ethical decision making (Hon, L. Grunig, & Dozier, 1992), and their leadership style (Aldoory, 1998a). This research has sought to add to the work that found women disadvantaged by organizations and used to achieve affirmative action goals such as was found in the velvet ghetto research.

The velvet ghetto studies were named after a *Business Week* article speculating that communication at least was a safe place, a "velvet ghetto," where women managers could be counted as such but would not threaten men for competition for top management jobs. *Business Week* reported on this tactic early on: "When is affirmative action not so affirmative? When companies load their public relations departments with women to compensate for their scarcity in other professional or managerial capacities that usually lead more directly to top management" ("PR: 'The Velvet Ghetto,'" 1978, p. 122).

Independently of the Velvet Ghetto study authors who used the *Business Week* term, sociologist Ghiloni (1984) conducted a case study of women in corporate public relations. She used the term "velvet ghetto" in her description of women stereotyped as second class partly by their freedom to choose their dress style. Women managers who could choose whether to dress more informally or follow the dress restrictions of a business suit communicated that they had less power in the organization.

Creedon (1993a) examined the velvet ghetto phenomenon by challenging systems theory as the paradigm for describing the public relations function of organizations. She posited that systems theory did not address gender, race, class, and heterosexism. She proposed that there was an organizational infrasystem of values and norms that preserved a system of male privilege. Her solution was to look at dissymmetry as symmetry in different directions so that "we may be able to build a flexible, encompassing paradigm for the field in which the goal of achieving mutual understanding can truly mean valuing diversity" (p. 164).

Hon's (1995a, 1995b) interviews with women in public relations revealed patterns of discrimination and second-class citizenship. Women reported that they earned less than subordinates and that their work had a marginalized status in general. "One media relations director said that practitioners are 'perceived as stupid'" (Hon, 1995a, p. 22-23). Although the women interviewed felt that men experienced the same stigma, they suspected that having a preponderance of women in public relations compounded the devaluation (p. 23).

Aldoory (1998a) advanced feminist research on the velvet ghetto phenomenon by looking at women who had become leaders in their public relations organizations and associations. Aldoory made available women's experiences and strategies in gaining their professional achievements. Her women leaders defined leadership as "vision and seeking to understand staff's personal lives" (p. 96). Their leadership language was interactive and emphasized a humanist approach. Her findings contributed to a feminist leadership model that could assist other women entering leadership positions and looking for guidance.

HOW WE CAN ACT ON WHAT WE HAVE LEARNED FROM FEMINIST RESEARCH

The feminist researchers who have developed our perspectives on women and public relations have made us look at the practice of public relations in a much different way from how we did in the past. They have confronted the increasing numbers of women entering the field by delivering more clearly how organizations make choices based not on merit but rather on gender.

Feminist research has contributed further action steps that will assist public relations people who want the best for their profession and who want to work in organizational environments that encourage excellent public relations. Among these steps are Hon's (1995a) suggestions that we in public relations must raise levels of awareness about sexism, must rethink the masculine ethic in organizations, and must address the marginalization of the function and devise specific strategies for overcoming the problem. Aldoory (in press) suggested that, for the practice of public relations, we must make requisite variety a reality. We might be able to influence hiring practices within our organizations or with the use of consultants and freelancers. We need to be aware of subtle discriminatory practices in organizations and find ways in which to address them. We must force ourselves to make checklists for all research projects; for example, we must determine whether race, class, sexuality, and gender of research participants were considered in all phases of the design (Aldoory, in press). When developing campaign messages, we must ask ourselves what audiences actually do in their lives, what they consider important, and how they view the world (Aldoory, in press). We cannot assume that our professional standpoints, whether in the practice of public relations, in educational institutions, or in research, make us knowledgeable. We have to constantly test our assumptions and question ourselves.

All public relations people have been touched by the gender transition of the field. Public relations people have been the early warning system for social changes that could affect their organizations and have been among the first to advise managers about policy decisions that affect society. They are in a position to create strategies to engage these social changes so that their organizations contribute rather than hinder the social dialogue. I hope that this chapter of the handbook will encourage them to do so.

CHAPTER 18

Public Relations Law

MICHAEL G. PARKINSON

DARADIREK EKACHAI

LAUREL TRAYNOWICZ HETHERINGTON

■ We live in a litigious society where all of us, including public relations practitioners, must be concerned with protecting our own work and avoiding any conduct that would result in legal action against us. Unfortunately, the trend toward frequent legal action in our culture forces all practitioners involved in public communication to know the laws that affect their profession. Knowledge of laws applicable to public relations should guide our conduct and help us to know when we should seek professional legal advice.

Despite the public nature of their profession and the increasing imposition of legal restrictions on all of those in public communication, public relations practitioners describe themselves as having little familiarity with the laws that are relevant to their profession. More than 80% of practitioners have attorneys review less than 25% of their work (Fitzpatrick, 1996a). Our experience would suggest that practitioners know even less about law than they think they know. The purpose of this chapter is to provide a brief introduction to those legal principles that affect the practice of public relations in the

United States. Because of the chapter's brevity, it introduces only general principles that can be used to guide a practitioner or student of public relations. Such a brief and general approach necessitates some imprecision and requires the omission of many rules and principles. Because this chapter might be used by those seeking answers to specific public relations practice questions, we consider it essential to begin by explaining what is *not* covered here and to make absolutely clear that even careful use of this single chapter cannot substitute for legal advice tailored to the practitioner's specific situation and based on the laws of the jurisdiction in which the practitioner works.

The major task in preparing this treatise was not finding information but rather deciding what information to include and what to exclude. In a single chapter, it is simply not possible to cover all the laws, regulations, codes, agreements, and professional standards that affect or limit the practice of public relations.

The chapter focuses exclusively on law. This means that many limitations on the conduct of public relations practitioners are not included. For example, we have opted not to address codes of ethics, professional standards prohibiting plagiarism, and phone company tariffs, all of which may either prohibit or restrict some of the conduct of public relations practitioners.

We also should emphasize that the United States has a federal government. This means that the U.S. courts are courts of limited jurisdiction. In many situations, state law prevails over federal law. Therefore, many of the principles presented here must be interpreted differently in various states. We do not attempt any state-by-state description of differences in the law. Rather, we present here general principles of law based on either federal law or laws that are applicable in most states.

Similarly, we do not make any attempt to address legal principles beyond Anglo-American law. Those practicing outside the United States or with clients or colleagues from other legal systems should be warned that countries differ significantly in their treatment of intellectual property and contract obligations. We hope that it also is apparent that all the principles of free speech arising from the First Amendment to the U.S. Constitution cannot be assumed to apply outside the United States.

It also should be noted that laws change. Legislatures and judges are free to create statutes or render decisions in response to new technology or changing public opinion. These changes present particular problems, especially when applying laws to Internet use. We have selected principles that have remained stable over time and that, we believe, will remain constant for the foreseeable future. However, none of us owns a "crystal ball," and the best assurance we can offer is that the principles presented here are accurate at the time of this writing.

This chapter focuses on four areas of law: the free speech and press rights arising from the First Amendment to the U.S. Constitution, limitations on free speech such as privacy and defamation, intellectual property law, and contract law. These four areas were selected for two reasons. First, these areas include the legal principles that most often affect the practice of public relations. Second, in a discussion of these four areas, it is possible to address nearly all the legal misconceptions and questions that have been presented to us by clients, colleagues, and students in public relations. Following the discussion of each of these four areas, we include a description of some current application to Internet use. These Internet applications are provided both to show the current state of law and to demonstrate how laws can and must change.

THE FIRST AMENDMENT AND PUBLIC RELATIONS

Public relations is one of those rare professions whose members can argue that they are essential to the function of their society and that the practice of their profession is constitutionally guaranteed. In the First Amendment, the authors of the U.S. Constitution clearly indicated that the free flow of ideas must be guaranteed:

> Congress shall make no law respecting an establishment of religion, or prohibiting the free exercise thereof; or abridging the freedom of speech, or of the press; or the right of the people peaceably to assemble, and to petition the government for a redress of grievances.

Our courts have recognized the "inherent value of free discourse" (*Dennis v. United States,* 1951) and even have argued that it is "essential to the security of the republic" (*Stromberg v. California,* 1931). Furthermore, the courts frequently have struck down laws that restricted the distribution of information in the traditional media of public relations. For example, *Lovell v. Griffin* (1938) struck down an ordinance requiring a permit to distribute literature, and *Talley v. California* (1960) voided a Los Angeles ordinance banning distribution of anonymous pamphlets or brochures. Of particular application to the practice of public relations, the courts have ruled that the right to be free from governmental restrictions on free speech extends to both individuals and corporations (*First National Bank of Boston v. Bellotti,* 1978).

When Free Speech Rights Do Not Apply

Even the constitutional protection does not guarantee the public relations practitioner the right to deliver any message in any medium. The First Amendment requires only that Congress make no law abridging free speech. Although the Fourteenth Amendment extends this requirement to the states and their subdivisions, it still is applicable only to governmental entities. There simply is no requirement that the private owner of a meeting hall, employee lunch room, or printing plant guarantee access to all. The First Amendment requires only that the governments of the United States and each of its individual states not create laws, ordinances, or practices that restrict free speech. It should be noted, for those of us who teach at state-supported universities, that these institutions are, as government entities, covered by the First Amendment.

Furthermore, it should be noted that the freedom of press guaranteed in the First Amendment is not a guarantee of special treatment. A reporter has only those communication rights that are held by every other citizen. The First Amendment prohibits any rule imposing special restrictions on the press, but under the Constitution a free press has no greater right to information or to communicate its messages than does every U.S. citizen (*Schaefer v. United States,* 1920).

Although the Constitution appears to provide an absolute guarantee of free speech, nearly every society, including our own, restricts free expression in some areas. These restrictions exist to meet other governmental obligations. Libel and slander laws protect individuals or groups against defamation, copyright laws protect authors and publishers, and statutes protect the community standard of decency and protect the state against treasonable and seditious expressions (Rivers & Work, 1986, p. 332).

The U.S. Supreme Court has recognized that governments have obligations that outweigh the interest in free speech and free press rights. Most notable among these is the recognition that governments have traditional police powers to protect the public's health and safety. Under these police powers, governments can restrict the time, place, or manner of communication. For example, *City of Los Angeles v. Preferred Communications Inc.* (1986) restricted access to cable television, *U.S. Postal Service v. Council of Greenburgh Civic Associations* (1981) upheld a prohibition against placing unstamped material in postal boxes, *Grayned v. City of Rockford* (1972) upheld an ordinance forbidding noisy demonstrations near schools, and *Adderly v. Florida* (1966) upheld the trespass conviction of demonstrators on a jail driveway. Each of these cases recognized that the government has some obligation that is incompatible with totally free speech. For example, the government does have obligations to regulate noise, secure funding for the postal service, and prevent jail escapes. However, it also should be noted that in each of these cases the imposition on free communication that was upheld carefully restricted only the time when a message could be delivered, the place where it could be delivered, or the manner in which it could be delivered. The courts did not impose any restriction on the content of the message itself.

The major exceptions to this prohibition against government restrictions based on message content arise from the government's obligations to protect public morality and to protect against fraud. These obligations manifest themselves in the government rules against obscenity and false advertising. In *Allen B. Dumont Laboratories Inc. v. Carroll* (1949), a Pennsylvania decision restricting obscenity on television was upheld by the U.S. Supreme Court. The Supreme Court, in *Winters v. New York* (1948), upheld regulations of specific words found to be lewd, indecent, obscene, or profane. And the Supreme Court, in *Donaldson v. Read Magazine Inc.* (1948), ruled that there is no freedom of press protection to raise money by deception of the public.

The need for limiting fraud and the related obligation of the federal government to regulate interstate commerce (as stated in Section 8 in Article I of the U.S. Constitution) has led the Supreme Court to create some specific rules allowing restrictions on the content of commercial speech. Although these rules usually do not apply to press releases, they almost always apply to advertising and direct mail pieces. For commercial speech to receive First Amendment protection at all, it must concern only a lawful activity and must not be misleading. Furthermore, any government restriction on it must advance a significant government interest, and the restriction must not be any broader than necessary to meet that interest (*Central Hudson Gas & Electric Corp. v. Public Service Commission of New York,* 1980). Clarifying the rule for false advertising or deceptive releases, misleading commercial speech simply receives no First Amendment protection at all.

Other significant limitations on free speech include prohibitions against defamation and rules protecting intellectual property. These laws are so extensive that they are addressed individually in the next main section on limitations on free speech.

Some Current Internet Applications

In 1996, the U.S. Congress passed the Communications Decency Act (CDA). The CDA was challenged almost immediately and was struck down as unconstitutionally vague and too broad (*ACLU v. Reno,* 1996). Although some argued that the CDA was simply the product of election year politics (Lessig, 1998), the passage of such a law was evidence of a concern by both the public and the legislature for unique problems presented by cyberspace. A reasonable user of the Internet would predict that new, more carefully tailored, and well-defended limitations on free speech will appear in the near future (D. Burke, 1996).

Traditional or existing rules require very narrow applicability for any limitation on free speech. Addressing the objective of the CDA specifically, this means that under current law one may not ban indecent material altogether to protect children from obscenity (*Butler v. Michigan,* 1957). However, the ubiquitous nature of personal computers and access to the Internet means that it is almost impossible for a legislator or "cybercop" to know who is receiving or may receive materials placed on the Internet. Put an-

other way, the traditional time, place, and manner restrictions used to meet the government's obligation to protect free speech and simultaneously protect the public's health, safety, and morality just do not work in cyberspace.

Every public relations practitioner placing information on the Internet should be aware that anyone, even a computer-literate child, can access that information. To protect oneself from penalties imposed by existing obscenity or fraud laws, particularly from those that we can anticipate in the future, the cautious practitioner will write and illustrate his or her Internet material for all including even those not in the target public.

LIMITATIONS ON FREE SPEECH AND FREE PRESS

Previously, we described some activities not protected by the constitutional prohibition against government restrictions on free speech. In addition, free speech rights can be limited by other specific laws that prohibit some communications. Principal among these limitations are the prohibitions against defamation and the laws protecting privacy.

Defamation

Anglo-American common law protected citizens from damage to their reputations through laws prohibiting libel and slander, and this protection is beyond First Amendment protection (*Beauharnais v. Illinois,* 1952; *Chaplinsky v. New Hampshire,* 1942). Traditionally, libel laws prohibited the publication of false statements, and slander prohibited oral false statements. This distinction arose primarily because of the greater damage that would be done by a written statement that could be read by a larger number of people than could hear an oral statement. Although there still are some differences between libel and slander, contemporary technology for audio and video recording and reproduction makes the distinction largely irrelevant. In addition, many jurisdictions have consolidated the laws of libel and slander into a single offense called defamation. Therefore, here we address, as a common rule, the prohibition against defamation. Also, defamation can be either civil or criminal, but here we focus on the civil offense because criminal defamation varies with jurisdiction and rarely is applied to the practice of public relations (Walsh, 1988, p. 77).

Although there are several definitions of defamation, all include the following common elements:

1. communication to a third person;
2. identification of the plaintiff;
3. a statement that holds the plaintiff up to hatred, contempt, or ridicule; and
4. the absence of truth. (*Gertz v. Robert Welch Inc.*, 1974)

We address each of these four elements separately.

Communication to a third person is essential for defamation. In other words, the courts recognize that a person's reputation cannot be damaged by statements made directly to him or her. For those who practice public relations, this element is essentially irrelevant because most of our communications are directed to groups and, therefore, almost always address more than just the person who might be defamed.

Identification of the plaintiff is required for an action in defamation. This requirement usually affects statements about either large groups or vague references. For an individual to successfully prosecute an action in defamation, the individual must show that he or she was specifically the target of the statement. As a general rule, members of large groups cannot sue for statements made about their groups (*Neiman-Marcus Co. v. Lait,* 1952). However, it is not necessary to use the individual's name in the defamatory statement. All that is required is that those who read or hear the statement could reasonably identify the individual (*Petsch v. St. Paul Dispatch Printing Co.,* 1989).

A statement that holds the plaintiff up to hatred, contempt, or ridicule is required. Such statements can cover a wide variety of topics or allegations, and there is no simple rule for what does and does not constitute a defamatory statement (*Newell v. Field Enterprises Inc.,* 1980); rather, when examining this element, the courts look to the context within which the statement was made and how reasonable members of the public or audience will react. Specific topics of criticism that have been found to be defamatory include the imputation of a crime or immorality (*Christopher v. American News Co.,* 1949), accusations of dishonesty or fraud (*Pullman Standard Car Mfg. Co. v. Local Union No. 2928 of United Steelworkers of America,* 1946), accusations of indebtedness or delinquency in paying debts (*Oberman v. Dun & Bradstreet Inc.,* 1972), and accusations that damage an individual's professional reputation (*Dorin v. Equitable Life Assurance Company of United States,* 1967).

The absence of truth is required—or, more accurately, truth is a defense in defamation. In other words, no matter how painful or damaging a statement, if the statement is true, then it is not defamation. Furthermore, it is not even necessary to show that the entire statement being challenged is true; it is only necessary to show that the part of the statement that imputes the individual is true (*Cantrell v. American Broadcasting Companies Inc.,* 1981).

The public relations practitioner should note that intent is not an element of defamation. To be liable for defamation of a private person, one does not have to intend any insult or harm, nor does one have to have intended his or her message to describe the individual harmed; one needs only to have been negligent (*Corringan v. Bobbs-Merrill Co.,* 1920). This rule is very different in the case of public figures. For a public figure to recover for defamation, the individual must show that the communication about him or her was made with malice. For this purpose, malice has been defined as actual knowledge that the statement is false or a reckless disregard for whether it is false or not (*New York Times Co. v. Sullivan,* 1964). The practitioner also should know that corporations or businesses, as well as individuals, can be defamed (*Bruno & Stillman v. Globe Newspaper Co.,* 1980).

There are other defenses against defamation that include fair comment and privilege. Fair comment generally refers to the publication or repetition of statements that are, in themselves, newsworthy. Privilege applies primarily to the actions of the courts and governmental agencies.

Privacy

Defamation is a long-standing protection against the harm to reputations that can arise from false statements. Privacy rights have been created much more recently by common law and some statutes. The right of privacy protects citizens from harm caused by the public dissemination of truthful but private information about them.

The invasion of privacy has been divided into four separate torts or legal actions: intrusion, disclosure, false light, and appropriation (McCarthy, 1998, sec. 1-18; Prosser, 1960). Statutes in most states add a fifth related right, often called the right to publicity, which protects every citizen's right to control the commercial use of his or her identity (McCarthy, 1998, sec. 1-2).

Intrusion regulates the techniques used to secure information. It specifically prohibits physical invasion of a citizen's solitude or private affairs. Publication is not an element of intrusion. In other words, simple acquisition of information by invasion is prohibited, regardless of what is done with that information (McCarthy, 1998, sec. 5-10).

Disclosure or, more accurately, public disclosure of private facts occurs when facts concerning the private life of a plaintiff are disclosed to a large number of persons when that disclosure would be highly offensive to a reasonable person and the facts are not of legitimate concern to the public (McCarthy, 1998, sec. 5-9(c)). For the public relations practitioner, it is particularly helpful to note that photos taken in public places and facts already made public by the plaintiff (*Sipple v. Chronicle Publishing Co.*, 1984) or facts from public records (*Pemberton v. Bethlehem Steel Corp.*, 1986) are not seen as private information. Therefore, publishing those facts cannot

be prosecuted as invasion of privacy. Also, the publication of photos taken in public places has been ruled not to invade a right of privacy (*McNamara v. Freedom Newspapers Inc.*, 1991).

False light invasion of privacy, unlike defamation, requires that the information be "widely publicized" (*Douglass v. Hustler Magazine,* 1985). Furthermore, the information must be either untrue or presented in a way in which a false impression is created (*Larsen v. Philadelphia Newspapers,* 1988). Like defamation, this privacy offense also requires that the plaintiff be sufficiently identified in the published material. The material must place the plaintiff in a false light that would be offensive to a reasonable person (*Godbehere v. Phoenix Newspapers Inc.*, 1989).

The appropriation form of invasion of privacy requires only two elements. First, the defendant must use some aspect of the plaintiff's identity in a way in which the plaintiff is identifiable. Second, the use of the plaintiff's identity must cause mental or physical distress to the plaintiff (McCarthy, 1998, sec. 5-8(b)).

The most significant difference between the appropriation form of invasion of privacy and the right of publicity is that the appropriation form of invasion of privacy focuses on the injury to the mental state or health of the plaintiff, whereas the right of publicity focuses on financial damages done to the plaintiff by the misappropriation of his or her identity or likeness (McCarthy, 1998, sec. 5-8(c)). For those who practice public relations, this simply means that the right of publicity belongs to those whose celebrity gives their names, images, or identities financial value but that noncelebrities also are protected if the use of their images, names, or likenesses causes them significant distress.

A Current Internet Application

A comparison of two apparently contradictory rulings suggests that a public relations practitioner encouraging his or her clients' use of the Internet might be subjected to serious defamation liability. *Cubby Inc. v. CompuServe Inc.*

(1991) was the first federally reported case involving an action for defamation against a commercial on-line service ("Defamation in Cyberspace," 1996). That case ended in summary judgment for the defendant, CompuServe. Shortly after *Cubby*, another action, *Stratton Oakmont Inc. v. Prodigy Services Co.* (1995), involving nearly identical facts produced a summary judgment for the plaintiff. Simply put, in 1991 a federal court in *Cubby* ruled that CompuServe could not be held liable for defamatory statements that its users posted on-line, whereas in 1995 another federal court ruled that Prodigy could be held liable in practically the same situation.

It is not the similarity between *Cubby* and *Stratton Oakmont*, but rather the very subtle differences, that should concern public relations practitioners. In the *Cubby* decision, the court noted that CompuServe, like a book publisher or a common carrier, had not made an effort to edit or monitor what was in its chat rooms or special interest forums. Therefore, CompuServe was not held responsible for what appeared in its database. On the other hand, the court in *Stratton Oakmont* noted that Prodigy had held itself out as a family-oriented network that exercised a level of editorial control over the content of its bulletin boards ("Defamation in Cyberspace," 1996, p. 1077).

For those of us in public relations, this means that the more we attempt to control, edit, or manage the contents of our employee chat rooms, bulletin boards, or other Internet postings, the more likely we are to be liable for anything placed in the database, even by an anonymous user.

INTELLECTUAL PROPERTY

The U.S. Constitution, in Section 8 of Article I, "promote[s] the progress of science and useful arts by securing, for limited times to authors and inventors, the exclusive right to their respective writings and discoveries." It is this provision of the Constitution that is the source of all patent, trademark, and copyright laws in the United States (Copyrights, 1996).

Patents rarely are a concern of those of us in public relations, but it is worth noting one requirement for a patent because it helps to explain a copyright requirement. Patents protect processes or methods of construction rather than the objects constructed. Copyrights, on the other hand, protect only intellectual property that has been reduced to a tangible form (Copyrights, 1996, sec. 102(b)). In other words, neither one's ideas nor those of a client for a press release or campaign can be copyrighted, but the written notes, photographs, printed verbiage, and/or recordings can (sec. 102(a)).

The other elements required for material to be copyrighted are notice and registration. Notice simply means that when the material is first published the author or copyright holder notified those who saw the work of the copyright holder's name and the fact that a copyright was claimed. Such notice must be placed or delivered in a way that is so obvious that it would be seen or heard by a reasonable observer (Copyrights, 1996, sec. 401(b)). Of course, abbreviations such as the letter "c" in a circle (©) or "Copr." to indicate a claim of copyright and well-known abbreviations for the author or copyright owner's name may be used (sec. 401(b)). For the public relations practitioner who realizes after mailing that he or she failed to attach notice, it might be helpful to note that the copyright holder may provide notice for up to 5 years after the original delivery (sec. 405(b)). However, the material published without notice can be used by any recipient until he or she receives the supplementary notice (sec. 405(a)).

We mention the last requirement, registration, primarily because we have heard innumerable arguments among colleagues about the advisability of registering copyrights. Although registration is not a requirement to claim a copyright and its protections, any prosecution for copyright infringement requires that the copyright be registered (Copyrights, 1996, secs. 407, 411). Registration simply means filing two copies of the material for which protection is sought along with a small registration fee and an application with the copyright office at the Library of Congress.

Even if the author takes all of these precautions, it still is possible for another to use or even reproduce small numbers of copies for what is called fair use. There is no concrete definition of fair use that would guide the public relations practitioner. However, general use of small parts of a copyrighted piece or single copies for criticism, news reporting, or education is permissible when that use has no impact on the market for the original material (Copyrights, 1996, sec. 107).

Copyrights are not immortal. Even carefully copyrighted material falls into the public domain and can be used without permission after a specified period of time. Generally, this time is the life of the author plus 50 years. For material copyrighted by corporations or organizations, the term generally is 75 years from first publication or 100 years from creation, whichever comes first (Copyrights, 1996, secs. 302(a), 302(c)). For materials created after January 1, 1998, these time limits have been extended by 20 years. For example, for a document written by an individual author after January 1, 1998, the copyright can be enforced for the life of the author plus 70 years. Particularly for those practitioners producing specific works for clients or firms, it also is important to note that an author might not be in a position to claim a copyright. The copyright of work performed by an employee within the scope of his or her employment typically belongs to the employer; the employer is, for the purposes of copyright law, presumed to be the author (secs. 101, 201(b)).

Trademarks should be mentioned here because their creation and use often fall within the purview of public relations practitioners. Trademarks are symbols that are associated in the public's mind with organizations, products, or services. They belong not to their authors but rather to the organizations with which they are associated, and trademark rights can survive forever so long as their association with the organizations remains in the public's mind (*Radio Shack Corp. v. Radio Shack,* 1950).

A Current Internet Application

Although there are several instances of existing litigation over Internet copyright infringements, most of these deal with material about the Internet rather than material taken from on-line sources (e.g., Wilke, 1998). Several legal scholars have argued that copyright law simply does not work for material taken from the Internet (e.g., Counts & Martin, 1996; Schlachter, 1997). Schlachter (1997) specifically identified several problems that make enforcing copyright laws on the Internet almost impossible. The problems he identified included economic problems, technological issues, and sociological phenomena.

Economic judgments against those prosecuted for making illegal copies off the Internet generally are limited to the financial injuries or lost profits of the copyright holders. Schlachter (1997) argued that the additional or marginal cost of each copy is very low and that there is little, if any, marginal profit associated with each use. The low profit and low cost leave copyright holders with no motivation to pursue prosecution. These low profits and costs also are reflected in common practices among those who legally place information on and retrieve material from the Internet. Many information systems offer copyrighted or copyrightable materials to Internet users in hopes that the "gifts" will lead to purchases of materials or services, and others offer the option to try software or information services before purchase decisions (p. 26).

These economic realities, along with simple ignorance on the part of many Internet users, frustrate attempts to enforce copyrights on the Internet. The ease of access to personal information and the opportunity to exchange information facilitate the formation of "communities" with mutual interests and a motivation to cooperate with one another. Internet users also are conditioned to expect "freebies" (Schlachter, 1997, pp. 29, 37). In short, many Internet users believe that they are doing friends a favor when they forward or download copyrighted materials for those in their Internet communities.

This belief in the propriety of exchange among friends is complicated by the collective legal ignorance of most Internet users. Specific to the type of information that a public relations practitioner is likely to place on the Web, Betts (1995) reported on a survey of information systems professionals indicating that 72% believed that they should be able to download on-line news articles and share them as they desired.

Technology such as copy protection, date bombs, and encryption exist to prevent or frustrate illicit reproduction of copyrighted material, but even the existence of these options seems to encourage infringement. Many Internet users seem to believe that the failure to impose effective technological barriers grants all comers a license to use otherwise copyrighted materials.

Economic realities that make copyright enforcement through traditional litigation unrealistically expensive, a technology that makes quality reproductions and anonymous infringement possible, and communities of Internet users that impose no social sanctions on copyright violators combine to create an environment in which traditional copyrights, for all practical purposes, are severely limited.

This reality has led some legal scholars to suggest that the elimination of copyright infringement on the Internet is neither possible nor desirable (Counts & Martin, 1996, pp. 1132-1133; Schlachter, 1997, p. 50). Regardless of one's opinion about the propriety of these positions, it is apparent that the practitioner who wants to protect against unauthorized use of materials placed on the Internet must consider options beyond traditional copyright litigation such as encryption and other technological protection.

CONTRACTS AND PUBLIC RELATIONS

Contract law usually is ignored in explanations of law and public relations. However, it appears to us that the creation of an enforceable contract might be the most important legal skill for a public relations practitioner. The releases that can exempt the practitioner from lawsuits for copy-

right infringement, defamation, or invasion of privacy are contracts and must be enforceable to provide any protection. Further contracts with employers, clients, printers, and media representatives frequently are negotiated and executed by practitioners. Therefore, we include a brief introduction to contract law here.

A contract is a "promise or set of promises for breach of which the law gives a remedy, or the performance of which the law recognizes as a duty" (American Law Institute, 1986, sec. 1). We all can make promises; the trick in contract law is knowing what makes a promise legally enforceable. The classic requirements are that there must be "two parties with capacity, consideration, mutual assent, and a lawful subject matter" (*Federal Home Building & Loan Association v. Blaisdell,* 1934).

Obviously, one cannot make a legally binding promise to oneself, so at least two parties are required. The parties can be what the law calls "natural persons" or corporations (*Taller & Cooper v. Illuminating Electric Co.,* 1949; *United Butane Sales Inc. v. Bessemer-Suburban Gas Co.,* 1968). Legal capacity means simply that the parties must be adults and must have the legal capacity to understand what they are doing (Lord, 1990, sec. 1:20). Although we cannot imagine a situation in which a practitioner would seek to contract with a person who is mentally incompetent, it is not unusual for practitioners to contract with minors. When entering into an agreement with a minor, it is imperative to understand that minors might have the freedom to disaffirm contracts. In other words, they can simply change their minds, and the contracts are not enforceable against them even if adult parties to the contracts have performed the minors' obligations. The details of creating effective contracts with minors vary significantly from state to state. For example, depending on the state, minors can be anyone up to the age of 18 or 21 years (Farnsworth, 1990). In some states, minors' right to disaffirm contracts might survive for several months or even years after the minors reach adulthood (Edge, 1967). In other states, minors are not permitted to disaffirm contracts for artistic services. Usually, a solution for contracting with a minor is to contract through a legal guardian, but even here the practitioner should be forewarned that the minor's parents often are not legal guardians. In short, when attempting to contract with a minor, it is advisable to seek the advice of a local attorney.

Because of the requirement for consideration, bare promises are not enforceable. There must be an exchange of a promise for something of value—the consideration. The consideration can be another promise. An exchange such as "I promise to endorse your product if you promise to pay $10,000 next week" does have consideration, as does "I promise to endorse your product if you promise to write press releases about my career." The only requirement is that the promises exchanged must have some value. Therefore, a promise to do something that already has been done or that the party already is legally obligated to do is not consideration (Farnsworth, 1990, sec. 2.7).

The requirement for mutual assent simply means that the parties must have agreed to the terms of the contract. To agree, they both must have understood the terms of the contract. Therefore, a mistake or misunderstanding might be grounds for avoiding a contract (Farnsworth, 1990, secs. 9.2, 9.3, 9.4). If either party seeks to avoid a contract obligation, that party often will argue that he or she simply misunderstood or did not agree to the terms of the contract. Because of this, written contracts are favored by lawyers and others to whom enforcing contract obligations might be important. However, it should be noted that for most contracts, there is no requirement for a written instrument. All that is required is sufficient evidence that the parties reached an agreement. Although there is no requirement for most contracts to be in writing, some types of agreements are seen as so important or so likely to be misunderstood that courts require a written contract for enforcement. This principle, called the statute of frauds, covers agreements to answer another person's obligation, agreements that take more than 1 year to perform, and agreements for the sale of goods (and sometimes services) over a statutory amount (Farnsworth,

1990, secs. 6.1-6.6). The statute of frauds also covers agreements to marry, prenuptial agreements, and land sales, but those matters are beyond the scope of this chapter.

The final requirement of a contract is that it must have legal subject matter and be enforceable. Of course, we all understand that we cannot go into a court in the United States and enforce a contract for the sale of an illegal substance because the subject of the contract was illegal. There is one type of potentially unenforceable contract that is worth mentioning for public relations practitioners—the personal services contract. Public relations practitioners often are contracted to perform specific services, or they hire celebrities to act as spokespersons. These contracts are financially enforceable. In other words, we can refuse to pay the employee who refuses to perform, we can sue that employee for the value of the contract lost because he or she failed to perform, or we can even enjoin the employee from working for any competitor. However, it is impossible, in the United States, to create a contract that actually forces anyone to perform a personal service for another (*Dallas Cowboys Football Club v. Harris,* 1961).

A Current Internet Application

Contracting about Internet services is in no way distinct from contracting for other media used in public relations. However, as e-mail and other electronic communication come to dominate client and media contacts, it is possible that actually forming a contract over the Internet will create problems. Of course, regardless of the medium used to communicate the agreement, the requirements for creation of a contract remain the same. In most cases, that is simply an agreement and some exchange of consideration.

Those contracts that fall under the statute of frauds do present an interesting problem. They must be in writing and must be signed. Edelstein (1996) presented an eloquent response to that requirement. He noted that in this context, there is no significant difference between a 100-year-old telegraph and the contemporary Internet. In 1869, the New Hampshire courts, addressing a contract evidenced by a telegram, ruled that it made no difference whether the writing was made

> with a steel pen an inch long attached to an ordinary pen holder or whether the pen was a copper wire a thousand miles long. In either case, the thought is communicated to the paper by the use of the finger resting upon the pen. (*Howley v. Whipple,* 1869)

It would appear that one may contract over the Internet and create all those obligations that could be created by a face-to-face meeting over traditional written documents.

An Internet contract does present problems not present in a traditional written contract. It is at least easier for a forger to reproduce a typed or an electronically transmitted signature than it would be to reproduce a manually written signature. Those public relations practitioners offering or accepting contracts over the Internet should explore encrypted or digital signatures (Fresen, 1997).

CONCLUSION

Concerns about litigation and public relations practitioners' legal rights have shaped, and still are shaping, our field. Unfortunately, the very size and growth of public relations practice might have contributed to an increased emphasis on legal rights and principles while decreasing the emphasis on trust and commonsense ethics. Regardless of the cause, it is apparent that both familiarity with applicable law and access to good legal counsel are important components of any successful public relations practice.

Despite their importance, it is simply impossible to detail all the laws that affect the practice of public relations in a single chapter. What we have attempted here is a brief introduction to those laws most likely to shape the profession. We hope that this provides some guidance and general principles. If nothing else, we also hope that we showed that laws vary by jurisdiction with such complexity that a practitioner would be advised to periodically consult a local attorney. Furthermore, we hope that the discussions of Internet applications demonstrated how law might continue to shape the practice of public relations in the future.

CHAPTER 19

Integrating Planning and Evaluation

Evaluating the Public Relations Practice
and Public Relations Programs

TOM WATSON

This chapter offers an overview on the nature of public relations evaluation, the attitudes of practitioners toward it, and the models on which it can be based. My aim is to guide the reader away from the discussion of specific methodology, which obsesses many practitioners, and toward the integration of planning and evaluation in the development of public relations programs.

The chapter begins with a discussion of evaluation and objective setting. It then considers the culture of public relations practice and the barriers to widespread use of evaluation techniques. Finally, it reviews existing models for evaluation and two new approaches that I developed.

A TOP PRIORITY

In a Delphi study conducted by White and Blamphin (1994) among U.K. practitioners and academics of public relations research priorities, the topic of evaluation was ranked number 1 in the development of public relations practice and research. But what is evaluation of public relations? Is it measuring output or monitoring progress against defined objectives? Is it giving a numerical value to the results of programs and campaigns? Is it the final step in the public relations process or a continuing activity?

When discussing this topic, there is considerable confusion as to what the term *evaluation* means. For budget holders, whether employers or clients, the judgments have a "bottom-line" profit-related significance. J. Grunig and Hunt (1984) wrote of a practitioner who justified the budgetary expenditure on public relations by the generation of a large volume of press coverage. He was flummoxed by a senior executive's question of "What's all this worth to us?" (p. 129). In the United Kingdom, articles in the public relations and marketing press refer to evaluation in terms of "justifying expenditure," which is similar to J. Grunig and Hunt's example. White

(1991) suggested that company managers have a special interest in the evaluation of public relations: "Evaluation helps to answer the questions about the time, effort, and resources to be invested in public relations activities; can the investment, and the costs involved, be justified?" (p. 141).

Many definitions emphasize effectiveness— "systematic measures of program effectiveness" (Cutlip, Center, & Broom, 1994, p. 406); "evaluation research is used to determine effectiveness" (Pavlik, 1987, p. 23); "the systematic assessment of a program and its results" (Blissland, 1990, p. 25); "measure public relations effectiveness" (Lindenmann, 1993, p. 7). A development of these definitions are those that are related to program or campaign objectives, a reflection on the management-by-objectives influence on public relations practice in the United States. Cutlip et al. (1994) concluded that evaluation research (a term interchangeable with *evaluation*) is "used to learn what happened and why, not to 'prove' or 'do' something" (p. 410). Definitions of evaluation, therefore, can be seen to fall into three groups: commercial (which is a justification of budget spend), simple effectiveness (which asks whether the program has worked in terms of output), and objectives effectiveness (which judges programs in terms of meeting objectives and creation of desired effects).

For effective evaluation to be undertaken, starting points must be set out, a basis of comparison must be researched, and specific objectives must be established. Weiss (1977) said that the

> purpose [of evaluation] should be clearly stated, and measurable goals must be formulated before questions can be devised and the evaluation design chosen. The start point and the objective must be set as part of the public relations program design. Its waypoints can be measured and the effectiveness and impact assessed. (p. 4)

White (1990) argued that "setting precise and measurable objectives at the outset of a program is a prerequisite for later evaluation" (p. 9).

Simplistic media measurement or reader response analysis considers only output—volume of "mentions"—and not effects. "Objectives" of, say, more mentions in the *Financial Times,* which might be sought by a quoted company, are little more than a stick with which to beat the public relations (or, more correctly, press relations) practitioner. Dozier (1985) referred to this approach as "pseudo-planning" and "pseudo-evaluation." Pseudo-planning is the allocation of resources to communications activities in which the goal is communication itself, and pseudo-evaluation is "simply counting news release placements and other communications" (p. 18).

Historically, the measurements of column inches of press cuttings or mentions on electronic media were seen as adequate evaluation techniques. They fail as objective measures because they cannot demonstrate the requirements for validity and reliability. They can be skewed by the subjectivity of different personalities undertaking the judgment, and they cannot be replicated. Some are little more than sales lead measures, and others that consider "tone" of articles (cf. rigorous content analysis), opportunities to see, or media ratings are judgments that are made to suit the client/employer rather than to measure the effectiveness of reaching target markets. Too often, the evaluation is determined after the campaign has been set in motion.

Another method of judgment is advertising value equivalents (also called advertising cost equivalents), where an advertising space value is given to media coverage. This is a measure often claimed from media coverage. The typical use of this measure is to observe the amount of exposure in time or column inches of the news or editorial coverage in a news story. For example, a British public relations consultancy might claim that a product it is promoting could receive the equivalent of £375,000 in advertising. The weakness of such conclusions is that they are not based on measures of the impact of this publicity. Such measures might include awareness, attitude formation, and attendance at a sponsored event.

McKeone (1993) said, "The whole concept of AVEs is based on false assumptions, and any conclusions based on them are misleading and dangerous" (p. 10). Wilcox, Ault, and Agee (1992) described this methodology as "a bit like comparing apples and oranges" (p. 211) because advertising copy is controlled by the space purchaser, whereas news mentions are determined by media gatekeepers and can be negative, neutral, or favorable. It also is inherently absurd to claim a value for something that never was going to be purchased.

PRACTITIONER CULTURE

Evaluation is a subject widely written about at the academic and practitioner levels. Pavlik (1987) commented that measuring the effectiveness of public relations has proven to be almost as elusive as finding the Holy Grail. Cline (1984) reviewed approximately 300 articles and reports during the mid-1980s and found no consensus of effective methodology. She commented, "There was a pervasive desire to reinvent the wheel" (p. 68) rather than to apply proven social science methodology.

The culture of public relations practitioners is a fundamental issue when considering attitudes toward evaluation and the methodology used. In textbooks and articles about public relations, writers and academics are almost unanimous in their advice that programs must be researched during preparation and evaluated during and after implementation. However, researchers have found that a minority of practitioners use only scientific evaluation methods.

J. Grunig (1983a) has a celebrated cri de coeur on the subject:

I have begun to feel more and more like a fundamentalist preacher railing against sin, the difference being that I have railed for evaluation in public relations practice; just as everyone is against sin, so most public relations people I talk to are for evaluation. People keep on sinning, however, and PR [public relations] people continue not to do evaluation research. (p. 28)

Dozier's research on evaluation over the past 15 years or so has encompassed local (San Diego), national (Public Relations Society of America [PRSA]), and international (International Association of Business Communicators [IABC]) samples (Dozier, 1981, 1984a, 1984b, 1985, 1990). One consistent finding of his studies has been that evaluation of programs increases as the practitioner's management function develops, whereas it either plateaus or falls away if the practitioner has a technician role (e.g., writing, media relations, production of communication tools). Dozier (1990) said,

Some practitioners do not engage in any program research, [whereas] others conduct extensive research. Practitioners vary in the kinds of research methods they use from intuitive, informal "seat-of-the-pants" research to rigorous scientific studies. Although little longitudinal scholarly research is available, the best evidence is that—over time—more practitioners are doing research more frequently. (p. 4)

Although there have been many small-sample studies, the main extensive national and international studies have been conducted by Dozier among PRSA and IABC members, by Lindenmann (1990) among a selected group of U.S. practitioners, and by Watson (1993, 1994) among Institute of Public Relations (IPR) members in the United Kingdom.

In 1988, Lindenmann (1990, pp. 7-9) undertook a nationwide survey among major corporations, large trade and professional associations, large nonprofit organizations, and the 20 largest public relations consultancies and academics. The key findings were that 57.4% believed that outcomes of public relations programs can be measured (41.8% disagreed). Fully 75.9% agreed that research is widely accepted by most public relations professionals as a necessary part of planning programs. In addition, 94.3% agreed that research still is more talked about than done (54.2% *strongly* agreed). Research was undertaken for the purposes of planning (74.7%), monitoring or tracking activities (58.1%), evaluating outcomes (55.7%), conducting publicity polls (41.1%), and tracking crisis issues (36.4%). (Multiple responses were sought for this question.)

The expenditure on research and evaluation showed wide variations. Many respondents, principally in large corporations, utilities, trade associations, and nonprofit organizations, claimed that it was included in budgets, but they were almost equally balanced by those who claimed not to have budgets for this activity. Lindenmann (1990) found that the 89 respondents who did allocate funds for research indicated that the sums were small; specifically, 22.5% said that it was less than 1% of the total public relations budget, 31.5% said that it was between 1% and 3% of the budget, 21.3% said that it was between 4% and 6% of the budget, and 12.3% said that it was at least 7% of the budget.

The issues that Lindenmann (1990) considered negative were

the acknowledgment by better than 9 out of every 10 PR professionals that research is still talked about in PR than is actually being done. Also of concern was the finding that, in the view of 7 out of every 10 respondents, most PR research that is done today is still casual and informal rather than scientific or precise. (p. 15)

Watson's (1994) survey among IPR members found that evaluation was viewed very narrowly and that they lacked confidence to promote evaluation methods to employers and clients. Practitioners claimed that they lacked time, budget, and knowledge of methods to undertake evaluation. They also feared evaluation because it could challenge the logic of their advice and activities. Yet, they said that public relations suffered as a communication discipline because of the inability to predict and measure results. It also was not easy to isolate its effects from other variables such as advertising and related promotional activity. They believed that future public relations performance would be aided by applied measures, probably based on software.

The most widely used techniques relied on some form of output measurement of media coverage. There was a reluctance to pretest or research when preparing public relations activities. Most often, practitioners relied on experience, knowledge of markets and the media, and client/employer imperatives. The picture that emerged was of the practitioner as a "doer" rather than as an adviser or a consultant.

There were some evaluation strategies occasionally undertaken such as "attending relevant meetings and hearings," "monitoring relevant meetings and hearings," and "interviews of the public to check impact." The bulk of responses indicated that output measurement was considered more relevant than either gauging impact or gaining intelligence to further improve programs.

The lack of knowledge or, possibly, the disinclination to learn about evaluation techniques also showed up as the most commonly offered reason why programs were not formally evaluated. This was followed by "cost," "lack of time," and "lack of budget." When the results for "cost" and "lack of budget" were added together as a global financial excuse, they became the dominant reason.

Motives for undertaking evaluation also were sought. By nearly double any other category, public relations practitioners nominated "prove value of campaign/budget," followed by "help campaign targeting and planning" and "need to judge campaign effects" and, as a distant fourth choice, "help get more resources/higher fees."

The use of evaluation techniques to improve programs or to judge the effects of current activities was considered to be half as important as "proving value," implying that practitioners were defensive about their activities. They aimed to present data on which they would be judged rather than to act proactively to improve or fine-tune campaigns.

Indications of the lack of self-confidence in the U.K. public relations profession are evidenced in an article in the *Financial Times* (Houlder, 1994). White (1991) argued that the need of practitioners to evaluate activities was "partly a matter of professional insecurity." Mike Beard, the 1994 president of the United Kingdom's IPR, agreed with White but pointed out that other professions rarely have standard evaluation systems: "Other professions are not obsessed by this issue, nor should we be" (cited in

Houlder, 1994). Taking a different tack, another prominent practitioner, Quentin Bell, then chairman of the United Kingdom's Public Relations Consultants Association, said, "Unless we can get clients to insist on evaluation, there will not be a PR consultancy business in 25 years' time" (Bell, 1992, p. 22).

An indicator of attitudes that might be slowly changing was the snapshot study undertaken by Blissland (1990) of entries in the PRSA's annual Silver Anvil case study competition. Blissland compared entries from 1988-1989 to those at the beginning of the decade in 1980-1981 to see whether there were changes in attitude toward evaluation methods over the period. A cosmetic change was that during the early 1980s, only one entrant used the term *evaluation,* but 88% used the term *results.* By 1988-1989, 83% used *evaluation* as the term to describe their outcomes sections. They also used more evaluation methods; this number increased from a mean of 3.60 methods/winner to 4.57 methods/winner.

The statistically significant changes were the use of behavioral science measures and two measures of organizational goal achievement: inferred achievement and substantiated achievement. Blissland (1990) concluded that by the end of the decade, there was marginally greater reliance on the output measure of media coverage, which rose from 70.0% to 79.2%. However, when this is linked to the inferred (i.e., unsubstantiated) achievement claims (which increased in winning entries from 53.3% to 87.5%), it is hard to agree with Blissland's conclusion that "clearly, progress has been made" (p. 33).

European research on evaluation, which can be compared to the U.K. study on practitioner attitudes, has been undertaken in Germany. Baerns (1993) studied attitudes among German in-house public relations managers in 1989 and 1992 and found results similar to those in Dozier's studies. She said, "Almost all West German public relations experts in managerial positions regarded analytical work as important in the context of public relations. However, almost all of them rarely analyzed and controlled what they had accomplished irregularly or never" (p. 67).

Baerns (1993) found that the majority of respondents (55%) regarded long-term public relations planning as "indispensable," whereas 39% referred to the priority of day-to-day events. A small number (7%) regarded planning in public relations as "impossible." Baerns then explored the ways in which planning took place and found a considerable gap between the reported attitudes toward planning and the reality of what took place.

Baerns (1993) found that 63% of respondents believed that "scientific findings" play only a minor part in public relations practice. This corresponds with the seat-of-the-pants attitudes identified in the United States and the United Kingdom by Dozier (1984, 1985, 1988b) and Watson (1993, 1994), respectively. Baerns's concluded that when evaluation or monitoring took place, it was "mostly as press analyses."

Among the U.S. studies are contributions from Chapman (1982), Finn (1982), Hiebert and Devine (1985), and Judd (1990). Chapman (1982) found that practitioners in Chicago relied less on the media for evaluation purposes, but there was a seat-of-the-pants category called "general feedback" used by 83% of respondents. Finn (1982) found that 38% of senior communications executives in major companies were studying the impact of programs. Judd (1990) found that 67% of PRSA members used formal research or evaluation and that regional practitioners in Texas were only marginally lower at 66%. He also cross-checked his results by analyzing whether those who said that they evaluate actually do so and was satisfied that there is a clear correlation between saying and doing. His results, however, are at variance with those of most U.S. and overseas practitioner studies. Hiebert and Devine (1985) found the reverse in an earlier study of government information officers in the United States, 85% of whom thought that evaluation "was either an important or very important activity" but who conducted almost no research.

Research in Australia by MacNamara (1992a) also detected a gap between saying and doing but, more significantly, detected a reliance on measurement of media indicators and the absence of objective research methods. He found that only 3 of 50 senior public relations consultancies surveyed could nominate an objective methodology used to evaluate media coverage even though 70% of respondents claimed that they undertook qualitative judgment of media coverage.

THE BARRIERS TO EVALUATION

There are many barriers to the more widespread evaluation of public relations activity, as has been demonstrated heretofore. Dozier (1985) indicated several reasons—previous working experience of practitioners, lack of knowledge of research techniques, the manager-technician dichotomy, and the practitioner's participation in decision making. Lindenmann (1990) believed that practitioners were "not thoroughly aware" of research techniques. He also found that respondents to his survey complained of a lack of money, with 54% spending 3% or less (often much less) on evaluation. Watson (1993, 1994) indicated that time, knowledge, budgets, and costs were the principal difficulties for U.K. public relations people. Baerns (1993) found similar barriers in Germany, with time, lack of personnel, inadequate budgets, and doubts about the process all being important. MacNamara's (1992a) research found that practitioners lacked knowledge of methodology but did not explore other explanations. In the United Kingdom, one strong reason advanced by Bell (1992) was money and client reluctance to spend it:

> And the problem I fear lies with money—too many clients are still not prepared to allocate realistic budgets to pay for the process. But I concede that it's a catch-22; until clients have become accustomed to what's possible on evaluation, they won't begin to demand it. That's the basic problem that our industry as a whole must aim to solve. (p. 22)

These barriers follow a circular argument. Most practitioners' education does not include social science research techniques; therefore, they do not use them but instead concentrate on

technician skills, and this means that they do not rise into the manager roles and participate in decision making. This would give access to budgets for planning and evaluation, thus creating programs and campaigns that can enhance their personal standing and meet the objectives of their clients or employers.

MODELS OF EVALUATION

When practitioners undertake evaluation, there is a tendency to take a narrow view of the methods used and to concentrate on simplistic methodologies. However, there are at least four models that are familiar to the more widely read practitioners. In this chapter, two more models are proposed, based on recent research. In the United States, one of the best known models is that of Cutlip et al. (1994), which has been included in many of the seven editions of their standard text, *Effective Public Relations*, widely used in undergraduate education.

Cutlip et al.'s (1994) evaluation model is widely taught to students in the United States. Known as *PII* (preparation, implementation, and impact), it is a step model that offers levels of evaluation for differing demands. It does not prescribe methodology. The authors make the key point that the most common evaluation error is substituting measures from one level for another. For example, an implementation measure such as the number of press releases disseminated is used to claim impact. This "substitution game" frequently is seen when reading articles in the trade press or when reviewing award entries.

Each step in the PII model, according to Cutlip et al. (1994), contributes to increased understanding and adds information for assessing effectiveness. The bottom rung of preparation evaluation assesses the information and strategic planning, the implementation evaluation stage considers tactics and effort, and the impact evaluation stage gives feedback on the outcome.

The PII model is valuable for its separation of output and impact and for counseling against the confusion of these different measures. It acts as a checklist and a reminder when planning evaluation. However, like many academic models, it assumes that programs and campaigns will be measured by social science methodologies that will be properly funded by clients/employers. As a model, it puts short- and long-term public relations activity together without allowing for their often very different methodologies and goals.

The importance of PII, through its widespread teaching, is highlighted by the next model discussed—MacNamara's (1992b) *macro* model. MacNamara's model, which he calls macro communication, is similar to PII and represents public relations programs and campaigns in a pyramidal form, rising from a broad base of inputs, to outputs, to results, with the pinnacle being "objectives achieved." The base inputs are similar to PII and include background information, appropriateness of media, and quality of message. In the middle of the pyramid is a sequence starting at message distribution and ending with data on readership. The results section is concerned with stages of research and ends with the judgment on whether or not objectives have been reached or problems have been solved.

The model separates outputs and results. For example, a news release can be evaluated as an output in terms of quality, readability, and timeliness but not as to whether a communication effect has been achieved. The macro model lists evaluation methodologies that can be applied to each of the steps in an attempt to develop a completed measurable process. MacNamara (1992b) claimed that it "presents a practical model for planning and managing evaluation of public relations" and that it recognizes communication as a multistep process.

Lindenmann's (1993) public relations *yardstick* model differs from the other models because its staging does not progress from planning to objectives. It encapsulates Lindenmann's experience in advising the international public relations consultancy and aims to make evaluation more accessible. He argued that it is possible to measure public relations effectiveness and that there is growing pressure from clients and employers to be more accountable. He added, "Measuring public relations effectiveness does not have to be either unbelievably expensive or laboriously time-consuming. PR measurement

studies can be done at relatively modest cost and in a matter of only a few weeks."

The yardstick model consists of a two-step process: setting public relations objectives and then determining at what levels public relations effectiveness is to be measured.

Three Levels gauge the extent of measurement. Level 1 is the basic level, which measures public relations "outputs"—the ways in which the program or campaign is presented through, typically, media relations. It is measured in terms of media placements and the likelihood of reaching the target groups.

Level 2 is termed by Lindenmann (1993) as the intermediate level, which uses "outgrowth" or "out-take" measures. These judge whether or not the target audience actually received the messages and so evaluates retention, comprehension, and awareness. Practitioners will use a mix of qualitative and quantitative data collection techniques such as focus groups, interviews with opinion leaders, and polling of target groups.

"Outcomes" are measured in Level 3. These include opinion, attitudes, and behavioral changes. Lindenmann wrote that this is where the role of pre- and posttesting comes into its own with the use of before-and-after polling, observational methods, psychographic analysis, and other social science techniques.

Lindenmann (1993) concluded his article with a statement that emphasized his practical approach in developing the yardstick model: "It is important to recognize that there is no one simplistic method for measuring PR effectiveness. Depending upon which level of effectiveness is required, an array of different tools and techniques is needed to properly assess PR impact" (p. 9).

UNIVERSALITY OF THE MODELS

The three models just discussed have varying provenances. Cutlip et al.'s (1994) PII is well known. MacNamara's (1992a, 1992b) macro model is much less well known. Lindenmann's

(1993) yardstick model has been publicized in the United States and the United Kingdom.

Research among practitioners (Watson, 1995) has found, however, that existing evaluation models are too complex, do not have an integral relationship with the creation of effects, and lack a dynamic element of feedback. These models all fit that hypothesis. They are essentially static, step-by-step processes that, to quote Cutlip et al. (1994), are "the final stage in the [public relations] process" (p. 410). Yet, public relations activity is not a "start/stop" communications process in which, for example, a company stops all interactions with its many publics while it measures the results of a media relations program.

To develop a more complete approach to planning (and subsequent evaluation), the "effects-based planning" theories put forward by Van Leuven and colleagues are valuable (Van Leuven, O'Keefe, & Salmon, 1988). These are closely associated with management-by-objectives techniques used widely in industry and government. Underlying Van Leuven's approach is the premise that a program's intended communication and behavioral effects serve as the basis from which all other planning decisions can be made. The process involves setting separate objectives and sub-objectives for each public. Van Leuven et al. (1988) argued that the planning becomes more consistent by having to justify program and creative decisions on the basis of their intended communication and behavioral effects. It also acts as a continuing evaluation process because the search for consistency means that monitoring is continuous and the process of discussion needs evidence on which to reach decisions. Effects-based planning, according to Van Leuven et al., means that programs can be compared without the need for isolated case studies.

TWO NEW EVALUATION APPROACHES

Taking into account the need for accessible dynamic models of evaluation, two models were

proposed by Watson (1995): the *short-term* model for short-time-span, largely media relations-based campaigns and activities that seek rapid results and the *continuing* model for long-term activities in which the consistent promotion of messages is a central strategy and the outcomes may occur after long periods (1 year or more) of continuous activities.

These models link with J. Grunig's four summations of public relations activity (J. Grunig & Hunt, 1984). The short-term model is similar to the press agentry and public information one-way summations in that it does not seek dialogue or feedback. The continuing model fits with the two-way asymmetric and two-way symmetric models that cover a broader band of communication methods and rely on feedback for campaign monitoring and modification of messages. These models can be expressed graphically.

The Short-Term Model

The short-term model (Figure 19.1) has a single-track, linear process with an outcome. It does not set out to measure effects, and because it does not have a continuing existence, there is no feedback mechanism. Typically, a public relations campaign has a simple awareness objective with one or two strategies. A common example of public relations practice in the public information summation is the distribution of news releases about products or services to the media. This is a technician skill of assembling information and photographs or drawings in the manner most acceptable to the media. Measuring achievement of the objectives can be by media analysis, sales responses, or phone research among the target audience.

Using the short-term model, the objectives could be set on the basis of obtaining coverage in specific media (chosen for relevance to target audiences), the number of sales responses (realistically set according to the appropriateness of the media and the attractions of product or service), or quantitative techniques such as phone research and mail surveys. The judgment of success or failure, therefore, is made on whether or not the targets are reached. If the client or em-

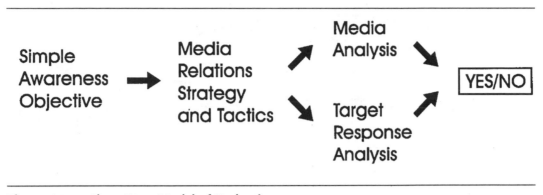

Figure 19.1. Short-Term Model of Evaluation

ployer sets unrealistic objectives, then this simple model will be as irrelevant as a step-by-step model or an informal seat-of-the-pants judgment. The quality of the model's results depends on the professionalism of the practitioner in designing the campaign.

The Continuing Model

The continuing model (Figure 19.2) has been designed for use in long-term public relations activities. In reviewing the case studies, the need for a dynamic model to cope with ever changing circumstances was identified. A program such as that for major land use changes (with long-term corporate and planning objectives) or for an industrial redevelopment (with a medium-term objective of planning permission and a long-term objective of improved relations with the local community) needed a flexible evaluation model.

The continuing model offers elements that have not been included in step-by-step models. It has an iterative loop and takes into account the effects that are being created by the program. An additional element is that it offers an opportunity to make a judgment on "staying alive"—the important stage in a long-term, issues-centered program when keeping the issue in the decision frame is important. The continuing model epitomizes Van Leuven et al.'s (1988) effects-based planning approach. By adopting these principles

within the continuing model, a dynamic and continuing evaluation process is created because the search for consistency means that monitoring is continuous.

The evidence from the long-term case studies reviewed in the research shows that the search for consistency is one of the most difficult practical issues facing public relations practitioners. The continuing model, using effects-based planning, offers a more disciplined approach that allows the parameters of the program to be more closely defined and enables continuous monitoring to replace after-the-event evaluation. The consistency of effects-based planning also aids validity and reliability of data.

The elements of the continuing model are an initial stage of research, the setting of objectives and choice of program effects, followed by the strategy selection and tactical choices. As the program continues, there are multiple levels of formal and informal analysis from which judgments can be made on progress in terms of success or "staying alive." The judgments are fed back to each of the program elements. These iterative loops assist the practitioner in validating the initial research and adding new data, adjusting the objectives and strategy, monitoring the progress to create the desired attitudinal or behavioral effects, and helping with the adjustment or variation of tactics. This model is a continuing process that can be applied to a specific program or to the overall public relations activities of an organization.

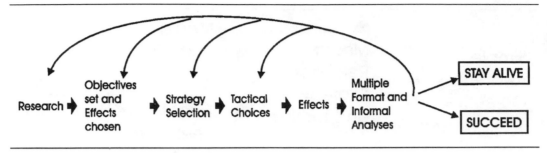

Figure 19.2. Continuing Model of Evaluation

CONCLUSION

The search for consistency is one of the most difficult practical issues faced by the public relations professional. A more disciplined approach will allow the parameters of the program to be more closely defined and for continuous monitoring to replace a single postintervention evaluation. It also will bolster the objectivity of the evaluation process.

Unless evaluation becomes less of a mystery and a more accessible process, it would appear that a generation of better educated practitioners is needed to break the technician mold.

Technicians always will be needed to carry out the operational aspects and tactical implementation of programs and campaigns, especially those that are based on media relations and publications.

If the evaluation models are simpler to operate, then technicians can participate in them. Given that they are producing many of the materials for the strategy, it makes sense for them to aid in the evaluation process. Money and time always will be in short supply, but simpler models to enable evaluation to take place more frequently would prove to be a more convincing case to employers or clients when budgets are set.

20

Media Effects Research for Public Relations Practitioners

BETH OLSON

■ The promise of understanding media effects can be seductive—a search for knowledge of cause and effect and the relationship between human behavior and consumption of media. This chapter explores the theory and research of media effects that may be applicable to public relations practitioners by defining media effects, presenting a historical overview of media effects models, outlining traditional categorizations of media effects (e.g., level of analysis, form vs. content), and exploring how the more powerful media effects models may be applied to the study and practice of public relations in an ever changing media environment.

DEFINING MEDIA EFFECTS AND EARLY EFFECTS MODELS

This section discusses both formal and informal definitions of media effects and examines shifts away from fear of dominant or direct effects. If these dominant effects did occur, then a public

relations practitioner with a sound grasp of media could essentially achieve what is called the magic bullet effect—load a message into a medium and pull the trigger. Whereas early understanding of mass media effects was grounded in the magic bullet model, subsequent research disproved key assumptions found in the model.

Discovering how mass media researchers define media effects is complex and typically is inferred from context. "Mass communication involves the scientific study of the mass media, the messages they generate, the audiences they attempt to reach, and their *effects* on these audiences" (Tan, 1985, p. 3, italics added). Effects can be broadly based, from effects on an individual to societal effects, ranging from a child's fear reaction to an R-rated film to undecided voters casting ballots for a third-party candidate. Effects generally include any of the psychological or sociological outcomes following mass media consumption. More specifically, media effects may be defined by a categorization scheme such as type of effect or duration of effect. The term *mass media* has grown to include print media, electronic media, and computer-generated media, with content ranging from advertising to news and to informational and entertainment programming.

Early intuition about media effects assumed a direct effects magic bullet model from the early 1900s to the 1940s. Most mass media were in their infancy, and the emergence of each new medium, from film to radio to television, was met with public fear about potentially harmful effects as the consequence of exposure. For example, the initial hysteria reported following the 1938 radio broadcast of Orson Welles' *War of the Worlds* added fuel to the public's growing concern that new media were capable of producing direct, and negative, effects (Hadley, 1940). The pendulum of media effects began at the far right.

Historically, the scientific empirical study of media effects has evolved from the fields of psychology and sociology, most notably the research work of psychologist Paul Lazarsfeld (Lazarsfeld, Berelson, & Gaudet, 1944). As a result, the majority of scientific investigations have been generated in the social science quantitative tradition. Lazarsfeld debunked early ideas about direct media effects and became a proponent of a limited effects model during the early 1950s, sending the pendulum from direct effects to weak or limited effects, swinging the pendulum to the extreme left.

The limited effects model led to the development of the two-step flow model (Lazarsfeld et al., 1944) and the uses and gratifications line of research (Katz, 1959). Both research theories postulated the importance of the individual's thoughtful use of media messages in the media communication process, thereby reducing the power of the media. The two-step flow model identified the importance of opinion leaders in diffusing media messages to individuals, whereas the uses and gratifications approach focused on the differences in the ways in which individuals sought and received gratifications from media use. However, the "front end" of the communication process often is overlooked. That is, the intent or purpose of those people that produce the messages seldom are investigated. As a result, little is known about the place of effects derived from a specific purpose such as the effect created when a public relations practitio-

ner successfully places a news item in a broadcast news program. The limited effects model also is supported by Klapper's (1960) work, which concluded that the media have very limited power and might only be capable of reinforcing preexisting ideas.

This tradition gave way during the 1970s to a powerful media effects model. The powerful effects model may be visualized as a softening or midway point of the media effects pendulum swinging back to center. The powerful effects model, which also has been referred to as a moderate effects perspective (Baran & Davis, 1995, p. 16), may be perceived as a compromise between the two extreme positions; under certain conditions for some people, the media can contribute to strong effects or outcomes.

CATEGORIZATION OF MEDIA EFFECTS

The theme in this section is that, on the one hand, the media can have a substantial impact, but that on the other, they might have limited effects. We may realize, therefore, that effects vary. The reasons for such variance may be informative to practitioners, and the variance can be grouped according to the following typologies. Basil (1997) offered five categories of media effects: level of analysis, type, nature, intention, and whether effects are the result of form or content. Level of analysis considers whether the research examined the media effects on individuals, groups, or societies. Type of effects may be split into one of three primary subcategories: affective, cognitive, or behavioral. Nature of effects includes the processes first identified by Lazarsfeld et al. (1944) when studying voter behavior. Does the consumption of media create activation (new belief), reinforcement (confirmation of existing belief), or conversion (change to a different belief)? Intention considers whether the effects were intended or unintended. This also may be extended to include long-term versus short term effects and manifest versus latent effects. Finally, form versus content examines the medium of delivery versus content. For example, most people would spontaneously report that reading is more cognitively engaging than viewing television, but studies on similar content have reflected little difference between cognitive processing (and subsequent learning) of print and cognitive processing of televised images (Meadowcroft & Olson, 1995).

Level of Analysis for Effects

Most of the research conducted that tests media effects assumptions includes the individuals as participants or survey respondents. However, effects may be present at the cultural and societal levels as well as at the individual level (Geiger & Newhagen, 1993). Group and societal studies occur less frequently, although most of the effects on individuals are extrapolated to the aggregate, namely society at large. However, results from experimental research typically conducted on individuals contain an inherent caveat against such extrapolation due to low external validity and small sample sizes. Responses of individuals are grouped to represent subgroups of society, which may serve to inform us about groups and societal attitudes and behavior. For example, individuals may be placed in subcategories for their responses to be reported, perhaps by demographic attributes such as gender, age, and ethnicity or by psychological attributes such as attitudes or comprehension levels. One example of research on the individual level that may be generalized found that the television viewing styles of individuals were correlated with comprehension of plot material, indicating that people who actually spent more time staring at the television screen were less likely to comprehend the plot (Hawkins, Pingree, Bruce, & Tapper, 1997). One interpretation of these results is that staring is part of passive viewing and, as a result, lowers comprehension levels. Active viewers, on the other hand, tend to "check in" and are able to recall more plot points.

The categorization of effects is applicable to public relations in a number of ways, centering on knowledge of target audience. Knowing that the audience was exposed to one's message in the media is no guarantee that it will produce the desired effects. Some audience members are more difficult to reach because of their individual styles of media use such as the passive "couch potato" viewer described earlier. As a result, messages designed for effective impact would best be placed in programs most watched by active selective viewers. In this manner, individualist data may be applied to larger groups. The individual level of analysis appears to be the most powerful tool of those interested in level of analysis because it may be generalized from smaller individual effects to larger group effects. Knowledge of the individual is the building block on which to construct knowledge of the audience.

Type of Effects

The categorization for type of effect includes the human responses of cognition, affect, and behavior. Cognition, when compared to affect, often is considered to be the result of a "stronger" central processing route in human thought and subsequent persuasion, whereas affect or emotional response is produced much more quickly and with less concentrated effort via the peripheral route (Petty & Cacioppo, 1986). Further investigation of the processes and their relationship to persuasive advertising messages indicated that use of product information (e.g., presenting a product in a problem-solution scenario) precipitated cognition but was negatively related to affect, as was the use of spokespersons (Chaudhuri & Buck, 1995). Commonly used advertising messages such as excitement, aggression, and sexual content were labeled as mood arousal (or affect) dimensions. These messages, along with status appeals (featuring a reward [for using the product] or a punishment [for not using the product]), were positively related to affect but negatively related to cognition, much the same as Fishbein and Ajzen's (1975) theory of reasoned action or Ajzen's (1991) theory of planned behavior (1991) and classical conditioning of association to product (see, e.g., Staats & Staats, 1958).

The issue of identification stands in contradiction to these findings. As Basil (1996) pointed out, identification (through the use of spokespeople) might be the single underlying factor among Bandura's (1977) social learning theory, Kelman's (1961) theory of opinion change, and Burke's (1950) dramatism theory. Social learning theory (Bandura, 1977) posits that identification with a model increases learning; Kelman's (1961) theory includes the components of compliance, identification, and internalization; and dramatism theory (Burke, 1950) offers speculation on the level of identification that a viewer has with a fictional character. Whereas the previous study (Chaudhuri & Buck, 1995) found the use of spokespeople to be considered less effective because it was a predictor of negative affect, Basil (1996) postulated that identification best explained effectiveness of celebrity endorsements. In his study following Magic Johnson's announcement of the basketball star's HIV status, respondents' predictor variables (age, gender, sexual experience, reliance on media, and media use) mediated the message; those who identified with Johnson reported more behavioral and attitudinal changes following the announcement. Identification, as a component of affect, might be most effective when employed by a celebrity spokesperson, although this study did not measure affect explicitly.

Other research findings proposed another contradiction: Affect (or emotion) might be placed in the central processing route because public service announcements (PSAs) with strong emotional appeals pertaining to AIDS produced higher recall levels (Lee & Davie, 1997). However, gender also was an important mediating variable for recall, a feat probably not replicated with other non-sexually related content. Female respondents recalled more of the emotional messages than did male respondents, whereas male respondents recalled more of the rational appeals than did female respondents. Both rational and emotional appeals were more engaging (depending on respondent gender); therefore, both could be considered as participating in the central processing route. An example of a PSA judged to consist of a rational appeal contained a visual of putting on a sock and accompanying narration, suggesting that a simple

act could save one's life. Emotional PSAs included people giving personal testimonials about how they thought they never could contract AIDS.

Behavioral responses are the single definitive manifestation of responses to media message consumption. Respondents typically are asked to report behaviors; direct observation of behavioral changes rarely is employed. For example, those people participating in the survey on attitudinal change following Johnson's announcement were asked their levels of agreement with statements such as "I will definitely limit my sexual activity in the future because of AIDS" and "I will likely get a blood test for HIV infection within the next 6 months," and they were asked to provide the number of sexual partners they likely would have during the subsequent 18 months (Basil, 1996, pp. 292-293). Researchers have been stymied by the findings that attitudinal change does not necessitate a subsequent behavioral change (see, e.g., Ajzen, 1988). In fact, behavior might not correspond to attitudinal beliefs, as health awareness campaign designers are well aware (see, e.g., Brown & Walsh-Childers, 1994). Fazio (1990) offered a counterexplanation: Behaviors are spontaneous and not carefully deliberated through the central processing route, especially when there is little risk involved in the decision. The ability of the presence of an attitude object to change a behavior suggests that behavior can be produced by either route—central or peripheral—which greatly adds to the complexity of understanding human behavior.

How can public relations practitioners use such research findings? Public relations practitioners should address audience characteristics in designing messages and in determining which component to be targeted—cognition, affect, or behavior. The central processing route appears to be the prized form of media consumption because it might be the strongest predictor of thoughtful behavioral choices. Practitioners can construct message content based on the effect desired such as sexual imagery for affective component, problem-solution format for cognitive component, and identification/modeling for behavioral change.

Nature of Effects

In research conducted on voter behavior in the 1940 presidential election, Lazarsfeld et al. (1944) determined three media functions: activation, reinforcement, and conversion. These three concepts make up the category of nature of effects. Activation occurred when voters who were predisposed to vote for a particular candidate did so after the media messages aroused interest in voting; this led to increased exposure, which in turn activated selective attention and the voting decision. Reinforcement occurred via selective attention when voters already knew their decisions and selected media messages to reinforce their decisions. Conversion was the smallest of the three effects; it occurred when people changed their vote from one candidate to another.

Conversion, more recently, has been found to be very likely when a voter attends to media coverage and does not have strong feelings for any of the candidates (Graber, 1989). Reinforcement actually might be more common than conversion because of the selective perception inherent in people who already have candidate preferences and party preferences (Lanoue, 1992). In addition, another type of reinforcement is indicated by the way in which experimental participants have reported who "won" a presidential debate; those inclined to favor a candidate were more likely to say that their favored candidate was the winner (McKinnon, Tedesco, & Kaid, 1997).

Here it becomes apparent that public relations practitioners, especially those working in the political arena, can be most successful when their job is partially completed before they begin—reinforcing attitudes that audience members already possess so as to lock in their preferences.

Intention for Effects

Categorization of intent of media messages includes distinctions such as intended effects versus unintended effects, short-term effects versus long-term effects, and manifest effects versus latent effects. The summative research conducted during the early years of the television program *Sesame Street* exploring the knowledge gap hypothesis may be considered an example of intended versus unintended effects. (Note that the knowledge gap hypothesis predicts that as media information becomes available, people from higher socioeconomic backgrounds tend to acquire the material at a faster rate than do people from lower socioeconomic backgrounds, thus creating a gap in the knowledge between the two groups [Tichenor, Donohue, & Olien, 1970].) The program's original purpose was to assist at-risk preschoolers in narrowing the achievement gap between them and more advantaged children (Ball & Bogatz, 1970) by teaching rudimentary skills in language and math for children 3 to 5 years of age. The summative research indicated that the program's content did accomplish this goal for the at-risk children who viewed the program (intended effect). However, the children from advantaged backgrounds watched the program too, and they watched more of it. As a result, these children made similar gains in their achievement scores, and this contributed to widening the knowledge gap between the two groups rather than reducing it (unintended effect) (Cook et al., 1975).

Unintended effects may arise from the most benign intent and, as such, might be nearly impossible to predict, as might manifest versus latent effects. The investigation of short-term effects versus long-term effects might best be approached by a longitudinal study, designed to assess attitude change over time. Researchers may investigate other contributing variables, such as audience characteristics, when creating, pretesting, and disseminating messages. In the case of *Sesame Street,* if creators had possessed the knowledge of their audience and also had known the effectiveness and popularity of the program, then they might have been able to predict the higher levels of use. However, as with most informational or educational media campaigns, the benefits to all outweigh the alternative of limiting access to some. Obviously, it would be impossible to prevent non-at-risk children from watching "too much" *Sesame Street.* However, it was possible to increase the viewing levels of the at-risk children and to offer supplementary instructional materials to narrow the gap.

Public relations practitioners will take care to note as many outcome scenarios as possible so as to prevent a campaign from being negated by unintended, latent, or unforeseen long-term effects. Again, knowledge of the target audience combined with knowledge of possible outcomes is advantageous.

Form versus Content for Effects

The "medium is the message," McLuhan's (1964) oft-cited quotation, is at the core of form versus content. The channel through which a message is sent might intuitively seem to have an effect, namely on cognitive processing, learning, memory, and subsequent behavior. Most people would automatically report that reading printed material is more cognitively engaging than viewing that same material presented via television. Singer (1980) maintained that humans are active information processors whose cognitive skills are facilitated by print characteristics, whereas the formal features of television, such as rapid pacing, make it more difficult to employ cognitive skills while processing the message. Television "trains us to watch it" by providing a constant stream of images to capture a viewer's attention, creates a "system overload" by presenting information in both audio and visual channels, and adheres to a pace over which the viewer has no control (Singer, 1980). Other research has indicated that reading results in a larger degree of invested mental effort because people expect it to be more difficult. These expectations, however, have been overcome in experimental conditions in which participants were instructed to allocate mental effort to a television watching task (Clark, 1983; Salomon, 1979).

In an effort to test these information-processing assumptions, four experimental treatment groups were exposed to one television condition and three print conditions that contained an identical stimulus from a 60-minute *NOVA* program on PBS about chaos theory (Meadowcroft & Olson, 1995). The edited version was approximately 12 minutes in length; the print conditions were exposed to transcriptions of the audio text and included one of three versions: no images, helpful photographs (taken from video screen) that contributed to understanding of the theory, and nonhelpful or unrelated photographs. Attention was measured by self-report of the amount of invested mental effort and a surrogate measure of attention that also assessed allocation of mental effort. The surrogate measure consisted of performing a secondary task—responding to randomly spaced audio tones—while engaging in the primary task of reading or watching television. The response time needed to push a button after tone presentation was converted to a reaction time. Consistent with Kahneman's (1973) theory, it is assumed that the quicker the reaction time, the less cognitively engaged one is in the material and vice versa. Form versus content might be a moot argument; results from participants indicated few differences in the ways in which readers and television viewers process information when examining attention, elaboration, memory of central content, enjoyment of content, and recall memory. However, readers did report more visualization of content than did television viewers (Meadowcroft & Olson, 1995). Given the informational/ educational nature of the PBS program and the information-processing assumptions surrounding content versus form, it is speculated that the results of this study may easily be extended to other printed or visual communication. In addition, the emergence of "blurmercials" (Mandese, 1993), living infomercials (Elliott, 1994), and "documercials" (Wells, 1993) is erasing the traditional boundaries among news, advertising, and entertainment programming (B. Stern, 1994), and this further muddies the distinctions.

Form versus content also may be broken down into other dimensions, and in so doing, other finite differences may be uncovered. For example, form versus content may be further dissected into dimensions of television and audiences. The characteristics of a medium also may be varied to produce an effect. Participants gave political candidates who appeared in fast-paced television political advertisements more positive evaluations than they did candidates in slower paced commercials featuring static images (Geiger & Reeves, 1991). Cognitive abilities of the audience also need to be considered. Form versus content did produce a difference when age was included as an independent variable. In particular, the elderly, as a growing segment of the population, present a challenge to determining message form and content because they have been shown to have difficulty in processing information (for learning and retrieval) regardless of form (Cole & Houston, 1987). Older audiences, who might have limited information processing skills, might learn less and recall less than do younger audiences and, in fact, had more difficulty than younger participants in processing information in a print media condition and learned less from the television condition (both stimuli consisted of news and advertising content) (Cole & Houston, 1987).

Public relations practitioners often might face the dilemma of deciding where their messages should be placed. The review of research findings reported in this section lead to several key conclusions. First, consumers approach media in a predetermined way, but this ultimately has a limited impact on information processing when the message is the same. Second, message designers should exploit the formal features of the chosen medium to maximize effectiveness (e.g., television messages use attention-getting production techniques, print is used to present complex information). Third, a target audience's cognitive abilities need to be assessed to aid in determining how the message is constructed.

Cost and size of audience might be the most pertinent criteria given that the research shows little processing differences across media. The increasing numbers of people who obtain information from the Internet pose an interesting problem for researchers concerned with form versus content. Are information-processing assumptions changed when printed text is presented in a more traditionally visual (monitor) format and information from a screen is downloaded and printed in text form?

POWERFUL EFFECTS THEORIES

This segment builds on the insights learned in the previous sections. It suggests that we might misunderstand the concepts of direct or limited effects when the goal is more accurately a powerful effect. A sharper insight into this phenomenon of powerful effects and its theories offers an important implication for public relations, namely the capacity for cumulative effects.

The theories of cultivation, agenda setting, and spiral of silence all may be considered powerful effects theories. Cultivation theory predicts that heavy media use will result in consumers expressing opinions and beliefs similar to those messages featured predominantly in the media such as a belief that the world is a mean and scary place (Gerbner, Gross, Signorielli, Morgan, & Jackson-Beeck, 1979). Agenda setting (McCombs & Shaw, 1972) postulates that media consumers will determine that issues predominant in media messages will be correlated with those issues they find to be important such as the danger of nuclear weapons (Miller & Quarles, 1984) and U.S. defense capability (Iyengar, Peters, & Kinder, 1982). Spiral of silence has a similar attitudinal/public opinion focus (Noelle-Neumann, 1973, 1980). It predicts that people who believe that their viewpoints are in the minority will be less willing to speak publicly about their viewpoints, leading to an increasingly larger group of people who choose not to voice their opinions. Opinions presented in the media as being those of the majority become stronger and face less and less vocal opposition, leaving the media as a powerful developer of public consensus.

All three of these are cognitively based theories; cultivation theory and agenda setting have been referred to as "theories of accumulation" because they predict cumulative effects over a long period of time (Jeffres, 1997). Cultivation theory's contribution to public relations comes in the form of its accrued creation of attitudes that correspond to media content. Cultivation speaks to the presence of broad-based ideological messages such as those messages supporting "consumption, materialism, individualism, power, and gender, race, and class status quo" (Shanahan, Morgan, & Stenbjerre, 1997, p. 309). For example, themes pervasive in content, such as the impact of science, technology, and pollution on the environment, produced a cultivation effect of general apprehension about the environment in heavy viewers. However, this group of heavy viewers also was less likely to make behavioral changes such as engaging in recycling behavior (Shanahan et al., 1997). Public relations practitioners could find that broad public information campaigns might conceivably produce a cultivation effect in viewers (particularly heavy viewers) who adopt the media message in developing a similar attitude, but behavioral consequences rarely are part of cultivation theory's prediction. Public relations practitioners might find the theory of agenda setting useful because once they are able to place issues on the news media agenda, the public's agenda theoretically will follow with increased importance subsequently allocated to those issues. Spiral of silence could be the weak point of a communication campaign; the so-called "silent majority" might sabotage any public relations efforts based on faulty beliefs about public opinion.

Much of Edward Bernays' public relations efforts appear to be aligned most closely with a powerful effects model, namely agenda setting, although when he began his early campaigns the magic bullet model was commonly assumed to be operating in conjunction with the budding mass media in this country. One of the earliest examples of a powerful media effect, the power of media promotion, and a successful Bernays campaign occurred in 1929 when elegant women were shown in evening gowns smoking Lucky Strikes in cigarette holders and espousing the slogan, "Reach for a Lucky instead of a sweet." Bernays spearheaded the campaign, which included hiring women to march in the New York City Easter parade and to smoke in public—something unheard of for women at that time and typically associated with prostitutes. The next day, the event made front-page headlines across the country (and the world) (Pollay, 1990), revolutionizing the social acceptability of women's consumption of cigarettes. Bernays relied on a Freudian analysis from a psychoanalyst to market cigarettes to women, invoking the personal freedom (and oral fixation) that cigarette use symbolized. At that time, cigarette smoking was synonymous with males, not females, and women's liberation was paralleled with the societal freedom that men already enjoyed (Brill, cited in Ewen, 1976). Bernays, as one of the earliest recognized practitioners of public relations, combined the field with psychology and sociology (i.e., media effects). However, not all observers were complimentary of this mix; one author called it the "science of ballyhoo" (Flynn, 1932). Bernays spent the latter part of his life trying, in a sense, to "undo" what he had accomplished in marketing tobacco use so successfully, stating, "No reputable public relations organization would accept a cigarette account since their cancer-causing effects have been proven" (quoted in Buffett, 1999, pp. 148-149). Media depictions of smoking continue to be criticized because cigarette use in the media still is considered to be the stuff that role models are made of. Fully 17 of 18 films examined from 1997 included at least 1 incident of smoking a cigarette, and half of them featured more than 15 scenes of smoking ("Smoking Seen," 1997).

A more recent example of a perspicuous publicity promotion started in July 1996 when the Tyco Toys public relations firm sent a Tickle-Me-Elmo doll to talk show host Rosie O'Donnell (for her then 1-year-old son) and another 200 dolls to the show's producer. However, the doll did not appear on the show until October, when O'Donnell threw it into the audience every time a guest (unknowingly) said the word "wall," in a takeoff on the Groucho Marx game show *You Bet Your Life*. Given that a portion of the audience demographics for *The Rosie O'Donnell Show* consists of stay-at-home mothers with preschool-age children, the marketing ploy, combined with knowledge of audience, hit the jackpot. The doll experienced another television promotional opportunity when *Today* host Bryant Gumbel held a Tickle-Me-Elmo doll on his lap for most of a show in November (the doll had been part of a segment on popular holiday gifts and was mentioned in passing as a gender-free toy). Prior to Christmas 1996, the furry red doll spun off from the *Sesame Street* character was so scarce that people were asking $2,000 per doll (it retailed for about $30). Sending the doll to O'Donnell was no spur-of-the-moment fluke. The public relations firm had successfully linked Cabbage Patch dolls to pregnant *Today* host Jane Pauley in 1983 and wanted to repeat the event with Tickle-Me-Elmo and O'Donnell. At the peak of the pre-holiday craze, Tyco Toys actually tried to halt the media effect and pulled its Tickle-Me-Elmo commercials off the air, fearing that the very sight of the toy would increase discontent among the children who did not have the toy (unintended effect) (Pereira, 1996).

Public relations practitioners can see from these illustrations that, regardless of the time period, public relations efforts can have wildly successful and powerful outcomes when content is carefully matched to an audience. Bernays' work provides an example of an unintended or long-term effect not originally foreseen—widespread knowledge of the health risks of tobacco use. Tickle-Me-Elmo's marketing created such a desire that, in some ways, it produced an unintended effect of discontent and frustration for children and parents who were unable to locate the toy or afford the inflated purchase price.

MEDIA ENVIRONMENT

As anyone even peripherally involved in observing the media industry will attest, the media environment is constantly transforming. The changing consumption patterns still display some consistent and intuitive findings related to socioeconomic status, age, and exposure to news and, ultimately, the path to potentially powerful media effects.

As Stempel and Hargrove (1996) noted, the mass media environment is changing, necessitating a continuing examination of the mass media audience. The authors specified the ways in which the media sphere has changed—(a) the prevalence of CNN and the proliferation of television news programs such as NBC's *Dateline,* (b) the addition of Internet and on-line news sources, (c) the ability of grocery store tabloids to set political agendas, and (d) the deregulation of radio during the 1980s and the subsequent elimi-nation of radio news. A national survey of adults who matched census figures was conducted in 1995 (Stempel & Hargrove, 1996) and evaluated the use of 11 media: local and network television news, television magazine programs (e.g., *Hard Copy, A Current Affair*), daily newspapers, radio news, radio talk shows, news magazines (e.g., *Newsweek, Time, U.S. News and World Report*), political magazines (e.g., *New Republic, National Review*), grocery store tabloids (e.g., *National Enquirer*), and Internet and on-line computer services (e.g., CompuServe, America Online).

Local television news was the most regularly used medium and was highly correlated with use of network television news. Demographically, media use increased with age for most media. Assuming that younger people use media more is likely a common misconception. Younger people, who began their educational careers by learning the ABCs from television, actually used media less. Print media and radio news use increased with higher levels of education; college graduates were less likely to view television magazine shows and less likely to read grocery store tabloids (or at least less likely to *say* that they read grocery story tabloids!). Use of newspapers, political magazines, and news magazines increased with income, whereas lower income respondents reported that they were regular users of television news magazines and grocery store tabloids. The traditional forms of media were the most used, and despite all the hyperbole, use of computer media lagged behind use of other media use and still would even if use of computer media tripled.

The high level of viewership in local television news is a plus for public relations practitioners who are particularly interested in getting video news releases (VNRs) on the air. Public relations practitioners, however, have some obstacles to overcome such as mistrust of information provided in a VNR and television news' emphasis on visual storytelling. Research indicates that approximately 80% of news directors use VNRs in television newscasts ("Nationwide Survey," 1990) and that 78% of television stations use VNRs in some fashion once a week ("Survey of News Directors," 1991). A content analysis of stories generated from a VNR on local television news indicated that extensive production costs probably were wasted. Results showed that most stations used portions of the VNR for the "America Responds to AIDS" campaign rather than the packaged story provided (Cameron & Blount, 1996). Stations used "B-roll" (video pictures that match reporter or anchor audio), mobilizing information, and sound bites from official sources that were placed closer to the beginning of the story than those sound bites toward the end of the story. Also, contrary to popular opinion positing that stations with limited resources are more likely to use VNR stories in their entirety, "resource-poor" stations did not use more of the packaged story when compared to their resource-rich counterparts (Cameron & Blount, 1996). An experiment testing viewer responses to VNRs indicated that participants reported that VNR-based messages were more credible than similar-source material and showed a positive relationship between the credibility of a newscast and VNR recall (Owen & Karrh, 1996).

News also may be an advantageous placement for public relations issues for several reasons, and news content is likely to be a product of public relation efforts. Conservative estimates place the percentage of news that is derived directly from public relations efforts at 40% (Stauber & Rampton, 1995). News content has been shown to facilitate more learning about political information when compared to learning from political advertisements, the rationale being that audiences have a greater chance of being exposed to the information in news than in ads (Zhao & Chaffee, 1995). Prior research from the 1972 presidential campaign had shown just the opposite; people learned more from the political ads because ads contained more issue-oriented information than did newscasts (Kern, 1989).

Although political advertisements are not PSAs, results from learning about issue-oriented content may be applied to PSAs because the average viewer might not have the visual literacy necessary to make the distinction between a commercial announcement and a PSA. News content, like advertising and PSAs, is one of the few media messages in which the message is more or less consistent across media. Its pervasiveness, therefore, is more likely to contribute to powerful media effects. That consistency and pervasiveness, combined with what we know

about socioeconomic and age-specific media consumption, have media selection implications for public relations.

CONCLUSION

Bernays' writing from more than 70 years ago continues to sound fresh and applicable for public relations and media effects. In *Crystallizing Public Opinion* (Bernays, 1923), and in a public address (Bernays, 1925), he summarized three points for public relations practitioners. First, the practitioner must be a careful student of media to know how people develop their "pictures of the world" (Bernays, 1923). Second, the practitioner should be knowledgeable about sociology and anthropology to know how attitudes are formed through culture and social structures (Bernays, 1925). Third, the practitioner should be knowledgeable of the individual's psychological processes; practitioners can then tailor their efforts for maximum effect (Bernays, 1923).

Understanding of direct, limited, and powerful effects models, coupled with a working categorization of effects (level of analysis, type of effect, nature of effect, intent of effect, and form vs. content), can serve to inform choices made by public relations practitioners. Research on the intersection of issues pertinent to practitioners, under the rubric of media effects, helps bring clarity to an unavoidably inexact science. This poses a challenge to academic researchers to further explicate theory into practice.

A recurring theme throughout this chapter has been the importance of knowing audience characteristics. People interested in media effects never can know too much about the audience under scrutiny. Unfortunately, much of what occurs in an audience's mind—the black box—is unknowable simply because individuals are unable to express their thought processes accurately; research on media effects has been based primarily on self-report measures (Geiger & Newhagen, 1993). Nevertheless, the audience is the necessary lynchpin underlying media effects.

Stewardship

The Fifth Step in the Public Relations Process

KATHLEEN S. KELLY

It is easier to keep a friend than to make a new friend. In terms of public relations, reinforcing attitudes and behaviors of individuals who already think and act in ways desired by an organization is a strategically sound objective. Yet, theories of how public relations is and should be practiced ignore the importance of *previously established* relationships. Specifically, models describing the process of public relations, such as Marston's (1979) popular RACE (research, action plan, communication, and evaluation) formula, end with the final step of evaluation, thereby implying that friendships resulting from one instance of programming are of little or no value to future efforts.

Contradictorily, contemporary definitions of public relations hold that the function is responsible for establishing and *maintaining* relationships between an organization and its key publics (Cutlip, Center, & Broom, 2000). Recent research on relationship management has shown that factors such as trust, involvement, and commitment—developed through multi-year efforts—differentiate members of publics who react positively toward an organization from those who react negatively (Ledingham & Bruning, 1998b). The findings support J. Grunig's (1993a) contention that the contribution of public relations to organizational success is dependent on practitioners "building long-term behavioral relationships with strategic publics" (p. 136).

Current process models, then, are seriously flawed because they ignore ongoing relationships. This chapter introduces a new model with the fifth step of stewardship, which prescribes maintenance of relationships and makes the public relations process truly cyclical; that is, the process does not begin each time with completely unknown publics. The five-step process of ROPES (research-objectives-programming-evaluation-stewardship) better explains what practitioners do—or should do—to make public relations effective and efficient.

ROPES PROCESS

ROPES originally was conceptualized as a descriptive and normative theory of fund raising, one of the specializations of public relations (Kelly, 1998). It draws from a public relations model by Hendrix (1998), ROPE, which does not include the stewardship step or account for the fund raising specialization. As explained shortly, stewardship of previous donors is essential to raising future gifts—a principle widely accepted by fund raisers. Literature suggests that practitioners in other specializations, such as investor relations, also devote much of their attention and time to known groups and individuals who have demonstrated their support of the organization in the past. In contrast to current models, ROPES provides a comprehensive theory of relationship management; that is, it explains how relations with all publics—whether donors, investors, community residents, government officials, members of the media, consumers, or others—are and should be managed. Figure 21.1 displays the ROPES process.

As shown in Figure 21.1, the public relations process begins with research in three areas: (a) the organization for which practitioners work; (b) the opportunity, problem, or issue faced by the organization; and (c) the publics related to the organization and opportunity. Failure to conduct research in all three areas dooms public relations to sporadic results that contribute little to organizational effectiveness. The second step in the process is setting objectives that are specific and measurable. They are of two types: output (which deals with public relations techniques or the work to be produced) and impact (which deals with the intended *effects* of programming). Both types of objectives flow from the organization's goals; that is, their attainment directly supports organizational plans.

The third step, programming, consists of planning and implementing activities designed to bring about the outcomes stated in the objectives. The fourth step is evaluation, which is conducted on three consecutive levels: messages and techniques are tested (preparation evaluation), programming is monitored and adjusted (process evaluation), and results are measured and compared to the set objectives (program evaluation). Finally, stewardship completes the process and furnishes an essential loop back to the beginning of managing relationships. Four elements are basic to stewardship: reciprocity, responsibility, reporting, and relationship nurturing.

A full description of stewardship is given later, followed by an overview of the other four steps in ROPES. Before doing so, the chapter first examines communication effects, recent research on relationship management, and the importance of previous behavior.

COMMUNICATION EFFECTS

Most process models require that objectives precede and govern programming decisions and that, in turn, evaluation is based on how well the programming met the set objectives. In other words, the intended effects of public relations are specified in the objectives chosen early in the process.

Communication scholars break down impact objectives, or those specifying intended effects, by creation, change, or reinforcement of cognitions, attitudes, and behavior. Cognitions are further broken down to concepts dealing with awareness, knowledge, and understanding, each a progressively higher order of thinking. J. Grunig and Hunt (1984) drew from theory and research to conceptualize a taxonomy of public relations objectives, which they grounded in McLeod and Chaffee's (1973) coorientation model. More recently, Hunt and J. Grunig (1994) refined and presented the five impact objectives for programming: awareness, accuracy, understanding, agreement, and behavior. The objectives—combined with creation, change, and reinforcement—represent all intended effects of communication and are increasingly difficult to achieve as they ascend from awareness to behavior.

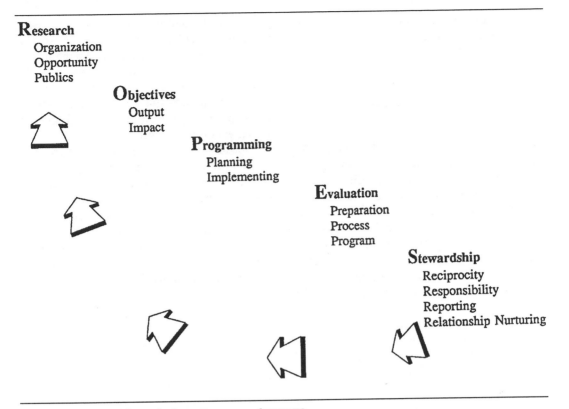

Figure 21.1. Public Relations Process of ROPES

Although it is relatively easy to get people to form new cognitions or to change them (e.g., a story in the mass media can create awareness), it is much more difficult to affect attitudes and behavior. Situations calling for creating *new* attitudes or behaviors are unusual (e.g., people's first exposure to new innovations such as Web sites). Changing them rarely is achievable through short-term programming. As Hunt and J. Grunig (1994) explained, communication can change attitudes and behaviors of publics, but the objectives often take years to accomplish. "Only simple behavior generally can be changed in the short run" (p. 17). "If bringing about a behavior is a must," J. Grunig and Hunt (1984) advised, then "identify the people who are already active publics for the behavior you want" (p. 366).

Despite such advice, public relations scholars pay little more than lip service to reinforcing ei-

ther attitudes or behavior, which are central to effectiveness. Hunt and J. Grunig (1994), for example, barely mentioned objectives dealing with reinforcement in their theoretical framework for public relations techniques. Although Broom and Dozier (1990) designated "repeat behavior" as a high-level effect in their program impact criteria, they provided weak justification for its inclusion, saying only that maintaining desired behaviors over an extended time "[is an outcome] sought by many public relations programs" (p. 86).

The stewardship step in ROPES ensures that the public relations process is continuous; it does not stop and then later start with entirely different and unknown publics. This additional step makes ROPES superior to other models, which ignore crossovers in situational publics and critical objectives of reinforcing positive attitudes and behavior. It offers greater congruency with findings now emerging from research on relationship management.

RELATIONSHIP MANAGEMENT

According to Ledingham and Bruning (1998a), the field of public relations is undergoing a paradigm shift as attention increasingly focuses on managing organization-public relationships rather than on producing communication activities. The authors explained, "The essence of public relations as relationship management . . . is to use communication strategically to create, develop, and *nurture* a relationship between an organization and its key public(s)" (p. 2, italics added).

The conceptual change began with Ferguson's (1984) work more than 15 years ago and has been advanced by scholars such as Broom, Casey, and Ritchey (1997); J. Grunig (1992a, 1993a); and Ledingham and Bruning (1998a, 1998b). For example, whereas J. Grunig and Hunt (1984) defined public relations during the mid-1980s as "the management of communication between an organization and its publics" (p. 6), J. Grunig (1992a) more recently described the purpose of public relations as "building relationships with publics that constrain or enhance the ability of the organization to meet its mission" (p. 20).

Recent studies have identified and tested factors contributing to successful relationships and have provided evidence that such relationships have beneficial consequences for organizations. Ledingham and Bruning (1998b), for example, found that among a telephone company's current customers, those who perceived high levels of trust, openness, involvement, investment, and commitment in the relationship likely would continue to purchase phone services from the company, whereas customers who perceived lower levels of the relationship variables would likely sign up with new providers or were undecided about what they would do. The researchers concluded, "Building trust, demonstrating involvement, investment, and commitment, and maintaining open, frank communication . . . im-

pacts the stay-leave decision in a competitive environment" (p. 61).

In subsequent research, Ledingham and Bruning (1998a) verified that perceptions of the relationship between an organization and members of a key public significantly influence loyalty to the sponsoring organization. They found that awareness of a company's performance on the relationship factors "creates a favorable *predisposition* toward the organization" (p. 9, italics added). In turn, favorable predispositions can positively affect an organization's financial well-being. Ledingham and Bruning argued, therefore, that relationship *building* should be a cornerstone of public relations practice. The importance that they assigned to existing relationships has long been acknowledged in fund raising and marketing.

IMPORTANCE OF PREVIOUS BEHAVIOR

A fund-raising principle given almost the status of law is the following: "The best prospects are previous donors." Consultant James Gregory Lord elaborated, "Experience shows that the best prospects for the immediate future are those who have given in the past" (Lord, 1983, p. 49). Previous donors have a higher probability of making gifts than do nondonors, regardless of all other factors. Furthermore, the more a person gives, the more likely he or she will give again (Seymour, 1966/1988). Conversely, Lord (1983) warned, "It's very difficult to turn a non-giver into a giver" (p. 85). Greenfield (1991) summarized practitioner wisdom: "Donors are and will always remain the best prospects for more giving" (p. 40).

Effects theory holds that changing behavior is more difficult than reinforcing behavior. Nichols (1992), drawing from theory and experience, argued that it takes five times as much work to acquire a new donor as it does to renew an existing one. Based on observation, practitioners estimate that about 75% of an organization's lower level donors renew their gifts the next year

(Mixer, 1993). Therefore, reinforcing repeat behavior is a fundamental objective for annual giving—one of the two primary programs of fundraising (Kelly, 1991). Practitioners also strongly assert that most major gifts, the second primary program, come from previous donors.

Repeat gifts cost significantly less to raise than do new gifts. Levis (1991), for example, estimated that the cost ratio for raising an average gift of $10 from new donors is 100%, whereas it is only 35% from renewed donors. An average gift of $1,000 from new donors costs 25%, but it costs only 10% from renewed donors. Based on systems theory, continued funding by repeat donors reduces financial uncertainty by providing a relatively dependable stream of dollars.

The critical difference in probability of giving between an organization's previous donors and nondonors was documented by Independent Sector (1994) in its biennial survey of U.S. giving and volunteering. It found that 85% of the respondents would be very likely or somewhat likely to make gifts in response to mail solicitations from organizations that they had regularly supported in the past, whereas only 45% would be very likely or somewhat likely to contribute to organizations that they had not previously supported.

Summarizing this discussion, a simple fact of fund raising is that most annual gifts, and nearly all major gifts, come from individuals, corporations, and foundations that have given to the organization in the past. Therefore, how donors are treated *after* they make their gifts largely determines future success. It also costs less to raise gifts from past donors than from new donors.

Touching briefly on marketing, common sense dictates the necessity of keeping customers in today's competitive global economy. For example, during 1998, Hyatt International Corporation concentrated on "retention marketing" to survive the downturn in the tourism industry caused by the Asian currency crisis. Sharon Barlow, Hyatt's corporate public relations manager, explained the strategy in a recent presentation: "Take care of those customers [who] we do have and offer value for their hard earned money. It is these customers who we look after today who will be loyal to us tomorrow" (Barlow, 1998).

Furthermore, marketing studies show that it costs seven times more to get a new customer than to keep a current one (Microsoft, 1997).

Public relations needs a process model that acknowledges the desirability of stewarding existing friendships.

STEWARDSHIP

According to Greenfield (1991), the purpose of stewardship in fund raising is to thank donors who have made gifts and to "establish the means for continued communication that will help to preserve their interest and attention to the organization" (p. 148). Worth (1993) added, "Because the best prospects for new gifts are past donors, programs that provide careful stewardship and provide donors with timely information on the impact of their gifts can pay significant dividends in continued support" (p. 13).

As noted earlier, the stewardship step in ROPES consists of four alliterative elements requiring the attention of fund raisers and other public relations practitioners: (a) *reciprocity,* by which the organization demonstrates its gratitude for supportive beliefs and behaviors; (b) *responsibility,* meaning that the organization acts in a socially responsible manner to those who have supported it; (c) *reporting,* a basic requirement of accountability; and (d) *relationship nurturing.* Embedded in the elements are ethical standards that hold moral duty above other considerations. In other words, the added step of stewardship not only ensures continuity in the public relations process but also promotes ethical behavior by practitioners and their organizations.

According to Jeavons (1994), stewardship is thought of too narrowly as dealing only with the management of contributed funds. The original meaning, he argued, is larger and fuller—responsibility for overall administration. "Steward speaks of a person who is concerned with the right ordering and management of all the affairs and concerns—including what we now call economic concerns—of a household or community" (p. 111).

As stewards, then, public relations practitioners are attentive to every aspect of the organization's behavior that might affect relations with supportive publics. They serve as agents of accountability and the organization's conscience. Jeavons (1994) explained, "Real stewardship has inescapably moral obligations and responsibilities" (p. 115).

Reciprocity

The norm of reciprocity, conceptualized by sociologist Alvin Gouldner, holds that "those whom you have helped have an obligation to help you" (Gouldner, 1960, p. 173). Therefore, Gouldner concluded, "If you want to be helped by others, you must help them; hence it is not only proper but also expedient to conform with the specific status rights of others and with the general norm" (p. 173).

According to Gouldner (1960), reciprocity is a universal component of all moral codes. Studies by anthropologists have shown that it is cross-cultural and fundamental to all people; human interaction requires stable practices of give and take (Becker, 1986b). For individuals, reciprocity is a mandatory virtue (Martin, 1994b); for organizations, it is the essence of social responsibility (J. Grunig & White, 1992). Therefore, when publics support organizations by adopting positive attitudes and behavior, the organizations receiving the support must reciprocate.

Repaying obligations helps to maintain social balance, and as M. W. Martin (1994) explained, "Mere taking upsets the balance" (p. 70). Becker (1986) further emphasized that reciprocity affects respect of self and the other party. When socially ingrained expectations of reciprocity are not met, respect is put at risk. Conversely, when expectations are met, they strengthen a sense of *equal worth*—a characteristic of symmetrical public relations. Lombardo (1995) elaborated, "An unbalanced relationship has been temporarily created, which can be put into balance through reciprocity" (p. 297).

At the applied level, reciprocity simply means that organizations show gratitude to those who have supported them. Gratitude is broken down by acts of appreciation and recognition. The most common and expected way of demonstrating appreciation is to say "thank you." Whereas marketers have adopted this basic rule of reciprocity to help keep customers, public relations practitioners rarely thank publics on whom the organization's success depends. As Howe (1991) advised fund raisers, "The more prompt and personal the expression of appreciation, the more favorable the carryover toward further giving" (p. 32).

According to Ryan (1994), "Recognition displays your institution's style and gratitude. It shows good stewardship. It says you're thoughtful, attentive, and caring" (p. 64). An effective and simple form of recognition is to personalize, whenever possible, all future communications to supportive publics, thereby recognizing their special status to the organization. More elaborate acts of appreciation and recognition also are recommended. For example, when community residents and government officials have supported expansion of a company's facility, the company can reciprocate by inviting members of the publics to a special event, such as an open house, at the completion of construction.

Scholars have found that patterns of reciprocity lead to further helping by exchange partners. An illustration is provided by Dayton Hudson, the Minneapolis, Minnesota-based conglomerate that owns more than 1,000 department and discount stores including Marshall Field's and Target. A longtime leader in corporate philanthropy, Dayton Hudson is one of the few large U.S. corporations that annually contributes 5% of its pretax income—a policy it adopted in 1946 (Gray & Moore, 1996). During the past 50 years, the corporation has given more than $350 million, or roughly $19,000 a day, to charitable organizations in the various communities in which it operates. Reciprocity, as well as other elements of stewardship, by the recipients encouraged repeated contributions. The long-term relationships paid off royally in 1987 when community organizations rallied to the corporation's aid and helped it survive a hostile takeover attempt by the Dart Group of Landover, Maryland.

According to Ann Barkelew, Dayton Hudson's then vice president of corporate public relations, in June 1987 the corporation confronted "the very real possibility of being taken over by people we knew would 'bust up' the corporation and sell off its assets to finance the takeover" (Barkelew, 1993, p. 8). The chief executive officer (CEO) of Dayton Hudson asked Minnesota's governor to call a special session of the legislature to tighten the state's anti-takeover laws, thereby providing greater protection for the company. Legislators took action just 7 days later, largely because of a groundswell of support from the media, other businesses, government officials, and, as stated in the *Minneapolis-St. Paul Star Tribune,* "groups that have received millions of dollars of contributions" (quoted in Barkelew, 1993, p. 8).

The experience reinforced Dayton Hudson's commitment to philanthropy, and community organizations continue to benefit from the corporation's giving program. Significantly, the normative model of public relations, the two-way symmetrical model, envisions public relations as a process of continual and reciprocal exchange between an organization and its key publics (J. Grunig, 1993a).

Responsibility

Stewardship demands that organizations act in a socially responsible manner to publics that have supported the organization and its goals in the past. The concept of social responsibility simply means that organizations act as good citizens. It is rooted in systems theory in that organizations are interdependent with people and other organizations in their environment.

At its most basic level, responsibility requires organizations to keep their word. Promises made when seeking support must be kept (e.g., a pledge to reduce air pollution). More generally, organizations must demonstrate through their actions that they are worthy of supportive attitudes and behaviors. Public relations practitioners counsel senior management about promises

and expectations that must be fulfilled if the organization is to succeed. Betraying public trust is expensive; building goodwill with people who already are aligned with the organization saves money.

Heath (1997) argued that achieving high standards of corporate responsibility is vital to strategic management, and he placed the obligation for meeting key publics' expectations on the public relations function. Congruent with the stewardship step, Wilson (1994) contended that the focus of public relations ought to be on the development of "relational responsibility."

Reporting

Organizations are required to keep publics informed about developments related to the opportunity or problem for which support was sought. Reporting to publics reinforces positive attitudes and behaviors, and it increases the probability that supportive publics will react similarly in future situations.

Organizations are accountable to specific publics as well as to society in general. Accountability is the degree to which organizations continually reinforce public confidence in the integrity and effectiveness of their performance (Dressel, 1980).

On a general level, accountability is closely related to the concept of social responsibility. All organizations—for-profit companies, government agencies, and nonprofits—have an obligation to serve societal needs because society grants them the opportunities to operate (J. Grunig, 1992a). As pointed out by J. Grunig and Hunt (1984), almost all discussion about social responsibility is concerned with companies, yet these authors rightfully asserted, "It is as important for governmental and nonprofit organizations to be socially responsible as for business firms" (p. 48). A former president of the General Electric Company explained the basic philosophy: "We know perfectly well that business does not function by divine right but, like any other part of society, exists with the sanction of the community as a whole" (Cutlip et al., 2000, p. 24).

On the specific level, an organization is answerable to constituencies that are affected by or may affect the organization's behavior. Of particular importance are those publics that have supported the organization in the past. Relationships cannot be maintained if the organization only communicates with friends when it seeks more help.

Relationship Nurturing

The head of fund raising for Carnegie Mellon University justified time and resources spent on stewardship: "It's easier to get a second gift from a donor who is treated well the first time than it is to get a new gift" (Dundjerski, 1994, p. 22). Treating publics well goes beyond reciprocity, responsibility, and reporting; relationships so critical to the organization's success must be nurtured. Grace (1991) said that whereas "traditional notions of stewardship refer to the gift and ensuring that it is spent wisely and in accordance with the donor's wishes," contemporary fundraisers have adopted "an expanded sense of stewardship, one that includes continued relationship building with the donor" (p. 158). "This new view of stewardship," she explained, "lets people know on a regular basis that you care about them, respect their support, appreciate their gifts, and want their interest and involvement" (p. 158).

As described earlier, recent research has documented the value of nurturing relationships with publics other than donors, and scholars have recommended that relationship building form a cornerstone for public relations practice. Culbertson, Jeffers, Stone, and Terrell (1993) provided the rationale: "There is reason to believe that involvement enhances genuine, long-term behavioral support" (p. 98).

The most effective means of nurturing relationships is quite simple: Accept the importance of supportive publics and keep them at the forefront of the organization's consciousness. Information and involvement are fundamental, and both should flow naturally from the organization's work. For example, publics that have been supportive in the past should receive copies of the organization's publications including its annual report. They should be among the groups represented when advisory boards are formed. Opportunities to nurture relationships are numerous and occur on a weekly basis.

Public relations and the organizations it serves can benefit from following fund raising and adopting stewardship as an essential component of relationship management. Lord (1983) summarized the thrust of this discussion as follows: "Good stewardship is well worth the extra effort it requires. It is the bedrock on which the future of an organization is built" (p. 93). The chapter concludes by presenting an overview of the four steps preceding stewardship in the ROPES process.

RESEARCH

Regardless of the emphasis here on stewardship, the most important step in the public relations process is the first—research. Without solid research, public relations is reduced to flackery—hit-and-miss activities without direction and with little respect. Research provides knowledge, formulates strategy, inspires confidence, and ensures that practitioners achieve desired results. As Cutlip et al. (2000) proclaimed, research "is the essential ingredient that makes public relations a management function as well as a managed function" (p. 364).

Following Hendrix (1998), the first step in ROPES is broken down into research in the three areas of organization, opportunity, and publics. Practitioners must be thoroughly familiar with the organization's history, finances, personnel, products and services, and past public relations efforts. They must develop a solid understanding of operations and industry issues.

A logical progression from knowledge about the organization is research on the opportunity, which is grounded in coorientation theory. Models of coorientation, such as Broom and Dozier's (1990) model, emphasize the importance of determining the degree of agreement and accuracy between an organization's views of an opportunity, problem, or issue and its constituencies' views before programming begins. If differences are found, then the organization must change its intended behavior or correct misperceptions.

Effective and efficient public relations demands that publics be matched to the organization and the opportunity, and this can be accomplished only through research. J. Grunig's situational theory of publics (e.g., J. Grunig & Repper, 1992) guides practitioners in identifying groups to which public relations should target its communications. The three predictor variables—problem recognition, level of involvement, and constraint recognition—distinguish publics that are active, aware, latent, and nonpublics. Logically, research on publics starts by determining the status of individuals and organizations that have been supportive in the past (i.e., those with whom relationships have been maintained and strengthened through previous stewardship). The research then extends outward to strangers.

OBJECTIVES

Goals of the public relations department evolve from the organization's goals. Based on the research step, goals are broken down into objectives. The objectives are formulated to state the results desired from programming. Paraphrasing fund raiser Joel Smith, without objectives derived from organizational goals, public relations is destined to be more random than rational—an amateurish effort around which serendipitous accomplishments occasionally will occur but by which they rarely are caused (Smith, 1981).

Goals are general statements that express broad desired results, whereas *objectives* are specific statements that express results as measurable outcomes. Objectives consist of five parts: an infinitive verb, a single outcome stated as re-

ceiver of the verb's action, the magnitude of the action expressed in quantifiable terms, the targeted public, and a target date or time frame for achieving the outcome. For example, one public relations objective might be as follows: To hold at least 20 meetings with leaders of civic and professional groups throughout the county to discuss tax policy between July 1, 200_ and June 30, 200_. Another objective might be: To increase the percentage of county residents who understand the company's position against higher property tax rates from 20% to 55% by November 1, 200_. These examples illustrate output and impact objectives, respectively.

Output objectives, according to Hendrix (1998), are "stated intentions regarding program production and effort (or output)" (p. 25). Impact objectives, on the other hand, "represent specific intended effects of public relations programs on their audiences" (p. 26). Whereas impact objectives deal with the five communication effects (awareness, accuracy, understanding, agreement, and behavior), output objectives focus on the public relations techniques used to communicate with publics (e.g., small group meetings, speeches, direct mail, special events, newsletters, story placements, public service announcements). Both types of objectives are valuable to the ROPES process, which contradicts the assessment of most authors: "In the best of all possible worlds, PR directors would use only impact objectives" (p. 25).

Output objectives do not address the consequences of one cycle of programming. If used appropriately, however, they do contribute to the eventual attainment of longer term goals. Stated another way, output objectives, strategically selected and based on research, increase probabilities for future success; specifically, they enhance the climate for changing attitudes and behaviors.

Such objectives are valued in fund raising and are used to guide an important part of programming known as *cultivation*. For example, practitioner wisdom holds that a major gift typically requires a minimum of nine cultivation contacts over a period of 2 to 3 years before solicitation (Kelly, 1998). Therefore, a common fund-raising objective is as follows: To meet with 25 nondonors who are prospects for major gifts to discuss mutual interests and needs by June 30, 200_. Astute fund raisers generally reserve the bulk of impact objectives for reinforcing the behavior of previous donors.

A general rule for public relations, then, is that output objectives should be used to direct programming that will contribute to future success, whereas impact objectives should be formulated to direct programming that will *create* awareness, *change* accuracy and understanding, and *reinforce* positive attitudes and behaviors.

Objectives must be reviewed and approved by senior managers. Not only does approval ensure that objectives support the organization's goals, but evaluation of public relations programs and practitioners' performance will be based on the extent to which the objectives are met.

PROGRAMMING

The programming step consists of two parts: planning and implementing. The first part results in a written public relations plan. A convenient format is to first divide the plan by programs or specializations, such as government relations or investor relations, and then to subdivide each by the related objectives. A synopsis of the research supporting and shaping each objective is given, followed by an outline of the activities and tasks required to accomplish the objective, including selected public relations techniques. (A decimal system explained by Kelly, 1998, is helpful.) Planning tools are used to present time lines and personnel assignments. The means by which the objective will be evaluated and plans for stewardship are described. Budgets are a fundamental component, including line items for contingency (10%), research (10%), and stewardship (3%).

Implementing programming is the most familiar part of the public relations process. To avoid repetition of common knowledge, the discussion skips over this major component and

moves to the evaluation step, which often is given short shrift by practitioners.

EVALUATION

Organizations are effective when the goals they formulated are met. As stated earlier, the public relations department's goals are formulated in support of the organization's goals, and measurable objectives are specified to meet departmental goals. Guided by the objectives, programming is planned and broken down by activities and tasks. When implementation is complete, programming is evaluated by the degree to which it accomplished the set objectives. If objectives are met, then goals will have been attained. In this systematic manner, the department advances the organization by helping it to achieve its overall goals and to fulfill its mission. In other words, the public relations department contributes to organizational effectiveness when it meets the goals and objectives it formulated to support the organization's goals.

Practitioners conduct preparation evaluation, testing messages and techniques for their appropriateness. For example, readability studies determine whether messages are written in a style suitable to the educational level of targeted publics. During programming, practitioners conduct process evaluation to monitor progress and to make adjustments when necessary. They use methods such as telephone surveys to periodically check the outcomes of activities. Once programming is completed, practitioners evaluate their efforts by comparing the results attained to the results sought, as expressed by the set objectives. Whereas in-house counting tells them whether output objectives were reached, survey research and other methodologies are needed to assess programming designed for impact objectives.

Findings of program evaluation document the contribution of public relations to organizational effectiveness and are used to improve future efforts. An add-on value of the fourth step is that by *listening* to publics through evaluative research, practitioners engage in two-way communication, and the research itself provides quality interaction; that is, research serves as a cultivation and stewardship activity.

CONCLUSION

The public relations process is incomplete without stewardship. The relationships established and developed through the steps just described should not be discarded. Publics who have demonstrated that they are friends of the organization are deserving of continued attention.

Public relations practitioners must ensure that expressions of appreciation are provided, recognition activities are planned, responsibility is monitored, a system of reporting is in place, and strategies for relationship nurturing are carried out. A key issue, however, is that others in the organization must be as concerned with stewardship as the public relations department. CEOs and other senior managers who deem relationships important when seeking support, but who do not take a role in stewardship after support is given, are acting under false pretenses. As in all steps of ROPES, public relations must be an advocate for both the organization and the publics on which the organization's success and survival depend.

CHAPTER 22

Activism

MICHAEL F. SMITH

DENISE P. FERGUSON

From the earliest days of the modern practice of public relations, activists and organizations have maintained a symbiotic but tense relationship. Near the turn of the 19th century, an activist media, led by writers whom Ewen (1996) called " 'Progressive publicists,' drummers on behalf of social reform" (p. 44), urged organizations and the government to ameliorate social problems. Journalistic muckrakers pressured organizations and the government to impose regulations on business, and one of the earliest public fights between an organization and activists was fought in 1884 when the American Medical Association debated anti-vivisectionists, foreshadowing today's animal rights movement (Cutlip, 1994; see also Cutlip, 1995, chap. 15). The surge in activism during the 1960s and 1970s resulted in a plethora of studies that attempted to explain and predict activist organizations' behavior—and, coincidentally, that highlighted the importance of public relations efforts to manage the issues raised by these groups.

Activism is such a part of public relations practice that some have suggested that public relations practitioners gain legitimacy and in-

crease their utility to an organization primarily in the presence of active publics. In summarizing their research on activism and corporate responses, J. Grunig and L. Grunig (1997) claimed that "activist pressure stimulates organizations to develop excellent public relations departments" (p. 25). Despite this, the relationship between activists and organizations is tenuous, and the history of conflict between these two entities suggests that much can be learned from studying activism and responses to it.

In this chapter, we examine the role of activism in public relations practice. We treat activists not only as challenges for public relations practitioners but also as practitioners themselves. In developing our views, we draw from studies in political science, sociology, communication, and public relations.

One of the first challenges in discussing activism is defining just what an activist organization is. Organized activists are variously referred to as special interest groups, pressure groups, issue groups, grassroots organizations, or social movement organizations (Smith, 1996a). L. Grunig (1992a) argued that an "activist group is a group of two or more individuals who organize in order to influence another public or publics through action.... Its members are committed and organized ... to reach their goals—which could be political, economic, or social" (p. 504). This definition, however, could describe many organizations. Berry (1984) suggested that activist groups are organized around a common goal and attempt to influence public policy to reach that goal. Smith (1997) suggested that activist organizations' primary purpose is to influence public policy, organizational action, or social norms and values. It is important to recognize that activists are *organized* and, therefore, face some of the same challenges as do other organizations. They also strategically use communication to achieve those goals (Ferguson, 1997).

In this chapter, we explore the dimensions of activism and the interaction between activists and those institutions or organizations that they target for change. To accomplish this, we (a) review various theories regarding the formation and development of activism, (b) examine the goals of activist organizations and the tactics used to achieve those goals, (c) study the responses of organizations targeted by activists, and (d) offer some observations regarding methodology and areas of future research.

FORMATION AND DEVELOPMENT OF ACTIVIST ORGANIZATIONS

One of the principal concerns of public relations researchers has been in determining how activist organizations form. From a corporate management perspective, understanding how activists organize can help public relations practitioners to predict how and when activism will create the need for public relations programs. For activists, this knowledge can help them to organize more effectively.

In this section, we review three general perspectives on how activist organizations form and develop. The first involves macro-level explana-

tions of the conditions that foster the formation of activist publics. The second explains activism from the standpoint of the activists themselves, arguing that groups of people form activist publics because they identify problems and believe that taking action can solve them. The third perspective builds on the other two and examines the stages through which activism and activist organizations develop.

Macro-Level Perspective

The first major perspective offers macro-level analyses of the formation of activist groups. One macro-level explanation suggests that a country's system of government, political climate, media, and culture provide the preconditions for activism (Ferguson, 1998; Sriramesh & White, 1992). Much of this research has examined public relations as practiced internationally, particularly in countries undergoing economic and political transformations. Researchers have investigated what political, economic, and cultural conditions were necessary before normative public relations principles can be practiced and, specifically, whether it even was possible to practice these generic principles in a socialist, centralized society (Vercic, L. Grunig, & J. Grunig, 1996). Several international studies have suggested that an "alert and challenging" media (Sriramesh, 1992a, p. 268), cultural values that favor freedom of expression and distribution of power, and the presence of activist organizations have been significant factors in the development of public relations (Ferguson, 1998; Sriramesh, 1992a). In these studies, not only did the cultural and media environment establish the conditions for activism, but activism also contributed to the nature of those countries' public relations practice.

In the United States, scholars have assumed that democratic values, freedom of expression, and a tradition of dissent laid the foundation for activism. Traditionally, activism in the United States has been viewed through the lens of class, and this suggested that groups of individuals with similar economic interests organized to obtain direct economic benefits. Hauser and Whalen (1997) noted,

> Prior to the mid-1960s, movement theorists of many stripes focused on those common perceptions of economic grievance, typical understandings of the sources of material injustice, and, perhaps most importantly, broad relationships of class in which social movement activity was seemingly rooted. (p. 124)

More recently, however, activism has appeared to cut across class lines, engaging publics from many social segments. Heath (1997) claimed that "activist groups, especially in recent years, routinely draw members from every economic and educational strat[um] of society" (pp. 155-156).

This trend is reflected in a second macro-level explanation, which has attempted to distinguish between types of activist organizations. For example, the differences between interest groups and issue groups, according to Tesh (1984), lie primarily in the nature of membership and the nature of benefits that members seek. Tesh suggested that an interest group is concerned primarily with securing private benefits that accrue to members (or to those whom members represent), who tend to comprise pre-existing occupational or demographic segments that stand to gain if the group's efforts to allocate resources are successful (Smith, 1996a). Rather than primarily seeking benefits for themselves, members of issue groups, according to Tesh, "appeal to moral convictions about the rightness of policies" (p. 31). Nonprofit and issue-oriented groups represent public purposes and popular interests rather than private economic interests of a particular industry or corporation (Scheuer, 1991).

The Publics Perspective

The second major perspective on activist group formation emphasizes the communicative process through which people identify common problems and argue for resolutions to those problems. The roots of this perspective may be found in Dewey's (1927) notion that publics emerge when groups of people perceive problems in similar ways and organize to resolve those problems, but it was developed most fully for public relations theory in J. Grunig's situational theory of publics. J. Grunig and others (J. Grunig, 1978, 1989c; J. Grunig & Hunt, 1984; J. Grunig & Repper, 1992) have identified independent variables (problem recognition, constraint recognition, and level of involvement) and dependent variables (information seeking and information processing) that indicate when an organization should direct communication to a public. In an early formulation of this theory, J. Grunig and Hunt (1984) suggested that high problem recognition, low constraint recognition, and high level of involvement characterize active publics.

Four generally enduring types of publics have been identified: all-issue, apathetic, single-issue, and hot-issue publics (J. Grunig, 1989c; J. Grunig & Hunt, 1984). Significantly, these publics are categorized based on their actions in regard to *issues*. Crable and Vibbert (1985) suggested that an issue is "created when one or more human agents attaches significance to a situation or perceived 'problem.' These interested agents create or recreate arguments which they feel will be acceptable resolutions to questions about the status quo" (p. 5). Similarly, Vasquez (1993) advocated a "homo narrans" paradigm for publics, suggesting that "a public represents individuals who have created, raised, and sustained a group consciousness around a problematic situation" (p. 209). More recently, Botan and Soto (1998) proffered a semiotic, or language-centered, approach that allows for publics that form reactively, as a result of a problem or an issue, *as well as* proactively, motivated by the internal needs of a public (e.g., a deeply held value) to set the agenda.

What J. Grunig's situational theory makes clear, however, is that some publics are more likely to become active than others and that those publics require information and will work to rectify their problems. In sum, this perspective privileges communication about issues as essential to the formation of active publics. For activist organizations, this implies that issues not only are the reason why organizations form but also can act as incentives to attract new members (J. Grunig, 1989c; Olson, 1965; Smith, 1995; Tesh, 1984).

The Developmental Perspective

The third perspective encompasses the first two but attempts to explain how activism develops from the initial stages of problem recognition to the interaction between active publics and target organizations or institutions. Here, activism is treated as a dynamic social phenomenon. Although it is difficult for scholars to apprehend the dynamic nature of activism (a methodological concern that we address later), the temporal dimension has been captured by the notion of a life cycle. This biological metaphor connotes not only growth but also change and, ultimately, decay. The analogy also suggests that activist organizations, like humans, face challenges throughout their lives.

Several conceptualizations of the life cycle of activism exist (Blumer, 1946b; Griffin, 1952; Hainsworth, 1990; Heath, 1997; Lofland, 1992; Stewart, Smith, & Denton, 1994). Each assumes discrete stages through which activism passes. Each stage is characterized by various challenges that, in turn, require various communication activities to address. Heath's (1997) cyclical model included five stages: (a) strain, when publics recognize issues, define them, and seek to gain legitimacy; (b) mobilization, when activists form organizations, establish communication systems, and begin to mobilize resources to pursue their goals; (c) confrontation, in which activists push corporations and/or the government to resolve problems; (d) negotiation, in which the various sides in the dispute exchange messages designed to reach some sort of compromise; and (e) resolution, in which the controversy is (at least temporarily) solved. For communication researchers, the real importance of activism stages is that they represent different rhetorical challenges for activists and their target organizations or insti-

tutions. In the following section, we examine the tactics used by both activists and the organizations that they target.

ACTIVIST GOALS AND TACTICS

When public relations thinkers write about the tactics of activists, it generally is to propose programs of action in response to those challenges. Here, we contend that activist organizations themselves face challenges that require public relations programs. Indeed, activist organizations use many of the same tactics as do other organizations. In this section, we first discuss the two major goals of activist tactics and then provide some examples of the range of tactics used to meet those goals.

Goals

Activists typically use public relations to achieve two overall goals. The first, and most recognizable, goal is to rectify the conditions identified by the activist publics. Thus, if an environmental organization believes that government policy would resolve an environmental problem, then it uses public relations tactics designed to generate support for legislative remedies. Activists face several challenges in pursuit of this goal. Issue management literature suggests that issue advocates must draw attention to the problem, position themselves as legitimate advocates, and successfully argue for their recommended resolutions to the problem (Crable & Vibbert, 1985; Heath, 1997; Vibbert, 1987). Through its public relations activities, an organization communicates its positions on issues, solicits support for action, and (ideally) engages target organizations in policy discussions.

The second, and related, goal is to maintain the organization established to pursue the activists' purposes. Although the avowed aim of many activists is to work themselves out of a job, in reality the struggle for social change is a long-term ongoing process. Activist organizations must maintain membership, thrive in what might be described as a competitive marketplace of ideas and issues, and adjust to changes in their environments. Simons (1970) argued that social movement organizations, a type of activist public, must "attract, maintain, and mold workers (i.e., followers) into an efficiently organized unit" (p. 1). Stewart (1980) noted that organizations

> must wage a continual battle to remain viable. More rhetorical energy may be expended on fund-raising, membership drives, acquisition of materials and property, and maintenance of . . . communication media than on selling ideologies to target audiences and pressuring the opposition. (p. 303)

One of the realities of activism is that simple survival requires a great deal of time and energy. The ideological intransigence that critics sometimes associate with activist organizations tends to fade as the reality of maintaining the organizations presents itself.

Making the task of maintaining the organization more difficult is the fact that most activist groups must compete with other activist organizations for attention and resources. McCarthy and Zald (1977) argued that a variety of organizations often arise around a particular issue and are linked by a common rubric. For example, both the Southern Christian Leadership Conference and the Black Panthers were perceived as civil rights organizations, although each had different policy agendas and tactics for pursuing those goals. The sum of the organizations involved in a particular movement comprise what McCarthy and Zald labeled a "social movement industry." Thus, like corporations in a tight marketplace, activist organizations not only must marshal resources to pursue particular issues but also must compete for limited resources with other organizations pursuing similar goals.

As they work to maintain viability, activist organizations, like their corporate cousins, must adapt to changes in their environments. The most important feature of an activist group's environment is the status of the issues that it advocates. Research has demonstrated that a major incentive for those who join activist organizations is the salience of the groups' goals—their issues. A group's position on its primary issue not only identifies particular sorts of policy goals but also embraces values that can be used to appeal to potential members and retain current members. Schlozman and Tierney's (1986) study of 20 activist groups cited the attractiveness of their issues as their most important resources. Hrebnar and Scott (1982) argued that activists "must rely on the attractiveness of 'the cause' or 'the goal' in order to attract or maintain membership" (p. 20).

If issues are the primary feature of an activist organization's environment, then what happens when that environment changes? Issues management theorists have contended that issues are cyclical; that is, they rise and fall in status on the public's agenda (Crable & Vibbert, 1985; Downs, 1972; Hainsworth, 1990; Jones & Chase, 1979). As issues gain status, activist organizations gain attention, members, and resources. When issues appear to be resolved or otherwise fall from the public's agenda, activist organizations suffer. To survive, activist organizations must adjust to changes in their issues environments (Jopke, 1991; Smith, 1995).

Now that we have examined the goals of ameliorating problematic conditions and maintaining the organizations formed, we turn to a discussion of the tactics that activists use.

Activist Tactics

In pursuing the goal of solving problematic conditions, activists generally attempt to either confront organizations directly or seek regulation from the government or administrative agencies (L. Grunig, 1992a). Some of the factors that may determine strategy choice include (a) the organization's resources including membership, money, and expertise; (b) the perceived efficacy of various courses of action; (c) the legitimacy of the problem, the proposed solution, and the organization advocating it; and (d) the interaction with the target of the activists' efforts (L. Grunig, 1992a; Heath, 1997; Jackson, 1982, Ryan, 1991). Jackson (1982) identified five general categories of tactics:

1. informational activities including interviews and other media relations techniques;
2. symbolic activities including boycotts;
3. organizing activities such as distributing leaflets, networking, and holding meetings;
4. legalistic activities such as petitions, lawsuits, filing legislation, testimony at hearings, [and] prodding regulatory and administrative agencies; and
5. civil disobedience such as sit-ins, blocking traffic, [and] trespassing. (p. 215)

In a review of 34 cases of activism, L. Grunig (1992a) concluded that activists' tactics ranged along a continuum and included contact with the media (see also Ryan, 1991), direct solicitation campaigns aimed toward the public or regulators, lobbying, public forums, petition drives, litigation, pseudo-events, public education, picketing, boycotts, and sit-ins. Depending on the group's resources, activists also may engage in issue advertising (Smith, 1997).

Several observations can be drawn from these lists of tactics. First, many studies have focused on the confrontational nature of some of these tactics (Bowers & Ochs, 1971; Cathcart, 1978; Gregg, 1971; Ritter, 1971; Short, 1991). In describing activist tactics, L. Grunig (1992a) wrote, "When it comes to a fight, the weapons in each activist's arsenal might vary. And as the battle drags on, the weapons might become more lethal" (p. 516). Although confrontations between activists and organizations are the most visible form of interaction, the most fruitful results more likely are accomplished through negotiation and compromise. Activists sometimes approach organizations directly, only to be rebuffed and, therefore, compelled to turn to methods that are more confrontational (Ryan,

1991). For example, when leaders from Operation PUSH initially approached Nike about its minority hiring practices, they were criticized publicly by the shoemaker's spokesperson. Operation PUSH promptly organized a boycott of Nike products that resulted in a great deal of publicity (Smith, 1992).

A second observation is that there seems to be disagreement among researchers and practitioners regarding the efficacy of certain strategies. For example, L. Grunig (1992a) found that in local disputes, activists received favorable media coverage. However, she also observed that, in general, media coverage is not unilaterally favorable to activists. Thus, although activists often are given credit for gaining media attention, they also appear to have some of the same complaints about media accuracy and fairness that mainstream organizations have (Ryan, 1991). Summarizing their work with Boston's Media Research and Action Project, Ryan, Carragee, and Schwerner (1998) argued that their cases "dispel romantic notions that movements and groups need only to employ the techniques of marketing or public relations to better advance their views in public discourse; these views ignore the structural obstacles that confront marginalized groups in U.S. society" (p. 179).

Receiving less scholarly attention are the tactics used to maintain activist organizations. Although this is accomplished primarily through internal publications aimed toward members, followers, or interested recruits, the success of the external strategies mentioned earlier also affects the ability of an organization to maintain itself. Like traditional corporate "house organs," internal publications attempt to keep members informed about organizational news and, more important, the organization's issues. Moe (1980) argued that newsletters act as a membership incentive "by emphasizing the number, value, and type of political goals [that an organization] seeks, the effectiveness of [an organization's] political methods, and the need for funds" (p. 41). Increasingly, technologies such as organizational Web sites, the Internet, and e-mail newsletters perform similar functions (Elliot, 1997).

With this understanding of the goals and tactics of activists, we now turn to a consideration of organizational responses.

ORGANIZATIONAL RESPONSES TO ACTIVISM

Interacting with activists is something that many organizations resist. Activists often are viewed as problems for organizations (L. Grunig, 1992a). Smith (1997) argued that activists often are treated as threats to other organizations because they might disrupt other organizations' routines, influence the development of issues that might be threatening to other organizations, use tactics that might appear threatening, and are perceived as being made up of members whose commitment to a cause is threatening. J. Grunig (1989c) argued, "When members of active publics join activist groups, they contribute to the constraints on organizational autonomy that create a public relations problem and bring about the need for a public relations program" (p. 3).

Despite this, there exist a number of normative frameworks suggesting that organizations have a variety of response options when dealing with activists (Crable & Vibbert, 1985; J. Grunig & L. Grunig, 1997; Heath, 1997; Jackson, 1982; Jones & Chase, 1979; Oliver, 1991). Most scholars suggest that responding to activists requires strategic planning, with consideration given to the desired outcomes and implications of a confrontation. Oliver (1991) outlined five strategic responses to outside pressure:

1. acquiesce, which includes complying with activists' demands;
2. compromise, which involves balancing the perspectives of multiple constituencies, pacifying outside critics, or bargaining to reach agreements;
3. avoid through concealing problems, changing activities, or building barriers between the organization and outside pressure;
4. defy by ignoring explicit norms and values, challenging new requirements, and attacking the sources of institutional pressure; and
5. manipulate through co-opting influential constituents, influencing perceptions of the organization, and controlling the processes by which the organization might be influenced.

Although not writing from a public relations perspective per se, Oliver's work does have some implications for practice. Compromise and defiance are two extremes of the types of tactics often employed by organizations (J. Grunig & L. Grunig, 1997; L. Grunig, 1992a). Although some organizations (e.g., Mobil) have gained a reputation for their public attacks on critics, these tactics sometimes can backfire. The Clorox Company, for example, received negative publicity when it was revealed that its crisis management plan recommended undermining the credibility of critics, one example of Oliver's defiance strategy (Stauber & Rampton, 1995).

Several factors may influence an organization's choice of strategy. Oliver (1991) suggested that strategic choices are influenced by the reason for activist pressure, the number and nature of constituents demanding change, the content of the requested changes, the means by which pressure is being exerted, and the environmental context in which demands are being made. Others (Heath, 1997; Jackson, 1982) have suggested that the nature of the issue under contention, the relative power of the parties involved, and the potential for confrontation to either disrupt or enhance the organization's goals can influence the decision to confront. Finally, J. Grunig and L. Grunig (1997) claimed that the expertise of the public relations practitioners determines the type of organizational response. Their argument was that greater expertise is required to engage in dialogue or negotiation with activists as opposed to one-way attacks or avoidance (Grunig, 1989e).

Perhaps the most important indicator of an organization's response is the approach of the dominant coalition to corporate social responsibility. An organization's understanding of this role is reflected in its relationships with and responses to activist publics. J. Grunig (1992a) defined social responsibility as requiring organizational management to keep "an eye on the effects of their decisions on society as well as on the organization" (p. 17).

Three approaches to public relations have addressed this concern with social responsibility. Rhetorical (Heath & Vasquez, 1996), symmetrical (J. Grunig, 1993d; J. Grunig, L. Grunig, & Dozier, 1995), and humanistic (Ferguson, Botan, & Sintay, 1996) perspectives share an emphasis on collaboration, trust, and mutual responsibility between parties, with subtle distinctions in their conceptualizations.

Heath and Vasquez (1996) argued that public relations "cannot be socially responsible without grounding in the nature of rhetoric as an inherent feature of humans working together in all contexts to form and maintain society that allows for individual and collective experience and activity" (p. 2). Rhetoric is the means through which organizations and activist publics use "symbols to achieve agreement, persuade, or induce cooperation" (Pearson, 1989b, p. 113). Through dialogue, participants "achieve degrees of agreement and disagreement . . . on matters related to public policy, organizational image, or the attractiveness of an organization's products, services, or community philanthropy" (Heath & Vasquez, 1996, p. 8).

In the International Association of Business Communicators *Excellence* project, J. Grunig (1992a) advocated the two-way symmetrical approach as a socially responsible normative theory to guide interaction between organizations and their publics (see also J. Grunig, 1989e). In summarizing their program of research on organizations and activism, J. Grunig and L. Grunig (1997) advocated the following normative organizational responses:

1. Listening to all strategic constituencies is an important way in which to learn the consequences that an organization has on those publics.
2. Disclosing information and telling the organization's story helps to establish trust and credibility.
3. Communicating with activists should be continuous, largely because of their shifting stances.
4. Recognizing the legitimacy of all constituent groups, large and small, is important because of the potential that even small activist groups have for engaging an organization (L. Grunig, 1992a; Olson, 1965).
5. Enacting two-way symmetrical responses requires skilled practitioners.
6. Determining long-term effectiveness is important in helping both the organization and the activists to remain patient during the extended time it takes to reach agreement.
7. Public relations practitioners who are close to the center of power in an organization are better able to shape the organization's response to activists.

In sum, the *Excellence* study emphasized communication skills employing a frank exchange of information and mutual respect.

A humanistic approach is characterized both by possessing a humanistic ethic—including facilitating free and informed choice, symbol use, rational decision making, dialogue, and sociality—and by making socially necessary information readily available (Ferguson et al., 1996; see also Johannesen, 1971; Langer, 1948). Within this view, for public relations to be socially responsible, organizations must be willing not only to provide publics with pertinent information but also to engage the public in their decision-making processes (Ferguson et al., 1996; Smith, 1996b). In this capacity, public relations has the effect of binding individuals to groups, binding groups to institutions, and binding institutions to society, not only weaving people and groups into existing sets of values but also enabling groups to work together in weaving a new part of the social fabric (Ferguson et al., 1996). Although it is true that few studies have demonstrated the long-term efficacy of a symmetrical approach to activism, an increasing number of scholars are advocating its use (Smith, 1996b; Susskind & Field, 1996).

In sum, although relationships between organizations and most activists are far from cordial, interaction can lead to mutual gains.

CONCLUSION

In this chapter, we have reviewed the major theories that attempt to explain the formation and development of activist organizations, examined the tactics of activists, and provided a review of organizational responses. The chief claim of this chapter was that both activists and "mainstream" organizations use public relations as a means to achieve their goals. Understanding this contributes to public relations practice in three ways. First, the communication challenges faced by activists are not dissimilar to those faced by all practitioners. Moreover, we suggest that all practitioners use similar strategies and tactics to meet these challenges, although we later suggest further research needs in this area. Understanding these similarities might help to raise the professional consciousness of all practitioners and to reduce some of the debates over tactics that sometimes are injected into disputes over issues. Second, this chapter argued that an organization's sense of social responsibility influences the type of tactics used. This finding contributes to the continually evolving sense that public relations practitioners' responsibilities lie not only with their employers but also with the public at large. Finally, the research on activism strongly suggests that the hallmarks of symmetrical communication, especially dialogue, negotiation, and collaboration, offer lower cost, ethical, and socially responsible ways in which to resolve disputes between organizations and activists.

In reviewing the literature on activism, we find two interrelated needs. The first need is for continued research into activism and the interaction between activists and other organizations. The second is for greater methodological diversity in studying the interaction between activists and other organizations.

More research is needed to test assumptions about activists and their tactics. As noted earlier, although some studies have indicated that activists enjoy relatively unfettered media access and influence (L. Grunig, 1992a), others have suggested that activists are reluctant to use the media (Ryan et al., 1998; Wirth, 1995). Just what are activists' attitudes toward the media? How do those attitudes influence their media relations strategies? J. Grunig and L. Grunig (1997) argued that one reason why their work did not focus more on activists' tactics was because they were not convinced that activists "do" public relations any differently from how other practitioners do it. However, we believe that further research is needed to test that assumption. More international case studies of activism are required to overcome any Western bias in current research (Ferguson, 1998; J. Grunig & L. Grunig, 1997). Another research area involves case studies of communication behavior between activists and organizations. Although many studies have examined either activist or organizational campaigns, it is the clash of messages between activists and organizations that produces and reproduces issue definitions and influences the development of the conflict (Smith, 1992). Greater understanding of this clash is required to understand and predict how relationships between activists and organizations may develop.

The second major need is to develop greater methodological diversity when studying activism. To fully apprehend the nature of activism requires methodologies that are longitudinal and multivocal. Longitudinal studies allow researchers to trace the cyclical movements of organizations and issues as well as the methods used to meet various challenges (Griffin, 1952; Smith, 1995, 1996a). Multivocal case studies can explicate the interaction between activists and organizations. Many case studies have examined primarily the discourse of single organizations through a focus on public relations "campaigns." We would argue that the interaction between and among messages from all the parties involved shapes issues and can lead to resolving those issues (Smith, 1992).

Rhetorical/critical methods provide ways in which to study individuals' and organizations' use of language (e.g., metaphor, myth, imagery) in building arguments and creating relationships between organizations and activist publics. Rhetorical/critical research focuses on the creation and interpretation of messages (Burke, 1950, 1957; Fisher, 1984; Heath, 1992a, 1992b), the historical/social/political context (Blair, 1984; Burke, 1957), the quality of the message (Weaver, 1953, 1970), the communicative processes (Foss,

1996; Solomon, 1985), and the impact of the discourse on the parties to the relationship and on society as a whole (Brummett, 1984; Schiappa, 1989; Zarefsky, Miller-Tutzauer, & Tutzauer, 1984). Thus, a rhetorical/critical approach helps practitioners to account for how organizations, as well as individuals, "acquire images, express personae, receive and supply information, make value judgments about their activities and policies, and advocate as well as yield" (Heath, 1993, p. 141) to other parties (i.e., publics) in an interaction or a series of interactions.

Many communication scholars agree that the use of multiple methods can provide significant advantages for researchers. The strengths of a method may be maximized while the weaknesses are neutralized in combination with other compatible methods (Deetz, 1982; Jick, 1979). Multiple methods are especially helpful in examining a group's communication processes, ideology, motivations, and the relationships among these aspects and others involving strategic communication outside the organization (Sriramesh, 1992a; Vasquez, 1993).

Further research and methodological diversity will help researchers and practitioners to understand the dynamic nature of activism and its influence on public relations practice and, ultimately, society itself. More than 50 years ago, Humphrey (1946) observed that public relations and social work were two fields that attempted to solve or rectify social problems: "Originally utilized exclusively by business leaders as a systematic body of knowledge and technique, [public relations] has more recently been adapted to the needs of educational, social work, and ameliorative social pressure organizations" (p. 12). From this rich tradition, public relations professionals of all stripes can work toward a practice that truly embraces the public good.

CHAPTER 23

Public Relations and Conflict Resolution

KENNETH D. PLOWMAN

WILLIAM G. BRIGGS

YI-HUI HUANG

In today's fast-paced global marketplace, organizational success depends on developing and maintaining relationships with strategic publics or stakeholders. Success also depends on reinforcing the organizational reputation or brand equity in the minds of these important stakeholders. Conflicts among stakeholders and organizations require immediate attention and resolution. As a result, the development of conflict management strategies in the field of public relations has become essential (Dozier, L. Grunig, & J. Grunig, 1995; Huang, 1997; Plowman, 1995; Vasquez, 1996). Public relations scholars have suggested that professionals, functioning in the roles of organizational boundary spanners and communication managers (J. Grunig & Hunt, 1984; L. Grunig, J. Grunig, & Ehling, 1992), often help an organization to manage its response to conflict and rapid environmental changes (White & Dozier, 1992). Improved understanding of the essence of conflict management has become imperative to

public relations scholars as well as the practice in general.

PURPOSE AND SCOPE

This chapter focuses on the operational terms of conflict management, *negotiation tactics*, as they apply to the practice of public relations. It traces those tactics through the two-way models and mixed motives, and it revisits recent studies on public relations and conflict resolution at the domestic and international levels. The results are a more complete set of tactics for public relations that can be used in its daily practice. Benefits are in building long-term relationships with strategic publics based on two-way communication, problem solving, trust, strategic planning, and control mutuality. Contributions to recent trends in the practice are noted including relationship marketing, corporate reputation, and branding.

TWO-WAY MODELS OF PUBLIC RELATIONS

Conflict resolution in public relations evolved from the four models of public relations (J. Grunig & Hunt, 1984). The most sophisticated of the four models are the two-way asymmetrical and two-way symmetrical models. The two-way asymmetrical model has been defined as scientific persuasion, empirically seeking feedback from stakeholders so that an organization can persuade its publics to its own views. The two-way symmetrical model is similar, except its goal is to manage conflict and promote mutual understanding instead of persuasion to its own ends. Public relations professionals can negotiate solutions to conflicts between their organizations and strategic stakeholders (Dozier et al., 1995).

As these two models of public relations evolved, J. Grunig (1989e) described the two-way symmetrical model as "public relations efforts [that] are based on research and evaluation and that use communication to manage conflict and to improve understanding with strategic publics" (p. 17). With the introduction of the word *conflict*, Ehling (1992) asserted that public relations management can realize this two-way model only by making its primary mission that of attaining or maintaining accord between the organization and its stakeholders. However, to attain that accord requires a continual effort to mediate and mitigate conflict between the organization and its environment.

The most recent model of public relations that incorporates these two models is the *new model of symmetry as two-way practices* (Dozier et al., 1995). This model is based on the *Excellence* study (J. Grunig, 1992c) and research by Murphy (1991) using game theory to examine the two-way models. In the new model of two-way communication practices, the win-win zone uses negotiation and compromise to allow organizations to find common ground among their separate and sometimes conflicting interests. The model subsumed the two-way asymmetrical and two-way symmetrical models. By doing so, it did not exclude the use of asymmetrical means to achieve symmetrical ends. Dozier et al. (1995) said, "Asymmetrical tactics are sometimes used to gain the best position for organizations within the win/win zone. Because such practices are bounded by a symmetrical worldview that respects the integrity of long-term relationships, the two-way model is essentially symmetrical" (p. 49).

MIXED MOTIVES

Although the two-way symmetrical model would seem to be the ideal model for conflict management (Ehling, 1984, 1985), it is difficult to determine the exact point for appropriate behavior on a continuous scale between two-way asymmetric and two-way symmetric communication (J. Grunig & L. Grunig, 1992; Hellweg, 1989). J. Grunig et al. (1991b) and Murphy (1991) suggested that a *mixed motive* version of the two-way symmetrical model might better describe what is happening in the actual practice of public relations because it incorporates both asymmetrical and symmetrical tactics. Although more recent studies have shown more use of the two-way symmetrical model (L. Grunig, Dozier, & J. Grunig, 1994; Rawlins, 1993), those studies have acknowledged that the more frequently practiced model is the one termed *mixed motives*.

Using mixed motives, Murphy (1991) said that each side in a stakeholder relationship retains a strong sense of its own self-interests, yet each is motivated to cooperate in a limited fashion to attain at least some resolution of the conflict. Parties in a conflict, an organization and its strategic publics, act as *cooperative antagonists* (Raiffa, 1982). They might be on opposite sides of an issue, but it is in their best interests to cooperate with each other. "They do not trust each other, nor do they believe everything communicated by the other side. However, they do trust each other enough to believe that each will abide by any agreement reached" (Dozier et al., 1995, p. 48).

A definition of public relations as a mixed-motive game helps to reconcile the divergence between the asymmetric and symmetric models. Mixed-motive games provide a broad third category that describes behavior as most public relations people experience it (L. Grunig et al., 1994)—a multidirectional scale of competition and cooperation in which organizational needs must be balanced against constituents' needs but never lose their primacy. Researchers have shown that most organizations appear to practice a blend of the three asymmetric models—press agentry, public information, and two-way asymmetrical—of public relations and symmetric communication styles (J. Grunig & L. Grunig, 1989).

MIXED-MOTIVE MODEL FOR PUBLIC RELATIONS

Most recently, Huang (1997) and Plowman (1995) established a number of negotiation tactics that fit into what Plowman called a mixed-motive model for public relations that encompassed the entire spectrum between the two-way asymmetrical and two-way symmetrical models. The original model included contention, avoidance, accommodation, compromise, cooperation, unconditionally constructive, and win-win or no deal. It now includes the additional tactics of principled and mediated or cultural, as shown in Figure 23.1. The box represents all the independent, complementary, and common core values or interests for both the organization and its strategic publics. The box also encompasses the nine negotiation tactics that can be employed by both parties. The arrows above the solid line extending through the win-win zone show that that these tactics can flow either way through the win/win zone from asymmetric to symmetric back to other asymmetric again. The only way in which to represent two ends in what more properly would be a matrix is to show one-way communication. Everything else in the box represents two-way communication.

The model was adapted from a number of sources that originated with Thomas's (1976) most complete version. In this model, dimensions were defined for *contending, cooperating, avoiding, accommodating,* and *compromising.* Plowman (1995) added two negotiation tactics: what Fisher and Brown (1988) termed *unconditionally constructive* and what Covey (1989) called *win-win or no deal.*

Unconditionally Constructive

In Plowman's (1995) study, problems arose when the opposition or a strategic public refused to come to agreement, even when both parties used cooperative tactics. The alternative action for getting around this impasse was the negotiating tactic of being unconditionally constructive. Being unconditionally constructive was used in the positive sense of Fisher and Brown (1988), that is, guidelines that "will be both good for the relationship and good for me *whether or not you follow the same guidelines*" (p. 37, italics in original). Even if the other party in the conflict does not reciprocate, the organization acts in reconciling the strategic interests of both the organization and its strategic public. Although the decision to take this altruistic tactic is unilateral, it remains two-way because the organization must have done research to determine the interests of its strategic public. It also is a win-win situation because both parties mutually benefit from the result of the tactic. The key lies in both parties' common interests. One party cannot be unconditionally constructive if the interests of the other party are not affected positively. Those common interests allow for a limited set of options to be unconditionally constructive (T. C. Schelling, personal communication, November 8, 1995).

Win-Win or No Deal

The second additional negotiation tactic in Plowman's (1995) study seemed to develop as an

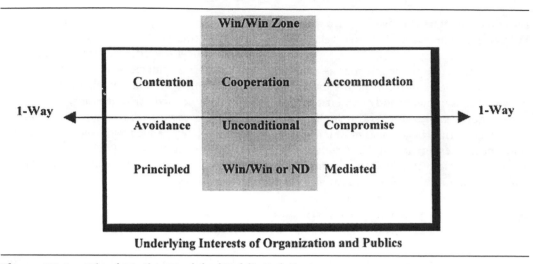

Figure 23.1. Mixed-Motive Model of Public Relations

alternative beyond unconditionally constructive to avoid stalemate in a negotiation. To get past a stalemate in a positive way for both parties, at least one party's best alternative to a negotiated agreement was the option of no deal at all. The only options in this situation were for both parties to either collaborate in mutually beneficial circumstances or hold off on any agreement until both parties were ready for a win-win deal to be struck.

Covey (1989) adapted the game theory terms of Deutsch (1973) into what Covey called "six paradigms of human interaction." Participants in Plowman's (1995) study did not mention these first five paradigms but instead directly emphasized the sixth paradigm—win-win or no deal. Covey (1989) said, "If these individuals had not come up with a synergistic solution—one that is agreeable to both—they could have gone for an even higher expression of win/win—win/win or no deal" (p. 213). The *no deal* addition to the term *win-win* means that if the parties cannot find a solution that would benefit both, then they would agree to disagree—no deal.

Third-Party Mediation

Huang (1997) extended the research in conflict resolution and public relations from two-party conflicts to multiple organizations in conflict and to the international arena. Her study of the Taiwanese legislature focused on the relationships among organization-public relationships, public relations strategies, and conflict management strategies. It revealed another negotiation tactic in the mixed-motive model—*third-party mediation.* This is where an outside, and usually disinterested, party arbitrates the dispute. Mediation has played a critical role in Chinese techniques of conflict resolution and even has integrated itself within the society (Sohn & Wall, 1993; Wall & Blum, 1991).

Wall and Blum (1991) maintained that China has a long history of community mediation. The characteristics of Chinese culture that emphasize harmony, relationships, and face can help to explain why mediation is a popular conflict resolution technique. First, Confucianism emphasizes a harmonious and orderly organism (Pye, 1981). Society generally was regarded as an expanded family (Ching, 1977), and people were expected to act as a unit. Second, Chinese society is one in which relationships among parties have been defined clearly. In this circumstance, the Chinese further developed a unique cultural characteristic—an emphasis on *kuan-hsi* (i.e., interpersonal relations or a third-person relationship) to resolve problems. This emphasis on kuan-hsi, which is associated closely with the

Chinese sense of dependency, has particular implications for Chinese conflict management (Sohn & Wall, 1993; Wall & Blum, 1991). Third, out of concern for relationships and harmony, a typical Chinese places special emphasis on face work such as face saving and face giving (Pye, 1992). Therefore, when a conflict situation occurs, a person often will use a third person to resolve conflict so as to save face.

In sum, Wall and Blum (1991) concluded that, for the Chinese, mediation is integrated within the society. They further compared the techniques of mediation in Western and Chinese societies and found that the Chinese techniques, unlike U.S. mediators, have "a distinct mediator-knows-best flavor" (p. 18). These mediators are considered a quasi-arm of the law and aggressively "persuade" the disputants to return to an appropriate harmonious relationship.

Principled

This tactic spans most of the other tactics already mentioned and is based on a term developed by Covey (1991) in *Principle-Centered Leadership.* The emphasis is on the word *principle,* and the term is *principled.* The basis for this term arose during a session of the April 1998 meeting of the Southern Communication Association. Principled means to hold to higher ethics that cannot be compromised. If a party takes a principled stance, then it is unilateral but may be beneficial or detrimental to the other party in the negotiation. Unlike unconditionally constructive, it does not do necessarily what is best for the relationship. In fact, the principle could even have a negative effect on the originating party. That party could simply "stand on principle" and not be moved from that position because it is a long-held core value or interest.

In a related discussion, Huang (1997) wrote of ethical communication in public relations, referring to two extremes. One referred to good or evil consequences that an action brings about, and the other considered the intrinsic features of intent or mental aspect of a contemplated action (Grcic, 1989). J. Grunig and L. Grunig (1996) termed these extremes *consequentialist* theories

and *nonconsequentialist* theories. In other words, public relations practitioners first should consider the impact of their communication behaviors on their strategic publics. Then, they should follow nonconsequentialist rules to be honest, truthful, and sincere when communicating (Reinsch, 1990).

These concepts of ethics in public relations lead to both an asymmetrical and a symmetrical view of principled negotiation. Symmetrical negotiation is one that considers consequences and the effect that they have on a relationship. It encapsulates social responsibility where public relations managers incorporate the effects that their organizations' behavior might have on their stakeholders or publics. Ethics could be asymmetrical if disclosure were involved and unilateral, that is, one-sided and nonconsequentialist in that one party could be honest and truthful without consideration for the consequences affecting the other party in a negotiation situation. Disclosure refers to advocacy in public relations, acting in the client organization's best interest. Bivins (1987) suggested that revealing the reasons for asymmetrical actions could secure ethical standards. The use of this rationale means that principled negotiation could be either asymmetrical or symmetrical.

These nine negotiation tactics represent the state of theory in public relations as informed by or discovered through its practice. These are tools that practitioners can use to develop relationships with both internal and external strategic publics or stakeholders.

IMPLICATIONS FOR PRACTITIONERS

As Carrington (1992) emphasized, there is a shortage of communicators with the conflict resolution and negotiation skills that chief executive officers (CEOs) of excellent organizations seek. Excellent organizations need public relations managers with skills in two-way communication and strategic planning (J. Grunig, 1992c). They can obtain those skills from knowledge and experience in the use of the mixed-motive model of public relations (Figure 23.1). Organizationally, a company can benefit if it is interested in improving its organization-public relationships, public relations strategies, and conflict management techniques.

The number one characteristic of communication excellence in organizations is manager role expertise, according to the recent *Excellence* study (J. Grunig, 1992c) and its follow-up case studies (L. Grunig et al., 1994). The expertise needed to be a communication manager is tied closely to the expertise needed to engage in negotiation tactics. Ehling (1987) described such activities to be in the public relations jurisdiction if they entailed the strategic means and ends of public relations. Strategic means entail communication and conflict resolution strategies. The "strategic end-state of public relations management is to achieve a non-conflict state via the means of a well-designed communication system" (p. 29), that is, establishing and/or maintaining relationships.

As Dozier et al. (1995) stated, the combination of asymmetrical and symmetrical tactics seemed paradoxical when examining their two extremes superficially. Indeed, Pruitt and Rubin (1986) believed that negotiation tactics could not be considered in a linear continuum because both contending and cooperating can be strong at the same time. They said, "People can be both selfish and cooperative (leading them to engage in problem solving in an effort to reconcile both parties' interests)" (p. 29). In addition, one could be principled or unprincipled, benefiting or not benefiting the other party in the negotiation as the situation demands.

In mixed motives, both parties still can pursue their own self-interests. Organizations and their strategic publics can be both selfish or contending and principled or cooperative. This leads the parties to engage in problem solving to reconcile their overlapping interests (Pruitt & Rubin, 1986). Raiffa (1982), and later Dozier et al. (1995), used the term *cooperative antagonists*. These parties actually are *cooperative protagonists* in the struggle to satisfy their own interests with the knowledge that satisfaction is best accomplished through satisfying each other's interests as well. The question is not one of mixed motives, where short-term asymmetrical tactics are combined with long-term symmetrical tactics as advocated by Dozier et al., but rather one of discovering the priority level of importance for the common interests of the strategic parties.

Experience with the use of mixed motives and these negotiation tactics leads to a number of abilities highly sought after by organizations and public relations practitioners. According to Huang (1997) and Plowman (1995), abilities include two-way communication, problem solving, trust building in long-term relationships, strategic planning, and control mutuality in relationships. Problem solving for organizations is derived directly from practitioners' ability and expertise to use the two-way models and the tactics of negotiation. Contributing to problem solving is the background of public relations managers including attributes such as natural ability, knowledge and experience in the field, and sound judgment. All of these factors contributed to a relationship of trust between the dominant coalition and public relations built over the long term.

Trust is critical to interpersonal relationships (Canary & Cupach, 1988) and in organizational conflicts in which risk is involved (Carlson & Millard, 1987; Krimsky & Plough, 1988). Likewise in the field of public relations, L. Grunig et al. (1992) emphasized the significance of trust and credibility inasmuch as trust from publics enables an organization to exist. Concerning long-term relationships, this is a factor for both interpersonal relationships with the dominant coalition or decision-making management group of an organization and those external strategic publics that are vital to the organization's existence. There is an *accumulation* of trust engendered and personal chemistry with the dominant coalition over time. This credibility also accrues with strategic publics and is vital to resolving management communication problems for the organization.

Any long-term relationship, whether it be between a public relations manager and the dominant coalition or between an organization and its strategic publics, depends mostly on activity that is reciprocally positive for its survival.

These studies have shown that short-term two-way asymmetrical or contending tactics can have their place in a long-term relationship. Longer term two-way symmetrical tactics, however, should take precedence over those activities.

This *building of relationships* in the long term also is an essential part of strategic thinking for public relations managers. It contributes greatly to creating the common ground for the solution of problems through mixed motives, negotiation tactics, and being unconditionally constructive. The ability of public relations managers to do strategic planning for the communications function is a top priority for upper management (Plowman, 1995, 1999). Strategic planning can occur either formally or informally, meaning that public relations could be part of the dominant coalition or could be in the form of a high-level counselor brought in when needed for advice on communication aspects of planning.

In essence, organizations are looking for public relations managers with knowledge and experience in public relations and the mixed motives of the new model of symmetry as two-way practices. This knowledge and experience include the nine negotiation processes of contention, avoidance, principled, mediated or cultural, compromise, accommodation, cooperation, unconditionally constructive, and win/win or no deal. Public relations can use this knowledge and experience with the addition of ability to do strategic planning and good judgment to solve problems for the organization in the mixed-motive model of public relations.

Furthermore, for most managers of public relations, both domestic and international, all of these negotiation tactics and results are not entirely symmetric. Instead, the typical practice of public relations involves mixed motives. Mixed motives is a process that can range from satisfying one party to satisfying all parties involved and possibly for the mutual benefit of these same parties. The concept of mutual benefit itself can be asymmetrical as to the degree of benefit for these parties as well. Mixed motives can stretch along the entire spectrum of the new model to include asymmetric communication from either the dominant coalition's or the strategic public's perspective.

The final ability that can prove positive for public relations is the concept of *control mutuality.* The term connotes mixed-motive, symmetrical, and asymmetrical characteristics. Stafford and Canary (1991) defined control mutuality as "the degree to which partners agree about which of them should decide relational goals and behavioral routines" (p. 224). They conceptualized this notion as whether the contending parties in a relationship agree that one or both may rightfully influence the other or whether the partners agree on the power balance in the relationship (Canary & Stafford, 1992). They also quoted Kelley (1979), further specifying that bilateral or mutual control is distinguished by unilateral attempts to control the partner (Canary & Stafford, 1992, p. 224). Control mutuality, then, can have asymmetrical results but with the agreement of the parties in the dispute, similar to the negotiation tactic of accommodation. In this case, it is not used as a tactic but rather is used as an ability resulting from the tactic that can benefit the practice of public relations.

Dozier et al. (1995) suggested that the use of any of these negotiation tactics would be more likely to result in favorable relationships, emphasizing the pressing need to "know much more about strategies that practitioners can and do use at different points" (p. 23). The research represented here provides specific guidelines for the ways in which different public relations tactics contribute to certain relational outcomes. For example, if an organization would like to build up trust with its publics, then two-way communication can help to achieve that goal. Also, for trust to develop between the practitioner—hopefully, the public relations manager—and the dominant coalition, it would require participating in long-term strategic planning and solving problems for the organization. Many of these abilities have been substantiated through principles articulated by the Program on Negotiation and Conflict Resolution at the Harvard Law School (Susskind & Field, 1996). Its mutual gains framework suggests the following organization-public relationships:

1. Acknowledge the concerns of the other side.

2. Encourage joint fact finding.
3. Offer contingent commitments to minimize impacts if they do occur. Promise to compensate unintended effects.
4. Accept responsibility. Admit mistakes and share power.
5. Act in a trustworthy fashion at all times.
6. Focus on building long-term relationships.

IMPLICATIONS AT THE INTERNATIONAL LEVEL

At the start of the 21st century, global mass communications and interdependent regions are expanding outward into a global economy dominated by interlocking transnational corporations and nongovernmental organizations as well as other nongovernmental organizations. No government or organization can survive in isolation today. Advocacy stakeholder groups have made it impossible for organizations to ignore comment and criticism.

Dealing with such global entities brings on a new set of challenges for public relations. Culture is a powerful force shaping thoughts, perceptions, behavior, and communication. Another model of public relations relevant to the extension of negotiation on a global scale is the *personal influence* model. Several studies documented the use of personal influence or interpersonal communication as the dominant model for practicing public relations at the international level (J. Grunig & L. Grunig, 1996; J. Grunig, L. Grunig, Sriramesh, Huang, & Lyra, 1995). By its very nature of uniqueness, culture initiates the negotiation tactics of contention or principled in many instances. The ability to successfully navigate and negotiate cross-culturally will be the key to successful public relations practice on the global scale in the future.

Widespread use of English as the language of business and global mass marketing projects a veneer of homogeneity, but that is misleading at best. "Differences in culture are an important consideration in the conduct of virtually all international negotiations; even a negotiation between a U.S. executive and a Canadian manager involves cultural differences. Yet, members of the business community have tended to slip into one or more mistaken assumptions about culture (Rubin & Salacuse, 1993).

According to Rubin and Salacuse (1993), mistaken cultural assumptions include thinking that culture is the only thing that matters in a negotiation or that culture is of no importance. Other mistakes include thinking that culture is only an obstacle or that cross-cultural negotiations can be improved by reading some "how to" book purchased at the airport boarding lounge. The authors argued that we must get beyond simplifying everything into stereotypes and find conditions that promote a relationship, that is, an awareness that one needs the other person if one is to reach his or her goals. Graham (1993), in his 15-year study of negotiation styles in 17 cultures, concluded that cultural differences are apt to cause misunderstanding and that the initial goal should be improving the efficiency and effectiveness of the negotiation by becoming aware that such differences lie not only in *what* is being said (content) but also in *how* it is being said (linguistic and nonverbal behaviors) and in the *social context* of the negotiation.

Cultural diversity makes communication more difficult. Communicating wants and needs cross-culturally is complex. Because knowledge is culture specific, the more a communicator understands cross-cultural differences, the easier the communication task becomes. Paradoxically, although communication cross-culturally is often more difficult, creating mutually beneficial options can become easier. According to Adler (1991), if negotiators can overcome communication barriers, then mutually beneficial solutions—the cooperative tactic and win-win solutions—might become easier. Differences, rather than similarities, can form the basis of mutually beneficial solutions. Obviously, in a multicultural environment, the differences are increased. Thus, the opportunities for mutual gain also are increased.

Occasionally, some negotiators go beyond mutually beneficial solutions to create synergistic agreements, where competitive advantage is deemphasized. Instead, synergistic solutions use differences as a resource, transforming the greatest source of cross-cultural problems into win-win solutions that otherwise would have been impossible (Adler, 1991). As communicators come to the negotiating table in the global village as cultural interpreters, they are entrusted with the reputations of their organizations and the concerns of their stakeholders over business, environmental, human rights, and peace issues. Public relations, still in its global adolescence, can now transcend media divisiveness and traditional advocacy roles in favor of a mutual gains approach that unites all of us.

NEW DIRECTIONS

The emphasis by Huang (1997) on relationships parallels recent trends in public relations. The literature in public relations is full of references to the focal concept "relationship" (Broom, Casey & Ritchey, 1997; Ferguson, 1984; J. Grunig, L. Grunig & Dozier, 1995; L. Grunig et al., 1992). Regis McKenna, a Silicon Valley public relations practitioner turned marketing guru, popularized the term *relationship marketing*. Emphasis on the relationship is almost a culture clash itself in the United States, where emphasis has been on quarterly earnings. Now, relationships underscore the practice of public relations, from issues management to crisis communication. Maintaining positive perceptions in the minds of stakeholders is the mission of public relations, which in another of its endless renamings often is referred to today as *reputation management*.

Maintaining the reputation of an organization ultimately might be the most important function of public relations. Historically, public relations has been scrutinized and criticized for its lack of accountability. In an environment where organizations have flattened and demand more from employees, contractors, and agencies alike, the need to measure and evaluate results reigns supreme. Borrowing a term from marketing, this is managing *brand equity,* the difference between an organization's fixed asset value and

its worth in the marketplace. Often 5 or 10 times greater—or even more—than the cash assets, brand equity is *the* bottom line. It is a company's most important asset. It is measurable. It is what boards of directors, CEOs, and shareholders care most about. Its management legitimizes the communication budget necessary to maintain it.

Ironically, in a global marketplace, brand equity takes on dramatic importance, with manufacturing infrastructure deemphasized and competition coming from all sides. Even more so than domestically, a brand is the manifestation of a company's character and personality; essentially, it is a guarantee of consistency, quality, and value (Bentley, 1998). Deciding where to do business is subject to the degree to which an organization is willing to adjust its marketing to meet the needs of those individual markets. As Burnett and Moriarity (1998) pointed out, some observers, such as Theodore Levitt of Harvard University, see segmenting markets by culture or geography as not cost-effective. Levitt urges companies to adopt a global orientation, view the world as one market, and sell global products. Others, such as Philip Kotler of Northwestern University, believe that products and promotional strategies must be designed to fit the local culture. Burnett and Moriarity pointed to a study showing 61% of non-food companies working toward a global strategy on existing brands. Although "think globally, act locally" seems like a good strategy for the present, the future might be driven by truly global markets.

The winners in global marketing will be those companies with high-quality, reasonably priced products and great reputations. Increasingly, the care of those reputations falls to culturally aware public relations practitioners, and that means increasingly more public relations people are sitting at the negotiation tables. Domestically and internationally alike, more and more of managers' time is spent identifying, establishing, and maintaining mutually beneficial relationships between organizations and stakeholders. Profitability and viability depend on it. Across the negotiating table, a pledge of one's reputation is a powerful demonstration of trust and commitment.

Humans everywhere respond favorably to organizations (and people) that they know and respect. For virtually all organizations, to be better known is to be better liked. As J. Grunig (1993d) said,

> If public relations is practiced according to the principles of strategic management, public responsibility, and the two-way symmetrical model, it is an important element of the global communication system—facilitating communication that helps [to] build relationships among organizations and publics and to develop policies that are responsible to those publics. (p. 157)

All of the negotiation tactics mentioned earlier are practical tools that lead to building such relationships and help to establish the branding of an organization's reputation. The brand, in turn, is a tool with which an organization can center most of its strategic publics. The totality of the brand is a relationship with any audience that has a stake in the brand—customers, employees, shareholders, suppliers, distributors, special interest groups, the media, or any other stakeholder group (Hines, 1998). This relationship motivates these strategic publics to do something positive for the relationship as in the negotiation tactics of unconditionally constructive, win-win or no deal, compromise, accommodation, cooperation (and sometimes even principled), and avoidance. The results in a brand relations model are similar to previous abilities that an organization values for public relations. In today's new highly competitive business arena, the value of a brand can be measured by its long-term profitable and market-savvy relationships. This is done by maintaining a strategic consistency through planning in all brand communications to stakeholders. The process is meaningful two-way communication that builds dialogue to shape the brand image that creates trust. All of this leads to long-term customer loyalties, the type of bond that brings a lifetime of customer value. The more that this mixed-motives type of communication takes place, the better able a company will be able to coorient to and respond to the needs of its strategic stakeholders and achieve the cooperation and mutually beneficial or synergistic solutions that it seeks.

Most recently, during 1998-1999, a study at San Jose State University surveyed members of the Business Marketing Association, the International Association of Business Communicators, and the Public Relations Society of America chapters in Silicon Valley. Individuals responded to the skills required of current communication practitioners in the intensely competitive nature of Silicon Valley. Their answers reflected their understanding of that environment and the combination of skill sets and academic background needed to best position themselves to take advantage of the opportunities for higher level management in that environment. Some 42% of respondents said that negotiation/conflict resolution was very important, whereas 36% said that it was somewhat important. If that skill set is viewed as a tactic to help achieve other skill sets, then those other skill sets represented most of the abilities sought by organizations in these public relations/conflict resolution studies. Marketing public relations, brand management, crisis communication, global communication strategies, and strategic planning all scored above 60%. These are the skills that public relations practitioners are looking for in Silicon Valley. Practitioners can obtain them through the development of two-way communication, mixed motives, specific negotiation tactics, and other cooperative strategies.

CHAPTER 24

Public Relations and the Ecology of Organizational Change

JAMES L. EVERETT

■ Over the past two decades, the view that public relations is a management function responsible for identifying and maintaining relationships between an organization and its social environment has come to represent one of the major perspectives to organize public relations theory and practice (Baskin, Aronoff, & Lattimore, 1997; Broom & Dozier, 1990; Crable & Vibbert, 1986; Cutlip, Center, & Broom, 1985, 1994; Heath, 1990; Long & Hazelton, 1987). The foundations for this ecological perspective on public relations were first articulated by Cutlip and Center in 1952 as the adjustment and adaptation model of public relations (Cutlip, 1991). This perspective posits the functional significance of public relations as helping organizations to "adjust and adapt to changes in their environments" (Cutlip et al., 1994, p. 199). This perspective and its analogs (particularly the "symmetric" model of practice detailed by J. Grunig & T. Hunt, 1984, and refined in J. Grunig & L. Grunig, 1992) are "ecological" perspectives because they locate the primary context of public relations practice in the relationship between an organization and its social environment (Everett, 1990, 1993).

In this context, the concept of ecology organizes the view that "public relations deals with the interdependence of organizations and others in their environments" (Cutlip et al., 1994, p. 199). Because of its dominance in the discipline's textbook tradition, the ecological perspective arguably constitutes "normal science" in public relations. J. Grunig and L. Grunig (1992) operationalized this position in their contention that the "two-way symmetrical model will be characteristic of excellent public relations programs" (p. 360).

ORGANIZATIONAL ECOLOGY

Coincident with these developments in public relations theory, since the late 1970s, a substantial body of theory and research has moved the study of organizational ecology into the mainstream of organizational theory (Aldrich & Mueller, 1982; Aldrich & Pfeffer, 1976; Astley, 1977, 1985; Carroll, 1984, 1988; Hannan & Freeman, 1977, 1989; Wholey & Brittain, 1986). The study of organizational ecology is based on the fundamental assertion that, under specific conditions, evolutionary and ecological theory can be used to describe both organizational and biotic populations. Hannan and Freeman (1977) argued a strong case for the interaction of biological and sociological theory. They contended, "The [biological and ecological] models lead to valuable insights regardless of whether the populations under study are composed of protozoans or organizations. We do not argue metaphorically" (p. 962). The major organizing framework for work in organizational ecology is the description and explanation of organizational diversity and discontinuity over time as it relates to the creation, failure, and change of organizations (Baum & Singh, 1994; Hannan & Freeman, 1989; Singh, 1990; Singh & Lumsden, 1990).[1]

CHAPTER OVERVIEW: ORGANIZATIONAL ECOLOGY AND PUBLIC RELATIONS

In spite of the concurrent developments of situating the task of public relations within the context of the organization-environment relationship and the growth of organizational ecology as a significant research domain in sociology and the management sciences, little of the work in organizational ecology informs public relations theory and practice. At the basic and arguably most significant level of theory, the discipline's textbook tradition, not one of the five major textbooks released since 1990 devotes any attention to theory and research in organizational ecology (Baskin et al., 1997; Cutlip et al., 1994; Newsom, Turk, & Kruckeberg, 1996; Seitel, 1998; Wilcox, Ault, & Agee, 1998). This omission is significant because these texts do contain fundamental claims about public relations theory and practice that are squarely embedded in the domain of organizational ecology. The most important of these claims is the use of the classic ecological concept of the organization-environ-

ment relationship to capture the primary theoretical context of public relations (Cutlip et al., 1994; Newsom et al., 1996; Seitel, 1998).[2]

Based on locating public relations in this ecological context, the texts emphasize the importance of the environment to organize discussions of the operational role of public relations. For example, Baskin et al. (1997) argued that "thorough knowledge of the environment of the organization in which the practitioner works is a prerequisite to public relations effectiveness" (p. xiii). In addition, these approaches use the fundamental ecological concept of adaptation to describe the outcome of organizational efforts to meet environmental demands (see, e.g., Baskin et al., 1997).

THE IMPERATIVES OF ECOLOGICAL RESEARCH AND THEORY

This chapter proceeds from two essential imperatives based on the view that the primary task of public relations is set in the context of the organization-environment relationship. First, locating the task of public relations in that relationship establishes a necessary, sufficient, and significant warrant to link theory and research in organizational ecology to public relations. Because the focus of organizational ecology is drawn from the organization-environment relationship, this literature provides important research and models for public relations researchers to analyze and extend. In addition, the literature can refine the use of fundamental conceptual tools in public relations theory such as organizational adaptation, equilibrium state, and niche.

Second, ecological perspectives of public relations make understanding the relationship between organizational change and the environmental context for such change an imperative for refining public relations practice. When public relations programs are evaluated on the basis of their efficacy in producing change to optimize the adaptive state of the organization-environment relationship, examination of the ecology of organizational change is fundamental to the practice of public relations. Such a claim is captured in the contention that "public relations is a management function that helps achieve organizational objectives, define philosophy, and facilitate organizational change" (Baskin et al., 1997, p. 5).

Given these imperatives, this chapter explores research on organizational change within the literature of organizational ecology to identify implications for public relations theory and practice. First, I describe the foundations for ecological models of public relations. From this discussion, I identify three keystone propositions around which ecological models of public relations are elaborated. Next, I relate these propositions to research in organizational ecology from the "selection" perspective. Finally, I discuss the implications of the assessment to ecological models of public relations. It is hoped that identification of these implications will serve to move them from the status of qualitative generalizations to testable hypotheses for empirical research in public relations. Ultimately, the goal of this initial exploration is to spark a greater interest in systematically integrating the literature of organizational ecology with public relations theory and practice.

ECOLOGICAL MODELS OF PUBLIC RELATIONS

Models of public relations that are ecological in their approach (i.e., that specify the organization-environment relationship as the focus for the task of public relations) share the central claim that the role of public relations is to monitor environmental conditions and to develop organizational and environmental change programs that facilitate a state of "adaptation" between the organization and its social environment (J. Grunig & L. Grunig, 1991, p. 269; Heath, 1990, p. 41; Long & Hazelton, 1987, p. 6; Wilcox et al., 1998, p. 4).

In these ecological approaches to public relations, *organizational adaptation* is a cornerstone term that specifies an ideal state for the organization-environment relationship (Figure 24.1). In the standard use of these models, adaptation is employed to capture the notion that effective change programs produce a balanced state of affairs or an equilibrium between the organization and its social environment (Cutlip et al., 1994, p. 213). Thus, adaptation is an idealized outcome to the processes that link the organization and the environment. The state of adaptation can be measured by transient outcomes to the relationship such as the direction of public opinion, the acceptability of a labor contract to management and labor, the consumer appeal and profitability of the organization's products, the effectiveness of the organization's management system, the productivity of the organization's employees, the community's acceptance of the organization's operations, and the regulatory climate for organizational operations.

Following the tenets of open systems models in systems theory, the concept of adaptation that drives ecological models in public relations is based on the idea that the relationship between the organization and its social environment is one of mutual dependency (Cutlip et al., 1994, p. 206). As a consequence of this interlocked dependency, adaptation is predicated on the capacity for reciprocal change between the organization and its social environment. For example, J. Grunig and L. Grunig (1992) noted that in symmetrical models the focus for public relations is on adjusting the relationship between the organization and its publics (p. 289). Cutlip et al. (1994) argued that "public relations management is charged with keeping organizational relationships in tune with the mutual interests and goals of organizations and their publics" (p. 209). In addition, it is assumed that change must be continuous to achieve and maintain "states of equilibrium and balance" between the organization and the environment (p. 213).

Thus, within the ecological perspective on public relations, the concept of adaptation sets the central task for public relations management as the effort to maximize the degree of adaptation between the organization and its social environment. This state of adaptation is achieved by actively monitoring the environment and then

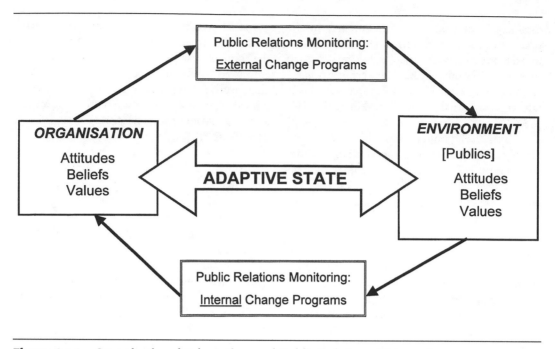

Figure 24.1. Organizational Adaptation and Public Relations Change Programs

developing and managing internal and external change programs targeted to components of the organization as well as to its external environment. For example, Cutlip et al. (1994) contended that "public relations' essential role is to help organizations adjust and adapt to changes in their environment" (p. 199). This suggests that no public relations effort can succeed in any ideal sense unless the practitioner understands and can influence the processes of organizational change. This premise clearly represents a fundamental challenge to "corporate journalism" conceptions of public relations in which one-way communication programs focusing on media placements are the primary program goals.

KEYSTONE PROPOSITIONS FOR ECOLOGICAL MODELS OF PUBLIC RELATIONS

Ecological models of public relations proceed by linking the primary concepts of environmental

monitoring, organizational change, adjustment of organizational-environmental relationships, and organizational adaptation. These concepts are linked in the following keystone propositions from which all ecologically based models of public relations are elaborated (Figure 24.2):

Proposition 1 (tight coupling of environmental tracking and organizational change): The relationship between environmental monitoring and organizational change must be tightly coupled to optimize the adaptive state between an organization and its environment.

Proposition 2 (continuous organizational change): Because environmental conditions can change continuously, an organization must be capable of adopting programs of continuous change to optimize the adaptive state between an organization and its environment.

Proposition 3 (increasing amount of organizational-environmental linkages): The linkages between an organization and its environment must increase over time to

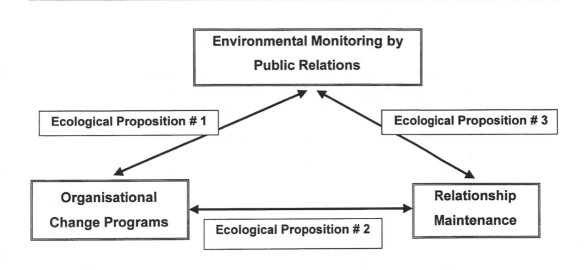

Figure 24.2. Relationships of Keystone Ecological Propositions in Ecological Models of Public Relations

optimize the adaptive state between an organization and its environment.

Together, these propositions provide the functional significance of public relations to the organization. First, public relations tracks environmental changes by monitoring the operational environment. Second, based on the information from environmental tracking, public relations develops internal and external change programs to optimize the adaptive state between the organization and its environment. Third, public relations programs increase the number and quality of linkages between the organization and its environment by identifying, building, and maintaining relationships with significant environmental elements. Kanter (1983) captured this "received view" of the relationship among the keystone propositions:

> The organizations now emerging as successful will be, above all, flexible; they will need to be able to bring particular resources together quickly on the basis of short term recognition of new requirements and the necessary capacities to deal with them. They will be organizations with more "surface" exposed to the environment and with a whole host of sensing mechanisms for recognizing emerging changes and their implications. In such an organization, more people with greater skills than ever before will link the organization to its environment. (p. 41)

THE SELECTION PERSPECTIVE OF ORGANIZATIONAL ECOLOGY

Propositions 1, 2, and 3 are the diagnostic propositions that organize ecological models of public relations. These models provide a view of public relations as a key operational bridge between environmental monitoring and the development of change programs that increase the probability of organizational survival. However, these keystone propositions receive a much different treatment from the perspective of organizational ecology.

A key analytical focus for organizational ecology is the "selectionist approach to organization-environment relationships" (Singh & Lumsden, 1990, p. 161). The "selection" perspective that dominates the literature of organizational ecology contrasts sharply with the "adaptation" perspective that organizes most of the models of public relations management (for a discussion, see Everett, 1993). Singh and Lumsden (1990) contended, "In contrast to the predominance of adaptation in the study of organizations, organizational ecology investigates the role of selection processes" (p. 62).

The selection perspective has come to represent the diagnostic analytical program for theories of organizational ecology (Aldrich & Mueller, 1982; Aldrich & Pfeffer, 1976; Astley, 1985; Freeman, 1982; Hannan & Freeman, 1977, 1989; McKelvey & Aldrich, 1983). An essential attribute of the selection perspective is its characteristic focus on organizational populations (i.e., organizations grouped as a function of confronting similar environmental conditions, structure, market niche, form, etc.) rather than on individual organizations (Freeman, 1982).[3] Unlike adaptation models of change that posit organizations tracking environmental conditions and responding by instituting change programs, the selection perspective is based on the view that "inertial forces" act on organizations to slow the effort to match adaptive response to shifting environmental conditions. According to Hannan and Freeman (1989), "Existing organizations, especially the largest and most powerful, rarely change strategy and structure quickly enough to keep up with the demands of uncertain changing environments" (p. 12). Organizational inertia can result from factors such as sunk costs of operating, internal political constraints to planned change, legal and financial barriers, barriers to information availability for decision making, and inappropriate modeling of adaptive behavior of other organizations. For public relations practitioners, these forces include the climate of public opinion within which the organization operates, the organization's culture that constrains attitudes toward change held by employees, shareholder beliefs about necessary actions to improve market share, and interpretations about management actions by financial reporters. The stronger the inertial forces acting on the organizational population, "the more

likely that the logic of environmental selection is appropriate" (Hannan & Freeman, 1977, p. 930).

Under the terms of the selection perspective, environmental forces such as the density of organizations within a population and resource competition among population members ultimately "select out" organizations that lack attributes appropriate to environmental conditions. As a general rule, because inertial forces inhibit the capacity for change, those organizations in a population with the highest levels of variation in form and process will have the highest probability of success over the longest period of time and across the largest range of environmental conditions. Unlike adaptation models in which organizations change over time to meet environmental demands, the selection perspective holds that those population members with *existing* variations appropriate to the challenges of selective forces will survive. Organizations within the population that lack a sufficient pool of variation to mediate or respond to selective forces face increased probabilities of failure.

IMPLICATIONS OF SELECTION TO ECOLOGICAL MODELS OF PUBLIC RELATIONS

Proposition 1

One of the most important empirical results of the selection perspective of organizational ecology is the work concerning the problem of inertial forces that act to slow the rate of organizational change that responds to shifting environmental demands. The terms of the selection perspective indicate that the tight coupling of environmental tracking and organizational change required by Proposition 1 is much less likely over time due to the twin dilemmas of organizational reliability and accountability. Hannan and Freeman (1989) argued that to ensure access to environmental resources and increase the chances for long-term viability, organizations must demonstrate that they have "the capacity to produce collective products of a given quality repeatedly" (the problem of reliability) and that "they can account for their actions rationally" (the problem of accountability) (p. 72). These key features provide legitimacy for organizational actions and, consequently, increase the probability of organizational survival. Hannan and Freeman contended that failure to demonstrate reliability and accountability

> threaten[s] an organization's ability to maintain commitment of members and clients as well as its ability to acquire additional resources. Thus we assume that selection in populations of modern organizations favors forms with high reliability and high levels of accountability. (p. 74)

Hannan and Freeman (1989) argued, "When adaptive change violates legitimacy claims, organizations incur costs. . . . The likelihood that adaptation will compromise legitimacy serves as a strong brake on fundamental change" (p. 69). To achieve these attributes, organizations must have stable and reproducible structures that are built by institutionalizing and standardizing routines and other aspects of organizational behavior. The need for stability produces a resistance to change as the organization pursues viability through reproducible structures and processes. Ultimately, "selection processes favor organizations with relatively inert structures, organizations that cannot change strategy and structure as quickly as their environments can change" (p. 25). Research on these hypotheses has been a central, if contentious, arena for research in organizational ecology (e.g., Boone & van Witteloostuijn, 1995).

To make the argument that inertial forces degrade the coupling between environmental tracking and organizational change programs, Hannan and Freeman drew a distinction between the core and peripheral structures of an organization. Core structures include elements such as goals, technology, and fundamental marketing strategy. Peripheral structures are those elements that buffer the core from environmen-

tal shocks and broaden the organization's connections to the environment (e.g., through joint ventures such as the partial funding of Apple Computer by Microsoft Corporation). Core structures are highly resistant to change (Hannan & Freeman, 1984, p. 156). Work by Kelly and Amburgey (1991) documented that environmental change was associated with a significant *decrease* in the probability of corporate-level change. In fact, the authors found strong evidence that "a change does not 'unfreeze' an organization but only unfreezes changes of the same type" (p. 606). In other words, the changes with the highest probability of occurrence were "changes that they had experienced in the past" (p. 608).

In these terms, public relations efforts clearly are part of the peripheral structures of the organization. The primary role of public relations is to help achieve legitimization for the operations of the organization and, thereby, increase the accountability of the organization (see, e.g., Heath, 1990, p. 30; Wilcox et al., 1998, p. 4). Thus, in terms of the selection perspective of organizational ecology, public relations operates as a peripheral organizational structure that produces programs to protect the core features of the organization. To the extent that public relations programs are effective, they will serve to *reduce the probability of change* in core features of the organization because those core features serve as the rationale for the role of public relations. This conceptualization presents a challenge to two-way symmetric models of public relations (J. Grunig & L. Grunig, 1992; J. Grunig & Hunt, 1984). These models are predicated on the idea of reciprocal change between the environment and the organization. Under these terms, public relations is successful to the extent that the organization is capable of changing itself to accommodate the needs and demands of its operating environment. However, if organizational change is least likely at the level of core features, then there is a limit to the adequacy of symmetric models of public relations based on reciprocal change. The adequacy of those models to describe the task of public relations ends at the point at which the changes threaten core features of the organization. Thus, the success of public relations change programs can be predicted based on the extent to which they threaten core features of the organization. A corollary to this idea is that the credibility of and support for the public relations function within the organization should vary as a function of whether public relations is seen as protecting or subverting the core features of the organization. It is unlikely that there would be much support for any internal function that acted to subvert the core features of the organization. Thus, from the selection perspective, the degrading of the tight coupling of environmental tracking and organizational change serves to reduce the quality of the adaptive state between the organization and its environment.

Proposition 2

This view of the decreasing potential for change over time also clearly is at odds with the required terms of Proposition 2. Given the assumption of interlocked mutual dependency in ecological models of public relations, this proposition requires that if the organization confronts environments that undergo continuous change, then the organization must be able to change itself continuously. In other words, the organization seeks to continuously "fine-tune" itself to meet environmental conditions (Boone & van Witteloostuijn, 1995). To the extent that continuous organizational change is not possible, then, under the terms of reciprocal dependency it is impossible for the organization to achieve an optimum state of adaptation with its environment.

From the context of the selection perspective, Hannan and Freeman (1989) hypothesized that each time an organization goes through a period of change (reorganization), the reliability of performance could be reduced. Just like a newly founded organization, there is a "liability of newness" for an organization that implements

changes. The changes can affect organizational performance, which in turn endangers the property of reliability. Moreover, Hannan and Freeman reasoned that because the length of time over which a reorganization is attempted also increases the costs of change, "the mortality rate of organizations attempting structural change rises with the duration of the reorganization" (p. 86). The work of Miner, Amburgey, and Stearns (1990) supports these hypotheses. Their work was set in the following argument:

> Structural inertia theory posits that fundamental change will increase the risk of failure. Modern environments favor organizations with high reliability of performance. Transformation disrupts the organization, produces more variability in outcomes, and therefore raises the risk of failure. Thus, even changes that might eventually reduce the risk of failure through aligning the organization better with its environment on particular dimensions will increase the short-term risk of failure. (p. 694)

In their study of Finnish newspapers, the authors found that organizational transformations significantly increased the probability of failure for all organizations in the population. In fact, the more efforts at change an organization undertook, the higher the likelihood of failure for the organization. At the same time, the authors found that during periods of "exogenous shocks" (e.g., severe disruptions in environmental conditions), the rate of multiple transformations for all organizations increased.

Thus, in terms of the requirement of continuous change stipulated in Proposition 2, the selection perspective suggests that even if the organization can overcome the degrading of the coupling between environmental tracking and organizational change, each successive change will act to increase the probability of failure for the organization. In this context, the requirement of continuous change stipulated by ecological models of public relations is a primary cause for reducing the adaptive state between the organization and its environment.

This work clearly has important implications for symmetrical models of public relations that hold reciprocal change as an essential goal in the effort to manage the organization-environment relationship. For example, the research of Miner et al. (1990) suggests that when public relations responds to significant changes in the operating environment of the organization (e.g., large-scale shifts in public opinion about the organization) by implementing organizational change, the public relations programs might actually *increase* the risk of failure for the organi-zation.

Proposition 3

The significance of Proposition 3 for ecological models of public relations is captured by J. Grunig and L. Grunig's (1992) contention that "public relations increases the effectiveness of organizations by managing the interdependence of the organization with the publics that restrict its autonomy. Organizations manage their interdependence by building long-term, stable relationships with those publics" (p. 313). The view that long-term linkages reduce the risk of failure was examined empirically in the research of Miner et al. (1990). They tested the hypothesis that linkages would act as a "transformational shield" (a resource that would deflect environmental shocks during change) and, thereby, influence organizational survival. In their study of a population of Finnish newspapers between 1771 and 1963, the researchers found that linkages increased the chances of transformation for the members of the population. In terms of the empirical merits of Proposition 3, they found that "organizations with linkages were more likely to fail after transformation than [were other members of the population]. Thus, a trait that generally lowers the chances of failure increased the chances of failure after transformation" (p. 710).

For public relations, such research suggests, for example, that building and maintaining long-term relationships with print and broadcast media while an axiomatic pillar of practice might actually serve to increase the risk of failure for an organization that has successfully implemented a change program. Such an eventuality challenges not only what gets done as media relations but also, more important, whether the long-term impact of the speciality is even beneficial to the organization. In light of such challenges, when program evaluation focuses on marginal measures such as "placements" and "top-of-mind" awareness (enduring hallmarks of media relations), the speciality never will provide much substance to the broader problems of organizational theory and behavior.

SUMMARY AND CHALLENGES FOR FUTURE RESEARCH

The selection perspective of organizational ecology represents an important challenge to ecological models of public relations theory and practice. The arguments and research reviewed here indicate the potential scope of the challenge. The challenge entails refining the propositional substrate of ecological models of public relations theory to improve their descriptive and explanatory mass. Clearly, one of the major problems in this challenge is to test and refine the assumptions of the adaptation perspective. Although adaptation continues to be an important explanatory term in organizational ecology (Baum & Singh, 1994), the expanding empirical foundation and consequent theoretical robustness of the selection perspective relegate Scott's (1987) maxim—"to survive is to adapt; to adapt is to change" (p. 91)—to the realm of glib oversimplification. However, the dominance of the adaptation perspective in ecological models of public relations theory is driven by Scott's maxim more than by the substance of the selection perspective.

The professional practice of public relations is framed by the employment of models of complexities such as audience response, media effects, public opinion, and organizational process. Historical momentum can entrench these models in the collective consciousness of practitioners and, consequently, drive ineffective practices for long periods of time. For example, practitioners continue to employ the program model in which the alchemy of audience "impressions" ultimately is conflated with "creating awareness" in that audience. This particular model of goal, strategy, and outcome reappears in substantial numbers each year in the program summaries submitted to the Silver Anvil competition held by the Public Relations Society of America. This type of truculent problem documents the importance of cross-disciplinary research in the effort to refine the practice of public relations. These problems cannot be resolved by national tests of practitioner experience and knowledge. In fact, the call for "professionalizing" the practice of public relations can best be accomplished by challenging fundamental models of practice with substantial and systematic research programs rather than by reifying such models in a "body of knowledge." Research that challenges the received view of public relations practice is the best hope to avoid ineffective programs that produce limited results or, at worst, actually reduce organizational effectiveness and survival. These types of threats to the effectiveness of the individual practitioner and to the survival of the organization constitute both the challenge and imperative of integrating theory and research in organizational ecology with the discipline of public relations.

NOTES

1. Following the perspectives of Singh (1990) and Winter (1990), this chapter proceeds from the perspective that organizational ecology subsumes work at the organizational, population, and community levels of analysis. The work of researchers on population ecology (e.g., Hannan & Freeman, 1989) is, therefore, a perspective within the domain of organizational ecology but not equivalent to it.

2. The influential two-way symmetric model of public relations (J. Grunig & L. Grunig, 1992; J. Grunig & Hunt, 1984) subsumes a number of important ecological propositions in its claims. The model places strong emphasis on organizational change programs that result from the "monitoring" of external environmental factors by public relations. This model is built from the central proposition that reciprocal change between the organization and its environment leads to mutual benefit.

3. Freeman (1982) argued that the selection perspective "is directed toward understanding the range of variation in morphological characteristics as displayed in some population or set of populations. Just as bioecologists do not often concern themselves with the behavior of individual organisms . . ., organizational ecologists do not concern themselves with individual firms" (p. 2).

The Centrality of Organizational Legitimacy to Public Relations Practice

MARIBETH S. METZLER

■ The premise of this chapter is that establishing and maintaining organizational legitimacy is at the core of most, if not all, public relations activities. Simply stated, organizational legitimacy is an organization's right to exist and conduct operations. Publics evaluate an organization's legitimacy based on its activities' relationship to social norms and values. Thus, legitimacy is based on the actions of an organization and responsible communication about them; it is not a mere perception or facade created and manipulated to weather the latest storm. Although in certain situations legitimacy clearly is the focus of communication efforts, communication activities in other situations typically have at least some relation to a public's belief that an organization is operating in an appropriate manner. As issue-oriented publics and the general public intensify their scrutiny of organizations and the latter's activities, direct disputes of organizational legitimacy will become more prevalent.

Given this centrality to public relations practice, the goal of the chapter is to present a framework that will be useful to both public relations scholars and practitioners for examining the discourse of organizations and publics and for examining and designing public relations activities. After explaining the theoretical basis of the framework, I illustrate it by examining elements of several legitimacy disputes that occurred at the U.S. Department of Energy's (DOE) nuclear weapons facility in Fernald, Ohio. Between 1952 and 1989, the plant produced purified uranium metal products that were shipped to other facilities for use in weapons manufacture. The operations at the Fernald site resulted in numerous types of environmental contamination, most notably uranium contamination of the air, soil, and drinking water supply. Since 1989, operations at the site have focused on cleaning up the many and varied environmental problems that stem from decades of concentration on produc-

AUTHOR'S NOTE: This chapter is drawn from the author's dissertation (Rensselaer Polytechnic Institute, 1996). She gratefully acknowledges the guidance of her adviser, Teresa M. Harrison, and committee members S. Michael Halloran, Jean A. Lutz, and James P. Zappen.

tion activities. Certain members of the local community have been outraged and active regarding contamination issues since the U.S. DOE revealed them late in 1984. Finally, I discuss the implications of this framework for public relations research and practice.

A FRAMEWORK OF
ORGANIZATIONAL LEGITIMACY

Organizational legitimacy is an organization's right to exist and conduct operations. It is established, maintained, challenged, and defended through dialogues between an organization and its various publics regarding organizational activities and their relation to social norms and values. Thus, organizational publics grant legitimacy to the organization and make the organization dependent on them in this respect. Communication scholarship has shown various connections between communication and legitimacy in boundary-spanning activities (Aldrich & Herker, 1977; Finet, 1993) as well as in image, issue, and crisis management (Allen & Caillouet, 1994; Benoit & Brinson, 1994; Hearit, 1991; Heath, 1997; Kernisky, 1994; Smith, 1994). These studies generally examine the effects that legitimacy has on organizations and the role of communication in producing these effects. But by examining only the immediate causes and effects of legitimacy disputes, many of these studies overlook the underlying processes involved in establishing and defending legitimacy. An understanding of these processes and the central role of communication in them will enrich the work of public relations scholars and practitioners in this crucial area.

Neilsen and Rao (1987) claimed that organizational legitimacy should be approached as a "complex process of socially constructing reality" (p. 525) and as the "*collective* making of meaning" (p. 524, italics in original). The collective construction draws on public and organizational expectations of activities that are based on localized social norms and values. This dynamic

aspect of legitimacy requires that organizations remain responsive to the views of the publics with which they act to construct their legitimacy. Participating in this process also provides organizations with the information they need to adjust organizational activities to fit the changing social standards of legitimacy or to influence those standards through policy initiatives based in issues management.

When a public questions an organization's legitimacy, four questions must be addressed to examine the dispute. The first question is, *What is the root issue of the dispute?* Beetham (1991) explained three dimensions of legitimacy that are useful in this regard. His first dimension of legitimacy, "legal validity of the acquisition and exercise of power" (p. 12), can be viewed as based in norms and values in several ways. A legal system is in essence a codified set of norms and values. However, the process of creating laws does not by itself create legitimacy. The social expectation that laws will be followed actually provides legitimacy to organizations that follow laws and is the basis for disputes of legal legitimacy when a law is violated.

This aspect of Beetham's (1991) framework actually is part of a larger category of organizational activities. In Ashforth and Gibbs's (1990) conceptualization of organizational legitimacy, legal issues are an aspect of role performance. As with laws, legitimate performance of organizational roles is based on the expectations of various publics. However, these expectations relate not only to the rules that society constructs for an organization but also to the "rules" and role that an organization establishes for itself, most notably through its mission. Even though organizations typically develop mission statements or goals internally, the statements cannot be created in a vacuum. Parsons (1956) pointed out that organizational goals must be framed within the larger social value system to be legitimate. Although the organization establishes these operational rules and roles, they must be "a function on behalf of the society as a system" (p. 68).

A role performance legitimacy dispute is based on the discrepancy between an organization's performance and social expectations of it.

In Beetham's (1991) second dimension, the legitimacy dispute focuses on a conflict between laws and a specific set of social norms and values. An organization usually tries to justify its actions based on laws, norms, or values. Obviously, if legitimacy stems from the expectation that organizations will follow laws *and* conform to social norms and values, then a discrepancy between the two can place an organization in a very awkward position. Does it comply with the laws and, thereby, preserve its legitimacy with those who enforce and support the laws? Or, does it follow the dictates of social norms and values and, thereby, maintain its legitimacy with other publics? In either instance, how does it justify its actions? Operators of abortion clinics face such questions every day.

Finally, disputes based in Beetham's (1991) third dimension, displays of dissent, can be either connected to a specific event, as are the first two dimensions, or more cumulative in nature. The key to understanding actions of dissent as a distinct dimension of organizational legitimacy, rather than simply as an outgrowth of other issues, is to remember that dissent involves some overt display of a public's views about an organization and/or its activities. As Beetham pointed out, actions of consent confer legitimacy, whereas "withdrawal or refusal of consent will . . . detract from it" (p. 19). In dissent, publics typically seek to orient the action of others or change their opinions.

As Habermas (1976/1979b) noted, legitimacy usually is not an issue until it is questioned: "The concept is used above all in situations in which the legitimacy of an order is disputed, in which, as we say, legitimation problems arise" (pp. 178-179). For example, actions evidencing consent to an organization's legitimacy probably will not receive much notice outside of a situation where legitimacy is being questioned. On the other hand, actions evidencing a withdrawal of consent or actual dissent (e.g., letter-writing campaigns, boycotts, demonstrations, strikes) usually are very noticeable, even to those outside an organization. Situations such as these are what public relations scholars and practitioners need to investigate.

The second question, *How does the communicative context affect the dispute?*, includes the publics involved in the dispute, any strategic interests they might have, and the communication forums used. Identifying not only who questions an organization's legitimacy but also what their relationship is to the organization and other publics and what their values are should be very useful in understanding the basis of their legitimacy challenges. Ice (1991) explained four categories of corporate publics that are important in this context. He described the categories as follows:

> Enabling publics control allocations of authority and resources and offer regulatory functions. . . . Functional publics supply inputs to and receive outputs from the corporation. . . . Normative publics incorporate norms for the corporation and represent publics that share similar interests with the corporation. . . . Diffused publics reflect unorganized publics who may be subject to the consequences of the corporation's activities, including communities near a corporate facility and "general publics." (p. 343)

One caveat is necessary here. Events that trigger legitimacy disputes might cause previously diffused publics to organize to address the problems. They also might attract the attention of special interest or advocacy groups. When Ice explained the normative public, he specifically referred to other organizations that were in the same business segment as the organization being studied. However, when a diffused public organizes to address a problem or an advocacy group becomes involved, it might approach an organization with different norms to guide activities. Broadening the normative category to include such groups more accurately reflects the current operating environment of organizations.

Relationships and strategic interests could guide the discourse toward certain issues and away from others. For example, a public might be trying to maintain or enhance its own legitimacy, might have other agendas that it is trying to further through the dispute, or might need the approval of one public to enhance its efforts with another. Such strategic management might color the way in which other parties view the dispute or how the issues are addressed. In addition, it could hinder the progress of the dispute. The particular forum in which a legitimacy dispute occurs also could have numerous effects on the dispute. Some forums are dictated by the nature of the issue, whereas the use of other forums may result from the choices or activities of various parties in the dispute. Obviously, groups will try to operate in forums that might benefit their particular points of view or that they can control. Taken together, these elements of communicative context might affect not only how a dispute is resolved but also the legitimacy and acceptance of that resolution.

The third question, *How are communication strategies used in organizational legitimacy disputes?*, is pivotal to understanding how a dispute progresses. Many studies have examined legitimation strategies as types of communication that can be characterized through certain quantitative measures. For example, Allen and Caillouet (1994) studied various strategies (excuses, justification, ingratiation, denouncement, and distortion) and examined their frequency of use and to whom each type was directed; Kernisky (1994) quantified the relationship between message theme and general structure (narrative or rational) and the perception of Dow Chemical's legitimacy; and Singh, Tucker, and House (1986) quantified the effects of legitimacy strategies on organizational survival. But as Neilsen and Rao (1987) noted, legitimacy is more than "something to be managed in a functional sense," a characterization that they claimed oversimplified the concept (p. 525). Although quantitative studies provide useful information regarding legitimation strategies, they too often neglect the processual aspects and normative and value basis of legitimacy. Therefore, in this framework, I approach strategies as rhetorical concepts and examine speaker choice, appeals to reason, and identification.

Choice of speaker in and of itself expresses what an organization or public values. Miller and Halloran (1993) observed that *ethos* reflects "the fact that the individual voice is always heard and interpreted against the background of the group character that gives it 'authority,' while the group character is, conversely, at stake in the performance of the individual" (p. 121). Group character is one aspect of what is at stake in a legitimacy dispute. By examining speaker choice, scholars and practitioners can assess what it reveals about the way in which a party is approaching the dispute and what constitutes an appropriate speaker in a given situation.

Habermas (1981/1984) explained the general circumstances of legitimacy disputes quite simply: They focus on "problems of grounding" (p. 268). From this perspective, discourse in legitimacy disputes can be analyzed using Toulmin's (1958) model of argumentation. Warrants and backing are the most important parts of Toulmin's model in a legitimacy dispute. They reveal the norms and values that each party provides as an appeal to the reason of the other parties (warrant) and as the foundation of its position (backing). The success of such appeals relies on the parties sharing those norms and values. By recognizing any differences between an organization and its publics at this level, scholars and practitioners can understand the basis of a dispute and why a particular line of discourse is or is not convincing to the other parties. This recognition also indicates the real issues that must be resolved to settle the dispute. In other words, the simple fact that an organization did not perform its role properly is not what ultimately is important; what that role performance indicates about the organization to its publics, as revealed in the warrants and backing of the publics' arguments, is what really matters in a legitimacy dispute.

Toulmin's (1958) strategy of logical structure applies only to certain arguments, not to all of the communication that occurs in a legitimacy dispute. Another effective and commonly used strategy is identification. As explained by Burke (1969b), identification is a connection, based in understanding shared values and communicating adherence to them, that a speaker makes with an audience so as to move the audience to action or to change an opinion. Dowling and Pfeffer (1975) maintained that organizations can achieve legitimacy by using communication to identify "with symbols, values, or institutions which have a strong base of social legitimacy" (p. 127).

Finally, identification probably is the clearest way in which to illustrate the interdependence of these strategies. As Farrell (1993) pointed out,

> Pivotal to Aristotle's understanding of rhetoric . . . is its peculiar inculcation of cognition, ethos, and emotion in the decisions and acts of collectivities. The norms and conventions of a culture thus find themselves employed as premises of both recognition and inference. (p. 76)

A speaker's ethos is persuasive because members of a public find elements of the speaker's character that they can identify with or that reflect their values. If a speaker has nothing in common with a public or is unable to strike some mutually agreeable bond, then he or she will not be able to move the public. In addition, the sharing of norms and/or values (an indicator of the consubstantiality of the parties [Burke, 1969b]) is the only way in which appeals to reason will work. If the speaker cannot establish this link, then the warrant will not hold and the argument will fall apart. In general, without a specific connection between the speaker and the public, all communication strategies will fail.

The final question, *How are legitimacy disputes resolved?*, brings together all of the dispute elements. The type of dispute influences which publics will be involved but is not an absolute predictor or determinant of them. Aspects of the communicative context can, in turn, affect the way in which the dispute is framed and progresses. The focus of the strategies is the publics to whom they are addressed, but the organization must consider all of the aspects in a legitimacy dispute to make strategy choices and try to bring the dispute to a resolution. Finally, all of the elements interact to influence the resolution of the dispute. To adequately understand and explain the basis, processes, and resolution of a legitimacy dispute, public relations scholars and practitioners must examine the various elements

operative in the dispute and their interdependence.

The four questions provide a framework for investigating and developing responses to legitimacy disputes. They are illustrated in the following sections with examples from several legitimacy disputes related to the environmental cleanup at the Fernald facility. I collected the majority of the data discussed here during the summer of 1993, which I spent observing various activities at the Fernald site. The site organization, referred to here as the Fernald Environmental Management Project (FEMP), is composed of both U.S. DOE and contractor personnel. The external publics of chief concern to the organization are the Environmental Protection Agency (EPA, both U.S. and Ohio) and a local citizens' group, Fernald Residents for Environmental Safety and Health (FRESH). I observed meetings held inside and outside the organization including the legally required public meetings regarding the cleanup and FRESH's monthly meetings. I collected a variety of documents and interviewed organizational members and people from various publics whom I had seen participate actively (mainly in meetings) in the Fernald situation. Since the period of my initial research, I have maintained contact with site personnel and FRESH members and have continued to collect site documents.

WHAT IS THE ROOT ISSUE OF THE DISPUTE?

The three types of legitimacy disputes, although possibly interrelated to varying degrees and all based in social norms and values, can be differentiated. Public relations scholars and practitioners must understand whether some aspect of role performance, a conflict between laws and social norms and values, or dissent is in dispute so as to focus on relevant communication activities. The interpretations of the dispute by the publics and by organizational members are of paramount importance here because they reflect the norms and values on which the dispute is based. This information reveals the specific normative and value characteristics of legitimate organizational activities in the instance being examined. Examples from Fernald are presented in chronological order in this section for continuity rather than in the order of types of disputes presented earlier.

The organizational legitimacy disputes relating to the Fernald operation began with the formation of FRESH, which was itself an act of dissent. Bitzer (1978) suggested that communication regarding issues and/or problems calls contemporary publics into being (p. 71). That is exactly what happened when the U.S. DOE began to reveal the environmental problems related to production at the Fernald site. FRESH formed in late 1984 in response to reports of radioactive dust leaks from the then operating Fernald plant. The public health issues related to these contaminant releases brought people together to discuss them, gather more information, and act.

One of the initial elements that sparked FRESH's dissent related to changing the entire manner in which environmental matters at the Fernald plant were regulated. FRESH wanted the U.S. DOE to be accountable, not autonomous. Testifying before a Senate subcommittee in 1985, FRESH asked that outside regulators be given authority over environmental matters at the site. As Kathy Meyer, FRESH founder, said, "The record at the Feed Materials Production Center is reprehensible. . . . It is eminently clear to us that this type of admission [radioactive dust leaks from the plant] is indicative of the need to replace DOE as the regulator" (U.S. Senate, 1985, p. 254). FRESH's position here was quite clear: The U.S. DOE had proven itself unable to regulate the plant in a manner that ensured the community's safety. This testimony represented dissent because one organizational public, FRESH, was trying to convince another organizational public, Congress (the U.S. DOE's ultimate enabling public), to act against the U.S. DOE and in support of FRESH. FRESH's evaluation of the U.S. DOE's efforts clearly indicates a lack of legitimacy in regulating the Fernald plant. The organization could not be relied on to protect the environment or people's health; therefore, FRESH called on Congress to act.

The underlying normative claim behind FRESH's dissent was that government in general, and its agencies in particular, should exist to protect the citizens, not to harm them. Regarding the Fernald plant, Vicky Dastillung, FRESH's vice president, told a congressional committee that

> while working to protect the nation, the government neglected to simultaneously protect the citizens' rights to a safe and healthy environment. . . . When our taxpayer dollars are spent on defense, the result must be the defense of our nation plus the defense of our health, our resources, and our future. (U.S. House of Representatives, 1988, p. 206)

The lack of citizen protection evidenced throughout the history of operations at the Fernald facility formed the basis of FRESH's dissent. The U.S. DOE needed to undergo a basic change in its operations and manner of dealing with the community to conform to this norm of protecting citizens and, thereby, become legitimate.

An example of a role performance legitimacy dispute occurred when FEMP failed to meet a milestone in its cleanup agreement. The milestones are the legal indicators by which cleanup progress is measured. This incident became a legitimacy problem because the milestones already had been renegotiated once because FEMP could not meet them. FEMP had assured the U.S. EPA, the Ohio EPA, and FRESH that it could meet the new milestones. At the first community meeting following the signing of the new agreement, Lisa Crawford, FRESH's president, stressed FRESH's perspective on the importance of the agreement:

> We don't want any more delays, we don't expect any more delays, we won't tolerate any more delays. This is it, *this is the last chance to prove yourselves.* A safe, diligent cleanup needs to start now and finish when the job is done and done correctly. Again, it's just a warning to remember that

the eyes of FRESH are going to be watching you and very closely. (community meeting transcript, October 29, 1991, italics added)

FRESH, as a normative public, clearly viewed the milestones as the performance measure by which FEMP had to prove its capability to conduct the cleanup. The organization had negotiated these milestones, acknowledged them as integral steps toward the goal of cleaning up the site (which is exactly what FRESH wants done), signed a legal agreement stating that it would abide by them, and assured FRESH that it could meet *this* set of milestones. The first new milestone came, and FEMP missed it. Taken as a whole, this situation created a role performance legitimacy problem for the FEMP organization with this very important normative public.

A legitimacy dispute based in a conflict between laws and social norms and values occurred as a result of the legal resolution of the milestone problem. In brief, to facilitate cleanup progress, the U.S. EPA approved, with the Ohio EPA's concurrence, FEMP's plan to pump uranium-contaminated groundwater out of the drinking water aquifer to stop the migration of the contamination. FEMP was allowed to discharge the contaminated groundwater into the Great Miami River with little or no treatment provided that other, more contaminated wastes were treated. FRESH and other members of the community viewed the discharge of contaminated water, regardless of the contaminant level, as counter to the norm that organizations should not pollute the environment and to the value that they placed on protecting their health and the environment. Thus, they were not pleased with this practice, even though it had been approved by the national and state EPAs (the equivalent of law for the site).

When this topic came up at a FRESH meeting, FEMP representatives endured a heated attack from FRESH members. The discussion mainly involved Ray Hansen, the U.S. DOE's assistant manager for site operations, and Norma Nungester, a FRESH member who is very concerned about pollution in the river. When Hansen pointed out that the EPAs had agreed to

the discharge, Nungester replied, "And it's the same thing as with the laws; if they're not right, change them" (FRESH meeting transcript, May 27, 1993). Hansen tried to use the EPA approval as law, but Nungester challenged the legitimacy of that approval. Because FRESH members objected to the terms of the agreement, they naturally would object to actions based on them. Later, Nungester said, "There is no safe level of that stuff. We don't want it shipped out to that river, is what it boils down to" (FRESH meeting transcript, May 27, 1993). Clearly, FEMP's right to handle the uranium-contaminated water in this manner, even though the plan was approved and legal, was in dispute because the agreement violated FRESH's normative and value positions. In FRESH's view, neither FEMP's actions nor the basis on which the actions were being taken was legitimate.

HOW DOES THE COMMUNICATIVE CONTEXT AFFECT THE DISPUTE?

The characteristics of the interactions between an organization and its publics constitute the communicative context of a legitimacy dispute. The importance of context lies in the fact that it influences, and in some cases even dominates, the communication efforts of both the organization and its publics. Without recognizing contextual aspects, only a superficial picture of the dispute is available for analysis. Scholars and practitioners must examine the relationships between an organization and its publics, the relationships between the publics, any strategic dimensions of a party's discourse, and (in some cases) the discourse forums of the dispute given that all of these contextual elements may affect communication efforts.

Although the members of FRESH were members of the local community and initially were part of the diffused public, when they organized and began to make normative demands on FEMP's operations, they took on the role of a normative public for FEMP. FRESH continues in that role today, constantly demanding that FEMP protect community health and the environment. In a specific example from the legitimacy disputes, FRESH insisted that FEMP perform to the standards not only that it had legally obligated itself to through the milestone agreement with the U.S. EPA, but also that it had repeatedly told FRESH and other members of the community that it would abide by: "When DOE puts their name on a consent agreement . . ., it should be a good faith effort on their part" (Crawford, FRESH meeting transcript, May 27, 1993). In my observations of and dealings with the members of FRESH, I noticed that they placed a premium on honesty and remaining true to one's word. Those were some of the norms of action they were requiring of FEMP in this situation and on which the legitimacy challenge was based.

FRESH played a different role with the EPAs from that played with FEMP. The EPAs act to protect the environment and the people who live in it. Therefore, FRESH is their functional public because it receives the benefits of their regulatory activities. In requiring the EPAs to fulfill their legislatively mandated roles, FRESH's approval became an important indicator of the legitimacy of the EPAs' actions at the Fernald site. Thus, in the milestone incident, FEMP's legitimacy was not the only one at stake; the legitimacy of the EPAs, particularly the U.S. EPA, also was at issue.

The relationship with FRESH and community approval in general were very important to the Fernald regulators. Graham Mitchell, the Ohio EPA's project manager for the Fernald operation, explained that when the Ohio EPA filed contempt charges against the site in 1990, "we felt we needed to maintain credibility for everyone because we need to do our job. The citizens need to see us doing the job" (personal interview, August 4, 1993). After having FRESH's explicit support in their fight to gain control over U.S. DOE operations, the regulators knew that the community looked to them to keep FEMP in line and that they had to provide evidence that they were fulfilling that role.

During the early years of the Fernald conflict, the relationships between the parties were dictated by their various strategic interests more clearly than at any other time. The primary strategic interests related to the fact that the U.S. DOE was trying to protect its authority and the EPAs were trying to take it. Of course, the larger issue for the U.S. DOE was not just the Fernald site but the entire weapons complex. Maintaining its self-regulator status would keep the U.S. EPA and the state EPAs out of its operations across the country. The U.S. and Ohio EPAs obviously wanted to expand their power and influence at the expense of the U.S. DOE. From the U.S. EPA's perspective, gaining authority in one group of federal facilities would give it a foot in the door at all federal facilities.

But strategic interests did not subside after Congress granted the EPAs regulatory authority over the U.S. DOE. When the U.S. EPA penalized FEMP with a fine and required a $2 million supplemental project for missing the milestone, the U.S. EPA exercised its regulatory authority in a very visible way. Jim Saric, the U.S. EPA's remedial project manager, felt that the fine and supplemental project were important to show that "we still have a handle over DOE. . . . I think it was important that we have a good perception with the public that EPA is being a regulator, and we're trying to keep DOE in line" (personal interview, August 19, 1993). Given FRESH's emphasis on the importance of the milestones, the U.S. EPA needed to fine FEMP in this situation to maintain its positive relationship and legitimacy with FRESH.

The last element of communicative context, the forum(s) of the dispute, has varying influence on the progression and resolution of a dispute. For example, after settling the milestone dispute between themselves, the main forums that FEMP and the EPAs used for communicating with FRESH regarding the resolution were community meetings and a special dispute resolution hearing. FEMP ran the community meetings. The format used at the time of this dispute had FEMP personnel giving presentations, followed by comments from the U.S. and Ohio EPAs. Then, FRESH would make a statement, followed by questions from the audience. In these instances, Jack Craig, the U.S. DOE's assistant manager for environmental remediation, presented the information regarding the dispute. The U.S. EPA conducted the dispute resolution hearing. During the hearing, Saric reviewed the events of the dispute and presented the details of the resolution. Then, he and Mitchell answered questions. Both of these forums privileged the role of the presenter by allowing him to establish the baseline of information for discussion. FRESH members certainly could, and sometimes did, bring up other topics, but these discussions stayed very close to the information that Craig, Saric, and Mitchell presented.

These forums ended up being fairly limiting for FRESH. There was no place for its input during the process of resolving the dispute. Thus, the key public in terms of the legitimacy implications of this dispute was simply handed the official resolution. In the overall context of resolving the legitimacy dispute, this situation had a negative impact on FEMP's ability to address this issue with FRESH. It also had detrimental effects for the EPAs. Although FRESH approved of the fine involved, its members objected to the discharge of uranium to the river and believed that the EPAs should have been tougher on FEMP regarding this issue. Although the EPAs, in particular the U.S. EPA, gained some benefit to their legitimacy through the fine, the lack of communication with FRESH during the resolution process had negative impacts for them as well.

The other main forum for all Fernald issues was FRESH meetings. Their structure is very different from those of the U.S. EPA public hearings and the community meetings. The control of this forum definitely belongs to FRESH, and the members seemed to like emphasizing that at times. A good example of this occurred at the meeting after the U.S. EPA milestone hearing. One of FEMP's agenda items was a discussion of the pump test for the groundwater extraction wells. At the first mention of the testing, FRESH took charge of the discussion and turned it away from the testing aspects to what was being done with the water. The questioning was heated and

reflected the members' confidence in being in their own forum. Most of the FEMP personnel, regardless of their topic, were on the defensive the entire evening. In general, FRESH members reacted differently in their own meetings from how they reacted in the other meetings that I observed. More of them attended the FRESH meetings, more of them asked questions, and their tone was more aggressive.

HOW ARE COMMUNICATION STRATEGIES USED IN ORGANIZATIONAL LEGITIMACY DISPUTES?

Appropriate communication strategies vary depending on the nature of the legitimacy dispute, the public(s) addressed, the operative norms and values, and the communicative context. For example, in a dispute regarding role performance, clear reasoning and justifications for actions presented by the person responsible for those actions might be the best strategy for an organization. Organizational publics might take a similar approach or counter with something different. The descriptions provided here reveal what norms and values the various parties recognize and give credence to and, thereby, provide insight into the resolution of the dispute.

Perhaps the most fundamental strategy is the choice of who speaks for the organization. We typically choose spokespeople based on organizational position, expertise, and/or rapport with the target public. But in the groundwater dispute, neither Hansen, the highest ranking DOE official on the site, nor Craig, who was in charge of the overall cleanup effort, had any success in dealing with the issue. However, when FEMP shifted to Dave Brettschneider as the speaker, progress began. FEMP moved from management personnel to the engineer in charge of this project. This change indicated FEMP's desire to deemphasize the managerial/legal aspects of the dispute (where it was clearly making no progress) and to focus on the importance of explaining the technical details of the project to the community.

Brettschneider turned out to be a very good choice in this instance. At the June 24, 1993, FRESH meeting, a FEMP representative followed up on groundwater issues. He said that Brettschneider would talk to anyone who had questions. Crawford commented, "He is a good person, and he'll explain it to you in a way that you understand." Others agreed. Brettschneider obviously had established a positive rapport with at least some of the members of FRESH during an earlier workshop on the groundwater cleanup and in his community meeting presentation. One sign of his success was that there was very little discussion of groundwater discharge at this FRESH meeting. FRESH apparently had heard all that it needed to hear at the two earlier meetings. Brettschneider was able to explain the technological limits of this project in a way that showed that FEMP was doing all that it could to address FRESH's concern about uranium in the water.

Appeals to reason can occur in any type of legitimacy dispute, but at the Fernald site they were most prominent in the role performance case. Basically, FEMP argued that it did not simply miss a milestone; rather, good cause existed that justified extending the milestone. FEMP developed interpretations of various provisions of the cleanup agreement and backed them with relevant norms and values as its primary strategy in arguing that good cause existed for the milestone extension. One such argument involved data issues. To write a cleanup report of the magnitude required here, FEMP had to collect a voluminous number of field samples and analyze them to characterize the contamination. These data also had to be compared for consistency of results and validated to ensure the quality of the results. Many of the U.S. and Ohio EPAs' concerns regarding the report pertained to such data issues, and resolving them would require FEMP to conduct more fieldwork and analysis (Craig, letter to Saric and Mitchell, February 2, 1993). FEMP agreed with the U.S. EPA's concerns regarding the data; its own results had revealed discrepancies. To make sound cleanup decisions, the scientific norm of accuracy required that

data inconsistencies be resolved. FEMP employed this norm, with which the U.S. EPA obviously identified, as part of the backing that justified its interpretation of the warrant as showing that there was good cause for an extension.

The U.S. EPA rejected FEMP's arguments. In addressing the data argument, the U.S. EPA relied heavily on actual language from the cleanup agreement or summaries of it. For example,

> In Section XVIII, Paragraph C.1., of the ACA [the agreement], U.S. EPA and U.S. DOE agreed that if, despite U.S. DOE's best efforts, additional sampling is required, good cause may exist for an extension. . . . However, "best efforts" requires something more than mere good faith and, in effect, requires U.S. DOE to show that delay due to additional sampling is necessary due to no fault on U.S. DOE's part. (Saric, letter to Craig, February 9, 1993)

Although the U.S. EPA obviously agreed that more sampling was necessary, its response to FEMP's argument hinged on the "best efforts" evaluation. The U.S. EPA did not reject the norms that FEMP used to back its arguments; however, it wanted FEMP's best efforts to meet an additional norm—timeliness. Recalling the U.S. EPA's strategic interests, it wanted the cleanup completed correctly but also on schedule to show Congress and FRESH that it could manage the effort properly.

The final strategy, identification, is one of the reasons why Brettschneider was successful with FRESH. Brettschneider identified with FRESH's desire to see the groundwater project proceed and the uranium discharge levels decrease. When he explained the concepts behind the project, he framed the technology as the only viable option for moving the project forward. Without it, the entire groundwater project, and perhaps others, would have been halted. He stressed the fact that FEMP, the EPAs, and FRESH all wanted this project to work, making the bond among them clear. He also portrayed the decreasing uranium discharge levels as a product of the technology, and although clearly based on the EPAs' and FRESH's demands, they appeared to be what

FEMP wanted as well. Given the technological constraints and the essential unity of all the parties on the purpose of the groundwater project, FRESH would have had a very difficult time posing objections at this point without appearing inconsistent.

FRESH was not unfamiliar with identification. Crawford, during her congressional testimonies, explicitly tied FRESH to Senators Glenn and Metzenbaum and to Congressman Luken. By referencing their statements and thanking them for their help in providing information, Crawford identified FRESH's position and values with those of people who were influential in this forum and who had some control over the U.S. DOE. By identifying with these legitimate participants, FRESH gained legitimacy for its standing as a public of the U.S. DOE and the dissent it was voicing. In addition, FRESH received support from its congressional representatives throughout the hearings. When Luken questioned Crawford at the 1986 hearing, he set her up with topics that enabled her to discuss the U.S. DOE's disregard for community health and its lack of basic knowledge about the community and the area. FRESH clearly had the consent and support of influential members of Congress, and this legitimated its position and made ignoring this organizational public very difficult for the U.S. DOE. At the same time, Luken's strong identification with FRESH maintained his, and through association Congress's, legitimacy with FRESH.

HOW ARE LEGITIMACY DISPUTES RESOLVED?

In essence, the response to this question tells us what constitutes an adequate response to a legitimacy dispute and why. In many ways, it is analogous to the evaluation efforts in a campaign. Addressing this question first requires examining the interaction of the aspect of legitimacy in dispute, the publics involved and overall communicative context of the dispute, and the manner in which communication strategies are used so as

to understand why the efforts of an organization did or did not resolve a legitimacy dispute and with which publics. Analysis should move beyond the obvious results (i.e., an organization loses its legitimacy and ceases to exist [Singh et al., 1986; Smith, 1994]) to more subtle issues. Scholars and practitioners should examine how the dispute process positions all of the parties for future actions. Few resolutions are final with an ongoing organization; they simply become a part of the history of a relationship between an organization and a public(s) and may strengthen or weaken the position of each, thereby changing the context in which the organization operates and communicates with its public(s).

The dissent case had the clearest resolution of the three disputes discussed here. FRESH's dissent strategies appear to have played a role in generating a response from Congress. Regarding the specific focus of FRESH's dissent, the U.S. DOE's status as an autonomous self-regulator, Congress did make all federal facilities subject to environmental laws and to regulation by the U.S. and state EPAs. This shift was a huge shock to the U.S. DOE. The changes were totally alien to the sheltered manner in which its facilities always had operated. In taking away its environmental regulatory authority, Congress was in essence saying that the U.S. DOE was not legitimate in this area of its operations. The U.S. and Ohio EPAs and FRESH obviously agreed.

The resolution of this dispute created a fundamental shift in the relationships between the parties at the Fernald site. Not only did the EPAs gain legitimate authority over cleanup operations, but FRESH gained a legitimate voice in them as well. One of the chief impacts of this outcome on FEMP was that future issues that the EPAs and FRESH might raise would have to be addressed. To ignore them could result in the U.S. DOE ultimately losing the right to conduct environmental activities at all of its facilities.

Regarding the role performance dispute, FEMP and the U.S. EPA resolved the milestone problem itself through stipulated dispute resolution procedures. Basically, for them a legal problem resulted in a legal solution—a negotiated settlement agreement. FEMP needed to resolve the milestone problem with the U.S. EPA and, to some extent, the Ohio EPA before moving to the legitimacy problem with FRESH. By successfully working through the dispute resolution process, FEMP managed to enhance its position for future dealings with the EPAs. In negotiating the settlement agreement, FEMP displayed continued good faith and cooperativeness by agreeing to accelerate several phases of the cleanup, even though the U.S. EPA had rejected this proposal as a good cause argument. FEMP's position clearly was one of willingness to get the cleanup completed in a timely manner, which was exactly what the U.S. EPA wanted.

But in regard to the legitimacy problem with FRESH over the milestones, the resolution with the U.S. EPA did not leave FEMP in a very strong position. In fact, it did not resolve the issue at all. It added one more missed milestone to the list, and the lack of meaningful communication with FRESH during the dispute with the U.S. EPA seemed only to have exacerbated the problem. After having the U.S. EPA reject its arguments, FEMP had few options left for dealing with FRESH on this issue. My discussions with FRESH members revealed that they still thought that the milestones were a major issue. When I asked Craig what effect he believed the milestone problem had with FRESH, he clearly was pessimistic: "I'm sure it wasn't good. Since these schedules have been renegotiated three times already, it just gives less credibility to DOE each time we have to renegotiate. They, like EPA, a lot of times don't want to hear any excuses" (personal interview, August 10, 1993). Only by meeting future milestones will FEMP be able to resolve this legitimacy problem with FRESH. FRESH demands actions, not just promises, when the role of cleaning up the Fernald site is at issue.

As should be clear from the discourse in the contaminated groundwater dispute, simply relying on the legal ground of "we have an agreement" never would have resolved the dispute. It did not work for Hansen and Craig or for Saric and Mitchell. Quite simply, when a law is in dispute, the law itself cannot be relied on to settle the dispute. FRESH and other community members felt that their norms and values had not been considered in the agreement regarding uranium discharges to the river. Therefore, relying on that agreement to justify discharge levels or actions simply made the problem worse. Both Saric and Brettschneider tried to show that the agreement had indeed taken community concerns into consideration. Brettschneider had more success because he could explain the technical reasons why those concerns could not be addressed more completely.

The interesting dimension of the resolution of this dispute is the shift in focus from the discharge agreement per se to its technological basis. Although FRESH still was not satisfied with the level of the uranium discharges to the river, the agreement remained unchanged. What FRESH members seemed to bow to were the technological inevitabilities of this situation. In essence, when Brettschneider shifted the discourse to technology, he was addressing FRESH's norms and values rather than just the agreement. He explained that given the current technological limitations, the discharge that FEMP and the EPAs had agreed to really was the best that could be done for cleaning up the site and protecting community health and the environment. Those are some of FRESH's chief concerns. Once Brettschneider addressed them, FRESH accepted the situation.

IMPLICATIONS

Regarding the situation at the Fernald site, legitimacy issues dominated the activities of the public relations staff for years. Practitioners there certainly handled all of the routine functions of a day-to-day public relations operation such as media relations and employee communications. But most staff members also were assigned to specific community groups (e.g., FRESH, township trustees) so that FEMP had constant up-to-date information on the concerns that were being expressed at various meetings in the area. A problem with FRESH often was enough to pull people off of their normal tasks to provide extra help to resolve the situation.

Today, although FRESH is far from quiet or totally supportive, the relationship between the group and FEMP is much more constructive. The legitimation strategy that eventually has enjoyed the most success is the choice of speaker or, more accurately, speakers. In 1994, the public relations office began its Envoy Program; community opinion leaders and anyone else who wants to participate are given an individual contact person within the FEMP organization. These contacts are not, for the most part, the public relations staff; rather, they are members of the site management team and environmental specialists. For example, the U.S. DOE's site manager is the envoy to a FRESH member. When Gary Stegner, who currently is in charge of public relations activities at the Fernald site, visited Miami University's Public Relations Student Society of America chapter in September 1997, he described how FRESH had supported the Fernald site when the *Cincinnati Enquirer* ran a potentially damaging series of articles about environmental activities at the site. FRESH members, in particular, felt that they had accurate information through their envoys and so did not believe the news stories; the series became a nonissue. Slick campaigns and high-tech tactics are not often the answer. FEMP returned to the basic strategy of making personal connections to enhance its legitimacy, and although this is resource intensive, it has paid huge dividends in the way in which community members respond to site activities and information about them.

In the broader spectrum of public relations scholarship and practice, legitimacy certainly is an issue that is gaining attention. The current situation with the tobacco industry is a prime example. The allegations made in 1994 congressional hearings of the tobacco industry's longstanding knowledge and cover-up of the dangers of smoking and of its manipulating nicotine content to make cigarettes more addictive continue to provide grounds for a major legitimacy crisis for the industry. Scholars and practitioners should examine not only high-profile cases such as this but also the everyday practices of their own clients/organizations and the views of their publics for indications of where the major problems of the future lie. Legitimacy problems are not problems that spring up overnight or that go away on their own; indeed, few of the problems that public relations addresses today are. But given their basis in social norms and values, legitimacy problems have the potential to devastate an organization and go to the very core of what it means to act in the public interest, as Article 1 of the Public Relations Society of America's Code of Professional Standards instructs us to do.

The framework presented here will enable scholars and practitioners to understand and address legitimacy problems in a productive and successful manner. Such activities will become vital to public relations as organizational publics increase the intensity and frequency of their examinations of organizations' activities. To deal successfully with legitimacy problems, efforts in this area should be integrated with an organization's issues management practices. Fernald's Envoy Program goes to the core of what Heath (1997) described as issues management: It "advance[s] organizational interests and rights by striking a mutual balance with those of stakeholders. It supports strategic business planning and management . . . by using two-way communication to foster understanding and minimize conflict" (p. 9). In the tobacco example, the lack of legitimacy of the industry already has generated numerous attack and counterattack issue advertisements and might lead to public policy changes. Legitimacy problems reveal areas in which public relations and issues management are needed; appropriate organizational actions could prevent, or at least mitigate, legitimacy problems. Coordinating these efforts should enhance the success of each.

Issues Management

The Paradox of the 40-Year U.S. Tobacco Wars

CORNELIUS B. PRATT

■ A concern of business communicators worldwide is the questionable relevance of much academic research to their strategic plans for growth and adaptation. In fact, broader questions about the application of academic programs and research to the professions are being raised, even within the academy (Hart, 1989; Tuggle & Sneed, 1998). Facetiously, they gnaw at the high-level theoretical orthodoxy of such research. More seriously, such concerns strike at the heart of the raison d'être for academic research.

Recently, in evaluating a research presentation given during an educators' session at an international conference, a practitioner said, "It's too theoretical." She obviously was alluding to her concern about how well the findings, conclusions, and recommendations of a research tome applied to the daily work experiences of communication professionals. The message: Academics beware! And work a little harder to make your work readily useful, not just to the academy but to the professions as well.

More than a half century ago, social psychologist Lewin (1944/1951) wrote, "Many psychol-

ogists working today in an applied field are keenly aware of the need for close cooperation between theoretical and applied psychology. . . . *There is nothing so practical as a good theory*" (p. 169, italics added). Similarly, German philosopher Kant (1793/1974) said that a crucial test of any theory is its capacity to guide *action* in fruitful ways. Both of those views challenge the loosely held assumption that there is indeed a chasm between theory and practice and that anything that is theoretical may have only a perfunctory relevance, if any at all, to everyday realities. But any meaningful theory cannot *not* be practical.

This chapter has two purposes. First, it defines public relations ideally as a practice that integrates issues management into strategic planning such as that for the tobacco industry. That case is examined in light of its more than 40 years of controversy regarding the positioning and marketing of tobacco and the managing of health risks associated with its use.

Second, the chapter argues that to the extent that the tobacco industry has substituted confrontation for dialogue and negotiation with its stakeholders, it has failed to benefit from the strategic use of issues management. Although we have no evidence that tobacco executives and staffers were oblivious to the strengths of issues management, there is evidence that their handling of the long drawn out industrial crisis was both insensitive to and in violation of issues management principles.

To achieve both of these purposes, this chapter does not engage in yet another theoretical analysis per se. Rather, it draws largely from issues management theory, applying it to an analysis of the tobacco debacle and elevating it in the strategic planning and management efforts of communication practitioners. As Heath (1997) noted, "Issues management enjoys prominence in the opinion of each organization's executives . . . to the degree that its practitioners know how to add value to their organizations while balancing the organizations' interests with the community of key stakeholders and stakeseekers" (p. x). In essence, this chapter is an attempt to help communication managers better understand how issues management can more readily be their preferred strategy for conducting their organizations' activities. Gaunt and Ollenburger (1995) reported that although a few major corporations have adopted issues management as a powerful strategic planning tool, it has failed to attract the widespread attention that it deserves.

This chapter also can help business communicators to reflect on the strengths, limitations, and challenges of a management tool whose contributions to public relations will be even more expansive in the increasingly competitive marketplace of the 21st century.

A focus on the U.S. tobacco industry is justified by its enormous influence both on the U.S. economy in general and on popular culture in particular, not least its creative, and occasionally disingenuous, use of public relations and advertising campaigns. Tobacco is the country's sixth-largest crop, fetching $2.5 billion for growers, and is the number one nonfood crop (Mollenkamp, Levy, Menn, & Rothfeder, 1998). The industry directly employs 600,000 Americans and generates $200 billion in revenues. It is one of the country's largest recruiters of lobbyists; in April 1998 alone, it spent $35 million to recruit 208

lobbyists to defeat anti-tobacco legislation. It is one of the largest donors to politicians (from 1987 to 1997, its political contributions amounted to $29.7 million); to professional sports; and to health and welfare, the environment, education, and the arts. It has an enormous influence on towns (e.g., Winston-Salem and Durham, North Carolina; Macon, Georgia), on city landmarks (e.g., "Joe Camel" billboard in New York City's Times Square; similar fixtures in Tobaccoville, North Carolina), and on regions (e.g., "Marlboro Man" country, the "tobacco country," the "Wild West").

APPLYING ISSUES MANAGEMENT

A new generation of issues managers is helping organizations to anticipate issues, project and communicate their probable impacts on the organizations, formulate policies and actions that implement their strategic thinking, and influence public policy debates. Heath (1997) described those activities as a part of organizational strategic planning that entails sophisticated issues monitoring and analysis, both of which can strategically and proactively enable organizations to avoid engaging in practices that can be offensive to key publics. The intent here is not merely to influence an organization's publics but also to change an organization's practices, making them more responsive to the public interest. The plan should formulate goals, strategies, and tactics that will result in an optimal "fit" between the deployment of an organization's resources and the opportunities for responding effectively to its environment (e.g., consumer interests) while actively engaged in the public policy process.

This chapter applies four functions commonly identified in issues management. These are (a) anticipate and analyze issues, (b) develop organizational positions on issues, (c) identify key publics whose support is vital to the public policy issue, and (d) identify desired behaviors of key publics (Heath, 1997). In brief, "those who want to be issues managers need to engage in smart planning, scout the terrain, get the house in order, and enact tough defense and smart offense" (p. 25). It is within the context of those four functions, then, that we present the paradox of the industry's strategies and tactics.

Anticipate and Analyze Issues

The first rule of issues management is to understand both the internal and external environments in which an organization operates and in which its products or services are distributed. In the parlance of issues managers, an organization should be equipped with "an early warning system." To what extent did the tobacco industry anticipate, not least analyze, emerging issues in its environment? Did it "scout the terrain" (Heath, 1997, p. 25), searching for potential trouble spots?

Perhaps no health-related controversy had tweaked the consciences of both the U.S. consumer and business, had stirred and perpetuated so much scientific debate and conflict, and had generated so much interest in research evidence as that regarding the effects of tobacco use on public health. The complex interplay between tobacco use and consumer health became the focus of public health agencies soon after tobacco was introduced into Spain and England by early 16th-century explorers. During the 17th century, England's King James said that tobacco was "loathsome to the eye, hateful to the nose, harmful to the brain, dangerous to the lungs" (quoted in Mackenzie, 1986, p. 13).

Since the early 20th century, experimental studies among lower animals have indicated possible links between exposure to smoke and the incidence of lung cancer, emphysema, and other health problems (e.g., Cooper, Lamb, Sanders, & Hirst, 1932). Among humans, retrospective and prospective studies conducted through the mid-1950s showed an association between tobacco smoking and lung cancer (Doll & Hill, 1952; Levin, Goldstein, & Gerhardt, 1950; McNally, 1932; Mills & Porter, 1950; Ochsner, 1954; Wynder & Graham, 1950; Wynder, Graham, & Croninger, 1953). Admittedly, some of the early literature on the subject showed results that were

inconclusive (Gies, Kahn, & Limerick, 1921; McConnell, Gordon, & Jones, 1952). Nonetheless, a number of health organizations, including the American Cancer Society, the Canadian National Department of Health and Welfare, and similar organizations in the Nordic countries, have warned the public about the health dangers of cigarette smoking.

What did the tobacco industry do early on? There were telltale signs of a product in trouble—of an industry in a caldron of a controversy—and the industry rose to the challenge by establishing the Tobacco Industry Research Committee (TIRC) on January 4, 1954. (The TIRC was renamed the Council for Tobacco Research U.S.A. Inc. [CTR].) There was an urgent need for scientific evidence on the ensuing questions about tobacco use and public health, and the CTR filled that need.

The industry gathered overwhelming scientific and marketing evidence on its products. That evidence, when made public, signaled an end to the U.S. tobacco industry's strategy of denial. For example, more than 4,000 pages of internal documents and memoranda from Louisville, Kentucky-based B&W, the third-largest U.S. tobacco company, and its parent company, BAT Industries PLC (formerly British-American Tobacco Company Ltd.), indicated deception. In one such document dated July 17, 1963, Addison Yeaman, B&W vice president and general counsel, wrote, "Nicotine is addictive. We are, then, in the business of selling nicotine, an addictive drug effective in the release of stress mechanisms."

The government's response to the growing controversy was articulated in June 1956, when Leroy E. Burney, U.S. surgeon general, authorized the U.S. Public Health Service to set up a scientific study group to appraise extant research on health and tobacco use. In accepting the group's report, Burney (1958) said, "It is clear that there is an increasing and consistent body of evidence that excessive cigarette smoking is one of the causative factors in lung cancer" (p. 44). That statement, made on July 12, 1957, set the stage for a 40-year conflict between "Big Tobacco" and the smoking public, consumer organizations, and health agencies. Two years later, based on new information, Burney said that smoking was the principal etiologic agent in the incidence of lung cancer and that, unless the use of tobacco could be made safe, a person's risk could be reduced by quitting smoking.

In 1962, U.S. Surgeon General Luther L. Terry established yet another study group, the Advisory Committee on Smoking and Health, to reevaluate the position of the Public Health Service, as enunciated by his predecessor and in light of additional studies indicating that smoking was associated with major health problems. The committee met from November 1962 to December 1963, and in its January 1964 report, it concluded that the hazards of cigarette smoking were of sufficient importance to warrant appropriate remedial action. Between 1967 and 1984, other surgeons general published reports that iterated earlier findings on the health hazards of smoking.

The industry's response to the growing scientific evidence on the health hazards associated with smoking was twofold. First, it established an institution whose primary responsibility was to gather hardcore scientific evidence. Second, from the public relations standpoint, it hired Hill & Knowlton, a New York City-based public relations agency, to develop a public relations program that made counterclaims suggesting that a controversy existed within the scientific community on the health issue. The agency also organized a Scientific Advisory Board that comprised scientists whose experiments showed contrary evidence, thereby suggesting that a medical controversy actually existed (Miller, 1992). In addition, the industry charged that findings about the health risks associated with smoking came from research done by a small group of overzealous scientists.

One could argue, however, that in light of issues management's premise of proactivity, the industry falls short in demonstrating leadership in searching for solutions to emerging issues before it was obligated—if not required—to search for them. As a recent case in point, on April 1, 1998, the Senate Commerce Committee overwhelmingly approved a draft tobacco bill sponsored by its chairman, Senator John McCain of Arizona. That bill overshadowed the proposed national agreement announced June 20, 1997. But the stricter terms of the bill blindsided the industry, which in mid-April (i.e., reactively) launched a $40 million television and radio campaign to defeat it. The bill had been so revised and extended that it was killed in Congress on June 17, 1998.

The industry could have been proactive, leading the scientific debate on the health risks associated with the use of its product and strategically influencing its fallout. Failure to be proactive has consequences, as Renfro (1993) observed: "Where a corporation, institution, or agency fails to respond to the public issues process 'voluntarily,' federal or state regulations can and, in most cases, will eventually force a response acceptable to the general public" (p. 27). That has been the experience of the industry, as the chronology of events outlined in the Appendix shows.

Develop Organizational Positions on Issues

Issues management casts problems and opportunities in the same mold, suggesting that issues managers respond to each with comparable promptness and fervor. That calls for formulating goals, objectives, and strategies that guide fomenting and advocating an organization's position on an issue. Such a response has two advantages. First, it provides additional methods for organizational stock taking, self-assessment, and redirection based largely on extant public debates on the issue. Public debates can enrich—or besmirch—the actions of an organization whose position, consequently, could be more clearly honed. Second, it provides additional outlets for strategically influencing issues-related public opinion and legislative actions.

What was the position of an industry that historically has been under siege? Perhaps no one said it more brazenly than Steven F. Goldstone, chairman and chief executive officer (CEO) of RJR Nabisco Holdings Corporation and the industry's point man. In a speech at the National Press Club on April 8, 1998, he said, "I have a business to run in an industry on which millions of people depend. We have to move on. So, we will continue to manage our business in the most responsible and competitive way we can." But Goldstone's use of the words "most responsible" is suggestive of his speaking true to a decades-old organizational goal: product marketing and profit making. Yet, in the long run, higher ethical standards make companies strong competitors (Reidenbach & Robin, 1989).

As early as January 4, 1954, the TIRC placed a full-page advertisement titled "A Frank Statement to Cigarette Smokers" in more than 400 newspapers nationwide, targeting 43 million Americans. In the ad, the TIRC claimed, inter alia, that there was no agreement among scientists on the cause of lung cancer and that "statistics purporting to link cigarette smoking with the disease could apply with equal force to any one of many other aspects of modern life. Indeed the validity of the statistics themselves is questioned by numerous scientists."

Early in the controversy, the CTR and the Tobacco Institute, a trade association founded in 1958, conducted full-tilt public relations (e.g., lobbying) on behalf of the industry. Both have since opposed legislation that they perceived unfavorably, have since funded research for their members' benefits, and have since promoted various other interests on behalf of their industry.

During the 1950s and 1960s, the research department of B&W privately acknowledged the dangers of smoking cigarettes and launched a variety of safe cigarette projects in hopes of using filters and additives to limit those dangers. In 1974, however, it scrapped those projects in preference for "defensive research" that would challenge scientific reports linking smoking to ill health. (Philip Morris, the largest U.S. tobacco company, shut down its research facility in 1970, and R. J. Reynolds, the industry's second-largest company, did so in 1983.) Industry officials publicly denied that there was any credence to the argument—which they described as "merely a hypothesis"—that cigarettes caused cancer.

Through the 1970s, the Tobacco Institute presented evidence that challenged findings linking cancer with tobacco. During the early 1980s, the industry focused on consumer awareness of the widely known risks associated with smoking. To extend and enrich the debate, it shifted the issue from product safety to freedom of choice and adopted the famously evasive (marketing) slogan, "Freedom of choice is the best choice."

In another vein, B&W's research results indicated that its cigarettes contained additives that were carcinogenic and that carbon monoxide could become increasingly regarded as a serious health problem for smokers, but those results were not widely publicized.

Unresolved contradictions are deceptive at best and potentially injurious to the public health at worst. As Pincus and DeBonis (1994) noted, consistency is the core ingredient of credibility. Its apparent absence suggests the connivance of industry officials with research and interest groups in attempts to protect tobacco industry interests. One of the terms of the June 1997 agreement was that the industry would "tell the truth" about the hazards of tobacco smoking. That the inspiration for such a disclosure eventually could come from proposed legislation rather than from the free will of the industry reinforces age-old questions about the latter's socially responsible conduct—or its lack thereof.

During an April 14, 1994, hearing in the House Subcommittee on Health and the Environment, each of the top executives from seven major U.S. tobacco companies said unequivocally under oath, "I believe that nicotine is not addictive." Yet, a confidential B&W study titled "A Tentative Hypothesis on Nicotine Addiction" dated May 30, 1963, and conducted for BAT by scientists at Battelle Memorial Institute in Geneva, Switzerland, acknowledged its addictive pharmacological effects. As Slade, Bero, Hanauer, Barnes, and Glantz (1995) wrote, "By 1963, scientists at B&W and BAT and executives at B&W readily acknowledged to each other that nicotine is addictive" (p. 225).

On June 6, 1995, the *Journal of the American Medical Association* posed the following statement and question to Tom Fitzgerald, manager of public affairs at B&W: "B&W knew that nicotine was addictive, and that tobacco smoke was biologically active, more than 30 years ago. . . . Does B&W still maintain that nicotine is nonaddictive?" (Graham, 1995, p. 255). The company's position was as follows: "We continue to believe that nicotine is not addictive because over 40 million Americans have quit smoking, 90 percent of them without any help at all" (p. 254). Yet, more than three decades earlier, its proprietary research presented contradictory findings.

The industry's public position was turned on its head when the Liggett Group Inc., which accounted for a mere 2% of the domestic cigarette market, broke ranks with Big Tobacco by admitting publicly on March 20, 1997, what everyone had long known—that smoking caused cancer; that, to boost the impact of nicotine, its levels were manipulated; and that nicotine was an addictive health hazard. It also broke new ground in its decision to include, on its cigarette packs, a warning about nicotine addictiveness.

What has the industry done? It has used a risky, if not ethically questionable, see-no-evil, hear-no-evil approach to articulating its position on a public issue. In part, that approach arises from the industry's belief that its public relations activities are being compromised by both anti-smoking activists and state and federal regulators. In part, it arises from the industry's attempt to strategically position the cigarette issue largely as one of consumer choice.

Identify Key Publics Whose Support Is Vital to the Public Policy Issue

Issues management is a public policy-driven process. Publicly, the CTR is the "sponsoring agency of a program of research into questions of tobacco use and health. . . . [It] awards research grants to independent scientists who are assured complete scientific freedom in conducting their studies" (cited in Glantz, Barnes, Bero, Hanauer, & Slade, 1995, p. 220).

Privately, however, the CTR "was organized as a public relations effort. . . . The industry research effort has included special projects designed to find scientists and medical doctors who might serve as industry witnesses in lawsuits or in a legislative forum" (cited in Glantz et al., 1995, p. 220).

Historically, three key publics have had a major influence on the tobacco debate. First, there are researchers and associations in the health professions—the American Cancer Society, the American Lung Association, the American Heart Association, and the American Medical Association. Miller (1992) observed that, even though these associations provided research grants to investigators, they left the reporting and the disseminating of research findings to the scientists, who were no match for the massive public relations and advertising offensive of the tobacco industry. Miller asserted, "The health groups' biggest advantage over the tobacco industry was credibility, but their lack of public relations expertise not only limited their effectiveness but actually harmed their cause" (p. 10).

Second, there are government officials whose legislation and city ordinances influence media public agendas on, and interpretations of, tobacco issues. The landmark Minnesota Clean Indoor Air Act of 1975, for example, restricted smoking in restaurants, offices, and public buildings and was adopted as model legislation by other states.

Finally, there are activist groups such as Californians for Nonsmokers' Rights, Americans for Nonsmokers' Rights, Action on Smoking and Health, the Group Against Smoking Pollution, and the California Restaurant Association.

Little wonder, then, that internal documents and memoranda that incriminated the industry were made public in 1994 through the anonymous distribution to three parties: (a) Stanton A. Glantz, a medical researcher at the University of California, San Francisco; (b) two congressmen, Ron Wyden of Oregon and Henry A. Waxman of California (chairman of the House Subcommittee on Health and the Environment); and (c) the news media. These three parties represent the public, policy, and media agendas, respectively. It is in the interest of the industry to influence the complex (triangular) interaction by applying (proactive) issues management principles that undergird the industry's (proactive) social responsibility behaviors.

Identify Desired Behaviors of Key Publics

In the end, it is the fourth of these functions that ideally should be the ultimate goal of the industry. But as stated early on, the intent here is not to merely change an organization's publics; it is to make the organization more responsive to them.

In a memorandum dated October 17, 1969, B&W's advertising agency, Post-Keyes-Gardner, announced a project inaptly code-named "Project Truth: It Can't Hurt You." One of its objectives was "to set aside in the minds of millions the false accusation that cigarette smoking causes lung cancer and other diseases, a conviction based on fanatical assumptions, fallacious rumors, unsupported claims, and the unscientific statements and conjectures of publicity-seeking opportunists" (cited in Hilts, 1994, p. 12; see also Post-Keyes-Gardner, 1969). It specifically attempted to influence public opinion on six myths:

Myth 1: Cigarette smoking causes cancer. The truth: No one has proved conclusively, scientifically, or otherwise that smoking causes cancer.

Myth 2: The 1964 surgeon general's report is conclusive. The truth: Pertinent unpublished aspects of the report are actually areas of doubt.

Myth 3: The statistics against cigarettes [are reliable]. The truth: They actually point to major fallacies and contradictions.

Myth 4: 100,000 doctors quit smoking. The truth: It was 835 doctors. And there are other examples of inflated statistics.

Myth 5: [There have been] 2,000 studies published since [the] 1954 surgeon general's report. The truth: Most of them respected earlier statements, many actually conflicted with the anti-smoking premise, and most [were not] even studies.

Myth 6: Smoking is a general health hazard. The truth: There is no demonstrated causal relationship between smoking and any disease (Post-Keyes-Gardner, 1969).

Other tactics used to influence public policy and consumer behavior were for the CTR to selectively fund "independent" research on tobacco use, that is, projects whose results were likely to endorse the industry's position. Furthermore, CTR lawyers reviewed proposals for funding as well as the findings of research they had funded before those findings were submitted for possible publication in scholarly journals.

Privately, Big Tobacco had indicated an interest in manufacturing "safer" cigarettes. This interest coincided with that of Jeffrey S. Wigand, a tobacco executive turned whistle-blower and a key player in the controversy. On January 1, 1989, he assumed a position as B&W's vice president for research and development in hopes of developing a product that would be less likely to cause diseases.

In an interview on the *60 Minutes* television program in November 1995, Wigand made several incendiary allegations against his former employer. He revealed, for example, that Thomas E. Sandefur, Jr., chairman and CEO of B&W, had privately acknowledged nicotine's pharmacologically addictive effects; that B&W knew that smoking could be lethal; that J. Kendrick Wells, B&W's staff attorney (and now the assistant general counsel of B&W), had deleted 12 pages from the minutes of a meeting in which discussions about developing a safer cigarette were held; and that when Wigand had indicated an interest in developing a safer cigarette, Sandefur considered that research proposal a bête noire. Wigand was fired March 24, 1993, because of, as he put it during a *60 Minutes* broadcast on February 4, 1996, "poor performance . . . and just not cutting it."

In November 1995, B&W sued Wigand, charging him with theft and a breach of the confidentiality agreement he had signed, following the termination of his appointment with the company. The company described him as "a Jekyll and Hyde personality"; it contracted the services of the Investigative Group Inc., a detective agency, to dig into his private life; and it created and publicized a 500-page dossier titled "The Misconduct of Jeffrey S. Wigand Available in the Public Record." In February 1996, Wigand became a witness in the U.S. Department of Justice criminal investigation of the tobacco industry.

On June 20, 1997, Mississippi Attorney General Michael Moore announced that if Big Tobacco had not agreed to drop all charges against Wigand, whom the attorneys general regarded as a martyr, then the national agreement of 1997 would not have been reached. He described Wigand as "a true American hero" in the government's case against the industry. But Wigand had to contend with a well-orchestrated smear campaign by his former employer, B&W; with a failed marriage caused by stress that he and ex-wife Lucretia Wigand had suffered from being hounded by B&W; and with threats to his life, particularly on the heels of his cooperating with state governments in building their case against tobacco executives.

To foment the desired change in consumer behavior, the industry consistently disseminated information that smokers wanted to hear from believable sources (Miller, 1992). It appealed to the self-interest of consumers by noting that freedom of choice was being compromised. Its lobbying arm, the Tobacco Institute, also had used massive public relations campaigns to fend off both governments and interest groups. It also engaged in a campaign that challenged earlier documented effects of tobacco use.

Credibility with publics always has been a key issue in the tobacco debacle. In April 1998, it launched a full-blown public relations campaign—and a legal offensive. On April 9, for example, it ran full-page advertisements in major national newspapers and on its Web site to outline reasons for backing out of a national agreement that it described as "dead."

Even so, the industry has had enormous difficulties in winning anti-smoking lobbies, and it has not influenced public policy to ensure its growth—at least domestically—not least because tobacco is responsible for more than 30% of all cancers, for nearly one in five deaths in the United States each year, and for an estimated $501 billion in additional health care costs. (The percentage of U.S. adult smokers dropped from 32% in 1986 to 27% in 1998, but among U.S. teenagers, the comparable percentages were 10% in 1986 and 25% in 1998.) The industry had sold genetically spiked, high-nicotine tobacco, even

as it reassured the federal government that it had stopped that practice 4 years earlier. It marketed its product aggressively, even though it knew that about 75% of the nation's 48 million adult smokers wanted to quit—and that only some 3% succeeded in doing so each year. The industry targeted young minorities, particularly those in predominantly black communities, in advertisements that capitalized on youth culture, even though it knew that 3,000 youths began smoking each day and even as 300 cities joined in a recent "Kick Butts Day" campaign to protest marketing cigarettes to minors. The industry continued to deny the pharmacological effects of smoking, even though it knew that more than 450,000 Americans died each year from tobacco-related diseases. Partly because of the exposure of the industry's secrets, it had little but a Hobson's choice—to reach an agreement with state governments. Even so, it fought several state governments over the release of more than 45,000 documents that held some evidence of the industry's unhealthful manufacturing, marketing, and advertising practices. However, it subsequently reached early agreements with four states: Mississippi, for $3.6 billion; Florida, $11.3 billion; Texas, $15.3 billion; and Minnesota, $6.6 billion.

Meanwhile, the industry upped the ante for three major reasons:

1. The number of lawsuits from individual smokers was increasing. For example, R. J. Reynolds' cases grew from 50 in 1994 to 540 in March 1998.
2. The industry's advertising and marketing strategies, its legal maneuvers, and the June 1997 settlement have spawned tobacco lawsuits in Canada, Brazil, France, Israel, Japan, and the United Kingdom.
3. The McCain Bill required the industry to pay about $148 million more than the amount agreed to in the June 1997 settlement. But more than that, it restricted cigarette advertising to a greater extent and required that the industry sign a protocol on marketing and advertising restrictions. For example, point-of-sale and Internet advertising and vending ma-

chine sales were prohibited, raising free speech issues.

Public relations programs or campaigns tend to have a minuscule impact on attitude and behavior change; J. Grunig and Hunt (1984) advised practitioners not to expect to affect more than 20% of the target group. For the industry to influence the behaviors of its key publics required a public demonstration of credibility; it had to air the noxious truth. Furthermore, it had to work more seriously with state governments, federal agencies, and interest groups to ensure greater sensitivity to consumer welfare—and in ways that were not undermined by its justifiable interest in profit making.

To force, as it were, organizational behavior change and compliance from Big Tobacco, the Clinton administration has iterated its resolve to seek tougher tobacco legislation and to ensure that U.S. youths no longer remain the bull's eye of the industry's advertising and marketing activities. The administration does not intend to put the industry out of business; rather, it is working to ensure that the historically irresponsible tactics of an industry be discouraged while the industry is being required to play by the manufacturing, advertising, and marketing rules of a civil society.

LESSONS AND IMPLICATIONS FOR THE INDUSTRY

Although it is impossible to predict the possible outcomes of the tobacco controversy if the industry had handled it differently, it is plausible to conclude that, if its actions had been predicated on the assumptions of issues management (particularly in a symmetrical context, i.e., responding to consumer interest in a manner that promotes dialogue and negotiation between organizations and their publics), then the fallout would not have been so long drawn out and costly. Thus, the argument in this chapter is that the ongoing tobacco wars could have been less

intense if the actions of the tobacco industry had been sensitive to the fundamental principles of issues management.

The wars are prominent in the annals of global business. For businesses in general, and for the U.S. tobacco industry in particular, the application of issues management has strong potential for making a difference in the outcome of the challenges they confront. In the tobacco case, well-trained industry public relations and advertising executives formulated campaigns geared toward raising questions on accumulating evidence of the health hazards of a product—and shoring whatever credibility the industry had among its key publics.

Thus, the major argument in this chapter is that, during four decades of crisis, the tobacco industry reneged on some of its responsibilities by not conducting its activities demonstrably in the public interest. The industry supports programs on health, on education, on the environment, and on the arts. However, even as the controversies regarding its product intensified, it used marketing and advertising programs to lure the young—the unsuspecting. Furthermore, internal corporate documents and recent legal decisions show, beyond a doubt, that the industry has had suckers for customers, making the merits of its widely touted personal responsibility and free choice strategies arguable.

In essence, the industry's marketing, advertising, and public relations programs suggest that issues management has been given short shrift. For example, its use of the Web has been criticized for its accessibility to underage smokers and for its inherently asymmetrical characteristics. Such sites tend to have fewer interactive devices that can facilitate two-way communication and have more transactional devices that usually are one-way (i.e., they are used to collect information from visitors). Another asymmetrical tool that is indicative of the industry's communications program is a quarterly magazine, *Unlimited,* launched in October 1996 by Philip Morris, manufacturers of Marlboro cigarettes. Its maiden issue had feature articles on arm wrestling and road trips, with hardly any contributions from the more than 2 million adult smokers to whom the magazine is mailed and without any column titled "Frequently Asked Questions."

Modern public relations still uses press agentry techniques pari passu with communication strategies whose roots lie in the practices of the public-be-damned robber barons of the early 20th century. Therefore, today's issues managers shoulder heavier responsibilities—to ride herd on professional misconduct and to create a business environment that nurtures corporate credibility, mutual relationships, and public support. The tobacco warfare threatens that environment, particularly in light of Big Tobacco's reluctance to admit publicly to any wrongdoing.

Lerbinger (1997) described Dow Corning's silicone gel breast implant crisis as "the most egregious case of deception" (p. 217), one that could have been avoided if the company had learned the lessons of the Johns-Manville Corporation and the A. H. Robins Company. In retrospect, perhaps Big Tobacco could have learned from the experiences of those companies; rather, it perpetuated a decades-long neglect of issues management principles.

A dangerous trend among tobacco companies is the control over their communication programs by corporate lawyers. The downside is that general counsel for such a company is more likely to focus almost exclusively on the legal ramifications of corporate communications and to foment controversy among tobacco researchers, leaving the public even more befuddled about an issue. The public relations practitioner, on the other hand, is more likely to apply consistency, clarity, and upfront principles to all communications.

CONCLUDING REMARKS

This chapter has argued that the failure of the tobacco industry to use issues management deprived it of its chances to contribute more meaningfully to U.S. public policy on smoking and health, that is, to influence the policy agenda. All in all, using public relations to foment campaigns that challenge the earlier documented ef-

fects of tobacco while concealing in-house evidence that holds contrary evidence is tantamount to a disregard of public health—and of the public interest. Similarly, shifting the corporate focus, after the mid-1970s, from biological testing to legal posturing so as to contradict results of years of nonindustry research into the hazards of cigarette use compromises the very essence of issues management. Using a research agency as a front for advocacy or denial is manipulative. Refusing to concede publicly that nicotine is addictive, even though corporate documents have held precisely that evidence for years, is misleading. And employing "public relations" and an investigative agency to orchestrate a smear campaign against a former employee is as indefensible as it is unprofessional.

The industry's strategies and tactics generate questions about its use of asymmetrical communications. By extension, those types of communications do not augur well for the reputation of a practice that, if used strategically and credibly, can increasingly serve both business and public interests symmetrically. Public relations practitioners, as issues managers, cannot afford to ignore the immanent challenges of the marketplace by not formally—and demonstrably—incorporating issues management into their organizations' operations.

APPENDIX

A Chronology of Events

1921	Links between smoking and cancer are inconclusive (Gies, Kahn, & Limerick, 1921).
1932	Experimental studies among lower animals by Cooper, Lamb, Sanders, and Hirst (1932) indicate possible links between exposure to smoke and the incidence of lung cancer and other health problems.
1932	Study among humans by McNally (1932) shows findings similar to those of the animal studies.

1950	Studies among humans (Levin, Goldstein, & Gerhardt, 1950; Mills & Porter, 1950; Wynder & Graham, 1950) show findings similar to those of 1932.
1952	Additional studies (e.g., Doll & Hill, 1952) report an association between smoking and lung cancer.
1952	Results of an association between smoking and cancer are inconclusive (McConnell, Gordon, & Jones, 1952).
1952	The American Cancer Society, the Canadian National Department of Health and Welfare, and similar organizations in the Nordic countries warn the public about the health dangers of cigarette smoking.
1953	Further research evidence on the health hazards of tobacco use is published (Wynder, Graham, & Croninger, 1953).
1954, January 4	Tobacco growers and manufacturers establish the Tobacco Industry Research Committee (renamed the Council for Tobacco Research U.S.A. Inc.). It gathers scientific evidence and starts "defensive research" on tobacco use and public health.
1956	Leroy E. Burney, U.S. surgeon general, authorizes the U.S. Public Health Service to set up a scientific study group to appraise extant research on the health controversy.
1957, July 12	Burney (1958) issues statement: "It is clear that there is an increasing and consistent body of evidence that excessive cigarette smoking is one of the causative factors in lung cancer" (p. 44). That statement formally set the stage for the 40-year U.S. tobacco wars.
1962	Luther L. Terry, U.S. surgeon general, establishes the Advisory Committee on Smoking and Health to reevaluate the position of the Public Health Service, as enunciated by his predecessor and in light of additional studies indicating that smoking is associated with major health problems.
1964	Terry's advisory committee concludes that the hazards of cigarette smoking are of sufficient importance to warrant appropriate remedial action.
1966	Cigarette advertisements and packages begin carrying the message, "Caution: Cigarette smoking may be hazardous to your health."
1967 and beyond	Other surgeons general publicly state earlier findings on the health hazards of smoking.
1970	Cigarette advertisements and packages begin carrying a stronger message: "Warning: The surgeon general has determined that cigarette smoking is dangerous to your health."
1970s	The American Tobacco Institute presents arguments that challenge U.S. government reports.
1979	The surgeon general releases another report that underscores the dangers of smoking.
1980s	The tobacco industry, in its attempt to obfuscate the debate over tobacco use, adopts a marketing slogan, "Freedom of choice is the best choice."
1988	The surgeon general says that cigarette smoking is addictive.
1994, April 14	Seven U.S. tobacco executives testify in Congress that they do not believe that nicotine is addictive.

1997, June 20	A landmark settlement is reached between the tobacco industry and 40 state governments. Industry agrees to pay $365.5 billion over 25 years.		approved April 1 in Senate committee. The industry launches a $40 million public relations and advertising offensive in which the bill is portrayed as a big tax, big government, tax-and-spend measure.
1997, July 3	The tobacco industry agrees to pay Mississippi, the first state to settle with it, $3.6 billion to cover smoking-related health care costs.	1998, May 8	Minnesota and co-plaintiff, Blue Cross-Blue Shield of Minnesota, reach a $6.6 billion settlement with the tobacco industry.
1997, July 10	R. J. Reynolds announces the retirement of its cartoon character, Joe Camel, from U.S. cigarette ads and billboards. It had been a promotional feature in the United States since 1987.	1998, June 10	A Jacksonville, Florida, court orders B&W to pay about $1 million to the family of a man who died after smoking Lucky Strike cigarettes for nearly 50 years.
1997, August 25	The tobacco industry agrees to pay Florida $11.3 billion for smoking-related health care costs.	1998, June 17	The tobacco bill sponsored by Senator John McCain of Arizona fails in the Senate.
1998, January 15	Texas reaches a $15.3 billion settlement with the tobacco industry.	1998, June 22	A 1996 judgment for $750,000 against B&W is overturned by a Tallahassee, Florida, appeals court. Claimant Grady Carter, who had smoked for 44 years, blames B&W for his lung cancer.
1998, April 1	The Senate Commerce Committee approves draft tobacco bill requiring that the tobacco industry pay $516 billion over 25 years, that an annual limit of $6.5 billion be set for private legal claims, and that about $29 billion of the settlement be used to compensate tobacco farmers, displaced workers, and their communities.	1998, November 20	A decisive $206 billion settlement is reached between the industry and 46 states, the District of Columbia, and five territories. Payments will be spread over 25 years. About $1.5 billion is allocated for anti-smoking research and education and for advertising against underage tobacco use.
1998, April 8	The tobacco industry declares the June 20, 1997, settlement "dead" in light of the draft tobacco bill		

Using the Collapse Model of Corporate Image for Campaign Message Design

MARY ANNE MOFFITT

■ Understanding how an organization creates and delivers its images to relevant audiences that relate to it obviously is of the utmost importance to the public relations professional. Understanding how these targeted audiences receive and process the organization's intended images also obviously is of great importance to the public relations professional. In fact, a comprehension of the power *and* the limitations of how the organization plans and delivers its images, and of how the audience members receive and process intended and unintended images, serves as a guiding principle and informs all that the public relations professional does. Managing a corporation's image is a core public relations concept that always has been accepted as a central issue to the teaching, researching, and practice of public relations. Accepting this fact, this chapter makes an effort to pick the image process apart—to investigate how people cognitively process a corporate image.

This chapter proposes that the complex process of corporate image communication can be explained by the collapse model of corporate image, which relates concepts of corporate image to concepts of campaign strategy and campaign message design. The collapse model provides the campaign professional with a model for conceptualizing corporate image from both the organization's and the receiver's points of view. With these concepts in mind, the campaign strategist is able to effectively design the campaign messages appropriate for each targeted audience within the course of a campaign.

To explain corporate image and its role in planning campaign strategy and in designing campaign messages, this chapter is divided into three sections. First, a detailed explanation of the collapse model is presented. Next, some research findings and case study applications of the collapse model are provided to demonstrate how it works. Finally, some practical applications for the public relations campaign strategist are provided along with some direct and hands-on instructions for how to operationalize theories of image to actual message design construction and campaign strategy.

THE COLLAPSE MODEL OF CORPORATE IMAGE

Recent research into corporate image has sought to understand how persons gain images of an organization. This research has led to an understanding of public relations campaign strategy in a distinctive, perhaps even unconventional, way compared to most accepted definitions of campaigns and most established ways of conducting campaigns. To understand the conceptualization, planning, and execution of a campaign based on the collapse model, this section first presents some "new" definitions for some "old" concepts. For the professional campaign strategist and communication specialist, these reworkings and reconceptualizations suggest some different considerations and some new applications of corporate images to the design of campaign messages.

To begin, the notion of "collapse" in the collapse model needs to be explained. The term signifies that the theoretical constructs of "image" and "public" are theorized as essentially related concepts that function in similar ways. They are collapsed into the same concept. By definition, then, the collapse model suggests that because notions of image and public operate in much the same way, they can be collapsed into the same construct, hence the collapse model of corporate image.

First, conceptualizations and definitions of corporate image are considered. Boulding's (1977) seminal study of image was referenced by more recent image theorists (Botan, 1993a; J. Grunig, 1991; L. Grunig, 1993; Moffitt, 1992, 1994b; Williams & Moffitt, 1997) who recognized that the organization can deliver its intended images but that a corporation's images ultimately are determined by the audiences that process them. In organizational research, and in public relations research in particular, findings have begun to view the locus of image in the audience members (Baskin & Aronoff, 1988; Cole, 1989, Denbow & Culbertson, 1985; J. Grunig, 1991; J. Grunig, Ramsey, & Schneider, 1985; Olins, 1991). Furthermore, Botan (1993a), Dervin (1989), and L. Grunig (1993) viewed corporate image as a dialogue between the organization and its audiences and agreed that images are in the individual and often are quite independent of the intended corporate image.

Adding to these studies are others finding that multiple factors—organizational, cultural, historical, and personal—affect images received by the audience (Alvesson, 1990; Baskin & Aronoff, 1988; Cole, 1989; Dowling, 1988; Fombrun & Shanley, 1990; J. Grunig, 1991; J. Grunig & Hunt, 1984). In addition, Haedrich (1993) posited image in the receiver and noted that many images of one corporation are possible—positive, negative, indifferent, and partial. These findings suggest that images in the receiver are ever changing and historically determined, that is, as products within a certain time and place.

Public relations' appreciation of the role of the organization in generating messages requires an equal commitment to understanding how the other half of the public relations communication process operates—the complicated and multifaceted image process that goes on inside the individual receiver. As suggested by these recent studies of corporate image, traditional assumptions of corporate image as decided and created by the organization and as a relatively singular construct (one global image of the organization) have been given up in favor of a concept of corporate image as multiple "images" that also are determined by the receiver and that always are open to change within the individual receiver. An image is conceptualized as any and all opinions, pieces of information, attitudes, and behaviors that an individual holds regarding an organization. That is, if a person has some positive and negative opinions of a company and, consequently, takes some positive and negative behaviors regarding the same company, then each positive opinion plus each negative opinion plus each positive and negative behavior is a singular and separate image regarding the organization.

In sum, multiple images are possible in each individual. These images are theorized as historical events or as products of personal, environmental, and organizational factors that are, nevertheless, changeable because they always are historically and culturally contextualized. This explains how a receiver can develop many images—positive, negative, indifferent, and/or partial—of one organization, with some images often different from corporate intention.

This *deconstruction* of global image created and managed by the organization into multiple corporate images in the receiver is crucial for understanding the collapse model and its relevance to campaign message design. This view of images as varied and multiple within the organization and within the individual also informs a new definition of public. To understand this revised explanation of public, specific definitions and distinctions between a population and a public need to be presented. To understand how new considerations of public affect the components of campaign message design and those major assumptions that guide the planning and execution of a campaign, the campaign strategist must have in mind the differences between a population and a public.

A population or an audience is defined as a group of individuals who share a relationship to the organization such as the employees, the customers, the stockholders, or the media. The terms *audience* and *population* are synonymous. Note that the audience or population is defined according to only one measurement—the sharing of a *relationship* to the organization. An organization's employees are arbitrarily grouped as a population because they all share the relationship that they work for the corporation; the community residents are a population related to the organization because they all live in the community in which the corporation is located; and the customers make up a population, or serve as a market or potential market, for the organization. The members within each population just mentioned might not know each other and probably have widely differing opinions and images regarding the organization. However, whether a population's members know each other or share any images does not matter for the definition of a population or an audience. *The only factor that assigns persons to the same population is that they all share the same relationship to the organization; they do not have to share any other factors such as beliefs, attitudes, demographics, or needs to be cat-egorized as a population.* Individuals are considered to be a population because they all share a relationship to the organization—all employees, all stockholders, or all customers—and that is the only thing they have to share to be considered a population or audience.

At the same time, within any given population are individuals who share a certain knowledge (a lot of information or just a little information regarding an organizational issue), an attitude (they like something a lot, are neutral, or intensely dislike something about the company), or a behavior regarding the corporation. For example, within an organization's population of stockholders are some persons who know a lot about the organization and some persons who know little. Within an organization's population of employees are those who like the company and like working for it, those who are indifferent toward the company, and those who genuinely dislike the company and their jobs. This notion of shared images and shared meanings among persons who might or might not know each other also was suggested by Heath (1993) in his concept of "zones of meaning"; zones of meaning, corresponding to shared public positions or shared images, not only can exist within a population but also, as Heath explained, are social meanings that can emerge between and among many target audiences at different times surrounding any organizational issue or policy.

The segmentation of persons *within any given population* who share a certain knowledge, attitude, or behavior traditionally have been viewed as publics or individuals who share a certain knowledge, attitude, or behavior. The term *public* almost always is used to identify a group of persons sharing some characteristic or set of attributes, for example, in J. Grunig and Hunt's (1984) terminology, *active, aware, latent,* or *nonpublic publics.*

However, it is time for a more careful definition and a more precise use of the term *public* than typically is used today. The definition of public has a direct impact on how the campaign manager plans strategy, creates messages, and makes communication choices. Even though today publics most often are defined as segments of a larger audience that share certain knowledge, attitudes, behaviors, and so on (J. Grunig & Hunt, 1984), in the collapse model this common definition of the term *public* is replaced with the term *public position.*

According to the collapse model, a public position also is any single factor—one opinion, one piece of information, or one behavior—held by an individual regarding an organization. That is, if a person has some positive and some negative opinions regarding a company and, consequently, takes some positive and some negative behaviors toward the same organization, then each opinion, each attitude, and each behavior corresponds to a singular and separate public position. In other words, rather than segmenting a population into groupings of persons who share a particular opinion, attitude, or behavior and identifying them as an active, aware, or latent public within the larger population, the collapse model identifies from the larger population the particular opinions, attitudes, or behaviors that are shared by all members across the entire population. Rather than grouping people according to an opinion, attitude, or behavior (or lack thereof) and placing them in a public based on that opinion, attitude, or behavior, the collapse model groups the similar opinions, attitudes, or behaviors of all members across the entire population. The concept of *segments of people as publics* within a population is replaced with a more precise and detailed view of *public positions as shared knowledge, attitudes, and behaviors* within a population. The theory of reasoned action (Ajzen & Fishbein, 1980; Fishbein & Ajzen, 1975) can offer some corroboration of multiple (and sometimes contradictory) attitudes affecting multiple varied behaviors. Fishbein and Ajzen's (1975) seminal theory recognizes that sets of beliefs held by the individual and by society can affect multiple attitudes that, in turn, affect intention and multiple varied behaviors in response to a given situation.

Given findings that beliefs, attitudes, intentions, and behavior are multiple, and given the new and revised definitions of image and public position as any singular attitude, belief, behavior, or knowledge of an organization, it is possible to conceptualize image and public position as similar concepts. Within the receiver are multiple images that are, in effect, also defined as multiple public positions. Because the collapse model conceptualizes image(s) and public position(s) as the same theoretical construct, they are collapsed as one in the collapse model.

One final illustration can demonstrate image and public position as analogous and identical concepts. Say, for example, that a campaign professional is conducting research on a certain population—the employees—to find out the employees' knowledge of the company, the company's product, and the company's reputation in the community as well as the employees' attitudes toward how the company treats them. Each employee interviewed will have a singular and respective answer for each question, possibly a positive, negative, and/or indifferent knowledge, attitude, or behavior on each measurement— company history, company product, company reputation, and perceived personal treatment. If we accept, according to the collapse model, that each knowledge, attitude, and behavior held by any one person is essentially an image and a public position within the individual, then how can one person be assigned to a public (in the traditional sense) when there are multiple image/ public positions within each individual? If a person has some positive, some negative, some strong, some weak, and some indifferent images/ public positions regarding the same organization, then it becomes impossible to group *persons* according to a shared corporate image.

What if one person with whom the researcher talked yesterday about the benefits of the corporation likes the corporation because of a good benefits package, but when the same person is asked today about the corporation's policy of not allowing unions, he or she expresses a negative opinion of the corporation? For the issue of benefits, the person has a positive image and public position; for the issue of unions, the person has a negative image and public position.

In sum, multiple images and public positions are possible in each individual. Public positions and images are theorized as any singular beliefs, attitudes, opinions, knowledge, or behaviors that an individual possesses regarding an organization. Furthermore, images and public positions, as historical events, function as products of personal, environmental, and organizational factors that are, nevertheless, changeable because they always are historically and culturally contextualized by the receiver. This explains how a receiver can develop many images/public positions—positive, negative, indifferent, or partial—of one organization, with some images/public positions often different from corporate intention.

CASE STUDIES AND RESEARCH SUPPORT COLLAPSE MODEL

The collapse model has been presented and explained, but a look at some research that has been done on actual organizations can evaluate its accuracy and utility as a measurement of corporate image processes. The first attempt to apply the collapse model to an actual organization was an ethnographic study of the image of State Farm Insurance in the home office community (Moffitt, 1994b).

Research findings from interviews with residents of Bloomington-Normal, Illinois, revealed that, indeed, multiple images of State Farm were held by the community residents. Although the research sample recognized the organization-controlled image ("Like a good neighbor, State Farm is there") intended by State Farm, many other negative, positive, indifferent, weak, and strong images were revealed in the study. Furthermore, an expected finding confirming the collapse model was that multiple images and public positions were both *within each individual* and shared *among the resident sample*. The picture of multiple personal, organizational, and social factors interacting and articulating images suggested a type of struggle for received corporate images in the study's sample of community residents.

For example, this study's respondents frequently demonstrated their multiple positive, negative, or indifferent images and public positions when discussing the various facets of State Farm:

Joyce: Oh, well, from what I understand, it's a great [employer]—the benefits they provide their employees, that type of thing.

Joyce: It's a great thing to have them here. If we didn't have them, it would be a different economic perspective in this town.

Joyce: Well, my daughter Karen did not like it, working for State Farm. So . . ., she said that working in insurance is not for everyone.

Joyce: One impact [that State Farm has] is on local housing, which makes me sick. They have people moving in from California who have sold these two- or three-hundred-thousand-dollar houses . . . and they don't want to pay capital gains, and they drive up our real estate prices. (Moffitt, 1994b, pp. 54-55)

Joyce's comments were representative of the study's sample of residents. She revealed multiple images regarding State Farm, and depending on what issue was discussed (employee benefits, economic impact on the community, her daughter's experiences, or real estate overpricing), she revealed a positive or negative image for each experience she has had with the organization. Joyce also demonstrated that multiple factors come together and articulated these images; personal knowledge through friends who are employees, knowledge of the economic impact of State Farm on the community, family experience of her daughter, and organizational experience of State Farm's impact on real estate overpricing all are factors—personal, social, family, and organizational—that influenced her images of State Farm.

A follow-up study expanded on the collapse model and confirmed again that multiple personal, organizational, and cultural factors influence multiple images and public positions in the receiver (Williams & Moffitt, 1997). A large telephone survey (427 residents) again was conducted on the images of State Farm in the home office community to explore and expand the concept of multiple factors interacting to create multiple images and public positions. The method of measurement used in the study suggested that some images were interrelated and not completely discrete images, suggesting that some type of overall image felt by the individual might, nevertheless, be supported by multiple images or public positions. The picture of multiple images of a corporation within the individual, however, cannot be denied.

Williams and Moffitt's (1997) study supported the model of multiple factors contributing to an overall corporate image—organizational, personal, and social factors. However, another very significant factor also emerged from the study—*business factors,* which included experience with the company as a customer or knowledge of the reputation of the organization's product.

Another new finding from this study was the importance of *personal factors* in articulating corporate image. Adding the elaboration likelihood model (Petty & Cacioppo, 1986; Petty, Cacioppo, & Goldman, 1981) to the collapse model led to an examination of personal motivation as a factor in processing and receiving images. This study's findings were that, even though personal factors had been recognized earlier as one of the major factors articulating meaning and images, personal networks were found to be very important in stimulating corporate images in the individual. Compared to other contributing factors such as media messages and second-hand information placed by the organization and business factors experienced by the individual, personal factors were identified as a powerful factor negotiating images of State Farm within its employees and among the community residents.

Three additional follow-up studies applied the collapse model to corporate image processing, in this case, in measuring the images of a large, midwestern, publicly supported university among the state's residents (Kazoleas & Moffitt, 1998). A pilot study of telephone surveys conducted across the state and two larger telephone survey studies of the state's residents ($N = 415$) and the university's faculty and staff ($N = 398$) were conducted.

Data and findings from all three university studies confirmed findings in the State Farm image studies. Support for multiple factors—organizational, social, personal, and business—articulating multiple images to relevant audiences was established. The importance of personal

contact as a factor creating and managing the university's images also was confirmed in the university studies. Indeed, results indicated that the greatest source of influence on images was not the media or other secondhand information but rather direct personal experience or experience through interpersonal networks. For the university image studies, factors such as geography/proximity to campus, personal experience, personal contact with family or friends who knew the university, employee status, media stories, and sports reports were contributing factors to multiple images. In turn, representative images revealed included high-quality graduate programs, a commitment to serving the community, a good science program, a "sleepy" university with no expertise, good sports teams, and good preparation for students.

In replicating the State Farm findings, these studies also found that a global image could be identified within the populations of residents, staff, and faculty, along with multiple supporting and contrasting images also noted by the respondents. The study solicited the global image by asking whether the respondents believed in a positive, neutral, or negative overall image of the university. Then, a correlation was established between the global image (how positive or how negative) and the supporting images (positive or negative to the global image). Additional findings were that all types of personal contact were strong factors affecting positive and negative images in the receivers—personal contact through employee relations, parent-to-child relationships, and friend-to-friend relationships.

Perhaps the most important contribution of all the State Farm and university studies is that among the populations' members, a somewhat global overarching image can dominate all of the received images, with other multiple images agreeing or disagreeing with the global image. However, research findings indicate that the concept of a singular, overall, organizationally determined image is inaccurate given that the global image—if there is one—ultimately is determined by the receiver.

This model of multiple factors supporting a global image or multiple images is consistent with Fishbein and Ajzen's (1975) and Ajzen and

Fishbein's (1980) theory of reasoned action, which suggests that sets of beliefs within an individual affect sets of attitudes and affect intentions and eventual behaviors. According to the collapse model, each of these beliefs, attitudes, intentions, and behaviors identified in the theory of reasoned action would be defined as a separate and discrete image or public position at work within the individual.

IMPLICATIONS FOR THE PROFESSIONAL CAMPAIGN STRATEGIST

The research that has applied the collapse model to actual organizations reasserts the collapse model's importance for the public relations campaign professional. First, recognition of multiple images, corresponding to each positive or negative belief, attitude, behavior, or knowledge the receiver possesses regarding the organization means that corporate image is not a singular construct determined and controlled by the organization. Related to this is the recognition that multiple factors (personal, organizational, social, and business), many of which often are outside the control of the organization, articulate various images to members of the population.

Research findings also indicate that personal networking cannot be ignored as a significant factor affecting a corporation's image. This suggests that the organization must not rely exclusively on media messages or on other secondhand sources to manage its intended images. As demonstrated in the preceding research, resources of the organization also should be put into the satisfaction of its employees, its community, its staff, and its administration, especially given the importance and power of these informal image networking channels in affecting the corporate images held by the populations relating to it.

Another implication is that, if varied corporate images are in both the organization and the receiver, then more and varied messages should be created to ensure more thorough and successful communication to the relevant populations. To appeal to the varied public positions experienced within a population, the campaign professional is obliged to include a multiplicity of messages that address the multiple images. This is not to argue that the organization does not have the power to present its own images; indeed, the organization remains as one of the important sources for its corporate images—along with personal, cultural, and business experiences of members of the related populations. Nevertheless, as indicated by the State Farm and university studies, more research needs to be done to explore the notion of global image and supporting images as well as their relationship to each other.

This model of multiple and changing images and public positions presents a challenge for the campaign professional—how to target all these potentially ever changing images *within each individual* and *across all the individuals in a population.* Remember that the project for the campaign manager shifts away from grouping individuals into a public and then delivering messages to this segment of persons. Instead, the campaign strategist is obliged to consider an entire population and to group the various shared public positions together—in Heath's (1993) terms, the opinions or attitudes that mark various zones of meaning. The campaign research identifies, among the entire population membership, those dominant images that are shared throughout the population. With this in mind, the campaign strategist's task is to create campaign messages to target the dominant and important images, public positions, and zones of meaning that emerge out of the population. Consequently, campaign messages are planned to target groupings of images/public positions and not groupings of people. The collapse model advocates using the tools of research to explore and reveal the multiple and diverse images or public positions revealed by the population's members so that strategies and messages can be created to appeal to the dominant and outstanding *images,* not to a *segment of persons* from within the population.

The recognition of potential multiple public positions dictates that an increased number of basic strategies, messages, and communication selections probably will need to be communicated by the organization throughout the course of a campaign. More and varied basic strategies (goals and objectives), more and varied message components (copy points and visualization factors), and perhaps more and varied communication selection choices will allow the targeting of the multiple and varied images within an audience.

Let me offer here an applied hands-on approach for creating the preceding strategies (Moffitt, 1998). The first step in creating campaign strategy is to plan the basic strategies from the formative research findings already conducted on the target populations. Basic strategies are made up of goals and objectives; a goal is any desired effect or change attempted in each targeted audience, and an objective is a statement of the number of pieces of information that will need to be communicated to support the goal. To accomplish each goal listed for a population, a listing of objectives also is constructed that will, hopefully, support the goal and achieve the desired change or effect set out in the goal.

For example, assume that formative research conducted on the community population indicates multiple images within the resident population. Research finds that members of the population are relatively conservative, possess strong family and church values, and have strong ties to school and sports activities. In response to these general image findings, the organization wants to enhance its image in the community through the following goal:

Goal: that the resident population will have a stronger image of the organization as a charitable organization and as an organization that cares about the children in the community

Some representative objectives to support this goal could be the following:

Knowledge objective: a total of 15 pieces of information about how the organization supports Toys for Tots at Christmas time

Knowledge objective: a total of 20 pieces of information about how the organization supports little league soccer and football

Attitude objective: a total of 20 pieces of information to encourage the opinion that it is desirable for the organization to support youth sports in the community

Behavior objective: a total of 10 pieces of information on how the community can get involved in coaching, refereeing, or participating in the city's sports leagues

Notice that these objectives relate to family values, school, and sports interests while at the same time supporting the goal that the community will believe that the organization is charitable toward community youths. This example is only one goal that might be appropriate for one population in the course of one campaign. Consider that the campaign manager, for each campaign, decides on a whole range of goals (desired changes in knowledge, beliefs, attitudes, and behaviors) and supporting objectives to match the currently held images in each relevant population in the campaign. The campaign strategist might want to enhance and strengthen some images found in a population or contradict some other images that are incorrect, or the strategist might want to create some new images desired by the organization or simply maintain desirable images. Depending on the size and scope of the campaign, this creative process might yield a set of 5 to 10 goals for each targeted population; these goals will suggest how many messages will need to be created to contain and communicate all these objectives within the course of the campaign as well as how many personal and media communication selection channels can get all the messages out to the various populations.

The matching of goals (desired effects) and objectives (message content) to the images, beliefs, attitudes, behaviors, and meanings of the targeted audience is what gets the audience's attention, facilitates persuasion, and accomplishes the goals of the organization. Consistent with theories of selective perception (Davison, Boylan, & Yu, 1976; Freedman & Sears, 1965), audience members tend to pay attention to message content that is consistent with already held beliefs. According to cognitive dissonance theory (Festinger, 1957), persons also will pay attention to contrary messages so as to confirm their already held beliefs. Creating strategy is, therefore, a matching exercise.

If the goals and objectives and the messages match the population's images and public positions, then the campaign manager has a better chance at having a greater impact on the receivers. As Fishbein and Ajzen's (1975) theory of reasoned action suggests, and as Petty and Cacioppo's (1986) and Petty et al.'s (1981) elaboration likelihood model suggests, the campaign professional is obligated not only to get the attention of the populations through basic strategies and message components but also to get the populations to process and accept the intended images.

The campaign professional is not obligated to create dramatic, clever, or cute messages that get people's attention—messages that might or might not persuade them to the organization's desired images. Rather, all the formative research conducted on the population members that reveals their images and public positions is what directs the campaign's basic strategies, message components, and communication selection channels. A campaign manager should not create messages with no regard for populations' currently held images and public positions. Messages can be clever and attention getting, but they also must represent the organization and match and enhance the audiences' multiple and varied images and public positions regarding the organization.

CHAPTER 28

The Workplace, Undergraduate Education, and Career Preparation

The Public Relations Academic and Practitioner Views

GAYLE M. POHL

DEE VANDEVENTER

■ Undergraduate students (traditional and non-traditional), parents, and employers see higher education as the ultimate answer to the students' employment futures. Members of the community are turning to their public universities for guidance, support, and help. Although academics do not consider themselves responsible for job training or vocational rehabilitation, they must provide students with realistic skills and knowledge for ultimate use in the marketplace. A college education, therefore, is seen as an important bridge from a fiscally dependent (or at least challenged) life to a fiscally independent one.

Universities sense this increased pressure from parents and students to provide marketable skills. Tuitions (and student loan amounts) have risen dramatically over the years, and "consumers" (i.e., parents and students) demand a solid return on their investment. Return on investment can be defined as marketable skills.

Galbraith (1991) asserted that society's current economic conditions are primarily responsible for the demand for an applicable and practical college education. Successful institutions and professors must respond to the changing economic climate and reflect the realities found in their communities. Educational missions must be modified to accommodate communities and their needs.

Although many liberal arts and science faculty do not consider preparing students for careers to be their most important goal as educators, most acknowledge its importance to students, parents, and constituents. Ironically, despite a vigorous interest in the material conditions of texts, societies, and people, liberal arts faculty often are unaware of the material conditions that dominate the workplaces that their students are preparing to enter. These faculty often are unaware of how different their students' experiences as workers will be from those in the classroom. In other words, most faculty are unaware of the skills that students actually need to succeed in the workplace. At the very least, faculty often are unsure whether the skills, concepts, and styles that they teach in the classroom still are being used on the job. The purpose of this chapter is to identify and discuss the skills and knowledge that undergraduate students need to enter the workplace to be effective entry-level practitioners.

DEFINITION OF PUBLIC RELATIONS

In 1979, Scott Cutlip, professor at the University of Georgia and a pioneer in public relations education, presented a lecture to the Foundation for Public Relations Research and Education in which he assessed public relations in American society. Cutlip (1980) listed three pluses of the public relations profession:

1. Public relations has made organizations more responsive to their publics by channeling feedback from publics to management.
2. Practitioners serve the public interest by providing an articulate clear voice in the public forum for every idea, individual, or institution.
3. Practitioners increase the public's knowledge by providing information through the media that the media themselves do not have the manpower or budget to provide.

Five years later, J. Grunig and Hunt (1984) suggested that the practice of public relations needed to be professionalized. Professionals possess a body of knowledge and have mastered communication techniques not known to the average citizen. They also have a set of values and a code of ethics that encourage the use of their knowledge and skills for the good of society. J. Grunig (1992c) indicated that professionalism is developed by creating a set of professional values, maintaining memberships in strong professional organizations, formulating professional norms and objectives, devising procedures for attaining accreditation, and offering professional development seminars (see also Grunig, 1989a).

At the dawn of the 21st century, public relations will lead business and other complex organizations. Its leadership will be defined by the public relations professional's ability to integrate at several levels of business and society and to create more integrated management processes. The value of integration as a public relations contribution emerges from the self-defined role of public relations building "relations" or integrating relationships between an organization and its publics (Caywood, 1997). Public relations will provide a new level of leadership for management to integrate relationships inside as well as outside an organization, using a wide range of management strategies and tactics.

Myriad definitions of public relations are quoted in academic and trade journals. J. Grunig and Hunt (1984) defined public relations as "management of communication between an organization and its publics" (p. 6). Black (1979) stated that the British Institute of Public Relations defined it as "the deliberate, planned, and sustained effort to establish and maintain mutual understanding between an organization and its public" (p. 3). Harlow (1976) emphasized all of the major elements of public relations, after reviewing journals and magazines and talking with practitioners, in his definition:

> Public relations is the distinctive management function which helps establish and maintain mutual lines of communication, acceptance, and cooperation between an organization and its publics; involves the management of problems or issues; helps management to keep informed on and responsive to public opinion; defines and emphasizes the responsibility of management to serve the public interest; helps management keep

abreast of and effectively utilize change, serving as an early warning system to help anticipate trends; and uses research and sound and ethical communication techniques as its principal tools. (p. 36)

Cutlip, Center, and Broom (1996) described public relations as a "planned effort to influence opinion through good character and responsible performance, based upon mutually satisfactory two-way communication" (p. 31). Nolte (1979) emphasized persuasion as two-way communication when he defined public relations as

> management function which adapts an organization to its social, political, and economic environment and which adapts that environment to the organization, for the benefit of both. This implies two types of activity. First, the public relations practitioner must persuade management to do the things to the organization that will make it worthy of public approval. Second, the public relations practitioner must convince the public that the organization deserves its approval. (p. 10)

Pohl (1995) stated, "Public relations is a management function which seeks to establish and maintain mutually beneficial relationships between and among its publics" (p. 1). Caywood (1997) emphasized the importance of integration in his definition: "Public relations is the profitable integration of an organization's new and continuing relationships with stakeholders, including customers, by managing all communication contacts with the organization that create and protect the brand and reputation of the organization" (p. xi).

Overall, J. Grunig and Hunt (1984), the British Institute of Public Relations, and Harlow (1976) all emphasized public relations as a management function. Cutlip et al. (1996) focused on the persuasive nature of public relations, whereas Nolte (1979) focused on the two-way persuasive nature of the practice. Pohl (1995) emphasized the establishment and maintenance of beneficial relationships, whereas Caywood (1997) focused on relationship integration. These theories provide the framework under

which students are taught and develop their public relations practitioner foundations. But are students being taught relevant to what profits and nonprofits need? Do practitioners appreciate the relevance of theory and grasp the changing role of public relations?

METHODOLOGY

Public relations professionals around the United States were surveyed to discover more about the public relations workplace and career preparation for entry-level practitioners. Participants had the opportunity to respond to the survey by phone, fax, mail, or e-mail. Fax and e-mail were the only two response methods chosen. Responses were then grouped using a cross-case analysis method (Patton, 1990). This method was described by Noblit and Hare (1988) as a "meta-ethnography." The challenge of this method is to retain the integrity, uniqueness, and holism of responses even when synthesized in translation. Results of survey responses were grouped by question and similar-themed ideas. (Questions serve as headings in the Findings section.)

Sample

For the purpose of this study, participants were defined as middle to upper level practitioners with 3 to 5 years of experience primarily performing public relations duties and activities. Selection criteria were based on a national sampling of practitioners from both for-profits and not-for-profits from the fields of education, health, agency, sports and entertainment, government, and the Fortune 500. A total of 57 practitioners were asked by phone to complete the survey, and 24 responses were received for a response rate of 42.1%. A demographic profile was established through information solicited in the survey.

FINDINGS

How Is Public Relations Defined?

When participants were asked how they defined public relations, certain themes flowed throughout their responses. Most said that public relations was relationship driven:

Public relations is relationship oriented. When dealing with the public, it is the relationship that the practitioner has with the customer that will predict the success of the venture.

[Public relations is] a management function that attempts to identify, establish, and maintain mutually beneficial relationships between all audiences involved.

Public relations was seen as reflecting the company's image and perhaps even defining it:

[Public relations is] anything that can affect the perception/image of the organization.

Public relations is a vital component of the marketing mix responsible for maintaining organizational image and reaching targeted audiences through strategic communications programs, developed in a cost-conscious fashion.

[Public relations] is an expression of your corporate identity.

And with that, many believed that public relations was an organized and purposeful function:

[Public relations] is developing strategies for an organization and letting people know and understand your mission and your achievements.

In addition to relationships, respondents defined public relations as a communications effort:

Public relations involves communication efforts—both internal and external. It includes printed and verbal and electronic communications to various publics. [It includes] a two-way process of communications: understanding your audiences, their concerns and interest; [and] knowing your objectives and then developing a program that will gain understanding, acceptance, and a behavior favorable to your objectives.

Unfortunately, a few participants still viewed public relations from somewhat of a propaganda and one-way communications model:

[Public relations is] communication and action that inform and influence public and key audience perceptions and attitudes about a company, individual, or issue.

There are many definitions, but I guess I prefer something along the lines of the following: Public relations is the art of identifying key audiences and applying a number of professional techniques to achieve positive perceptions from those key audiences.

Overall, respondents defined public relations as a function of relationship and image building, using strategic planning.

Do You Use a Formal Strategy for Campaign Development?

Practitioners were asked whether they used a formal strategy to develop a campaign. Nearly half (45%) of the respondents indicated that some form of campaign development strategy was used. Most strategies described included the formulation of goals and objectives, based on research and understanding of the client's business, implementation tactics, and feedback. One respondent stated,

Strategic planning . . . includes a thorough understanding of the client's business, environment, customers, [and] competition; [it] is based on establishing measurable performance-based objectives [and] tactical plans of action and measurement tied to the objectives.

Surprising to academics but not so to practitioners, no formal evaluation measurements were
specifically identified. This often neglected element of the planning process was the reality of
most public relations practices. Ever increasing
performance achievement demands left little
time for evaluation.

What Roles Do Marketing and Advertising Play in Public Relations?

Public relations, marketing, and advertising
often were used interchangeably. The die-hard
public relations practitioners and academics
were appalled at this "lack of understanding of
the disciplines." Practitioners who responded to
the interview guide said that public relations is a
subset of marketing and advertising:

> We view marketing as the all-inclusive word for
> what we do—public relations, publication, and
> advertising.

> Much of what we do supports our marketing ef-
> forts.

> Public relations should support and amplify mar-
> keting and advertising messages. Public relations
> opportunities are also byproducts of marketing
> activities and advertising relationships with me-
> dia.

Overall, public relations activities were considered under the purview of marketing.

How Is Integrated Communication Defined, and Does It Play a Role in Your Practice?

Integrated communication was defined by
some practitioners as the "bringing together of
all communication disciplines to work together
to solve an organizational problem." One practitioner related integrated communication back to
the definition of public relations by saying,

It not only means that all communications
carr[y] similar themes and values regardless [of]
the department issuing them or the media used or
the target audience; it also means invariably allowing participation and involving feedback.

Half of the respondents, however, were unfamiliar with the term.

More than half (63%) of the respondents did
not use integrated communication, but those
who did said that they used it to key similar messages to all internal and external audiences so
that an opportunity to have a voice in the organization was offered.

Do You Deal With the Media?

A more vital aspect of the practice of public
relations was media relations. Fully 91% reported varying degrees of media contact on a
regular basis. Respondents stated that media relations was essential and that practitioners
needed to be advocates for the media:

> We deal with media on an almost daily basis. For
> most clients, our relationships with local, re-
> gional, and national media are very important.

Some reported that it was critical:

> Media relations is one of our primary functions
> and of vital importance.

> Know the media and what they need, respect their
> deadlines, be honest, establish integrity, and edu-
> cate the media about your organization.

> Give the media everything they need to complete
> a story. Be honest and straightforward.

How Do You Budget and Allocate Dollars?

Managing a budget, however, was a priority
for only 75% of the surveyed practitioners. The
remaining 25% indicated that budget dollars
were not available to them. Fund-raising and do-

nations were the only means of obtaining dollars. When budget dollars were allocated, practitioners believed that those dollars needed to be tied to the organization and campaign goals and objectives:

> Budget allocations must be made according to marketing goals.

> [I] need to work with an inside-out allocation system. I make budget allocations after I identify the target measure, sales capability, projected revenues, and company benchmarks. Then I spread the money accordingly.

Another preferred method of allocation was zero-based budgeting:

> We can zero-base a budget working from our best approach to solving a client's communication need, regardless of the final cost.

> [It is] based on business objectives; set priorities on the most important strategies/activities needed. Zero-based is best.

A third method of allocation was looking to the bottom line:

> The bottom line is the main concern, so when allocating money, look to the bottom line and what will generate the greatest return on the dollar.

Do You Have a Crisis Communication Plan?

It came as no surprise that only 35% of the respondents had a crisis communication plan in place. Students are taught that organizations need a crisis contingency plan. Practitioners generally considered it to be a good idea, although only one third actually had a formal written plan in place:

> The plan includes every possible scenario: a description of it, corporate philosophy, audience affected, how to communicate with them best, who communicates, follow-up necessary, by whom, and extensive appendices of reference materials.

The plan was developed by a management team who focused on a situation requiring reaction, response, and explanation; attracting external questions and examination; where the organization was no longer in control; in which decisions needed to be made instantaneously; [and] focused on unsolicited media attention on the company.

> [The] crisis communication plan involved potential scenarios, lists of media and other key people, staffing considerations, policymaking infrastructure, [and] guidelines on who is authorized to talk to the media.

Only 33% of the respondents without a normalized crisis communication plan apparently saw the need for one.

What Role Does Technology Play?

Of the practitioners surveyed, all indicated a growing need for technology in the profession, but only three organizations reported frequent and broad access. The practitioners' access to technology was limited because the firm had only four computers. Those who did have access to technology used it for person-to-person information transfer and instant feedback, detailed research, media contact, branding, and monitoring competition:

> We have a news digest that sends our news releases to a growing list of . . . customers. And we are also making increasing use of the Internet to communicate with reporters and directly with the public.

> I access the Web a number of times a day to monitor company news and other business news. Also, a fair amount of research can be done on the Web, although at some point, for detailed research, more sophisticated databases, such as Lexis/Nexis and Dow Jones News Retrieval, are required.

Where Do You See Technology Heading?

Technology was viewed as still in its infancy. Each day brought more advances:

[Technology] will only accelerate, and we cannot even imagine all the ways we will be using it in 3 to 5 to 10 years.

In a nutshell, computer technology is eliminating distance and ignorance. With the Web and other tools, all the information you would ever need about any subject will be almost instantaneously available. Someone once said that the Internet is like a massive tidal wave roaring across the Pacific, and we're sitting in a canoe off the coast of California.

One respondent indicated that practitioners need to realize that when global communication of information is important, public relations will use it widely:

But as Bill Gates said, it will never replace face-to-face relationship building. So, technology, like media, becomes [a] reinforcement tool to maintain vital relationships, which are created face-to-face.

Another practitioner recognized both the advantages and disadvantages of technology:

It will grow as a source of information and communication but will not replace personal relationships with journalists. It will, however, make more information available to much broader numbers of people in differing areas. Also, [it will] dramatically increase the speed of communication—for example, a release of a divestiture careening across the newswires before your side was ready to make a statement—Panic City.

How Will Technology Affect Public Relations?

The impact of technology on the practice of public relations was viewed as very strong:

[It will] extend one's market.

Messages will be sent and received much faster, and they will be more interactive and more visible (e.g., photos on the Internet).

Some practitioners believed that technology will change media dissemination:

My future argument is that the media as we know it will cease to exist as a disseminator of information as people grow more accustomed to gathering information via other technology means. This is a great opportunity and a great fear.

I believe newspapers will eventually fade away; the Internet is infinitely more interesting and user-friendly. Newspapers gain 40% of their revenues from classified ads, but on the Internet, by typing in a key word, you can find in several seconds what it would take you much longer to find in the "want ads." I believe that technology will dramatically change the face of media, and as public relations practitioners, this will have an enormous impact on how we do business.

Are You Involved in Strategic Planning and Research? What Kinds of Research Do You Do?

Two areas that are very important to academics are research and strategic planning. The research and strategizing process allows practitioners to counsel clients/organizations. More than half (60%) of the respondents reported varying degrees of strategic planning and research in their practice:

Practitioners provide strategic counseling to [chief executive officers]. The research is necessary to provide this counseling and to know all you can about the publics, consumer environment, organization, and competing products and services.

[Strategic planning] teams meet periodically throughout the year to ensure that programs are strategically on track and that we're understanding all the relevant opportunities. Research is a part of all client/agency programs and can take any forms—both qualitative and quantitative. We use it to understand the client's marketplace and position, to develop programs, [and] to evaluate results of individual program aspects and annual initiatives.

The types of research conducted included secondary research, focus groups, surveys, focused feedback, and mall intercepts.

How Is Ethics Defined?

When asked how practitioners defined ethics, the most prominent responses mentioned honesty, integrity, and fairness:

We must always be truthful and help others in seeking the truth. Our conduct must always conform to the highest standards of honesty and fairness. We treat each other, the people in our constituencies, and our contacts in the news media as we wish to be treated.

[Follow] the Golden Rule: Do unto other individuals, organizations, and publics as you would like them to do unto you.

Protect client information, give the clients their money's worth, and make your ideas original.

Credibility and integrity are fundamental in dealing with the press and public. This does not mean we must tell all. But responses and positions must be honest and honorable and at the appropriate level of depth to inform and protect the company.

One practitioner stressed that ethics needs to be given more attention:

I believe that public relations needs to spend a great deal more effort in adhering to the code of ethics because, otherwise, the field cannot have credibility. Practitioners are all too quick to act unethically when it suits them or when their companies/clients tell them to do so. I believe that when practitioners begin quitting jobs over mat-

ters of principle or blowing the whistle on unethical behavior on the part of their clients/ companies, the field will begin to be respected. The [Public Relations Society of America] Code of [Professional Standards] is a good start, but I'd wager that most practitioners couldn't even tell you what is in it.

Are You Involved in International Public Relations? Where Is It Heading?

A growing area in the field is international public relations. Appropriately, half of the respondents had some, but limited, involvement in global relations. Work in international public relations was viewed as ever expanding:

In our fast-shrinking world connected by the Internet and satellites, etc., I believe there soon will not be a separate entity called "international public relations."

Almost all public relations is international now.

[It is] getting bigger and encompassing every facet of our work.

Globalization had been somewhat confined to areas such as government, education, and health care until today:

Instantaneous news and information is bringing to the public issues faced by public service agencies, educational institutions, and health care into the global arena now populated primarily by government and corporations.

With globalization also comes the need for consistency:

[We] need to have consistent images and messages around the globe. [We also need] consistent fundamentals with local adaptability. [And we] need to have control plus local action . . ., [which is] hard to achieve.

If an agency cannot offer [international public relations] through a network, corporate clients will go elsewhere to find it.

How Is Partnering Defined?

In addition to international public relations, the concept of partnering has become a growing trend in the profession. Approximately half of the respondents were not familiar with the term, but the other half considered partnering to be less essential to the survival and success of public relations:

[Partnering is] a relationship between two or more companies which mutually benefit from the relationship.

[Partnering is] working collaboratively with other freelancers or agencies to get the job done. [It] also involves the client.

[Partnering is] organizations on the same footing united in some project or cause. If not equal footing, it's a vendor relationship.

The 21st-century marketplace will be defined by and thrive on the convergence phenomenon. To be able to compete effectively in this area, it will be necessary to partner.

Partnering can be defined as two organizations working jointly to promote a product or service.

[Partnering involves] strategic relationships that serve the interests of all included—[for] example, corporate partner to nonprofit.

Who Have You Established Partnerships With in Your Practice?

When asked with whom they partnered, practitioners responded with a variety of answers:

[We partner with] sports teams, colleges, and [the] entertainment field.

[We partner with] several research field houses, printing and video partners, computer programming firms, other PR [public relations] firms through an international network, and over 25 virtual members of the firm on an as-needed counsel basis, located around the nation and beyond.

[We partner with] travel agencies, attorneys, artists, writers, strategists, educators, venture capitalists, etc.

What Are the Benefits of Partnering?

Practitioners saw the benefits of partnering as combining strengths, saving costs, and broadening expertise:

Each organization has a different set of attributes to offer to the other. Each can increase income by offering their strengths to the other and create a very strong team in the process.

[The benefits of partnering are] synergy, brains, and viewpoints [that] neither side could afford; mutual client sharing; mutual extra hands or outsourcing; [and] profitable coalitions.

Another practitioner stated that a larger market and more resources also are benefits and added,

Partnering with companies who have the same philosophy and good name recognition helps in the "battle for the mind" in the marketplace.

Partnering allows you to get more done faster and more effectively.

What Skills Are Essential for an Entry-Level Practitioner?

To academics, one of the most important questions asked was about the skills and/or knowledge that an entry-level practitioner needed to possess. Responses did vary but can be summarized by a list of skills that were consistently mentioned—oral and written communication, self-discipline, research, interpersonal, strategic/critical thinking, design, photography, marketing, organizational, Internet knowledge, and computer skills:

> Excellent reporting and writing skills, at least a grudging respect for the rules of grammar and punctuation, and, increasingly, computer and Web skills [are important].

> Writing, research, [and] an outgoing/friendly attitude [are important, as are] a "get it done" attitude [and being] creative—able to come up with new ideas.

> Knowledge of human behavior, understanding of organizational life, ability to think through a situation, ability to gather data, [and] writing skills— not journalism, but thought-provoking for writing issue analyses, reports, plans, and the other documents vital to PR practice[—all are important].

> Good communication and interpersonal skills [and] knowledge of how and where PR fits into an organization [are important].

What Entry-Level Opportunities Are Available?

If an entry-level practitioner possesses the requisite skills, then opportunities available to him or her include account coordinator, assistant account manager, and fund-raising and copywriting positions. One practitioner believed that entry-level practitioners should work for nonprofits because they provide excellent training and the practitioners get to do a variety of projects.

How Is Public Relations Evolving?

The final question asked of practitioners was where they saw the field of public relations heading. The majority of the respondents answered that public relations was going to become more

media oriented, more global, more relationship oriented, and more strategic counseling oriented. The public is and will be the heart of the campaign. One practitioner elaborated,

> [Public relations will head] away from information transfer and manufacturing communication products [and] into strategy, counsel, and training exec[utives]. And front-liners [will] be communicators, customer delegators, and relationship-builders. [We will go] toward face-to-face emphasis, whether in ally development or community relations or grassroots lobbying—meaning larger, but far different, staffing patterns. [We will see] acceptance as a profession. [We will be] out of the traditional link with journalism or communication schools [and] into speech or management liberal arts entities. PR practitioners are not in-house journalists, and many are fed up with the shabby treatment PR is receiving—especially when in most programs it's the PR students who [are] the majority or nearly so. [Finally, we will receive] acceptance as an integral part of the . . . decision-making coalition at the top rung.

IMPLICATIONS AND CONCLUSION

Respondents indicated their belief that public relations was about relationship building, but they also considered it a subset of marketing. Public relations needs to be a profession unto itself. Public relations, marketing, and advertising each needs to be considered a separate field from the others. Each field has specific functions that can operate in conjunction with the others but are distinctly separate. Public relations is a profession seeking to strategically foster mutually beneficial relationships between and among clients, organizations, people, and the like. Successful public relations often leads to marketing of products, services, and ideas and can use advertising to disseminate specific messages about those products, services, or ideas. Those who consider themselves practitioners need to use the term *public relations* correctly and need to educate their staffs and clients. The end result will be members of the public who consider public relations to be a legitimate profession in itself and not just an add-on term that sounds good.

Practitioners also stated that integrated communication sometimes is needed but rarely is used. The reason why integrated communication is such an anomaly to practitioners is that they, once again, considered the profession to be under the purview of marketing. Recognizing advertising, public relations, and marketing practitioners as distinct and separate professionals eventually will lead to the successful understanding and use of integrated communication. Media relations was believed to be a primary function of public relations. Practitioners need to be honest, establish integrity, educate the media about their organizations, respect media deadlines, and give the media what they need to write their stories. Both academics and practitioners believed that media relations is not as important as face-to-face relationship building with clients/constituencies/customers/vendors and the like. There was a general agreement between academics and practitioners in five areas:

1. All public relations activities—campaign strategy development, publications, budgets, special events, fund-raising, and the like—need to be closely tied to the organization's goals, objectives, and values.
2. A successful public relations program must include a crisis communications plan, informal and/or formal research, and strategic planning. (These often are overlooked due to lack of time and money.)
3. Technology is a growing necessity in today's global marketplace. Messages will be sent and received rapidly, and media dissemination will be global.
4. Ethics is defined as honesty, integrity, and fairness. The PRSA Code of Professional Standards clearly lays out the ethical responsibilities of the practitioner.
5. Partnering is an evolving concept that soon will be commonplace for all organi-

zations. It is especially important in a global marketplace. Agencies and organizations can partner with global organizations to produce a worldwide and all-encompassing campaign that targets publics on both sides of the globe.

Results of this study place an enormous responsibility on colleges and universities teaching public relations. All students need to be proficient in writing, speaking, conducting formal and informal research, thinking strategically, understanding how an organization functions, being self-disciplined, and being flexible enough to work either independently or in a group. Professionals also are requiring certain technical skills such as layout, design, and photography. Basic skills need to be pre-possessed by the entry-level practitioner, placing an emphasis on practical experiences outside the classroom.

Public relations is becoming a strategic planning and relationship-building profession that launches products, ideas, and services. Most important, academics and practitioners strongly agreed that for the field of public relations to survive the coming years, students need to have a firm understanding of what public relations is, what it can do for a company or an organization, and the value of the practice beyond that of a subset of marketing and advertising.

Results of this study indicate that the field of public relations needs the following from practitioners:

1. to use advanced technology and keep up with the daily advances made;
2. to use partnering as a strategy when working with clients (because it works);
3. to develop evaluation procedures for every campaign (because it can heighten the credibility of the profession);
4. to strive to make public relations a profession unto itself rather than a subset of marketing and/or advertising;
5. to reconsider integrated communications (because it is not universally used); and
6. to teach entry-level practitioners oral and written communication, strategic think-

ing, and computer skills (specifically, Web design and Internet use).

The future of public relations is bright, according to respondents who painted a pleasant scenario. Public relations will be an integral part of the organizational decision-making coalition, more involved in strategic planning, and accepted as a profession. Academics must understand the needs and prepare their students accordingly.

CHAPTER 29

Accreditation

Is There Access to the Process for All Public Relations Academic Programs—If Desired?

BONITA DOSTAL NEFF

"Accreditation, to the public, means institutions have met external standards," stated a Stanford University representative ("Fight Intensifies," 1998). Accreditation bodies per se emphasize that certain disciplines are critical to society, and a process like accreditation encourages "sound educational programs in these fields" and provides administrators and faculty with the stimulation that comes from "exchanging viewpoints with persons outside their own institutions and outside the academy" ("The Purposes," 1998). Others purport that accreditation recognition is the basis for funding access. In some cases, administrators believe that the privileges of resources and recognition enhances the recruitment of students and faculty. The incentive list is long.

However, the accreditation process also is fraught with controversy. What is the cost of the accreditation process in terms of real dollars and frustration? What is the true measure of this re-

cognition? Consider this statement from Christ's book on *Assessing Communication Education:*

> Many believe accreditation is in trouble. In 1992, the U.S. Congress very nearly removed the restriction that only students attending accredited institutions could receive federal financial aid. . . . In 1993, the Council on Postsecondary Accreditation voted to disband, noting its inability to bring together disparate accrediting agencies. (Arnold, 1994, p. 335)

Other critics look at the process as outdated and "geared to large research universities," and they view standards as "inappropriately prescriptive" (Arnold, 1994, p. 335). Ultimately, the test should focus on the quality of the students "produced." Does accreditation improve the results? Or, a more global issue views the role of accreditation as sustaining the employment market. So, what is driving the accreditation movement? How does one assess whether accreditation works?

THE ASSESSMENT CARROT

Some believe that accreditation drives assessment and that accreditation is necessary to ensure that assessment is conducted. An interesting statement considering the 1997 update on a longitudinal study from the Fitch-Hauser and Neff (1997) study on public relations programs established that a high level of program review currently is being conducted. However, to those believing in this connection, the reasons given seemingly are clear at first glance. Teachers are too busy to conduct thorough assessments (Fitch-Hauser, Barker Roach, & Barker, 1988). Other teachers are not interested in assessments. Some teachers do not have the backgrounds or skills to develop an effective assessment program. In some instances, the administrative body overseeing the program does not provide leadership in assessment. It seems, then, that accreditation can provide the framework for setting standards for assessment.

Several studies cited by Christ, McCall, Rakow, and Blanchard (1997) on this issue described the following:

> There are not many faculties who would willingly give up teaching preparation or research time to devote their energies to the large time-consuming commitment needed to do assessment well. That is why the current assessment movement seems to be fueled more by outside forces and real fears of retrenchment, program elimination, and accreditation guidelines than by faculty needs. (p. 23)

So, assessment is the carrot that makes accreditation inviting. What also is inherited is the imposed value system of the accreditation system. However, this might not be the best "fit" for the department or for the field of study as a whole. For example, when comparing two accrediting bodies in their approach to the field of advertising, the results are quite different. The Accrediting Council on Education in Journalism and Mass Communication (ACEJMC) has a liberal arts approach, whereas the American Assembly of Collegiate School of Business (AACSB) (business-oriented accreditation) focuses more on professional courses. Here, the course requirements for each accrediting body demonstrate the striking differences (Applegate, 1997, p. 336):

ACEJMC	Semester system	90 hours outside major; 65 hours in the liberal arts and sciences; 6 hours can be applied from major toward liberal arts and sciences section
	Quarter system	131 hours outside major; 94 hours in liberal arts and sciences

Accreditation in business schools focuses more on courses in business. Accreditation outside of business schools, such as the ACEJMC, focuses on the liberal arts and restricts the professional sequence offerings. Different agendas develop from accrediting bodies. When considering accreditation enforcement originating from the state, regional, and national levels, the complexity of the process seems to be a major challenge.

The Link to Other Rewards

So, why should faculty and administrators be driven to assessment? Is it not just pure joy to conduct evaluation and play with data, or is it, at best, to meet a legal requirement imposed by a large body? Unfortunately, the answer is not that simple. More and more assessment is tied to resources and funding. There are many links to resources (e.g., extra faculty, equipment) as well as out-and-out funding that make assessment so attractive. These are factors that cannot be overlooked. In an age when cutbacks are frequent, hiring is tight, and good teachers are hard to find, additional resources can breathe life into a program that otherwise might wither and die. Survival is a factor that can draw one into assessment. So, access to accreditation can be a matter of survival. The denial of access can lead to the consideration of alternatives.

PUBLIC RELATIONS: FORCED TO DEAL WITH ALTERNATIVES?

To understand why there is a growing body of public relations professionals looking seriously at accreditation, one needs to review the development of its history per se. This history reflects the growth of public relations as a field of study and as a discipline evolving to greater degrees of complexity. Public relations professionals—both academics and practitioners—have a stake in the profession. The relationship is somewhat of a complex entity.

Early Public Relations Training

Early public relations practitioners were trained in journalism. This academic home for the first formally trained public relations practitioners was, at best, awkward. Journalists opting to move into the public relations profession often were considered to be not as ethical or as professional as their journalism colleagues. This tension remains today on some levels.

Over the years of practicing public relations, practitioners grew to understand that public relations practice is quite different from journalism practice ("Public Relations Education," 1982). In *The New York Times,* Dean Cleghorn indicated that "it was essentially a marriage of convenience that took place many years ago, when journalism and public relations programs were sprouting up at universities throughout the country," but Cleghorn did not view these programs "as requiring the same skills or having the same professional values" (Rosenberg, 1998, p. C7). Public relations does not adhere to the same guidelines or professional codes as does journalism. So, the debate over academic train-

ing has become more oriented toward the type of training that is best for the public relations professional, whether as a future academic or future practitioner.

Accreditation of Public Relations Tied to Journalism

Unfortunately, academic training in public relations is greatly affected by the accreditation designation. Accreditation is tied to the public relations programs in journalism and/or mass communication departments/schools by the actions of the ACEJMC. First, according to the *Public Relations Accreditation Proceedings* published by the National Communication Association (NCA), "The U.S. Department of Education Accreditation division allows only *one* designated group to accredit programs" (cited in Neff, 1987, p. 3). The ACEJMC has literally "locked out" all public relations programs (now the majority of the academic programs) associated with departments of speech and/or communication. Other organizations desiring to accredit programs in public relations found the ruling prohibitive in another way. For example, when the Public Relations Society of America (PRSA) was interested in accrediting public relations programs, it chose to use the word *certified* (Certified in Education for Public Relations—CEPR) (Neff, 1987). Supposedly, it was believed that the word *accreditation* was the sole propriety of ACEJMC. However, the Department of Education claims not to have propriety rights over the use of the word accreditation and so the spirit of accreditation designation lives outside the ACEJMC purview.

PUBLIC RELATIONS GROWTH IN OTHER AREAS

College Curriculum

Public relations programs have flourished in departments outside of journalism and mass communication despite not being recognized by the ACEJMC accreditation body. In 1975, Dennis Wilcox identified at least 300 academic institutions offering "courses, sequences, and majors in public relations" in U.S. higher education institutions (cited in Trent & Trent, 1976, p. 292). Trent and Trent (1976), in their article on public relations education, noted the opportunities for speech communication. They summarized their findings with the following challenge:

> Public relations practitioners and speech communication students and faculty can benefit mutually from association. The practitioners can use the knowledge and skills our students possess because their trade is communication. Speech communication students can benefit by preparing for a specific career. Both students and faculty can benefit from having a specific field that regularly applies principles we study and teach. The practitioners represented by the Public Relations Society of America have made it clear that they would support the development of academic programs. Speech communication departments can respond to this support with rigorous public relations programs which have a broad communication base. (p. 298)

More than a decade later, in a 1987 study, 582 higher education institutions were identified as offering public relations courses, sequences, and majors (Neff, 1989, p. 159). This study substantiated the curriculum growth by reviewing university catalogs. Every course that listed public relations in the title or in the content description as the focus of the course was counted. This guideline for identifying public relations courses was established by the 1987 Commission on Undergraduate and Graduate Public Relations. Because college catalogs are considered legal documents in a court of law, the documentation of sequences is material evidence. Having a reliable source would add further authenticity to the research. Lastly, the specific data on course sequences in Table 29.1 have not been previously published and detail the extent or curriculum depth of public relations programs located in communication departments by 1987.

Table 29.1 shows that public relations sequences (i.e., three or more courses) in 1987 were significantly more present in communication departments than in journalism or mass communication departments. A total of 78 communication departments offered three or more classes in public relations. Combining journalism and mass communication departments (the category of departments where accreditation is allowed), only 62 departments offered three or more classes in public relations. Neff's (1989) findings established that speech/communication departments contributed significantly to the education of public relations practitioners in 1987. This finding is contrary to the stated assumption of public relations as primarily in journalism schools, as cited in the 1987 commission report (Neff, 1987, p. 5) and as reported in public relations textbooks (e.g., Seitel, 1998; Wilcox, Ault, & Agee, 1998) and professional publications (e.g., *The Strategist*). Always reported is the magic number of 200 public relations programs in the colleges of journalism and mass communication (Seitel, 1996, p. 1). Why does this myth persist?

A member of the 1987 commission stated that the "opinion" was that communication departments had public relations courses but not enough for sequences. So, at that time, no one bothered to look or ask about the courses in departments outside of journalism and mass communication. Indeed, there were 108 communication departments with only one course offered. But in journalism and mass communication departments in 1987, 60 departments also offered only one course. If someone had closely examined the public relations curriculum in speech/communication departments and acknowledged the sequence offerings (three or more courses in public relations), then the frequency of the single-course offering would not be deemed a negative. One course at least gives students a survey of, or basic offerings in, public relations. Now, more than a decade later, public relations *sequences* continue to flourish in speech/communication departments by building on the one initial course. Meanwhile, another development has greatly affected the journalism schools.

In 1982, Trent and Trent noted a trend in academic public relations that affected their earlier perspective:

TABLE 29.1

Numbers of Departments Offering Public Relations Sequences in 1987

Department Type	Number of Courses					
	0	1	2	3	4	5[a]
Communication	0	108	54	36	21	21
Journalism	0	48	33	15	15	13
Business	0	87	9	2	1	1
Interdisciplinary	0	12	13	9	6	5
Mass communication	0	12	6	7	3	9
Miscellaneous	0	16	3	3	1	0
Public Relations[b]	3	2	3	0	2	3

SOURCE: Data taken from 582 college catalogs.
a. Number of departments offering five or more courses.
b. A public relations sequence is listed in the program description for an interdisciplinary degree in public relations. Each department involved contributes one or more courses that do not contain the words *public relations* in the title or in the course description.

Whereas only a small portion of journalism students in 1976 considered themselves to be preparing for public relations careers, the most recent national census of majors in all journalism sequences shows that 70% . . . perceive public relations or advertising as their career goal. (Trent & Trent, 1982, p. 50)

This great reversal in student goals is one very clear reason why retaining accreditation for public relations is viewed as critical in the journalism and mass communication departments. What Trent and Trent did not fully realize was that the rapid growth of public relations in speech communication already was taking place. (*Speech communication* is just a subarea today, and often the umbrella term for most departments is *communication.*) The leadership in public relations curriculum offerings continues in communication, and the growth is further supported by the establishment of public relations interest groups (PRIGs)/divisions in academic associations in communication (NCA, International Communication Association [ICA], and regional communication associations).

A truly singular event punctuating the myth of where public relations should be located occurred when the public relations sequence was dropped from the School of Journalism and Mass Communication at the University of Maryland and was relocated in the School of Communication within the same institution. The communication faculty offered the opportunity of additional public relations faculty, graduate assistantships, and other needed resources. The headline in *The New York Times* read "Finding a Home for Public Relations" and told of public relations' move to the College of Arts and Humanities. This single act demonstrated most profoundly the presence of public relations within communication departments. The reverberations were being felt in the accreditation agencies that, up to this time, refused to include communication departments in the accreditation pro-

cess by definition. In fact, the debate to be accredited, or to seek accreditation, has been led
mainly by the academic associations up to this
point, with the primary accrediting agency,
ACEJMC, refusing to allow program reviews
outside the journalism and mass communication departments.

Academic Associations

National/International

The first academic effort to establish a PRIG
outside of AEJMC was officially initiated by Pete
Hamilton in 1984 with other founding members
(George Foster, John Madsen, and Bonita Dostal
Neff). The ICA-PRIG held the first interest
group presentation on research at the International Communication Conference in Hawaii
in 1985.

By 1987, the Public Relations Commission
(now a Public Relations division) for NCA (formerly the Speech Communication Association)
was established by Neff, who served as chair for
the first 2 years. During the 2nd year, the PRide
Award was established recognizing outstanding
research in public relations education. The NCA
Public Relations division grew to 480 members
by 1998. The ICA-PRIG now has 203 members
and attained division status in 1997. The more
than 30-year-old Public Relations division in the
AEJMC had 405 members in 1998. The development of public relations divisions in speech/
communication associations is another sign of
the public relations growth in communication
academic associations.

Regional

In 1987, the Central States Communication
Association (CSCA) approved the petition submitted by Neff to establish a PRIG. Neff initiated
the CSCA-PRIG's petition to the board as the
first appointed chair, and now the interest group
holds an annual competitive paper session and
refereed panel session along with an undergraduate honor research panel for students. The
Southern States Communication Association

similarly established a PRIG, and joint meetings
are held between the two regional associations
every 5 years.

THE ACCREDITATION DEBATE

In response to the growing frustration with the
lack of representation for public relations programs in accreditation other than in journalism
and mass communication departments, the
ICA-PRIG surveyed its membership. In April
1987, Hamilton, the initiator of organizing the
committee of founders and acting as the first
chair of PRIG, presented his research, an internal
survey on program accreditation and possible
action by PRIG, at the meeting of the Central
States Speech Association in St. Louis, Missouri.

Hamilton's (1987) findings represented 30
completed questionnaires or "approximately 50
to 60 percent of the colleges and universities
which have at least one faculty member holding
ICA-PRIG membership" (Hamilton, 1987). The
results in Table 29.2 often included open-ended
responses.

Two directions were suggested by the research. First, the respondents were strongly in favor of approaching ACEJMC to consider opening up accreditation to those currently excluded
by the guidelines. The second direction was to
support PRIG in undertaking a study to determine what advantages, if any, there would be in
having a public relations program accredited.
The respondents generally seemed to be "not
sure" about establishing their own accreditation
process, which is a bit difficult to initiate under
the circumstances.

SECOND STUDY BY THE PRIG

By May 1987, at the ICA business meeting in
Montreal, the Public Relations Accreditation
Task Force, established by PRIG, proposed set-
ting up an accreditation system through PRIG.

TABLE 29.2

ICA-PRIG Accreditation Survey, 1987

Q1   Is your PR program certified by the ACEJMC?
      Yes: 30.0%   No: 70.0%

Q2   If NO: Have you ever attempted to have your PR program certified?
      Yes: 00.0%   No: 100.0%

Q3   Are you planning to apply for ACEJMC certification in the future?
      Yes: 30.0%   No: 30.0%   Not sure: 40.0%

Q4   Would you be interested in having some sort of certification procedure established by our interest group?
      Yes: 20.0%   No: 30.0%   Not sure: 50.0%

Q5   Would you attempt to have your program certified by the ACEJMC if your program qualified?
      Yes: 30.0%   No: 13.3%   Not sure: 40.0%   No answer: 16.7%

Q6   Would you support a certification procedure that used the Commission on Undergraduate Public
      Relations Education's guidelines as certification standards?
      Yes: 43.4%   No: 16.6%   Not sure: 40.0%

Q7   Would you be interested in any/all of the following plans?

Q7.1 The PRIG should approach the ACEJMC to work toward including PR programs currently not eligible for
      certification in its certification procedures.
      Yes: 62.1%   No: 17.2%   Not sure: 20.7%

Q7.2 The PRIG should explore the establishment of its own certification procedures.
      Yes: 34.5%   No: 17.2%   Not sure: 48.3%

Q7.3 The PRIG should approach the SCA (now NCA) PR interest group to explore certification of non-
      journalism PR programs.
      Yes: 48.3%   No: 20.7%   Not sure: 31.0%

Q7.4 The PRIG should undertake a study to determine what advantages, if any, there are to having a PR
      program certified.
      Yes: 82.1%   No: 7.1%   Not sure: 10.8%

      Would you be willing to serve on such a commission?
      Yes: 57.1%   No: 28.6%   Not sure: 14.3%

NOTE: ICA = International Communication Association; PR = public relations; ACEJMC = Accrediting Council on Education in Journalism and Mass Communication; PRIG = Public Relations Interest Group; SCA = Speech Communication Association; NCA = National Communication Association.

The proposal was *tabled indefinitely* (Hamilton, 1987). A new task force was formed to redirect efforts toward assessing the membership interest and needs regarding accreditation and was accomplished through the interest group's newsletter and distributed at PRIG's business meeting in New Orleans, Louisiana, in May 1988. A total of 13 were completed; the responses to the questions are detailed in Table 29.3.

Overall, the Public Relations Accreditation Task Force reached two major conclusions from the second survey. First, given the low response rate, the committee wondered whether people (a) were not concerned with accreditation issues or (b) did not know enough about the issues to even begin to respond to the questionnaire. Second, those who completed the survey felt that the issue of educational standards was an important one but expressed very little agreement about how well the ACEJMC's accreditation process served public relations needs or what the PRIG should be doing next. A logical response to both of these concerns seems to be more education for members as to what accreditation is, what is involved, who the key players are, and the like. The ICA special task force, therefore, decided to sub-

TABLE 29.3

ICA-PRIG Accreditation Survey, 1988

Q1   Should ICA-PRIG address the issue of educational standards in a session of the next convention?

    Yes: 8   No: 4   Maybe: 1   Total: 13

Q2   Does ACEJMC's accreditation process for public relations reflect the concerns found in departments other than journalism/mass communication (e.g., speech communication, business)?

    Yes: 3   No: 5   Maybe: 3   Don't know: 1   No answer: 1   Total: 13

The three people who answered "maybe" elaborated on their answers. One indicated that he or she did not know how the accreditation process was conducted but thought that the process might be a concern depending on whether the ACEJMC accredits departments or sequences. The second one noted that the application of the "75%-25% rule" to programs in arts and sciences sometimes was problematic. The third suggested that ACEJMC was run by too many "green-eye-shaded news-ed types." The person who responded "don't know" indicated a need for more information about the accreditation process.

Q3   Should the ICA-PRIG endorse the concept of accreditation (or sanction) by some organization as an alternative to the ACEJMC?

    Yes: 5   No: 6   Maybe: 1   Don't know: 1   No answer: 0   Total: 13

Q3a If "yes": Should this priority be considered high or low?

    High: 2   Low: 2   No answer: 1   Total: 5

Q3b What organization(s) would you suggest as appropriate to sanction PR programs?

Two people wrote responses to this question. One indicated that the PRSA should sanction with cooperation from the ICA, SCA, and AEJMC. Another suggested that the program be conducted by a joint ICA-SCA group.

NOTE: ICA = International Communication Association; PRIG = Public Relations Interest Group; ACEJMC = Accrediting Council on Education in Journalism and Mass Communication; PR = public relations; PRSA = Public Relations Society of America; SCA = Speech Communication Association.

mit a special report to members on accreditation issues.

At the 1988 annual meeting in New Orleans, the results presented from the membership survey revealed little awareness about the accreditation process. Approaches and letters to the ACEJMC indicated that the board was not willing to have a discussion on speech/communication department accreditation. Neff, as chair of the Public Relations Accreditation Task Force, was asked to send a letter expressing PRIG's concerns about accreditation of public relations to the U.S. Department of Education's Accreditation division. The letter addressed ACEJMC's failure to provide public relations representation on the Accrediting Committee. In October 1988, Neff visited the U.S. Department of Education Accreditation division and COPA or the Council on Postsecondary Accreditation (the latter of which is now defunct; replaced by the Council for Higher Education Accreditation or CHEA). The government investigated the PRIG concern and concluded that *there is representation for public relations on the council.* After a lengthy telephone conversation with John Lavine, head of ACEJMC, Neff was directed to the council's public representative, Carol Reuss of the University of North Carolina. Reuss affirmed that public relations was represented on the council. She also discussed PRSA's certification plan that was approved by PRSA Educational Affairs Committee at the 1988 annual meeting in Cincinnati, Ohio. Betsy Plank countered that the ACEJMC must realize that *how* public relations is represented is a major issue. The rationale for the PRSA certification program, for example, stresses that because of "unit" accreditation, specific programs are not accredited but rather are carried along in the accreditation of a larger program (Certification for Education in Public Relations—CEPR-PRSA). Several statements here summarize the issues.

Issue: How public relations is represented in the accreditation process is a point of contention.

Clearly, the journalism model being supported by ACEJMC's accreditation does not require a specific number of courses, whereas specific content areas are proposed by the 1987 Commission on the Design of an Undergraduate Public Relations Program. Plank, as co-chair of the 1987 commission, intended to establish a more ideal public relations curriculum model, one that ICA-PRIG endorsed by assigning a task-force member to initiate the possibilities of a program review process through PRSA.

By the late 1990s, a second commission was established to examine the status of public relations. This was not to be just a review of the 1987 commission report but rather an entirely new effort to grapple with the public relations growth and practice in both academia and the professional world. A joint commission composed of academics and practitioners agreed to accept NCA's offer to start with a grassroots approach. The NCA co-sponsored a public relations conference in the summer of 1998 with PRSA in Washington, D.C. The conference focused on outcomes, curriculum, pedagogy, and assessment from both undergraduate and graduate perspectives. A major survey was conducted to provide a database for the analysis of the findings and this report is available on NCA's Website under "conferences"—1998 summer conference proceedings (www.natcom.org).

Issue: The fact remains that communication departments are excluded from ACEJMC's accreditation.

In November 1988, at a forum sponsored by the Public Relations division of the Speech Communication Association in New Orleans, John Lavine stated that communication departments are excluded by definition from ACEJMC accreditation. Lavine further stated evidence indicating that communication departments' compliance with accrediting guidelines would not change the exclusionary policy.

The U.S. Department of Education interpreted the request by the Public Relations Accreditation Task Force of the PRIG as a legitimate basis for requesting communication departments to be considered for accreditation. In fact, the committee was advised on the legal procedures to pursue. However, action was not taken. Two reasons dictated that action would not be prudent. First, in the fall of 1988, the NCA's Public Relations division was only 1 year old, and the ICA's Public Relations division still was a very young and small group. Second, the follow-up survey to determine the knowledge of accreditation by the PRIG membership indicated that an informational process had to occur first before significant discussion could result. Obviously, there was not enough organized support to follow through on major action. There was documented evidence of the rapid growth of public relations in communication departments (Neff, 1989, pp. 167-171), but the departments did not need accreditation to proceed and perhaps perceived that accreditation might slow progress. So, interest in pursuing accreditation was very minimal.

A decade later, in 1998, the public relations membership was well organized, and a second Commission for the Study of Undergraduate and Graduate Curriculum in public relations is completed. (See *Port of Entry: The Report of the Commission on Public Relations Education,* October 1999, www. prsa.org under "Public Relations in the 21st Century.") The 1998 summer conference had representatives from journalism, mass communication, communication, human communication, speech communication, and other departments present for a working conference of 120 participants. Chairs and/or co-chairs for each area (outcomes, curriculum, pedagogy, and assessment) presented reports on each group's work and then formed integrated teams to provide insight to how this looked from professional and/or theoretical types of programs from both undergraduate and graduate perspectives. There was much positive feedback on how well the different disciplines worked with each other. The database was integrated into the conference work, and the agreement between academics and practitioners was not expected to be as strong as the findings indicated. So, given this monumental joint accomplishment among the disciplines, where is the accreditation debate?

THE ACCREDITATION DECISION

A college program's decision to go through accreditation is not always an easy one. The accreditation process is a lengthy and a time-consuming documentation process, and it sometimes can bring overweighing negatives to the supposedly positive benefits of having a public relations program accredited. For some, the decision is a moot point.

The open-ended responses to Hamilton's 1987 questionnaire were quite informative on this. In fact, the balance between positive and negative factors in accreditation appears quite even when one examines the list of pro and con factors contributed by respondents in Table 29.4.

The two columns listed seem to be in sharp contrast on some points. One respondent viewed accreditation as a "sign of quality," whereas another respondent believed that it designates the opposite—"a rigid, out-of-date program." So, accreditation obviously does not guarantee credibility.

The value of "uniformity" was countered with "lack of creativity." Others viewed a standard of conformity as a constraint. Some believed that the "enhancement of student recruitment" is not a positive; public relations has grown steadily, and the job market had a 46% growth rate over the period from 1991 to 1996 (Rappleyea, 1998). The market incentive is there, so who needs accreditation? In addition, many public relations students have no clue as to whether a program is accredited or not and have little sense of the relevance of accreditation. Most important, the majority of respondents

asked who was going to pay for the extra expense and the overload of work on faculty (if not administrators as well). So, even if accreditation is available, the positive impact of the decision still is in question. What can possibly inspire public relations academics to desire accreditation enough to protest the rule of where public relations is housed? There are several factors to be considered.

ACCREDITATION CONTROLS

Some clues to the accreditation situation were revealed by a 1997 longitudinal study updating a 10-year-old study. Two populations were studied. A total of 198 surveys were returned by the Association of Schools in Journalism and Mass Communication (ASJMC) and 83 were returned by the Association for Communication Administrators (ACA), indicating that their programs offered either a major or a major emphasis in public relations. On the question of "where public relations is taught," the sample was divided between speech/communication and multidisciplinary for a total of 43.0% and journalism and mass communication for 42.1%. Only 17.0% reported a decline in student enrollment; of these declining programs, 46.7% were in journalism departments and 20% were in speech/communication or mass communication departments. Periodic self-study was reported by 93.8% of the ACA respondents and by 93.6% of the ASJMC respondents, and 42% of these were on a 1- to 3-year rotation review or one every 4 to 6 years (Fitch-Hauser & Neff, 1997, pp. 1-6) (Table 29.5).

To establish the status of speech/communication in regard to accreditation in 1997 (10 years after the review of 587 higher education programs offering public relations), a question was asked in the Fitch-Hauser and Neff (1997) study "of whether or not a program was housed in a unit accredited by AEJMC" and the response was strongly influenced by the association membership of the responding institution. An examination of those public relations programs that reported being affiliated with an AEJMC-

TABLE 29.4

Pros and Cons of ICA-PRIG Accreditation Survey

Advantages	Disadvantages
Attracts students	Little practical meaning (in a field like public relations, where most practitioners are not members of any common professional organization [e.g., IABC, PRSA] and where practitioners come from a variety of backgrounds, certification might pull little weight in the hiring or career potential of graduates)
Provides program credibility	
Makes standards uniform across universities	
Educates them to needed curriculum changes	
Helps to secure more faculty positions	
Helps to secure more financial support for program	
Increases students' confidence in their major	Red tape with no payoff to students or school
Recognition, accountability, standardization	Lack of support from our administration for use of my time
Has credibility and established reputation	Takes large amount of time to prepare for (faculty already are overloaded)
Recognizes value of liberal arts	
Allows justification for program development on department level	Subjects our program to a national "norm" that might not adequately recognize the particular mission of our institution and clientele
Students sense more professionalism	
Creates distinctions: certified and not certified	Overstates and overweighs the significance of an external team or group that only touches the surface in a short period of time
Enhances student internship possibilities	
Enhances recruitment of students	
Enhances chance for getting additional funding to support program expansion	Participation would unnecessarily compound workload
	Dual programs conceivably would depreciate the value of both
Index of quality for programs (this might be especially useful in cases where programs are under review by state agencies given that "objective" measures such as certification often are valued)	Certification would be duplicative of the AEJMC
	Certification would require programs with limited faculty to teach two versions of very similar courses in some cases
	We attract plenty of majors without certification, so the extra effort required would not generate additional students or faculty here
Aids in student recruitment ("good" students might be drawn to programs that are certified)	
Mark of professionalism (certification might help to ensure high standards for programs and demonstrate that programs are of "professional" caliber)	Expense
	It slows down innovation by the entanglements of bureaucracy
Improvement in facilities	It does not ensure that the reviewers will be competent to review, evaluate, and certify
Improvement in salaries	
Improvement in student-teacher ratio	Cost of administration (certifying programs will take time and effort, and it will involve some expense; who will pay?)
Gives credibility to us as educators and gives us greater strength with our respective professional groups)	Under current ACEJMC standards, accreditation is actually perceived by many to mean that your program is not of high quality because standards are so out-of-date
Provides some guidelines for program planning	
Aids in promoting program	Restricts what we can do in program
Attracts high-quality faculty if/when program expands	Paperwork and bureaucracy both increase
Prestige with colleagues (both in and out of public relations, particularly non-public relations colleagues in our department and in our college)	We might become less responsive to community and student needs because we fear losing accreditation
	Restrictive offerings
Retains students in program and prevents transfers to other schools	Lack of creativity and change
	Staffing distractions
Benefits to our students in resultant self-respect and recruitment	It does not ensure a good program
	It does not increase employability
Could give students edge in the workplace	
Could help PRSSA chapters—a decided benefit	
Might help to sell administration on the need for resources to develop additional casework	
Helps program to attain credibility in the academic organization of which it is a part	
Improves quality of program through input of certification team (process produces insights and suggestions)	
Contributes external impetus and encouragement for improvement and change	

NOTE: ICA = International Communication Association; PRIG = Public Relations Interest Group; IABC = International Association of Business Communicators; PRSA = Public Relations Society of America; ACEJMC = Accrediting Council on Education in Journalism and Mass Communication.

TABLE 29.5			
Accredited by the ACEJMC in 1997 (percentages)			
Accredited?	*ACA*	*ASJMC*	*Combined*
Yes	25.8	58.7	46.8
No	71.0	38.5	50.3
Not applicable	3.2	2.8	2.9

NOTE: ACEJMC = Accrediting Council on Education in Journalism and Mass Communication; ACA = Association for Communication Administrators; ASJMC = Association of Schools in Journalism and Mass Communication.

TABLE 29.6	
Programs Accredited by Department in 1997 (percentages)	
Speech/communication	1.3
Mass communication	20.0
Journalism	43.8
Combination	21.3
Other	13.8

NOTE: 1.3% = one department.

accredited unit (Table 29.6) reveals that only one speech/communication program reported being accredited, thus lending credence to the previously mentioned assumption that ACEJMC accreditation standards are biased (Fitch-Hauser & Neff, 1997).

So, not much has changed with the accreditation situation since 1989. As mentioned earlier, during a forum sponsored by the Public Relations division of the Speech Communication Association (now NCA), an ACEJMC representative indicated that "communication departments are not accredited, and he did not see the council allowing communication departments to be audited in the future" (Neff, 1991, p. 6). More than a decade later, this statement best describes the current accreditation policy: exclusionary and restricted to journalism and mass communication programs. Any future change will depend on (a) the degree of cooperation among public relations professionals (both academics and practitioners), (b) the growth in recognition of PRSA's independent program review process, and (c) the interest in resolving the quandary over ACEJMC's dual membership in CHEA and the Department of Education while condoning a biased and exclusionary review system which denies speech and communication departments, Arts and Sciences, business, etc., access to program review opportunities, privileges, and accreditation recognition.

CHAPTER 30

Case Studies and Their Use in Public Relations

JOHN J. PAULY

LIESE L. HUTCHISON

■ To a remarkable degree, the profession of public relations understands itself through case studies. Both practitioners and educators treat cases as the condensed wisdom of the profession. Agencies keep case histories on file to preserve institutional memories of techniques used and problems solved. Professional and scholarly journals publish cases that testify to the successes and failures of public relations. Emerging specialties, such as crisis communication, use cases to display and legitimize practitioners' newfound expertise (Fearn-Banks, 1996a; Fishman, 1996). The Public Relations Society of America (PRSA) bestows its annual award, the Silver Anvil, on the basis of case studies that organizations submit.

Educators have come to depend on such materials to train and socialize students. Textbooks have included some form of case studies since at least the 1950s (Canfield, 1952), and textbooks devoted to cases now are common (Center & Jackson, 1995; Hendrix, 1995; Simon & Wylie, 1994). The curriculum guidelines of the Public Relations Student Society of America (1999) re-

quire sponsoring departments to offer coursework in "strategy and implementation," which often means a cases course or an integrated cases and campaigns course. Cases socialize students by encouraging them to imagine public relations in the same terms as do working professionals, especially when the textbooks include examples from the Silver Anvil competition. Even historians often treat cases as milestones—the major events by which one might track the field's origins and progress (Cutlip, 1995; Hiebert, 1966). Histories of public relations memorialize famous cases in the same way as popular histories of journalism memorialize famous exposés and as popular histories of advertising memorialize famous campaigns.

Although they use case studies regularly, public relations practitioners and educators have not thought systematically about what it means to investigate, write, read, or teach a case. We consider this lack of attention a lost opportunity. Cases already are central to public relations practice and education. If crafted more artfully, case studies could become a valuable means to monitor and improve education, theory, and practice. Aptly written cases could help the public relations professional to become what Schön (1983) called a "reflective practitioner." Schön argues that any profession depends on an "irreducible element of art" (p. 18). Reflective practitioners know how to use their experience and learning to respond to new problems by drawing on "a *repertoire* of examples, images, understandings, and actions" (p. 138, italics in original). Case studies could help public relations professionals to build that repertoire.

To make the best use of cases, however, practitioners and educators need to pay closer attention to their narrative form. By *narrative form,* we mean the literary strategies by which writers construct and readers interpret case studies. Little in the current theory or practice of public relations tells practitioners and educators how to write a case study. Even the simplest questions elude easy answers. For example, what type of a story is a case study? Is it a news story? A business report? An ethnography? A history? A memoir? What genre conventions should it follow? If I am the writer, how do I decide which facts to include or exclude? How do I imagine the plot of that story? What roles do I cast for its characters? What point of view do I assume as the narrator, and how do I handle my own relation to the events described? If I am the reader, how do I expect the story to be told? What other stories does the case allude to, in either its echoes or its silences? What role does the case invite me to play in relation to the events described? What do practitioners and educators think they are up to when they write case studies, teach them to students, or invoke them as parables of ethical practice?

As a narrative form, the case study confronts us with a paradox. It is a fiction, written after the fact, invented to make the practice of public relations more real. Cases are stories that claim to be more than just stories. They promise reality. Public relations practitioners, teachers, and students all value case studies for their presumed authenticity, and they consider made-up or disguised cases a poor substitute. Through case studies, public relations imagines its work. A case study, well told, makes public relations intelligi-ble and compelling for practitioners, educators, and students.

At the end of this chapter, we provide modest suggestions about how practitioners and educators might construct, teach, read, and evaluate case studies in a more self-reflective way. But first, we need to explore what it means to understand case studies as a form of narrative. We start by surveying other professions' use of cases in research and teaching. Then, we note the distinctive problems that practitioners and educators face in constructing public relations case studies. Finally, we argue that better case studies could improve both professional practice and pedagogy. Understanding case studies as stories would encourage us to think of public relations as an interpretive profession rather than as a mode of advocacy—a conceptual shift that would benefit society as well as the profession.

CASE STUDIES IN RESEARCH AND TEACHING

Scholars in the social sciences, law, medicine, education, and business all use case studies, but what counts for a case study has varied from field to field. Sometimes, the term denotes a social scientist's decision to collect in-depth data about a single instance rather than aggregate data about many instances. Sometimes, the term denotes any situation or condition that presents itself to a medical, legal, or therapeutic professional. One version of the term, *case method,* denotes a technique used by business or law school teachers to walk students through real or life-like situations. This range of uses poses no particular problem given that each discipline creates case studies to suit its purposes. Public relations practitioners and educators, however, never have been entirely clear about their own uses. What types of case studies best serve their purposes? And what might practitioners and educators learn by examining other professions' use of case studies?

When sociologists use the term *case study* (Feagin, Orum, & Sjoberg, 1991; Hamel, Dufour, & Fortin, 1993), they typically mean the field studies and life histories written during the early 20th century at the University of Chicago or the community or neighborhood studies such as *Middletown* (Lynd & Lynd, 1929) and *Street Corner Society* (Whyte, 1943). Quantitative and qualitative sociologists often have debated the value of such case studies as a form of knowledge (Ragin & Becker, 1992). Quantitative researchers typically use the term *case* to denote each empirical unit in a data set; they search for patterns of similarity or covariation across each set of cases (Ragin, 1992, pp. 4-5). Qualitative researchers, by contrast, define a case as an ensemble of social behaviors recognizably bounded by time, place, or circumstance. Becker (1992) has proposed that researchers treat the term *case* as a theoretical and rhetorical claim—as an argument that particular social behaviors demand our attention. For Becker, a case is the story that takes shape in the interaction of ideas and evidence as the researcher begins to argue for the significance of a set of facts, a pattern of relationships, a system of ideas, or a collection of observations.

Medicine and psychology have used the term *case study* for clinical purposes, referring to individuals who present themselves for diagnosis and treatment. They classify each case as one instance of a disease or condition found in varying frequencies within a larger population. In diagnosing a patient, doctors and psychologists look for symptoms that they already know how to decipher. They cast the patient as a character in a story whose plot and likely climax already are written. Cases show students how professionals use tests and scientific reasoning to consider and reject alternative stories, eventually finding one that justifies a line of treatment. This tradition of case analysis has even produced its own literary genre, developed early by Freud and continued today by physician-writers such as Sacks (1985, 1995). As a literary form, the medical case study often borrows the conventions of the detective story—the case of the man who mistook his wife for a hat, to borrow one of Sacks's most famous titles—to reconstruct the physician's acts of discovery.

Legal education has developed an analogous use of case studies. Within the law, a case signifies a violation, tort, or interpretive conflict that ended up before a judge or regulatory body. Law professors use cases to demonstrate to students the relations between new situations and existing constitutions, statutes, precedents, rulings, and traditions. Conceived ideally as a Socratic (and not sadistic) method of education, this method requires each student to come to class prepared to analyze and argue the significance of the cases. In law, as in medicine and business, case method helps students to understand the artful process through which professionals arrive at their judgments. Cases help students to understand lawyering, not just the law per se.

Case method has been most thoroughly developed and capitalized in graduate business schools, especially the Harvard Business School. The average M.B.A. student in the Harvard Business School analyzes 500 case studies over the course of his or her graduate education (Harvard Business School, 1998), often covering 20 or more case studies in a single course. Harvard markets its cases to other business programs around the country through a publishing subsidiary. Each year, the business school faculty produce about 700 new cases for their classes, many of them based on their experiences as consultants (Harvard Business School, 1998). The case method has become part of the mythic lore of the Harvard Business School, with former students, faculty, and administrators pointing to it as the secret of the school's success (Andrews, 1953; Barnes, Christenson, & Hansen, 1995; Ewing, 1990; McNair, 1954; Towl, 1969).

Even if we slightly discount this enthusiasm or express reservations about the method, as some critics have done (e.g., Argyris, 1980), the business school approach suggests some useful principles for public relations education. Business school cases offer problems, not solutions. Whereas public relations cases describe what someone else did, business school cases ask students what *they* would do. The case method integrates research and teaching, showing students the practical value of theoretical study. In its ideal form, case method asks "What did students learn?" not "What did the teacher teach?" (Rangan, 1995).

Public relations practitioners and educators could learn something from each of these traditions of research, analysis, and pedagogy. Like sociologists, public relations case writers could reflect on the theoretical and rhetorical claims that they make whenever they investigate, write, or teach a case. Like physicians and psychologists, public relations case writers could help students learn to place a problem within a larger universe of practices and precedents. And like their colleagues in business, law, and medicine, public relations teachers could use case method to integrate theory into practice to help students learn to become more reflective practitioners.

CASE STUDIES AS NARRATIVES

The quality of public relations cases in textbooks and journals clearly has improved over the past 40 years. Gone are the blatant ideological biases that allowed an early case writer such as Canfield (1952) to propose an anti-union campaign to convince a milk company's employees that "free enterprise is the privilege of every American" (p. 68). More authors now include relevant social and cultural contexts or attempt comparative analyses in their cases (Seitel, 1998). More case writers now ground their analyses in theory, as a number of scholars have recommended (Botan & Hazleton, 1989; Culbertson, Jeffers, Stone, & Terrell, 1993; Elwood, 1995; Toth & Heath, 1992). With few exceptions (Fishman, 1996; Mickey, 1995; Newsom, 1996; Newsom, Turk, & Kruckeberg, 1996, pp. 485-488; Simon & Wylie, 1994, pp. vii-x), however, practitioners and teachers have written little about the problems of investigating, writing, reading, and teaching public relations cases. By comparison, dozens of scholars have spent the past 20 years studying news as a narrative form, trying to understand the conditions of its making (Darnton, 1975; Edelman, 1988; Ettema & Glasser, 1998; Fishman, 1980; Gans, 1979; Tuchman, 1978).

As we have noted, practitioners, educators, and students all value the case study for its presumed realism. But what makes a case real? The case study, like other forms of storytelling, achieves its sense of authenticity by deploying familiar literary conventions that the reader will take to be real. A case establishes its realness by putting it in writing.

Case studies employ some familiar narrative strategies for making themselves real. Sometimes, as with news stories (Tuchman, 1978), the public relations case equates the real with the factual. By this standard, a case study would be unreal only if it made counterfactual claims about people, times, places, organizations, or events. In a similar way, some cases are assumed to be real because they are famous. Examples such as the Exxon *Valdez* oil spill and the Tylenol murders show the profession at its most dramatic moments. Such examples appeal to students, who are more likely to have heard about newsworthy events, as well as to teachers, who appreciate the way in which famous cases spark student interest. But this habit of equating the real with the famous introduces its own distortions. One function of the profession, crisis communication, comes to represent the whole. The emphasis on the extraordinary might obscure the routine bureaucratic habits that have led to some of the worst disasters (Edelman, 1988; Mitroff & Pauchant, 1990; Vaughan, 1996). Crises also overemphasize the importance of media relations within the repertoire of public relations work. This emphasis on managing the media, in turn, inadvertently favors an older definition of public relations as a profession in which former journalists massage the perspectives of current journalists.

When trying to make less famous events seem real, public relations case writers sometimes treat their storytelling techniques as natural and taken for granted. Center and Jackson (1995), for example, said that they have presented their cases "in narrative form rather than outline" because a narrative "most closely approximates the way information comes to practitioners" (p. 31). They offer sound pedagogical reasons for avoiding a RACE/ROPE (research-action-communication-evaluation/research-objectives-programming-evaluation) outline; they want students to think through the cases themselves. Yet there is nothing more natural or real about that choice. They have simply traded one set of narrative conventions for another.

Similarly, Seitel (1998) frequently uses feature writing techniques. His cases often start with delayed leads or descriptions of the settings. In many of them, Seitel uses exposition to set up dramatic quotes, as any good journalist would. He and other case writers might reasonably justify these feature techniques as a way of making their cases more interesting to students. Yet this choice also carries consequences. To write a case as a feature story is to frame events within journalists' assumptions about what counts for a story, how one tells a story, where the storyteller stands in relation to the events described, and how students (as an audience) ought to be addressed.

To make public relations practice *usefully* real, cases must struggle for and argue (rather than just assume) their sense of reality. As matters now stand, most case writers borrow familiar literary conventions with little sense of how those conventions frame the evidence. Given how many public relations practitioners and educators have written for the news media, it is no surprise that case writers fall back on the journalistic storytelling they know best. Like the guest lecturer who invokes the claim that "I was there," the case writer is simply looking to make the analysis authentic and authoritative. These and other strategies of narrative realism have been studied extensively by media scholars (Gans, 1979; Tuchman, 1978), literary critics (Jameson, 1981; Mitchell, 1981), social scientists (Clifford & Marcus, 1986; Geertz, 1988; Polkinghorne, 1988; Van Maanen, 1988), historians (Cronon, 1992; White, 1987), philosophers (Ricoeur, 1984-1988), and rhetoricians (Burke, 1941; Fisher, 1987).

Even the most minimal case study depends on literary artifice to achieve its sense of reality. For example, the RACE/ROPE formula used in the Silver Anvil competition as well as in some textbooks, implicitly portrays every campaign as well planned, task oriented, efficient, and systematic. Cases written in this formula exemplify perfectly the symbolic process that Weick (1995) has called "sensemaking," whereby humans retrospectively create narratives that make complex events intelligible and preserve them for future discussion. In the RACE/ROPE formula, the *story* of the campaign moves calmly from research to objectives, planning, execution, and evaluation, even when the campaign itself stumbled in a panic from one deadline to another.

As a narrative convention, the RACE/ROPE formula also answers to the practical needs of the Silver Anvil competition. The PRSA (1998b) has regulated the most obvious forms of self-promotion by requiring a standard format—each submission in an unembellished three-ring binder, no more than three inches thick, on letter-sized paper. The goal, presumably, is to base the judging on fact rather than on promotional skill. Yet these guidelines do not eliminate rhetoric; they simply change the rhetorical rules that case writers must follow to be successful. In their submissions, organizations must simultaneously promote their work and downplay their efforts at self-promotion. Narratives must strike the right balance between persuasion and exposition, trumpeting the entrants' accomplishments in a restrained factual style that will attract notice. In a sense, the RACE/ROPE formula is public relations' equivalent of the inverted pyramid, a narrative style widely accepted as a straightforwardly factual account of reality.

Whether using famous cases, invoking personal experience, employing tricks of the news trade, or reducing chaos to a spare minimalist formula, the case writer shapes the evidence by using narrative conventions that stand outside of and prior to the events of the case. From a wide repertoire of cultural forms, the writer chooses a genre, and that genre frames what issues are at stake, establishes assumptions about what interests the reader, and points to styles of argument that the reader will find convincing.

Understood as a narrative form, case studies in public relations reveal all the anomalies and contradictions that dog the profession. Consider the strategic silences that fill many case studies. Cases rarely describe the decision-making processes that created the campaigns. Most say little or nothing about where the public relations function fits within the organizations—a factor that practitioners have long argued greatly affects their credibility. Cases rarely tell whether organizations' actions reflected the best advice of practitioners or represented decisions contrary to practitioners' advice or a compromise between conflicting strategies. In general, the small-group processes within a public relations department, or between departments, remain invisible. Cases pay too little attention to defective bureaucratic routines, or to the role of organizational culture, in making some strategies implausible. Most cases do not report the costs of public relations activities. Very few admit, in the end, that practitioners would have done things differently if given a second chance.

THREE USES OF CASES

Writing a case study is a more complicated task than it appears to be. Although we would like to see practitioners and educators dramatize their work with other literary forms, in the short run the case study probably will remain the profession's preferred form of self-presentation. So, to help improve public relations teaching, research, and practice, we propose a typology of case studies. We can imagine three related but distinct uses of public relations cases: as summaries of campaigns past and present, as a mode of teaching, and as a mode of research. We summarize each of these types and its advantages in Table 30.1.

Campaign Summaries

Cases that show how public relations professionals put together campaigns might more accurately be called *campaign summaries.* Many of the case studies in current textbooks fall into this category, as do some of the cases in professional journals. The term *summaries,* in this use, would include both present and past campaigns. Some current textbook writers (Center & Jackson, 1995; Newsom et al., 1996) use the term *case histories* for past campaigns and the term *case studies* for contemporary campaigns. But this history/study distinction does not articulate the differences in narrative strategy that interest us

the most. Cases written as campaign summaries value narrative closure. They provide endings because their purpose is to teach students how to plan, deploy, and connect all the stages of complex campaigns, from identifying goals and tactics, to analyzing publics, to planning events, to evaluating results.

Case Method

Because they condense, simplify, and dramatize professional practices, campaign summaries will remain an indispensable part of public relations education. But because they focus on practitioners' answers to problems, case summaries might not ask enough questions. Summaries say too little about the theoretical contexts in which cases might be understood or about the organizational processes that led to particular decisions. This is why, in teaching case studies, public relations educators often ask students to conduct additional outside research so as to extend and deepen textbooks' presentations of the cases.

Public relations educators who want to encourage students' skills in strategic analysis, critical thinking, and effective argumentation need cases that lend themselves to *case method* teaching. Case method requires open-ended fact sets that stimulate analysis and discussion. Some public relations textbooks have experimented with open-ended cases, or have included examples of faulty practices, to allow more room for student critiques (Simon & Wylie, 1994). But using the case method probably will require educators to develop new case materials as well as new styles of classroom instruction (Kreps & Lederman, 1985). A case written for this method of teaching must defer any final story or simple solution and must compel students to find their own way through a mass of contradictory or incomplete evidence.

Case Study

We suggest reserving the term *case study* to describe a mode of research (Hamel et al., 1993;

TABLE 30.1		
Three Uses of Public Relations Cases		
	Goal	*Use(s)*	*Questions to Ask*
---	---	---	---
Campaign summary	Describe the steps involved in planning, implementing, and evaluating a public relations campaign.	Show students how to assemble and conduct a campaign.	What was the purpose of this campaign?
		Record a department's or an agency's public relations activities for future reference.	What happened in this campaign and why?
Case method	Teach public relations students to think strategically and critically.	Show students how a reflective practitioner solves problems.	What would the student do under these circumstances?
Case study	Analyze the theoretical significance of some set of public relations activities by placing them in historical, social, economic, political, or ethical context.	Deepen knowledge of public relations as a communication practice.	Why are these public relations activities worthy of study?

Yin, 1994), whether historical or contemporary. This use would follow the general practice of the social sciences, where the term *case study* signifies sustained in-depth analysis of a group, event, or setting. Public relations has not produced ethnographies as candid or revealing as those found in sociology and anthropology. It offers no body of organizational studies that compares with the literature on newsroom routines (Berkowitz, 1997) or with the growing literature on organizational culture (Sypher, 1990, 1997).

Practitioners and academic researchers would learn much from in-depth case studies. Public relations agencies already compile summaries to document the ensemble of strategies they used in particular campaigns. But the case study might be imagined, more ambitiously, as a white paper—a postmortem analysis of the strategic thinking that went into a campaign or the organizational problems and missed opportunities experienced during it. Seen in this way, the case study could become the mode through which an agency or department evaluates and improves its work. Such case studies could be used to envision the future, not just remember the past. Large agencies could even hire ethnographers to write case studies while campaigns are in progress.

Beyond recognizing the possibilities and limits of these three modes of case writing, public relations practitioners and educators might experiment more with the case study as a literary genre. For example, what would an oral history of a public relations campaign look like? Who would the researcher talk to? How would one write up the results? What might one learn from such an oral history? As a genre, the public relations case study tends to accept the crisis, campaign, or organization as its unit of analysis. Textbooks often match their cases to the system of professional distinctions—investor relations, community relations, crisis communication, public affairs, or internal communication. Case studies, however, could start in a different place. A case could study one public relations agency across several campaigns. Or, it could study a particular function, such as media relations, within an organization or across organizations.

Or, it could compare the effects of different organizations' public relations activities within a single community. Or, it could examine the use of a similar campaign strategy by the same organization at different moments or by different organizations at the same moment. All of these examples would count for legitimate case studies in the social sciences. But such cases are rare in public relations today.

Here, as has so often been the case, public relations' historical ties to journalism have made it difficult to theorize the problems facing the profession. Public relations might do better to emulate organizational communication, a field that has made the case study an invaluable research tool. Some organizations, such as W. L. Gore, have even hired ethnographers to document their current social practices, as other companies have long hired historians to document their pasts. Recently, rhetorical approaches to public relations have done much to deepen our understanding of public relations as a symbolic practice (Elwood, 1995; Toth & Heath, 1992). But case studies in organizational communication typically provide more insight into internal decision-making processes, pay more attention to conflicts, acknowledge structural forces, and listen to a wider range of voices.

Public relations case studies testify to the dilemmas of identity and purpose that vex the profession. Given the chance to tell its story, public relations reverts to the simple journalistic forms that its youngest practitioners learn. It remains in thrall to the ambitions of pioneers such as Edward Bernays, who wished to make his profession a mode of advocacy—of equal importance to legal counsel. It advertises itself as a mediating interpretive profession, but it struggles against the organizational pressures that force it to identify with managerial authority, even when conducting theoretical analyses of its work.

Cultivating the arts of case study teaching and research could help public relations practitioners and educators to approach these problems with nuance and care. If public relations professionals hope to become reflective practitioners in Schön's (1983) sense, then they must nurture their interpretive talents. A profession that is more self-conscious about its use of cases will be better prepared to meet that challenge.

CHAPTER 31

PUBLIC RELATIONS ETHICS

Public Relations and Social Responsibility

EMMA L. DAUGHERTY

The public relations practice has evolved greatly from its early beginnings of press agentry. Nobly, the practice has become more focused on the development of strong relationships, consensus building, and socially responsible behavior. Business and societal forces appear to influence the nature of public relations, but practitioners have not always seized opportunities to recommend and shape socially responsible policy. This chapter examines the practice of public relations as it involves social responsibility, the importance of stakeholders, the essentiality of ethical behavior, the need for issues management, and the role of practitioners in the development of socially responsible acts.

MEETING SOCIETAL DEMANDS

Global activism and the growing number of special interest groups place public relations practitioners in the role of community builders responsible for helping to link socially, politically, geographically, culturally diverse, and often competing interests. Community involvement and the strengthening of communities are important issues for management to address in the new millennium (Thomsen, 1997). Futurists predict that organizations will be judged more on their social policies than on their delivery of products and services, and key publics will become more influential. "Consumers, investors, employees, environmentalists, and the general public are emerging as attention-getters and stakeholders of corporate America" (Abdeen, 1991, p. 26). To be socially responsible, corporations also must cooperate with other groups—such as competitors, nonprofits, and government agencies—to help solve social problems (Bowie, 1991).

Business exists at the pleasure of society, and its behavior must fall within the guidelines set by society (Wartick & Cochran, 1985). Therefore, an organization needs to be a positive contributing member of society in order to flourish (Watson, 1991). "The public increasingly will hold institutions accountable for their actions, and effective management will require an enhanced sensitivity to shifts in public and societal expectations and demands" (Pagan, 1989, p. 14). Indeed, societal expectations are higher than they were 30 years ago (Heath, 1997). Organizations are expected to do more for society.

> Corporations are granted status as special citizens in the social system. They have certain rights and obligations. Their social obligations now extend beyond compliance with the law and providing profits, jobs, and services or goods. Society expects a just use of power and support of public policy. (Judd, 1995, p. 40)

Business interests are served by a just and peaceful society.

> Few corporations can be profitable in the long run in a world without social, political, and economic justice. . . . Companies with strong social records perform better financially in the long run than those that behave irresponsibly. Social investing is therefore not only ethically aware, it is also financially responsible. (Van Buren, 1995, pp. 51-52)

Activities that tarnish companies' images will result in lost sales and benefits from government (Reich, 1998). Organizations that do not consider public expectations might suffer from considerable legislative or regulatory penalties (Heath, 1997). As social creations, organizations exist on the willingness of society to endure and support them. Corporations' profits also afford growth and enable society to achieve a variety of social objectives (Reich, 1998), but society still expects business to treat employees, customers, and suppliers fairly by making reasonably safe products and by compensating individuals who are wronged by goods or services (Wokutch & Spencer, 1987).

Issues relating to human rights, forced labor, the environment, and safe working conditions will remain high on the agenda of corporations as communities press for socially responsible corporate policies (Schilling & Rosenbaum, 1995). Companies function best when they merge their business interests with the interests of their stakeholders—customers, employees, suppliers, neighbors, investors, and other groups

affected (directly or indirectly) by their operations (Makower, 1994).

Public hostility surfaces when a gap occurs between society's expectations of an organization and the actual performance of the organization. Corporations and nonprofits are social institutions that depend on society's acceptance of their roles and activities to survive and grow. "Institutions are expected to respond to the expectations of society, and if an institution's performance does not meet these expectations, a gap develops between expectations and performance, and pressures begin to build around specific issues of concern to the public" (Buchholz, 1982, p. 429). A widening gap between the performance of an organization and society's expectations of it causes the organization to lose its legitimacy, thereby threatening its survival. This legitimacy gap can be narrowed by focusing on certain business strategies including efforts to alter the public's perception of the organization through education, use of different symbols to explain organizational performance, and changing actual organizational performance to meet society's expectations (Sethi, 1977).

To avoid a legitimacy gap, issues managers can focus on potential problematic areas such as fair pricing practices, product quality, responsible advertising, timely resolution of customer complaints, community responsiveness, and environmental management (Heath, 1997).

Because it makes good business sense to be socially responsible, public relations executives, acting as the corporate conscience, should constantly strive for corporate policies and actions that are responsive to societal needs (Ryan, 1986) so as to avoid a legitimacy gap.

DEFINING PUBLIC RELATIONS

This orientation toward the need for greater emphasis on social responsibility has far-reaching effects on the ever evolving practice of public relations. Definitions of public relations have changed over time to reflect the growing sophistication and maturation of the practice. Cutlip and Center (1971) defined public relations as "the planned effort to influence opinion through good character and responsible performance, based on mutually satisfactory two-way communication" (p. 2). Even the earliest public relations counselors understood the importance of good deeds and responsible performance. Ivy Lee, considered the father of public relations, saw the need for organizations to respond to public opinion and to align themselves with the public interest (cited in Wilcox, Ault, & Agee, 1998). Lee told prospective clients that he would advise them on ways in which to correct their public policies so that they would get favorable coverage. He is credited with recognizing that good publicity is generated from good work and performance (Cutlip & Center, 1971). Likewise, Edward Bernays called for "a movement toward public responsibility in private business" (cited in Cutlip, Center, & Broom, 1985, p. 49). He believed that organizations need to recognize changes in their social settings and respond to those changes so as to meet a common ground (Cutlip, Center, & Broom, 1994).

More recently, Cutlip et al. (1994) defined public relations as "the management function that establishes and maintains mutually beneficial relationships between an organization and the publics on whom its success or failure depends" (p. 6). Wilcox et al. (1998) believed that key words best describe public relations—*deliberate, planned, performance, public interest, two-way communication,* and *management function.*

> Effective public relations is based on actual policies and performance. No amount of public relations will generate goodwill and support if the organization is unresponsive to community concerns. . . . Public relations activity should be mutually beneficial to the organization and the public; it is the alignment of the organization's self-interests with the public's concerns and interests. (p. 6)

Other definitions of public relations include concepts such as engaging in relationship building, managing communication between an organization and its publics, advocating a position, and engaging in consensus building.

In a survey conducted by the *Public Relations Journal* in 1993, public relations practitioners were asked whether they believed that they were advocates, consensus builders, or both. Among the respondents, 21% believed that public relations practitioners were advocates for their organizations, 7% viewed their role as consensus builders, and 57% said that they were both advocates and consensus builders. Those who believed that their role was to advocate indicated that they win support and acceptance of clients' products and services or of the issues or policies they favor (Katzman, 1993).

Consensus builders cited a need to gain mutual trust and understanding by listening to, negotiating with, and actively responding to key publics through communication programs and special projects. Those who believed that practitioners are both advocates and consensus builders acknowledged that public relations no longer is a one-dimensional function. Mutuality among key publics and organizations must be established so that the public interest—and the interest of the organizations—is served (Katzman, 1993).

Still, Kruckeberg and Starck (1988) "maintain that public relations practitioners do not understand their most important role in society. That role is to serve not only their clients but society at large" (p. xii).

The dangers that threaten society also threaten productivity and profits. Organizations need to consider their social, political, and economic environments to identify the needs of the organizations' publics; evaluate the products and services designed to help meet the needs of the publics; and interpret probable future growth, decline, or change of those needs (Culbertson & Jeffers, 1992).

A study by Judd (1989) found that public relations practitioners viewed themselves as the consciences of their organizations. Fully 65% of the respondents indicated that responsibility to society was more important than responsibility to employers or clients. Judd also found a significant positive relationship between practitioner participation in important policy decisions and public relations actions of social responsibility.

> When practiced ethically and responsibly, public relations provides a vital communication function for organizations, nations, and even the world, helping to develop an understanding among groups and eventually reduce conflict. When practiced unethically and irresponsibly, however, public relations can manipulate and deceive. (J. Grunig, 1993d, p. 138)

Wilson (1994) described foundations for the "new" public relations, which is an ethics-based practice instead of the past manipulative and unethical practices of press agentry and publicity. Foundations for the new practice include a people orientation, a value orientation, integrity, and communication.

Relationships between organizations and their publics develop because organizations' actions have consequences for publics. To have good relationships with their publics, organizations must be responsible. Thus, public relations is the practice of public responsibility. According to J. Grunig (1993d), the quality of the relationship depends on the model of public relations practiced by the organization. Because negotiation, compromise, and openness are practiced in the two-way symmetrical model, it is considered more ethical than the other models of public relations.

FOCUSING ON SOCIAL RESPONSIBILITY

During the industrial revolution of the 19th century, business was concerned with profit making and had little interference from the government. The concept of social responsibility began to evolve during the 1960s in response to society's changing social values (Buchholz, 1982; Chrisman & Carroll, 1984). The public policy debates of the 1960s and 1970s raised awareness of social issues. Legislative agencies were established. Corporations had new legal responsibilities, and

public expectations for the social accountability of business heightened (Mau & Dennis, 1994). Prominent social issues surfaced such as equal employment opportunities, the environment, and product safety. Federal cutbacks during the 1980s forced business to expand and redefine its obligation to society. Business not only must engage in social causes but also must consider the social consequences of its economic activities. Therefore, business evolved from a purely economic instrument of society to a socioeconomic instrument (Chrisman & Carroll, 1984).

Social responsibility is the development of processes to evaluate stakeholder and environmental demands and the implementation of programs to manage social issues (Thomas & Simerly, 1994). Corporate social responsibility has been associated with ethical codes, corporate philanthropy, community relations programs, and law-abiding actions (Wood, 1991).

Corporations are responsible for effectively producing and distributing goods and services for consumer consumption and for generating profits for shareholders. However, society also feels that corporations should contribute to worthy causes addressing social concerns (Cavanagh & McGovern, 1988; Kruckeberg & Starck, 1988). Corporations are viewed as not only economic institutions but also social institutions. As social institutions, corporations have responsibilities to society (Bick, 1988).

> American business institutions function within a social system. The system confers legitimacy on business institutions [and] defines the bounds and rules of their performance. . . . The conclusion is inescapable that the corporation receives its permission to operate from a society and ultimately is accountable to the society for what it does and how it does it. (Anshen, 1980, p. 6)

Thus, corporations have an obligation to solve some of society's most pressing social problems and to devote some of their resources to the solution of these societal problems. Milton Friedman, the Nobel Prize-winning economist, believed that corporations have no responsibility to society that goes beyond adhering to the law and maximizing profits for shareholders. Executives must maximize the return to shareholders. Friedman did not suggest that corporate charitable giving be reduced if the activity contributes to profit making. Being perceived as socially responsible can be an element in attracting customers and employees—an investment that increases future profitability (Lee & McKenzie, 1994).

Drucker (1995), however, argued that although economic performance is the first responsibility of a business, it is not its only responsibility.

> Economic performance is the base without which a business cannot discharge any other responsibilities, cannot be a good employee, a good citizen, a good neighbor. . . . So the demand for socially responsible organizations will not go away; rather, it will widen. . . . Every organization must assume full responsibility for its impact on employees, the environment, customers, and whomever and whatever it touches. That is its social responsibility. (p. 84)

According to Drucker, however, organizations should not engage in activities that hinder their ability to accomplish their missions or pursue responsibilities where they have limited competence or expertise.

Some corporate leaders realize the need for social and moral responsibilities, but organizations must determine when and to what extent to accept such responsibility. The responsibilities of a corporation are complex. Of primary importance are responsibilities for customers, employees, and investors. Secondary responsibilities include those to suppliers, the local community, and the physical environment. Tertiary responsibilities encompass issues facing the country or the world such as unemployment (Cavanagh & McGovern, 1988).

Indeed, Drucker (1974) believed that social impacts and social responsibilities—those dealing with quality of life issues—are major tasks for managers. That is, managers of all organizations are responsible for the impact of legitimate business activities on people, society, and the physical environment. Organizations are responsible for intentional or unintentional impacts of their existence such as inescapable by-products caused by their operations. For example, students attending classes might cause traffic jams around a university campus, or a manufacturing plant might emit foul odors into the atmosphere. On the other hand, businesses, hospitals, and schools have difficulty remaining healthy in a sick society even if society's sickness is not caused by these organizations. Society expects organizations to anticipate and resolve social problems (Drucker, 1974).

Epstein (1993) saw the need for corporations to be socially responsible but suggested that contributions be made in areas where there is a comparative advantage. In a survey asking shareholders how they wanted corporations to spend money related to social issues, he found that they ranked cleaning up corporate facilities and efforts to stop pollution as most important. Improving product safety was second in importance, and distributing additional funds as dividends was third. Fully 91% of the shareholders saw product or service quality as the most important criterion when determining whether a company was a good corporate citizen. Environmental responsibility ranked second (85%). Other high rankings included following regulations, caretaking of employees, and contributing to the economy. Only 36% thought that contributing to charitable organizations was important.

In a 1994 nationwide survey, researchers found that 70% of consumer respondents were much more likely to buy from a socially responsible company. Half (50%) said that they would not buy from a company that is not socially responsible. Respondents ranked business practices, community support, and employee treatment as indicators of a company's social responsibility (Gildea, 1994-1995).

Instead of social responsibility, Buchholz (1982) advocated public responsibility.

> The philosophy of management that makes the most sense in responding to the changing role of business in society is one of public responsibility, a concept that implies business's willingness to become more actively involved in public issues, even those that are not necessarily directly related to the immediate self-interest of the company but

that are of major concern to society. Involvement in public issues means the development of a capacity to identify and research public issues, the willingness to debate these issues in the public arena, and the ability to work with other groups in society, particularly government, that have other ideologies and other incentives, to solve these problems. (p. 436)

Carroll (1991) suggested that corporate social responsibility encompasses economic, legal, ethical, and philanthropic responsibilities. Economic responsibilities provide the foundation for the others. A corporation has a responsibility to be profitable. Moreover, a corporation must obey the laws and be ethical by being fair and avoiding harm. A corporation must be a good corporate citizen by contributing resources to the community and improving the quality of life.

Reder (1995) established several criteria to rate the socially responsible corporation—provides steady employment, designs company facilities that maximize social benefit, offers goods and services needed by the community, improves quality of life in the community, pays its fair share of taxes, behaves ethically (lives by the Golden Rule), has adequate emergency procedures and equipment, encourages employees to be good citizens, and contributes to the community philanthropically.

> Social responsibilities are determined by society, and the tasks of the firm are: (a) to identify and analyze society's changing expectations relating to corporate responsibilities, (b) to determine an overall approach for being responsive to society's changing demands, and (c) to implement appropriate responses to relevant social issues. (Wartick & Cochran, 1985, p. 763)

Corporate responsibility is constantly redefined when stakeholders and activists demand new standards, industry groups want higher operating performance of their members or another industry, or government regulators enforce codes of operation. In other words, the ideology of society reshapes the standards of behavior.

In addition, absolute standards of corporate responsibility do not exist. They may change with each generation. Standards also may vary among stakeholders, and stakeholder interests may conflict (Heath, 1997; Ryan and Martinson, 1985). Moreover, corporations cannot simply adhere to the law so as to be socially responsible. The public is able to decipher the differences between legal and ethical behavior (Heath, 1997).

Public relations practitioners are instrumental in helping corporations to be socially responsible. Ryan (1986) found that most public relations practitioners agreed that the development of programs beneficial to society is good business, that a company's pursuit of social goals strengthens its profit-making potential, that social responsibility enhances a corporation's credibility, that social responsibility entails consistent actions in the public's best interest, that practitioners act as corporate consciences, and that practitioners should be heavily involved in defining social roles for the corporation.

Ryan and Martinson (1985) concluded that public relations practitioners want to be involved in policy decision making and are not satisfied with being management representatives who serve as mere technicians. Nearly all of the respondents in their study believed that public relations practitioners should work with management to change policies they viewed as not in the public's best interest. Respondents also indicated that responsible public relations practitioners represent two publics: management and the outside public.

Judd (1989) found a significant positive relationship between practitioners recommending socially responsible actions and their participation in policymaking. Fully 65% of the respondents indicated that responsibility to society was more important than responsibility to their employers or clients.

Society is evolving in humanistic terms, and individuals are empowered by technology. Thus, a responsible corporation will become active in legislative and regulatory matters and will budget for corporate responsibility. Public relations practitioners are experts on stakeholder relationships and offer a unique service to their organizations (Bovet, 1994). Public relations practitioners should serve as their organizations' radar by establishing relationships with stakeholders, understanding stakeholders' needs and demands, and formulating their organizations' responses (Mau & Dennis, 1994).

UNDERSTANDING THE IMPORTANCE OF STAKEHOLDERS

An organization's stakeholders are those who use its products and services, earn its wages, and share its environment (Heath, 1988b). Stakeholders are considered as any individuals or groups that can affect or are affected by the organization's operations. Also called claimants, stakeholders supposedly have some type of claim on the organization (Watson, 1991). They can be customers, employees, investors, government officials, the local community, suppliers, environmentalists, media, competitors, consumer advocates, unions, trade associations, and members of special interest groups (Freeman, 1984).

An organization enters into a social partnership when it makes a commitment to achieve harmony with its stakeholders (Freeman, 1984; Heath, 1988b). Guiding principles help to develop and maintain the organization's social partnership. The organization must include ethics in its strategic planning process. Employees must be evaluated and rewarded for maintaining those standards. They must be clear about the organization's mission and performance standards. The organization's success is tied closely to the policies it sets because they affect stakeholders (Heath, 1988b).

A business organization must create a sense of community among its constituents for the proper functioning of that organization. The development of community will engender an environment that will lead to an increase in profits, productivity, and all of the other traditional indices by which the success of a business have been measured. . . . Community can only evolve through moral commitment. Business organizations that discover the means to foster this commitment will experience a dedicated and loyal constituency. (Heerema & Giannini, 1991, pp. 90-91)

Organizations must undertake systematic analyses of their stakeholders, values, and societal issues. Freeman (1984) suggested identifying stakeholders; the effects that the institution has on them in political, economic, and social terms; and the stakeholders' perceptions of these effects. He recommended determining the dominant organizational values, the values of the key executives and board members, and the values of the stakeholders. Furthermore, he advised organizations to identify the economic, political, social, and technological issues that face society during the next 10 years and to determine how these issues affect the organizations and their stakeholders.

Market and public policies appear to be based on dominant issue motivators such as security, equality, esthetics, and fairness. Some security issues are worker safety, environmental safety of surrounding communities, product use safety for the consumer, investment safety for the investor, and interindustry safety so that manufacturers buy safe goods for the production of their own products (Heath, 1988b). Esthetics focus on issues dealing with the environment, and fairness is related to value and exchanges made for that value such as the pricing of a product or service. Equality issues concern the fair and equal treatment of individuals (Heath, 1997).

Drake and Drake (1988) developed four recommendations for managing a more responsible corporate culture:

1. Be realistic in setting values and goals about employment relationships, and do not promise what cannot be delivered.

2. Encourage input from all levels throughout the organization about appropriate values and practices.

3. Explore methods that provide for diversity and dissent such as grievance and review procedures.

4. Provide practical training for managers implementing corporate values.

Nongovernmental organizations have increasingly become authors of public agenda and policy. A new era of social and consumer activism has emerged. Special interest groups and activist organizations use technology to put their causes onto the public agenda. They force the hand of corporations and pressure government to react. Business must respond to these challenges and take an active role in setting the public agenda.

> Corporations can find a way to retrieve eroded public trust, can be dynamic participants in the debates of our time, and can fairly balance the social contract between themselves and consumers. . . . In an age of instant information, globally networked activism, a sensitized public, and a growing cynicism about business, it is no longer adequate to use public affairs specialists as designated hitters. . . . Business must be part of the debate; it must identify and get to know the players. When developing issues are ignored, corporate opportunity narrows, room to maneuver becomes constricted, and corporate liability increases. (Pagan, 1989, pp. 14-16)

Activists are successful in getting access to policymakers, are popular among consumers, and understand how to get media attention. Their ability to get media attention through impassioned statements gives them power (Heath, 1997). Therefore, public relations practitioners must profile activist groups in terms of key players and size, be responsive to activist concerns and advocate alternative solutions to the problems, offer a human side to the issues by using personal stories to get media and policymaker attention, and get other credible organizations to help tell their sides of the stories (Rose, 1991a). Unfortunately, most managers use justification responses, which convey that the standards used by protest groups to evaluate their conduct are inappropriate. The public views protests by consumer and social groups as a right, but when organizations engage in such tactics to defend practices, they face a less supportive public (Garrett, Bradford, Meyers, & Becker, 1989).

ACCEPTING ETHICAL BEHAVIOR

Ethics is derived from a philosophical term of the Greek word *ethos,* which means character or custom. Ethical behavior is morally acceptable as right instead of wrong or good instead of bad (Sims, 1992). Ethics is the study of moral judgments. Applied ethics is the practice of what is understood to be good or right to a particular institution. Business ethics is the application of what is understood to be good or right in the pursuit of business activity (Bick, 1988).

Ethical behavior is that which serves both the organization's and public's interests. Ethical behavior contributes to bottom line results. Public relations practitioners must convince management that ethical behavior will have a direct influence on the bottom line. "Remember, ethical corporate behavior is the only way to win—and to enjoy—the continued public acceptance and approval, [and] that will *allow* bottom line success" (Wylie, 1991, p. 12, italics in original). Ethical behavior serves the interests of both the organization and its stakeholders.

Standards of ethical performance are developed by monitoring the opinion of key publics, updating and enforcing codes of conduct, and integrating issues management into strategic planning processes (Heath, 1997).

Organizations may be unethical for a variety of reasons such as out-of-touch managements, a bottom line mentality that forces short-term solutions that are financially sound but cause ethical dilemmas, and excusing poor behavior because it appears to be best for the organizations. Most managers appear to practice utilitarian ethical theories, where correct conduct is determined by the usefulness of its consequences, instead of a theory of rights, which attempts to ensure respect for the rights of all, or a theory of justice, which is predicated on decisions based on equity, fairness, and impartiality (Premeaux & Mondy, 1993).

Four types of management orientations toward stakeholders are recognized. The immoral management exploits stakeholders. Ethical misconduct may include cheating and misleading customers and disregarding the local community by violating ordinances. Amoral management bases its actions on profit making and abiding by the law. Ethical considerations are given little thought. Moral management, however, views stakeholders as equal partners. Organizations with moral management treat customers fairly by providing full information and taking steps to achieve customer satisfaction. They are active in and supportive of community institutions, and they view community goals and company goals as mutually interdependent (Carroll, 1991).

During the 1980s, many businesses developed codes of conduct. Most focused on internal issues such as bribery, the use of expense accounts, and conflicts of interest. Early codes rarely mentioned external concerns relating to stakeholders (Van Buren, 1995). Some organizations continue to adopt ethical codes. Some issues addressed in these codes include purchasing guidelines, conflicts of interest, equal opportunity, and relations with the community. The pros and cons of such statements are debated. Ethical codes offer some protection to an organization and give guidance to employees about what constitutes appropriate behavior. Codes, however, might be unable to encompass all potential problems and might be costly to communicate to employees. If they are too detailed, then they might be inflexible and unlikely to be read (Buchholz, 1982). On the other hand, managements can use codes to assist them in their strategic planning and daily operations (Heath, 1997).

Organizations must establish an ethical climate. Society demands that organizations adhere to high ethical and moral standards. Chief executives must establish an ethical climate from the top down. Effective managers ensure that their employees know how to deal with the ethical issues facing them. Employee feedback about the practices of ethical behavior must be encouraged so that all views are represented. Ethics training programs for employees must be implemented. Formal procedures must be established to support and reinforce ethical behavior, and employees must believe that their actions will be supported by top management (Sims, 1992). Heath (1997) suggested activities to enhance ethical performance such as monitoring stakeholder opinion to appraise changing standards of social expectations, integrating issues management into strategic planning, updating codes of ethical conduct, and informing stakeholders about the achievement of standards.

MANAGING ISSUES

Issues management focuses on the identification of and response to developments that might affect organizations. Socially responsible organizations anticipate public issues and attempt to respond to them before the issues become politicized (Buchholz, 1982). Issues managers take a competitive proactive stance by meeting or exceeding stakeholder expectations and lessen unwanted interference by fostering mutual interests and developing harmonious relationships with stakeholders (Heath, 1997). For more effective management of issues, organizations have moved toward a greater reliance on cooperative and coalition-building strategies to achieve their goals (Littlejohn, 1986).

Standards of corporate responsibility vary by organization and differ for each stakeholder. Heath (1997) suggested several steps for issues managers to follow as they define standards of corporate responsibility: Understand the expectations of key stakeholders; compare those standards to the organization's standards; determine whether differences exist and, if so, whether they strain the relationship; ascertain whether the differences are perceptual or factual; change operating standards to lessen the legitimacy gap; develop policies to better serve the public interest; communicate to stakeholders to eliminate misunderstandings or disagreements; incorporate corporate responsibility standards into strategic planning; make standards a part of performance evaluations; use standards of corporate responsibility as a competitive advantage; and inform stakeholders about the achievement of standards through communication tools. In addition, involvement of all areas of management in the development and implementation of socially responsible standards is important.

ENLISTING THE SUPPORT OF LEADERSHIP

To help ensure the success of socially responsible programs, the commitment and participation of organizations' top executives are vital (Anshen, 1980; Heath, 1997; Pagan, 1989; Paluszek, 1974; Sethi, 1994; Wylie, 1991). The loss of public confidence in corporate management's competence is a big challenge for public relations practitioners because corporate leaders are seen as arrogant and not in touch with customers and employees (Thomsen, 1997). Now more than ever, the compensation of America's top corporate executives is tied to company stock prices, but society needs executives who act responsibly because they consider themselves society leaders (Reich, 1998). Corporate executive officers need to be encouraged to broaden the vision of their role in society and be positioned as important public figures. The selection of a chief executive officer (CEO) should be a vital social decision requiring extensive discussion and exposure. The CEO should be installed in a ceremonious fashion and should declare specific policies to improve the quality of relationships with stakeholders. Furthermore, a systematic process to report socially responsible activities should be implemented (Sethi, 1994).

Issues managers face internal politics when executives are unwelcoming of criticism from external forces voicing opposition or concern outside of their areas of expertise. Executives are more likely to adopt new standards of ethical performance if they are able to see how business could be improved by doing so. Moreover, operations officers are likely to fear that new standards will interfere with their performance. Therefore, issues managers must have the commitment of

executives to implement appropriate changes in standards of ethical performance (Heath, 1997).

"Top management, specifically the chief executive officer and the board of directors, must be responsible for the decision to commit an organization to a philosophy and program of coordinating economic and social performance" (Anshen, 1980, p. 145). When formulating social performance policies and programs, the CEO should involve senior management. The involvement of these managers will heighten their sensitivity to such issues and strengthen their commitment to them.

Business leaders who led aggressive social responsibility programs during the early 1970s recommended that the CEO must make a personal and total commitment to the program; assess the company's unique business environment; select the most talented personnel to tackle the task; provide adequate resources; set clear policies; make the process accountable with specific goals, time lines, and outcome measurements; and continuously communicate the company's commitment throughout the organization and to its publics (Paluszek, 1974).

A corporation's social policies partially reflect its management. Managers whose responsibilities are mostly internal appear to be less sensitive to stakeholder needs. Moreover, the background of the CEO appears to affect the level of sensitivity. Firms with high corporate responsibility ratings had more CEOs with marketing and sales backgrounds. On the other hand, firms with low corporate responsibility ratings had more executives with backgrounds in manufacturing and engineering. Firms with high ratings also had CEOs who had worked at their organizations for longer periods of time, thereby suggesting that they had better grasps of the needs of stakeholders (Thomas & Simerly, 1994).

The leadership for this openness to the emerging public agenda must, as always, come from the top. The larger vision will play its necessary role in the formation of company strategy when chief executive officers come to value public policy as much as they do profitability and leadership in the industry. (Pagan, 1989, p. 16)

ENGAGING IN PHILANTHROPIC ACTIVITIES

Strategic charitable giving can be good business for companies, and nonprofit organizations can offer a way for corporations to contribute to their communities. One benefit of corporate giving is image. Thus, if a corporation is seen as ethical, then consumers might be more inclined to give the organization the benefit of the doubt if a controversy occurs (Mullen, 1997).

Nonprofit organizations provide resources that enhance the quality of life. In turn, healthy communities create a prosperous economy, but fewer than 30% of all corporations give money to philanthropic activities (Reder, 1995).

Although organizations want to ensure that philanthropic activities are aligned with their missions and visions and are integrated with their business goals, many are taking more of a market-driven, strategic management, and bottom line approach to philanthropy. Results are measured like other functions of business. In addition, these types of charitable activities require their own strategic plans, are assessed regularly, have set giving guidelines, and need staffing to support the charitable endeavors (Mescon & Tilson, 1987).

Corporate charity takes several different forms—social venture giving, cause-related marketing, surplus inventory and in-kind gifts, and employee giving campaigns (Reder, 1995). Social venture giving is a form of long-term investment in which companies support social activities that appeal to their self-interests. For example, an aerospace corporation might donate money to a university's engineering program in hopes of strengthening education in the field and better preparing a future workforce.

Cause-related marketing is an aspect of charitable giving that is growing in popularity because it is tied to the bottom line. As a strategy for selling, cause-related marketing activities come from marketing budgets and are tax-deductible business expenses (Williams, 1986). With cause-related marketing, the more a product or service is sold, the more money that goes to charity.

Indeed, cause-related marketing is seen as a way in which to help achieve marketing objectives while fulfilling social responsibilities and enhancing a corporate image. In a study by Smith and Alcorn (1991), respondents believed that it was important to purchase products from companies supporting charitable causes. About 46% of the respondents indicated that they were somewhat or very likely to switch brands to support a company that donates to charity.

Walker (1987) claimed that corporations minimize the importance of charitable giving and see it primarily as a tax benefit. On the other hand, contributions of employee time and talents provide more public relations and marketing benefits. This form of volunteerism is seen as more sincere and provides additional benefits for employees who share a unified goal outside of the workplace. It can improve morale and enhance employees' confidence.

Corporate charitable giving must be promoted to ensure visibility of such good deeds. By doing so, the company demonstrates its commitment to social responsibility and enhances its position in the marketplace.

> More and more corporations have realized that helping others not only can be good for the community but also good for business. Increasing sales and spreading goodwill need no longer be mutually exclusive objectives but can instead be goals which complement each other. (Mescon & Tilson, 1987, p. 59)

In a study by Wokutch and Spencer (1987), companies with records of no crimes and high philanthropic contributions were considered socially responsible. The authors found that corporate philanthropic activity is expected if firms are to be perceived as good corporate citizens. Organizations that do not act as society expects will suffer financially. Wokutch and Spencer also concluded that firms that had committed crimes but made large philanthropic contributions performed better than did companies that simply obeyed the laws.

REPORTING COMMITMENT TO SOCIAL RESPONSIBILITY

Abdeen (1991) recommended disclosing nonfinancial information that documents an organization's commitment to social responsibility in annual reports so as to increase the credibility of the information and to widen the message's audience. He believed that social responsibility disclosure will increase employee and consumer trust and loyalty.

Marx (1992-1993) surveyed 139 U.S. companies during 1991-1992 to determine their methods of reporting their social concern activities to the public. Fully 90% said that they never published comprehensive reports of the major social issues affecting their organizations. Some companies published smaller reports and publications, mostly in the form of single-issue reports and inserts in annual reports, to communicate better with and keep their constituencies informed, to influence their publics and call on them for assistance, to get credit for their good deeds, and to avoid relying on a feeling that the public knew that they were good corporate citizens.

The most important key publics in Marx's (1992-1993) study were ranked in the following order: employees, stockholders, the general public, federal government, local and state government officials, the media, academia, and local communities where companies operate.

The number one issue was the environment. Philanthropic activities were ranked second, followed by a discussion of management's goals and philosophy. Health, minorities, and plant safety followed in importance. Issues of lesser importance included energy, employee development, local community, business conditions, education, product safety, and literacy.

STRENGTHENING THE ROLE OF PUBLIC RELATIONS

Organizations must constantly adapt to the changing needs and expectations of society. Therefore, public relations practitioners must monitor and evaluate social attitudes and expectations; analyze the significance of social attitudes and expectations for existing and potential corporate policies, programs, and actions; make recommendations for maintaining or changing existing policies and developing new ones; participate in strategic planning; become involved in the assessment of performance; develop communication strategies; and prepare executives for playing responsible roles in communicating with stakeholders (Anshen, 1980).

Jacoby (1974) recommended measures to help corporations respond to social needs. These included developing "social sensors" to identify and measure changes in public values, attitudes, and expectations that could affect company performance; implementing systems of feedback within the organization to evaluate and act on information; establishing two-way channels of communication with social groups; creating a "social account" or a systematic record of company activities that improve the quality of life; and conducting an annual social audit that would measure the effectiveness of the company's social programs.

Unfortunately, public relations practitioners are not playing key roles in ethics and policymaking for their organizations. In a study of ethics officers, Fitzpatrick (1996b) found that only 6.7% worked in public relations. About 28% were lawyers, 25% worked in human resources, and 11.5% had positions in finance. Another 5.8% worked in accounting, and 2.9% were in marketing or advertising. Ethics officers ranked complying with the law as the most important factor for fulfilling social responsibility. Other important activities included providing a safe workplace, providing equal employment opportunities, and avoiding harm to constituents. Little importance was given to community involvement and philanthropic activities.

Perhaps public relations functions are increasingly being placed in the hands of other individuals because many public relations practitioners are unprepared to handle the responsibilities of continuously monitoring attitudes and expectations of stakeholders, preparing executives to develop strong relationships with stakeholders, and truly understanding the relationship between an organization and its many constituents.

On the one hand, Wilson (1994) concluded that management is turning to public relations practitioners to help solve problems of the organization's community by building relationships with the organization's publics. As community specialists, expert public relations practitioners understand all the organization's publics. "Public relations provides the vision, the decision expertise, and the functionary communication skills to serve the corporation, its publics, and its community in building the relationships and resolving the problems blocking the achievement of organizational goals" (p. 337).

Public relations practitioners must work toward achieving company goals; adhering to professional standards; and advocating just, ethical, and responsible behavior in the eyes of society (Judd, 1995).

To survive, organizations must address social responsibility as seriously as they do marketing, production, and other aspects of doing business. Issues such as providing equal employment opportunities, enhancing health and safety in the workplace, promoting economic development in disadvantaged communities, and protecting the environment should be some of the priorities on their business agendas.

> Companies function best over the long run when located in healthy communities where the quality of life includes such factors as a below-average crime rate, adequate education and health care facilities, pools of qualified workers, robust economic activity, a healthy environment, and viable cultural and community institutions. (Makower, 1994, p. 18)

Transnational businesses face even broader challenges. They have global influence and a global responsibility to require compliance from their vendors as well as an obligation to respect human rights in their global workplaces.

Long-term profitability and organizational stability are protected and enhanced if managers address employee health, safety, and family needs; treat customers with dignity; develop strong, long-term relationships with suppliers; and engage in civic activities in the local community (Bowie, 1991). Furthermore, a responsible organization is one that not only protects employees' right to criticize current practices but also actively encourages employees to question and clarify their own values as well as the values of the corporation (Drake & Drake, 1988).

Public relations executives must be members of the dominant coalition, those individuals in an organization who hold the most power, to participate in strategic management, influence policymaking, and practice the two-way symmetrical model of public relations that is most ideal for the implementation of standards of social responsibility. They must be consensus builders and keenly aware of stakeholders' interests.

To achieve social responsibility, public relations practitioners need to define their stakeholders; understand their stakes; analyze the challenges and opportunities presented by stakeholders; determine their organizations' economic, legal, ethical, and philanthropic responsibilities to stakeholders; and develop strategies and tactics to fulfill those responsibilities (Carroll, 1991). Public relations practitioners must foster mutually beneficial relationships with all stakeholders to achieve harmony, and organizations must meet or exceed the expectations of key publics and create policies in the mutual interest of all parties (Heath, 1997). Public relations practitioners can greatly influence the profitability of their organizations by safeguarding interests, thereby moving toward a better world and remembering that key publics—the stakeholders—are the real judges of organizational behavior. Public relations practitioners should embrace the concept of social responsibility to ensure a better society and business environment for the organizations they represent.

CHAPTER 32

Public Relations Ethics

An Overview and Discussion of Issues
for the 21st Century

KENNETH D. DAY

QINGWEN DONG

CLARK ROBINS

Unethical behavior on the part of public relations practitioners has been a continuing concern both within and outside of the field. Nelson's (1989) *Sultans of Sleaze* and Stauber and Rampton's (1995) *Toxic Sludge Is Good for You!* are recent, highly critical narratives of public relations practice. Even public relations practitioners themselves have been shown to rate the ethics of public relations practitioners below that of business executives and journalists (Judd, 1989). Improving public relations ethics has been seen as a key component in achieving greater professionalism in the field.

This chapter provides background on public relations ethics by summarizing a number of different approaches to ethics, a brief overview of some of the research on the ethics of public relations practitioners, and significant concepts from the work of two of the most influential scholars on public relations. Brief consideration is given to current approaches to raising the ethical conduct of public relations practitioners. The chapter concludes by proposing three important areas of ethics that public relations must address particularly as it enters the new millennium. It also provides a discussion of the importance of dialogic communication in future practice in the field.

TYPES OF ETHICAL SYSTEMS AND PRINCIPLES

Ethical systems and principles traditionally have been classified into a number of categories. One of the best known is deontological or duty ethics.

Deontological ethical principles and systems treat actions themselves as always right or wrong. Not disseminating false information is an example of a deontological principle that might be followed by a public relations practitioner.

Teleological ethical principles and systems are different in that they stress the end result of an action rather than the action itself. Utilitarianism, an ethical philosophy stressing that actions should be decided based on which action provides the greatest good for the greatest number of people, is an example of a teleological approach to ethics. The assertion that public relations practitioners' actions should serve the public interest is an example of this approach. Ethical theories of public relations practice that stress acting in the best interests of a client also would fall under the teleological classification.

Situation or situational ethics differs from both of the two previous approaches to ethics in that ethical decision making is seen as depending on the specific circumstances of each situation. This approach can be sensitive to the fact that there may be a number of conflicting ethical responsibilities in each situation as well as the fact that blindly following deontological duties can, in some circumstances, yield considerable harm. Some forms of situational ethics involve balancing deontological principles with teleological principles as applied to the specific situation. Withholding requested information from the press when disclosure of that information would be harmful to one's client is an example of ethical decision-making in this style.

A more extreme approach, subjectivism or individual relativism, sometimes is lumped into the situational category. This approach asserts that there are no objective ethical principles and that people must simply do what they believe is right. Of the four approaches to ethics, this approach usually is seen as the least ethical. Ryan and Martinson's (1984) finding that public relations professionals respond differently to the same ethical situations can be seen as evidence of the prevalence of this form of situational ethics view in actual practice.

SELECTED RESEARCH ON THE ETHICS OF PUBLIC RELATIONS PRACTITIONERS

Empirical research on the ethics of public relations practitioners began systematically in 1984 with the study by Ryan and Martinson. Their survey raised significant concerns about the lack of consistency of ethical decision-making by public relations professionals and the lack of objective standards of ethical conduct.

Some evidence exists that members of a professional association such as the Public Relations Society of America (PRSA) report more ethical conduct (McKee, Nayman, & Lattimore, 1975), but accredited members do not seem to report higher ethical behavior than do non-accredited members (Pratt, 1991a).

One variable that has been found to correlate with endorsement of ethical beliefs and ethical conduct is age, suggesting that ethical conduct increases with maturity. Pratt (1991a) found older practitioners to rate a variety of behaviors as more unethical than did younger practitioners. Shamir, Reed, and Connell (1990) also found a moderate correlation between age and the extent to which practitioners reported following professional ethics. Following professional ethics also was found to be correlated with years of experience.

A stronger predictor of subscription to professional ethics is the extent to which one adheres to personal ethics. Shamir et al. (1990) found that PRSA members who scored high on a measure of professional ethics also scored high on a measure of personal ethics. Wright (1985) also claimed to have data supporting this relationship.

Newsom, Ramsey, and Carroll (1993), in a survey of public relations students, educators, and practitioners, found that responsibilities of the practitioner were ranked in the following order: the client, the client's relevant publics, the self, the society, and the media. This study was designed to replicate a 1972 study by the Public Relations division of the Association for Education in Journalism and Mass Communication. Both studies found the client to be rated as the first responsibility. However, responsibility to relevant publics was the responsibility in last place in the 1972 study, whereas it was in second place in the study two decades later. Raising some concern was the drop of the society from second to fourth place in the more recent survey.

The heavy reliance of public relations research on endorsement of belief and self-reported behavior raises serious questions regarding the validity of much of this research. The use of lists of PRSA members as a means of constructing samples also raises questions as to the generalizability of the results to the public relations profession in general.

SOME IMPORTANT CONTRIBUTIONS TO PUBLIC RELATIONS ETHICS

Although seldom cited today in writings on public relations ethics, the work of Albert Sullivan has made, and might continue to make, an important contribution to the thinking on public relations ethics. Appearing mostly during the 1960s as several chapters in a book on issues relating to public relations, Sullivan's work, according to Pearson (1989c), has been the most complete theory on ethical public relations practice.

Sullivan (1965a) proposed that public relations as a profession deals with images of reality just as medicine as a profession deals with the human body. Although skeptical about the possibility of accurate images because of their partial nature and the distortions that result from encoding and decoding messages in language, Sullivan insisted that public relations professionals must strive to provide true information to the public.

Sullivan (1965b) also proposed that public relations was influenced by and must address three value systems: technical, partisan, and mutual. Technical values were defined as having to do with pride in one's work and efficient use of public relations techniques. Partisan values were

tied to loyalties such as commitment, trust, and obedience. Mutual values were those that considered the rights and well-being of others. Stemming from mutual values, Sullivan (1965b) recognized a right of mutuality that insisted on the responsibility of public relations practitioners to recognize the rights of others. Here, Sullivan seemed to be anticipating the dialogic principles advocated by other public relations scholars, most notably J. Grunig and Pearson.

J. Grunig and Hunt (1984) proposed that ethical practice in public relations calls for a dialogic communication model, which they called the two-way symmetric model. According to J. Grunig (1989e), only when public relations professionals engage in two-way communication with their publics, where the organization responds to its publics, can public relations be truly ethical. J. Grunig's work has been widely received within public relations. Pearson (1989b) provided a more extensive philosophical grounding for dialogic communication and placed the development of the concept in historical context. The utility of this idea for public relations ethics is demonstrated later in this chapter.

THE ROLE OF ETHICS CODES AND ACCREDITATION IN PUBLIC RELATIONS ETHICS

Whereas professional education is an important contributor to raising professional and ethical conduct in public relations, professional and ethical codes and professional accreditation also have been given a great deal of emphasis. The three best-known ethical codes for public relations are the Code of Professional Standards (revised most recently by the PRSA in 2000), the Code of Ethics (adopted by the International Association of Business Communicators [IABC] in 1961), and the Code of Athens (first adopted by the International Public Relations Association [IPRA] in 1968). Wright (1993) pointed to the lack of enforceability as the primary problem of ethical codes. For example, from 1950 to 1985, there were more than 150 complaints regarding violations of the PRSA code by its members filed with the PRSA, and only 10 of these cases resulted in reprimands (Budd, 1991).

Kruckeberg (1989) argued for the value of ethical codes, suggesting that they do provide guidelines for practitioners, set expectations for the performance of practitioners, and provide both grounds for charges of wrongdoing and defenses. Day (1991) argued that written ethical codes still are the best way in which to encourage practitioners not to rely on merely subjective judgments.

Bernays (1979, 1980) has had few followers in advocating the state licensing of public relations practitioners. Wright (1993) noted that fears of governmental abuse outweigh the benefits that would result from such greater accountability.

The certification of practitioners by professional associations has received stronger support. Both the PRSA and IABC offer such certification. According to Cutlip, Center, and Broom (1994), approximately half of the eligible members of the PRSA (i.e., those in practice 5 or more years) are accredited by the organization. Certification examinations for these organizations require demonstrated knowledge and understanding of the organization ethic codes. However, even with the high rate of certification by the PRSA, only a small proportion of practitioners (fewer than 1 in 15) belong even to this largest of public relations professional associations (Pratt, 1991a).

SIGNIFICANT ISSUES FOR THE 21ST CENTURY

As the practice of public relations faces the 21st century, a number of significant ethical issues need to be addressed. These include the complex nature of truth, the role of public relations within a society, and the special problems of public relations ethics in intercultural contexts. Without careful consideration of these issues, public relations risks rejecting all but the most minimal ethical principles or generating ethical discourses that justify nearly all public relations practices as serving the greater good. One can hope that most corporate public relations professionals do not endorse Friedman's (1987) position that anything goes in business so long as there is no fraud or deception. On the other hand, all public relations practice does not serve the greater good of all sectors of society. The dialogic approaches of J. Grunig (1989e) and Pearson (1989b) to public relations ethics might indeed have something to offer for all of these concerns.

Most discussion of truth in public relations practice seems to treat truth as amply addressed if there is no false or misleading information. Both the PRSA and IABC codes include statements regarding avoiding such statements, and Ewen (1996) described the history of the ethical discourse of "facticity" through the history of public relations practice.

Few would argue that concern for factually correct information should not be a significant ethical concern in the practice of public relations. But even this ethical principle presents dilemmas for public relations practitioners. As Heath (1992a) pointed out, public relations professionals might lack the technical expertise to accurately report on the activities of their client organization or might not have direct access to information.

Similarly, if a non-misleading presentation of information is to occur, then disclosure of all relevant information would seem to be required. Yet, Englehardt and Evans (1994) argued that concealment is necessary in the practice of public relations.

However, beyond these concerns is the serious error of equating accurate information with the truth, an error that is derived from a simplistic objectivist view of reality and language. As Sullivan (1965a) noted, public relations practice deals in images. Such images are a construction of a particular way of viewing "reality" that first serves the best interests of the client organization. Public relations messages are persuasive rhetorical messages and, as such, are not mere presentations of data. As Weaver (1970) noted, words are sermonic; they invoke particular values.

At the same time, the presentation of visual images in public relations messages presents even greater problems in overreliance on the discourse of facticity. As Postman (1986) noted, much of present-day television and magazine advertising and promotions cannot be evaluated in terms of its factual correctness; rather, these can be evaluated only in terms of whether we like or dislike what is presented.

The responsibilities of public relations to the society within which the client organization operates also is an area that requires more careful consideration. The apparent shift in ranking with the rise in importance of relevant publics and the decline in importance of society in terms of responsibilities can be seen as both good and bad. The recognition of the importance of groups external to the organization shows maturity in the conceptualization of public relations practice. At the same time, the decline in ranking of responsibility to society suggests a decline in concern for the greater good.

Organizations potentially provide significant service to society through providing employment and acts of philanthropy. But the contact points between an organization and communities expands well beyond these areas.

K. Leeper (1996) suggested the value of a communitarian perspective to ethical public relations practice. More than simply guiding ethical conduct, she suggested that a genuine communitarian approach can aid organizations in more effectively and appropriately responding in crisis situations. Although communitarianism would seem to have some genuine merit for application in American society, it might be most workable for smaller organizations located in specific communities. National and international organizations might simply have headquarters too far away from the communities they serve for management to feel any membership in these communities.

For American society, the area of greatest concern might well be the impact of public relations practice on the democratic process. Ewen (1996) presented a revealing social history of the thinking of professional communicators working for government and the private sector during the 20th century. Prevalent in this thinking were ideas that American democracy could not function based on the rational thinking of the common man. Mobilizing the nation in ways deemed best by those who deemed themselves superior was seen as following an ethical principle that superseded deception and unconscious manipulation of the public.

Nelson (1994) expressed concern about the increased participation of public relations in issues communication and advocacy. While accepting the legitimate right of corporations to present their views and noting that the legitimate airing of these views has potential social utility, Nelson showed concern that corporations follow ethical guidelines.

So long as issues communication and advocacy are clearly labeled as to their source, a major ethical concern is satisfactorily addressed. Ewen (1996), however, expressed concern about attempts by public relations practitioners to manufacture what appears to be grassroots-level support for issues while concealing the organization that lies behind the action.

Ethics in international public relations is a rapidly growing area as international diplomacy, trade, and business continue to expand. Kruckeberg (1989) has been one of the most vocal advocates for an international ethics code for public relations. Considering existing codes (including that of the IPRA) to be inadequate because they do not describe specific practices, Kruckeberg (1998a) recently offered predictions of the coming development of such codes.

Kruckeberg (1996b) argued for a universal ethical code for international business and public relations, but one slightly tempered to adjust to the moral taste of each country. He suggested that, in conducting international business, one might need to decide whether or not to abstain from an alcoholic beverage to avoid offending a Muslim colleague or to decide whether or not to pass a bribe with one's passport to expedite receiving a visa. However, one should keep intact the ethical guidelines that one considers to be important.

One problem with discussion of international ethics codes in public relations is that too little attention has been given to questions of ethics in public relations communications as opposed to merely business practices. Day (1998) demonstrated how seemingly universal ethical codes that describe communication behavior might reflect the values and culture of the individual who drafts the code. He suggested that people from one culture are likely to be insensitive to the norms of communication in another culture. An even more significant problem may be that communicators from Western countries might feel that they have superior access to political, social, scientific, and religious truth, thereby resulting in elitist and monologic communications. He argued that the best guide to ethical communication in international and intercultural situations is for people to attempt to engage in dialogue. In this situation, no individual is granted special access to the truth. Each can state only what he or she believes to be true, not what is necessarily true.

We believe that J. Grunig (1989e) was correct in proposing dialogic communication as the most basic principle of ethical public relations practice. This principle is useful in addressing all three of the preceding problem areas and in providing the most basic standard for public relations practice for the 21st century. The final and closing section of this chapter considers what dialogic communication has to offer as well as the problems associated with concept in practice.

DIALOGIC COMMUNICATION AS ETHICAL PUBLIC RELATIONS PRACTICE

According to Heath (1988a), companies have not only the right to discuss issues of corporate performance with their publics but also the responsibility to do so. Indeed, he suggested that dialogic communication might be important to the survival of business organizations. Dialogue with publics might be the only effective alternative to costly legal or legislative actions stemming from public anger and discontent. As Pearson (1989b) suggested, the time has passed when companies can merely present their points of

view with the certainty of being morally and ethically correct or with the arrogance that results from the subjectivist view that, because there are no absolute ethical standards, the companies' viewpoints and practices are as ethical as those of the companies' critics. During a postmodern age where absolute "truth" and universalist ethics have evaporated, the only means of arriving at shared truth and standards of ethics is through dialogue between communities grounded in a historical context. It is through such dialogue that organizations will need to determine what is and is not ethical practice.

Organizations have a genuine right to present images of the world from their own perspectives. This must, however, be done in a way that acknowledges that the organizations themselves are speaking and that allows publics to respond with opposing points of view. If there is to be an overall truth, then it must be one that is produced by all parties in the dialogue.

Dialogic communication will be helpful in more ethical relations between organizations and communities in letting community members communicate their concerns about practices of organizations. Philanthropic efforts would be better guided by community members indicating ways in which organizations could provide genuine service to the communities. Dialogue at the international and intercultural level would similarly offset problems in inappropriate public relations messages and in making international corporations more accountable for their actions.

But how is dialogical communication to be achieved? Habermas (1984) has been the most influential recent philosopher on the conditions for ethical dialogue. Burleson and Kline (1979) summarized Habermas as requiring the following:

1. Participants must have an equal chance to initiate and maintain discourse.
2. Participants must have an equal chance to make challenges, explanations, or interpretations.
3. Interaction among participants must be free of manipulations, domination, or control.

4. Participants must be equal with respect to power. (p. 423)

Issues management practices that rely on research on publics to alter corporate practice and guide the construction of corporate communications do not qualify as dialogue. J. Grunig (1989e) would classify this model of public relations practice as two-way asymmetric.

Dialogic communication requires that participants engage each other. Public forums such as the editorial pages of newspapers and public meetings called by corporations with representatives from their various publics potentially provide such conditions. Newly emerging technologies such as the Web and Internet offer public discussion lists on which both members of organizations and members of their various publics can enter into discussions. Correspondence and face-to-face private meetings between appropriate members of organizations and representatives of their publics also may qualify as truly dialogic.

To the extent that interaction with publics is used only to educate and persuade the members of these publics, true dialogue will not have occurred. Organizations will need to be open to compromise and change.

But there are challenges in putting dialogue into practice. Who legitimately speaks for a public? How should a corporate decision be made when dialogue with key publics yields no consensus among the members of a particular public or no consensus across a number of key publics? When a lack of consensus among key publics is found to exist, which public should be more influential in guiding corporate decision making? These are issues that will need to be addressed in future practice.

Organizations that engage in dialogue with their publics and that evaluate organizational performance on ethical standards developed in dialogue with publics should gain in positive reputations with their publics. As such, publicity regarding dialogic activities will become a part of public relations practice. A danger here is that public relations practitioners will be tempted to stage dialogic encounters or arrange them only with representatives of publics known to be in agreement with current organizational practices. The staging of encounters between political candidates and the public is a well-known example of such contrived dialogic encounters. True dialogue will require interaction with those who hold points of view in opposition to current organizational practice.

As we move further into the 21st century, the role of public relations practitioners will need to change from one of merely wielding self-serving influence, crafting communications, and researching publics. Ethical practice for the field of public relations will require practitioners to be facilitators of dialogue and listeners as much as speakers. Strong leadership will be needed from high-profile organizations that exemplify best practices in opening their own practices and decision-making to public criticism.

CHAPTER 33

Ethics in Public Relations

Theory and Practice

PATRICIA A. CURTIN

LOIS A. BOYNTON

Few fields can invoke as much debate over ethics as can public relations. In *Toxic Sludge Is Good for You*, Stauber and Rampton (1995) labeled much public relations "contrived," "undemocratic," "manipulative," "misleading," and "phony." That the book is in its third printing, however, might testify more to the vibrancy of the discussion about public relations ethics today than to the accuracy of its claims. In just the past 5 years, public relations ethics has been the topic of more than 10 professional seminars and more than 20 articles and books.

Because how one defines public relations in part determines how one defines ethical public relations practice, much of the contemporary discussion originates in the debate about the function of public relations. Is public relations a profession and, therefore, bound by professional codes? Is its primary function to inform, to persuade, or to negotiate and accommodate? What weight should be given to conflicting individual, group, and societal obligations? This chapter outlines the philosophical principles underlying

ethics and relates them to models of public relations practice to demonstrate how form and function mutually inform public relations ethics.

PHILOSOPHICAL AND THEORETICAL BASES OF ETHICAL DECISION MAKING

Teleological versus Deontological Reasoning

Broadly speaking, ethical thought can be divided into teleological and deontological approaches. Teleology emphasizes outcomes; simply put, the ends justify the means. Ethical actions are those that result in the greatest good. Restricted forms of teleology calculate the consequences only for a particular person or group such as family or firm. Universal teleology, or utilitarianism, stresses consequences to society as a whole—the greatest good for the greatest number. Critics of teleology note that knowing the consequences of actions before the fact can be difficult, that not all things can be assigned a numerical value (e.g., human life), and that looking only at short-term consequences can be shortsighted.

Deontologists believe that good consequences are not in and of themselves sufficient to guarantee good actions; some acts must be done regardless of their consequences. Rule deontology stresses following rules when making ethical decisions such as the Golden Rule, the Ten Commandments, or a professional code of ethics. Critics note, however, that sometimes correct actions have disastrous consequences. For example, some individuals would not lie when asked by Nazi interrogators where Jews were hidden. Act (or mixed) deontology weighs both acts and their consequences to determine ethical action, relying on rigorous application of concepts of duty, justice, and rights. This approach is inherently difficult to apply, however, and often results instead in ethical relativism, where each situation is approached individually and no consistent guidelines are applied.

A Typology of Moral Decision Making and Public Relations Models

Kohlberg's (1981b, 1984) typology of six stages of moral reasoning provides a useful basis for discussion of the differing approaches to public relations ethics. Kohlberg's *preconventional* level (Stages 1 and 2) comprises a restricted teleological view focusing on self-interest. Persons who employ Stage 1 reasoning act out of fear of reprisal, obeying those who have power over them such as practitioners who comply with all management orders for no reason other than fear of losing their jobs if they do not. This type of thinking is characterized by commitment to personal goals rather than societal ones, use of situational consequences rather than universal principles, and emotional reaction rather than reasoned action (Kohlberg, 1981b, 1984).

Persons using Stage 2 reasoning exploit situations for personal gain. Individuals act for personal reward, using manipulation and deception as necessary to achieve the desired end. Short-term rewards are emphasized over long-term consequences (Kohlberg, 1981b, 1984). Practitioners employing this type of moral reasoning would exploit situations to achieve promotion within their firm or organization such as the promotional activity often associated with P. T. Barnum. In terms of J. Grunig and Hunt's (1984) four models of public relations, the propaganda model, with its emphasis on personal gain over societal well-being, equates with Kohlberg's typology at this level.

At the *conventional* level (Stages 3 and 4), principles are based on conformity to commonly accepted expectations or standards. Individuals using Stage 3 reasoning promote the interests of their culture, peer group, or organization such as practitioners who place the goals of their company or organization above all else. The reasoning may encompass both deontological and teleological principles provided that they are principles held by the group or result in actions that benefit the group (Kohlberg, 1981b, 1984).

Persons employing Stage 4 reasoning obey the letter of the law because it represents legitimate power accruing from position or legal standing. Correct action consists of obeying the laws and fulfilling duties to maintain the group and allow it to function, a form of rule deontology (Kohlberg, 1981b, 1984). Practitioners employing such reasoning would rely on written codes, such as those of the Public Relations Society of America (PRSA) or International Association of Business Communicators (IABC), because they represent legitimate authority within the profession. With their emphasis on promoting the interests of the primary reference group, J. Grunig and Hunt's (1984) journalist-in-residence and two-way asymmetric models align roughly with Kohlberg's typology at the conventional level (Stages 3 and 4) of moral reasoning.

The *postconventional* level (Stages 5 and 6) is marked by personal autonomy and critical reflection. Stage 5 reasoning is universal teleology or utilitarianism; consequences for general societal well-being are crucial to ethical decision making (Kohlberg, 1981b, 1984). Practitioners using this reasoning make ethical decisions based on the overall consequences for society and not based solely on the benefits to their client or organization. J. Grunig and Hunt's (1984) two-way symmetric model, based on equality among organizations and their publics, roughly aligns with Kohlberg's postconventional type of reasoning.

Stage 6 principled reasoning is a form of act deontology in which each decision is weighed based on its benefit to society in terms of universal principles such as equity, justice, and fairness. People are seen as ends in themselves, not as a means to an end or even as the ends of society as a whole. Decisions are made based on principles freely chosen but that the chooser would be willing for everyone to live by as well (French & Granrose, 1995). Kohlberg, a developmental psychologist, termed true Stage 6 reasoning theoretical only; he believed that most people could not achieve the rigor of thought necessary to employ it with any consistency (Colby, Gibbs, Kohlberg, Dubin-Speicher, & Candee, 1980).

Relating J. Grunig and Hunt's models to Kohlberg's typology, based on the relevant domain of validity for both, illustrates how differing views of the function of public relations equate with differing types of ethical reasoning. It must be stressed, however, that the models are used here as a typology only and not to argue, as J. Grunig (1992c) did, that one model represents a better form of practice than does another model. Similarly, Kohlberg's numbered stages represent a typology only and do not indicate that one stage is better than another stage (Colby et al., 1980).

Empirical tests of Kohlberg's typology demonstrate that although individuals rely predominantly on one type of moral reasoning, they use a combination of types to a certain extent (Colby et al., 1980), much as J. Grunig (1992c) found that organizations use a combination of models of public relations, with one model often predominating. Kohlberg also found that most adults use conventional-level reasoning predominantly, much as J. Grunig (1992c) found that the corresponding journalist-in-residence

and two-way asymmetric models predominate in practice. This interrelated structure of ethical theory and public relations function provides a basis for the examination of different schools of thought in public relations ethics.

SCHOOLS OF THOUGHT IN PUBLIC RELATIONS ETHICS

Coorientation

The coorientation model uses teleological reasoning; practitioners should strive to achieve a convergence of perspectives between an organization and its key publics (Broom, 1977). The emphasis on shared group norms makes coorientation theory consistent with Kohlberg's Stage 3 reasoning. Much of the literature has emphasized the media relations function and defined journalists as the key public. Aronoff (1975) found that journalists typically do not view practitioners as credible. Journalists, however, have greater respect for practitioners with whom they regularly work than for the public relations profession in general. How journalists classify practitioners differs based on whether the image was formed from general perception (social norm level) or through personal experience (functional level) (Jeffers, 1977). Conversely, practitioners typically have a better image of the journalism profession than of individual reporters. Journalists and practitioners define lying similarly and agree that declining comment or being evasive does not equate with telling a lie (Ryan & Martinson, 1991). Because both journalists and practitioners view practitioners as less forthright due to their advocacy role, journalists might believe that public relations professionals are less trustworthy.

The coorientation model assumes convergent norms, but public relations practitioners often are measured against the journalistic standard as an absolute. This inequality may be attributed to the large number of practitioners who began their careers as journalists (Meyer, 1983). Some fear that by not embracing journalistic ethics, they will alienate those who control important news channels (Nayman, McKee, & Lattimore, 1977; Seib & Fitzpatrick, 1995), a form of Kohlberg's Stage 3 reasoning.

Because coorientation theory is based on the presupposition that journalists and practitioners perform similar job functions and, therefore, should follow similar professional norms, the theory is applicable only to those practitioners working in media relations and following a journalist-in-residence model of practice. In addition, because the emphasis has been placed on journalistic norms rather than on a convergence of perspectives, critics argue that the coorientation model will forever condemn public relations to being perceived as inherently unethical (McBride, 1989). For example, journalists justify the use of unethical practices as a means of obtaining truth and serving the public interest, but they perceive practitioners as roadblocks to the public interest, serving the corporate interest instead (Bishop, 1988; Ryan & Martinson, 1991). If, however, publics other than the media are the ends in question, then advocacy can be viewed as an ethical function.

Advocacy

Advocacy ethics stems from the social responsibility theory of the press and from persuasion, rooted in Greek philosophy as a legitimate means of conveying a position or argument (Heath, 1997; Toth & Heath, 1992). The approach is primarily teleological, valuing organizational goals, but fundamental, rules-based guidelines may be applied (Nelson, 1994), consistent with Kohlberg's (1981b, 1984) conventional-level reasoning.

The social responsibility theory of the press (Siebert, Peterson, & Schramm, 1956) has implications for all communicators because of its emphasis on the necessity of allowing all ideas to compete in the free marketplace of ideas. Some even suggest that public relations arose from a lack of media responsibility (Wright, 1976) because of the need for practitioners to make public information that otherwise was going unpublished during the public-be-damned business era. Since Ivy Lee, many practitioners consider

social responsibility not only to make good business sense but also to be a categorical imperative (Seib & Fitzpatrick, 1995).

Whereas Lee emphasized the public's right to know, Edward Bernays stressed the advocacy nature of public relations, thereby sharply differentiating it from the journalistic function in the minds of many journalists, as noted in the previous subsection (McBride, 1989). Proponents of advocacy theory note that in a democratic society based on free expression, a persuasion ethic is both acceptable and necessary for the emergence of truth (Barney & Black, 1994; Bernays, 1986). Much like attorneys, who function as advocates for their clients, practitioners serve as organizational advocates, whether presenting the benefits of products or designing persuasive health care messages (Wallack, Dorfman, Jernigan, & Themba, 1993; Witte, 1994). Advocacy allows members of the public to make informed decisions of their own free will, permitting "voluntary change" in attitudes or behaviors (Nelson, 1994). Final responsibility for informed choice, then, lies not with the practitioner but rather with the public.

Persuasion is considered unethical, however, when deliberate lying, distortion, or deception is used to mask intentions such as in the case of blatantly irresponsible communication campaigns (J. Grunig & Hunt, 1984; Nelson, 1994; Olasky, 1985a, 1985b), but at times the ethical implications might be difficult to discern (Guttman, 1997). Critics argue that persuasion never can be considered a sound ethical basis because the true end is not public welfare but rather organizational profit. Thus, J. Grunig (1992c) argued in excellence theory that only a two-way symmetrical public relations approach that gives equal weight to company/client and public interests, as opposed to manipulative one-way techniques, can guide ethical practice.

Such an approach might be naive because in practice most employers expect practitioners to be organizational advocates as part of their contractual work. Although practitioners also may function as the organizational conscience, with socially responsible practitioners guiding management toward strategies that reflect the public interest (Theus, 1995), employers often equate advocacy with loyalty (Spicer, 1997). Many practitioners rank responsibility to the public above their responsibility to the organization (Judd, 1989), but they also find that ethical demands of the employing organization, the society, and the self might contradict, creating confusion within the public relations profession as well as misunderstanding and mistrust among the public (Parsons, 1993; Shamir, Reed, & Connell, 1990; Stacks & Wright, 1989; Wright, 1989).

A more fundamental critique stems from the critical/cultural paradigm, which brands social libertarianism as a hegemonic notion, encouraging the idea of a free marketplace of ideas and informed citizenry while in fact promoting the status quo to maintain inherent power differentials. Under this view, the public relations practitioner is not the champion of the activist voice unheard by journalists but rather the source of expertise available only to those who can afford it, meaning that many voices remain relatively unheard (L'Etang, 1996a).

Professionalism

Professionalism typically employs rule deontology (Kohlberg's Stage 4 reasoning) to determine the scope of acceptable principles through codes, accreditation, and licensing. Professional associations and a growing number of companies have codified ethics to define daily decision-making standards and reflect practitioner responsibility to the public (Bovet, 1993; Hunt & Tirpok, 1993; Jurgensen & Lukaszewski, 1988; Seib & Fitzpatrick, 1995). Codes also may reinforce ethical expectations to public relations novices and deter government intervention, thereby enhancing professionalism (Wright, 1993).

Many industry associations, including the IABC and International Public Relations Association (IPRA), have member codes. The PRSA formalized ethics standards nearly a half century ago and has updated its Code of Professional Standards every decade since. The code addresses public interest, honesty, integrity, accuracy, truth, disclosure, conflict of interest, gifts, confidence and privacy, professional reputa-

tions, and enforcement terms (Bovet, 1993). Professional organizations also have instituted a universal accreditation process, formally acknowledging mastery of public relations practices and ethics, to signal greater professionalism (Marston, 1968; Pavlik, 1987).

Practitioner dedication to professional norms, however, is relatively unsubstantiated (Cameron, Sallot, & Curtin, 1997). Although some evidence exists that accredited PRSA members show greater professional orientation than do non-accredited members regarding some occupation values, results are not conclusive (Wright, 1981). Accreditation of individual practitioners is not enough to ensure societal acceptance of the value of public relations (Jackson, 1988; Sharpe, 1986) or to ensure accountability (Wright, 1993). Proponents of licensing point to the need to advance beyond codes and accreditation to enable performance standards to be enforced extensively and uniformly (Forbes, 1986), a move that most practitioners resist as inviting government interference (Hunt & Tirpok, 1993). Promoting codes beyond the public relations ranks might help engender public acceptance of professionalism, with or without licensing.

Reliance on professional ethics codes leads to criticisms that they are vague, unenforceable, or applied inconsistently (Hunt & Tirpok, 1993; Kruckeberg, 1993b; Seib & Fitzpatrick, 1995; Wright, 1993). For example, the PRSA code clearly proscribes lying, but it does not give clear guidance on when withholding information is justified, an ethical dilemma experienced by most practitioners (Ryan & Martinson, 1984; Saunders, 1989). Calls have been made to give elements of the PRSA code operational definitions to make the standards less vague (Sharpe, 1986), but doing so could make the code so situationally specific as to render it useless in practice and legalistically problematic (Seib & Fitzpatrick, 1995). As globalization has evolved, others have suggested the development of universal or international codes based on the belief that certain moral elements are basic to all humanity despite cultural differences (Kruckeberg, 1989, 1993b; Sharpe, 1986). Many cultures, however, do not embrace written codes of ethics, making such a code unlikely to gain wide acceptance and necessarily so broad as to lack pragmatic application (French & Granrose, 1995).

Codes of ethics, then, might be better at providing an image of professionalism than at actually guiding action (Wright, 1993). In fact, in one study, practitioners who said that they relied on codes of ethics also believed that they did not face ethical dilemmas in their work, suggesting that codes might be applied more as a professional prop than as a tool for thoughtful decision making (Saunders, 1989).

Game Theory

Game theory proposes that social interactions can be analyzed using mathematics to determine beneficial actions (von Neumann & Morgenstern, 1944). Applied to public relations, game theory expands Ehling's (1984, 1985) decision theory model, in which individuals identify possible actions and weigh their outcomes to resolve conflict, by placing individual decision strategies in the context of other players (Murphy, 1989). The resulting purely teleological ethics, a type of cost-benefit analysis, weighs the consequences of possible actions by all actors by assigning numerical values to each. Much as individuals often use simple cost-benefit analysis to make decisions about everyday things such as consumer purchases (French & Granrose, 1995), proponents of game theory stress the ability of this more complex form of cost-benefit analysis to allow practitioners to make systematic rational decisions not just based on the organizations for which they work but also taking into account their publics, particularly in instances where clear-cut choices might not be obvious (Murphy, 1989). By weighing the "what ifs" for all players, game theory enables practitioners to better understand coalition formation and behavior and to proceed with more confidence in strategic planning (Folger, Poole, & Stutman, 1993).

Critics of game theory point to the problems inherent in any purely teleological approach. Determining all possible consequences and players beforehand can be difficult (if not impossible), assigning numeric values to all possible actions

and outcomes can be arbitrary at best, and achieving the best outcome might require inherently unethical action such as lying. In addition, although true game theory requires that all players be considered, cost-benefit analysis often is used in a restricted teleological form. For example, Ford Motor Company analysts used cost-benefit analysis in their decision not to recall the Pinto and fix its gas tank despite the hazard to human life. Management, then, may stress the financial bottom line over intangibles such as public faith and goodwill, to which it is inherently more difficult to assign a dollar value, when calculating outcomes, particularly in times of crisis (French & Granrose, 1995; Rest, 1979). If not carefully applied, game theory degenerates into gamesmanship in which personal assertiveness is high, cooperation is low, and other players are disempowered (Folger et al., 1993). Depending on the breadth of application, then, game theory can embody Kohlberg's (1981b, 1984) Stage 2, Stage 3, or Stage 5 reasoning.

Corporate Responsibility

Corporate responsibility has been approached from two different theoretical backgrounds. One is *enlightened self-interest*, a restricted form of teleology consistent with Kohlberg's Stage 3 reasoning. A corporation recognizes that doing good results in doing well, and being seen as a responsible corporate citizen benefits the bottom line (Cutlip, Center, & Broom, 1994; K. Leeper, 1996). Consumer advocacy and awareness have forced businesses to be more accountable to society (Wright, 1976). Thus, corporate philanthropy represents good action because of the resulting goodwill that it buys for the company or organization. Ethical action is determined using cost-benefit analysis to further the company's goals in the belief that what benefits the organization will have wider consequences and eventually will benefit society as well.

Recently, this approach to corporate responsibility has fallen in favor of an approach based in social contract theory and the notion that social responsibility goes beyond good business practice; it encompasses the rights of publics and corporations' duties to those publics (Heath, 1997; Martinson, 1994, 1995-1996). As such, this formulation combines aspects of coorientation, advocacy, professionalism, and game theory, culminating in a form of act deontology in which principles are delineated to guide actions and communications with publics. Publics themselves are viewed as stakeholders and are treated as ends in themselves and not as means to ends (L'Etang, 1996a). Stakeholder ethics emphasizes an organization's obligations to both internal and external publics, with the realization that these interests often will conflict and that principles of balancing these interests, such as not harming others, must be developed (Cunningham & Haley, 1998; Heath, 1997). Ethical action, then, involves respecting the rights of others and upholding the organizational duty to those others by not compromising ethical principles. Proponents point to the process of issues management to demonstrate stakeholder ethics and corporate responsibility in action. Organizations monitor their environments and identify publics and their interests to determine courses of action that will respect the rights of all stakeholders (Heath, 1997; Heath & Ryan, 1989; L'Etang, 1996a).

In practice, however, this approach often is not easy to achieve, in large part because public relations practitioners frequently are left out of organizational ethical decision making, leaving them powerless to enact corporate philosophies (Fitzpatrick, 1996b; Heath & Ryan, 1989). Because it requires changes in organizational behavior, it is easier to practice socially responsible public relations when that already is management's philosophy (Heath, 1997; Wright, 1976). Empirical studies suggest that external publics all too often are discounted, and corporate responsibility reverts from actions performed out of obligation to publics and long-term planning to those performed in enlightened self-interest serving the short-term bottom line (Heath & Ryan, 1989; L'Etang, 1996a; Martinson, 1995-1996).

Critics suggest that major social reform is necessary to strengthen the relational links among individuals, organizations, and their shared environments. Such approaches often are based in communitarian ethics, which stresses the role of the community in forging ethical people and organizations as well as the equal empowerment of all members of the community—individual, corporate, and otherwise—consonant with J. Grunig's (1992c) excellence theory of public relations (Culbertson & Chen, 1997b; K. Leeper, 1996). Other approaches suggest that such change can originate within corporations themselves (Heath, 1997) and that most successful businesses already are using self-regulation to operate under such a model. Lacking a clear strong motivation for corporate responsibility, however, equal empowerment of stakeholders probably will remain an ideal but not a functional norm (L'Etang, 1996a).

Structural/Functional Approach

A structural-functional approach to public relations ethics is based in systems theory, which stresses the role of organizational environment and purpose, to delineate differing ethical standards according to job function (Bivins, 1987, 1989a, 1989b; Judd, 1989) based on Dozier's (1983) identification of two main public relations roles: communication technician and communication manager. This division results in an ethical decision-making hierarchy in which technicians, functioning as advocates for their organization, first employ rule deontological principles such as codes of ethics; if codes are unavailable or incomplete, then practitioners turn to teleological principles (Bivins, 1989a, 1989b, 1992). But because managers function as advisers, they follow the opposite route, as befits a more autonomous and objective status. Both approaches fall within Kohlberg's (1981b, 1984) conventional-level reasoning.

A strength of this approach is its ability to provide a unified ethical system for differing public relations functions. Although the order of application varies, the same principles are used by advocates and advisers, resulting in similar outcomes (Bivins, 1987, 1989a, 1989b, 1992). Empirical tests have found a significant correlation between the adviser function and an emphasis on social responsibility (Judd, 1989), although it is unclear whether this relationship is a result of job role, age, or experience. However, professionals rank the public image of practitioners' sense of social responsibility as poor (Judd, 1989; Pratt, 1991b). Thus, a functional basis for ethical development could be inadequate if a shared notion of the adviser function is not publicly held, which might reduce motivation to conform to its standards.

Additional lack of motivation stems from the hierarchical ordering of the functions, which makes ethics a luxury of those with autonomy. Because the technician functions as an advocate whose primary loyalty is to the employer, questioning the employer's ethics can result in loss of employment, leading proponents of this approach to suggest that these types of ethical calls are best left to advisers (Bivins, 1987, 1989a, 1989b). Thus, the approach assumes that, at the technician level at least, professional norms can be separated from personal values, an assumption not supported by empirical tests (Shamir et al., 1990; Stacks & Wright, 1989; Wright, 1989). Those who propose that advocates should hold to personal principles despite company loyalty suggest that such individuals become whistle-blowers as necessary (Schick, 1996)—a course of action that lacks inherent motivation. The fundamental critique of structural/functional approaches, then, is their assumption that the function is inherently ethical rather than examining the ethical basis of the function itself.

Accommodation/Discursive Approach

Whereas the structural/functionalist approach emphasizes the strategic goal achievement aspects of systems theory, the accommodation/discursive approach emphasizes the relational aspects. Sullivan (1965a, 1965b) outlined three types of public relations values: technical, which he viewed as morally neutral; partisan, comprising commitment, loyalty, and trust in the organization; and mutual, comprising institutional obligations to the public based on principles of mutuality and rationality. Sullivan placed the locus of ethical issues at the intersection of partisan and mutual values, highlighting the tension that often exists in practice between organizational and broader societal interests, and stressed the need for practitioners to facilitate communication between the two (Pearson, 1989c).

In addition, the approach employs the discourse ethics of Habermas (1979a, 1996) to resituate ethics in the process of communication rather than in communication outcomes. Building on Kohlberg's typology of moral reasoning, Habermas (1979a) specified discourse rules ensuring that discussion participants are best able to advance their interests and weigh them critically against those of the larger community (Huspek, 1997). This philosophy is embodied in Item 7 of the IPRA code of ethics: Members "shall undertake to establish the moral, psychological, and intellectual conditions for dialogue in its true sense."

Pearson (1989a) and R. Leeper (1996) outlined a communication system that promotes negotiation between equal and rational communicators, equating it with J. Grunig's ideal model of public relations practice, the two-way symmetric communication model. The role of the practitioner is to ensure the possibility of and enactment through a collaborative decision-making process within the systems perspective (Pearson, 1990). Under this approach, advocacy is inherently unethical because it is based on content, not process, and on monologue, not dialogue (J. Grunig, 1993d; J. Grunig & L. Grunig, 1992). The approach makes moot the question of whether clients are so unethical that a practitioner cannot represent them in good faith (J. Grunig, 1993d) because unethical clients often refuse to submit to such a process.

Critics note that the process requires rational application of procedural rules, yet not all organizations are interested in rational decision making, leaving open the question of whether using persuasion to convince them to enter into negotiation would not be more ethical than simply leaving them outside the bounds of practice (Cheney & Dionisopoulos, 1989). In addition, empirical evidence suggests that few employers are willing to pay practitioners to perform as negotiators for equally empowered conflicting publics, a condition termed *managerial bias* in organizational communications (Hellweg, 1989).

One answer to these difficulties has been suggested by development of the mixed-motives model of public relations practice, in which elements of game theory and systems theory are combined to suggest a continuum between the two-way asymmetric and two-way symmetric models (Dozier, L. Grunig, & J. Grunig, 1995; J. Grunig & L. Grunig, 1992; Murphy, 1991; Pavlik, 1989). Within this model, organizations strive to forward their own interests and increase their autonomy while reaching results acceptable to their publics (J. Grunig & L. Grunig, 1992). Excellent or normative public relations practice, however, still is equated with the two-way symmetric model despite admissions that the model contains some asymmetric elements (J. Grunig & L. Grunig, 1992; Dozier et al., 1995).

The result of the mixed-motives theoretical development is to once again stress the functional elements of systems theory over relational aspects, reducing it to a hierarchical structural/functional approach in which persuasion is applied first, followed by negotiation if persuasion fails. Again, ethics becomes a privilege of the few practitioners who have managed to acquire adviser roles in socially responsible companies. For the majority of practitioners, the model may serve instead as an excuse for always falling short of ethical action.

Contingency Theory

Contingency theory, a relatively new development in public relations theory, arose from perceived difficulties with J. Grunig's excellence theory of public relations as outlined earlier. Recognizing that many internal and external factors could constrain relations with publics, contingency theory suggests that organizations weigh these factors to determine which style of public relations practice is most appropriate under the circumstances (Cancel, Cameron, Sallot, & Mitrook, 1997; Leichty & Springston, 1993). Accommodation, then, is not always possible or even desirable. Instead, a large number of factors

must be carefully weighed and systematically applied in any given situation.

To date, limited empirical testing of the model has been performed (e.g., Cameron, Mitrook, & Cancel, 1997), and full ethical development has yet to take place. A decision-making framework consonant with a contingency approach expands on the Potter Box, in which agents prioritize values and publics by defining the situation, identifying values, selecting principles, and choosing loyalties (McElreath, 1996). This approach, rather than forcing a choice, combines deontological and teleological principles in a similar four-step framework:

1. Confront ethical dilemma.
2. Determine individual motivation to act.
3. Consider rules, principles, and duties as well as predictions concerning causes and consequences of actions.
4. Reach decision and take appropriate action.

The result suggests a true situation ethics in which moral decisions are based on detailed knowledge of each relevant situation and both principled action and a weighing of consequences (Vasquez, 1996). Care should be taken here to distinguish true situation ethics, comprising Stage 6 reasoning in Kohlberg's typology and requiring the most cognitive effort (French & Granrose, 1995), from situational ethics, which often is misused as a synonym for ethical relativism (see, e.g., Jurgensen & Lukaszewski, 1988).

Empirical work has found that practitioners find both strict teleological and strict (rule) deontological approaches to be insufficient in and of themselves, preferring a true situation ethic (Englehardt & Evans, 1994). Pratt (1993), after reviewing classic utilitarian and deontological approaches, also espoused what he termed an "eclectic ethical approach" in which each situation is carefully weighed against principles of duty and justice and in terms of their consequences to decide what constitutes ethical action in that instance. Because both are forms of act deontology, the contingency approach suggests an ethics similar to that formulated by

Heath (1997; see also Toth & Heath, 1992) under the corporate responsibility model, attributable in large part to the fact that both approaches treat public relations not as a singular function or set of discrete functions but rather as a multifaceted process. Further testing of contingency theory is necessary, however, to determine whether the two approaches are fully consonant.

As noted earlier, however, act deontological principles are difficult to apply consistently, and Kohlberg believed that most people were incapable of the sustained cognitive effort that such reasoning requires. When not consistently applied, situation ethics degenerates into ethical relativism. Thus, it might be no accident that empirical research to date, including interviews, experiments, and surveys, suggests that ethical relativism predominates in the profession, with no one set of ethical principles applied consistently (Olasky, 1985a, 1985b; Ryan & Martinson, 1984; Saunders, 1989). When situation ethics degenerates into ethical relativism, it allows practitioners to rationalize inappropriate behaviors (Jurgensen & Lukaszewski, 1988).

IMPLICATIONS FOR PUBLIC RELATIONS PRACTICE

Responding to Environmental Factors

As the preceding discussion illustrates, the definitions of the function of public relations and ethical public relations practice are mutually informative. Empirical research demonstrates that no one ethical approach dominates in practice, in large part because no one functional definition of public relations exists (Pratt, 1994). What is evident, however, is that public relations is operating in an increasingly complex environment, and as in any robust profession, new environmental factors renew debate. Witness the medical profession's attempts to distribute donated organs fairly or to conduct genetic research. Similarly, many environmental factors have contributed to the recent development of public relations—information overload and new technology, the increasing emphasis on

public opinion for policy formation, the global economy, the rise of consumerism and environmentalism, increasing government regulation, and the proliferation of publics and decline of mass media (Heath, 1997; Wilcox, Ault, & Agee, 1998).

From these trends, a clear ethical directive has emerged. Organizations no longer can hold onto the false belief that they can function as independent entities divorced from society at large. Unidimensional ethical theories that take only the organization into account, such as simple forms of coorientation, advocacy, professionalism, or corporate social responsibility, are not adequate to inform modern practice. As interior and exterior publics become more diverse and more empowered, public relations practice must embrace new techniques and expand its ethical reasoning to handle conflicting stakeholder claims while defining and redefining organizational relations on an ongoing basis (Vasquez, 1996). Thus, public relations practice must become more proactive, engaging in environmental scanning and issues management to gauge and meet the changing needs of the organization and its publics. To reach the ever increasing diversity of publics, practitioners must engage in narrowcasting and develop new technology channels as a means of empowering publics through two-way information and communication flow. To support public relations as a proactive management function, a more complex ethical framework is required, one that expands from organizational to societal viewpoints—or, in Kohlberg's terms, from conventional to postconventional thought—such as those suggested by the relational dynamics of contingency theory and more complex forms of corporate social responsibility.

Reconciling Normative Theory With Practical Application

If management does not support proactive public relations practice, however, then tension develops between the norms of ethical theory and what practitioners can achieve pragmatically, resulting in a lack of motivation for practitioners to advocate ethical stances. Because the current focus of much of public relations ethical theory is on individual decision making (Ferre, 1990; L'Etang, 1996a), the political context in which those decisions are made has been deemphasized. Not only are more complex forms of ethics that can adjust to environmental factors necessary, then, but practitioners must convince management of the benefits of such approaches in terms of long-term gains. Concurrent with the need to demonstrate to management the benefits of proactive public relations practice is the need for practitioners to develop well-defined standards by which to operate and evaluate their practice and their organization's responsiveness to the larger environment (Heath, 1997).

Another difficulty lies in the inherent complexity of accurately gauging fluid environments. Such approaches demand that certain principles, such as universality, be applied, yet the specific relational aspects of each situation, such as competing stakeholder claims, must be weighed as well for such an approach not to deteriorate into ethical relativism. Kohlberg believed such sustained complexity of thought to be beyond the capacity of much of the adult population. For this reason, reports on educating business managers and ethics in higher education speak of the need to stimulate the moral imagination to develop people's inherent moral capacity (Hastings Center, 1980a, 1980b). Yet, public relations textbooks lack any in-depth conceptual discussion of ethical systems (Bivins, 1989a, 1989b; Harrison, 1990a), and only one in four colleges or universities offers courses devoted to communication ethics (Harrison, 1990b). The texts often used in these courses generally focus on journalism (Pratt, 1991b); they typically include a single chapter on public relations, usually treating it in terms of advocacy ethics only (see, e.g., Fink, 1995). The ethical challenges of the modern workplace demand that changes in curriculum as well as in practice be made if practitioners are to confront ethical challenges in an informed manner.

Despite these inherent difficulties in application, to conclude—as Stauber and Rampton (1995) did in *Toxic Sludge Is Good for You*—that public relations is a morally bankrupt profession is to ignore the evolving function of public relations in modern managerial practice. A continuation of today's vibrant debate on ethics is needed to inform day-to-day practice and to expand public and managerial awareness of the scope of public relations practice.

CHAPTER 34

Public Relations Between Universality and Particularity

Toward a Moral-Philosophical Conception of Public Relations Ethics

TANNI HAAS

Public relations has been, and indeed should be, defined as "the management function that identifies, establishes, and maintains mutually beneficial *relationships* between an organization and the various publics on whom its success or failure depends" (Cutlip, Center, & Broom, 1985, p. 4, italics added). Yet, if the essence of public relations is relationship management, then how is a corporation to ensure that its relationships with publics are managed in an ethical manner? It is to this important issue that the present chapter is dedicated. More specifically, this chapter considers whether it is possible for a corporation to interact with publics as groups of people with equal rights to have their interest claims represented within its internal decision-making processes while at the same time acknowledging that those interest claims are likely to be based on dif-

ferent, and potentially mutually conflicting, underlying values. This conception of the ethical responsibilities of the corporation vis-à-vis its publics poses serious challenges to the practice of public relations. As is elaborated during the course of this chapter, the corporation must address a number of important issues relating to its relationships with publics and, in particular, to the modes of discourse to be applied during interaction. First, should the corporation focus attention on salient commonalities among its publics to treat them as equal moral agents? Or, alternatively, should the corporation focus attention on salient differences among its publics to attend to individuating differences? Furthermore, should the corporation apply a higher order (synthetic) mode of discourse to subject potential differences among its publics to rational-

AUTHOR'S NOTE: An earlier version of this chapter was presented as a "Top Three Competitive Paper" at the annual convention of the International Communication Association, Public Relations Division, Jerusalem, Israel, July 1998. E-mail: thaas@brooklyn.cuny.edu.

critical mediation? Or, alternatively, should the corporation apply multiple (syncretistic) modes of discourse to provide its publics with opportunities to articulate irreducible differences among them?

In recent years, a number of prominent public relations scholars have turned to German moral philosopher Jürgen Habermas for inspiration to address similar ethical issues (Cheney & Dionisopoulos, 1989; German, 1995; J. Grunig & White, 1992; R. Leeper, 1996; Pearson, 1989a, 1989d). Scholars have argued that Habermas's discourse ethics, and especially his notion of an ideal speech situation, is important to public relations because it directs attention to the process, rather than the substance, of the interactions between a corporation and its publics (Pearson, 1989a). This focus has been said to help facilitate a shift from a situational to a universalistic approach to public relations ethics (R. Leeper, 1996). This chapter argues that although Habermas's discourse does indeed have important implications for the practice of public relations, it is based on an underlying conception of self-other relations that ultimately renders it unsuitable as the conceptual basis for a public relations ethics.

Habermas's discourse ethics is based on an underlying conception of self-other relations that requires the corporation (as a self) to interact with its publics (as others) in their capacity as generalized others. This implies that both the corporation and its publics must abstract their interest claims from the underlying values on which they are based. Although this is feasible hypothetically in a traditional homogeneous society associated with considerable value consensus both between the corporation and its publics and among the corporation's publics internally, it is problematic in a modern heterogeneous society, such as the United States, associated with considerable value dissensus. Consequently, the application of Habermas's discourse ethics is likely to result in interactions associated with various types of systematic distortion and, importantly, the distinction between the corporation (as a self) and its publics (as others) is likely to collapse.

As a viable alternative to Habermas's discourse ethics, Benhabib's (1992) suggestions for a more contextually sensitive approach to ethics are discussed. Benhabib's reconsideration of Habermas's discourse ethics is based on an underlying conception of self-other relations that requires the corporation (as a self) to interact with its publics (as others) simultaneously in their capacity as generalized and concrete others. This implies that both the corporation and its publics must articulate the values underlying their interest claims during interaction. From the perspective of the corporation, this entails conceptualizing all of its publics as having equal rights to have their interest claims represented within its internal decision-making processes (in their capacity as generalized others) while at the same time conceptualizing each of its publics as having irreducible, yet legitimate, differences in values in need of representation (in their capacity as concrete others). Consequently, Benhabib's reconsideration of Habermas's discourse ethics provides the conceptual basis for the development of a public relations ethics that is universalistic, yet contextually sensitive.

Finally, some important practical problems associated with assuming the standpoint of the concrete other in practice are discussed. Although the assumption of the standpoint of the concrete other ideally requires the corporation and its publics to be situated in the context of spatio-temporal co-presence, interacting with one another through face-to-face dialogue, the corporation often may be forced to apply either mediated interaction or mediated quasi-interaction instead. Whereas both types of interaction are problematic from the standpoint of concern with the concrete other, the application of mediated interaction provides the most potential for assuming this standpoint because it entails a dialogical mode of interaction aimed at specific others.

HABERMAS'S DISCOURSE ETHICS

Habermas (1984, 1987), following Austin's (1962) and Searle's (1969) speech act philosophy, argued that whenever people engage in interaction, they implicitly raise, and at the same time become accountable for, four types of validity claims that relate to four different types of speech acts: truth (constatives), correctness (regulatives), sincerity (representatives), and intelligibility (communicatives). These four validity claims, in turn, correspond to four different domains of reality: the external world, human relations, the individual's internal world, and language. Therefore, every instance of interaction (a) presupposes the representation of facts (the external world), (b) establishes legitimate social relations (human relations), (c) discloses the speaker's point of view (the individual's internal world), and (d) is intelligible (language). The ideal speech situation (Habermas, 1973), or what Habermas (1990) subsequently termed the universal and necessary communicative presuppositions of argumentative speech, represents a communication situation in which participants may redeem all four of these validity claims. Whenever one or more of these validity claims are breached by the participants, their interactions may be characterized as systematically distorted (Habermas, 1970).

Habermas's (1984, 1987) discussion has important implications for the practice of public relations. Most important, the ideal speech situation stipulates certain ethical ideals in terms of which the interest claims of the corporation and its publics must be represented within the corporation's internal decision-making processes. From the perspective of the corporation, only when the force of the better argument rather than various types of systematic distortion govern its interactions with publics may the corporation be said to provide its publics with genuine opportunities to represent their interest claims. In practice, this would require the corporation to satisfy the following four conditions vis-à-vis its publics:

1. It must provide publics with opportunities to represent their particular interest claims rather than limit representation to certain publics and types of interest claims.

2. It must provide publics with opportunities to question its interest claims rather than keep those interest claims off-limits.

3. It must acknowledge the underlying values on which its interest claims are based rather than claim that those interest claims are value neutral.

4. It must provide publics with opportunities to apply modes of discourse suitable for the representation of their interest claims rather than valorize modes of discourse that make it difficult to represent those interest claims.

The Moral Point of View

Although Habermas's (1984, 1987) conception of ethical interaction has important implications for the practice of public relations, it also is associated with weaknesses that ultimately render it unsuitable as the conceptual basis for a public relations ethics. This becomes clear when considering in closer detail the conditions under which the ideal speech situation applies.

Habermas (1990, 1993) argued that the ideal speech situation does not apply to all types of discourses (and interest claims). In elaborating his conception of the moral point of view, Habermas distinguished between moral-practical discourses (about universalistic principles of justice and rights), which are amenable to rational-critical discourse under the conditions stipulated by the ideal speech situation, and ethical-existential discourses (about particularistic conceptions of the good life), which are amenable to rational-critical discourse only within the unproblematic horizon of a concrete historical form of life. For this reason, Habermas (1993) argued that his discourse ethics may more accurately be termed a discourse theory of morality than a discourse ethics proper.

Habermas (1990, 1993) distinguished between moral-practical discourses, to which the ideal speech situation applies, and ethical-existential discourses, to which the ideal speech situation does not apply, because in modern heterogeneous societies associated with considerable value dissensus among different societal groups, achieving a consensus about their underlying values, such as what represents the good life, has become increasingly difficult. Under such conditions, Habermas (1993) argued, the ethical basis for interaction may be located only in the structure of the interactions themselves through rational-critical discourse about generalizable interest claims: "[Moral]-practical reason is thereby transformed from a context-dependent faculty of prudent deliberation that operates within the horizon of an established form of life into a faculty of pure reason operating independently of particular contexts" (p. 120).

Habermas's (1990, 1993) distinction between moral-practical and ethical-existential discourses is problematic from a public relations perspective. Most important, this distinction suggests that the corporation and its publics must abstract their interest claims from the underlying values on which they are based during interaction. Although this is feasible hypothetically in a traditional homogeneous society associated with considerable value consensus both between the corporation and its publics and among the corporation's publics internally, it is problematic in a modern heterogeneous society, such as the United States, associated with considerable value dissensus. Therefore, it is only partly correct, as Pearson (1989a) argued, that Habermas's discourse ethics directs attention to the process, rather than the substance, of the interactions between a corporation and its publics. Whereas the ideal speech situation stipulates certain processual ideals in terms of which their respective interest claims must be represented within the corporation's internal decision-making processes, it also stipulates certain limitations as to which types of interest claims are suitable for representation in the first place.

The Standpoint of the Generalized Other

The emphasis that Habermas (1990, 1993) placed on generalizable interest claims is problematic from a public relations perspective. For an interest claim to qualify as generalizable, it must to be abstracted from the underlying values of the participants. As such, it is associated with a conception of self-other relations in which the participants must interact with one another in their capacity as generalized others (Mead, 1934) in the sense that they are to adopt a standpoint of moral impartiality and neutrality concerning the values underlying their interest claims. This may be accomplished, Habermas (1993) argued (following Mead, 1934), through the application of ideal role-taking, "which requires everyone to take the perspective of all others" (p. 174). To view something from the moral point of view, Habermas argued, "means that we do not elevate our own understanding and worldview to the standard by which we universalize a mode of action but instead test its generalizability also from the perspectives of all others" (pp. 174-175).

The conception of self-other relations underlying Habermas's (1990, 1993) discourse ethics (the other as a generalized other) is problematic from a public relations perspective. First, and most important, to assume the standpoint of the generalized other implies that the corporation (as a self) and its publics (as others) must abstract their interest claims from the underlying values on which they are based. Such an abstraction would not represent a problem in a traditional homogeneous society associated with considerable value consensus both between the corporation and its publics and among the corporation's publics internally. But in a modern heterogeneous society (e.g., the United States) associated with considerable value dissensus, it becomes problematic. Specifically, it is likely to result in interactions associated with various types of systematic distortion. If the corporation and its publics must abstract their interest claims from the underlying values on which they are based, then it becomes possible for the corporation to claim that its interest claims are value neutral, a type of systematic distortion known as neutralization (Deetz, 1992). From a public relations perspective, it becomes possible for the corporation to hide the values underlying its interest claims and, thereby, to prevent its publics from assessing whether, and to what extent, they would endorse those values if given the opportunity to evaluate them.

Furthermore, it becomes possible for the corporation to dismiss the interest claims of its publics as not being suitable for representation within its internal decision-making processes on the basis that these concern evaluative conceptions of the good life that are amenable to rational-critical discourse only within the unproblematic horizon of a concrete historical form of life that differs fundamentally from that of the corporation. When the interest claims differ among the corporation's publics internally, it becomes possible for the corporation to claim that a common ground for their rational-critical mediation is too difficult to identify. This becomes especially problematic if some of the corporation's publics attempt to represent interest claims of a noneconomic character. Needing a seemingly value-neutral (or impartial) means of conflict resolution, it becomes possible for the corporation to reduce noneconomic conflicts of interest to questions of economic character in ways that further the (primarily economic) interests of its owners/stockholders. From a public relations perspective, it becomes possible for the corporation not only to dismiss the interest claims of certain publics prior to their representation within the corporation's internal decision-making processes but also, and importantly, to reduce interest claims already admitted for representation to questions of economic character, even when those interest claims are of a noneconomic character.

To require the corporation and its publics to abstract their interest claims from the underlying values on which they are based not only is unethical but also is likely to be associated with negative epistemic consequences. If the nature of the interest claims deemed suitable for representation within the corporation's internal decision-making processes is determined in advance of interaction, then important types of interest claims likely never will reach the corporation's internal decision-making processes.

Although the application of Habermas's discourse ethics, as R. Leeper (1996) rightly argued, might facilitate a shift from a situational to a universalistic approach to public relations ethics, it does so at a costly price. Specifically, it is likely to result in a public relations ethics that is universalistic, yet contextually insensitive.

BENHABIB'S RECONSIDERATION OF HABERMAS'S DISCOURSE ETHICS

Benhabib's (1992) reconsideration of Habermas's (1990, 1993) discourse ethics represents an attempt to transcend his narrow conception of the moral point of view and the associated distinction between moral-practical discourses (about universalistic principles of justice and rights), to which Habermas argued his discourse ethics applies, and ethical-existential discourses (about particularistic conceptions of the good life), to which Habermas argued his discourse ethics does not apply. Whereas Benhabib's reconsideration has been developed in terms of a feminist emancipatory agenda (Haas & Deetz, 2000), several aspects are important from a public relations perspective. Most important is Benhabib's contention that Habermas's narrow conception of the moral point of view, based as it is on a limited conception of self-other relations (the other as a generalized other), limits the scope of application of his discourse ethics considerably.

The Generalized and the Concrete Other

A broadened conception of the moral point of view might be developed, Benhabib (1992) argued, by attending to two different conceptions of self-other relations that delineate different moral perspectives and norms of interaction: the standpoint of the generalized other (a term originating with Mead, 1934, and applied by Habermas, 1990, 1993) and the concrete other (for a similar emphasis on the other as a concrete other, see Manning, 1992; Noddings, 1984; Wood, 1994). According to Benhabib, these two moral perspectives reflect traditional dichotomies between autonomy and nurturance, between independence and bonding, between the public sphere and the private sphere, and (more broadly) between universalistic principles of justice and rights and particularistic conceptions of the good life. For Benhabib, to assume the standpoint of the generalized other

> requires us to view each and every individual as a rational being entitled to the same rights and duties we would want to ascribe to ourselves. In assuming this standpoint, we abstract from the individuality and concrete identity of the other. We assume that the other, like ourselves, is a being who has concrete needs, desires, and affects, but that what constitutes his or her moral dignity is not what differentiates us from each other but rather what we, as speaking and acting rational agents, have in common. Our relation to the other is governed by the norms of formal equality and reciprocity; each is entitled to expect and to assume from us what we can expect and assume from him or her. The norms of our interactions are primarily public and institutional ones. (pp. 158-159)

To assume the standpoint of the concrete other, on the other hand,

> requires us to view each and every rational being as an individual with a concrete history, identity, and affective-emotional constitution. In assuming this standpoint, we abstract from what constitutes our commonality and focus on individuality. We seek to comprehend the needs of the other, his or her motivations, what [he or] she searches for, and what [he or she] desires. Our relations to the other [are] governed by the norms of equity and complementary reciprocity; each is entitled to expect and to assume from the other forms of behavior through which the other feels recognized and confirmed as a concrete, individual being with specific needs, talents, and capacities. Our differences in this case complement rather than exclude one another. The norms of our interaction are usually, although not exclusively, private, non-institutional ones. (p. 159)

The problem associated with assuming only the morally impartial and neutral standpoint of the generalized other is, Benhabib (1992) argued, that it entails a conception of self-other relations that makes individuating among different selves difficult. The other as distinct from the self, or the otherness of the other, is likely to disappear because the criteria for individuating among different selves are lacking. Neither the concreteness nor the otherness of the other may be recognized, Benhabib argued, in the absence of the voice of the other. The characteristics of the concrete other emerge as distinct only as the result of self-definition on the part of the other.

Therefore, the understanding of the self implied by the concept of the generalized other is, Benhabib (1992) argued, incompatible with the criteria of reversibility of perspectives and universalizability advocated by universalistic moral philosophers, that is, universalistic moral perspectives exemplified by Habermas's (1990, 1993) appropriation of the Meadian concept of ideal role-taking (Mead, 1934) or Rawls's (1971) concept of the veil of ignorance in terms of an original position. To conceptualize and interact with the other only in his or her capacity as a generalized other implies, Benhabib argued, a conception of otherness whereby the other achieves a definitional identity but does not appear to the self as an embodied and embedded individual. Consequently, Benhabib argued, "One consequence of limiting procedures of universalizability to the standpoint of the generalized other has been that the other as distinct from the self has disappeared in universalizing moral discourse" (p. 10).

Habermas (1993) responded directly to Benhabib's (1992) argument that to assume the standpoint of the concrete other becomes impossible in terms of his discourse ethics. Specifically, Habermas argued that the impression that his discourse ethics makes the assumption of this standpoint impossible may be attributed to a preoccupation with questions of justification: "The unique disposition of a particular case that calls for regulation, and the concrete characteristics of the people involved, come into view only after problems of justification have been resolved" (pp. 153-154). Consequently, Habermas argued, "[Moral]-practical reason is not fully realized in discourses of justification. Whereas in justifying norms [moral]-practical reason finds expression in the principle of universalization, in the application of norms it takes the form of a principle of appropriateness" (p. 154).

Habermas's (1993) distinction between a universalistic justification of norms and a contextually sensitive application of norms does not, however, adequately address the issue at stake. To assume the standpoint of the concrete other requires one to articulate individuating characteristics of the other from the outset rather than to introduce their articulation during any subsequent decision about how to interact with the other in an ethical manner. Habermas's approach, on the contrary, entails an initial abstraction from individuating characteristics of the other that makes it impossible to introduce their subsequent articulation. Therefore, Habermas's approach is associated with the problematic contention that one initially should assume the (universalistic) standpoint of the generalized other, followed by the assumption of the (contextually sensitive) standpoint of the concrete other. In other words, it is a problematic two-step process: "In justificatory discourses, it is necessary to abstract from the contingent contextual embeddedness of a proposed norm only to ensure that the norm, assuming it withstands the generalization test, is sufficiently open to context-sensitive application" (p. 58).

The Moral Conversation

For Benhabib (1992), a broadened conception of the moral point of view requires one to simultaneously assume the standpoint of the generalized and the concrete other. In turn, this requires a shift from a substantialistic to a discursive conception of rationality. This may be accomplished, Benhabib argued (following Habermas's [1990, 1993] discourse ethics), by engaging in open-ended and reflective moral conversations that require the adherence to two underlying principles: (a) the principle of universal moral respect (the recognition of the rights of all individuals capable of speech and action to be participants in moral conversations), and (b) the principle of egalitarian reciprocity (the recognition that within such moral conversations all

participants have the same symmetrical rights to various speech acts, to initiate new topics, to ask for reflections about the presuppositions of the conversations, etc.). Although these principles are derived from Habermas's discourse ethics, the approach no longer is general and universalistic but rather is concrete and contextually sensitive.

The purpose of engaging in moral conversations, Benhabib (1992) argued in a critique of Habermas's (1990, 1993) discourse ethics, is not to reach a rationally motivated consensus among the participants concerning their respective values and interest claims. Such a consensus is likely to imply their transcendence whereby the distinction between self and other collapses. Rather, Benhabib argued (following Arendt, 1961), the objective should be "the anticipated communication with others with whom [one] must finally come to some agreement" (p. 9). Consequently, engagement in a moral conversation does not guarantee that a consensus ultimately may be reached among the participants. Rather, Benhabib argued, to engage in moral conversations "demonstrates the will and readiness to seek understanding with the other and to reach some reasonable agreement" (p. 9). Therefore, moral conversations that are genuinely open-ended and reflective, and that do not rely on any epistemic limitations, might lead to a mutual understanding of the otherness of the participants. They actualize dialogues "among actual selves who are both generalized others, considered as equal moral agents, and concrete others, that is, individuals with irreducible differences" (p. 169).

For Benhabib (1992), this way of conceptualizing the moral conversation represents a transcendence of the classical moral-philosophical distinction between universalistic principles of justice and rights and particularistic conceptions of the good life: "If in discourses the agenda of the conversation is radically open . . ., then there is no way to predefine the nature of the issues discussed as being public ones of justice versus private ones of the good life" (p. 110). Rather, Benhabib argued, such a distinction should be drawn only "subsequent and not prior to the process of discursive will formation" (p. 110).

Toward a Universalistic, yet Contextually Sensitive, Public Relations Ethics

Benhabib's (1992) reconsideration of Habermas's (1990, 1993) discourse ethics has important implications for the practice of public relations. First, Benhabib's reconsideration suggests that if a corporation (as a self) is to interact with its publics (as others) in an ethical manner, then the corporation must interact with them simultaneously in their capacity as generalized and concrete others in terms of a moral conversation.

To assume the standpoint of the generalized other requires the corporation to conceptualize all of its publics as being similar in the sense of having valid interest claims in need of representation within its internal decision-making processes. In Benhabib's (1992) vocabulary, the corporation must conceive of its publics as representing equal moral agents (through adherence to the principle of universal moral respect) by focusing attention on what they have in common rather than on what distinguishes them from one another. Yet, as Benhabib rightly argues, it is not sufficient to assume the standpoint of the generalized other. By focusing attention on what its publics have in common, the corporation risks ignoring salient differences among them as perceived from the perspectives of those publics themselves. In Benhabib's vocabulary, the corporation risks suppressing the otherness of each public. Thus, it is possible that seemingly identical interest claims are based on different, and potentially mutually conflicting, underlying values. Consequently, the corporation also must assume the standpoint of the concrete other.

To assume the standpoint of the concrete other requires the corporation to conceptualize all of its publics as being different in the sense that their interest claims may be based on different, and potentially mutually conflicting, underlying values. In Benhabib's (1992) vocabulary, the corporation must conceive of its publics as representing groups of people with irreducible differences (through adherence to the principle of egalitarian reciprocity) by focusing attention on what distinguishes them from one another

rather than on what they have in common. Because the corporation's publics are likely to adhere to different, and potentially mutually conflicting, underlying values, it is unethical to pursue the Habermasian ideal of a rationally motivated consensus. Such a consensus is likely to imply their transcendence whereby certain values are valorized over other potentially equally legitimate ones. Instead, the objective should be to achieve what Benhabib termed a mutual understanding of the otherness of each public.

Second, and equally important, Benhabib's (1992) reconsideration suggests that if the interactions between a corporation and its publics are to be considered genuinely open-ended and reflective, then the corporation must provide its publics with opportunities to apply multiple (syncretistic) modes of discourse such as public/institutional and private/noninstitutional ones. It is only when the corporation satisfies this obligation that its publics may apply modes of discourse suitable for the representation of their particular values. Yet, the corporation also must provide its publics with opportunities to apply a higher order (synthetic) mode of discourse whereby it is possible to mediate among those different modes of discourse. That is, whereas the application of different modes of discourse might provide the corporation and its publics with opportunities to articulate the values on which their interest claims are based, the application of a higher order mode of discourse might provide the means to subject salient differences among those values to rational-critical mediation. The application of such a higher order mode of discourse should be seen as a meta-value that is independent of the particular values to which the corporation and its publics subscribe. It might enable interactions that are aimed at achieving not a transcending common interest but rather a consensus on how to interact on what is in their common interest in an ethical manner.

When those ethical ideals are considered together, it should be clear why Benhabib's (1992) reconsideration of Habermas's (1990, 1993) discourse ethics is important to the practice of public relations. Most important, Benhabib's reconsideration provides a viable response to the ethical issue discussed in the introductory paragraphs of this chapter: Is it possible for a corporation to interact with its publics as groups of people with equal rights to have their interest claims represented within the corporation's internal decision-making processes while at the same time acknowledging that those interest claims are likely to be based on different, and potentially mutually conflicting, underlying values? From Benhabib's perspective, the corporation may successfully address this issue by simultaneously interacting with its publics in their capacity as generalized and concrete others. This would, in turn, require the corporation to conceptualize all of its publics as having equal rights to have their interest claims represented within its internal decision-making processes (in their capacity as generalized others) while at the same time conceptualizing each of its publics as having irreducible, yet legitimate, differences in values in need of representation (in their capacity as concrete others).

To require the corporation and its publics to articulate, rather than abstract from, the values underlying their interest claims not only represents a more ethical stance than the one endorsed by Habermas but also is likely to be associated with positive epistemic consequences because it is not associated with limitations as to the types of interest claims deemed suitable for representation within the corporation's internal decision-making processes.

THE CONCRETE OTHER AND THE PROBLEM OF SPATIO-TEMPORAL DISTANCIATION

The preceding discussion suggests that to simultaneously assume the standpoint of the generalized and the concrete other in terms of a moral conversation should be considered the ethical ideal for interaction between a corporation and its publics. Although this ideal might be worthy

of consideration, it is likely to be difficult to realize in practice. In an important sense, to assume the standpoint of the concrete other requires the corporation and its publics to be situated in the context of spatio-temporal co-presence, interacting with one another through face-to-face dialogue. Without the context of spatio-temporal co-presence, it is arguably difficult for the corporation to achieve a recognition of the otherness of each of its publics in all of their complexity. The modern corporation, however, is increasingly structured in such a way that it is situated at a distance from its publics, maintaining relationships with them through the application of different technical means of communication (e.g., the transnational or international corporation). Therefore, the basis on which publics may actively participate within the corporation's internal decision-making processes is increasingly based less on spatio-temporal co-presence and more on what Thompson (1995) termed *spatio-temporal distanciation.*

Mediated Interaction and Mediated Quasi-Interaction

The important question, then, is whether the corporation might be able to assume the standpoint of the concrete other vis-à-vis its publics in the context of spatio-temporal distanciation. To shed some light on this issue, it is useful to distinguish between two modes of interaction that Thompson (1995) termed *mediated interaction* and *mediated quasi-interaction.* Mediated interaction represents a dialogical mode of interaction, facilitated by technical media of communication such as letter writing and telephone conversations, that permits messages to be transmitted between participants who are situated in different spatio-temporal contexts. This mode of interaction is oriented toward specific others. Mediated quasi-interaction, on the other hand, represents a monological mode of interaction facilitated by media of mass communication such as newspapers, radio, and television. This mode of interaction is oriented toward an indefinite range of potential receivers.

Thompson's (1995) mediated interaction/ mediated quasi-interaction dichotomy is important from a public relations perspective. Specifically, it suggests that whereas both modes of interaction are problematic from the standpoint of concern with the concrete other, because the corporation and its publics are not situated in the context of spatio-temporal co-presence, mediated interaction offers the most potential for assuming this standpoint. This mode of interaction is both dialogical in character, permitting the corporation and its publics to engage in actual dialogues, and directed toward specific others, permitting a reciprocal recognition of individuating differences. Mediated quasi-interaction, on the other hand, is inherently problematic. This mode of interaction is both monological in character and oriented toward an indefinite range of receivers, for which reason it becomes difficult to assume the standpoint of the concrete other.

From a public relations perspective, the mediated interaction/mediated quasi-interaction dichotomy suggests that the corporation should carefully consider which modes of interaction to apply when interacting with publics. Specifically, it suggests that when the interest claims of the corporation and its publics differ in important respects, the corporation should engage its publics in mediated interaction. It is only through mediated interaction, or the conduct of actual dialogues, that the corporation might be able to achieve a complex understanding of its publics' particular interest claims and, especially, of how those interest claims conflict with its own. Alternatively, when the interest claims of the corporation and its publics do not conflict, it might be sufficient for the corporation to engage publics in mediated quasi-interaction.

Direct and Indirect Social Relationships

The application of mediated interaction is useful not only as a means of identifying important differences among the interest claims of the corporation and its publics but also as a means of establishing social relationships that resemble what Calhoun (1995) termed *direct social relationships*. Calhoun argued that a distinction should be drawn between the experiences gleaned from nonmediated interpersonal relationships (direct social relationships) and mediated mass communicational relationships (indirect social relationships) that are established when social actions affect others through the mediation of media of mass communication, interpersonal markets, or complex organizations. When social relationships are mediated, such as by media of mass communication, understandings of others are likely to be based not on a recognition of the nature of their relationships to oneself but rather on categorical differences. Although these categories may imply certain concrete modes of conceptualizing others, the abstract category is likely to take precedence.

Calhoun's (1995) direct/indirect social relationship distinction is important from a public relations perspective. Specifically, it suggests that although it might be possible for the corporation to establish direct social relationships with publics through the application of mediated interaction, the application of mediated quasi-interaction allows for the establishment only of indirect social relationships. Indirect social relationships are problematic because they make it difficult for publics to clearly perceive the nature of their relationships with the corporation.

Approximating the Ideal

Although it might be difficult for a corporation to assume the standpoint of the concrete other vis-à-vis its publics in an ideal sense, there is much the corporation can do in practice to approximate this ideal. Perhaps most important, it might be useful for the corporation to challenge entrenched ways of conceiving of its relationships with publics. Fundamental to such a reconception is the realization of a different way of understanding the purpose of engaging in interaction with them. Rather than conceiving of interaction as a means for successful self-expression, it might be useful for the corporation to conceive of interaction as a means for successful self-destruction. By interaction as self-destruction, I mean attempts on the part of the corporation to open itself up to its publics and, especially, to the various ways in which those publics would like to define their relationships. In practical terms, this would require the corporation to denaturalize and deneutralize ways in which it so far has conceived of its relationships with publics. Rather than considering those relationships to be natural in the sense of being given by nature or neutral in the sense of being free of underlying values, the corporation should acknowledge that those relationships might be defined more accurately as the results of numerous (value-laden) micro-interactions occurring on a day-to-day basis. By opening itself up to its publics, and by providing them with opportunities to challenge entrenched ways of defining their relationships, their interactions might over time become productive rather than reproductive. By productive interactions, I mean interactions that enable the corporation and its publics to produce new and more mutually satisfying relationships together rather than to reproduce old and unsatisfying ones.

CONCLUSION

Historically, discussions among public relations scholars about which ethical perspective should guide the practice of public relations have clustered around two mutually conflicting approaches: deontology and utilitarianism (L'Etang, 1996a). Whereas proponents of deontology argue that it is the intentions underlying an act that determine whether or not it should be considered ethical, proponents of utilitarianism argue that it is the consequences of an act that determine whether or not it should be considered ethical. Both perspectives, however, are problematic. The deontological approach is problematic because an assessment of the intentions underlying an act will by necessity be based on certain contestable values. The utilitarian approach is problematic because the consequences of an act are difficult to measure objectively.

Perhaps more important, neither the deontological nor the utilitarian perspective offers

much guidance as to how a corporation should interact with its publics as equal moral agents while at the same time acknowledging that those publics represent groups of people with irreducible differences. As the preceding discussion suggests, this particular issue has become increasingly important to consider because of the heterogenization of society and the associated emergence of societal groups with different, and potentially mutually conflicting, underlying values.

If public relations scholars were to address this important issue, then they might find it useful to turn to Habermas's (1990, 1993) discourse ethics for inspiration. As the preceding discussion suggests, Habermas's discourse ethics embodies discursive ideals in terms of which the interactions between a corporation and its public might be conducted in an ethical manner. Yet, Habermas's discourse ethics ultimately is unsuitable as the conceptual basis for a public relations ethics because it is based on an underlying conception of self-other relations that requires the corporation (as a self) to interact with its publics (as others) in their capacity as generalized others. This implies that both the corporation and its publics must abstract their interest claims from the underlying values on which they are based. Although this provides the corporation with opportunities to interact with publics in their capacity as equal moral agents, it does not allow for a recognition of individuating differences.

Benhabib's (1992) reconsideration of Habermas's (1990, 1993) discourse ethics succeeds in overcoming some of the weaknesses associated with Habermas's approach. Specifically, by arguing that one should simultaneously assume the standpoint of the generalized and the concrete other in terms of a moral conversation, Benhabib implied not only that the corporation should provide all of its publics with opportunities to participate within its internal decision-making processes but also, and equally important, that the corporation should attend to salient differences among its publics without attempting to transcend those differences in pursuit of a rationally motivated consensus.

CHAPTER 35

The Measurement of Ethics

Instruments Applicable to Public Relations

KATHIE A. LEEPER

■ The importance of ethical issues to public relations was articulated by Ivy Lee in 1906 in his "Declaration of Principles." Historically, the centrality of ethics has been recognized. In 1950, the Public Relations Society of America (PRSA) developed its first version of a Code of Ethics, a document that continues to be updated. In 1965, the International Public Relations Association also developed a code of ethics. This focus is essential because, as McElreath (1996) explained, "the hallmark of professionals is their adherence to a common set of values, principles, and loyalties—to a common set of ethical guidelines" (p. 5).

Surveys of businesses and business journals indicate that organizations and business increasingly have developed their own codes of ethics and have hired ethics officers to establish standards for what is right and wrong, or good and bad, within the organizations.

Paralleling the increased interest in ethics in business has been an increased interest in theory and research in public relations ethics. McElreath (1996) explained, "Public relations managers are being held to ever higher standards of ethics and accountability" (p. 4).

In response, organizations such as the PRSA have focused programs as well as entire conventions on ethics and credibility. Academically, numerous scholarly articles have been published on ethics in public relations. Descriptive and theoretical studies have been conducted to identify where the field is and to lay the foundation for where the field should be moving during the coming decades. Given the increasing emphasis on ethics, both practitioners and academics can benefit from awareness of tools available for the measurement of ethics.

One step in the process of applying ethical theory is the development of instruments to measure ethics. Such instruments enable researchers or practitioners to quantify differences among individuals as well as changes across time. The purpose of the present chapter is to identify instruments currently available to measure ethics from a public relations perspective. It presents the results of a survey of public relations research and business ethics conducted to identify the primary paper-and-pencil instruments developed and used predominantly to quantify ethics. Only those studies reporting development or testing of an instrument applicable to the public relations area are included in the discussion that follows. As a result of this study, practitioners will have a source for identifying instruments that they might want to employ, and researchers will be more likely to conduct studies comparing and contrasting these instruments.

SCOPE OF THE STUDY

To identify instruments available to measure ethics, I reviewed those studies in the public relations literature that used some type of paper-and-pencil instrument to quantify ethics. In addition, business research literature was reviewed for similar instruments in management and marketing. Eight separate instruments representing varying levels of sophistication and relationship to ethical theory were identified through this survey.

The instruments identified include the first edition of Allport and Vernon's *Study of Values* (Vernon & Allport, 1931; see also Allport, Vernon, & Lindzey, 1960), Crissman's (1942) instrument, Clark's (1966) questionnaire, Rokeach's (1973) terminal and instrumental value scales, Newstrom and Ruch's (1975) instrument to measure managerial ethics, Rest's (1979) Defining Issues Test, Harris's (1988) Business Practice Questionnaire, and Reidenbach and Robin's (1990) Multidimensional Ethics Scale. The chapter traces the historical development and use of each instrument.

EARLY WORK

In 1931, Allport and Vernon published the first edition of their *Study of Values* (Vernon & Allport, 1931; see also Allport et al., 1960). According to Vernon and Allport (1931), the Allport-Vernon scale was based on Eduard Spranger's work, "Types of Men," a 1928 English translation of the fifth edition of his work. Spranger's work identifed the basis that each in-

dividual uses in making evaluative judgments. This instrument provided a numeric representation of the relative prominence of six values—theoretical, economic, aesthetic, social, political, and religious—for each individual. The instrument "consists of a number of questions, based upon a variety of familiar situations, to which two alternative answers (in Part I) and four alternative answers (in Part II) are provided" (p. 236). The self-administered test resulted in a profile on each of the six values. Validity was assumed but not specifically tested.

The Allport-Vernon scale was used in 1933 and 1938 studies by Whitely designed to determine consistency in the value profile over 100 days in the first study (Whitely, 1933) and consistency over each of 4 years of college for a group of 84 students in the latter study (Whitely, 1938). In both studies, Whitely found "a relatively high degree of constancy of the mean scores for the successive administrations of the test" (Whitely, 1938, p. 406). This helped to demonstrate the reliability of the instrument and the consistency of individuals' value priorities.

Bender (1958) was able to retest Whitely's group of 84 individuals in 1956. Although he found consistency with the group's scores from 18 years earlier, he also found a "highly significant increase in religious value" (p. 41). His conclusion regarding this change was that "the temper of the times in which we live influences the religious value more than does the maturity of the men" (p. 45). The Allport-Vernon scale identified the primary value focus for evaluation but did not provide a basis for determining a level of ethics.

Crissman (1942) sought to study the moral judgments of college students through development of a 50-item Likert-type inventory based on "some relatively familiar and concrete situation(s) or item(s) of behavior" (p. 29). The purpose of this instrument was to indicate a general level of ethics. Respondents were asked to judge behavior in terms of "rightness" or "wrongness" on a scale of 1 to 10. Comparing responses from university students in 1929 and 1939, Crissman found a correlation of .963 when the items were compared for rank difference. As a result, the reliability of this questionnaire also was demonstrated; however, a specific relationship to a theoretical basis was not presented.

Extending Crissman's (1942) work, Rettig and Pasamanick (1959) compared student responses to scores obtained by Crissman. Their factor analysis of the same data resulted in six factors: Factor A, a general factor "of basic morality" (p. 860); Factor B, a group factor that "pertains to religious morality" (pp. 860-861); Factor C, a bipolar factor that "is family related" (p. 861); Factor D, a group factor that "pertains to a form of puritanical morality in condemnation of conduct that is in disrepute" (p. 861); Factor E, which "may involve an exploitative-manipulative, socially disengaged type of attitude" (p. 861); and Factor F, which "expresses an economic sense of morality" (p. 861). Results indicated that the items remained fairly consistent in ratings of rightness and wrongness between 1929 and 1958, again giving an indication of reliability.

Applying Crissman's (1942) work specifically to public relations, Wright (1985) modified some items "to present values more meaningful six decades after the instrument was first used" (pp. 53-54). Although he did not explain the methods used for classifying responses, the responses were "examined in terms of five seven-item scales measuring basic morality, economic morality, religious morality, basic honesty, and legal issues" (p. 54). His grouping of items under these categories, however, did not match with the factor analysis of Rettig and Pasamanick (1959).

Wright (1989) also conducted a factor analysis of the Crissman (1942) scale. It produced six factors that met the study's primary loading guidelines. He identified these as a socioeconomic morality, which included items such as arson, armed robbery, and falsifying income tax returns; a sense of religious morality, which included items such as not believing in God, committing suicide, and getting divorced; basic morality "such as honesty, law, treatment of others, and so forth" (p. 26); puritanical morality, which included items such as making huge profits and using birth control methods; a belief in basic social responsibility, which included not voting in primaries and elections and not giving money to charities when able to do so; and financial morality, which included selling below cost to crowd out a weaker competitor and charging interest above a fair rate when lending money.

Wright concluded that these six factors may define "the structure of moral values in the North American public relations person" (p. 31).

The two factor analyses (Rettig & Pasamanick, 1959; Wright, 1989) did not result in a clear-cut set of factors. Items that loaded on one factor in the initial analysis did not necessarily load in the second analysis. As a result, more specific work on the validity of this questionnaire might be needed.

USE OF CASE STUDIES

Clark (1966) developed a questionnaire to determine "the content of a personal ethical creed, the recognition or lack of recognition of moral parameters by the business executive" (pp. 84-85). He selected 11 cases to evaluate "the respondent's commitment to a specific ethical ideal" (p. 87) including commitment to "personal integrity and honesty . . . and to the observation of laws governing business activity" (p. 88). In addition, 7 cases evaluated responsibility for "ethical concern for the welfare of those to whom one owes no direct legal obligation and a concern for the responsibility of business to the community as a whole" (p. 88). The actual questionnaire set out 26 cases, and respondents were asked whether they approved, somewhat approved, somewhat disapproved, or disapproved of the action of a specific individual in each case. These responses represented a range "from the choice of personal gain through the choice of total support of the social value" (p. 134).

Harich and Curren (1995) used Clark's (1966) questionnaire to "compare current American business executives' ethical standards with those prevalent thirty years ago" (Harich & Curren, 1995, p. 58). They found that, in general, American business ethics "have remained relatively stable over the last three decades" (p. 66). Along with Clark's work to establish reliability and validity of the instrument, the authors' use of the instrument served to validate the appropriateness of the instrument 30 years later.

Rokeach (1973) suggested another way of looking at the issue. His work with values suggested that they act as "standards that guide on-going activities and of value systems as general plans employed to resolve conflicts and to make decisions" (p. 12). Rokeach's value survey, which alphabetically arranged a list of 18 terminal values and 18 instrumental values, enabled researchers to "make quantitative statements about the value priorities of a whole society and of various segments of society" (p. 323).

Using Rokeach's (1973) value survey, Heath (1976) studied changes in value structures as a result of situational differences. When provided with a specific scenario, participants significantly changed the rankings of certain value priorities consistent with various situational demands. Heath suggested that individuals may "respond to appeals and select a hierarchy of values which meets the situational exigencies and their intrapersonal needs and which accords with peer expectations" (p. 333).

Van Leuven (1980) used Rokeach's (1973) value survey to identify the value hierarchies of nine major interest groups that were involved in the Environmental Policy Act of 1969. Although he did not find that the survey adequately predicted attitude change, Van Leuven (1980) did find it to be beneficial "as an early warning device for gauging the impacts of particular policy alternatives on various interest groups" (p. 56).

In an attempt to explore construct validity of Rokeach's (1973) value survey, Weber (1993) studied the relationship between Rokeach's value survey and the stages of moral reasoning identified by Kohlberg (1981a). Weber (1993) found that "the association of these two theories provides an interactive, two-step conceptual framework where values express the individual's basic belief system as well as an operational process where the individual's basic value preferences are activated in a moral reasoning mode" (p. 456).

Finegan (1994) looked at the relationship between Rokeach's (1973) value survey and judging the morality of five ethical scenarios. She found that differences in the value hierarchies among individuals were related to differences in perceptions of targeted behaviors and in willingness to rectify an unethical situation.

In another instrument, Newstrom and Ruch (1975) surveyed literature for examples of possible ethical items. From this initial group, they developed a list of 17 factors "that seem[ed] to encompass all of the major forms of intra-organizational 'cheating'" (p. 30). Respondents evaluated each item on a 5-point Likert-type scale ranging from *very unethical* to *not at all unethical*. In addition, each respondent evaluated the extent to which "they thought their business *peers* would consider it unethical, whether they thought their *top management* would believe it to be unethical, how frequently *they* engaged in that behavior, and how frequently they believed their *peers* practiced that behavior" (p. 31, italics in original). Specific data on reliability or validity were not presented, nor was the relationship of the items to ethics theory specifically indicated.

Applying this instrument to public relations, Pratt (1991a) developed a questionnaire modeled on 12 of the 17 items from the instrument developed by Newstrom and Ruch (1975). Pratt (1991a) changed some items "minimally to make them applicable to public relations" (p. 148). Pratt's goal was to measure "the reported ethical beliefs and behaviors of practitioners . . . and compare their beliefs and behaviors with their perceptions of those of their peers and top management" (p. 145). He explained, "The instrument consisted of 12 items in each of three belief and two behavioral situations, and 12 items concerning the likelihood that management would take disciplinary action should an unethical behavior be discovered" (p. 148) as well as some background information for a total of 78 items. As with the Newstrom and Ruch scale, respondents were asked to indicate ethicality on a 5-point scale.

Based on the suggestion that "practitioners' perceptions of statements on *personal* and business ethics will indicate their ethics in *professional* situations," Pratt (1992, p. 261) factor analyzed the results from the preceding survey. He explored "the correlates and predictors of practitioners' self-reported beliefs about and behaviors in unethical situations" (p. 259) and found two factors: "passive beliefs about unethical situations . . ., activities [that] do not require active participation, only passive acceptance" and "beliefs about active, intentional, unethical situations" (p. 261). He suggested, "Practitioners' beliefs need to be ascertained; then, if change is necessary, programs should be targeted at beliefs" (p. 266).

Harris (1988) developed an instrument based on 15 short scenarios "presenting various ethical situations confronting today's business managers" (p. 32). Participants indicated their levels of approval or disapproval of each on a 5-point scale. In addition, participants were asked to identify "which of four ethical maxims best described their ethical reasoning process" (p. 32). Harris stated, "This approach measures ethical values across five separate constructs, generally named (1) fraud, (2) coercive power, (3) influence dealing, (4) self-interest, and (5) deceit" (p. 31). Data indicating means used to establish validity or reliability of the instrument were not presented.

In a follow-up study, Harris (1990) used his 1988 instrument to determine whether individuals at different levels of the organization demonstrated the same value priorities. The instrument demonstrated that gender, education, and tenure with the organization could be assessed for their impacts on ethical evaluations. He found that his instrument indicated that "top managers are observably less tolerant (more disapproving) of fraudulent practices than others within the organization" (p. 744). Tests to demonstrate construct validity were not included.

Jean Piaget and Lawrence Kohlberg are two of the most recognized experts in the study of moral development. Whereas Piaget focused on ethical development in childhood, Kohlberg developed a six-stage model of moral development that focused on adults. Thus, Kohlberg's work has been the basis for much of the research in business ethics. Rather than a paper-and-pencil test, he and his colleagues developed a standardized interview and scoring manual with acceptable reliability and validity (Colby et al., 1990). Although his work is important from a theoretical standpoint, it was not a paper-and-pencil test.

Rest (1979) developed a non-interview measurement instrument, the Defining Issues Test (DIT), based on an adaptation of the theoretical model of Kohlberg. The DIT consisted of six hypothetical dilemmas. For each, the participant checked whether a specified action should be taken or should not be taken (or whether he or she could not decide). For each situation, 12 considerations were listed for the participant to evaluate in terms of their importance in reaching a decision. The participant then ranked the four most important considerations (pp. 289-296). Support for the theoretical development of the instrument, as well as the reliability and validity of the instrument, was presented.

Elm and Weber's (1994) analysis of Rest's (1979) DIT and Kohlberg's (1981a) moral judgment interview compared what they identified as "the two primary means of assessing moral reasoning used today" (p. 354). They reaffirmed the reliability and construct validity of the two instruments and the fact that "both instruments positively compare to other measures assessing moral reasoning as well as numerous external criterion variables" (p. 352). This instrument would appear to offer the possibility for research specifically applied to public relations.

In another attempt to develop an instrument firmly grounded in philosophical literature of ethics, Reidenbach and Robin (1990) developed a scale based on what they identified as the "conceptual core" of "contemporary normative philosophies." They selected 33 items representing major concepts from those philosophies. Three scenarios were selected to represent ethical problems within a business setting. Results from their factor analysis were presented, as were the reliability and validity tests. The dimensions they discussed included a moral equity dimension, a relativism dimension, and a contractualism dimension. The factor analysis of the results identified the three dimensions and considered its strength to be that this instrument is a multidimensional ethics scale. As such, it recognized that ethical decision making often is based on more than one rationale and that "the importance of those rationales is a function of the problem situation faced by the individual" (p. 639).

In a refinement of Reidenbach and Robin's (1988) study, these same authors found that their multidimensional scale demonstrated "substantial reliability and validity for evaluating the perceptions of the ethical content of business activities" (Reidenbach & Robin, 1990, p. 649). Their findings suggested that "individuals tend to rely on a broad sense of moral equity dominated by concerns for fairness and justice, tempered by relativistic and social contract dimensions" (p. 649). Because the authors suggested that this instrument could "provide information as to why a particular business activity is judged unethical" (p. 650), it could provide valuable application to public relations.

Cohen, Pant, and Sharp (1993) extended Reidenbach and Robin's (1990) work. Using participants from across the United States and other countries in the accounting area, they demonstrated the applicability of the instrument to a wider group of participants and called for further research on specific adaptations.

CONCLUSION

This chapter has reviewed instruments currently available for the measurement of ethics in the public relations area. The instruments demonstrate several approaches to measuring ethics and increasing sophistication in measurement techniques. However, these instruments need further study. Significant research remains to be done in comparing and contrasting these instruments within public relations situations as well as in developing an instrument specifically focused on public relations. Additional work could study development of students' ethical understanding during their educational process, the bases for ethical choices among professionals, and the development of ethical understanding during a career. The suggestion by Reidenbach and Robin (1990) that their instrument could be used to identify how and why a public views a specific situation as unethical presents policy and communication implications. As our ability to quantify public relations ethics increases, we can better test and strengthen our theoretical approaches.

The instruments identified here should provide a basis for significant research in public relations ethics. This will improve our ability to identify that "common set of values, principles, and loyalties" or that "common set of ethical guidelines" that McElreath (1996) discussed as the "hallmark of professionals."

IN SEARCH OF BEST PRACTICES

Learning Best Practices From Experience and Research

ROBERT L. HEATH

■ Public relations is a practical applied discipline. To the extent that research and theory lose sight of that reality, they become dysfunctional. All of the sections of the handbook give attention to the principles that drive the application of professional practice. Section III is specifically devoted to that objective as it examines *best practices*. What can and should be done to perform or practice public relations in an effective, responsible, and ethical fashion? That question brings us to examine best practices that can be applied universally as well as to individual contexts of the practice.

The theme of best practices drives the discipline. Much of what is written, especially in the "professional" literature, centers on the question: What do we need to know to improve the ways in which we practice our profession and, thereby, increase our ability to influence outcomes on behalf of employers and clients? That crass theme might offend and frustrate some, but it is a reality that we cannot ignore, dismiss, or condemn.

Best practices evolve through experiences and judgments of leading practitioners. They may be defined and researched by practitioners and academics. Some best practices arise from the research and theory of academics. For this reason, it is in the practice where practitioners and academics ultimately meet one another.

This section would be stronger if it had a single contribution for each of the applied contexts that are part of professional practice. Accomplishing that end might require a handbook of its own. In response to the call for contributions, many proposals came in. Many proposals were accepted; some did not mature to completion. Some pieces on best practices were commissioned; some never were written. Some discussed topics that might not seem to be mainstream. But all applications of skills to contextual challenges define the nature of the discipline and urge us to better understand the myriad options for best practices.

Thus, this section tends to be more illustrative than definitive. The lines of analysis and the chapters presented in this section can demonstrate themes that give us reason to stop and consider what the best practices are for all of the contexts in which practitioners operate.

Some key best practices are featured in this section. They include structuring/planning the public relations function, crisis, community and other relationships, education, and similar applications.

The section begins appropriately with consideration of best practices in structuring and planning the public relations function. Drawing on his years of professional practice, Hutchins (Chapter 36) sheds light on the best practices that result in and arise from the creation of the corporate public relations function as a revenue center rather than a cost center. Hinrichsen (Chapter 37) describes the mechanics of agencies. She addresses the policies, procedures, and personnel issues that can differentiate success from failure for the agencies and persons who practice in them. Both of these chapters address the key issue: What needs to be done by practitioners to add value to the organizations they serve?

Hallahan (Chapter 38) addresses that question by examining the mix and strategic use of media. He makes many interesting points, one of which is the notion that although we are keen on developing relationships, we still need—because of, or in spite of, our sense of public relations—a strong insight into how to structure and plan public relations tactics to use media. Vital to the structuring and planning functions are audits—formative and evaluative assessments. Kazoleas and Wright (Chapter 39) offer insights into best practices for designing, using, and interpreting communication audits as a vital part of structuring and planning public relations. Their interest is the application of research and theory to better understand the communication needs of employees and to develop research tools that can assess those needs and an organization's ability to satisfy them.

Crisis has been a dominating topic in the recent search to develop best practices. Part of the incentive for that interest is driven by consultants who have prospered from the cottage industry of crisis planning and response. Media have helped to create that cottage industry. Academics and practitioners are intrigued by the nature of crisis that serves as an incentive to discover the best practices in crisis preparation, management, and response. Crises can threaten the viability and legitimacy of organizations.

The effort to understand the best practices of crisis response includes the need to define *crisis*. Not all media attention, even negative attention, is a crisis. Some organizations and industries do not like to use the term *crisis,* which suggests that they are or might be unprepared to respond appropriately and quickly. These persons often prefer the concept of *emergency response.* An emergency is something that an organization can anticipate and plan to respond to resolve appropriately and quickly. A crisis, by contrast, is an event that exceeds normal planning and truly is of the magnitude that the organization's legitimacy is on the line. In any event, lots of attention has been devoted to developing rationales and strategies for protecting the image and interest of organizations during difficult periods.

To address some of those issues, Fearn-Banks (Chapter 40) draws on the systems and symmetry literature to suggest how organizations should plan for and respond to media inquiries that interrupt the organizations' normal activities. Planning, practicing, and being proactive are central themes in the development of crisis best practices.

Carrying the theme of planning a step further, Olaniran and Williams (Chapter 41) suggest that the best crisis response depends on the foundation of looking for crises, planning for them, and communicating about them before they happen. That is a highly proactive stance.

Hearit's (Chapter 42) attention focuses more on the message strategies that can be employed during and after the crisis. He is interested in the rhetorical processes that occur around a crisis. Media reporters and critics of the event often try to portray the event with its most negative meaning. Organizations have options to use in response. Hearit suggests ways in which organizational spokespersons can engage with reporters and other critics in dialogue to frame the appropriate interpretation of the event.

That theme is brought to bear on issues of race causing crisis. Baker (Chapter 43) suggests that one reason why race matures into crisis is that business operations often are not designed to appreciate diversity in the interpretation of what could be offensive. Therefore, crisis-producing behaviors and policies result from this lack of sensitivity to cultural diversity. She suggests best practices that ask organizations to be willing to accept the existence of or potential for racial problems to become a crisis. Business managers and others in strategic planning and communication positions need to take the appropriate measures to avoid the crisis by doing the right thing.

A concept that is receiving increased attention in the literature is the virtue of creating relationships as part of public relations. That can become a buzzword that is not easily translated into practice. Moving us closer to a sense of the appropriate best practices, Wilson (Chapter 44) and Ledingham and Bruning (Chapter 45) suggest best practice strategies that are founded on research findings that can increase organizations' ability to create mutually beneficial relationships with key markets, audiences, and publics.

The practice of public relations has many universal best practices. Some, however, are tailored more narrowly and strategically to the specific relationship, information-sharing, collaborative decision-making, and persuasive influence requirements of certain types of organizations. One of those is education. When one thinks of the huge number of people engaged in various types of public relations, the practice in support of educational institutions might not readily come to mind.

Educational public relations requires many of the same best practices that are found to be useful for other organizations, according to Henderson (Chapter 46). They need to be sensitive to various routine situations as well as more unsettling ones. They need to be able to analyze the situations and needs of their constituents and to respond accordingly. In addition, practitioners are required to engage in media relations and crisis management planning and response. The ultimate goal is to create organizations that meet community expectations for the dissemination of education in ways that satisfy the needs of various constituents. Wise educational public relations practitioners see themselves as building collective goodwill for the institutions by positioning them to meet community constituent needs.

Educational organizations tend to be unwieldy structures despite the fact that people often think that they are monolithic and speaking with one voice. DeSanto and Garner (Chapter 47) address the difficulties that institutions of higher education have as they work to achieve internal communication unity as a first step toward communicating externally. Such unity is vital to their efforts to create and sustain relationships. External audiences, publics, and markets look to such organizations to speak with one voice and to present a consistent and agreeable persona. Viewed in this way, public relations not only can help the organization to achieve one voice but also can be the boundary spanner that allows the flow of information into and from the organization as relationships build and mature.

One unique need of educational institutions is to supply information about their sports programs. As Neupauer (Chapter 48) explains, for better or for worse, education and sports more often than not are a closely knit package. For this reason, the sports information director plays a key role in understanding what the community wants in the way of information about the sports program and providing it to build a bond or a relationship of goodwill between the community and its sports-minded constituents.

The presidency is as much, or even more, image than it is substance. To a large extent, that can be said for all of politics. Public relations is one discipline that helps to create image as well as exchange information with constituents. It is a means by which politicians can understand and appreciate the positions and interests of their constituents. McKinnon, Tedesco, and Lauder (Chapter 49) gathered data that give insights into the roles, purposes, and ethical performances of practitioners in support of politicians. They conclude that public relations is an indispensable part of the political process. As much as that is a blessing, it also is a mandate for careful stewardship.

In 1998, employees struck UPS, a well-managed organization that had achieved a high degree of employee satisfaction. One explanation of the union's success in mounting its strike was its willingness and ability to employ professional public relations. Hansen-Horn (Chapter 50) explores the role of public relations in labor relations. If corporate interests are prone to use public relations against unions, then unions are prudent to respond by employing their own professional public relations help. Such choices might polarize labor and management conflicts into hard-fought and unproductive battles. But if public relations can be a conflict-resolving, collaborative decision-making, and relationship-building practice, then it might manage this strife in the interests of the union; the corporation; and their markets, audiences, and publics.

The final context explored in this section is the best practices of the health care industry. That complex industry is fraught with marketplace and public policy arena challenges. Hetherington, Ekachai, and Parkinson (Chapter 51) argue that when practitioners employ best practices, they can make a difference in the future of members of the industry and build relationships with the stakeholders and stakeseekers who focus their attention on the health care industry. As is true of the practice for other types of organizations, practitioners need to understand the industry and the pressures it suffers. They need excellent communication skills, high ethics, and a commitment to building a positive future for the health care industry, its components, and the persons who turn to it for care.

Out of this section, one could generate a list of best practices. The reader might even expect a list to emerge and be "codified" at the end of this introduction or the section itself. One of the benefits of bringing the voice of so many interested advocates together is to give them the chance to agree and disagree. From that dialogue, each reader is encouraged to prepare his or her own list of best practices. In that regard, we may ask ourselves several questions. To what extent are certain practices universal? Are some unique to each context? Are we maturing in the list that emerges? In that regard, do we feature the best practices of communication that foster mutually beneficial relationships?

CHAPTER 36

A New Order for Public Relations

Goodbye Cost Center, Hello Profit Center

H. R. HUTCHINS

■ In its brief modern history, public relations essentially has paralleled the tumultuous growth of corporate America. From its flackery reputation earned during the Great Depression to its new role of strategic "relationship management" (Shayon, 1996, p. 7) during the 1990s, public relations has lived a confused history.

Gary Grates, chief executive officer (CEO) of communication specialists Boxembaum & Grates, called it the "maturation" of public relations (Grates, 1997, p. 3). During the 1960s and 1970s, Grates maintained that management called on public relations after a problem arose and asked "What do I say?" The focus was on words. During the 1980s, management progressed to asking public relations "How do I say it?" The focus was on spin. Today, Grates argued that public relations is being challenged with "What do I do?" The focus is on action (p. 3).

Now, with the dawn of the new millennium, public relations has finally arrived as "a management function concerned with the relationship between the organization and its external environment" (Nagelschmidt, 1982, p. 290).

Whereas Grates (1997) and Nagelschmidt (1982) aptly described significant evolutionary events, I would argue that there is yet another major bump to navigate on the road to maturation of public relations. It goes well beyond today's relationship role or the "What do I do?" focus on action. The new question is "How do I add value?" My premise is that today's public relations organization will not survive as an expense or overhead cost in the new corporate business model. The new business model demands that public relations be accountable—that it actually contribute to the net income of the business. More to the point, in the new business order, public relations cannot exist or survive as a cost center. It must become a profit center.

That is what is happening at Shell Oil Company in the corporate public relations area. Since 1995, Shell's public relations function has been transforming—no past tense here because it still is evolving—from a traditional corporate expense to running as a business. As manager of corporate communications, responsible for a broad range of internal and external communi-

445

cations programs, I find myself right in the thick of it.

Our transformation had its genesis in the trauma of a major Shell restructuring in 1991 when deregulation and market forces drove profits to an all-time low—$21 million net income for a company with more than $20 billion in assets. During the subsequent 3 years, improved operating performance, restructured assets (including a workforce reduction from 33,000 to 22,000 employees), and selective new investments helped to lift Shell back to respectable profitability. But it still was not enough.

The winds of change worldwide continued to increase in force with intensified competition, new technology, globalization, and rising societal expectations. When Phil Carroll, a veteran Shell operating and administrative executive, assumed the presidency in 1994, he put it very simply: "Change is not an option if we [Shell] are to survive and prosper in the new global marketplace" (Staff, 1994, p. 3).

And change we did. Shell, not unlike the other major integrated oil companies, was characterized as a hierarchical, asset-based organization. Executive vice presidents, reporting to the CEO, led the upstream (exploration and production), downstream (manufacturing and marketing), and administrative functions. Decision making was top-down, and information essentially cascaded from senior management to lower levels (Figure 36.1).

Carroll and a new Leadership Council succeeded the traditional corporate board of directors. The Leadership Council was formed to provide forums for Shell's senior leaders to discuss areas of mutual interest and to nurture the transformation across the company. In turn, they introduced a new governance model emphasizing independent business units with individual boards of directors. Four new independently operated companies were formed: Shell Exploration and Production Company (SEPC), Shell Oil Products Company (SOPC), Shell Chemical Company (SCC), and Shell Services Company (SSC). Each operating company had its own CEO and board of directors with the freedom to run, and the accountability for running, its business as an independent entity.

In addition to the principal businesses, the tax, legal, planning, finance, human resources, and public relations organizations were restructured into four professional firms designed to provide services to the corporate center, to the businesses, and to each other.

The new governance model emphasized less command and control and more shared responsibility and individual accountability. Shell's organizational structure began to look more like a constellation of alliances as the businesses' new independence led to a number of joint ventures and partnerships with industry kin such as Mobil, Texaco, Amoco, and Exxon (Figure 36.2).

As more and more joint ventures were formed, the "glue" bonding these "satellites" together were Shell's mission, vision, and core values. Briefly, Shell's mission is to excel in the oil, gas, and petrochemical and related businesses in the United States and, where Shell adds value, internationally. We set our sights high. Our vision is to become the premier company in the United States by the year 2002 with sustained world-class performance in all aspects of our business.

If "premier" is our destination, then our core values are the guides that will get us there. As part of our transformation, we identified five values—belief in people, trustworthiness, excellence, innovation, and a sense of urgency—as guiding principles powerful enough to lead us to our destination.

So, where did public relations fit within Shell's new framework of a networked community? For better or for worse, public relations in 1994 became part of one of the four professional firms, specifically Planning, Finance, and Investment Services (PF&IS). Why with Shell's corporate planners and number crunchers and not with the CEO's office or as a stand-alone firm? That is a good question, and one that still is being debated today. But that is a chapter for another book. The important point is that public relations and all other former corporate staff cost centers suddenly were thrown into a whole new world and were told to run essentially as a business. The services of the firms were to be market based, with each of Shell's businesses deciding the range and quantity of services it wished to use and pay for. The firms would bill for their ser-

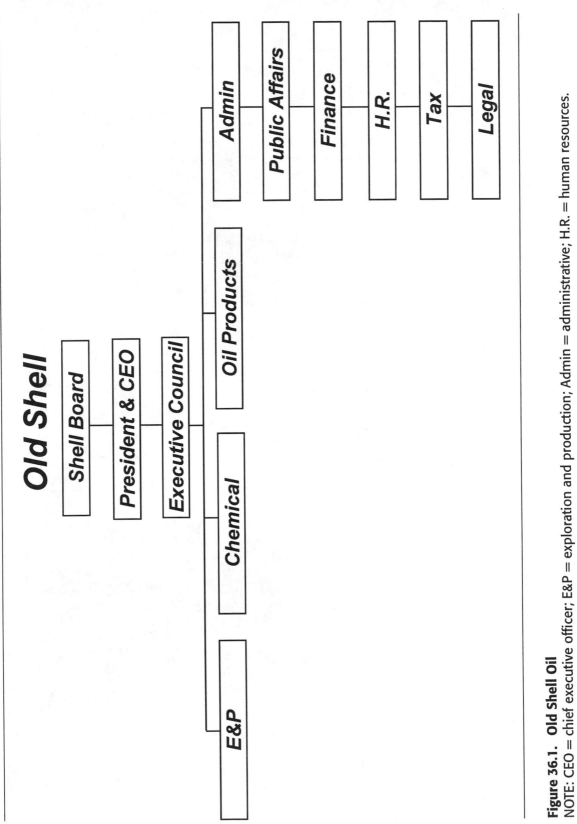

Figure 36.1. Old Shell Oil
NOTE: CEO = chief executive officer; E&P = exploration and production; Admin = administrative; H.R. = human resources.

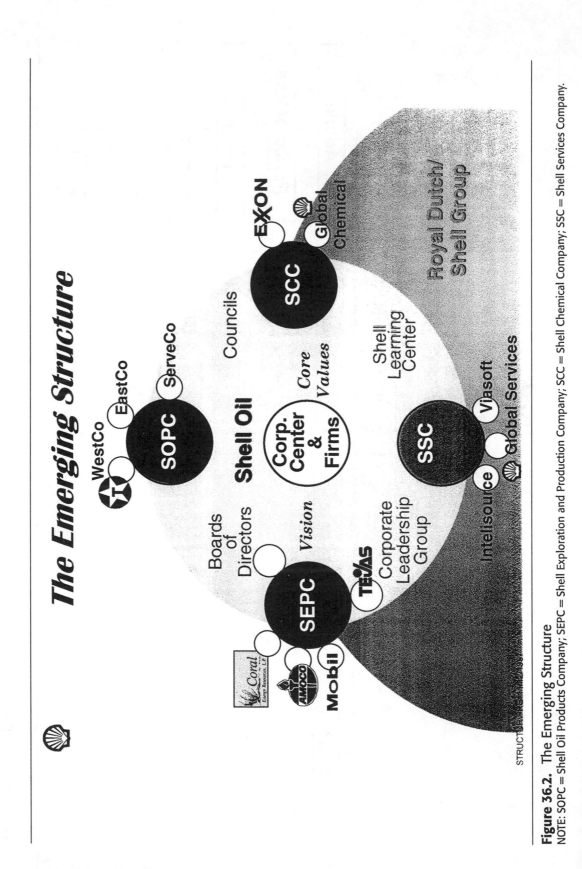

Figure 36.2. The Emerging Structure

NOTE: SOPC = Shell Oil Products Company; SEPC = Shell Exploration and Production Company; SCC = Shell Chemical Company; SSC = Shell Services Company.

vices on an hourly basis at rates competitive with independent professional firms.

For public relations, we were told that to survive in the new Shell, we must add value to the bottom line and be profitable. No longer could the publication editor, the community relations manager, or the media relations specialist simply wait for the next business project to come across the transom. The reality of Shell's new governance model gave the businesses the freedom to seek the most cost competitive and highest quality work wherever they could find it, inside or outside of Shell. No longer were any of Shell's businesses or professional firms required to use the company's in-house public relations or creative services. We would have to compete for the business.

For Shell public relations, running as a business meant establishing a value proposition and setting financial beacons such as revenue and profitability growth targets. Identifying the value proposition was essential. In the old cost center or services environment, public relations value was measured by the number and type of communication tools or projects developed such as the amount of media coverage or column inches garnered for the company's latest accomplishment. Today, Shell's public relations value proposition means that we will help the businesses and professional firms to meet their respective business objectives by providing innovative, cost-effective communications and public affairs resources. As for financial beacons, annual target minimums were set at 10% revenue growth and 12% net income before taxes.

It did not take much of a leap for the leadership level of Shell's public relations group to recognize that if we were being told by management to run as a business, then we had best reconstruct ourselves in the image of a successful public relations business in the external market.

The first place that public relations looked for best practices was our own backyard—the corporate sector. Surely, we were not the only corporate public relations group faced with the challenge of being a profit center rather than a cost center.

We found AT&T's Creative Services Group, an industry pioneer in making corporate public relations activities more bottom line oriented. Formed back in 1989, Creative Services is a stand-alone part of AT&T's public relations organization. It operates as a full-cost recovery business, not to make a profit but just to recover costs or break even. AT&T's approach was not consistent with what Shell's management was asking us to be.

Dick Malloy described the evolution of U.S. West's communications group as "having to win business in head-to-head competition with outside firms, and we had to generate enough revenue to cover our expenses" (Malloy, 1998, p. 33). Again, this was not to make a profit but just to recover costs or break even.

Several years and countless phone calls and benchmarking visits later, we still are looking for a corporate equivalent of the successful professional public relations firm that measures success by revenue growth as well as profitability.

With no best practices success from the corporate sector, we turned to the professional public relations agency/counselor side of the business. The Burson-Marstellers and Hill & Knowltons of the world certainly know how to run like a business and make handsome profits. After several months of extensive information-sharing sessions with national, regional, and even boutique agencies, we had the needed answers to reconstruct Shell's public relations organization to run as a business.

Within the PF&IS firm, we became the Communications and Reputation practice area with 45 partners, not employees, dedicated to enhancing Shell's image by providing diverse communication services and products to our customers. Our major business service lines include community and constituent corporate center relations and CEO support, corporate communications, investor relations, media relations/monitoring, and philanthropic initiatives. We used market-based rates for setting individual partner fees for professional services including markups for pass-through items such as outside printing and production expenses. Our customer billing rates range from $60 per hour for administrative-type services to $350 per hour for senior service line managers. Our average billing rate across all 45 partners is approximately $150 per hour. All partners are required to record their time on a computer-based timekeeping program, and each partner is expected to bill daily at least 70% of his or her time to a revenue/income-producing activity. We have an operating plan and monthly profit-and-loss statements that essentially mirror Shell's corporate operating plan.

We measure success through the use of value drivers. In the purest sense, a value driver is a measurement of work output relative to financial results or the ratio of output (product or service) over input (billable hours). In a simpler sense, think of it as miles per gallon (MPG) for the gallons of gasoline that one puts into his or her car. One puts gallons in and expects a certain MPG in return—input/output. Suddenly, one notices that MPG is going down. Something has changed—most likely the value. What is causing or driving it? Analyze and fix it.

Is our still evolving profit center transformation working? Although Carroll has retired and there is a new leadership structure in place at Shell, my answer is a resounding *yes* in several respects. Most obvious is our profitability. Since our official start in 1995 as a practice area, we have met or exceeded revenue and profitability targets. More important, we have learned to be adaptable, accountable, and competitive. No longer do we sit idly by, waiting for the next assignment to come our way unsolicited. All 45 partners now embrace a "client obsession" attitude (Duhon, 1998, p. 2) that manifests itself in being so tuned in to our customers that we know what they want or need before they know themselves.

This brief look at Shell's journey to run its public relations organization as a business is intended as a wake-up call. The restructuring of corporate America never is over. It is just a matter of when and how extensive the next downsizing will be. I have argued that today's public relations organization will not survive as an expense or overhead cost in the current corporate business model. I believe that public relations professionals who do not take the initiative to add value—not just recovery of costs but also *profit*—will end up on the junk heap of last year's model. The implications for the public relations profession are enormous. In the future, we will face some radical new demands about how we think about our roles and about the leadership role that public relations can play in helping corporate institutions evolve to be successful in a global economy. We are going to have to rethink and reinvent many of the traditional organizational ways for public relations as well as the skill and knowledge base that support the structures. If public relations can shed its past soft and squishy image and be recognized for adding value to the bottom line, then it will earn a legitimate place at the table with the dominant coalition.

CHAPTER 37

Best Practices in the Public Relations Agency Business

CATHERINE L. HINRICHSEN

In a parallel universe, one probably can find a public relations agency where the clients call every day to say "thank you," the employees cannot wait to get to work in the morning, and the firm's financial officers whistle merrily as they look at the books. But here in our world, it is tough to make all of those things happen simultaneously. The best agencies balance the need to provide excellent client service with the demands of running a successful business.

In this chapter, I look at some of the best practices in the public relations agency environment. First is a discussion of what it is like to work in a public relations agency. Just as it is tough to describe the typical agency—there are thousands of them—the typical agency job might not exist. But there are some common factors among agencies; they tend to be fast-paced, exciting, demanding, and challenging.

THE AGENCY: A LOOK INSIDE

In rows of cubicles, smartly dressed young people talk to journalists on the phone, tap at their computer keyboards, or pore over spreadsheets. Occasionally, one hears running feet in the hallway, especially if it is time for express mail pickup. Meanwhile, behind closed doors, the senior counselors advise clients on a crisis, a pending merger, or a major shareholder announcement. This is a public relations firm. But so is this: a desk and computer in the corner of a living room, where a young woman in pajamas sips coffee and reads her e-mail.

Public relations agencies differ in size and structure, but they have this in common: The public relations firm (or agency) consists of one or more public relations professionals whose purpose is to counsel others in their communication and relationship-building activities in exchange for a fee.

The companies that agencies represent are known as the *clients*, and a client's program or project is called the *account*. People in agencies often use the term *the client* when referring to both the client company and the contact person. The senior-level people on the account might prefer to be called *counselors*.

Companies seek public relations counsel for several reasons, ranging from the need for senior-level counseling to the need for extra people

451

to get the work done. The firm generally has expertise that the clients have no access to internally. Clients might seek fresh ideas and an objective outlook. Some also might appreciate the prestige of being affiliated with a respected firm (Wilcox, Ault, & Agee, 1989).

Practitioners differ on whether the term *agency* or *firm* is more appropriate. To some, *agency* refers to a place where advertising accounts are handled, whereas a public relations company is a *firm*. Many use the terms interchangeably. Some object to the use of *agency* because they believe that public relations is a management counseling function that cannot be delegated to others, as the term *agent* or *agency* implies (Wilcox et al., 1989).

Agencies are prospering. Fee income for the nation's 50 largest public relations agencies rose 10.3% in 1997 to a record $1.71 billion (Elliott, 1998). The trend is for most public relations activities to be handled by firms (Seitel, 1998). That makes agencies a hot prospect for jobs (Goldman, 1998).

The Advantages of Working in an Agency

If public relations is seen as a glamorous field, then public relations firms may be viewed as "Glamour Central." There can be prestige and excitement, and there always is a fast pace. Some other advantages are the following.

Variety. One is likely to hear that an advantage of working in an agency is the variety. But this is another example of how agencies can differ. An account person might be assigned to anything from one major account to a dozen small clients, which might be too much variety. A large account might have a program that changes little from year to year—not much variety there.

Big budgets. In agencies, the program budgets can be larger than in other settings, so the account person can get experience on tactics that are cost-prohibitive elsewhere. Satellite media tours, video news releases, syndicated feature stories, photo shoots, splashy publications, videoconferencing, large-scale special events—these are big-budget items that agencies are more likely to handle than are nonprofit organizations or small to medium-sized corporations.

Team of professionals. Perhaps the greatest advantage is being able to work with peers who understand public relations. In this collection of professionals, there always is someone to learn from, even for the "top dog." Many of the most skilled practitioners work in agencies, and the collegial atmosphere can be stimulating and motivating.

The Disadvantages of Working in an Agency

On the flip side, agency life also can be rigorous, stressful, and demanding. Some of the issues are the following.

The long hours. People in an agency usually work late in the day and on weekends. There are two reasons for this: client service and income generation. First, one's responsibility is to the client, and that means if the client calls with a request as an agency person is about to leave for the day, then the agency person probably will stay late. Second, the public relations firm earns its money by billing the client based on the time that the account team devotes to the client. Therefore, each account person is expected to work a specific number of billable hours—time that can be billed to the client—and this often is 7.5 to 8 hours per day. That means time spent working directly for the client, not time going to staff meetings, reading e-mail, attending seminars, taking that elusive lunch break, or having chats at the water fountain. As a result, it is tough to work "9 to 5" in an agency.

Pressure. The agency environment is like a pressure cooker, with what can seem like constant hammering to stay billable, produce excellent work under a time crunch, stay on budget, satisfy the client, and manage the ever-changing work-load. And this can lead to turnover.

Turnover. Agencies tend to have high turnover rates. This could be attributed to resignations over the working conditions or, as some agency presidents believe, the high demand for people with agency experience. Then again, some agencies must let people go if they lose big accounts. An agency might not be the right place for someone who needs job security, although few jobs offer great stability these days (Seitel, 1998).

How Agencies Make Money

An excited young college student came back to his public relations class after an agency visit and reported, "The pay is really good in an agency. The entry-level people make $65 an hour!" Actually, the entry-level person at that agency had a $65 per hour *billing rate*—not salary. There is quite a difference.

Many agencies earn their money by billing clients on an hourly basis. Each employee has an hourly billing rate, and for each hour the employee works on behalf of the client, the company charges the client. The hourly rate should be based on the employee's annual salary plus benefits, the agency's overhead (cost of doing business, such as office space), and the agency's desired profit percentage (Croft, 1996). Therefore, that envied entry-level salary probably is only one-fifth to one-fourth of that $65 per hour billing rate.

Agencies may use timesheets to track employee hours. Each employee fills out a timesheet periodically, indicating the number of hours worked on each account. At the end of the billing period, the client is billed for the number of hours multiplied by the billing rates for each person plus out-of-pocket (non-time) costs for travel, telephone calls, and other expenses. There also might be markup charged for printing and other outside vendor expenses.

Other payment arrangements include monthly retainers for counseling only and a flat rate per project.

How Agencies Use Research

Research is fundamental to the public relations program, and agencies typically use it in three ways: to recruit a new client, to develop a custom program for the client, and to evaluate the program's success.

During the new business pitch. The firm approaching a potential new client should do its homework first and learn the prospect's business, industry, markets, and competitors (Croft, 1996).

In developing the new public relations plan. It is particularly important to establish a benchmark of attitude or behavior among target publics before the plan is implemented. Later, the results can be measured by comparing the target audience's attitudes or behaviors to the benchmark data. The agency also might undertake a research project as a tactic that serves as an end product and use the research results as an announcement that generates public attention (Booth, 1988; Hicks, 1994).

As evaluation. To measure results, the agency should conduct research to determine behavioral change. Research, the desired starting and ending point, is largely dependent on the budget. Unless a public relations firm has its own research department conducting up-to-date consumer research, the cost of research is built into the budget, meaning that the client pays for it. It is the account team's responsibility to persuade the client of the value of investing in that research.

The New Business "Pitch": How Agencies Recruit Clients

In the changing business world, few successful companies can sit back on their laurels serving the same clients year after year. Budget cuts, mergers, and poor client-agency relationships can cause agencies to lose clients. To remain viable, agencies need to replace lost clients by soliciting "new business."

The pitch. Working on a new business "pitch" can be exhausting but exhilarating. Some agencies allot time during the workday to new business, whereas others expect staff to work on it after hours. Depending on the account, the business might be brought in with a simple phone call or lunch meeting, or it might require an all-out presentation that costs the firm hundreds of thousands of dollars and thousands of hours.

After all the work, the account might go to someone else—or the investment might pay off. Of course, the best—and most cost-effective—way in which to bring in new business is to increase the work that one does for existing clients. Happy clients often will increase their budgets or agree to new programs.

THE ROLE OF THE AGENCY IN THE PUBLIC RELATIONS FIELD

Some Historical Highlights

The nation's first public relations firm was the Publicity Bureau, organized in mid-1900 by former newspaperman George Michaelis (although the firm's chief function was publicity, not full-service public relations). A few years later, in 1904, Ivy Lee and George Parker founded what is commonly credited as the first true public relations firm (Cutlip, 1994).

Some other major agencies of the 20th century include Carl Byoir and Associates (purchased by Foote Cone & Belding and later Hill & Knowlton), Burson-Marsteller (founded in 1953 and today the world's largest public relations firm), and Ketchum Public Relations and Hill & Knowlton (the only two major public relations agencies created during the post-World War I era to survive today).

The most important sole practitioner was Edward Bernays, one of the most influential figures of the 20th century (Cutlip, 1994). Bernays is thought to be the first to use the term *counselor* to describe his services (Burson, 1989).

Ethical Issues in the Public Relations Agency

Public relations firms confront ethical dilemmas on a regular basis. It often is said that public relations people cannot do a good job unless they believe in what they do. The public relations person must go to work every day willing to resign from a job or an account over principle (Croft, 1996; Lesly, 1998). This is especially true in an agency. The account person must believe in the client. Not everyone can choose what accounts he or she would like to work on, but if there is a client to which an account person objects on moral grounds, then that person should make the objections known and should not be forced to work on that account.

Some believe that everyone is entitled to public relations representation. That has led some agencies down a dangerous path. Even the Nazi Germany government sought the advice of American public relations experts, Lee and Byoir, to help moderate growing anti-Nazi sentiments in the United States during the late 1930s; the counselors were heavily criticized (Cutlip, 1994). Public relations professionals are expected to act for the good of the public, so when agencies accept controversial clients, a public outcry can be expected.

High-profile, controversial accounts. In perhaps the icon of a controversial ethical issue involving an agency, the major international firm Hill & Knowlton came under fire for bending the truth so skillfully that it might have helped bring about U.S. participation in the Gulf War. In 1990, Hill & Knowlton's office in Washington, D.C., represented a group called "People for a Free Kuwait," which had been presented as a grassroots citizen group but actually was 90% funded by the Kuwaiti royal family. Among the most controversial strategies was the use of congressional testimony by a teenage girl named Nayirah, who claimed to have witnessed Iraqi atrocities such as removing babies from incubators. Later, it was revealed that Nayirah was the daughter of the Kuwaiti ambassador to the United States and had not even been in Kuwait during the time of the alleged atrocities (Lipman, 1992). Hill & Knowlton's exact role in this deception is not clear, but in the aftermath, the new chairman and chief executive officer acknowledged that although everyone might be entitled to representation, Hill & Knowlton is not obligated to represent anybody (Shell, 1994a). The same is true of any firm of integrity.

Code of Ethics. The Public Relations Society of America (PRSA, 1998a) has a 17-part Code of Professional Standards, which guides its more than 18,000 members in their practices. Several are particularly relevant to agencies. Members are instructed to conduct their professional lives in accord with the public interest, to identify publicly the clients for whom they are working, to avoid representing clients that appear to support announced causes but actually serve others, to scrupulously safeguard confidences and privacy rights of clients, and to avoid serving competing or conflicting clients.

The Changing Agency Environment

The public relations agency environment has undergone great change during the past 10 years. Trends affecting agencies today include the following.

International focus. Because the world is "shrinking" with widespread use of electronic communication, agency practitioners often find themselves looking beyond the U.S. borders. The agency might have overseas clients or clients based in this country who do business overseas. To serve this global client base, many agencies have offices in countries around the world. They send employees from U.S. offices to work overseas or recruit from among the local profession-

als. An agency might even be owned by a foreign company. As of 1998, four of the top five U.S. firms were owned by European companies.

Ad agency ownership. Another trend is ownership of public relations firms by large advertising agencies. Of the top 10 U.S. public relations firms, 7 are owned by advertising agencies, including Burson-Marsteller, Hill & Knowlton, and Porter Novelli (O'Dwyer, 1997). This is seen as detrimental by some counselors, who are concerned over what they see as the danger of ad agencies placing too much emphasis on marketing functions (Lesly, 1998) and applying financial pressures that can result in moral lapses (Cutlip, 1994). Others see this as a natural evolution toward integrated marketing communications.

Virtual account teams. Technology is bringing new options. Far-flung specialists are united by the Internet, so agencies can link clients with counselors in other offices ("Corporations Leading," 1997; Shell, 1994b; Stateman, 1998).

Outsourcing. Corporate downsizing is making its mark on the agency scene as well. Many senior executives are setting up shop after losing high-level corporate public relations positions. Opportunities for freelancers can abound in this environment as well. In fact, a young person starting out in public relations today should expect to have at least one period of working as an entrepreneur (Goldman, 1998). The trend toward hiring outside consultants, or *outsourcing*, is expected to continue well into the new millennium (Bisbee, 1998).

BEST PRACTICES IN THE AGENCY ENVIRONMENT

The best agencies are those that can provide excellent client service while operating as successful businesses and providing enriching work environments. Here are a few practices that keep top agencies (both large and small) successful.

Client Service

The account person must be devoted to client service, keeping the client's best interests in mind and sharing the client's passion for business goals. Harold Burson, founder of Burson-Marsteller, put it this way: "When someone sticks the client with an icepick, I bleed" (Burson, 1989).

Maturity and good judgment are crucial. Account people must represent themselves, the firm, and the client professionally on and off the job.

It is an ongoing challenge to continually demonstrate the firm's value. Consequently, the account team constantly needs to work to impress the client with its savvy, industriousness, brainpower, and wisdom.

Striving for perfection is an overarching goal. Here is a good reason why: In a survey of nearly 2,300 clients who had fired their agencies, the number-one reason cited was "sloppy work" ("Survey Sheds," 1996). That is amazing. It is a great reminder that when the client pays a lot of money for high-quality work, the client expects flawless execution—better than what the client is capable of doing internally—and that even minor errors can erode confidence.

Sometimes, conflict between the interests of the client and those of the firm cannot be resolved, and the result is a parting of the ways. A firm might resign because of demands for service that make the account unprofitable, unsavory client practices (Lesly, 1998), unrealistic client expectations, or client mistreatment of account people.

But in the best-case scenario, the agency-client relationship is so strong that it makes history. For example, the handling of the Tylenol crisis in 1982 was the result of the bond between Johnson & Johnson and its firm, Burson-Marsteller. This case is widely recognized as one of the most important in the history of the practice of public relations (Seitel, 1998), and the goodwill garnered by the public relations practitioners in that case can affect the perception of the entire industry.

Nurturing the Client-Agency Relationship

The ability to build a strong client-agency relationship is one of the most important skills a practitioner can offer (Canfield, 1998). As Burson (1989) noted, "I can't overemphasize the need for developing a strong personal relationship." Free-flowing communications between agency and client help to make the relationship operate more smoothly (Seitel, 1995).

In the ideal agency-client relationship, there is mutual respect, trust, understanding of the client's needs, and willingness to compromise on both sides. How can one find that ideal relationship? Some senior counselors have shared the following advice.

From counselor Marilyn Hawkins of Hawkins & Company in Seattle, Washington, come the following tips for a being a "great consultant":

1. Start off by relaxing; this sets a tone of confidence and collaboration.
2. Never complain to the client about how busy you are.
3. Always listen before you talk.
4. Determine early on how the client wants to be updated.
5. Learn how to disagree agreeably.
6. Get a grip on your ego; let the client discover how smart you are on its own.

And finally, "Your clients will love you . . . only after they trust you . . . only after they respect you . . . only after they see your competence" (Hawkins, 1996, p. 5).

To this list of qualities, add these from a survey of Fleishman-Hillard staff by Anne Sutton Canfield, senior vice president of the firm's office in Kansas City, Missouri. The top five client service practices were the following (there was a tie for first place):

1. Keep your commitments.
1. Get results; meet or exceed objectives.
3. Stay in regular contact and keep the client informed—no surprises.
4. Provide strategic insight and counsel.
5. Have a "no problem" attitude. (Canfield, 1998)

"This is a problem-solving business," said Burson, who added that the counselor's main objective is to identify and deal successfully with problems. Burson (1989) also advised taking advantage of opportunities, developing a set of options and a range of their upsides and downsides, being able to get up to speed fast on a problem, being able to listen, and knowing the client's business.

Another useful piece of advice: "Underpromise, overdeliver" (Gaschen, 1998).

Not Just Fulfilling Requests: Counseling

The most valuable commodity that the agency can offer is its counsel—the ability to advise the client on the proper course of action. The ability to counsel comes with experience, but it also means being able to sift through issues and information and to make a recommendation. Even the most junior-level staff member can demonstrate this skill.

Sometimes, counseling means being able to persuade a client that is not open to what the agency has to say. When the agency and client disagree, then the agency must decide whether to try pushing to persuade—or challenging—the client. It takes a delicate touch to know when to take that stand. Some clients view the agency as "order takers," whose people they can tell what to do as if they were making a selection in a diner. They resist the agency's advice. As one account

supervisor at a northwestern agency put it, "I don't think this client likes to be challenged; I don't even think she likes *expertise!*" The client merely wanted the agency to carry out her requests regardless of whether those actions were in the client's best interest.

But ideally, the client appreciates and draws on the agency's level of expertise and expects the agency to provide direction. An account supervisor at Burson-Marsteller's New York headquarters office kept a hand-scrawled note taped to her wall: "Recommendations, not options. Take risks!" This was an admonition from her group vice president after the team had submitted a draft program with a menu of ideas rather than strong recommendations. She urged her account team to propose a carefully analyzed course of action tailored to the client rather than listing the evening's specials.

It Is a Business too

Clients might be quite delighted if their firm provided excellent service and then never sent a bill. But such a firm would not be able to provide that great service for long. Therefore, a firm also must focus on profitability. According to A. C. Croft, author of a book on running a successful agency, "A PR [public relations] firm also has only one purpose [with client service being its main function]: to achieve and maintain levels of income that will assure a reasonable financial return to its owners and fair and competitive compensation to its employees" (Croft, 1996, p. 7). Croft's book is filled with excellent information on agency profitability and is highly recommended.

A Great Place to Work

Agencies are notorious for turnover. Most clients are unhappy when they are constantly handed from one account person to another; they believe that they always are spending money to bring new people up to speed. Keeping employees satisfied is key to the firm's ability to provide client service.

Employee training is a must, especially on account management. In addition, the employee must learn about the client's business. An agency that is willing to cover the cost of sending an account person to an industry trade show or other educational opportunity on behalf of the client creates immense goodwill.

New business presentations are another great way for a junior staff person to learn more about the business, according to Sue Bohle of The Bohle Company in Los Angeles. Sometimes, a firm is reluctant to involve its younger staff, especially in the face-to-face presentation itself, when there is greater-than usual concern about the impression that the agency makes and when a slip of the lip can cost the agency the account. But, said Bohle, "Any risk to the agency is far outweighed by the benefits. Meanwhile, the young person hears how the agency presents itself, gets exposure to a prospective client, and gains self-assurance for the next situation. The sophisticated client also appreciates seeing the whole team, from senior to junior members" (personal communication, June 2, 1998).

Some companies try to increase job satisfaction with experiments designed to increase employee satisfaction. A Los Angeles firm, Laer Pearce and Associates, combined practices such as "flextime" with simpler but effective tactics such as "sleep-in passes" as a reward for hard work or late-night meetings, early paydays, and casual dress day every day (Pearce & Martin, 1998).

Flextime and part-time hours are increasingly popular. Some firms, such as Ketchum Public Relations, have found that valued female employees appreciate part-time schedules that enable them to spend time with their children. Working Mother magazine called public relations one of the 10 hottest careers for working women and featured a Ketchum account supervisor on its cover ("Advice," 1998).

Now that home office resources are affordable and convenient, agency employees also can work from home and still keep their visibility with the client.

It is a great time to look for work in a firm.

GETTING AND KEEPING AN AGENCY JOB

Finding an Agency Job

Here are some ways in which one can put himself or herself in a better position for an agency job:

- Do informational interviews. Ask good questions. What are the job responsibilities for someone at my level? (Ask to see a job description, if available.) How many accounts do your employees work on? What is your turnover rate for both clients and employees? What happens when you lose a big account? What contacts could you refer me to? Ask to have your resumé, portfolio, and cover letter critiqued. Realize that when an account person takes an hour to talk to you, that is an hour of billable time that must be made up somewhere. The client certainly cannot be billed for it. Thank the agency people and do not waste their time.
- Be available for freelance work. Sometimes, agencies cannot commit to hiring full-time people but need help on certain projects. Doing freelance work for them introduces them to your talents.
- Read the business news and find out who has just landed new accounts. They might need to "staff up."
- If you still are in college, do an internship. Agencies sometimes hire former interns. It also is good exposure to the agency experience.

Moving Ahead

The account person can grow by developing a deeper understanding of the client's business, growing proficient at account management, and continuing to polish counseling skills.

Read the trade magazines, business publications, and books on the client's business and on public relations. Attend trade shows. Invest in frequent visits to the client and its retail, manufacturing, and/or remote locations. Join a professional organization, such as PRSA and its Counselors Academy, and an organization related to the client's business. Look into materials from the PRSA's Professional Practices Center in New York. Attend professional development seminars. Talk to your colleagues throughout the organization. Work on new business. If your company has no training program or resource library, then ask to start one. Look into professional accreditation programs.

CHAPTER 38

Strategic Media Planning

Toward an Integrated Public Relations Media Model

KIRK HALLAHAN

Media play a central role in public relations as channels of communication between an organization and its key publics. Surprisingly, public relations practitioners and researchers have devoted conspicuously little attention to the question of how to select communications media in public relations programs (Schwartz & Glynn, 1989; Van Leuven, 1986).

Media planning is emerging as an important new specialty in public relations. Its growth is being spurred by the rapidly growing number of new channels available to deliver public relations messages. Although public relations media planning has a long way to go before it rivals the sophistication of advertising media planning, public relations media planners must now address some of the same questions that confront advertisers. What media best meet a program's objectives? How can media be combined to enhance program effectiveness? What media are the most efficient to reach key audiences?

RECENT TRENDS IN PUBLIC RELATIONS MEDIA

For many years, public relations media planning strategies required little forethought. In general, programs focused on obtaining publicity in mass media—newspapers, magazines, radio, and television. Sometimes, these efforts were supplemented with collateral materials or occasional special events. The incremental expenditures of money or staff time to get additional placements or to handle incidental assignments were small. Today, however, the situation is starkly different. The sheer number of publicity outlets has expanded, increasing the direct costs to provide materials and making it difficult to approach every potential outlet effectively. Meanwhile, other changes are occurring in the public relations media environment.

New technologies have provided many more media options for delivering messages—the Web, Internet chat rooms, e-mail and listservs, videoconferencing, and CD-ROMs, to name a few (Johnson, 1997; O'Keefe, 1997; Sherwin & Avila, 1998). The traditional information brokering role of the press also has been usurped. Politicians and other newsmakers have discovered that they can circumvent die-hard journalists to take their messages directly to the populace via sprightly talk shows, satellite news conferences, appearances on entertainment shows, sponsored programs on cable networks, and video brochures (Hallahan, 1994).

Direct spending related to the delivery of public relations messages, as a proportion of total campaign expenditures, is on the rise. Clients are willing to invest directly in the production and distribution of information in media where they can control both the timing and content of messages. The conventional view that public relations seeks "free" exposure no longer applies. Significantly, as spending levels have increased, clients and practitioners alike have begun to consider the need for using cost-benefit analysis. Their concern is to justify expenditures and to analyze the *trade-offs* among different types of media.

Mass media audiences have become increasingly fragmented. Whereas once it was possible to reach large segments of the U.S. population through newspapers or network television, the percentages of Americans who use these media regularly have declined. This splintering of the American audience now requires placements in larger numbers of different outlets merely to reach the same number of audience members possible in the past. At the same time, public relations programs are targeting more narrowly defined audience segments than ever before. These audiences are highly involved and knowledgeable, and they want specific or often highly technical information on topics. As such, the media needed to deliver those messages have become highly specialized.

The information expectations of publics have risen. Technological advancements (e.g., remote broadcasts, facsimiles, homepages, 800 telephone numbers) have taught audiences to *expect* immediate access to news and information. Once complacent audiences now want information on demand. As a result, control over the timing of information delivery has shifted from message *producers* to *audiences*. Many public relations operations have become purveyors of information 24 hours a day and serve audiences worldwide.

The functions performed by public relations media themselves have changed. Traditionally, media were used in public relations only to gain exposure or to disseminate information. Other techniques were employed by practitioners to solicit feedback such as monitoring press coverage, opinion surveys, and personal contacts. Today, interactive media serve as conduits for instantaneous responses from audiences and facilitate both *incoming* and *outgoing* communications. Thus, media now facilitate the practice of what normative theorists term *excellent public relations*, which emphasizes two-way symmetric communication (J. Grunig, 1989e, 1992c; J. Grunig & Hunt, 1984).

Many familiar media distinctions have become blurred. For example, the modern idea that media content falls neatly into separate compartments of news, entertainment, and advertising is being usurped by the advent of hybrid messages (Balasubramanian, 1991; Mitroff & Bennis, 1989). Today's postmodern media environment is filled with ambiguous formats where the intent of messages is not readily clear to audiences—advertorials, infomercials, video news releases, home shopping shows, product placements, and promotional events co-sponsored by media that are reported as legitimate news. Previous differentiations between external and internal media similarly are under challenge. In increasing numbers, employees hear announcements about major developments at their companies from the news media, not from internal sources. Much to the chagrin of managers, it also has become impossible to prevent public distribution of what once were considered internal or company confidential, communications. Finally, the demarcations that once separated public relations, advertising, and marketing are being dismantled in some organizations with the rise of "change agents" and integrated marketing communication (IMC) programs (Schultz, Tannenbaum, & Lauterborn, 1993; Thorson & Moore, 1996). Although IMC is controversial in many public relations circles, two clear messages have evolved from the IMC movement. First, successful communication for a client involves using a full range of communications tools and media. Second, public relations as a discipline cannot define itself in terms of any specific communication tool or technique.

AN INTEGRATED PUBLIC RELATIONS MEDIA MODEL

In light of this rapidly changing media landscape, public relations program planners need to reexamine their traditional approaches to the practice and think about media *broadly* and *strategically*. An effective public relations program must employ techniques ranging from broad-based traditional mass communication to highly individualized interpersonal communication. Moreover, the process of selecting media must be *rationalized*.

The underdeveloped state of thinking about public relations media is readily evident by examining introductory public relations textbooks. Most provide little guidance about the circumstances when a particular medium is appropriate. Some texts provide cursory comparisons of the advantages and disadvantages of different media (usually mass media only). Others use classification systems that categorize media tools as external versus internal or controlled versus uncontrolled. Still others differentiate media tactics based on the primary modalities of media, that is, whether they rely on written, visual, or spoken communication. Few books have made an effort to classify media multidimensionality (Norton & Hughey, 1987, cited in Simmons, 1990; Wilson, 1995).

As an alternative, this chapter outlines an integrated model of media that public relations people can use strategically and efficiently in program planning. The model is purposefully comprehensive and parsimonious, and it focuses particularly on how to select different *types* of media. It suggests that all media used in public relations can be grouped into one of five broad categories: public media, interactive media, controlled media, events/group communication, and one-on-one communication.

The premise for this model is that media planning is inextricably linked to the *strategic uses* that media are best suited to serve in a public relations program. Other unique characteristics of media or benefits of specific vehicles (e.g., a newspaper such as *The New York Times*) should be secondary considerations in the planning process. Table 38.1 provides an overview of these five categories along with exemplars of media found in each group. Table 38.2 compares some of the key characteristics that distinguish the media in each group. A brief discussion of each category follows.

Public Media

Public media represent all channels owned and operated by third-party media organizations. These include the major mass media as well as out-of-home advertising media. Public media (with the exception of public broadcasting) are in the business of *creating audiences* and primarily serve as conduits for commercial message sponsors to reach potential purchasers of goods and services. Secondarily, public media provide a vital link between audiences and *information sponsors,* such as public relations clients, who want to reach large audiences with news and information at a low cost per impression or at no direct cost at all.

Public media can be employed in public relations in three ways. Publicity, the longtime mainstay of the public relations field, involves obtaining editorial coverage in the news and information portions of mass media. Public media have become dependent on public relations sources to obtain material deemed important or interesting to audiences while at the same time reducing the cost of gathering information. Gandy (1982, 1992; Turk, 1986) referred to this as a subsidization of media operations. Publicity has been considered particularly valuable in

	TABLE 38.1				
	An Integrated Public Relations Media Model				
	← Mass Communication			Interpersonal Communication →	
	Public Media	*Interactive Media*	*Controlled Media*	*Events/Group Communication*	*One-on-One Communication*
Key uses in a public relations program	Build awareness	Respond to queries; exchange information	Promotion; provide detailed information	Motivate attendees; reinforce existing beliefs and attitudes	Obtain commitments; resolve problems
Principal examples	Newspapers Magazines Radio Television Out-of-home media Directory advertising Special media Movie trailers	*Telephone based:* Automated response systems Audiotext *Computer based:* Internet, Intranets, Extranets Databases (e.g., telnet, file transfers, gopher) E-mail and listservs Newsgroups, chat rooms, and bulletin boards Electronic kiosks CD-ROMs	Brochures Newsletters Sponsored magazines Annual reports Books Direct mail Point-of-purchase displays Ad specialties Videobrochures	Speeches Trade shows Exhibits Meetings/ conferences Demonstrations/ rallies Sponsorships Observations/ anniversaries Sweepstakes/ contests Recognition/ awards programs (Supported by audiovisuals and multimedia)	Personal visits Lobbying Personalized letters Telephone calls Telemarketing solicitation

public relations because of the higher credibility of news messages, but recent research evidence provides only mixed support for such arguments (Hallahan, 1996b, 1999a, 1999b).

Entertainment programming is being used with increasing frequency to heighten public consciousness of a wide range of ideologies, issues, and products. These range from the dangers of nuclear proliferation to the benefits of a vacation at Disneyland. Producers are willing to cooperate with information sponsors who want to promote particular ideas in entertainment

fare because the producers believe in the causes or have been convinced by sponsors that issues such as the dangers of alcohol are socially relevant or will endear them to audiences. During recent years, entertainment producers have institutionalized product placements, that is, the incidental inclusion of products in storylines or scenes as a way in which to defray rising production costs for movies, television game shows, and prime-time entertainment shows. Public acceptance of such techniques has contributed to the expanded use of other entertainment-based for-

TABLE 38.2

Comparison of Five Major Media Groups

	Public Media	*Interactive Media*	*Controlled Media*	*Events/Group Communication*	*One-on-One Communication*
Nature of communication	Nonpersonal	Nonpersonal	Nonpersonal	Quasi-personal	Personal
Directionality of communication	One-way	Quasi-two-way	One-way	Quasi-two-way	Two-way
Technological sophistication	High	High	Moderate	Moderate	Low
Channel ownership	Media organizations	Common carrier or institution	Sponsor	Sponsor or other organizer	None
Messages chosen by	Third-parties and producers	Receiver	Sponsor	Sponsor or joint organizer	Producer and audience
Audience involvement	Low	High	Moderate	Moderate	High
Reach	High	Moderate to low	Moderate to low	Low	Low
Cost per impression	Extremely low	Low	Moderate	Moderate	High
Key challenges to effectiveness	Competition and media clutter	Availability and accessibility	Design and distribution	Attendance and atmosphere	Empowerment and personal dynamics

mats, including infomercials and sponsored programs, which are produced and paid for by public relations clients and other information sponsors.

Finally, paid image, issue, financial, and event advertising is being used with greater regularity by both for-profit and not-for-profit entities that previously considered purchasing time or space as an anathema. These information sponsors are attracted by the ability to control both the timing and content of strategically important messages as well as by a desire to increase the frequency with which audiences receive messages. These are shortcomings inherent in using publicity, donated public service time or space, and entertainment programming.

Key challenge: Capturing audience attention. The primary challenge in using public media—news, entertainment, or advertising—is capturing the attention of audiences in a highly competitive and cluttered message environment. Gaining attention in the public media arena involves infusing a client's story with either news or entertainment values (or both) and, thereby, making the story or idea attractive to media producers. Such strategies are consistent with recent persuasion research that emphasizes the need to enhance an audience's motivation, ability, and opportunity to process mediated messages (MacInnis & Jaworski, 1989; MacInnis, Moorman, & Jaworski, 1991).

Key use: Building awareness. From a strategic perspective, the primary value of public media lies in the ability to create broad public *awareness,* or a generalized knowledge, of organizations, causes, products, and services. This applies whether the message appears as news, entertainment, or advertising because there is little difference among the three approaches strategically and because audiences make few distinctions among them. Public media also remain critical to clients who must disseminate information quickly in emergencies as well as all clients who want to reach extremely large audiences with high efficiency. Significantly, audiences are exposed to messages in public media through a process of *incidental exposure,* whereby audience members read newspapers, watch television, and drive past billboards as part of their daily lives. Attention to messages in public media involves little special effort by audiences.

Interactive Media

Interactive media include the growing array of communications options that allow people to communicate with organizations using telephones and personal computers. Modern audiences can use interactive media technology to make inquiries, to perform routine tasks, or to exchange information with organizations electronically.

Touch-tone telephones, now installed in about 90% of U.S. homes, enable individuals to access automated telephone response systems, voice mail, and audiotext systems operated by a wide range of organizations. Meanwhile, personal computers with modems, now found in about 40% of American households, allow access to the Internet and other on-line information services. Still in the development stage, interactive television will allow future audiences to access similar services and information sources using sophisticated television remote controls.

Interactive media operate in ways that are fundamentally different from public media. Although some interactive media systems are owned and operated by corporations and other large organizations for use by their employees and customers, the interactive media systems are concentrated in the burgeoning information services industry. On-line information services (e.g., America Online) market their own proprietary content, and Internet service providers help clients produce attractive and functional Web pages. However, the most important function that these organizations (along with telecommunications firms) provide is the computer access necessary between information sponsors and audiences. These firms operate largely as common carriers and exercise little control over practitioner-generated material that is distributed.

The use of interactive media by audiences also is fundamentally different from that of public media. Users of interactive media, by definition, are actively involved in the communication process. Users *initiate* communications and purposefully use interactive media to fulfill some personal need, whether informational, entertainment, or social in nature. Interactive media users are both *producers* and *receivers* of messages and, therefore, are unlike passive public media audiences, whose members sometimes have little or no interest in topics to which they are exposed.

Key challenges: Availability and accessibility. In contrast to public media, the key challenges of using interactive action in a public relations program are to ensure that potential users are able to (a) *locate* and then (b) *access* the information they desire. The availability of telephone access or Web sites in cyberspace must be actively promoted and must be easily locatable through directories or computerized search engines, depending on the circumstances. Once accessed, interactive media must be easy to use. Unlike other forms of media, messages in interactive media are parsed into electronic fragments and stored randomly. Producers of interactive messages must guide users to desired information with clear and logical voice prompts or hypertext links. And because users can access the same information via a variety of different pathways, information must be self-contained and make no contextual assumptions about what users might have heard or seen previously.

Key uses: Handling queries and sharing information. Interactive media are user driven. Thus, they are not well suited to creating broad awareness in the same way as public media. However, they are a potentially powerful and low-cost way for organizations to handle queries and to provide routine and individualized information to users on demand, varying in their degrees of media richness, that is, the ability to simulate the quality of human exchanges found in interpersonal communication (Rice, 1989, 1993). Similarly, they are excellent ways in which to share information with a reasonably well-defined group of technologically savvy people with a high level of interest and involvement in a particular topic. Users can quickly become part of virtual communities through participation in computer-based chat rooms, bulletin boards, and listservs dedicated to particular topics.

Controlled Media

Controlled media represent all categories of media that are physically produced and delivered to the recipient by the sponsor and can include any object that carries a client's name or message.

Unlike either public or interactive media, information sponsors assume total responsibility for the design, production, manufacturing, inventory, and distribution of controlled media. Sponsors often retain outside vendors to perform key tasks related to design, production, or distribution. However, as the name implies, sponsors retain total creative license over content and control distribution. Sponsors are unfettered by creative or ideological restrictions imposed by third-party gatekeepers, such as news editors and entertainment producers, who play a pivotal role in public media. Similarly, controlled media enable sponsors to control the order of presentation and the integrity of information provided—subtle problems inherent in interactive media.

Controlled media permit messages to be directed to highly pinpointed audiences. This capability is possible with the advent of database systems, which also permit specific content to be individualized for recipients. Although controlled media can contain response mechanisms, such as bounce-back cards in brochures, feedback often is delayed compared to the instanta-neous feedback possible with interactive media, events/group communication, and one-on-one communication.

Key challenges: Distribution and design. Audiences do not consume controlled media messages as part of a daily media routine or in an effort to seek information. Instead, controlled media must be purposefully placed in the hands of audience members, who must then be encouraged to attend to the message. Special attention must be paid to distribution to ensure that materials reach targeted audiences in a timely and efficient manner. Once audiences receive controlled media, the design of the material is critical. Engaging copy and presentational devices—graphics, photography, sound, video, and the like—is essential to entice audiences and maintain their interest.

Key uses: Promotion and providing detailed information. Controlled media are particularly well suited to communicate promotional messages and to provide detailed information that goes beyond the mere general awareness possible via public media or the sometimes fragmentary information provided through interactive media. Messages can be as detailed as necessary because controlled media can offer greater message capacity and can deliver more complex messages than are possible using public media, where time or space is limited. Similarly, controlled media are packaged in a single, self-contained bundle, unlike interactive media that require users to ferret out information in sometimes obscure locations.

Events/Group Communication

An event involves direct interpersonal communication between the representative of a client organization and a group of people. A meeting among three or more persons is the simplest example. Events, as used here, represent legitimate efforts to communicate directly with attendees and can be distinguished from *pseudo-events* and *stunts* staged merely to gain news coverage through public media (Boorstin, 1964; Fuhrman, 1989).

Venues for events can include the premises of the sponsor, public streets and parks, and public event facilities (e.g., auditoriums, stadiums, hotels, convention centers). Some events, such as teleconferences, can link participants from remote locales electronically. Program planners generally must assume responsibility for organizing the entire activity but often work cooperatively with another organization. Such cooperation is evident in the typical sponsored speech, where a representative of one organization appears at a meeting, conference, or exposition organized by another organization. Another example of cooperative events is the growing number of fund-raising and lifestyle events staged by nonprofit organizations with the support of for-profit entities seeking positive exposure through association with a worthwhile cause.

Key challenges: Attendance and atmosphere. As with each of the other media categories, events pose particular challenges. For an event to be effective, an audience first must be in attendance. Recruiting can be a problematic task in itself. Once the target group is at the event site, the challenge then becomes the creation of a conducive *atmosphere.* Although audiences listen to presentations (oral communication is the primary mode of communication at events), event participants gain as many insights and form impressions by observing the overall festivities, by talking with other participants, and by observing their own reactions. Indeed, events are primarily experiential media, and the success of events is predicated on eliciting favorable *emotional responses,* which can be leveraged into a state of *emotional contagion* as attendees interact. Common devices used to create favorable emotional responses include symbolic settings, festive staging, audiovisuals, entertainment, music, and food.

Key uses: Motivation and reinforcement of existing beliefs and values. Although events sometimes are used for educational or information-sharing purposes, the real value of events lies in their

unique ability to *motivate* individuals to take action and to crystallize the *already extant* beliefs or attitudes of attendees. Events can be used best to inspire individuals to engage in particular behaviors, as witnessed in events such as college pep rallies and political demonstrations. For other audiences, events serve as ritualistic exercises that impart little new knowledge and encourage no change in behavior but can be highly effective in validating what attendees already know or cherish.

One-on-One Communication

The final group of public relations media includes all forms of *dyadic communication,* that is, communications that take place on an interpersonal level between a representative of an organization and an individual member of a public. One-on-one communications involve highly individualized communications that often are unstructured, unplanned, and ephemeral in nature. As with events, the primary form of communication involves face-to-face contact using oral communication. However, interpersonal media—telephones and correspondence—also can be deployed.

The contexts in which one-on-one communications occur vary. These can include face-to-face solicitations of major donors by fund-raising executives, responses to customer complaints by consumer affairs staff members, lobbying of lawmakers by government relations representatives, conflict negotiations by community relations specialists, and counseling or bargaining by employee relations personnel.

Key challenges: Empowerment and personal dynamics. Dealing effectively with individuals on a one-on-one basis requires organization representatives to be empowered with the *authority* to represent the organization and, as necessary, to make commitments or grant concessions. Success also is highly dependent on the personal dynamics that evolve in the interaction between the parties. The organization's representative must be able to nurture a positive rapport with the target audience and use interpersonal communication skills effectively.

Key uses: Obtain commitments and resolve problems. The deployment of one-on-one communications in public relations programs generally is limited to special situations that involve *negotiations,* that is, highly interactive and sometimes volatile discussions between the organization and members of key publics. Sometimes these negotiations involve the organization obtaining desired commitments from individuals in positions of power or influence. Examples might include obtaining a multi-million-dollar commitment from a donor, soliciting the support of key legislation by a lawmaker, and obtaining the endorsement of an influential organization in a controversy. One-on-one communications also are used to resolve problems involving disgruntled customers or activists. Such negotiations often center on shortcomings in the organization's performance, whether real or perceived. Audience members believe that the focal problem has created high levels of uncertainty or risk in their lives, and they seek one-on-one meetings with the organization to resolve the problem. Organizations often are forced to participate because the audiences confront them and demand that they do so.

COMBINING MEDIA
IN AN INTEGRATED
PUBLIC RELATIONS PLAN

The preceding discussion suggests that the media found within each of these five major media groups operate in ways that are fundamentally different from those in other categories. In addition, the media in these groups share similar challenges that must be addressed to use them effectively. Most important, the media within each of these categories are particularly suited to meet specific types of program objectives.

This model provides a valuable starting point for public relations media planning by fo-

cusing attention on the *strategic differences* among types of media. In using the model, public relations media planners can begin the media selection process by first examining the *explicit objectives* in a program and then matching them to the key use(s) suggested in the model for each media category. Then, looking *within* the category with the key use that most closely matches the stated objective, media planners can choose specific media deemed most appropriate to employ. Among second-level factors that can then be taken into account are a particular medium's availability, reach, frequency, cost, modality, and prestige. Other considerations involve the producer's abilities to meet production deadlines, to time the distribution of messages to desired dates, to segment audiences, and to individualize messages. Media planners also will want to be sure that the selected medium matches the audience's literacy skills and extant media use patterns and that it is appropriate for meeting the audience expectations about the messages found in a particular medium.

Implications

Several valuable insights about public relations media planning quickly become apparent from a closer examination of this model.

One is the *hierarchical* nature of these media groups and their corresponding objectives. As suggested earlier, these five groups represent the full range of communication options in public relations—from nonpersonal mass communication (the domain of public media) to highly individualized interpersonal communication (represented by one-on-one communication). Public media, interactive media, controlled media, events/group communication, and one-on-one communication represent progressively more ideal ways in which to communicate with publics. They are increasingly *personalized* and *involving,* as well as *less technologically driven,* forms of communication. Moreover, the suggested ideal uses or purposes for each category successively address objectives that bring audience members closer to *taking action* and correspond closely to the stages of the adoption cycle suggested in various hierarchy of effects models (Lavidge & Steiner, 1961; Rogers, 1962; Strong, 1925). Whereas the exact nomenclature varies from writer to writer, the hierarchy of effects notion suggests that individuals follow a process in which they first become aware of a topic and then acquire knowledge, formulate attitudes, and develop convictions before taking action. Such a process clearly applies to decisions that are important to an individual, although decisions that have little relevance or consequences might be made without systematic or effortful thought (Chaiken, 1980; Petty & Cacioppo, 1986). The hierarchy idea suggests that different media have different roles to play as audiences become aware, interested, and convinced before they actually vote for a candidate, purchase a product, or accept the position articulated by a company on an environmental controversy.

This model also dramatizes the central role that *media integration* should play in a public relations media plan. Media integration refers to the planned and coordinated use of multiple media to achieve a desired result. The idea of integration is not new. In a public relations context, the concept can be traced back to at least the 1920s (Wilder & Buell, 1923). This model provides a simple operational definition of integration by suggesting that an integrated public relations media plan *combines media from two or more of these five media categories to achieve closely related but separate objectives that together are intended to achieve an overall program goal.* For example, during the earliest stages of a campaign, creating mere awareness through public media exposure might be very appropriate. Later, however, it might become essential to provide additional information through interactive or controlled media or to prompt desired audience action through events/group communication or one-on-one communication.

A final notion that emerges logically from this model is the need for public relations planners to *optimize* the use of media. The failure to deploy the right media for an appropriate purpose could have deleterious consequences by diluting either the effectiveness or efficiency of the program. *Effectiveness* refers to the ability to achieve the desired goal, whereas *efficiency* refers to obtaining a desired goal at the lowest possible cost. Effective public relations media planning involves striking a balance between these two concerns.

Dilution of efficiency occurs whenever higher order media are used to achieve objectives that could be achieved using lower order, more cost-efficient media choices. For example, one-on-one communications could be used to build awareness, respond to inquiries, provide detailed information, and reinforce existing beliefs or attitudes. However, except in circumstances where the target audience is exceptionally small, such an approach is time-consuming and costly—and might needlessly deplete program resources.

Dilution of *effectiveness,* by contrast, can occur whenever lower order media are expected to achieve unrealistic higher order objectives that require the use of more powerful media. Research suggests that mere exposure in public media alone generally is not adequate to elicit direct behavioral change (Pfau & Parrott, 1993) but should be reinforced with other forms of communication such as interpersonal influence. Similarly, as sales personnel and fund-raising veterans can attest, a person's mere attendance at an event might be highly motivating but might not result in a commitment without one-on-one contact. Effective public relations media planning involves ensuring that the program has sufficient promotional power to achieve desired objectives but does not waste resources, thereby maximizing results.

Improving Corporate and Organizational Communications

A New Look at Developing and Implementing the Communication Audit

DEAN KAZOLEAS

ALAN WRIGHT

■ The purpose of this chapter is to present a new model for developing and implementing an internal communication audit. The process and model presented is based on organizational communication and public relations theory and has been tested in a number of medium-sized and large organizations. The focus of this chapter is to bridge the gap between academic research and the needs of the public relations practitioner. The current model was developed by public relations scholars/practitioners who specialize in management-employee communication and who found that a number of commonly used audits could not provide answers to some simple communication-based problems. To that extent, this chapter offers a mix of theoretical, strategic, and tactical suggestions as well as a template that can be used by the public relations practitioner.

In this chapter, an emphasis is placed on the notion that this audit process is an evaluative/ diagnostic technique that can solve problems, plan processes, and be used as a tool to drive organizational change. Whereas assessing and "reengineering" internal communications is vital, getting management to support changes and "buy-in" to the restructuring process also is critical.

This chapter is divided into several sections and focuses on providing a "hands-on" approach that is coupled with a theory- and research-based model. The first section offers a brief discussion of the impact that communication has on corporate and employee performance and well-being. This portion also presents some of the symptoms of poor communication and discusses how these often are easily predicted by theory and prior research. A second section examines the process of building the audit. This section includes specific factors that should be included, processes to be followed, and suggestions for situational variations that allow for customization. The third and final section deals with the implementation of the audit and makes suggestions regarding communication reengineering that can significantly improve communications up, down, and across the organization.

THE IMPORTANCE OF GOOD COMMUNICATION

To a communication scholar, the value of effective efficient communication always is at the forefront. However, this might not be the case in the eyes of the corporate executive or mid-level manager. A critical function of the communication professional often is persuading "management" that a focus on building effective communication is a top priority that warrants time, staffing, and funding. To examine the value of good communication, the issue needs to be discussed in two contexts: the impact of communication on the organization and the impact on the employee as an individual.

Impact of Communication on the Organization

Corporate communication has a large impact on organizational performance, culture, and well-being. Large organizations are made up of interacting units that coordinate their efforts to produce products, serve clients, and maintain organizational structure. Lack of communication can have disastrous results leading to decreased performance, decreased productivity, problems with safety and morale, and (in some industries) regulatory and statutory violations.

With communication playing such a pivotal role, it is surprising at times to hear executives conceptualize it as a "soft" variable, that is, not connected to the bottom line. When faced with myriad symptoms and problems that are indicative of communication failure, managers often look for any other explanation than the one that is most apparent: There is no effective means of communication. This skepticism, although at times frustrating, should be expected and is easily understood. As with any complex problem, there are times when the root cause cannot be directly observed but can be deduced only by looking for the presence of a series of related symptoms. Similarly, corporate communication professionals often do not see the immediate impacts of poor communication; instead, they see and hear the complaints of others. From a practitioner's perspective, the terms used by clients usually are surprisingly similar, from the claim that employees and managers are working from "functional silos" or that "one hand doesn't know what the other is doing," to the complaint that "we can't seem to get the point across" or, even worse, "productivity is down because we have to 'redo' work frequently." These all communicate a lack of coordination as well as problems with internal communications. The bottom line for organizations is that poor communication slows productivity, reduces quality, can create turnover, and can contribute to a negative culture/climate.

The Impact of Communication on Employees

Research that explains the relationship among employee needs, perceptions, and communication can be of substantive value when developing a system to accurately assess communication needs and problem areas and to provide recommendations that can be used to reengineer communication systems. From the practitioner's standpoint, the names of the theories might sound somewhat unfamiliar. However, when working with clients and conducting research in organizations, the story told by employees almost always is the same. Frustration, fear, uncertainty, dissatisfaction, and a sense of hopelessness often coexist in organizations with poor communication systems.

No one can disagree that employees need information. They need it to do their jobs and to reduce uncertainty in the face of ambiguity or crisis. It is not surprising, then, that when employees do not have access to needed information, the result often is anxiety and frustration. The research on uncertainty reduction and ambiguity (see, e.g., Berger & Calabrese, 1975; R. Burke, 1996) provides an effective understanding of employee anxiety when faced with this situation. Similarly, theory can predict the needs that employees have in terms of having access to accurate and timely information so that they can do their jobs effectively. Many professionals know of these needs but are faced with communication systems and hierarchies that do not meet these simple needs and, even worse, contain such obstacles that the systems themselves become "demotivating" to employees. Not surprisingly, the frustration, irritation, and lack of motivation felt by employees within organizations with poor communication systems has been explained and predicted by theories such as Herzberg's (1966, 1976) motivator-hygiene theory. This theory posits that structures, actions, and policies within organizations can serve as either motivators or demotivators for employees. In this case, a lack of the information needed to do one's job over time basically demotivates employees, resulting in apathy, frustration, and employee turnover (if other options are available) (Miller, Ellis, Zook, & Lyles, 1990). These examples demonstrate that although theory might appear to be "irrelevant" to many practitioners, it often is of paramount value in diagnosing symptoms related to communication problems and in providing effective remedial recommendations.

These theories also can explain some of the relationships found between effective communication and so-called soft variables such as employee satisfaction and morale. For example, Kazoleas, Levine, and Wright (1998) examined the relationship between perceptions of keeping employees informed and employee satisfaction and morale in two large organizations. Consistent with past research and the predictions of uncertainty reduction and motivator-hygiene theory, a moderate positive statistically significant relationship was found to exist between these variables. Simply put, when employees are kept informed, they tend to be more satisfied with their jobs, exhibit a higher level of morale, and are more motivated to be productive employees.

One of the unique factors about the audit measure presented in this chapter is that its foundation rests on a knowledge of these needs and on the application of uses and gratifications theory from the mass media research area (for a review, see Rubin, 1986, 1994). This theory posits that individuals use certain media to fulfill/gratify certain needs and to perform certain necessary functions. The media choices available in most organizations are no different from those in the regular "mass media." The key is to recognize that employees in an organization have preferences in using media types to obtain specific types of information. To that extent, employees often have developed "informational" habits that, as with any habitual behavior or practice, can be difficult to change. The lesson for the practitioner is that the most pragmatic approach is to place information on specific topics in the communication vehicles that are preferred by the target public. This not only increases the probability that needed or desired information will be available but also increases the likelihood that somewhat aware (moderately involved) publics that might scan these media also will be exposed to the information.

BUILDING A BETTER COMMUNICATION AUDIT

An effective communication audit begins with a receiver-oriented, as opposed to a sender-focused, model. The problems of relying on a sender-based approach are best exemplified by noting an excerpt of a conversation that one of us once had with a corporate executive on the topic of internal communications. When asked whether the manager had relayed some needed information to employees, the manager responded that he had "sent a memo." When asked again whether he knew the information had been received, the response was the same: "I don't know. . . . I sent a memo." Finally, when asked about the number of memos sent to employees during the week, a response of "I don't know—about 30 to 40" was obtained. This example highlights the danger of a sender-oriented approach, that is, the assumption of "If I sent it, then it must have been received," ignoring the possibility that the message might not have been received, understood, or acted on.

The audit discussed in what follows is based in part on the research and ideas forwarded by a number of public relations and communication scholars who suggest that research and practitioners examining internal organizational communication should focus on the receiver as well as the sender of information (Cameron & McCollum, 1993; J. Grunig & Hunt, 1984; Pavlik, Nwosu, & Ettel-Gonzalez, 1982; Pavlik, Vastyan, & Maher, 1990).

The application of a uses and gratifications approach to public relations research and practice is not a new suggestion. For example, Cameron and McCollum (1993) examined corporate culture, corporate communication, and the degree to which management and employees had a shared understanding and definition of corporate structure and culture. Interestingly, they found that employees tended to prefer direct interpersonal communication over mediated communication when obtaining information on those topics. They concluded by stating, "Public relations practitioners should focus more on ways to facilitate the two-way communication between management and employees than on creating top-down communication programs" (p. 248). Similar conclusions regarding employee preferences for specific media were reported by Pavlik et al. (1982, 1990).

This approach also is consistent with J. Grunig's two-way symmetrical model of public relations (J. Grunig, 1984; J. Grunig & Hunt, 1984), which reflects a situation in which feedback is used to modify organizational goals, strategies, and/or policies in an attempt to develop more understanding and a better relationship with a particular public. In this instance, employee feedback is used to improve communication up, down, and across the organization, thereby strengthening the relationship between the organization and all its relevant internal publics.

Focusing on Employee Needs and Preferences

By definition, a receiver-based approach focuses on the needs of employees at all levels. Furthermore, a balanced approach has to be taken where employee preferences are incorporated at both a global and a more tactical level. Thus, employees have input into global-level communication structures and also the communication and decisional functions that can be served by a particular communication vehicle.

Because of reliance on employee input, the process of using research to build the audit is central to success. Many practitioners would like to use a measure that they pull "off the shelf," but frequently this practice leads to missed information and does not allow for the development of comprehensive solutions. No two organizations are exactly alike. Even if organizations are structured similarly, or identically in the case of branch offices or franchises, different groups of individuals may develop different informal networks and/or develop different preferences in terms of choosing informational media. A balanced approach requires an in-depth research-oriented strategy that examines all communication vehicles, systems, and networks across the client organization.

What Makes This Audit Different?

What differentiates this audit measure from several other more commonly known audits is that it allows a greater level of receiver involvement, specifically in that it matches content with vehicle selection across a large number of areas. One of the more well-known audit tools came out of the International Communication Association's (ICA) organizational communication audit (Goldhaber, Dennis, Richetto, & Wiio, 1979; Goldhaber, Porter, & Yates, 1977; Goldhaber & Rogers, 1979). To develop this audit, the ICA undertook a longitudinal survey that exam-

ined applied organizational communication research and the measures and techniques used to
conduct those investigations. The results of the
ICA audit forwards Wiio's organizational communication audit (OCD) as a model for conducting internal communication audits. Wiio's
(1979) model also has been included as a
"model" audit in a "sourcebook" of communication measures (Rubin, Palmgreen, & Sypher,
1994).

To some extent the OCD survey developed
and validated by Wiio (Rubin et al., 1994) does
examine the degree to which employees prefer to
receive overall information via a certain channel.
However, the measure does not allow employees
to indicate the extent to which they could get
specific information from specific channels or
media. That is, employees are given little choice
over the function that each communication vehicle serves. For example, if an employee would
prefer to get information about plant productivity and scheduling from a newsletter rather than
from a computer bulletin board system, the
OCD audit measure does not allow the employee
to indicate so. The employee is asked only to
make global ratings of how much information he
or she receives on a particular topic and of how
much he or she would prefer to receive. Although
Wiio's OCD audit adequately assesses global informational needs and media preferences, the
lack of specificity in allowing employees to
match informational needs and content with
specific media means less power and flexibility
when reengineering corporate communication
systems. But in defense of Wiio's model, it is accurate to say that although it is somewhat less
powerful, the audit measure is fairly brief, which
sometimes is an important factor in performing
applied research. In addition, its brevity makes it
less cumbersome to analyze and easier to interpret outcomes.

The Internal Corporate
Communication Audit

The research process used to develop the audit measure could best be described as an induc-
tive process that can use a wide variety of qualita-

tive and quantitative techniques. This audit
model, outlined in Tables 39.1 and 39.2, uses a
multistage approach that assesses all current
communication vehicles in any given organization in terms of their usefulness, actual use, accuracy, timeliness, and perceived effectiveness. If
preliminary research indicates a lack of trust,
then factors such as perceived trust and honesty
of the information/vehicle are added. These factors, as well as current vehicle use, and informa-
tion/topic areas are ascertained with preliminary
research, usually through a series of interviews
and focus groups with both high- and mid-level
managers as well as with "frontline" employees.
If necessary, brief preliminary surveys can be
used to narrow the number of vehicles examined
and the diversity of topics assessed.

Assessing Current
Communication Vehicles

The first section of the audit focuses on assessing the vehicles used to convey information
within the organization (Table 39.1). This section can be used to examine any or all of the
methods to communicate up, down, and across
the organization. Vehicles can be assessed on factors such as use, usefulness, effectiveness, accuracy, timeliness, perceived trust, and compre-
hensiveness. Again, these factors are just a
sample of the types of information that can be
included to assess current vehicles. Factor
choices should be made only after making an initial assessment of organizational communication needs that are compiled, which usually comes out of the preliminary research process. In
the end, the analyzed results from the first section of the audit will allow the communication
professional to make judgments regarding which
vehicles should and can be redesigned and which
(if any) can be eliminated.

Assessing Informational Needs
and Vehicle Preferences

A second stage (Table 39.2) in the audit examines information needs in specific areas that

TABLE 39.1					
Example of First Section of Communication Audit: Assessing Current Communication Vehicles					

Please rate the ACME Inc. newsletter:

Not useful	1	2	3	4	5	Very useful
Inaccurate	1	2	3	4	5	Accurate
Ineffective	1	2	3	4	5	Very effective
Untimely	1	2	3	4	5	Timely
Dishonest	1	2	3	4	5	Honest

NOTE: This listing represents only a sample of possible vehicle assessment factors. Others can be used as deemed necessary.

are identified by preliminary research. These areas can be identified by the use of interviews, focus groups, or preliminary surveys. The measure assesses individual satisfaction with the amount of information employees are receiving on the topic relative to needs, the understandability and usefulness of the information, and overall preferences of modality (e.g., face-to-face, electronic). Included in this section is a series of questions asking employees where they currently get information (checklist) and, more important, where they would prefer to get that information. Again, it should be noted that the topics, vehicles, and factors presented in Table 39.2 are only an example. Any or all key topics (e.g., safety, business environment, compensation) can be assessed, all vehicles can be listed, and information flow can be assessed along a wide variety of factors.

An analysis of the results from this second section can instantly provide data on key informational need areas, make suggestions regarding the structure of the communication on the given topic, and provide indications of where employees prefer to get information on that topic. It is important to note that this is one of the key differences between this audit and others like it. Armed with the results of this audit, the communication professional can place information in

media that the employees use regularly or would prefer to use. Crossing this information with break-outs or using cross-tabs, the communication professional can make recommendations to increase information flow to any particular group in the organization using its preferred media. In contrast to top-down-generated approaches, this process forgoes the added steps of informing and "training" employees on where to look for information as well as the expensive "roll-out" campaigns that often accompany such efforts.

The end result of this audit is that the effectiveness of every vehicle is determined, information needs are ascertained, and preferences for information flow are identified. This is especially important for internal publics that might be latent in nature and, thereby, might only scan for information. The use of the main audit components, coupled with break-outs by demographics, allows the practitioner to identify needs with pinpoint accuracy at almost any level of the organization. In addition, it identifies vehicles to deliver the information that maximizes the probability of any given message being received in an accurate and timely manner.

For added flexibility and diagnostic power, a series of open-ended questions can be attached at the end of the audit measure. Questions ascer-

---

TABLE 39.2

Example of Second Section of Communication Audit:
Assessing Specific Informational Needs and Media Preferences

Operations (NOTE: This category is just one of many possible topics that can be assessed):
Operations information refers to information that is related to day-to-day operations, production, schedules, and use of resources.

How satisfied are you with the amount of information on operations that you receive?
(Please circle the number that best reflects your response.)

Very dissatisfied   1   2   3   4   5   Very satisfied

How understandable is the information on operations that you receive?
(Please circle the number that best reflects your response.)

Not at all understandable   1   2   3   4   5   Very understandable

In general, how would you prefer to receive information on operations?
(Please check your desired response.)

[ ] Through written materials   [ ] Through one-on-one interactions
[ ] Through group meetings   [ ] Verbally over the phone

The following section is designed to find out where you currently get information on operations and where you would prefer to get that information. Please check all of the boxes that apply and feel free to write in any sources of information that you currently use or ones that you would like to see used.

I currently get information on operations from: I would prefer to get information on operations from:

[ ] The company newsletter   [ ] The company newsletter
[ ] Weekly meetings   [ ] Weekly meetings
[ ] Weekly status reports   [ ] Weekly status reports
[ ] E-mail   [ ] E-mail
[ ] Intranet   [ ] Intranet
[ ] Supervisor updates   [ ] Supervisor updates
[ ] Other   [ ] Other

---

taining general communication problems, what works, what does not work, and/or what employees would like to see often can generate very useful insights and suggestions. This is highly recommended in cases where access for preliminary research has been difficult or where organizational structure makes preliminary assessments of all groups difficult.

AUDIT IMPLEMENTATION AND COMMUNICATION REENGINEERING

The audit model offered in this chapter is designed to be administered via survey and can be either sent home with employees or, for the best results, completed by employees while on the job. Be forewarned that if an organization has a large number of communication vehicles and/or a large number of critical information targets, then the audit measure can be quite long. To some extent, brevity is the advantage that many more globally oriented audits can offer. However, length does not necessarily preclude participation. Response rates to measures such as the one outlined here usually can be expected to be more than 50%, especially if employees are given an opportunity to complete the audit on company time. In truth, many individuals usually relish the opportunity to provide feedback on an area that often lends itself to frustration, lost effort, and demoralization.

Using the results of the audit to reengineer communications is fairly straightfoward. Based on an analysis of the data, vehicles can be reengineered, discarded, or created. Information needs can be prioritized by topic and job function or by any other demographic or geographic factor and matched with employee preferences. The end result is the first stages of a communication system that has clearly identified priorities and needs as well as a sense of direction.

The key to successful communication reengineering is to create a communication system that provides the strategic and tactical information resources that all members of the organization need to coordinate activities, provide direction, reduce uncertainty, and do their jobs in an efficient and productive manner. From a more simplistic perspective, a communication system that allows information to be moved up, down, and across the organization has to be designed. The information has to be accessible, on time, and of use to employees.

The results of an internal communication audit can contribute to these efforts in two different ways. First, the audit results identify key need areas, preferred modes of communication, and vehicle-specific ratings of effectiveness. Second, the results of the communication audit can work to help obtain management's buy-in for the necessity and implementation of a new and improved communication system. This last factor should not be overlooked. Assessment tools such as this audit do have the ability to diagnose problem areas and provide critical information for developing organizations that operate at optimum levels. However, a report that sits on a shelf does not drive change. To that extent, the results of the assessment have to be packaged in such a manner that they not only communicate empirical findings but also energize the organization and provide the impetus for change.

BEST PRACTICES IN CRISIS COMMUNICATION

Crisis Communication

A Review of Some Best Practices

KATHLEEN FEARN-BANKS

Since the term *public relations* was coined early in the 20th century, the profession has been crisis driven. Most public relations programs are developed either to prevent a crisis or to recover from a crisis. As we enter the 21st century, we are more aware of the importance of protecting organizations (including companies and public individuals) from a greater number and a greater magnitude of threats to their well-being.

Advances in technology, especially relating to the news media, have made it possible to deliver messages to the public faster than even a decade ago, and unfortunately, these messages are not always accurate. The "watchdog" media also can be the "attack" dog media. Whether the messages are accurate or not, they can be damaging enough to interrupt normal operations and, sometimes, even put an organization out of business.

People today are increasingly aware that crisis management and communications are an important factor in the business mix. They know that organizations need to be prepared to cope with crises and need to prevent, if possible, the occurrence of crises. Support of stakeholders

and publics is crucial to an organization's existence. Publics demand to know what issues and problems threaten the success of the organization, what prodromes (warning signs) to impending crises may develop, and what communication is used to thwart the problems. Key publics have grown up with inquiring minds fed by an abundance of communication tools—television, radio, newspapers, books, magazines, and the Internet. There is a widespread atmosphere of "Don't misuse or abuse me," "Give me my money's worth," "Don't make my life any harder than it is," and "I want my piece of the pie." Anyone who interferes with these demands is in a crisis. Therefore, organizations are increasingly seeing the need for crisis communication. Crisis communication is a necessity, not a frill or a procedure or policy that is developed *if* a company has a skilled employee with spare time. But what practices can an organization embrace on an ongoing basis that will help it to prevent a crisis? Some crises might be unavoidable; nature and human failure never are controlled. What are an organization's best practices to help it return to normalcy as soon as possible after a crisis? What practices help the organization suffer minimal damage to reputation during a crisis? These are the questions I seek to answer in this chapter.

First, there are terms that need to be understood. A *crisis* is a major occurrence with a potentially negative outcome affecting an organization as well as its publics, services, products, and/or good name. It interrupts normal business transactions and can, at its worst, threaten the existence of the organization. Not all crises spell absolute doom, as Fink (1986) indicated; a crisis is a "turning point," not necessarily laden with irreparable negativity but rather "characterized by a certain degree of risk and uncertainty" (p. 15). It is possible for an organization to make a turn for the better during a period of crisis.

Crisis management is strategic planning to prevent and respond during a crisis or negative occurrence, a process that removes some of the risk and uncertainty and allows the organization to be in greater control of its destiny. The process of *crisis communication* is the verbal, visual, and/or written interaction between the organization and its publics (often through the news media) prior to, during, and after the negative occurrence. Many professionals speak of the media as a public in themselves, but the media are more of a route through which one reaches the publics. True, certain practices must take place. And true, there is an art to doing this well. However, if one makes a point with reporters and reporters do not disseminate the messages, then there is failure. Actually, the public relations person does not care what the reporter personally believes; the idea is to get the reporter to act in the way that the public relations person wishes and to deliver the organization's message accurately and adequately to print and broadcast publics. Crisis communication is designed to minimize damage to the reputation of the organization (Fearn-Banks, 1996b).

A crisis has five stages. The first stage, detection, was referred to by Barton (1993) as the prodromal stage when the organization is watching for warning signs or prodromes. The second stage is preparation/prevention, that is, heeding the warning signs and making plans to avoid the crisis through a proactive campaign or preparing a reactive campaign to cope with the crisis. The third stage, containment, is the effort to limit the duration of the crisis or to keep it from becoming more serious or more damaging. The fourth stage, recovery, refers to the efforts to return to normalcy—to business as usual. The fifth stage, learning, is the process of evaluating the crisis and determining what is lost and what is gained (if anything) and how to turn the crisis into a prodrome for the future.

CRISIS COMMUNICATION THEORY

Some crisis communication theories find that organizations with specific practices tend to suffer less financial and reputational damage than do organizations without those practices or without what professionals might call best practices. These practices refer to the second stage of crisis, preparation/prevention. This list of best practices is developed by the works of Fearn-Banks (1996b); J. Grunig and L. Grunig (1992); J. Grunig, L. Grunig, and Ehling (1992); J. Grunig and Hunt (1984); J. Grunig and Repper (1992), and Marra (1992). Their works are built largely on the excellence theory of public relations credited primarily to J. Grunig (1992c). The theory is based on four models, with Model 1 the least desirable and Model 4 the most desirable practices in public relations.

Again, researchers say that if an organization maintains the following practices on an ongoing precrisis basis, then either it is in a better position to prevent a crisis or it will suffer less and recover more rapidly from a crisis. These are the practices of excellent organizations with stellar precrisis public relations programs:

1. The public relations head is an important part of top management.
2. Programs are designed to build relationships with all key stakeholders.
3. Public relations, through research, identifies key stakeholders, segments the stakeholders, and ranks them in importance.

4. An ongoing public relations plan is developed for each key stakeholder.
5. Public relations develops strong relationships with the news media.
6. Issues management is part of a two-way symmetrical program handled by the public relations department.
7. An ongoing two-way symmetrical crisis communication plan is developed as a response to a crisis.
8. A practice of risk communication activities is developed.
9. The organization has ideologies that encourage, support, and champion crisis management preparations.
10. The organization, through crisis inventory, anticipates the type of crisis that it is likely to suffer.
11. The organization maintains a reputation for having an overall "open and honest" policy with publics at all times.

Heath's (1997) work centered on an issues management approach to crisis communication. He believed that the two are inextricably linked—crises can create issues, and issues can become crises. His hypothesis was as follows:

If a company is engaged in issues management before, during, and after a crisis (in other words, ongoing), it can mitigate—perhaps prevent—the crisis from becoming an issue by working quickly and responsibly to establish or re-establish the level of control desired by relevant stakeholders. (p. 289)

This coincides with Practice 6.

Mitroff and Pearson (1993) identified crisis management actions in an ideal situation. In the areas of communication, they agreed with the featured crisis communication theorists in two major actions: "increased relationships with intervening stakeholder groups" and "increased collaboration among stakeholders" (p. 114). This action concurs with Practices 2 through 5.

Pauchant and Mitroff (1992b) discussed two types of organizations—the crisis prone and the crisis prepared—and said that the difference between the two is responsibility. In the area of preparation, in addition to espousing the same actions attributed to Mitroff and Pearson (1993), Pauchant and Mitroff (1992b) said that the organization should look for "signs of weakness before a determined adversary does so and evaluate whether the total set of relationships . . . has become too complex or too tightly coupled" (p. 137). In other words, they suggested a shared purpose and bond between stakeholders and management. Pauchant and Mitroff primarily concurred with Practices 2, 3, and 9.

Following are explanations and examples of the practices listed. All of the practices are pre-crisis steps. Cases cited come from direct communications with public relations professionals for the organizations experiencing crises (Fearn-Banks, 1996a).

Practice 1: The Public Relations Head Is an Important Part of Top Management

J. Grunig, L. Grunig, and Ehling (1992) called this "being a member of the dominant coalition." The key reason is that it is imperative that the public relations department be privy to and part of all major decision making as well as be aware of issues that might become crises.

Some professionals argue that it is only necessary for a member of the public relations staff to have a liaison to top management and that the link does not have to be the head of the public relations department. Although it is possible for that relationship to exist, it is more likely in plans for organizational hierarchy that the most senior member of the public relations department will have the strongest link to the head of the organization.

This needed link can be a problem in a company that hires a public relations agency only when there is a problem, an issue, or a crisis. The public relations agency is not an ongoing part of top management decisions and is privy only to what the company permits it to know. This also is a problem in a company that has a public relations department but the chief executive officer (CEO) and top executives are in one geographical location and the public relations department is in another (sometimes the two are on different U.S. coasts). A third problem is when public relations is several steps below the CEO in the organizational hierarchy, for example, if the head of public relations reports to the head of marketing, who reports to the corporate manager, who reports to the CEO. In such an organization, the importance of public relations obviously is not recognized as a vital component of crisis planning and response.

Progress in this area was indicated when the Public Affairs Group conducted a study of 530 companies and reported in *Phillips PR News* ("Corporate Communication," 1999) that more than half of the top-ranking communication officers reported directly to corporate CEOs. Only 28% reported to vice presidents or lower positions in the corporate hierarchies.

Practices 2 and 3: Programs Are Designed to Build Relationships With All Key Stakeholders Who Are Identified Through Research, Segmented, and Ranked According to Importance

Stakeholders are people who have an interest in the organization and are affected by decisions made by it. The organization always should know who its stakeholders are, know which are most important, rank them according to importance, and strive to develop and maintain strong relationships with them. *Segmenting* the stakeholders defines and categorizes them into manageable and reachable bodies of people for ongoing communication.

In 1990, the University of Florida suffered a news-making crisis when several students were killed on successive days by a then unknown assailant. The public relations director had a close relationship with the university president, who was a member of the crisis team (Practice 1). The team was thoroughly familiar with the key stakeholders—students, parents, faculty, staff, and neighbors. Each public was segmented. For example, students were segmented according to who lived on campus, who lived off campus,

who was from out of the country, and who had relevant disabilities. Relevant disabilities would mean that if written material was the communication tool for the student body, then sight-impaired students would require another form of communication. If radio was the tool of choice, then hearing-impaired students would require another form. The safety of the university community was first and most important, and communication processes were developed for these stakeholders first. The news media sought responses to questions, but more intimate communications were developed for the stakeholders.

Similarly, during Johnson & Johnson's 1982 crisis in which five people died from taking cyanide-laced Tylenol capsules, the company looked to its credo for guidance. The credo spelled out the company's priorities in order—consumers (including medical personnel), employees, communities, and stockholders. The company already had strong relationships with all of its publics. The company credits these strong relationships with saving its reputation during the crisis, and public relations history concurs. All of the stakeholders stood by Johnson & Johnson and remained loyal. This case remains one of the prime examples of how relationships and honesty can help an organization through difficult times.

Practice 4: An Ongoing Public Relations Plan Is Developed for Each Key Stakeholder

These pre-crisis proactive programs necessarily go beyond media relations and one-way programs (Models 1 and 2) to two-way asymmetric or symmetric programs (Models 3 and 4), which sometimes can either prevent crises or lessen the severity of crises. A continuing dialogue with publics marked by a give-and-take between both sides helps to build strong relationships, eliminates the gulf between the organization and its stakeholders, and makes the stakeholders feel like an integral part of the organization. This dialogue is the essential practice that defines Model

4 public relations programs—those J. Grunig (1992c) calls *excellent.* Many times, organizations experience crises and then realize that their relationships are not effective or that their public relations campaigns directed at key stakeholders need to be planned more carefully. This was a problem in the 1992 United Way of America crisis in which the CEO, William Aramony, was accused of overzealous spending. A most important stakeholder was the organization's board of directors. As the crisis developed, the head of the national nonprofit's public relations department realized that the containment stage of the crisis was prolonged because the board directed its loyalty to the CEO under fire, not to the organization. The public relations department wanted the board to ask the CEO for his resignation so that all of the United Way agencies around the country would not be hampered in getting donations to operate the charity and so that the member agencies would continue to pay dues to national headquarters to keep it functioning. As it happened, many individuals withheld donations to the member agencies, and the member agencies withheld dues from headquarters and made efforts to function independently. The public relations staff believed that the fiasco could have been avoided if either Aramony had volunteered to step down earlier or the board had asked him to resign. In hindsight, it was apparent that a pre-crisis public relations program designed to make the board realize its responsibility to the organization and not the CEO would have been effective.

Practice 5: Public Relations Develops Strong Relationships With the News Media

Starbucks Coffee Company, based in Seattle, Washington, found that its relationships with the news media paid off when a crisis developed in 1996 involving a line of Easter candy that had been on the shelves of its stores for only a few days. An anonymous letter warned that the candy was poisoned. The company immediately recalled all of the candy. The local media had en-

joyed a professional and ethical relationship with Starbucks and were supportive of the company's plight. News stories indicated that Starbucks had been victimized and had taken the proper steps in the situation. No poisoned candy ever was found. The recall resulted in a loss of revenue, but the company's reputation remained intact among consumers.

Practice 6: Issues Management Is Part of a Two-Way Symmetrical Program Handled by the Public Relations Department

A public makes an issue when it perceives that a problem is not being solved. In *issues management,* the public relations department anticipates the issues that are potential crises and ranks them in order of possible damage to the organization. Then, a crisis prevention campaign is developed for the most likely and most damaging potentialities. The canned tuna industry averted a boycott after StarKist, followed by other companies, examined issues. Environmentalists were concerned that dolphins were being killed in the tuna netting. Schoolchildren made appeals to stop killing the dolphins. Stockholders expressed their hesitation to own tuna stocks. Retailers threatened to take the tuna off their shelves. Any of these would sorely affect the tuna industry, so it was forced to adopt dolphin-safe policies.

Practice 7: An Ongoing Two-Way Symmetrical Crisis Communication Plan Is Developed as a Response to a Crisis

The crisis communication plan may be part of an overall crisis management plan, or it may be independent. It should be developed prior to a crisis, but often it is not. The plan should identify the crisis team, the spokespersons, the duties of the team, how to contact key stakeholders, and key points or *talking points.* When Pepsi-Cola was hit with the bizarre syringe-in-the-can crisis in 1993, the home office put to use its product tampering crisis communication plan with the

CEO, Craig Weatherup, as spokesperson. Pepsi had a customer relations plan that included two-way communications to retail stores, bars, restaurants, and individual consumers. The people who sell Pepsi always were encouraged by Pepsi management to express their observations of problems and issues, trends among consumers, and any factors that might affect sales. Pepsi management discusses the information and makes decisions that may institute changes in the product, the merchandising, or anything relating to the consumer. The vendors serve as eyes and ears for the company, and both are served by the effective communication. When sales are up, both the vendors and Pepsi benefit. There also was a two-way employee relations plan in which employees were encouraged to provide feedback. In addition, Pepsi had a plan for working with the legal department and a media relations plan to inform the masses. In a short time, the crisis was history and sales soared again.

Practice 8: A Practice of Risk Communication Activities Is Developed

The term *risk communications* frequently is used in connection with health and environmental crises or disasters. According to Marra, the argument goes beyond these issues; he indicated that "all organizations face risk, and it's better to determine possible risks before rather than during a crisis" (personal communication). He emphasized the importance of realizing the difference between actual and perceived risks: "That's where lots of crisis communication campaigns mess up" (F. J. Marra, personal communication, March 1999).

In a broad sense, Marra's discussion of *risk communication* prescribes activities that are similar to those espoused by J. Grunig and Repper's (1992) *issues management* treatment. The basic lesson here is that an organization should make efforts to eliminate risks or issues before crises develop. A children's pajama manufacturer, for example, should be aware that if pajamas are made of flammable fabric, then if a crisis occurs, the company runs the risk of reputation damage

as well as lawsuits. So, not only would the pajama company select less risky fabrics, but it also would engage in activities to communicate this action to its stakeholders.

Practice 9: The Organization Has Ideologies That Encourage, Support, and Champion Crisis Management Preparations and Two-Way Symmetrical Communications Practices

Marra's position is that all of these practices should be ongoing practices so as to possibly prevent crises. Few organizations have ongoing two-way programs, although Johnson & Johnson, in the Tylenol tampering case, had an ongoing two-way symmetrical practice with the medical community that was one of its main strengths during the crisis. At the time, it did not have crisis communication preparations, although it did live by the company credo that served as a crisis guideline. As time passes and the profession of public relations becomes more recognized, practitioners will be more informed of best practices and will implement them.

Many organizations in crises use a two-way communications ideology for crises only, as Pepsi did with the consumer public during the syringe-in-the-can crisis. Consumers could telephone Pepsi on hotlines and talk with staff about the issue. The U.S. Postal Service, after several incidents of violence in its offices, developed these hotlines in an effort to learn about potentially violent employees. The Postal Service agrees that the hotlines, available to all employees, are an improvement in its employee relations program. Management can make efforts to get counseling or other help for irate employees as soon as other employees recognize signs of serious emotional instability. Of course, it is impossible to say whether the communication has prevented violent incidents, but if the work atmosphere is less tense and stressful, then that in itself is progress. In some of these cases, the two-way communication is merely feedback (Model 3), whereas in others, it may be a situation in which the organization might make changes to adjust to the public's demand (Model 4). The latter is preferable to the former, but any two-way communication is better than none.

Practice 10: The Organization, Through Crisis Inventory, Anticipates the Type of Crisis That It Is Likely to Suffer

The organization that not only prepares a crisis communication plan but also plans it for the precise type of crisis that the company might experience, recovers faster and with less damage. In some cases, the company gains admiration and a better reputation. The United Way of America suffered because it had no plan for a crisis caused by its CEO. Pepsi-Cola, although unaware that greedy consumers would place hypodermic needles in cans, was prepared for a product tampering crisis and emerged successfully.

Practice 11: The Organization Maintains a Reputation for Having an Overall "Open and Honest" Policy With Publics at All Times

At first, Johnson & Johnson spokesmen, in the Tylenol tampering case of 1982, told the news media that there was no cyanide in its plants. When they discovered that there was cyanide present, rather than ignore it, they called the media and informed them. The media could (and the sensational news media of the 1990s probably would) make the fact a big story. But the media, in this case, did not play up that fact because all indications were that the tampering was done elsewhere. Johnson & Johnson's communications were with metropolitan newspapers that, even today, tend to be less sensational than television news broadcasts.

CONCLUSION

All of the organizations mentioned in this chapter credited one or more of the practices identified by crisis theories for helping them to suffer less financial, emotional, and/or perceptual damage during their crises. In most cases, the organizations in the learning stage of the crises adopted additional practices to prevent future crises.

The main points to be made in crisis communication are the following. First, crises can and will happen. Second, the organization recovers best when it is prepared for a crisis and when the overall ideology is one of ethical and professional behavior. Third, a detailed crisis communication plan is a good preparation for a crisis. Fourth, a strategic proactive public relations plan is the best crisis prevention.

41

Anticipatory Model of Crisis Management

A Vigilant Response to Technological Crises

BOLANLE A. OLANIRAN

DAVID E. WILLIAMS

Industrial crises, the likes of the Three Mile Island nuclear accident, Chernobyl nuclear disaster, Exxon *Valdez* oil spill, Bhopal toxic chemical leakage, Johnson & Johnson Tylenol tampering, AT&T power outages, silicone gel breast implant problems, ValueJet crash, and (very recently) Odwalla fruit juice poisoning, are organizational crises with a common factor—technology. As industrialized nations attempt to improve productivity, they continue to depend on modern technologies. The dependency on technology is not without its problems given that some organizations have become complacent with the idea that technology is foolproof. The complacency heightens a rather crucial problem—the failure to plan for crisis. Some organizations hold the assumption that with the installation of sophisticated technologies, the probability of failure is reduced or eliminated completely (for a list of

misleading assumptions, see Pearson & Mitroff, 1993). However, evidence has shown that one of the top four leading causes of crises experienced by Fortune 100 companies involves technology or computer breakdowns (Mitroff, Pauchant, & Shrivastava, 1989; Pauchant & Mitroff, 1992a; Udwadia & Mitroff, 1991).

To complicate crisis management efforts, some organizational decision makers believe that no matter what they do, the potential for catastrophic accidents is imminent. Only 28% of the organizations responding to a 1993 National Society for Human Resource Management survey had crisis management programs (Anfuso, 1994; Coco, 1998). A majority of the senior management officials in the surveyed *Fortune* 100 companies reported that it will take a major disaster to get them to prepare for crises (Mitroff et al., 1989). Even Lerbinger (1997) recently claimed, "Like natural disasters, technological accidents will inevitably occur because they follow the laws of chance" (p. 91). This attitude coincides with Perrow's (1984) view on "normal accidents" that some systems especially (i.e., technology) with catastrophic potential possess elements of risk regardless of the attempts to make them safe. Often, the financial requirement and low probability of technological crises lead to inadequate preparation for crises. Perhaps it is this assumption about technology that prompts most organizations to focus on post facto crisis management. To challenge such complacency, this chapter focuses on crisis management and challenges public relations' and other disciplines' vigilant response to crises by stressing precrisis (i.e., anticipation) management.

The goal of this chapter is to present an anticipatory model of crisis management for prevention or deescalation of adverse crisis consequences. First, the chapter addresses the current status of crisis management communication. Then, it presents the anticipatory model of crisis management. Three specific crises are used to illustrate or explain the model, and general implications for organizational decision makers are provided.

Research on crisis management has been popular over the past 10 to 15 years, with a notable increase over the past 5 years. During this span, the research has moved from essentials of media management and public image restoration to the beginnings of theory proposal and model development. The anticipatory model is an example of the latter.

Earlier crisis management research provided the public relations practitioner with somewhat predictable advice for the handling of crisis situations. Researchers explained the role of the media in crisis situations and how the crisis manager must be able to interact with these gatekeepers during the earliest stages of the crisis response (Albrecht, 1996; Fink, 1986; Lerbinger, 1997). The proactive stance was deemed critical in that it allowed the institution to have the initial word about the crisis, thereby gaining the advantage in initial public perception. Benson (1988) credited the proactive stance as being a key in Johnson & Johnson's management of the Tylenol tampering case.

The proactive stance was combined with suggestions and guidelines for the creation of crisis teams, the selection of spokespersons, and the conducting of crisis audits as primary tools for the public relations practitioner working in crisis management. Littlejohn (1983) hinted at the emergence of the anticipatory model in his discussion of the crisis audit. He viewed the crisis audit as "a systematic approach to identifying crisis issues by gathering information on the internal and external environments and establishing priorities on these issues" (p. 41). This stage of crisis management research provided the essential components for practitioners who would be responsible for safeguarding their company against the potential losses to be felt from a crisis event. This research also provided the impetus for current research, which is simultaneously moving toward both a specialization in response strategy and a broader view of theory development.

Recent works in crisis response strategy have been offered by Benoit (1997), Heath and Abel (1996b), Heath and Gray (1997), Sellnow (1993), and Sellnow and Ulmer (1995). Sellnow has recognized the use of specific strategies such as strategic ambiguity and scientific argument in crisis response situations. Heath and others have led the way in revealing the interconnectedness of risk communication and crisis communication. This research gives the crisis manager an insight into the more technical elements of working with technological and environmental crises. Benoit's research has developed a focus on image restoration strategies. The strategies of denial, evading responsibility, reducing offensiveness, correcting action, and mortification are placed in a taxonomy appropriate for evaluation of a particular crisis response situation. These researchers and others have helped to move the response strategy approach from a prescriptive set of procedures to the recognition that crisis management communication can be initiated from a variety of rhetorical perspectives. Lerbinger's (1997) recent work continued the response strategy approach. He detailed best responses for crisis ranging from natural causes to management misconduct.

Theory and model development is the newest level of complexity tapped by crisis management research. Work by Heath (1997), for example, explained how the rhetoric of apologies and the narrative perspective can be insightful frameworks for approaching crisis communication. Coombs and Holladay (1996) contributed a symbolic model of crisis communication that is based on attribution theory and neo-institutionalism. Gonzalez-Herrero and Pratt (1996) constructed a crisis lifestyle with appropriate response strategies to guide the crisis practitioner.

The anticipatory model that is offered in this chapter blends the traditional approach with the realities of technological growth. The anticipatory model borrows from the early crisis work and the notion of preparation that is brought to life with the audit. However, the model and its components are discussed in terms of technological dependency and faulty reliance on its presumed perfection.

ANTICIPATORY MODEL OF CRISIS MANAGEMENT AND TECHNOLOGY

As already indicated, the decision to implement technology in most organizations is based on cost-benefit factors. According to Sethi (1987), the criteria for introducing complex and potentially dangerous technologies are based on potential benefits to those introducing the technologies. The danger of this approach lies in the fact that many stakeholders are unaware of the dangers to which they are being subjected. This suggests an emphasis on potential benefits that ignore imminent dangers for the relevant environment of such technologies. Consequently, decision makers make no effort to avert the impending disaster. The key issue, however, is not whether technology will fail but rather when and how it will fail. Therefore, answering the questions of when and how technology will fail is central to the anticipatory model in solving the puzzle of effective crisis management and prevention. To answer these questions, we look at the assumptions of the anticipatory model.

Understanding and Anticipation

The notion of anticipation in our conceptualization of the crisis management model derives from the works of scholars such as Mitroff and Kilmann (1984) and Weick (1988). From Mitroff and Kilmann (1984), we subscribe to the argument that although one might not be able to alleviate all tragedies from occurring, prevention should be a primary concern. Similarly, we draw from Weick's (1988) *enactment perspective,* which focuses on the prevention of error occurrences in an effort to reduce the magnitude of those errors.

Therefore, with the anticipatory model, we share with these scholars the position that although human errors cannot be eliminated in their entirety, it still is our responsibility to engage prevention efforts that require anticipation of these errors. Sethi (1987) argued that one can anticipate nearly all the unthinkables before they become realities. To this end, the anticipatory model argues that effective crisis management is prevention oriented because it is hard to cope with a crisis for which one has not prepared.

First, it is assumed that the less attention devoted to understanding the nature of a crisis, the more likely the crisis will escalate. Furthermore, Weick (1988) warned, "The very action which enables people to gain some understanding of these complex technologies can also cause those technologies to escalate and kill" (p. 308). Consequently, an understanding of the technology and organizational environment is essential. By *understanding,* we mean a thorough working knowledge of the technologies and their complexities. Technologies are as fallible as humans because they are designed by humans and, as a result, fallibility is embedded in their designs. This reasoning finds some justification in that the majority of industrial disasters are linked to technological failures that are aggravated by human errors (see also Sethi, 1987; Shrivastava, 1987; Shrivastava & Mitroff, 1987; Shrivastava, Mitroff, Miller, & Miglani, 1988; Udwadia & Mitroff, 1991; Weick, 1988, 1996). One does not have to look far to notice that a human act always is one of the principal elements that set crises into motion (Weick, 1988). Therefore, a crisis management model must take into account human errors or human acts that could heighten crisis situations.

Setting Understanding Into Motion With the Anticipatory Model

Two relatively similar concepts, enactment and expectations, set the tone for "understanding" in the anticipatory model. Enactment is defined as a process in which a specific form of action is brought about (Smircich & Stubbart, 1985). Weick (1988) extended the notion of enactment by addressing not only actions but also the consequences imposed by actions. He stated, "The term 'enactment' is used to preserve the central point that when people act, they bring events and structures into existence and set them in motion" (p. 306). Enactment constitutes a retrospective sensemaking process such that the notion of *anticipation* (of crisis) in and of itself is an action given that it determines the choice that an organization makes based on derived information. Justification of this argument lies in the fact that decision makers often find themselves in situations where they have to be able to anticipate opportunities, threats, and weaknesses in their environment and then take appropriate measures to safeguard their interests. Furthermore, it should be noted that individuals' or decision makers' actions or lack of actions result in different (i.e., crisis) outcomes. When people act one way versus another way, they are faced with different types of problems, opportunities, and constraints (Kilduff, 1996; Weick, 1988, 1995, 1996).

Expectations

Expectations are assumptions that people make about certain events or objects. Assumptions made about an occurrence determine whether or not an error results in a crisis of catastrophic proportions. In essence, assumptions by decision makers about technologies represent a critical starting point in crisis prevention. However, assumptions also could bring about the realization of a self-fulfilling prophecy. For example, when organizational decision makers assume

that a technology is foolproof, they might relax safety measures and avoid the necessary redundant procedures. In other words, a technological disaster with an occurrence probability perceived to be nonexistent could not be justified as worthy of prevention. This assumption may be devastating; for example, it has been established that technology becomes more interactively complex as "slack" (e.g., maintenance) decreases (Perrow, 1984). To this end, decision makers set in motion actions that are consistent with their assumptions (Weick, 1988, 1996).

In sum, it is clear from the preceding that crisis prevention requires a thorough understanding of the technology and the context in which the technology is being used. However, there are two essential components that must be present to facilitate the understanding process: enactment and expectation. Whereas enactment consists of specific actions, expectation about an object determines the type of actions taken in the enactment process.[1] Together, these factors constitute the crisis anticipation process, where an occurrence of a crisis is foreseen and an effort is made to eliminate or reduce the degree of the catastrophe. After all, the aim of crisis management is to help organizations avoid crises and manage them more effectively when they happen (Pearson, Clair, Misra, & Mitroff, 1997). The process involved in the anticipatory model is illustrated in Figure 41.1.

ANTICIPATION AS A VIGILANT RESPONSE

Although the process of enactment and expectation, as presented in the model, are potentially crucial in any crisis prevention, by no means do they constitute an automatic vigilant response to crisis. Therefore, this section addresses other concerns relevant to vigilant decision making.

The vigilant decision-making process suggests that decision makers should be able to move through the decision-making process in an efficient manner by carefully analyzing the situation, setting goals, and evaluating the outcomes (Hirokawa & Rost, 1992; Williams & Olaniran,

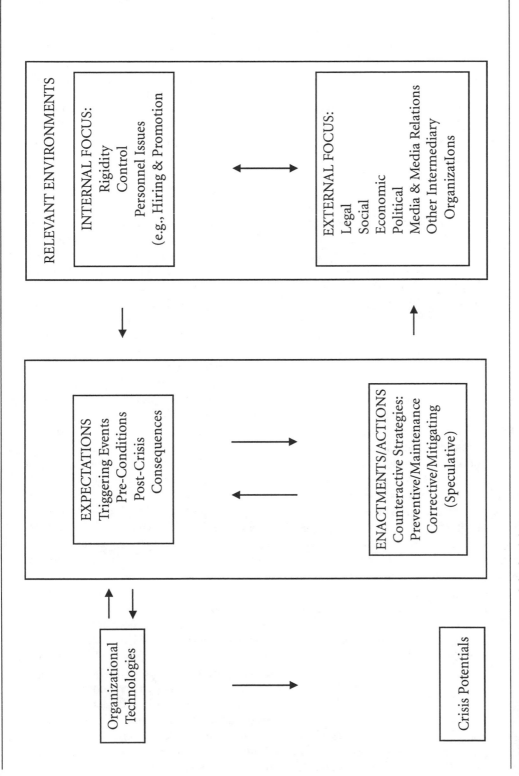

Figure 41.1. Anticipatory Model of Crisis Management

The anticipatory model guides practitioners toward a position in which they can proactively investigate their organizations to determine the most likely causes of technological crisis. With a foundation in anticipation and empowerment, the model optimizes the precautionary abilities of the organization to prevent crisis.

1994). Therefore, the decision-making process centers on the internal communication behaviors within an organization.[2] A vigilant decision-making process is, however, better facilitated under a stress-free environment. Anticipating a crisis focuses on prevention, which implies preparatory practices that can reduce uncertainties when crises do occur. Pearson et al. (1997) concluded, "Practice does not necessarily make perfect, but it does seem to lead to clearer thinking and smoother action under duress" (p. 53).

Anticipating crises would constitute a vigilant response only when the process has managed to scrutinize all the imaginable potential causes of a technological failure/distress. Shrivastava et al. (1988) referred to this process as identifying the "triggering event"—specific events identifiable according to place, time, and agents (p. 288). Although triggering events might have a low probability of occurrence (as the case may be in some technologies), they signal the occurrence of a catastrophic disaster (Kates, 1977; Pearson et al., 1997; Pearson & Mitroff, 1993; Udwadia & Mitroff, 1991). Research has found that crises with the most consequences occur because nobody thinks about them (Mitroff, Harrington, & Gai, 1996; Pearson et al., 1997). Therefore, technology must be scrutinized for places and conditions in which a minute degeneration could escalate exponentially. Technologies are interactively complex; thus, by anticipating smaller problems, one can address them before they spread through the system and develop into a crisis. Because stress accompanies all crises, the goal is to counteract and consequently reduce the stress level in any crisis management. In an effort to facilitate a stress-free environment for decision makers, attention to two key issues during the anticipation process would be beneficial for enhancing a vigilant response. The two issues involve the elements of *rigidity* and *control* as designed by decision makers.

Rigidity

Rigidity consists of the degree of inflexibility that is built into a particular action or process. Thus, the degree of rigidity that is exercised by a decision maker could determine how vigilant a crisis response is. Weick (1988) illustrated the notion of rigidity by looking at the relationship between enactment and commitment. He indicated that as actions become "public" and "irrevocable," they become difficult to change. He stated that these actions also become more "volitional," which in turn makes their explanation more tenacious. This view is consistent with vigilant interaction theory, which argues that how individuals view problems, available options, and consequences will determine the quality of the choices made (Hirokawa & Rost, 1992).

Tenacious justifications that involve rigid explanations about certain actions (Salancik, 1977) could be advantageous in crisis situations for clarifying ambiguity and confusion (Staw, 1980). Furthermore, justification provides structure for maintaining accurate views and analyzing available options (Weick, 1988). However, the principle of rigidity creates a "blinder effect" that prevents individuals from considering competing alternatives. In such cases, one fails to acknowledge that a decision or an explanation provided could adversely intensify the crises. For example, organizational decision makers often are convinced that so long as a regulatory standard for technological upkeep is maintained, they are absolved of liability (Troutwine, 1990). When this happens, decision makers fail to recognize that death or losses attributable to organizational crises may not be dismissed on the basis of simple adherence to the minimal safety standards because different rules and factors come into play depending on the member of the relevant environment affected. Some scholars have addressed this concern in suggesting that organizational responsibility in crisis situations should be decided on the extent to which a crisis could have been anticipated and prevented (Buckey, 1984, 1986; Mitroff, 1986; Pearson et al., 1997; Sethi, 1987). The following statement illustrates a potential danger imminent with rigidity: When a person is committed to the view that fluctuations in electricity cause 90% of variances in electronic gauges, the possibility that a much different percentage is possible will not be entertained until crisis is at the advanced stage (Weick, 1988).

Control

Control can be viewed as the degree of influence that organizational members have at their disposal. Control often is elusive because it has to do with individual perception, especially when the influence is "indirect" in nature, which often is the case.

Control influences crisis in the sense that it affects how individuals respond to crisis situations. For example, when individuals see themselves as having the ability and authority to do something about a crisis, it is more likely that they will take action. Thus, ability and authority go hand in hand and constitute empowerment, which could extend to a vigilant response in crisis management.

Empowering organizational members in crisis management programs provides an opportunity for those members to be able to exercise control in their behaviors by exploring their personal abilities. It is believed that if people are given the opportunity to handle a variety of issues (expanded roles) based on their expertise, then they will be willing to do more than if they are restricted to their formalized job descriptions. Weick (1988) indicated that empowerment creates the belief among employees that they should pay more attention to their surroundings and important issues. Empowerment also leads to greater abilities to control and cope with the environment. When organizational members are empowered, they can respond more quickly to crisis-triggering events as they unfold. For example, in the earlier illustration, an employee looking at the high fluctuations in "gauges" might choose to report to the appropriate quarters or to a technician rather than dismissing the variances as simple fluctuations in electricity, thereby preventing a crisis from occurring. By contrast, an individual with specialized expertise will have a narrow focus that could prevent him or her from seeing the incident as a crisis-triggering event and could miss the chance to prevent a crisis (Perrow, 1984).

Giving organizational members greater control implies that the control in an organization will have to be redistributed. Top-level organizational members should be willing to relinquish some of their control to the lower level members; this could be accomplished by facilitating a cooperative climate and working relationships among members (Kreps, 1990; Quinn & Spreitzer, 1996). Individuals who are closer to the proximity of triggering events should be allowed to attend to the situation rather than having to wait for approval of others in another part of the organizational echelon before they can take action (Olaniran, 1993; Perrow, 1984; Quarantelli, 1997; Tabris, 1984). Furthermore, this process addresses the need for organizational leaders to determine the optimal span of control for specified tasks (Clarke & Perrow, 1996; Quinn & Spreitzer, 1996). This process stresses decentralization contrary to the centralized information dissemination that is prevalent in crisis management literature; the two are not necessarily in contradiction. Centralization addresses information and actions geared toward individuals who are external to the organization such as the public and the media (Shallowitz, 1987). Given the need for consistency, centralization is prudent. However, decentralization of information and action is stressed because of the internal focus of crisis prevention, whereas centralization will only complicate issues by delaying actions due to a greater span of control resulting from different organization constituents and job responsibilities (Quarantelli, 1988; Tabris, 1984). To this end, it is recommended that a small span of control be used in the anticipatory crisis management model due to the interdependent and nonroutinized nature of tasks (Clarke & Perrow, 1996).

Decentralization emphasizes the importance of the career path in organizations and their crisis management. Weick (1995) stressed that decision makers who moved up the organizational ladder via technical ranks usually possessed hands-on experience and the expertise to sense troubleshooting areas in the technological environment. In addition, this experience could help decision makers to recognize the importance of letting people who are closer to the source of the problem attend to it. This strategy assumes that technicians who are closer to the problem source are in the best position to initiate preventive actions pending the availability of top management. Another implication is the need to restructure organizational management promotion and tenure policies. For example, in a crisis-prone organization, it might be beneficial for the management to promote people with technical expertise into decision-making positions when those positions are available (Shrivastava & Mitroff, 1987; Weick, 1988). Relinquishing control might not be an easy task at first. However, having executives anticipate and assess possible perception by various stakeholders in time of crisis might help realize the need to relinquish control to people with expertise, especially when crisis vulnerabilities reveal "unflattering perspectives" (Pearson & Mitroff, 1993). The key is to exercise "duty of loyalty," which suggests not seeking personal gain at the company's expense (Troutwine, 1990).

More significant is the effect of both rigidity and control on the interaction patterns within organizations. Excessive rigidity and inappropriately distributed control would result in one of the following faulty decision-making schemes: (a) failing to recognize positive qualities of alternate decision options, (b) overlooking critical negative aspects of a decision choice, (c) exaggerating positive aspects of a decision option, and (d) overestimating negative consequences of a decision option (Hirokawa & Rost, 1992). Crisis decision processes resulting in one or more of these problems will hinder the decision outcome and render crisis management procedure as a mere "fantasy document" (Clarke & Perrow, 1996). However, avoiding these problems facilitates vigilant decision making (Hirokawa & Rost, 1992).

IMPLICATIONS FOR CRISIS MANAGEMENT

As stated earlier, the general perception of crisis management resides in the view of actions embarked on when crises have escalated and the concern is with postcrisis management. This perspective represents a passive and reactionary view of crisis management. However, what this chapter has done is present a proactive view of crisis management in which efforts are made to avert and eliminate some crises altogether. When crises eventually occur, the proactive measures should be able to minimize the eventual consequences. Therefore, the anticipatory model of crisis management is designed to aid in the preparation and analysis of potential crises. Public relations personnel can then better maintain a positive public image for their company by preventing future crises.

This section examines some implications of the model for some crisis events of our time. Following are three crisis scenarios that could be characterized as either well managed or poorly managed. We evaluate them against the requirements of the anticipatory crisis management model to determine what could have been done differently.

The Tylenol Tampering

September 1982 saw five deaths in the Chicago area resulting from Tylenol capsules laced with cyanide. The finding that cyanide-laced capsules were traced to multiple lots complicated an already tense situation. A public that was shocked by the deaths became more leery, with the fear of more tragedy to come. Consequently, the manufacturer (McNeil Laboratories) had to notify its retailers to withdraw 11 million bottles of regular and extra-strength Tylenol from shelves (Shrivastava et al., 1988). The crisis for Johnson & Johnson (the parent company of McNeil Laboratories) did not end there because the Food and Drug Administration testing after the fact indicated another case of contaminated Tylenol in California. This claim forced an additional recall of Tylenol. Shrivastava and associates (1988) noted that, in total, 31 million bottles of Tylenol were recalled by Johnson & Johnson at an estimated cost of $100 million in addition to multi-million-dollar lawsuits. No culprit was apprehended in the case. Johnson & Johnson was able to bounce back and regain its market share within 8 months. In its efforts to assure consumers of safety, Tylenol was repackaged in a "triple tamper-resistant" package.

About 3½ years later, another death from cyanide-laced Tylenol was reported in the New York area. The capsules were traced to manufacturing plants in Pennsylvania and Puerto Rico, and the incident led to another costly recall of Tylenol products and eventual replacement of Tylenol capsules with caplets. Johnson & Johnson also redesigned its production facilities. The total cost of handling the second crisis was more than $150 million (Shrivastava et al., 1988). Therefore, decision makers at Johnson & Johnson should have imagined the unthinkable and moved to caplets and tamper-proof packaging before rather than after the crisis.

Tylenol's case management was selected because it has been labeled as one of the best examples of crisis management in recent history (Mitroff & Kilmann, 1984). Applying the anticipatory model of crisis management suggests that improvements could have been made. Regarding the anticipation issue, Tylenol poisoning could have been predicted ahead of time. There were cases of medication and food poisoning prior to the Tylenol case. Therefore, decision makers and the public relations experts at Tylenol should have addressed the possibility of whether this could have happened to them. There also remains the question of why Johnson & Johnson waited until the occurrence of the second incident before it replaced capsules with caplets. The explanation will reveal that Johnson & Johnson's decision-making process could have been more effective with a vigilant response to the crisis situation.

It seemed plausible that the decision makers had anticipated that the poisoning episode could recur, and that is why the triple tamper-resistant packaging was implemented. However, the decision was less than adequate, as evidence later indicated with the second episode of tampering. Shrivastava et al. (1988) concurred when they argued that Johnson & Johnson created a precondition for another poisoning by dropping the investigation without finding the source of the first poisoning episode. This argument justifies the human error factor that always is in place in a system/process development. Furthermore, one might question whether the Tylenol manufacturer became complacent with the fact that the

public was sympathetic given that the incident was due to sabotage that was no fault of Johnson & Johnson. The public relations staff at this point should have noted that the technological flaw still was undetected and that public sympathy might wane with a second crisis. The triggering element of the model would have alerted the public relations staff to this possibility. It is uncertain whether, but quite possible that, Johnson & Johnson based its decision not to withdraw capsules from the market purely on financial reasons. Tylenol accounted for 7% of world sales, and the capsule was responsible for between 15% and 20% of the profit in the industry (Shrivastava et al., 1988). The rigid commitment to the Tylenol capsule as a "cash cow" product within the industry might have been simply too important for it to be terminated. Previous research also speaks to the Tylenol situation by indicating that prior experience with crises often results in organizational behavior that makes the company less ready to cope with future crises (Reilly, 1987). Staw, Sandelands, and Dutton (1981) characterized this as the "threat-rigidity" effect based on the assumption that a crisis with low probability of occurrence is less likely to repeat itself, resulting in the perception that money spent in preparation for something that probably never will happen is wasteful (Reilly, 1987).

In summary, the expectations component of the anticipatory model would have indicated to Tylenol's public relations staff that they were in a comfort zone with the assumption that the capsules were safe. Other food poisoning cases could have triggered the proactive response to anticipate possible problems. This places a big responsibility on the public relations staff to be aware of and knowledgeable about the technology used by their company as well as similar technology in use by the competition. This vigilance will help to identify where expectation and rigidity might be problematic for the company.

Exxon Valdez Oil Spill

March 24, 1989, witnessed one of the worst oil spills in history when the Exxon *Valdez* oil tanker hit a reef off Prince William Sound, causing more than 240,000 barrels of oil to spill into the water and along the shore (Shabercoff, 1989; Williams & Olaniran, 1994). To complicate the terrible spill, Exxon found itself battling myriad negative publicity and public perceptions on how it managed the crisis. Just a day after the incident, environmentalists and marine biologists began to place animals on "in danger" lists. Public outcry from various special interest groups began a negative campaign predicting lasting damage from the grounding. The media added to Exxon's woes as they were quick to capitalize on the company's silence by condemning Exxon for the spill while also focusing on its contributory negligence (Small, 1991). The media alleged that the tanker's captain was not at the helm and speculated on the possibility of the captain being intoxicated at the time of the accident. Exxon spent a significant amount of money in the cleanup process and in subsequent multi-million-dollar lawsuits. Small (1991) described Exxon's scenario as an example of how an organization could spend a billion dollars in cleanup and still wind up with a black eye.

Exxon's case has been characterized as among the worst managed crises of the decade (Small, 1991; Williams & Treadaway, 1992). The Exxon case further illustrates the implication of control in crisis management. Like the Tylenol scenario, the question facing Exxon is whether the oil spill could have been prevented. The response to this question is clear from the following explanation.

Certainly, an oil spill of even this magnitude was foreseeable. History has shown similar accidents such as the *Burma Agate* tanker in Galveston Bay. There also were spills in both the Persian Gulf and the Gulf of Mexico where more than 183 million gallons were spilled in each episode. The Amoco *Cadiz* incident in France, and the collision of the *Atlantic Express* near Trinidad spilled 68 million and 92 million gallons of oil, respectively (Small, 1991). Therefore, the question of whether this type of misfortune could happen to Exxon was moot. As a result, Exxon was in a good position to anticipate the spill well in advance of the accident. There also were clear precedents set for how the external focus on legal, social, economic, and media aspects would

affect the company. Public relations staff should have had a detailed plan of action for responding to this spill.

Another issue of importance is why the Alyeska Pipeline Service company anticipated a spill of only 200,000 barrels of oil over a 10-hour period to be the worst-case scenario. The *Valdez* spill resulted in 250,000 barrels during the first 3 hours of the accident (Calloway, 1991). Based on historical evidence, a number in excess of well over a third of the cargo-carrying capacity of the tanker is more prudent. Exxon's chairman himself attested to the inadequacy of Alyeska preparedness and the need for a better handling of the spill as a whole: "When you get 240,000 barrels of oil on the water, you cannot get it all up. But we could have kept up to 50% of the oil from ending up on the beach somewhere" (quoted in Levenson, 1989, p. 51).

In another point of view, Harold, Marcus, and Wallace (1990) concurred and argued that, based on existing technology and experience in past oil spills, it is unreasonable to assume that in a major oil spill more than 15% to 30% of the oil will be picked up mechanically, treated with dispersants, or burned. A significant portion of the oil will hit the beach (p. 23). Although the cleanup team did not foresee the spill potential, Exxon public relations staff should have been able to at least have a better public response.

Rather, Exxon resorted to burden-sharing and blame-shifting strategies. A case in point is the blame placed on the Alaskan Department of Environmental Conservation for not allowing the use of dispersants until the oil spill had gotten out of control in the postcrisis management. Exxon also attributed the delay to the environmentalists advising the government. These two factors should have been dealt with during Exxon's crisis preparation. The anticipatory model directs attention beyond the immediate geographical boundary. Outcry from multiple stakeholders such as environmentalists and local fishermen, is telling. Therefore, the antagonism generated by the need to test the dispersants before application was something that could have been avoided by having the department's and environmentalists' approval for the dispersants well in advance of the grounding. Consequently, administering the dispersants right away could have been done without the need for approval from the Alaskan authorities.

The events following the *Valdez* oil spill reveal some problems concerning the issue of control and rigidity within Exxon. Regarding control, Exxon made no meaningful effort to communicate to the public that it was on top of the situation and that efforts were under way to remedy the situation. In the first instance, its chairman and chief executive officer, Lawrence Rawl, did not appear in public to address the problem until about a week after the spill. Another criticism concerns Rawl's decision to send lower rank executives to Alaska instead of going there himself and taking control. The timing of this decision was inappropriate; in essence, Rawl and Exxon decision makers missed a crucial "window of opportunity" (which usually is the first couple of hours following the crisis) to establish control of the situation. An opportunity to demonstrate concern to the affected stakeholders and win public sympathy (as in the Tylenol case) was lost. Exxon also demonstrated the lack of control over and inadequacy of its crisis preparation plan in the way it depended on the wire service for its information instead of using the media to relay its stories.

According to John Scanlon, a senior vice president at the public relations firm Daniel Edelman Inc., corporations the size of Exxon are known to be rigid by exhibiting a "monolithic bureaucracy" tendency that is slow to act (cited in Small, 1989). Rawl's communication style confirmed this tendency for Exxon. The blaming and shifting of burden are common strategies often employed when one is not willing to accept an alternate view of responsibility. This was demonstrated in several instances where Rawl chose to blame the government and coast guard for delay in the cleanup. Rawl's unyielding behavior was evidenced in his insistence on justification and defense of Exxon's action based on the amount of compensation paid to victims and money spent on the cleanup. Rawl either was unconcerned with or failed to anticipate how the public perceived his comments and presentations. Clearly, this strategy falls short of the recommendation that calls for rhetorical strategies

deemphasizing both technical and financial issues but focusing on safety and humanitarian aid to stakeholders for repairing relationships with the public during crises (Austin, 1998; Ice, 1991; Quarantelli, 1996, 1997).

The decision to restrict the flow of information to Alaska during the early stages of the crisis is presumed to be too rigid and restrictive. Small (1991), reflecting on Fink's (1986) comments, suggested that establishing a news center clearinghouse at a place like New York would have facilitated greater access to information given that New York represents one of the most proficient news centers in the world.

If the anticipatory model had been followed by Exxon public relations experts, then the company would have recognized the preconditions that make a large-scale oil spill possible. The company also would have been aware of its inherent rigidity and how to counter it in case of a spill. Finally, the company would have been better equipped to handle the public reaction of all stakeholders from the external environment.

AT&T Network Outage

AT&T experienced a software glitch that caused a power outage that disrupted its nationwide services for 9 hours in January 1990. The problem was attributed to a software problem that corrupts itself by transmitting different messages among its nodes (Hargadon, 1990). A little less than a month after the incident, AT&T experienced another network outage when a network technician making routing changes forgot to program the routing changes into a control point. It was reported that approximately 200 800 numbers were affected including those of the Internal Revenue Service (IRS) and General Electric. The IRS estimated that thousands of their customers were affected by the event, which lasted for about 2 hours (Keller, 1990). History repeated itself in a third outage that occurred on September 17, 1991, when a switchover to a central office generator failed and the battery-powered backup went dead while technicians were away at a company-sponsored event. Also, the emergency alarm system that was supposed to sound when the battery system was engaged failed to operate. The third outage lasted 6 hours. Among the hardest hit by the third outage was the Federal Aviation Administration; more than 90% of its communications were paralyzed, and the "domino effect" resulted in jammed airports nationwide, with 550 cancellations affecting about 38,000 passengers (Thyfault, Medina, & Hoffman, 1991). In the final analysis, several million private and business calls were either blocked or canceled.

First is the issue of why a few hours of halted services constitutes a crisis. The answer is twofold. The first deals with the fact that most businesses or organizational operations are phone dependent. The second is similar to the first in that a few hours of disruption in phone service could create problems that have a lasting effect.

There are debates as to how well AT&T managed these crises. It was argued that people whose businesses were paralyzed are more likely to see things differently. It was noted, however, that the timing and quick response by the AT&T crew prevented these crises from having a far-reaching deleterious effect. This fact notwithstanding, the whole episode still gives the entire nation something to worry about, such that angry stakeholders demand investigations and the establishment of better reliability standards (Thyfault et al., 1991). One question that needs a closer look is whether this crisis could have been anticipated and prevented.

The occurrence of three consecutive network outages at AT&T preempts the questionability of the company and its crisis management program. Despite the idiosyncratic nature of each of the events, there is an underlying factor common to all of them—technology and human error. Thus, it is difficult to comprehend that these problems or their foreseeability were missed. First, it is suggested that AT&T should have anticipated this problem and that the reason it did not could be attributed to the fact that the company was unprepared. AT&T had been considered to be a reliable company. Part of its reliable reputation stems from its rigorous software testing (Coy & Lewyn, 1990; Finneran, 1990). AT&T, to some extent, must have initiated a certain level of anticipation, with the installation of self-cor-

rective software to ensure that no single failure could shut down the system. However, a lack of thorough reconnaissance of its system still is missing. Software could be corrupted, and the software design created interconnections that exacerbate a prominent problem and prevent quick isolation of troubles. Coy and Lewyn (1990) indicated that the January power outage points to the fact that self-corrective software can go wrong and take systems out of service when there is no evidence of a problem. This particular event points to the fact that AT&T's decision making failed to identify all potential troubleshooting areas of its software. Some argue that the company's reliability might have slipped given the external pressure by competitors and that its reliability is not keeping up with the pace to design "fault-tolerant" technologies (Coy & Lewyn, 1990; Xenakis, 1991). This accentuated the fact that technologically oriented organizations are becoming more and more complacent and cost sensitive to the neglect of crisis prevention programs. The problem, however, is that the advances in computing and communication technologies increase users' susceptibility to technological breakdowns. Xenakis (1991) described the magnitude of the technology-related crisis when he noted that a fiber-optic network cable failure could have negative ramifications for hundreds of thousands of consumers, compared to just a few interruptions by a failure in the old telephone cable system. Stan Welland, a manager of General Electric's telecommunications, put things into perspective: "It used to be when the telephone company messed up your call, they gave you your dime back. We're not talking dimes anymore. We're talking millions of dollars" (quoted in Thyfault, 1991, p. 40).

As part of any vigilant crisis anticipation program, a plan that sets in motion an effort to reduce the negative problems of contributory human error is a must (Pearson & Mitroff, 1993). The second episode raises questions as to why there were not people in place to evaluate and inspect each other's work. For example, it would be prudent to have someone double-check the work of the system's programmer to ensure that the job was done according to specification; this would have prevented the fiasco. As for the third episode, AT&T should have had technicians in place to deal with problems as the crisis symptoms developed (e.g., generator switchover). This problem no doubt would have been corrected before the 6-hour battery power supply elapsed and the crisis escalated to affect the public. The alarm system failure also could have been avoided if the company had explored contingency plans for the alarm failure. The AT&T chairman's statement also emphasized the need for crisis anticipation. He stated after the first incident, "We're going back to Ground Zero . . . on every aspect of this failure" (Coy & Lewyn, 1990, p. 40). Why after the fact? Why was this not done ahead of time? With this statement of action, one must question the occurrences of the subsequent crises. Given that several stakeholders are dependent on the company for their livelihoods, and given the company's claim to reliability, it seems prudent that the company would attempt to protect its reputation and credibility. Instead, consumers lost faith, AT&T's reputation was bruised, and the assumption of its reliability was jeopardized (Finneran, 1990).

AT&T also made some errors in its postcrisis management by not immediately releasing the access codes for switching networks to its customers while repairs or corrections were being made (Hargadon, 1990). AT&T was either rigid or fearful that a temporary switch to competing telecommunication services would become permanent. Not releasing access codes to its users could backfire in a way that prevents stakeholders from understanding and sympathizing with AT&T and its problem. It is suggested that an organization accept responsibility for problems even when the source of the crisis eventually could be traced to an external factor beyond organizational control. In addition, a vigilant anticipatory crisis model should put in place a program that consistently adopts the policy of providing stakeholders with something positive to talk about in an attempt to mitigate the negative publicity (Austin, 1998). The decision not to approve the Federal Communications Commission-imposed backup plan until after the third outage also was not prudent (Thyfault, Bartholomew, & Violino, 1991). A responsible company and vigilant crisis decision makers should

self-monitor the company's affairs such that the self-imposed restrictions in terms of safety and other disaster prevention standards are above and beyond those of the government. Consequently, AT&T's crisis response was not vigilant.

AT&T's crisis episodes emphasize the importance of having a good anticipatory crisis management program. From these cases, one could see how crises have an interdependent effect on other organizations. This raises an important question as to why AT&T's stakeholders do not have in place a plan to remedy an outage. Finneran (1990) provided the explanation that when something breaks regularly, people expect it to break; however, when something never breaks, no one expects it to break (as in the case of telephone services that had been faultless for years).

Each case proves that technology and human errors often are involved in crisis situations. More important, however, is the increasing interactive complexity that is involved in technological designs that increase the potential for crises. Thus, vigilant decision making would include a crisis management plan that anticipates potential sources of crises and deals with them before they grow into major catastrophes. Perhaps an important implication from the anticipatory model of management can be likened to the law of probability indicating that the less frequent the occurrence of an event, the greater the probability that the event will occur in the future. Therefore, organizations should and must continue to evaluate reliance on technology and to prepare for crises in advance. The anticipatory model of crisis management suggests the possibility that crises could be held in check through an understanding of preconditions and instituting action plans to counteract the precondition effects (Pearson & Mitroff, 1993). The importance of this fact cannot be overstated given that instituting action against crisis preconditions could simplify tasks while also subduing potentially catastrophic crises. Weick (1988) indicated that task simplification is important when one considers the fact that stress accompanies all crises but with less effect on simple task performance and that many crises escalate due to the secondary effect of stress-induced crisis decision making. Task simplification effects could be realized when one prepares for the occurrence of one major disaster such that when faced with a crisis, even when the crisis differs from the one anticipated, one can draw some useful information from the anticipated crisis (Mitroff et al., 1989; Pauchant & Mitroff, 1992a). The anticipatory model of crisis management extends beyond organizational boundaries to communities and nations at large. For example, less developed countries are new targets of technology crisis and disaster in terms of nuclear waste dumps and other environmental hazards. With the anticipatory model, a society can empower itself to plan for the risks. With this approach, societies will learn to assess and prepare for crises through the experiences of other communities that have gone through such crises (Shrivastava, 1995).

The model places more power in the hands of public relations practitioners. In exacting this model, public relations experts are asked to move beyond traditional communication responsibilities and to develop skills in researching the company and industry history (with regard to the crisis) and forecasting potential problems with even remote stakeholders. It is believed that the extra burden in preparation would pay dividends if and when a crisis occurs.

To assist practitioners in using this model, a call is made for periodic safety inspections and maintenance audits of technologies and their environments for vulnerability analysis and assessment to identify possible sources of failure in technology and the general social systems (Pearson & Mitroff, 1993; Shrivastava & Mitroff, 1987). Specifically, it is indicated that the most vigilant way of responding to crises and eliminating their catastrophic nature is to reduce interactive complexity design in a system. This implies paying attention to the interactions of human, technological, and general management factors that exacerbate crises (Shrivastava & Mitroff, 1987; Weick, 1988). Indeed, the fact that no system could be failure-proof and that one cannot prevent all crises (Pauchant & Mitroff, 1992a; Perrow, 1984) should not hinder us from anticipating the problems and taking actions to prevent crises from happening. To adopt the anticipatory model of crisis management is to be crisis prepared. Being prepared requires having self-awareness knowledge, realizing one's vulnerability to crisis, and engaging a plan of action that counteracts the risk of crisis (Udwadia & Mitroff, 1991). No additional warnings are needed to prove to decision makers their organizational vulnerability to crises. Events of recent years are sufficient.

NOTES

1. To say that expectation engaged the enactment process is not to make a linear assumption about the two components. Thus, an assumption of interdependency between the two factors is assumed given that the enactment process could result in, or set into motion, a condition in which the expectation is made based on the action taken during the enactment.

2. The emphasis on the internal factors does not lessen the importance of external factors; rather, it assumes that the external factors, as indicated in Figure 41.1, are constant variables that always are present regardless of specific internal strategies. They are not discussed in this chapter due to space limitations and because they have been covered extensively elsewhere (e.g., Shrivastava et al., 1988).

Corporate Apologia

When an Organization Speaks in Defense of Itself

KEITH MICHAEL HEARIT

In November 1992, the ABC News program *PrimeTime Live* aired a broadcast charging that the North Carolina-based Food Lion tolerated unsanitary conditions in its grocery stores, often repackaging and selling old meat and other products. Shortly after the program aired, Food Lion filed a lawsuit against ABC News. In its suit, the chain did not deny the truthfulness of the allegations but countercharged that the news organization had engaged in fraud in that its producers had misrepresented their identities to secure positions at Food Lion and had used hidden cameras to videotape alleged wrongdoing at the grocery chain. A jury agreed, fining ABC News $5.5 million in punitive damages, an amount later reduced to $315,000 ("Food Lion Award," 1997).

The aforementioned *apologetic* exchange between ABC News and Food Lion is paradigmatic of the charges and countercharges faced by organizations that operate in the turbulent contemporary environment. Driven by the need to protect their multi-million-dollar investments in products and reputations, coupled with the accompanying trend of media organizations (now increasingly corporate owned and bottom line oriented) to pursue dramatic stories so as to generate higher ratings, organizations regularly challenge one another's integrity and contemporaneously defend themselves against such allegations. This chapter explores such contexts and their appurtenances to arrive at an understanding of the distinctive characteristics of corporate response to wrongdoing. In view of this purpose, the chapter first defines the key terms of apologetic inquiry and then analyzes the circumstances likely to result in apologetic discourse. It then details the substantive conventions that inhere in this form of communication. Finally, it draws a series of conclusions for both scholars and practitioners.

DEFINITIONAL ISSUES

Originally characterized as a genre of discourse that explicated how individuals respond to charges of wrongdoing, the study of apologia increasingly has been applied to organizational contexts. Indeed, a number of theorists have argued that the nature of discourse during the 20th century changed, undergoing a paradigmatic shift from an individualist form to a corporate one. These theorists have concluded that discourse increasingly emanates from an institutional source, is prepackaged and focus group tested, and is designed to appeal to a constituency as opposed to a generalized or universal audience (Crable, 1986; Sproule, 1988). Concomitant with this trend, due to the heavily mediated environment that characterizes Western culture, organizations (be they for-profit, not-for-profit, or governmental) increasingly find themselves the targets of criticism that challenges their legitimacy or social responsibility (Hearit, 1995b).

Although the criticism of organizations is not a recent phenomenon (witness Tarbell's [1904] *A History of the Standard Oil Company*), the modern criticism of organizations has become more prolific, more widespread, and often more vitriolic. It is against such a backdrop that organizations respond to charges of wrongdoing with apologiae. An apologia is not an apology, although the terms do share the same etymological root (Tavuchis, 1991). Rather, an apologia is a response to criticism that seeks to present a compelling competing account of organizational actions (Hearit, 1994). Although the nature of this type of "defense" has many permutations, common to all responses is that an organization seeks to "clear its name," having as its motive the purification of its image (Benoit, 1995a; Fisher, 1970; Goffman, 1971; Snyder, Higgins, & Stucky, 1983).

Although a number of scholars have attempted to address the issue (Ryan, 1982; Ware & Linkugel, 1973), perhaps the fullest articulation of what determines the nature of apologetic situations was offered by Kruse (1981). She concluded that three factors must be present in a situation for it to be considered apologetic: It must feature an ethical charge of wrongdoing, it requires the purification of one's reputation as the primary motive for responding (a response in which an audience expects a message to be apologetic), and it must be delivered by the self in defense of the self. Although Kruse dismissed the possibility of a *corporate* apologia, when one considers that organizations are recognized before the law as *juristic* persons coupled with the fact that they seek to construct singularly distinct social personae, it follows that corporations are indeed capable of apologiae and do fulfill Kruse's three criteria (Dionisopoulos & Vibbert, 1983). Corporate apologiae are a response to ethical charges in which organizations have as their primary motive the defense of their reputations and to which they offer discourse in *self*-defense that explains, denies, or justifies their actions.

In exploring the nature of the ethical charge against organizations qua organizations, Hearit (1995b) proposed that the role of the situation be reconceptualized as a legitimation crisis. Social legitimacy theory proposes that organizations are legitimate to the degree that their values are reflective of larger societal values (Dowling & Pfeffer, 1975). Consequently, when organizational actions are construed to have violated normative public values, the organizations face legitimacy crises:

> A clear indicator of a social legitimacy crisis is the emergence of public animosity toward the corporation. This hostility is a form of social sanction by which the supra-system (e.g., media, opinion leaders, consumers, etc.) in effect says, "We don't approve of what you have done." (Hearit, 1995b, p. 3)

Although these conceptualizations are useful to delineate the valuative and conditional nature of what constitutes apologetic discourse, little work has been done to articulate the contexts in which organizational apologiae occur. Indeed, apologia scholars must turn to the work of crisis researchers for development of the situations to which organizations are likely to face criticism for their actions. Drawing from the models of Marcus and Goodman (1991) and Coombs (1995), this analysis suggests four contexts that substantively describe the situations likely to result in apologetic discourse. First, *accidents* describes those one-time events that typically occur with little warning and count innocents as their victims. Although unintentional, they frequently have systemic causes (Perrow, 1984). Conversely, *scandals and illegalities* characterizes the context that surrounds the disclosure that a company intentionally engages in unethical and/ or illegal acts that bring damage to its reputation and often result in social sanction. Third, *product safety incidents* tend to emerge in an opposite manner to accidents; instead of occurring randomly and unexpectedly, they emerge over time as evidence from variable sources begins to appear. A final category, *social irresponsibility,* encompasses those contexts in which critics have redefined company actions to violate current social and community norms. This could be as simple as an unfortunate misstatement by a chief executive officer (CEO) or as developed as the act of moving a company plant to a cheaper labor market.

SUBSTANTIVE AND STYLISTIC ISSUES

Message Strategies

Much is known about the "factors" or "strategies" exercised by apologists that face ethical criticism. Indeed, the most prolific line of research, the cataloging of message strategies, has resulted in a number of competing taxonomies. Perhaps the most famous and widely used recounting of message strategies was articulated by Ware and Linkugel (1973). They proposed that apologists caught in a wrongdoing use one or a combination of the following four strategies: denial, bolstering, differentiation, and transcendence. Denial, of course, is a simple rejection of charges that characterizes them as untrue; those who cannot deny an act are likely to deny that they *intended* to commit an act, for intent is a key factor in the judgment of culpability. Bolstering is an identificational strategy in which constituents are reminded of past relationships. Differentiation is a redefinition strategy that divides a singular context into two distinct meanings. Transcendence occurs when an apologist is able to redefine the context of the alleged wrongdoing into a broader and more abstract context.

These strategies are directly applicable to the corporate context, although some revision of their use is necessary. Denial frequently is an attempt to claim that an incident or accident was not a corporation's responsibility (Benoit & Lindsey, 1987; Ice, 1991; Schultz & Seeger, 1991), whereas bolstering occurs when organizations attempt to connect themselves to their publics through identification (Ice, 1991). A primary way in which corporations bolster is to remind constituents of the number of jobs the firm brings to a community. Differentiation, conversely, is a strategy that attempts to change public perceptions by separating and redefining issues. Perhaps transcendence is the most difficult to apply to the corporate context. Ice (1991) defined transcendence as a vehicle that apologists use to identify "abstract principles that supersede the present public issues" (p. 344). One such example of transcendence, according to Dionisopoulos (1986), occurred when the atomic power industry, in its post-Three Mile Island discourse, attempted to redefine atomic power from simple use of electricity to a vehicle that reduced dependence on foreign oil. Hearit (1996) attempted to maintain the moral undercurrent in Ware and Linkugel's (1973) use of transcendence, explicating its use by Johnson Controls in defense of the company's fetal protection policy that sought to justify discrimination against women because of the "greater good" of protecting unborn children.

Benoit (1995a) and Brinson and Benoit (1996) offered fuller descriptions of the message strategies used by corporate apologists. Benoit's theory of image restoration strategies argued that individuals and organizations, when charged with wrongdoing, seek to save face. They do so by using one or a combination of the following strategies: denial, evading responsibility, reducing offensiveness, corrective action, and mortification.

Denial occurs when a corporation chooses to dispute having committed an alleged act (Brinson & Benoit, 1996) or at least to deny that it was responsible (Benoit, 1995a). A variant of denial occurs when a company tries to "shift the blame" or to scapegoat another, perhaps its employees or a union.

Evasion of responsibility transpires when an organization seeks to attenuate its responsibility for an offensive act (Benoit, 1995a). One way in which the company does this is by claiming that it was provoked. A second approach to evading responsibility is to use a strategy of defeasibility; here, the accused corporation claims that events really were beyond its control. A third method is to assert that the outcome was the result of an accident. A final approach is to claim that the company had good motives or intentions, even though the outcome was bad.

Reducing the offensiveness of an event happens when a company uses one of six strategies to make its wrongdoing appear to be less serious. One way in which to do this is to bolster—a strategy that attempts to "strengthen . . . positive feelings toward the accused" (Brinson & Benoit, 1996, p. 31). A company also can use minimization to reduce offensiveness by seeking to reduce the magnitude of the anger directed at the organization. Drawing from Ware and Linkugel (1973), Benoit (1995a) proposed that organizations use both differentiation, which seeks to distinguish the act from other similar acts, and transcendence, which changes the context through an appeal to a higher value system for judgment as vehicles by which to lessen the offensiveness of an act. Two other strategies are available to a company to reduce offensiveness. One is to attack its accusers, in particular their credibility, and the second is to offer to pay compensation to help mitigate suffering and reduce ill will.

Another mechanism that an organization can draw on to repair its damaged image is a strategy of corrective action. Here, the apologist promises to correct a problem in such a way that it is unlikely to recur (Benoit, 1995a). This strategy is critical because it reassures key publics that the problem has been isolated and resolved and that the chances of its return are remote (Hearit, 1995b). Benoit astutely observed that an organization can draw on this strategy without ever admitting guilt (Benoit, 1995a; Benoit & Lindsey, 1987).

Mortification occurs when a corporation apologizes and asks for forgiveness (Benoit, 1995a). Here, the organization admits responsi-

bility and seeks a pardon. When a company takes this tact, it frequently couples it with corrective action (Benoit, 1995a).

Postures

Although explicating the message strategies available to corporate apologists is a necessary step to fully develop understanding of apologia, such an approach does not provide an awareness of how such strategies are combined in actual apologetic discourse. In light of this fact, researchers since Ware and Linkugel (1973) have attempted to develop the postures enacted by apologists when they respond to allegations of wrongdoing. Drawing on the research of a number of scholars (Benoit, 1995a; Fitzpatrick & Rubin, 1995; Hearit, 1994), it is possible to conclude that corporations regularly take one of five stances when dealing with the problem of their guilt: denial, counterattack, differentiation, apology, or legal. Each of the five stances is rooted in the notion that the fundamental problem in apologetic situations is that of guilt and that the motive for apologists is to distance (or dissociate) themselves from their guilt (Benoit, 1995a; Fisher, 1970). Put another way, all apologetic efforts rely on dissociations, which are reality-changing strategies whereby apologists attempt to bifurcate previously unitary concepts by claiming that the charges leveled against the organizations are "mere appearances" (i.e., false) and do not represent the "true reality" of the situations (Perelman & Olbrechts-Tyteca, 1969).

Denial

Apologists caught in wrongdoing need to examine the context carefully and plan their strategic responses based on a calculus that takes into account the perceived levels of their guilt and public antipathy. In this first form, corporations assume a posture of denial because either (a) they are not guilty, (b) they are in a position to deny that the actions were intentional (and therefore of limited culpability), or (c) they choose a defensive strategy out of fear of liability in which they deny guilt regardless of the public evidence. All three rationales have as a guiding principle the belief that a strategy of denial will assist organizations in distancing themselves from the wrongdoing.

When using a denial posture, companies in effect profess that "We're not guilty" or "We want to make it clear that it never was our intention for anything bad to happen." At such times, they use an opinion-knowledge dissociation to deny guilt by "claiming that current discussions . . . are mere 'opinions' that do not represent 'actual knowledge' of the events" (Hearit, 1994, p. 119). Such was the tact taken by Johnson & Johnson in 1982 when it was disclosed that seven people had died after taking Tylenol, which had been contaminated with cyanide (Benoit & Lindsey, 1987). The use of denial worked well for Tylenol due to the fact that third-party sources quickly concluded that the company was not at fault. A similar stance was taken by Chrysler in 1987 when critics charged that it had engaged in consumer fraud by driving vehicles with unhooked odometers for a period of time before rehooking them and selling the vehicles as new (Hearit, 1994). Chrysler claimed that its critics' charges were opinions and that those who had real knowledge of the situation knew that the auto maker really was engaged in a "valid quality assurance program" (p. 119).

The use of denial is not without problems. First, individuals are skeptical of corporate speech to begin with and are unlikely to believe it absent some third-party corroborating evidence that legitimizes corporations' claims such as in the aforementioned Tylenol episode (Bradford & Garrett, 1995). Brinson and Benoit (1996), for example, found that in response to allegations that Dow Corning's silicone breast implants were unsafe, the company's initial stance of outright denial was a failure and that the company's image restoration efforts began to improve only when it tried a more conciliatory approach. Similarly, Huxman and Bruce (1995) concluded that Dow Chemical Company faced image problems rooted in the 1960s napalm controversy in which the company maintained a denial stance and was unwilling to try more accommodating or explanative approaches. Perhaps the best counsel for companies that use denial is to couple it with

a corrective action strategy to assure customers that any potential for problems has been rendered safe (Benoit, 1995a; Hearit 1995b).

Counterattack

A variant of denial that has appeared more frequently of late is the use of counterattack. In such occurrences, organizations not only deny that they are guilty of the charges but also take the criticism one step further and allege that their critics are ethically suspect for having leveled false charges. This type of an approach was taken by the Suzuki Corporation in 1988 when it responded to allegations by *Consumer Reports* magazine that the Samurai was prone to rollover by labeling the charges "defamatory" (Hearit, 1995a, p. 122). Here, organizations deal with the problem of guilt by denying it and subsequently attempting to transfer it to the accusers. This strategy is powerful rhetorically because it inverts the direction of the exchange; instead of the advantage being held by the critics, it enables the accused to regain some definitional hegemony and argumentative momentum (Hearit, 1996). Unfortunately, companies do not have to be "not guilty" to employ the counterattack strategy; in fact, it is a tool for unethical companies that seek to extricate themselves from criticism—or at least to muddy the waters a bit. Such was the approach taken by Sears to allegations by the California Department of Consumer Affairs in 1992 that the company had systematically overcharged customers in its auto repair business. The approach failed for Sears and made the company look more guilty (Benoit, 1995b).

Due to the fact that allegations of wrongdoing increasingly come from corporate-owned media institutions, companies—regardless of their degree of guilt—level the following countercharges to draw rhetorical blood: (a) that reporters used preconceived storylines; (b) that the media edited the stories unfairly; and/or (c) that the media, rather than acting in the public interest, hyped stories to generate high ratings and profits (Hearit, 1996). Such a strategy is highly risky and portrays companies as aggressive. To hedge against this fact, Dionisopoulos and Vibbert (1988), in their study of the counterattack by Mobil Oil to allegations by CBS that the company had engaged in "creative bookkeeping" to inflate profits, observed that corporations that level countercharges do so by claiming to act in the "public interest."

Differentiation

The most frequently used stance by those accused of wrongdoing by far is the use of a differentiation posture. This occurs frequently not because it is the most rhetorically powerful but rather because corporate acts seldom are guilt free. More often than not, companies bear *some* level of responsibility for the alleged wrongdoing, although the degree to which they are guilty is not always entirely clear. In instances such as these, organizations are most likely to engage in some form of an individual-group dissociation in which they find scapegoats and then argue that individuals acted on their own behalf without organizational sanction (Hearit, 1994, 1995a, 1995b). In so doing, guilt is transferred from the organizations qua organizations and located in individuals who can then be disciplined, fired, and/or prosecuted by the authorities. This leaves the organizations to play the role of innocents.

Such was the strategy taken by American Airlines in 1990 when it responded to criticism for canceling 11% of its flights during the busy holiday season by claiming that it was due to an "illegal sick-out" coordinated by the Allied Pilots Association (Hearit, 1995a). Here, the company scapegoated its employees—its pilots—for a company-wide failure, claiming that "most of our 100,000 employees are dedicated to that goal [superior service]" (Hearit, 1995a, p. 125). A similar strategy was chosen by AT&T in 1991 when the company lost the capacity to direct long-distance calls into and out of New York City for several hours. AT&T's initial strategy was to transfer the blame to low-level employees, charging that they failed to notice alarms that would have alerted the company to pending problems and would have allowed it to prevent them (Benoit & Brinson, 1994).

Employees are not the only target; corporations have been known to shift blame to their subsidiaries. Union Carbide claimed that the leak of methyl isocynate, which caused the deaths of more than 2,000 Indians in 1984, was not due to a failure on the part of Union Carbide in general but rather was the fault of the locally controlled Union Carbide India Ltd. that administered the plant in which the gas leak occurred (Ice, 1991). Similarly, after it was disclosed that Toshiba had sold "top secret" milling equipment to the then Soviet Union in 1987, thereby enabling the Soviet military to produce submarines more difficult to detect by U.S. sonar, the company went to great lengths to claim that the act was perpetrated by its subsidiary, the Toshiba Machine Company, and that the Toshiba Corporation had no knowledge of the act and subsequently was outraged when it was discovered (Hearit, 1994). In other words, this strategy draws a distinction between a corporation and its subsidiaries, claiming that they are two altogether different entities (Hearit, 1994).

Not all efforts at a differentiation posture enact a strategy of shifting the blame. In 1988, when the Chrysler Corporation was accused of violating its commitment to continue building automobiles in its aging plant in Kenosha, Wisconsin (Schultz & Seeger, 1991), it used a strategy of defeasibility. Here, the company admitted that it had changed its plans from an earlier agreement but justified doing so by claiming that the current market conditions had made the 85-year-old plant no longer viable. The company's CEO, Lee Iacocca, claimed that if the company was "guilty" of any charge, it was that management was a group of "cockeyed optimists" who believed that an outdated plant could still be profitable (p. 56).

Apology

In another posture enacted to respond to criticism, organizations deal with the problem of their guilt by acknowledging it largely because they have no other choice. When doing so, they use an act-essence dissociation to claim that "accidents" were isolated acts and should not be taken as representative of the companies' essences. The use of apologies by corporations, however, seldom offers clear statements that seek forgiveness; rather, due to liability concerns, they tend to make use of statements of regret in which companies extend how sorry they are that the accidents occurred while carefully avoiding any acknowledgments that they are indeed responsible (Hearit, 1994).

Probably the most famous corporate apology is the case of Exxon, which, in response to the *Valdez* oil spill in Prince William Sound in 1989, took out a full-page advertisement in more than 100 magazines and newspapers to apologize to the people of Alaska (Hearit, 1995b). In its "open letter," CEO Lawrence Rawl defined the spill as an "accident" and was careful *not* to assume full responsibility (Tyler, 1997, p. 58; Williams & Olaniran, 1994). Not all uses of the apology stance avoid the question of responsibility so directly. During the aforementioned AT&T crisis, after company officials concluded that a differentiation posture was ineffectual, the company switched to a more direct stance of apology and concessions, a move that Benoit and Brinson (1994) argued helped AT&T to resolve the crisis more quickly and with less damage to the company's image.

In this case, corporate use of discourse benefits from the ambiguities inherent in language. When the term *apology* is used, it gives the impression of a close parallel between individual and corporate apologies. This is unfortunate, for unlike the case with an individual, when a corporation apologizes, it does not expect that an incident will be forgotten; rather, given the gross inequities of size, the primary purpose of a corporate apology, as opposed to an interpersonal apology, is to put on the public record an acknowledgment that the company is responsible for an act (Tavuchis, 1991).

Legal

In this final posture, rather than taking an aggressive public posture, corporations adopt a legal stance toward their alleged wrongdoing. Typical use of this posture occurs when corporations encounter product safety incidents in which the threat of liability judgments is considerable. Because of this, these organizations adopt denial strategies, using an opinion-knowledge dissociation to argue that those who criticize the integrity of their products do so without full understandings of "all the facts" (Hearit, 1994). This strategy, more than most, suggests that organizations have recognized that their problems will be long term and, consequently, have turned over the handling of the problems to legal staffs that will adjudicate their cases. In their analysis of how organizations enact this posture, Fitzpatrick and Rubin (1995) described the components of traditional legal strategy:

> (1) say nothing; (2) say as little as possible and release it as quietly as possible; (3) say as little as possible, citing privacy laws, company policy, or sensitivity; (4) deny guilt and/or act indignant that such charges could possibly have been made; or (5) shift or, if necessary, share the blame with the plaintiff. . . . Never admit blame. (p. 22)

Such was the approach taken by a number of organizations faced with product safety cases. In defending its Pinto from charges that it was prone to explode in rear-impact collisions, the Ford Motor Company conducted its public defense primarily through the courtroom (Kaufmann, Kesner, & Hazen, 1994). Similarly, A. H. Robins, in its defense of the Dalkon Shield during the 1970s, took a legal approach that accommodated public demands only when forced to do so (Mintz, 1985). Due to liability fears, the company did not publicly acknowledge a problem with the device, nor did it extend a recall. In such instances, corporations take a posture of silence unless significant court thresholds are crossed and news is generated (Hearit, 1994). In addition, corporations that use this approach often are inclined to settle out of court; when they do so, they cite the costs of litigation (both financial and personal) as the rationale and sign agreements with confidentiality clauses and acknowledgments that no guilt is admitted. Research conducted by Fitzpatrick and Rubin (1995) found that the legal approach is the strategy most frequently adopted by companies.

CEO/Persona

Apologiae are a form of *self*-defense in which individuals respond to accusations against their characters (Kruse, 1981). Although corporations are not individuals but rather juristic persons before the law, the current trend is for corporations to make use of the personae of CEOs to deliver their apologiae (Fox, 1982; Seeger, 1986). The cases surveyed in this chapter are illustrative. CEO Richard Allen delivered the AT&T apologia (Benoit & Brinson, 1994). Iacocca delivered the apologia for Chrysler, as did the CEO for the Toshiba Corporation (Hearit, 1994). Similarly, Rawl spoke in defense of Exxon (Tyler, 1997), and Ed Brennan defended Sears from allegations of fraud (Benoit, 1995b). Such a move has two effects. First, apologiae are, at root, character-based defenses in which people measure the degree to which individuals have changed, and the use of CEOs assists auditors in gauging corporate sincerity. Second, if apologiae fail, then there are ready-made scapegoats of individuals (i.e., the CEOs) who have publicly taken responsibility for the situations.

Ideological Analysis

Ideologically, corporations draw on cultural myths that they invoke in their responses to allegations of wrongdoing. The first, the myth of managerial rationality, suggests that organizations are capable of learning from their errors; that is, after acts have been committed, the use of social sanctions by consumers, whether it be the cutting up of credit cards, pickets outside of companies' headquarters, or simply lack of future patronization, "sends a message" to companies that their acts are not going to be tolerated and that they had better "learn" from their wrongdoing (Hearit, 1995b).

A second myth that organizations use is the fiction that surrounds the use of technology. Ice (1991) was one of the first to note that corpora-

tions invoke technology as an argumentative form to justify their actions. They do this by moving the locus of arguments from a public sphere to a technical sphere, one that privileges their positions (Goodnight, 1982). In so doing, technology obscures the argumentative playing field in that it is possessed only by the offending corporations; hence, there is no way in which to verify the legitimacy of the arguments (Hearit, 1995b).

Not only is technology invoked to privilege the arguments made by corporations, but the myth of technological restoration is a powerful resource used by organizations to reassure key publics and critics that the problems have been taken care of so that they do not reappear (Hearit, 1995b). A corrective action strategy draws on this myth by offering a vehicle by which organizations are able to "undo" their wrongdoing by harnessing the redemptive power of technology and lessening their long-term culpability (Brown & Crable, 1973). After the oil spill in Prince William Sound, for example, Exxon sought to use Corexit 9527, a bioremediation technology that would break down the oil, to claim that it could expunge the harm from the spill of oil (Hearit, 1995b).

Legal and Liability Issues

Surprisingly undeveloped in the research on apologia is an understanding of the role of liability as it affects the choices made by corporations (Kaufmann et al., 1994). Indeed, preliminary inquiries suggest that the threat of liability is paramount in nearly all apologetic situations (Tyler, 1997). The problem is perhaps best conceptualized by Tyler (1997), who argued that although corporate officials are inclined to take responsibility for their actions, the prospect of liability prohibits them from doing so because their primary legal responsibility is to their shareholders. Complicating this situation is the fact that whereas activist groups, victims, consumers, and the media clamor for public apologies, the companies' stockholders expect strong statements of denial that, as Marcus and Goodman (1991) have shown, result in a positive effect on equity value. Consequently, organizations are caught in a classic Hobson's choice: Do they apologize and violate their legal responsibility to their shareholders, or do they not apologize and risk alienation of key publics and consumer groups?

The subsequent impact on corporate communication is easy to ascertain. Tyler (1997), for example, argued that the subsequent effect is that corporations communicate equivocally. The more likely consequence is that organizations issue statements of regret that offer remorse for what has occurred or its consequences without acknowledging that they are responsible for causing the actions (Fitzpatrick, 1995; Hearit, 1994). Such a difficult position leaves companies in the paradoxical position of apologizing for what they have not done and instituting changes to ensure that it does not recur.

This is not to say that liability issues affect all corporate communicative situations. There are instances in which organizations accused of wrongdoing face contexts in which the threat of lawsuits, particularly ones with high punitive damage potential, is limited. In such cases, organizations are much more inclined to claim responsibility and reap the public relations benefit for "doing the right thing." Examples include the aforementioned AT&T apology for a technical failure (Benoit & Brinson, 1994; Tyler, 1997) and the situation faced by Volvo in 1990 when it was accused by the Texas attorney general of using misleading advertising in communicating the strength of its vehicles to withstand repeated drive-overs by a "monster truck" (Hearit, 1994). A second situation in which organizations may accept responsibility with little fear of liability, according to Wagatsuma and Rosett (1986), is when apologies can be used to mitigate damages in defamation suits as part of settlements or punishments.

RESEARCH ISSUES

Having considered the substantive and situational nature of the research on corporate apologia, I now draw a number of conclusions as to the character of the research inquiry, the scope of the research program, and the yield that the past decade of vigorous research on the subject has rendered.

One of the fundamental questions that provides an invaluable line of research with which scholars have yet to wrestle is the question as to the fundamental nature of organizations. To what degree are organizations singular social actors or a not yet understood form of *corporate* actors? Organizations are made up of large numbers of individuals, but they are much more than aggregates of the individuals. For example, they take on a singular social quality and are recognized by the law as individual social actors. They also have been shown to have lives often long beyond those of their employees; they pursue survival and seek to self-perpetuate themselves. To date, only Cheney (1992) has attempted to address these fundamental issues.

Although scholars know a great deal of the message strategies used by corporate apologists, comparatively little is known about *when* they say what they say. Fink (1986), for example, argued persuasively that crises typically go through four identifiable stages: crisis buildup, crisis breakout, abatement, and termination. During these different stages, corporations tend to vary their message strategies to fit the contexts and frequently change strategies to find those that are effective. One suspects, for example, that the initial impulse during a crisis is to begin with a strategy of denial and to try other approaches only once it is clear that denial no longer will work for the company. In the current research on apologia, whereas the different strategies that organizations use are exhaustively cataloged, there is a comparatively unsophisticated sense of how organizations tend to favor one strategy over another at different stages of the life cycles of crises. In other words, a weakness of this line of research is that scholars tend to treat the responses of organizations as static and linear when in reality they are dynamic and variable.

Closely related to this point is that the research development of the nature of the context that results in apologetic discourse has remained relatively unexplored. Most scholars seem to treat the situation as solely a defense to a charge.

Little is known (beyond a sentence or two) as to how the contexts to which apologists respond differ, nor is there an understanding of how the different contexts of criticism have an impact on the rhetorical stances chosen by companies. To date, Coombs (1995) and Marcus and Goodman (1991) have offered the fullest development of the contexts of crises that is applicable to apologetic discourse. This chapter offers a hybrid of the two, proposing that corporations face media criticism for four different types of wrongdoing: accidents, scandals and illegalities, product safety incidents, and social irresponsibility. Research is needed to determine whether this category system is exhaustive enough to apply to all apologetic discourse and whether certain types of apologetic contexts tend to result in specified communication choices. For example, one suspects that organizations are more likely to apologize when they have accidents because accidents are by their nature unintentional. Similarly, one imagines that scapegoating probably occurs when corporations are engaged in legal scandals and, hence, people can be fired.

Perhaps one of the most glaring research weaknesses is the relatively scant attention paid to the effect of liability on the rhetorical choices of apologists when they respond to allegations. Although a few scholars have offered conclusions that corporations carefully craft their messages to avoid lawsuits (Fitzpatrick, 1995; Hearit, 1995b; Kaufmann et al., 1994; Tyler, 1997), little work has been done to arrive at a complete understanding of what probably is the core determinant that apologists consider when formulating their responses to criticism.

The final criticism that offers a potentially fruitful line of research is methodological in nature. Scholars know a great deal about the strategies that apologists draw on when charged with wrongdoing, but relatively few inquiries have attempted to develop which of these message strategies are likely to find success with key publics or the means to measure success (Bradford & Garrett, 1995; Coombs, 1995). Put another way, qualitatively little is known from a social scientific perspective concerning the effectiveness of these strategies or of the results that come from changes in actions and policies, particularly

from a strategic issues management perspective (Heath, 1997).

PRACTITIONER ISSUES

The research of the past decade has witnessed the emergence of a number of major programs of research that have thoroughly explored the substantive dimensions of this form of corporate speech, arriving at a rich understanding of what it is that apologists say when they are criticized (Benoit, 1995a; Coombs, 1995; Hearit, 1995b). One virtue of this research program is its direct relevance to practitioners. As this chapter has shown, corporate apologists have available to them a wide variety and well-cataloged repertoire of strategies from which to draw when defending their reputations. They can deny, counterattack, shift the blame, propose corrective action, and/or apologize.

The cataloging of message strategies has meaning to professionals only when one considers the role that the problem of guilt plays in determining which message strategy to enact. Consequently, a calculus that takes into account the level of guilt sustained by organizations offers prescriptions for organizational response. To those organizations that perceive themselves as not guilty of the allegations, for example, a stance of denial or even counterattack is the preferred choice. Conversely, for those organizations that clearly are guilty, a strategy of apology offers the only way in which to attenuate their culpability. It is likely that most organizations fall somewhere in the middle—that they are indeed responsible for the alleged acts to some degree, although the degree to which the causes were their explicit policies is unclear. In such instances, research suggests that most companies choose to use a differentiation strategy whereby they acknowledge some level of guilt while seeking a less blameworthy posture.

Regardless of the level of guilt, the extant research on apologia counsels practitioners to make use of two strategies. First, a statement of regret or concern for victims, be they personal or environmental, projects an image of companies that are concerned about more than just the bottom line (Hearit, 1994). Such a strategy is an effective vehicle by which to diffuse hostility. Due to liability concerns, however, organizations are prudent to avoid direct statements of responsibility. Second, a strategy of corrective action, in which organizations describe changes in policies to ensure that future problems do not recur (whether or not they have chosen to accept responsibility for the current problems), assures key publics that the problems that precipitated the alleged wrongdoing have been isolated, addressed, and resolved.

Strategies are available for practitioners to employ in their attempts to lessen culpability. Nevertheless, it is prudent for practitioners to counsel organizations to be forthcoming and frank. Indeed, preliminary research in corporate responses to criticism suggests that ethical action and honest communication by organizations are most likely to result in positive images, even in crises of companies' own doing. Benoit and Drew (1997) and Bradford and Garrett (1995), for example, reported findings showing that organizations that take a conciliatory rather than combative stance do less damage to their public images in crises. In the end, communication professionals must act in an ethical manner and in the best interests of their organizations.

CONCLUSION

Most of the criticism and crisis situations that organizations face are rooted *not* in external agents, such as terrorists and psychopaths, but rather in their own misdeeds. These misdeeds bring unwanted public scrutiny, and if organizations' responses are judged to be uncompelling, then social sanctions ensue on the part of disgruntled stakeholders and special interest groups. This chapter has attempted to address the multifaceted nature of corporate apologetic speech. In so doing, it sought to explicate the different contexts that result in apologetic discourse, to delineate the repertoire of strategies and postures available to corporate apologists, and to draw a number of conclusions that prescribe the scope and direction of future scholarly and practitioner inquiry.

CHAPTER 43

Race and Reputation

Restoring Image Beyond the Crisis

GAIL F. BAKER

■ No organization is immune to crisis. A precipitous increase in corporate crises over the past decade has fueled myriad books and articles, spawned training programs, and created awareness that a crisis can do irreparable harm to an organization. Many now view the management of crises as both an art and a science, no longer an unusual specialty but rather an imperative skill for public relations practitioners (Maggart, 1994). In the best situations, crises can be averted through a combination of strategic planning and proactive behavior. When ignored, crises can develop into full-fledged wars that polarize groups, cost time and resources, and forever change the organization's relationship with its stakeholders.

Unfortunately, many organizations find themselves responding to crises rather than preventing them. When the smoke finally clears, those without clear-cut crisis communications strategies are left struggling with ways in which to repair the severe damage often done to their reputations.

INTRODUCTION

Crisis Defined

Although scholars and practitioners universally accept no single definition of crisis, there are some characteristics that help identify out-of-the-ordinary events.

Much of the literature concentrates on organizational conflicts that lead to crises. Other articles focus on crisis survival. Barton's (1993) comprehensive view of crisis incorporates the impact of an emergency situation on all aspects of the organization. He defined crisis as "a major unpredictable event that has potentially negative results. The event and its aftermath may significantly damage an organization and its employees, products, services, financial condition, and reputation" (p. 2).

One area that has not been given much attention by public relations researchers is the management of crisis emanating from events involving race (e.g., charges of racism against an organization, the use of racial slurs by corporate officials or other employees, lawsuits alleging discrimination on the basis of race). Yet, many organizations face these types of problems and concerns. A random Lexis/Nexis search of articles under the descriptor "racial discrimination" yields more than 500 titles annually.

Members of all racial minorities, including African Americans, Asian Americans, Latino Americans, and American Indians, make formal and informal charges. The objects of the complaints are organizations representing nearly every major industry. Corporate giants such as Texaco, American Airlines, Pillsbury, AT&T, General Motors, Eddie Bauer, and Denny's all have received negative publicity surrounding racial issues. Charges are made against municipal governments, churches, local grocery stores, media outlets, and hospitals. Sports teams and department stores also are included. Few industries, if any, can escape allegations of racial discrimination. Yet, the literature does not reveal major interest among scholars or practitioners on the most effective methods for avoiding a racial crisis, managing a racial crisis, and restoring the tarnished image that most assuredly will linger after the crisis has officially ended.

A Matter of Race

It was projected that non-whites would comprise 28% of the U.S. population by the year 2000. That number is expected to rise to 39% by 2030 and to 48% by 2050 (Andorfer, 1996). As participants in policy development for organizations, public relations professionals have an obligation to keep their companies aware of emerging trends and the impact of those trends on the ways in which business is conducted. Organizations can ill afford the financial burdens caused by charges of racism. Of even greater consequence, issues of race can cause significant damage to organizations' images among critical stakeholders.

Denny's restaurant chain paid $46 million to settle discrimination charges ("Denny's Settles,"

1994). It cost Pillsbury $3.6 million to settle a class action suit brought by 14 employees ("Pillsbury to Pay," 1990). Charges of racial discrimination forced Shoney's restaurant chain into paying a $100 million settlement (Duke, 1993). Other companies, including Publix, Avis, and USAirways, have found themselves embroiled in costly racial crises.

Recent attacks on affirmative action also have a significant impact on organizations as they attempt to determine fair and equal policies without clear guidance from the government. Broad and liberal interpretations of what constitutes discrimination surely will open the door for more complaints, lawsuits, and charges of racism, making this category of crisis even more popular.

Two high-profile cases involving racial incidents are analyzed in this chapter. Because media coverage helps practitioners to examine public perceptions of organizations' responses to crises, press reports of the events serve as the basis for investigating and critiquing the performance of the organizations involved.

Reputation management theory provides a backdrop for the discussion of how organizations are perceived by their constituencies and how a crisis undermines the public trust. The recently developed theory of image restoration discourse is used as the foundation for an examination of image repair strategies.

WHAT IS REPUTATION?

"Reputation is real" (Jackson, 1997). It is not an image because image can be based on false perceptions. Organizations have to communicate true reputations to their publics so that the publics will trust enough to give the organizations the support they need.

Reputation is composed of many elements. At the core are impressions and perceptions that the organizations' publics attribute to the organizations. Reputation is the publics' judgments of the organizations' behavior. The sum of these components is credibility of what the companies say and do and establishes future expectations (Greyser, 1995). Sound reputations are required to protect the organizations against existing and potential confrontations such as those that arise when racial incidents occur. According to Young (1995-1996), "There are two common characteristics in every instance of reputation damage control: (1) management is forced to spend nonproductive time on a negative event and (2) each case potentially has serious ramifications for an organization's reputation with one or more stakeholder groups" (p. 7). Therefore, the potential time and money that an organization could spend dealing with reputation damage control is immeasurable.

Young (1995-1996) believed that organizations spend so much time in reputation damage control because they have not engaged in enough time planning and preparing for potential crises. He asserted that there are early warning signs of impending crises and steps that can be taken to build and maintain reputations in the face of these potentially dangerous circumstances.

Young (1995-1996) further suggested that organizations can listen and pay attention to what their publics are saying. In the area of racial crisis, being aware of the social and political climates and determining audience perceptions might go a long way toward avoiding all-out crisis situations.

Based on what Young (1995-1996) and other public relations counselors have said about reputation and the need to understand its origin and meaning, organizations should consistently assess the perceptions of all their stakeholders including minority constituents. A failure to do so might place organizations in a position of having to repair their reputations rather than maintaining them.

Image Restoration

Much of the literature on image restoration focuses on individuals and their efforts to save face or their reputations. Brinson and Benoit (1996) asserted that organizations, like individuals, must develop, maintain, protect, and restore images. When images are threatened, as they are during crises, organizations are forced to respond. They attempt to regain consumer confidence, minimize negative publicity, and return the companies to the economic stability they enjoyed before the crises began.

According to Brinson and Benoit (1996), there are five categories of image repair strategies: denial, evading responsibility, reducing offensiveness, correcting action, and mortification.

The denial strategy is self-explanatory. The institution accused of wrongdoing simply refuses to accept the blame. Take, for example, the case of the Northern Trust Bank of Illinois. In the face of hundreds of discrimination charges by potential black and Latino customers, the bank claimed that not a single denied loan could be traced to racism (Glater, 1995). Organizations that employ the denial strategy also are likely to shift the blame to other sources.

The evasion of responsibility strategy is related to denial but is considerably more complex. It is tantamount to the "devil made me do it" defense in which the objects of complaints admit to wrongdoing but claim to be the victims of others' indiscretions. This strategy also is used when organizations claim not to have had all the information required to make the right decisions or to take the proper actions. Calling the incidents "accidental" and stating that "good intentions" lead to unfortunate consequences also are variations on the evasion of responsibility theme.

Organizations that find themselves embroiled in crises involving race also might use the reduction of offensiveness strategy of image restoration. A number of tactics are thought to help. Organizations can bolster their images by reminding the audiences of their long-term performance. They can downplay the significance of the occurrences. Under the reduction of offensiveness strategy, the accused also can attempt to distinguish their actions from similarly offensive behaviors in an effort to make their behaviors seem less offensive. In addition, organizations can attempt to attack the accusers or offer them compensation.

In the corrective strategy, organizations promise to fix the problems. They admit to the problems and announce programs aimed at repairing the existing ills.

The most straightforward of all image restoration strategies is mortification. Organizations accused of wrongdoing make sincere confessions and seek forgiveness for the offensive actions in the hope that their publics will not judge their behaviors too harshly.

These strategies provide a framework for examining, discussing, and comparing the corporate responses of two corporations plagued with controversial racial crises: Eddie Bauer and American Airlines.

THE EDDIE BAUER CASE

In 1995, two African American teenagers shopping in an Eddie Bauer clothing outlet outside of Washington, D.C., found themselves being followed by a uniformed Prince George's County police officer. One of the youths was wearing an Eddie Bauer shirt he had purchased the day before. The officer asked the 16-year-old to produce a receipt for the clothing, and when the youth was unable to comply, he was told to take the shirt off, go home, get the receipt, and return to the store. The humiliated teen left the store without the shirt he already had purchased.

The story about Eddie Bauer's treatment of the black youths was first published in *The Washington Post,* bringing immediate national attention to the issue. Critics, activists, media celebrities, and lawyers quickly became involved in the case.

Eddie Bauer's Restoration Strategies

The company used a number of restoration strategies in an effort to minimize the impact of the crisis. In its initial response to the accusations, Eddie Bauer management used both denial and evasion of responsibility strategies. A company spokesperson called the incident "minor" and "typical," claiming that it had been blown way out of proportion. In addition, the company offered no apology to the offended shoppers (Milloy, 1995).

During this initial stage of the crisis, a store manager also attempted to evade responsibility by claiming that the police officer was to blame and that his behavior was not related to Eddie Bauer policy. She called the incident a police matter and suggested that reporters talk with police about it.

After weeks passed and Eddie Bauer had taken no specific action to rectify the matter, the youths were advised to sue the company for $85 million, claiming false imprisonment, defamation, and violation of civil rights ("Eddie Bauer," 1997). With the lawsuit came additional negative publicity for the company. Still, there was no official apology and no real efforts to reduce the offensiveness of the company's behavior. Another corporate spokesperson made the company appear even more insensitive and unresponsive when she said that the company gave the youth the benefit of the doubt in letting him keep the shirt (Milloy, 1995).

When it appeared that the company did not take the issue seriously, black leaders rushed to the side of the teens and their parents, calling the case an example of subtle and pervasive racist behavior. Community groups, including the National Association for the Advancement of Colored People (NAACP), sent a letter to Eddie Bauer headquarters, launched protests, and called for a boycott of the popular clothing stores.

Two months after the actual incident, Eddie Bauer hired public relations giant Hill & Knowlton to help manage its communications. After the agency was employed, the company made its first step toward corrective action. Eddie Bauer President Rick Feresh made an official statement in which he admitted wrongdoing and vowed to fix it. He met with NAACP officials in December 1995, the same month in which the company distributed Eddie Bauer clothing to homeless shelters in Prince George's County.

The NAACP's Washington director, Wade Henderson, demonstrated skepticism about the company's behavior, suggesting that Eddie Bauer was simply responding to criticisms thrown at it by black leaders (Evans, 1995).

The Bottom Line

A federal jury awarded one of the youths $850,000 and two others $75,000 apiece. The negative publicity surrounding the case lasted for months and is revisited annually by the news media. Although it is impossible to clearly connect the incident with sales, Eddie Bauer stores have not performed up to expectations ("Spiegel's Eddie Bauer," 1998).

THE AMERICAN AIRLINES CASE

During an investigation of a 1995 American Airlines crash, a pilot's manual containing a section called "Survival in Latin America" was made public. In it, special references were made to Latin American passengers:

> They expect not to depart on time. In fact, it's rumored that they will call in a false bomb threat to delay a departure if they think they'll be late. They like a drink in the plane prior to takeoff. Unruly and/or intoxicated passengers are not infrequent. ("American to Change," 1997)

Predictably, public outrage was swift and severe. Politicians, consumers, and community organizations challenged the company to explain and rectify its actions immediately.

American Airlines' Restoration Strategies

Because the information was clearly printed in the pilot's manual, American Airlines could not employ the denial strategy. It had indeed made offensive comments about one of its valuable customer groups. Therefore, the company accepted that the incident had taken place and immediately removed the manual from circulation.

However, American Airlines did not accept full responsibility for its actions. In a press conference held 3 days after the manual was made public, a Latino senior vice president, Peter Dolara, claimed that the airline had received reports on passenger behavior from Eastern Airlines when it took over that company's routes in 1989. Nevertheless, he issued an apology on the part of the company's employees ("American to Change," 1997).

Negative publicity, threatened boycotts, and harsh words from community leaders prompted American Airlines to act quickly. A Latino congresswoman, Nydia M. Velazquez of New York, said, "If attitudes like these persist, American Airlines will learn the hard way that insensitivity can be very costly" (Velazquez, 1997). The League of United Latin American Citizens demanded diversity training and expressed disappointment that the incident had come to light by mere happenstance.

American Airlines did not attempt the reduction of offensiveness strategy; there were no efforts made to minimize the offensiveness of the action. It did, however, move quickly toward corrective action, beginning with the removal of the manual. It went further by agreeing to hire more minorities, increasing its donations to Hispanic causes, and promising to review all manuals and remove any offensive references. American Airlines entered into a partnership with the National Council of La Raza in which it promised to donate travel for community and youth organizations. Prominent Latino leaders were quick to applaud American Airlines for its actions.

The Bottom Line

American Airlines was not sued by any Latino group following the pilot's manual incident. The negative publicity lasted less than 1 week, and American continues to dominate the Latin American airline market.

COMPARING EDDIE BAUER AND AMERICAN AIRLINES

Comparisons of these two cases offer some insight into which restoration strategies are most effective in providing an organization with useful tools in a crisis. If actual financial cost to the organization is to be considered a measure of effectiveness, then American Airlines is the clear winner. The company was not forced into court by disgruntled consumers and actually received a vote of confidence from a major Latino organization. By contrast, Eddie Bauer was ordered to pay $850,000 to one litigant and $75,000 to two others for its lack of response to charges of racism.

In analyzing the cases using the image repair framework, it is clear that a number of factors contributed to the markedly different outcomes experienced by the two organizations.

Eddie Bauer used *denial* strategy while American Airlines did not. In all fairness, American Airlines' action was undeniable, forcing the company to move quickly to another, more acceptable strategy.

The denial strategy probably is ineffective in racial crises because most victims of racism recognize its existence and consider an unconditional denial to be an outright lie.

Both companies attempted to use the evasion of responsibility strategy, but each employed different tactics to explain its behavior. Eddie Bauer blamed a security guard, making it appear that the company did not care enough about its customers to carefully screen and train its contractors. American Airlines shifted some of its responsibility to the carrier from which it assumed the Latin American routes, thereby making it appear that American Airlines was not the only insensitive airline. American Airlines' action, although unacceptable, caused consumers to consider what offensive rhetoric might be in the manuals of other companies.

Eddie Bauer did not attempt to restore its image using the reduction of offensiveness strategy, but American Airlines did. Eddie Bauer returned the shirt to its purchaser and offered no apology, whereas American Airlines reminded its customers of the company's respect for them by issuing a strong and unwavering apology.

Both companies promised to correct their behaviors, but the time frames in which they did so were different, and this possibly influenced the outcomes of the incidents. After 2 months of negative publicity, an $85 million lawsuit, and a hostile letter from the NAACP, Eddie Bauer's president responded and promised policy changes. It took American Airlines just 3 days to issue an apology, withdraw the offensive material, and forge an alliance with a highly visible Latino organization.

Finally, both companies employed the mortification strategy, but again, it appears that speed influenced how well this strategy was accepted. American Airlines apologized within 72 hours, whereas Eddie Bauer's official apology took 2 months.

A FRAMEWORK FOR MANAGING RACIAL CRISES

Crises surrounding racial incidents tend to fall into three major categories: actions, words, and symbols. Each type of crisis requires a distinct response. In the Eddie Bauer case, the incident was caused by action, whereas American Airlines faced a crisis based on written words. In the absence of actions or words, it sometimes is a symbol that creates racial conflict. The Sambo's restaurant chain was forced to change its name to Sam's because of negative imagery associated with the word *sambo*, which is a term used to describe coon-like black characters from the 19th century who possessed exaggerated physical features and little intelligence.

An AT&T internal publication, in which a monkey was used to depict customers in Africa, is an example of the role that symbolism can play in creating a racial crisis. Following considerable criticism, AT&T ceased publication of the magazine.

In planning for and managing crises emanating from racial issues, it also is important to understand the sources of the complaints. There are basically two major areas from which complaints emerge: from inside organizations or from external individuals or groups. Different strategies should be considered to communicate throughout crises based on who originates discussion about the problems. Internal stakeholders (e.g., employees) bring a particular perspective to the charges. The potential for harm to organizations' images is greater because employees are likely to be perceived as having firsthand knowledge.

Following are some recommendations for dealing with racial crises based on type of crises:

1. Racial incidents resulting from actions or behaviors are best managed by measured and calculated responses.
2. Racial incidents resulting from words (e.g., racial slurs) are most effectively handled by apologies and swift dissociation from the individuals or groups responsible for the behaviors.
3. Racial crises that erupt over the use of symbols are best managed by modifying the symbols.

In the case of a racial crisis that begins with an actions or a behavior, no response at all or a knee-jerk reaction can bring unwanted extra attention to the situation. Instead, an organization must carefully review how much credibility and reputation are likely to be lost and whether they can be repaired. A single charge of racism, although potentially serious, should not cause an organization to completely revamp its policies unless, of course, they are unethical and/or illegal. On the other hand, such a charge gives the organization an opportunity to review and evaluate its policies.

Because there is no justification for the use of a racial slur, the organization has no choice but to apologize and move away from the person or behavior post haste. When a radio announcer in Washington, D.C., made comments apparently supporting the brutal killing of a black man in Texas, station management suspended him later that day. The reaction time was deemed as slow by many African Americans who thought that the suspension was too light a punishment and that he should have been pulled from the airwaves immediately.

Under the best of circumstances, an organization that finds itself faced with a racial problem based on words will quickly dissociate itself from the racist language, accept the fact that wrongdoing took place, and handle the incident in accordance with company policy. In cases where a policy does not exist, the organization can view the incident as an opportunity to create one.

No doubt, companies have tremendous financial and (sometimes) emotional investments in symbols. Organizations also have moral and social responsibilities to respect the cultures of individuals outside their doors. Enlightened organizations recognize that times change, as do social norms and mores. Images portraying slavery that were acceptable during the middle of the 19th century are reprehensible today. Few mainstream companies would consider using depictions of women as hysterical or subservient creatures, as they often were viewed 100 years ago.

Sports teams regularly change uniforms, build new facilities, and move away from the cities in which they were founded. Could the change of a mascot or a symbol be any more costly? The real issue for organizations in this situation is to measure long-term standing with stakeholders against short-term gain. Will the organizations help to pave new roads, or will they be flattened by the steamroller of change?

CONCLUSION

How well an organization responds to crises involving race is closely linked to its willingness to accept the existence of a racial problem and respond accordingly. Both of the cases discussed in this chapter indicate that it is dangerous for organizations to attempt to ride out the storm or to issue arrogant and insensitive statements. The highly charged atmosphere that surrounds any crisis is likely to be exacerbated by the introduction of race, which remains an area of considerable conflict and disagreement in American society.

In the art and science that is crisis management, public relations practitioners have a responsibility to view the entire landscape and provide informed counsel. In situations involving race, it might be prudent for public relations professionals to advise management to immediately acknowledge offensive behavior, take swift corrective action, and review all company policies in an effort to prevent such incidents from arising again. Even better advice would be to take a close look at policies, behaviors, and actions and to implement changes *before* someone makes a damaging accusation from which there might be no retreat.

BEST PRACTICES IN RELATIONSHIP BUILDING

Relationships Within Communities

Public Relations for the New Century

LAURIE J. WILSON

In 1992, the Global Scenario Planning division of the Royal Dutch/Shell Group of Companies published a set of updated global scenarios for the next three decades. The scenarios are based on exhaustive research and the collaboration of some of the most prestigious experts in virtually every field of endeavor and study. The purpose of the scenarios is to predict the global future so as to facilitate corporate strategic planning.

The scenario planning group identified two patterns fundamentally changing the world in which we live: increasing liberalization and increasing globalization (Jaworski, 1996). The group members termed the 1990s decade a "hinge of history," with two diametrically opposing alternatives emerging. They labeled one alternative *new frontiers* because of the possibilities of global cooperation and inclusive economic reform. It is a possibility of a new international order because individuals, groups, and governments see beyond short-term interests and display generosity and care that broadens their interests to encompass the entire global human experience.

The group members labeled the other alternative *barricades* because people, groups, and nations erect barriers to protect themselves from instability emerging from greed, exploitation, suspicion, racism, and fear. It paints a dismal picture of a world beset with problems that have been so neglected that relations have deteriorated and the world is on the verge of global conflict and collapse of overwhelming proportions.

One of the most interesting dimensions of both scenarios is the part played by the business sector. Corporations clearly were identified as the entities to direct the path to be taken at this hinge of history. According to the Royal Dutch/Shell Group, the greatest hope for the solutions to problems plaguing our society is the cooperation of business with other actors in interdependent communities (Jaworski, 1996).

In the current American business environment, however, that is not a role assumed by corporate entities. It would require a shift from typically bottom-line thinking and evaluation to a more communitarian approach to business and society.

This chapter examines the requirements and ramifications of that approach, the role of organizational public relations in its implementation, and the best practices that would result. If adopted, they will fundamentally change the ways in which we do business and live our lives in the society of the 21st century. This approach is, at its core, a shift from focusing on financial gain as a primary social good that is distributed to relatively few to an emphasis on the interdependent relationship and role of business as a participant in a community that consists of a variety of actors, both individual and organizational, all cooperating for a common good that extends far beyond solely financial factors.

THE DEVELOPMENT OF THE DENIAL OF RELATIONSHIPS AS AN ORGANIZING PRINCIPLE

The argument of the past couple of decades seems to be whether or not it is the responsibility of the corporation to function for the benefit of the other actors in society. The obligation of corporate social responsibility is much debated. According to world-renowned economist Milton Friedman, the social responsibility of business is "to maximize its profits" (Friedman, 1970). That position has caused many corporations to assert that their contributions to communities and society are limited to economic factors and outcomes. They provide jobs, goods, and services to the free marketplace, and they provide tax revenues to government. Any further expectation of citizenship is unrealistic and, in fact, a threat to the world capitalist system that is responsible for the tremendous growth and development of society and the comfort of our lives.

This purely economic rationale has spawned an economic counterpoint that being socially responsible ultimately is in the best interest of the organization's bottom line. Those of us deceived by the assertion of a purely economic role for the corporation in society, or indeed for the function of work itself, have been led to argue that relationships with other actors directly or indirectly affect the profit-making status of a company. Unhappy employees strike, unhappy communities withdraw tax breaks, unhappy government agencies regulate, and unhappy consumers boycott—all making it more difficult for the corporation to operate profitably.

The argument is not without merit, but it is inherently flawed. It is flawed because it is based on the assumption that economics is primary and social relationships are secondary, that the latter are of significance in the grand scheme of society only if they can be elevated to the status of economics. The argument asserts that the only relationship of real importance is the one that a corporation has with its bottom line, subordinating even investors themselves to its ultimate power and justification.

During recent years, however, the deception has begun to unravel. In the words of Ralph Estes, resident scholar and co-founder of the Center for the Advancement of Public Policy, "Our system is marked by a relatively small number of individuals, with no accountability, controlling great power for the benefit of narrow interests, while the broad public interest is carried along as a captive passenger, a hostage" (Estes, 1996, p. 77).

Accordingly, other actors in society have become increasingly impatient with a business sector that claims rights but abdicates responsibilities. Recognizing the resources of business, they have begun to apply the type of pressure that encourages, even demands, more active participation in all facets of society including a role in solving the social problems that a corporation increasingly finds affecting the productivity of its workforce. As observed elsewhere,

> Since . . . traditional strategic management principles with their over-emphasis on the short-term bottom line are failing to mediate those issues, management is turning to public relations to build relationships with the organization's publics to solve the problems facing the organization's community. (Wilson, 1994, p. 336)

How did the corporate world, and by extension our society, arrive at the point of using relationship building as the approach of last resort?

The error lies within two critical misperceptions mentioned earlier that have led to one of the greatest fallacies of our time. The first misperception is that business has a purely economic role and that only the yardstick of the bottom line can measure success. The second is that the corporation exists solely to make a profit. Although both misperceptions are widely accepted in today's business and social circles, they ignore the historically fundamental purpose for the establishment of the corporation in society. Corporations were "first chartered in the public interest to meet a public need, to provide a public service. They were seen as extensions of the government, doing government—that is, state or public—business" (Estes, 1996, p. x).

The fallacy perpetuated by these two misperceptions is the denial of the reality that relationships are at the very core of the structure and operation of our physical and social worlds. It is a convenient denial. It allows corporations, and potentially other types of groups and individuals, to justify acting without morality or conscience. It "makes good people do bad things" (Estes, 1996, p. xi).

But as Jaworski (1996) found in his survey of the physical and social sciences from physics to business management, "*relationship* is the organizing principle of the universe" (p. 184, italics in original). Nothing exists in isolation. Nothing functions in isolation. All people and processes are fundamentally interconnected. Given this reality, the question is not whether or not we have relationships in society but rather what the status and quality of those relationships are.

Because prevailing American business management principles are established on a "bottom-line philosophy" (Hampden-Turner & Trompenaars, 1993; Peters & Austin, 1986; Peters & Waterman, 1982; Wilson, 1994), corporate leaders—managers, accountants, and attorneys, typically trained in America's business and law schools established on that philosophy—are largely untrained and unskilled in building, assessing, and maintaining relationships with any of an organization's publics except its investors. Building relationships with other publics most often has been viewed as the job of public relations staffers, a "feel good" tactic to be tolerated

during times of plenty and eliminated during times of budget constraints. But the relationship builders are far more essential to the corporation than has been believed. Their role now, at the dawn of the 21st century, will be at the heart of corporate strategy and operation if the corporation is to survive.

THE COMMUNITARIAN ALTERNATIVE

In 1989, a group of scholars and other individuals engaged in the study and practice of public policy formed a new organization dedicated to the support and promotion of a communitarian perspective in our society. Believing fundamentally that "neither human existence nor individual liberty can be sustained for long outside the interdependent and overlapping communities to which all of us belong" (Etzioni, 1998, p. xxv), they began to champion an approach viewing society as a "pluralistic web of communities" (p. xiv) and individuals as possessing multiple memberships.

While affirming democratic and capitalist principles and individual rights and responsibilities, the *responsive communitarian platform* also "recognizes that communities and polities, too, have obligations—including the duty to be responsive to their members and to foster participation and deliberation in social and political life" (Etzioni, 1998, p. xxv).

Characteristics of Communitarian Relationships

The philosophy of communitarianism does not advocate a communal society in its traditional sense. The philosophy celebrates individual rights but asserts that the provision of such rights requires responsibility on the part of all members of the community. No participant (i.e., no profit-making organization) is sacrificed for the gain of the other participants, but all actors assume a share of responsibility. If it were not so, then rights could not be provided. The analogy is given of the bricks in an arch (Etzioni, 1995, p. 19). Without bricks, there is no arch; without the arch, the bricks remain in a pile. There is tension in the structure that maintains the arch—a balanced give-and-take.

The new communitarian philosophy rejects the individualist solutions to societal problems pursued through the master strategies of the free market, on the one hand, or the state, on the other (Bellah, 1998). According to Bellah (1998),

> The lifeworld missing in these conservative and liberal ideologies is the place where we communicate with others, deliberate, come to agreements about standards and norms, pursue in common an effort to create a valuable form of life—in short, the lifeworld is the world of community. (p. 17)

The role of both the market and the state is to serve the community, not dominate it.

Given this definition of the role of community, Bellah (1998) identified four values on which communitarian relationships are based. The first is the sacredness of the individual and the rejection of any type of oppression combined with the realization that "strong, healthy, morally vigorous communities are the prerequisite for strong, healthy, morally vigorous individuals" (p. 18).

The second value is solidarity, meaning that we are who we are because of our relationships. Third, the communitarian relationship is complementary to the multiplicity of memberships of participant individuals and organizations. Finally, participation in the community is both a right and a responsibility. Membership has a distributive good only when all actors participate in supporting the community and solving the problems within it.

Making the Shift to a Relationship Approach

In the new communitarian philosophical approach, today's corporation and its public relations function are fundamentally different from what they have been to date. Business approaches that have focused predominantly on profit and have formed relationships with internal and external publics for primarily manipulative purposes are doomed to fail in today's evolving business ecosystems (Moore, 1996). Probably with rare exceptions, corporate success in the 21st century will be based on the quality of the relationships built. Relationship building will be a strategic function directed by public relations but engaged in by key corporate leaders who participate in building productive relationships emphasizing communities of mutual support and cooperation. This strategy will not be just a "feel good" public relations tactic. In the new century, it will determine corporate survival.

Organizational public relations personnel are in the best position to counsel management on making this shift in strategy. Progressive public relations practitioners have learned to synthesize their strategic communications planning and management function (in the American business management style) with well-developed relationship-building skills imperative for their success with the publics targeted by the public relations function (Wilson, 1996). Because they know how to build relationships, they naturally will be called on to direct, counsel, and advise other organizational leaders in that effort. Organizational public relations personnel will help the corporation to take four key actions—best practices—in organizing its efforts to survive in a cooperative and communitarian environment.

First, they will lead the organization in a philosophical shift that helps the organization's leaders to view the world in fundamentally different ways. No longer can corporate managers perpetuate a solely economic perspective on business and society. In the new century's environment, organizations will make a philosophical shift by accepting the undeniable pervasiveness of relationship as an organizing principle of the universe and of the world of work.

The philosophical shift is operationalized by expanding the view of the role of the corporation in its community. Public relations counselors' role will be to ensure that the organization recognizes and accepts its responsibility to its employees, customers, and neighbors to engage in cooperative action for the growth, benefit, and improvement of the community. Corporate participation in the community will be driven by the strategic pursuit of an improved quality of life for all community participants, not because it is financially profitable but rather because it is the morally responsible course. In this role, public relations counselors will become the organization's conscience in ways never before imagined.

Second, the corporation will realize the greatest benefit by committing itself to the pursuit of common good (including its own) within the context of the multiplicity of relationships that represent the corporate reality. This means that public relations counselors will be key in helping the organization to recognize that the community consists of more than investors and/or stockholders; it also consists of stakeholders—employees, customers, neighbors, competitors, suppliers, regulators, and a host of other publics with whom relationships must be cultivated.

Third, because a relationship approach is largely foreign to the practices of American business management as taught in most business schools, corporate leaders will be unfamiliar with evaluation techniques to gauge success. By committing itself to the common good, the corporation will effectively evaluate progress toward its mission only by changing the "scorecard" by which it measures success. Public relations counselors, the traditional organizational relationship builders, are best equipped to aid in the development of new standards and measures to evaluate corporate success. Estes (1996) asserted that effective measures would include accountability to customers, workers, communities, and society as well as to investors. Evaluations will extend beyond the financial measures to include standards that measure broader success in the community such as customer and employee satisfaction and the reduction or elimination of social problems.

The final best strategic public relations practice resulting from a shift to the communitarian approach will be the establishment of a set of corporate values on which the organization's relationships with its publics (members in its communities) will be established. Now in a recognized strategic role, public relations counselors become key in shaping the value set because of their intimate (and often exclusive) knowledge of the organization's publics.

Peters and Waterman (1982) found that in organizations with strong overriding corporate values truly governing policy and practice at all levels, the corporate value set usually consisted of those core values personally held by the chief executive officer. That reality reinforces the argument that business is more than just a profit-making venture; it has a complex relational role in a society made up of individuals as well as organizational units.

Relationships are fundamentally based on trust. Research has shown that loyalty toward an organization in a community is strengthened by the community members' perceptions of the organization's openness and its involvement and investment in, as well as its commitment to, the community (Ledingham & Bruning, 1998b). Adopting those values will be a solid beginning.

THE ROLE OF PUBLIC RELATIONS IN THE NEW CENTURY

Given the global scenarios posited for the next few decades and the evolution of the corporate role in society, the question then becomes not whether or not an organization's public relations effort engages in community relations but rather what types of relationship building the organization pursues with its strategic cooperative communities (Wilson, 1996). As public relations practitioners, we would do well to begin to view all of the organization's publics in terms of the communities we have in common. Doing so will enable us to cultivate the characteristics of community—and benefit from the success of cooperation within the community—with each and every organizational public.

As noted previously, the emerging realities of business and society have moved the corporate public relations counsel into an enviable position. We have achieved, through the impetus of societal change, what we had been unable to achieve·through persuasion—a seat at the table with the strategic managers. We will retain that seat so long as we play to our strength—long-term relationship building based on the broader (than economic) role of the organization in its communities.

CHAPTER 45

Managing Community Relationships to Maximize Mutual Benefit

Doing Well by Doing Good

JOHN A. LEDINGHAM

STEPHEN D. BRUNING

The community is a key public for organizations that practice strategic public relations. Not only do communities represent geographic publics, they also encompass key constituencies that share a relationship with local organizations. Such constituencies include customers, stakeholders, suppliers, employees, and local governmental officials. The nature of that relationship is symbiotic. Organizations may benefit from tax incentives, favorable zoning rulings, and loyalty to the organizations' products and services from local citizens. Communities also may benefit through organizational sponsorship of community activities and events, investment in community infrastructure, support for educational initiatives, and so on. But although the relationship is mutually dependent, it is not *necessarily* mutually beneficial. Managing the relationship for the benefit of both the organization and the community is the basis of modern community relations. Moreover, the notion of mutual benefit represents an appropriate paradigm

for both the study and the practice of community relations.

Community relations has been described as "an institution's planned, active, and continuing participation with and within a community to maintain and enhance its environment to the benefit of both the institution and the community" (Peak, 1998, p. 117). Leading public relations texts include community relations as part of the mix that defines public relations. Community relations is seen as a way in which to redress organizational wrongs, as a means of demonstrating support for communities, and as a vehicle for gaining official and public support for the organization. Wilcox, Ault, and Agee (1998) noted,

> Because a corporation relies on local governments for construction permits, changes in zoning laws, even tax concessions, a good working relationship with city hall and community groups is important. A vigorous program also helps in the

recruitment of employees and gives the company influence in community affairs. (p. 301)

Seitel (1998) suggested that most organizations today recognize a responsibility to the welfare of the communities in which they operate and that community relations can play a role in meeting that responsibility: "More and more, companies and other organizations acknowledge their responsibilities to the community: helping to maintain clean air and water, providing jobs for minorities, and, in general, enhancing everyone's quality of life" (p. 350). The notion of corporate social responsibility has been further reinforced by scholars such as Wilson (1994), who sees community relations as a vehicle with which to correct organizational excesses, and by Kruckeberg and Starck (1988), who maintained that the primary function of all public relations activities should be the building and maintenance of community.

This chapter provides an overview of the scholarship and practice of community relations. In so doing, it reports on the use of community relations initiatives by practitioners from a broad range of industries as well as on recent research concerning the societal and economic benefits that effective community relations programs can provide for communities. Such research suggests that community relations initiatives not only can help an organization to fulfill its responsibility to community support but also can influence levels of community member loyalty toward the sponsoring organization. Finally, the material reviewed in this chapter serves as the basis for development of guidelines for those charged with the responsibility of developing strategic community relations programs for their organizations.

BACKGROUND

Community relations initiatives were not always designed with the notion of generating mutual benefit for organizations and communities. The roots of community relations can be traced to the latter part of the 1800s and early 1900s, an era of extraordinary growth in American manufacturing, transportation, and retailing. Unencumbered by regulatory controls and fueled by unparalleled economic growth, some corporations acted with little regard for the welfare of their workers or society in general. As has been noted, "Much of public relations history is woven into the unending struggle between employer and employee" (Cutlip, Center, & Broom, 1994, p. 97). That observation certainly holds true for community relations. Continued corporate abuses ultimately led to a public outcry, spurred by a crusading public press, for governmental intervention. In response, some corporations turned to early publicity agents in an effort to turn around negative public opinion. As part of that effort, many corporate leaders were encouraged to establish libraries, foundations, and other community-supportive initiatives to serve as the basis for favorable press reports.

As governmental regulations began to balance the interests of corporations with those of the public welfare, many organizations continued to engage in community relations to generate goodwill in their communities in the hopes that it would result in preferential treatment. Today, community relations is part of an overall strategy that not only supports the business interests of an organization but also contributes to organizational efforts to meet its responsibility to support the welfare of the community.

Seitel (1998) noted that the concept of corporate social responsibility has emerged only within the past three decades. He suggested,

The social and political upheavals of the 1960s forced organizations to confront the real or perceived injustices inflicted on certain social groups. The 1970s brought a partial resolution of those problems as government and the courts moved together to compensate for past inequities, to outlaw current abuses, and to prevent future injustice. In the 1990s, the conflict between organizations and society became one of setting priorities—of deciding which community group deserved to be the beneficiary of corporate involvement. Today, most organizations accept their role as an agent for social change in the community. (p. 351)

PROFESSIONAL AND SCHOLARLY RESEARCH

The literature of community relations is replete with suggestions for the practice of community relations as well as a limited amount of scholarly literature. For example, Braman (1980) concluded that community feedback is a necessary component of effective community relations programs, and Wright (1979) suggested ongoing sampling of community members as a way in which to formalize the feedback process. The need for direct citizen involvement is another theme that runs through the literature of community relations. In that regard, Price (1994) found that bringing citizens into the community relations process helps to resolve public fears in a potentially volatile situation. Similarly, Arnstein (1994) reported that involving citizens in problem resolution contributes to long-term public relationships and enhanced organizational credibility with community members. Moreover, a number of organizations reportedly have created community advisory panels to help resolve organization-community tension in environmentally threatening situations (Fairley, 1997; Mullin, 1997; Rotman, 1997). Also, Mau and Dennis (1994) suggested that failure to respond to the concerns of *shadow constituencies,* such as environmental, arts, and education groups, can adversely affect organizational operations, and Arenson (1998) emphasized the need for organizations to fully inform communities of current and future organizational operations. In terms of new media, Metcalfe (1997) recommended using the Internet to increase dialogue between organizations and community members. In a more strategic vein, Sutula (1981) recommended that organizations seeking to create organization-community relationships match their particular expertise to community needs

(e.g., a hospital providing CPR training), and Kelly (1984) recommended that organizations serving numerous communities decentralize community relations programs to encourage local managers to develop relationships with their constituent communities. To determine the impact of community relations programs, Laird (1996) urged that community relations managers quantify the results of their initiatives, whereas Judd (1989) suggested that a mutually beneficial approach to community relations programs provides opportunities for community relations practitioners to participate in organizational policymaking. In terms of community relations training, Cox and Mosser (1975) reported on Gulf Oil's programs in which the petroleum company created a mythical community where community relations trainees are brought in for day-long exercises in which they are presented with a series of community relations problems and asked to solve them.

In discourses and research reports with obvious implications for the practice of community relations, Coombs (2000) argued that a mutually beneficial approach to organization-public relationships can minimize the impact of crises when they occur, whereas Putnam (1980) and Ledingham and Bruning (1997) suggested that practitioners focus their community relations activities on a single community need so as to maximize organizational impact. Moreover, J. Grunig (1993a) drew a distinction between symbolic relationships (those linked to communication) and behavioral relationships (those concerned with organizational behavior). He contended that both are necessary for building long-term organization-public relationships. In a quantitative test of that notion, Ledingham and Bruning (1998b) determined that effective organization-public relationships are the result of organizational behavior *and* communication through a multistep process in which an organization first identifies the needs of the community, initiates programs responsive to those needs, and then disseminates information on those initiatives to community members through planned communication programs. Moreover, repeated research (Bruning &

Ledingham, 1998, 2000a; Ledingham & Bruning, 1997, 1998b, 2000; Ledingham, Bruning, Thomlison, & Lesko, 1997; Ledingham, Bruning, & Wilson, 1999) clearly has demonstrated that programs grounded in the identified organization-relationship dimensions of openness, trust, community involvement, community investment, and community commitment generate mutual benefit for organizations and constituent communities. With regard to the communication portion of the process, J. Grunig (1990) urged practitioners to develop segmentation strategies as an alternative to reliance on mass media alone as communication vehicles.

THEORETICAL PERSPECTIVE

Modern theories of community relations have grown beyond the manipulative persuasive paradigms that once dominated the practice of community relations. Today's organization cannot operate simply to adapt the environment to the needs of the organization; it also must act to adapt the organization to the environment. Moreover, community relations practitioners, as well as scholars, operate from stated or implied theoretical perspectives that serve as the basis for program planning. Some assume that the third-party objectivity implied by press coverage serves as an endorsement of an organization's activities and may legitimatize those activities in the minds of community members. Thus, it is believed that enhancing the organization's reputation, or *image,* in the public consciousness may smooth the way for opportunities for the organization. Recent declines in public perceptions of media credibility, however, have raised serious questions regarding that assumption (Hallahan, 1999b). Others view the organization as part of a system in which changes in one part (the organization) result in changes in other parts (the community). In that perspective, organizational practitioners are cognizant that a decline in community will negatively affect the welfare of the organization (for a discussion of the systems perspective, see Cutlip et al., 1994, pp. 206-224). Lowengard (1989) contended that community

relations is driven by two imperatives: a marketing opportunity and a *commercial obligation* grounded in the notion of societal responsibility. Finally, there is the perspective that community relations programs—and all public relations endeavors—need to strive for balance between the interests of the organization and those of the community. Thus, the desired outcome of effective community relations programs is mutual benefit.

One theoretical framework that serves as the framework for scholarly research and practice in the area of community relations is that of social exchange theory. The social exchange perspective posits that social relationships involve the exchange of resources such as "status, information, goods, services, money, security, and love" (Knapp, 1984, p. 44). Much like a marketing model, the giving and receiving of physical and psychological resources can be viewed as *costs* and *rewards*. However, in this case, costs are defined as physical and mental effort, whereas rewards include matters such as pleasure, satisfaction, and gratification of a need (Kelly & Thibaut, 1959). This perspective contends that each partner in a relationship has a standard or an expectation of the other. When a partner meets or exceeds that standard or *comparison level,* satisfaction with the relationship occurs. When the standard or expectation is not met, dissatisfaction occurs. Moreover, partners continually weigh the rewards and costs of the relationship. How much costs over rewards one will accept and remain in a relationship depends on that individual's *comparison level for alternatives.* In other words, if there are other equally attractive or more attractive choices available, then there will be less tolerance for anything below a person's standard for satisfaction. Moreover, having other viable choices available will reduce an individual's acceptance of anything less than his or her expectation for satisfaction. Of course, level of commitment to the relationship and how much one has invested in the relationship will affect how much attention one will pay to other available choices. Having numerous options also is seen as tending to modify the comparison level or standard for satisfaction. According to social exchange theory, then, unless our expectations are met or exceeded, we will select other viable alternatives if they are available. Proponents of social exchange theory also view interpersonal relationships as *transactional* in much the same way as they consider a marketplace exchange transactional. An individual expects to get something when he or she gives something. When what the individual gives seems out of balance with his or her internal ledger, the relationship is considered unsatisfactory. Thus, if one can determine (a) the choices available to those in the relationship, (b) the comparison level, and (c) the levels of satisfaction of those in the relationship, then it is theoretically possible to predict when the relationship will terminate.

RECENT RESEARCH

The social exchange perspective is the theoretical framework for a stream of recent research focused on the notion of organization-community relationships. In research with community members, Ledingham et al. (1997) found that the elements of satisfying relationships that research shows drive interpersonal relationship satisfaction also operate within the context of organization-public relationships. In subsequent research, Ledingham and Bruning (1998b) found that an organization's community relations initiatives, as well as its recognition of those initiatives, influences the choice behavior of individual community members. Based on that research, Ledingham and Bruning suggested that "organizational . . . support of the community in which it operates can engender loyalty toward an organization among key publics when that involvement/support is known by those key publics" (p. 63). They also found that public perceptions of the organization with regard to the organization-public relationship dimensions of trust, openness, community investment, community commitment, and community involvement act as predictors of perceptions of the organization-public relationship and of public choice behavior. Of those five organization-public relationship dimensions, three (community investment, community involvement, and community commitment) traditionally are seen as operating

under the purview of community relations. A companion study by Bruning and Ledingham (2000a) concerning organizations and community businesses produced similar results. Moreover, subsequent analysis found that time in the relationship affects perceptions of the relationship in an organization-public context, just as it does in an interpersonal relationship (Ledingham et al., 1999), and, furthermore, that perceptions of the organization-public relationship influence respondent levels of satisfaction (Bruning & Ledingham, 1998).

Additional research tested the results of Ledingham and Bruning's findings in a quasi-experimental setting (Ledingham & Bruning, 2000). The researchers found that respondent perceptions of the organization-public relationship and key public expressions of loyalty toward the sponsoring organization improved when community members were aware of the organization's community investment, community involvement, and community commitment.

The organization that served as the basis for that research was a telephone company that was the historic provider of local telephone service to the community. Because local telephone service was provided in a competition-free environment, many company executives and governmental regulators took the position that community relations activities were needless or even extravagant. The company's community relations practitioners held that even without competition, maintaining good community relations had immediate and long-term benefits for both the organization and the communities served by the organization. They cited the need for the company to interact with local governments, state regulators, and local businesses and consumers. As the result of regulatory changes, the telephone company recently began to experience competition from other telephone service providers. The situation served as an opportunity to examine the influence that organization-community relationships exert on consumer perceptions and resulting choice behavior (Ledingham & Bruning, 2000).

The study used a research design encompassing a benchmark, an intervention, and a retest of the perceptions and intended behavior of community members. The survey instrument that was developed also explored community member perceptions of the organization with regard to dimensions of the organization-public relationship identified in the prior research—trust, openness, community involvement, community investment, and community commitment. Other issues that were explored included company image, consumer media diet, advertising recall, and respondent demographics. As a result of a survey, Ledingham and Bruning (2000) collected data from 448 community respondents. Once the benchmark was completed, the telephone company initiated a public information campaign in which the company's contributions to the community's well-being were highlighted. As a part of that initiative, company spokespersons served as guests on local radio talk shows and made presentations at local club functions, and the company's contributions to the community infrastructure were the subject of a full-page story in the Sunday edition of the local newspaper. Moreover, the organization used mailers, billing inserts, and billboards as an additional method of communicating messages concerning its support for the welfare of the community.

Some 4 months after the benchmark, and 1 month after the intervention, the original respondents again were surveyed, and interviews were completed with 136 of them. In the second wave of interviews, respondents again were asked their perceptions of the organization-public relationship as well as their intentions with regard to selection of a local telephone service provider. Analysis revealed significant increases in respondent perceptions of the organization-public relationship and a 10% increase in public members who said that they would opt to stay with the historic provider of telephone service, even if a competitor offered to provide the same service at 10% less cost.

DISCUSSION

The results from the review of the professional and scholarly literature, as well as from the recent research reported herein, clearly demonstrate the important role that community relations plays in an organization's overall public relations strategy. Community relations exerts an influence on respondent perceptions of the organization and of the organization-public relationship. Moreover, community relations influences loyalty toward a sponsoring organization by community members. Community relations can serve to generate benefits for both organizations and communities. Community gains include economic, societal, civic, and environmental benefits, whereas organizational gains engender community support for organizational goals. The research further suggests that long-term organization-community relationships are driven by a mutually beneficial approach rather than one that merely meets the needs of the organization.

The literature also indicates that building organization-community relationships is a multistep process in which the organization (a) identifies the needs of the community, (b) develops initiatives that respond to those needs, and (c) communicates organizational support of those initiatives to community members. A number of methods to identify community needs are suggested including the use of focus groups with community members and business leaders, development of community advisory panels, and ongoing surveys of community members. Moreover, the importance of well-planned communications programs to inform community members of the organization's support for the community is reflected in Ledingham and Bruning's (1998) observation that "organizational . . . support of the community in which it operates can engender loyalty toward an organization among key publics when that involvement/support is known" (p. 63). Thus, the accumulated research demonstrates that organization-public relationships can and should be managed for mutual benefit. The community benefits from the organization's community involvement, community investment, and community commitment. The organization, in turn, benefits from increased loyalty toward the organization among community members when those members are aware of the organization's activities. Clearly, that awareness should be the goal of community relations practitioners' communication efforts.

GUIDELINES

Community relations represents a way in which organizations can build long-term relationships with the communities in which they operate. We suggest that those charged with responsibility for developing and maintaining this key relationship follow a five-step relationship management process as outlined here:

Step 1: Analyze the Situation

a. List all *key constituencies* in the community that can influence the organization economically, socially, politically, and culturally.

b. Circulate the list of key constituencies *throughout the organization* to gain input and to ensure that all key constituencies have been identified.

c. Circulate the list to *key community members* to ensure that the community perspective is represented and that community input is sought early in the process.

d. Using a Likert-type scale, ask organizational members their *perceptions of the relationship* with each key constituency to provide a basis for comparing organizational ratings to those of community members.

e. Identify the *needs of the community* as well as community perceptions of the organization through the use of qualitative and quantitative research.

   i. Conduct *focus groups* with community members and *roundtable discussions* with internal publics to probe community needs and the organization-community relationships, particularly with regard to the dimensions of *openness, trust, community involvement, community investment, and community commitment.*

   ii. Using a Likert-type scale, *survey community members* and quantify their perceptions of community needs and the organization-community relationship dimensions.

   iii. Compare the *perceptions of the relationship* of the organization members to those of community members so as to identify areas of agreement as well as those where perceptions diverge.

Step 2: Planning

a. Create an *advisory panel for organization-community relationships* of community members and organizational members.

   i. The purpose of the panel is to *review the information* gathered through the use of roundtables, focus groups, and surveys.

   ii. The members of the panel should meet at least *quarterly* to provide continuous feedback and to suggest necessary adjustments to community-building initiatives.

b. In conjunction with the advisory panels, *develop organizational initiatives* that are responsive to community needs.

c. Design *communication programs* to disseminate information regarding the organization's plans with regard to community support.

   i. Emphasize the notions of *openness, trust building,* and the organization's *involvement in, investment in, and commitment to the community* in communication messages.

   ii. *Pretest* strategic initiatives with a randomly selected sample of members of key constituencies.

d. Design programs so that *key organizational personnel* are associated with community relations initiatives.

i. Encourage corporate executives to act as *spokespersons* for the community relations initiatives.

Step 3: Implementation

a. Initiate *behavioral and communication* initiatives.

b. *Inform community members* of the community- building initiatives through traditional communication channels such as media advisories, speaker's bureaus, and new media opportunities such as the Internet.

Step 4: Monitoring

a. Periodically *monitor the impact* of community relations initiatives.

   i. Track the *changes that take place in community perceptions* of the organization.

   ii. Track the degree to which the community *believes that its needs are being met* through organizational initiatives.

b. *Modify* community programmatic initiatives as suggested by responses from community members.

Step 5: Evaluation

The evaluation phase should focus on answering the following five questions:

1. Are the initiatives of the organization meaningfully affecting the needs of the community?
2. Should the organization continue to focus on those needs, or are there different needs that the organization should be addressing?
3. Are the initiatives positively affecting the organization-community relationship?
4. Are there positive gains in perceptions of the organization-community dimensions?
5. Are the initiatives generating benefit for the organization as well as for the community? If so, how?

RECOMMENDATIONS

Some experts believe that the highest level of a relationship is signaled by a public declaration of support (Knapp, 1984). With that in mind, we suggest to community relations practitioners that community members responsible for achieving the greatest improvements in organization-community relationships be singled out for special recognition. This can be achieved through an annual recognition awards function or a similar type of activity. Be sure to articulate how their efforts contributed to the welfare of the community.

Also, establish a regularly scheduled report of the results of the strategic initiatives to be disseminated to internal audiences. This builds internal support for community relations and helps to establish community relations as part of the organization's culture. Communication should use available vehicles including e-mail, memos, bulletin board postings, and newsletters. Likewise, the results of community-building initiatives should be communicated to those outside the organization as part of an ongoing reporting process designed to inform the community of the organization's support. Be sure to explain the value of community input to making community relations work for everyone.

Effective community relations meets the needs of both the organization and its key community constituencies. Failure to keep this in mind results in programs that serve only to meet the needs of the organization. By definition, that is not a relationship.

Educational Public Relations

JULIE KAY HENDERSON

In the United States, there are 136,012 public and private schools as well as 3,681 colleges and universities (Moody, 1998; Rodenhouse, 1997). All of them have relations with their publics, whether or not they have public relations departments or staff.

Today, good public relations is vital to the successful functioning of any educational institution. At the K-12 level, educators face community concerns about violence in schools, sex education, the role of religion, salary negotiations, books in the library, and countless other issues. Bonding measures, which provide more capital for schools, are turned down more often than they are approved by voters, in part because they provide rare opportunities for taxpayers to vote down taxes.

Higher education has its own challenges. Critics call it too expensive, charging that money is wasted and graduates cannot get jobs. Universities face competition for students and dwindling resources. Universities usually have three charges to fulfill: teaching, service, and research. Many people are not aware of the last two. It is part of a public relations practitioner's job to create that awareness.

Universities' need for public relations is quite different from that in 1900, when only 4% of high school graduates went on to attend college. Today, alumni provide a majority of donations, but they also represent an expanding number of people who believe they have a vested interest in their alma maters and, therefore, should have a say in their operations.

Educational public relations practitioners work for elementary and high schools, district offices, colleges and universities, and state and federal governments. Literally volumes could be written about the practice of educational public relations. This chapter briefly reviews the four-step process as it applies to this area plus two key aspects of educational public relations: community relations and media relations (the latter in crisis and noncrisis situations). The chapter concludes with an overview of the structure of public relations in education.

THE FOUR-STEP PROCESS IN EDUCATIONAL PUBLIC RELATIONS

No matter what level they serve, all educational public relations professionals strive to be more proactive than reactive—to anticipate problems and opportunities rather than always reacting to crises. One way in which to achieve this is by following a four-step public relations process beginning with research or the gathering of information, followed by planning, follow-through, and then evaluation. And, like other public relations practitioners, those in education make sure that their public relations plans fit in with the overall strategic plans of their organizations.

Step 1: Research

What is the current situation? How did we get here? What do we need to know? What problem do we need to address?

A reflection of the current situation, a situation analysis, sets the stage for further action. Once it is completed, the gathering of necessary information begins. But first, it often is helpful to determine who are the most important publics to be addressed. This requires systematically looking at all groups inside and outside the organization that have direct contact with or influence on it. Some publics for elementary schools, high schools, and universities overlap, but each level also has its own unique publics with which it must deal.

Figure 46.1 illustrates some of the more common external publics of educational institutions. External publics are groups outside an organization, whereas internal publics are those within an organization. Neither can be ignored. In a school, the staff (e.g., bus drivers, cooks, clerks) might have the most regular and/or daily contacts with the students. Outside the school, they talk to their neighbors, friends, and family and, therefore, can spread a message about where they work—for better or for worse.

Internal publics for all educational institutions include the students, faculty, staff, and administration. But even within one public, characteristics cannot be assumed to be universal. For example, the public of *students* for a college includes recent high school graduates, older than average students, those who are employed, those who are parents themselves, commuters, dormitory residents, and many others. Each subgroup has its own geographical, racial, and cultural

mix. Obviously, all of these groups have differing needs and expectations of their educational experiences and have differing viewpoints on various issues. Thus, identifying publics in broad strokes often is only the starting point. The more that can be learned about each, the better.

Typical methods of gathering information about the target publics include mailing questionnaires, administering telephone polls, conducting focus groups, interviewing opinion makers, doing student surveys, and analyzing the "grapevine." Open-ended questions should be included to learn not only the respondents' opinions on current issues but also what they consider to be crucial needs for the future.[1]

Not all research has to be reinvented. Secondary research, or that which has been gathered by someone else, often can fill needs in a more economical manner. Research on education abounds. For example, *First Things First* is a report based on a nationwide survey of parents, nonparents, and focus group interviews. It found that parents want their children taught three things: to read and write English; to do simple arithmetic by hand; and to have a common knowledge of science, history, and geography. The survey also found that three fourths of Americans say that drugs and violence are serious problems in schools. This type of research, already conducted, can help school public relations directors to establish their own baselines (cited in Carey, 1996).[2]

Local chambers of commerce also can provide schools with information on the biggest employers in town and the socioeconomic, ethnic, and geographic divisions of the citizens. Other sources used by educators include the census bureau, city and county agencies, and realtor organizations. Sometimes, local colleges or universities also have faculty who study demographics.

The image of an institution is affected by many things such as daily news, the school's own publications, the physical condition of the buildings, the curriculum, SAT scores, other test scores, dropout rates, teen pregnancy rates, drug use, athletic programs, school and business partnerships, and student or staff volunteers in the community. Research on any or all of these areas

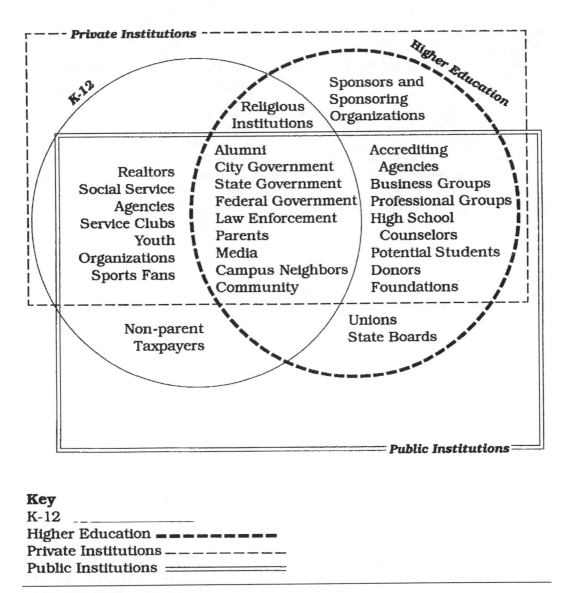

Key
K-12 _____
Higher Education ━━━━━━
Private Institutions ─ ─ ─ ─ ─ ─
Public Institutions ══════

Figure 46.1. External Publics

might be needed. A communication audit for the institution itself also might be helpful. The audit lists and evaluates all of the school's current methods of communication.

Research points the rest of the public relations effort in the right direction and indicates which of the many publics are priorities. Sometimes, research findings support previous concepts. Sometimes, they refute them. In either case, the research is beneficial. Research also

might support ideas already held but tweak them a bit. For example, administrators at a college might believe that faculty are unhappy because travel allowances for them have been reduced. Research might indicate that this indeed is true but that the faculty are unhappy because of the accompanying change in how the funds are allocated. The two situations would require different solutions. Research keeps the public relations plan on course.

Step 2: Planning

What do we want to accomplish? If there is a problem, how will we solve it?

Once all the information that is necessary has been gathered, a plan can be developed. The plan should encompass the whole school team. This also is an opportunity to sort out an organization's public relations priorities and to identify emerging issues and problems.

A public relations plan includes a goal, objectives that address that goal, strategies for meeting the objectives, and tactics for implementing the strategies. Objectives identify the target audience, the time factor, and the measure of success (this is used again in the evaluation process [Step 4]). The following might be an example:

Goal: To increase enrollment for evening classes

Objective: To increase media coverage of evening class offerings by 20% by September 1, 2001

Strategy: Target weekly newspapers within a 50-mile radius

Tactic: Write feature news releases on success stories such as students seeking college degrees at night

Tactic: Prepare individualized news releases on local graduates

At this point in the process, it is relevant to reflect on the school or college itself. There is no point in attempting to communicate that a school is a warm and loving place to be if it is not. The role of public relations is not to make a bad situation look good. To develop a positive public relations plan that will be successful, it is necessary to have all employees behind it, and the key to that is establishing a healthy work environment. In the preceding example, it will not profit the university to raise interest in evening classes if professors do not want to teach them; if the bookstore, library, and computer labs cannot remain open to serve the new students; or if the admissions office does not have the staff to fill the new requests.

Step 3: Communication

How do we accomplish our strategies? What tools and techniques can we use?

Educational public relations tools run the gamut available to other practitioners. In any communication to any public, it is important to speak in a language that the target public can understand, avoiding acronyms and educational jargon. Some of the most common public relations tools are cited in Table 46.1.

Each public relations office also will use the public relations techniques that best fit its needs. For example, private schools often have turned to paid advertising to attract new students; public schools have done less so.

Middle schools have taken a lesson from colleges that have a freshman orientation day. The middle schools conduct the same type of event for elementary school students who are about to make the difficult transition. Many schools also anchor special events around national events such as American Education Week (November), Lutheran Schools Week (March), and Children's Book Week (November).[3]

Some schools, and most universities, now sponsor Web sites on the Internet. Universities include information about departments, requirements for graduation, faculty, financial aid, and how to apply for entrance—basically any information that also appears in college catalogs. Public schools at the K-12 level include information on the schools' philosophies or mission statements, school year calendars—again, anything that can appear on paper. Because of the time involved, most schools find it more difficult to keep current information, such as the week's school menu, constantly updated. But as the technology improves, updating will become easier.

Step 4: Evaluation

How did we do? Did we meet our goals?

Evaluation is a necessary step to measure success and to provide a basis for information for

TABLE 46.1		
Standard Public Relations Tools		
	Internal	*External*
K-12	Bulletin board for achievements	Home visits by teachers
	Newsletters	Annual reports
	Memos	Menus (with room for comments)
	Handbooks and manuals	Newsletters
	Face-to-face communication	News releases
	Group meetings	Monthly calendars
	Letters	Letters to the editor
	Yearbooks	Public service announcements
		Op-ed pieces
		Paid advertisements
		Letters
		Parent volunteers in school
		Sports broadcasts
		Literature drops
		Cable access television shows
		Public speaking engagements
		Special events
		Notes
		Open houses
Higher education	Memos	Brochures
	Handbooks	Letters to the editor
	Newsletters	Public service announcements
	Fliers	News releases
	Letters	Op-ed pieces
		Annual reports
		Paid advertisements
		Direct mail
		Speakers bureau
		Special events
		Newsletters
		Sports broadcasts

the next cycle of research. Evaluation standards should be set at the beginning of the program, not at the end, so that it will be possible to accurately gauge the program's success.

Two types of evaluation helpful in educational public relations are formative and summative. Formative evaluation is done during the course of a program so that changes can be made as they are needed. Summative evaluation is conducted at the end of a program to determine whether goals have been met.

For example, a high school might sponsor a program discouraging students from smoking cigarettes. The goal is to decrease the number of students who start to smoke during the year by 10%. A formative evaluation done during the middle of the year might involve asking students whether the program is working. Changes suggested by the students then could be incorporated into the program. The summative evaluation, done at the completion of the campaign, would determine whether the goal had been met.

Evaluation methods include nearly every type of activity conducted for research such as questionnaires and observations. The information gained during evaluation is used during the next cycle, again beginning with research.

COMMUNITY RELATIONS

Any entity—from the police department, to the corner market, to a multinational corporation—benefits from having good relations with its home community. But for schools, positive community relations is a lifeline.

Since 1974, the Gallup Poll has surveyed the American public on questions regarding its schools. Respondents give schools in their own communities higher grades than they do the nation's schools. Parents give schools in a community higher grades than do nonparents. The findings seem to indicate that familiarity does not breed contempt; rather, it breeds respect (Rose, Gallup, & Elam, 1997). Because the proportion of households without children attending school now exceeds that of households with children attending school, in some cities as much as 75% to 25%, a school without a strong community relations program has little hope of ever convincing its residents that a school bond issue should be passed or that the school system in general is worth supporting. See Table 46.2 for ideas regarding community relations.

MEDIA RELATIONS

As just stated, the Gallup Poll indicates that people think that their own schools are good but that the nation's schools are wanting. Part of the reason for this divergence of opinion is the source of information. Most people learn about their community schools from other people, whereas most people learn about the nation's schools from the media. This illustrates the impact that the media have on forming public opinion on which schools thrive or wilt.

Media relations frequently is a large part of a public relations practitioner's duties. Media relations, which chiefly refers to working with the news departments at the various media, can include sending information to the media (e.g., in the form of news releases), suggesting stories to reporters (called *pitching*), and dealing with inquiries from the media. Unfortunately, research has shown that although the public reportedly acknowledges the need for a constant flow of information using every available medium both from the schools to the public and from the public to those operating the schools, neither schools nor the media have been very successful at maintaining this constant flow (Hynds, 1989).

A recurring theme of research findings through the 1970s regarding news coverage of education was a lack of consensus between reporters and educational leaders, especially in terms of reporters criticizing educators for not understanding what news is and what the function of the news media is. In addition, neither schools nor the media appeared to be successful in providing coverage of the topics in which the

---

TABLE 46.2

Community Involvement: Ten Ways in Which to Improve Community Involvement

---

1. "Principal for a Day" or "Teacher for a Day" brings local community leaders into the school for a day and allows them to witness what goes on at a school firsthand. Invitees can include businesspeople, professionals, parents, local journalists, and local politicians.

2. School staff speak at the service clubs that are so numerous and always in need of speakers.

3. Service and professional groups, such as Rotary and Lions, are invited to meet at the school, either one time or on a monthly or regular schedule.

4. Community forums are held.

5. Advisory committees are composed of community leaders and alumni.

6. Information booths are placed at obvious and not so obvious places and events—street or art fairs, airports, or shopping centers (especially during the back-to-school sales).

7. Schools frequently publish newsletters or inserts for the local newspapers at least once a year. A list of equipment, books, and/or materials needed can be included in a "Wish We Had This" type of list.

8. A classroom is adopted by a business. The business can get recognition through an office display at the school, articles in the school publications, or a display of a class photograph and a certificate at its own headquarters. To show their thanks, the children can send artwork to the business or perform at Christmas or other special times.

9. The Gallup Poll of 1997 cited earlier found that 69% of the respondents would be willing to work as unpaid volunteers at their communities' public schools. The "wish list" cited in Item 7 above also could include a list of talents or special knowledge needed.

10. Begin each school board meeting on a positive note. Highlight some success at the school such as a student achievement, a new course, or a project.

---

public indicated interest (Farley, 1952; Fleming, 1960; Gerbner, 1967; Jacobson, 1978; Jelinek, 1955; Kemp, 1941; Stout, 1951).

During the 1970s, research took a different turn, critiquing the output of the journalists more than the efforts of the educators. This possibly was a result of a more general movement to critique news coverage following the Watergate scandal. Or, it might have been a result of more people specifically trained in public relations moving into the positions, thereby fulfilling their responsibilities better than in the past.

Briefly, the recurring themes that have appeared during the past 10 to 20 years in regard to the critical examination of education news coverage are the following:

- Coverage of education lacks context and perspective.
- Articles tend to focus on anecdotes and true-to-life vignettes rather than on broader trends.
- Reporters are poorly prepared to scratch beneath the surface or to frame current events into a broader perspective.
- The media personalize the news.
- The media present news that is shallow and disjointed. (Bracey, 1985; Drake, 1991; First, 1986; Haberman, 1987; Hynds, 1989; Kaplan, 1992; McQuaid, 1989; Rhoades and Rhoades, 1991; Savage, 1989; Schoonmaker, 1985; Zakariya, 1987)

These themes occurred in research specifically regarding educational reporting, but are similar to critiques of general news coverage of any topic.

Educational public relations practitioners learn from research such as that just cited. They also take advantage of general guidelines to working with the news media that apply to all public relations practitioners. For example, when trying to get news coverage, a school will have more success if it can tie into a current event—what is already being discussed in the news columns, on the editorial page, or on talk radio.

Working with the news media can be frustrating if the media are perceived to be a school's public relations arm. The news media have their job, and educational public relations practitioners have theirs. The relationship does not have to be adversarial, but it should be based on two groups of professionals doing their jobs professionally.

Crisis Management

Working with the news media often is a significant part of any crisis management. No matter how well prepared an institution is, crises may hit at any time. They may be natural or manmade, but they never can be totally prevented.

School crises can include natural disasters such as fires or earthquakes, emergencies such as shootings, other acts of violence, food poisoning, or bus accidents. Crises situations also may arise if employees are accused of embezzlement or administrators are accused of sexual harassment.

A crisis plan is helpful in dealing with the situation effectively. A plan will cover *who* is responsible for telling *what information* to *what publics* through *what channels of communication*. For example, the first public to be informed of any crisis situation should be the internal publics—employees, faculty, and students. A crisis plan will determine whether this will be done in small groups, face-to-face, via telephone or e-mail, or through a telephone tree. Employees never should learn something about their school from the media. Internal communication is crucial.

Next, key publics should be informed. A crisis plan should identify who they are (e.g., parents, the media) and who will be responsible for talking to them. Usually, one person is designated as the spokesperson to the news media. That person must have all the information available. Public relations professionals know that a "no comment" usually is translated as a "guilty." If information is not known or is not available, then the spokesperson will say so and agree to get the information for the reporter. Saying "I don't know" is not a crime.

The key to handling a crisis is communication, which should be quick and consistent. A plan helps to accomplish this.

ROLES AND TITLES

An individual public school at the K-12 level might not have a public relations department or even one person doing public relations. Frequently, the public relations activities are shared among several administrators and teachers. A district-level office is more likely to have a public relations professional on staff. In addition, consultants might be hired on an as-needed basis.

Multiple Roles

At the postsecondary level, the practice of public relations more frequently is done by professionals, but they still might be called on to fill various roles. These include the management of information, community relations, employee relations, government liaison, media relations, issues management, marketing research, publication management (now including the Internet), fund-raising, special events coordinating (e.g., homecoming, graduation, dedications), research, evaluation, and crisis management. The variety of titles of offices used at the college level indicates this range of duties—alumni relations, information services, university relations, news bureau, news office, information office, media relations, public affairs, public information office, college relations, community relations, fund-raising, and institutional advancement.

CONCLUSION

Several organizations exist to help people who work in educational public relations. They can provide more information on the field. They include the National School Public Relations Association, Public Relations Society of America (Educators Academy), and Council for the Advancement and Support of Education (formerly American College Public Relations Association and American Alumni Council).

NOTES

1. Information on conducting surveys, including writing questionnaires, sampling, interviewing, and analyzing data, is available from the Phi Delta Kappa Center for Professional Development and Services in Bloomington, Indiana. The PACE (Polling Attitudes of the Community on Education) manual is designed to help schools conduct scientific polls of attitudes and opinions about education.

2. The Phi Delta Kappan publishes the results of the Phi Delta Kappa/Gallup Poll of the Public's Attitudes Toward the Public School in its September issue each year. The magazine's address is Box 789, Bloomington, Indiana 47402.

3. Several books, including Chase's Calendar of Events, publish a list of all special days and weeks. Chase's, for example, cites nearly 100 events under "Education, Learning, Schools." Chase's is published by Contemporary Books in Chicago.

Strength in Diversity

The Place of Public Relations in Higher Education Institutions

BARBARA J. DeSANTO

R. BROOKS GARNER

From colonial Harvard University to today's on-line courses, higher education, whether public or private, has occupied an important place in U.S. social, cultural, and political spectrums. It signifies citizen commitment to the next generation's future as well as an avenue to produce knowledge for current use.

Perhaps because education has been such a valued commodity, the mission and methods of educating future generations enjoyed somewhat sacred underpinnings. After all, the people who comprise higher education institutions should know more than any other component of society given that their "product" is knowledge.

Throughout the centuries, American higher education developed into a diverse conglomeration of public and private entities, from 2-year community college to 4-year research institutions, influenced by national, regional, and local forces from politics and consumer demand to affirmative action. Today, however, the long insu-

lated position of higher education, like other professions such as law and medicine, is undergoing public scrutiny in all parts of its complex operations.

Such a change, from enjoying revered unquestioned status to being pushed into a high-profile arena populated by media, special interest groups, empowered consumers, and other vocal entities, presents new challenges for higher education public relations practitioners.

This chapter offers practitioners involved in higher education communication key points to consider in planning for, communicating with, and evaluating the results of their relationships with the increasingly complex network of entities, from students and parents to provosts and regents, that make decisions about the future of higher education. Specifically, the chapter focuses on building the necessary internal communication unity for developing and maintaining external relationships.

CONCERNS AND CHALLENGES FOR HIGHER EDUCATION

Because the historical structure within higher education institutions evolved quietly, often without widespread public attention, the new demand by outside groups for accountability might seem like a new threat for higher education. Cutlip, Center, and Broom's (1985) description of closed and open systems aptly illustrates higher education's transitory stage. The traditionally closed system premise of many higher education institutions emphasized bringing the internal and external stakeholders in line with the organization with little regard for how the interaction of the component parts appeared to work together or conflict, hence the "ivory tower" image. By contrast, the open system premise viewed external and internal stakeholder interaction as critical to adapting to and flourishing in today's changing environment, something higher education is finding it must do.

A variety of external pressures affect higher education.[1] One recent study elaborated on the public's perception that higher education must be more responsive to the needs of its constituents including being more accessible to different types of students, more aware of and responsive to educational costs, and more concerned with the relevance of higher education to the demands of the marketplace. The National Center for Public Policy and Higher Education (1998) study found that 89% of Americans believed that qualified students should not be denied college educations because of cost. In addition, 75% believed that a college education is more important today than it was 10 years ago. Newsom, Turk, and Kruckeberg (1996) cited the 1960s American realization that people with money are another key factor in consumerism, which highlighted ordinary citizens' rights and resulted in people demanding voices in decisions that affected them. Along with the flood of baby boomers, education saw more women, minorities, and nontraditional students enrolled, and it saw graduates with one degree returning to school to retool

and/or obtain second degrees. Van Patten's (1996) higher education case study book also illustrated how consumerism created a demand for more accountability from education's variety of stakeholders including faculty and administrative productivity, student retention, more academic programs and offerings at all levels, improved allocation and use of resources, and greater responsiveness to business and industry. Add to the list the often skewed or misleading media coverage of the cost of higher education, headlines about binge drinking and drug use among students, and lead stories about athletic scandals. What emerges is an often unflattering picture of the environment in which higher education operates. The new millennium emphasis will continue to stress the individual's responsibility and power of choice, from selecting and questioning his or her own health care options to demanding quality and relevance from higher education institutions.

The internal structure of higher education also is chaotic, with many different factions balancing their goals with others while competing for resources and visibility. Graduate education versus undergraduate education, finite and often diminishing resources versus increasing resources, administration versus faculty on issues such as academic freedom and governance, academics versus athletics, affirmative action and diversity mandates versus funding established directives, technological innovations versus traditional course and information delivery systems—the structure often is compared with a multitude of fiefdoms squabbling under the nose of the king.

As higher education institutions grew and became more fragmented internally, functions became compartmentalized and seemed to operate without any knowledge of what other parts of the institutions were doing. Warner (1996) detailed the often disjointed development of higher education as separate offices to deal with media relations, development and alumni, sports promotion, publications, video services, and (most recently) Web sites for external audiences. All of these coexist with internal faculty and staff audiences, resulting in a plethora of seemingly unrelated, and often contradictory, external and internal messages. Now more than ever, higher education institutions not only must become aware of how many public relations efforts are going on in their respective institutions but also must step back and coordinate those efforts within their structures before going out to external audiences. As Berube (1996) wrote, "The most important thing is that we need to reevaluate our priorities internally if we're going to understand how we might be revalued externally" (p. 17).

APPLYING PUBLIC RELATIONS CONCEPTS TO HIGHER EDUCATION STRUCTURES

Unlike public information, which J. Grunig and Hunt (1984) described as basic, truthful one-way communication techniques to dispense information, public relations is best when defined as proactively building ongoing relationships with individuals and groups not only necessary to an organization's survival but also imperative to an organization's success. For colleges and universities, it means presenting consistent congruent messages developed from an internal, university-wide set of agreed-on internal goals supported by appropriate measurable objectives that, when presented, all contribute to the overall image, reputation, and substance of a university. The key element in attaining this congruency is two-way, mutually beneficial negotiation. The function of negotiation should be to arrive at these agreed-on goals through discussion and participation among all those responsible for communication, from college or university leaders (e.g., the president) to the different communication functions (e.g., development and recruitment), before each different unit sets its own goals and objectives to create and distribute its information. Only then can each communication practitioner know where his or her efforts need to be directed to achieve both the organizational goals and the individual unit objectives. For educational institutions, this means that the traditional practice of sending out one-way, independently   produced   and   distributed

information may well still be the end objective and output of the various units, but the internal structure of the university now will share in developing the overarching mission and goals for the institution. Higgins (1983) concluded,

> Institutions prosper because they possess a unique identify, a coherent sense of self, and a unified purpose. This purpose guides decision making and sets the institution's hierarchy of values and priorities. The task of public relations involves achieving and articulating the institution's sense of self. . . . There must be an honest evaluation of what it has done well or poorly and a determination of a common set of values for its publics. (p. 25)

The traditional public relations process includes collectively conducting research and developing objectives before messages are ever crafted, and it means critically evaluating the effects of any action during the action and after it has taken place. It means building and maintaining the publicity age externally while moving to the strategy age internally. Whereas much has been written about how to plan and carry out specific functions in a general context such as conducting fund-raising, maintaining alumni relations, recruiting new students, and promoting athletics, very little has been written about getting the internal public relations components together to develop an all-encompassing internal strategy before going outside the university's ivy-covered walls. Quirke (1996) described this type of communication as "boxitis." "Either the right hand doesn't know what the left hand is doing, or worse, the right hand is actively fighting the left hand" (p. 14). Quirke pointed out,

> Without remembering or understanding the whole picture, functions and factions inevitably start competing with each other. With all the best intentions in the world, the organization pulls itself apart pursuing different objectives. This leads inevitably to mixed messages and conflicting priorities. [One] cannot simply overlay a customer-focused culture . . . as a move away from the hierarchy mentality. (pp. 13-15)

HANDS-ON COORDINATED PLAN ELEMENTS

Six elements, based on the unique structure of higher education moving from a closed to an open system, comprise this model of higher education public relations practice:

1. working from set goals that are compatible and synchronized internally to mesh with and support the overarching institutional short and long-term mission, goals, and plans;
2. identifying and prioritizing key stakeholders for each unit's goals as well as the overall mission of the institution;
3. identifying opinion leaders crucial to the overall success of the institution as well as each unit's success;
4. communicating with one clear institutional voice;
5. conducting and sharing ongoing evaluations with all other relevant institutional units—an ongoing report card that allows corrections and grades; and
6. recognition of public relations as the boundary-spanning, coordinating force leading the collaborative internal effort.

1. Synchronized Goals

Historically, educational institutions have mission statements that offer institutional goals in fairly broad terms. Likewise, each unit should have its own mission statement and goals in writing using clear and well-defined language. The challenge here is not only sharing these goals among institutional units but also understanding and cooperating among units. Territorial protection—turf wars—too often prevents cooperation from developing among entities that depend on each other for survival. In this age of justifying existence, cooperation among different parts of the same organization often is sacrificed for continued individual existence at the expense of the organization's overall efforts. But

sharing information will get all units involved in relationship building and communication and allow each to see its contributing pieces to the whole picture, to see where they might overlap, to see where they might appear to contradict each other (or actually do), and to see what is not being addressed by anyone. This sort of organizational mapping helps to develop one theme that presents a united front to the outside world.

Internally, practitioners then can use this information to refine their own team-building strategy so that it meshes with management goals. For example, if one of the institution's goals is to raise more community support for athletic events, then one cannot afford to have ongoing negative coverage of the university's handling of unruly students' behavior after an athletic victory or loss. If the school's housing office sends out harsh-sounding rules and regulations about dorm policies, then those messages need to be reconciled with the friendly campus atmosphere that the admissions office is promoting.

To be understood and evaluated, goals must be practically written as impact statements rather than as output tactics. Impact objectives focus on setting standards against which to measure information, attitude, and/or behavior changes in key stakeholder groups. Without having those standards to measure against, evaluation often becomes simply counting how many brochures were produced and sent out.

2. Stakeholders

After each entity has developed its own goals and objectives, it should identify and prioritize its key internal and external stakeholders. These are the groups of people that each entity cannot live without—from alumni, to voters, to athletes. In higher education, stakeholders are as varied as the units within the institutions. Newsom et al. (1996) stressed, "The key to identifying target publics is research—finding out who these publics really are and what they actually think" (p. 144). By identifying these stakeholders, practitioners will find that many individual institutional efforts have stakeholders in common and that some stakeholders might be overlooked. For example, alumni often are contacted for general school and specific department fund-raising, to buy season athletic tickets, or to provide internships for current students. The important thing to realize is that often the same stakeholders are important to a variety of internal educational units, and often the rivers of seemingly unrelated one-way information at best annoy, or at worst turn off, stakeholders to all institutional efforts. Similarly, a plethora of messages that do not address any stakeholders' self-interests might turn them off entirely.

After all stakeholders are identified, each unit should prioritize its key constituents. Ranking these individuals or groups will help to focus efforts on the segments most important to achieving the unit's individual goals. This coordinated effort helps each unit to make the most of its often limited resources and allows diverse units to specialize in what they do best rather than trying to be all things to all stakeholders or appearing to be at odds with other parts of the organization.

3. *Opinion Leader Development*

Identifying and prioritizing stakeholders provides practitioners with the natural opportunity to develop "assistants" or echoes in the form of opinion leaders—key individuals and/or groups that spread information and add credibility to an institution's strategy and messages. Opinion leader programs, as described in *PR Reporter,* are used in several universities with reported success. Sams (1998) said, "Higher education is fortunate that we have people who are very interested in us and will give us their time and expertise for free—because they are alumni or because they hire our graduates" (p. 1). Clemson University has developed a Board of Visitors whose members volunteer to evaluate university messages and give feedback, and the Commission on the Future of Clemson, an advisory group that brings outside perspectives to the university's planning efforts. The University of Illinois and Macomb (Illinois) Community College have developed similar sounding board programs.

The key here is to have each internal unit identify and engage internal and external opinion leaders who can advise, provide perspective during planning and evaluation, and carry messages as additional credible sources to other stakeholders.

4. *Communicating With One Voice*

Once goals, objectives, and key stakeholders are agreed on, individuals and groups must recognize that they are not operating "alone" or as the "only voice" for their organizations. An organization's key messages must be communicated in relation to its overall theme—what Heath (1994) called *voice.* Heath described voice as "all of the actions one entity makes that are meaningful to itself and to others" (p. 21). Whereas each internal unit undoubtedly is aware of its place and function in the internal hierarchy, to the outside world each appears as "the school." The absence of one institutional voice or theme often leads to a disjointed portrayal of an organization, much like the Keystone Cops falling all over each other. For example, does the institution have one standard logo and typeface that unites all publications? In addition to appearance, are messages congruent in philosophy? A review of all the institution's publications and video clips will provide a fact-based snapshot of how the institution appears in the stakeholders' eyes and will let the public relations practitioners know whether a unified "theme" or "mission" is being understood as the institution intended. Heath described this desired state as follows: "What employees say and do will be similar and complementary, thereby becoming the desired voice" (p. 50).

This examination also shows the gaps or contradictions in the institution's image. If one does not know what the admissions office is presenting to prospective students or what athletic promotions are in place, then one cannot communicate with one voice or coordinate additional information from other units to reinforce one's own message. Conversely, when negative messages are splashed across a newscast, the time that one has invested in speaking with one voice and building goodwill with key stakeholders can carry through by dipping into what Al Golin, vice president of public relations for McDonald's, termed "the reservoir of goodwill" (Golin, 1997, p. 1).

5. Evaluation

Evaluation must tie directly back to the goals set in the umbrella plan and developed specifically for each unit. Evaluation must be ongoing and must be specified in the planning stage before any action is taken. If the organization believes that it cannot afford evaluation, then it needs to reevaluate the plan components. Evaluation takes time and money, but it allows practitioners to determine at any time whether they are on track. Reaching key stakeholders as the organization planned, making changes and/or midcourse corrections during implementation, and providing hard data to justify accomplishments to other management entities—both internally and externally—is the only way in which to gain credibility with each of these diverse publics. Evaluating well-written impact objectives demonstrates accomplishments in direct relation to efforts expended. The same objectives written out in the planning phase should appear again in the evaluation phase, followed by data to support what was accomplished.

6. Public Relations as a Boundary Spanner and Change Agent

Gillis (1997) studied the relationship of public relations officers with top university leaders and concluded that it is essential that the public relations coordinator have the trust of, and access to, the educational organization's top officers and play a key role as a member of the president's advisory staff. Being left out of the policy- and decision-making loops makes meshing communication plans and actions with top management's overall goals and objectives difficult, if not impossible.

Crucial to internal evaluation, collaborative goal setting, and developing voice is having a leader—a boundary spanner, an internal consultant. Quirke (1996) wrote that the consultant's main task is to understand all the issues the organization faces and "to be expert in reorganizing communication to help remove barriers to success" (p. 274). The idea is not to control communication but rather to coordinate and guide it to get the best results. The strength, according to Jackson (1995), is "having the positive relationships, effective communication methods, mutual trust, and teamwork in place before change initiatives are launched—so fear, resistance, sabotage and other negative outcomes are largely avoided" (p. 2).

CONCLUSION

This chapter has discussed how important it is for higher education institutions to develop internal cohesion in purpose and meaning among its many important communication components before attempting any external communication strategies and actions. Although the end objectives of the educational communication process may indeed be more one-way than two-way communication with external audiences, the internal components must have a high degree of internal understanding of both purpose and meaning to ensure that the variety of necessary external messages, although different, present a unified institution with unified themes.

The following process highlights five steps that practitioners can implement to build internal unity in voice and meaning. The steps focus on two-way communication based on employee involvement at each step. This helps to ensure employee understanding and support—shared meaning—when practices are implemented.

A Practitioner's Guide to Best Practices in Internal Communications in Higher Education

Step 1: Enlist the support and understanding of the top managers in your educational organization—the president and any other key decision makers.

Step 2: Identify all internal educational organizational units involved in public relations and/or publicity tasks—from producing newsletters, to recruiting students, to lobbying legislators.

Step 3: Have each of these identified units prepare a written assessment of the following:

- ◻ its main internal goals;
- ◻ its main external goals;
- ◻ its main internal stakeholders/audiences;
- ◻ its main external stakeholders/audiences;
- ◻ its main internal messages;
- ◻ its main external messages; and
- ◻ its evaluation efforts and techniques.

Step 4: Invite all of these identified units to a planning session to share this information. As a group, identify the overlapping efforts, the neglected efforts, the contradictory efforts, and the complementary efforts. From this input, identify the strengths and weaknesses seen not only in their own efforts but in the efforts of other units as well. Use this information to develop an umbrella plan including all units' public relations efforts.

Step 5: Provide for ongoing communication among these groups and schedule periodic evaluation sessions in which each unit can share its successes and concerns.

The complex, compartmentalized, diverse, and sometimes turf-bound components of higher education will continue to be scrutinized in this age of heightened consumer power and often superficial sound bite journalism. Working through the five steps using the six key concepts focused on building internal unity before venturing outside the institution will help public relations practitioners to combine their diverse strengths into a coherent network that can provide the right message to the right stakeholder in the right format at the right time. In diversity, there can be strength.

NOTE

1. A review of the most recent 6-month index of the *Chronicle of Higher Education* and the past several years of *Academe,* the American Association of University Professors magazine, presents an interesting list of what the higher education trade press considers important.

CHAPTER 48

Sports Information Directing

A Plea for Helping an Unknown Field

NICHOLAS C. NEUPAUER

█ As we enter the 21st century, two of the most dynamic growth industries in the United States have been computer science and sports administration (Helitzer, 1996; Isch & Fowler, 1997). Although computer science has received a great deal of attention in our society, little is known about sports publicity and promotion—tasks performed at the collegiate level by the sports information director (SID). So little is known, in fact, that sports information directing has been mentioned in only one of the four best-selling college public relations textbooks (Wilcox, Ault, & Agee, 1995)[1] and often is misunderstood by sports reporters who believe that SIDs use the press agentry model of public relations.

Some scholars, however, have contributed to the literature that defines the SID field. McCleneghan (1995, 1996) developed important median demographics for SIDs and stated that the SID is a public relations practitioner in trouble. Neupauer analyzed personality traits of SIDs (Neupauer, 1997a, 1999), the importance of including SID courses in public relations curricula (Neupauer, 1997b), and women in the male-dominated world of SIDs (Neupauer, 1998). Isch

and Fowler (1997) discovered that burnout from the job is a common problem. Lambrecht (1998) analyzed the levels of job satisfaction for the SID. Although some theses from sports management programs have focused on the area (Harwick, 1981; James, 1976; Roy, 1980; Smith, 1976), scholarship on the SID profession has been sorely lacking.

Even undergraduate education has ignored this specialized public relations field (Neupauer, 1997b). Approximately 200 colleges and universities in the United States, as well as many overseas, offer public relations sequences and degree programs. Yet, few offer SID courses, let alone sequences and/or degrees. Some graduate programs, such as those at Ohio University, West Virginia University, the University of Connecticut, and the University of Massachusetts, offer solid degrees in sports management, but most undergraduate students have to stick with basic public relations courses and wait until graduate school or internships to gain the experience.

The question begging to be asked is why the SID is so unknown when the profession has grown tremendously over the past 40 years.

In 1996, the College Sports Information Directors of America (CoSIDA) listed 2,196 members serving in such a collegiate capacity (CoSIDA, 1996). When considering professional and amateur sports, Mark Tudi, a sports executive recruiter, estimated that there are 1.5 million marketing and 300,000 media front-office personnel positions (Helitzer, 1996).

The purpose of this chapter is to provide an understanding of the SID and his or her unique job responsibilities by summarizing the history of the field, analyzing the demographics and qualifications needed, describing the culture and atmosphere associated with the position, and concluding with suggestions for the future.

HISTORY OF THE SID

The origins of sports public relations can be traced back to the decade of the 1920s, often described as the "golden era of sports." Although newspapers and magazines were devoting space to sports coverage dating back to the late 19th century, it was during the post-World War I years that sportswriting started to evolve rapidly (Anderson, 1994).

Those who handled the public relations for professional and collegiate teams during that period were dubbed either press agents or publicity men. As time went on, these professionals have been given various titles ranging from public relations director to director of media relations, from press director to promotions director, from director of communication to media director, and so on.

The variety of titles actually has been one of the big problems confronting the SID field over the years. Such vagueness leads to a lack of uniformity, consistency, and understanding of what the SID actually does. Although such problems still exist today, if it were not for the foresight of 102 individuals meeting in Chicago in August 1957, the SID still would be in complete disarray, both professionally and at the collegiate level (CoSIDA, 1997).

Up until the decade of the 1950s, collegiate promotions specialists were part of the American College Public Relations Association. The public relations side of collegiate administration had been around for a long time, but an athletic niche was relatively new. Realizing that a separation between the two had to be made, those attending the Chicago convention tabbed their niche "sports information" and their professional organization the "College Sports Information Directors of America."

With solid membership and annual conventions in different regions across the United States, CoSIDA has done its part in establishing ground rules, frameworks, workshops, and support systems for SIDs since its origination more than 40 years ago. Highlights from the organization during that time period include Fred Stabley of Michigan State University becoming the first vice president and program chairman (1957-1958), small college representatives becoming part of the executive committee (1960-1961), Rosa Gatti of Brown University becoming the first female member of the board (1979-1980), and June Stewart of Vanderbilt University becoming the first female president (1990-1991) (CoSIDA, 1997).

DEMOGRAPHICS AND QUALIFICATIONS

McCleneghan (1996) discovered that the average profile of a SID at the National Collegiate Athletic Association (NCAA, Divisions I, I-AA, II, and III) and National Association of Intercollegiate Athletics levels was the following: 38.5 years old, held a bachelor of arts degree in journalism (public relations emphasis) but no advanced degree, earned $38,500 annually, was employed 10 years at his or her present institution, belonged to CoSIDA but not the Public Relations Society of America (PRSA) or the International Association of Business Communicators (IABC), and served 3 years as an assistant SID. Other findings included SIDs having a median of only 1.5 years of prior media experience (usually with newspapers) and having interned at their respective schools' SID offices as undergraduates.

Helitzer (1996) stated that the best route to the professional sports public relations level is to gain the experience in the collegiate ranks. During the past few years, it has become equally obvious that no one can be involved in pro sports without intimate knowledge of sports public relations. The average SID college staff consists of 2.5 full-time professionals and 15 to 20 interns. Together, they produce 118 publications, send out 5,000 individual news and feature releases, and work with 100 to 200 different media reporters and editors, on average.

Remarkable to some might be the fact that journalism skills today are only about 40% of the SID's required tasks. One of the biggest differences between the SID and other public relations professionals is the SID's wide scope of duties. Among the primary responsibilities the SID has to perform, Helitzer (1996) listed the following:

publications: media guides, programs for all home games, schedule cards, mail-order brochures, recruiting kits, annual reports, and booster club newsletters;
publicity: news and feature releases, news conferences and backgrounders, photography, media interviews, and media tours;
game management: public address announcers, scoreboard operations, telephone hookups, scorers, officiating facilities, press box seating and credentials, broadcast facilities, video facilities, travel, and lodging; and
game supervision: crowd participation and safety, uniform insignia, giveaways, contests, promotions, sponsorships, halftime exhibitions, honors and awards, music, U.S. flags, and team banners.

Secondary responsibilities listed by Helitzer (1996) included the creation and placement of advertising, league meetings, conventions and workshops, booster club activities, fund-raising, fan surveys, budgets, scheduling, equipment negotiations, licensing, and merchandising.

Other job characteristics set the SID profession apart from other public relations positions. The SID often works 7 days a week, 12 to 20 hours a day. Because most sporting events take place during the evening hours or on weekends, and because half are played on the road, the SID gets to spend little time away from the job. Even when he or she is at home taking a breather, it is not uncommon for fellow professionals or even sportswriters to phone the SID's home with questions or requests.

The SID might not be affiliated with the college's or university's public relations department but instead might be affiliated with the athletic department. Considering that some athletic directors know little about public relations—or, worse, like to believe that they know a lot—one can imagine the difficulties this presents.

Unlike other public relations practitioners, the SID boasts about the opposition. The better the opposition, the better the fan interest and ticket sales.

The SID not only must be good at what he or she does (e.g., reliability of postgame statistics) but also must be quick at churning out his or her material given that deadlines from the various mass media and wire services must be met. If an individual cannot meet deadlines on a consistent basis, then the SID profession is not for him or her.

THE CULTURE OF THE SID

In analyzing the job satisfaction of sports information personnel, Lambrecht (1998) discovered that SIDs are moderately satisfied with their jobs, with no significant differences in levels of satisfaction among the various NCAA division sizes or among the various management levels (e.g., director, associate director, assistant director). Lambrecht's results were consistent with the findings of earlier studies of sport management personnel in professional sports (Hutson, 1995), private sport and athletic club management

(Lambrecht, 1996), and NCAA athletic directors (Lunde, 1996).

Not only are many in the profession only moderately satisfied with their jobs, but Isch and Fowler (1997) discovered that the long hours, low pay, and lack of respect from administrators also was causing burnout for some SIDs. Those in the profession cited budget cutbacks, funding, and gender equity concerns as the biggest obstacles that SIDs face.

On the topic of gender, Neupauer (1998) analyzed the lack of female membership in CoSIDA. Although 54% of the jobs in public relations are held by females, women account for just 22% of the SID population. Compared to other professional organizations such as the IABC (62%) and PRSA (52%), the proportion is low. The reason, according to Neupauer's study, is twofold. First, the rigors and demands of the profession (e.g., time commitments, travel, weekend work) do not cater to women who are the primary caretakers of their households. Second, considering that men administer about 97% of intercollegiate athletic programs, the lack of females is status quo in the male-dominated world of college sports. Quite simply, men hire men, who then hire more men, and so on.

CONCLUSION

One of the biggest problems facing the SID today is obscurity. Not only is the profession overlooked in undergraduate education, but professional associations such as the PRSA make no mention of sports information.

The PRSA's (1987) *Report of the Commission on Undergraduate Public Relations Education* described the importance of public relations specializations in publicity and media relations, community relations, employee relations, consumer relations, financial/shareholder relations, public affairs, fund-raising, and international public relations. The PRSA ignored sports information directing as a public relations specialization worthy of attention in undergraduate edu-

cation. Nine years later, the PRSA (1996a) again overlooked the SID in its *Design for Undergraduate Public Relations Education.*

Despite such oversights, there appears to be a new generation of undergraduate public relations majors who want to assume the SID role. Therefore, educators, scholars, athletic directors, and even SIDs themselves need to focus on a few areas. First, they need to define the role of the SID in today's intercollegiate athletics arena. Is the SID part of the athletic department or of the college's or university's public relations staff? Exactly where does the SID fall in the formal hierarchy—as a manager or as a subordinate? Should CoSIDA serve as an isolated organization—with its own publication contests, awards, and ethics codes—or should it work on a formal relationship with the PRSA or even the IABC? Given that Lambrecht (1998) pointed out that SIDs are only moderately satisfied with their jobs and Isch and Fowler (1997) discovered that SIDs suffer from a lack of respect from administrators and from burnout on the job, addressing these questions could go a long way toward rectifying such problems.

Second, educators, scholars, athletic directors, and SIDs need to document the qualifications that aspiring SIDs need to have. More scholarly articles need to address this overlooked public relations area. An undergraduate curriculum with detailed textbooks for the *novice* to the field, in addition to graduate-level texts, needs to be written.

Finally, educators, scholars, athletic directors, and SIDs need to make sure that those aspiring to enter the field are prepared to handle the job by providing appropriate coursework and training. At Marist College in Poughkeepsie, New York, for example, the School of Communication and the Arts is originating a sports communication certificate that can be coupled with the undergraduate student's communication major. The 15-credit (five-course) certificate will consist of three tracks: sports public relations, sportswriting, and sports broadcasting. Specialized courses in sports reporting, sports public relations writing, sports journalism writing, sports broadcasting, and sports case studies—in addition to introductory classes in public relations, journalism, and broadcasting—will give the undergraduate student a leg up on the field rather than being forced to rely on graduate-level schooling.

By addressing these needs and others now and during the coming years, the road to becoming a SID will be a less bumpy one.

NOTE

1. The other best-selling college public relations textbooks that make no mention of the sports information field are Cutlip, Center, and Broom (1994); Newsom, Scott, and Van Slyke (1993); and Seitel (1998).

CHAPTER 49

■ BEST PRACTICES IN CONTEXT

Political Power Through Public Relations

LORI MELTON McKINNON

JOHN C. TEDESCO

TRACY LAUDER

■ Since the birth of American democracy, public relations practices have played a key role in shaping our politics. In fighting for our independence from England, early colonists adopted the campaign slogan "No taxation without representation." Samuel Adams organized committees of news correspondents to disseminate anti-British information throughout the colonies. One of the earliest special events, the famous Boston Tea Party, was staged as colonists dressed as Indians dumped imported tea into the harbor and created a true media event. Furthermore, public relations pieces such as Paine's pamphlet *Common Sense;* Hamilton, Madison, and Jay's *The Federalist Papers;* and Madison's draft of the *Bill of Rights* helped to band colonists together and to ratify the U.S. Constitution and its first 10 amendments (Cutlip, Center, & Broom, 1994; Seitel, 1995). Thus, these early attempts at swaying public opinion established a strong precedent for advocacy and presented Americans with important examples of the power of public relations.

As the U.S. political system has evolved, public relations practices have continued to grow in importance as those pursuing or wielding political power seek ways in which to communicate their messages to the voting public. The purpose of this chapter is to provide an overview of the role of public relations in American politics. Not only does the chapter highlight the historical origins of public relations in the political process, but it also focuses on the changing face of political public relations in the media age.

Without doubt, the use of public relations in politics has been around since the time of the ancient Greek and Roman leaders. As Gaby (1980) pointed out in his historical discussion of early American politicians, "It was correctly believed that if you didn't have a keenly developed sensitivity to people and a capacity to communicate effectively, you had no business being a politi-

AUTHORS' NOTE: We thank the following expert panelists for their time, participation, and opinions: Rick Farmer, Donna Lucas, Stephen C. Craig, Victor Kamber, Carol Arscott, Chris Wilson, "Doc" Sweitzer, and Phillip Fremont-Smith (see Note 1 for affiliations and biographies).

cian" (p. 11). Whereas "PR savvy" has long been a crucial characteristic for all political candidates, the use of paid political consultants is a more recent requirement. In 1829, President Andrew Jackson selected the first presidential press secretary, Amos Kendall, to serve in his administration. A former journalist and editor, Kendall performed nearly all White House public relations tasks including speech writing, creating state papers, sending official messages and press releases, and conducting opinion polls. He coined and publicized the term *kitchen cabinet* to represent Jackson's key advisers, and he even created a newspaper, the *Globe,* to represent the views of the administration (Cutlip et al., 1994; Seitel, 1995). In response to President Theodore Roosevelt's attempt to win public support for his programs through a network of publicity experts, Congress passed the Gillett Amendment of 1913 to limit the practice of public relations in government. Worried about the possibly unlimited persuasive power of the president, an amendment passed stating that appropriated funds could not be used to pay a publicity expert unless specifically earmarked for that purpose. Several years later, Congress passed the gag law, which prohibited using appropriations for services, messages, or publications designed to influence any member of Congress. As Seitel (1995) explained, "Even today, no government worker may be employed in the practice of public relations [in title]. However, the government is flooded with public affairs experts, information officers, press secretaries, and communications specialists" (p. 375). These political communication professionals serve as official spokespersons for the administration or for the candidate. Because elected officials and the process of electing them are hot topics for media coverage, the importance of public relations support and counsel at the local, state, and national levels has become an increasingly valued commodity.

Whereas public relations techniques have been used within a political context for many years to promote candidates and key campaign issues, to stage political events, to provide media contacts, to prepare promotional materials (e.g., news releases, ads, brochures, posters), to counsel clients in media relations, to spin political information to candidates' advantage, and to offer advice on packaging political policies, there are several more immediate trends in public relations that are worthy of note. More and more, American politics is experiencing a blurring of political media. Traditional political public relations (e.g., advertising, debates, rallies, news coverage) are interacting with each other and are creating a new political dialogue (Jamieson, 1992; Kaid, Tedesco, & McKinnon, 1996; Tedesco, McKinnon, & Kaid, 1996; West, 1993). Political press secretaries are leaving government to work for commercial public relations firms, and practitioners are leaving agencies to serve as public affairs officers (McAvoy, 1987). News outlets are reducing political sound bites to a mere 8 seconds, making it imperative for consultants to package political information in a concise and catchy fashion that fits into the horse race nature of modern coverage (Jamieson, 1992). Practitioners are using the Internet as a way in which to communicate campaign objectives with voters and as a way for voters to provide immediate feedback to candidates (Tedesco, Miller, & Spiker, 1999). In addition, professionals are relying more heavily on research to shape political campaign goals and strategies (Judd & Hellinger, 1995). Some of these trends, along with others, might be helping to reshape the traditional role of public relations in politics. Through our Delphi panel of experts, we strive to establish what are the best practices of public relations in support of politics.

METHOD

Allen (1978) described the social science methodology of the Delphi technique as a tool used by policymakers to forecast and make plans for the future. The Delphi technique allows some flexibility on the part of the researchers, depending on the scope and magnitude of their research questions. Most Delphi panels involve at least a two-stage design in which panelists respond to initial researcher questions in Round 1 and then provide commentary and reaction to the other panelists' responses in Round 2. Consistent with most Delphi methods, our panel of experts was targeted purposefully for their known reputations in political public relations, keeping partisan interests of the professionals in mind. Eight expert panelists were located from *The Political Resource Directory* (Hess, 1997) and were selected for our Delphi study: five political and public relations consultants, two academicians, and a pollster.[1] In the first round, panelists were asked to respond to seven open-ended questions,[2] and in the second round, respondents commented on the other panelists' answers and evaluated them using a 7-point Likert-type scale (ranging from *strongly agree* to *strongly disagree*). The Delphi technique enabled practitioners to provide us with their perceptions of the current and future roles of public relations in American politics. Answers remained confidential at all times so that panelists could feel comfortable giving honest responses and fair evaluations.

RESULTS

Whereas answers to the first round of questions appeared diverse, the second-round responses to the initial questions were overwhelmingly rated with agreement. In most cases, panelists either strongly agreed or moderately agreed with their cohorts' responses. Thus, the general themes from each question are presented. However, when appropriate, important caveats or points of disagreement also are noted. Due to space limitations, we do not report on the final question regarding tools that students should develop to enable them to succeed in the changing world of public relations. However, we briefly address that question in the discussion section.

How Important Is the Role of Public Relations in Politics?

All panelists agreed that the role of public relations in politics is becoming more important with the increase in media competition. Panelists strongly agreed with the comment, "Having someone in a campaign or in an elected official's office who knows the media, who takes the time

to develop relationships with individual reporters, and who understands what makes them tick is going to make a politician's life a lot easier." One panelist made a particular point to distinguish "public relations as encompassing 'free' and 'earned' media" from paid media. Most panelists strongly agreed with the comment, "It is clear that press coverage is increasingly central to campaign strategies and increasingly critical to the success (or failure) of candidates." There was one caveat pointed out by a panelist:

> The importance of public relations in politics varies by campaign. In those campaigns which generate the heaviest press coverage, public relations is most essential; voters will get as much or more information from the news than from ads. In those campaigns in which there is significant paid media and minimal press coverage, public relations is at its least important. And in those campaigns in which paid media either [are] nonexistent or insignificant, public relations again gains more importance. In other words, there is a curve of sorts, in which public relations is most critical on both ends (i.e., president and dog catcher) but less so in the middle (i.e., many state legislative races).

Respondents generally agreed that public relations is very important to the political process and that the context of the campaign has an impact on the public relations strategies and effects.

Describe the Position That Public Relations Holds in the Political Campaign Process

Panelists strongly agreed with the comment, "Public relations is central to a political campaign." An example from the 1996 presidential campaign was provided to show the strategic hold that public relations has over campaigns:

> In 1996, Senator Bob Dole's presidential campaign staff temporarily refused to accept a financial contribution from a gay group because they feared it would create an unfavorable public perception. At a time when money is often cited as the most important element of politics, it is in-

structive that public relations considerations were primary. In a political campaign, almost every decision is driven by public relations considerations, particularly as they relate to voters.

Although the panelists represented both Republican and Democratic consulting firms, they did not let partisanship stand in the way of their evaluation of responses. In fact, although a few panelists made special notes about their disagreement about whether the 1993 documentary *The War Room* is a superb film, they overwhelmingly agreed with the following:

> Perhaps the penultimate example is the role George Stephanopoulos played in the 1992 Clinton campaign (for documentation, watch the superb film *The War Room*). His job was essential PR [public relations] strategy—"spin," if you will. His role was to be at the confluence of politics and policy and to use that to position the campaign so it generated the most positive earned media coverage. A key part of that process was to dictate the messages used in paid advertising and to ensure consistency between paid and earned media. This function—the preeminence of PR in determining campaign strategy—is ideal, I believe. Message development—the essence of good PR—should drive paid advertising and every other aspect of any campaign. To do otherwise is to let the tail wag the dog.

Panelist responses indicate that whether the candidate is running ahead or behind certainly dictates the public relations techniques. A campaign that falls behind in the public relations fray could spend more time fighting fires than building support with the constituents.

List Five Ways in Which Public Relations Is Used and/or Misused to Shape Politics (explain if necessary)

Interestingly, panelists did not make a point to distinguish how public relations strategies are misused in the political process. Most panelists included some detail about defining oneself,

one's opponent, and/or the issues of the campaign or ballot initiative. Although respondents had different terminology for the public relations strategies used in campaigns, five general uses appearing in most answers were (a) message development, (b) research, (c) earned media (both proactive and reactive), (d) advertising, and (e) constituent relations and coalition building. Panelists agreed that issue and candidate definition, complete research on issues and opponents, media events and spin, consistency of advertising appeals with other public relations messages, and endorsements from surrogates are the key tools for public relations in political campaigns.

To What Degree Do Public Relations Professionals Maintain Accountability in the Political Process?

The question of accountability raised the most discrepant answers in the first round and the most disagreement among evaluations in the second round. One respondent stated, "The bottom line is that there is no accountability beyond your professional reputation and the law." This response was not evaluated highly by the other panelists.

Accountability was deemed to rest with different sources such as the voters, the public relations professional, the candidate, and the media. Several panelists pointed out that because public relations and media consultants are unknown to the vast amount of the public, the candidate ultimately bears the brunt of responsibility. Based on evaluations of the responses to this question, it appears that there are many different levels of accountability—the consultants are accountable to the candidate, the candidate is accountable to the voters, and the media also are accountable to the voters. One panelist reported, "The unfortunate fact is that the media has a selective process of screening for accountability." This answer received all favorable evaluations except for one *moderately disagree* response.

Partisan interests flared on this question, as a few consultants were identified for unethical treatment of candidates and issues. In fact, one respondent stretched the point by claiming, "There is a great deal of accountability on the Republican side, less on the Democratic side." As one would expect, this response was evaluated according to the respective partisan interests of most of the panelists.

Panelists agreed that there need to be additional mechanisms in place for accountability, and they overwhelmingly agreed with the following response:

> When campaign rhetoric degenerates into mud-throwing about trivial or personal issues which do not have much relevance to the lives of voters, then the voters' ability to make an informed choice diminishes and democracy suffers. But I do not know of a mechanism to force campaign consultants and staff to be held to this type of accountability, short of the news media and the voters themselves exercising critical judgment and not voting for campaigns which engage in "poison politics."

Although one panelist identified the efforts of the Committee on Ethics and the Profession within the American Association of Political Consultants, the enforcement powers of that organization are limited. Proposed legislation that attempts to control and monitor unethical campaign activity within several states was dismissed as ineffective for improving accountability and charged with padding the size of bureaucracy.

Where Is the Line Drawn Between Informing Voters and Selling a Political Candidate or Campaign Message?

Responses to this question were fairly standard, with the following overwhelming opinion: "The line is drawn between truth and lies." However, one panelist noted, "With every election cycle, the line moves," suggesting that voters, the media, and the candidates push the threshold of tolerance with each election. One response that included the statement, "The goal of the PR pro-

fessional is to sell the candidate and has no responsibility to inform unless that helps sell the candidate," received one *moderately disagree* response; all other respondents agreed or responded neutrally. Although the panelists agreed that negative campaigning would remain a staple in public relations and politics, they believed that so long as the campaign messages were truthful, negativity was acceptable.

Forecast What You See to Be the Future of Public Relations in Politics

Perhaps the most interesting aspect of this look into political public relations is the information that the panelists provided about their perceptions of the future of the field. The panelists generally agreed that political public relations would become increasingly more complex if trends in media development continue. Multiple cable channels, Web TV, and the Internet were cited as information sources that will continue to diversify the audience and multiply the number of media within which practitioners must work. Panelists also agreed that, in the future, message development might be less important than speed of message delivery. Two panelists envisioned a fast-paced, almost crisis environment for future political campaigns, with one stating, "The pace of technology is making deliberative democracy an endangered species." Panelists also agreed with the following comment:

> The Clinton White House has given all political professionals a model to emulate. They are so darned good that the country's best reporters do nothing but admire their spinning skills. I doubt, however, that any other president (or elected official—or campaign) would get away with the same brazen tactics.

Unfortunately, no media experts were included on the panel to respond to their ability to critically evaluate campaign spin.

DISCUSSION

The high-speed communication revolution certainly is changing the nature of political public relations. Our panelists envisioned a future environment in which message construction in public relations campaigns might be less crucial than the pure speed of message responses to opponent communication. In fact, the response-rebuttal-reply aspect of political advertising during the 1996 presidential campaign was so immediate that candidates Clinton and Dole were waging almost daily dialogue through their ad campaigns. Meanwhile, the candidates and their staff were spinning the ads and waging public relations campaigns that appeared redirected almost every day.

So, how does the student of public relations prepare for success in this field? Our panelists, above and beyond any other advice, indicated that writing skills never would go out of style. Although message construction might not be as crucial in the future, weak writing skills certainly will lead to failure. The other resounding advice was to practice in the field. Many panelists indicated that internships are essential for students to learn about the trade and sharpen their skills necessary for the quick public relations game. Furthermore, knowledge of new communication technologies is a must.

One limitation of this Delphi panel is the absence of media professionals. Although our purpose was to report on perceptions of the changing role of public relations in the political process, the media certainly play an important role in that process. Several of our panelists mentioned the media's role in their responses, and it would have been interesting to see how media professionals envisioned the future of political public relations. Moreover, this study focused primarily on how public relations functions in the campaign process. Future researchers might want to examine the public relations role as it relates to government agencies, lobbyists, and political media professionals.

Despite its limitations, this study provides an important overview of the historical origins of political public relations as well as insight into current and future trends for the role of public relations in the political process. Indeed, public relations is an indispensable component of modern American politics, and opportunities are expanding for current and future practitioners in the political arena.

NOTES

1. **Rick Farmer** is an assistant professor of political science and a fellow in the Ray C. Bliss Institute of Applied Politics, University of Akron, specializing in campaign management and political parties. He has published in *Social Science Quarterly, Oklahoma Politics,* and *Almanac of Oklahoma Politics.* **Donna Lucas** is chief executive officer and president of Nelson Communications Group, which represents Fortune 500 companies, political figures, and national associations. She served as California media director for the 1992 and 1996 Republican National Conventions, as California press secretary for President George Bush's 1988 campaign, and as press secretary to former Governor George Deukmejian. She is an officer of the American Association of Political Consultants. **Stephen C. Craig** is a professor of political science at the University of Florida and is the director of the university's Graduate Program in Political Campaigning. He is author of *The Malevolent Leaders: Popular Discontent in America* (1993), editor of *Broken Contract? Changing Relationships Between Citizens and Their Government in the United States* (1996), and coeditor of *After the Boom: The Politics of Generation X* (1997). He also has published numerous articles on the nature of American public opinion, has worked extensively with both academic and political surveys, and continues to do polling and focus group research for clients in Florida and elsewhere. **Victor Kamber** is president and founder of The Kamber Group, one of the nation's largest independently owned communications consulting and public relations firms. Prior to starting his firm, he served as assistant to the president of the Building and Con-

struction Trades Department, AFL-CIO, and as director of the AFL-CIO Task Force on Labor Law Reform. He is author of *Giving Up on Democracy: Why Term Limits Are Bad for America* (1995) and is co-author (with Brad O'Leary) of *Are You a Conservative or a Liberal?* (1996). **Carol Arscott** is a vice president at Mason-Dixon Political/Media Research Inc. in Columbia, Maryland. Before joining the firm, she served as legislative aide to the minority leader of the Maryland House of Delegates for 14 years and was press secretary for the Maryland House Republican Caucus. She was chairman of the Howard County (Maryland) Republican Party for five years, managing the successful coordination of local campaigns. She also was a delegate to the 1992 Republican National Convention and was press secretary for the Bush-Quayle 1992 Maryland campaign. **Chris Wilson** is president and chief operating officer of SWR Worldwide, a public affairs research arm of Shandwick. He was cited as a "rising star" in American politics by *Campaigns & Elections* magazine. **Thomas M. "Doc" Sweitzer,** cofounder and partner of The Campaign Group, is one of the most successful political/media consultants for Democrats. He has represented more than 30 members of the House and Senate including Vice President Al Gore. He writes and produces commercials and also provides management and marketing advice to political clients. A former media buyer, he is a frequent speaker for political and business groups. He has consulted numerous newspaper associations regarding political marketing and money-making advertising plans. **Phillip Fremont-Smith,** a full partner at Alfano Production, has worked in politics for more than six years helping to design some of the highest profile campaigns of the 1990s. After running several successful campaigns to elect Republicans in his home state of Massachusetts, he was hired to design and direct Mitt Romney's bid to unseat Senator Ted Kennedy in 1994. He also has worked on the campaigns of U.S. Senator Alfonse D'Amato, New York Governor George Pataki, presidential candidate Steve Forbes, the National Federation of Independent Business, Empower America with Bill Bennett and Jack Kemp, Massachusetts Governor Bill Weld, and the National Republican Congressional Committee's Rapid Response Program.

2. The seven questions are listed individually as the subsection headings in the results section.

CHAPTER 50

Labor and Public Relations

The Unwritten Roles

TRICIA HANSEN-HORN

☐ Can public relations learn anything from studying labor and its public relations activities? The management team of United Parcel Service (UPS) claims that we can. The Teamsters union recently used public relations techniques to best the efforts of UPS management:

> "One thing is certain," says Ken Sternad, vice president of corporate public relations for UPS. "We will never again underestimate an opponent to such an extent. If there is ever a next time, we will be better prepared. We were, in some ways, outmaneuvered by the Teamsters' PR [public relations] machine and may have lost the battle of public opinion." (quoted in Jiles, 1997, p. 1)

Unfortunately, scholars of public relations have largely neglected the study of the public relations triumphs and challenges of labor (Miller, 1995), even though "much of public relations history—constructive and destructive—is woven into this unending struggle between employer and employee that today is fought with publicists, not Pinkertons" (Cutlip, 1995, pp. 204-205). Because much of public relations

scholarship is driven by interests within the larger field of communication, the neglect of organized labor might well be an extension of neglect within that arena (Botan & Frey, 1983; Hansen, 1993; Hansen-Horn, 1996; Hansen-Horn & Vasquez, 1997; Redding, 1966, 1992). The neglect also may be influenced by the "us versus them" mentality (evidenced in the preceding quote where Sternad speaks of underestimating an opponent) that dominates business-oriented thinking. Most public relations teachings are framed from a business perspective; hence, if organized labor is one of "them," then why focus on the lessons its public relations activities can teach us? In addition, the relationships between public relations and the media may play a role in the neglect. Pomper (1959) began the argument long ago that "because of the pattern of the mass media, the union member and leader are not recognizable elements in popular culture" (p. 495). Perhaps we *are* guilty of being influenced by what is popular. Dozier and Lauzen (1998) argued that we need to study nonpopular groups such as activists "for ways their practices are not accounted for in contemporary public relations theories, models, norms, and practices" (p. 28). Labor activities are popularly tied to activism.

The neglect of organized labor is real. The neglect is undesirable. The communication discipline, especially that of organizational communication, is particularly well suited to its study (Botan, 1990; Botan & Frey, 1983; Brock, Botan, & Frey, 1985; Hansen-Horn, 1996; Hansen-Horn & Vasquez, 1997). It is not a far reach to claim that public relations is particularly well suited to its study as well. This chapter argues that public relations scholars should stop neglecting the study of organized labor given that there is much to be learned. A review of the literature is presented and critiqued for what it does and does not highlight about labor and public relations. A suggested list for future research is presented.

REVIEW OF THE LITERATURE

A review of the literature addressing organized labor and public relations suggests that there still is much to be done. Miller (1995) reviewed the public relations strategies used by both organized labor and management during the national steel strike of 1946. Specifically, Miller focused on the struggle that occurred between the United Steelworkers of America and the Steel Institute. She articulated the story of the 1946 struggle between management and workers from a machine tool manufacturing company in Madison, Wisconsin. She positioned her story within the following premise:

> Since industrialization, both management and labor have used public relations programs to attempt to manipulate their own and each other's image. Numerous studies have found entertainment and news media biases against unions, and labor leaders in the U.S. have prescribed "an ongoing media relations effort" to help combat the public's negative perceptions of organized labor. Analysis of the image of big business indicates

that anti-corporate sentiment decreased over time, and scholars have analyzed campaigns, such as those conducted by the National Association of Manufacturers, which sought to discredit unions. (p. 305)

Miller addressed the public relations efforts of both sides of the steel strike. The efforts were evident in the front-page news of both of the town's daily newspapers. She argued that public relations was seen by both parties as a means of managing public opinion. Miller's study is the most recent review of which I am aware that was directed specifically at labor and public relations. However, labor is not totally absent in public relations history.

When writing *Public Relations History*, Cutlip (1995) briefly mentioned the union-busting tactics of "big business" and the historical role of public relations in the "unending struggle between employers and employees" (p. 204). As mentioned in the introduction of the study, Cutlip suggested that much of the history of public relations lies within this struggle.

Cutlip (1994) made more specific mention of organized labor in *The Unseen Power*. He addressed "the union-busting tactics of such pioneers as Ivy Lee and John Price Jones" (pp. 57-61, 234-236; see also Miller, 1995, p. 306) as well as the activity of John Wiley Hill (Cutlip, 1994, pp. 458-523). The Rockefellers hired Lee to provide public relations counsel during the aftermath of the Ludlow Massacre. Father and son "were under heavy verbal assault from the nation's press and public for their brutal strike-breaking tactics in their Colorado Fuel and Iron Co. (CF&I) strike" (p. 57). The Rockefeller mining company had authorized troopers and mine guards to assault miners and their families through the use of firearms. Both women and children were killed. The Rockefellers turned to Lee, whose public relations counsel was successful in "skillfully muffling . . . the criticism of the Rockefellers in the wake of [the Ludlow Massacre]" (p. 58). Later in history, Lee and his firm were retained by West Virginia coal operators "to counter the ugly publicity that had flowed from their use of a large armed force to crush a miners' march against union organizers" (p. 119). Lee and his firm used a series of publicity tactics to attempt to stem the tide of negative publicity directed at the coal operators.

Cutlip (1994) addressed John Price Jones as well. Like Lee, Jones was involved in strike-breaking tactics. His firm participated in the anti-United Mine Workers campaign during the early 1900s and later again in the efforts surrounding the 1937 Johnstown Steel Strike. Again, like Lee, Jones was hired as a public relations counselor.

Finally, Cutlip (1994) addressed "John Wiley Hill's public relations practices and ethical standards" (p. 458). Hill was involved with the steel industry and worked specifically with the American Iron and Steel Institute in its efforts to win "the labor and legal battles of the steel industry from mid-November 1933 until the end of his active involvement in Hill and Knowlton" (p. 458). He provided public relations counsel to the steel industry for three decades. Cutlip generally addressed labor from the lens of how public relations historically has been used in favor of management and against labor.

Cutlip, Center and Broom (1994) also provided organized labor recognition in their textbook *Effective Public Relations*. Miller (1995) applauded their text for containing one "section specifically on public relations for unions" (p. 306). Cutlip et al. (1994) asserted that "organized labor . . . symbolizes and speaks for working men and women in the United States" (p. 539), and as such, public relations plays an instrumental role in organized labor's efforts toward that end:

> Labor public relations uses press contacts, preparation and distribution of materials on specific subjects, television spots, and interviews and press conferences to get labor's point of view across. Of increasing importance are the estimated 5,000 union publications on the national and local level. (p. 541)

Cutlip et al. argued that because of "serious problems besetting the economy in the 1990s, it follows that there has been a decline in public confidence in unions" and that, therefore, "pub-

lic relations has taken on added emphasis as the movement's political, educational, and community involvement has increasingly supplemented its traditional role in labor-management negotiations" (p. 306). They also discussed "the problem of strikes" (p. 541) and the negative impacts that strikes can have. Strikes can cause difficulties—real or perceived—to strikers and nonstrikers alike. Cutlip et al. suggested that organized labor must use public relations tactics to explain the "public inconvenience caused by strikes" (p. 541).

Douglas (1986), although perhaps not considered to have written mainstream public relations scholarship, authored a noteworthy book, *Labor's New Voice: Unions and the Mass Media*. She argued that "few avenues have been overlooked in labor's attempt to inform and persuade its audiences" (p. 2). She focused specific effort toward providing an understanding of "the broad context or total environment in which labor operates in terms of its public relations" (p. 3). As indicated by the subtitle of her book, Douglas's definition of public relations is limited to media relations. However, Douglas's work provides interesting contexts for many types of public relations analyses. She addressed the historical public relations foundations of the AFL-CIO, quoting a 1955 report of the First Constitutional Convention Proceedings to demonstrate that organized labor is, and has been, aware of "the need for attaining and maintaining good public relations" (p. 17). Douglas argued that organized labor had to use public relations to stem the flow of negative publicity directed toward it as an institution. She saw this as a justifiable attempt on the part of unions based on the following argument:

> American institutions are evaluated largely in terms of their perceived relationship to democracy and a capitalist economy. To those who view industrial growth as a sign of a thriving, healthy economy, and who have a strong belief in the free market, the protection of the rights of private property, and the traditional concept of individualism, the labor unions, with their persistent emphasis on the right to organize and to bargain col-

lectively, must appear generally threatening if not subversive. (p. 17)

Douglas (1986) then addressed the public relations activities of specific international labor unions such as the International Ladies' Garment Workers Union; the United Automobile, Aerospace, and Agricultural Implement Workers of America; the International Association of Machinists and Aerospace Workers; and the American Federation of State, County, and Municipal Employees. She addressed the public relations efforts of these internationals to demonstrate how they, or even the efforts of local unions, often supplemented or even supplanted the public relations efforts of the AFL-CIO.

Douglas (1986) also examined the role of public relations and organized labor on another level. She reported the results of a 1981 survey directed toward international unions and "designed to provide information on the structure and function of public relations departments and on policy and opinions of labor leaders concerning the media relationships of their own unions, of labor in general, and of the AFL-CIO" (p. 110). She found that the majority of responding unions had 1 or more staff members devoted to public relations; some had as many as 12 public relations staff members. The unions reported a variety of important publics including "their own members and officers, potential members, members and officers of other labor unions, government officials and legislators, the general public, and the AFL-CIO" (p. 111). The survey results also addressed international union perception of the public relations efforts of the AFL-CIO, use of the mass media, response to the Fairness Doctrine, and participation in advertising.

Crable and Vibbert (1986) recognized the institution of organized labor in the chapter of their text devoted to "Review of Public Relations Environments: Past and Present." They suggested that labor plays a role in the current and complex "industrial/economic context of public relations activity" (p. 80) and that labor unions "realized the power . . . [that] public appeals could hold" (p. 92) during the period from 1940

to 1950. Crable and Vibbert also cited the Supreme Court ruling in 1982 in the case of *Massachusetts v. Hunt* as "the decision that differentiated union activity from 'conspiracy' and opened the way for public unions which would require public communication programs" (p. 98).

Brock et al. (1985) performed a rhetorical analysis of a prescription for union busting. They suggested, "Labor unions are direct attempts to organize workers, and such efforts rely upon using communication both as a process and as a product. Workers organize to communicate their needs, while communication is used to organize workers" (p. 52). Brock et al. argued that efforts to stop organizing (certification) or to do away with institutionalized unions (decertification) also are communicative efforts. As such, "certification and decertification campaigns are persuasive communication campaigns. . . . Therefore, these elections . . . are similar to other persuasive campaigns in society—advertising, merchandising, political, *public relations,* and public policy" (p. 52, italics added).

IMPLICATIONS OF THE LITERATURE

The texts reviewed in the preceding section can be looked at again for the specific purpose of articulating what organized labor-public relations perspectives are present and absent. Sometimes, what is not present is as valuable as what is present. In other words, when scholars articulate one account or story, there exists the potential for another account or story that, although deferred for the moment, also can be told. Smith and Turner (1995) suggested, "If scholars neglect their own grounds and/or invoke foundationalist criteria, they become closed to the idea that their own characterizations are also constructions and, as such, are always open to reconstruction" (p. 159). The reviewed texts are first examined for what perspectives are present.

Public Relations and the Presence of Labor

Miller (1995) pursued an understanding of public relations and labor within one context and time frame. She focused specifically on the public relations strategies used by both management and labor at the local and national levels to manipulate public opinion during the 1946 steel strike in Madison. Cutlip (1995) simply suggested that much of public relations history lies within the struggle between management and labor. Cutlip (1994) surveyed the public relations activities of Lee, Jones, and Hill in their efforts to provide counsel to big business leadership of their day. Cutlip et al. (1994) defined unions as a mouthpiece for working men and women. They cast unions as dependent on public relations for successful organizing. They also stressed the role that public relations plays in negating the negative effects of strikes on union members, on unions themselves, and on concerned communities. Douglas (1986) sought to bring labor's pervasive use of the media to light. She highlighted the role of public relations (taken as media relations) in countering negative publicity aimed at organized labor as an institution, in reaching a variety of publics considered important by organized labor, and as a constituent of the image of the AFL-CIO as perceived by internationals. Crable and Vibbert (1986) cited organized labor as part of the environment in which public relations activities must take place, and they made mention of the fact that public communication programs are part of contemporary labor's activities. Brock et al. (1985) cast public relations as a constituent force in the certification and decertification of unions.

Public Relations and the Absence of Labor

Miller (1995) focused on only one strike and one time frame. Cutlip (1995) credited the labor-management struggle with much of public relations history but did not articulate that history. Cutlip (1994) subordinated organized labor concerns and its use of public relations strategies against the efforts of Lee, Jones, and Hill to dis-

cussions of how Lee, Jones, and Hill used public relations strategies against labor. Cutlip et al. (1994) neglected to ask the self-reflexive questions as to whether labor's traditional role really was primarily negotiations between workers and management and whether nonunion efforts have used, and still do use, public relations to magnify public inconveniences caused by strikes. In addition, Cutlip et al. asserted, "The American labor movement is credited with helping bring about many of the changes and legislation in civil rights, health, education, and employee rights that have occurred since the death of President Franklin Roosevelt" (p. 529). They did not, however, cite the source of this assumption, nor did they encourage scholarly effort to articulate how organized labor has used public relations theory and techniques to accomplish these changes. Finally, they articulated the assumption that unions spoke for working men and women but failed to articulate how unions used public relations strategies to speak for both men and women. It appears that Cutlip et al. considered the needs of men and women to be the same and to have been equally represented by union activity. Specific articulation was not given to how working men's needs or working women's needs have been represented. Crable and Vibbert (1986) began a discussion of organized labor and public relations, but they did not continue it. They pointed to, but did not develop, labor's role in the industrial/economic arena of public relations activity. They also did not develop a framework for understanding how labor has facilitated powerful public appeals. Brock et al.'s (1985) exploration of the rhetoric of union busting subordinated public relations as a subset of communicative activity instead of focusing on public relations as a powerful constituent of union-busting success.

SUGGESTIONS FOR FUTURE RESEARCH

There are many directions for future analysis. Some of these can be developed from what this reviewed literature already has begun, pointed to, or presented through absence. Table 50.1 contains a list of suggested areas, both historical and contemporary, for further pursuit.

We can learn from the study of labor on at least two levels. The first is the level of analyzing the challenges that labor efforts present for client organizations. We can learn lessons such as those that Jiles (1997) claims UPS did from the efforts of the Teamsters—that (a) the media fight does matter a lot, (b) it is important to wage a proactive and aggressive media campaign, (c) it is important to avoid rumors by providing facts, and (d) winning the press battle often depends on the emotion that messages impart. If UPS can learn, then all public relations scholars and practitioners can learn.

The second level involves learning from labor's triumphs in organizing workers in the face of massive challenges from huge conglomerates (from the turn of the 20th century to the present) and from labor's ability to create issues and rally individuals around them in a manner leading to difference making. Triumphal efforts of this process are recorded in historical accounts of things such as the efforts to abolish child labor practices and to secure fair labor standards for all working people. Lessons like these might prove valuable to issues management and activist understanding. We also can draw on these historical lessons to understand more clearly the potential of democracy as well as the place public relations efforts have in creating that potential. Public relations strategies historically have been used by the labor movement to change the way in which big business is done. Perhaps proponents of community building and corporate social responsibility can gain insight from the study of labor and help to change the face of big business even more. We also can study the image-making efforts, successes, and defeats of the AFL-CIO. The AFL-CIO has a long history of struggling with

TABLE 50.1
Suggested Areas for Future Organized Labor-Public Relations Research

Organized labor and:
- organizing efforts
- institutionalization
- worker strikes
- strategic media use
- political lobbying
- the public goodwill
- the representation of masculine interests
- the representation of feminine interests
- gendered public relations
- civil rights
- health issues
- education
- employee rights
- the history, presence, and image of public relations

Nonunion efforts and:
- resistance to the institutionalization of labor
- the deterrence of organizing
- worker strikes
- lobbying against organized labor's political goals
- the facilitation of anti-labor public perception

union member and nonmember perception. The lessons we learn here might transfer well into the current dialogue about image.

Public relations scholars have neglected the study of organized labor. As demonstrated in this chapter, however, there is much to be learned from directing focus to historical and contemporary organized labor-public relations activities and relationships. The review of the literature presented here, and the search for what it says and does not say, points the way for future studies of labor and public relations.

Public Relations in the Health Care Industry

LAUREL TRAYNOWICZ HETHERINGTON

DARADIREK EKACHAI

MICHAEL G. PARKINSON

Frankly, it's hard for me to tell you where health care PR [public relations] is going because I can't see where health care organizations are going.

—Anonymous public relations professional
(quoted in Lewton, 1995, p. 1)

Health care is changing at unprecedented levels. Former models of care that feature the physician providing medical treatment have been largely replaced by health care team models promoting prevention and wellness (Dziabis & Lant, 1998; Marino & Ganser, 1997). Furthermore, current intricacies based on changes in reimbursement, clinical and operational practices, the management of health care processes and information, and the very structure of health care organizations combine to challenge even the most astute public relations practitioner.

In this chapter, the theory and practice of public relations in the health care industry are examined. The practice of health care public relations, formerly described as similar to that of other service industries (Zeithaml, Parasuraman, & Berry, 1992), has changed along with the dramatic transformation of health care itself. In a sense, public relations in health care might be no different than that in any other service industry given that the overall aim of public relations still is one of "harmonizing long-term relationships" (Seitel, 1995) and "reputation management" (Newsom, Turk, & Kruckeberg, 1996). In the current health care environment, traditional public relations practitioners who are skilled in writing, research methods, and analysis remain invaluable.

Yet, health care is a unique industry. Starr (1982) claimed that medicine is different from any other industry because of the product (life, death, and healing), the rapid and profound changes in the health care system (from physician as solo practitioner to multiconglomerates of layered health care processes and reimbursement scenarios), and the interaction of client (patient) with suppliers (health care providers within a defined system). Furthermore, the motivation to improve the health care industry is not fixed on cost reduction—a universally cited rationale in other service industries. Rather, the desire to improve health care processes is motivated by providers who seek to provide a higher quality of care in a coordinated manner (Beed, 1994). Thus, public relations practitioners who are responsible for promoting and conveying improvements and systemwide transformation within the health care industry must walk the tenuous line between motivation for purposes of profit and care.

The stance we take is that health care is, first and foremost, an industry. It has products, processes, suppliers, vendors, customers, and outcomes. It is unique, as are other industries, and its suppliers (physicians, other health care providers, and internal agents such as hospital workers) view themselves as unique (Oddo, 1992). During this era of transition to managed care within the health care industry, public relations represents a series of processes by which the various health care publics adapt to and cooperate with each other. Yet, the common and fundamental public relations principles remain.

CHANGING NATURE OF HEALTH CARE AND ITS PUBLIC RELATIONS

Lewton (1995), in a history of health care public relations, indicated that the "good times" of health care public relations spanned the 1950s and 1960s. During that time, health care public relations practitioners "felt little need to create awareness or preference because health care organizations had always received public support and favor" (p. 2). Public relations did not need to be proactive to "maintain and build on public confidence" (p. 2). Rather, public relations roles were prescribed and limited to the communication of information and positive image.

During the 1970s, however, noticeable shifts emerged in health care delivery, reimbursement, and the public's insistence on high-quality care at lower costs (James, 1989). The modern delivery of health care was being examined by critics who questioned the high cost of getting and staying well. "In short, payers were beginning to ask questions" (Lewton, 1995, p. 3). Marketing departments in health care organizations took on greater responsibilities thanks to a new emphasis on generating health care revenues from sources different from traditional sources—individual patients. Some within the health care industry have called the dramatic change in health care provision over the past 20 years a "paradigm shift," consistent with Kuhn's (1970) discussion of what happens when foundations of knowing transform. The traditional public relations tasks of promoting positive image and placing appropriate news items expanded to include conducting administrative briefings on how to manage new levels of consumer criticism and training internal publics on the team-centered nature of internally derived communication about the organization.

The 1970s and 1980s marked a time of financial difficulties for traditional health care providers as employers strove to reduce their health care costs. Increasingly, physicians were slowly losing control of the health care system in favor of reimbursers and third-party payers (Pearson, 1996). Out of necessity, those hospital administrators who had not already done so began to seek out public relations and communication professionals so as to maintain a two-way relationship between the hospital or health care organization and its publics (Lewton, 1995).

Currently, at the turn of the 21st century, health care public relations is continuing to be influenced significantly and irrevocably by four major business changes: the arrival of managed care, the transition from a medical model to a wellness model, the emergence of continuous quality improvement initiatives, and the genesis of health care networks and systems.

Managed Care

Managed care, the health care reimbursement system that has restructured health care delivery and payment processes, is fast becoming the norm in the United States (Pearson, 1996). Managed care is perhaps the most dramatic change experienced within the health care industry within the past two decades. Through managed care plans, patients are encouraged to stay well, and providers are financially motivated to avoid costly medical tests. Managed care bases reimbursement on capitation, which means that providers receive a certain amount of money each month based on number of health plan subscribers (patients per capita) rather than money for each test and procedure (also known as a fee-for-service plan).

The Wellness Model

The health care industry formerly relied on what is known as a medical model. A patient became sick and sought the medical attention of a health care provider—usually a physician. The doctor's office and the hospital were places where people went for treatment, diagnoses, surgery, and other medical procedures. Patients also saw physicians for "well checks" such as immunizations and annual physician examinations, but the emphasis remained one of treatment. With the advent of managed care, the health care industry moved from the medical model, which emphasized solving health problems, to a wellness model emphasizing prevention of illness and injury.

Continuous Quality Improvement

The genesis of health care public relations has moved hand-in-glove with the changing fabric of American health care practices. The one-way public relations models of the 1950s and 1960s have dissolved in favor of more aggressive two-way models attuned to the needs of the vari-ous health care delivery system publics. Current emphases on values-based and values-driven management (Thomsen, 1997) are consistent with continuous quality improvement (CQI) methods that are emerging in health care systems across the world.

Of greatest concern for health care systems is the emphasis on the patient in a CQI environment (Carleton, 1997; Luciano, 1997; Wintersteen, 1997). This patient-centered focus usually shows up formally in health care organizations' vision and/or mission statements. In addition, research and quantification of clinical and operational results, a hallmark of CQI initiatives, continue to take center stage for those responsible for communicating within the industry (Spath, 1989). Furthermore, emphasis is increasingly being placed on patient-centered solutions to managed care challenges (Joint Commission on Accreditation of Healthcare Organizations [JCAHO], 1992). Addressing routine and acute patient problems in a medically responsible but cost-effective manner always has been a concern of the medical community, but now reimbursers, third-party payers, and accrediting agencies are adding to the challenge in ways not seen previously.

Health Care Networks and Systems

DeMuro (1994) discussed the advent of the health care delivery system, which has replaced or is quickly replacing the hospital-based or hospital-centered model of health care delivery. Integrated delivery systems include medical groups, physician-hospital organizations, and medical services organizations. Their aim almost always is related to the desire to coordinate the provision of care (McCarthy, 1997). A fully integrated delivery system, according to DeMuro (1994), is "an organization or group of affiliated organizations that provides physician and hospital services to patients" (p. 30). Systems may include standard services as well as mental health care, long-term care, home health care, and rehabilitation.

THE RESPONSE OF PUBLIC RELATIONS TO HEALTH CARE INDUSTRY CHALLENGES

The transformation in health care delivery has significant effects on all who enter and sustain health care systems, and it includes patients, providers, reimbursers, and vendors. As the health care field evolves, so do the public relations theories, models, strategies, and tactics that surround and define it. Past work in health care public relations has focused on strategies and tactics engaged by health care organizations, with an archer-target stance prevailing (Smith & Schaaf, 1995). Previously, public relations was considered as something to "use" rather than as a process through which an organization could meet many goals as well as its aim of building a loyal and satisfied customer base (see, e.g., Giordano, 1997; Johnston, 1997). This perspective promotes an asymmetrical one-way view of the role of public relations in health care.

Although public relations professionals recognize that changes occurring in the health care field call for public relations transitions (Bardin, 1994; Green, 1994; Greenberg, 1994), subsequent working models of health care public relations practice are scarce. Health care's future—focused on patient-centeredness, prevention, and systems based on capitation rather than on fees for services—calls for new ways in which to manage and address public opinion. Published case studies (Comrie, 1997) provide evidence of the dynamic nature of public relations practitioners and constituencies. Yet, two-way symmetrical models proposed and advocated by J. Grunig and his colleagues (J. Grunig, 1992a) are not found in substantial numbers in actual practice situations.

Traditional approaches to health care public relations have not vanished but rather have transformed as changes continue to occur within health care systems. Public relations practitioners continue to perform the mainstay activities of the profession—writing, research, and planning. With the continually increasing emphasis on health care relationships and systems, the center of public relations practice in the 21st century is relationship building and maintenance. The communication principles that describe and predict healthy long-term relationships are no less relevant in health care public relations than they are in everyday dyadic relationships. Thus, principles of reciprocity, equality, respect, and trust take on renewed meaning in the context of health care business relationships. With the patient at the center, vendors and providers such as physicians, pharmaceutical companies, managed care companies, and third-party payers find themselves in a unique public relations conundrum.

Lewton (1998) suggested that the role of public relations in health care systems is increasingly one of requiring listening rather than one of emphasizing sending messages. Proactive assertive methods of promoting and communicating health care images, such as through educational initiatives, are in line with the new health care emphasis on preventing problems instead of waiting to fix them when they occur.

The state of health care reform, and the ever present possibility of national health care, raises additional issues for health care and public relations practitioners who seek to predict the future of this industry. New technologies such as telemedicine are making an entrance into routine health care delivery, and third-party payers are holding the verdict on reimbursement pending additional clinical trials. Capitation systems, in which insurance companies pay providers based on the number of enrolled patients rather than using a fee-for-service system, currently are incapable of absorbing the costs of some of the health care innovations on the horizon.

LESSONS FOR AND FROM PUBLIC RELATIONS PRACTITIONERS

Case Studies

Recently published case studies convey the tenor of change within health care public relations. Four themes predominate: the value of cooperation during this era of health care systems and managed care, the success that systems experience when communication is timely and lavish, the importance of education during change, and the role of involvement in establishing enduring improvements.

Several case studies converged on a popular contemporary public relations lesson: A struggling organization can become competitive through cooperation. Laurel Health System in Tioga County, Pennsylvania, did just this. The system formed a partnership with community groups (including churches, lending institutions, governments, and schools) as one method by which to analyze customer needs and meet health care demands (Sandrick, 1995). By relinquishing some degree of control over system features and having other groups provide resources for the assessment that the health system desired, Laurel Health System now is one partner in a community-wide system that has community health as its aim.

The lessons of communication and education resonated in the case study of the Nebraska Health System. Warneke (1998) provided a case study of the involvement of public relations in the merger of two health care organizations, Clarkson Regional Health Services and the University of Nebraska Medical Center, into the Nebraska Health System. The role of public relations in this case was both internal and external, and it focused equally on communication and education. Internally, employees required information due to the uncertainty involved in any potential merger. Building a base of mutual employee support across the two organizations proved to be a complicated task for human resources and public relations officers. Externally, customers and suppliers required information about the merger and its effects. Employees from both organizations formed cross-disciplinary teams with the greater good of the ultimate external customer (the patient) at the heart of the transition.

Additional case studies revolve around large health care systems that underwent major CQI initiatives. Oddo (1992) provided detailed summaries of the clinical and operational changes that took place when two large medical centers,

the University of Michigan Medical Center (Ann Arbor, Michigan) and Intermountain Health Care (Salt Lake City, Utah), adopted CQI initiatives as a way in which to improve quality and lessen health care costs. Although the organizational details differed across these two corporations, the basic public relations premises remained the same: Communicate changes thoroughly and quickly to internal and external audiences, provide ample education and training during the change initiative, and involve as many individuals as possible during the process.

A Model of Health Care Relationships

A model relevant to the concerns of health care public relations practitioners is depicted in Figure 51.1. This model illuminates the changing relationships between the patient and health care providers, as buffered by the influence of the managed care environment (the health maintenance organization), and is compatible with a two-way symmetrical view of public relations.

The model centers on public relations in the current patient-focused environment. As discussed previously, a body of recent research indicates that the patient-centered health care network constitutes the new way of doing business in the 21st century. Unlike the medical model, which places the physician at the center of business, the wellness model places the patient at the center.

Clearly, there is an interdependence between the public relations practiced within a specific health care organization and its constituencies—including what previously were considered "competitors" such as local health care systems. The notion of cooperation where there once existed competition among health care systems will be discussed as a critical feature of the public relations models taking center stage in the 21st century of health care transformation. Various power control theories (L. Grunig, 1992b) explain former views rather than current and future views of health care public relations.

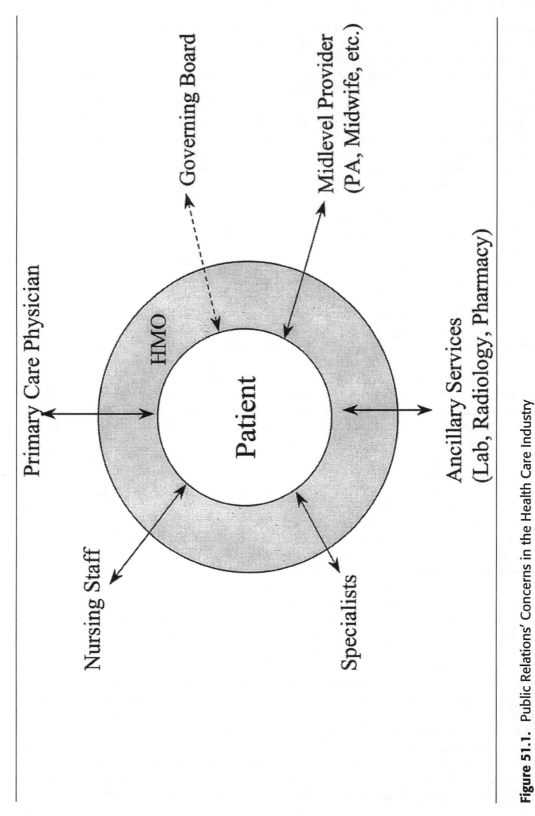

Figure 51.1. Public Relations' Concerns in the Health Care Industry

NOTE: HMO = health maintenance organization; PA = physician's assistant.

Best Practices for Public Relations Practitioners

Several public relations lessons are pertinent to the health care public relations practitioner. These best practices are gleaned from a historical and critical reading of health care management and public relations literature; from experiences of public relations professionals; and from the future forecasting being done now by financial analysts, health care providers, public relations practitioners, and managed care experts.

1. Two-way public relations models work.

One-way models and power control theories will not work in a managed care CQI systems environment. The nature of patient-centered care, by definition, negates the utility of one-sided models. Two-way models, such as those proposed by J. Grunig (1992a), continue as the public relations practitioner's prototype, with minimally a two-way asymmetrical model employed in health care settings. Symmetry remains a goal, although it is difficult to attain based on constraints such as patient privacy, confidentiality, and risk management issues.

2. Cooperation is needed among former competitors.

Public relations practitioners must take a leadership role in encouraging cooperation between and among health care entities that now must work together in an integrated delivery system. As boundary agents who cross department and organizational lines, public relations persons will find this quest for cooperation a common thread in their work during the early years of the 21st century.

3. Public relations must take a leadership role with CQI initiatives.

CQI is accepted by health care, management, and accrediting principals as a necessary part of health care organizations' futures. Current business trends are reinforced by requirements of external accrediting agencies such as JCAHO and the Health Care Financing Administration. Public relations will continue to play a prominent role in the internal and external rollout of CQI initiatives.

4. Internally, public relations must continue to work with education, communication, and recognition components of health care system reform.

Public relations also must remain or become integrally involved with organizational and strategic planning as well as with the relations between the health care system and accrediting bodies. This is an important point to stress because normally health care accreditation is seen by health care administrators as a function taking place between the accrediting agency and medical staff (including quality management and physicians).

5. Continue with the accepted tenets of "good public relations."

The roles of writing, research, planning, community and media relations, internal and external relations, and other such public relations functions remain invaluable even in a rapidly changing health care environment. These traditional public relations functions vary little in essence from their roles in other service industries, but the context in which they are engaged (e.g., managed care, CQI) has changed. Specific knowledge of the health care and managed care context is critical to accomplish traditional public relations tasks.

6. In practice, health care public relations can and must continue to operate in a complementary fashion with marketing and integrated marketing communications.

The theory of public relations is conceptualized differently from the various practices and components of integrated marketing communications. This point was made by L. Grunig (1992b) and continues to be advocated today in modern public relations textbooks (McElreath,

1996). Yet, as we put on our "downsized reality of 21st-century health care public relations" hats, there is no room for public relations specialists who do not do marketing or integrated marketing communications. Wearing more than one hat will remain an important facet of how the health care public relations practitioner accomplishes his or her work. The actual configuration of public relations in health care system components, such as in medical centers and hospitals, must change from separate departments labeled *communication, marketing, staff development,* and *community relations* to interdependent departments stemming from a larger communication and public relations base.

7. New public relations hires must be continually educated in health care management principles.

The best way in which to use new hires will be in traditional roles—writing, research, and community relations. But new hires and other members of the public relations staff must be educated regularly in the business of health care change to keep the public relations function ahead of the curve in a demanding environment.

8. The patient-centered focus of the health care system must be prominent in promotion efforts.

Any type of promotion or communicative efforts of the health care system will be best if it speaks about an innovative, quality-conscious, reasonably priced, continuously improving system that values external and internal customers. Not doing so jeopardizes the future of the organization in terms of the marketplace (patients) but also in terms of accrediting bodies. Such promotion must, of course, come from senior management decisions and be voiced through the uppermost layer of the system.

9. Public relations models must change continuously.

Within the realm of two-way public relations models, change will occur regularly. This is an important mind-set for the public relations practitioner, who is responsible for leadership and communication efforts that respond to new demands and practices in the industry.

10. Public relations practitioners must retain a sensitivity to, and an awareness of, where we have been and where we are going.

Similar to any other industry in which public relations is practiced, the health care practitioner must remain committed to continuous education in health care industry changes. To maintain credibility with internal and external customers, a sensitivity to health care's past will prove important.

Health care often is described as a complex business with an uncertain future (Lewton, 1995). Public relations professionals responsible for the planning, implementation, and promotion of health care business strategy are sure to continue the wild ride begun during the latter part of the 20th century. As the paradigm shift continues in health care provision and reimbursement, the public relations practitioners who will survive are those who continually educate themselves and their colleagues in the business of health care provision and who become integrated with the systems thinking so foundational to modern health care practices.

PUBLIC RELATIONS IN CYBERSPACE

The Frontier of New Communication Technologies

ROBERT L. HEATH

■ One of the greatest challenges facing practitioners and academics interested in public relations will be in understanding and prudently using the new communication technologies that are being developed at a staggering rate. Although previous generations have had to adapt to technological change, they had a time line learning curve luxury that simply does not exist today. Before one can prudently understand and master some or all of the new communication technologies, more change occurs.

Of related importance is the likelihood that not only is the technology changing at a rapid rate, but so are the principles and practices that affect how people will use them. During previous years, the dominant predictor of technological change has been that as change has occurred, there has tended to be concomitant changes in professionalism. Advances in technology have been spurred by the growing capabilities of computers. This is the root cause of the ability for the phenomenal growth in the challenges and opportunities for increased ability to communicate on behalf of, and in sharp criticism of, organizations. In specific instances today, especially the Internet, that simply is not the case.

Whatever is explained and discussed in this section might not be true—or even in existence—in days, weeks, or months after the handbook is published. For that reason, one might read this section with a sense of understanding and sympathy that differs from the other sections because this truly is an uncharted frontier. It was that reason that led this to be a stand-alone section rather than a subsection of one of the other sections of the handbook.

Lordan (Chapter 52) offers an overview of the technologies that are used to collect, assemble, and disseminate information in public relations. One of the results of this growth has been an increase in the ways or places in which public relations messages can be disseminated. It also constitutes an increased array of opportunities for critics of an organization to place and disseminate messages that can concern the activities of the practitioners. More information can flow more quickly to a wider array of interested persons than has been the case previously.

One of the most important advances offered by new technologies has been the size and content of databases. A vast array of information on topics relevant to the content and process of public relations is available to knowledgeable users. Users often can add to databases as well as use their contents to understand an issue or to segment markets, audiences, or publics. One use of such databases is to provide on-line newspaper copy. Copy of electronic news, for example, also is on-line. One type of database that an organization can employ in its public relations effort is its own Web page. There, information about the organization and its issues and marketing positions can be supplied for the interested reader and viewer. Such material is in an accessible place that can be obtained by cognitively involved users on a 24-hour, 7-days-a-week basis.

Through databases, public relations can provide and obtain information. So can the critics of an organization. In this regard, the standard elements of public relations communication might not change much but can take on a new look and a cyberspace character through the use of new technologies.

Focusing her attention a bit more narrowly, Gaddis (Chapter 53) concentrates on several on-line research techniques. The standard research techniques include surveys and interviews. These can be done quite successfully on-line within the parameters characteristic of the Internet. This means that the researcher can reach only persons who use the Internet. This tends to be biased toward young affluent males. Such work can, however, be tailored in different ways if the time and cost related to the research project can be expended to create more targeted research. With this new technology, public relations practitioners have another research data-gathering tool. It also can be employed by scholars.

Springston (Chapter 54) provides insights into the use of the Internet for research and other data-gathering activities, but he also suggests challenges that can occur and will have to be met through the use of the Internet. One of the significant effects of the Internet is to drift or catapult toward niche research opportunities as well as "narrowcasting" abilities. The Internet allows for a type of speed and narrowness of information flow that is unparalleled. Practitioners use the Internet to monitor issues but believe that their skills are inadequate to take full advantage of what the Internet offers as an information-gathering resource and a source of information that can be supplied to interested markets and publics.

Cozier and Witmer (Chapter 55) use a structuration approach to examine the role that publics play on the Internet. Expanding the definition of public beyond that which treats them as being interested in a problem, the authors suggest that publics consist of individuals who share common experiences and meanings. One of the ways in which publics create and maintain relationships is through sharing information via the Internet. Thus, through their interaction patterns and the shared meaning that results from them, publics form via the interaction that is made possible through the Internet. In this way, each public develops and maintains an ideology as a means for developing and maintaining relationships among its members. To engage many of these publics, public relations practitioners cannot assume that they can provide information to publics but must engage in the interaction—the dialogue—that transpires among the members of the dialogue. In this way, new communication technologies are changing the power and meaning formation processes in society.

Less is known about the marketplace and public policy arena impact of new communication technologies than is necessary to fully grasp their impact and the implications that they hold for the future of the profession. The chapters in this section touch on some of the thought-provoking issues that suggest directions for academic research and practitioner skill development. Each new communication technology has had a significant impact on society. Such is the case for the technologies of today, which are unique because of the power given to communicators through the role that computers play. This set of dynamics offers a new terrain, one that changes quickly and challenges the adaptive resources of practitioners.

Cyberspin

The Use of New Technologies in Public Relations

EDWARD J. LORDAN

Over the past 20 years, an increasing array of communications technologies have been introduced into every area of the public relations profession, from the research process used to develop new business proposals to the final evaluation phase of campaigns. This chapter provides an overview of the technologies used to collect, assemble, and disseminate information in public relations. It explains why new technologies have been introduced in public relations; what the technologies are, how they are used, and the advantages and disadvantages of each; and management implications for the technologies. It also provides a summary of the use of the technologies in relation to the overall process of public relations.

TRENDS AFFECTING TECHNOLOGICAL GROWTH

In discussing perspectives of new technology, Johnson (1997) noted,

Public relations practitioners began using computers for word processing, budgeting, and media database management but soon were using them for public relations program evaluation and communication with colleagues. . . . Now public relations has entered the 'fourth wave' of technological change in the field. (p. 213)

The adoption of new technologies in public relations is the result of unparalleled growth in six interrelated areas: the number of media outlets available, the speed of transmission of information, the amount of information available, the size of organizations using public relations, the size of the public relations organizations themselves, and the amount and variety of new technologies applicable to the industry.

The growth of media outlets, particularly news media outlets, is evident in both print and broadcast. As Katzman (1995) noted, "The increasing number of video outlets has created a need for more and more programming, which public relations people are eager to supply" (p. 7). Both print and broadcast outlets have seen a blending of information and entertainment programming as well as a blending of the media themselves such as the MSNBC network and on-line newspapers. These fundamental changes are creating even more public relations opportunities.

In terms of speed of transmission, new technologies have redefined the idea of "in time" delivery of information. Regimented news delivery models, based on the regular evening news on television and the daily delivery of the morning newspaper, gave way to a new paradigm when CNN began offering 24-hour news service on cable television during the 1970s and newspapers began offering information on-line during the 1980s. During the 1990s, this model gave way to an even faster form—what Thomsen (1995) called a "hyperspeed process" that forces the practitioner to stay ahead of, or even with, other news consumers by conducting "pro-search." He noted,

> Most online services, even those that update the databases every 24 hours, still only archive what *has* happened. The new focus of issues tracking and issues management for these practitioners is to "capture" the "news" before it may actually be published in [the] mainstream daily or trade press. (p. 110)

This technology also has produced increased storage capacity for information, resulting in an astounding increase in the amount of information available to news consumers. The knowledge base that had accumulated by the year 1600 doubled by 1950 and then doubled again by 1980. It now doubles every 7 years and might be doubling every 35 days by the year 2010. Faced with such growth, public relations practitioners increasingly rely on advanced technologies to collect, organize, and prioritize information.

The growth of organizations that use public relations has kept pace with the growth of information, and each has been further fueled by advances in technology. The first half of the 20th century witnessed the growth of regional organizations, followed by transportation and communication improvements during the second half of the century that pushed such groups toward a national approach. As the century came to a

close, the scope of leading organizations had matured into a worldwide perspective for materials, labor, and markets. The evolution of these organizations had been matched by growth in the public relations firms, as agencies had ratcheted up their personnel, expertise, and technological capabilities to deal with international clients and audiences.

A final trend that contributes to the growth of information technology in public relations is the growth of the technology itself. That is, there are more information technology products available than ever before, fueling a significant, and sometimes erratic, increase in use.

OVERVIEW OF THE NEW TECHNOLOGIES

"New technologies have made former ways of organizing what practitioners do outdated," noted Johnson (1997, p. 215). The very definition of new technology has been framed differently by a variety of researchers. Such disparity inevitably leads to differences of opinion as to what technologies should be included in the discussion. This chapter focuses on computer-related and interactive technologies including e-mail, desktop publishing, the Internet and World Wide Web, on-line databases and media monitoring systems, internal databases, and teleconferencing systems.

Regardless of the complexity and haphazard evolution of these technologies, they still are used primarily to gather, package, and disseminate information. These three basic public relations functions are by no means discrete, and the new technologies allow the practitioner to provide a range of services that go beyond the capabilities of traditional public relations, but they remain primary functions.

Information Gathering

The most significant application of new technologies in public relations has been the increased use of databases for collecting and storing information about prospects, clients, audiences, media, competitors, and industries. Databases allow practitioners to collect more information, in more detail, faster and cheaper than ever before. These advantages can create types of analyses that would be almost impossible using more traditional methods of storing and sorting information. Petrison and Wang (1993) noted that, through creative applications of databases, an examination of customers' "demographics, lifestyles, buying behaviors, credit history, and media exposure could lead to a more sophisticated understanding of the consumers' buying process" (p. 237).

Databases include internal (self-supporting) and external (on-line) sources. Internal databases, which are created and maintained by the agency or client, offer privacy, control over data, increased storage capacity, and an increased ability to distribute relevant data throughout the organization. Petrison and Wang (1993) summarized a possible scenario for internal database use:

> The public relations department can create a database to keep track of all information as it is accumulated. One section of the database may include information on media such as reporter and publication names, addresses, types of computers owned, whether review copies of products are requested, types of products (business or entertainment) covered, a subjective estimate of the reviewer's importance to the company, and an estimate of how frequently products are covered. The database system may also be used to keep track of other data such as product information, review copies and news releases mailed, media coverage received, and competitor information. (p. 242)

The practitioner should consider the following questions when considering whether or not to use an internal database:

1. What information can a database provide that I am not already getting?
2. How much time and money will a database save?

3. What other advantages and disadvantages does a database provide in relation to other systems already in place?

A number of software programs are available for developing and maintaining internal databases including DataEase, Paradox, and DBase II. Although most of these systems are relatively simple to use, managers of public relations organizations must determine whether system maintenance will be handled as an administrative or clerical function. Some organizations hire or appoint one person to be in charge of their systems, some make the maintenance and supervision of the databases a responsibility shared by various members of the organizations, and some delegate the entire operation to an outside source.

The practitioner should consider the limitations and disadvantages of such an internal database before adopting one because a considerable expenditure of time and energy is needed to bring the database up to speed. Once the basic database is in place, the organization must devote resources (e.g., space, personnel, money) on an ongoing basis to maintain it. Finally, public relations managers must be extremely sensitive in using information developed for databases because audiences, including consumers and members of the media, are extremely sensitive to privacy issues.

On-line databases offer many of the advantages of in-house databases as well as greater scope and unique early-detection and monitoring capabilities. These databases offer high-speed transmission, breadth of coverage, and the ability to tap into information sources continuously or on a schedule convenient to the user.

The disadvantages of on-line databases are the inability to control the information received and the varying degrees in authenticity and truthfulness of the information. The biggest disadvantage, however, might be the overwhelming amount of information and lack of cohesion in its organization.

The earliest on-line database systems covered limited media outlets and were primarily reactive, but a growing range of on-line database services has greatly improved the scope and speed of the services. State-of-the-art on-line systems recognize the dual challenges related to the growth in the amount and speed of transmission of information. For example, the DataTimes system provides access to 200 major daily newspapers in the United States, with updates every 24 hours. Another system, NewsEdge, not only provides access to more than 100 news sources (e.g., wire services, newspapers, broadcast transmissions) but also allows the user to customize the system so that stories on a particular topic are automatically downloaded to the individual's computer. WordPerfect's Mainstream takes the monitoring and sorting process to the next logical step: Using customized profiles of user interests, it scans a variety of news outlets for appropriate stories and converts them into e-mail form delivered directly to the user's computer— within seconds of the time they are placed on the wire and hours before they appear in print. The most sophisticated database search-and-retrieval software systems offer wide coverage, almost instantaneous transmission of information as it is made available, and (perhaps most important) a method of organizing the immense amount of information in a way that is useful to the practitioner and the client.

Additional on-line database systems now are being designed specifically for public relations purposes. For example, on-line systems such as edcals.com, from Bacon's and Media Map, summarize and synthesize editorial calendars to increase reach and improve organization of media tracking.

The practitioner who is considering the purchase or lease of an on-line database should consider the following questions:

1. What are the specific goals (e.g., monitoring media, prospecting for new clients, examining trends) that I would achieve through the use of the database?
2. What existing systems could be replaced through the use of the database?
3. How fast do I need the information?
4. In what form do I want the information?

On a smaller scale, public relations practitioners also have begun using on-line services to reach specific audiences through the use of "chatrooms" and focus groups. Chatrooms allow the practitioner to monitor, and participate in, a free-flowing discussion of a variety of subjects including those related to the client or product. The drawback to this technique is that these conversations can be disorganized, unfocused, and unmanageable—sometimes producing too few useful results. The more coordinated (and thus more useful) version of the chatroom is the on-line focus group. A researcher can contact a range of participants, through the Internet or through more traditional systems, and establish a time and place on the on-line system to conduct a focus group. This approach can save time and money by allowing a variety of people spread over a geographic area to participate simultaneously and in real time in a directed discussion. A more important factor might be a by-product of the privacy afforded by the medium: On-line focus groups can yield data that might not show up in a face-to-face focus group because participants are less restricted by inhibitions and social mores that might keep them from giving truthful answers in a face-to-face setting.

Information Packaging

Desktop publishing systems combine hardware (computers and high-quality printers) with software used for word processing, graphics, and page making. Whereas IBM and IBM-compatible computers dominate American business as a whole, Mac and Mac-compatible personal computers and support software remain the preferred systems in graphic arts.

Desktop publishing programs have a number of advantages over more traditional scenarios used to produce print products. The entire process, from initial concept to camera-ready copy, can be done in-house. Turnaround time and communication errors among departments can be reduced, and in many cases, overall costs can be reduced.

The maturation of desktop publishing and, more significantly, the capacity to download materials directly from the Internet have expanded the capabilities of this industry. CD-ROM catalogs and Web sites designed to assist the graphic designer make it possible to import photographs, clip art, fonts, and so on, making publishing almost as versatile as the offerings of traditional print shops that used to be central to the public relations process.

The practitioner who is considering implementing or expanding a desktop publishing system should consider the following questions:

1. What specific projects will I be producing?
2. What advantages, in terms of time, cost, and flexibility, will I gain?
3. Do I want to take on the additional responsibilities of creating the final product in-house?

Information Dissemination

The three growth areas in information dissemination for public relations are homepages on the Internet, video news releases, and teleconferencing systems.

Homepages on the Internet offer a number of advantages. The costs generally are limited to content development; traditional distribution costs such as photocopying and postage in public relations or media buying in advertising are minimized or eliminated. The homepage is available 24 hours a day, 365 days a year. Speed of transmission is improved because users can gain access to information as soon as it is posted. There is some limited advantage in tracking the distribution of information, but this might be restricted to the most basic data—the number of "hits" by users. As practitioners become more sophisticated in homepage techniques, they are beginning to develop systems that distinguish between users who are consumers, members of the media, general browsers, or competitors.

Most of the disadvantages of the Internet can be traced to the fact that it is a new and quickly evolving technology. The Web is disorganized, and as demand increases, the bottlenecks that occur keep some consumers from getting online. Universal access to posting information has reduced the quality and credibility of all sites.

Finally, the user group is skewed toward college-educated males in the 18- to 30-year age range, appropriate for some clients and useless to others. The Internet user profile is evolving rapidly, but it remains a relatively limited audience.

Early use of the Internet mirrored the distribution systems already in place, but this reactive approach has evolved as practitioners have grasped the unique possibilities offered by this new medium—the potential to offer services that are reactive, interactive, and proactive. For example, many sites now include hypertext and homepage links that make it possible for a consumer to use the page as a starting point for contacting a variety of sources; both depth and breadth are possible. The most sophisticated sites allow the user to customize and order information, converting the homepage into an individualized delivery system for relevant information. For example, a homepage might allow a reporter to request the automatic distribution of a company's new product releases in the form most useful to the reporter (e.g., fax, e-mail, conventional "snail" mail). This innovative approach makes the fullest use of the technology by truly fulfilling the facilitator role of the practitioner: A reporter can receive only the information he or she wants, in a timely fashion, in the most useful form. Although 90% of reporters still prefer to receive information by conventional mail, an ever increasing number are taking advantage of alternative information dissemination methods.

The practitioner who is considering developing a Web page for an organization should consider the following questions:

1. What nontraditional audiences will the Web page reach?
2. Can I use the Web page to offer increased interaction?
3. Who will be the page's Webmaster—the person responsible for maintaining and updating the Web page?
4. How will the Web page be integrated into the overall message delivery system?

A second technology that has proven to be successful is the video news release (VNR), which saw an annual growth rate of approximately 25% during the 1990s. This distribution system presents the broadcast media with the message in a form identical to what is shown on the air, increasing control by the practitioner and acceptance by broadcasters. The VNR technology now is used to reach nonmedia audiences as well in annual reports, employee newsletters, and other forms of controlled communication.

One of the older, and less adopted, dissemination technologies is teleconferencing, which includes videoconferencing, audioconferencing, and groupware, a software system allowing multiple computer users to simultaneously work together on different documents. Teleconferencing systems were introduced during the mid-1960s, but high costs, system incompatibilities, poor picture quality, and the failure of potential users to fully comprehend and use the systems have kept them from achieving widespread use.

During the 1990s, a number of these obstacles have been reduced. Initial system costs for teleconferencing are dropping but remain prohibitively high; a desktop unit costs as much as $55,000. This has led to an increase in public retail videoconferencing, in which organizations rent two or more spaces and connecting communications equipment for approximately $300 per hour. The increasing availability of integrated services digital network lines has increased the rate of signal transmission, improving the picture quality. Improvements have led to more creative uses of teleconferencing as practitioners employ them for internal activities (e.g., discussion sessions among members of a widely dispersed organization) and external activities (e.g., satellite media tours). Many practitioners remain skeptical about teleconferencing, however, and the technology will need further improvements to reach a point of critical mass.

MANAGEMENT AND ADMINISTRATION

Applications of new technologies in management and administration of public relations combine information gathering, packaging, dissemination and a number of additional useful functions.

Databases can introduce more and better information into the public relations organization faster and at a lower cost than before. That information can then move through the organization via computer systems, specifically e-mail systems, more efficiently through effective file management and shared project files. Videoconferencing and audioconferencing have improved internal communication while reducing travel costs. Effective use of internal information management systems also can reduce general administrative expenses and improve tracking and evaluation of the work itself. For example, administrative software can be used to make the accounting function more detailed, and automated time sheets can be used to speed up the billing process. Some agencies even have introduced automated billing and direct deposit on approval from clients, potentially reducing payment problems and delays.

CONCLUSION

New technologies will not replace the traditional tools used in public relations, but the fast-paced growth in the amount of information and the variety of technology available—as well as increases in client, media, and audience expectations about new technologies—are creating tremendous pressure on public relations practitioners to increase their use of emerging systems. Anderson and Reagan (1992) noted, "The costs involved in adopting new technologies are substantial. But the real cost to the practitioner is losing his or her competitive edge to those who have mastered computer-age technology" (p. 165).

Practitioners also must recognize that a commitment to technology assumes permanent ongoing expenditures. Half of the public relations organizations using computers upgrade their hardware every 2 years, and 85% renovate their systems on a 3-year cycle.

This chapter is designed to help the practitioner to recognize the inevitable myriad technological changes occurring in all facets of the public relations process. The challenge for practitioners is to determine the short-term and long-term needs of their organizations and to weigh the overall costs and benefits of these evolving technologies while operating in an exceptionally dynamic atmosphere for clients, audiences, and members of the media. By implementing the theories and evaluation techniques presented in this chapter, the public relations practitioner not only can identify and apply appropriate applications of an ever evolving range of technological offerings but also can work to identify present and future needs and opportunities that can be addressed, partially or totally, through the application of new technologies.

Practitioners must resist the overuse of technologies such as bombarding media with multiple forms of the same message simply because it is convenient to do so. The practice of public relations will be advanced not by applying emerging technologies to collect, process, and distribute more information but rather by using the appropriate technologies to handle information more efficiently and effectively so that clients, colleagues, members of the media, and members of specific audiences receive the most up-to-date and useful information possible.

On-Line Research Techniques for the Public Relations Practitioner

SUSANNE ELIZABETH GADDIS

■ Understanding how research can be conducted over the Internet is particularly important to public relations practitioners as the field enters the 21st century. Why? Among other reasons, Internet research has been shown to be quick, easy, and inexpensive when compared to traditional research methods (Bittle, 1995). Also, with the continued increase in Internet users, the Internet offers a viable addition or alternative to traditional methods for gathering information from local, national, and international publics.

The value of Internet research is just beginning to be recognized and understood. In a 1996 study conducted by the Council of American Survey Research Organizations (CASRO), it was discovered that "about 17% of marketers who work in some of the 2,000 largest U.S. companies have used data from online surveys" (Edmondson, 1997, p. 10). Another report, the 1997 Media in Cyberspace Study, found that 98% of all journalists surveyed used on-line tools for researching and reporting (Ross & Middleberg, 1997).

To illustrate how on-line research is being used, four brief examples follow:

1. Greenfield Online Research Center in Westport, Connecticut, a company specializing in on-line research, recently used the Internet to put up an on-line study on Good Friday. By Monday morning, it had received 2,400 completed forms (Edmondson, 1997).

2. Odwalla Inc., a California-based juice company, hired the Edelman Public Relations agency to keep an eye on public opinion in the midst of a crisis caused by an e-coli outbreak. Edelman accomplished this by monitoring discussions in newsgroups and chatrooms and by recommending the creation of a Web site specifically designed to communicate the latest information about the crisis. The Web site received 19,000 "hits" during the first 48 hours (Edelman Public Relations, 1997).

3. Janice Gjersten, director of marketing for on-line entertainment company WP-Studio, conducted on-line focus groups to gauge reaction to a new Web site. Instead of the 4 weeks normally required for re-

sults, Gjersten was able to receive a full report in 1 day (Schafer, 1996).

4. During the first 12 months of being posted on-line, the Net Traveler Survey, designed to study the travel and tourism characteristics of Internet users, received more than 17,700 survey responses from 81 countries (Schonland & Williams, 1996).

These cases represent only a fraction of the ways in which the Internet is being used for research. These and other research techniques are presented in this chapter. Specifically, the chapter examines on-line interviews, e-mail surveys, and Web surveys. It also demonstrates how newsgroups and listservs can be valuable additions to a public relations practitioner's "research toolbox."

LIMITATIONS

Before one might come to believe that the Internet offers a research cure-all, the limitations of on-line research should be noted. First, the Internet is not representative of the entire population. Rather, it is biased toward young affluent males. Therefore, on-line research is at best representative of the on-line population only. Generalizing or projecting the results of Internet research is questionable (Foster, 1994). However, as the number of Internet users grows, the demographic profile will "become more similar to that of the average American" (Edmondson, 1997, p. 10).

Sampling bias is another limitation. Respondents often will self-select to participate in Internet surveys (Foster, 1994). Additional sampling errors are encountered when individuals complete surveys more than once (Edmondson, 1997). Surveys with promotional tie-ins are particularly susceptible to such sampling bias.

Caution also should remain regarding the validity of data collected over the Internet (Persichitte, Young, & Tharp, 1997). Data collected from anonymous individuals might be tainted with half-truths, gross exaggerations, and/or inaccuracies (Solomon, 1996).

Despite these limitations, the Internet does offer a plethora of research opportunities. It opens doors to get in touch with subjects previously inaccessible (Persichitte et al., 1997). It makes it possible to locate a highly specific target group without screening a large random sample (Edmondson, 1997). On-line research also has been shown to sidestep the noncooperation problem frequently seen with direct mail and telephone surveys. This might be due to the novelty of the medium. Or, it might be because Internet research is less intrusive, is voluntary, and often is completed by respondents at their leisure (Edmondson, 1997).

INTERNETS AND INTRANETS

By definition, an internet is a network of computer networks. The first internet, ARPANET, was developed in 1969 by the U.S. Department of Defense. As a result of the success of ARPANET, which eventually became known as the Internet (with an uppercase *I*), a number of smaller internets (with a lowercase *i*), including America Online, CompuServe, and Prodigy, were formed. In addition, smaller networks called intranets were formed. An intranet is defined as a private network within an organization. Firewalls, or machines that control access from the outside, often serve to keep Internet traffic off intranets (Hale, 1996).

Each of these networks offers new opportunities for conducting research. Over an intranet, researchers can gather information from employees and enter into a dialogue with them about ideas, issues, and problems (Hallett, 1995). Similarly, intranets can be used to conduct internal communication audits and to distribute company surveys.

Research over an internet or the Internet can take many forms including on-line interviews, e-mail surveys, Web surveys, and on-line focus groups. Similarly, on-line research can include issues tracking, which can be accomplished by monitoring newsgroup and listserv postings. The remainder of this chapter covers each of these on-line research techniques.

ON-LINE INTERVIEWING

On-line interviews are a "useful new research methodology" (Heflich, 1997, p. 14). An on-line interview can be conducted via e-mail, newsgroups, Internet relay chat, CU-SeeMe, or an Internet phone.

Like a traditional interview, an on-line interview calls for an individual to respond to a series of questions. On-line, this can occur synchronously or asynchronously depending on the chosen method. Proven to be quick, inexpensive, and convenient, the on-line interview has other advantages including the following.

No gatekeeper. On-line interviews let researchers bypass potential gatekeepers and communicate directly with the decision makers. Individuals who will not return phone calls often are more likely to send e-mail. For example, Bill Gates, notorious for maintaining a low profile and declining personal interviews, is known to conduct e-mail interviews with magazine writers (Hart, 1996).

Interviewer bias. Persichitte et al. (1997) found that with many forms of on-line interviews, the researcher is unable to give evaluative nonverbal responses. Similarly, the researcher cannot interrupt the interviewee. Because of this, the interviewee and the interviewer are afforded the time to be thoughtful and careful in their responses.

Time considerations. With many forms of on-line interviews, appointments need not be scheduled. Interruptions also are of less importance (Persichitte et al., 1997). An interview can be completed at the interviewee's convenience anytime day or night.

Longitudinal consideration. On-line interviews provide "the ability to continue the interview process until the researcher is satisfied that a saturation point has been reached" (Persichitte et al., 1997, p. 281).

Persichitte et al. (1997), who conducted a series of e-mail interviews, recommended the following methodological guidelines when conducting e-mail interviews:

1. Select the sample carefully using specific criteria and with the understanding that sampling bias will likely exist. . . .
2. Establish guidelines a priori with the interviewees regarding time between communications, whether any other type of communications may be expected (e.g., telephone, regular mail), full disclosure that they are participating in a research project and the correlated ethical issues, and other issues related to using interview protocols.
3. Prior to actual interviewing, establish a rapport with the interviewees by "chatting." This state of the pre-interview process will also help to establish standardized electronic mail response patterns for both [you] and the interviewee.
4. Be timely with responses, especially when clarifications, illustrations, explanations, or elaborations are needed.
5. Use acronyms and symbols that communicate feelings, emotions, and the like. Encourage interviewees to do the same. Ask for explanations when new expressions are introduced.
6. Summarize the interviewee's responses to previous questions and return the summary to the interviewee immediately for verification. This will demonstrate understanding and concern for careful representation while allowing for clarification of misinterpretation.
7. Check for messages from interviewees regularly.
8. Limit the length of messages to interviewees. Break questions into small parts and ask only a few questions at a time. . . .

9. Be alert for misunderstandings. Be attentive to changes in "tone" of responses, unusual lag, symbols that are inconsistent with previous dialog, and any other clues that might lead you to question the credibility of a response.
10. Be prepared to refocus the discussion on the interview topic(s)....

...

[11]. Be an ethnographer. Study the culture of electronic mail, and be careful not to be offensive. Subscribe to a listserv, if necessary, and spend some time "lurking" so that "netiquette" will not be a problem when you begin your research. (pp. 281-282)

Although these recommendations specifically address e-mail interviews, many of these suggestions can be used for other methods of online interviewing as well.

E-MAIL SURVEYS

With e-mail being one of the most widely used services on the Internet (Lescher, 1995), e-mail surveys offer a viable option for collecting data from many target populations. Viewed as "more important, more interesting, more enjoyable, and more relaxing than paper-based surveys" (Chisholm, 1995, p. 13), e-mail surveys also benefit by the fact that when people check their e-mail, they are psychologically prepared to read and respond. E-mail surveys also may make a good alternative to traditional phone surveys that, due to misuse, often are less representative and more expensive (Oppermann, 1995). Other advantages of e-mail surveys found in the literature include the following.

Immediate return of undeliverables. A researcher no longer has to wait a week to determine which surveys were undeliverable. E-mail offers an immediate "undeliverable" message when an e-mail address no longer is valid. This is an "important feature especially when surveys are targeted at a highly mobile population" (Oppermann, 1995, p. 33).

Higher response rate. Oppermann (1995) reviewed a number of studies that compared traditional mail surveys to e-mail surveys. In all but one case, e-mail response rates were found to be superior to those of traditional mail surveys.

Speed. The response speed of e-mail is much quicker than that of a traditional mail survey. In one study, Oppermann (1995) polled 500 members of the Association of American Geographers. Within 2 days, Oppermann had a 23.6% response rate. After resending the survey again to nonrespondents, Oppermann had a 48.8% response rate within 14 days.

Cost. E-mail surveys are very economical because the need for postage, phone, and manual data entry is eliminated. Unlike traditional mail surveys, the costs of e-mail surveying are not proportional to the number of respondents. E-mailing a survey to a dozen costs about the same as e-mailing a survey to thousands. "Thus, more respondents can be included in surveys, yielding more complete data" (Chisholm, 1995, p. 11). Because an e-mail survey is in electronic form, it also is easy to modify. Eliminating the need to send a survey to the printer further reduces costs (Oppermann, 1995).

Interviewer bias eliminated. Because e-mail surveys are self-administered, interviewer bias is eliminated. Also, because e-mail surveys yield written transcripts, there is less room for human error than when transcribing handwritten or spoken words (Chisholm, 1995; Oppermann, 1995).

Clarification requests. Depending on the design of the e-mail study, respondents may use the interactivity the Internet offers to request clarification about the meaning of specific questions.

Similarly, they may pose other questions (Oppermann, 1995).

Prior to conducting an e-mail survey, the researcher should be aware of the potential disadvantages:

Incorrect addresses. Even e-mail lists that have been recently compiled can contain 10% to 20% undeliverable addresses (Business Research Lab, 1998; Schuldt & Totten, 1994). This problem is compounded by individuals having more than one e-mail account, only one of which is checked on a regular basis.

Spam. Spam is unsolicited e-mail that, according to "netiquette" (i.e., Internet etiquette), is not recommended. According to the Business Research Lab (1998), however, sending unsolicited e-mail to a customer is acceptable. E-mail surveys "appear to be most suited to panels of people who have agreed to participate or with whom the researcher has some connection, thus ensuring compliance" (Schonland & Williams, 1996, p. 84).

Ease of deletion. Right now, e-mail surveys are novel, but "sooner or later e-mail subscribers may become calloused pressers of the 'delete' key who pitch your questionnaire, unread, into the electronic world's equivalent of the circular file" (Parker, 1992, p. 54). This might be particularly true as the prevalence of e-mail surveys continues to rise. With their increase, people might ignore them, which will have a significant effect on how representative e-mail surveys will be in the future (Business Research Lab, 1998).

Incompatibility between systems. System incompatibility and the low sophistication level of some e-mail software can present a problem. Some older versions of e-mail software do not feature a "response" function, which can impede the use of e-mail questionnaires. Older systems also might not be able to see the various optical enhancements that can negatively affect response rates (Oppermann, 1995).

An e-mail survey may be designed in a number of ways. The simplest design consists of sending a series of questions in a single e-mail delivered to respondents' e-mail inboxes. To return the e-mail questionnaire, respondents need only to press the "reply" command, answer the questionnaire, and return the questionnaire to the researcher's inbox.

Of course, it is not always necessary for respondents to fill out the e-mail survey on screen. Respondents can be instructed to print the survey and fax it back or to call in to a completely automated telephone survey (CATS) that uses interactive voice response technology to complete the interview. To use a CATS, respondents answer fixed-response questions by pressing numbers on their push-button telephones. They also give verbal open-ended responses that are recorded for transcription and coding (DePaulo & Weitzer, 1994).

Surveys of a sensitive nature can be returned through an automatic remailer service. This assures respondents of complete confidentiality given that the remailer strips the e-mail of all original information contained in the header. Backard (1996) provided a comprehensive review of remailers in her "Anonymous Remailer FAQ" (http://www.well.com/user/abacard/remail.html).

In addition to designing simple e-mail surveys, a number of companies have developed commercially available e-mail survey software. This survey software offers a number of advanced features. Decisive Technology Corporation (http://www.decisive.com), for example, markets on-line survey software that allows the researcher a chance to view charts, tables, statistics, and cross-tabs as soon as the first survey responses arrive.

Oppermann (1995) offered several points that need to be considered in the design of an e-mail survey including that (a) respondents should be provided with directions on how to complete and return the survey, (b) line lengths in the survey should not exceed 70 characters per line (due to incompatibilities in formatting), (c) the first screen of the survey should include the number of questions and the estimated time needed to complete the survey, (d) respondents should be assured of their confidentiality, and (e) a reminder notice should be e-mailed several days after the original survey was sent to people who have not responded.

WEB SURVEYS

By using forms in hypertext markup language, Web surveys can be designed to be a part of a larger Web site, or they can be designed to stand alone. When designed as part of a larger Web site, respondents usually will access a Web survey through a hyperlink. But recently, "companies such as Burke Inc. of Cincinnati, Ohio, have created applications that route every *n*th Web site visitor to a survey section" (Edmondson, 1997, p. 12). In this way, self-selection bias is reduced.

The advantages and disadvantages to Web surveys almost directly correspond with those found in on-line e-mail surveys. They have been found to be "fast, effective, and cost-efficient" (Davis, 1997, p. 31). They also allow for the inclusion of graphics, color, and special formatting that can increase a survey's visual appeal.

Gaddis (1998) suggested that the effectiveness of Web surveys could be increased by following key design principles. Many of these principles are found in the traditional survey design, whereas many are new and applicable only to an on-line environment. Among other suggestions, Gaddis stated that the design of a Web survey should include the following.

The title of the survey. A clear title reflecting the survey's content should appear both at the top of the survey and in the title bar of the survey's homepage. This is accomplished by placing the title in between the opening and closing title commands. According to Gaddis, doing so should increase a survey's likelihood of being included in search engines.

Screening questions. With the large and extremely diverse population that can locate and complete an on-line survey, upfront screening questions can effectively screen out nonqualifying respondents.

An introduction. A brief introduction always should be included to help orient respondents who could have accessed the survey in a number of ways. This introduction should include information regarding confidentiality. It also should include the number of questions asked and the approximate amount of time that it should take to complete the instrument.

A "clear option." Respondents should have a way to clear items, just as they would have a chance to erase responses in a traditional pencil-based survey.

Skip patterns. On-line surveys can be designed with built-in skip patterns. Different sections of the survey can be delivered based on respondents' input. In this way, on-line surveys are much more dynamic than paper-based surveys.

In addition to these suggestions, Schonland and Williams (1996) suggested that surveys be designed to include pull-down menus, which make surveys appear shorter and make it easy for "respondents to select preformatted answers from a menu of questions" (p. 82).

In addition to Web-based surveys, one of the newest additions to survey design is the banner survey. To conduct banner survey research, a company purchases banner advertising space on popular search engines. Then, instead of using the typical "click through" design, the company uses the banner to conduct a quick one-question survey.

FOCUS GROUPS

As with traditional focus groups, on-line focus groups may be used "as a qualitative tool to supplement ongoing research activities" (Miller, 1994, p. 14). During on-line group sessions, the discussion usually is informal and friendly (Solomon, 1996). On-line focus groups are good for brainstorming, tapping the thinking of employees, and testing and evaluating new products and campaigns.

Research has shown on-line focus groups to be "most productive when the subject matter is rational and straightforward and less productive when the subject matter is highly emotional or psychological" (Jacobson, 1996-1997, p. 29). This is largely due to the respondents' inability to see each other's nonverbals, making it impossible to interpret the subtleties that might exist.

By definition, an on-line focus group differs from a traditional focus group in that the former "is conducted entirely online—everything from recruitment and screening (which the recruiter does via e-mail) to the moderation of the discussion itself" (Solomon, 1996, p. 10).

During an on-line focus group, all group interaction usually takes place using a form of Internet chat or discussion software. Although a variety of chat software exists, the typical chat is designed so that all communication appears in a single screen. As respondents enter and post comments, these comments are viewed by all group participants.

On-line groups are moderated. Because an on-line group requires total concentration from the moderator, it is recommended that an on-line session should last no longer than 90 minutes. Limiting the time to 90 minutes tends to keep response quality high. It also helps to alleviate screen fatigue among participants (Jacobson, 1996-1997).

An on-line group ideally should consist of six to eight panelists (Jacobson, 1996-1997). This is recommended because groups of this number have been shown to "lead to a more realistic, balanced, and considered viewpoint" (Peebles, 1996, p. 5). Groups consisting of more than eight panelists also tend to produce too many "threads" for the moderators to follow.

For their time, respondents normally receive an average of $50 per hour to participate (Montague, 1994). However, respondents have

been known to be paid as little as $15 and as much as $90 per session (Miller, 1994). In lieu of monetary payment, participants might be offered various incentives for participation including prizes, awards, and products. In addition to a monetary or incentive payment, those not having the necessary software normally are provided it free of charge.

The advantages of on-line focus groups as shown in the literature include the following.

Real-time results. The speed at which on-line focus group studies can be carried out and analyzed is one of on-line focus groups' biggest advantages. Greenfield Online Research Center reported that "projects can be recruited, confirmed, and conducted within as few as three days" (cited in Jacobson, 1996-1997, p. 28). Part of Greenfield Online's success at such quick turnaround time is that it recruits participants from its proprietary database of more than 100,000 on-line users.

Cost. One major factor in the rising popularity of on-line focus groups is the cost (Bittle, 1995).

> For a traditional market research project, a corporate client might pay $10,000 in travel costs for two facilitators to fly to one or more cities to meet with five or six focus groups. The total cost, including a report of findings, might be $30,000. On-line focus groups typically run one-fifth to one-half that cost. This makes them ideal groups to run before traditional ones. (Parks, 1997, p. 28)

The elimination of facility overhead fees (e.g., space rental, food, equipment) and the fact that panelist incentives often can be lower also contribute to reduced costs (Jacobson, 1996-1997).

Instant transcripts. The majority of chat software on the market allows for group conversation to be recorded directly to a file, allowing for instant transcripts. This file can then be loaded directly into a content analysis program or printed, saving valuable analysis time.

Respondent comfort. The on-line focus group allows people in diverse geographic locations to participate from the comfort of their own homes or offices. Thus, people can be studied in their natural habitats (Jacobson, 1996-1997, p. 28).

Respondent honesty. With on-line focus groups, people are more honest, at ease, frank, and spontaneous (Schafer, 1996; Solomon, 1996). They also tend to self-disclose more (Persichitte et al., 1997). Respondent anonymity is of special benefit when group members are asked to discuss topics of a sensitive nature.

Multiple conversations. Chat allows for the free flow of ideas from respondents. Therefore, several conversations can proceed simultaneously, and individuals can contribute their ideas without having to wait their turns.

Idea testing. Because the on-line focus group is being delivered electronically, participants can be directed to Web sites on which they can view background information or see a variety of images and graphics. Because of the interactive nature of the medium, respondents can "see the immediate results of their decisions and change their minds if they like. All is recorded and becomes a part of your raw data" (Parks, 1997, p. 28). "For more tangible items (e.g., a food flavor or product packaging), a product can be mailed to the respondent to be discussed online after the consumer has tested the product" (Solomon, 1996, p. 11).

Leveling out. With on-line focus groups, a leveling effect is seen among participants. In face-to-face groups, one or two enthusiastic individuals may "dominate the discussion. The tendency for this type of group dynamic to occur in [the] on-line focus group is lessened by the fact that each respondent answers the moderator's question simultaneously behind the 'safety' of a screen name" (Solomon, 1996, p. 10).

Mixing group members. "In the virtual world, researchers can combine gender and age ranges,

with fewer downside group dynamic effects" (Jacobson, 1996-1997, p. 28). With on-line focus groups, researchers can mix and match different types of people—rich and poor, older and younger, men and women—in ways that would not work in person (Edmondson, 1997).

Client interaction. With an on-line focus group, a client can log in to watch the discussion. When necessary, the client can use instant messaging, a feature included in most chat software, to communicate in private with the moderator.

Private interactions. Instant messaging can be used by the moderator to hold private conversations with group members. The moderator can send a private message asking a group member to "speak up" or to "clarify a comment" in private.

Post-group commentary. An on-line focus group allows the moderator a chance to illicit post-group commentary from group members. Through e-mail, the moderator can contact respondents and ask them for clarification or elaboration on issues raised during the group discussion.

The disadvantages of on-line focus groups include the following.

No nonverbals. Perhaps the biggest drawback to on-line focus groups is that "researchers can't watch the body language, facial expressions, and interaction between the people—those 'touchy-feely elements' that qualitative research is supposed to yield" (Miller, 1994, p. 2). One way in which researchers can address this issue is to educate group members about "emoticons" or keyboard symbols used to exhibit emotion. Group members also can be instructed about how to "yell" (e.g., by typing in all uppercase letters) or how to include acronyms such as BTW (by the way) and LOL (laughing out loud) in their written communications.

Technology problems. "Every now and then, the old technology breaks down. It's a little like the

Wild West" (Miller, 1994, p. 2). Operating under a worst-case scenario, group members should be told what to do if the technology breaks down in the middle of the discussion. They should be provided with instructions about how to rejoin the group, if possible, and what the protocol is for reporting technical difficulties.

Message overload. Because of the nature of on-line focus groups, conversational threads sometimes are difficult for members to follow, and conversational chaos can result. Also, key input can be missed as individuals focus on keying in their own comments. This makes it important for the moderator to periodically summarize input and to ask for clarification when needed. In addition, chat screens currently are designed so that each entry "appears to have equal weight, so it is sometimes difficult to distinguish the moderator's 'voice' from that of other participants" (Collins & Murphy, 1997, p. 45).

Time consideration. Because chats are synchronous in nature, all participants must be present on-line at the same time. This can be difficult for people who are dispersed over time zones or on different time/work schedules (Collins & Murphy, 1997).

Typing skills necessary. People need to be able to type to communicate. Individuals with poor typing skills find it very hard to make comments in a timely fashion (Collins & Murphy, 1997).

On-line focus group members may be recruited in a number of ways. Messages can be posted on pertinent listservs or newsgroups. By posting a message announcing a study, a researcher often can target a hard-to-reach group with relative ease (Edmondson, 1997). Individuals can be contacted via e-mail, an especially effective method for internal research where the researcher can secure a current mailing list. Recruiting through Web sites or through Web banners also can be effective.

Another way of recruiting group members is to create a panel or to contact a research firm already possessing a database of Internet panelists in place. Several companies now offer databases of individuals. Examples include Cyber Dialogue (http://www.cyberdialogue.com), which has a database of more than 10,000 people that it draws on for focus groups (Schafer, 1996), and Market Facts Inc. (http://www.marketfacts.com), which has teamed up with Juno Online Services to create a panel of 20,000 individuals. Based on client needs, these companies use their databases to draw individuals who fit the desired demographic and psychographic characteristics.

If panels are not used, then it is important that demographic and psychographic information be obtained prior to inviting individuals to participate. This can be done through a survey delivered via e-mail or throughout the Web (Miller, 1994).

Once respondent characteristics have been gathered, selected individuals should be sent the Web address of the chat site along with a password allowing them to log into the password-restricted site.

NEWSGROUPS

Newsgroups can be a powerful research tool. Newsgroups can be monitored for content, used as a place to gather information, and used as a place to recruit new respondents for a research study. They can serve as a place to collect creative ideas and to gain information about the competition.

Usenet consists of more than 15,000 subject-oriented interest groups. Through Usenet, individuals may access newsgroups and read, respond to, and post messages. Through newsgroups, an individual can actively participate in the conversation or learn by eavesdropping (Finch, 1997).

According to Ross (1995), Usenet discussion groups "accumulate 4 gigabytes of scrawlings every 2 weeks" (p. 260). Because misinformation can take many forms on the Internet, companies that fail to monitor Usenet and other forms of Internet traffic such as listservs might be headed for public relations disasters (Paine, 1995). Ulfelder (1997) suggested that companies frequently plug in their company names or the names of their best known products in the Usenet search engine Deja.com (http://www.deja.com) to see whether they are the targets of Internet smear campaigns.

LISTSERVS

Listservs offer another alternative for on-line research. Also referred to as mailing lists, listservs are an advanced form of the electronic bulletin board. Like newsgroups, listservs usually revolve around set topics, offering places where individuals can read, post, and respond to list postings.

Membership is required to participate in a listserv. Subscribing and all subsequent correspondence is done through e-mail. Once a member, an individual can read and respond to other postings on the list. As postings are added, threads develop. In addition to monitoring listservs for content, listservs can be used for recruitment and information gathering.

NEWSGROUP AND LISTSERV METHODOLOGY

To get the most out of newsgroup or listserv research, Finch (1997) offered a step-by-step process.

1. *Identify potential newsgroups.* Typing in the search term "newsgroups" in any Web search engine will result in a list of newsgroup-related sites. Deja.com also is a good starting point. Other newsgroup list sites include Tile.net News (http://tile.net/news), Usenet Info Center

Launch Pad (http://sunsite.unc.edu/usenet-b/home.html), and Infoseek Guide (http://guide.infoseek.com).

2. *Extract product-oriented conversations.* After searching through indexes of Usenet newsgroup names, monitor those newsgroups and save all interesting messages.

3. *Continually monitor Usenet.* A search tool called Reference.com (http://www.reference.com) will search Usenet messages, based on a user's set criteria, and will e-mail the results daily.

4. *Identify relevant mailing lists.* Although there is no "one-stop" location on the Internet to find a comprehensive index of mailing lists, there are several good places to start. Liszt (http://www.liszt.com) is a Web site that indexes more than 60,000 mailing lists and discussion groups. Inter-Links (http://www.nova.edu/inter-links/cgi-bin/lists) and Tile.net Lists (http://tile.net/listserv/viewlist.html) also are good starting points for identifying mailing lists.

5. *Extract listserv information.* Once a pertinent mailing list is found, try to locate its archives. Many mailing lists archive all messages at a Web site, allowing for keyword searches.

6. *Use the information.* Information from newsgroups and listservs can be used to determine customer wants and needs, gain information about the competition, and monitor public opinion about a company or product.

CONCLUSION

Despite its current limitations, the Internet offers a viable way in which to facilitate interviews, conduct surveys, and monitor public opinion. Whether used on its own or as an addition to a traditional research method, on-line research offers public relations practitioners a quick and inexpensive way to gather information.

As the Internet continues to evolve, so too will on-line research. Increased bandwidth, faster connections, advances in software, and additional individuals joining the on-line community all will affect on-line data collection. Similarly, public attitude toward on-line research will evolve as well.

As we look toward the future, on-line research is certain to grow. Therefore, public relations professionals possessing knowledge of these new on-line techniques for gathering data are at a distinct advantage as the field enters the 21st century.

54

Public Relations and New Media Technology

The Impact of the Internet

JEFFREY K. SPRINGSTON

■ The Internet and related computer technologies are revolutionizing the way in which individuals and organizations communicate. The Clinton administration and many others have embraced the new capabilities with enthusiasm and optimism indicative of the notions of McLuhan's (1964) utopian "global village." Others view this revolution more darkly, reflecting Mumford's (1979) fears of the loss of privacy, the loss of autonomy, and estrangement from community. No doubt, there is some truth to both positions. In 1998, IntelliQuest Information Group estimated that up to 62 million people in the United States were using the Internet (Weber, 1998). Given the exploding growth in this area, research and theoretical development are critical.

The transformation to digital technology has far-reaching implications for the practice of public relations. Capabilities are expanding while equipment prices are dropping. On a computer system costing about $1,000, a public relations practitioner can create multimedia programs or even live video images and deliver them instantly worldwide over the Internet. The ease, cost, and capability of the computer are stretching and changing the boundaries, roles, and relationships of public relations practitioners inside and outside their organizations.

Traditionally, public relations practice and research have been informed, to a great extent, by traditional mass media research. However, Schudson (1992) and other scholars have noted that the convergence of technologies made possible by the computer strains traditional notions of mass media. As Morris and Ogan (1996) pointed out,

> When the Internet is conceptualized as a mass medium, what becomes clear is that neither mass nor medium can be precisely defined for all situations but instead must be continually rearticulated

AUTHOR'S NOTE: The survey reported in this chapter was funded by the Bureau of Media Research at Indiana University. I thank Jennifer Dolce for her assistance on this project.

depending on the situation. The Internet is a multifaceted mass medium; that is, it contains many different configurations of communication. Its varied forms show the connection between interpersonal and mass communication. (p. 42)

CHANGING MODELS OF COMMUNICATION

Holtz (1996) argued that two fundamental models of communication have been altered by the ability to communicate and access information via computer: who provides information and how audiences get the information they need. Public relations practitioners traditionally have been hired to facilitate in the delivery of organizations' messages. This communication usually takes the form of either *one-way communication* (e.g., sending out brochures through direct mail), *two-way communication* (e.g., a company negotiating with an activist coalition), or *multidirectional communication* (e.g., a charitable group such as the United Way encouraging other organizations and groups to interact with their memberships and other groups to support United Way's cause). Each of these models involves a communication gatekeeper. However, anyone with a computer and a modem now can access and distribute information, often directly and with no gatekeepers involved. This effectively shifts the sender-based information model to a receiver-based model. The implications are enormous. Traditional notions of informational power and access are fundamentally altered.

December (1996) pointed out that a message on the Internet can be distributed in the following ways:

- **I** *Point to point:* A single user sends a message to a single receiver.
- **I** *Point to multipoint:* A single user sends a message to a server, which can then be accessed by anyone with appropriate software.

- **I** *Point to server narrowcast:* A single user sends a message to a server, which is then available to only a specific group of users who have log-in names and passwords.
- **I** *Server broadcast:* A server contains stored information that is available to any user with an appropriate software client.
- **I** *Server narrowcast:* A server provides information to only a specific set of authorized users. (p. 22)

The net effect of the new technology and the expansion of communication models means change for the public relations field in a variety of ways. Johnson (1997) interviewed 17 public relations professionals regarding the impact of new technology on the field. Her study revealed important changes in terms of (a) productivity and efficiency, (b) the potential for research and evaluation, (c) information retrieval and distribution, (d) implications for public relations roles, and (e) challenges to incorporating new technologies. This chapter further explores these issues and also examines (f) the ability to tailor information to specific audiences through interactivity and (g) the ability to explore power and information control issues that are likely to arise as a result of a shift from a sender-based model to a receiver-based model. This exploration is done in three ways: a review of existing literature, a content analysis to identify specific aspects of technology being discussed on a popular public relations e-mail discussion list, and a regular mail survey of public relations practitioners regarding the use and impact of Internet technology on the profession.

IMPLICATIONS OF NEW TECHNOLOGY ON PUBLIC RELATIONS

Productivity and Efficiency

Technology has been touted for some time as enabling public relations practitioners to do more work in less time. Productivity has been enhanced by tools such as e-mail to clients, employees and other publics, electronic calendars, and electronic databases (Johnson, 1997; Petrison & Wang, 1993). The speed of transmission and increased timeliness of messages are consistent pluses to Internet technology. There is strong evidence that public relations agencies are increasingly seeing the Internet as an important tool for increasing productivity, efficiency, and effectiveness. In a recent study conducted by the Los Angeles-based Bohle Company, nearly all agencies surveyed provided account executives with Internet-connected computer systems, and 85% upgraded their equipment at least once every 3 years ("The Internet's Continued Impact," 1998).

However, not everyone agrees that computers are enhancing productivity. There is a growing sense that information overload is becoming a serious problem. Dern (1997) noted, "As anyone who has come even near the Internet is probably all too aware, we are drowning in data. We're reaching our threshold of how much total news we can or want to consume or even be aware of" (p. 23). Indeed, not only practitioners are faced with information overload in scanning their environments; so too are journalists and members of many other publics. Finding ways in which to slice through this glut of information to reach target publics probably will be a growing challenge for public relations professionals. In addition to information overload, other aspects of computer technology bring increases in efficiency and productivity to question. Sichel (1997) argued that computers become obsolete too rapidly, making it necessary to buy a new one just when the old one starts helping productivity. Computer consultant William Holliday commented that this perpetual process of hardware and software updating forces employees into the "futz factor," which he translated to mean trying to make personal computers work properly (cited in Fernandez, 1997).

Research and Evaluation

New technology provides an expanded avenue for conducting research. Practitioners in Johnson's (1997) study found on-line surveying a particularly good way in which to do research because of its speed and economy. As one respondent noted, "We didn't do research before because it was too slow" (p. 229). With the click of a mouse, a survey can be distributed to an internal or external public without the expense of postage, and the survey will arrive almost immediately. If the survey is built into a Web site, then responses can be automatically entered into a database as respondents complete the survey. This eliminates the labor and time required to code data. It also enables the researcher to do up-to-the-minute analysis as data are received.

In addition to conducting on-line surveys, many advances are being made in conducting research and evaluation of both new media and conventional media coverage. Software products such as ClipSCAN and SpinControl[1] provide ways for public relations practitioners to manage media lists, distribute press releases, and track their publicity either on-line or over conventional media. Conducting audience research on-line is becoming big business for new companies such as Cyberscan and eWatch. These companies monitor on-line newsgroups and discussion lists and also provide reports to clients in much the same way as companies such as Burrelle's monitor magazines and newspapers. Web audience measurement services also are becoming a very big business. Industry giants such as Nielsen and Arbitron, as well as new companies such as WebTrack, Digital Planet, and Next Century Media, all are working on ways in which to effectively measure on-line Web site traffic (Carveth, 1996). Not only is it feasible to determine the number of people visiting a Web site, but systems are being developed that measure the amount of time spent in a site, how much user interaction takes place, and how many menu levels the user goes down within the site (Mandese, 1995).

The Internet also provides tremendous access to archival data, allowing practitioners and scholars to comb through data in ways that were inconceivable before the computer and the Internet. With targeted key word searching, on-line information services such as Lexis/Nexis provide access to hundreds of magazines, journals, newspapers, and wire services. Although services such as Lexis/Nexis are fee based, most locations on the Web, as well as most Usenet sites and discussion lists, are free. A wealth of information is available on-line. The danger, however, is that the information is strictly of the "buyer beware" variety. A number of studies have documented that much of the information on the Web is erroneous (e.g., Levins, 1997; Wolff, 1994).

Information Retrieval and Distribution

New media technology offers a wide array of methods for retrieving and distributing information, and it is having an impact on all levels of the profession. A recent survey conducted by the Florida-based Institute for Public Relations Research and Education and funded by MCI Communications Corporation found that more than 90% of public relations executives think that e-mail is a fundamental means for internal and external communication ("The Internet's Continued Impact," 1998). The growing popularity of distributing and receiving information via e-mail, the Web, and file transfer protocol (FTP) sites is not hard to understand. These technologies offer the ability to transfer and archive information simultaneously. Reporters and other individuals can receive up-to-the-minute information, and if an organization has archives available on-line, then interested parties also can scan old press releases, position papers, or whatever else the organization chooses to make available. Often, links to other locations of interest are built into the Web sites.

Information no longer is restricted to text or static graphic images either. Webcasting audio now is commonplace. With the appropriate software, a user now can log onto a large number of Web sites that offer either live or archived information and music in CD-quality sound. Many radio stations now Webcast their programs, and some organizations Webcast speeches and interviews on their Web sites. Webcasting is not just restricted to audio. As a recent headline in *Public Relations Tactics* proclaimed, "Webcasting: Internet Videoconferences Come of Age" (1998, p. 20). Although videoconferencing technology has been around for some time, the cost of buy-ing or leasing the technology was expensive. A conventional videoconference typically involves owning or leasing a room specifically equipped with one or more video cameras and microphones for each linked site. The signals are transmitted via telephone lines or satellite uplink and downlink.

Overall costs for equipment and transmission use can amount to hundreds of dollars per hour even if the equipment and space are being leased. Webcasting changes this. For less than $100, a person can purchase a video camera that connects to his or her computer. With the appropriate inexpensive software, individuals or groups can send and receive live video images over the Internet. Now, practically anyone can afford to conduct videoconferences. In addition, because the technology runs on a personal computer, the need for specialized videoconferencing rooms often is eliminated. However, whereas Webcast audio quality is excellent, Webcast video image quality currently is nowhere near broadcast quality. This is because the amount of data required to create a moving video image is far greater than that required for audio, text, or still images. Conventional phone lines are not consistently capable of handling the amount of data necessary for full-screen full-motion video. Therefore, to deliver recognizable images, the visual frame size usually is transmitted in a quarter screen.

This probably will change, however, in the not too distant future. There are many technological, business, and political forces creating demand for high-performance access to cyberspace. Helmore (1999) concluded that because of these forces, widespread high-performance access to cyberspace is inevitable. As data compression techniques improve and high-bandwidth channels become available, high-quality full-motion video soon will be a reality. It also will be possible to transfer vast amounts of other types of information.

Implications for Public Relations Roles

There is growing evidence that new technology is enhancing, and to some degree changing, public relations roles. One important aspect of the Internet technology is the ability to efficiently search vast amounts of information, greatly enhancing the issues management function (Hauss, 1995; Ramsey, 1993; Thomsen, 1995). Emerging issues can be detected more quickly than ever before. With the use of database spreadsheets and other tools, more power is placed in the hands of practitioners to process and present information to superiors and subordinates (Masterton, 1992). The nature of communicating with a variety of key publics including the media, employees, and customers is changing because of technology (Davids, 1994; Dorf, 1995; Fulk, 1993; Shell, 1995). For example, although many journalists still prefer to receive information in more traditional ways, recent research has shown that more than a third of journalists prefer to receive information via e-mail (Bovet, 1995).

An effective on-line presence can aid crisis and risk managers. For example, because reporters were able to get up-to-the-minute information from a state-run Web site, the Michigan Emergency Management Service (EMS) experienced a dramatic drop in the expected number of calls from reporters during a rash of tornadoes that hit the state in 1996 (Springston & Brown, 1998). Michael Prince, public information officer for the Michigan State Police, explained that the Web site provided several important advantages. The drop in reporters' calls freed up EMS personnel for other duties, information was disseminated in a more consistent and timely manner, and many members of the media expressed a high degree of satisfaction with receiving disaster information via the Internet.

Challenges to Incorporating New Technologies

Although new technology provides an expanded horizon for the public relations field, there are many challenges to incorporating this technology into practice. These challenges come in a variety of forms. One challenge is how cyberspace is perceived inside and outside organizations. As Smethers (1998) noted, industry and social paranoia traditionally have accompanied the introduction of all mass communica-

tion technologies. However, there are some legitimate concerns about new technology. Public relations has been forced to deal with problems such as information sabotage ("How Do You Police Cyberspace?," 1996); privacy and copyright concerns (Kimball, 1995; Tedesco, 1996; Teinowitz, 1996); and the negative image of the Internet portrayed in the traditional media regarding the free flow of sexual, racist, or other politically unpopular information.

Another major challenge to incorporating new technology pertains to cost and ease of use. A recent national survey revealed that Internet users generally were wealthier and more highly educated than nonusers (Katz & Aspden, 1997). The study also found that even experienced Internet users find it difficult to navigate cyberspace. In addition, navigation requires much less expertise than does authoring, designing, and managing Web sites and other new technologies—elements necessary to successfully use the Internet for public relations. Johnson (1997) found that a lack of practitioner education about new technology was a major impediment to its incorporation in public relations practice. This is backed up by a recent report indicating that although most public relations agencies now provide their account executives with Internet-connected computers, nearly a third of the agencies surveyed provide no technical support and half of the practitioners surveyed reported having no technology training ("PR Agencies," 1998).

Using Interactivity to Facilitate Two-Way Communication and Tailor Information

Organizations and public relations firms are increasingly recognizing the Internet as a way in which to reach a psychographically unique, computer-oriented array of publics (Dorf, 1995). One key reason is the ability to build interactivity into programs and to tailor information to very specific publics. Interactive media have been used as both an informational tool and a sales tool (Davids, 1994; Sheth & Sisordia, 1993; Solberg, 1995). However, there is evidence that the interactive nature of the new technology has not been used to its full advantage. As Carveth

(1996) noted, "Many of the first group of firms setting up shop on the Web have merely created electronic versions of print-based materials. . . . Moreover, most are struggling to figure out just who they are trying to reach and are getting confused in the process" (p. 79). Negroponte (1995) indicated that many developers of new media have focused on the display aspects of communication rather than concentrating on the content and audience needs. He noted that the best Internet content is that which recognizes Internet users as active rather than passive.

Power and Information Control

The Internet has transformed mass communication from a sender-based model to a receiver-based model. This transformation has important implications for power and information control in society. Previously, much of the information power in society was in control of large, well-financed broadcast and publishing companies. As Bremser (1998) noted,

> For the first time, independent publishing may have just as much of a chance at reaching the public as the most corporate of corporate media. From radio to movies, tight corporate control consistently forces those people with ideas but no money outside the mainstream. The Web, on the other hand, has consistently acted as the great equalizer by liberating individuals with a passion for expression and allowing them to broadcast their views without the restrictions of big-wig radio producers and TV execs.

This shift certainly is not restricted to the broadcast and publishing industries. The Internet potentially exposes organizations of all types to new threats and challenges from individuals, opposition groups, and competitors large and small. Literally anyone connected to the Internet can distribute and exchange information worldwide. However, this shift in information power need not be viewed negatively. As Kruckeberg and Starck (1988) argued, an important function of public relations is to build com-

munity. Bessette (1997) argued that the Internet provides a mechanism to facilitate communication interchange and enable community discussion in ways that were impossible 15 years ago. Clearly, the Internet provides both opportunities for and challenges to organizations.

To this point, we have looked at what the literature reveals about the impact of Internet-related technology on public relations. However, as Johnson (1997) pointed out, rigorous public relations research about the use of new technologies has been limited. Her qualitative study interviewing 17 public relations practitioners was a good first step at identifying some of the core issues. The next logical step is to conduct a larger quantitative inquiry into the issues discussed thus far in this chapter. The next section outlines the methods and results of a two-part study to build on existing literature.

DATA COLLECTION

Content Analysis

Two methods of primary research were conducted. The first was a content analysis identifying the types of technology discussed on the PRFORUM, an Internet discussion list. The PRFORUM was co-created in 1993 by me and the late Bill Lutholtz, corporate communications manager for Indianapolis Power and Light. The list ranges from 1,200 to 1,600 members and is comprised primarily of public relations practitioners and academicians from around the world. The PRFORUM provides its members with the opportunity to exchange information and debate issues affecting the profession. It is not uncommon for the list to generate more than 50 messages a day. Discussion of technology and its impact is a common topic on the list.

The purpose of the content analysis was to identify what types of technologies have been discussed since the creation of PRFORUM. This was done to gain a sense of the technologies of interest to practitioners and scholars. First, several books on communication technology were reviewed to generate a list of search terms (Bridges, 1997; Holtz, 1996; McGuire, Stilborne, McAdams, & Hyatt, 1997; Reddick & King, 1997). More than 100 terms were entered into the list search engine to identify the number of messages that contained each term. Whereas most of the terms were related to some aspect of the Internet, other types of technology also were included in the search (e.g., video, fax-on-demand, voice mail). The search uncovered 72 of the terms used in messages. These terms are divided into nine basic categories: information retrieval/files, distribution methods, on-line behavior, on-line interaction, search functions, software, technical/hardware, World Wide Web, and a miscellaneous category. Although some terms overlap categories, the divisions are intended to aid discussion.

As Table 54.1 displays, World Wide Web and On-line Interaction were by far the most mentioned categories, generating approximately 9,000 to 10,000 messages each. References to the Web (WWW) and to e-mail comprised most of the numbers. A sampling of message content revealed that most messages containing WWW involved members passing along Web site addresses of interest, although some discussion revolved around effective Web page design or strategies for publicizing Web sites and gaining priority placement in various search engines. E-mail was mentioned primarily as a means of providing contact information (e.g., e-mail me at johndoe@anycorp.com), although there was some discussion of e-mail software and using e-mail to interact with the media and other publics. With exception to technical and hardware concerns, the other categories generated roughly equivalent numbers of messages, ranging from approximately 1,200 to 1,800 messages each. There were a lot of requests for information about, and recommendations for, all types of software. Queries were common about Internet search engines and operations of on-line resources such as the Web and on-line information services. Discussion of on-line behavior also was a common theme. This discussion usually focused on assessments of appropriate behavior on the PRFORUM. The Technical/Hardware category and the few miscellaneous items reflected relatively little discussion in comparison to the other categories.

Mail Questionnaire

The second method was a mail questionnaire sent to 750 public relations practitioners throughout all 50 states. The survey queried respondents about the impact of the Internet on themselves, their organizations, and the public relations field. In the case of agency practitioners, respondents were instructed to answer the questions in relation to their "typical" clients. In addition to factors already discussed, the survey was developed to integrate the elements suggested by Rafaeli (Newhagen & Rafaeli, 1996; Rafaeli, 1988). He proposed that communication on the Internet and related technologies should be studied in terms of five basic concepts: multimedia, hypertextuality, packet switching, synchronicity, and interactivity. Multimedia refers to the overall sensory appeal and use of text, voice, pictures, animation, video, and so forth. Hypertextuality refers to the nonlinearity potential of various aspects of the Internet such as the Web. Packet switching refers to the concept of gatekeeping and communication routes or the lack thereof. The Internet is designed to be route oblivious. This fact has an impact on everything from pricing and legislation to social relations or "netiquette." Synchronicity refers to the notion that the Internet allows both real-time communication and time-delayed or archived information simultaneously, making it a concern of both process and effects. Finally, interactivity refers to the extent that a user can make choices and actively respond to the program.

In addition, questions regarding uses and gratifications of new technology were integrated into the questionnaire. Infante, Rancer, and Womack (1993) suggested that the uses-and-gratifications approach promises to be a useful way in which to study Internet-related communication behavior. The Internet offers a wide range of communication possibilities such as en-

TABLE 54.1

Frequency of Technology Topics Discussed on the PRFORUM

Topic	Frequency	Topic	Frequency
On-line Interaction		Transfer	42
Chat	409	FTP	153
Discussion list	514	GIF	4
E-mail	7,867	Info retrieval service	3
Internet phone	73	JPEG	9
Usenet	196	Lexis/Nexis	91
		TIFF	60
World Wide Web		Upload	52
WWW	7,015		
Hotlist	2	**Distribution Methods**	
Hypertext	32	Broadcast distribution	39
URL	1,615	CD-ROM	490
Web page	954	Corporate radio	3
Webmaster	234	E-zine	112
		Electronic BBS	20
Search Functions		Electronic newsletter	33
Archie	17	Fax-on-demand	23
Browser	204	Mailing list	453
Gopher	153	Teleconference	15
Links	425	Video	524
Mosaic	53	Video news release	98
MS Internet Explorer	17		
Netscape	169	**Technical/Hardware**	
Search engine	210	Modem	193
Searchable	99	ISDN	14
Surf	379	LAN	32
Veronica	8	WAN	12
		PPP	23
On-line Behavior		SLIP	40
Emoticon	21	UNIX	40
Flame	425	Shell accounts	1
Lurk	358	Terminal	30
Netiquette	100	Baud	29
Spam	301	Firewall	21
		WAIS	21
Software		VRML	4
Groupware	5	Telnet	33
Java	66	Node	54
Shareware	48		
Shockwave	6	**Miscellaneous**	
Software	1,384	Digital video editing	11
		User ID	44
Information Retrieval/Files		Virtual reality	49
Databases	691		
Download	422		

tertainment, work-related information, and social interaction. As Newhagen and Rafaeli (1996) put it, "Because of the Internet's chameleon-like character . . ., uses and gratifications offers a vehicle to lay out a taxonomy of just what goes on in cyberspace" (p. 11). Because the Internet accommodates and usually requires that a consumer actively seek information to fulfill some need, this approach holds much promise for research to advance our understanding of both the consumption and development of public relations activities on the Internet.

A number of typologies exist that identify gratifications people can gain from communication. Wenner (1986) developed a taxonomy that might be particularly useful in studying Internet communication development and use including surveillance, entertainment/diversion, interpersonal utility, and parasocial interaction. Surveillance refers to communication monitoring activity in which an individual would engage to gather information useful in daily work or personal life. Entertainment/diversion would be information seeking specifically to escape from work or other cares and problems. Interpersonal utility refers to gathering information useful in interpersonal discussion or in personal career development. Parasocial interaction is that activity sought for its human interaction qualities, often used as a substitute for face-to-face relationships and interaction.

Participants were selected from the membership directories of the Public Relations Society of America and the International Association of Business Communicators using a random selection procedure. The questionnaire design and mailing followed guidelines developed by Dillman (1978). Each questionnaire was accompanied by a cover letter introducing and explaining the survey. A repeat mailing was done 2 weeks after the initial mailing to increase the number of surveys returned. Of the 32 questions comprising the questionnaire, 8 were categorical questions and 24 were Likert-type questions placed on a 5-point scale ranging from 1 = *strongly agree* to 5 = *strongly disagree*. A total of 303 usable surveys were returned, representing a 40% return rate. This return rate is comparable with the average response rate reported by Yu and Cooper (1983) in their survey of 93 social science journal articles using mail surveys published over a 20-year period.

RESULTS

Results indicated that 94% of respondents had access to the Internet and that 63% of respondents' organizations had Web sites. A vast majority (76%) of the Web sites were programmed by organizations' information technology (IT) departments or were subcontracted out to technical support firms. Public relations departments programmed only 16% of the Web sites, with the remaining Web sites being created by other departments (e.g., marketing, human resources). However, a substantial percentage of practitioners (86%) indicated that public relations had a significant role in working with IT to design and maintain their organizations' Web sites. Only 6% of respondents indicated that their organizations had used Webcast technology to transmit audio or video speeches or other events live, and only 12% indicated that their organizations had used Internet relay chat (IRC) technology. Only 9% of respondents indicated that their organizations subscribed to services that monitor on-line newsgroups (e.g., eWatch).

As Table 54.2 displays, practitioners were neutral, leaning toward negative attitudes about the effectiveness of their organizations' use of multimedia capabilities (mean = 3.42), and had similar feelings about their own competency in creating multimedia materials (mean = 3.39). Respondents were neutral about their organizations' use of hypertext capability (mean = 3.09) and generally did not agree that their organizations had successfully converted existing materials to a hypertext format (mean = 3.81).

Practitioners did indicate fairly strong agreement that the Internet provides an opportunity for individuals and smaller organizations to compete with larger organizations (mean = 1.87) and that the Internet provides individuals and groups opposed to their organizations' positions significant opportunities to influence pub-

TABLE 54.2

Responses to Questions About Public Relations and Technology

Question/Comment	Mean	Standard Deviation
Your organization effectively uses the multimedia capabilities of the computer (combining text, sound, graphics, and video) on its Web site.	3.42	0.91
You are competent in developing multimedia materials for electronic distribution.	3.39	0.77
Your organization effectively uses hypertext capability in new material created for the Internet (i.e., the ability to link users to other relevant material from within a particular document) on your Web site.	3.09	1.07
Your organization has successfully converted existing materials from a linear format to a hypertext format.	3.81	0.81
The Internet provides an opportunity for individuals and smaller organizations to compete with larger organizations in the marketplace.	1.87	0.63
The Internet provides an opportunity for individuals and groups opposed to your organization's positions to significantly influence public opinion.	2.12	0.80
Individuals and groups opposed to your organization's positions have significantly influenced public opinion via the Internet.	3.97	0.55
The ability to Webcast and archive information simultaneously is a valuable tool for public relations (e.g., broadcasting the audio of a speech as it occurs).	2.23	1.71
The ability to tailor information to specific audiences is a major strength of computer technology.	2.02	0.65
Your organization effectively uses computer technology to tailor information to specific audiences.	3.73	0.78
Computer technology offers an effective way for members of various publics to interact with your organization.	1.74	0.95
Your organization effectively uses computer technology to enable members of various publics to interact with the organization.	2.98	0.90
You often use the Internet to monitor trends and issues in the environment.	1.89	0.58
You believe you are well trained in using the Internet to its full potential.	3.88	0.76
You find that information available on the Internet enhances your career.	2.77	0.98
Because of new technology, you frequently experience information overload.	1.38	0.86
You spend a substantial amount of time trying to make your computer work properly.	1.59	0.93
You use the Internet to maintain personal ties with other public relations professionals.	2.52	0.67
It is important for public relations materials available on the Internet to be entertaining.	3.99	0.52

NOTE: Likert scale values ranged from 1 = *strongly agree* to 5 = *strongly disagree.*

lic opinion (mean = 2.12). However, practitioners expressed reasonably strong disagreement with the notion that opposition groups actually had influenced public opinion (mean = 3.97). Respondents tended to agree that the ability to Webcast and archive information simulta-neously is a valuable tool to public relations (mean = 2.23). There was fairly strong agreement that the ability to tailor information to specific audiences is a major strength of computer technology (mean = 2.02), but many in the sample disagreed that their organizations were effectively taking advantage of this capability (mean = 3.73). Practitioners generally agreed with the notion that computer technology offers an effective way for members of the public to interact with their organizations (mean = 1.74) but were largely neutral regarding their organizations' use of computer technology to interact with their publics (mean = 2.98) (Table 54.2).

It appears that practitioners routinely used the Internet to monitor trends and issues in the environment (mean = 1.89), but many appear to believe that they need more training to use Internet resources more effectively (mean = 3.88). Practitioners strongly agreed that information overload is a problem because of new technology (mean = 1.38) and that a substantial amount of time is spent on trying to make their computer systems work properly (mean = 1.59). Respondents were somewhat neutral about the impact of the Internet with regard to enhancing their careers (mean = 2.77). They did tend to agree with the statement that they used the Internet to maintain personal ties with other public relations professionals (mean = 2.52). Finally, there was fairly strong disagreement with the notion that public relations materials available on the Internet need to be entertaining (mean = 3.99) (Table 54.2).

DISCUSSION

The literature and the results of the two studies presented in this chapter indicate that Internet technology is having a significant impact on public relations. Overall, the findings of the content analysis and the mail survey support the existing literature. E-mail and the Web appear to be the most important aspects of the Internet. Their use appears to be fully integrated into public relations practice. As analysis of the PRFORUM revealed that although there is some discussion about the best e-mail software or Web browser to use, most references to the technology are simply routine conversations exchanging addresses. Although viewing Web sites might be routine for public relations professionals, creating them is a different matter. Results of the survey indicate

that computer specialists, rather than public relations specialists, create most organizational Web sites. It is encouraging to note, however, that although public relations specialists do not often create Web sites, they are routinely consulted in the creation process and involved in updating content on the sites.

Although e-mail and Web site use appears common, many of the features and multimedia capabilities of the new technology appear to be underused. For example, although the ability to Webcast speeches and other activities were deemed important for public relations, few organizations appear to actually use this capability. Few organizations appear to use IRC technology as well. The data also suggest that the hypertext capability of the new media technology is being underused, supporting Carveth's (1996) observation that much of the material on the Internet is just an electronic version of conventional print material. Also, it appears that organizations are not exploiting the potential of new media technology to improve two-way communication with publics to the degree that practitioners believe is possible.

There is recognition by practitioners that the Internet has the capability of leveling the playing field between large and small organizations. There is some recognition that individuals and groups opposed to one's organization can use new media technology to significantly affect public perception about the organization, although few in this study appear to have personally experienced this. Given that only 9% of respondents indicated that their organizations subscribed to services to monitor electronic newsgroups, there might not be a full appreciation of the potential impact of this type of communication. However, the potential threat is very real. For example, at the end of the O. J. Simpson murder trial, a rumor began circulating that Mrs. Fields' Original Cookies supplied free cookies at Simpson's victory party. Although completely false, the rumor perpetuated on-line to the point where a boycott of Mrs. Fields' cookies was mounted, and the company reported a significant loss in sales as a result (Copilevitz, 1997; Stahl, 1998).

The literature and this study remain mixed regarding new media technology's impact on the efficiency and productivity of public relations practitioners. As in other studies (e.g., Thomsen, 1995), respondents in this study reported routine use of the Internet to scan the environment for issues and developing trends. However, practitioners appeared relatively neutral regarding the role of new media technology in enhancing their careers. This sentiment might be due, in part, to a lack of confidence in their training and ability to use the new technologies. Respondents in this study indicated that they needed more technology training. This sentiment also might be recognition that one will have to stay abreast of new technology just to maintain position. There is evidence that the new technology is somewhat overwhelming to many practitioners. Information overload was identified as a problem, and professionals also indicated that they spend substantial amounts of time just getting their computers to work properly. Not all of this time appears to be work related, however. Practitioners appear to use the Internet in parasocial ways, maintaining personal contact with other public relations professionals. It is not clear what impact the parasocial aspects of Internet use have on productivity, career enhancement, and information overload.

THE FUTURE

Abrahamson (1998) recently noted, "It is not possible for anyone to predict the scope and/or effect of something as profound as the Internet" (p. 17). However, he and other scholars have offered glimpses of that future. One likelihood is that the concept of mass audience will continue to be supplanted with niche publics demanding high-value information. The rejection by practitioners in this study to the notion that public relations material on the Internet needs to be entertaining might be recognition of the needs of these niche publics. As we leave what Stephens (1998) termed "the age of insufficient information," public relations professionals will increasingly need to learn ways in which to slice through the growing glut of information to identify and provide information to these niche publics.

The form of that information also is likely to change. Stephens (1998) argued that in the future, Web sites will increasingly be filled with video. Public relations educators need to prepare students to understand and develop video and other aspects of multimedia and interactivity. A byproduct of this will be the increasing importance of working in teams. Developing multimedia requires so many different skills that one person cannot realistically do it all. Research in group and interpersonal communication will become increasingly salient to public relations. Carey (1998) noted that predictions of the future always have been more about creating self-fulfilling prophecies than about clairvoyance. Predictions serve as ways in which to "domesticate the future . . . to bring it under rational, predictable control" (p. 28). Public relations practitioners and scholars need to work together to help guide the future of the Internet in ways that are beneficial to the profession, to our clients, and to the greater society.

NOTE

1. ClipSCAN and SpinControl are registered trademarks of SpinWARE Software Publishing Inc.

The Development of a Structuration Analysis of New Publics in an Electronic Environment

ZORAIDA R. COZIER

DIANE F. WITMER

Public relations officers believe that establishing positive relationships with the media is critical to an organization's public relations function and communication role. Reaching the media first and controlling the content and quality of messages is considered essential to the maintenance of a "positive image" (see, e.g., Cheney & Vibbert, 1987; J. Grunig, 1993c; Haedrich, 1993). Corporations systematically develop messages that are designed to influence stakeholders and opinion leaders (Heath, 1994). These efforts now include the use of computer-mediated communication systems (CMCS) to create Web sites, to form user groups for feedback from publics, and to use e-mail to communicate more quickly with an organization's publics (Bobbit, 1995; Capps, 1993; Marken, 1995). However, new communication technolo-gies create alternative venues for individuals to develop "computer-mediated communities" (Jones, 1995) and for publics to evolve.

Whereas electronic commerce, Web pages, and on-line ads tend to be the focus of using CMCS for public relations, the emergence of more than 15,000 newsgroups, an indeterminate number of electronic mailing lists (often called *listservs* in reference to a specific type of e-mail distribution software), and a multitude of private access groups have spawned innumerable on-line social organizations. Thus, public relations efforts may be counteracted by the voices embedded in the interactive discourse of CMCS.

The emergence of unregulated on-line social organizations has generated concerns over the possibilities of a "cybercrisis" in public relations (Middleberg, 1996). Consequently, public rela-

AUTHORS' NOTE: A more comprehensive version of this chapter was presented to the Public Relations Interest Group at the meeting of the International Communication Association, May 1997, Montreal, and is available on request from the first author.

615

tions researchers have proposed the development of Web site surveillance systems (J. Alexander, 1996) to monitor the Web and scrutinize unregulated on-line discourse. However, other aspects of the Internet, including interactive meeting spaces (e.g., MUDs, MOOs, MUSHes, and chat rooms),[1] Usenet newsgroups, listservs, and electronic bulletin boards, also offer unprecedented opportunities for public relations officers and scholars to monitor multiple dimensions of on-line social organizations. This presents a need for an exploration of on-line discursive spaces to provide insight into the communicative nature of these social relationships and organizations.

The role of technology in social interaction has drawn interest from scholars and practitioners for some time. Gumpert and Cathcart (1986) posited that media played a role in the formation, maintenance, and dissolution of interactions. Gumpert and Drucker (1993) later argued that electronic space acts as a public venue for social interaction. Historically, technological innovations such as telephone and print mechanisms have facilitated the growth of interpersonal communication networks (Ferrara, Brunner, & Whittemore, 1991; Wellman & Tindall, 1993). What distinguishes the CMCS information revolution from previous eras is that the interactive technology allows people to communicate freely in an often unregulated, uncensored, multinational, and public environment.

This chapter extends the traditional concept of a public's communication as a set of organized actions around issues and negotiational processes surrounding a particular problematic state and addresses the ontological status or communicative nature of a public. A public's communication is not to be equated solely with a set of actions; rather, it is a "medium of intersubjectivity" (Giddens, 1993) via the public's discursive and institutional practices. To present an alternative conceptualization and analytic framework of publics, we first present a brief description and critique of significant theoretical ideations of publics. We then explicate the theoretical and methodological limitations of those concepts in relation to the emerging electronic environment. Finally, we propose an

alternative analysis of on-line publics that is undergirded by Giddens' (1979, 1984, 1987, 1990, 1993, 1995) structuration theory.

SITUATIONAL THEORY: A PREDOMINANT TYPOLOGY OF PUBLICS

The typology of publics used most often by public relations researchers is drawn from the situational theory of publics (J. Grunig, 1989b, 1989c; J. Grunig & Repper, 1992), which is grounded in a systems perspective of public relations. The situational theory of publics is significant because it centralizes the communication behavior of publics and public participation in public relations research. This approach entails an analysis of the levels of a public's organized cognitions about an issue (Dyer, 1996; J. Grunig, 1989b, 1989c) or a public's public opinion and issues orientation (Berkowitz & Tunmire, 1994). Strategic publics tend to be defined in terms of actions regarding consensus or dissensus with an organization's policies or positions (J. Grunig, 1992b; J. Grunig & Hunt, 1984).

Situational theory construes publics as external systems that interpenetrate the focal organization or the adaptive subsystem (J. Grunig & Hunt, 1984). The situational theory of publics addresses a public's cognition in terms of a group's information processing and information seeking (J. Grunig, 1989b, 1989c; J. Grunig & Repper, 1992) and how these variables influence a group's communication behavior (J. Grunig, 1989b, 1989c). Public relations theorists can categorize or segment publics in an attempt to predict their communication behaviors (Broom & Dozier, 1990; J. Grunig 1989b, 1989c, 1992b; J. Grunig & Hunt, 1984).

Situational theory has been incorporated into a theory of strategic management through a normative approach to public relations (J. Grunig & Repper, 1992). This approach distinguishes between stakeholders and publics. First, there is a stakeholder stage where a group's actions have consequences for an organization or where an organization's mission or procedures affect a public. These stakeholders become a public when they "recognize one or more of the consequences of a problem and organize to do something about it" (J. Grunig & Repper, 1992, p. 124). This approach argues that when the public organizes around issues or "creates issues" (J. Grunig & Repper, 1992, p. 124), the public moves into the issue stage.

LIMITATIONS OF SITUATIONAL THEORY FOR ANALYSIS OF PUBLICS

The situational perspective establishes a foundation for the study of communication behaviors of a public. It does not focus solely on a one-way orientation in which an organization's communication goals take precedence. However, it has certain theoretical and methodological limitations for explicating the communicative nature of publics as social systems and the ways in which social systems are created and re-created, both on- and off-line.

The first theoretical limitation stems from assumptions concerning the organizational-environmental interface (i.e., public-institutional interaction) that undergird the definitions of publics from a situational perspective. The assumption that an organization and its publics are discrete entities situates publics as possessions of the focal organization. This assumption discounts human agency in the creation of organizational-environmental interfaces, and it restricts the research focus to a linear and top-down analysis of how environmental contingencies affect organizational structure (for an overview of environmental scanning research, see Dozier, 1990). However, an organization and its publics are not discrete bounded entities. There is, instead, a recursive relationship between them.

A second theoretical limitation of the situational perspective is its tendency to overemphasize the view that a public is centered on a problem or issues. This neglects publics or stakeholders that emerge around a sense of shared experiences or re-creation of experiences (Branham, 1980; Branham & Pearce, 1985). The predominant conceptual framework of publics and public participation presents an underdeveloped explication of the communicative nature of a public. Significant theoretical developments in the field of public relations have addressed the need to explore the range and changeability of publics (Lauzen & Dozier, 1992), sensitivity of publics over time (Thomsen, 1995), and motives of both a public and a focal organization (Dozier, 1992; Dozier, L. Grunig, & J. Grunig, 1995; Murphy, 1989, 1991). The reliance on traditional conceptualizations of publics does not allow for an adequate description of the human communication processes that constitute a public's communication, both on- and off-line. Therefore, there is a need for a segmentation approach that illuminates the levels of cognition, underlying motives, and meaning systems of a public's constituents.

There also is a need to identify and explore the constituent and precipitating factors that influence the development of a public's dominant ideological stance. The dominant stance has the potential to either marginalize or delegitimate alternative ideological meaning systems (Deetz & Mumby, 1990; Mumby, 1989) over time and to close off "certain possible perceptions and courses of action" (Mumby, 1989, p. 302). Consequently, methodological implications of situational theory include a lack of descriptive studies that observe the emergence and local organization (Sacks, Schegloff, & Jefferson, 1978) of a public's communicative nature.

In sum, the predominant conceptualization of publics overemphasizes the view that a public is centered around a problem or issues and neglects the emergence of publics around a sense of shared experiences or a re-creation of experiences (positive and negative) in which human communication processes are central to the development of the public's ideological stance. A theory of publics needs to move away from considering a public's cognition as information processing, from equating a public's seeking of issues, and from situating motives in a public's action or position on issues in the public arena. Public relations researchers need to employ a framework that shifts the locus of analysis to the public's communicative practices in interactional settings. The growing use of Internet and Web technologies by individuals and organizations alike underscores the need.

THE ELECTRONIC ENVIRONMENT AND EMERGENT NEW PUBLICS

Computer-based communication technologies present significant challenges to public relations practitioners who rely on information-based approaches to define, identify, and analyze publics. The presentation of the Internet solely as a vehicle that allows organizations to create informed publics (Bobbit, 1995; Capps, 1993; Chew, 1994; Murdock & Golding, 1989) negates the influence of public participation and discounts the political function of day-to-day communicative practices in on-line interactions. Information-based approaches situate public participation at the end of the reception channel and limit the analysis of a public's participation to the use of and response to the media.

The Internet offers vivid illustrations that people discursively develop, maintain, and dissolve relationships. A number of CMCS researchers (Baym, 1995; Beninger, 1987; Bizzell, 1982; Ferrara et al., 1991; Finlay, 1987; Giddens, 1987, 1990; Gumpert & Cathcart, 1986; Murray, 1988; Parks & Floyd, 1996; Rheingold, 1993; Rice, 1989) have argued that on-line communicative interactions can result in the formation of new collectivities. Parks and Floyd's (1996) study of four major newsgroup hierarchies, for example, showed that friendships have flourished in newsgroup discussion. Baym's (1995) study of gossip in a soap opera newsgroup used a structuration approach that moved beyond the treatment of communication in CMCS as a conduit model and explored the newsgroup's communicative practices and its time and space relations. Of particular interest to public relations researchers are the implications of this study, which showed that the newsgroups did not emerge around a problematic situation but

rather through a sense of shared experiences or a re-creation of shared experiences.

The role that genres of discourse play in the formation of social relationships has been studied extensively by only a handful of linguistic scholars (Bizzell, 1982; Ferrara et al., 1991; Hymes, 1986; Noon & Delbridge, 1993; Wilkins, 1991), and even less often by communication scholars (Baym, 1995; Parks & Floyd, 1996). The CMCS literature shows that the Internet facilitates the emergence of reproduced practices in communicative and social interaction as well as how these communicative interactions form social organizations. Studies of CMCS that have addressed the features of on-line interactions and collectivities have focused on a variety of social and organizational issues including infrastructure (Baym, 1995; Rheingold, 1993); interpersonal-mediated communication (Cathcart & Gumpert, 1983); formation of virtual communities (Beamish, 1995; Beninger, 1987; Rheingold, 1993); segmentation of audiences (Rice, 1989); closed user groups (Finlay, 1987); trust (Giddens, 1987, 1990); turn taking and alteration of co-presence (Bizzell, 1982; Ferrara et al., 1991; Murray, 1988; Wilkins, 1991); participation status (McLaughlin, Osborne, & Smith, 1995); and the synchrony, transmission, and textual nature of dyadic connections (Culnan & Markus, 1987; Garton & Wellman, 1991).

Of particular importance to this chapter is the perpetuation function in which maintenance strategies serve as social lubricants. Kurtz (1997) reported that these functions of talk are evident in on-line support groups, just as they are in traditional telephone networks and off-line support groups. Similarly, Thomsen (1995) indicated that participants in a public relations listserv relayed their experiences through discourse and established a supportive network. It seems clear that, given the ways in which on-line social organizations are formed and sustained, on-line social organizations can constitute publics and stakeholders that are active participants of a campaign, whether or not they commit to actions in the public policy or social arenas. In this chapter, we refer to such collectivities as *new publics*. The term denotes a critical/political perspective that is drawn from Finlay (1987) and distinguishes our structuration approach from the situational approach.

One consequence of traditional public relations research and practices in CMCS is that the public is treated as an end-state of an interaction in a series of point-to-point or point-to multipoint communication endeavors or data transmissions (December, 1996). Finlay (1987) argued that pacification of a public situates it as an "object, opponent, or receiver" (p. 89). The success of new communication technologies relies on the treatment of a public solely as a consumer. Consequently, the hype surrounding the Internet has situated the public as (a) a body of consumers who never have been exposed to ads previously; (b) individuals with tabula rasae who must be educated to make informed choices; and (c) a body devoid of morals that never has been exposed to the profanity, indecency, and immoral acts that can be found on the Internet. These approaches serve to treat publics as victims or passive audiences rather than as collectivities of reflexive individuals. Hence, the role of human agency in on-line interactions is discounted.

New publics represent new challenges of identification and analysis for public relations theorists and practitioners. Particularly important to a discussion of new publics is Goffman's (1981) proposal that "when a word is spoken, all those that happen to be within a perceptual range of an event will have some participation status relevant to it" (p. 3). Researchers cannot dismiss the nonparticipants (known as *lurkers*) of Internet-based groups. Neither can researchers consistently access lurkers' identities or discourse. In Usenet newsgroups, for example, lurkers leave no trace of their silent participation. Furthermore, researchers have no way of tracking the extent to which lurkers might send private posts to individual members of a newsgroup or mailing list, repeat newsgroup discussions to private on-line groups, or carry online conversations to off-line groups.

Our concept of new publics is an attempt to move away from the use of mass communication approaches and social-psychological variables (e.g., information processing) and is consistent both with Toth's (1995) proposal to apply inter-personal and organizational communication perspectives to the field of public relations and with Heath's (1994) assumption that interactions affect public presentation. We address a new public's communicative practices in everyday interactions, which serve to constitute and enact a particular ideological stance that motivates individuals to act or refrain from acting (for similar critiques of mass communications, see Lupton, 1994, and Yates & Orlikowski, 1992). Our approach views a new public's ongoing discursive and institutional practices as means of producing and reproducing dominant ideological meaning systems (Deetz, 1996; Mumby, 1989, 2001). Drawing from Giddens' (1979) work, we view ideology as discourse as well as "involvements of beliefs within 'modes of lived existence'" (p. 183). The ideological aspects of symbol systems enact four political functions. Three of the functions of ideology, set forth by Giddens are (a) naturalization of the present (reification), (b) denial or transmutation or contradictions, and (c) representation of sectional interests as universal ones (pp. 193-195). Mumby's (1987) concept of hegemonic control constitutes a fourth political function.

A structurationist approach to the analysis of new publics offers a description of a public that is not limited to the a priori categories set forth in the predominant typology of publics, which treats communication as non-context dependent. Structuration also permits a reconceptualization of the public-institutional interaction that acknowledges the ability of a an organizational facet to become a public and that recognizes a recursive relationship between the dominant meaning systems of a public and those of an organization.

STRUCTURATION AND NEW PUBLICS

Structuration theory (Giddens, 1979, 1984, 1987, 1990, 1993, 1995) addresses the temporal, structural, and spatial aspects of social systems. The central theme of structuration revolves around the ways in which the patterning of social relations is understood as reproduced practices (Giddens, 1984, 1990) "via the actors' reflexive monitoring of system production and the articulation of discursive 'history' " (Giddens, 1987, p. 153). Social systems are to be construed not as bounded entities but rather in terms of degrees of systemness such as the permeability of boundaries (Giddens, 1984). Structuration theory, therefore, situates organizational environments as continually created and enacted in each social interaction.

Structuration theory assumes that social organizations can act as "disembedding mechanisms" that overcome time and space (Giddens, 1991). The notion of a disembedding mechanism allows for a reconceptualization of the organization-environmental interface such that the organization and the public are not separate bounded entities but rather exist through relationships that extend beyond co-presence. There is a reflexive relationship between the meaning systems of both. A Usenet newsgroup, for example, can take the form of disembedding mechanism as participants disembed local practices from external organizations and from on-line interactions and re-embed them within the context of the newsgroup postings. Similarly, lurkers and visible participants alike can disembed structures from the on-line organizations to recreate publics both on- and off-line. Thus, new publics emerge through shared or re-created experiences and have both discursive and nondiscursive (lurking) aspects.

The public nature of on-line newsgroup discourse challenges the notion of static publics because it allows for an analysis of the new public's communicative practices in everyday settings. This further informs the researcher about the political functions of a public's practices and that public's ability to act as a disembedding mechanism. Furthermore, an institutional analysis would entail an analysis of the meaning systems between the local and global organizations.

Structuration posits that in social interactions, reflexive actors draw on rules and resources that enable them to proceed (Giddens, 1984). These structures include the use of experiences lodged in interpretive schemes to consti-

tute meaning (structures of signification), the enactment of a normative order to sanction modes of conduct (structures of legitimation), and the mobilization of resources to enact power relationships (structures of domination). In social interactions, "the structural properties of social systems are both the medium and outcome of the practices they recursively organize" (p. 25). The theory presumes that human consciousness takes on two forms: discursive and practical consciousness. Human agents access tacit knowledge that they cannot articulate through the practical consciousness. This accounts for "repressed forms of cognition impulsion" (p. 4). Discursive consciousness constitutes knowledge that an actor can articulate.

Giddens' (1984) model provides insight into an actor's motivations. Although an actor cannot always explicitly account for his or her motives, the actor continually engages in a reflexive monitoring of his or her own activities, and this can lead to both intended and unintended consequences. Reflexivity is evident in an actor's conduct. The consequences of action account for a feedback loop into one's motivation for action. The person then reconstitutes his or her motivation for action. Thus, the actor can articulate the reasons or grounds (accountability) for action via the rationalization of action. Because structuration focuses on the interactions of reflexive actors recursively creating and re-creating social systems, it provides an ontological framework (Banks & Riley, 1993; Witmer, 1997) that explicates a new public's motivational context and meaning constitution; its communicative nature; and its production, reproduction, and transformation.

Structuration theory also offers the theorist at least two levels of analysis. First, any social system can be analyzed in terms of strategic conduct in which "the focus is placed upon modes in which actors draw upon structural properties in the constitution of social relations" (Giddens, 1984, p. 288). A strategic conduct analysis (Giddens, 1979, 1984) of a new public's practices can address an actor's motivations, knowledgeability, and desires. A strategic context analysis (Stones, 1991) can illuminate "the social nexus of interdependencies, rights and obligations, and asymmetries of power" (p. 676).[2] This can be followed by an institutional analysis in which aspects of the first analysis are bracketed, with the focus on how "structural properties are treated as chronically reproduced features of social systems" (Giddens, 1984, p. 288). The patterns and themes in each new public's discursive and institutional practices, therefore, can be analyzed in terms of three guiding research questions:

1. How do the dominant ideological meaning systems constituted in a new public's discursive and institutional practices serve to rhetorically construct a shared reality?
2. How do a new public's dominant ideological meaning systems affect its public communication efforts with relevant and conflicting publics?
3. Does a new public act as a disembedding mechanism that has the potential to construct and reconstruct publics on- and off-line?

These three questions explore the participation framework of a public to identify the communicative nature of a new public and the potential for lurkers and posters to create and re-create publics both on- and off-line. This analysis has implications for the conceptualization of a new public, for new public-institutional interactions, and for how a new public's communicative practices can engender both visible and invisible (e.g., lurker) participation.

RELEVANCE TO PUBLIC RELATIONS

Normative conceptualizations of organizational public relations, particularly the management approaches, position the role of the public relations practitioner in a boundary-spanning role between management and publics. This implies that public relations communication is inextricably linked to communication roles and communication outcomes (see, e.g., Dozier, 1992;

Dozier & Broom, 1995, J. Grunig, 1993c; Lauzen & Dozier, 1992).

Structuration theory challenges role theory and role prescriptions at the boundaries of organization and environment because "social systems are not constitutive of roles but of (reproduced) practices, and it is practices, not roles, which (via the duality of structure) have to be regarded as the 'points of articulation' between actors and structures" (Giddens, 1979, p. 117). This proposition conceptualizes the communicative role (as opposed to the communication role addressed in Dozier, 1992, and Dozier & Broom, 1995) as a discourse-based activity in which public relations communication continues beyond the public-institutional interaction.

Public relations communication, which is subsumed by the communicative role, evolves from the ongoing production and enactment of dominant ideological meaning systems. Therefore, the communicative role and public relations communication can be seen as separate but interrelated human communication processes. This proposal is congruent with both Giddens' (1979, 1984) and Mumby's (1987, 1988, 1989) approaches to the relationship between ideology and discourse as well as with Giddens' (1984, 1993) treatment of language as situated practices in day-to-day interactions.

A public's public relations communication needs to be viewed as a series of locally situated accomplishments rather than as solely an exchange of messages or meanings. Furthermore, a public's communicative role needs to be situated as a practical achievement rather than equated with a typology of communication outcomes in the public arena. Hence, this reconceptualization aims to depict the ontological status of the new publics that are continually emerging through new communication technologies.

The everyday function of public relations requires an understanding of a public's ideological meaning systems. On-line discursive organizations are not isolated from each other or from social systems in society. They interact with others and influence each other's meaning systems. A structurationist approach to organizations, as noted by Witmer (1997), allows researchers to "focus on the ways in which organizational members recursively reproduce social structures while, at the same time, [structuration] is sensitive to the organizational/environmental interconnections that both create and are created by the organization and its members" (p. 345). Thus, a structuration analysis of new publics can help the researcher to determine a public's level of openness, its perspectives on interdependent organizations, its ideological meaning systems, the motivations that influence its production and enactment of communication, the perceived communicative constraints and enablements of its communicative role, and its possibility of creating other publics both on- and off-line. Thus the practitioner can investigate the communicative practices of new publics and generate new insights about how to better understand and segment them.

An ideology critique (Giddens, 1979) and analysis of a new public's motivations to engage in or refrain from external interactions can be conducted after the researcher explores the structures of the social system. This analysis can offer an explication of the emergence of new publics, insight into how structural properties influence the philosophical perspectives of new publics' members, and understanding of the impact of those members' external interactions and public communication efforts. This can be accomplished by addressing how members of a public perceive choices about the possible courses of action and how they view the communicative constraints and enablements of potential public-institutional interactions.

Empirical work is needed to explore the three guiding research questions described earlier. Other areas of interest include when a discursive organization becomes a new public, when a discursive organization brings a social organization into the participation framework, and the levels of interdependency between a new public and other organizations. A structuration analysis does not entail a cursory view of a new public's discourse. This chapter calls for extensive naturalistic inquiry to investigate a new public's communicative practices over time. Unfortunately, both the ethics of participant observation and the need for informed consent in on-line settings

still are being debated (see, e.g., Reid, 1996; Thomas, 1996).

On-line communication has global implications because the discourses of new publics are available worldwide and facilitate new publics' abilities to influence others, mobilize individuals to action, and create additional new publics. An analysis of new publics can provide public relations scholars and practitioners with knowledge about constitutive factors (including cognition, motivation, and meaning systems) of a new public's communication as it relates to public relations and the enactment of the public's ideological stance. This serves to enact a motivational context that provides a new public with views of the communicative constraints and opportunities associated with its communication and interactions with other organizations. Thus, there is a need for exploration of a broader participation framework in which the communicative nature of an organization influences the production and reproduction of social systems, both on- and off-line.

CONCLUSION

This chapter has presented an alternative approach to the study of social organizations in an electronic environment. An analysis of on-line communities requires a conceptualization of systems as comprised of reproduced practices. In the proposed structurationist approach, a social organization is conceived as having both visible and invisible (to the researcher) participants. To identify the emergence of new publics in an electronic environment, the public relations researcher needs to move beyond the systems approach in which a public refers to a group of individuals who emerge around a problematic situation. To be more proactive, the researcher needs to view new publics as emergent through the creation and re-creation of shared experiences that are embedded in discursive and institutional practices.

Social systems on-line have generated a new organizational environment that is comprised of an indeterminate number of new publics. A structuration analysis of the communicative practices of a discursive organization can generate knowledge about the internal dynamics of a group and members' mobilization of resources to attain a dominant ideology. A structuration approach calls for a move away from a deductive analysis of text or interactive discourse of a public because a deductive analysis serves to decontextualize the richness of discourse. The treatment of a public's day-to-day talk solely as information offers little theoretical import into how a public is mobilized or constrained. There is a need to address language (as an array of practices) in which social reality is constructed, reified, and perpetuated in a public's internal interactions.

Analysis of the dynamic nature of a new public's meaning systems over time and the micropolitics embedded in its on-line interactions can assist the public relations researcher in the development of an emic description of the new public's perspective and insight into its communicative nature. Uncensored communication over the Internet facilitates the scrutiny of what once was private discourse in everyday interactions and analysis of a new public's on-line discursive and institutional practices. This permits an examination of how ideology creates and maintains a dominant meaning system through social interaction. Because ideology serves to mobilize, sustain, and constrain a public, such analysis may help public relations researchers to discern the dominant meaning systems of a new public and the consequences of that public's practices

that have implications, both negative and positive, for the focal organization.

As noted earlier, what is rendered problematic in the public relations literature is the overemphasis on a public's actions and its disruptive nature to an organization. Analyzing the ongoing communicative practices of a social organization (typically associated with a latent, closed public, or a nonpublic) is more proactive than waiting for a group to contest issues relevant to an organization's mission as prescribed in the situational theory of publics (J. Grunig, 1989b, 1989c; J. Grunig & Repper, 1992). Publics do not have to act on issues or publicly commit themselves to problems that affect the focal organization to be granted significance in organizational public relations. It is clear that as new publics continue to proliferate, researchers and practitioners need to develop processes and methods for analyzing them.

NOTE

1. MUD is an acronym for multiuser dungeon (or multiuser dimension), which is similar to a chat room but supports role-playing activities. The first MUDs were based on adventure games such as *Dungeons and Dragons*. MOOs and MUSHes are similar. MOO stands for MUD, object oriented, and MUSH stands for multiuser shared hallucination.

2. See Stones (1991) for a discussion of a strategic context analysis as an extension to Giddens' strategic conduct analysis.

GLOBALIZING PUBLIC RELATIONS

Globalization— The Frontier of Multinationalism and Cultural Diversity

ROBERT L. HEATH

■ One of the ironies of the era of globalization is the feeling that the globe is simultaneously shrinking as it expands into an enlarging kaleidoscope of people, languages, cultures, governmental structures, and economic systems. A few years ago, the key question before most persons who thought about international public relations was whether an organization should try to hire and train people who were conversant with people in various countries or whether the better strategy was to use agencies in those countries. Today, the more compelling issue is whether a global organization (business, nonprofit, or governmental) can meet or exceed the expectations of a Babel of voices and cultures without losing its identity by trying to be everything to all markets and publics.

This section addresses some of the key issues related to international public relations. For the most part, the focus is on the multinational engaging in global activities. At first glance, the thought of the multinational brings to mind gigantic corporations, massive activist groups, and embracing governmental agencies. However, even very small organizations of these types are likely to have strategic plans that are affected by global issues and the players that drive and are driven by those issues.

Of related interest is the discussion in several chapters that feature the best practices in key countries or geographical locations around the globe. One of the themes that runs throughout the discussion is a choice between being local while acting and thinking globally and being global while acting and thinking locally.

The section begins with a solid overview by Taylor (Chapter 56). She examines the ways in which the J. Grunig-Hunt model and assumptions can be found to prevail in the practice of professionals in various countries. Research suggests that each of the four parts of the model may be emphasized or deemphasized in various countries. Additional research might suggest the variables that lead to these differential approaches to practitioner styles. In addition, Taylor reviews the best practices that differ in idiosyncratic ways across countries. Such conclusions have implications for the training and ethical acuity of practitioners who operate in a global society/marketplace and public policy arena.

In all, the future of public relations cannot escape the global influence. Theories and best practices that seem to work well in the United States might have to be reexamined and refined by international practitioners. All of this suggests that standard quandary of the academic and astute practitioner: The more we learn, the more we realize what we need to learn.

Wakefield (Chapter 57) provides research data suggesting that typical practitioners are lacking in the knowledge and skills required for effective practice in global situations. Thus, they tend to either extend what they would do on the domestic scene or see dramatic differences between their domestic practices and the mysterious challenges of globalization. Although many similarities exist between what one would do domestically and what one would do globally, the differences can make or break the ability of organizations to meet their strategic plans. The new paradigm starts with a clear and careful definition of the organization. It needs to be tailored to fit all circumstances that require its reputation and operations to meet or exceed the expectations of all who are touched by them.

How will the challenge of international practice be met by the academy? Newsom, Turk, and Kruckeberg (Chapter 58) suggest some broad areas of study that should be included in students' academic preparation. Recommended subject areas include behavioral and communication theories, mass media structures and uses, interpersonal communication systems, research methodologies, and an understanding of markets and public policy arenas. Such educational topics carry students beyond a familiarity with domestic media relations and insights into basic public relations best practices and skills that may be localized to a country. In this education, one of the most important topics that needs to be understood is culture and cultural differences. A blend of best practices, sound theory, research skills, and a profound interest in culture and cultural differences can lead students toward the levels of professional preparation that can arm them for successful careers in a global practice on behalf of organizations that operate in myriad countries. Students need not leave their domestic skills behind as they go global. By the same token, they need to realize in profound ways the differences in their practices that will result from meeting cultural differences.

To add insights into cultural differences, several chapters focus on practices that are typical of countries and regions. Motion and Leitch (Chapter 59) address practices and theory that characterize the practice in New Zealand under the influence of the Public Relations Institute of New Zealand (PRINZ). In its inception, PRINZ was influenced by the Public Relations Society of America and the International Association of Business

Communicators. Practitioners have, until recently, risen through the ranks via on-the-job experience as a substitute for academic education. That trend is changing. One of the strong influences over the practice is the marketing discipline. Challenges to the ethical side of the practice are guided by the PRINZ Code of Conduct. As is true of many other countries, the organizations based in New Zealand are challenged to practice both domestically and internationally. Both of these challenges require insights into practices and cultures that require substantial sensitivity to differences as a basis for creating harmonious relationships among organizations, publics, and markets.

China, Russia, and the United States cover a lot of territory and have substantial populations. Although their economies are quite different, their origins as modern nations share the fact that each has been shaped by the influence of activist rhetorical challenges to the establishment. This premise underpins the analysis provided by McElreath, Chen, Azarova, and Shadrova (Chapter 60). Although the marketplaces and public policy arenas are substantially different in these countries, the best practices that have been honed in the United States typically are exported to China and Russia. To explore this thesis, the authors look at parallel developments in these three countries using the J. Grunig-Hunt model as a structure and analytic point of view. As we enter the new century, public relations is emerging in China and Russia largely based on efforts to attract and shape markets. The efforts of practitioners in these countries are being strengthened by education in their schools rather than through training abroad. They are realizing the advantage of more symmetrical approaches to the practice. Balanced relationships are replacing a more manipulative top-down approach to marketplace and public policy influence.

The European Union (EU) was one of the most fascinating economic and public policy experiments during the last half of the 20th century. Miller and Schlesinger (Chapter 61) discover that one of the stumbling blocks to the development of the EU is the absence of a genuine public sphere. At the moment, public relations and lobbying are engaged in a frenzy of activities designed to shape markets and public policy decision-making principles and practices. Various countries and multinational organizations are drivers in this effort, employing some of the largest public relations firms in the world in their efforts to gain advantages. The trend at the moment is to have public relations and lobbying serve the interests of elites. The product of this trend, the authors conclude, is to create a democratic deficit that will have to be overcome before the EU is fully functioning.

Although the paradigm is to think of international as occurring in other people's countries, true globalization is based on the world as a single marketplace and public policy arena with many individual and localized opportunities for the practice of public relations. One dramatic example of that principle occurred, according to Samra (Chapter 62), as an event designed by a U.S. university to bring together key players in the Middle East controversy. Dialogue replacing monologue—that is the emerging paradigm of effective public relations. As we think of public relations as relationship building rather than as manipulation, we can appreciate the efforts that can be expended in one locale to effect changes elsewhere. The dialogue between Middle East spokespersons is one example of such dialogue.

As the daunting challenges of difference and diversity become more apparent, efforts are being undertaken to understand and develop best practices that can bridge national cultural boundaries. Markets and public policy decisions are reshaping the globe. Public relations is finding many challenges and is learning to adapt to those obstacles to bring to bear the principles that are needed to forge and sustain mutually beneficial re-lationships. That is the challenge of globalization. It is a task that calls for the best think-ing and careful strategic choices by academics and practitioners from all parts of the world. In this way, the relationship-building potential of public relations is reshaping international marketplaces and public policy forums.

56

International Public Relations

Opportunities and Challenges for the 21st Century

MAUREEN TAYLOR

■ Public relations communication with international publics is quickly becoming a reality for small and large organizations alike. As new communication technologies and the globalization of business occur, more and more public relations practitioners will need to be able to communicate to a wide array of international audiences (Epley, 1992). Although this international and intercultural communication might, at first glance, seem like a daunting task, there has been considerable research and discussion by public relations researchers to guide practitioners in this endeavor.

WHY INTERNATIONAL PUBLIC RELATIONS IS IMPORTANT

Public relations is in the business of altering or negotiating relationships between organizations and publics (Botan, 1992). Moreover, because of

the profession's research skills, public relations serves as the eyes, ears, and voice of organizations. When organizations move into the global economy, practitioners will need to adjust to see, listen, and speak to international publics. An internationalization of public relations is both an opportunity and a challenge for professionals.

The need for public relations practitioners to operate in an international context is an exciting opportunity. Because the practitioner is able to serve the organization during a time of transition and uncertainty, astute practitioners will become valuable resources for their organizations. Public relations also has opportunities to positively affect the developing nations of the world through participation in development communication (Newsom, Carrell, & Kruckeberg, 1993), nation building (Taylor, 1998), and avoiding war between states (Kunczik, 1990; Signitzer & Coombs, 1992).

Yet, for all of these opportunities, there also are many challenges ahead. Societal culture might be one of the most difficult challenges.

Sriramesh and White (1992) suggested that international public relations will have to reflect the cultural and societal norms of the host nation. This will create unique public relations situations in every society. Language probably also will present other problems. Corporate slogans, marketing, and advertising themes, and the translation of organizational materials, all will need to be checked and rechecked for international audiences. Everyone remembers the Nova manufactured by Chevrolet and its demise in South America. It is only through research and cultural awareness that this situation will not happen again. Media also will present challenges for public relations professionals because in many parts of the world governments continue to dominate media ownership and content. Thus, organizations might have to pay to have stories published, and this will change the dynamics of media relations. Finally, issues of ethics will continue to challenge public relations practitioners in the international arena. Cultural variation, different norms of conduct, and different levels of social-political development all will demand different approaches to the practice.

These opportunities and challenges will make the practice of international public relations a dynamic activity. Fortunately, a growing body of scholarship and commentary has addressed the theory and practice of international public relations. This chapter organizes this body of research into four distinct paths and shows the various opportunities and challenges that await public relations practitioners as they communicate with international publics. The first line of international public relations research that is discussed in this chapter extends the idea of public relations as a symmetrical communication activity as proposed by J. Grunig. The second trend in international research contextualizes and describes the practice of public relations in different nations of the world. A third way in which scholars have approached the study of international public relations focuses on the ethical and educational foundations of the practice. The final approach lays the groundwork for developing new theories of public relations that can transcend national boundaries. All four paths contribute to our understanding of the theories and practices of public relations.

Extensions of Symmetrical Research

The first path of international public relations scholarship can be identified as an extension of the symmetrical approach. Symmetrical communication (J. Grunig, 1989e; J. Grunig & Hunt, 1984) between an organization and its publics continues to be a concern in the field of public relations research. Several studies that focus on the international practice of public relations have attempted to extend the International Association of Business Communicators (IABC) Excellence Project (J. Grunig, 1992c) and have documented the practice of two-way symmetrical communication.

Chen (1996) conducted an exploratory study of public relations practitioners in mainland China and found that "practitioners who emphasized management roles practiced two-way symmetrical public relations" (p. 150). Continuing the IABC study, J. Grunig, L. Grunig, Sriramesh, Huang, and Lyra (1995) conducted metaresearch of previous studies that examined public relations practices in India, Greece, and Taiwan. The findings of the metaresearch analysis showed that there is "at least preliminary evidence that the models must be generic to all cultures and that an approach to public relations that contains at least elements of the two-way symmetrical model may be the most effective in all cultures" (p. 182). The role of a "cultural translator" also is becoming an important role for practitioners as they guide their organizations through the cultural variations of different nations.

The personal influence model, coined by Sriramesh (1992b, 1996), extended J. Grunig and Hunt's (1984) models. This fifth model of public relations described practitioners cultivating good relationships with external publics to restrict government regulation, secure government approval, and ensure positive press coverage. Thus, public relations practitioners perform "personal influence relations" (Sriramesh, 1992b, p. 207). Moreover, Sriramesh (1992b) noted that, in many nations in the developing world, organizations tend to ignore the attitudes of mass publics and instead focus specifically on the attitudes of journalists and government officials. Personal influence is a "pervasive public relations technique" in many nations (Sriramesh, 1996, p. 186). Practitioners traveling to countries with hierarchical cultures should keep this in mind when developing public relations strategies.

The practice of public relations in Slovenia has been studied extensively. Vercic, L. Grunig, and J. Grunig (1996) reported on the status of the IABC Excellence Project in Slovenia. The researchers found that Slovenia, like the United States, Canada, and the United Kingdom, shares similar views about excellent public relations. However, excellent public relations is not practiced as often in Slovenia as in the West. This may be attributed to the lack of practitioner involvement in strategic communication and planning.

Sriramesh, J. Grunig, and Dozier (1996) explored the relationship between organizational culture and public relations and found that organizations can be categorized by dimensions of organizational culture. A participatory culture allows organizational members to have input into organizational decision making. Alternatively, authoritarian cultures rely on tradition and use trial and error in decision making. The authors concluded that "culture is neither a necessary nor a sufficient condition of excellent public relations practice" (p. 257). Whereas an authoritarian culture may practice excellent public relations, "a participatory culture . . . provides the most nurturing environment" (p. 257) for symmetrical relationship building.

Vasquez and Taylor (1999) integrated J. Grunig and Hunt's (1984) instrument with Hofstede's cultural variables in an attempt to internationalize quantitative public relations research. Hofstede's dimensions of culture—collectivism/ individualism, masculinity/femininity, uncertainty avoidance, and power distance—offer a means to examine practices in different cultures. Other attempts to extend the discussion of symmetrical public relations include that of Signitzer and Coombs (1992), who integrated models of public relations with the models of traditional European diplomacy. Public diplomacy occurs when governments attempt to influence other nations through strategic communication efforts. Signitzer and Coombs found that "public relations and public diplomacy are in a natural process of convergence" (p. 146) and that each seeks "similar objectives and use[s] similar tools to reach those objectives" (p. 145).

The extension of symmetrical communication path of research shows us that scholars attempt to advance our knowledge of the models into the international arena. Although more evidence is needed to show that symmetrical communication occurs in other parts of the world, we know more than ever before that it is the contextual factors such as the economy and political and societal systems that play important roles in the development of public relations. The next path in international public relations research explores these factors.

Contextualized Research

A second path to studying international public relations, defined here as contextualized or comparative research, has described the practices of public relations in diverse countries around the world. A recent book edited by Culbertson and Chen (1996) offered many chapters of contextualized research. Europe is one area that was examined extensively in both the book and the field.

Hiebert (1994) explored advertising and public relations in the nation of Hungary and observed that public relations as a profession often is misinterpreted as advertising. Hiebert reported that employee relations and internal communications are becoming "even more important than public and media relations" because of cross-cultural communication problems (p. 365). According to Hiebert (1992), two change agents— new technology and public relations—are influencing the nature of public communication in former Communist states. Public relations will change much of the post-Communist world because it will allow organizations and political figures to "assess public attitudes and communicate effectively" (p. 119). In Hiebert's vision of the post-Communist world, public relations generates information through new media technologies, and this information contributes to development. Moreover, public relations will contribute directly to democratic political systems because "the more a nation has a variety of communication sources and a variety of target audiences, with developed media and responsive feedback systems, the more effective will be the communication system of the nation" (p. 125).

In another discussion of European public relations, Turk (1996) described the birth of public relations in Romania. Public relations started as a one-woman public relations, advertising, and marketing agency. Today, there are "more than 50 [agencies], most of them either local affiliates of major Western European or U.S. firms or small specialized 'boutique' firms" (pp. 342-343). Turk surveyed practitioners in Romania and found that public relations continues to reflect propagandistic practices. This can be attributed to the many years that Romania lived under communism. A second related finding shows that even though practitioners rely on persuasion to achieve goals, they seek to "develop mutual understanding between the management of the organization and the publics the organization affects" (p. 346). Although these might appear to be two contradictory goals, they no doubt reflect Romania's past experiences and future potential.

Senior practitioner and author Carole Howard offered similar comments on the practice of public relations in the post-Communist world. This region has emerging political and economic systems, and these systems often constrain the practice of public relations. Howard (1991-1992) suggested that practitioners must have a good understanding of the culture and business environment and approach public relations from a "back-to-basics" approach. That is, practitioners need to focus on research, maintaining a consistent message, and an attention to details (p. 18). Gruban (1995) further explained public relations in Central and Eastern Europe and outlined tips for practitioners including not to bribe, not to skimp on paying for quality services, and not to use émigrés as translators because their language skills might be too outdated for successful communication (p. 23).

Bentele and Peter (1996) described public relations practice in what once was known as East Germany (now part of the Federal Republic of Germany). Public relations was considered a tool of the Communist regime; therefore, it has negative connotations. Although public relations today is gaining credibility with German organizations and publics, many Germans in the eastern part of the nation consider public relations to be merely advertising/marketing. Public relations, however, is uniquely situated to help people in the eastern region to learn more about democracy, participate in government, and integrate themselves into social and economic development.

Haug and Koppang (1997) explored the proliferation of lobbying practices in Europe and noted that governments in Western European nations affect private corporations in four ways. Because of large public sector spending, the intertwine of private business and government, the enormity of red tape, and a system of government subsidies, there is a growing need for corporations to use "lobbying as a tool to gain maximum influence" (p. 238). In a study that looked closely at lobbying in Norway, Haug and Koppang found that "all companies [in the study] had lobbying efforts directed at civil servants or national politicians" (p. 238). Moreover, lobbying efforts often were conducted by both the chief executive officer (CEO) and the public relations management. Lobbying efforts were hierarchical in that the CEO would speak with high-level government officials and public relations managers were responsible for monitoring information and communicating with civil servants. Haug and Koppang's study is valuable for organizations that wish to lobby European officials because it advised organizations to send their high-level members to these important relationship-building meetings. Moreover, their study reinforces the long-held belief that public relations practitioners need to be included in the highest levels of decision making for organizations to best use their skills to guide organizational policy. Corbett (1991-1992) also discussed public relations communication in the new European Union (EU). There are multiple challenges for public relations as nations in Europe combine their economic systems. Problems that the EU might face include immigration, unemployment, and inflation. However, advantages such as the "building of new bridges to free and open communication and commerce" are exciting opportunities (p. 11).

One final study in contextualized research was by Coombs, Holladay, Hasenauer, and Signitzer (1994). The authors compared public relations practices in Austria and Norway to those in the United States. The study examined professional orientation, fulfillment, and practitioner roles and looked for cultural variation in these categories. Coombs et al. found that Austrian and Norwegian practitioners appear less interested in prestige and more focused on uncertainty avoidance. Moreover, Austrian practitioners appear to be concerned about career fulfillment and education, whereas American and Norwegian practitioners are not. The findings of this research project showed that public relations practice is influenced by cultural variation.

These studies all showed that European public relations practices will require highly skilled and adaptable practitioners. Practitioners who will operate in the European environment will have many resources to consult for guidance in public relations. Other regions of the world, however, have not been as fully explored. Indeed, the region of Africa, although larger than Europe in size and population, has been the subject of only a few articles that discuss public relations. Scholars and practitioners interested in government public relations can learn from Pratt's (1985, 1986) examination of public relations in Nigeria. Pratt studied public relations practitioners who worked in the Nigerian government and found that they contributed to Nigerian nation building.

Van Leuven and Pratt (1996) also explored public relations practices in southern Africa. Public relations practices reflect the political and economic development of the region. Although the region shows great potential, "there is little opportunity for practicing public relations in the Western sense of the term" (p. 95). Professional organizations, such as the Federation of African

Public Relations Associations, exist. But for public relations to truly develop, social, economic, and political factors must improve on the continent.

Asia is at a different level of economic and social development from Africa. Thus, many case studies and research projects have described and critiqued the practice of public relations in the region. Public relations practices in Thailand can be traced back to government efforts to "inform and educate the Thai people abut the new political system and the government's policies" (Ekachai, 1995, p. 326). Slowly, public relations professionalism and education have emerged. The dominant role behaviors of Thai practitioners fit into J. Grunig and Hunt's (1984) conception of the press agentry and public information models. Thai technicians view their job as sending out news releases, clipping news stories, and disseminating information to a target public. Using Broom's public relations roles, Ekachai (1995) found that practitioners were slowly moving toward management roles.

Beng (1994) surveyed public relations practitioners in Singapore and found that many organizations have not yet realized the value of strategic public relations. The Southeast Asian nation of Malaysia also has been the topic of much public relations research. Public relations often has been used for nation building in Malaysia. That is, public relations campaigns attempt to foster relationships between the government and the people and also attempt to build relationships between previously unrelated ethnic publics as part of the development process (Taylor, 1998; Taylor & Botan, 1997; Van Leuven, 1996). However, public relations rarely is a static activity. Public relations in Malaysia and Singapore now focuses on building markets and trade relations (Van Leuven & Pratt, 1996; Wee, Tan, & Chew, 1996). In the Philippines, public relations also is expected to help build democracy and energize people for economic and social development (Jamias, Navarro, & Tuazon, 1996).

International interest in China has generated much research into Chinese public relations. Chen and Culbertson (1992) found that the Chinese government practices two approaches to public relations: symmetric public relations and "old time propaganda, press agentry, and image building plus modern marketing strategy" (p. 36). Chen and Culbertson (1996) also interviewed Chinese female practitioners. They found that achievement of many professional, personal, and social goals rests on a concept of *gao guanxi*. This term means "establishing connections, creating obligations and favors among interactants, and enjoying privileges through relationships" (p. 280). Public relations practitioners often perform the gao guanxi role. Chen and Culbertson (1996) found that in China, female practitioners feel constrained by their role as guest relations. In Japan, female public relations practitioners experience similar obstacles (Cooper-Chen & Kaneshige, 1996).

Many organizations are reaching out to Central and South America for business opportunities. Unfortunately, nations in Central and South America have been underrepresented regions in contextualized research in international public relations. Only a few studies have explored this vast region. Gonzalez and Akel (1996) reported how public relations efforts in and around Costa Rica have helped to protect the nation's rain forests from deforestation. Public relations traditionally has been viewed as part of the political election process, yet in Costa Rica the profession benefits from a societal desire for freedom of expression, minimal government intervention, and swift economic development. In another analysis of Latin America, Luer and Tilson (1996) suggested that so long as media and commercialization continue to expand in Latin America, public relations will expand as well.

The Middle East also needs more research. Alanazi (1996) examined the evolution of public relations in Saudi Arabia and noted that public relations is greatly influenced by cultural and religious traditions. That is, because women's roles in Saudi Arabia are limited, most public relations practitioners are males. Al-Enad (1992) also explored public relations in Saudi Arabia and found that practitioners there attempt to serve the public and the organization's interests. Zaharna (1995) studied source credibility in Saudi Arabia and found that the person who delivers messages carries greater significance than what is said. In other words, organizational messages will be accepted as credible so long as credible spokespersons are behind the messages. This is important for consultants who advise Arab clients and multinationals that operate in the region.

The studies just described have shown Western scholars how social, political, and economic contexts influence the practice of public relations. The contextualized research path offers both scholars and practitioners insight into the practice of public relations in different nations and regions. Multiple challenges and opportunities exist for practitioners who will communicate with publics in these regions and for the scholars who will explore public relations practices, education, and ethics. Indeed, the education and ethical issues of public relations professionals in these nations are very important for the future development of the field. The next section explores this path in international public relations research.

Pedagogy and Ethics

A third path in the Western public relations scholarship has focused on pedagogical and ethical issues. This educational approach to international public relations has examined the various bodies of knowledge that guide practitioners in other parts of the world (Sommerness & Beaman, 1994). For example, public relations education and training in India have been explored. Newsom and Carrell (1994) reported that public relations education in India suffers from a short supply of qualified teachers. Public relations courses often are taught in "open universities" that serve office and industrial workers. One of the major causes for concern in Indian public relations education is the lack of professors' experience and exposure to communication theory and the behavioral sciences.

Ekachai and Komolsevin (1996) described public relations education in Thailand and suggested that Thai teachers develop their own texts and teaching materials so that students not only can learn about Western theories and practices but also can begin to develop a Thai approach to public relations.

Even nations in the developed world need to improve their education for public relations. Hatfield (1994) described public relations education in the United Kingdom and found that little undergraduate education in public relations exists and that formal graduate education is only a decade old. Public relations is taught through management studies in which students learn about general business curriculum because, unlike in the United States, journalism and mass communication majors do not exist.

In addition to pedagogy, ethics has been a focus in the international public relations literature. Codes of ethics for public relations communicators are a major topic in the literature, and many professional groups have them. However, Hunt and Tirpok (1993) argued for a universal code of ethics that will show external publics that communication professionals share a common standard for ethical practice. Roth, Hunt, Stravropoulos, and Babik (1996) also explored ethics and offered a set of principles for international practice of public relations. Roth et al. (1996) challenged practitioners to "review their code of ethics from the standpoint of the 'others' with whom practitioners are increasingly doing business" (p. 159). Likewise, in a long line of commentary, Kruckeberg (1989, 1993b, 1996a, 1996b) charged public relations professionals with the task of serving as cultural and ethical interpreters for corporations in the future of globalization. Kruckeberg viewed the role of practitioners as professionals who need to know their own values, belief systems, and ideologies to better serve both their own organizations and the various publics that they serve. Kruckeberg argued extensively for a universal code of public relations ethics that strives for community-building practices.

These discussions of pedagogy and ethics in international public relations not only strengthen our understanding of public relations in international settings but also strengthen our understanding of American educational and ethical issues. Indeed, without an understanding of ethics, education, and contextualized studies, international public relations theory never will grow and its practices never will evolve. Some scholars have begun the difficult task of building theory for international public relations. The next section explores how public relations theory has been advanced by exploring the presuppositions of the international practice of public relations.

Exploring Presuppositions

The final path of international public relations scholarship identified in the literature is the presupposition path. J. Grunig (1989e) argued that the field of public relations should carefully examine its presuppositions to understand where the field currently is and, more important, where it is going. The area of international public relations is not exempt from this introspection, and some scholars have looked beyond the U.S. understanding of public relations to question the assumptions underlying cross-cultural public relations theory and practices. For example, Botan (1992) discussed how culturally biased assumptions obscure how public relations can help organizations to better understand their publics. He challenged scholars and practitioners to look beyond their cultural biases to see new and useful ways in which to practice public relations. Simoes (1992) followed this path and questioned the conception of public relations as a communication and promotion function. He instead articulated a political function of public relations from a Latin American viewpoint. Whereas many scholars assume the function of public relations to be that of a relationship builder, Simoes claimed that the assumption guiding his view of public relations is conflict. Conflict as a function of public relations can "make sure that unfair policies are changed," but it also "is the loss of time and energy" (p. 194). Either way, Simoes argued that relationships between organizations and publics create political dimensions to organizational decisions.

Banks (1995) also offered scholars and practitioners suggestions for improved intercultural public relations. Banks suggested that public relations assumptions be flexible and adaptable to whatever the intercultural situation presented. Wakefield (1996) suggested that cultural, management, societal, and communication theories will help us to better understand the practice of public relations in an international context. Wakefield concluded that "new theories could incorporate available theories from other disciplines as well as from public relations" (p. 28). One example of this approach is that of Nessmann (1995), who identified the underlying assumptions of European public relations theorists and practitioners in the German-speaking countries. Nessmann found that many of the European assumptions about public relations are based on philosophers such as Sigmund Freud and Jurgen Habermas. Discussions such as Nessmann's show that examining the assumptions behind theory serves to enrich our knowledge of the underlying communicative and human relationships in the practice of public relations at home and abroad.

Wilson (1990) examined issues management and found that "the underlying assumptions, which have not yet been questioned in the literature on issues management, focus the efforts to date on corporate activities of the Western developed world" (p. 41). In response, Wilson (1996) created a matrix approach for issues analysis for international issues management. This matrix broadens issues management and ensures that corporations act with social responsibility in decision making.

The assumption of relationships between publics and organizations prompted Taylor and Kent (1999) to explore the assumption that publics, composed of regular citizens, actually have and can exert power to influence the fate of organizations. Although publics might have power in the United States and in other Western nations, Taylor and Kent found that "multiple publics may be an important part of public relations communication in the developed world, but in the developing world, specific publics such as journalists and government officials may actually be more important publics" (p. 134).

The research path that examines the presuppositions underlying public relations theory and practice is an important step toward articulating useful theories of public relations. There are many more assumptions about Western public relations that need to be explored, and no doubt the next few years will bring the field closer to the introspection it needs to better develop theories and practices for international public relations.

CONCLUSION

International public relations is having an important influence on the development of all forms of public relations practice and scholarship. As the four paths discussed in this chapter show, the reality of international public relations forces practitioners and theorists to look beyond their own assumptions, environments, legal and ethical standards, and theories. Consideration of questions such as "How will public relations be different in other parts of the world?" and "How will we have to adapt to communicate with international publics?" makes us step back and analyze the field from a more holistic perspective. Such introspection not only is good for the field but also is necessary for its further development.

Each of the four paths of research into international public relations is making important contributions to our understanding of the field. When combined together, the four paths offer a broad picture of what we know and do not know about the practice. The paths also show that successful public relations will require an understanding of theory, context, and ethics as well as a critical look at the assumptions that guide our understanding of the functions and roles of public relations.

Some tentative conclusions can be made about our knowledge of international public relations. First, the extensions of the symmetrical path remind us that the frameworks that guide evaluations of U.S. practices might not hold up in other cultures. The contextualized path shows that unique social, political, and economic factors will shape the practice of successful public relations. The pedagogy and ethics path shows that more education is needed to prepare all practitioners for ethical communication. Finally, the presuppositions path reminds us that every assumption that we make about public relations needs to be critically examined when we communicate with international publics.

The study and practice of international public relations already are shaping theory development. As Botan (1992) noted, the international turn in public relations practice can only benefit scholars and practitioners. By reflecting on our own cultural and social norms, we become more sensitive, critical, and open to new approaches. Moreover, theorists can learn about public relations development by studying nations with fledgling public relations activities. Instead of studying the development of public relations as a historical event, by looking at public relations in other nations, we can actually watch it evolve. This is an exciting opportunity.

International public relations also is shaping Western practices because it opens up new approaches and functions of public relations. Public relations for nation building and national development shows us that public relations and strategic communication no longer are merely the domain of profit-making organizations. Instead, public relations is available for any group or organization that wishes to build, alter, and maintain relationships with targeted publics.

The chapter shows that there are opportunities and challenges ahead for public relations practitioners who will communicate with international publics. Some areas of the world are very well researched (e.g., Asia, Slovenia, Europe, India, China), and this information should help practitioners, managers, and scholars to better formulate their actions in these regions. After reading these articles, public relations professionals should be able to successfully represent their organizations and strategically plan communication within these regions. Unfortunately, many regions (e.g., Latin America, the Middle East, Africa) have not yet been adequately studied. As economic and social development occurs in these regions, public relations research no doubt will follow.

Public relations will be affected by the internationalization of communication, new technologies, instantaneous communication, and international politics. All of these factors will force public relations professionals to evaluate their own assumptions and actions. Public relations no doubt will be affected by technologies and processes such as the Internet. Instantaneous communication will reduce the time that public relations professionals have to react to organizational problems and environmental disasters. Thus, new methods and specialties might emerge, and traditionally closed organizations will have to open communication with new publics to survive.

The practice of public relations in the 21st century presents both opportunities and challenges for practitioners. Increased education, cultural sensitivity, and increased professionalism are the best responses to these challenges. We still have a lot to learn about international public relations. Because public relations has the ability to build relationships, however, it no doubt will serve as an important tool for organizations in the 21st century.

Effective Public Relations in
the Multinational Organization

ROBERT I. WAKEFIELD

■ As the world careens into the 21st century, public relations people are being swept into a whole new global arena. Public relations no longer is just a domestic enterprise. With nearly 40,000 multinational entities and thousands more considering the global marketplace, the implications of the world inevitably confront all organizations—even those that do not want to "go global" but face the reality of foreign competitors in their own backyards.[1]

The convergence of financial markets, technologies, and communication is fostering unprecedented interaction between people and societies. The world becomes more and more interdependent as we seek solutions to global problems such as the environment, health, human rights, and other mutual challenges. But although the interactions of diverse cultural groups can foster harmony, they also can produce opposite effects such as more entrenched stereotypes and increased suspicions, misunderstandings, tribalism, and conflict.

All of this shows the need for better communication across cultures and, for public relations people, the need to help our organizations think and act appropriately beyond our own borders. However, little is known about how the field should address globalization. Research in this area of public relations is starkly insufficient, and most of the treatises on *international public relations* either examine public relations practices in specific countries or offer simple anecdotes that explain how certain organizations handled given situations. Precious little information exists to help multinational organizations to understand the global nature of their public relations or to guide them as they develop resources not only to get their messages out to increasingly cross-cultural publics but also to anticipate and respond to behaviors by those publics that could affect the organizations. This chapter specifically addresses the issue of effective public relations in the multinational—as opposed to the purely domestic—entity.

THE EVOLUTION OF PUBLIC RELATIONS IN MULTINATIONALS

In the past, those who operated in foreign environments relied on their own intuition. But intuition devoid of any reliable road maps can result in mistakes that "jeopardize millions of dollars" in revenues (Harris & Moran, 1991, p. 21). To avoid these calamities, international public relations people must be guided by sound knowledge about cross-cultural practice. They must know how to maintain consistent communication and protect their entities' reputations around the world. At the same time, multinationals need to understand the nuances of public relations between countries, or even in different regions within countries, and how misunderstandings of those nuances can bring problems on a global scale.

Most multinational entities have gone through evolutionary stages as they have expanded overseas (Adler, 1997). As they added a few international units, they often have tried to keep everything coordinated from headquarters. But they found this increasingly difficult to do as their geographic reach brought in more and more languages and cultures. So, most then created autonomous local units to respond to the varying sociocultural and political differences in markets. Then, as they saw the extreme costs and challenges of uniquely addressing each market, they sometimes abandoned local autonomy in favor of a least-cost (i.e., centralized) approach to getting homogeneous products to all markets.

Now there is an emerging global phase characterized by geographic reach—many corporations operate in more than 50 countries—and multiculturalism. But globalism is about philosophy more than size. As Morley (1998) said, "Becoming a global corporation requires speaking with a global voice" (p. 24). It means keeping a strong competitive advantage through innovative thinking from a multicultural employee force. In a truly global entity, headquarters and regional offices would resemble a United Nations as the best and brightest talent is drawn from anywhere in the world (Kanter, 1995).

Morley (1998) argued, however, that only a "handful of corporations" have achieved this balance to become "global in the fullest sense" (p. 24).

Unfortunately, public relations and other human elements of organizations have lagged behind as international evolution followed the bottom-line demands of markets, production, and finance. Organizations typically conducted "worldwide management of people as if neither the external economic and technological environment nor the internal structure and organization of the firm had changed" (Adler, 1997, p. 5). Such a philosophy also is apparent in the public relations programs of many multinationals as they spread throughout the world.

At the 1998 national conference of the Public Relations Society of America (PRSA), Larry Foster, long-time vice president of public relations for Johnson & Johnson, said, "Of all the areas of public relations . . ., the international sector is the most difficult to manage. It is more complex, [is] more unpredictable, and generates more risk than most domestic-based public relations" (Foster, 1999, p. 1). Then, Foster sent an ominous message to public relations officers about international practice:

> There are . . . some dark and disturbing clouds on the horizon. The darkest is the tendency of many large multinational companies to make international public relations management the victim of benign neglect.
>
> As a result of this neglect, the international public relations/public affairs function has not developed in large corporations as it should. While this may seem to bode well for the public relations agencies and consultancies that are filling the void, I believe that over the long term it can spell trouble. (p. 3)

With such an assessment, it should be no surprise that most public relations people, at least in the United States, feel unprepared to practice internationally. In a study reported in *Public Relations News,* half of all public relations officers responded that the field has insufficient expertise to conduct global programs ("International PR on Rise," 1993). In another study, three fourths of the respondents admitted that they themselves lacked the necessary competence (Fitzpatrick & Whillock, 1993). Despite this, international public relations positions often are filled by employees promoted from within the organizations (including public relations firms) who have little or no previous experience outside of their own countries.[2] No wonder they feel underqualified, as the latter study showed.

Lacking international savvy, managers usually resort to one of two approaches to international public relations. Some merely extend their domestic practices to other countries with a few minor modifications. This approach ignores the subtle factors in other cultures that mandate departures from traditional programs. The alternative is to view international public relations as so mysterious that it must be entirely separated from domestic programs (and often is placed under international marketing). When this happens, the organization loses consistency in reputation and global communication processes. Thus, both approaches are destined to fail because they misunderstand the realities of international public relations.

NEW WAYS OF THINKING REQUIRED

What public relations needs is a "paradigm shift" to reflect its emerging globalization. This change should replace the misguided choices just described with a more comprehensive integrated approach to public relations in the multinational. International practitioners should understand that it no longer is acceptable for corporations to impose their centralized mandates that do not fit local situations, as per the "think global, act local" philosophies of the recent past (Morley, 1998). On the other hand, allowing local managers free reign to conduct their affairs without central guidance or global consistencies also bodes trouble. The new paradigm ought to account for a more comprehensive approach that creates thinking and acting at both the local and global levels of the organization.

This new paradigm should bridge a seemingly contradictory reality: International public relations is essentially the same as domestic public relations but also is significantly different. This might seem confusing, but a brief explanation can clear up the apparent contradiction. And when the dual reality is understood, it becomes possible to organize a full-scale, effective public relations program within the multinational that accounts for both sides of the equation.

The remainder of this chapter sets forth a discussion on how to make public relations effective within the multinational. Through this explanation, the chapter should contribute to the literature on international public relations. It starts with a discussion of how domestic and international public relations are both similar to and different from each other.

Similarities Between Domestic and International Public Relations

There is mounting (but still inconclusive) evidence that many of the basics of public relations are more or less universal. The specific tactics certainly change from country to country, but strategic public relations seems to be valued among practitioners worldwide, at least on the surface. Some form of media relations occurs almost everywhere, as do advertising, promotionals, communication with targeted publics, issues and crisis management, and a growing amount of community relations. Often, these functions have been introduced by multinational corporations and public relations firms or by local practitioners who were educated in the United States or the United Kingdom.

Even standards of ethical conduct seem to be converging. In countries where pay-offs for publicity have been the modus operandi in the past, media and public relations people are changing ethical norms and eliminating this practice. Behavioral codes, such as the Universal Declaration of Human Rights and the International Public Relations Association's Code of Athens, are gaining acceptance. Recently, I sat in on a fascinating debate in the Baltics on the ethics of public relations in the tobacco industry. The range of opinions paralleled what could be found in the United States on the same topic.

But perhaps the greatest argument for similarity comes from why public relations exists in the first place. All entities, whether domestic or multinational, strive to preserve their reputations from internal or external threats. They all try to identify and build relationships with vital publics. They anticipate problems and seek to eliminate them or reduce the adverse effects. They want to be like Coca-Cola, whose logo is globally consistent and, for example, is recognized by 80% of all consumers in China.[3] Such goals are basic to any organization and never should be decentralized, whether domestic or international.

Differences Between Domestic and International Public Relations

At a PRSA conference a few years ago, one speaker observed, "There aren't many differences between cultures, but those differences make all the difference in the world." So it is with international public relations; it is easy to list similarities between countries—and just as easy to dismiss the differences. But organizations get into trouble by not recognizing that the international arena is exponentially more complex than domestic fronts, as Foster (1999) stated. This complexity lies both in organizations themselves and in the added cross-cultural factors of each country, most of which are human elements that can fall into the realm of public relations.

Maddox (1993) described how multinational entities differ from domestics in a way that shows implications for public relations. First, multinationals face multiple regulatory arenas governing products, language, employees, taxation, and so forth. This then affects employee relations, promotional materials, translations, claims, and other public relations activities. Second, multinationals have multicultural employee forces with diverse perspectives on work hours, use of time and space, managerial styles, and other work-related attributes. This makes internal communication much more difficult.

Externally, there are dispersed publics that often mistrust multinationals and that now can effect great global pressure through the mass media or the Internet. There also are cross-border problems, such as pollution and labor, whose resolutions require intercultural communication. All of these factors are faced by managers who might have years of experience in the domestic setting but are entirely out of their comfort zones in the international environment.

Distinctions also are seen in public relations practices between countries. For example, some countries have national communication systems, whereas others are highly local or regional. Media campaigns can be nightmarish in India, which has more than a dozen official languages. In Romania, typical public relations can be interpreted as "relations with the public," which parallels customer relations or "the ombudsman." Practicing public relations in Brazil requires a license, but to obtain publicity one needs a journalist's license. Even practice in Canada can be hazardous if one is not sensitive to the cultural and legal ramifications of the volatile "French" situation.[4] For these and other reasons, senior practitioner John Reed advocated a "first rule" of international public relations: "Get responsible local help" (Reed, 1999, p. 31).

A Comprehensive Approach for Balancing Global and Local

It seems possible, then, to reconcile the apparent contradiction that international and domestic public relations are both similar and different. All public relations should exist to preserve a consistent reputation and build relationships. These overall goals should be similar throughout the world, but they can be fulfilled in different ways from one culture to the next. Achieving these goals is much more difficult in the global arena due to cultural and language differences, regulatory environments, political and economic systems, media, and other local variables that must be considered. But with the proper organizational thinking, it is possible to respond to all of these factors while at the same time preserving the local and global mandates.

Adler (1997) said that multinationals finally are casting off domestic myopia: "Rather than global management being a subset of traditional domestic management approaches, single-culture, domestic management has become a limited subset of global, cross-cultural management" (p. 10). In other words, organizations finally are creating structures in which global imperatives supersede the "domestic first, international second" mentalities of the past.

This is the aforementioned "paradigm shift" that should be occurring in public relations: The global should become the strategic umbrella by which all domestic programs are carried out. Managers should eschew notions that international work is just an extension of the domestic traditions or that international public relations is so different that it must be a completely separate operation. But to date, such global vision occurs in just a few of the major entities while the rest struggle to put together less visionary programs that they think will work.

EFFECTIVE PUBLIC RELATIONS IN THE MULTINATIONAL

When talking about international public relations, there is no one best prescription. All multinational entities work in the same global arena, but each has its unique traits and challenges. For example, a few corporations are huge and dispersed, whereas others are in relatively few countries. Many are product oriented, whereas others are in the service mode. Companies in the heavy manufacturing industries can face significantly more activism than can those in technology.

Despite these differences, I believe that certain minimum standards must exist within any multinational organization for it to be effective in its public relations. Therefore, the remaining paragraphs risk proposing some of these minimum standards. Some managers might say that the guidelines do not apply to their organizations, but nevertheless, the suggestions that follow should offer possible foundations and road maps to start taking international practitioners

beyond the dangerous realm of intuition. So, in general, what comprises effective public relations in the multinational entity? Following are some suggestions.

Balancing the Global and the Local

The majority of organizations still struggle with "either/or" mentalities about international management. They give their host offices significant autonomy to handle the local mores, or they peddle their one-size-fits-all products and management concepts. With either mode of thinking, public relations can suffer. In the first case, senior local managers assume complete authority over all host country activities including public relations, even though they most likely know nothing about public relations. In the other case, strong central policies tend to destroy local flexibility and can be so marketing driven that public relations is reduced to mere promotional support.[5] Unfortunately, there are numerous horror stories of entities that have tipped the balance and lost their markets through either neglect or rebellion (Wakefield, 1997, pp. 25-27).

To be effective, public relations must retain a broad base in the multinational, identifying and communicating with all critical publics and not just consumers. It also must balance this global function with local strategies that address local demands. But why should these decisions be left to international marketing managers or local senior executives who do not understand public relations? The people who can make the best decisions on the correlation of global and local public relations are those who are genuinely qualified to practice it at both levels.

Public Relations in One Unit

In a groundbreaking study, *integration* was identified as critical to effective public relations (J. Grunig, 1992c). Instead of splitting into various units of the organization, public relations is more valuable when it is in a single coordinated department. Then, the function can strategically build communication and preserve the reputation for the entire entity rather than satisfying the diverse, and often contradictory, whims of managers in separate divisions.

What holds domestically is even more important in the multinational; effective public relations combines the best domestic and international programs in one unified worldwide function. Practitioners with international expertise should be retained both globally and locally, and they should work closely together. When they understand the global nature of reputation, communication, and activism, they will anticipate and respond to opportunities and challenges anywhere in the world. They will create global strategies to preserve the entity's reputation, to retain consistent messages and identity, and to anticipate and handle problems that might cross borders. The competent people in each country will operate effectively within the local cultural context and will maintain constant feedback and idea exchange loops for the broader unit (for a more complete listing of possible central and local responsibilities, see Table 57.1).

How is this integration reconciled with host country executives who insist on local control? Barbara Burns, a past chair of the Public Relations Society of America's International Section who has practiced internationally for more than 20 years, has suggested *dual responsibility* (personal communication, March 1995). In this arrangement, local practitioners are able to work closely with their country managers, advising them on public issues and carrying out programs in their own markets. But they also serve on this macro public relations team, where they monitor and provide grassroots input on issues, share ideas, and help to solve public relations problems on a global scale.

Horizontal and Team-Oriented Structure

Successful public relations in the multinational is not "top-down." For years, the axiom has been "think global, act local." This recognizes global imperatives and local sensitivities but also implies headquarters strategy and host country implementation—as if the local unit cannot do anything until it receives marching orders. But what if local factors require distinct strategies? These should be encouraged so long as they do not conflict with the overall mission of the organization. And what if problems cross borders? Headquarters had better act, not just think. The phrase also suggests that only headquarters people are able to think—that no matter how bright the local forces might be, they cannot benefit the overall planning and problem-solving processes. Such a situation creates an unfortunate waste of talent.

Morley (1998) proposed the alternative stance of "think local, act global" (p. 32). As such, entities can avoid perceptions of "imperialism" and address the reality that, in the end, "all public relations is local." When local units can think and not just act, they become free to effectively satisfy "local history, customs, rituals, taboos, and prejudices" (p. 33).

Morley (1998) was on the right path, but he did not fully explain "acting global." It means that the entity anticipates and is prepared to respond quickly to problems that can cross borders. And although messages must be written specifically for each local public, they should not contradict global themes. Therefore, if a corporation values human rights, then its local unit should not say that labor unions are harmful or that the homeless people outside the plant are a menace and must be hauled away. To build and protect corporate reputation globally, these instances require a transnational vision from someone who is capable of holistic thinking and whose interests (or paychecks) are not exclusively local.

Global public relations, then, is best executed as a cross-cultural international team. The team functions laterally, and everyone has a strategic role in executing the public relations mission. Central officers interact with senior executives to understand and influence the entity's strategic actions. They also communicate corporate goals to their public relations team. Local officers on the team provide constant feedback to help corporate executives stay abreast of their environment worldwide. They also work with their own local executives to satisfy stakeholder

TABLE 57.1

Balance of Global and Local Functions

Activities at Headquarters	*Activities in Host Countries*
▯ Work with senior executives to ensure that they value two-way communication.	▯ Set up and carry out local public relations programs that are appropriate for the value systems and logistics of the specific country.
▯ Advise senior executives on all global business decisions that have public relations implications and carry out public relations goals in compliance with corporate mission.	▯ Ensure that local activities do not directly contradict global goals.
▯ Work with senior executives to ensure that public relations is integrated worldwide.	▯ Establish local research mechanisms to identify publics and monitor potential local issues.
▯ Ensure that all local public relations officers work closely with their local executives.	▯ Adapt messages from headquarters into appropriate local messages.
▯ Conduct training for all line managers so that they can understand global reputation and support integrated public relations.	▯ Advise local senior executive on business decisions that have public relations implications.
▯ Establish broad but flexible guidelines on public relations activities and opinion research.	▯ Help train local senior executive to understand goals and missions of public relations and to effectively represent the entity in the host country (with media and other important publics).
▯ Establish and implement public relations training for all public relations officers worldwide.	▯ Participate on the global public relations team by providing feedback on local issues and helping to exchange ideas and solve potential transnational problems.
▯ Foster teamwork, information sharing, and idea exchange processes among members of global public relations team.	
▯ Work with global team and senior line executives to build issues anticipation and crisis communication procedures.	
▯ Establish and monitor accountability programs for global public relations unit.	
▯ Ensure that global guidelines allow for important local flexibility.	

expectations while reinforcing the corporate mission and communication needs. When issues threaten to transcend borders, the team members work together to monitor and resolve the issues if necessary. Such a structure might best be described by the more comprehensive philosophy, "think global *and* local, act global *and* local."

Team Leader, Not Manager

No one in this system has a monopoly on knowledge, and no authoritative manager is dictating procedures. Rather, there is a team leader who can communicate global perspectives and is capable of building essential camaraderie among team members. In other domains, such a person has been called a *cultural integrator* (Maddox, 1993). Kanter (1995) said that integrators "have the vision, skills, and resources to form networks that extend beyond the home base." They "can see beyond obvious differences among countries and cultures . . ., resolve conflicts among local ways, and . . . bring the best from one place to another" (p. 88). Kanter certainly did not have public relations in mind, but this statement could apply well to a qualified team leader in a global public relations program.

Consideration of Agencies

Most multinational entities eventually consider whether to use public relations firms and, if they do, what types best fit their needs. A thorough discussion of this topic cannot possibly be provided here, but some basic questions can be contemplated. The main issue is whether to hire external resources on a global, regional, or local basis. If the need is worldwide, then it is typical to select a global firm (e.g., Burson-Marsteller, Edelman) that owns offices in dozens of countries or a global agency network (e.g., Pinnacle, Worldcom) that connects independent agencies around the world.

Whatever choice is made, the multinational always should control its global public relations programs internally with someone who has daily access to top management and can stay abreast of constant changes within the organization that require public relations decisions or counsel. This senior public relations person should work closely with the public relations agency but should not abdicate control to that outside resource.

A 1998 study found that 44% of multinationals organize their own local resources.[6] These networks created by the multinationals can include internal staff, local agencies, or both. In larger and more profitable markets, it makes sense to hire an internal staff that can devote full-time energies to the organization. Still, the local office may retain an outside firm to help with major promotional events, crisis communication, and other projects that might overly stretch the capabilities of the internal staff. In smaller markets, it might be more appropriate to retain an outside agency than to have a full-time staff. In this case, the decision is whether to use an affiliate of a global firm or network or to use an independent local firm that is not affiliated with a larger entity. But whether inside or outside of the organization, the local resource should be part of the global public relations team discussed earlier.

CONCLUSION

As should now be apparent, there are many challenges in creating effective public relations for the multinational entity. Those just listed really are just a few of the major organizational challenges. It is not as easy as extending traditional domestic activities into the global realm. To be effective as described, multinational public relations presupposes qualified personnel. A team leader should be well versed in international issues and events, skilled in cultural integration, and knowledgeable about public relations strategizing. Local officers should be experienced in local public relations and also able to make valuable contributions to the overall strategies of a global public relations unit.

In today's real world, such an ideal program is a stretch for most companies. As was shown earlier, the majority of practitioners in the United States view international public relations as somewhat mysterious and feel unprepared to practice in this arena. So, there still is much work to do. More studies are needed to determine principles of effectiveness, both globally and country by country. We must identify what comprises effective training for those who will practice in the global context. And more and better examples of how organizations successfully balance their global and local imperatives are needed.

NOTES

1. A 1993 U.N. investment report estimated a total of 37,000 multinationals. The Foreign

Trade Council said that 80% of U.S. firms face foreign competition domestically (cited in Adler, 1997).

2. This is based on my discussions with several headhunters and global public relations officers.

3. This is according to a recent survey by the Gallup Organization ("Business Is Far From Spotlight," 1998).

4. All of these examples are based on my personal conversations with numerous practitioners and scholars in each of the countries cited.

5. In a 1998 visit to Romania, I reviewed a global guidebook that all public relations people in a huge multinational were required to follow. It covered every imaginable contingency in 100-plus pages, but it addressed only one stakeholder group—consumers. There was no recognition that government, media, activists, competitors, and other potential stakeholders were important.

6. Laura Ralstin, while a Ph.D. candidate at the University of Alabama, surveyed 50 global public relations managers on several issues. Along with those who create their own networks, 15% said they use global firms and 22% said they use agency networks.

International Public Relations

A Focus on Pedagogy

DOUG NEWSOM

JUDY VANSLYKE TURK

DEAN KRUCKEBERG

Public relations now is being taught world-wide, and increasingly so in universities. Yet, what is this subject? Is it an art, a craft, or a social science? Is it pre-professional in nature, or does it require professional training? Uncertainty about public relations as an area of study has had much to do with the many variations of its practice that have grown up in all sorts of ways throughout the world.

Despite the ubiquity of public relations practice, there still is debate about what public relations people do—a legacy of how public relations evolved into today's practice from propaganda, promotion, publicity, and press agentry. In addition, defining and describing the practice of public relations is complicated because many techniques and tactics are confused with the modern role of public relations practitioners as counselors and strategists. Yet, as people are hired the world over to fulfill a public relations function, there are expectations about their role and function. Where confusion exists regarding the role and function of public relations, misunderstandings doom the public relations practitioner to failure.

Yet, a lack of understanding about public relations—what it is and what it does—has not slowed the demand for public relations education through university courses, public relations professional associations' certification programs, and workshops that are being taught throughout the world by both educators and practitioners (McDermott, 1991, 1998). Public relations educators also are being approached with requests for international consulting and speaking engagements. Students and practitioners are studying abroad and practicing abroad.

The pedagogical demands of teaching public relations internationally require that public relations practitioners and educators consider the following criteria for a profession: an international body of knowledge, standards for entry into the field, shared ethical values of practitioners, professional competencies that can be taught at different levels, and a foundation of knowledge that gives practitioners a reason to turn to universities for continuing education in the same tradition of the professions of law and medicine.

There is no denying the need for basic skills, but these are much broader than the publicity and promotion skills that once were viewed as synonymous with public relations. Today's global environment demands a greater sensitivity to cultural nuances, especially considering that public relations efforts for even a local market can have an international impact. Regardless of how many basic communication skills are needed to execute tactics, today's public relations practitioners spend more of their time developing strategies.

Practitioners are working closely with their organizations and publics as well as with markets so that management can achieve its goals with the permission and support—or at least the understanding—of every organizational stakeholder. Public relations persons also are responsible for helping to resolve issues before they become crises. This suggests that public relations education must include a knowledge of, and an appreciation for, diverse socioeconomic and political systems as well as an understanding of the impact that these systems have on cultures and on media that are used to communicate in these cultures. Fortunately, a body of knowledge exists to guide the teaching of public relations in an international environment, even though this knowledge has not been codified.

The purpose of this chapter is to argue for global adoption in teaching of a topical body of knowledge, a topical syllabus, a recognition of cultural-government-media differences, and a research agenda by academics and practitioners that examines research needs created by the global environment and a testing of traditional and new research methods to cope with different infrastructures.

A TOPICAL BODY OF KNOWLEDGE

What might have been a formidable task in the past—access to common knowledge by teachers and students of public relations throughout the world—is being facilitated by the Internet. Although many important early public relations documents still must be added, more than enough current material is available to be categorized on-line from journals and international conferences.

This internationalized body of knowledge needs no editor or gatekeeper. Teachers and students simply need good computer search engines and basic archival research skills. However, what is needed is the commitment of public relations practitioners and educators to share information by placing these materials on-line.

Previous efforts to establish a printed body of knowledge have been unsuccessful. Two organizations, the Public Relations Society of America and the International Public Relations Association, have made extraordinary efforts to codify the body of knowledge that is essential to the professional practice of public relations.[1] Just keeping up with all of the materials is a massive undertaking. Furthermore, the politics of choosing what goes in and what does not is formidable. Finally, awareness and availability of the resulting annotated bibliographies have been limited.

A better approach would be the designation of subject areas that are essential to public relations so that these could form the general guides for Internet searches. Drawing from previous categories, the following seem to be logical choices: behavioral and communication theories (across social science disciplines and countries), mass media structures and uses (internationally, which would incorporate folk media as well as government-run media systems), interpersonal communication systems (with an emphasis on international and cultural differences), research methodologies (primarily from the social sciences but also including marketing and polling applications), management techniques and strategies (for all types of organizations across a range of international settings), markets—business and consumer (global financial markets and international companies as well as literature about the cultural impact of business on people and nation-states), imaging (public perceptions of products, organizations, situations, and individuals), and crises (perceptions of crises by international audiences, using a matrix to categorize crises as violent or nonviolent and as whether they are acts of nature or human acts that are either intentional or accidental).

A TOPICAL SYLLABUS

Like the topical body of knowledge, the development of a useful worldwide topical syllabus must result in an outline that lends itself to adaptation to and explication of specific circumstances without diluting the specific areas that must be covered:

- ▢ definitions of public relations and explanations of its use;
- ▢ public relations' management role and its strategic communication functions;
- ▢ the environment for public relations practice in terms of socioeconomic, political, and cultural characteristics; and
- ▢ the expectations of public relations efforts and the measurement of outcomes.

Although both broad and general, these topics would allow discussion of critical subtopics under each category such as research for planning, issues monitoring, and counseling under the management topic as well as discussion of all types of internal and external communication under the strategic communication functions topic. Also, the environment topic would allow discussion of ethical and legal issues as well as particulars such as campaigns and cases. Discussion of the behavioral changes that public relations can effect would demonstrate how the practice has evolved and expanded from simple media relations as well as how public relations can document its value to management.

Although theory can and should undergird each of these areas, there is a risk in attempting to apply to international situations the communication theories that arise from either one national environment (e.g., the United States) or one generalized experience (e.g., Western nations). A fundamental reason for a culturally specific body of knowledge is the ability to access theory from other countries as well as from a variety of disciplines such as anthropology, sociology, and psychology (Pavlik, 1987). Also, theories can be built from descriptions of public relations in various countries using "thick description" (Geertz, 1973).

Despite the ability to build generalizable theory by incorporating multiple cultures and disciplines, differences among cultures must be addressed. What works in one country might not work well in another country because of national culture, political and economic infrastructure, media systems, and research protocols. Suggestions for acclimatizing public relations practitioners to these differences follow.

CONSIDERATION OF CULTURAL DIFFERENCES

Cultural differences have to be addressed on two levels (Hall, 1995). The first is organizational; even across national boundaries, certain organizational types and structures share an identifiable culture. The second type of cultural difference is national and individual; people in one nation individually and collectively share a culture different from that of people in another country. Both differences are critical to understanding the environment in which public relations is practiced.

All organizations function along a spectrum of open to closed communication. One of the most striking features of organizational culture is the prevailing communication system. The more closed a system is, the more likely it is that communication is top-down and that the system takes a management-by-objectives approach. The more open a system is, the more participative it is and the more likely that it is aligned with total quality management principles.

ORGANIZATIONAL CULTURES AND INDIVIDUALS

In addition to having a distinct communication style, each organization has a cultural style. Four basic cultural styles were identified by Hall (1995): low assertive/low responsive, low assertive/high responsive, high assertive/high responsive, and high assertive/low responsive (p. 75).

When the culture is low assertive/low responsive, the organization's approach is methodical, precise, cautious, factual, and quantitative. When the culture is low assertive/high responsive, harmony is valued, the environment is loyal and trusting, and there is room for compromise. When the culture is high responsive/high assertive, the culture is individualist, quick moving, unpredictable, challenging, and quick changing. When the culture is high assertive/low responsive, the culture is task oriented, authoritarian, demanding, and pushy, with a controlling attitude (p. 58). Implicit in these descriptors are values because certain types of behavior and work outcomes are more valued in one organizational culture than in another. Awareness of these values creates some assumptions on the part of employees, affecting their behavior (Fisher, 1993, p. 51).

The culture usually is maintained by the employer, which chooses people who "fit" the culture, and also by employees, who are likely to choose to work in an organization in which they feel comfortable. Individual styles fit the organizational cultural descriptors. For example, in the low assertive/low responsive culture, individuals are analytical; in the high assertive/high responsive culture, they are expressive; in the low assertive/high responsive culture, they are amiable; and in the high assertive/low responsive culture, they are drivers (Hall, 1995, p. 101).

The organization often maintains a corporate culture for many years. One event that can change a corporate culture is selection of a new management team that imposes a new culture and that recruits or transfers into the organization individuals who are a good fit. Others from the "old culture" often resign or are let go. Mergers and acquisitions also lead to change and make for troublesome adjustments when a dominant culture emerges in which not everyone is comfortable.

When companies move beyond their geographic borders, their organizational cultures go with them. Depending on similarities between old and new environments, situations are likely to occur in which the organizations' home cultures clash with those of their new geographic regions. If adjustments are not made, the organizations usually are not successful in maintaining the locations.

NATIONAL AND REGIONAL CULTURES

Culture clashes occur because national and regional patterns usually do not change, at least not rapidly. When changes do occur, they are throughout an extended period, even centuries. Although some researchers have used the same descriptors as cited earlier to delineate national cultures, most researchers find few truly national characteristics but many regional eccentricities (Chen, 1996, p. 124).

A good example for someone who knows the United States would be to compare the states of Texas and New York. In India, one could compare the cities of Bangalore and Madras or could compare either of those to New Delhi. In Japan, one could look at the differences between the cities of Tokyo and Kyoto. In China, one could compare the cities of Beijing with Nanjing. These metropolitan areas, although in the same nations, are strikingly dissimilar. Furthermore, whether the nations are small or large, these differences are more than just the differences between rural and urban areas. In fact, regions in different countries might resemble each other more than they do other regions in their own countries.

Culture and tradition impose a style of communication and result in certain types of behavior ("Being Global," 1997). Traditions are rooted in values. These traditions have a strong impact on ethical issues, which figure significantly in communication and in other aspects of business (Culbertson & Chen, 1996). For example, a tradition of discrimination is a major factor in communication patterns, whether it is based on gender, social class, religion, or race. Also influencing culture are attitudes toward women or toward people of a race or religion different from the dominant one. This also is true of the treatment of social classes or of people in linguistic groups different from the dominant one; the way in which children are regarded and their role in the workplace, and the way in which animals are treated, can have significant implications for communication in particular cultures.

Another area in which values differ from culture to culture is how people are compensated for their services beyond payment for costs. A simple example is the practice of tipping people who perform services. In some countries, tipping might be considered an insult. Companies, especially those in service industries such as hotels and restaurants, have to adjust wages and employee benefits to compensate for these differences when their businesses cross borders.

Advance payment in anticipation of services occurs in many business situations, but usually early payment is a part of the stated cost for a purchase or repair. However, there is an unstated custom in some cultures that a gratuity is required before taking delivery on a purchase or service. Some countries (e.g., the United States) would call this a "bribe" and might outlaw it. In other countries, such a gratuity is so common that it is simply seen as an ethical part of doing business.

The nuances of a culture are an important part of building relationships. Public relations practitioners must understand and appreciate cultural differences and be responsive to them. Teaching students how to discover and appreciate these differences and to use that information in practicing public relations is critical.

GOVERNMENT ORGANIZATION AND THE ECONOMICS AND POLITICS OF PUBLIC RELATIONS PRACTICE

Understanding a nation's government is the linchpin for grasping both its economic and political structures. The key word is *understanding*. A democracy is not the same form of government everywhere. For example, one could look at Canada, the United States, and Australia. All three are democracies using a federal system, but they are quite different in the ways in which the three governments are organized. One could

compare these countries to India, also a democracy but one that uses a quasi-federal system like that of Germany, or to the governments of Great Britain, Italy, and France. The differences are in the distribution of power.

The source of power is fairly clear in military governments as well as in religious states, although the latter can change as various factions rise to power. Most nations have documents, usually called constitutions, defining the distribution of power, although such is not always the case in religious states. However, many aspects of a constitution can be unwritten, as is the case with Great Britain. Furthermore, even written constitutional provisions sometimes are ignored, for example, "freedom of speech" in some totalitarian regimes.

Public relations practitioners need to know who has the power to do what under which circumstances. Knowing how and where laws are made and being enforced is essential if an organization expects to function within a country's borders.

Laws also affect the economics of a nation. Who owns what and how that ownership is acquired and maintained are essential bits of knowledge. For example, can non-nationals buy property and own it with a legal deed? Can people essentially take ownership of private property simply by settling on it? Who hires and fires safety officers (e.g., firefighters, police officers) and maintains community services? What social benefits (e.g., medical care, education) are open to anyone living in the country? How are personal communication tools (e.g., telephones, computers) owned and regulated?

Public relations practitioners must understand both the public and private sectors of the countries with which their organizations might become involved, for example, nations that are changing from having pervasive government economic controls to market economies in which whole segments of the economies are being privatized.

Public relations practitioners often overlook government control over media (Merrill, 1995). Control is direct when the government owns and operates some media and might not allow competition ("Press Freedom," 1997). Control is indirect when the government has a firm hand on media economics such as allotments of newsprint, assignment of airwaves, and placement of government advertising. To stay out of trouble and realize opportunities, internationally educated practitioners have to understand the ways in which governments control what happens within their borders.

A VIEW OF DIFFERENT MEDIA (MASS AND SPECIALIZED), THEIR CULTURAL USE, AND THEIR EFFECTIVENESS

Just because mass media may be easily recognized does not mean that one medium is like others in its general category. For example, in some countries, political parties own many newspapers while governments own still others, making it difficult to generalize from one newspaper to another. Also, governments or religious groups, not private individuals or corporations, own some news-gathering organizations. This is not to denigrate any form of ownership but merely to emphasize that knowledge, not assumptions, must govern judgment in using media as sources and disseminators of information.

Specialized media are equally diverse. They can be special interest publications or media that are used only by members of certain groups such as trade associations, specific industries, and activist groups. Media that are limited to organizations' employees or other special publics are other examples, and they may take many forms—anything and everything from intranets, to closed-circuit television, to publications.

What public relations practitioners must understand is that any of these, even those intended for internal audiences, can "go global" at any time. Cultural awareness and political savvy must be considered when preparing everything from annual reports to an e-mail messages. The way in which an organization presents itself often influences or affects how other media—mass or specialized—mirror that organization, resulting in either a reasonably faithful image or a

gross distortion. This understanding goes beyond the tactics of media relations to the broader strategy of counseling management and planning. It requires a thorough knowledge of how an organization's message presents itself and how it is likely to be reflected in the opinions of different publics including a media public.

When a public relations practitioner is using media systems for an organization's purposes, it helps to know that many countries use nontraditional media to communicate. (This does not mean indigenous-language mass media. Mass media in the languages of subgroups still are part of a nation's mass media spectrum. Some of these indigenous-language print and broadcast media may be identified as specialized because they are the products of religious groups. Nevertheless, they are easily recognized as mainstream media.) In some nations, especially in developing countries where a multiplicity of languages and dialects is a problem, nontraditional media are used. An example is India, where performances of plays or puppet shows in some areas are used to inform as well as to entertain. Many countries that are considerably less developed than India use other types of performances to communicate such as songs and dances.

Creative use of media always is a challenge. In some cases, the more nontraditional the media are, the more difficult it is to measure impact. An international practitioner must be educated to develop a system for determining the effectiveness of folk media as well as traditional media.

RESEARCH CHALLENGES FOR INTERNATIONAL PUBLIC RELATIONS EDUCATION

Preparing public relations practitioners for the research needs that they will encounter in an international environment means making them aware of the accessibility and reliability of secondary information and the political implications of that information. Furthermore, the primary research skills that most U.S.-educated students possess might or might not work elsewhere because of these countries' limitations in infrastructure and differences of culture. Yet, the demand for research in international settings is increasing (Synnott & McKie, 1997, pp. 280-282).

Secondary Information

Gathering basic background data on a population in the United States is relatively easy because so much information exists in libraries including public databases such as census reports and several institutions' published polling data. In addition, there is little difficulty in supplementing published materials with reliable information that is available electronically, although some electronic data might be available only by subscription to on-line publications such as the on-line *Wall Street Journal.* Nevertheless, the information is there, and its reliability is reasonably good, at least when facts are triangulated (i.e., checked against at least two other sources) so that there is some confirmation of accuracy.

Information about other countries also is available in data banks, but it is important to know how this information was gathered. Some countries believe that they are politically vulnerable concerning statistical data describing their populations such as life expectancy, annual income, and other demographic data that might put these countries in an unfavorable light. Sometimes, it is difficult to locate reliable sources for accurate data in these countries, and it is even more difficult to get access to this information. And if a government objects to that type of research, then an unpleasant situation could develop from seemingly innocuous data gathering.

Obtaining current information from secondary sources seems more difficult than gathering historical secondary information, which might appear to be more accessible. Perhaps there are fewer political consequences for making historical information public. However, government structure is a major factor in obtaining secondary information, whether historical or current. Some governments require all sorts of documentation concerning the intended use of

such information before releasing it. Others are quite open and regularly publish information or freely relinquish it to researchers. Occasionally, information retrieval means just knowing where to look and not giving up easily. One Asian country prided itself on its democratic structure, but obtaining simple statistics from bureaucrats was a daunting challenge. However, a local librarian was an excellent source. The information that was sought actually was publicly available, but the bureaucrats either did not know that or did not want to be identified as the ones who had released the information.

The lesson to be taught in public relations education is this: Do not take gathering secondary information for granted. The information might not be available. Even when it is available, such information might not be accurate, having been adjusted to ensure a better image of the country.

Primary Research

As mentioned earlier, both infrastructure and culture can be major obstacles to conducting primary research. A government simply might not permit research that it has not initiated. Furthermore, in some countries where there have been political upheavals or religious conflicts, many people are uncomfortable responding to phone interviews or to completing questionnaires. There is some uncertainty about who will have access to this information and what the consequences might be. This is true even when the research focus seemingly is innocuous such as surveys about use of media or products.

Infrastructure problems include some resources that researchers in the United States take for granted such as reasonably reliable telephone and mail address directories. In many countries, these simply do not exist. Even when they do exist, they might not be accurate or up-to-date. In one country where obtaining a phone line requires a wait of 1 year or more, people simply use the phone lines that were in the residences or offices before they moved in. So, looking for such a person's name is useless unless you know the name of the former resident under which the phone line had been contracted. Business lines are almost as bad as residential lines in this regard. Also, in some countries where getting a phone line is difficult, people simply use cell phones. Getting those numbers from a source other than the user is a challenge. What all this means is that randomly selected telephone interviews or mailings probably will not work.

In most countries where these problems exist, researchers resort to cluster interviews of samples chosen by city blocks or land areas. However, in some cities, local maps are not available. Cities with considerable tourist trade might have maps, but these usually are promotional maps with most streets missing. Of course, cities do have maps in their municipal planning offices, but getting these is time-consuming at best. One municipal official told a researcher that municipal maps were available only to police, fire, and other emergency personnel because of the possibility that bombs could be planted in various places. (No maps were available to nonviolent researchers.)

Cultural differences also can create difficulties in gaining access to some populations and in phrasing questions that are socially and politically acceptable. Even getting permission to ask the questions is problematic, especially in governments that are highly sensitive to criticism.

Access problems occur in countries where women are not allowed unrestricted contact with the outside world. An advertising agency trying to get information about a product for women found access to the product's users barred because of cultural barriers. In another less restrictive situation where a woman was permitted to be interviewed so long as a male member of the household was present, the woman was not allowed to answer the questions. The male answered the questions for her.

Another often inaccessible group is children. Even where polling is accepted in a culture, efforts are made to keep children away from researchers by limiting access in schools and requiring parental consent for interviewing. In many countries, children simply are not available except for street children or perhaps working children who might be accessible through their employers.

Language and literacy levels also might be barriers. If the interviewer or the questionnaire does not use the language of the respondent, then distortions can occur. Translators must be able to convey the intent of the questions, which might not be literal translations. The same is true of questionnaires that have been translated. Questionnaires always should be pretested by someone fluent in the languages of both the questioner and the respondent.

Misunderstood or misinterpreted questions can result in more than unreliable answers. A misstated question can incur hostility and possible government intervention if enough people get upset. Some of the most sensitive questions concern personal or political matters. An example is a drug company that tried to discover how many women knew about the company's birth control pills. The questions had to be revised many times to elicit information without offending. (And this was in a country whose government supports birth control.) Some religious governments might not even permit that type of questioning, even though the drug might be available to citizens.

Another cultural difficulty can occur when local interviewers are hired to perform research. In some countries, the social class or religion of the interviewers might impede the process. Interviewers might be uncomfortable talking to those in lower classes or from different religious groups. In addition, the interviewees might not be willing to talk to the researchers. Structuring this type of research means being sensitive to situations where one or both would be uncomfortable or inaccessible or where the answers would be unreliable because of social dynamics.

Traditionally, survey respondents are asked whether they want to see the results of the study, which is a type of compensation for their participation. In some international settings, getting a copy of results might jeopardize a person's social, religious, or political situation. An example is a Christian who had been interviewed at church and who received survey results at home in a largely non-Christian village where there was little privacy. Although she was an acknowledged member of a minority-faith community, recognition that she had given "voice" to her beliefs on related issues created serious problems for her in the community.

A more likely scenario would be action taken against the researcher if the government or those in the dominant faith in the community take exception to the published results. Some international scholars have great difficulty in obtaining permission from governments to perform research because published findings in the past have been unflattering. And if the government is the faith community, then this can be quite serious because religious law—not civil law—is the law of the land.

This is not to say that research cannot be done in some countries or cultures. But in their curricula, educators must alert researchers to the problems that are likely to arise.

CONTINUING EDUCATION FOR PUBLIC RELATIONS

Any number of professionals, such as certified public accountants, physicians, and lawyers, have returned to universities for continuing education classes and seminars. They expect to put cutting-edge knowledge that they have learned to immediate use in their practices. How many public relations practitioners return to universities for such updating? In fact, recent college graduates in public relations often find that practitioners are using archaic practices because they have not pursued continuing education.

Partly as a result of this deficiency, many public relations practitioners have limited knowledge of strategic planning other than what they might have acquired on the job. Why is that? Universities are not being tapped as a source of cutting-edge research and applicable information for practitioners, many of whom never have enrolled in a public relations course. (And some practitioners say this with pride.)

Many agencies/firms provide on-site learning experiences for their employees because they do not have confidence in universities and because on-site education is in some ways easier to finance and control. Large agencies/firms can gather their employees from offices throughout the world to be taught by internationally experienced experts from their own companies. Smaller organizations cannot provide that type of opportunity, and their public relations practitioners cease to grow, perhaps not in terms of business but often in terms of effectiveness. Many national professional associations try to compensate by offering seminars and workshops, some in connection with scheduled conferences and others that are "road shows" that can be offered in major cities.

Universities, however, are perhaps best equipped to offer cutting-edge research and critical assessments of traditional public relations practice (Atlbach & DeWit, 1997). However, this research must be cutting-edge, and the critical analysis must come from educators who are thoroughly familiar with public relations practice; otherwise, it has no value.

In actuality, many public relations practitioners not only do not perform research, they do not even understand it. Others simply write off research as being a marketing tool (which, of course, it is, but not solely). Furthermore, many practitioners do not understand the Internet. If they do use the Internet, then they often depend on technical people—not communicators—to install Web pages or e-mail systems, and they ignore the countless other ways in which the Internet can be used in their work, particularly for research.

Practitioners also are less likely to take a critical look at the effectiveness of what they are doing. In some appalling examples, attempted evaluations have been based on the crudest of measures such as counting the number of inches of newspaper clippings or the amount of television or radio air time for a client and multiplying that by the medium's commercial rate. Others have not only permitted but actually recommended that clients use focus group research methodology to gather data for major management decisions and sometimes even policy changes. Practitioners often blame the clients for not providing enough money and time for research, but practitioners should be in a position to make sound recommendations and to be unrelenting in explaining what is necessary to do the job right. Practitioners might not be on firm ground, however, because of their lack of knowledge of research methods and of an understanding of when research is needed.

The advantage of bringing public relations practitioners back into the university setting for continuing education is that they will not only learn from but also make a contribution to the public relations body of knowledge. Some practitioners returning to the university might be former students who want to upgrade their competencies. Universities are missing an opportunity to improve their own statuses by failing to help these former students.

MEETING THE NEED

Global education for public relations is in its infancy, but demand for such education is critical. This demand comes from educators throughout the world who want help in determining what to teach and in finding resources to do that. Further demand comes from practitioners, especially those outside the United States, most of whom have had no formal education in public relations. In addition, there are today's students from the United States who are studying abroad, traveling abroad, or perhaps even doing internships abroad without any forewarning about what to look for as they function in their new environments.

By creating parameters for an international body of knowledge and for academic study in public relations that respects differences across societies, governments, and cultures, public relations educators and practitioners can build a global understanding of public relations as an international profession.

NOTE

1. The International Public Relations Association (IPRA) has published 12 "Gold Papers" that are listed in the IPRA directory and can be ordered from the IPRA secretariat (fax: 011-44-181-481-7648; e-mail: iprasec@compuserve.com). The IPRA also publishes *International Public Relations Review.* This journal provides some of the best information on the status of public relations in different parts of the world. Also, selected proceedings from several IPRA world congresses have been published. The first formal report that outlined the books, periodicals, databases, bibliographies, curricula, principles, practices, and ideas defining the public relations body of knowledge was that of Walker (1988). Preparation of a new body of knowledge publication began during the fall of 1998. Also, the *Public Relations Bibliography* has been published regularly since 1957; since 1976, it has been published annually as a special issue of *Public Relations Review.* In addition, the Public Relations Society of America published an annual *Bibliography for Public Relations Professionals* each February until it was discontinued in 1995, in part because of the proliferation of on-line publication search engines.

New Zealand Perspectives on Public Relations

JUDY MOTION

SHIRLEY LEITCH

■ The creation of an all-encompassing body of theory has been the primary goal of much public relations scholarship. This goal was apparent, for example, in the "Body of Knowledge" project initiated by the Public Relations Society of America in 1986 (Cutlip, Center, & Broom, 1994). The desire has been to establish a theoretical foundation on which to base both practice and higher education programs in public relations. In the process, cultural, regional, and other differences have been rendered largely invisible by this drive for academic and professional legitimacy. Such legitimacy cannot, however, be derived from an impoverished body of theory that does not recognize differences. This section of the handbook poses an overt challenge to the creation of a grand narrative for public relations precisely because national differences constitute the central theme.

The focus of this chapter is on the practice and theorization of public relations in a New Zealand context. Its purpose is to distinguish the unique characteristics of such theory and practice as well as the commonalities with other national and international experiences. The chapter draws on the findings of the New Zealand Public Communication Survey of New Zealand's top 100 companies and on interviews with 12 of the in-house public relations practitioners who worked for these companies (Leitch, 1995). It also draws on interviews with senior public relations consultants (Motion, 1997, 1998). The survey was designed to map the features of in-house public relations practice in New Zealand. Follow-up interviews were intended to enable practitioners to tell their personal stories and to reflect on the past, present, and future of public relations practice in New Zealand.

AUTHORS' NOTE: A version of this chapter was rewritten for the 1999 inaugural issue of the *Asia Pacific Public Relations Journal*.

THE HISTORY OF PUBLIC RELATIONS IN NEW ZEALAND

The public relations industry in New Zealand originally developed through the efforts of demobilized army and air force press officers following the end of World War II (J. Trenwith, personal communication, April 1998). In June 1954, five of these practitioners met in the Star Hotel in Auckland to form the group that now is the Public Relations Institute of New Zealand (PRINZ). Their primary goals were to share knowledge about what they viewed as their craft and to create a network among all those engaged in public relations work. The concept that a Code of Practice was required to guide their work was accepted from the beginning. These early practitioners knew little about developments in the United States or Europe, but they were hungry for any information that became available and circulated articles and books among the group members. In the absence of any formal public relations training, new practitioners were recruited from the ranks of senior journalists. These journalists readily made the transition into higher paying public relations jobs because media relations was the major function of early public relations departments and consultancies.

The establishment of PRINZ marked the beginning of the emergence of public relations as a profession in its own right. The PRINZ membership, however, always was divided on this point—over whether public relations was a profession or simply a craft for "wordsmiths." The introduction by PRINZ of accreditation examinations as a prerequisite for full membership in the organization led to a split in the ranks. Some senior practitioners left PRINZ and joined the International Association of Business Communicators, which did not require such an examination. Today, the split is less marked, mainly because the value of formal qualifications is more widely accepted.

Currently, PRINZ has grown to include some 500 members. Its membership is divided evenly between public relations consultants and in-house practitioners. PRINZ hosts an annual conference in New Zealand and a joint conference with its Australian equivalent, the Public Relations Institute of Australia, every other year. In addition to administering the accreditation process, PRINZ organizes educational seminars for members, particularly when top international practitioners or academics become available. The goal is to continuously update the knowledge of New Zealand practitioners and to ensure that they are aware of best practices internationally.

A new development for PRINZ has been the use of the Web. Through its Web site, PRINZ provides information about the organization and its activities. The Web site also contains information about the accreditation process and the universities and technical institutes that offer public relations qualifications. As is the case with many organizations, PRINZ is actively exploring the possibilities that the Web holds for the public relations industry.

PUBLIC RELATIONS EDUCATION

The recent genesis of public relations education in New Zealand has meant that many senior practitioners still are without formal qualifications in the area. In place of public relations qualifications, some practitioners have degrees in journalism or other, often unrelated areas. The New Zealand Public Communication Survey of in-house practitioners conducted during the mid-1990s, for example, found that only 56% had any type of public relations training or education (Leitch, 1995). Moreover, 67% of those with training identified on-the-job training or short seminars as the sole source of their public relations knowledge. Only 20% had university or technical institute qualifications, and few of these were in public relations. Moreover, only one practitioner had undertaken the PRINZ accreditation examinations. This figure would be somewhat higher if the survey were repeated today. However, in-house practitioners always have been less likely to undertake the PRINZ accreditation examinations than have consultants. Perhaps consultants have more need of the independent endorsement of their expertise that is represented by PRINZ accreditation.

The low number of tertiary qualified public relations practitioners is explained by the relatively short history of public relations education in New Zealand. During the late 1960s, the country's first public relations course was launched by the Wellington Polytechnic in conjunction with PRINZ. This part-time course focused on media relations and promotion, and it was undertaken by many of the public relations practitioners working for the capital city's major corporations, government departments, and politicians. Today, public relations courses are offered at universities and technical institutes throughout New Zealand. The majority of these programs are indistinguishable in content from those found in many North American institutions. Their theoretical orientation is positivist and rooted in the systems approach. By contrast, the largest public relations program in New Zealand, at the University of Waikato, is critical and draws on rhetorical and discourse theory.

Scholars at the University of Waikato have worked to theorize public relations in a way that fits the New Zealand context. Drawing on the rhetorical and critical approaches of Toth and Heath (1992) and the poststructuralist discourse approaches of Fairclough (1992, 1995a, 1995b), Foucault (1972, 1987, 1988), and others (Hall, 1986; Moffitt, 1994a), they have begun to build an indigenous body of public relations theory (see, e.g., Leitch & Neilson, 1997; Leitch & Roper, 1998; McKie, 1997; Motion, 1997; Motion & Leitch, 1996). In particular, they have been concerned about understanding the role that public relations practitioners have played in major social, cultural, and political events in recent New Zealand history. Rhetorical and discourse theory has provided the foundation for empirical work on public relations and the creation of a New Zealand perspective on public relations. From this perspective, public relations practitioners can be seen as "actively involved in the research, redesign, and training dimensions of discursive struggles to maintain or transform sociocultural practices" (Motion & Leitch, 1996, p. 301). The extent to which this theory might apply elsewhere remains to be tested in other national and cultural contexts.

NEW ZEALAND IN THE INTERNATIONAL CONTEXT

Many aspects of New Zealand public relations practice, however, follow standard international patterns. There is, for example, a strong relationship between marketing and public relations in many New Zealand organizations. Public relations scholars have expressed concern about what they perceive to be "imperialism and encroachment" (Lauzen, 1991, p. 245) by marketing on the "conceptual domain and operational turf" (Broom, Lauzen, & Tucker, 1991, p. 219) of public relations. Gordon Chesterman, past president of PRINZ, does not share this view. In an interview conducted in 1996, Chesterman moved easily between the two disciplines, employing whichever was appropriate to meet the needs of his clients (Motion, 1998). When designing a political campaign, for example, Chesterman stated that he assessed individuals for their "product benefits" and "points of differentiation" (p. 174) and then used the techniques of market research, public relations, and marketing to construct a campaign.

Another international practice followed by New Zealand is that the professional association, PRINZ, has a Code of Conduct. This code sets out ethical standards to which member practitioners must adhere. The efficacy of the code had a very public testing in 1996 when PRINZ received a complaint over the behavior of a prominent practitioner, Michelle Boag. A major scandal in recent New Zealand history, known as the "Winebox Affair," concerned the alleged large-scale tax avoidance by major New Zealand corporations. The complaint to PRINZ against Boag concerned her role in the unauthorized filming of a senior politician at a judicial inquiry. The politician was Winston Peters, New Zealand's deputy prime minister, who had instigated a judicial inquiry into the Winebox Affair. The unauthorized filming had occurred while Peters was giving evidence. Boag's response to the PRINZ inquiry into her conduct was to resign from PRINZ (Chesterman, 1996). PRINZ then was unable to investigate further because it was deemed inappropriate to sit in judgment on a

person who was not a PRINZ member. Therefore, a central weakness of the Code of Conduct
was revealed: Any member could avoid a PRINZ
inquiry simply by resigning. This case mirrors
that involving Anthony Franco, former president
of the Public Relations Society of America.
Franco also resigned in the face of an attempt by
his professional body to investigate his actions
(Wright, 1993, p. 14). In both countries, resignation from the professional bodies does not prevent individuals from continuing to work in the
field. In practice, then, the primary role served by
such codes might be symbolic in that they signal
the collective view on appropriate conduct
rather than serve as disciplinary frameworks.

Acceptance of the collective wisdom represented by the PRINZ Code of Conduct might
not, however, be widespread among New Zealand practitioners. Interviews conducted with
New Zealand practitioners over the past 7 years
indicate that adherence to any professional code
of conduct is seen as problematic by many practitioners, who tended to view ethics as a personal
choice. One in-house practitioner stated, "I prefer to abide by my own organisation and my own
personal beliefs as to what is right and proper"
(quoted in Leitch, 1995, p. 28). In a similar vein, a
senior consultant stated, "I won't promote anyone at all unless I believe in him or believe in her
or believe in the organisation. . . . I think ethics
and values are everything" (quoted in Motion,
1998, p. 166). It was the personal belief systems of
practitioners or what one practitioner referred
to as values that came "from your parents"
(quoted in Leitch, 1995, p. 28), rather than an abstract professional code, that guided public relations practice. Clearly, PRINZ still has much
work to do in convincing some practitioners that
a code of conduct is an essential defining element
of their professionalism.

PRINZ also has work to do in terms of the
public image of public relations in New Zealand.
One senior consultant, reflecting on the status of
public relations practitioners, stated,

> I think generally they are perceived as being pur-
> veyors of snake oil and hokum. It is partly the

glass and glitz . . . in terms of corporate launches
. . . and also public relations is very much associated with some of the more distressing or more
unpopular government policies. . . . I think public
relations as a whole has become discredited and
identified with those things in the popular mind.
(quoted in Leitch, 1994)

Although other practitioners did not express this
view quite so candidly, there appeared to be a
general consensus among the in-house practitioners that public relations practice was not well
respected in New Zealand (Leitch, 1994).

The practitioner view just quoted, concerning the prominent role that public relations people had played in government and politics, is indicative of another international trend that also
may be found in New Zealand. The relationship
among politicians, media, and public relations
practitioners creates what Tiffen (1989) referred
to as "coterie communication" (p. 93). Tiffen likened coterie communication to a "hall of mirrors" in which the coterie "are audience one minute, actors the next; targets of some messages,
sources of others" (p. 93). The New Zealand public relations practitioners interviewed identified
the cultivation and utilization of friendships
with media personnel as a key tactic in their media strategies, particularly with reference to political public relations (Motion, 1998). These
close relationships develop at least partly because so many senior journalists in New Zealand
have moved into public relations. That the first
stage of the switch between journalism and public relations often is a stint as a media officer for a
politician also is an important factor in coterie
communication.

EMERGING TRENDS

Increasingly, New Zealand public relations practitioners have become aware both that most of
their clients operate in an international environment and that New Zealand is a multicultural

microcosm. Each of these emerging trends is discussed in this section. The internationalization of New Zealand business is a well-documented trend (Enderwick, 1996, 1997), and public relations consultancies are no exception. Some, such as Baldwin Boyle, have opened offices in other Asia-Pacific countries. Others, such as Wellington-based Logos, have allowed themselves to be bought out by companies with worldwide networks (in Logos' case, Omnicom). Still others, such as the Sigma Group, have chosen to affiliate with U.S.-based firms (in Sigma's case, the Bozell Sawyer Miller Group). This trend has been exacerbated by international companies, such as Saatchi and Saatchi, widening the scope of their activities globally to include public relations. Despite these developments, the majority of New Zealand public relations consultancies listed in the PRINZ directory still are small businesses employing just two or three consultants. Moreover, all of the listed agencies purport to offer all public relations services as opposed to one or two specialties (Dunlop, 1998).

In the New Zealand context, multiculturalism has two main strands. The first strand, known as biculturalism, relates to New Zealand's indigenous population of Maori people. Maori constitute approximately 10% of the overall population, and recognition of traditional Maori rights is legally enshrined. For example, Maori and English are the two official languages in New Zealand. There are no primarily Maori public relations consultancies and few Maori practitioners. However, practitioners generally are becoming increasingly aware of the need to adapt their communication strategies to speak meaningfully to Maori. The dearth of information on how practitioners might engage in such cross-cultural communication was highlighted during the recent campaigns surrounding a nationwide referendum on a proposed compulsory superannuation scheme. Wellington's leading daily newspaper, *The Dominion,* noted in a headline, "More Research Needed on How to Target Maori" (1997, p. 2). The difficulty of conducting such research is exacerbated by the fact that there is no unified Maori culture. For example, Maori are divided into a number of tribal and subtribal groupings. Each group has its own history, customs, and culture. There also are growing divisions between rural Maori, who tend to have strong family and tribal links, and urban Maori, for whom such links might have been lost.

The second strand of multiculturalism has arisen because of the growing number of immigrant groups in New Zealand. Auckland, New Zealand's largest city, has a significant proportion of residents who originate from the Pacific island states such as Tonga, Samoa, the Cook Islands, and Fiji. During the past 10 years, there also has been a growing number of Asian immigrants to New Zealand. Just as consultants are having to learn to develop campaign strategies for the Asia-Pacific region, so too are they having to acknowledge that a growing proportion of the national audience does not have English or Maori as its first language. This trend toward greater ethnic diversity shows no signs of reversing. Expertise in intercultural communication will, therefore, become an essential area of expertise for public relations practitioners.

CONCLUSION

In this chapter, we have briefly mapped the topography of New Zealand public relations. In the process, we drew out some of the key distinguishing features of the New Zealand experience. These features include the relatively recent genesis of public relations as a recognized area of expertise, the use of rhetorical and discourse theory as a foundation for public relations education and scholarship, and the growing importance of biculturalism and multiculturalism in New Zealand public relations practice and theory. Our central purpose in mapping out these features was to demonstrate that public relations theory must take account of differences. As the context in which public relations is practiced changes, so too must scholarship move to theorize differences.

The Development of Public Relations
in China, Russia, and the United States

MARK McELREATH

NI CHEN

LYUDMILA AZAROVA

VALERIA SHADROVA

Public relations has a long history in China, Russia, and the United States. Heavy-handed propaganda and staged publicity events by activist publics played a role in establishing each nation. For each country, public communication campaigns sponsored by governmental and nongovernmental organizations were important for national development. Public relations defined as the management of organizational communication activities designed to build relationships among stakeholders is a relatively new concept in all three countries. Only during the late 20th century have research-based public relations campaigns become commonplace in these countries—during the past 40 to 50 years in the United States and during the past 10 to 20 years in China and Russia.

Environmental and organizational factors help to explain and predict the evolution of the concept. In the United States, senior executives have learned that they have to communicate more and be more engaged with stakeholders to succeed in its increasingly competitive, product-saturated, service-oriented marketplace. In Russia, following the collapse of the control of the Communist Party, public relations practices reflected those in the United States at the turn of the 20th century; the growth of capitalism and new media opportunities allowed the practice of public relations to be highly successful, even though it often was unethical by today's standards. In China, within the past few decades, controls on the economy have been loosened to allow more free market activities including advertising and public relations. The practice of public relations has become a significant part of each country as it enters the 21st century.

As the global economy becomes more market oriented and interdependent, the practice of public relations has spread worldwide. Practitioners are identifying best practices around the world and applying them as soon as possible in their own countries. Consequently, the development of public relations in newly emerging market economies will be accelerated compared to what happened in the United States, which one scholar called public relations' "country of origin" (Goregin, 1996). What has taken more than a century to develop in the United States might now occur in other countries in just a few years.

Based in part on the J. Grunig and Hunt (1984) four-stage model, public relations can be described as developing through the following stages:

- *initial introduction and development:* most often using former journalists as press agents with an emphasis on one-way communication and too often an emphasis on unethical media manipulation;
- *an upsurge or "take-off" in the practice of public relations:* less manipulation and more emphasis on disseminating accurate news and public information, especially as other organizations recognize the competitive advantage of good public relations;
- *a period of rethinking by members of the dominant coalition about the role and function of public relations:* more managers placing an emphasis on research and two-way asymmetrical communication, and more professional organizations and "in-house" specialists displacing outside consultants; and
- *sustained growth and increasing emphasis on two-way communication:* a wide range of public relations practices including an increasing but limited emphasis on genuine two-way symmetrical communication.

We describe public relations practices at each of these stages based on research that we have conducted in each of these countries. We are part of faculty exchange programs among Towson University in the United States, the Electrotechnical University in Russia, and the Wuxi University of Light Industry in China. We discuss the status of higher education in public relations in China, Russia, and the United States. In addition, we discuss changing roles of public relations practitioners including the role of women in the profession.

THE "MANIPULATION" STAGE: THE INITIAL DEVELOPMENT OF PUBLIC RELATIONS

United States

The history of public relations in the United States is well documented elsewhere (Cutlip, 1994). Others have described the early practice of public relations in the United States as the "manipulation stage" (Baskin, Aronoff, & Lattimore, 1997). The founding fathers of the United States were masters of the media of their day, not only knowing how to write and publish articles (e.g., the *Federalist Papers*) but also knowing how to stage events (e.g., the Boston Tea Party) to attract the attention of the press and opinion leaders on both sides of the Atlantic. The U.S. Constitution guaranteed press freedoms and encouraged associations and private businesses to engage in lobbying and public communication campaigns.

Publicity campaigns by major landowners, especially exaggerated claims about western properties, were one factor in the United States' rapid western expansion during the 1800s. P. T. Barnum was famous for his hype about "the greatest show on earth" and his creatively staged media events that attracted so much attention to his roving circuses at the end of the 19th century. The initial use of public relations by major capitalists at the turn of the 20th century clearly was heavy-handed one-way communication designed to dominate and suppress opposition.

China

Although the term *public relations* is relatively new in China, the practice can be traced back over more than 2,000 years of Chinese history, encompassing 13 dynasties. All emperors recognized the importance of establishing and maintaining harmonious relationships between the ruler and the subjects. It was said that good rulers viewed their subjects as water—something that could not only carry the imperial boat but also turn it over (Chen, 1994). Most rulers emphasized relationship building; hence, public relations can be said to have been practiced in ancient China. For example, Confucius, the great Chinese philosopher, encouraged harmonious communication as a way in which to smooth relationships and reduce conflicts within the social system.

The People's Republic of China was established in 1994. For about three decades (up to the late 1970s), the political system in China was dominated by a small political elite headed by Mao Zedong. These leaders ruled primarily through direct Communist Party control, propaganda manipulation, military might, and police brutality, with a minimum of mass participation (Chen & Culbertson, 1992). The Chinese people primarily experienced one-way communication from their leaders until the early 1980s, when China's new leadership adopted an "open door" policy and began its economic reforms. Nevertheless, as one official of the Beijing Public Relations Association noted, nothing of consequence could be done in public relations in China without the support of the Communist Party (Goregin, 1996).

With the economic reforms in China came an understanding by the elite that these leaders needed to engage in more two-way asymmetrical communication. It still was one-sided communication, but more research was done prior to formulating communication campaigns (Chen, 1990). For example, the municipal government of Tianjin was among the first in the nation to get feedback from citizens prior to establishing public policies. It engaged in a range of activities designed to allow leaders to hear more from citizens. The municipal government gained public support for its activities by engaging in more two-way asymmetical communication activities, soliciting citizens' input, and forming public policies based on the publics' suggestions (Fu, 1990; Gao, 1991). The central government in Beijing continues to engage most often in one-way (or, more infrequently, two-way) asymmet-

rical communication activities with its publics, especially those outside China (Kristof, 1990).

The Chinese government's use of two-way asymmetrical communication during the 1980s parallels that seen in the United States during the 1930s, when the U.S. government initiated a number of new programs and the public began to demand greater governmental accountability. Feedback from citizens was seen as essential for effective government programs. The assumption was that government could not meet the needs of the people unless it first established what those needs were. Needs assessment research was considered very important to establishing viable government programs. In China, questions already have been raised about what the people's needs are and how those needs are changing. Consequently, more research on people's attitudes, people's opinions, and lifestyle issues is being conducted. A movement toward more two-way asymmetrical communication activities clearly is under way.

Russia

Russia's first printing presses and newspapers were established more than 800 years ago. The Russian church and state have a long history of controlling, taxing, and managing mass communication in that country. During the 19th century, using the name of the czar or other elite rulers in books or newspaper articles without expressed permission (and without, e.g., the payment of an appropriate tax) was not permitted. Dostoyevsky learned this the hard way (McElreath & Azarova, 1995).

The Bolshevik Revolution in 1917 was accomplished with a lot of effective propaganda and street demonstrations. The revolution's leader, Vladimir Lenin, was a strong advocate of using the media to agitate the public. Lenin wrote essays on the importance of elite decision makers using and controlling the media to bring about change and reform in society. During the Josef Stalin years, the leaders of the Communist Party strongly controlled mass communication throughout the massive country in an attempt to shape public opinion and suppress opposing points of view in the Soviet Union (Ganley, 1996).

During the late 1980s, Mikhail Gorbachev's policy of openness, called *perestroika,* powerfully changed public communication within Russia. Former U.S. President Richard Nixon said of Gorbachev's sophisticated use of modern media, "He may have a Ph.D. in economics, but he has a master's degree in public relations." Gorbachev hired Western-based public relations specialists to help him alter the image of Russia in the West (Goregin, 1996).

Since the collapse of communism and the introduction of free market reforms in Russia, the practice of advertising, marketing, and public relations in the country has been strongly influenced by Western practitioners, especially by the major public relations agencies and multinational corporations establishing operations in Russia. For example, during the early 1990s, more than 40 million Russians were issued vouchers that they could use to purchase shares in formerly state-owned enterprises being privatized. After more than 70 years of Communist rule, most Russians knew next to nothing about the rights and responsibilities of shareholders. In 1993, Burson-Marsteller, one of the world's largest public relations agencies, assumed the role of prime communication adviser to the Russian Ministry of Privatization, which was responsible for conducting a nationwide campaign to build support for the government's privatization efforts. The campaign strategy was to elicit a commitment from citizens by increasing their awareness and understanding of privatization issues and to move citizens to action by giving them an opportunity for discussion, trial adoption, and personal experience that would generate new knowledge and greater confidence in their new behaviors as stockholders. The agency conducted research throughout the nation, drafted a national declaration of shareholder rights that was endorsed by the Russian opinion leaders, engaged in a nationwide advertising campaign, and created training programs at the local level to support the work of activist groups knowledgeable about corporate governance and shareholder rights. As a result of these actions, there was no organized national backlash to the privatization program, the declaration of shareholder rights was incorporated into national law, and more than two dozen shareholder rights groups were established (McElreath, 1996).

The privatization process by formerly centralized, state-controlled economies is one factor driving the spread of public relations around the world. Public understanding and acceptance of government-sponsored privatization programs makes effective public relations an essential component to the success of privatization programs.

Privatization of state-owned properties and the movement toward democracy are under way in both Russia and China, with each country on its own timetable. History indicates that democracy both requires and contributes to communication between a government and its publics. This, in turn, encourages attention by government officials to public needs and wants. Democracy requires public participation in decision making. An informed public with a taste of freedom eventually begins to demand two-way symmetrical communication. Most often, what the people in Russia, China, and the United States continue to experience is one-way or two-way asymmetical communication from most of the dominant organizations and groups in their societies. Even in the freest of free market economies, it is rare for genuine two-way symmetrical communication to be engaged in by the major organizations. Most large-scale organizations—the ones most likely to hire public relations specialists—engage in one-way and two-way asymmetrical communication activities; it is a fact of life around the world.

THE UPSURGE AND "TAKE-OFF" STAGE: NEW HORIZONTAL AND CONTINUED VERTICAL DEVELOPMENT OF PUBLIC RELATIONS

United States

As public relations developed vertically in the United States within the railroad, steel, and oil industries owned by capitalist "robber barrons" at the beginning of the 20th century, the practice also developed horizontally, spreading its influence from one sector of the economy to others. Especially when the new media of the day—first national magazines and then radio and movies—came into play in the marketplace, other sectors of the economy saw the advantage of having public relations as part of the marketing mix.

Hyperbole and exaggerated claims were part of the mix as the practice of public relations spread in the United States. Media manipulation and exaggerated claims by public relations practitioners were part of the set of problems that created the unrealistic expectations by investors leading to the stock market crash in 1929 (Cutlip, 1994).

China

In China, the practice of public relations spread from the joint venture manufacturing corporations involved with Western partners to an increasing number of service-oriented (and relatively small) organizations (Chen, 1996). State ownership of major large-scale organizations constrained the growth of public relations in the public sector. The army and other major institutions in society, however, used public information specialists. But the rapid growth of public relations occurred primarily among the tens of thousands of small businesses that quickly recognized the advantages of public relations for generating free publicity and goodwill among key stakeholders.

Russia

In Russia during the 1990s, many of the first wave of public relations practitioners were either trained in the West or former journalists from Russian media. Many of the former Russian journalists established "press services" or "press centers" and offered their clients media relations services primarily focused on generating free publicity. Because many of the economically strained media organizations demanded "under-the-table" payments for the placement of press releases, the early Russian public relations practitioners often paid bribes as part of their media relations work. Later, as more Western-

based agencies began to run more substantial campaigns throughout the nation (and were able to demonstrate to local media the value of working with major public relations campaigns), the media learned to distinguish between paid advertising and legitimate news releases.

The media coverage of government and business was chaotic during the early 1990s. Government and business leaders recognized that the media could distort information or ignore important news. They had to use more effective public relations practices to offset the chaos being generated by the exploding number of media outlets. From the late 1980s to the early 1990s, the number of media outlets in Russia increased by the tens of thousands. Many lasted only a few months. Only a few will survive economically to be operating well into the 21st century. Out of this surge of new media in Russia came an increased need for information subsidies from public relations practitioners.

Another factor driving the initial growth of public relations in Russia was the number of political parties competing in Russia's first free presidential election in 1993. More than 50 political parties competed for the public's attention. The surprising popularity of supporters of the Communist Party, especially Vladimir Zhirinovsky (the leader of an ultra-nationalist party), concerned reform-minded government and business leaders. The members of the dominant coalitions backing economic reforms recognized the need for more accurate public opinion surveys and the importance of practical advice from public relations specialists.

THE RETHINKING STAGE: MEMBERS OF THE DOMINANT COALITIONS RECONSIDERING THE FUNCTIONS AND ROLES OF PUBLIC RELATIONS AND THE RISE OF PROFESSIONALISM

United States

World War I brought a profound change to the practice of public relations. Around the world, nation-states incorporated propaganda into their war machines as never before. The U.S. propaganda in support of that country's war effort has been described as the greatest public relations effort in history up to its time (Baskin et al., 1997). Public relations practitioners from various industries within the economy were recruited to work with government to disseminate public information and mobilize the "homefront." At the end of the war, the hundreds of practitioners trained by their experience in government propaganda and public information returned to the private sectors with a new understanding of the role and power of effective public relations.

Based in part on the productive experiences of the wartime public information specialists, codifying and disseminating the body of knowledge in public relations began in the United States during the 1920s. Edward Bernays wrote the first book about public relations, *Crystallizing Public Opinion,* and taught the first college-level course in public relations in 1923 (Bernays, 1923). These initial efforts toward professionalism, however, were not enough to offset the wave of unethical and illegal public relations practices at the time, especially defrauding the investing public by disseminating false claims about companies listed on the stock market.

The 1929 stock market crash in the United States led to major reform in corporate reporting requirements. Federal legislation during the early 1930s established the principle of full and timely disclosure of material facts about publicly owned corporations that could affect the decisions of investors to either buy or sell stock in those companies. This profoundly redefined the role and function of public relations. No longer could public relations practitioners disseminate exaggerated claims about corporations. Now it was the law in the United States that corporations had to be accurate in disclosing information to the investing public. For the major corporations, senior public relations practitioners moved permanently into the corporate boardrooms and were part of the dominant coalition.

Public relations higher education in the United States followed the development of journalism and mass communication education. Many of the undergraduate programs offering a

sequence of courses in public relations were at universities receiving federal funds to develop agricultural extension programs that included a major emphasis on public information. Many of these universities were in the "heartland" of the United States. Other university programs were established at urban universities. The undergraduate curriculum typically consisted of courses in principles, writing, and campaigns, with students encouraged to pursue internships. More advanced programs required students to take research methods, law, and ethics. Programs were accredited that met these standards (and more) including the requirement that students take the majority of their university coursework outside the public relations, journalism, or communication major. There are more than 300 university-based public relations programs in the United States today.

China

In China, the rethinking stage began after June 1989. The shock to the power elite resulting from the 1989 student democracy movement and the government's crackdown caused the leadership to call for the reconsideration of all ideas imported from the West. A new policy stressed the definition of socialist public relations with Chinese features; it emphasized strengthening the Communist Party's supervision over public relations practices (An, 1990; Men, 1990). The new policy affected the development and usefulness of public relations to some degree.

Deng Xiaoping's visit to China's southern coastal cities in 1992 and his post-tour speech set the tone for the continuation of his "open door" policy. He emphasized that "whatever it takes"— be it capitalism, socialism, or some mix of economic/political ideologies—should be encouraged so long as it increased China's productivity (Yuan & Han, 1992). Xiaoping's policy stopped debate about how best to control the practices of public relations. Since then, public relations practices have grown more widespread and are becoming more professional.

An estimated 1 million Chinese are employed in the public relations field (personal interviews with Guangwei Jia, general manager of the Shanghai office of Fleishman-Hillard, and Hongyi Li, associate professor and director of public relations teaching and research office at Wuxi University of Light Industry, June 1998). Professional organizations for public relations practitioners exist in nearly all cities and in every province. Hundreds of public relations publications are available including professional books, trade magazines, scholarly journals, and newsletters. Public relations agencies have opened in most of the large cities. All of the major global public relations firms have offices in China. It is estimated that there are more than 1,200 public relations firms in China employing more than 30,000 people (Strenski & Yue, 1998).

Based on survey data collected in Beijing, Nanjing, Shanghai, and Guangzhou, there is a clear distinction between Chinese practitioners engaged in more two-way communication activities and performing manager roles and those engaged in one-way communication activities and performing technician roles (Chen, 1996). A significant percentage of public relations practitioners in China perform problem-solving manager roles. Most individuals who claim to be in manager roles are engaged in communication-related decision making and policymaking. Few have participated in the overall strategic decision-making process (personal interviews with selected directors of corporate communication in Guangzhou, Shanghai, Shenzhen, and Wuxi, January 1999).

In China, female practitioners outnumber male practitioners, especially in technician roles. Chinese women have not advanced as far as men in the field of public relations (Bernstein, 1986; Chen, 1995; Hon, L. Grunig, & Dozier, 1992). *Guest relations* constitutes an important technician role for Chinese women in public relations (Chen & Culbertson, 1996). In the United States, no such similar role has emerged in surveys of practitioners. In China, guest relations is not a trivial role. It focuses on the subtle interpersonal relationships so important in the Chinese culture. Unfortunately, too often guest relations in China means making clients happy and entertaining them. And too often, women assigned to guest relations are not encouraged or expected to advance to higher levels in the public relations

practice. Physical attractiveness is important for Chinese women entering the public relations practice. The "glass ceiling" that keeps people from advancing into management positions in public relations appears to be much harder to crack for women in China than for women in the United States.

In both China and Russia, the training of local public relations practitioners involved tutoring by Western practitioners involved in joint venture projects. Then, short-term workshops and seminars were sponsored by the growing number of professional associations. Later, university courses and degree programs were established (Wang, 1992).

In 1985, China's first public relations majors and sequences were established at Shenzhen University (Black, 1992). To date, most colleges, universities, and even military and political academies offer public relations courses. At present, about 300 universities in China offer some public relations courses, and certificate or degree programs are available at 70 universities. More than 300,000 people have been trained, and some 30,000 currently are studying public relations at Chinese universities (personal interviews with Jia and Li, June 1998).

Public relations higher education in China is divided into levels. The first level is the training offered by public relations associations. At the second level, public relations is provided through distance learning via the Chinese Central Television station and university-based correspondence courses. At the third level, public relations education is provided by specialized vocational schools offering 2-year degree programs in public relations. At the fourth and highest level, education is offered through 4-year university degree programs in public relations (Chen, 1994).

A 4-year degree in public relations at a Chinese university usually is made up of 60% to 70% required courses. Each student is expected to be fluent in the English language, complete a practicum or an internship, and write a thesis. Some of the required courses include public relations principles, case studies, writing, organizational communication, mass communication, marketing, modern management, interpersonal communication, psychology, speech, advertising campaigns, corporate culture, research methodology, negotiation techniques, public opinion, mass media law, ethics, logic, and aesthetics (Staff, 1995).

Russia

Higher education in public relations is offered at various levels in Russia. Professional associations and private companies offer short-term workshops and seminars. Most practitioners and professional associations in Russia are located in Moscow or St. Petersburg. Consequently, the education of most practitioners in Russia occurs in these two cities.

The first full-time courses in public relations were offered during the early 1990s at Moscow State University and its Institute of Foreign Relations. Later, the university's journalism department offered separate courses in public relations. Russia's first university-based degree program was established in 1993 at the Electrotechnical University in St. Petersburg. Modeled after the undergraduate degree program at Towson University in the United States, the Electrotechnical University offers the following courses: introduction to advertising and public relations, principles, writing, campaigns, international advertising, marketing, organizational communication, internship/practicum, media law, and ethics. Each graduating senior must write a thesis. Each student is required to be fluent in the English language to enter the program and must be fluent in a third language before he or she graduates. Many of the elite students speak four or five languages (McElreath & Azarova, 1995).

LATEST STAGE: SUSTAINED GROWTH AND GROWING BUT LIMITED EMPHASIS ON TWO-WAY COMMUNICATION ACTIVITIES

Public relations still is a relatively new concept and a young practice in China. As such, it still is

facing problems and challenges. Public relations often is relegated to a product promotion function within marketing. Public relations too often is seen as guest relations involving women in roles as functionaries. However, the competitive advantage of good public relations is driving the growth of public relations in China, as more managers are seeing the advantage of strategic two-way communication with key stakeholders.

In Russia, the major institutions and organizations continue to engage in one-way and two-way asymmetrical communication. These are the dominant modes of communication for most large mixed-mechanical organizations, not only in Russia but also around the world.

Two-way symmetrical communication allows small complex organizations to be flexible and competitive. Russian entrepreneurs and Chinese small businesses are discovering the competitive advantage of effective public relations.

In the United States, the concept of integrated communication is becoming more popular. Integrated communication is more than integrated marketing communication because of the emphasis that the former places on internal organizational communication (Caywood, 1997). In Russia and China, where less emphasis is placed on employee communication, public relations often is involved in integrated marketing communication. In the United States, an increasing number of practitioners are involved equally in internal and external public relations.

Codes of ethics for public relations practitioners have been established by associations in the United States, China, and Russia. The Universal Accreditation Board, established by the Public Relations Society of America and others, is involved in examining the common values and principles expressed in codes of professional public relations associations around the world. Common to all are concerns for telling the truth, avoiding harm, and establishing mutually beneficial relationships and understandings.

The types of organizations dominant within an economy and cultural differences help to explain and predict the types of public relations practiced in China, Russia, and the United States.

Because a free market economy has been operating in the United States longer than in China or Russia, public relations is more commonplace and entrenched in the United States. As free market reforms ebb and flow in the Russian and Chinese economies, public relations practices will change to fit the marketplaces.

CONCLUSION AND RECOMMENDATIONS

The four stages described in this chapter are likely to apply to other countries as well. More research needs to be done to further refine what occurs in these stages including comparable data sets from each country, comparable data sets within specific industries operating within each country, longitudinal data, and improved theoretical models.

Because two-way communication activities are associated with the growth of free markets and democracy, public relations will continue to grow and develop as free market economies and democratic institutions continue to expand. As in the United States, Russia, and China, wherever public relations is practiced, it most likely will go through the following stages: an initial wave of media manipulation, a more substantial stage of public information, a readjustment period as the practice takes root, and a final stage of sustained growth.

The Changing Shape of Public Relations in the European Union

DAVID MILLER

PHILIP SCHLESINGER

■ Lobbying and public relations in the European Union (EU) have dramatically expanded during the past decade.[1] This is a consequence of the increasing transfer of power from member states to the supranational level. The expanding lobbying community forms one part of a developing EU policy community. This chapter documents the increased importance of lobbying and public relations at the European level, sets out some of their characteristics, and underlines the Anglophone preponderance in lobbying provision and elite media. It is argued that there still is no genuine "public sphere" in which European matters are discussed; rather, to the extent that there is a common communicative space, this is dominated by a variety of elite interests.

CHARACTERISTICS OF THE EU SCENE

Considered as a quasi-polity, the EU consists of four main institutions: the European Commission, the European Council of Ministers, the European Parliament, and the European Court of Justice. Together, these constitute a unique institutional arrangement.

The Commission is the "motor of the integration process" (Christiansen, 1996, p. 78). It formulates policy and implements EU legislation; therefore, it is the main focus of lobbying activities. Commission officials increasingly rely

AUTHORS' NOTE: This research was conducted as part of a study of "Political Communication and Democracy" funded under the Economic and Social Research Council's "Media Economics and Media Culture" program. We thank Deirdre Kevin and Will Dinan for their research assistance.

on groups and firms to supply them with good information and expertise and to suggest workable policy solutions (Mazey & Richardson, 1993). Lobbying groups with an interest in the policy area will "befriend" such people, gain their trust, and supply them with expertise.

Whereas the Commission pushes the political and legislative agenda, it is the Council of Ministers (drawn from all the member states) that is the key forum for intergovernmental bargaining. The Council's procedures are, however, more secretive than those of the Commission because of the intergovernmental nature of negotiations. Member states want to be able to put their own spin on proceedings and to play down any element of compromise. This makes the Council less accessible to lobbying groups; therefore, this body tends to be more dependent on national civil servants (Mazey & Richardson, 1992). What we learn of these decision-making processes through national media allows member-state governments to give the impression of victories and a lack of compromise over other EU countries. When asked about access to the institutions of the EU, British journalists claimed that it was most difficult to get information about the decisions made by the Council (Morgan, 1995).

The Parliament is the only directly elected body in the EU. Since the Single European Act of 1987, and even more so since the Treaty of European Union of 1991, the Parliament has had an increased role in "co-deciding" legislation with the Council of Ministers (Earnshaw & Judge, 1996). Its increased power has made it more of a focus for lobbying activities. The Parliament often transmits the causes of interest groups and lobbyists by pressuring the Commission, the Council, and national members of Parliament (MPs).

A key example of the Parliament recently flexing its muscles was its inquiry into bovine spongiform encephalopathy (BSE, or so-called "mad cow disease") during 1996-1997. The Commission was indicted for a cover-up of the risks of BSE so as to protect the beef industry. This is seen in the Commission and in the Parliament as a key historical moment in a longer term process. As Ken Collins, member of the European Parliament (MEP), chair of the Parliament's Agriculture Committee, and member of the BSE Inquiry team, put it, "BSE is unique.... There hasn't ever been a crisis like that before. It affected [political relations with the Commission] more than anything else I have ever known" (interview, May 25, 1998). As a result of the inquiry, several Commission officials were removed from their posts, and there was an organizational change that gave the Consumer Affairs Directorate much greater powers while removing some of the powers of the Agriculture Directorate ("Committee of Inquiry," 1997). The constitutional effect was to increase the Parliament's influence in such matters in the future.

The Court of Justice is perceived by many analysts as having made a substantial contribution to the process of European integration by its judicial activities, decisions on the interpretation of EU legislation, challenges to member states over the nonimplementation of regulations, and the resolution of arguments between the institutions over the legal basis of regulations. Citizens and interest groups from the member states also have taken cases to the Court of Justice challenging member states' implementation of legislation. Many cases are referred by national courts to the Court of Justice for clarification of EU legislation that, according to some commentators, allows the Court of Justice considerable scope in interpreting the intentions of the original treaty. Its interaction with other institutions and interests in developing both community law and policy has been crucial for European integration (Wincott, 1996, p. 183).

An indication of the impact of EU legislation on the national political space—to take the British case—and the extent to which power has moved beyond national boundaries can be seen from the following figures presented in a recent "think tank" report. It is claimed that 80% of economic and social legislation and 50% of all legislation is decided at the EU level, that 20% to 30% of civil service time is taken up with EU matters, and that 90% of EU decisions are made by national civil servants behind closed doors. As with other member states, EU law has precedence over U.K. law, impinging on all areas except housing, civil liberties, and domestic crime (Leonard, 1997).

The emergent European public sphere and its core constituent, the EU policy community, occupy a paradoxical position: The European polity suffers from a severe "democratic deficit," whereas the policy process in Brussels, Belgium, is extremely transparent in comparison to that of member states such as the United Kingdom. As David Earnshaw, director of government relations at SmithKline Beacham (and a former lobbyist and researcher for a leading Labour MEP), put it,

> Everybody says . . . that Brussels is the most open transparent political system you are ever going to work with. . . . This is a very open, transparent, participatory, political system. It is why one can have an influence not just on tactical things going through the legislative system, but even on the design of the thing. (interview, May 26, 1998)

Such sentiments are shared by many nongovernmental organizations (NGOs) and interest groups. Yet, at the same time, the results of the process both in terms of the lack of democratic influence on policy outcomes and in terms of the dominance of sectional business interests, tend to speak of a policy arena that is closed. Furthermore, the limits of secrecy in EU institutions have been contested. *The Guardian's* Brussels correspondent John Carvel, backed by his newspaper and by the Danish and Dutch governments, took a successful case against the European Council for denying him access to documents "which should have been available under its freedom of information code" to establish the trail of ministerial accountability (Carvel, 1995, p. 17). A subsequent Council report on rules for disclosure of information was itself the subject of information management by both the Council and the Commission when it first was declared secret and then released ("EU: Secrecy Report," 1996).

In essence, the system is very open for those able to participate in it. Our research in Brussels showed that access to senior civil servants and other policy actors was comparatively easy. The emergent Euro-elite, however, mainly comprises business and political interests together with a range of NGO and interest group representatives. There is a marked lack of integration of the wider civil society into the European policy arena. Strikingly, this lack of widespread public engagement contrasts with the relative openness of the Euro-political institutions to those who actually gain access to them.

THE POLITICO-BUSINESS ELITE AND ITS MEDIA

Aside from the particularized activity of political exchange, there is a general framework of communications available to a European policy elite. There are newspapers and magazines that self-consciously address a European (as well as a global) elite audience conceived as composed of political and economic decision makers whose common language is English. The *Financial Times*, with a 9% share of the elite's "important business reading," is the most widely read daily newspaper in the 15 EU countries, Norway, and Switzerland. For this purpose, Europe's elite is defined as "the top 4 percent in terms of income and executive activity" (Research Services Ltd., 1996, p. 17).

The *Financial Times* is owned by Pearson PLC and is based in London. Although the newspaper has globalized its marketplace, Europe undoubtedly is a crucial regional market for the *Financial Times*, which publishes in the United Kingdom, France, Germany, Sweden, and Spain. Within Europe, among senior people in the continent's largest businesses, the newspaper outsells its daily competitors in 17 countries. In the key EU member states, especially France and Germany, members of the economic elite are willing to read a newspaper published *in English* because of its international standing. Inside the EU, the *Financial Times* is "usually cited as being favoured by official sources" because of its "European-wide readership" (Morgan, 1995, p. 333). Despite its global reach and ambitions, the newspaper's European edition contributes to a common agenda for a fraction of Europe's elite.

Along with the Benelux countries, France and Germany are the continental states of greatest interest to *The Economist*, owned by the London-based The Economist Newspaper Ltd. Like the *Financial Times* but in the weekly market, *The Economist* is the most widely read newspaper of its category across Europe, amounting to 3% of the potential readership. The company holds that there is "a pan-European business-government elite . . . speaking English on a daily basis, using it in business and personal life." For *The Economist,* the EU's development offers "transnational cultural opportunities" for selling its product (interview with Simon Philips, marketing executive of *The Economist,* April 21, 1998). Survey figures support these views: Of the top 4% of employees across 14 of the richest European countries examined (a mere 5.7 million people), 68% speak or read English, and of these, more than 38% use some English at work, albeit with major variations among countries (Research Services Ltd., 1995, p. 11).

The Economist Newspaper Ltd. also has recognized the potential of the political microculture in Brussels described earlier, launching *European Voice* in October 1995 based on the model of Washington, D.C.'s *Roll Call. European Voice* is a weekly newspaper with a "village feel" to it aimed at all the top people in the Brussels micropolity. The publication has "the exclusive cooperation of the European Commission, the Council of Ministers, and the European Parliament, who circulate 7,000 individually addressed copies of the newspaper to commissioners, their cabinets, MEPs, and A grade civil servants." Other targets are registered lobbyists, the business community, and the press, with a total circulation reaching 16,000 (http://www.european-voice.com/advertise/2.p15, January 1999; interview with Hugh McCahey, marketing executive of *The Economist,* April 21, 1998).

THE PUBLIC RELATIONS INDUSTRY IN EUROPE

The public relations industry in Europe is very unevenly developed. In 1996, 13 of the top 15 European consultancies were U.S. or British owned. The world's largest advertising, marketing, and communications conglomerates (e.g., Lopex, Cordiant, Grey Advertising, Young and Rubicam, McManus Group, Interpublic) each owns 1 of the top 15 European agencies, and the very largest corporations (e.g., Omnicom, WPP) each owns more than 1.[2]

The public relations market in Britain is far bigger than those in other European nations (Table 61.1). Part of the explanation for this lies in historical, political, and economic differences among Western European states along with cultural differences in policy styles. However, the size and development of the public relations industry in the United States and Britain is a key reason why British and U.S. firms dominate the market in most member states of the EU. In 1995, only the Netherlands had more than 6 independent agencies in the top 20, and Italy had only 1.[3] The lobbying scene in Brussels, the seat of the European government, is also dominated by U.S.- and British-owned or Anglophone consultancies. Most of the bigger agencies are Anglophone in origin and operating language (although nearly all Brussels lobbyists are at least bilingual).

Concentration of ownership is also occurring. Many of the leading Brussels lobbyists are subsidiaries of multinational communications corporations. For example, GPC Market Access is owned by Omnicom, European Strategy is owned by Lopex, and APCO is owned by Grey Advertising. In 1998, one of the biggest and most respected independent lobbying firms, Adamson Associates, was taken over by Charles Barker BSMG, itself a subsidiary of the U.S. giant, True North. This move probably signaled the beginning of the end for independent public relations or lobbying consultancies of any significant size in the Brussels arena, although the strength of the accountancy, law, and management consultancy sectors might slow down the takeover process. Lobbying and public affairs in Brussels have acquired a specific character because of these professions. Although much of the impetus to develop the consultancy industry came from specialization within public relations as well as from the more traditional development of ex-ministers, MPs, MEPs, and civil servants acting as lobbyists, the heightened complexity of regu-

TABLE 61.1

Relative Sizes of Public Relations Agencies in Europe, the United States, and Japan

Country	ICO Members, 1991	ICO Members' Employees, 1991	Members' Fee Income, 1991 (thousands of ECUs)	Fee Income of Top 10 Agencies Combined, 1995 (thousands of British pounds)	Estimated Fee Income of Industry as a Whole, 1997 (billions of dollars)
Belgium	16	187	12,640	16,494	
Denmark	12	60	4,920		
Finland	24	119	12,000		
France	26	589	43,620	55,813	0.7
Germany	30	975	66,359	54,981	0.9
Greece[a]	16	64	2,300		
Holland	50	396	27,326	20,400	
Ireland	25	250	13,200		
Italy	21	440	34,098	18,199	
Norway	12	40	2,800		
Portugal[a]	4	45	1,060		
Spain	16	250	19,444	15,671	
Sweden	23	182	20,000		
Switzerland	11	228	20,780	22,416	
United Kingdom	163	4,145	239,400	133,255	3.1
United States				642,221	16.6
Japan					2.4

SOURCES: Figures in the first three columns are from the International Communications Organization cited in Mazur (1992). Figures in the fourth column are from "Europe: Top European Consultancies" (1996); figures for United States are from O'Dwyer's Web page (http://www.odwyerpr.com/rankingspagecopy.htm). Figures in the fifth column are from WPP Group PLC (1998).
NOTE: ICO = International Communications Organization; ECUs = European Currency Units.
a. *Observer.*

latory regimes in the EU has meant that some law practices have become specialists in advocacy and regulatory analysis. In addition, the lobbying and public affairs industries in countries such as France and Germany owe much more to these professions than is the case in Britain. More than 150 law practices and a similar number of accountancy firms are active in Brussels, many in some form of lobbying (Landmarks, 1997).

In Britain, the public relations consultancy sector expanded nearly 10-fold in real terms between 1979 and 1997 (Miller & Dinan, 2000). Most medium-sized to large British public relations consultancies now offer advice on European policy and legislation. Most of the bigger global consultancies also have public relations or lobbying offices in Brussels (e.g., Burson-Marsteller, Hill & Knowlton, Grayling Group, GCI, Fleishman-Hillard Shandwick, Edelman, Countrywide Porter Novelli).

In 1988, the total number of lobbyists in consultancies was estimated to be 500 (van der Straten Waillet, 1989, p. 11), and by the end of the 1980s, Berry (1991) reported that "only a small number" of British consultancies had "gone to the lengths of establishing associate offices in Brussels" (p. 213). The Single European Act of 1985 and the Treaty of European Union of 1991 have been crucial markers of the rise in lobbying capacity both in the consultancy and the in-house or trade association sectors. By the mid-1990s, the lobbying presence had increased dramatically. Estimates vary, but most suggest that there were between 10,000 and 15,000 full-time lobbyists working in Brussels for consultancies and also, more important, for companies, trade associations, and the like (Benoit, 1998; Clarke, 1996). In the early 1990s, Mazey and Richardson (1993, p. 14) estimated that there were 3,000 organizations and 10,000 lobbyists.

Staff levels doubled during the 5 years between 1993 and 1998, and the figure could double again by 2005. In 1998, half of the top 10 lobbying consultancies had been in Brussels only since 1990 or later, and only 2 had been in existence for more than 11 years (Benoit, 1998; Gardner, 1991, p. 56). Indeed, some notable players on the British lobbying and public relations scene, such as APCO and Shandwick, arrived in Brussels as late as 1995 (Bevan, 1995; "Boosting Own Brands," 1995).

Lobbyists apparently spend between 7 billion and 10 billion Belgian francs (between $190 million and $270 million) a year in Brussels (Benoit, 1998, p. 10). As a consequence, the Belgian public relations market is made up of a relatively high proportion of consultancies with high fee income. Only the Belgium, Switzerland, and U.K. markets included consultancies with more than £10 million fee income in 1997 (Hollis Directories Ltd., 1998, p. 26). Unsurprisingly, Belgium also has the highest proportion of consultancies that conduct European campaigns (p. 28). There

was a marked upturn in the pace of public relations and lobbying activities following the Treaty of European Union in 1991 (Hollis Directories Ltd., 1994, p. 41). However, even the bigger lobbyists do not necessarily bring in huge fees, and profits often are modest by public relations standards. Lobbying and public relations consultancy activities focused on the European institutions currently are undergoing marked growth. According to our sources in lobbying and public relations in Brussels, budgets topping £1 million may be spent by multinational corporations or collective interests in a single lobbying campaign. This is not surprising given the impact of EU regulations on cost structures in the European marketplace.

One of the key factors in the rise of the public relations and lobbying scene in Brussels was the early recognition of the significance of the European marketplace by U.S. multinationals. Large corporations, such as Coca-Cola, Alcoa, Dupont, Monsanto, Ford, IBM, and General Motors, set up government relations teams in Europe and began hiring public relations consultancies. "Of the 500 companies with [in-house] lobbying/government relations offices in Brussels, one third are American" (Benoit, 1998, p. 10). In addition, the flood of U.S. multinationals quickly led to U.S.-based public relations companies setting up offices in London, Brussels, and other European capitals (Mazur, 1992). Setting up offices in London was an obvious choice for many U.S. consultancies given the proximity of language and other cultural similarities as well as the significance of the city as a European financial center. However, some multinationals, such as IBM, also set up operations in Brussels. It is likely that the Anglophone dominance in public relations and lobbying will strengthen as new member states are admitted to the EU. Large companies in countries such as Sweden have tended to opt for English-speaking consultancies when entering the EU given their linguistic preferences (interview with Steven Atack, executive search consultant and editor of *Public Affairs Newsletter*, October 15, 1997). The lobbying and public relations industries targeting the EU have not yet faced the type of criticism aimed at their British equivalents (Greer, 1997; Leigh &

Vulliamy, 1996). However, lobbying activities and the outside interests of MEPs also have become an issue debated by the European Parliament since the early 1990s. In early 1996, MEPs voted in favor of a code outlawing the acceptance of gifts from outside interests and introduced a register of lobbyists that is notable for the lack of rigor with which it is enforced (Butler, 1996, p. 2; for a discussion, see Greenwood, 1998).

LOBBYING IN PRACTICE

The extensive "Europeanization" of governmental processes is reflected in the development of a truly transnational European political community. It is apparent that a supranational public space has indeed evolved around the policymaking actors in the various institutions. There are certain organizations that play an active role in policymaking and, therefore, have a more Pan-European approach to their activities than do others. These include the Union of Industries in the European Union and the European Trade Union Confederation, both of which are regularly consulted by the EU. Many other organizations have expanded, and in some cases have initiated, their advocacy activities to influence EU legislation. But even here, much of this activity ultimately relates back to national or regional interests.

This can be illustrated by reference to British business interests. Small and medium-sized British businesses and their representatives, such as the Institute of Directors, have been less enthusiastic about the EU than have larger corporations, particularly in the financial sector, and organizations such as the Confederation of British Industry. Their skepticism has, in some cases, led to a reliance on national government as a bulwark against Europe (PR Central, 1996). One consequence of this is that some British companies are less reliant on public relations and lobbying in Brussels than might be expected. Gerry Wade, a public affairs consultant with extensive in-house lobbying experience in Brussels, set up his consultancy in London:

We had a very serious discussion about opening our office in Brussels because it was our view that that is where the action was going to be longer term. Thank God we didn't because we would have been out of business very, very quickly. (interview, January 29, 1998)

The officially recognized regions of member states tend to have representative offices in Brussels. Despite criticism of this development by the national governments of some member states, the European Commission established a Consultative Council of Regional and Local Authorities, which is consulted on policies regarding regional development (Mazey & Richardson, 1992). In 1995, it was estimated that there were some 60 territorial offices in Brussels (Mitchell, 1995). These actors often cooperate with particular industries important for their regions. According to Gardner (1991), the involvement of regional representatives in a lobbying campaign "can impart a European 'spin' to an issue" (p. 67). Canel's (1994) analysis of the activities of EU regional agencies argued that the majority of the work involves "information mediation" in that the agencies provide details of EU policies and plans to other bodies at the national level as well as to regional governments in different countries. In general, regional bodies, such as other sectoral and industrial groups, have to establish liaisons with central government representatives in the EU on common lobbying strategies (Mazey & Mitchell, 1993).

EU information initiatives also are intended to work through regional links for reasons of "subsidiarity" and to recognize the growing legitimacy and voice of regions at the EU level. A good example of such regional articulation is Scotland Europa, which represents a variety of both public and private sector interests but mainly serves as an information office. Many sectoral interests do not operate through Scotland Europa, largely because relevant competencies remain with central government. Consequently, some Scottish interests have been expressed through U.K. representation, leaving it up to relevant British ministers, especially the Scottish secretary, to exert influence on the line taken at the EU level (Mazey & Mitchell, 1993;

Mitchell, 1995). Now that Scotland and Wales have devolved, their regional representation in the EU will develop in line with the changes in governance in those countries.

Non-EU interests also are extremely visible. As noted, U.S.-based multinationals have long seen Europe as a single marketplace, albeit one with different cultural and national sensitivities and regulations. According to nearly every writer on the subject (e.g., Gardner, 1991; Greenwood, 1997; Mazey & Richardson, 1993), the most important operator is the EU committee of the American Chamber of Commerce, widely noted as an extremely skilled and effective lobbyist for the interests of U.S. capital.

Although U.S. and other multinationals do have a privileged role in the EU arena, other interests also are at play. The case of the EU's Cocoa Directive highlights the increased complexity of lobbying inside the European Union and draws attention to the crucial role of both coalition building and resources in lobbying.[4] The Cocoa Directive has been one of the longest running lobbying battles in the EU arena. It revolves around the attempt to harmonize European-level policy on the constituents, definition, and labeling of chocolate. In 1973, when the United Kingdom joined the EU's precursor, the European Economic Community, it obtained an exemption from the general rule that chocolate had to contain only cocoa butter. This allowed British manufacturers to include up to 5% of non-cocoa vegetable fat and still call the product chocolate. The issue has been whether to move to the U.K. standard or to retain the Belgian/French standard.

The arguments have involved the chocolate manufacturers in each European country, their national trade associations, Europe-wide trade associations, and European umbrella associations of national trade associations. The European Parliament and the European Commission also have been involved. Countries that export much of the cocoa butter or, alternatively, the vegetable oil also have a direct interest in the debate. So, developing countries such as the Ivory Coast, Niger, and Mali have been involved in the debates, as have development and fair trade interest groups such as Oxfam. The lobbying effort

since 1973 has been immense, involving a wide range of Brussels-based and wider European public relations and lobbying consultancies together with the government relations officials of corporations and various trade associations and business interest groups (Mann & White, 1998).

Such debates and the mediation of interests that accompanies them are extremely complex and take up extensive resources and effort on the part of the interested parties. Yet, a telling symptom of the democratic deficit is that they are barely reported in member states and certainly do not become major issues in the domestic media.

CONCLUSION

Lobbying and public relations activities in the EU are increasing in scope and intensity. They also are diversifying by targeting not just the EU institutions (although that is their primary arena) but also national and regional governments in the member states. Trade associations, corporations, and interest groups also are increasingly finding themselves the subjects of lobbying and coalition building by the growing cohorts of promotional professionals.

Lobbyists and public relations people form a key part of the emergent European political elite. Their personal and professional histories are intertwined with other elements of both the European and member states' political elites. Many key actors have experience in party politics, have occupied research positions for politicians, have lobbied in consultancies, or have worked in civil service or journalism. Lobbying and public relations are largely undertaken for corporate and other sectional interests, and they increasingly mediate between these and the EU's institutions.

At present, the dominant trend in the evolution of EU-centered public relations and lobbying appears to be reinforcing intense interaction within a relatively closed policy community. This tendency is further supported by developments in some Europe-wide media sustaining a restricted communicative space that, above all, serves the European elites (Schlesinger, 1999; Schlesinger & Kevin, 2000). Consequently, the EU's "democratic deficit" appears more likely to increase than to decrease.

NOTES

1. The European Union consists of the following 15 member states: Austria, Belgium, Denmark, France, Finland, Germany, Greece, Ireland, Italy, Luxembourg, the Netherlands, Portugal, Spain, Sweden, and the United Kingdom.

2. WPP-owned agencies include Hill & Knowlton and Ogilvy, Adams, and Rhinehart (ranked 5th and 14th, respectively), and Omnicom owns Porter Novelli International, Fleishman-Hillard Europe, and Ketchum PR Europe (ranked 2nd, 10th, and 11th, respectively).

3. Figures on European companies are from "Europe: Top European Consultancies" (1996) and "Europe: Top European Agencies" (1997), both *PR Week* supplements.

4. Information on the Cocoa Directive is from interviews, especially with Andrew Johnson of Charles Barker, May 27, 1998; as well as from Mann and White (1998) and PR Central (1996).

Middle East Public Relations

A New Frontier in the United States

RISË JANE SAMRA

After years of observing the war-torn nations of the Middle East, significant events during the 1990s decade offered a new perspective to the world. Although considerable turmoil prevails, the current peace process brings hope. The signing of the Middle East peace agreement between warring nations on September 13, 1993; *The Fundamental Agreement Between the Holy See and the State of Israel* on December 30, 1993; and the awarding of the Nobel Peace Prize to Palestinian leader Yasser Arafat, late Israeli Prime Minister Yitzak Rabin, and former Israeli Foreign Minister Shimon Peres on October 13, 1994, were not only symbolic gestures but the beginning of a long journey toward reconciliation and peace.

To join in the understanding of differences and to promote the peace process, Barry University, a Roman Catholic institution with a Dominican tradition located in Miami, Florida, hosted its first Middle East peace conference titled "The Road to Peace: The Challenge of the Middle East" on March 22, 1994. Subsequently, a second conference titled "The Holy Land: Peace or Jihad?" was held on February 13, 1996. This was an ideal location for Middle East peace conferences because Barry has been engaged in an ongoing concerted dialogue with the Jewish community in South Florida.

Former Massachusetts Governor Michael Dukakis (the keynote speaker); several other prominent speakers; more than 700 faculty, staff, and students from Barry University, the University of Miami, Florida International University, and Florida Atlantic University; and interested people from the South Florida community participated in this day-long event.

This chapter discusses the highlights and lessons from the two peace conferences as prototypes for the Western public relations practitioner.

APPLICATION

I began by assembling an advisory board comprised of Jewish community leaders, Christian Lebanese, and Roman Catholic clergy. We met four times to plan the program format, content, publicity, and logistics. We made every effort to make sure that all sides of the issue were represented. Once the speakers were selected, we had to pursue them and their differences vigorously. The Likud and Labor parties of Israel, different factions of Muslims, and Christian Arabs of the region needed to be represented. Dealing with these different factions was analogous to the interaction that takes place in the Middle East except that it was happening on American turf. For example, representatives from the Israeli Likud party were not pleased with the peace agreement, whereas the Labor party wanted to push the peace initiative. The Muslim Arabs from the region had varied opinions among themselves depending on their regard or disregard for Hamas or Hezbollah. Palestinians were inclined to regard themselves as victims of occupation by the Jews. If they were Christian Lebanese, then they were inclined to believe that they were victims of occupation by both Palestinians and Jews. Thus, the scenario was very complex, and so was the challenge of allowing each speaker the opportunity to voice his or her opinion in a limited amount of time. These challenges were met, but the order of the program had been arbitrarily set by the advisory board to fit the format and schedule. When all the speakers participated on the large panel at the end of the day, it was intriguing to watch many of them vying for the last word. Indeed, they represented the microcosm of the true Middle East conflict, but with a sense of civility as each participant sat side by side.

It should be mentioned that security at the event was a big factor. Campus security, local police, and federal agents were ordered by the U.S. state department. Fortunately, there were no recorded incidences.

The Program Format and Content

Because the designated speakers represented three major faiths and many political viewpoints of the Middle East, innovations were recited by a Syrian Orthodox priest, an imam, a rabbi, and a Roman Catholic monsignor.

Dukakis, the keynote speaker, espoused "the case for optimism in the Middle East":

> I congratulate Barry on doing this. I would like to think this is a reflection of a new spirit brought about in the world and especially in the Middle East. . . . A few things have happened since [the Middle East peace agreement], and if you let them get to you, it can have a terrible effect on our sense of optimism. Given the background and the history of the Middle East during the last century, [however], . . . there is great room for cause for optimism. (Dukakis, 1994)

Subsequent noted speakers with the following panel topics ensued.

ISRAEL: ITS GOVERNMENT AND OPPOSITION

Ruhama Hermon, former consul general of Israel, said,

> I am optimistic, although there are many difficulties and we're facing so many obstacles. But there is no other way. There is no alternative . . . for us or for them. What is [a] peace? Now, this is the time to talk to them [the Arabs]. (Hermon, 1994)

Manfred Lehmann, national vice president of the Religious Zionists of America, said,

> There is no opposition when it comes to the question of peace. We all want peace. . . . The question is what kind of peace. Hundreds and hundreds of generals are opposed to peace. There are many alternatives. . . . Israel needs a majority unity government taking in all elements of the Jews of Israel, and in that case we can look forward to secure peace and not [a peace] fraught with many dangers as we see now. (Lehmann, 1994)

THE PALESTINE LIBERATION ORGANIZATION AND ITS OPPOSITION

James Zogby, executive director of the Arab American Institute, said,

The tendency in approaching the Arab-Israeli conflict is for each side to do history and then do it very badly. Sadat said it best in Jerusalem: . . . "We each have our history, and we could stand here . . . and do nothing with each other but say, here's my story, all the things that have happened to me; and I could come forward and do the same, and we could have Arabs and Jews arguing what happened in '29, '48, '67 . . ., whatever, you name the year. You got a story, we got a story. But the point is, we're stuck in the mud together now. And what happened to get us in the mud almost doesn't matter as much as if we don't reach out together and get out of the mud together, we're both going to drown and die." (Zogby, 1994)

Nihad Awad, former editor of the *Muslim World Monitor*, said,

The most important thing is to appreciate the fact [that] victims [on both sides] have been . . . exchanging labels and accusations. Everyone will say at [what] price; each one has to compromise. And I believe the handshake that shook the world should not shake the fact of history. . . . I am a victim of occupation. I was born in a refugee camp. Until the age of 4 years old, I did not have shoes to put on. We did not receive proper health care or education. . . . We have been traumatized, and the question in my mind [is] always, why me? Oppression produces violence, but this violent attitude is temporary . . . because I sincerely believe that every faith—Christianity, Islam, and Judaism—preaches justice. (Awad, 1994)

Robert Stern, secretary general of the Catholic Near East Welfare Association, said,

[Pursuant to the Middle East peace agreement, *The Fundamental Agreement Between the Holy See and the State of Israel*] was a clear affirmation of the part of the Holy See in Israel about the freedom of religion . . . and the rights of conscience and the repudiation of anti-Semitism and every form of discrimination against Jews. It also was an agreement that both the Roman Catholic Church and the state of Israel . . . have sovereign rights and then went on to say how the rights of the Roman Catholic Church would be exercised in the state of Israel—a very interesting challenge for the state of Israel to develop legislation about the presence and prerogatives [of] minority religions in the Jewish [state], a new enterprise [there].

One of the healthy developments [from the peace process] is the realization that we have to stop *demonizing* and start seeing the dignity of every person whether we agree with his political views or not. . . . We're not just concerned with negotiated solutions but [also are concerned with] the ultimate reconciliation, which comes from pardoning . . . pardoning someone who has offended you. . . . Peace is really the fruit of the process of reconciliation and of pardoning, and peace is also the climate of the future development of a person. (R. Stern, 1994, italics in original)

RELIGIOUS DIALOGUE

Lawrence Boadt, editor at Paulist Press, said, "We have this ecumenical opportunity [now]" (Boadt, 1994).

David Carroll, director of programs for the Catholic Near East Welfare Association, said, "We know full well [that] just as religion can be a *case* for conflict, it too can be a *cause* for conflict" (Carroll, 1994, italics in original).

Hassan Sabri, resident imam for the Islamic Center of South Florida, said,

As Muslims, we believe that God has created us as human beings in the best manner. . . . [However,] . . . we might reach or negotiate an agreement that both [of us] will sign, but when we go to our peoples, we'll find that we're in one valley and our people are totally in another valley. (Sabri, 1994)

Jack Bemporad, director of the Center for Christian-Jewish Understanding at Sacred Heart University, said,

> There is no real faith dialogue as long as one faith community [is] interested in converting the other; and there is no real dialogue as one faith community thought it covered the market on truth.... One has to give credit to the recent developments in the Catholic Church . . . in trying to rectify . . . the teaching of contempt in respect to Jews and Judaism. (Bemporad, 1994)

ETHNIC/RELIGIOUS MINORITIES

Walid Phares, associate professor of international relations at Florida Atlantic University, said,

> Real peace is beyond that [peace paper]. The farther we are from the region, the less knowledgeable we are. Without history, there is no presence. Dozens of mega-Hebrons are being perpetrated. Millions of people are suffering in the Middle East. (Phares, 1994)

Keith Roderick, secretary general of the Coalition for the Defense of Human Rights in Islamic Countries, said, "Any peace must arise from the region because those [its inhabitants] are the people who have vested interest, and that must include all parties, and the peace cannot be imposed from outside" (Roderick, 1994).

EVALUATION

It is true that peace begins within each one of us, but then it needs to graduate to the next level—imparting the peace concept to others. In a time when we, as a country, are so immense in popula-

tion and strapped by bureaucracy, sometimes it is easier to reap more immediate rewards by working out our differences at the local level. Obviously, the Barry University community initiated the peace discussion, but it was the receptivity of our distinguished guest speakers, the Miami community, and the community's great curiosity that made this such a fruitful event. As one participant wrote, "Oh, if only such congenial debates could be part of the [peace process] in the Middle East itself!" (Carroll, personal communication, April 25, 1994). Still another participant wrote the following, as published in *The Miami Herald:*

> Diverse and contending views were presented regarding peace possibilities not only between Israelis and Arabs, but [also] for the region. Partisans for each side of the . . . peace accords disagreed not only with the other side, but [also] with their compatriots. Across the more severe divides was a reading of history, a telling of their story that left little room for the other party. . . . A Catholic monsignor raised by a Jewish father and a Catholic mother told how natural it was to experience the two traditions in the harmony of a family. A Palestinian Muslim journalist disowned terrorism and, in adherence to Islam, believed that he was obligated to live in peace with Jews and Christians. A Lebanese Maronite Christian said it's naive for us in the West to believe that suddenly everyone in the Middle East would embrace enlightenment and peace would arrive. He preferred to sit down with the Islamic fundamentalist and seek how each could be faithful to his own tradition and yet accept the other. (DelColle, 1994, p. B3)

In view of the positive and uplifting response to all who took part in the 1994 conference, I coordinated the second Middle East peace conference in 1996. Local experts on the Middle East were invited to speak on this subject at Barry. Four of the speakers originated from the Middle East: a Christian Lebanese, a Muslim Lebanese representing Hamas, a Jew from the Likud party, and a Jew from the Labor party. One participant was a Christian from the Sudan. Participants exchanged controversial points of view in a heated discussion spurred by the audience. Things became especially intense when some of the American-born Jews in the audience confronted the Hamas panelist regarding terrorism. He, in turn, read from the Quran to substantiate these acts. The Christian Sudanese panelist also confronted the Hamas panelist when he elaborated with statistics on the persecution of Christians in the Sudan. Years later, these people still are talking about these events, as revealed through their articles published in American, Israeli, and Arabic newspapers as well as through their phone calls and correspondence to the university and me.

For the Western public relations practitioner, the Middle East peace process could be taking place right in one's own community, as was the case in South Florida. Where there are multiethnic groups that play a significant role in the religious and sociopolitical spectrum, there is opportunity abounding for public relations practitioners to implement their skills beginning at the local level. To begin, they could assume the role of educating and reeducating the American public on the Middle East. The mutual benefits to this include (a) deeper appreciation of Middle Eastern history and its contribution to Western civilization, (b) better understanding of the behaviors of its people and culture, (c) ongoing religious and political dialogue, (d) leadership and participation in the peace process, and (e) financial gains to Arabs and Jews by expanding economic ties. Thus, the successful completion of the peace process would add to the stability of the Middle East in multifaceted ways.

So, how do we pave the way to this new frontier to the Middle East? It is with willingness and tenacity that we do so. In spite of the signing of these peace agreements, isolated attacks by extremist factions and the assassination of Israeli Prime Minister Rabin in 1995 challenged the peace process. However, these events did not and should not stand in the way of progress. As witnessed on October 23, 1998, in Maryland, Palestinian leader Yasser Arafat and Israeli Prime Minister Benjamin Natanyahu signed the American-brokered Wye River peace accord, which was drafted to address land, law, and security in the Middle East. This event seemed truly remarkable because Netanyahu has represented the ultra-religious and Zionist right who have hindered the peace process. Perhaps this event came too late for Netanyahu's political career. On May 17, 1999, a sweeping backlash to Natanyahu's conservative views elected Ehud Barak, Rabin's protégé, as Israel's new prime minister (Sontag, 1999). Furthermore, King Abdullah Hussein of Jordan promised to pursue the peace process that his father upheld (Morris, 1999).

The peace conferences could present a very exciting challenge to those of us in the public relations field, giving us the opportunity to explore a new frontier with new techniques. We have the tools and the means to organize similar events, in the process creating awareness of our society and its international geopolitical structure of which we all are a part.

REFERENCES

Abbott, A. (1988). *The system of the professions: An essay on the division of expert labor.* Chicago: University of Chicago Press.

ABC News. (1998, June 1). Trumped by a widow: Woman refuses to surrender her home [online]. Available: http://www.abcnews.com/onair/2020/transcripts/2020-casino0601

Abdeen, A. M. (1991). Social responsibility disclosure in annual reports. *Business Forum, 16,* 23-26.

Abrahamson, D. (1998). The visible hand: Money, markets, and media evolution. *Journalism & Mass Communication Quarterly, 75*(1), 14-18.

ACLU v. Reno, 929 F. Supp. 824 (E.D. Pa. 1996).

Adams, J. (1995). *Risk.* London: UCL Press.

Adderly v. Florida, 385 U.S. 39 (1966).

Adler, N. J. (1991). *International dimensions of organizational behavior.* Boston: PWS-Kent.

Adler, N. J. (1997). *International dimensions of organizational behavior* (3rd ed.). Cincinnati, OH: South-Western.

Advice for soon-to-be working mothers. (1998, May). *Public Relations Tactics,* p. 30.

Aitkin, I. (1993). *Film and reform: John Grierson and the documentary film movement.* London: Routledge.

Ajzen, I. (1988). *Attitudes, personality, and behavior.* Chicago: Dorsey.

Ajzen, I. (1991). The theory of planned behavior. *Organizational Behavior and Human Decision Processes, 50,* 179-210.

Ajzen, I., & Fishbein, M. (1980). *Understanding attitudes and predicting social behavior.* Englewood Cliffs, NJ: Prentice Hall.

Alanazi, A. (1996). Public relations in the Middle East: The case of Saudi Arabia. In H. M. Culbertson & N. Chen (Eds.), *International public relations: A comparative analysis* (pp. 239-256). Mahwah, NJ: Lawrence Erlbaum.

Albrecht, S. (1996). *Crisis management for corporate self-defense.* New York: American Management Association.

Aldoory, L. (1998a). The language of leadership for female public relations professionals. *Journal of Public Relations Research, 10,* 73-102.

Aldoory, L. (1998b). *The need for meaningful health communications: Female audience interpretation analysis of mass media health messages.* Unpublished dissertation, Syracuse University.

Aldoory, L. (in press). The standard white woman in public relations. In E. L. Toth (Ed.), *The gender challenge to media: Diverse voices from the field.* Cresskill, NJ: Hampton.

Aldoory, L., & Toth, E. L. (in press). Two feminists, six opinions: The complexities of feminism in communication scholarship today. In W. B. Gudykunst (Ed.), *Communication yearbook 24.* Thousand Oaks, CA: Sage.

Aldrich, H., & Herker, D. (1977). Boundary spanning roles and organization structure. *Academy of Management Review, 2,* 217-230.

Aldrich, H., & Mueller, S. (1982). The evolution of organizational forms: Technology, coordination, and control. *Research in Organizational Behavior, 4,* 33-87.

Aldrich, H., & Pfeffer, J. (1976). Environments of organizations. *Annual Review of Sociology, 2,* 79-105.

Aldrich, J. H., Sullivan, J. L., & Borgida, E. (1993). Foreign affairs and issue voting. In R. G. Niemi & H. F. Weisberg (Eds.), *Controversies in voting behavior* (pp. 167-186). Washington, DC: Congressional Quarterly.

Al-Enad, A. H. (1992). Values of public relations conduct in Saudi Arabia. *Public Relations Review, 18,* 213-221.

Alexander, J. M. (1996, November). Setting up a Website surveillance system. *Public Relations Tactics,* p. 6.

Alexander, S. (1996, September). *How to survive in a digital society.* Paper presented at the Public Relations Institute of Australia National Convention, Adelaide.

Allee, V. (1997). *The knowledge evolution: Expanding organizational intelligence.* Boston: Butterworth-Heinemann.

Allen B. Dumont Laboratories Inc. v. Carroll (D.C. Pa. 1949) 86 F. Supp. 813, *affirmed* (CA3) 184 F. 2d 153, *certiorari denied* 340 U.S. 929.

Allen, M. W., & Caillouet, R. H. (1994). Legitimation efforts: Impression management strategies used by an organization in crisis. *Communication Monographs, 61,* 44-62.

Allen, T. H. (1978). *New methods in social science research.* New York: Praeger.

Allen, V. L. (1975). Social support for non-conformity. In L. Berkowitz (Ed.), *Advances in experimental social psychology* (pp. 133-175). New York: Academic Press.

Allport, F. H. (1924). *Social psychology.* Boston: Houghton Mifflin.

Allport, F. H. (1937). Toward a science of public opinion. *Public Opinion Quarterly, 1,* 7-23.

Allport, G. W., Vernon, P. E., & Lindzey, G. (1960). *Study of values* (3rd ed.). Boston: Houghton Mifflin.

Alvarez, P. H. (1995). *A house divided: Communicating to a fractured society* (Vernon C. Shranz Distinguished Lectureship in Public Relations). Muncie, IN: Ball State University.

Alvesson, M. (1990). Organization: From substance to image? *Organization Studies, 11,* 373-394.

Amburgey, T. L., Kelly, D., & Barnett, W. P. (1993). Resetting the clock: The dynamics of organizational change. *Administrative Science Quarterly, 38,* 51-73.

American Law Institute. (1986). *Restatement (second) of contracts.* Washington, DC: Author.

American to change offensive language. (1997, August 20). *United Press International* [newswire].

An, G. (1990). Chuangban you Zhongguo tese de gongguan [Establish public relations with Chinese features]. *Gonggong Guanxi* [Public Relations Journal], *2,* 4-5.

Andersen, P. A., & Guerrero, L. K. (Eds.). (1998). *The handbook of communication and emotion.* San Diego: Academic Press.

Anderson, D. A. (1994). *Contemporary sports reporting* (3rd ed.). Chicago: Nelson-Hall.

Anderson, R. B. (1995). Cognitive appraisal of performance capability in the prevention of drunken driving: A test of self-efficacy theory. *Journal of Public Relations Research, 7,* 205-229.

Anderson, R., & Reagan, J. (1992). Practitioner roles and uses of new technologies. *Journalism Quarterly, 69,* 156-165.

Andorfer, B. (1996, March 31). The changing face of America: Soon majority will be a minority. *Gainesville Sun,* p. A6.

Andrews, K. R. (Ed.). (1953). *The case method of teaching human relations and administration.* Cambridge, MA: Harvard University Press.

Anfuso, D. (1994). Deflecting workplace violence. *Personnel Journal, 73*(10), 66-67.

Anshen, M. (1980). *Corporate strategies for social performance.* New York: Macmillan.

Applegate, E. (1997). Advertising. In W. G. Christ (Ed.), *Media education assessment handbook* (pp. 319-339). Mahwah, NJ: Lawrence Erlbaum.

Arendt, H. (1961). *Between past and future: Six exercises in political thought.* New York: Meridian.

Arenson, M. C. (1998, June). Not in our back yard. *Nursing Homes,* pp. 24-30.

Argyris, C. (1980). Some limitations of the case method: Experiences in a management development program. *Academy of Management Review, 5,* 291-298.

Aristotle. (1952a). Politics (B. Jowett, Trans.). In R. M. Hutchins (Ed.), *Great books* (Vol. 2, pp. 445-548). Chicago: Encyclopaedia Britannica.

Aristotle. (1952b). Rhetoric (W. R. Roberts, Trans.). In R. M. Hutchins (Ed.), *Great books* (Vol. 2, pp. 593-675). Chicago: Encyclopaedia Britannica.

Aristotle. (1954). *The rhetoric* (W. R. Roberts, Trans.). New York: Modern Library.

Arnold, J. E. (1994). Using accreditation for assessment. In W. Christ (Ed.), *Assessing communication education* (pp. 333-350). Hillsdale, NJ: Lawrence Erlbaum.

Arnstein, C. (1994). How companies can rebuild credibility and public trust. *Public Relations Journal, 50*(4), 28-29.

Aronoff, C. (1975). Credibility of public relations for journalists. *Public Relations Review, 1*(2), 45-56.

Arrow, K., Anderson, P., & Pines, D. (1988). *The economy as an evolving complex system.* Reading, MA: Addison-Wesley.

Ashforth, B. E., & Gibbs, B. W. (1990). The double-edge of organizational legitimation. *Organization Science, 1,* 177-194.

Astley, W. G. (1977). Central perspectives and debates in organizational theory. *Administrative Science Quarterly, 22,* 245-273.

Astley, W. G. (1985). The two ecologies: Population and community perspectives on organizational evolution. *Administrative Science Quarterly, 30,* 223-241.

Athanasiou, T. (1996). *Divided planet: The ecology of rich and poor.* Boston: Little, Brown.

Atlbach, P. G., & DeWit, H. (1997, Fall). U.S. risks losing competitive edge. *Medallion,* pp. 6-7. (Phi Beta Delta Honor Society for International Scholars)

Austin, J. (1962). *How to do things with words.* Cambridge, MA: Harvard University Press.

Austin, N. K. (1998, May). When buzz goes bad: Some tips on how to operate in a crisis. *Inc.,* pp. 44-53.

Avineri, S., & de-Shalit, A. (1992). Introduction. In S. Avineri & A. de-Shalit (Eds.), *Communitarianism and individualism* (pp. 1-11). Oxford, UK: Oxford University Press.

Awad, N. (1994, March). *The PLO and its opposition.* Panel discussion at the conference, "The Road to Peace: The Challenge of the Middle East," Miami, FL.

Backard, A. (1996, November 15). *Anonymous remailer FAQ* [on-line]. Available: http://www.well.com/user/abacard/remail.html

Badaracco, C. H. (1998). The transparent corporation and organized community. *Public Relations Review, 24,* 265-272.

Baerns, B. (1993, May). *Understanding and development of public relations in Germany, East and West.* Paper presented at the Second European Seminar for Teachers, Practitioners, and Researchers, Prague, Czech Republic.

Baker, L. W. (1993). *The credibility factor: Putting ethics to work in public relations.* Homewood, IL: Irwin.

Bakhtin, M. M. (1981). *The dialogic imagination: Four essays by M. M. Bakhtin* (M. Holquist, Ed.; C. Emerson & M. Holquist, Trans.). Austin: University of Texas Press.

Balasubramanian, S. K. (1991). *Beyond advertising and publicity: The domain of hybrid messages* (Report No. 91-131). Cambridge, MA: Marketing Science Institute.

Bales, R. F. (1970). *Personality and interpersonal behavior.* New York: Holt, Rinehart & Winston.

Bales, R. F. (1988). A new overview of the SYMLOG system: Measuring and changing behavior in groups. In R. B. Polley, A. P. Hare, & P. J. Stone (Eds.), *The SYMLOG practitioner: Applications of small group research* (pp. 319-344). New York: Praeger.

Bales, R. F., & Cohen, S. P. (1979). *SYMLOG: System for the Multiple-Level Observation of Groups.* New York: Free Press.

Ball, S., & Bogatz, G. A. (1970). *The first year of Sesame Street: An evaluation.* Princeton, NJ: Educational Testing Service.

Bandura, A. (1977). *Social learning theory.* Englewood Cliffs, NJ: Prentice Hall.

Banfield, E. (1958). *The moral basis of a backward society.* New York: Free Press.

BankDirect. (1998). [Description and advertising for on-line banking services.] Available: http://www.bankdirect.co.nz/kiosk

Banks, S. P. (1995). *Multicultural public relations: A social-interpretive approach.* Thousand Oaks, CA: Sage.

Banks, S. P., & Riley, P. (1993). Structuration theory as an ontology for communication research. In S. A. Deetz (Ed.), *Communication yearbook 17* (pp. 167-196). Newbury Park, CA: Sage.

Baran, S. J., & Davis, D. K. (1995). *Mass communication theory: Foundations, ferment, and future.* Belmont, CA: Wadsworth.

Bardin, M. D. (1994). Taking the pulse of health care reform. *Public Relations Journal, 50*(3), 14-16, 29.

Barkelew, A. H. (1993). *Building bridges: The public relations challenge in the public and private sector* (Vernon C. Schranz Distinguished Lectureship Monograph). Muncie, IN: Ball State University, Department of Journalism.

Barlow, S. L. (1998). The ox, the tiger, and El Nino: All instigators who have led us to where we are today. In *Proceedings of International Symposium 2.* Gainesville: University of Florida, Institute for Public Relations Research and Education.

Barnes, B. (1988). *The nature of power.* Urbana: University of Illinois Press.

Barnes, L. B., Christenson, C. R., & Hansen, A. J. (1994). *Teaching and the case method: Text, cases, and readings* (3rd ed.). Boston: Harvard Business School Press.

Barney, R. D., & Black, J. (1994). Ethics and professional persuasive communications. *Public Relations Review, 20*, 233-248.

Barton, L. (1993). *Crisis in organizations: Managing communications in the heat of chaos.* Cincinnati, OH: South-Western.

Bartunek, J., Gordon, J. R., & Weathersby, R. P. (1983). Developing "complicated" under-standing in administrators. *Academy of Management Review, 8*, 273-284.

Basil, M. D. (1996). Identification as a mediator of celebrity effects. *Journal of Broadcasting & Electronic Media, 40*, 478-495.

Basil, M. D. (1997). A new world of media effects. In L. W. Jeffres (Ed.), *Mass media effects* (2nd ed., pp. 1-18). Prospect Heights, IL: Waveland.

Baskin, K. (1998). *Corporate DNA: Learning from life.* Boston: Butterworth-Heinemann.

Baskin, O., & Aronoff, C. (1988). *Public relations: The profession and the practice* (2nd ed.). Dubuque, IA: Wm. C. Brown.

Baskin, O., & Aronoff, C. (1992). *Public relations: The profession and the practice* (3rd ed.). Dubuque, IA: Wm. C. Brown.

Baskin, O., Aronoff, C., & Lattimore, D. (1997). *Public relations: The profession and the practice* (4th ed.). Madison, WI: Brown & Benchmark.

Baudrillard, J. (1983). *In the shadow of the silent majorities.* New York: Semiotext(e).

Baum, J. A. C., & Singh, J. V. (Eds.). (1994). *Evolutionary dynamics of organizations.* New York: Oxford University Press.

Baxter, L. A. (1994). A dialogic approach to relationship maintenance. In D. J. Canary & L. Stafford (Eds.), *Communication and relational maintenance* (pp. 233-254). San Diego: Academic Press.

Baym, N. K. (1995). The emergence of community in computer-mediated communication. In S. G. Jones (Ed.), *Cybersociety: Computer-mediated communication and community* (pp. 138-163). Thousand Oaks, CA: Sage.

Beamish, A. (1995). *Communities on line: Community-based computer networks.* Unpublished dissertation, Massachusetts Institute of Technology. Available: http://alberti.mit.edu/arch/4.207/anneb/thesis/toc.html

Beauharnais v. Illinois, 343 U.S. 250 (1952).

Becker, H. (1992). Cases, causes, conjunctures, stories, and imagery. In C. C. Ragin & H. S. Becker (Eds.), *What is a case? Exploring the foundations of social inquiry* (pp. 205-216). Cambridge, UK: Cambridge University Press.

Becker, H. S., Greer, B., Hughes, E. C., & Strauss A. L. (1961). *Boys in white.* Chicago: University of Chicago Press.

Becker, L. C. (1986). *Reciprocity.* New York: Routledge & Kegan Paul.

Beed, E. T. (1994, June 28). *Total quality management: Can its principles improve health care delivery, especially to the urban poor?* Testimony to the Subcommittee on Technology, Environments and Aviation Committee on Science, Space, and Technology, House of Representatives, 103rd Congress, 2nd session. Washington, DC: Government Printing Office.

Beetham, D. (1991). *The legitimation of power.* Atlantic Highlands, NJ: Humanities Press International.

Beiner, R. (1992). *What's the matter with liberalism?* Berkeley: University of California Press.

Being global means going multi-lingual and multi-cultural. (1997, October 20) *PR Reporter,* pp. 1-2.

Bell, Q. (1992). Evaluating PR. In *Institute for Public Relations Handbook* (pp. 21-22). London: Kogan Page.

Bellah, R. N. (1998). Community properly understood: A defense of "democratic communitarianism." In A. Etzioni (Ed.), *The essential communitarian reader* (pp. 15-19). Lanham, MD: Rowman & Littlefield.

Bellah, R. N., Madsen, R., Sullivan, W. M., Swidler, A., & Tipton, S. M. (1985). *Habits of the heart: Individualism and commitment in American life.* Berkeley: University of California Press.

Bellah, R. N., Madsen, R., Sullivan, W. M., Swidler, A., & Tipton, S. M. (1992). *The good society.* New York: Vintage Books.

Bemporad, J. (1994, March). *Religious dialogue.* Panel discussion at the conference, "The Road to Peace: The Challenge of the Middle East," Miami, FL.

Bender, I. E. (1958). Changes in religious interest: A retest after 15 years. *Journal of Abnormal and Social Psychology, 57,* 41-46.

Beng, Y. S. (1994). The state of public relations in Singapore. *Public Relations Review, 20,* 373-394.

Benhabib, S. (1992). *Situating the self: Gender, community, and postmodernism in contemporary ethics.* New York: Routledge.

Beninger, J. R. (1987). Personalization of mass media and the growth of pseudo-community. *Communication Research, 14,* 352-371.

Bennett, W. L. (1980). *Public opinion in American politics.* New York: Harcourt Brace Jovanovich.

Benoit, B. (1998, June 15-21). Lobbyists swarm to Europe's Washington D.C. *The European,* p. 10.

Benoit, W. L. (1995a). *Accounts, excuses, and apologies: A theory of image restoration strategies.* Albany: State University of New York Press.

Benoit, W. L. (1995b). Sears' repair of its auto service image: Image restoration discourse in the corporate sector. *Communication Studies, 46,* 89-105.

Benoit, W. L. (1997). Image repair discourse and crisis communication. *Public Relations Review, 23,* 177-186.

Benoit, W. L., & Brinson, S. L. (1994). AT&T: "Apologies are not enough." *Communication Quarterly, 42,* 75-88.

Benoit, W. L., & Drew, S. (1997). Appropriateness and effectiveness of image repair strategies. *Communication Reports, 10,* 153-163.

Benoit, W. L., & Lindsey, J. J. (1987). Argument strategies: Antidote to Tylenol's poisoned image. *Journal of the American Forensic Association, 23,* 136-146.

Benson, J. A. (1988). Crisis revisited: An analysis of strategies used by Tylenol in the second tampering episode. *Central States Speech Journal, 39,* 49-66.

Bentele, G., & Peter, G. M. (1996). Public relations in the German Democratic Republic and the new federal German states. In H. M. Culbertson & N. Chen (Eds.), *International public relations: A comparative analysis* (pp. 349-366). Mahwah, NJ: Lawrence Erlbaum.

Bentham, J. (1962). *The works of Jeremy Bentham.* New York: Russell & Russell. (Original work published 1838)

Bentley, D. (1998, October). Stand by your brand. *Hemispheres.* (United Airlines)

Berg, P. O. (1986). The symbolic management of human resources. *Human Resource Management, 25,* 557-579.

Berg, P. O. (1989). Postmodern management? From facts to fiction in theory and practice. *Scandinavian Journal of Management, 5*(3), 201-217.

Berg, P. O., & Gagliardi, P. (1985). *Corporate images: A symbolic perspective of the organization-environment interface.* Paper presented at the Standing Committee on Organizational Symbolism Conference on Corporate Images, Antibes, France.

Berger, C. R., & Calabrese, R. J. (1975). Some explorations in initial interaction and beyond: Toward a developmental theory of interpersonal communication. *Human Communication Research, 1,* 99-112.

Berger, M. A. (1983). In defense of the case method: A reply to Argyris. *Academy of Management Review, 8,* 329-333.

Bergquist, W. H. (1993). *The postmodern organization: Mastering the art of irreversible change.* San Francisco: Jossey-Bass.

Berkowitz, D. (1997). *Social meanings of news: A text-reader.* Thousand Oaks, CA: Sage.

Berkowitz, D., & Tunmire, K. (1994). Community relations and issues management: An issue orientation approach to segmenting publics. *Journal of Public Relations Research, 6,* 105-123.

Bernays, E. L. (1923). *Crystallizing public opinion.* New York: Boni & Liveright.

Bernays, E. L. (1925). *Crystallizing public opinion for good government.* Address presented at the joint meeting of the National Municipal League and the American Civic Association, Pittsburgh, PA.

Bernays, E. L. (1965). *Biography of an idea: Memoirs of public relations counsel Edward L. Bernays.* New York: Simon and Schuster.

Bernays, E. L. (1979). The case for licensing and registration for public relations. *Public Relations Quarterly, 24*(2), 26-28.

Bernays, E. L. (1980). Gaining professional status for public relations. *Public Relations Quarterly, 25*(2), 20.

Bernays, E. L. (1986). *The later years: Public relations insights, 1956-1986.* Rhinebeck, NY: H&M Publishers.

Bernstein, J. (1986, January 27). Is PR field being hurt by too many women? *Advertising Age,* pp. 66-67.

Bernstein, R. J. (1983). *Beyond objectivism and relativism: Science, hermeneutics, and praxis.* Philadelphia: University of Pennsylvania Press.

Berry, J. M. (1984). *The interest group society.* Boston: Little, Brown.

Berry, S. (1991). *The growth and development of the commercial lobbying industry in Britain during the 1980s.* Unpublished Ph.D. dissertation, Birkbeck College, University of London.

Berube, M. (1996). Public perceptions of universities and faculty. *Academe, 82*(4), 10-17.

Bessette, G. (1997). Empowering people through information and communication technology: Lessons from experience? *Journal of Development Communication, 17,* 1-26.

Betts, M. (1995, June). On-line pay per view. *Computer World,* p. 58.

Bevan, S. (1995, July 28). Single Europe, single agency. *PR Week,* p. 41.

Biagi, S. (1998). *Media/impact: An introduction to mass media* (3rd ed.). Belmont, CA: Wadsworth.

Bick, P. A. (1988). *Business ethics and responsibility: An information sourcebook.* Phoenix, AZ: Oryx Press.

Bisbee, J. (1998, February). The survey says . . .: Outsourcing of PR activities on the rise. *Public Relations Tactics,* p. 13.

Bishop, R. I. (1988). What newspapers say about public relations. *Public Relations Review, 14*(2), 50-52.

Bittle, S. (1995, December 14). Surveying consumers on the Internet. *Travel Weekly,* p. 23.

Bitzer, L. F. (1968). The rhetorical situation. *Philosophy and Rhetoric, 1,* 1-15.

Bitzer, L. F. (1978). Rhetoric and public knowledge. In D. M. Burks (Ed.), *Rhetoric, philosophy, and literature: An exploration* (pp. 67-93). West Lafayette, IN: Purdue University Press.

Bivins, T. H. (1987). Applying ethical theory to public relations. *Journal of Business Ethics, 6,* 195-200.

Bivins, T. H. (1989a). Are public relations texts covering ethics adequately? *Journal of Mass Media Ethics, 4,* 39-52.

Bivins, T. H. (1989b). Ethical implications of the relationship of purpose to role and function in public relations. *Journal of Business Ethics, 8,* 65-73.

Bivins, T. H. (1992). A systems model for ethical decision making in public relations. *Journal of Business Ethics, 18,* 365-383.

Bizzell, P. (1982). Cognition, convention, and certainty: What we need to know about writing. *Pre/Text, 3,* 213-243.

Black, S. (1979). Introduction. In S. Black (Ed.), *Public relations in the 1980's: Proceedings of the eighth annual Public Relations World Congress* (p. xi). Oxford, UK: Pergamon.

Black, S. (1992). Chinese update. *Public Relations Quarterly, 37*(3), 41.

Blair, C. (1984). From "All the President's Men" to every man for himself: The strategies of post-Watergate apologia. *Central States Speech Journal, 35,* 250-260.

Blank, W. (1995). *The 9 natural laws of leadership.* New York: American Management Association.

Blewett, S. (1993). Who do people say that we are? *Communication World, 10*(7), 13-16.

Blissland, J. H. (1990). Accountability gap: Evaluation practices show improvement. *Public Relations Review, 16*(2), 25-35.

Blumer, H. (1946a). Elementary collective groupings. In A. M. Lee (Ed.), *New outlines of the principles of sociology* (pp. 178-198). New York: Barnes & Noble.

Blumer, H. (1946b). Social movements. In A. M. Lee (Ed.), *New outlines of the principles of sociology* (pp. 199-220). New York: Barnes & Noble.

Blumer, H. (1948). Public opinion and public opinion polling. *American Sociological Review, 13,* 542-554.

Boadt, L. (1994, March). *Religious dialogue.* Panel discussion at the conference, "The Road to Peace: The Challenge of the Middle East," Miami, FL.

Boal, I. A. (1995). A flow of monsters: Luddism and virtual technologies. In J. Brook & I. A. Boal (Eds.), *Resisting the virtual life: The culture and politics of information* (pp. 3-15). San Francisco: City Lights.

Bobbitt, R. (1995). An Internet primer for public relations. *Public Relations Quarterly, 40*(3), 27-32.

Boje, D., & Dennehy, R. F. (1994). *Managing in the postmodern world: America's revolution against exploitation* (2nd ed.). Dubuque: IA: Kendall/Hunt.

Boje, D., Gephart, R., Jr., & Thatchenkery, T. J. (1996a). Postmodern management and the coming crisis of organizational analysis. In D. Boje, R. Gephart, Jr., & T. J. Thatchenkery (Eds.), *Postmodern management and organization theory* (pp. 1-18). London: Sage.

Boje, D., Gephart, R., Jr., & Thatchenkery, T. J. (Eds.). (1996b). *Postmodern management and organization theory.* London: Sage.

Bok, S. (1995). *Common values.* Columbia: University of Missouri Press.

Bonoma, T. V., & Shapiro, B. P. (1983). *Segmenting the industrial market.* Lexington, MA: Lexington Books.

Boone, C., & van Witteloostuijn, A. (1995). Industrial organization and organizational ecology: The potentials for cross-fertilization. *Organization Studies, 16,* 265-298.

Boorstin, D. J. (1964). *The image: A guide to pseudo-events in America.* New York: Harper Colophon.

Boosting own brands. (1996, July 26). *PR Week,* p. vii. (Top European consultancies supplement).

Boote, A. (1981). Market segmentation by personal values and salient product attributes. *Journal of Advertising Research, 21,* 29-35.

Booth, A. L. (1985). Who are we? *Public Relations Journal, 41*(6), 14-20, 44.

Booth, A. L. (1988). Strength in numbers. In R. E. Hiebert (Ed.), *Precision public relations* (pp. 111-118). White Plains, NY: Longman.

Booth, W. C. (1981). Mere rhetoric, rhetoric, and the search for common learning. In E. I. Boyer (Ed.), *Common learning: A Carnegie colloquium on general education* (pp. 23-55).

Washington, DC: Carnegie Foundation for the Advancement of Teaching.

Bormann, E. G. (1972). Fantasy and rhetorical vision: The rhetorical criticism of social reality. *Quarterly Journal of Speech, 58,* 396-407.

Bormann, E. G. (1982). Colloquy I: Fantasy and rhetorical vision—Ten years later. *Quarterly Journal of Speech, 68,* 288-305.

Bormann, E. G. (1983). The symbolic convergence theory of communication and the creation, raising, and sustaining of public consciousness. In J. I. Sisco (Ed.), *The Jensen Lectures: Contemporary communication studies* (pp. 71-90). Tampa, FL: University of South Florida, Department of Communication.

Bormann, E. G. (1985). Symbolic convergence theory: A communication formulation. *Journal of Communication, 35*(4), 128-138.

Bormann, E. G. (1986). Symbolic convergence theory and communication in group decision-making. In R. Y. Hirokawa & M. S. Poole (Eds.), *Communication and group decision-making* (pp. 219-236). Beverly Hills, CA: Sage.

Bormann, E. G. (1996). Symbolic convergence theory and communication in group decision making. In R. Y. Hirokawa & M. S. Poole (Eds.), *Communication and group decision making* (2nd ed., pp. 81-113). Thousand Oaks, CA: Sage.

Bormann, E. G., Cragan, J. F., & Shields, D. C. (1992, November). *In defense of symbolic convergence theory: A look at the theory and its criticism after two decades.* Paper presented at the meeting of the Speech Communication Association, Chicago.

Bostdorff, D., & Vibbert, S. L. (1994). Values advocacy: Enhancing organizational images, deflecting public criticism, and grounding future arguments. *Public Relations Review, 20,* 141-158.

Boswell, J. (1990). *Community and the economy: The theory of public cooperation.* London: Routledge.

Botan, C. H. (1987). Theory development in public relations. In C. H. Botan & V. Hazleton, Jr. (Eds.), *Public relations theory* (pp. 99-110). Hillsdale, NJ: Lawrence Erlbaum.

Botan, C. H. (1990). Industrial relations communication. In D. O'Hair & G. L. Kreps (Eds.), *Applied communication theory and research* (pp. 61-75). Hillsdale, NJ: Lawrence Erlbaum.

Botan, C. H. (1992) International public relations: Critique and reformulation. *Public Relations Review, 18,* 149-159.

Botan, C. H. (1993a). A human nature approach to image and ethics in international public relations. *Journal of Public Relations Research, 5,* 71-81.

Botan, C. H. (1993b). Introduction to the paradigm struggle in public relations. *Public Relations Review, 19,* 107-110.

Botan, C. H. (1996). Communication work and electronic surveillance: A model for predicting panoptic effects. *Communication Monographs, 63,* 293-313.

Botan, C. H., & Frey, L. R. (1983). Do workers trust their labor unions and their messages? *Communication Monographs, 50,* 233-244.

Botan, C. H., & Hazleton, V., Jr. (Eds.). (1989). *Public relations theory.* Hillsdale, NJ: Lawrence Erlbaum.

Botan, C. H., & Soto, F. (1998). A semiotic approach to the internal functioning of publics: Implications for strategic communication and public relations. *Public Relations Review, 24,* 21-44.

Boulding, K. D. (1977). *The image: Knowledge in life and society.* Ann Arbor: University of Michigan Press.

Bourdieu, P. (1987). What makes a social class? On the theoretical and practical existence of groups. *Berkeley Journal of Sociology: A Critical Review, 32,* 1-18.

Bovet, S. F. (1993). The burning question of ethics: The profession fights for better business practices. *Public Relations Journal, 49*(11), 24-25, 29.

Bovet, S. F. (1994). Make companies more socially responsible. *Public Relations Journal, 50*(10), 30-31, 34.

Bovet, S. F. (1995). Hi-tech editors lead charge into cyberspace. *Public Relations Journal, 51*(1), 40.

Bowers, J. W., & Ochs, D. (1971). *The rhetoric of agitation and control.* Reading, MA: Addision-Wesley.

Bowie, N. (1991, July-August). New directions in corporate social responsibility. *Business Horizons, 34*(4), 56-65.

Bracey, G. W. (1985). Is education newsworthy? *Phi Delta Kappan, 66,* 654-655.

Bradford, J. L., & Garrett, D. E. (1995). The effectiveness of corporate communicative responses to accusations of unethical behavior. *Journal of Business Ethics, 14,* 875-892.

Bradsher, K. (1996, April 26). Ford announces recall of 8.7 million cars and trucks. *The New York Times,* p. D1.

Braman, D. (1980). Feedback in community and government relations. *Public Relations Quarterly, 25*(2), 16-19.

Branham, R. J. (1980). Ineffability, creativity, and communication competence. *Communication Quarterly, 28*(3), 11-20.

Branham, R. J., & Pearce, B. (1985). Between text and context: Toward a rhetoric of contextual reconstruction. *Quarterly Journal of Speech, 71,* 19-36.

Braverman, H. (1974). *Labour and monopoly capital: The degradation of work in the twentieth century.* New York: Monthly Review Press.

Bremser, W. (1998, January). Webcasting 101: Pump up the volume! *On-line Computer Life* [on-line]. Available: http://www.zdnet.com/complife/clo-home.html

Bridges, J. (1997). *An Internet guide for mass communication students.* Madison, WI: Brown & Benchmark.

Brinson, S. L., & Benoit, W. L. (1996). Dow Corning's image repair strategies in the breast implant crisis. *Communication Quarterly, 44,* 29-41.

Brock, B., Botan, C. H., & Frey, L. R. (1985). The rhetoric of union busting: Analysis of a management journal for union decertification campaign. *Michigan Association of Speech Communication Journal, 20,* 51-63.

Brody, E. W. (1992). We must act now to redeem PR's reputation. *Public Relations Quarterly, 37*(3), 44.

Brody, E. W. (1994). PR is to experience what marketing is to expectations. *Public Relations Quarterly, 39*(2), 20-22.

Brody, E. W., & Stone, G. C. (1989). *Public relations research.* New York: Praeger.

Brook, J., & Boal, I. A. (Eds.). (1995). *Resisting the virtual life: The culture and politics of information.* San Francisco: City Lights.

Broom, G. M. (1977). Coorientational measurement of public issues. *Public Relations Review, 3*(4), 110-119.

Broom, G. M. (1982). A comparison of sex roles in public relations. *Public Relations Review, 8*(3), 17-22.

Broom, G. M., Casey, S., & Ritchey, J. (1997). Toward a concept and theory of organization-public relationships. *Journal of Public Relations Research, 9,* 83-98.

Broom, G. M., & Dozier, D. M. (1986). Advancement for public relations role models. *Public Relations Review, 12*(1), 37-56.

Broom, G. M., & Dozier, D. M. (1990). *Using research in public relations: Applications to program management.* Englewood Cliffs, NJ: Prentice Hall.

Broom, G., Lauzen, M., & Tucker, K. (1991). Public relations and marketing: Dividing the conceptual domain and operational turf. *Public Relations Review, 17,* 219-225.

Broom, G. M., & Smith, G. D. (1979). Testing the practitioner's impact on clients. *Public Relations Review, 5*(3), 45-49.

Brown, J. D., & Walsh-Childers, K. (1994). Effects of media on personal and public health. In J. Bryant & D. Zillmann (Eds.), *Media effects: Advances in theory and research* (pp. 389-416). Hillsdale, NJ: Lawrence Erlbaum.

Brown, S. (1995). *Postmodern marketing.* London: Routledge.

Brown, S. (1998). *Postmodern marketing two: Telling tales.* London: International Thomson Business Press.

Brown, S. L., & Eisenhardt, K. M. (1998). *Competing on the edge: Strategy as structured chaos.* Boston: Harvard Business School Press.

Brown, W. R., & Crable, R. E. (1973). Industry, mass magazines, and the ecology issue. *Quarterly Journal of Speech, 59,* 259-272.

Brummett, B. (1984). Rhetorical theory as heuristic and moral: A pedagogical justification. *Communication Education, 33,* 97-107.

Brummett, B. (1990). Relativism and rhetoric. In R. A. Cherwitz (Ed.), *Rhetoric and philosophy* (pp. 79-103). Hillsdale, NJ: Lawrence Erlbaum.

Brummett, B. (1995). Scandalous rhetorics. In W. N. Elwood (Ed.), *Public relations inquiry as rhetorical criticism: Case studies of corporate discourse and social influence* (pp. 13-23). Westport, CT: Praeger.

Bruning, S. D., & Ledingham, J. A. (1998). Organization-public relationships and consumer satisfaction: The role of relationships in the satisfaction mix. *Communication Research Reports, 15,* 199-209.

Bruning, S. D., & Ledingham, J. A. (2000a). Business to business relationships. In J. A. Ledingham & S. D. Bruning (Eds.), *Relationship management: A relational approach to public relations.* Mahwah, NJ: Lawrence Erlbaum.

Bruning, S. D., & Ledingham, J. A. (2000b). Organization and key public relationships: Testing the influence of the relationship dimensions in a business to business context. In J. A. Ledingham & S. D. Bruning (Eds.), *Relationship management: A relational approach to public relations* (pp. 159-173). Mahwah, NJ: Lawrence Erlbaum.

Bruno & Stillman v. Globe Newspaper Co., 633 F. 2d 583 (1980).

Bryant, D. C. (1953). Rhetoric: Its function and its scope. *Quarterly Journal of Speech, 39,* 401-424.

Bryce, J. (1888). *The American commonwealth.* London: Macmillan.

Buber, M. (1965). *Between man and man* (R. G. Smith, Trans.). New York: Macmillan.

Buchholz, R. A. (1982). *Business environment and public policy: Implications for management.* Englewood Cliffs, NJ: Prentice Hall.

Buckey, K. F. (1984, February 27). Why more corporations may be charged with manslaughter. *Business Week,* p. 62.

Buckey, K. F. (1986, January). Corporate criminal liability. *Corporate Board,* p. 147.

Budd, J. F., Jr. (1991). *Ethical dilemmas in public relations* (International Public Relations Association, Gold Paper No. 8). Bourenmouth, UK: Roman Press.

Budd, J. F., Jr. (1995). Commentary: Communications doesn't define PR, it diminishes it. *Public Relations Review, 21,* 177-179.

Buffett, W. (1999). Smokers' hacks. In K. B. Massey, (Ed.), *Readings in mass communication: Media literacy and culture* (pp. 142-150). Mountain View, CA: Mayfield.

Burke, D. D. (1996). Cybersmut and the First Amendment: A call for a new obscenity standard. *Harvard Journal of Law and Technology, 9,* 87-145.

Burke, K. (1937, January 20). Synthetic freedom. *New Republic,* p. 365.

Burke, K. (1941). *The philosophy of literary form.* Baton Rouge: Louisiana State University Press.

Burke, K. (1946, October 22). [Letter to Malcolm Cowley.] Kenneth Burke file, Pennsylvania State University.

Burke, K. (1950). *A rhetoric of motives.* Englewood Cliffs, NJ: Prentice Hall.

Burke, K. (1951). Rhetoric—Old and new. *Journal of General Education, 5,* 202-209.

Burke, K. (1957). *Philosophy of literary form* (rev. ed.). New York: Vintage Books.

Burke, K. (1961). *Attitudes toward history.* Boston: Beacon.

Burke, K. (1965). *Permanence and change* (2nd rev. ed.). Indianapolis, IN: Bobbs-Merrill.

Burke, K. (1966). *Language as symbolic action.* Berkeley: University of California Press.

Burke, K. (1968). *Counter-statement.* Berkeley: University of California Press.

Burke, K. (1969a). *A grammar of motives.* Berkeley: University of California Press.

Burke, K. (1969b). *A rhetoric of motives.* Berkeley: University of California Press.

Burke, K. (1973a). *The philosophy of literary form* (3rd ed.). Berkeley: University of California Press.

Burke, K. (1973b). The rhetorical situation. In L. Thayer (Ed.), *Communication: Ethical and moral issues* (pp. 263-275). New York: Gordon & Breach.

Burke, K. (1983). Counter-gridlock: An interview with Kenneth Burke. *All Area*, pp. 4-35.

Burke, R. J. (1996). Communication patterns in a professional services firm. *Psychological Reports, 78*, 384-386.

Burleson, B. R., & Kline, S. L. (1979). Habermas' theory of communication: A critical explication. *Quarterly Journal of Speech, 65*, 412-438.

Burnett, J., & Moriarity, S. (1998). *Introduction to marketing communication: An integrated approach.* Upper Saddle River, NJ: Prentice Hall.

Burney, L. E. (1958). Lung cancer and excessive cigarette smoking: Statement by Surgeon General Leroy E. Burney of the Public Health Service. *Ca Bulletin of Cancer Progress, 8*, 44.

Burrage, M. (1990). Introduction: The professions in sociology and history. In M. Burrage & R. Torstendahl (Eds.), *Professions in theory and history: Rethinking the study of the professions* (pp. 1-23). Newbury Park, CA: Sage.

Burson, H. (1989). *Counseling tips from the chairman* (remarks from the Critical Counseling Seminar, Glen Cove, NY). Report prepared by Burson-Marsteller, New York.

Business is far from spotlight at China summit. (1998, June 29). *International Herald Tribune*, p. 13.

Business Research Lab. (1998). *Market research and the Internet: E-mail surveys* [on-line]. Available: http://busreslab.com/tips/tip37.htm

Butler, K. (1996, July 18). MEPs ban gifts in bid for high ground. *Independent*, p. 2. (London)

Butler v. Michigan, 352 U.S. 380 (1957).

Caillouet, R. H., & Allen, M. W. (1996). Impression management strategies employees use when discussing their organization's public image. *Journal of Public Relations Research, 8*, 211-227.

Cairnes, J. E. (1887). *Some leading principles of political economy newly expounded.* London: Macmillan.

Calhoun, C. (1988). Populist politics, communications media, and large scale societal integration. *Sociological Theory, 6*, 219-241.

Calhoun, C. (1992). Introduction. In C. Calhoun (Ed.), *Habermas and the public sphere* (pp. 1-48). Cambridge, MA: MIT Press.

Calhoun, C. (1995). *Critical social theory: Culture, history, and the challenge of difference.* Oxford, UK: Blackwell.

Calloway, L. J. (1991). Survival of the fastest: Information technology and corporate crises. *Public Relations Review, 17*, 85-92.

Cameron, G. T. (1997). The contingency theory of conflict management in public relations. In *Proceedings of the Conference on Two-Way Communication* (pp. 27-48). Oslo: Norwegian Central Government Information Service.

Cameron, G. T., & Blount, D. (1996). VNRs and air checks: A content analysis of the use of video news releases in television newscasts. *Journalism & Mass Communication Quarterly, 73*, 890-904.

Cameron, G. T., & McCollum, T. (1993). Competing corporate cultures: A multi-method, cultural analysis of the role of internal communication. *Journal of Public Relations Research, 5*, 217-250.

Cameron, G. T., Mitrook, M., & Cancel, A. E. (1997, May). *Testing the contingency theory of accommodation in public relations.* Paper presented at the meeting of the International Communication Association, Montreal.

Cameron, G. T., Sallot, L. M., & Curtin, P. A. (1997). Public relations and the production of news: A critical review and a theoretical framework. In B. R. Burleson (Ed.), *Communication yearbook 20* (pp. 111-155). Thousand Oaks, CA: Sage.

Campbell, K. K. (1996). *The rhetorical act* (2nd ed.). Belmont, CA: Wadsworth.

Campbell-Johnson, A. (1956). A consultant's point of view. *Public Relations, 8*(4), 52-53.

Canary, D. J., & Cupach, W. R. (1988). Relational and episodic characteristics associated with conflict tactics. *Journal of Social and Personal Relationships, 5*, 305-325.

Canary, D. J., & Stafford, L. (1992). Relational maintenance strategies and equity in marriage. *Communication Monographs, 59*, 243-267.

Canary, D. J., & Stafford, L., (Eds.). (1994). *Communication and relational maintenance.* San Diego: Academic Press.

Cancel, A. E., Cameron, G. T., Sallot, L. M., & Mitrook, M. A. (1997). It depends: A contingency theory of accommodation in public relations. *Journal of Public Relations Research, 9,* 31-63.

Cancel, A. E., Mitrook, M. A., & Cameron, G. T. (1999). Testing the contingency theory of accommodation in public relations. *Public Relations Review, 25,* 171-197.

Canel, M. J. (1994). *Lobbying and communication: Regional bodies in the European Union.* Working paper, University of Navarra, Pamplona, Spain.

Canfield, A. S. (1998). Building client relationships by the numbers. *Public Relations Strategist, 4*(4), 33-34.

Canfield, B. R. (1952). *Public relations principles and problems.* Homewood, IL: Irwin.

Cantrell v. American Broadcasting Companies Inc., 529 F. Supp. 746 (1981).

Caplow, T. (1954). *Sociology of work.* Minneapolis: University of Minnesota Press.

Cappella, J. N. (1987). Interpersonal communication: Definitions and fundamental questions. In C. R. Berger & S. H. Chaffee (Eds.), *Handbook of communication science* (pp. 184-238). Newbury Park, CA: Sage.

Capps, I. (1993). What the "new technology" really means for communication professionals. *Public Relations Quarterly, 38*(2), 24-25.

Carey, A. (1995). *Taking the risk out of democracy: Propaganda in the U.S. and Australia.* Sydney: University of New South Wales Press.

Carey, J. (1996, January). Listen up! Do you hear what I hear? *Thrust for Educational Leadership, 25*(3), 6-8.

Carey, J. W. (1998). The Internet and the end of the national communication system: Uncertain predictions of an uncertain future. *Journalism & Mass Communication Quarterly, 75*(1), 28-34.

Carleton, S. (1997, May). Health reform rediscovers the patient. *Business & Health,* pp. 4-11.

Carlone, D., & Taylor, B. (1998). Organizational communication and cultural studies: A review essay. *Communication Theory, 8,* 337-367.

Carlson, W. B., & Millard, A. J. (1987). Defining risk within a business context: Thomas A. Edison, Eliihu Thomson, and the A.C.-D.C. controversy, 1885-1900. In B. B. Johnson & V. T. Covello (Eds.), *The social and cultural construction of risk* (pp. 275-293). Dordrecht, Netherlands: D. Reidel.

Carrington, J. (1992). Establishing a more strategic role in PR practice: Why, how, and when? *Public Relations Quarterly, 37*(1), 45-47.

Carroll, A. B. (1991, July-August). The pyramid of corporate social responsibility: Toward the moral management of organizational stakeholders. *Business Horizons, 34*(4), 39-48.

Carroll, A. (1994, March). *Religious dialogue.* Panel discussion at the conference, "The Road to Peace: The Challenge of the Middle East," Miami, FL.

Carroll, G. R. (1984). Organizational ecology. *Annual Review of Sociology, 10,* 71-93.

Carroll, G. R. (1988). *Ecological models of organizations.* Cambridge, MA: Ballinger.

Carr-Saunders, A. M., & Wilson, P. A. (1933). *The professions.* Oxford, UK: Clarendon.

Carruthers, S. (1995). *Winning hearts and minds: British governments, the media, and colonial counter-insurgency, 1944-60.* Leicester, UK: Leicester University Press.

Cartwright, D. (1949). Some principles of mass persuasion. *Human Relations, 2,* 253-267.

Carvel, J. (1995, October 20). Now read all about it. *The Guardian,* p. 17.

Carveth, R. (1996). Communication via interactive media: Communication in a new key? *New Jersey Journal of Communication, 4*(1), 71-81.

Castells, M. (1996). *The rise of the network society.* Cambridge, MA: Blackwell.

Casti, J. L. (1997). *Would-be worlds: How simulation is changing the face of science.* New York: John Wiley.

Cathcart, R. S. (1978). Movements: Confrontation as rhetorical form. *Southern Speech Communication Journal, 43,* 233-247.

Cathcart, R., & Gumpert, G. (1983). Mediated interpersonal communication: Toward a new typology. *Quarterly Journal of Speech, 69,* 267-277.

Cavanagh, G. F., & McGovern, A. F. (1988). *Ethical dilemmas in the modern corporation.* Englewood Cliffs, NJ: Prentice Hall.

Cawson, A. (1986). *Corporatism and political theory.* Oxford, UK: Basil Blackwell.

Caywood advocates integrated communications. (1997, November). *O'Dwyer's PR Services Report,* pp. 64-66.

Caywood, C. (Ed.). (1997). *The handbook of strategic public relations and integrated communications.* New York: McGraw-Hill.

Center, A. H., & Jackson, P. (1995). *Public relations practices: Managerial case studies and problems* (5th ed.). Englewood Cliffs, NJ: Prentice Hall.

Central Hudson Gas & Electric Corp. v. Public Service Commission of New York, 447 U.S. 557 (1980).

Chaffee, S. (1981). Mass media in political campaigns: An expanding role. In R. E. Rice & W. J. Paisley (Eds.), *Public communication campaigns* (pp. 181-198). Beverly Hills, CA: Sage.

Chaiken, S. (1980). Heuristic versus systematic information processing and the use of source versus message cues in persuasion. *Journal of Personality and Social Psychology, 39,* 752-766.

Chandler, R. L., & Drucker, G. (1993). You can't live by brand alone: Making something old look new. *Public Relations Quarterly, 38*(1), 36-37.

Chaplinsky v. New Hampshire, 315 U.S. 568 (1942).

Chapman, R. (1982). Measurement: It is alive and well in Chicago. *Public Relations Journal, 38*(4), 28-29.

Chaudhuri, A., & Buck, R. (1995). Affect, reason, and persuasion: Advertising strategies that predict affective and analytic-cognitive responses. *Human Communication Research, 21,* 422-441.

Chen, N. (1994). Public relations education in the People's Republic of China. *Journalism Educator, 49*(1), 14-22.

Chen, N. (1995, November). *Women in Chinese public relations.* Paper presented at the Global Conference on Poverty Alleviation and Social Development, Las Vegas, NV.

Chen, N. (1996). Public relations in China: The introduction and development of an occupational field. In H. M. Culbertson & N. Chen (Eds.), *International public relations: A comparative analysis* (pp. 121-153). Mahwah, NJ: Lawrence Erlbaum.

Chen, N., & Culbertson, H. M. (1992). Two contrasting approaches of government public relations in mainland China. *Public Relations Quarterly, 37*(3), 36-41.

Chen, N., & Culbertson, H. M. (1996). Guest relations: A demanding but constrained role for lady public relations practitioners in mainland China. *Public Relations Review, 22,* 279-296.

Chen, Y. (1990, September 10). Kaizhan zhenfu gongguang, shuli lianghao xingxao [Practice public relations in government institutions to establish good image]. *Beijing Gongguang Bao* [Beijing PR Newspaper], p. 21.

Cheney, G. (1991). *Rhetoric in an organizational society: Managing multiple identities.* Columbia: University of South Carolina Press.

Cheney, G. (1992). The corporate person (re)presents itself. In E. L. Toth & R. L. Heath (Eds.), *Rhetorical and critical approaches to public relations* (pp. 165-183). Hillsdale, NJ: Lawrence Erlbaum.

Cheney, G., & Christensen, L. T. (2001). Identity at issue: Linkages between "internal" and "external" organizational communication. In F. M. Jablin & L. L. Putnam (Eds.), *The new handbook of organizational communication.* Thousand Oaks, CA: Sage.

Cheney, G., & Dionisopoulos, G. N. (1989). Public relations? No, relations with publics: A rhetorical-organizational approach to contemporary corporate communications. In C. H. Botan & V. Hazleton, Jr. (Eds.), *Public relations theory* (pp. 135-157). Hillsdale, NJ: Lawrence Erlbaum.

Cheney, G., Garvin-Doxas, K., & Torrens, K. (1999). Kenneth Burke's implicit theory of power. In B. L. Brock (Ed.), *Kenneth Burke and the twenty-first century* (pp. 133-150). Albany: State University of New York Press.

Cheney, G., & McMillan, J. J. (1990). Organizational rhetoric and the practice of criticism.

Journal of Applied Communication Research,
18, 93-114.

Cheney, G., & Vibbert, S. L. (1987). Corporate discourse: Public relations and issues management. In F. M. Jablin, L. L. Putnam, K. H. Roberts, & L. W. Porter (Eds.), *Handbook of organizational communication* (pp. 165-194). Newbury Park, CA: Sage.

Cherwitz, R. A., & Hikins, J. W. (1986). *Communication and knowledge: An investigation in rhetorical epistemology.* Columbia: University of South Carolina Press.

Chesterman, G. (1996, September). A question of ethics. *Report,* pp. 1-2. (Public Relations Institute of New Zealand)

Chew, F. (1994). The relationship of information needs to issue relevance and media use. *Journalism Quarterly, 71,* 676-688.

Ching, J. (1977). *Confucianism and Christianity.* New York: Kodansha International.

Chisholm, J. (1995, December). Surveys by e-mail and Internet. *Unix Review,* pp. 11-16.

Chrisman, J. J., & Carroll, A. B. (1984). SMR Forum: Corporate responsibility—Reconciling economic and social goals. *Sloan Management Review, 25*(4), 59-65.

Christ, W. C., McCall, J., Rakow, L., & Blanchard, R. O. (1997). Integrated communication programs. In W. G. Christ (Ed.), *Media education assessment handbook* (pp. 23-53). Mahwah, NJ: Lawrence Erlbaum.

Christensen, L. T. (1994). Talking to ourselves: Management through auto-communication. *MTC Kontakten, Jubilœumstidsskrift,* pp. 32-37.

Christensen, L. T. (1995). Buffering organizational identity in the marketing culture. *Organization Studies, 16,* 651-672.

Christensen, L. T. (1997). Marketing as auto-communication. *Consumption, Markets & Culture, 1*(2), 197-227.

Christensen, L. T., & Cheney, G. (in press). Self-absorption and self-seduction in the corporate identity game. In M. Schultz, M. J. Hatch, & M. H. Larsen (Eds.), *The expressive organization.* Oxford, UK: Oxford University Press.

Christiansen, T. (1996). A maturing bureaucracy? The role of the commission in the policy process. In J. Richardson (Ed.), *European Union: Power and policy making* (pp. 75-95). London: Routledge.

Christopher v. American News Co., 171 F. 2d 275 (1949).

Cissna, K. N., & Anderson, R. (1998). Theorizing about dialogic moments: The Buber-Rogers position and postmodern themes. *Communication Theory, 1,* 63-104.

City of Los Angeles v. Preferred Communications Inc., 106 S. Ct. 878 (1986).

Clark, J. W. (1966). *Religion and the moral standards of American businessmen.* Cincinnati, OH: South-Western.

Clark, R. (1983). Reconsidering research on learning from the media. *Review of Educational Research, 66,* 445-449.

Clarke, H. (1996, July 11-17). The "honest brokers" of Brussels. *The European,* p. 40.

Clarke, L., & Perrow, C. (1996). Prosaic organizational failure. *American Behavioral Scientist, 39,* 1040-1056.

Clegg, S. R. (1990). *Modern organizations: Organization studies in a postmodern world.* London: Sage.

Clegg, S. R., & Hardy, C. (1996). Introduction: Organizations, organization, and organizing. In S. R. Clegg, C. Hardy, & W. R. Nord (Eds.), *Handbook of organization studies* (pp. 1-28). London: Sage.

Clegg, S. R., Hardy, C., & Nord, W. R. (Eds.). (1996). *Handbook of organization studies.* London: Sage.

Clemons, J. G. (1994). A communication office in the year 2010. *Communication World, 11*(1), 42-43.

Clifford, J., & Marcus, G. E. (Eds.). (1986). *The politics and poetics of ethnography.* Berkeley: University of California Press.

Cline, C. (1984). *Evaluation and measurement in public relations and organizational communications: A literature review.* San Francisco: IABC Foundation.

Cline, C. G., Toth, E. L., Turk, J. V., Walters, L. M., Johnson, N., & Smith, H. (1986). *The velvet ghetto: The impact of the increasing percentage of women in public relations and business communication.* San Francisco: IABC Foundation.

Cobb, R. W., & Elder, C. D. (1971). The politics of agenda-building: An alternative perspective for modern democratic theory. *Journal of Politics, 33,* 892-915.

Cobb, R. W., & Elder, C. D. (1972). *Participation in American politics: The dynamics of agenda-building.* Baltimore, MD: Johns Hopkins University Press.

Cobb, R. W., & Elder, C. D. (1983). *Participation in American politics: The dynamics of agenda-building* (2nd ed.). Baltimore, MD: Johns Hopkins University Press.

Cobb, R. W., Ross, J. K., & Ross, M. H. (1976). Agenda building as a comparative political process. *American Political Science Review, 70,* 126-138.

Coco, M. P., Jr. (1998). The new war zone: The workplace. *SAM Advanced Management Journal, 63,* 15-20.

Cohen, J. (1994). The earth is round ($p < .05$). *American Psychologist, 49,* 997-1003.

Cohen, J., & Arato, A. (1992). *Civil society and political society.* Cambridge, MA: MIT Press.

Cohen, J., Pant, L., & Sharp, D. (1993). A validation and extension of a multidimensional ethics scale. *Journal of Business Ethics, 12,* 13-26.

Colby, A., Gibbs, J., Kohlberg, L., Dubin-Speicher, B., & Candee, D. (1980). *The measurement of moral judgment.* Boston: Harvard University, Center for Moral Education.

Colby, A., Kohlberg, L., Speicher, B., Hewer, A., Candee, D., Gibbs, J., & Power, C. (1990). *The measurement of moral judgment* (Vols. 1-2). Cambridge, UK: Cambridge University Press.

Cole, C. A., & Houston, M. J. (1987). Encoding and media effects on consumer learning deficiencies in the elderly. *Journal of Marketing Research, 24,* 55-63.

Cole, R. T. (1989). Improving your small organization's image. *Public Relations Journal, 45*(6), 26-27.

College Sports Information Directors of America. (1996). *College sports information directors directory.* Kingsville, TX: Author.

College Sports Information Directors of America. (1997). *College sports information direc-*

tors of America 40th anniversary guide. Kingsville, TX: Author.

Collins, M. P., & Murphy, K. L. (1997). Reducing conversational chaos: The use of communications conventions in instructional electronic chats. In C. Olgren (Ed.), *Competition, Connection, and Collaboration* (Proceedings of the 13th annual Conference on Distance Teaching and Learning (pp. 43-50). Madison: University of Wisconsin.

Committee of Inquiry Into Bovine Spongiform Encephalopathy. (1997). *Report of the Committee on BSE.* Brussels, Belgium: European Parliament.

Comrie, M. (1997). Media tactics in New Zealand's Crown Health Enterprises. *Public Relations Review, 23,* 161-182.

Conover, P. J., & Feldman, S. (1984). How people organize the political world: A schematic model. *American Journal of Political Science, 28,* 95-126.

Conrad, C. (in press). Perspectives on organizational communication. In F. M. Jablin & L. L. Putnam (Eds.), *The new handbook of organizational communication.* Thousand Oaks, CA: Sage.

Cook, T. D., Appleton, R. F., Conner, R. F., Shaffer, A., Tamkin, G., & Weber, S. J. (1975). Sesame Street *revisited: A case study in evaluation research.* New York: Russell Sage.

Coombs, W. T. (1993). Philosophical underpinnings: Ramifications of a pluralist paradigm. *Public Relations Review, 19,* 111-119.

Coombs, W. T. (1995). Choosing the right words: The development of guidelines for the selection of the "appropriate" crisis-response strategies. *Management Communication Quarterly, 8,* 447-476.

Coombs, W. T. (1998a). An analytic framework for crisis situations: Better responses from a better understanding of the situation. *Journal of Public Relations Research, 10,* 177-191.

Coombs, W. T. (1998b). The Internet as potential equalizer: New leverage for confronting social irresponsibility. *Public Relations Review, 24,* 289-304.

Coombs, W. T. (1999). *Ongoing crisis communication: Planning, managing, and responding.* Thousand Oaks, CA: Sage.

Coombs, W. T. (2000). Crisis management: Advantages of a relational perspective. In J. A. Ledingham & S. D. Bruning (Eds.), *Relationship management: A relational approach to public relations*. Mahwah, NJ: Lawrence Erlbaum.

Coombs, W. T., & Holladay, S. J. (1996). Communication and attributions in a crisis: An experimental study of crisis communication. *Journal of Public Relations Research, 8*, 279-295.

Coombs, W. T., Holladay, S., Hasenauer, G., & Signitzer, B. (1994). A comparative analysis of international public relations: Identification of similarities and differences between professionalization in Austria, Norway, and the United States. *Journal of Public Relations Research, 6*, 23-39.

Cooper, E. A., Lamb, F. W. M., Sanders, E., & Hirst, E. L. (1932). The role of tobacco-smoking in the production of cancer. *Journal of Hygiene, 32*, 293-300.

Cooper, R., & Burrell, G. (1988). Modernism, postmodernism, and organizational analysis: An introduction. *Organization Studies, 9*(1), 91-112.

Cooper-Chen, A., & Kaneshige, M. (1996). Public relations practice in Japan: Beginning again for the first time. In H. M. Culbertson & N. Chen (Eds.), *International public relations: A comparative analysis* (pp. 223-238). Mahwah, NJ: Lawrence Erlbaum.

Copilevitz, T. (1997, January 13). Rumors spread on Internet via word-of-mouth. *Dallas Morning News*, p. C1.

Copyrights, 17 U.S.C.A. (1996).

Corbett, W. J. (1991-1992). EC '92: Communicating in the new Europe. *Public Relations Quarterly, 37*(4), 7-13.

Cornell, D. (1991). *Beyond accommodation: Ethical feminism, deconstruction, and the law*. New York: Routledge.

Corporate communication officers reporting to the top, most to CEO. (1999, January 25). *Phillips PR News*, p. 1.

Corporations leading the Internet pack. (1997, April). *Public Relations Tactics*, p. 9.

Corringan v. Bobbs-Merrill Co., 228 N.Y. 58 (1920).

Coser, L. A. (1956). *The functions of social conflict*. New York: Free Press.

Cottone, L. P. (1993). The perturbing worldview of chaos: Implications for public relations. *Public Relations Review, 19*, 173-174.

Counts, C. L., & Martin, C. A. (1996). Libel in cyberspace: A framework for addressing liability and jurisdictional issues in this new frontier, *Albany Law Review, 59*, 1083-1133.

Covello, V. T. (1992). Risk communication: An emerging area of health communication research. In S. A. Deetz (Ed.), *Communication yearbook 15* (pp. 359-373). Newbury Park, CA: Sage.

Coveney, P., & Highfield, R. (1995). *Frontiers of complexity: The search for order in a chaotic world*. London: Faber & Faber.

Covey, S. R. (1989). *The seven habits of highly effective people: Restoring the character ethic*. New York: Fireside.

Covey, S. R. (1991). *Principle-centered leadership*. New York: Fireside.

Cox, W. R., & Mosser, T. J. (1975). Preparing for the communication crunch. *Public Relations Journal, 31*(4), 44-47.

Coy, P., & Lewyn, M. (1990, January 29). The day that every phone seemed off the hook. *Business Week*, pp. 39-40.

Crable, R. E. (1986). The organizational "system" of rhetoric: The influence of *Megatrends* into the twenty-first century. In L. W. Hugenberg (Ed.), *Rhetorical studies honoring James L. Golden* (pp. 57-68). Dubuque, IA: Kendall/Hunt.

Crable, R. E., & Vibbert, S. L. (1983). Mobil's epideictic advocacy: "Observations" of Prometheus-bound. *Communication Monographs, 50*, 380-394.

Crable, R. E., & Vibbert, S. L. (1985). Managing issues and influencing public policy. *Public Relations Review, 11*(2), 3-16.

Crable, R. E., & Vibbert, S. L. (1986). *Public relations as communication management*. Edina, MN: Bellwether.

Cragan, J. F., & Shields, D. C. (1977). Foreign policy communication dramas: How mediated rhetoric played in Peoria in Campaign '76. *Quarterly Journal of Speech, 63*, 274-289.

Cragan, J. F., & Shields, D. C. (1981). *Applied communication research: A dramatistic approach.* Prospect Heights, IL: Waveland.

Cragan J. F., & Shields, D. C. (1990, July). *The uses of narrative in market research and advertising.* Paper presented at the Narrative of the Human Sciences Conference, University of Iowa, Iowa City, IA.

Cragan, J. F., & Shields, D. C. (1992). The use of symbolic convergence theory in corporate strategic planning: A case study. *Journal of Applied Communication Research, 20*(2), 199-218.

Cragan J. F., & Shields, D. C. (1995). *Symbolic theories in applied communication research: Bormann, Burke, and Fisher.* Cresskill, NJ: Hampton.

Creedon, P. J. (1991). Public relations and "women's work": Toward a feminist analysis of public relations roles. In L. A. Grunig & J. E. Grunig (Eds.), *Public relations research annual* (Vol. 3, pp. 67-84). Hillsdale, NJ: Lawrence Erlbaum.

Creedon, P. J. (1993a). Acknowledging the infrasystem: A critical feminist analysis of systems theory. *Public Relations Review, 19,* 157-166.

Creedon, P. J. (Ed.). (1993b). *Women in mass communication* (2nd ed.). Newbury Park, CA: Sage.

Crissman, P. (1942). Temporal change and sexual difference in moral judgments. *Journal of Social Psychology, 16,* 29-38.

Croft, A. C. (1996). *Managing a public relations firm for growth and profit.* Binghamton, NY: Haworth.

Cronon, W. (1992). A place for stories: Nature, history, and narrative. *Journal of American History, 78,* 1347-1376.

Cubby Inc. v. CompuServe Inc., 776 F. Supp. 135 (S.D. N.Y. 1991).

Culbertson, H. M. (1989a). Breadth of perspective: An important concept for public relations. In J. E. Grunig & L. A. Grunig (Eds.), *Public relations research annual* (Vol. 1, pp. 3-26). Hillsdale, NJ: Lawrence Erlbaum.

Culbertson, H. M. (1989b). Role taking and sensitivity: Keys to playing and making public relations roles. In J. E. Grunig & L. A. Grunig (Eds.), *Public relations research annual* (Vol. 3, pp. 37-65). Hillsdale. NJ: Lawrence Erlbaum.

Culbertson, H. M., & Chen, N. (Eds.). (1996). *International public relations: A comparative analysis.* Mahwah, NJ: Lawrence Erlbaum.

Culbertson, H. M., & Chen, N. (1997a). Communitarianism: A foundation for communication symmetry. *Public Relations Quarterly, 42*(2), 36-41.

Culbertson, H. M., & Chen, N. (1997b). Public relations' role in defining corporate social responsibility. *Journal of Mass Media Ethics, 4,* 21-38.

Culbertson, H. M., & Jeffers, D. W. (1992). Social, political, and economic contexts: Keys in educating true public relations professionals. *Public Relations Review, 18,* 53-65.

Culbertson, H. M., Jeffers, D. W., Stone, D. B., & Terrell, M. (1993). *Social, political, and economic contexts in public relations: Theory and cases.* Hillsdale, NJ: Lawrence Erlbaum.

Culnan, M. J., & Markus, M. L. (1987). Information technologies. In F. M. Jablin, L. L. Putnam, K. H. Roberts, & L. W. Porter (Eds.), *Handbook of organizational communication* (pp. 420-443). Newbury Park, CA: Sage.

Cunningham, A., & Haley, E. (1998, August). *Preparing students for real-world ethical dilemmas: A stakeholder approach.* Paper presented at the meeting of the Association for Education in Journalism and Mass Communication, Baltimore, MD.

Cupach, W. R., & Metts, S. (1994). *Facework.* Thousand Oaks, CA: Sage.

Cutlip, S. (1980). Public relations in American society. *Public Relations Review, 6*(1), 3-17.

Cutlip, S. M. (1991). Remarks. *Public Relations Review, 17,* 377-385.

Cutlip, S. M. (1994). *The unseen power: Public relations, a history.* Hillsdale, NJ: Lawrence Erlbaum.

Cutlip, S. M. (1995). *Public relations history: From the 17th to the 20th century—The antecedents.* Hillsdale, NJ: Lawrence Erlbaum.

Cutlip, S. M., & Center, A. H. (1971). *Effective public relations* (4th ed.). Englewood Cliffs, NJ: Prentice Hall.

Cutlip, S. M., Center, A. H., & Broom, G. M. (1985). *Effective public relations* (6th ed.). Englewood Cliffs, NJ: Prentice Hall.

Cutlip, S. M., Center, A. H., & Broom, G. M. (1994). *Effective public relations* (7th ed.). Englewood Cliffs, NJ: Prentice Hall.

Cutlip, S. M., Center, A. H., & Broom, G. M. (2000). *Effective public relations* (8th ed.). Englewood Cliffs, NJ: Prentice Hall.

Cvetkovich, G., & Earle, T. C. (1994). Construction of justice: A case study of public participation in land management. *Journal of Social Issues, 50,* 161-178.

D'Aveni, R. A., with Gunther, R. (1994). *Hypercompetition: Managing the dynamics of strategic maneuvering.* New York: Free Press.

Dahl, R. (1956). *A preface to democratic theory.* Chicago: University of Chicago Press.

Dahl, R. (1961). *Who governs?* New Haven, CT: Yale University Press.

Dahlgren, P. (1995). *Television and the public sphere: Citizenship, democracy, and the media.* London: Sage.

Dake, K. (1992). Orienting dispositions in the perception of risk. *Journal of Cross-Cultural Psychology, 22,* 61-82.

Dallas Cowboys Football Club v. Harris, 348 S.W. 2d 37 (Tex. Civ. App. 1961).

Darnton, R. (1975). Writing news and telling stories. *Daedalus, 104,* 175-194.

Davids, M. (1994). The interactive solution. *Journal of Business Strategy, 15,* 52-59.

Davis, G. (1997, April 14). Are Internet surveys ready for prime time? *Marketing News,* p. 31.

Davis, S., & Meyer, C. (1998). *Blur: The speed of change in the connected economy.* Reading, MA: Addison-Wesley.

Davison, W. P., Boylan, J., & Yu, T. T. C. (1976). *Mass media systems and effects.* New York: Holt, Rinehart & Winston.

Day, K. D. (1998). The problem of ethics in intercultural communication. In K. S. Sitaram & M. Prosser (Eds.), *Civic discourse, Vol. 1: Multiculturalism, cultural diversity, and global communication* (pp. 1-30). Norwood, NJ: Ablex.

Day, L. (1991). *Ethics in mass communications: Cases and controversies.* Belmont, CA: Wadsworth.

de Tocqueville, A. (1945). *Democracy in America.* New York: Knopf. (Original work published 1835)

Deatherage, C. P., & Hazleton, V., Jr. (1998). Effects of organizational worldviews on the practice of public relations: A test of the theory of public relations excellence. *Journal of Public Relations Research, 10,* 57-71.

December, J. (1996). Units of analysis for Internet communication. *Journal of Communication, 46*(1), 14-38.

Deetz, S. A. (1982). Critical interpretive research in organizational communication. *Western Journal of Speech, 46,* 131-149.

Deetz, S. A. (1992). *Democracy in the age of corporate colonization: Developments in communication and the politics of everyday life.* Albany: State University of New York Press.

Deetz, S. A. (1996). Describing differences in approaches to organization science: Rethinking Burrell and Morgan and their legacy. *Organization Science, 7,* 191-207.

Deetz, S. A., & Mumby, D. K. (1990). Power, discourse, and the workplace: Reclaiming the critical tradition. In J. Anderson (Ed.), *Communication yearbook 13* (pp. 18-47). Newbury Park, CA: Sage.

Defamation in cyberspace: Reconciling Cubby Inc. v. CompuServe, Inc., and Stratton Oakmont v. Prodigy Services Co. (1996). *Marquette Law Review, 79,* 1065-1082.

Defining public relations. (1992, August). *The Ragan Report,* pp. 1-2.

DelColle, R. (1994, April 5). Our different histories can unify us. *Miami Herald,* p. B3.

DeMuro, P. R. (1994, January). Provider alliances: Key to healthcare reform. *Healthcare Financial Management, 48,* 27-32.

Denbow, C. J., & Culbertson, H. M. (1985). Linkage beliefs and diagnosing an image. *Public Relations Review, 11,* 29-37.

Dennis v. United States, 341 U.S. 494 (1951), *rehearing denied* 342 U.S. 842, *rehearing denied* 355 U.S. 936.

Denny's settles claims in discrimination complaints for record $46 million. (1994, June 13). *Jet,* p. 6.

Denzin, N., & Lincoln, Y. (Eds.). (1994). *Handbook of qualitative research*. Thousand Oaks, CA: Sage.

DePaulo, P. J., & Weitzer, R. (1994, January 3). Interactive phone technology delivers survey data quickly. *Marketing News, 28*(1), 15.

Derber, C. (Ed.). (1982). *Professionals as workers: Mental labor in advanced capitalism*. Boston: G. K. Hall.

Dern, D. P. (1997, May). Drowning in data: Information overload on the Internet. *Digital Media*, p. 23.

Dervin, B. (1989). Audience as listener and learner, teacher, and confidante: The sense-making approach. In R. E. Rice & C. K. Atkin (Eds.), *Public communication campaigns* (2nd ed., pp. 73-112). Newbury Park, CA: Sage.

Deutsch, M. (1973). *The resolution of conflict*. New Haven, CT: Yale University Press.

Developing one-on-one relationships for improved customer support and loyalty: URL *http://iac.fcla.edu/cgi-bin/cgiwrap/ÿ7Efcliac/cgi2iac/UF?20049479*

Dewey, J. (1927). *The public and its problems*. New York: Holt, Rinehart & Winston.

Diamond, A. H. (1993). Chaos science. *Marketing Research, 5*(4), 9-14.

Dillman, D. A. (1978). *Mail and telephone surveys: The total design method*. New York: John Wiley.

Dingwall, R. (1983). Introduction. In R. Dingwall & P. Lewis (Eds.), *The sociology of the professions* (pp. 1-13). New York: Macmillan.

Dionisopoulos, G. N. (1986). Corporate advocacy advertising as political communication. In L. L. Kaid, D. Nimmo, & K. R. Sanders (Eds.), *New perspectives on political advertising* (pp. 82-106). Carbondale: Southern Illinois University Press.

Dionisopoulos, G. N., & Vibbert, S. L. (1983, November). *Refining generic parameters: The case for organizational apologia*. Paper presented at the meeting of the Speech Communication Association, Washington, DC.

Dionisopoulos, G. N., & Vibbert, S. L. (1988). CBS vs. Mobil Oil: Charges of creative bookkeeping in 1979. In H. R. Ryan (Ed.), *Oratori-cal encounters* (pp. 241-251). New York: Greenwood.

Dionne, E. J. (1991). *Why Americans hate politics*. New York: Simon & Schuster.

Doll, R., & Hill, A. B. (1952). A study of the etiology of carcinoma of the lung. *British Medical Journal, 2*, 1271-1286.

Donaldson v. Read Magazine Inc., 333 U.S. 178 (1948).

Donato, K. M. (1990). Keepers of the corporate image: Women in public relations. In B. F. Reskin & P. A. Roos (Eds.), *Job queues, gender queues: Explaining inroads into male occupations* (pp. 129-143). Philadelphia: Temple University Press.

Dorf, P. (1995). High-tech firms launching clients into cyberspace. *Public Relations Journal, 51*(5), 28-31.

Dorin v. Equitable Life Assurance Co. of United States, 382 F. 2d 72 (1967).

Douglas, M. (1982). *Essays in the sociology of perception*. London: Routledge & Kegan Paul.

Douglas, M. (1996). *Thought styles*. London: Sage.

Douglas, M., & Wildavsky, A. (1982). *Risk and culture*. Berkeley: University of California Press.

Douglas, S. U. (1986). *Labor's new voice: Unions and the mass media*. Norwood, NJ: Ablex.

Douglass v. Hustler Magazine, 769 F. 2d 1128 (7th Cir. 1985).

Dover, C. J. (1995). The shearing of the lambs: An irreverent look at *Excellence*. *Journal of Management Advocacy Communication, 1*(1), 38-44.

Dowling, G. R. (1988). Measuring corporate image. *Journal of Business Research, 17*, 27-34.

Dowling, J., & Pfeffer, J. (1975). Organizational legitimacy: Social values and organizational behavior. *Pacific Sociological Review, 18*, 122-136.

Downes, L., & Mui, C. (1998). *Unleashing the killer app: Digital strategies for market dominance*. Boston: Harvard Business School Press.

Downs, A. (1972). Up and down with ecology: The "issue attention cycle." *Public Interest, 12*, 38-50.

Dozier, D. M. (1983, May). *Toward a reconciliation of role conflict in public relations research.* Paper presented at the meeting of the Western Communications Educators Conference, Fullerton, CA.

Dozier, D. M. (1984a, June). *The evolution of evaluation methods among public relations practitioners.* Paper presented at the meeting of the International Association of Business Communicators, Educators Academy, Montreal.

Dozier, D. M. (1984b). Program evaluation and roles of practitioners. *Public Relations Review, 10*(2), 13-21.

Dozier, D. M. (1985). Planning and evaluation in public relations practice. *Public Relations Review, 11*(2), 17-25.

Dozier, D. M. (1988a). Breaking public relation's glass ceiling. *Public Relations Review, 14*(3), 6-14.

Dozier, D. M. (1988b, July). *Organic structure and managerial environment sensitivity as predictors of practitioner membership of the dominant coalition.* Paper presented at the meeting of the Association for Educators in Journalism and Mass Communication, Public Relations Division, Portland, OR.

Dozier, D. M. (1990). The innovation of research in public relations practice: Review of a program of studies. In L. A. Grunig & J. E. Grunig (Eds.), *Public relations research annual* (Vol. 2, pp. 3-28). Hillsdale, NJ: Lawrence Erlbaum.

Dozier, D. M. (1992). The organizational roles of communications and public relations practitioners. In J. E. Grunig (Ed.), *Excellence in public relations and communication management* (pp. 159-185). Hillsdale, NJ: Lawrence Erlbaum.

Dozier, D. M., & Broom, G. M. (1995). Evolution of the manager role in public relations practice. *Journal of Public Relations Research, 7,* 3-26.

Dozier, D. M., & Ehling, W. P. (1992). Evaluation of public relations programs: What the literature tells us about their effects. In J. A. Grunig (Ed.), *Excellence in public relations and communication management* (pp. 159-184). Hillsdale, NJ: Lawrence Erlbaum.

Dozier, D. M., Grunig, L. A., & Grunig, J. E. (1995). *Manager's guide to excellence in public relations and communication management.* Mahwah, NJ: Lawrence Erlbaum.

Dozier, D. M., & Lauzen, M. M. (1998, August). *The liberation of public relations: Activism and the limits of symmetry in the global market.* Paper presented at the meeting of the Association for Education in Journalism and Mass Communication, Baltimore, MD.

Drake, B. H., & Drake, E. (1988). Ethical and legal aspects of managing corporate cultures. *California Management Review, 30*(2), 107-123.

Drake, N. M. (1991). What is needed most—school reform or media reform? *Phi Delta Kappan, 73,* 57.

Dressel, P. L. (1980). *The autonomy of public colleges.* San Francisco: Jossey-Bass.

Drobis provides new terminology for roles of practitioner. (1998, June 22). *PR Reporter,* p. 3.

Drucker, P. F. (1974). *Management: Tasks, responsibilities, practices.* New York: Harper & Row.

Drucker, P. F. (1995). *Managing in a time of great change.* New York: Truman Talley Books/Dutton.

Duhon, J. (1998). *PF&IS first quarter marketing plan.* Houston, TX: Shell Oil Company.

Dukakis, M. (1994, March). *The case for optimism in the Middle East.* Speech delivered at the conference, "The Road to Peace: The Challenge of the Middle East," Miami, FL.

Duke, L. (1993, March 12). Cofounder of Shoney's quits following racial bias lawsuit. *The Washington Post,* p. A4.

Duncan, T. (1993, September). *A marketing perspective on IMC.* Paper presented at the Perspectives on Integrated Marketing Communication seminar (sponsored by International Association of Business Communicators, District IV), Des Moines, IA.

Duncan, T., Caywood, C., & Newsom, D. (1993). *Preparing advertising and public relations students for the communications industry in the 21st century.* Boulder: University of Colorado Press.

Duncan, T., & Moriarty, S. (1998). A communications-based marketing model for managing relationships. *Journal of Marketing, 62*(2), 1-13.

Dundjerski, M. (1994, October 18). Carnegie Mellon's fund-raising shake-up. *Chronicle of Philanthropy,* pp. 22-25.

Dunlop, M. (1998, April). *The business of communications.* Paper presented at the meeting of the Public Relations Institute of New Zealand, Rotorua, New Zealand.

Durkheim, E. (1933). *The division of labor in society* (G. Simpson, Trans.). New York: Free Press.

Dutton, J. E., & Dukerich, J. M. (1991). Keeping an eye on the mirror: Image and identity in organizational adaptation. *Academy of Management Journal, 34,* 517-554.

Dyer, S. C. (1995). Getting people into the crisis communication plan. *Public Relations Quarterly, 40*(3), 38-41.

Dyer, S. C. (1996). Descriptive modeling for public relations environmental scanning: A practitioner's perspective. *Journal of Public Relations Research, 8,* 137-150.

Dziabis, S. P., & Lant, T. W. (1998). Building partnerships with physicians: Moving outside the walls of the hospital. *Nursing Administration Quarterly, 22*(3), 1-5.

Earle, T. C., & Cvetkovich, G. T. (1995). *Social trust: Toward a cosmopolitan society.* Westport, CT: Praeger.

Earnshaw, D., & Judge, D. (1996). From co-operation to co-decision: The European Parliament's path to legislative power. In J. Richardson (Ed.), *European Union: Power and policy making* (pp. 96-126). London: Routledge.

Eckersley, R. (1992). *Environmentalism and political theory: Towards an ecocentric approach.* Albany: State University of New York Press.

Eddie Bauer taken to court. (1997, September 30). *United Press International.*

Edelman, D. J. (1996). Let's hold fast to the term public relations. *Public Relations Quarterly, 41*(2), 35.

Edelman, M. (1964). *The symbolic uses of politics.* Urbana: University of Illinois Press.

Edelman, M. (1988). *Constructing the political spectacle.* Chicago: University of Chicago Press.

Edelman Public Relations. (1997). *A case study of crisis communication management.* San Francisco: Author.

Edelstein, S. J. (1996, October). Litigating in cyberspace: Contracts on the Internet. *Trial,* pp. 16-23.

Edge, R. G. (1967). Voidability of minor's contracts: A feudal doctrine in a modern economy. *Georgia Law Review, 1,* 205, 227-232.

Edmondson, B. (1997, June). The wired bunch. *American Demographics,* pp. 10-15.

Ehling, W. P. (1984). Application of decision theory in the construction of a theory of public relations management [Part I]. *Public Relations Research & Education, 1*(2), 25-38.

Ehling, W. P. (1985). Application of decision theory in the construction of a theory of public relations management [Part II]. *Public Relations Research & Education, 2*(1), 4-22.

Ehling, W. P. (1987, May). *Public relations function and adversarial environments.* Paper presented at the meeting of the International Communication Association, Montreal.

Ehling, W. P. (1992). Public relations education and professionalism. In J. E. Grunig (Ed.), *Excellence in public relations and communication management* (pp. 439-464). Hillsdale, NJ: Lawrence Erlbaum.

Ehling, W. P., White, J., & Grunig, J. E. (1992). Public relations and marketing practices. In J. E. Grunig (Ed.), *Excellence in public relations and communication management* (pp. 357-393). Hillsdale, NJ: Lawrence Erlbaum.

Eight men in search of an answer. (1953). *Public Relations, 6*(1), 11-20.

Eisenberg, E. M., & Goodall, H. L., Jr. (1997). *Organizational communication: Balancing creativity and constraint* (2nd ed.). New York: St. Martin's.

Eisenhart, T. (1989). Playing together: Marketing and communications catch the team spirit. *Business Marketing, 74*(7), 40-46.

Ekachai, D. (1995). Applying Broom's role scales to Thai public relations practitioners. *Public Relations Review, 21,* 325-336.

Ekachai, D., & Komolsevin, R. (1996). Public relations in Thailand: Its functions and practitioners' roles. In H. M. Culbertson & N. Chen (Eds.), *International public relations: A com-*

parative analysis (pp. 155-170). Mahwah, NJ: Lawrence Erlbaum.

Elliot, C. M. (1997). *Activism on the Internet and its ramifications for public relations.* Unpublished master's thesis, University of Maryland, College Park.

Elliott, P. (1972). *The sociology of the professions.* London: Macmillan.

Elliott, S. (1994, January 14). Advertising: When a stranger offers to buy a drink at the bar, is it flattery or a walking commercial for cognac? *The New York Times,* p. D21.

Elliott, S. (1998, March 5). Public relations fee income a record. *The New York Times,* p. D5.

Ellis, R. J. (1998). *The dark side of the left: Illiberal egalitarianism in America.* Lawrence: University of Kansas Press.

Ellis, R. J., & Thompson, F. (1997). Seeing green: Cultural biases and environmental preferences. In R. J. Ellis & M. Thompson (Eds.), *Culture matters* (pp. 169-190). Boulder, CO: Westview.

Elm, D. R., & Weber, J. (1994). Measuring moral judgment: The moral judgment interview or the defining issues test. *Journal of Business Ethics, 13,* 341-355.

Elwood, W. N. (Ed.). (1995). *Public relations inquiry as rhetorical criticism: Case studies of corporate discourse and social influence.* Westport, CT: Praeger.

Enderwick, P. (1996). *Fast forward: New Zealand business in world markets.* Auckland, New Zealand: Longman Paul.

Enderwick, P. (1997). *Foreign investment: The New Zealand experience.* Palmerston North, New Zealand: Dunmore Press.

Endres, T. G. (1989). Rhetorical visions of unmarried mothers. *Communication Quarterly, 37,* 134-150.

Englehardt, E. E., & Evans, D. (1994). Lies, deception, and public relations. *Public Relations Review, 20,* 249-266.

Epley, J. S. (1992). Public relations in the global village: An American perspective. *Public Relations Review, 18,* 109-116.

Epstein, M. J. (1993). The fall of corporate charitable contributions. *Public Relations Quarterly, 38*(3), 37-39.

Estes, R. (1996). *Tyranny of the bottom line: Why corporations make good people do bad things.* San Francisco: Berrett-Koehler.

Ettema, J. S., & Glasser, T. L. (1998). *Custodians of conscience: Investigative journalism and public virtue.* New York: Columbia University Press.

Etzioni, A. (1969). *The semi-professions and their organization: Teachers, nurses, and social workers.* New York: Free Press.

Etzioni, A. (1993). *The spirit of community: The reinvention of American society.* New York: Touchstone.

Etzioni, A. (Ed.). (1995). *New communitarian thinking: Persons, virtues, institutions, and communities.* Charlottesville: University Press of Virginia.

Etzioni, A. (Ed.). (1998). *The essential communitarian reader.* Lanham, MD: Rowman & Littlefield.

EU: Secrecy report "secret," then released. (1996, September-October). *Statewatch,* pp. 22-23.

Europe: Top European Agencies, 1997. (1997, July 25). *PR Week.*

Europe: Top European Consultancies, 1996. (1996, July 26). *PR Week.*

Evans, J. (1995, December 30). Eddie Bauer's tarnished image. *The Washington Post,* p. C1.

Everett, J. L. (1990). Organizational culture and ethnoecology in public relations theory and practice. In J. E. Grunig & L. A. Grunig (Eds.), *Public relations research annual* (Vol. 2, pp. 235-251). Hillsdale, NJ: Lawrence Erlbaum.

Everett, J. L. (1993). The ecological paradigm in public relations theory and practice. *Public Relations Review, 19,* 177-185.

Ewen, S. (1976). *Captions of consciousness: Advertising and the social roots of consumer culture.* New York: McGraw-Hill.

Ewen, S. (1996). *PR! A social history of spin.* New York: Basic Books.

Ewing, D. W. (1990). *Inside the Harvard Business School: Strategies and lessons of America's leading school of business.* New York: Times Books.

Fairclough, N. (1989). *Language and power.* London: Longman.

Fairclough, N. (1992). *Discourse and social change.* London: Polity.

Fairclough, N. (1993). Critical discourse analysis and the marketization of public discourse: The universities. *Discourse and Society, 4,* 133-168.

Fairclough, N. (1995a). *Critical discourse analysis.* London: Longman.

Fairclough, N. (1995b). *Media discourse.* London: Edward Arnold.

Fairhurst, G. T., & Putnam, L .L. (1999). Reflections on the organization-communication equivalency question: The contributions of James Taylor and his colleagues. *Communication Review, 3,* 1-19.

Fairley, P. (1997, July 2). The community advisory dinner. *Chemical Week,* p. 48.

Farley, B. M. (1952). *What to tell people about the public school.* New York: Columbia University, Teachers College, Bureau of Publications.

Farnsworth, E. A. (1990). *Contracts* (2nd ed.). New York: Aspen.

Farrell, T. B. (1993). *Norms of rhetorical culture.* New Haven, CT: Yale University Press.

Fazio, R. H. (1990). Multiple processes by which attitudes guide behavior: The MODE model as an integrative framework. In M. Zanna (Ed.), *Advances in experimental social psychology* (Vol. 23, pp. 75-109). San Diego: Academic Press.

Feagin, J. R., Orum, A. M., & Sjoberg, G. (1991). *A case for the case study.* Chapel Hill: University of North Carolina Press.

Fearn-Banks, K. (1996a). *Crisis communications: A casebook approach.* Mahwah, NJ: Lawrence Erlbaum.

Fearn-Banks, K. (1996b). Crisis communication theory and ten businesses hit by news-making crises. In S. G. Amin & S. Fullerton (Eds.), *Global business trends* (pp. 55-62). Cumberland, MD: Academy of Business Administration.

Featherstone, M. (1990). Global culture: An introduction. *Theory, Culture, & Society, 7*(2-3), 1-14.

Featherstone, M., Lash, S., & Robertson, R. (Eds.). (1995). *Global modernities.* Thousand Oaks, CA: Sage.

Federal Home Building & Loan Association v. Blaisdell, 240 U.S. 398 (1934).

Felstiner, W., Abel, R. L., & Sarat, A. (1981). The emergence and transformation of disputes: Naming, blaming, and claiming. *Law & Society Review, 15,* 631-654.

Ferguson, D. P. (1997). *A "people of faith" movement: An ethnographic and rhetorical analysis of the Christian Coalition.* Unpublished manuscript, Purdue University.

Ferguson, D. P. (1998). From Communist control to glasnost and back? Media freedom and control in Eastern Europe and the former Soviet Union, and the implications for public relations. *Public Relations Review, 24,* 165-182.

Ferguson, D. P., Botan, C. H., & Sintay, S. (1996, May). *Humanism as a basis for socially responsible public relations.* Paper presented at the meeting of the International Communication Association, Chicago.

Ferguson, M. A. (1984, August). *Building theory in public relations: Interorganizational relationships as a public relations paradigm.* Paper presented at the meeting of the Association for Education in Journalism and Mass Communication, Public Relations division, Gainesville, FL.

Fernandez, B. (1997, October 7). Productivity paradox: Evidence of computers' benefits hard to find in Labor Department data. *Fort Worth Star-Telegram,* p. C10.

Ferrara, K., Brunner, H., & Whittemore, G. (1991, January). Interactive written discourse as an emergent register. *Written Communication, 8*(1), 8-34.

Ferre, J. P. (1990). Communication ethics and the political realism of Reinhold Neibuhr. *Communication Quarterly, 38,* 218-225.

Festinger, L. (1957). *A theory of cognitive dissonance.* Stanford, CA: Stanford University Press.

Fight intensifies over accreditation of teacher-education programs. (1998, October 9). *Chronicle of Higher Education,* p. A12.

Finch, B. J. (1997, May). A new way to listen to the customer. *Quality Progress,* pp. 73-76.

Finegan, J. (1994). The impact of personal values on judgments of ethical behavior in the workplace. *Journal of Business Ethics, 13,* 747-755.

Finet, D. (1993). Effects of boundary spanning communication on the sociopolitical delegitimation of an organization. *Management Communication Quarterly, 7,* 36-66.

Fink, C. C. (1995). *Media ethics.* Boston: Allyn & Bacon.

Fink, S. (1986). *Crisis management: Planning for the inevitable.* New York: American Management Association.

Finlay, M. (1987). *Powermatics: A discursive critique of new communication technology.* New York: Routledge & Kegan Paul.

Finn, P. (1982). Demystifying public relations. *Public Relations Journal, 38*(5), 12-18.

Finneran, M. (1990). AT&T's software-defined outage. *Business Communications Review, 20,* 77-78.

Firat, A. F. (1992). Postmodernism and the marketing organization. *Journal of Organizational Change Management, 5*(1), 97-83.

Firat, A. F., & Shultz, C. J. (1997). From segmentation to fragmentation: Markets and marketing strategy in the postmodern era. *European Journal of Marketing, 31*(3/4), 183-207.

First National Bank of Boston v. Bellotti, 435 U.S. 765 (1978).

First, P. F. (1986). Here's how press coverage can boost (or bust) your next school referendum. *American School Board Journal, 173*(11), 42.

Fishbein, M., & Ajzen, I. (1975). *Belief, attitude, intention, and behavior: An introduction to theory and research.* Reading, MA: Addison-Wesley.

Fisher, D. (1993). *Communication in organizations.* St. Paul, MN: West.

Fisher, R., & Brown, S. (1988). *Getting together: Building relationships as we negotiate.* New York: Penguin Books.

Fisher, W. R. (1970). A motive view of communication. *Quarterly Journal of Speech, 56,* 131-139.

Fisher, W. R. (1984). Narration as a human communication paradigm: The case of public moral argument. *Communication Monographs, 51,* 1-22.

Fisher, W. R. (1985). The narrative paradigm: An elaboration. *Communication Monographs, 52,* 347-367.

Fisher, W. R. (1987). *Human communication as narration: Toward a philosophy of reason, value, and action.* Columbia: University of South Carolina Press.

Fisher, W. R. (1989). Clarifying the narrative paradigm. *Communication Monographs, 56,* 55-58.

Fishman, D. (1996). Crisis communication, authority, and the narrative paradigm: Tylenol and Exxon revisited. In L. Barton (Ed.), *New avenues in crisis management* (pp. 16-31). Las Vegas: University of Nevada, Small Business Center.

Fishman, M. (1980). *Manufacturing the news.* Austin: University of Texas Press.

Fiske, A. P. (1991). *Structures of social life: The four elementary forms of human relations.* New York: Free Press.

Fiske, A. P., & Tetlock, P. E. (1997). Taboo trade-offs: Reactions to transactions that transgress the spheres of justice. *Political Psychology, 18,* 255-297.

Fitch-Hauser, M., Barker-Roach, D., & Barker, L. L. (1988, November). *A survey of public relations education in the U.S. and Canada.* Paper presented at the meeting of the Speech Communication Association, New Orleans, LA.

Fitch-Hauser, M., & Neff, B. D. (1997, November). *Where public relations is taught: A 1997 update on a longitudinal study.* Paper presented at the meeting of the National Communication Association, Chicago.

Fitzpatrick, K. R. (1995). Ten guidelines for reducing legal risks in crisis management. *Public Relations Quarterly, 40*(2), 33-38.

Fitzpatrick, K. R. (1996a). Public relations and the law: A survey of practitioners. *Public Relations Review, 22,* 1-6.

Fitzpatrick, K. R. (1996b). The role of public relations in the institutionalization of ethics. *Public Relations Review, 22,* 249-258.

Fitzpatrick, K. R., & Rubin, M. S. (1995). Public relations vs. legal strategies in organizational crisis decisions. *Public Relations Review, 21,* 21-33.

Fitzpatrick, K. R., & Whillock, R. K. (1993, November). *Assessing the impact of globalization on U.S. public relations.* Paper presented at the meeting of the Public Relations Society of America, Orlando, FL.

Fitzpatrick, M. A. (1988). *Between husbands and wives: Communication in marriage.* Newbury Park, CA: Sage.

Fitzpatrick, M. A., & Badinski, D. M. (1994). All in the family: Interpersonal communication in kin relationships. In M. L. Knapp & G. R. Miller (Eds.), *Handbook of interpersonal communication* (2nd ed., pp. 726-771). Thousand Oaks, CA: Sage.

Fiur, M. (1988). Public relations faces the 21st century. In R. E. Hiebert (Ed.), *Precision public relations* (pp. 337-356). New York: Longman.

Fleischer, C. (1998, October). *The state of public relations.* Working paper, School of Management, University of Waikato, Hamilton, New Zealand.

Fleisher, C. S., & Blair, N. M. (1998, July). *Tracing the parallel evolution of public affairs and public relations: An examination of practice, scholarship, and teaching.* Paper presented at the Fifth International Public Relations Research Symposium, Bled, Slovenia.

Fleming, T. F. (1960). Further appraisal of the manner in which the American press handles material relevant to education. *Journal of Educational Research, 54*(3), 92-98.

Flynn, J. T. (1932). Edward L. Bernays: The science of ballyhoo. *Atlantic Monthly, 149,* 562-571.

Folger, J. P., Poole, M. S., & Stutman, R. K. (1993). *Working through conflict: Strategies in relationships, groups, and organizations* (2nd ed.). New York: HarperCollins.

Fombrun, C., & Shanley, M. (1990). What's in a name? Reputation building and corporate strategy. *Academy of Management Journal, 33,* 233-258.

Food Lion award from Capital Cities trimmed to $315,000. (1997, September 2). *The Wall Street Journal,* p. B10.

Forbes, P. S. (1986). Why licensing is an opportunity for public relations. *Public Relations Review, 12*(4), 9-11.

Foss, K. A., Foss, S. K., & Griffin, C. L. (1999). *Feminist rhetorical theories.* Thousand Oaks, CA: Sage.

Foss, S. (1996). *Rhetorical criticism: Exploration and practice.* Prospect Heights, IL: Waveland.

Foss, S. K., & Foss, K. A. (1988). What distinguishes feminist scholarship in communication studies? *Women's Studies in Communication, 11,* 9-11.

Foss, S. K., Foss, K. A., & Trapp, R. (1991). *Contemporary perspectives on rhetoric* (2nd ed.). Prospect Heights, IL: Waveland.

Foster, G. (1994). Fishing the Net for research data. *British Journal of Educational Technology, 25*(2), 91-97.

Foster, L. G. (1999). *Building global bridges: 1998 Atlas Award lecture on international public relations* (International Section monograph). New York: Public Relations Society of America.

Foucault, M. (1972). *The archaeology of knowledge* (A. M. Sheridan Smith, Trans.). London: Routledge. (Original work published 1969)

Foucault, M. (1984). *The Foucault reader* (P. Rabinow, Ed.). New York: Pantheon.

Foucault, M. (1987). *The history of sexuality: The use of pleasure* (Vol. 2, R. Hurley, Trans.). London: Penguin.

Foucault, M. (1988). Technologies of the self. In L. H. Martin, H. Gutman, & P. H. Hutton (Eds.), *Technologies of the self* (pp. 16-49). Amherst: University of Massachusetts Press.

Fox, J. F. (1982). Communicating on public issues: A changing role for the CEO. *Public Relations Quarterly, 27*(2), 19-26.

Fox, S., & Moult, G. (1990). Postmodern culture and management development. *Management Education and Development, 21*(3), 161-268.

Frank, R. E., Massy, W. F., & Wind, Y. (1972). *Market segmentation.* Englewood Cliffs, NJ: Prentice Hall.

Freedman, J. L., & Sears, D. O. (1965). Selective exposure. In L. Berkowitz (Ed.), *Advances in experimental social psychology* (Vol. 2, pp. 57-97). New York: Academic Press.

Freedom and community: The politics of restoration. (1994, December 24). *The Economist,* pp. 33-36.

Freeman, J. L. (1982). Organizational life cycles and natural selection processes. In B. Staw & L. Cummings (Eds.), *Research in organiza-*

tional behavior 4 (pp. 1-32). Greenwich, CT: JAI.

Freeman, R. E. (1984). *Strategic management: A stakeholder approach.* Boston: Pitman.

Freidson, E. (1970a). *Medical dominance.* Chicago: Aldine-Atherton.

Freidson, E. (1970b). *Profession of medicine.* New York: Harper & Row.

Freidson, E. (1986). *Professional powers: A study of the institutionalization of formal knowledge.* Chicago: Univerity of Chicago Press.

Freidson, E. (1994). *Professionalism reborn: Theory, prophecy, and policy.* Cambridge, UK: Polity.

Freivalds, J. (1993). Creating a verbal identity. *Communication World, 10*(11), 32-33.

French, J. R., & Raven, B. (1968). The bases of social power. In D. Cartwright & A. Zander (Eds.), *Group dynamics* (3rd ed., pp. 259-269). New York: Harper & Row.

French, W. A., & Granrose, J. (1995). *Practical business ethics.* Englewood Cliffs, NJ: Prentice Hall.

Fresen, G. W. (1997). What lawyers should know about digital signatures. *Illinois Bar Journal, 85,* 170-173.

Friedman, M. (1970, September 13). The social responsibility of business is to increase its profits. *The New York Times Sunday Magazine,* p. 146.

Friedman, M. (1982). *Capitalism and freedom.* Chicago: University of Chicago Press.

Friedman, M. (1987). The social responsibility of business is to increase its profits. In D. Poff & W. Waluchow (Eds.), *Business ethics in Canada* (pp. 7-11). Scarborough, Ontario: Prentice Hall Canada.

Frohnen, B. (1996). *The new communitarians and the crisis of modern liberalism.* Lawrence: University of Kansas Press.

Frye, N. (1957). *Anatomy of criticism.* Princeton, NJ: Princeton University Press.

Fu, M. (1990). Zhenfu gongguang chutan [A brief study of government public relations]. *Gonggong Guangxi* [Public Relations Journal], *3,* 8-10.

Fuhrman, C. J. (1989). *Publicity stunt! Great staged events that made the news.* San Francisco: Chronicle Books.

Fukuyama, F. (1995). *Trust: The social virtues and the creation of prosperity.* New York: Free Press.

Fulk, J. (1993). Social construction of communication technology. *Academy of Management Journal, 36,* 921-950.

Gaby, D. M. (1980). Politics and public relations. *Public Relations Journal, 36*(10), 10-12.

Gaddis, S. (1998, June). How to design online surveys. *Training & Development,* pp. 67-71.

Galbraith, M. (1991). *Facilitating adult learning: A transactional process.* Malabar, FL: Krieger.

Galitzine, Y. (1960). The philosophy of public relations. *Public Relations, 12*(4), 49-55.

Gandy, O. H., Jr. (1982). *Beyond agenda setting: Information subsidies and public policy.* Norwood, NJ: Ablex.

Gandy, O. H., Jr. (1992). Public relations and public policy: The structuration of dominance in the information age. In E. L. Toth & R. L. Heath (Eds.), *Rhetorical and critical approaches to public relations* (pp. 131-163). Hillsdale, NJ: Lawrence Erlbaum.

Ganley, G. (1996). *Unglued empire: The Soviet experience with communication technologies.* Norwood, NJ: Ablex.

Gans, H. (1979). *Deciding what's news: A study of CBS Evening News, NBC Nightly News, Newsweek, and* Time. New York: Random House.

Gao, X. (1991). Zhenfu gongguang de Fanli [A case study of government public relations]. *Gonggong Guangxi* [Public Relations Journal], *1,* 26-27.

Gardner, J. (1991). *Effective lobbying in the European Community.* Deventer, Netherlands: Kluwer.

Garnett, A. A. (1951). That definition [letter to the editor]. *Public Relations, 3*(3), 16.

Garrett, D. E., Bradford, J. L., Meyers, R. A., & Becker, J. (1989, July). Issues management and organizational accounts: An analysis of corporate responses to accusations of unethical business practices. *Journal of Business Ethics, 8,* 507-520.

Garton, L., & Wellman, B. (1991). Social impacts of electronic mail in organizations: A review of the research literature. In B. R. Burleson (Ed.), *Communication yearbook 18* (pp. 434-453). Newbury Park, CA: Sage.

Gaschen, D. J. (1998, July). Managing the growth of your business (and getting a good night's sleep). *Public Relations Tactics*, pp. 12-13.

Gaunt, P., & Ollenburger, J. (1995). Issues management revisited: A tool that deserves another look. *Public Relations Review, 21*, 199-210.

Geertz, C. (1973). *The interpretation of cultures: Selected essays.* New York: Basic Books.

Geertz, C. (1988). *Works and lives: The anthropologist as author.* Stanford, CA: Stanford University Press.

Geiger, S., & Newhagen, J. (1993). Revealing the black box: Information processing and media effects. *Journal of Communication, 43*(4), 42-49.

Geiger, S., & Reeves, B. (1991). The effects of cuts and semantic relatedness on attention to television. In F. Biocca (Ed.), *Television and political advertising* (pp. 125-144). Hillsdale, NJ: Lawrence Erlbaum.

Geison, G. L. (1984). Introduction. In G. L. Geison (Ed.), *Professions and the French state, 1700-1900* (pp. 1-11). Philadelphia: University of Pennslvania Press.

Gell-Mann, M. (1994). *The quark and the jaguar: Adventures in the simple and the complex.* New York: Freeman.

Gerbner, G. (1967). Newsmen and schoolmen: The state and problems of educational reporting. *Journalism Quarterly, 44*, 213-224.

Gerbner, G., Gross, L., Signorielli, N., Morgan, M., & Jackson-Beeck, M. (1979). The demonstration of power: Violence profile No. 10. *Journal of Communication, 29*(3), 177-196.

German, K. M. (1995). Critical theory in public relations inquiry: Future directions for analysis in a public relations context. In W. N. Elwood (Ed.), *Public relations inquiry as rhetorical criticism: Case studies of corporate discourse and social influence* (pp. 279-294). Westport, CT: Praeger.

Gertz v. Robert Welch Inc., 418 U.S. 323 (1974).

Ghiloni, B. S. (1984). Women, power, and the corporation: Evidence from the velvet ghetto. *Power and Elites, 1*(1), 37-49.

Gibson, D. C. (1991-1992). Theory instruction through case studies. *Public Relations Quarterly, 36*(4), 45-46.

Giddens, A. (1979). *Central problems in social theory: Action, structure, and contradiction in social analysis.* Berkeley: University of California Press.

Giddens, A. (1984). *The constitution of society.* Berkeley: University of California Press.

Giddens, A. (1987). *Social theory and modern sociology.* Stanford, CA: Stanford University Press.

Giddens, A. (1990). *The consequences of modernity.* Stanford, CA: Stanford University Press.

Giddens, A. (1991). *Modernity and self-identity: Self and society in the late modern age.* Stanford, CA: Stanford University Press.

Giddens. A. (1993). *New rules of sociological methods: A positive critique of interpretive sociologies* (2nd ed.). Cambridge, UK: Polity.

Giddens. A. (1995). *A contemporary critique of historical materialism* (2nd ed.). Stanford, CA: Stanford University Press.

Gies, W. J., Kahn, M., & Limerick, O. V. (1921). The effect of tobacco on man. *New York Medical Journal, 113*, 809-811.

Gildea, R. L. (1994-1995). Consumer survey confirms corporate social action affects buying decisions. *Public Relations Quarterly, 39*(4), 20-21.

Gillis, T. (1997). Change agency and public relations officers in small colleges and universities. *Dissertation Abstracts International, 58*, No. AAT 9735944. Available: http://www.lib.umi.com/dissertations/fullcit?129597

Gillman, F. (1978). Public relations in the United Kingdom prior to 1948. *International Public Relations Association Review*, pp. 43-50.

Ginsburg, B. (1986). *The captive public: How mass opinion promotes state power.* New York: Basic Books.

Giordano, B. P. (1997). It's time to send the public the right message about perioperative nursing. *AORN Journal, 66*, 391, 394.

Glantz, S. A., Barnes, D. E., Bero, L., Hanauer, P., & Slade, J. (1995). Looking through a keyhole at the tobacco industry: The Brown and Williamson documents. *Journal of the American Medical Association, 274,* 219-224.

Glater, J. D. (1995, June 2). Chicago bank settles lending bias case for $700,000. *The Washington Post,* p. F1.

Glendon, M. A. (1991). *Rights talk: The impoverishment of political discourse.* New York: Free Press.

Godbehere v. Phoenix Newspapers Inc., 162 Ariz. 335 (1989).

Goerner, S. J. (1995). Chaos and deep psychology. In F. D. Abraham & A. R. Gilgen (Eds.), *Chaos theory in psychology* (pp. 3-18). Westport, CT: Praeger.

Goffman, E. (1959). *The presentation of self in everyday life.* New York: Overlook.

Goffman, E. (1971). *Relations in public.* New York: Basic Books.

Goffman, E. (1981). Replies and responses. In E. Goffman (Ed.), *Forms of talk* (pp. 5-77). Philadelphia: University of Pennsylvania Press.

Goldberg, J. (1998, June 21). Big tobacco's end game. *The New York Times,* p. F36.

Goldhaber, G. M., Dennis, H. S., Richetto, G. M., & Wiio, O. (1979). *Information strategies: New pathways to corporate power.* Englewood Cliffs, NJ: Prentice Hall.

Goldhaber, G. M., Porter, D. T., & Yates, M. (1977). *ICA communication audit survey instrument: 1977 organizational norms.* Paper presented at the meeting of the International Communication Association, Berlin.

Goldhaber, G. M., & Rogers, D. P. (1979). *Auditing organizational communications systems: The ICA communication audit.* Dubuque, IA: Kendall/Hunt.

Goldman, E. (1998). 21st-century sea change in public relations careers. *Public Relations Strategist, 4*(1), 43-45.

Golin, A. (1997). Golin/Harris, McDonald's provide food for body, soul in Chicago. *Public Relations Update, 32*(1), 1-2.

Gonring, M. P. (1994). Putting integrated marketing communications to work today. *Public Relations Quarterly, 39*(3), 45-48.

Gonzalez, H., & Akel, D. (1996). Elections and earth matters: Public relations in Costa Rica. In H. M. Culbertson & N. Chen (Eds.), *International public relations: A comparative analysis* (pp. 257-272). Mahwah, NJ: Lawrence Erlbaum.

Gonzalez-Herrero, A., & Pratt, C. (1996). An integrated symmetrical model for crisis communications management. *Journal of Public Relations Research, 8,* 79-105.

Goodnight, G. T. (1982). The personal, technical, and public spheres of argument: A speculative inquiry into the art of public deliberation. *Journal of the American Forensic Association, 18,* 214-227.

Gordon, J. C. (1997). Interpreting definitions of public relations: Self-assessment and a symbolic-interactionist alternative. *Public Relations Review, 23,* 57-66.

Goregin, A. (1996). *Common elements in Russian public relations and international practice of American public relations specialists.* Unpublished master's thesis, Oklahoma State University.

Gouldner, A. W. (1960). The norm of reciprocity: A preliminary statement. *American Sociological Review, 25*(2), 161-178.

Graber, D. A. (1989). *Mass media and American politics* (3rd ed.). Washington, DC: Congressional Quarterly.

Grace, K. S. (1991). Managing for results. In H. A. Rosso & Associates (Eds.), *Achieving excellence in fund raising: A comprehensive guide to principles, strategies, and methods* (pp. 140-160). San Francisco: Jossey-Bass.

Graham, J. L. (1993, April). The Japanese negotiation style: Characteristics of a distinct approach. *Negotiation Journal, 9*(2), 123-140.

Graham, T. (1995). The Brown and Williamson documents: The company's response. *Journal of the American Medical Association, 274,* 254-255.

Grates, G. F. (1997). *The maturation of public relations.* New York: Boxenbaum Grates Inc.

Gray, B. (1989). *Collaborating: Finding common ground for multiparty problems.* San Francisco: Jossey-Bass.

Gray, S., & Moore, J. (1996, July 11). Big gifts from big business. *Chronicle of Philanthropy*, pp. 1, 12-20.

Grayned v. City of Rockford, 408 U.S. 104 (1972).

Grcic, J. (1989). *Moral choices: Ethical theories and problems*. St. Paul, MN: West.

Green, R. (1994). Healthcare public relations shifts gears. *Public Relations Quarterly, 39*(2), 33-36.

Greenberg, K. E. (1994). Reform moves fuel advocacy fever. *Public Relations Journal, 50*(3), 16-18.

Greenfield, J. M. (1991). *Fund-raising: Evaluating and managing the fund development process*. New York: John Wiley.

Greenwood, J. (1997). *Representing interests in the European Union*. Basingstoke, UK: Macmillan.

Greenwood, J. (1998). Regulating lobbying in the European Union. *Parliamentary Affairs, 51*, 587-600.

Greer, I. (1997). *One man's word*. London: Andre Deutsch.

Gregg, R. B. (1971). The ego-function of the rhetoric of protest. *Philosophy and Rhetoric, 4*, 71-91.

Grenstad, G., & Selle, P. (1997). Cultural theory, postmaterialism, and environmental attitudes. In R. J. Ellis & M. Thompson (Eds.), *Culture matters* (pp. 169-190). Boulder, CO: Westview.

Greyser, S. (1995). *Greyser: Reputation is an aid to growth* [on-line]. Available: http://www.prcentral/com/rmif95greysr.html

Griffin, L. M. (1952). The rhetoric of historical movements. *Quarterly Journal of Speech, 38*, 184-188.

Griffin, W. G., & Pasadeos, Y. (1998). The impact of IMC on advertising and public relations education. *Journalism and Mass Communication Educator, 53*(2), 4-18.

Grönroos, C. (1981). Internal marketing: An integral part of marketing theory. In J. H. Donnelly, Jr., & W. R. George (Eds.), *Marketing of services* (pp. 236-238). Chicago: American Marketing Association.

Grönroos, C. (1990). Relationship approach to marketing in service contexts: The marketing and organizational behavior interface. *Journal of Business Research, 20*, 3-11.

Gruban, B. (1995). Performing public relations in Central and Eastern Europe. *Public Relations Quarterly, 40*(3), 20-23.

Grunig, J. E. (1975). Some consistent types of employee publics. *Public Relations Review, 1*(1), 17-36.

Grunig, J. E. (1976). Organizations and public relations: Testing a communication theory. *Journalism Monographs*, No. 46.

Grunig, J. E. (1978). Defining publics in public relations: The case of a suburban hospital. *Journalism Quarterly, 55*, 109-118.

Grunig, J. E. (1982). The message-attitude-behavior relationship: Communication behaviors of organizations. *Communication Research, 9*, 163-200.

Grunig, J. E. (1983a). Basic research provides knowledge that makes evaluation possible. *Public Relations Quarterly, 28*(4), 28-32.

Grunig, J. E. (1983b). Communication behaviors and attitudes of environmental publics: Two studies. *Journalism Monographs*, No. 81.

Grunig, J. E. (1983c). Washington reporter publics of corporate public affairs programs. *Journalism Quarterly, 60*, 603-615.

Grunig, J. E. (1984). Organizations, environments, and models of public relations. *Public Relations Research & Education, 1*(1), 6-29.

Grunig, J. E. (1987). *When active publics become activists: Extending a situational theory of publics*. Paper presented at the meeting of the International Communication Association, Montreal.

Grunig, J. E. (1989a). Communication, public relations, and effective organizations: An overview of the book. In J. E. Grunig & L. A. Grunig (Eds.), *Public relations research annual* (Vol. 1, pp. 27-61). Hillsdale, NJ: Lawrence Erlbaum.

Grunig, J. E. (1989b). Publics, audiences, and market segments: Segmentation principles for campaigns. In C. T. Salmon (Ed.), *Information campaigns: Balancing social values and social change* (pp. 199-228). Newbury Park, CA: Sage.

Grunig, J. E. (1989c). Sierra club study shows who become activists. *Public Relations Review, 15*(3), 3-24.

Grunig, J. E. (1989d). A situational theory of environmental issues, publics, and activists. In L. A. Grunig (Ed.), *Environmental activism revisited: The changing nature of communication through organizational public relations, special interest groups, and the mass media* (pp. 50-82, Monographs in Environmental Education and Environmental Studies). Troy, OH: North American Association for Environmental Education.

Grunig, J. E. (1989e). Symmetrical presuppositions as a framework for public relations theory. In C. H. Botan & V. T. Hazelton, Jr. (Eds.), *Public relations theory* (pp. 17-44). Hillsdale, NJ: Lawrence Erlbaum.

Grunig, J. E. (1990). Theory and practice of interactive media relations. *Public Relations Quarterly, 35*(3), 18-23.

Grunig, J. E. (1991, January). *On the effects of marketing, media relations, and public relations.* Paper presented at the Second Symposium of the Herbert Quandt Communication Group, Berlin.

Grunig, J. E. (1992a). Communication, public relations, and effective organizations: An overview of the book. In J. E. Grunig (Ed.), *Excellence in public relations and communication management* (pp. 1-28). Hillsdale, NJ: Lawrence Erlbaum.

Grunig, J. E. (1992b). The development of public relations research in the United States and its status in communication science. In H. Avenarius & W. Armbrecht (Eds.), *Ist public relations eine wissenschaft?* (pp. 103-132). Opladen, Germany: Westdeutscher Verlag.

Grunig, J. E. (Ed.). (1992c). *Excellence in public relations and communication management.* Hillsdale, NJ: Lawrence Erlbaum.

Grunig, J. E. (1993a). Image and substance: From symbolic to behavioral relationships. *Public Relations Review, 19,* 121-139.

Grunig, J. E. (1993b). Implications of public relations for other domains of communication. *Journal of Communication, 43*(3), 164-173.

Grunig, J. E. (1993c). On the effects of marketing, media relations, and public relations: Images, agendas, and relationships. In W. Armbrecht, H. Avenarius, & U. Zabel (Eds.), *Image und PR: Kann image gegenstand einer public relations-wissenschaft sein?* (pp. 263-295). Wiesbaden, Germany: Westdeutscher Verlag.

Grunig, J. E. (1993d). Public relations and international affairs: Effects, ethics, and responsibility. *Journal of International Affairs, 47,* 137-162.

Grunig, J. E. (1994). Worldview, ethics, and the two-way symmetrical model of public relations. In W. Armbrecht & U. Zabel (Eds.), *Normative aspekte der public relations* (pp. 69-90). Opladen, Germany: Westdeutscher Verlag.

Grunig, J. E. (1997). A situational theory of publics: Conceptual history, recent challenges, and new research. In D. Moss, T. MacManus, & D. Vercic (Eds.), *Public relations research: An international perspective* (pp. 3-48). London: International Thomson Business Press.

Grunig, J. E., & Childers, L. (1988). *Reconstruction of a situational theory of communication: Internal and external concepts as identifiers of publics for AIDS.* Paper presented at the meeting of the Association for Education in Journalism and Mass Communication, Portland, OR.

Grunig, J. E., & Grunig, L. A. (1989). Toward a theory of the public relations behavior of organizations: Review of a program of research. In J. E. Grunig & L. A. Grunig (Eds.), *Public relations research annual* (Vol. 1, pp. 27-63). Hillsdale, NJ: Lawrence Erlbaum.

Grunig, J. E., & Grunig, L. A. (1990, August). *Models of public relations: A review and reconceptualization.* Paper presented at the meeting of the Association for Education in Journalism and Mass Communication, Minneapolis, MN.

Grunig, J. E., & Grunig, L. A. (1991). Conceptual differences in public relations and marketing: The case of health-care organizations. *Public Relations Review, 17,* 257-278.

Grunig, J. E., & Grunig, L. A. (1992). Models of public relations and communications. In J. E. Grunig (Ed.), *Excellence in public relations and communication management* (pp. 285-326). Hillsdale, NJ: Lawrence Erlbaum.

Grunig, J. E., & Grunig, L. A. (1996, May). *Implications of symmetry for a theory of ethics and social responsibility in public relations.* Paper presented at the meeting of the International Communication Association, Chicago.

Grunig, J. E., & Grunig, L. A. (1997, July). *Review of a program of research on activism: Incidence in four countries, activist publics, strategies of activist groups, and organizational responses to activism.* Paper presented at the Fourth Public Relations Research Symposium, Bled, Slovenia.

Grunig, J. E., Grunig, L. A., & Dozier, D. M. (1995, November). *Combining the two-way symmetrical and asymmetrical models into a contingency model of excellent public relations.* Paper presented at the meeting of the Association for the Advancement of Policy, Research, and Development in the Third World, Las Vegas, NV.

Grunig, J. E., Grunig, L. A., & Dozier, D. M. (1996). Combining the two-way symmetrical and asymmetrical models into a contingency model of excellent public relations. In G. Bentele, H. Steinmann, & A. Zerfass (Eds.), *Dialogorientierte unternehmenskommunikation* (pp. 199-228). Berlin: Vistas.

Grunig, J. E., Grunig, L. A., Dozier, D. M., Ehling, W. P., Repper, F. C., & White, J. (1991a). *Excellence in public relations and communication management: Initial data report and practical guide.* San Francisco: International Association of Business Communicators Research Foundation.

Grunig, J. E., Grunig, L. A., Dozier, D. M., Ehling, W. P., Repper, F. C., & White, J. (1991b). *Initial results of survey to confirm value of communication and the components of excellent public relations* (report to the IABC Research Foundation). New York: International Association of Business Communicators.

Grunig, J. E., Grunig, L. A., & Ehling, W. P. (1992). What is an effective organization? In J. E. Grunig (Ed.), *Excellence in public relations and communication management* (pp. 65-90). Hillsdale, NJ: Lawrence Erlbaum.

Grunig, J. E., Grunig, L. A., Sriramesh, K., Huang, Y. H., & Lyra, A. (1995). Models of public relations in an international setting. *Journal of Public Relations Research, 7,* 163-186.

Grunig, J. E., & Huang, Y. H. (2000). From organizational effectiveness to relationship indicators: Antecedents of relationships, public relations strategies, and relationship outcomes. In J. A. Ledingham & S. D. Bruning (Eds.), *Public relations as relationship management: A relational approach to the study and practice of public relations* (pp. 23-53). Mahwah, NJ: Lawrence Erlbaum.

Grunig, J. E., & Hunt, T. (1984). *Managing public relations.* New York: Holt, Rinehart & Winston.

Grunig, J. E., & Ipes, D. A. (1983). The anatomy of a campaign against drunk driving. *Public Relations Review, 9*(2), 36-52.

Grunig, J. E., Nelson, C. L., Richburg, S. J., & White, T. J. (1988). Communication by agricultural publics: Internal and external orientations. *Journalism Quarterly, 65,* 26-38.

Grunig, J. E., Ramsey, S., & Schneider, L. A. (1985). An axiomatic theory of cognition and writing. *Journal of Technical Writing and Communication, 15,* 110-130.

Grunig, J. E., & Repper, F. C. (1992). Strategic management, publics, and issues. In J. E. Grunig (Ed.), *Excellence in public relations and communication management* (pp. 117-157). Hillsdale, NJ: Lawrence Erlbaum.

Grunig, J. E., & White, J. (1992). The effect of worldviews on public relations theory and practice. In J. E. Grunig (Ed.), *Excellence in public relations and communication management* (pp. 31-64). Hillsdale, NJ: Lawrence Erlbaum.

Grunig, L. A. (1988). A research agenda for women in public relations. *Public Relations Review, 14,* 48-57.

Grunig, L. A. (1992a). Activism: How it limits the effectiveness of organizations and how excellent public relations departments respond. In J. E. Grunig (Ed.), *Excellence in public rela-*

tions and communication management (pp. 503-530). Hillsdale, NJ: Lawrence Erlbaum.

Grunig, L. A. (1992b). How public relations/communication departments should adapt to the structure and environment of an organization . . . and what they actually do. In J. E. Grunig (Ed.), *Excellence in public relations and communication management* (pp. 467-482). Hillsdale, NJ: Lawrence Erlbaum.

Grunig, L. A. (1993). Image and symbolic leadership: Using focus group research to bridge the gaps. *Journal of Public Relations Research, 5,* 95-125.

Grunig, L. A. (1995). The consequences of culture for public relations: The case of women in the Foreign Service. *Journal of Public Relations Research, 7,* 139-161.

Grunig, L. A., Dozier, D. M., & Grunig, J. E. (1994). *IABC excellence in public relations and communication management, Phase 2: Qualitative study, initial analysis—Cases of excellence.* San Francisco: International Association of Business Communicators Research Foundation.

Grunig, L. A., Grunig, J. E., & Dozier, D. M. (in preparation). *Excellent public relations and effective organizations: A study of communication management in three countries.* Mahwah, NJ: Lawrence Erlbaum.

Grunig, L. A., Grunig, J. E., & Ehling, W. (1992). What is an effective organization? In J. E. Grunig (Ed.), *Excellence in public relations and communication management* (pp. 65-90). Hillsdale, NJ: Lawrence Erlbaum.

Gumpert, G., & Cathcart, R. (Eds.). (1986). *Intermedia: Interpersonal communication in a media world.* New York: Oxford University Press.

Gumpert, G., & Drucker, S. L. (1993). Media development and public space: The legislation of social interaction. In J. R. Schement & B. D. Ruben (Eds.), *Between communication and information: Information and behavior* (Vol. 4, pp. 435-452). New Brunswick, NJ: Transaction Publishers.

Guth, D. W. (1995). Organizational crisis experience and public relations roles. *Public Relations Review, 21,* 123-136.

Guttman, N. (1997). Ethical dilemmas in health campaigns. *Health Communication, 9,* 155-190.

Haas, T., & Deetz, S. A. (2000). Between the generalized and the concrete other: Approaching organizational ethics from feminist perspectives. In P. Buzzanell (Ed.), *Rethinking managerial and organizational communication from feminist perspectives* (pp. 24-46). Thousand Oaks, CA: Sage.

Haberman, M. (1987). What the media teach the public about education. *Education Digest, 53*(3), 5-8.

Habermas, J. (1970). On systematically distorted communication. *Inquiry, 13,* 205-218.

Habermas, J. (1973). Wahrheitsteorien. In H. Fahrtenbach (Ed.), *Wirklichkeit und Reflexion.* Pfullingen, Germany: Neske.

Habermas, J. (1979a). *Communication and the evolution of society* (T. McCarthy, Trans.). Boston: Beacon.

Habermas, J. (1979b). Legitimation problems in the modern state. In *Communication and the evolution of society* (T. McCarthy, Trans.) (pp. 178-205). Boston: Beacon. (Original work published 1976)

Habermas, J. (1984). *The theory of communicative action, Vol. 1: Reason and the rationalization of society* (T. McCarthy, Trans.). Boston: Beacon. (Original work published 1981)

Habermas, J. (1987). *The theory of communicative action,* Vol. 2: *Lifeworld and system* (T. McCarthy, Trans.). Boston: Beacon.

Habermas, J. (1990). *Moral consciousness and communicative action.* Cambridge, MA: MIT Press.

Habermas, J. (1991). *The structural transformation of a public sphere: An inquiry into a category of bourgeois society* (T. Burger & F. Lawrence, Trans.). Cambridge, MA: MIT Press. (Original work published 1962)

Habermas, J. (1993). *Justification and application: Remarks on discourse ethics.* Cambridge, MA: MIT Press.

Habermas, J. (1996). *Between facts and norms* (W. Regh, Trans.). Cambridge, MA: MIT Press.

Hadley, C. (1940). *The invasion from Mars: A study in the psychology of panic.* Princeton, NJ: Princeton University Press.

Haedrich, G. (1993). Image and strategic corporate and marketing planning. *Journal of Public Relations Research, 5,* 83-93.

Hainsworth, B. E. (1990). The distribution of advantages and disadvantages. *Public Relations Review, 16*(1), 10-15.

Hainsworth, B. E., & Wilson, L. J. (1992). Strategic program planning. *Public Relations Review, 18*(1), 9-15.

Hale, C. (Ed.). (1996). *Wired style: Principles of English usage in the digital age.* San Francisco: Hardwired.

Hall, S. (1986). On postmodernism and articulation. *Journal of Communication Inquiry, 10*(2), 45-60.

Hall, W. (1995). *Managing cultures: Making strategic relationships work.* New York: John Wiley.

Hallahan, K. (1994). Public relations and circumvention of the press. *Public Relations Quarterly, 39*(2), 17-19.

Hallahan, K. (1996a, August). *"Community" as the foundation for public relations theory/practice.* Paper presented at the meeting of the Association for Education in Journalism and Mass Communication, Anaheim, CA.

Hallahan, K. (1996b). Product publicity: An orphan of marketing research. In E. Thorson & J. Moore (Eds.), *Integrated communication: Search for synergy in communication voices* (pp. 305-330). Mahwah, NJ: Lawrence Erlbaum.

Hallahan, K. (1999a). Content class as a contextual cue in the cognitive processing of publicity versus advertising. *Journal of Public Relations Research, 11,* 293-320.

Hallahan, K. (1999b). No, Virigina, it's not true what they say about publicity's "implied third-party endorsement" effect. *Public Relations Review, 25,* 331-350.

Hallett, J. (1995, December). What the Internet means to the future of PR. *Public Relations Tactics* [on-line]. Available: http://www.prsa.org

Hamel, J., Dufour, S., & Fortin, D. (1993). *Case study methods.* Newbury Park, CA: Sage.

Hamilton, P. (1987, May). *Program accreditation.* Research presented at the International Communication Association Conference, Public Relations Interest Group, Montreal.

Hampden-Turner, C., & Trompenaars, A. (1993). *The seven cultures of capitalism: Value systems for creating wealth in the United States, Japan, Germany, France, Britain, Sweden, and the Netherlands.* New York: Doubleday.

Handy, C. B. (1985). *Gods of management: The changing work of organizations.* London: Pan Books.

Hannan, M., & Freeman, J. (1977). The population ecology of organizations. *American Journal of Sociology, 82,* 929-964.

Hannan, M., & Freeman, J. (1984). Structural inertia and organizational change. *American Sociological Review, 49,* 149-164.

Hannan, M., & Freeman, J. (1989). *Organizational ecology.* Cambridge, MA: Harvard University Press.

Hansen, T. L. (1993, November). *The ideology of the "organizing model" of unionism: Preliminary understandings.* Paper presented at the meeting of the Speech Communication Association, Miami, FL.

Hansen-Horn, T. L. (1996). *Searching for alternative organizational communication voices: The inscription of an organized labor perspective.* Unpublished doctoral dissertation, Purdue University.

Hansen-Horn, T. L., & Vasquez, G. M. (1997). Union advocacy: Power, organizing, and change. In J. D. Hoover (Ed.), *Corporate advocacy: Rhetoric in the information age* (pp. 187-203). Westport, CT: Quorum Books.

Harding, S. (1986). *The science question in feminism.* Ithaca, NY: Cornell University Press.

Harding, S. (Ed.). (1987). *Feminism and methodology.* Bloomington: Indiana University Press.

Hargadon, T. (1990, March). A lack of communication and what it can cost. *Office,* p. 27.

Harich, K. R., & Curren, M. T. (1995). A longitudinal examination of American business ethics: Clark's scales revisited. *Business & Professional Ethics Journal, 14,* 57-68.

Harlow, R. F. (1976). Building a public relations definition. *Public Relations Review, 4*(2), 34-42.

Harold, J. R., Marcus, H. S., & Wallace, W. A. (1990). The Exxon Valdez: An assessment of crisis prevention and management systems. *Interfaces, 20,* 14-30.

Harré, R., & Gillett, G. (1994). *The discursive mind.* Thousand Oaks, CA: Sage.

Harris, J. R. (1988). A comparison of the ethical values of business faculty and students: How different are they? *Business & Professional Ethics Journal, 7,* 27-49.

Harris, J. R. (1990). Ethical values of individuals at different levels in the organizational hierarchy of a single firm. *Journal of Business Ethics, 9,* 741-750.

Harris, P. R., & Moran, R. T. (1991). *Managing cultural differences* (3rd ed.). Houston, TX: Gulf Publishing.

Harris, T. L. (1991a). *The marketer's guide to public relations.* New York: John Wiley.

Harris, T. L. (1991b). Why your company needs marketing public relations. *Public Relations Journal, 47*(9), 26-27.

Harrison, B. (1994). *Lean and mean: Why large corporations will continue to dominate the global economy.* New York: Guilford.

Harrison, S. L. (1990a). Ethics and moral issues in public relations curricula. *Journalism Educator, 45*(3), 32-38.

Harrison, S. L. (1990b). Pedagogical ethics for public relations and advertising. *Journal of Mass Media Ethics, 5,* 256-262.

Hart, A. (1996, November). Howdy, partner: Home-office workers and small companies can find business partners via the Net. *Internet World* [On-line]. Available: http://www.internetworld.com/print/monthly/1996/11

Hart, J. (1989, March). Cool it: Profs and pros have skewered one another too long, to no one's benefit. *The Quill,* pp. 32-35.

Harvard Business School. (1998). *MBA curriculum: The case method* [on-line]. Available: http://www.hbs.edu/mba/program/case_method.html

Harwick, J. (1981). *Factors that influence college basketball game coverage.* Unpublished master's thesis, West Virginia University.

Hassard, J., & Parker, M. (Eds.). (1993). *Postmodernism and organizations.* Newbury Park, CA: Sage.

Hastings Center. (1980a). *Ethics in the education of business managers.* Hastings-on-Hudson, NY: Author.

Hastings Center. (1980b). *The teaching of ethics in higher education.* Hastings-on-Hudson, NY: Author.

Hatch, M. J., & Schultz, M. (1997). Relations between organizational culture, identity, and image. *European Journal of Marketing, 31*(5/6), 356-365.

Hatfield, C. R. (1994). Public relations education in the United Kingdom. *Public Relations Review, 20,* 189-199.

Haug, M., & Koppang, H. (1997). Lobbying and public relations in a European context. *Public Relations Review, 23,* 233-247.

Hauser, G. A. (1998). Vernacular dialogue and the rhetoricality of public opinion. *Communication Monographs, 65,* 83-107.

Hauser, G., & Whalen, S. (1997). New rhetoric and new social movements. In B. Kovacic (Ed.), *Emerging theories of human communication* (pp. 115-140). Albany: State University of New York Press.

Hauss, D. (1995). Technology gives early warning of news breaks. *Public Relations Journal, 51*(4), 18-22.

Hawkins, M. (1996, January). How to be a great client . . . and a great consultant. *Public Relations Tactics,* p. 5.

Hawkins, R. P., Pingree, S., Bruce, L., & Tapper, J. (1997). Strategy and style in attention to television. *Journal of Broadcasting & Electronic Media, 41,* 245-264.

Hayles, M. (1982). *Science or society: The politics of the work of scientists.* London: Pan Books.

Hayles, N. K. (1990). *Chaos bound: Orderly disorder in contemporary literature and science.* Chicago: University of Chicago Press.

Hazleton, V., Jr., & Botan, C. H. (1989). The role of theory in public relations. In C. H. Botan &

V. Hazleton, Jr. (Eds.), *Public relations theory* (pp. 3-15). Hillsdale, NJ: Lawrence Erlbaum.

Hazleton, V., Jr., & Kruckeberg, D. (1998, July). *Numerical significance: Jacob Cohen, critical statistics, and public relations.* Paper presented at the meeting of the International Communication Association, Jerusalem.

Hearit, K. M. (1991, November). *Organizations and legitimacy: Cooperation or co-optation?* Paper presented at the meeting of the Speech Communication Association, Atlanta, GA.

Hearit, K. M. (1994). Apologies and public relations crises at Chrysler, Toshiba, and Volvo. *Public Relations Review, 20,* 113-125.

Hearit, K. M. (1995a). From "we didn't do it" to "it's not our fault": The use of apologia in public relations crises. In W. N. Elwood (Ed.), *Public relations inquiry as rhetorical criticism* (pp. 117-131). New York: Greenwood.

Hearit, K. M. (1995b). "Mistakes were made": Organizations, apologia, and crises of social legitimacy. *Communication Studies, 46*(1/2), 1-17.

Hearit, K. M. (1996). The use of counter-attack in apologetic public relations crises: The case of General Motors vs. Dateline NBC. *Public Relations Review, 22,* 233-248.

Hearit, K. M. (1997). On the use of transcendence as an apologia strategy: The case of Johnson Controls and its fetal protection strategy. *Public Relations Review, 23,* 217-231.

Heath, R. L. (1976). Variability in value system priorities as decision-making adaptation to situational differences. *Communication Monographs, 43,* 325-333.

Heath, R. L. (1980). Corporate advocacy: An application of speech communication perspectives and skills—and more. *Communication Education, 29,* 370-377.

Heath, R. L. (1986). *Realism and relativism: A perspective on Kenneth Burke.* Macon, GA: Mercer University Press.

Heath, R. L. (1988a). Conclusion. In R. L. Heath & Associates (Eds.), *Strategic issues management* (pp. 387-394). San Francisco: Jossey-Bass.

Heath, R. L. (Ed.). (1988b). *Strategic issues management: How organizations influence and respond to public interests and policies.* San Francisco: Jossey-Bass.

Heath, R. L. (1990). Corporate issues management: Theoretical underpinnings and research foundations. In J. E. Grunig & L. A. Grunig (Eds.), *Public relations research annual* (Vol. 2, pp. 29-65). Hillsdale, NJ: Lawrence Erlbaum.

Heath, R. L. (1991). Effects of internal rhetoric on management response to external issues: How corporate culture failed the asbestos industry. *Journal of Applied Communication, 18*(2), 153-167.

Heath, R. L. (1992a). Critical perspectives on public relations. In E. L. Toth & R. L. Heath (Eds.), *Rhetorical and critical approaches to public relations* (pp. 37-61). Hillsdale, NJ: Lawrence Erlbaum.

Heath, R. L. (1992b). The wrangle in the marketplace: A rhetorical perspective of public relations. In E. L. Toth & R. L. Heath (Eds.), *Rhetorical and critical approaches to public relations* (pp. 17-36). Hillsdale, NJ: Lawrence Erlbaum.

Heath, R. L. (1993). A rhetorical approach to zones of meaning and organizational prerogatives. *Public Relations Review, 19,* 141-155.

Heath, R. L. (1994). *Management of corporate communication: From interpersonal contacts to external affairs.* Hillsdale, NJ: Lawrence Erlbaum.

Heath, R. L. (1995). Corporate environmental risk communication: Cases and practices along the Texas Gulf Coast. In B. R. Burleson (Ed.), *Communication yearbook 18* (pp. 255-277). Thousand Oaks, CA: Sage.

Heath, R. L. (1997). *Strategic issues management: Organizations and public policy challenges.* Thousand Oaks, CA: Sage.

Heath, R. L. (1998a). New communication technologies: An issues management point of view. *Public Relations Review, 24,* 273-288.

Heath, R. L. (1998b, November). *Rhetorical enactment theory: Another piece in the paradigm shift.* Paper presented at the meeting of the

National Communication Association, New York.

Heath, R. L., & Abel, D. D. (1996a). Proactive response to citizen risk concerns: Increasing citizens' knowledge of emergency response practices. *Journal of Public Relations Research, 8,* 151-171.

Heath, R. L., & Abel, D. D. (1996b). Types of knowledge as predictors of company support: The role of information in risk communication. *Journal of Public Relations Research, 8,* 35-55.

Heath, R. L., & Bryant, J. (1992). *Human communication theory: Concepts and contexts.* Hillsdale, NJ: Lawrence Erlbaum.

Heath, R. L., & Douglas, W. (1990). Involvement: A key variable in people's reaction to public policy issues. In J. Grunig & L. Grunig (Eds.), *Public relations research annual* (Vol. 2, pp. 193-204). Hillsdale, NJ: Lawrence Erlbaum.

Heath, R. L., & Douglas, W. (1991). Effects of involvement on reactions to sources of messages and message clusters. In L. Grunig & J. Grunig (Eds.), *Public relations research annual* (Vol. 3, pp. 179-194). Hillsdale, NJ: Lawrence Erlbaum.

Heath, R. L., & Gray, C. D. (1997). Risk communication: Involvement, uncertainty, and controls effects on information scanning and monitoring by experts' stakeholders. *Management Communication Quarterly, 10,* 342-372.

Heath, R. L., Liao, S. H., & Douglas, W. (1995). Effects of perceived economic harms and benefits on issue involvement, use of information sources, and actions: A study in risk communication. *Journal of Public Relations Research, 7,* 89-109.

Heath, R. L., & Nelson, R. A. (1986). *Issues management.* Beverly Hills, CA: Sage.

Heath, R. L., & Ryan, M. (1989). Public relations' role in defining corporate social responsibility. *Journal of Mass Media Ethics, 4,* 21-38.

Heath, R. L., & Vasquez, G. M. (1996, May). *Rhetoric as a basis for a socially responsible public relations.* Paper presented at the meeting of the International Communication Association, Chicago.

Heerema, D. L., & Giannini, R. (1991). Business organizations and the sense of community. *Business Horizons, 34*(4), 87-91.

Heflich, D. A. (1997, March). *Online interviews: Research as a reflective dialogue.* Paper presented at the meeting of the American Educational Research Association, Chicago.

Helitzer, M. (1996). *The dream job: Sports publicity, promotion, and marketing* (2nd ed.). Athens, OH: University Sports Press.

Hellweg, S. A. (1989, May). *The application of Grunig's symmetry-asymmetry public relations models to internal communications systems.* Paper presented at the meeting of the International Communication Association, San Francisco.

Helmore, E. (1999, January 10). Internet online for new revolution. *The Observer,* p. 8.

Hendrix, J. A. (1995). *Public relations cases* (3rd ed.). Belmont, CA: Wadsworth.

Hendrix, J. A. (1998). *Public relations cases* (4th ed.). Belmont, CA: Wadsworth.

Herbst, S. (1993). *Numbered voices.* Chicago: University of Chicago Press.

Hermon, R. (1994, March). *Israel: Its government and opposition.* Panel discussion at the conference, "The Road to Peace: The Challenge of the Middle East," Miami, FL.

Herzberg, F. (1966). *Work and the nature of man.* Cleveland, OH: World Publishing.

Herzberg, F. (1976). *The managerial choice: To be efficient and to be human.* Homewood, IL: Irwin.

Hess, A. (1950). Conference speeches. *Public Relations, 3*(2) 5.

Hess, C. (Ed.). (1997). *The political resource directory.* Burlington, VT: Political Resource Inc.

Hewitt, J. P. (1989). *Dilemmas of the American self.* Philadelphia: Temple University Press.

Hicks, N. (1994, November). Transforming surveys into news. *Public Relations Tactics,* pp. 14-15.

Hickson, D. J., & Thomas, M. W. (1969). Professionalisation in Britain: A preliminary measurement. *Sociology, 3,* 37-53.

Hiebert, R. E. (1966). *Courtier to the crowd: The story of Ivy Lee and the development of public relations.* Ames: Iowa State University Press.

Hiebert, R. E. (Ed.). (1988). *Precision public relations.* New York: Longman.

Hiebert, R. E. (1992). Global public relations in a post-Communist world: A new model. *Public Relations Review, 18,* 117-126.

Hiebert, R. E. (1994). Advertising and public relations in transition from communism: The case of Hungary, 1989-1994. *Public Relations Review, 20,* 357-372.

Hiebert, R. E., & Devine, C. M. (1985). Government's research and evaluation gap. *Public Relations Review, 11*(3), 47-56.

Higgins, J. (1983). Public relations' role in strategic planning for higher education. *Public Relations Journal, 39*(5), 25-26.

Hilts, P. J. (1994, June 18). Grim findings on tobacco and a decade of frustration. *The New York Times,* pp. A1, A12.

Hines, B. H. (1998). Unleashing the power of the brand. *Public Relations Strategist, 4*(2), 24-26.

Hirokawa, R., & Rost, K. (1992). Effective group decision making in organizations. *Management Communication Quarterly, 5,* 267-288.

Hirschman, A. O. (1991). *The rhetoric of reaction: Perversity, futility, and jeopardy.* Cambridge, MA: Belknap.

Hofstede, G. (1984). *Culture's consequences: International differences in work-related values.* Beverly Hills, CA: Sage.

Holbrook, M. B. (1987). Mirror, mirror, on the wall, what's unfair in the reflections on advertising? *Journal of Marketing, 51*(3), 95-103.

Holcomb, J. M. (1996). Citizen corporations, public policy, and corporate responses. In L. B. Dennis (Ed.), *Practical public affairs in an era of change* (pp. 209-225). Lanham, MD: Public Relations Society of America.

Hollis Directories Ltd. (1994). *Hollis Europe: The directory of European public relations and PR networks* (5th ed.). London: Author.

Hollis Directories Ltd. (1998). *Hollis Europe: The directory of European public relations and PR networks* (9th ed.). London: Author.

Holtz, S. (1996). *Communication and technology: The complete guide to using technology for organizational communication.* Chicago: Lawrence Ragan Communications.

Hon, L. C. (1995a). Feminism and public relations. *Public Relations Strategist, 1*(2), 20-25.

Hon, L. C. (1995b). Toward a feminist theory of public relations. *Journal of Public Relations Research, 7,* 27-88.

Hon, L. C. (1998). Demonstrating effectiveness in public relations: Goals, objectives, and evaluation. *Journal of Public Relations Research, 10*(2), 103-135.

Hon, L. C., Grunig, L. A., & Dozier, D. M. (1992). Women in public relations: Problems and opportunities. In J. E. Grunig (Ed.), *Excellence in public relations and communication management* (pp. 419-438). Hillsdale, NJ: Lawrence Erlbaum.

Hotchkiss, G. B. (1940). *An outline of advertising: Its philosophy, science, art, and strategy.* New York: Macmillan.

Houlder, V. (1994, September 8). Getting the measure of PR. *Financial Times,* p. 13.

How do you police cyberspace? (1996, February 5). *Business Week,* p. 97.

Howard, C. M. (1991-1992). Perestroika from Pleasantville: Lessons learned launching Reader's Digest in the Soviet Union and Hungary. *Public Relations Quarterly, 37*(4), 15-20.

Howard, C. M. (1994). Advertising and public relations. *Vital Speeches, 60*(9), 269-272.

Howe, F. (1991). *The board member's guide to fund raising: What every trustee needs to know about raising money.* San Francisco: Jossey-Bass.

Howley v. Whipple, 48 N.H. 487 (1869).

Hrebnar, R. J., & Scott, R. K. (1982). *Interest group politics in America.* Englewood Cliffs, NJ: Prentice Hall.

Huang, Y. H. (1997). *Public relations strategies, relational outcomes, and conflict management strategies.* Unpublished doctoral dissertation, University of Maryland, College Park.

Hughes, E. C. (1958). *Men and their work.* New York: Free Press.

Hughes, E. C. (1971). *The sociological eye: Selected papers.* Chicago: Aldine.

Humphrey, N. D. (1946). Social problems. In A. M. Lee (Ed.), *New outline principles of sociology* (pp. 3-67). New York: Barnes & Noble.

Hunt, M. L., & McKie, D. (1998). Banking on the wrong domain: Generation MM, marketing, and public relations. *Australian Journal of Communication, 25*(3), 97-111.

Hunt, T., & Grunig, J. E. (1994). *Public relations techniques.* Fort Worth, TX: Harcourt Brace.

Hunt, T., & Tirpok, A. (1993). Universal ethics code: An idea whose time has come. *Public Relations Review, 19,* 1-11.

Huspek, M. (1997). Toward normative theories of communication with reference to the Frankfort School: An introduction. *Communication Theory, 7,* 265-276.

Hutson, M. W. (1995). *Job satisfaction in sport management personnel, employed by professional sport organizations in the United States and Canada.* Unpublished master's thesis, Northern Illinois University.

Hutton, J. G. (1994, November 7). Excellence study: Political and narrow. *The Ragan Report,* p. 1.

Hutton, J. G. (1996a). Integrated marketing communications and the evolution of marketing thought. *Journal of Business Research, 37,* 155-162.

Hutton, J. G. (1996b). Integrated relationship-marketing communications: A key opportunity for IMC. *Journal of Marketing Communications, 2,* 191-199.

Hutton, J. G. (1996c). Making the connection between public relations and marketing: Building relationships, corporate equity, and a "culture-to-customer" business philosophy. *Journal of Communication Management, 1*(1), 37-48.

Hutton, J. G. (1998, May). *The nature and scope of public relations.* Paper presented at the Conference on Corporate Communications, Madison, NJ.

Huxman, S. S., & Bruce, D. B. (1995). Toward a dynamic generic framework of apologia: A case study of Dow Chemical, Vietnam, and the napalm controversy. *Communication Studies, 46,* 57-72.

Hymes, D. (1986). Models of the interaction of language and social life. In J. L. Gumpert & D. Hymes (Eds.), *Directions in sociolinguistics* (pp. 35-71). London: Bessell Blackwood.

Hymowitz, C., & Schellhardt, T. D. (1986, March 24). The glass ceiling: Why women can't seem to break the invisible barrier that blocks them from the top jobs. *The Wall Street Journal,* pp. D1, D4.

Hynds, E. C. (1989). Survey finds large daily newspapers have improved coverage of education. *Journalism Quarterly, 66,* 692-698.

Ice, R. (1991). Corporate publics and rhetorical strategies: The case of Union Carbide's Bhopal crisis. *Management Communication Quarterly, 4,* 341-362.

Independent Sector. (1994). *Giving and volunteering in the United States: Findings from a national survey* (Vol. 1). Washington, DC: Author.

Infante, D. A., Anderson, C. M., Martin, M. W., Herington, A. D., & Kim, J. (1993). Subordinates' satisfaction and perceptions of superiors' compliance-gaining tactics, argumentativeness, verbal aggressiveness, and style. *Management Communication Quarterly, 6,* 307-326.

Infante, D. A., Rancer, A. S., & Womack, D. F. (1993). *Building communication theory* (2nd ed.). Prospect Heights, IL: Waveland.

International PR on rise: Corporations giving business to global and local firms. (1993, October 18). *Public Relations News,* pp. 1-2.

Irvine, R. B., & Millar, D. P. (1996). Debunking the stereotypes of crisis management: The nature of business crises in the 1990's. In L. Barton (Ed.), *New avenues in risk and crisis management* (Vol. 5, pp. 51-63). Las Vegas: University of Nevada, Las Vegas, Small Business Development Center.

Isch, L., & Fowler, G. (1997, April). *Sports information directors assess their job, their skills, their futures: Burn-out is here!* Paper presented at the meeting of the Western Social Science Association, Albuquerque, NM.

Isocrates. (1929). Antidosis (G. Norlin, Trans.). In *Isocrates* (Vol. 2, pp. 182-365). Cambridge, MA: Harvard University Press.

Iyengar, S. (1987). *News that matters.* Chicago: University of Chicago Press.

Iyengar, S., Peters, M. D., & Kinder, D. R. (1982). Experimental demonstrations of the "not-so-minimal" consequences of television news programs. *American Political Science Review, 76,* 848-858.

Jackson, P. (1982). Tactics of confrontation. In J. S. Nagelschmidt (Ed.), *The public affairs handbook* (pp. 211-220). New York: American Management Association.

Jackson, P. (1988). Demonstrating professionalism. *Public Relations Journal, 44*(10), 27-29.

Jackson, P. (1995, October 23). Defining public relations' precise role as change agent. *PR Reporter,* pp. 1-2.

Jackson, P. (1997). Reputation management: Who needs an image? Developing one-on-one relationships for improved customer support and loyalty. *Techniques, 72*(6), 26-27.

Jacobson, D. Y., & Tortorello, N. J. (1990). PRJ's fifth annual salary survey. *Public Relations Journal, 46*(6), 18-25.

Jacobson, D. Y., & Tortorello, N. J. (1991). PRJ's sixth annual salary survey. *Public Relations Journal, 47*(6), 14-21.

Jacobson, D. Y., & Tortorello, N. J. (1992). PRJ's seventh annual salary survey. *Public Relations Journal, 48*(8), 9-21, 26-30.

Jacobson, H. K. (1978). Needed improvements in education news coverage as perceived by media and education gatekeepers. *Journal of Educational Research, 66,* 274-278.

Jacobson, P. (1996-1997, Winter). Focus on the consumer. *American Advertising,* pp. 28-29.

Jacoby, J. (1998, June 4). Keeping score is forbidden in a politically correct world. *Louisville Courier-Journal,* p. A11.

Jacoby, N. H. (1974). The corporation as social activist. In S. P. Sethi (Ed.), *The unstable ground: Corporate social policy in a dynamic society* (pp. 224-244). Los Angeles: Melville.

Jacques, R. (1996). *Manufacturing the employee: Management knowledge from the 19th to the 20th centuries.* Thousand Oaks, CA: Sage.

Jagtenberg, T., & McKie, D. (1997). *Eco-impacts and the greening of postmodernity: New maps for communication studies, cultural studies, and sociology.* Thousand Oaks, CA: Sage.

James, B. C. (1989). *Quality management for health care delivery.* Chicago: Hospital Research and Educational Trust.

James, P. (1976). *Guidelines for establishing a sports information office for women.* Unpublished master's thesis, Ball State University.

James, W. (1890). *The principles of psychology.* New York: Henry Holt.

Jameson, F. (1981). *The political unconscious: Narrative as a socially symbolic act.* Ithaca, NY: Cornell University Press.

Jamias, J. F., Navarro, M. J., & Tuazon, R. R. (1996). Public relations in the Philippines. In H. M. Culbertson & N. Chen (Eds.), *International public relations: A comparative analysis* (pp. 191-206). Mahwah, NJ: Lawrence Erlbaum.

Jamieson, K. H. (1992). *Dirty politics: Deception, distraction, and democracy.* London: Oxford University Press.

Jarausch, K. H. (1990). The German professions in history and theory. In G. Cocks & K. H. Jarausch (Eds.), *German professions, 1800-1950* (pp. 9-24). Oxford, UK: Oxford University Press.

Jaworski, J. (1996). *Synchronicity: The inner path of leadership.* San Francisco: Berrett-Koehler.

Jeavons, T. H. (1994). Stewardship revisited: Secular and sacred views of governance and management. *Nonprofit and Voluntary Sector Quarterly, 23*(2), 107-122.

Jeffers, D. W. (1977). Performance expectations as a measure of relative status of news and PR people. *Journalism Quarterly, 54,* 299-306.

Jeffres, L. W. (1997). *Mass media effects* (2nd ed.). Prospect Heights, IL: Waveland.

Jelinek, J. (1955). A comparison of newspaper coverage of topics of school news and the relative importance of those topics according to certain lay and professional groups. *Journal of Educational Research, 49,* 301-305.

Jick, T. (1979). Mixing qualitative and quantitative methods: Triangulation in action. *Administrative Science Quarterly, 24,* 602-611.

Jiles, J. (1997, November). Lessons learned from the UPS strike. *Public Relations Tactics,* pp. 1, 17.

Johannesen, R. L. (1971). The emerging concept of communication as dialogue. *Quarterly Journal of Speech, 57,* 373-382.

Johnson, M. (1996). Strategy "off the shelf." *Long Range Planning, 29,* 405-411.

Johnson, M. A. (1997). Public relations and technology: Practitioner perspectives. *Journal of Public Relations Research, 9,* 213-236.

Johnson, T. (1972). *Professions and power.* London: Macmillan.

Johnston, C. (1997, June 2). The boom in healthcare PR. *Marketing,* pp. 18-19.

Joint Commission on Accreditation of Healthcare Organizations. (1992). *An introduction to quality improvement in health care.* Oakbrook Terrace, IL: Author.

Jones, B. L., & Chase, W. H. (1979). Managing public issues. *Public Relations Review, 5*(2), 3-23.

Jones, S. G. (1995). *Cybersociety: Computer-mediated communication and community.* Thousand Oaks, CA: Sage.

Jopke, C. (1991). Social movements during cycles of issue attention: The decline of the anti-nuclear energy movements in West Germany and the USA. *British Journal of Sociology, 42*(1), 43-60.

Judd, D. R., & Hellinger, D. (1995, September). Persuasion industry and media join in manipulating public. *St. Louis Journalism Review,* pp. 1-3.

Judd, L. R. (1989). Credibility, public relations, and social responsibility. *Public Relations Review, 15*(2), 34-40.

Judd, L. R. (1990). Importance and use of formal research and evaluation. *Public Relations Review, 16*(4), 17-28.

Judd, L. R. (1995). An approach to ethics in the information age. *Public Relations Review, 21*(1), 35-44.

Jurgensen, J. H., & Lukaszewski, J. E. (1988). Ethics: Content before conduct. *Public Relations Journal, 44*(3), 47-48.

Kahle, L. (1986). The nine nations of North America and the value basis of geographic segmentation. *Journal of Marketing, 50,* 37-47.

Kahle, L., Beatty, S., & Homer, P. (1986). Alternative measurement approaches to consumer values: The list of values (LOV) and lifestyle values (VALS). *Journal of Consumer Research, 13,* 405-409.

Kahneman, D. (1973). *Attention and effort.* Englewood Cliffs, NJ: Prentice Hall.

Kaid, L. L., Tedesco, J. C., & McKinnon, L. M. (1996). Presidential ads as nightly news: A content analysis on 1988 and 1992 televised adwatches. *Journal of Broadcasting & Electronic Media, 40,* 297-308.

Kalish, D. (1990, Fall). The new advertising. *Agency,* pp. 28-33.

Kant, I. (1974). *On the old saw: That may be right in theory but it won't work in practice* (E. B. Ashton, Trans.). Philadelphia: University of Pennsylvania Press. (Original work published 1793)

Kanter, R. M. (1983). *The change masters.* New York: Simon & Schuster.

Kanter, R. M. (1995). *World class.* New York: Simon & Schuster.

Kaplan, G. R. (1992). *Images of education: The mass media's version of America's schools.* Arlington, VA: National School Public Relations Association. (ERIC Document Reproduction Service, No. ED 340081)

Karlberg, M. (1996). Remembering the public in public relations research: From theoretical to operational symmetry. *Journal of Public Relations Research, 8,* 263-278.

Kates, R. W. (1977). *Managing technological hazard: Research needs and opportunities* (Monograph No. 25). Boulder: University of Colorado, Institute of Behavioral Science.

Katz, A. R. (1987). 10 steps to complete crisis planning. *Public Relations Journal, 43*(11), 46-47.

Katz, D. M. (1994, April 4). Benefits managers are drowning in a sea of jargon. *Cash Flow,* pp. 7-8.

Katz, E. M. (1959). Mass communication research and the study of popular culture: An editorial note on a possible future for this journal. *Studies in Public Communication, 2,* 1-6.

Katz, J., & Aspden, P. (1997, October). *Motivations for and barriers to Internet usage: Results of a national public opinion survey.* Paper presented at the 24th annual Telecommunications Policy Research Conference, Solomon, MD.

Katzman, J. B. (1993). What's the role of public relations? Profession searches for its identity. *Public Relations Journal, 49*(4), 11-16.

Katzman, J. B. (1995). Interactive video gets bigger play. *Public Relations Journal, 51*(1), 6-12.

Kaufmann, J. B., Kesner, I. F., & Hazen, R. L. (1994, July). The myth of full disclosure: A look at organizational communication during crises. *Business Horizons, 37*, 29-39.

Kazoleas, D., Levine, K., & Wright A. (1998, November). *The effects of keeping internal stakeholders informed: A comparison and review of real world data.* Paper presented at the meeting of the National Communication Association, Applied Communication division, New York.

Kazoleas, D., & Moffitt, M. A. (1998, November). *Exposing the myth of organizational image: It's not a question of one but a question of how many.* Paper presented at the meeting of the National Communication Association, New York.

Kearns, K. D., & West, A. L. (1996). Innovations in public affairs programming: Collaborative planning and beyond. In L. B. Dennis (Ed.), *Practical public affairs in an era of change* (pp. 355-370). Lanham, MD: Public Relations Society of America.

Keller, J. J. (1990, February 13). AT&T's 800 service disrupted Friday, in another embarrassing breakdown. *The Wall Street Journal, p.* A4.

Kelley, H. (1979). *Personal relationships: Their structures and processes.* Hillsdale, NJ: Lawrence Erlbaum.

Kelly, D. C. (1984). Decentralized public relations. *Public Relations Journal, 40*(2), 32-33.

Kelly, D., & Amburgey, T. L. (1991). Organizational inertia and momentum: A dynamic model of strategic change. *Academy of Management Journal, 34*, 591-612.

Kelly, H. H., & Thibaut, J. W. (1959). *The social psychology of groups.* New York: John Wiley.

Kelly, K. S. (1991). *Fund raising and public relations: A critical analysis.* Hillsdale, NJ: Lawrence Erlbaum.

Kelly, K. S. (1998). *Effective fund-raising management.* Mahwah, NJ: Lawrence Erlbaum.

Kelman, H. C. (1961). Processes of opinion change. *Public Opinion Quarterly, 25,* 57-78.

Kemmis, D. (1990). *Community and the politics of place.* Norman: University of Oklahoma Press.

Kemp, W. M. (1941, October). A weakness in school publicity. *The Nation's Schools,* p. 30.

Kennedy, G. (1963). *The art of persuasion in Greece.* Princeton, NJ: Princeton University Press.

Kennedy, G. (1991). *Aristotle: A theory of civic discourse.* Oxford, UK: Oxford University Press.

Kent Wright, C. (1936). Intelligence and public relations: Local authorities. *Public Administration, 14,* 49-58.

Kern, M. (1989). *30-second politics: Political advertising in the eighties.* New York: Praeger.

Kernisky, D. A. (1994, May). *A critical analysis of the ethicality of organizational legitimation strategies: Dow Chemical's issues management bulletins—1979-1990.* Paper presented at the National Communication Ethics Conference, Gull Lake, MI.

Kersten, A. (1994). The ethics and ideology of public relations: A critical examination of American theory and practice. In W. Armbrecht & U. Zabel (Eds.), *Normative aspekte der public relations* (pp. 109-130). Opladen, Germany: Westdeutscher Verlag.

Key, V. O., Jr. (1961). *Public opinion and American democracy.* New York: Knopf.

Key, V. O., Jr. (1966). *The responsible electorate.* Cambridge, MA: Belknap.

Kilduff, M. (1996). Making sense of sensemaking: Into the jungle with Karl Weick. *Journal of Management Inquiry, 5,* 246-249.

Kim, Y., & Hon, L. C. (1998). Craft and professional models of public relations and their relation to job satisfaction among Korean public relations practitioners. *Journal of Public Relations Research, 10,* 155-175.

Kimball, J. G. (1995, November 27). What's yours could be mine. *Advertising Age,* p. 32.

Kisch, R. (1964). *The private life of public relations.* London: MacGibbon & Kee.

Klapper, J. T. (1960). *The effects of mass communication.* New York: Free Press.

Kleiner, A. (1996). *The age of heretics: Heroes, outlaws, and the forerunners of corporate change.* New York: Doubleday.

Kliman, M. (1936). Correspondence with the public. *Public Administration, 14,* 276-290.

Knapp, M. L. (1984). *Interpersonal relationships: Their structures and processes.* Boston: Allyn & Bacon.

Knapp, M. L., & Vangelisti, A. L. (1996). *Interpersonal communication and human relationships* (3rd ed.). Needham Heights, MA: Allyn & Bacon.

Kocka, J. (1990). "Burgeratum" and professions in the nineteenth century: Two alternative approaches. In M. Burrage & R. Torstendahl (Eds.), *Professions in theory and history: Rethinking the study of the professions* (pp. 62-74). Newbury Park, CA: Sage.

Kogan, M. (1996). Blah, blah, blah. *Government Executive, 28*(9), 52-57.

Kohlberg, L. (1981a). *Essays in moral development: The philosophy of moral development.* New York: Harper & Row.

Kohlberg, L. (1981b). *The philosophy of moral development: Moral stages and the idea of justice* (Vol. 1). New York: Harper & Row.

Kohlberg, L. (1984). *The psychology of moral development: Moral stages and the life cycle* (Vol. 2). New York: Harper & Row.

Kornhauser, W. (1959). *The politics of mass society.* New York: Free Press.

Korten, D. C. (1995). *When corporations rule the world.* West Hartford, CT: Kumarian Press.

Kotler, P. (1972). A generic concept of marketing. *Journal of Marketing, 36*(2), 46-50.

Kotler, P. (1986). Megamarketing. *Harvard Business Review, 64*(2), 117-124.

Kotler, P. (1991). *Marketing management: Analysis, planning, implementation, and control* (7th ed.). Englewood Cliffs, NJ: Prentice Hall.

Kotler, P. (1992, September). Total marketing. In *Business Week's advance briefs.* (Mailed to selected *Business Week* subscribers)

Kotler, P., & Anderson, A. R. (1987). *Strategic marketing for non-profit organizations.* Englewood Cliffs, NJ: Prentice Hall.

Kotler, P., & Levy, S. (1969). Broadening the concept of marketing. *Journal of Marketing, 33*(1), 10-15.

Kotler, P., & Mindak, W. (1978). Marketing and public relations: Should they be partners or rivals? *Journal of Marketing, 42*(3), 13-20.

Kovacs, R. S. (1998). *Pressure group strategies and accountability in British public service broadcasting.* Unpublished doctoral dissertation, University of Maryland, College Park.

Kreps, G. L. (1990). *Organizational communication: Theory and practice* (2nd ed.). New York: Longman.

Kreps, G. L., & Lederman, L. C. (1985). Using the case method in organizational communication education: Developing students' insight, knowledge, and creativity through experience-based learning and systematic debriefing. *Communication Education, 34,* 358-364.

Krimsky, S., & Plough, A. (1988). *Environmental hazards: Communicating risks as a social process.* Boston: Auburn House.

Kristof, N. D. (1990, November 6). China's leaders try to improve their images abroad. *The New York Times,* p. A5.

Kruckeberg, D. (1989). The need for an international code of ethics. *Public Relations Review, 15*(2), 6-18.

Kruckeberg, D. (1993a). Ethical values define public relations community. *Public Relations Update, 2*(2), 1-2.

Kruckeberg, D. (1993b). Universal ethics code: Both possible and feasible. *Public Relations Review, 19,* 21-32.

Kruckeberg, D. (1996a). A global perspective of public relations ethics: The Middle East. *Public Relations Review, 22,* 181-190.

Kruckeberg, D. (1996b). Transitional corporate ethical responsibilities. In H. M. Culbertson & N. Chen (Eds.), *International public relations: A comparative analysis* (pp. 81-92). Mahwah, NJ: Lawrence Erlbaum.

Kruckeberg, D. (1998a). Future reconciliation of multicultural perspectives in public relations ethics. *Public Relations Quarterly, 43*(1), 45-48.

Kruckeberg, D. (1998b). The future of PR education: Some recommendations. *Public Relations Review, 24,* 235-248.

Kruckeberg, D., & Starck, K. (1988). *Public relations and community: A reconstructed theory.* New York: Praeger.

Kruse, N. (1981). The scope of apologetic discourse: Establishing generic parameters. *Southern Speech Communication Journal, 46,* 278-291.

Kuhn, T. S. (1970). *The structure of scientific revolutions* (2nd ed.). Chicago: University of Chicago Press.

Kunczik, M. (1990). *Images of nations and international public relations.* Bonn, Germany: Friedrich-Ebert Stiftung.

Kunczik, M. (1994). Public relations: Angewandte Kommunikationswissenschaft oder ideologie? Ein Beitrag zur ethik der offentlichkeitsarbeit. In W. Armbrecht & U. Zabel (Eds.), *Normative aspekte der public relations* (pp. 225-264). Opladen, Germany: Westdeutscher Verlag.

Kurtz, L. F. (1997). *Self-help and support groups: A handbook for practitioners.* Thousand Oaks, CA: Sage.

L'Etang, J. (1995, July). *Clio among the patriarchs: Historical and social scientific approaches to public relations—A methodological critique.* Paper presented at the Second International Public Relations Symposium, Bled, Slovenia.

L'Etang, J. (1996a). Corporate responsibility and public relations ethics. In J. L'Etang & M. Pieczka (Eds.), *Critical perspectives in public relations* (pp. 82-105). London: International Thomson Business Press.

L'Etang, J. (1996b). Public relations and rhetoric. In J. L'Etang & M. Pieczka (Eds.), *Critical perspectives in public relations* (pp. 106-123). London: International Thomson Business Press.

L'Etang, J. (1996c). Public relations as diplomacy. In J. L'Etang & M. Pieczka (Eds.), *Critical perspectives in public relations* (pp. 14-34). London: International Thomson Business Press.

L'Etang, J. (1998a, July). *The development of British public relations in the twentieth century.* Paper presented at the meeting of the International Association of Mass Communication Research, History division, Glasgow, Scotland.

L'Etang, J. (1998b, September). *Public relations education in Britain, 1948-73.* Paper presented at the Public Relations Educators' Forum, Leeds, UK.

L'Etang, J. (1998c). State propaganda and bureaucratic intelligence: The creation of public relations in 20th century Britain. *Public Relations Review, 24,* 413-441.

L'Etang, J. (1999, January). *Grierson's influence on the formation and values of the public relations industry in Britain.* Paper presented at "Breaking the Boundaries: The Stirling Documentary Conference," Stirling, Scotland.

Lac Courte Oreilles Band v. Voight, 700 F.2d 341 (7th Cir., 1983).

Laclau, E., & Mouffe, C. (1985). *Hegemony and socialist strategy: Towards a radical democratic politics.* London: Verso.

Laird, N. (1996, May). Quantify, quantify: Can government and public affairs staffs measure their impact on the bottom line? *Electric Perspectives,* pp. 70-82.

Lambrecht, K. W. (1996). *Job satisfaction of sport and athletic club directors.* Unpublished manuscript, Northern Illinois University.

Lambrecht, K. W. (1998). Job satisfaction of sports information personnel (CoSIDA) employed in athletic departments in colleges and universities in the United States. *CoSIDA Digest, 48*(3). (College Sports Information Directors of America)

Landmarks. (1997). *The European public affairs directory.* Brussels: Author. Available: http://www.landmarks.be/epad/index.htm

Langer, S. (1948). *Philosophy in a new key.* New York: New American Library.

Lanoue, D. J. (1992). One that made a difference: Cognitive consistency, political knowledge, and the 1980 presidential debate. *Public Opinion Quarterly, 56,* 168-184.

Larsen v. Philadelphia Newspapers, 543 A. 2d 1181 (Pa. Sup. 1988).

Larson, M. S. (1977). *The rise of professionalism: A sociological analysis.* Berkeley: University of California Press.

Laufer, R., & Paradeise, C. (1990). *Marketing democracy: Public opinion and media formation in democratic societies.* New Brunswick, NJ: Transaction Books.

Lauzen, M. M. (1991). Imperialism and encroachment in public relations. *Public Relations Review, 17,* 245-255.

Lauzen, M. M., & Dozier, D. M. (1992). The missing link: The public relations manager role as mediator of organizational environments and power consequences for the function. *Journal of Public Relations Research, 4,* 205-220.

Laver, P. (1996, September). *The OkTedi project.* Paper presented at the Public Relations Institute of Australia National Convention, Adelaide.

Lavidge, R. J., & Steiner, G. A. (1961). A model for predictive measures of advertising effectiveness. *Journal of Marketing, 25*(5), 59-62.

Lazarsfeld, P. F., Berelson, B., & Gaudet, H. (1944). *The people's choice: How the voter makes up his mind in a presidential campaign.* New York: Duell, Sloan, & Pierce.

Leahigh, A. K. (1985-1986). If you can't count it, does it count? *Public Relations Quarterly, 30*(4), 23-27.

Lechte, J. (1994). *Fifty key contemporary thinkers: From structuralism to postmodernity.* New York: Routledge.

Ledingham, J. A. (1993). The kindness of strangers: Predictor variables in a public information campaign. *Public Relations Review, 19,* 367-384.

Ledingham, J. A., & Bruning, S. D. (1997). Building loyalty through community relations. *Public Relations Strategist, 3*(2), 27-29.

Ledingham, J. A., & Bruning, S. D. (1998a, June). *Community relations and relationship dimensions: Measuring the impact of a managed communication program.* Paper presented at the First International Interdisciplinary Research Conference, College Park, MD.

Ledingham, J. A., & Bruning, S. D. (1998b). Relationship management in public relations: Dimensions of an organization-public relationship. *Public Relations Review, 24*(1), 55-65.

Ledingham, J. A., & Bruning, S. D. (2000). A longitudinal study of organization-public relationship dimensions: Defining the role of communication in the practice of relationship management. In J. A. Ledingham & S. D. Bruning (Eds.), *Relationship management: A relational approach to public relations.* Mahwah, NJ: Lawrence Erlbaum.

Ledingham, J. A., Bruning, S. D., Thomlison, T. D., & Lesko, C. (1997). The transferability of interpersonal relationship dimensions to an organization-public context. *Academy of Managerial Communications Journal, 1,* 23-43.

Ledingham, J. A., Bruning, S. D., & Wilson, L. (1999). Time as an indicator of the perceptions of behavior of members of a key public: Monitoring and predicting organization-public relationships. *Journal of Public Relations Research, 11,* 167-183.

Lee, D. R., & McKenzie, R. B. (1994). Corporate failure as a means to corporate responsibility. *Journal of Business Ethics, 13,* 969-978.

Lee, J. M. (1972). The dissolution of the EMB. *Journal of Imperial and Commonwealth History, 1,* 51.

Lee, J., & Davie, W. R. (1997). Audience recall of AIDS PSAs among U.S. and international college students. *Journalism & Mass Communication Quarterly, 74,* 7-22.

Leeper, K. A. (1996). Public relations ethics and communitarianism: A preliminary investigation. *Public Relations Review, 22,* 163-179.

Leeper, R. V. (1996). Moral objectivity, Jurgen Habermas's discourse ethics, and public relations. *Public Relations Review, 22,* 133-150.

Lehmann, M. (1994, March). *Israel: Its government and opposition.* Panel discussion at the conference, "The Road to Peace: The Challenge of the Middle East," Miami, FL.

Leichty, G. (1997). The limits of collaboration. *Public Relations Review, 23,* 47-56.

Leichty, G., & Springston, J. (1993). Reconsidering public relations models. *Public Relations Review, 19,* 327-339.

Leigh, D., & Vulliamy, E. (1996). *Sleaze: The corruption of Parliament.* London: Fourth Estate.

Leitch, S. (1994). [New Zealand communication survey results.] Unpublished raw data, School of Management, University of Waikato, Hamilton, New Zealand.

Leitch, S. (1995). Professionalism in New Zealand public relations. *International Public Relations Review, 18*(3), 24-31.

Leitch, S., & Motion, J. M. (1999, June). The *"discipline" of corporate identity.* Paper presented at the Corporate Identity International Symposium, Strathclyde, Scotland.

Leitch, S., & Neilson, D. (1997). Reframing public relations: New directions for theory and practice. *Australian Journal of Communication, 24*(2), 17-32.

Leitch, S., & Roper, J. (1998). Genre colonisation as a public relations strategy: A framework for research and analysis. *Public Relations Review, 24,* 203-218.

Lentz, C. S. (1996). The fairness in broadcasting doctrine and the Constitution: Forced one-stop shopping in the "marketplace of ideas." *University of Illinois Law Review, 271,* 1-39.

Leonard, M. (1997). *Politics without frontiers: The role of political parties in Europe's future.* London: Demos.

Lerbinger, O. (1997). *The crisis manager: Facing risk and responsibility.* Mahwah, NJ: Lawrence Erlbaum.

Lescher, J. F. (1995). *Online market research.* Reading, MA: Addison-Wesley.

Lesly, P. (1988). Public relations numbers are up but stature is down. *Public Relations Review, 14*(4), 3-7.

Lesly, P. (1996). The Balkanizing of public relations. *Public Relations Strategist, 2*(3), 41-44.

Lesly, P. (1998). The place and function of the public relations counsel. In P. Lesly (Ed.), *Lesly's handbook of public relations and communications* (pp. 697-715). Lincolnwood, IL: NTC Business Books.

Lesly, P., Budd, J., Cutlip, S., Lerbinger, O., & Pires, M. A. (1987, April 20). Diverse titles splinter image of field: Report of PRSA's special committee on terminology. *Tips & Tactics,* pp. 1-2.

Lessig, L. (1998). Reading the Constitution in cyberspace. In J. L. Swanson (Ed.), *First Amendment law handbook, 1997-98 edition* (pp. 85-122). St. Paul, MN: Clark, Boardman, Callaghan.

Levenson, A. D. (May 8, 1989). In ten years you'll see nothing. *Fortune,* pp. 50-54.

Levin, M. L., Goldstein, H., & Gerhardt, P. R. (1950). Cancer and tobacco smoking: A preliminary report. *Journal of the American Medical Association, 143,* 336-338.

Levine, J. (1993, March 15). Teaching elephants to dance. *Forbes,* pp. 100-101.

Levins, H. (1997, January 4). Time of change and challenge. *Editor & Publisher,* pp. 58-60.

Levins, I. (1993). Can public relations actually move product? *Public Relations Quarterly, 38*(1), 18-19.

Levis, W. C. (1991). Investing more money in fund raising wisely. In D. F. Burlingame & L. J. Hulse (Eds.), *Taking fund raising seriously: Advancing the profession and practice of raising money* (pp. 257-271). San Francisco: Jossey-Bass.

Lewin, K. (1951). *Field theory in social science.* New York: Harper & Row. (Original work published 1944)

Lewton, K. L. (1995). *Public relations in health care: A guide for professionals* (2nd ed.). Chicago: American Hospital Publishing.

Lewton, K. L. (1998, March). From costs to confidence: Resuscitating health care. *Public Relations Tactics,* pp. 1, 6.

Lindenmann, W. K. (1990). Research, evaluation, and measurement: A national perspective. *Public Relations Review, 16*(2), 3-16.

Lindenmann, W. K. (1993). An "effectiveness yardstick" to measure public relations success. *Public Relations Quarterly, 38*(1), 7-9.

Lindenmann, W. K. (1997). Setting minimum standards for measuring public relations effectiveness. *Public Relations Review, 23,* 391-408.

Lipman, J. (1992, January 7). Hill & Knowlton faces new attacks over its PR tactics. *The Wall Street Journal,* p. B6.

Lippmann, W. (1922). *Public opinion.* New York: Harcourt Brace Jovanovich.

Lippmann, W. (1925). *The phantom public.* New York: Harcourt Brace Jovanovich.

Lipset, S. (1960). *Political man.* Garden City, NY: Doubleday.

Lipset, S. (1967). *The first new nation.* Garden City, NY: Doubleday.

Lissack, M. (1997). Mind your metaphors: Lessons from complexity science. *Long Range Planning, 30,* 294-298.

Littlejohn, R. (1983). *Crisis management: A team approach.* New York: American Management Association.

Littlejohn, S. E. (1986). Competition and cooperation: New trends in corporate public issue identification and resolution. *California Management Review, 29*(1), 109-123.

Littlejohn, S. W. (1983). *Theories of human communication* (2nd ed.). Belmont, CA: Wadsworth.

Littlejohn, S. W. (1989). *Theories of human communication* (3rd ed.). Belmont, CA: Wadsworth.

Littlejohn, S. W. (1992). *Theories of human communication* (4th ed.). Belmont, CA: Wadsworth.

Livesey, S. (1999). McDonald's and the Environmental Defense Fund: A case study of a green alliance. *Journal of Business Communication, 36,* 5-39.

Lockhart, C. (1997). Political culture and political change. In R. J. Ellis & M. Thompson (Eds.), *Culture matters* (pp. 91-104). Boulder, CO: Westview.

Lofland, J. (1992). The soar and slump of polite protest: Interactive spirals and the eighties peace surge. *Peace and Change, 17*(1), 34-59.

Lombardo, B. J. (1995). Corporate philanthropy: Gift or business transaction? *Nonprofit Management & Leadership, 5*(3), 291-301.

Long, L. W., & Hazelton, V., Jr. (1987). Public relations: A theoretical and practical response. *Public Relations Review, 13*(3), 3-13.

Lord, J. G. (1983). *The raising of money: Thirty-five essentials every trustee should know.* Cleveland, OH: Third Sector.

Lord, R. A. (1990). *Williston on contracts* (4th ed.). Rochester, NY: Lawyers' Cooperative Publishing.

Lovell v. Griffin, 303 U.S. 444 (1938).

Lowell, A. L. (1913). *Public opinion and popular government.* New York: Longmans Green.

Lowengard, M. (1989). Community relations: New approaches to building consensus. *Public Relations Journal, 45*(10), 24-30.

Luciano, L. (1997, September). Can consumers capture the essence of quality? *Business & Health,* pp. 12-15.

Luer, C., & Tilson, D. (1996). Latin American PR in the age of telecommunications, JC Penney, and CNN. *Public Relations Quarterly, 41*(3), 25-27.

Lukaszewski, J. E. (1987). Anatomy of a crisis. *Public Relations Journal, 43*(11), 45-46.

Lukaszewski, J. (1998, July 20). How to develop the mind of a strategist. *Jim Lukaszewski's Strategy,* pp. 1-4.

Lukes, S. (1978). Power and authority. In T. Bottomore & R. Nisbet (Eds.), *A history of sociological analysis* (pp. 633-676). New York: Basic Books.

Lunde, J. M. (1996). *Job satisfaction of athletic directors in the National Collegiate Athletic Association.* Unpublished master's thesis, Northern Illinois University.

Lupton, D. (1994). Toward the development of critical health communication praxis. *Health Communication, 6*(1), 55-67.

Lutz, W. (1996). *The new doublespeak: Why no one knows what anyone's saying anymore.* New York: HarperCollins.

Lynd, R. S., & Lynd, H. M. (1929). *Middletown: A study in American culture.* New York: Harcourt, Brace.

Macdonald, K. (1995). *The sociology of the professions.* Thousand Oaks, CA: Sage.

MacInnis, D. J., & Jaworski, B. J. (1989). Information processing from advertisements: An integrative framework. *Journal of Marketing, 53*(1), 1-23.

MacInnis, D. J., Moorman, C., & Jaworski, B. J. (1991). Enhancing and measuring consumers' motivation, opportunity, and ability to process brand information from ads. *Journal of Marketing, 55*(1), 32-53.

MacIntyre, A. (1984). *After virtue: A study in moral theory.* Notre Dame, IN: University of Notre Dame Press.

MacIntyre, A. (1988). *Whose justice? Whose rationality?* Notre Dame, IN: University of Notre Dame Press.

MacIntyre, A. (1990). *Three rival versions of moral enquiry: Encyclopaedia, genealogy, and tradition.* Notre Dame, IN: University of Notre Dame Press.

MacIntyre, A. (1994). The privatization of good: An inaugural lecture. In C. F. Delaney (Ed.), *The liberalism-communitarianism debate: Liberty and community values* (pp. 1-17). Lanham, MD: Rowman & Littlefield.

Mackenzie, R. (1986, May 19). From Sir Walter Raleigh on: The who and why of smoking. *Washington Times* (Insight section), pp. 13-14.

MacNamara, J. (1992a). Evaluation of public relations: The Achilles' heel of the PR profession. *International Public Relations Review, 15*(2), 19-28.

MacNamara, J. (1992b, May). *Macro communication: A model for integrated strategic marketing and corporate communication.* Paper presented at Marcom Asia '92, Singapore.

Maddox, R. C. (1993). *Cross-cultural problems in international business: The role of the cultural integration function.* Westport, CT: Quorum Books.

Maggart, L. (1994). Bowater incorporated: A lesson in crisis communication. *Public Relations Quarterly, 41*(3), 29-31.

Makower, J. (1994). *Beyond the bottom line: Putting social responsibility to work for your business and the world.* New York: Simon & Schuster.

Malloy, D. (1998). Thriving as an in-house agency. *Public Relations Strategist, 4*(1), 33-35.

Mandese, J. (1993, October 4). Not ad, not show—It's blurmercial: TV networks, advertisers link to create hybrid formats. *Advertising Age,* p. 16.

Mandese, J. (1995, March). "Clickstreams" in cyberspace. *Advertising Age,* p. 18.

Mann, M., & White, D. (1998, May 2). After 25 years, British chocolate nears victory. *Independent on Sunday,* p. 31 (Business section).

Mannheim, K. (1936). *Ideology and utopia: An introduction to the sociology of knowledge.* London: Routledge & Kegan Paul.

Manning, R. (1992). *Speaking from the heart: A feminist perspective on ethics.* Lanham, MD: Rowman & Littlefield.

Marconi, J. (1992). *Crisis marketing: When bad things happen to good companies.* Chicago: American Marketing Association.

Marcus, A. A., & Goodman, R. S. (1991). Victims and shareholders: The dilemmas of presenting corporate policy during a crisis. *Academy of Management Journal, 34,* 281-305.

Marino, B. L., & Ganser, C. C. (1997, April). Sensitivity of patient report of care to organizational change. *Journal of Nursing Administration, 27,* 32-36.

Marken, G. A. (1995). Getting the most from your presence in cyberspace. *Public Relations Quarterly, 40*(3), 36-37.

Marken, G. A. (1997). Marketing position needs new look, new emphasis. *Public Relations Quarterly, 42*(3), 41-42.

Markus, G. B. (1993). The impact of personal and national economic conditions on the presidential vote: A pooled cross-sectional analysis. In R. G. Niemi, & H. F. Weisberg (Eds.), *Controversies in voting behavior* (pp. 152-166). Washington, DC: Congressional Quarterly.

Marra, F. J. (1992). *Crisis public relations: A theoretical model.* Unpublished doctoral dissertation, University of Maryland, College Park.

Marston, J. E. (1963). *Nature of public relations.* New York: McGraw-Hill.

Marston, J. E. (1968). Hallmarks of a profession. *Public Relations Journal, 24*(7), 8-10.

Marston, J. E. (1979). *Modern public relations.* New York: McGraw-Hill.

Martin, M. (1994, November 4). HHCl rethinks to reclaim the integrated initiative. *Campaign London,* p. 11.

Martin, M. W. (1994). *Virtuous giving: Philanthropy, voluntary service, and caring.* Bloomington: Indiana University Press.

Martinson, D. L. (1994). Enlightened self-interest fails as an ethical baseline in public relations. *Journal of Mass Media Ethics, 9,* 100-108.

Martinson, D. L. (1995-1996). Client partiality and third parties: An ethical dilemma for public relations practitioners? *Public Relations Quarterly, 40*(4), 41-44.

Marx, T. G. (1992-1993). Corporate social performance reporting. *Public Relations Quarterly, 37*(1), 38-44.

Massy, W. F., & Weitz, B. A. (1977). A normative theory of market segmentation. In F. M. Nicosia & Y. Wind (Eds.), *Behavioral models of market analysis: Foundations for marketing action* (pp. 121-144). Hinsdale, IL: Dryden.

Masterton, J. (1992). Discovering databases: On-line service puts research at pratitioner's fingertips. *Public Relations Journal, 48*(11), 12-19, 27.

Mattelart, A. (1994). *Mapping world communication: War, progress, culture.* Minneapolis: University of Minnesota Press.

Mau, R. R., & Dennis, L. B. (1994). Companies ignore shadow constituencies at their peril. *Public Relations Journal, 50*(5), 10-11.

Maynard, R. (1993, December). Handling a crisis effectively. *Nation's Business,* pp. 54-55.

Mazey, S., & Mitchell, J. (1993). Europe of the regions: Territorial interests and European integration: The Scottish experience. In S. Mazey & J. Richardson (Eds.), *Lobbying in the European Community.* Oxford, UK: Oxford University Press.

Mazey, S., & Richardson, J. (1992). British pressure groups in the European Union. *Parliamentary Affairs, 45,* 92-107.

Mazey, S., & Richardson, J. (Eds.). (1993). *Lobbying in the European Community.* Oxford, UK: Oxford University Press.

Mazur, L. (1992). *Why you need public relations: Management guides* (Special Report No. PB-P654). London: Economist Intelligence Unit.

McAvoy, J. (1987). Mainstreaming. *Public Relations Journal, 43*(12), 12-16.

McBride, G. (1989). Ethical thought in public relations history: Seeking a relevant perspective. *Journal of Mass Media Ethics, 4,* 5-20.

McCarthy, J. (1975). *Basic marketing: A managerial approach.* Homewood, IL: Irwin.

McCarthy, J. D., & Zald, M. N. (1977). Resource mobilization and social movements: A partial theory. *American Journal of Sociology, 82,* 1212-1239.

McCarthy, J. T. (1998). *The rights of privacy and publicity.* St. Paul, MN: West.

McCarthy, R. (1997, September). Do integrated delivery systems do it better? *Business & Health,* pp. 39-43.

McCleneghan, J. S. (1995). The sports information director: No attention, no respect, and a PR practitioner in trouble. *Public Relations Quarterly, 40*(2), 28-32.

McCleneghan, J. S. (1996, November). *A national benchmark study: The sports information director.* Paper presented at the Southwest Journalism and Mass Communication Symposium, Northeast Louisiana University, Monroe.

McCombs, M. E., & Shaw, D. L. (1972). The agenda-setting function of mass media. *Public Opinion Quarterly, 36,* 176-187.

McConnell, R. B., Gordon, K. C. T., & Jones, T. (1952). Occupational and personal factors in the aetiology of carcinoma of the lung. *Lancet, 263,* 651-656.

McDermott, P. M. (1991). International public relations in the United States: First steps in a global journey. *International Public Relations Review, 14,* 37-43.

McDermott, P. M. (1998). Survey shows increase in international PR education at U.S. universities. *PR Educator, 1*(2), 1-3.

McDougal, W. (1920). *The group mind.* New York: Putnam.

McElreath, M. P. (1980). *Priority research questions in public relations for the 1980s.* New York: Foundation for Public Relations Research and Education.

McElreath, M. P. (1993). *Managing systematic and ethical public relations.* Dubuque, IA: Wm. C. Brown.

McElreath, M. P. (1996). *Managing systematic and ethical public relations campaigns* (2nd ed.). Madison, WI: Brown & Benchmark.

McElreath, M. P., & Azarova, L. (1995). *An introduction to advertising and public relations: A reader from the Russian consumer's point of view.* St. Petersburg, Russia: Electrotechnical University.

McElreath, M. P., & Blamphin, J. M. (1994). Partial answers to priority research questions—and gaps—found in the Public Relations Society of America's Body of knowledge. *Journal of Public Relations Research, 6,* 69-103.

McFarland, D. D. (1985). Self-image of law professors: Rethinking the schism in legal education. *Journal of Legal Education, 35,* 232-260.

McGee, M. C. (1975). In search of "the people": A rhetorical alternative. *Quarterly Journal of Speech, 61,* 235-249.

McGoon, C. (1992). Putting the employee newsletter online. *Communication World, 9*(4), 16-18.

McGuire, M., Stilborne, L., McAdams, M. & Hyatt, L. (1997). *The Internet handbook for writers, researchers, and journalists.* New York: Guilford.

McKee, B. K., Nayman, O. B., & Lattimore, D. L. (1975). How PR people see themselves. *Public Relations Journal, 31*(8) 47-52.

McKelvey, B., & Aldrich, H. (1983). Populations, natural selection, and applied organizational science. *Administrative Science Quarterly, 28,* 101-128.

McKeone, D. (1993, July 24). Paying a price for false comparisons. *PR Week,* p. 10.

McKie, D. (1997). Shifting paradigms: Public relations beyond rats, stats, and 1950s science. *Australian Journal of Communication, 24*(2), 81-96.

McKie, D. (1998, July). *Postwar public relations theory: An A to Z of virtual absences.* Paper presented at the meeting of the International Communication Association, Jerusalem.

McKinnon, L. M., Tedesco, J. C., & Kaid, L. L. (1997). The effects of presidential debates: Channel and commentary comparisons. In L. W. Jeffres (Ed.), *Mass media effects* (2nd ed., pp. 205-244). Prospect Heights, IL: Waveland.

McLaughlin, M. L., Osborne, K. K., & Smith, C. B. (1995). Standards of conduct on Usenet. In S. G. Jones (Ed.), *CyberSociety: Computer-mediated communication and community* (pp. 138-163). Thousand Oaks, CA: Sage.

McLeod, J. M., & Chaffee, S. H. (1973). Interpersonal approaches to communication research. *American Behavioral Scientist, 16,* 469-500.

McLuhan, M. (1964). *Understanding media: The extensions of man.* New York: McGraw-Hill.

McNair, M. P. (Ed.). (1954). *The case method at the Harvard Business School.* New York: McGraw-Hill.

McNally, W. D. (1932). The tar in cigarette smoke and its possible effects. *American Journal of Cancer, 16,* 1502-1514.

McNamara v. Freedom Newspapers Inc., 802 S.W. 2d 901 (Tex. App. 1991).

McQuaid, E. P. (1989, January). The rising tide of mediocre educational coverage. *Phi Delta Kappan Special Report,* pp. K1-K8.

McQuitty, S. (1992). An examination of chaos theory and its relation to marketing. *Marketing Theory and Applications, 3,* 474-483.

Mead, G. H. (1934). *Mind, self, and society.* Chicago: University of Chicago Press.

Meadowcroft, J. M., & Olson, B. (1995, August). *Television viewing vs. reading: Testing information processing assumptions.* Paper presented at the meeting of the Association for Education in Journalism and Mass Communication, Washington, DC.

Medialink. (1990, February 22). *Nationwide survey of TV news directors conducted by Nielsen Media Research for Medialink* [news release].

Melucci, A. (1988). Social movements and the democratization of everyday life. In J. Keane (Ed.), *Civil society and the state* (pp. 245-260). London: Verso.

Men, X. (1990). *Zhongguo guongguan de xianzhuang yu weilai* [The present state and the future of Chinese public relations: A discussion of Chinese PR with Socialist features]. Paper presented at the meeting of the Public Relations Associations, Guangzhou, China.

Merrill, J. C. (Ed.). (1995). *Global journalism: Survey of international communication.* New York: Longman.

Mescon, T. S., & Tilson, D. J. (1987). Corporate philanthropy: A strategic approach to the bottom line. *California Management Review, 29*(2), 49-61.

Metcalfe, B. (1997, April 21). "Filtered forums" let you decide what's witty and insightful, who's a bozo. *InfoWorld,* p. 109.

Metzger, J., & Springston, J. K. (1992). The skillful, the loving, and the right: An analysis of ethical theories and an application to the treaty rights debate in Wisconsin. *Howard Journal of Communication, 4*(1), 75-91.

Meyer, J. W., & Rowan, B. (1977). Institutional organizations: Formal structure as myth and ceremony. *American Journal of Sociology, 83,* 340-363.

Meyer, P. (1983). *Editors, publishers, and newspaper ethics.* Washington, DC: American Society of Newspaper Editors.

Mickey, T. J. (1995). *Sociodrama: An interpretive theory for the practice of public relations.* Lanham, MD: University Press of America.

Mickey, T. J. (1997). A postmodern view of public relations: Sign and reality. *Public Relations Review, 23,* 271-285.

Microsoft. (1997, October). *The bigger day.* Redmond, WA: Author.

Middleberg, D. (1996, November). How to avoid a cybercrisis. *Public Relations Tactics,* pp. 1, 15.

Milbraith, L. (1965). *Political participation.* Chicago: Rand McNally.

Millar, F. E., & Rogers, E. (1987). Relational dimensions of interpersonal dynamics. In M. E. Roloff & G. R. Miller (Eds.), *Interpersonal processes: New directions in communication research* (pp. 117-139). Newbury Park, CA: Sage.

Miller, A. H. (1991). Party identification, realignment, and party voting: Back to the basics. *American Political Science Review, 85,* 557-568.

Miller, A. H., Wattenberg, M. P., & Malanchuk, O. (1986). Schematic assessments of presidential candidates. *American Political Science Review, 80,* 521-540.

Miller, C. (1994, July 4). Focus groups go where none has been before. *Marketing News,* pp. 2-14.

Miller, C. R., & Halloran, S. M. (1993). Reading Darwin, reading nature: Or, on the ethos of historical science. In J. Selzer (Ed.), *Understanding scientific prose* (pp. 106-126). Madison: University of Wisconsin Press.

Miller, D. A. (1988). Women in public relations graduate study. *Public Relations Review, 14*(3), 29-35.

Miller, D. A., & Dinan, W. (1998, July). *Public relations and promotional culture.* Paper presented at the meeting of the International Association of Mass Communication Research, Political Communication division, Glasgow, Scotland.

Miller, D., & Dinan, W. (2000). The rise of the PR industry in Britain, 1979-98. *European Journal of Communication, 15*(1), 5-35.

Miller, G. R. (1989). Persuasion and public relations: Two "Ps" in a pod. In C. H. Botan & V. Hazleton, Jr. (Eds.), *Public relations theory* (pp. 45-66). Hillsdale, NJ: Lawrence Erlbaum.

Miller, H. (1960). A private view of public relations. *Public Relations, 13*(1), 37.

Miller, K. (1992). Smoking up a storm: Public relations and advertising in the construction of the cigarette problem, 1953-1954. *Journalism Monographs,* No. 136.

Miller, K. (1995). National and local public relations campaigns during the 1946 steel strike. *Public Relations Review, 21,* 305-319.

Miller, K., Ellis, B., Zook, E., & Lyles, J. (1990). An integrated model of communication, stress, and burnout in the workplace. *Communication Research, 17,* 300-326.

Miller, M. M., & Quarles, J. P. (1984). Dramatic television and agenda setting: The case of *The Day After.* In W. J. Severin with J. W. Tankard, Jr. (Eds.), *Communication theories: Origins, methods, uses* (2nd ed., pp. 275-276). New York: Longman.

Millerson, G. (1964). *The qualifying associations: A study in professionalization.* London: Routledge & Kegan Paul.

Milloy, C. (1995, November 15). Teen stripped of more than just a shirt. *The Washington Post,* p. D1.

Mills, C. A., & Porter, M. M. (1950). Tobacco smoking habits and cancer of the mouth and respiratory system. *Cancer Research, 10,* 539-542.

Mills, C. W. (1956). *The power elite.* Oxford, UK: Oxford University Press.

Milne, S. (1997, June 10). No one is sacred. *The Bulletin,* pp. 14-17. (ACP Publishing, Sydney, Australia)

Miner, A. S., Amburgey, T. L., & Stearns, T. M. (1990). Interorganizational linkages and population dynamics: Buffering and transformational shields. *Administrative Science Quarterly, 35,* 689-713.

Mintz, M. (1985). *At any cost: Corporate greed, women, and the Dalkon Shield.* New York: Pantheon.

Mintzberg, H. (1983). *Power in and around organizations.* Englewood Cliffs, NJ: Prentice Hall.

Mitchell, J. (1995). Lobbying Brussels; The case of Scotland Europa. *European Urban and Regional Studies, 2*(4), 287-298.

Mitchell, R. K., Agle, B. R., & Wood, D. J. (1997). Toward a theory of stakeholder identification and salience: Defining the principle of who and what really counts. *Academy of Management Review, 22,* 853-886.

Mitchell, W. J. T. (Ed.). (1981). *On narrative.* Chicago: University of Chicago Press.

Mitroff, I. I. (1986). Prevention: Teaching corporate America to think about crisis prevention. *Journal of Business Studies, 6,* 40-48.

Mitroff, I. I., & Bennis, W. D. (1989). *The unreality industry.* New York: Oxford University Press.

Mitroff, I. I., Harrington, K., & Gai, E. (1996). Thinking about the unthinkable. *Across the Board, 33*(8), 45-48.

Mitroff, I. I., & Kilmann, R. (1984). *Corporate tragedies: Product tampering, sabotage, and other disasters.* New York: Praeger.

Mitroff, I. I., & Pauchant, T. C. (1990). *"We're so big and powerful nothing bad can happen to us": An investigation of America's crisis prone corporations.* New York: Carol Publishing.

Mitroff, I. I., Pauchant, T., & Shrivastava, P. (1989). Can your company handle a crisis? *Business & Health, 7*(5), 41-44.

Mitroff, I. I., & Pearson, C. (1993). *Crisis management: A diagnostic guide for improving your organization's crisis preparedness.* San Francisco: Jossey-Bass.

Mixer, J. R. (1993). *Principles of professional fundraising: Useful foundations for successful practice.* San Francisco: Jossey-Bass.

Moe, T. M. (1980). *The organization of interests.* Chicago: University of Chicago Press.

Moffitt, M. A. (1992). Bringing critical theory and ethical considerations to definitions of a "public." *Public Relations Review, 18,* 17-30.

Moffitt, M. A. (1994a). Collapsing and integrating concepts of "public" and "image" into a new theory. *Public Relations Review, 20,* 159-170.

Moffitt, M. A. (1994b). A cultural studies perspective toward understanding corporate image: A case study of State Farm Insurance. *Journal of Public Relations Research, 6,* 41-66.

Moffitt, M. A. (1998). *Campaign strategies and message design: A practitioner's guide from start to finish.* Westport, CT: Praeger.

Mollenkamp, C., Levy, A., Menn, J., & Rothfeder, J. (1998). *The people vs. Big Tobacco.* Princeton, NJ: Bloomberg.

Moloney, K. (1997). Teaching organizational communication as public relations in U.K. universities. *Corporate Communication: An International Journal, 2,* 138-142.

Monge, P., & Contractor, N. (2001). Emergence of communication networks. In F. M. Jablin & L. L. Putnam (Eds.), *The new handbook of organizational communication.* Thousand Oaks, CA: Sage.

Montague, C. (1994, July-August). A cyberspace odyssey. *Marketing Tools* [on-line]. Available: http://www.demographics.com/publications/mt/94_mt/9407_mt/mt207.htm

Moody, W. (Ed.). (1998). *Patterson's American education* (Vol. 44). Mount Prospect, IL: Educational Directions.

Moore, J. F. (1996). *The death of competition: Leadership and strategy in the age of business ecosystems.* New York: HarperBusiness.

More, T. (1965). Utopia (G. C. Richards, Trans.). In E. Surtz, S. J. Hexter, & J. H. Hexter (Eds.), *The complete works of Sir Thomas More* (pp. 1-197). New Haven, CT: Yale University Press.

More research needed on how to target Maori. (1997, November 1). *The Dominion,* p. 2. (Wellington, New Zealand)

Morgan, D. (1995). British media and European news. *European Journal of Communication, 10,* 321-343.

Morgan, G. (1997). *Images of organization* (2nd ed.). Thousand Oaks, CA: Sage.

Morgan, R., & Hunt, S. (1994). The commitment-trust theory of relationship marketing. *Journal of Marketing, 58*(3), 20-38.

Morley, M. (1998). *How to manage your global reputation: A guide to the dynamics of international public relations.* London: Macmillan.

Morris, M., & Ogan, C. (1996). The Internet as mass medium. *Journal of Communication, 46*(1), 39-50.

Morris, N. (1999, June 3). Rifts among Arabs hinder efforts for united voice at Mideast talks. *Miami Herald,* p. A23.

Motion, J. (1996). *Identity and image: A discursive public relations perspective.* Paper presented at the meeting of the Australian and New Zealand Communication Association, Brisbane, Australia.

Motion, J. (1997). Technologising the self: An art of public relations. *Australian Journal of Communication, 24*(2), 1-16.

Motion, J. (1998). *Technologies of the self: A public identity framework.* Unpublished Ph.D. thesis, University of Waikato, Hamilton, New Zealand.

Motion, J., & Leitch, S. (1996). A discursive perspective from New Zealand: Another worldview. *Public Relations Review, 22,* 297-309.

Mulhall, S., & Swift, A. (1992). *Liberals and communitarians.* Oxford, UK: Blackwell.

Mullen, J. (1997). Performance-based corporate philanthropy: How "giving smart" can further corporate goals. *Public Relations Quarterly, 42*(3), 42-48.

Mullin, R. (1997, July 2). CAPs confront the downside of trust. *Chemical Week,* p. 38.

Mumby, D. K. (1987). The political function of narrative in organizations. *Communication Monographs, 54,* 113-126.

Mumby, D. K. (1988). *Communication and power in organizations: Discourse, ideology, and domination.* Norwood, NJ: Ablex.

Mumby, D. K. (1989). Ideology and the social construction of meaning: A communication perspective. *Communication Quarterly, 37,* 291-304.

Mumby, D. K. (2001). Power, politics, and organizational communication. In F. M. Jablin & L. L. Putnam (Eds.), *The new handbook of organizational communication.* Thousand Oaks, CA: Sage.

Mumford, L. (1979). The all-seeing eye. In J. G. Burke & M. C. Eakin (Eds.), *Technology and change* (pp. 22-36). San Francisco: Boyd & Fraser.

Munshi, D. (1998, July). *Not under Western eyes: Reviewing requisite variety with subaltern studies.* Paper presented at the meeting of the International Communication Association, Jerusalem.

Munshi, D. (1999a). *A multicultural critique of managerial discourses.* Unpublished doctoral dissertation, University of Waikato, Hamilton, New Zealand.

Munshi, D. (1999b). Relating to the other: Public relations and the management of diversity. *Asia-Pacific Public Relations Journal, 1*(1), 39-51.

Murdock, G., & Golding, P. (1989). Information poverty and political inequality: Citizenship in the age of privatized communications. In M. Siefert, G. Gerbner, & J. Fisher (Eds.), *The information gap: How computer and other new communication technologies affect the social distribution of power* (pp. 180-195). New York: Oxford University Press.

Murphy, P. (1987). Using games as a model for crisis communication. *Public Relations Review, 13*(4), 19-28.

Murphy, P. (1989). Game theory as a paradigm for public relations process. In C. H. Botan & V. Hazleton, Jr. (Eds.), *Public relations theory* (pp. 173-192). Hillsdale, NJ: Lawrence Erlbaum.

Murphy, P. (1991). The limits of symmetry: A game theory approach to symmetric and asymmetric public relations. In L. A. Grunig & J. E. Grunig (Eds.), *Public relations research annual* (Vol. 3, pp. 115-131). Hillsdale, NJ: Lawrence Erlbaum.

Murphy, P. (1996). Chaos theory as a model for managing issues and crises. *Public Relations Review, 22,* 95-113.

Murphy, P., & Dee, J. (1992). Reconciling the preferences of environmental activists and corporate policymakers. *Journal of Public Relations Research, 8,* 1-34.

Murphy, R. (1990). Proletarianization or bureaucratization: The fall of the professional? In R. Torstendahl & M. Burrage (Eds.), *The formation of the professions: Knowledge, state, and the strategy* (pp. 71-96). London: Sage.

Murray, D. E. (1988). The context of oral and written language: A framework for mode and medium switching. *Languages in Society, 17,* 351-373.

Nagelschmidt, J. S. (Ed.). (1982). *Public affairs handbook.* New York: American Management Association.

Naisbitt, J. (1997). *Megatrends Asia: The eight Asian megatrends that are changing the world.* London: Nicholas Brealey.

Naisbitt, J., & Aburdene, P. (1990). *Megatrends 2000.* London: Pan Books.

Narasimha Reddi, C. V. (1996). *Public relations: The state of the art in India.* Unpublished paper.

National Center for Public Policy and Higher Education. (1998). *The price of admission: The growing importance of higher education.* Washington, DC: Heather Jack.

Nayman, O., McKee, B. K., & Lattimore, D. L. (1977). PR personnel and print journalists: A comparison of professionalism. *Journalism Quarterly, 54,* 492-497.

Neal, P., & Paris, D. (1990). Liberalism and the communitarian critique: A guide for the perplexed. *Canadian Journal of Political Science, 23,* 419-440.

Neff, B. D. (1987, April). *Background on the trends in the profession.* Paper presented at the joint meeting of the Central States Speech Association and the Southern Speech Communication Association, St. Louis, MO.

Neff, B. D. (1989). The emerging theoretical perspective in PR: An opportunity for communication departments. In C. H. Botan & V. Hazleton, Jr. (Eds.), *Public relations theory* (pp. 159-172). Hillsdale, NJ: Lawrence Erlbaum.

Neff, B. D. (1991, April). *Public relations accreditation in the throes of change: Academics suggest new directions for program accreditation.* Paper presented at the meeting of the Central States Communication Association, Chicago.

Negroponte, N. (1995). *Being digital.* New York: Random House.

Neilsen, E. H., & Rao, M. V. H. (1987). The strategy-legitimacy nexus: A thick description. *Academy of Management Review, 12,* 523-533.

Neiman-Marcus Co. v. Lait, 13 F.R.D. 311 (D.C. N.Y. 1952).

Nelson, J. (1989). *Sultans of sleaze.* Monroe, ME: Common Courage Press.

Nelson, R. A. (1994). Issues communication and advocacy: Contemporary ethical challenges. *Public Relations Review, 20,* 225-231.

Nessmann, K. (1995). Public relations in Europe: A comparison with the United States. *Public Relations Review, 21,* 151-160.

Neupauer, N. C. (1997a, April). *Individual differences in sports information directors.* Paper presented at the meeting of the Eastern Communication Association, Baltimore, MD.

Neupauer, N. C. (1997b). Sports information: The most coveted, ignored profession. *Public Relations Strategist, 3*(3), 35-37.

Neupauer, N. C. (1998). Women in the male-dominated world of sports information directing: Only the strong survive. *Public Relations Quarterly, 43*(1), 27-30.

Neupauer, N. C. (1999). A personality traits study of sports information directors at big vs. small programs in the East. *Social Science Journal, 36,* 163-172.

New York Times Co. v. Sullivan, 376 U.S. 254 (1964).

Newell v. Field Enterprises Inc., 91 Ill. App. 3d 735 (1980).

Newhagen, J. E., & Rafaeli, S. (1996). Why communication researchers should study the Internet: A dialogue. *Journal of Communication, 46*(1), 4-13.

Newsom, D. (1996). Review of public relations literature: Case books. *Public Relations Review, 22,* 387-391.

Newsom, D. A., & Carrell, B. J. (1994). Professional public relations in India: Need outstrips supply. *Public Relations Review, 20,* 183-188.

Newsom, D. A., Carrell, B. J., & Kruckeberg, D. (1993, November). *Development communication as a public relations campaign.* Paper presented at the meeting of the Association for the Advancement of Policy, Research, and Development in the Third World, Cairo, Egypt.

Newsom, D. A., Ramsey, S. A, & Carroll, B. J. (1993). Chameleon chasing II: A replication. *Public Relations Review, 19,* 33-47.

Newsom, D., Scott, A., & Van Slyke, T. J. (1993). *This is PR: The realities of public relations* (5th ed.). Belmont, CA: Wadsworth.

Newsom, D. A., Turk, J. V., & Kruckeberg, D. (1996). *This is PR: The realities of public relations* (6th ed.). Belmont, CA: Wadsworth.

Newstrom, J. W., & Ruch, W. A. (1975, Winter). The ethics of management and the management of ethics. *MSU Business Topics, 23,* 29-37.

Nichols, J. E. (1992). *Targeted fund raising: Defining and refining your development strategy.* Chicago: Precept Press.

Niemi, R. G., & Weisberg, H. F. (1993). *Controversies in voting behavior* (3rd ed.). Washington, DC: Congressional Quarterly.

Noblit, G., & Hare, R. D. (1988). *Meta-ethnography: Synthesizing qualitative studies.* Newbury Park, CA: Sage.

Noddings, N. (1984). *Caring: A feminist approach to ethics and moral education.* Berkeley: University of California Press.

Noelle-Neumann, E. (1973). Return to the concept of powerful mass media. In H. Eguchi & K. Sata (Eds.), *Studies in broadcasting: An international annual of broadcasting science* (pp. 67-112). Tokyo: Nippon Hoso Kyokai.

Noelle-Neumann, E. (1980). Mass media and social change in developed societies. In G. C. Wilhoit & H. de Bock (Eds.), *Mass communication review yearbook* (Vol. 1, pp. 657-678). Beverly Hills, CA: Sage.

Noelle-Neumann, E. (1984). *The spiral of silence: Public opinion, our social skin.* Chicago: University of Chicago Press.

Nolte, L. W. (1979). *Fundamentals of public relations: Professional guidelines, concepts, and integrations.* New York: Pergamon.

Noon, M., & Delbridge, R. (1993). News from behind my hand: Gossip in organizations. *Organization Studies, 14,* 23-35.

Norris, C. (1982). *Deconstruction: Theory and practice.* London: Methuen.

Norton, D. L. (1991). *Democracy and moral development: A politics of virtue.* Berkeley: University of California Press.

Norton, R., & Hughey, J. (1987, November). *Understanding the exigency in order to craft the rhetorical response: Health-promoting behavior relating to the AIDS virus in a low-prevalence state.* Paper presented at the meeting of the Speech Communication Association, Boston.

Novak, M. (1996). *Business as a calling: Work and the examined life.* New York: Free Press.

NUA Internet Surveys. (1998, March 24). *NUA Limited, 3*(10) [on-line]. Available: http://www.nua.ie/surveys

O'Dwyer, J. (Ed.). (1997). *O'Dwyer's directory of public relations firms.* New York: Author.

O'Hair, D., Friedrich, G. W., Wiemann, J. M., & Wiemann, M. O. (1995). *Competent communication.* New York: St. Martin's.

O'Keefe, G. J., & Reid, K. (1990). The uses and effects of public service advertising. In J. E. Grunig & L. A. Grunig (Eds.), *Public relations research annual* (Vol. 2, pp. 67-94). Hillsdale, NJ: Lawrence Erlbaum.

O'Keefe, S. (1997). *Publicity on the Internet.* New York: John Wiley.

O'Sullivan, T., Hartley, J, Saunders, D., Montgomery, M., & Fiske, J. (1994). *Key concepts in communication and cultural studies* (2nd ed.). London: Routledge.

Oberman v. Dun & Bradstreet Inc., 460 F. 2d 1381 (1972).

Ochsner, A. (1954). *Smoking and cancer: A doctor's report.* New York: Julian Messner.

Oddo, F. (Ed.). (1992). *Putting the "T" in health care TQM: A model for integrated TQM—Clinical care and operations* (GOAL/QPC Health Care Application Research Committee report). Boston: GOAL/QPC.

Offe, C. (1990). Reflections on the institutional self-transformation of movement politics: A tentative stage model. In R. Dalton & N. Kuechler (Eds.), *Challenging the political order: New social and political movements in Western democracies* (pp. 232-250). New York: Oxford University Press.

Ogilvy, D. (1963). *Confessions of an advertising man.* New York: Atheneum.

Olaniran, B. A. (1993). Integrative approach for managing successful computer-mediated communication technological innovation. *Ohio Speech Journal, 31,* 37-53.

Olasky, M. N. (1984, August). *The aborted debate within public relations: An approach through Kuhn's paradigm.* Paper presented at the meeting of the Association for Education in Journalism and Mass Communication, Qualitative Studies division, Gainesville, FL.

Olasky, M. N. (1985a). Bringing "order out of chaos": Edward Bernays and the salvation of society through public relations. *Journalism History, 12,* 17-21.

Olasky, M. N. (1985b). Ministers or panderers: Issues raised by the Public Relations Society code of standards. *Journal of Mass Media Ethics, 1,* 43-49.

Olasky, M. N. (1987). *Corporate public relations and American private enterprise: A new historical perspective.* Hillsdale, NJ: Lawrence Erlbaum.

Olasky, M. N. (1989). The aborted debate within public relations: An approach through Kuhn's paradigm. In J. E. Grunig & L. A. Grunig (Eds.), *Public relations research annual* (Vol. 1, pp. 87-96). Hillsdale, NJ: Lawrence Erlbaum.

Olins, W. (1991, March). Corporate identity: Do we have it all wrong? *Across the Board,* pp. 29-34.

Oliver, C. (1991). Strategic responses to institutional processes. *Academy of Management Review, 16,* 145-179.

Olson, M. (1965). *The logic of collective action.* Cambridge, MA: Harvard University Press.

Oppermann, M. (1995, Summer). E-mail surveys: Potentials and pitfalls. *Marketing Research,* pp. 28-33.

Osgood, C. P. (1972). Graduate unilateral initiatives for peace. In A. Wright (Ed.), *Preventing World War III* (pp. 47-72). New York: Simon & Schuster.

Owen, A. R., & Karrh, J. A. (1996). Video news releases: Effects on viewer recall and attitudes. *Public Relations Review, 22,* 369-378.

Pagan, R. D., Jr. (1989, May-June). A new era of activism: Who will frame the agenda? *The Futurist,* pp. 12-16.

Paine, K. D. (1995, August). Measuring publicity on the Internet. *Public Relations Tactics,* p. 18.

Paluszek, J. L. (1974). Organizing for corporate social responsibility. In S. P. Sethi (Ed.), *The unstable ground: Corporate social policy in a dynamic society* (pp. 267-278). Los Angeles: Melville.

Paluszek, J. L. (1996). Public affairs and the community: Corporate social responsibility now. In L. B. Dennis (Ed.), *Practical public affairs in an era of change* (pp. 187-208). Lanham, MD: Public Relations Society of America.

Park, R. E. (1972). *The crowd and the public, and other essays* (C. Elsner, Trans.). Chicago: University of Chicago Press. (Original work published 1904)

Parker, L. (1992, July). Collecting data the e-mail way. *Training and Development,* pp. 52-54.

Parker, M., & Slaughter, J. (1988). *Choosing sides: Unions and the team concept.* Boston: South End.

Parkin, F. (1974). *The social analysis of class structure.* London: Tavistock.

Parks, A. (1997, May 12). Online focus groups reshape market research industry. *Marketing News,* p. 28.

Parks, M. R., & Floyd, K. (1996). Making friends in cyberspace. *Journal of Communication, 46*(1), 80-97.

Parsons, P. H. (1993). Framework for analysis of conflicting loyalties. *Public Relations Review, 19,* 49-57.

Parsons, T. (1939). The professions and the social structure. *Social Forces, 17,* 457-467.

Parsons, T. (1956). Suggestions for a sociological approach to the theory of organizations [Part I]. *Administrative Science Quarterly, 1,* 63-85.

Pasqua, T., Buckalew, J., Rayfield, R., & Tankard, J. (1990). *Mass media in the information age.* Englewood Cliffs, NJ: Prentice Hall.

Patton, M. Q. (1990). Humanistic psychology and qualitative research: Shared principles and processes. *Person-Centered Review, 5*(2), 191-202.

Pauchant, T. C., & Mitroff, I. I. (1992a). Management by nosing around: Exposing the dangerous invisibility of technologies. *Journal of Management Inquiry, 1,* 70-78.

Pauchant, T. C., & Mitroff, I. I. (1992b). *Transforming the crisis-prone organization.* San Francisco: Jossey-Bass.

Pavlik, J. V. (1987). *Public relations: What research tells us.* Newbury Park, CA: Sage.

Pavlik, J. V. (1989, May). *The concept of symmetry in the education of public relations practitioners.* Paper presented at the meeting of the International Communication Association, San Francisco.

Pavlik, J. V., Nwosu, I. E., & Ettel-Gonzalez, D. (1982). Why employees read company newsletters. *Public Relations Review, 8*(3), 23-33.

Pavlik, J. V., Vastyan, J., & Maher, M. F. (1990). Using readership research to study employee views. *Public Relations Review, 16*(2), 50-60.

Peak, W. J. (1998). Community relations. In P. Lesley (Ed.), *Lesley's handbook of public relations and communications* (pp. 113-136). Englewood Cliffs, NJ: Prentice Hall.

Pearce, L., & Martin, L. (1998, May). *The secret of employee retention: Better management and higher profit.* Paper presented at the meeting of the Public Relations Society of America, Counselors Academy, Palm Springs, CA.

Pearce, W. B., & Cronen, V. E. (1980). *Communication, action, and meaning.* New York: Praeger.

Pearson, C. M., Clair, J. A., Misra, S. K., & Mitroff, I. I. (1997). Managing the unthinkable. *Organizational Dynamics, 26,* 51-71.

Pearson, C. M., & Mitroff, I. I. (1993). From crisis prone to crisis prepared. *The Executive, 7,* 48-59.

Pearson, L. J. (1996, January). Annual update of how each state stands on legislative issues affecting advanced nursing practice. *Nursing Practice, 21,* 10-70.

Pearson, R. (1989a). Beyond ethical relativism in public relations: Coorientation, rules, and the ideal of communication symmetry. In J. E. Grunig & L. A. Grunig (Eds.), *Public relations research annual* (Vol. 1, pp. 67-87). Hillsdale, NJ: Lawrence Erlbaum.

Pearson, R. (1989b). Business ethics as communication ethics: Public relations practice and the idea of dialogue. In C. H. Botan & V. T. Hazelton, Jr. (Eds.), *Public relations theory* (pp. 111-131). Hillsdale, NJ: Lawrence Erlbaum.

Pearson, R. (1989c). Reviewing Albert J. Sullivan's theory of public relations ethics. *Public Relations Review, 15,* 52-62.

Pearson, R. (1989d). *A theory of public relations ethics.* Unpublished doctoral dissertation, Ohio University.

Pearson, R. (1990). Ethical values or strategic values? The two faces of systems theory in public relations. In L. A. Grunig & J. E. Grunig (Eds.), *Public relations research annual* (Vol. 2, pp. 219-234). Hillsdale, NJ: Lawrence Erlbaum.

Pearson, R. (1992). Perspectives on public relations history. In E. Toth & R. Heath (Eds.), *Rhetorical and critical approaches to public relations* (pp. 111-130). Hillsdale, NJ: Lawrence Erlbaum.

Peebles, J. (1996, March 11). Online technology creates research tools. *Marketing News,* p. 5.

Pemberton v. Bethlehem Steel Corp., 66 Md. App. 133 (1986).

Pereira, J. (1996, December 16). Toy story: How shrewd marketing made Elmo a hit. *The Wall Street Journal,* pp. B1, B5.

Perelman, C., & Olbrechts-Tyteca, L. (1969). *The new rhetoric* (J. Wilkinson & P. Weaver, Trans.). Notre Dame, IN: University of Notre Dame Press.

Perrow, C. (1984). *Normal accidents: Living with high risk technologies.* New York: Basic Books.

Persichitte, K. A., Young, S., & Tharp, D. D. (1997, February). *Conducting research on the Internet: Strategies for electronic interviewing.* Paper presented at the meeting of the Association for Educational Communications and Technology, Albuquerque, NM. (ERIC Document Reproduction Service, No. ED 409 860)

Personal competency and guts will prepare the future of PR. (1998, June 1). *PR Reporter,* pp. 1-2.

Peters, T. J. (1988). *Thriving on chaos: Handbook for a management revolution.* London: Pan Books.

Peters, T. J., & Austin, N. (1986). *A passion for excellence: The leadership difference.* New York: Warner Books.

Peters, T. J., & Waterman, R. H. (1982). *In search of excellence: Lessons from America's best-run companies.* New York: Harper & Row.

Petrison, L. A., & Wang, P. (1993). From relationships to relationship marketing: Applying database technology to public relations. *Public Relations Review, 19,* 235-245.

Petsch v. St. Paul Dispatch Printing Co., 40 Minn. 291 (1989).

Petty, R. E., & Cacioppo, J. T. (1986). *Communication and persuasion: Central and peripheral routes to attitude change.* New York: Springer-Verlag.

Petty, R. E., Cacioppo, J. T., & Goldman, R. (1981). Personal involvement as a determinant of argument-based persuasion. *Journal of Personality and Social Psychology, 41,* 847-885.

Pfau, M., & Parrott, R. (1993). *Persuasive communication campaigns.* Boston: Allyn & Bacon.

Phares, W. (1994, March). *Ethnic/religious minorities.* Panel discussion at the conference, "The Road to Peace: The Challenge of the Middle East," Miami, FL.

Pieczka, M. (1995, July). *Symmetry in communication and public relations.* Paper presented at the Second International Public Relations Symposium, Bled, Slovenia.

Pieczka, M. (1996a). Paradigms, systems theory, and public relations. In J. L'Etang & M. Pieczka (Eds.), *Critical perspectives in public relations* (pp. 124-156). London: International Thomson Business Press.

Pieczka, M. (1996b). Public opinion and public relations. In J. L'Etang & M. Pieczka (Eds.), *Critical perspectives in public relations* (pp. 54-64). London: International Thomson Business Press.

Pillsbury to pay $3.6 million to settle discrimination suit. (1990, October 10). *The Washington Post,* p. C2.

Pimlott, J. A. R. (1951). *Public relations and American democracy.* Princeton, NJ: Princeton University Press.

Pincus, J. D. (1997a). Changing how future managers "view" us. *Public Relations Strategist, 3*(1), 27-29.

Pincus, J. D. (1997b). The jargon IS the message or . . . communicator, hear thyself! *Communication World, 14*(6), 33-35.

Pincus, J. D., & DeBonis, J. N. (1994). *Top dog.* New York: McGraw-Hill.

Pincus, J. D., Ohl, C. M., & Rayfield, B. (1994). Public relations education in MBA programs: Challenges and opportunities. *Public Relations Review, 20,* 55-71.

Planalp, S. (1999). *Communicating emotion: Social, moral, and cultural processes.* New York: Cambridge University Press.

Plato. (1952). Gorgias (B. Jowett, Trans.). In R. M. Hutchins (Ed.), *Great books* (pp. 252-294). Chicago: Encyclopaedia Britannica.

Plowman, K. D. (1995). *Congruence between public relations and conflict resolution: Negotiating power in the organization.* Unpublished doctoral dissertation, University of Maryland, College Park.

Plowman, K. D. (1998). Power in conflict for public relations. *Journal of Public Relations Research, 10,* 237-262.

Plowman, K. D. (1999). *Strategic management, conflict, and public relations.* Unpublished manuscript, San Jose State University.

Plummer, J. (1993, August). [Oral presentation.] Part of panel discussion titled "Managerial Perspectives on Relationship Marketing," Annual Educators Conference of the American Marketing Association, Boston.

Pohl, G. (1995). *Public relations: Designing effective communications.* Dubuque, IA: Kendall/Hunt.

Polkinghorne, D. (1988). *Narrative knowing and the human sciences.* Albany: State University of New York Press.

Pollay, R. W. (1990). Propaganda, puffing, and the public interest. *Public Relations Review, 16*(3), 40.

Polley, R. B. (1988). Group field dynamics and effective mediation. *International Journal of Small Group Research, 4,* 55-75.

Pomper, G. (1959). The public relations of organized labor. *Public Opinion Quarterly, 23,*
483-495.

Post-Keyes-Gardner. (1969). *Brown & Williamson collection* [On-line]. Available: http://
gema.library.ucsf.edu/tobacco/docs/html/
2110.02/2110.02.1.html or http://gema.li-
brary.ucsf.edu/tobacco/docs/html/2110.03/
2110.03.1.html

Postman, N. (1986). *Amusing ourselves to death:
Public discourse in the age of show business.*
New York: Penguin Books.

Powell, W. N. (1990). Neither market nor hierarchy: Network forms of organization. *Research in Organizational Behavior, 12,* 295-
336.

Powell, W. W., & DiMaggio, P. J. (1991). *The new
institutionalism in organizational analysis.*
Chicago: University of Chicago Press.

PR agencies are getting wired. (1998, May). *Public Relations Tactics,* p. 8.

PR Central. (1996, May-June). Are British
bosses turning their backs on Europe? *Reputation Management.* Available: http://www.
prcentral.com/rmmj96uk.htm

PR: "The velvet ghetto" of affirmative action.
(1978, May 8). *Business Week,* p. 122.

Pratt, C. B. (1985). Public relations in the Third
World: The African context. *Public Relations
Journal, 41*(2), 11-16.

Pratt, C. B. (1986). Professionalism in Nigerian
public relations. *Public Relations Review,
12,*(4), 27-40.

Pratt, C. B. (1991a). PRSA members' perceptions
of public relations ethics. *Public Relations
Review, 17,* 145-159.

Pratt, C. B. (1991b). Public relations: The empirical research on practitioner ethics. *Journal of
Business Ethics, 10,* 229-236.

Pratt, C. B. (1992). Correlates and predictors of
self-reported ethics among U.S. public relations practitioners. *Psychological Reports, 70,*
259-267.

Pratt, C. B. (1993). Critique of the classical theory of situational ethics in U.S. public relations. *Public Relations Review, 19,* 219-234.

Pratt, C. B. (1994). Research progress in public
relations ethics: An overview. *Public Relations Review, 20,* 217-224.

Premeaux, S. R., & Mondy, R. W. (1993). Linking
management behavior to ethical philosophy.
Journal of Business Ethics, 12, 349-357.

Press freedom makes headway in Kenya: Kenyan
media still have government restrictions.
(1997, December). *Freedom Forum and New-
seum News,* pp. 1, 6.

Price, S. V. (1994). Learning to remove fear from
radioactive waste. *Public Relations Quarterly,
39*(3), 32-34.

Price, V. (1992). *Public opinion.* Newbury Park,
CA: Sage.

Prior-Miller, M. (1989). Four major social scientific theories and their value to the public relations researcher. In C. H. Botan & V.
Hazleton, Jr. (Eds.), *Public relations theory*
(pp. 67-81). Hillsdale, NJ: Lawrence
Erlbaum.

Pritchitt, J. (1992). If image is linked to reputation and reputation to increased use, shouldn't
we do something about ours? *Public Relations Quarterly, 37*(3), 45-47.

Prosser, W. L. (1960). Privacy. *California Law Review, 48,* 383-423.

Pruitt, D. G., & Rubin, J. Z. (1986). *Social conflict:
Escalation, stalemate, and settlement.* New
York: McGraw-Hill.

Public relations education: Two surveys. (1982).
Public Relations Journal, 38(2), 33-34.

Public Relations Society of America. (1987). *Report of the Commission on Undergraduate
Public Relations Education: A design for undergraduate public relations education.* New
York: Author.

Public Relations Society of America. (1990).
Public relations body of knowledge. New York:
Author.

Public Relations Society of America (1996a). *Design for undergraduate public relations education.* New York: Author.

Public Relations Society of America. (1996b).
Salary survey of public relations professionals.
New York: Author.

Public Relations Society of America. (1997).
*Forging consensus: Your side, my side, our
side—Workshop workbook.* New York: Author.

Public Relations Society of America. (1997-1998). *Public relations tactics: The blue book.* New York: Author.

Public Relations Society of America. (1998a). Code of professional standards for the practice of public relations. In *Public relations tactics: The blue book* (pp. A11-A23). New York: Author.

Public Relations Society of America. (1998b). *How to prepare your Silver Anvil entry* [On-line]. Available: http://www.prsa.org/silveranvil/prepare.html

Public Relations Society of America. (1998-1999). *Public relations tactics: The blue book.* New York: Author.

Public Relations Society of America. (1999). *What public relations is* [On-line]. Available: http://www.prsa.org/pressroom/aboutpr.html

Public Relations Student Society of America. (1999). *PRSSA new chapters* [On-line]. Available: http://www.prssa.org/framer.htm

Pullman Standard Car Mfg. Co. v. Local Union No. 2928 of United Steelworkers of America, 152 F. 2d 493 (1946).

The purposes and benefits of accreditation [on-line]. (1998, November 12). Available: http://www.ukans.edu/~acejmc

Putnam, B. (1980). How to build a community relations program. *Public Relations Journal, 36*(2), 28-31.

Putnam, L. L. (1990). Reframing integrative and distributive bargaining: A process perspective. In B. Sheppard, M. Bazerman, & R. Lewicki (Eds.), *Research on negotiation in organzations* (Vol. 2, pp. 3-30). Greenwich, CT: JAI.

Putnam, L. L., & Holmer, M. (1992). Framing, reframing, and issue development. In L. Putnam & M. Roloff (Eds.), *Communication and negotiation* (pp. 128-155). Newbury Park, CA: Sage.

Putnam, L. L., & Roloff, M. E. (1992). Communication perspectives on negotiation. In L. L. Putnam & M. E. Roloff (Eds.), *Communication and negotiation* (pp. 1-20). Newbury Park, CA: Sage.

Putnam, R. D. (1993). *Making democracy work: Civic traditions in modern Italy.* Princeton, NJ: Princeton University Press.

Putnam, R. D. (1995). Bowling alone: America's declining social capital. *Journal of Democracy, 6*(1), 65-78.

Pye, L. W. (1981). *The dynamics of Chinese politics.* Cambridge, MA: Legeschlarger, Gumn, & Halin.

Pye, L. W. (1992). *Chinese negotiating style.* Westport, NY: Quorum Books.

Quarantelli, E. L. (1988). Disaster crisis management: A summary of research findings. *Journal of Management Studies, 25,* 373-385.

Quarantelli, E. L. (1996). Basic themes derived from survey findings on human behavior in the Mexico City earthquake. *International Sociology, 11,* 481-499.

Quarantelli, E. L. (1997). Ten criteria for evaluating the management of community disasters. *Disasters, 21*(1), 39-56.

Quinn, R. E., & Spreitzer, G. M. (1996). Seven questions every leader should consider. *Organizational Dynamics, 26,* 37-50.

Quintilian, M. F. (1951). *The institutio oratoria of Marcus Fabius Quintilianus* (C. E. Little, Trans.). Nashville, TN: George Peabody College for Teachers.

Quirke, B. (1996). *Communicating corporate change: A practical guide to communication and corporate strategy.* New York: McGraw-Hill.

Radio Shack Corp. v. Radio Shack, 180 F. 2d 200 (C.A. Ill. 1950).

Rafaeli, S. (1988). Interactivity: From new media to communication. In R. P. Hawkins, J. M. Wiemann, & P. Pingree (Eds.), *Advancing communication science: Merging mass and interpersonal processes* (Vol. 16, pp. 110-134). Newbury Park, CA: Sage.

Ragan, L. (1994, September 13). It's time to look more closely at IABC's $400,000 *Excellence* report. *The Ragan Report,* p. 2.

Ragin, C. C. (1992). Introduction: Cases of "What is a case?" In C. C. Ragin & H. S. Becker (Eds.), *What is a case? Exploring the foundations of social inquiry* (pp. 1-17). Cambridge, UK: Cambridge University Press.

Ragin, C. C., & Becker, H. S. (Eds.). (1992). *What is a case? Exploring the foundations of social inquiry.* Cambridge, UK: Cambridge University Press.

Raiffa, H. (1982). *The art and science of negotiation.* Cambridge, MA: Harvard University Press.

Rakow, L. F. (1989a). From the feminization of public relations to the promise of feminism. In E. L. Toth & C. G. Cline (Eds.), *Beyond the velvet ghetto* (pp. 287-298). San Francisco: IABC Foundation.

Rakow, L. F. (1989b). Information and power: Toward a critical theory of information campaigns. In C. T. Salmon (Ed.), *Information campaigns: Balancing social values and social change* (pp. 164-184). Newbury Park, CA: Sage.

Ramprogus, V. (1995). *The deconstruction of nursing.* Aldershot, UK: Avebury.

Ramsey, S. A. (1993). Issues management and the use of technologies in public relations. *Public Relations Review, 19,* 261-275.

Rangan, V. K. (1995). *Choreographing a case class* (Report No. 9-595-074). Boston: Harvard University, School of Business Administration.

Rappleyea, W. (1998, July 10). Celebrating the entrepreneurial spirit. *USA Today,* p. B5.

Rawlins, B. L. (1993, August). *Organizational factors that contribute to practicing "excellent" public relations.* Paper presented at the meeting of the Association for Education in Journalism and Mass Communication, Kansas City, MO.

Rawls, J. (1971). *A theory of justice.* Cambridge, MA: Harvard University Press.

Readings, B. (1996). *The university in ruins.* Cambridge, MA: Harvard University Press.

Reagan, J., Anderson, R., Sumner, J., & Hill, S. (1990). A factor analysis of Broom and Smith's Public Relations Roles Scale. *Journalism Quarterly, 67,* 177-183.

Reddick. R., & King, E. (1997). *The on-line journalist.* Fort Worth, TX: Harcourt Brace.

Redding, W. C. (1966). The empirical study of human communication in business and industry. In P. E. Reid (Ed.), *The frontiers in experimental speech-communication research* (pp. 47-83). Syracuse, NY: Syracuse University, Division of the Summer Sessions.

Redding, W. C. (1992, November). *The strange case of the missing organization: Labor unions and the study of organizational communication.* Paper presented at the special meeting on "Labor Discourse in American Society" of the Speech Communication Association, Chicago.

Reder, A. (1995). The wide world of corporate philanthropy. *Business and Society Review, 92,* 36-42.

Reed, J. (1999, February). An international sensitivity. *Public Relations Tactics,* p. 31.

Reich, R. B. (1998). The new meaning of corporate social responsibility. *California Management Review, 40*(2), 8-17.

Reid, E. (1996). Informed consent in the study of on-line communities: A reflection on the effects of computer-mediated social research. *Information Society, 12,* 169-174.

Reidenbach, R. E., & Robin, D. P. (1988). Some initial steps toward improving the measurement of ethical evaluations of marketing activities. *Journal of Business Ethics, 7,* 871-879.

Reidenbach, R. E., & Robin, D. P. (1989). *Ethics and profits: A convergence of corporate America's economic and social responsibilities.* Englewood Cliffs, NJ: Prentice Hall.

Reidenbach, R. E., & Robin, D. P. (1990) Toward the development of a multidimensional scale for improving evaluations of business ethics. *Journal of Business Ethics, 9,* 639-654.

Reilly, A. H. (1987). Are organizations ready for crisis? A managerial scorecard. *Columbia Journal of World Business, 22,* 79-88.

Reinsch, N. L. (1990). Ethics research in business communication: The state of the art. *Journal of Business Communication, 27,* 251-272.

Renfro, W. L. (1993). *Issues management in strategic planning.* Westport, CT: Quorum.

Research Services Ltd. (1995). *The Pan European Survey: The results of the 1995 fourteen country survey.* Harrow, UK: Author.

Research Services Ltd. (1996). *The European Business Readership Survey 1996.* Harrow, UK: Author.

Reskin, B. K. (1989). Occupational resegregation. In S. Rix (Ed.), *The American woman:*

1988-89—A status report (pp. 258-263). New York: Norton.

Reskin, B. K., & Roos, K. (Eds.). (1990). *Job queues, gender queues: Explaining women's inroads into male occupations.* Philadelphia: Temple University Press.

Rest, J. R. (1979). *Development in judging moral issues.* Minneapolis: University of Minnesota Press.

Rettig, S., & Pasamanick, B. (1959). Changes in moral values among college students: A factorial study. *American Sociological Review, 6,* 856-863.

Reynolds, T. J., & Jolly, J. (1980). Measuring personal values: An evaluation of alternative methods. *Journal of Marketing Research, 17,* 531-536.

Rhee, Y. (1999). *Confucian culture and excellent public relations: A study of generic principles and specific applications in South Korean public relations practice.* Unpublished master's thesis, University of Maryland, College Park.

Rheingold, H. (1993). *Virtual community: Homesteading on the electronic frontier.* Reading, MA: Addison-Wesley.

Rhoades, L., & Rhoades, G. (1991). Helping the media add depth to education news. *Education News, 64,* 350-351.

Rhody, R. E. (1996). The CEO's role in nurturing public affairs. In L. B. Dennis (Ed.), *Practical public affairs in an era of change* (pp. 229-238). Lanham, MD: Public Relations Society of America.

Rice, B. (1988, March). The selling of lifestyles. *Psychology Today,* pp. 46-50.

Rice, R. E. (1989). Issues and concepts in research on computer-mediated communication systems. In J. A. Anderson (Ed.), *Communication yearbook 12* (pp. 436-476). Newbury Park, CA: Sage.

Rice, R. E. (1993). Media appropriateness. Using social presence theory to compare traditional and new organizational media. *Human Communication Research, 19,* 451-484.

Riche, M. F. (1990, June). New frontiers for geodemographics. *American Demographics,* p. 20.

Ricoeur, P. (1984-1988). *Time and narrative* (Vols. 1-3). Chicago: University of Chicago Press.

Ritter, K. W. (1971). Confrontation as moral drama: The Boston Massacre in rhetorical perspective. *Southern Speech Communication Journal, 42,* 114-136.

Rivers, W. L., & Work, A. R. (1986). *Freelancer and staff writer: Newspaper, features, and magazine articles* (4th ed.). Belmont, CA: Wadsworth.

Robertson, R. (1992). *Globalization: Social theory and global culture.* London: Sage.

Rodenhouse, M. P. (1997). *Higher education directory.* Falls Church, VA: Higher Education Publications.

Roderick, K. (1994, March). *Ethnic/religious minorities.* Panel discussion at the conference, "The Road to Peace: The Challenge of the Middle East," Miami, FL.

Rogers, E. M. (1962). *Diffusion of innovations.* New York: Free Press.

Rogers, N. (1958). The birth of the institute. *Public Relations, 10*(2), 9-12.

Rokeach, M. (1973). *The nature of human values.* New York: Free Press.

Roloff, M. E. (1981). *Interpersonal communication: The social exchange approach.* Beverly Hills, CA: Sage.

Rorty, R. (1979). *Philosophy and the mirror of nature.* Princeton, NJ: Princeton University Press.

Roschwalb, S. (1994). The Hill & Knowlton cases: A brief on the controversy. *Public Relations Review, 20,* 267-276.

Rose, L. C., Gallup, A. M., & Elam, S. M. (1997). The 1997 Gallup Poll of the public's attitudes toward the public schools. *Phi Delta Kappan, 79,* 42-56.

Rose, M. (1991a). Activism in the 90s: Changing roles for public relations. *Public Relations Quarterly, 36*(3), 28-32.

Rose, M. A. (1991b). *The post-modern and the post-industrial: A critical analysis.* Cambridge, UK: Cambridge University Press.

Rose, P. B., & Miller, D. A. (1994). Merging advertising and PR: Integrated marketing communications. *Journalism Educator, 49,* 52-53.

Rosenau, P. M. (1992). *Post-modernism and the social sciences: Insights, inroads, and intrusions.* Princeton, NJ: Princeton University Press.

Rosenberg, M. (1998, November 9). Finding a home for public relations. *The New York Times,* p. C7.

Rosenbloom, N. L. (1989). Pluralism and self-defense. In N. L. Rosenbloom (Ed.), *Liberalism and the moral life* (pp. 207-226). Cambridge, MA: Harvard University Press.

Ross, I. (1959). *The image merchants: The fabulous world of public relations.* New York: Doubleday.

Ross, P. E. (1995, December). Garbage recycler. *Forbes,* pp. 260-262.

Ross, S. S. (1995). Public relations in cyberspace. *Public Relations Journal, 5*(1), 36-38.

Ross, S. S., & Middleberg, D. (1997). *The Middleberg/Ross media in cyberspace study* [On-line]. Available: http://www.mediasource.com/intro.htm#Profession

Rosseau, J. J. (1968). *The social contract* (M. Cranston, Trans.). Harmondsworth, UK: Penguin. (Original work published 1762)

Roth, N. L., Hunt, T., Stavropoulos, M., & Babik, K. (1996). Can't we all just get along: Cultural variables in codes of ethics. *Public Relations Review, 22,* 151-161.

Rotman, D. (1997, July 2). It's a group effort. *Chemical Week,* pp. 48-50.

Rowley, T. J. (1997). Moving beyond dyadic ties: A network theory of stakeholder influences. *Academy of Management Review, 22,* 887-910.

Roy, M. (1980). *Examination of the techniques used by Southeastern Conference sports information directors in promoting their football players in All-American honors.* Unpublished master's thesis, University of Florida.

Rubin, A. M. (1986). Uses, gratifications, and media effects research. In D. Zillmann & J. Bryant (Eds.), *Perspectives on media effects* (pp. 281-298). Hillsdale, NJ: Lawrence Erlbaum.

Rubin, A. M. (1994). Media uses and effects: A uses and gratifications perspective. In D. Zillmann & J. Bryant (Eds.), *Media effects:*

Advances in theory and research (pp. 417-437). Hillsdale, NJ : Lawrence Erlbaum.

Rubin, J. Z., & Salacuse, J. W. (1993). Commentary, culture, and international negotiation: Lessons for business. *Alternatives to the High Cost of Litigation—Center for Public Resources, 11*(7), 95-99.

Rubin, R. B., Palmgreen, P., & Sypher, H. E. (1994). *Communication research measures: A sourcebook.* New York: Guilford.

Rueschemeyer, D. (1964). Doctors and lawyers: A comment on the theory of professions. *Canadian Journal of Sociology and Anthropology, 1,* 17.

Russell, D. (1982). The Causal Dimension Scale: A measure of how individuals perceive causes. *Journal of Personality and Social Psychology, 42,* 1137-1145.

Ryan, C. (1991). *Prime time activism.* Boston: South End.

Ryan, C., Carragee, K. M., & Schwerner, C. (1998). Media, movements, and the quest for social justice. *Journal of Applied Communication Research, 26,* 165-181.

Ryan, H. R. (1982). Kategoria and apologia: On their rhetorical criticism as a speech set. *Quarterly Journal of Speech, 68,* 254-261.

Ryan, J. P. (1994, March). Thanks a million: You need strong recognition programs to foster healthy donor relations. *CASE Currents,* p. 64.

Ryan, M. (1986). Public relations practitioners' views of corporate social responsibility. *Journalism Quarterly, 63,* 740-747, 762.

Ryan, M., & Martinson, D. L. (1984). Ethical values, the flow of journalistic information, and public relations persons. *Journalism Quarterly, 61,* 27-34.

Ryan, M., & Martinson, D. L. (1985). Public relations practitioners, public interest, and management. *Journalism Quarterly, 62,* 111-115.

Ryan, M., & Martinson, D. L. (1991, August). *How journalists and public relations practitioners define lying.* Paper presented at the meeting of the Association for Education in Journalism and Mass Communication, Boston.

Sabri, H. (1994, March). *Religious dialogue.* Panel discussion at the conference, "The Road to

Peace: The Challenge of the Middle East," Miami, FL.

Sacks, H., Schegloff, E. A., & Jefferson G. (1978). A simplest systematics for the organization of turn taking for conversation. In J. Schenkein (Ed.), *Studies in the organization of conversational interaction* (pp. 7-55). New York: Academic Press.

Sacks, O. (1985) *The man who mistook his wife for a hat: And other clinical tales.* New York: Summit Books.

Sacks, O. (1995). *An anthropologist on Mars: Seven paradoxical tales.* New York: Knopf.

Salancik, G. R. (1977). Commitment and the control of organizational behavior and belief. In B. M. Staw & G. R. Salancik (Eds.), *New directions in organizational behavior* (pp. 1-54). Chicago: St. Clair.

Sallot, L. M. (1997, November). *Interpersonal communication in public relations: A review of research.* Paper presented at the meeting of the National Communication Association, Chicago.

Sallot, L. M., Cameron, G. T., & Lariscy, R. A. (1997). Professional standards in public relations: A survey of educators. *Public Relations Review, 23,* 197-216.

Salomon, G. (1979). *Interaction of media, cognition, and learning.* San Francisco: Jossey-Bass.

Sampson, A. (1969). *The anatomy of Britain.* London: Book Club.

Sams, C. (1998, April 13). Colleges are a study in starting opinion leader programs. *PR Reporter,* pp. 1-4.

Samuelson, R. J. (1998, November 30). The amazing smokescreen. *Newsweek,* p. 47.

Sanchez, R. (1997). Strategic management at the point of inflection: Systems, complexity, and competence theory. *Long Range Planning, 30,* 939-946.

Sandel, M. J. (1982). *Liberalism and the limits of justice.* Cambridge, UK: Cambridge University Press.

Sandel, M. J. (1984). The procedural republic and the unencumbered self. *Political Theory, 12,* 81-96.

Sandel, M. J. (1996). *Democracy's discontent: America in search of a pubic philosophy.* Cambridge, MA: Harvard University Press.

Sandman, P. M. (1986). Getting to maybe: Some communications aspects of siting hazardous waste facilities. *Seton Hall Legislative Journal, 9*(2), 437-465.

Sandrick, K. (1995, July 5). If you want to play you've got to pay: Community outreach is the name of the game, but how do hospitals pay for it? *Hospitals & Health Networks,* pp. 25-27.

Saunders, M. D. (1989). Ethical dilemmas in public relations: Perceptions of Florida practitioners. *Florida Communication Journal, 17*(2), 23-27.

Savage, D. (1989, August). *The press and education research: Why one ignores the other.* Paper presented at the Colloquium on the Interdependence of Educational Research, Educational Policy, and the Press, Charlottesville, VA. (ERIC Document Reproduction Service, No. ED 311464)

Schaefer v. United States, 251 U.S. 466 (1920).

Schafer, S. (1996). Communications: Getting a line on customers. *Inc.* (Suppl. 17), p. 102.

Scheuer, J. (1991). Special interests and public discourse. *Dissent, 38,* 415-418.

Schiappa, E. (1989). The rhetoric of nukespeak. *Communication Monographs, 56,* 253-272.

Schick, T. A. (1996). Technician ethics in public relations. *Public Relations Quarterly, 41*(1), 30-35.

Schiller, H. I. (1969). *Mass communication and American empire.* New York: A. M. Kelley.

Schiller, H. I. (1989). *Culture, Inc.: The corporate takeover of public expression.* New York: Oxford University Press.

Schiller, H. I. (1995). The global information highway: Project for an ungovernable world. In J. Brook & I. A. Boal (Eds.), *Resisting the virtual life: The culture and politics of information* (pp. 17-33). San Francisco: City Lights.

Schilling, D. M., & Rosenbaum, R. (1995). Principles for global corporate responsibility. *Business and Society Review, 94,* 55-56.

Schin, D. A. (1987). *Educating the reflective practitioner.* San Francisco, CA: Jossey-Bass.

Schlachter, E. (1997). The intellectual property renaissance in cyberspace: Why copyright law could be unimportant on the Internet. *Berkeley Technology Law Journal, 12,* 15-51.

Schlesinger, A. M. (1992). *The disuniting of America: Reflections on a multicultural society.* New York: Norton.

Schlesinger, P. (1999). Changing spaces of political communication: The case of the European Union. *Political Communication, 16,* 263-279.

Schlesinger, P., & Kevin, D. (2000). Can the European Union become a sphere of publics? In E. O. Eriksen & J. Fossum (Eds.), *Democracy in Europe: Integration through deliberation* (pp. 206-229) London: UCL Press.

Schlozman, K. L., & Tierney, J. T. (1986). *Organized interests and American democracy.* New York: Harper & Row.

Schön, D. A. (1983). *The reflective practitioner: How professionals think in action.* New York: Basic Books.

Schön, D. A. (1987). *Educating the reflective practitioner.* San Francisco: Jossey-Bass.

Schonland, A. M., & Williams, P. W. (1996). Using the Internet for travel and tourism survey research: Experiences from the Net traveler survey. *Journal of Travel Research, 35*(2), 81-87.

Schoonmaker, M. E. (1985). The beat nobody wants: Everyone says education is important—But you wouldn't know it from reading most papers. *Columbia Journalism Review, 42*(1), 7-40.

Schudson, M. (1992). Was there ever a public sphere? If so, when? Reflections on the American case. In C. Calhoun (Ed.), *Habermas and the public sphere* (pp. 143-163). Cambridge, MA: MIT Press.

Schuldt, B. A., & Totten, J. W. (1994). Electronic mail vs. mail survey response rates. *Marketing Research, 6*(1), 36-39.

Schultz, D. E. (1993a, August 16). Four basic rules lay groundwork for integration. *Marketing News,* p. 5.

Schultz, D. E. (1993b, April 26). Why ad agencies are having so much trouble with IMC. *Marketing News,* p. 12.

Schultz, D. E., & Barnes, B. E. (1995). *Strategic advertising campaigns.* Lincolnwood, IL: NTC Publishing.

Schultz, D. E., Tannenbaum, S. I., & Lauterhorn, R. F. (1993). *Integrated marketing communications.* Lincolnwood, IL: NTC Publishing Group.

Schultz, P. D., & Seeger, M. W. (1991). Corporate centered apologia: Iacocca in defense of Chrysler. *Speaker and Gavel, 28,* 50-60.

Schumpeter, J. (1942). *Capitalism, socialism, and democracy.* New York: Harper.

Schwartz, D. F., & Glynn, C. J. (1989). Selecting channels for institutional public relations. *Public Relations Review, 15*(4), 24-36.

Schwartz, M., & Thompson, M. (1990). *Divided we stand: Redefining politics, technology, and social choice.* Philadelphia: University of Pennsylvania Press.

Sclove, R. E. (1995). Making technology democratic. In J. Brook & I. A. Boal (Eds.), *Resisting the virtual life: The culture and politics of information* (pp. 85-101). San Francisco: City Lights.

Scott, J. C., & O'Hair, D. (1989). Expanding psychographic concepts in public relations: The composite audience profile. In C. H. Botan & V. Hazleton, Jr. (Eds.), *Public relations theory* (pp. 203-219). Hillsdale, NJ: Lawrence Erlbaum.

Scott, R. L. (1976). On viewing rhetoric as epistemic: Ten years later. *Central States Speech Journal, 27,* 258-266.

Scott, W. R. (1987). *Organizations: Natural, rational, and open systems* (2nd ed.). Englewood Cliffs, NJ: Prentice Hall.

Searle, J. (1969). *Speech acts.* Cambridge, MA: Cambridge University Press.

Seeger, M. W. (1986). CEO performances: Lee Iacocca and the case of Chrysler. *Southern Speech Communication Journal, 52,* 52-68.

Seeger, M. W., Sellnow, T. L., & Ulmer, R. R. (1998). Communication, organization, and crisis. In M. E. Roloff (Ed.), *Communication yearbook 21* (pp. 230-275). Thousand Oaks, CA: Sage.

Seib, P., & Fitzpatrick, K. (1995). *Public relations ethics.* Fort Worth, TX: Harcourt Brace.

Seitel, F. P. (1992). *The practice of public relations* (5th ed.). New York: Macmillan.

Seitel, F. P. (1995). *The practice of public relations* (6th ed.). Englewood Cliffs, NJ: Prentice Hall.

Seitel, F. P. (1996). From the publisher. *Public Relations Strategist, 2*(3), 1.

Seitel, F. P. (1998). *The practice of public relations* (7th ed.). Upper Saddle River, NJ: Prentice Hall.

Sellnow, T. L. (1993). Scientific argument in organizational crisis communication: The case of Exxon. *Argumentation and Advocacy, 31,* 138-150.

Sellnow, T. L., & Ulmer, R. R. (1995). Ambiguous argument as advocacy in organizational crisis communication. *Argumentation and Advocacy, 31,* 138-150.

Sellnow, T. L., Ulmer, R. R., & Snider, M. (1998). The compatibility of corrective action in organizational crisis communication. *Communication Quarterly, 46,* 60-74.

Selznick, P. (1992). *The moral commonwealth: Social theory and the promise of community.* Berkeley: University of California Press.

Sen, F., & Egelhoff, W. G. (1991). Six years and counting: Learning from crisis management in Bhopal. *Public Relations Review, 17,* 69-83.

Sennett, R. (1998). *The corrosion of character: The personal consequences of work in the new capitalism.* New York: Norton.

Sereni, S. A., Toth, E. L., Wright, D. K., & Emig, A. G. (1997). Watch for falling glass . . .: Women, men, and job satisfaction in public relations—A preliminary analysis. *Journal of Public Relations Research, 9,* 99-117.

Serini, S. A., Toth, E. L., Wright, D. K., & Emig, A. G. (1998). Power, gender, and public relations: Sexual harassment as a threat to the practice. *Journal of Public Relations Research, 10,* 193-218.

Sethi, S. P. (1977). *Advocacy advertising and large corporations: Social conflict, big business image, the news media, and public policy.* Lexington, MA: D. C. Heath.

Sethi, S. P. (1987). Inhuman errors and industrial crisis. *Columbia Journal of World Business, 22,* 101-107.

Sethi, S. P. (1994). Conversion of a corporate CEO into a public persona. *Business and Society Review, 91,* 42-46.

Seymour, H. J. (1988). *Designs for fund-raising: Principles, patterns, techniques.* Rockville, MD: Fund-Raising Institute. (Original work published 1966)

Sha, B. L. (1999). *Cultural public relations: Identity, activism, globalization, and gender in the Democratic Progressive Party on Taiwan.* Unpublished Ph.D. dissertation, University of Maryland, College Park.

Shabercoff, P. (1989, March 31). Captain of tanker had been drinking, blood tests show. *The New York Times,* pp. A1, A12.

Shaffer, J. (1997). Reinventing communication. *Communication World, 14*(3), 20-23.

Shaffer, J. (1998, September-October). A vision: Employee communication tomorrow. *Journal of Employee Communication Management,* pp. 11-19.

Shallowitz, D. (1987, April 13). Preparation needed to handle catastrophes. *Business Insurance,* p. 30.

Shamir, J., Reed, B. S., & Connell, S. (1990). Individual differences in ethical values of public relations practitioners. *Journalism Quarterly, 67,* 956-963.

Shanahan, J., Morgan, M., & Stenbjerre, M. (1997). Green or brown? Television and the cultivation of environmental concern. *Journal of Broadcasting & Electronic Media, 41,* 305-323.

Shannon, C., & Weaver, W. (1949). *The mathematical theory of communication.* Urbana: University of Illinois Press.

Shapere, D. (1977). Scientific theories and their domains. In F. Suppe (Ed.), *The structure of scientific theories* (2nd ed., pp. 518-565). Urbana: University of Illinois Press.

Sharpe, M. E. (1996, November 21). The tyranny of the bottom line: Why corporations make good people do bad things [book review]. *Challenge, 39*(6), 60.

Sharpe, M. L. (1986). Recognition comes from consistently high standards. *Public Relations Review, 12*(4), 17-26.

Shayon, D. R. (1996). *Public affairs in the 21st century.* Philadelphia: Hotel Resource Network.

Shell, A. (1994a, August). Howard Paster: Turning around Hill & Knowlton. *Public Relations Tactics*, pp. 14-15.

Shell, A. (1994b, December). The PR firm of tomorrow. *Public Relations Tactics*, pp. 30-31.

Shell, A. (1995, June). CyberRelations: The race to be No. 1 in cyberspace. *Public Relations Tactics*, p. 6.

Sherwin, G. R., & Avila, E. N. (1998). *Connecting online: Creating a successful image on the Internet.* Grants Pass, OR: Oasis Press.

Sheth, J. N., & Sisordia, R. S. (1993). The information mall. *Telecommunications Policy, 17,* 376-389.

Short, B. (1991). Earth First! and the rhetoric of moral confrontation. *Communication Studies, 42*(2), 172-188.

Shrivastava, P. (1987). *Bhopal: Anatomy of crisis.* Cambridge, MA: Ballinger.

Shrivastava, P. (1995). Democratic control of technological risks in developing countries. *Ecological Economics, 14,* 195-208.

Shrivastava, P., & Mitroff, I. I. (1987). Strategic management of corporate crisis. *Columbia Journal of World Business, 22,* 5-11.

Shrivastava, P., Mitroff, I. I., Miller, D., & Miglani, A. (1988). Understanding industrial crises. *Journal of Management Studies, 25,* 285-303.

Sichel, D. (1997). *The computer revolution: An economic perspective.* Washington, DC: Brookings Institution.

Siebert, F. S., Peterson, T., & Schramm, W. (1956). *Four theories of the press.* Urbana: University of Illinois Press.

Signitzer, B. H., & Coombs, W. T. (1992). Public relations and public diplomacy: Conceptual convergences. *Public Relations Review, 18,* 137-147.

Sim, S. (Ed.). (1995). *The A to Z guide to modern literary and cultural theorists.* Englewood Cliffs, NJ: Prentice Hall.

Simmons, R. E. (1990). *Communication campaign management: A systems approach.* New York: Longman.

Simoes, R. P. (1992). Public relations as a political function: A Latin American view. *Public Relations Review, 18,* 189-200.

Simon, R., & Wylie, F. W. (1994). *Cases in public relations management.* Lincolnwood, IL: NTC Business Books.

Simons, H. W. (1970). Requirements, problems, and strategies: A theory of persuasion for social movements. *Quarterly Journal of Speech, 56,* 1-11.

Sims, R. R. (1992). The challenge of ethical behavior in organizations. *Journal of Business Ethics, 11,* 505-513.

Singer, J. L. (1980). The power and limitations of television: A cognitive-affective analysis. In P. H. Tannenbaum (Ed.), *The entertainment functions of television* (pp. 31-65). Hillsdale, NJ: Lawrence Erlbaum.

Singh, J. V. (Ed.). (1990). *Organizational evolution: New directions.* Newbury Park, CA: Sage.

Singh, J. V., & Lumsden, C. J. (1990). Theory and research in organizational ecology. *Annual Review of Sociology, 16,* 161-195.

Singh, J. V., Tucker, D., & House, R. (1986). Organizational legitimacy and the liability of newness. *Administrative Science Quarterly, 31,* 171-193.

Sipple v. Chronicle Publishing Co., 154 Cal. App. 3d 1040 (1984).

Slack, J. (1996). The theory and method of articulation in cultural studies. In D. Morley & K-H. Chen (Eds.), *Stuart Hall: Critical dialogues in cultural studies* (pp. 112-130). New York: Routledge.

Slade, J., Bero, L. A., Hanauer, P., Barnes, D. E., & Glantz, S. A. (1995). Nicotine and addiction: The Brown and Williamson documents. *Journal of the American Medical Association, 274,* 225-233.

Small, W. (1991). Exxon Valdez: How to spend billions and still get a black eye. *Public Relations Review, 17,* 9-26.

Smelser, N. J. (1963). *Theory of collective behavior.* New York: Free Press.

Smethers, S. (1998). Cyberspace in the curricula: New legal and ethical issues. *Journalism and Mass Communication Educator, 52*(4), 15-23.

Smircich, L., & Stubbart, C. (1985). Strategic management in an enacted world. *Academy of Management Review, 10,* 724-736.

Smith, D. (1976). *A study of sports media/sports information director relations in the Southwest Athletic Conference.* Unpublished master's thesis, University of Texas at Austin.

Smith, D. A. (1994, May). *An ethical examination of the A. H. Robins legitimizing strategies during the 21 year Dalkon Shield crisis.* Paper presented at the National Communication Ethics Conference, Gull Lake, MI.

Smith, E. (1993). Changes in the public's political sophistication. In R. G. Niemi & H. F. Weisberg (Eds.), *Controversies in voting behavior* (pp. 99-113). Washington, DC: Congressional Quarterly.

Smith, J. P. (1981). Rethinking the traditional capital campaign. In F. C. Pray (Ed.), *Handbook for educational fund raising: A guide to successful principles and practices for colleges, universities, and schools* (pp. 60-68). San Francisco: Jossey-Bass.

Smith, M. F. (1992). *Public relations as negotiation: Issue definition and development.* Paper presented at the meeting of the National Communication Association, Chicago.

Smith, M. F. (1995). Sane/Freeze, issue status, and rhetorical diversification. In W. N. Elwood (Ed.), *Public relations inquiry as rhetorical criticism* (pp. 191-212). Westport, CT: Praeger.

Smith, M. F. (1996a). *Issue status and social movement organization maintenance: Two case studies in rhetorical diversification.* Unpublished doctoral dissertation, Purdue University.

Smith, M. F. (1996b). *Public relations as a locus for workplace democracy.* Paper presented at the meeting of the National Communication Association, San Diego.

Smith, M. F. (1997). *Public relations from the "bottom-up": Toward a more inclusive view of public relations.* Paper presented at the meeting of the National Communication Association, Chicago.

Smith, P. P., & Schaaf, R. E. (1995). How public relations techniques are used by medical practices in the managed health care marketplace. *Public Relations Quarterly, 40*(4), 19-23.

Smith, R. (1993). *Images of organizational communication: Root-metaphors of the organization-communication relation.* Paper presented at the annual meeting of the International Communication Association, Washington, DC.

Smith, R. C., & Turner, P. (1995). A social constructionist reconfiguration of metaphor analysis: An application of "SCMA" to organizational socialization theorizing. *Communication Monographs, 62,* 152-181.

Smith, S. M., & Alcorn, D. S. (1991). Cause marketing: A new direction in the marketing of corporate responsibility. *Journal of Consumer Marketing, 8*(3), 19-35.

Smoking seen in 17 of 18 movies surveyed. (1997, October 29). *USA Today.* Available: http://167.8.29.16/life/enter/movies/lef451.htm

Snyder, C. R., Higgins, R. L., & Stucky, R. J. (1983). *Excuses: Masquerades in search of grace.* New York: John Wiley.

Soderlund, M. (1990). Business intelligence in the postmodern era. *Marketing Intelligence and Planning, 8,* 7-10.

Sohn, D., & Wall, J. A., Jr. (1993). Community mediation in South Korea: A city-village comparison. *Journal of Conflict Resolution, 37,* 536-543.

Soja, E. (1989). *Postmodern geographies.* London: Verso.

Solberg, R. (1995). Electronic malls match consumers with products. *Interactive Public Relations: Marketing Communications and PR in the Age of Cyberspace, 1*(2), 4-6.

Solomon, M. (1985). The rhetoric of dehumanization: An analysis of medical reports of the Tuskegee Syphilis Project. *Western Journal of Speech Communication, 49,* 233-247.

Solomon, M. B. (1996, Summer). Targeting trendsetters. *Marketing Research: A Magazine of Management & Applications,* pp. 9-11.

Sommerness, M. D., & Beaman, R. (1994). Back to the future: International education in public relations. *Public Relations Review, 20,* 89-95.

Sontag, D. (1999, June 25). Israel, guerrillas trade retaliatory fire. *Miami Herald,* p. A21.

Sorrell, M. (1998). Last word: Assessing the state of public relations. *Public Relations Strategist, 3*(4), 48.

Spangler, E., & Lehman, P. M. (1982). Lawyering as work. In C. Derber (Ed.), *Professionals as workers: Mental labor in advanced capitalism* (pp. 63-99). Boston: G. K. Hall.

Sparks, S. D. (1993). Public relations: Is it dangerous to use the term? *Public Relations Quarterly, 38*(3), 27-28.

Spath, P. L. (Ed.). (1989). *Innovations in health care quality measurement.* Chicago: American Hospital Publishing.

Spicer, C. (1997). *Organizational public relations: A political perspective.* Mahwah, NJ: Lawrence Erlbaum.

Spiegel's Eddie Bauer February sales down. (1998, March 5). *Reuters* [newswire].

Spragens, T. A. (1995). Communitarian liberalism. In A. Etzioni (Ed.), *New communitarian thinking: Persons, virtues, institutions, and communities* (pp. 37-51). Charlottesville: University Press of Virginia.

Springston, J. K. (1997a). Application of public relations theory to breast cancer screening: A worksite study. In J. Biberman & A. Alkhafaji (Eds.), *Business research yearbook: Global business perspectives* (pp. 762-766). Slippery Rock, PA: International Academy of Business Disciplines.

Springston, J. K. (1997b). Assessing the group field. In J. Biberman & A. Alkhafaji (Eds.), *Business research yearbook: Global business perspectives* (pp. 767-771). Slippery Rock, PA: International Academy of Business Disciplines.

Springston, J. K., & Brown, J. W. (1998, April). *Using public relations field dyanimcs in risk communication.* Paper presented at the meeting of the American Society for Business and Behavioral Sciences, Las Vegas, NV.

Springston, J. K., & Keyton, J. (1996). *Crisis management and the role of the group field.* Paper presented at the meeting of the Speech Communication Association, Public Relations Division, San Diego.

Springston, J. K., Keyton, J., Leichty, G. B., & Metzger, J. (1992). Field dynamics and public relations theory: Toward the management of multiple publics. *Journal of Public Relations Research, 4,* 81-100.

Sproule, J. M. (1988). The new managerial rhetoric and the old criticism. *Quarterly Journal of Speech, 74,* 468-486.

Sproule, J. M. (1990). Organizational rhetoric and the rational-democratic society. *Journal of Applied Communication Research, 18,* 129-140.

Sriramesh, K. (1992a). *The impact of societal culture on public relations: An ethnographic study of South Indian organizations.* Unpublished doctoral dissertation, University of Maryland, College Park.

Sriramesh, K. (1992b). Societal culture and public relations: Ethnographic evidence from India. *Public Relations Review, 18,* 201-211.

Sriramesh, K. (1996). Power distance and public relations: An ethnographic study of Southern Indian organizations. In H. M. Culbertson & N. Chen (Eds.), *International public relations: A comparative analysis* (pp. 171-190). Mahwah, NJ: Lawrence Erlbaum.

Sriramesh, K., Grunig, J. E., & Dozier, D. M. (1996). Observation and measurement of two dimensions of organizational culture and their relationships to public relations. *Journal of Public Relations Research, 8,* 229-262.

Sriramesh, K., & White, J. (1992). Societal cultural and public relations. In J. E. Grunig (Ed.), *Excellence in public relations and communication management* (pp. 597-614). Hillsdale, NJ: Lawrence Erlbaum.

Staats, A. W., & Staats, C. K. (1958). Attitudes established by classical conditioning. *Journal of Abnormal and Social Psychology, 57,* 37-40.

Stacey, R. D. (1996a). *Complexity and creativity in organizations.* San Francisco: Berrett-Koehler.

Stacey, R. D. (1996b). Emerging strategies in a complex environment. *Long Range Planning, 29,* 182-183.

Stacks, D. W., & Wright, D. K. (1989). A quantitative examination of ethical dilemmas in public relations. *Journal of Mass Media Ethics, 4,* 53-67.

Staff. (1994). *A report to the people of Shell Oil.* Houston, TX: Shell Oil Company.

Staff. (1995). *Zhongsuan Daxue Gonggong Guanxi Zhuanye Jianjie* [Zhongshan University: Its public relations curriculum]. Zhongshan, China: Zhongshan University Press.

Stafford, L., & Canary, D. J. (1991). Maintenance strategies and romantic relationship type, gender, and relational characteristics. *Journal of Social and Personal Relationships, 8,* 217-242.

Stahl, L. (1998, June 28). *The rumor mill: The Internet may contain many rumors and conspiracies which may look like fact to the casual observer* (CBS News transcript). Boston: Burrelle's Information Services.

Stanton, E. M. (1991). PR's future is here: Worldwide, integrated communications. *Public Relations Quarterly, 36*(1), 46-47.

Starr, P. (1982). *The social transformation of American medicine.* New York: Basic Books.

Stateman, A. (1998, May). PR agencies are getting wired. *Public Relations Tactics,* p. 8.

Stauber, J., & Rampton, S. (1995). *Toxic sludge is good for you! Lies, damn lies, and the public relations industry.* Monroe, ME: Common Courage Press.

Staw, B. (1980). Rationality and justification in organizational life. In L. Cummings & B. Staw (Eds.), *Research in organizational behavior* (Vol. 2, pp. 45-80). Greenwich, CT: JAI.

Staw, B., Sandelands, L., & Dutton, J. (1981). Threat rigidity effects in organizational behavior: A multilevel analysis. *Administrative Science Quarterly, 26,* 501-524.

Stempel, G. H., III, & Hargrove, T. (1996). Mass media audiences in a changing media environment. *Journalism & Mass Communication Quarterly, 73,* 549-558.

Stephens, M. (1998). Which communications revolution is it anyway? *Journalism & Mass Communication Quarterly, 75,* 13-19.

Stern, B. B. (1994). A revised communication model for advertising: Multiple dimensions of the source, the message, and the recipient. *Journal of Advertising, 13*(2), 5-15.

Stern, R. (1994, March). *The fundamental agreement between the Holy See and the state of Israel.* Speech delivered at the conference, "The Road to Peace: The Challenge of the Middle East," Miami, FL.

Stewart, C. J. (1980). A functional approach to the rhetoric of social movements. *Central States Speech Journal, 31,* 298-305.

Stewart, C. J., Smith, C. A., & Denton, R. E., Jr. (1994). *Persuasion and social movements* (3rd ed.). Prospect Heights, IL: Waveland.

Stewart, L. J. (1988). Women in foundation and corporate public relations. *Public Relations Review, 14*(3), 20-23.

Stocker, K. P. (1997). A strategic approach to crisis management. In C. L. Caywood (Ed.), *The handbook of strategic public relations and integrated communications* (pp. 189-203). New York: McGraw-Hill.

Stone, A. (1997). Foreword. In D. Zohar (Ed.), *Rewiring the corporate brain: Using the new science to rethink how we structure and lead organizations* (pp. ix-xiv). San Francisco: Berrett-Koehler.

Stones, R. (1991). Strategic context analysis: A new research strategy for structuration theory. *Sociology, 25,* 673-695.

Stout, D. G. (1951). The citizen's corner. *Journal of Education, 56*(1), 204.

Stratton Oakmont Inc. v. Prodigy Service Co., W.L. 323710 (N.Y. Sup. Ct. 1995).

Strenski, J., & Yue, K. (1998). China: The world's next public relations superpower. *Public Relations Quarterly, 43*(2), 24-26.

Stromberg v. California, 283 U.S. 359 (1931).

Strong, E. K. (1925). *The psychology of selling.* New York: McGraw-Hill.

Suchman, M. C. (1995). Managing legitimacy: Strategic and institutional approaches. *Academy of Management Review, 20,* 571-610.

Sullivan, A. J. (1965a). Toward a philosophy of public relations: Images. In O. Lerbinger & A. J. Sullivan (Eds.), *Information, influence, and communication: A reader in public relations* (pp. 240-249). New York: Basic Books.

Sullivan, A. J. (1965b). Values of public relations. In O. Lerbinger & A. Sullivan (Eds.), *Information, influence, and communication: A reader in public relations* (pp. 412-439). New York: Basic Books.

Sullivan, W. M. (1986). *Reconstructing public philosophy.* Berkeley: University of California Press.

Suppe, F. (1977). *The structure of scientific theories* (2nd ed.). Urbana: University of Illinois Press.

Survey sheds new light on why clients hire and keep PR firms. (1996, November). *Public Relations Tactics,* p. 4.

Susskind, L., & Field, P. (1996). *Dealing with an angry public: The mutual gains approach to resolving disputes.* New York: Free Press.

Sutula, D. A. (1981). Community education as a communications tool. *Public Relations Journal, 37*(2), 27-28.

Sweeney, P. (1994, April 3). Polishing the tarnished image of investor relations executives. *The New York Times,* p. F5.

Sweep, D., Cameron, G. T., & Weaver Lariscy, R. (1994). Rethinking constraints on public relations practice. *Public Relations Review, 20,* 319-331.

Swift, P. (1997). How to become a first-rate crap detector. [review of the book *The New DoubleSpeak*]. *Public Relations Quarterly, 42*(2), 3-4.

Synnott, G., & McKie, D. (1997). International issues in PR: Researching and prioritizing priorities. *Journal of Public Relations Research, 9,* 259-282.

Sypher, B. D. (Ed.). (1990). *Case studies in organizational communication.* New York: Guilford.

Sypher, B. D. (Ed.). (1997). *Case studies in organizational communication 2: Perspectives on contemporary work life.* New York: Guilford.

Tabris, M. D. (1984). Crisis management. In B. Cantor (Ed.), *Experts in action: Inside public relations* (pp. 57-73). New York: Longman.

Tallents, S. (1955). *The projection of England.* London: Olen Press. (Original work published 1932)

Taller & Cooper v. Illuminating Electric Co., 172 F. 2d 625 (1949).

Talley v. California, 362 U.S. 60 (1960).

Tam, S. Y., Dozier, D. M., Lauzen, M. M., & Real, M. R. (1995). The impact of superior-subordinate gender on the career advancement of public relations practitioners. *Journal of Public Relations Research, 7,* 231-258.

Tan, A. S. (1985). *Mass communication theories and research* (2nd ed.). New York: John Wiley.

Tapsell, S. (1998, May). Brickless banks. *New Zealand Management,* pp. 38-40.

Tarbell, I. (1904). *A history of the Standard Oil Company.* New York: McClure, Phillips.

Tarde, G. (1903). *The laws of imitation.* New York: Holt.

Tavuchis, N. (1991). *Mea culpa: A sociology of apology and reconciliation.* Stanford, CA: Stanford University Press.

Taylor, C. (1985a). Atomism. In C. Taylor (Ed.), *Philosophy and the human sciences: Philosophical papers* (pp. 187-210). Cambridge, UK: Cambridge University Press.

Taylor, C. (1985b). The diversity of goods. In C. Taylor (Ed.), *Philosophy and the human sciences: Philosophical papers* (pp. 230-247). Cambridge, UK: Cambridge University Press.

Taylor, C. (1989a). Cross-purposes: The liberal-communitarian debate. In N. L. Rosenbloom (Ed.), *Liberalism and the moral life* (pp. 159-182). Cambridge, MA: Harvard University Press.

Taylor, C. (1989b). *Sources of the self: The making of the modern identity.* Cambridge, MA: Harvard University Press.

Taylor, C. (1992). *Multiculturalism and the politics of recognition.* Princeton, NJ: Princeton University Press.

Taylor, C. (1994). Justice after virtue. In J. Horton & S. Mendus (Eds.), *After MacIntyre: Critical perspectives on the work of Alasdair MacIntyre* (pp. 16-43). Notre Dame, IN: University of Notre Dame Press.

Taylor, C. (1995). Liberal politics and the public sphere. In A. Etzioni (Ed.), *New communitarian thinking: Persons, virtues, institutions, and communities* (pp. 183-217). Charlottesville: University Press of Virginia.

Taylor, D. A., & Altman, I. (1987). Communication in interpersonal relationships: Social penetration processes. In M. E. Roloff & G. R. Miller (Eds.), *Interpersonal processes: New directions in communication research* (pp. 257-277). Newbury Park, CA: Sage.

Taylor, J. R., & Cooren, F. (1997). What makes communication "organizational"? How the many voices of a collectivity become the one voice of an organization. *Journal of Pragmatics, 27,* 409-438.

Taylor, J. R., Cooren, F., Giroux, N., & Robichaud, D. (1996). The communicational basis of organization: Between the conversation and the text. *Communication Theory, 6,* 1-39.

Taylor, M. (1998). Strategic management of communication: An analysis of campaign planner intent in Malaysia. In L. C. Lederman (Ed.), *Communication theory: A reader* (pp. 267-274). Dubuque, IA: Kendall/Hunt.

Taylor, M., & Botan, C. H. (1997). Public relations campaigns for national development in the Pacific Rim: The case of public education in Malaysia. *Australian Journal of Communication, 24*(3), 115-130.

Taylor, M., & Kent, M. L. (1999). Challenging assumptions in international public relations: When government is the most important public. *Public Relations Review, 25,* 131-144.

Taylor, O. L. (1989, August). *The education of journalists and mass communications for the 21st century: A cultural perspective.* Paper presented at the meeting of the Association for Education in Journalism and Mass Communication, Washington, DC.

Tedesco, J. C., McKinnon, L. M., & Kaid, L. L. (1996). Advertising watchdogs: A content analysis of print and broadcast adwatches. *Press/Politics, 1*(4), 76-93.

Tedesco, J. C., Miller, J. L., & Spiker, J. (1999). Presidential campaigning on the information superhighway: An exploration of content and form. In L. L. Kaid & D. Bystrom (Eds.), *The electronic election* (pp. 51-64). Hillsdale, NJ: Lawrence Erlbaum.

Tedesco, R. (1996, October 28). World Wide Web: Established media are searching for the unique identity that is cyberspace. *Broadcasting & Cable,* pp. 30-32.

Tedlow, R. S. (1979). *Keeping the corporate image: Public relations and business, 1900-1950.* Greenwich, CT: JAI.

Teinowitz, I. (1996, June 10). FTC chairman seeking voluntary Web rules. *Advertising Age,* p. 42.

Tesh, S. (1984). In support of "single-issue" politics. *Political Science Quarterly, 99,* 27-44.

Thayer, L. (1968). *Communication and communication systems.* Homewood, IL: Irwin.

The Internet's continued impact. (1998, June). *Public Relations Tactics,* p. 8.

Theus, K. T. (1995, May). *To whom is moral duty owed? Obligation, blame, and publics.* Paper presented at the meeting of the International Communication Association, Albuquerque, NM.

Thomas, A. S., & Simerly, R. L. (1994). The chief executive officer and corporate social performance: An interdisciplinary examination. *Journal of Business Ethics, 13,* 959-968.

Thomas, J. (1996). Introduction: A debate about the ethics of fair practices for collecting social science data in cyberspace. *The Information Society, 12,* 107-117.

Thomas, K. (1976). Conflict and conflict management. In M. Dunnette (Ed.), *Handbook of industrial and organizational psychology* (pp. 889-936). Chicago: Rand McNally.

Thompson, J. (1995). *The media and modernity: A social theory of the media.* Stanford, CA: Stanford University Press.

Thompson, M. (1982). The problem of the center: An autonomous cosmology. In M. Douglas (Ed.), *Essays in the sociology of perception* (pp. 302-328). London: Routledge & Kegan Paul.

Thompson, M., Ellis, R., & Wildavsky, A. (1990). *Cultural theory.* Boulder, CO: Westview.

Thomsen, S. R. (1995). Using online databases in corporate issues management. *Public Relations Review, 21,* 103-122.

Thomsen, S. R. (1997). Public relations in the new millennium: Understanding the forces that are reshaping the profession. *Public Relations Quarterly, 42*(1), 11-17.

Thorson, E., & Moore, J. (1996). *Integrated communication: Synergy of persuasive voices.* Mahwah, NJ: Lawrence Erlbaum.

Thyfault, M. (1991, September 23). Reliability ruckus: Latest outage reaffirms cry for network reliability standards. *Information Week,* p. 40.

Thyfault, M., Bartholomew, D., & Violino, B. (1991, September 30). AT&T approves backup plan. *Information Week,* p. 15.

Thyfault, M., Medina, D., & Hoffman, T. (1991, September 23). Strike three: AT&T outage hits New York. *Information Week,* pp. 12-13.

Tichenor, P. J., Donohue, G. A., & Olien, C. N. (1970). Mass media flow and differential growth in knowledge. *Public Opinion Quarterly, 34,* 159-170.

Tiffen, R. (1989). *News and power.* Sydney, Australia: Allen & Unwin.

Toch, H. (1965). *The social psychology of social movements.* Indianapolis, IN: Bobbs-Merrill.

Tolbert, P. S., & Moen, P. (1998). Men's and women's definitions of "good jobs": Similarities and differences by age and across time. *Work and Occupations, 25*(2), 168-194.

Tomlinson, J. (1991). *Cultural imperialism: A critical introduction.* Baltimore, MD: Johns Hopkins University Press.

Tortorello, N. J., & Wilhelm, E. (1993). Salary survey. *Public Relations Journal, 49*(7), 10-19.

Toth, E. L. (1987). Making peace with gender issues in public relations. *Public Relations Review, 14*(3), 36-47.

Toth, E. L. (1992). The case for pluralistic studies on public relations: Rhetorical, critical, and systems perspectives. In E. L. Toth & R. L. Heath (Eds.), *Rhetorical and critical approaches to public relations* (pp. 3-15). Hillsdale, NJ: Lawrence Erlbaum.

Toth, E. L. (1995, November). *Interpersonal communication and organizational communication: Contributions to the study and practice of public relations.* Paper presented at the meeting of the Speech Communication Association, San Antonio, TX.

Toth, E. L. (1996). Confronting the reality of the gender gap. *Public Relations Strategist, 2*(3), 51-53.

Toth, E. L., & Cline, C. G. (Eds.). (1989). *Beyond the velvet ghetto.* San Francisco: IABC Foundation.

Toth, E. L., & Cline, C. G. (1991). Public relations attitudes toward gender issues: A benchmark study. *Public Relations Review, 17,* 161-174.

Toth, E. L., & Grunig, L. A. (1993). The missing story of women in public relations. *Journal of Public Relations Research, 5,* 153-175.

Toth, E. L., & Heath, R. L. (Eds.). (1992). *Rhetorical and critical approaches to public relations.* Hillsdale, NJ: Lawrence Erlbaum.

Toth, E. L., Serini, S. A., Wright, D. K., & Emig, A. G. (1998). Trends of public relations roles: 1990-1995. *Public Relations Review, 24,* 145-163.

Toulmin, S. (1958). *The uses of argument.* Cambridge, UK: Cambridge University Press.

Towl, A. R. (1969). *To study administration by cases.* Boston: Harvard University, School of Business Administration.

Traub, J. (1996). Can associations of businesses be true community-builders? *The Responsive Community, 6*(2), 29-38.

Trenholm, S., & Jensen, A. (1996). *Interpersonal communication* (3rd ed.). Belmont, CA: Wadsworth.

Trent, J. D., & Trent, J. S. (1982). Speech communication and public relations: The prospect for the 1980's. *Association for Communication Administration Bulletin, 42,* 50-52.

Trent, J. S., & Trent, J. D. (1976). Public relations education: An opportunity for speech communication. *Communication Education, 25,* 292-298.

Troutwine, J. T. (1990). Management liability: A growing crisis. *Foundary Management & Technology, 118*(3), 41-42.

Trudel, M. R. (1991). Consumer marketing synergy: PR comes of age. *Public Relations Quarterly, 36*(1), 18-19.

Tuchman, G. (1978). *Making news: A study in the construction of reality.* New York: Free Press.

Tuckman, B. (1965). Developmental sequence in small groups. *Psychological Bulletin, 63,* 384-389.

Tuckman, B. W., & Jensen, M. A. C. (1977). Stages of small-group development revisited. *Group & Organization Studies, 2,* 419-427.

Tuggle, C. A., & Sneed, D. (1998). Faculty in professional programs: The mix of experience and degrees. *Journalism & Mass Communication Educator, 53,* 14-22.

Turk, J. V. (1986). *Information subsidies and media content: A case study of public relations influence on the news* (Journalism Monographs, No. 100). Columbia, SC: Association for Education in Journalism and Mass Communication.

Turk, J. V. (1989). Management skills need to be taught in public relations. *Public Relations Review, 15*(1), 38-52.

Turk, J. V. (1996). Romania: From publicitate past to public relations future. In H. M. Culbertson & N. Chen (Eds.), *International public relations: A comparative analysis* (pp. 341-348). Mahwah, NJ: Lawrence Erlbaum.

Turnbull, N. (1996). *The millennium edge: Prospering with Generation MM.* Sydney, Australia: Allen & Unwin.

Turner, B. (1976). The organizational and interorganizational development of disasters. *Administrative Science Quarterly, 21,* 378-397.

Tyler, L. (1997). Liability means never being able to say you're sorry: Corporate guilt, legal constraints, and defensiveness in corporate communication. *Management Communication Quarterly, 11,* 51-73.

Tymson, C. L., & Sherman, B. (1996a). *The new Australian and New Zealand public relations manual.* Birkenhead, New Zealand: Millennium Books.

Tymson, C. L., & Sherman, B. (1996b). *The new Australian public relations manual* (3rd ed.). Sydney, Australia: Millennium Books.

U.S. Department of Commerce. (1998). *Statistical abstract of the United States, 1998: The national data book* (117th ed.). Washington, DC: Government Printing Office.

U.S. House of Representatives. (1988). *Hearings before the Subcommittee on Transportation, Tourism, and Hazardous Materials of the Committee on Energy and Commerce regarding cleanup at federal facilities* (Serial No. 100-201). Washington, DC: Government Printing Office.

U.S. Postal Service v. Council of Greenburgh Civic Associations, 453 U.S. 114 (1981).

U.S. Senate. (1985). *Hearing before the Subcommittee on Energy, Nuclear Proliferation, and Government Processes of the Committee on Governmental Affairs regarding management and operation of the U.S. Department of Energy's Fernald, OH, Feed Materials Production Center* (Senate Hearing 99-00). Washington, DC: Government Printing Office.

Udwadia, F. E., & Mitroff, I. I. (1991). Crisis management and the organizational mind: Multiple models for crisis management from field data. *Technological Forecasting and Social Change, 40,* 33-52.

Ulfelder, S. (1997, July 14). Lies, damn lies, and the Internet. *Computerworld,* pp. 75-77.

United Butane Sales Inc. v. Bessemer-Suburban Gas Co., 281 Ala. 664 (1968).

Valazquez, N. M. (1997, August 20). *Insensitivity can be very costly* [congressional press release]. Washington, DC: Federal Document Clearing House.

Van Buren, H. J., III. (1995). Business ethics for the new millennium. *Business and Society Review, 93,* 51-55.

Van der Meiden, A. (1993). Public relations and "other" modalities of professional communication: Asymmetric presuppositions for a new theoretical discussion. *International Public Relations Review, 16*(3), 8-11.

Van der Straten Waillet, C. (1989). Lobbying in the European Community: An address to the 11th Public Relations World Congress, Melbourne, April 1988. *International Public Relations Review, 12*(3), 10-16.

Van Leuven, J. K. (1980). Measuring values through public participation. *Public Relations Review, 6*(1), 51-56.

Van Leuven, J. K. (1986, August). *A planning matrix for message design, channel selection, and scheduling.* Paper presented at the meeting of the Association for Education in Journalism and Mass Communication, Norman, OK.

Van Leuven, J. K. (1996). Public relations in South East Asia from nation-building campaigns to regional interdependence. In H. M. Culbertson & N. Chen (Eds.), *International public relations: A comparative analysis* (pp. 207-222). Mahwah, NJ: Lawrence Erlbaum.

Van Leuven, J. K., O'Keefe, G., & Salmon, C. (1988, July). *Effects-based planning for public relations campaigns.* Paper presented at the meeting of the Association for Education in Journalism and Mass Communication, Public Relations division, Portland, OR.

Van Leuven, J. K., & Pratt, C. B. (1996). Public relations' role: Realities in Asia and in Africa south of the Sahara. In H. M. Culbertson & N. Chen (Eds.), *International public relations: A comparative analysis* (pp. 93-106). Mahwah, NJ: Lawrence Erlbaum.

Van Maanen, J. (1988). *Tales from the field: On writing ethnography.* Chicago: University of Chicago Press.

Van Patten, J. (1996). *The culture of higher education: A case study approach.* Lanham, MD: University Press of America.

Van Zoonen, L. (1994). *Feminist media studies.* London: Sage.

Vasquez, G. M. (1993). A homo narrens paradigm for public relations: Combining Bormann's symbolic convergence theory and Grunig's situational theory of publics. *Journal of Public Relations Research, 5*(3) 201-216.

Vasquez, G. M. (1994). Testing a communication theory-method-message-behavior complex for the investigation of publics. *Journal of Public Relations Research, 6,* 291-316.

Vasquez, G. M. (1995). *Perspectives on "the public": A communication reformulation.* Paper presented at the Speech Communication Convention, San Antonio, TX.

Vasquez, G. M. (1996). Public relations as negotiation: An issue development perspective. *Journal of Public Relations Research, 8,* 57-77.

Vasquez, G. M., & Taylor, M. (1999). What cultural values influence American practitioners? *Public Relations Review, 25*(4), 433-449.

Vaughan, D. (1996). *The Challenger launch decision: Risky technology, culture, and deviance at NASA.* Chicago: University of Chicago Press.

Verba, S., & Nie, N. H. (1993). The rationality of political activity. In R. G. Niemi & H. F. Weisberg (Eds.), *Classics in voting behavior* (pp. 24-42). Washington, DC: Congressional Quarterly.

Vercic, D. (1997). Toward fourth wave public relations: A case study. In D. Moss, T. MacManus, & D. Vercic (Eds.), *Public relations research: An international perspective* (pp. 264-279). London: International Thomson Business Press.

Vercic, D., Grunig, L. A., & Grunig, J. E. (1996). Global and specific principles of public relations: Evidence from Slovenia. In H. M. Culbertson & N. Chen (Eds.), *International public relations: A comparative analysis* (pp. 31-66). Mahwah, NJ: Lawrence Erlbaum.

Vernon, P. E., & Allport, G. W. (1931). A test for personal values. *Journal of Abnormal and Social Psychology, 26,* 231-248.

Verschaffel, B., & Verminck, M. (1993). *Zoology on (post)modern animals.* Dublin, Ireland: Lilliput Press.

Vibbert, S. L. (1987, May). *Corporate discourse and issue management.* Paper presented at the meeting of the International Communication Association, Montreal.

Vinson, D., Scott, J. E., & Lamont, L. (1977). The role of personal values in marketing and consumer behavior. *Journal of Marketing, 41,* 44-50.

Vollmer, H. M., & Mills, D. L. (Eds.). (1966). *Professionalization.* Englewood Cliffs, NJ: Prentice Hall.

Von Neumann, J., & Morgenstern, O. (1944). *Theory of games and economic behavior.* Princeton, NJ: Princeton University Press.

Wagatsuma, H., & Rosett, A. (1986). The implications of apology: Law and culture in Japan and the United States. *Law & Society Review, 20,* 461-498.

Wakefield, R. I. (1996). Interdisciplinary theoretical foundations for international public relations. In H. M. Culbertson & N. Chen (Eds.), *International public relations: A comparative analysis* (pp. 17-30). Mahwah, NJ: Lawrence Erlbaum.

Wakefield, R. I. (1997). *International public relations: A theoretical approach to excellence based on a worldwide Delphi study.* Unpublished doctoral dissertation, University of Maryland, College Park.

Walker, A. (1987). The good that they do: The case for corporate in-kind contributions. *Public Relations Quarterly, 32*(2), 15-20.

Walker, A. (1988). *The public relations body of knowledge.* New York: Foundation for Public Relations Research and Education.

Wall, J. A., Jr., & Blum, M. (1991). Community mediation in the People's Republic of China. *Journal of Conflict Resolution, 35,* 3-20.

Wallace, K. R. (1963). The substance of rhetoric: Good reasons. *Quarterly Journal of Speech, 49,* 239-249.

Wallack, L., Dorfman, L., Jernigan, D., & Themba, M. (1993). *Media advocacy and public health: Power for prevention.* Newbury Park, CA: Sage.

Walsh, F. D. (1988). *Public relations and the law.* New York: Foundation for Public Relations Research and Education.

Walzer, M. (1995). The communitarian critique of liberalism. In A. Etzioni (Ed.), *New communitarian thinking: Persons, virtues, institutions, and communities* (pp. 52-70). Charlottesville: University Press of Virginia.

Wang, C. (1992). Lun Putong Cenci de Gongguang Jiaoyu [A look at different types of public relations training and education]. In J. Din (Ed.), *Gonggong Guanxi yi Gaigei Kaifang* [Public relations and reforms] (pp. 43-58). Anhui, China: Anhui People's Publisher.

Wang, J. (1997). *Becoming global, becoming local: The multinatonal advertising industry in China.* Unpublished doctoral dissertation, University of Iowa.

Ware, B. L., & Linkugel, W. A. (1973). They spoke in defense of themselves: On the generic criticism of apologia. *Quarterly Journal of Speech, 59,* 273-283.

Warneke, K. (1998, March). Why can't we be friends? Two health care organizations come together. *Public Relations Tactics,* pp. 20-21.

Warner, G. (1996). The development of public relations offices at American colleges and universities. *Public Relations Quarterly, 41*(2), 36-39.

Wartick, S. L., & Cochran, P. L. (1985). The evolution of the corporate social performance model. *Academy of Management Review, 10,* 758-769.

Wasson, C. R. (1983). *Marketing management: The strategy, tactics, and art of competition.* Charlotte, NC: ECR Associates.

Watson, C. E. (1991). Managing with integrity: Social responsibilities of business as seen by America's CEOs. *Business Horizons, 34*(4), 99-109.

Watson, T. (1993). Output measures rule in evaluation debate. *IPR Journal, 12*(5), 13-14.

Watson, T. (1994, July). *Public relations evaluation: Nationwide survey of practice in the United Kingdom.* Paper presented at the International Public Relations Research Symposium, Bled, Slovenia.

Watson, T. (1995, July). *Evaluating public relations: Models of measurement for public relations practice.* Paper presented at the International Public Relations Research Symposium, Bled, Slovenia.

Weaver, R. M. (1953). *The ethics of rhetoric.* Chicago: Henry Regnery.

Weaver, R. M. (1970). *Language is sermonic* (R. L. Johannsen, R. Strickland, & R. T. Eubanks, Eds.). Baton Rouge: Louisiana State University Press.

Webcasting: Internet videoconferences come of age. (1998, June). *Public Relations Tactics,* p. 20.

Weber, J. (1993). Exploring the relationship between personal values and moral reasoning. *Human Relations, 46,* 435-463.

Weber, T. E. (1998, April 16). Who, what, where: Putting the Internet in perspective. *The Wall Street Journal,* p. B12.

Wee, C. H., Tan, S., & Chew, K. (1996). Organizational response to public relations: An empirical study of firms in Singapore. *Public Relations Review, 22,* 259-277.

Weick, K. E. (1979). *The social psychology of organizing.* Reading, MA: Addison-Wesley.

Weick, K. E. (1987). Theorizing about organizational communication. In F. M. Jablin, L. L. Putnam, K. H. Roberts, & L. W. Porter (Eds.), *Handbook of organizational communication: An interdisciplinary perspective* (pp. 97-122). Newbury Park, CA: Sage.

Weick, K. E. (1988). Enacted sensemaking in crisis situations. *Journal of Management Studies, 25,* 305-317.

Weick, K. E. (1995). *Sensemaking in organizations.* Thousand Oaks, CA: Sage.

Weick, K. E. (1996). Speaking to practice: The scholarship of integration. *Journal of Management Inquiry, 5,* 251-260.

Weinberg, S. (1994). *Dreams of a final theory.* New York: Vintage Books.

Weiner, B., Perry, R. P., & Magnusson, J. (1988). An attribution analysis of reactions to stigmas. *Journal of Personality and Social Psychology, 55,* 738-748.

Weiner, R. (1996). *Webster's new world dictionary of media and communications* (rev. ed.). New York: Macmillan.

Weiss, C. H. (1977). *Evaluation research: Methods of assessing program effectiveness.* Englewood Cliffs, NJ: Prentice Hall.

Wellman, B., & Tindall, D. (1993). How telephone networks connect social networks. In W. D. Richards, Jr., & G. Barnett (Eds.), *Progress in Communication Sciences* (Vol. 12, pp. 63-94). Norwood, NJ: Ablex.

Wells, M. (1993, November 15). Tums to offer half-hour calcium "documercial." *Advertising Age, p. 12.*

Wenner, L. A. (1986). Model specification and theoretical development in gratifications sought and obtained research: A comparison of discrepancy and transactional approaches. *Communication Monographs, 53,* 160-179.

West, D. M. (1993). *Air wars: Television advertising in election campaigns, 1952-1992.* Washington, DC: Congressional Quarterly.

West Glen Communications. (1991, May 6). *Survey of news directors/assignment editors by West Glen Communications, Inc.* [news release].

What next, now that tactical PR has become a commodity? (1998, May 11). *PR Reporter,* pp. 1-2.

Wheatley, M. J. (1994). *Leadership and the new science: Learning about organization from an orderly universe.* San Francisco: Berrett-Koehler.

Wheelan, S. A., & Hochberger, J. M. (1996). Validation studies of the Group Development Questionnaire. *Small Group Research, 27,* 143-170.

Wheelan, S. A., & Kaeser, R. M. (1997). The influence of task type and designated leaders on developmental patterns in groups. *Small Group Research, 28,* 94-121.

Whipp, R. (1996). Creative deconstruction: Strategy and organizations. In S. Clegg, C. Hardy, & W. Nord (Eds.), *Handbook of organization studies* (pp. 261-275). Thousand Oaks, CA: Sage.

White, A. J. S. (1965). *The British Council: The first 25 years, 1934-59.* London: British Council.

White, H. (1987). *The content of the form: Narrative discourse and historical representation.* Baltimore, MD: Johns Hopkins University Press.

White, H. C. (1981). Where do markets come from? *American Journal of Sociology, 87,* 517-547.

White, J. (1988). The vantage point problem of public relations. *Public Relations Review, 14*(2), 3-11.

White, J. (1990). *Evaluation in public relations practice.* London: Cranfield Institute of Management/Public Relations Consultants Association.

White, J. (1991). *How to understand and manage public relations.* London: Business Books.

White, J., & Blamphin, J. (1994). *Priorities for research into public relations practice in the United Kingdom.* London: City University Business School/Rapier Marketing.

White, J., & Dozier, D. M. (1992). Public relations and management decision making. In J. E. Grunig (Ed.), *Excellence in public relations and communication management* (pp. 91-107). Hillsdale, NJ: Lawrence Erlbaum.

White, W. (1961). *Beyond conformity.* New York: Free Press.

Whitehead, H. (1933). Salesmanship in the public service: Scope and technique. *Public Administration, 11,* 267-276.

Whitely, P. L. (1933). A study of the Allport-Vernon test for personal values. *Journal of Abnormal and Social Psychology, 28,* 6-13.

Whitely, P. L. (1938). The constancy of personal values. *Journal of Abnormal and Social Psychology, 33*, 405-408.

Wholey, D. R., & Brittain, J. W. (1986). Organizational ecology: Findings and implications. *Academy of Management Review, 11*, 513-533.

Whyte, W. F. (1943). *Street corner society: The social structure of an Italian slum.* Chicago: University of Chicago Press.

Wiio, O. (1979). *Contingencies of organizational communication: Studies in organization and organizational communication.* Helsinki, Finland: Helsinki School of Economics.

Wilcox, D. L., Ault, P. H., & Agee, W. K. (1989). *Public relations: Strategies and tactics* (2nd ed.). New York: HarperCollins.

Wilcox, D. L., Ault, P. H., & Agee, W. K. (1992). *Public relations strategies and tactics* (3rd ed.). New York: HarperCollins.

Wilcox, D. L., Ault, P. H., & Agee, W. K. (1995). *Public relations: Strategies and tactics* (4th ed.). New York: HarperCollins.

Wilcox, D. L., Ault, P. H., & Agee, W. K. (1998). *Public relations strategies and tactics* (5th ed.). Reading, MA: Addison-Wesley.

Wildavsky, A. (1987). Choosing preferences by constructing institutions: A cultural theory of preference formation. *American Political Science Review, 81*, 3-21.

Wilder, R. H., & Buell, K. L. (1923). *Publicity: A manual for the use of business, civic, and social organizations.* New York: Ronald Press.

Wilensky, H. L. (1964). The professionalization of everyone? *American Journal of Sociology, 70*, 137-158.

Wilke, J. R. (1998, June 26). Who owns the name "Internet Explorer"? (hint: not Microsoft). *The Wall Street Journal*, pp. A1, A6.

Wilkins, H. (1991). Computer talk: Long-distance conversations by computer. *Written Communication, 8*(1), 56-78.

Williams, D. E., & Olaniran, B. A. (1994). Exxon's decision-making flaws: The hypervigilant response to the Valdez grounding. *Public Relations Review, 20*, 5-18.

Williams, D. E., & Treadaway, G. (1992). Exxon and the Valdez accident: A failure in crisis communication. *Communication Studies, 43*, 56-64.

Williams, M. J. (1986, June 9). How to cash in on do-good pitches. *Fortune*, pp. 71-72, 76, 80.

Williams, S. L., & Moffitt, M. A. (1997). Corporate image as an impression formation process: Prioritizing personal, organizational, and environmental audience factors. *Journal of Public Relations Research, 9*, 237-258.

Willnat, L., He, Z., & Xiaoming, H. (1997). Foreign media exposure and perceptions of Americans in Hong Kong, Shenzhen, and Singapore. *Journalism & Mass Communication Quarterly, 74*, 738-756.

Wilson, L. J. (1990). Corporate issues management: An international view. *Public Relations Review, 16*, 40-51.

Wilson, L. J. (1994). Excellent companies and coalition-building among the Fortune 500: A value and relationship-based theory. *Public Relations Review, 20*, 333-343.

Wilson, L. J. (1995). *Strategic program planning for effective public relations campaigns.* Dubuque, IA: Kendall/Hunt.

Wilson, L. J. (1996). Strategic cooperative communities: A synthesis of strategic issue management and relationship-building approaches in public relations. In H. M. Culbertson & N. Chen (Eds.), *International public relations: A comparative analysis* (pp. 67-80). Mahwah, NJ: Lawrence Erlbaum.

Wilson, L. J. (1997). *Strategic program planning for effective public relations campaigns* (2nd ed.). Dubuque, IA: Kendall/Hunt.

Wilson, R., & Dissanayake, W. (Eds.). (1996). *Global/local: Cultural production and the transnational imaginary.* Durham, NC: Duke University Press.

Wilson, S. R., Cruz, M. G., Marshall, L. J., & Rao, N. (1993). An attribution analysis of compliance-gaining interactions. *Communication Monographs, 60*, 352-372.

Wincott, D. (1996). The Court of Justice and the European policy process. In J. Richardson (Ed.), *European Union: Power and policy making* (pp. 170-199). London: Routledge.

Winter, S. G. (1990). Survival, selection, and inheritance in evolutionary theories of organization. In J. V. Singh (Ed.), *Organizational evolution: New directions* (pp. 269-297) Newbury Park, CA: Sage.

Winters v. New York, 333 U.S. 507 (1948).

Wintersteen, L. (1997). Marketing with a patient focus. *Journal of the American Dental Association, 128,* 1657-1659.

Wirth, P. (1995, September-October). Working with mainstream media: Are activists missing the boat? *The Nonviolent Activist,* pp. 16-17.

Witmer, D. F. (1997). Communication and recovery: Structuration as an ontological approach to organizational culture. *Communication Monographs, 64,* 324-349.

Witte, K. (1994). The manipulative nature of health communication research. *American Behavioral Scientist, 38,* 285-293.

Wokutch, R. E., & Spencer, B. A. (1987). Corporate saints and sinners: The effects of philanthropic and illegal activity on organizational performance. *California Management Review, 29*(2), 62-77.

Wolfe, A. (1989). *Whose keeper? Social science and moral obligation.* Berkeley: University of California Press.

Wolff, J. (1994, November). Opening up on-line. *Columbia Journalism Review,* pp. 62-65.

Wolter, L. (1993, September 13). Superficiality, ambiguity threaten IMC's implementation and future. *Marketing News,* pp. 12, 21.

Wood, D. J. (1991). Toward improving corporate social performance. *Business Horizons, 34*(4), 66-73.

Wood, J. (1994). *Who cares? Women, care, and culture.* Carbondale: Southern Illinois University Press.

Wood, S.H. (1936). Intelligence and public relations. *Public Administration, 14,* 41-48.

Worth, M. J. (Ed.). (1993). *Educational fund raising: Principles and practice.* Phoenix, AZ: American Council on Education.

WPP Group PLC. (1998). *Annual report and accounts 1997.* London: Author.

Wright, D. K. (1976). Social responsibility in public relations: A multi-step theory. *Public Relations Review, 2*(3), 24-36.

Wright, D. K. (1979). Some ways to measure public relations. *Public Relations Journal, 35*(7), 17-18.

Wright, D. K. (1981). Accreditation's effects on professionalism. *Public Relations Review, 7*(3), 48-61.

Wright, D. K. (1985). Can age predict the moral values of public relations practitioners? *Public Relations Review, 11,* 51-60.

Wright, D. K. (1989). Examining ethical and moral values of public relations people. *Public Relations Review, 15*(2), 19-33.

Wright, D. K. (1993). Enforcement dilemma: Voluntary nature of public relations codes. *Public Relations Review, 19,* 13-20.

Wright, D. K., Grunig, L. A., Springston, J. K., & Toth, E. L. (1991). *Under the glass ceiling: An analysis of gender issues in American public relations* (PRSA Foundation Monograph Series). New York: Public Relations Society of America.

Wuddock, S., & Boyle, M. E. (1994, October 10). Study reinforces centrality of community relations in PR. *PR Reporter,* pp. 1-2.

Wyatt, R. O., Smith, S. S., & Andsager, J. L. (1996). Spanning the boundaries: Support for media rights among public relations practitioners, journalists, and the public. *Journal of Public Relations Research, 8,* 123-135.

Wylie, F. W. (1991). Business and ethics—and long term planning. *Public Relations Quarterly, 36*(3), 7-12.

Wylie, F. W. (1994). Commentary: Public relations is not yet a profession. *Public Relations Review, 20,* 1-3.

Wynder, E. L., & Graham, E. A. (1950). Tobacco smoking as a possible etiologic factor in bronchiogenic carcinoma: A study of six hundred and eighty-four proved cases. *Journal of the American Medical Association, 143,* 329-336.

Wynder, E. L., Graham, E. A., & Croninger, A. B. (1953). Experimental production of carcinoma with cigarette tar. *Cancer Research, 13,* 855-864.

Xenakis, J. J. (1991, September 30). Want to buy a bridge? Route diversity and "infrastructure failure" are lessons of AT&T outage. *Information Week,* p. 37.

Yarbrough, C. R., Cameron, G. T., Sallot, L. M., & McWilliams, A. (1998). Tough calls to make: Contingency theory and the Centennial

Olympic Games. *Journal of Communication Management, 3,* 39-56.

Yates, J., & Orlikowski, W. J. (1992). Genres of organizational communication: A structurational approach to studying communication and media. *Academy of Management Review, 17,* 299-326.

Yin, R. K. (1994). *Case study research: Design and methods* (2nd ed.). Thousand Oaks, CA: Sage.

Young, D. (1995-1996). Looking at your company's fragile reputation. *Public Relations Quarterly, 40*(4), 7-13.

Young, I. M. (1990). *Justice and the politics of difference.* Princeton, NJ: Princeton University Press.

Yu, J., & Cooper, H. (1983). A quantitative review of research design effects on response rates to questionnaires. *Journal of Marketing Research, 20,* 36-44.

Yuan, S., & Han, Z. (1992). *Deng Xiaoping Nanxun hou de Zhongguo* [China after Deng Xiaoping's visit to southern regions]. Beijing: Gaige Press.

Zaharna, R. S. (1995). Understanding cultural preferences of Arab communication patterns. *Public Relations Review, 21,* 241-255.

Zakariya, S. (1987). Improving relations between schools and the press. *Education Digest, 53*(3), 8-11.

Zand, D. E. (1997). *The leadership triad: Knowledge, trust, and power.* Oxford, UK: Oxford University Press.

Zarefsky, D., Miller-Tutzauer, C., & Tutzauer, F. (1984). Reagan's safety net for the truly needy: The rhetorical uses of definition. *Central States Speech Journal, 35,* 113-119.

Zeithaml, V. A., Parasuraman, A., & Berry, L. L. (1992). *Delivering quality service: Balancing customer perceptions and expectations.* New York: Free Press.

Zhao, X., & Chaffee, S. H. (1995). Campaign advertisements versus television news as sources of political issue information. *Public Opinion Quarterly, 59,* 41-65.

Ziff, W. B. (1992). The crisis of confidence in advertising. *Journal of Advertising Research, 32*(4), 2-5.

Zimmerman, M. E. (1994). *Contesting Earth's future: Radical ecology and postmodernity.* Berkeley: University of California Press.

Zogby, J. (1994, March). *The PLO and its opposition.* Panel discussion at the conference, "The Road to Peace: The Challenge of the Middle East," Miami, FL.

Zohar, D. (1997). *Rewiring the corporate brain: Using the new science to rethink how we structure and lead organizations.* San Francisco: Berrett-Koehler.

Zotti, E. (1985). Thinking psychographically. *Public Relations Journal, 41*(5), 26-30.

INDEX

ABOUT THE CONTRIBUTORS

Lyudmila Azarova is Associate Professor and Chair of the Department of Public Relations at the Electrotechnical University in St. Petersburg, Russia. She is co-editor of *Introduction to Public Relations and Advertising: A Reader From a Russian Consumer's Point of View* (1995).

Gail F. Baker (Ph.D., University of Missouri), APR, is University of Florida Vice President for Public Relations and Associate Professor in the Department of Public Relations, College of Journalism and Communications. Her experience includes positions with IBM and International Harvester. She was a reporter and managing editor for the *Chicago Daily Defender* newspaper. Her major consulting clients include DIVA Advertising and Graphic Design, WGCI Radio, and Southwestern Bell Telephone. She is the author of *Advertising and Marketing to the New Majority* and co-author of *Exploding Stereotypes: Milestones in Black Newspaper Research.*

Lois A. Boynton earned an A.B. in history from Lenoir-Rhyne College in Hickory, North Carolina, and an M.A. from the University of North Carolina at Chapel Hill (UNC-CH), School of Journalism and Mass Communication, focusing on public relations. She currently is a Park doctoral fellow at UNC-CH, studying ethics and nonprofit organizations in public relations practice. She received the William Francis

Clingman, Jr., Ethics Award from UNC-CH in 1998.

William G. Briggs, Ed.D., is Professor of Public Relations at San Jose State University. A past director of the International Association of Business Communicators, he has studied cross-cultural communication at the East-West Center in Honolulu, Hawaii, and participated in the Harvard Law School Program on Negotiation and Conflict Resolution. He is a frequent international presenter on global strategic communication themes.

Stephen D. Bruning, Ph.D., is affiliated with the Department of Communication at Capital University in Columbus, Ohio. He conducts research on organization-public relationships with a variety of organizations and industries. His work has appeared in many scholarly and industry publications. He acts as a consultant to national and international corporations.

Ni Chen is Assistant Professor in the Department of Mass Communication and Communication Studies at Towson University. She is co-editor (with Hugh Culbertson) of *International Public Relations: A Comparative Analysis* (1996).

George Cheney (Ph.D., Purdue University) is Professor and Co-Director of Graduate Studies in the Department of Communication Studies at the University of Montana–Missoula. He also is Adjunct Professor in the Department of Management Communication at the University of Waikato in Hamilton, New Zealand. His research, teaching, and service interests cover areas such as power and identity in organizations, workplace democracy and employee participation, and business ethics in light of economic globalization. He is the author of two books and more than 50 journal articles, book chapters, magazine articles, and reviews. He has lectured extensively in North America, Europe, Latin America, and Australia.

Lars Thøger Christensen (Ph.D., Odense University) is Research Professor at the Department of Intercultural Communication and Management at the Copenhagen Business School. He specializes in the study of market-related communications—in the broadest sense of the term—issued and organized by corporate bodies, private as well as public. His theoretical perspective is meaning based and rooted in the socioanthropological tradition. His primary research interests are managerial discourse, corporate communications, advertising, semiotics, image/identity formation, and issues management.

W. Timothy Coombs is Associate Professor in the Department of Communication at Wayne State University. His Ph.D. in issues management and public affairs is from Purdue University. He has written a number of articles and book chapters about crisis management focusing on communication's role in the process. He is author of *Ongoing Crisis Communication: Planning, Managing, and Responding* (1999).

Zoraida R. Cozier is a doctoral candidate at Purdue University. She holds a master's degree in organizational public relations from Syracuse University and a bachelor's degree in human communication from the State University of New York at Fredonia. Her research interests include organizational communication, conflict resolution strategies, and structuration theory as an approach to organizational public relations. Her research has earned top honors in the pub-

lic relations divisions of the National Communication Association and the International Communication Association.

Fritz Cropp is Assistant Professor in the Department of Advertising, School of Journalism, University of Missouri. He taught in the public relations sequence at the S. I. Newhouse School of Public Communications, where he earned a Ph.D. in 1996. His professional experience includes 13 years in journalism, public relations, and marketing communications. His dissertation involved international advertising, and his master's thesis examined perceptions of public relations practitioners among newspaper journalists.

Patricia A. Curtin is Assistant Professor in the public relations sequence, School of Journalism and Mass Communication, University of North Carolina at Chapel Hill. She earned a Ph.D. at the University of Georgia in 1996. Her research includes public relations history, ethics, and agenda building. Recent publications focus on the role of market forces in agenda building and historical studies of agenda building in the *Journal of Public Relations Research, Communication Yearbook,* and *American Journalism.*

Emma L. Daugherty, APR, is Associate Professor and head of public relations in the Department of Journalism at California State University, Long Beach. She also taught at California State University, Fullerton; Michigan State University; Chapman University; and Carlow College. She formerly was an account supervisor at Greg Smith & Partners and was public relations director for the Pittsburgh Symphony Society. She received a bachelor's degree in public relations from West Virginia University and a master's in advertising from Michigan State University.

Kenneth D. Day (Ph.D., Indiana University, 1980) is Associate Dean of the College of the Pacific and Associate Professor in the Department of Communication at the University of the Pacific. His research interests include communication ethics, the relationship between mass communication and culture, the role of theory in mass communication, and pragmatic differences in language use in different cultures. Two of his articles on ethical issues in intercultural communication have appeared in *Cultural Diversity and Global Communication.*

Barbara J. DeSanto, Ed.D., APR, is Assistant Professor in the School of Journalism and Broadcasting at Oklahoma State University. Her research interests focus on public relations education, public relations research and strategic planning, and international public relations. Recent publications include public relations practitioners and research. She is researching best public relations practices in the United Kingdom.

Qingwen Dong (Ph.D., Washington State University) is Chair and Assistant Professor in the Department of Communication at the University of the Pacific, where he teaches courses in mass communication and communication research methods. His research interests include the psychological, social, and cultural effects of mass media. His research has been published in *Journalism Quarterly, Journal of Broadcasting and Electronic Media,* and *Communication Monographs.*

Daradirek Ekachai is Associate Professor in the Department of Speech Communication at Marquette University. Her education includes a B.A. in French from Chulalongkorn University in Thailand, an M.A. from the University of Wisconsin–Madison, and a Ph.D. from Southern Illinois University. Her research focuses on international/intercultural public relations, university image and communication, and the Internet and public relations. Her recent publications in *Public Relations Review* address public relations practitioners' roles and education in Thailand.

James L. Everett (B.A., University of Michigan; M.A., Ph.D., University of Colorado) is Associate Professor at Queensland University of Technology. Faculty appointments include the University of Hartford, Washington State University, the University of Wisconsin, and the University of Idaho. Professional experience includes development of operational policies, supervision of public relations/public information, publications, program evaluation, graphic design, and audiovisual services. His research interests are organizational evolution and ecology, organizational culture, and knowledge management.

Kathleen Fearn-Banks is Associate Professor at the University of Washington. She is author of *Crisis Communications: A Casebook Approach* and co-editor of *People to People: An Introduction to Mass Communications.* She was elected "1998 PR Professional of the Year" by the Seattle chapter of the Public Relations Society of America and was the 1998-1999 chair of the Professional Freedom and Responsibility Committee of the Association for Education in Journalism and Mass Communication. She spent 25 years in the communications industry.

Denise P. Ferguson, Ph.D., is Assistant Professor in the Department of Communication at the University of Indianapolis. She teaches courses in public relations, newswriting, magazine journalism, and graphic communication. Her research interests include public relations and issues management in nonprofit organizations and the role of media in the public sphere.

Susanne Elizabeth Gaddis, Ph.D., is Assistant Professor of Communication at the University of Houston–Clear Lake, where she teaches public relations, interpersonal communication, Internet communication, and Web design. Her research focus includes on-line research techniques and mediated communication. She holds a Ph.D. from Florida State University.

R. Brooks Garner, APR, is Associate Professor in the School of Journalism and Broadcasting at Oklahoma State University. He gained public relations experience with Southwestern Bell Telephone, Phillips Petroleum Company, and Oklahoma Gas & Electric. He began his career as a news reporter for the *Daily Oklahoman.* He holds membership in the Association for Education in Journalism and Mass Communication.

James E. Grunig is Professor of Public Relations in the Department of Communication at the University of Maryland, College Park. He is co-author of *Managing Public Relations, Public Relations Techniques,* and *Manager's Guide to Excellence in Public Relations and Communication Management.* He is editor of *Excellence in Public Relations and Communication Management.* He has published or presented more than 185 articles, books, chapters, papers, and reports. He has won the Pathfinder Award for excellence in public relations research of the Institute for Public Relations Research and Education; the Outstanding Educator Award of the Public Relations Society of America (PRSA); and the Jackson, Jackson, and Wagner Award for behavioral science research of the PRSA Foundation. He directed a $400,000 research project for the International Association of Business Communicators Research Foundation on excellence in public relations and communication management.

Tanni Haas (Ph.D., Rutgers University, 1999) is Assistant Professor in the Department of Speech Communication Arts and Sciences at Brooklyn College, New York. He has written two other chapters on organizational communication ethics in *Rethinking Organizational and Managerial Communication From Feminist Perspectives* (2000) and *The Foundations of Management Knowledge.*

Kirk Hallahan, Fellow PRSA, is Assistant Professor in the Department of Journalism and Technical Communication at Colorado State University. He previously taught at the University of North Dakota and the University of Wisconsin–Madison, where he received a Ph.D. in mass communications. He has 19 years of professional experience in the field. An earlier version of his chapter won a Top Three Faculty Paper Award presented by the Public Relations Division of the Association for Education in Journalism and Mass Communication in cooperation with the International Association of Business Communicators.

Tricia L. Hansen-Horn (Ph.D., Purdue University) is Assistant Professor of Communication at Central Missouri State University. Her primary research interests concern social constructionist/critical perspectives and public relations issues. Of specific interest is the need to articulate nondominant voices.

Keith Michael Hearit is Associate Professor in the Department of Communication at Western Michigan University. His research interests are in nontraditional forms of external organizational communication including the areas of corporate apologia and issues management. He has published a number of articles in *Public Relations Review* and *Communication Studies.* In 1996, he received the PRIDE Award for the outstanding research article from the Public Relations division of the National Communication Association.

Robert L. Heath (Ph.D., University of Illinois) is Professor of Communication at the University of Houston, Director of the Institute for the Study of Issues Management, and Advisory Director of Research for Bates Churchill Southwest. With co-editor Elizabeth Toth, he won the PRIDE Award in 1992 for *Rhetorical and Critical Approaches to Public Relations.* He won the Pathfinder Award in 1992 and the Jackson, Jackson, and Wagner Award in 1998. His other books are *Management of Corporate Communication: From Interpersonal Contacts to External Affairs* (1994); *Human Communication Theories and Research: Concepts, Contexts, and Challenges* (1992, with Jennings Bryant); *Strategic Issues Management* (1988); *Realism and Relativism: A Perspective on Kenneth Burke* (1986); *Issues Management: Corporate Public Policymaking in an Information Society* (1986, with Richard Alan Nelson); and *Strategic Issues Management* (1997), which also won a PRIDE Award.

Julie K. Henderson, APR, Ph.D., is Associate Professor of Journalism at the University of Wisconsin–Oshkosh. She holds degrees from Moorhead State University, North Dakota State University, and the University of North Dakota. Her doctoral dissertation addressed the importance of media relations to universities in crisis. She was named an American Society of Newspaper Editors Institute for Journalism Excellence fellow in 1998 and a University of Wisconsin System teaching fellow in 1999.

Laurel Traynowicz Hetherington (Ph.D., University of Iowa) is Associate Professor in the Department of Communication at Boise State University. She has worked in industry and academics over the past 20 years and specializes in designing and implementing continuous quality improvement initiatives for service organizations. She collaborates with rural health organizations in their quality improvement efforts. Her research agenda includes organizational transformation, rural health quality management, construction of identity, and relational communication.

Catherine L. Hinrichsen, APR, learned the agency ropes at Burson-Marsteller in New York. She founded her own firm, C&C Communications, in 1997. Previously, she was account supervisor at Evans Group (now Publicis) in Seattle, Washington. A practitioner since 1980, she has also worked in the corporate and nonprofit sectors. She earned an M.A. in communications from the University of Washington and a B.A. in journalism/public relations from the University of Nevada, Reno.

Yi-Hui Huang is Associate Professor in the School of Communications at the National Cheng-chi University in Taiwan. She holds a Ph.D. from the University of Maryland. Her research interests center on public relations theories, public relations, strategies, organization-public relationships, conflict management, and crisis management.

H. R. Hutchins is Manager of Corporate Communications for Shell Oil Company USA. He has served as media relations manager and as secretary and education grants officer of the Shell Oil Company Foundation. Prior to joining Shell, he spent 20 years in corporate communications with several forest products companies. A former newspaperman, he is a journalism graduate of the University of Oregon. He earned an M.A. in public relations at the University of Houston

in 1994. He is Adjunct Professor in the School of Journalism at the University of Houston.

Liese L. Hutchison, APR, is Assistant Professor of Communication at Saint Louis University, where she earned an M.A. in communication. She teaches courses in public relations principles, campaigns, and writing; advises the department's PR Club; and oversees the publication of the alumni newsletter. An active public relations consultant and business writer, she has more than 12 years of public relations experience, including work in agency, corporate, and nonprofit settings.

James G. Hutton teaches marketing and communications at Fairleigh Dickinson University. His Ph.D. in marketing is from the University of Texas, where he was a university fellow and dean's doctoral fellow. He was a manager of corporate and financial communications for three major multinational corporations. He is a consultant and author of numerous professional and academic publications including *Marketing Communications: Integrated Theory, Strategy, and Tactics* (2000).

Dean Kazoleas, APR, is Associate Professor of Public Relations in the Department of Communication at Illinois State University. He specializes in employee communication and relations, media relations, and campaigns. He received a Ph.D. in communication campaigns and research from Michigan State University. He is a senior partner in Insight Consulting and Research, a management consulting firm specializing in communication audits, culture assessment and transformation, and organizational change.

Kathleen S. Kelly (Ph.D., University of Maryland), APR, Fellow PRSA, is Hubert J. Bourgeois Endowed Research Professor and Coordinator of the Public Relations Degree Program at the University of Louisiana, Lafayette. She is author of two award-winning books, *Effective Fund-Raising Management* and *Fund Raising and Public Relations: A Critical Analysis.* Her research earned her the 1995 Pathfinder Award from the Institute for Public Relations Research and Education and the 1999 Jackson, Jackson, and Wagner Award from the PRSA Foundation.

Joann Keyton (Ph.D., Ohio State University) is Professor of Communication at the University of Memphis. Her research on group communication, sexual harassment, and organizational culture has appeared in *Small Group Research, Journal of Applied Communication Research, Southern Communication Journal, Management Communication Quarterly, Journal of Business Ethics, Communication Studies, Journal of Public Relations Research*, and *Mid-Atlantic Almanac*. She has served on the editorial boards of *Small Group Research, Communication Monographs*, and *Communication Studies*. She is author of *Group Communication: Process and Analysis*.

Dean Kruckeberg (Ph.D., University of Iowa), APR, Public Relations Society of America (PRSA) Fellow, is Coordinator of the Public Relations Degree Program and Professor in the Department of Communication Studies at the University of Northern Iowa. He has worked at Lutheran General Hospital in Chicago and the Agricultural Extension Service at the University of Minnesota. He has taught at the University of Minnesota–St. Paul, the University of Iowa, and Northwest Missouri State University. He has consulted or taught in the United Arab Emirates, Russia, Latvia, and Bulgaria. His research deals with international public relations. He is co-author of *Public Relations and Community: A Reconstructed Theory* and author of several book chapters and articles. He is co-author of the sixth and seventh editions of *This Is PR: The Realities of Public Relations*. His awards include the 1995 national "Outstanding Educator" of PRSA and the 1997 Pathfinder Award of the Institute for Public Relations.

Jacquie L'Etang is Director of the full-time M.S. in Public Relations at the University of Stirling and a member of the Stirling Media Research Institute. She has degrees in American and English History (B.A.), Commonwealth History (M.A.), Social Justice (M.Phil.), and Public Relations (M.S.). She has published in *Journal of Business Ethics, Public Relations Review, Australian Journal of Communication*, and is co-editor of *Critical Perspectives in Public Relations* (ITBP,1996). She is currently working on a book on the history of public relations in the UK.

Tracy Lauder is a graduate research assistant in the College of Communication at the University of Alabama. She has worked in public relations and various editorial departments at Southern Progress Corporation, a magazine publishing company based in Birmingham, Alabama. She ran a freelance writing and consulting business in Birmingham while teaching print journalism courses at Samford University. Her research focuses on messages found in media targeted to women.

John A. Ledingham, Ph.D., is affiliated with the Department of Communication at Capital University in Columbus, Ohio. His specialization concerns the management of relationships between organizations and publics as well as organization-media relationships. His work has appeared in numerous scholarly and professional journals. He serves as a consultant to national and international organizations.

Kathie A. Leeper (Ph.D., Indiana University), APR, is Professor of Communication at Concordia College in Moorhead, Minnesota. She has written articles that have appeared in, among other journals, *Public Relations Quarterly, Journal of Intergroup Relations*, and *Public Relations Review*.

Roy Leeper is Professor in the Department of Communication/Theatre Arts at Northwest Missouri State University. His research interests involve communitarianism and its implications for the public relations field and for freedom of expression issues.

Greg Leichty is Associate Professor of Communication at the University of Louisville. He teaches courses in public relations, organizational communication, research methods, and interpersonal communication. His areas of research are public relations theory, public relations and corporate social responsibility, and public relations and culture.

Shirley Leitch is Associate Professor of Management Communication and Associate Dean of the Waikato Management School at the University of Waikato in New Zealand. On joining the Waikato Management School in 1990, she founded what has become New Zealand's most comprehensive public relations program. She has a doctorate in political communication from the University of Auckland, and her professional experience includes several years in a senior public relations role with the New Zealand government.

Edward J. Lordan teaches newswriting, public relations, and mass media history at Temple University. He writes for a variety of newspapers and has published research on news presentation and comprehension. He has taught at Villanova University and St. Louis University, and he consults with businesses and nonprofit organizations. He holds a B.A. degree from West Chester State College, an M.A. from Temple University, and a Ph.D. from Syracuse University.

Mark P. McElreath is Associate Professor in the Department of Mass Communication and Communication Studies at Towson University. He is author of *Managing Systematic and Ethical Public Relations Campaigns* (1997), a member of the Universal Accreditation Board, and a member of the Commission on Public Relations Education.

David McKie is Associate Professor of Management Communication at the University of Waikato. He co-authored *Eco-Impacts and the Greening of Postmodernity: New Maps for Communication Studies, Cultural Studies, and Sociology* (1997) and has published on communication, cyberfutures, environmental issues, media, national identities, policy and globalization, transnational public relations, and virtual reality. Current research projects include management creativity, postmodern leaderships, and public relations scenarios.

Lori Melton McKinnon (Ph.D., University of Oklahoma) is Associate Professor of Advertising and Public Relations in the College of Communication at the University of Alabama. Her research interest is mediated political communication. Her work has appeared in the *Journal of Applied Communication Research, Harvard International Journal of Press/Politics, Journal of Broadcasting and Electronic Media, Journal of Political Communication, Journalism and Mass Communication Quarterly, Electronic Journal of Communication,* and *Argumentation and Advocacy.* She is a contributing author to books on national and international political communication, broadcasting, and magazines.

Maribeth S. Metzler (Ph.D., Rensselaer Polytechnic Institute) is Assistant Professor at Miami University. She has worked in environmental public affairs for the U.S. Air Force and as an environmental consultant. Her work has appeared in *Communication Studies* and *Responsible Communication: Ethical Issues in Business, Industry, and the Professions.*

David Miller is a member of the Stirling Media Research Institute. He is author of *Don't Mention the War: Northern Ireland, Propaganda, and the Media* (1994); co-author of *The Circuit of Mass Communication: Media Strategies, Representation, and Audience Reception in the AIDS Crisis* (1998); and editor of *Rethinking Northern Ireland: Culture, Ideology, and Colonialism* (1998). He is working on a book on public relations and promotional culture.

Mary Anne Moffitt is Associate Professor in the Department of Communication at Illinois State University. Her public relations management courses focus on corporate image strategies, message design for campaigns, and the execution of public relations campaigns. Her research centers on understanding how organizations deliver corporate images and on how audiences process corporate images. She is author of *Campaign Strategies and Message Design: A Practitioner's Guide From Start to Finish.*

Judy Motion is Senior Lecturer in Management Communication at the University of Waikato in New Zealand. Her professional public relations experience includes work for an environmental group. Her research interests include personal public relations and corporate identity. Her doctorate from the University of Waikato was titled *Technologies of the Self: A Public Identity Framework*.

Bonita Dostal Neff is Associate Professor in the Department of Communication at Valparaiso University. Trained as a policy fellow in the Institute for Educational Leadership, she is president of Public Communication Associates, an agency that consults in health, higher education, mass communication, public relations, and nonprofit endeavors. She serves on the steering committee for the Commission on Public Relations Education contributing to the final report *Port of Entry: Public Relations Education for the 21st Century*. She has published in *Public Relations Review* and was the lead author on PR "Outcomes" developed during the Summer 1998 PR conference. She contributes to *The Strategist*.

David Neilson is Lecturer in Political Science and Public Policy at the University of Waikato in New Zealand. He teaches political economy, public policy, and democratic theory. His research interests include regulation theory, state theory, and the New Zealand experience. He has a doctorate in political theory from the University of East Anglia in the United Kingdom.

Nicholas C. Neupauer (Ph.D., West Virginia University) is Assistant Dean of Humanities and Social Sciences at Butler County (Pennsylvania) Community College. A former sports reporter and assistant sports information director (SID), he has written articles on the SID field for *Public Relations Strategist*, *Public Relations Quarterly*, and the *Social Science Journal* in addition to presenting a number of convention papers on the subject. He earned an M.S. from Clarion University of Pennsylvania and a B.A. in print journalism from Pennsylvania State University.

Doug Newsom, Ph.D., APR, Public Relations Society of America Fellow, is Professor at Texas Christian University. She is co-author of three textbooks: *This Is PR* (with Judy VanSlyke Turk and Dean Kruckeberg), *Public Relations Writing* (with Bob Carrell), and *Media Writing* (with the late James Wollert). She is co-editor of a book of women's colloquium papers, *Silent Voices* (with Bob Carrell). She is a public relations practitioner and has taught in 10 countries outside the United States.

Bolanle A. Olaniran (Ph.D., University of Oklahoma) is Associate Professor in the Department of Communication Studies at Texas Tech University. His research focuses on communication technologies and organizational communication.

Beth Olson (Ph.D., Indiana University) is Director of Graduate Studies and Associate Professor in the School of Communication at the University of Houston, where she teaches media effects, broadcast newswriting, and gender and media. Her research interests include the psychological aspects of media consumption, media content, and gender issues. She has published in the *Journal of Broadcasting & Electronic Media, Journalism & Mass Communication Quarterly*, and *Sex Roles*.

Michael G. Parkinson (Ph.D., University of Oklahoma; J.D., Southern Illinois University), APR, is Associate Professor in the School of Mass Communications at Texas Tech University. He has worked and taught in public relations for 30 years. He is licensed to practice law before state courts of Illinois and Oklahoma and before both federal district and appellate courts. Recent publications have discussed international copyright law and Anglo-American contract law for Japanese businesses.

John J. Pauly (Ph.D., University of Illinois) is Professor of Communication and American Studies and Chair of the Department of Communication at Saint Louis University. His work on the history and sociology of the mass media and on qualitative research methods has appeared in *American Journalism, Communication, Communication Research, Critical Studies in Mass Communication, Journalism Monographs, Media Studies Journal*, and *American Quarterly*.

Magda Pieczka is Director of the Distance Learning M.S. in Public Relations at the University of Stirling and a member of the Stirling Media Research Institute. She has a degree in English (Jagiellonian University, Krakow, Poland) and postgraduate degrees in English literature (University of Glasgow) and Publishing (University of Stirling). She has published in the *Australian Journal of Communication* and *Journal of Public Relations Research* and is co-editor of *Critical Perspectives in Public Relations* (ITBP, 1996).

J. David Pincus, Ph.D., APR, recently left his post as Director of the M.B.A. Program and Research Professor of Communication at the University of Arkansas to work on a sequel to *Top Dog,* his widely acclaimed book about the chief executive officer's changing communication role and its relationship to corporate leadership. He taught public relations at California State University, Fullerton, for 12 years, and in the executive M.B.A. program at the University of Southern California for 2 years.

Kenneth D. Plowman, Ph.D., is Associate Professor and Coordinator of the Graduate Program in Journalism and Mass Communications at San Jose State University. The focus of his dissertation at the University of Maryland was public relations, strategic management, and conflict resolution. He specializes in those fields as well as high technology. He spent 15 years in the field, mostly on Capitol Hill in Washington, D.C.

Gayle M. Pohl, APR, is Associate Professor at the University of Northern Iowa and Faculty Adviser for the Public Relations Student Society of America. She has been a public relations practitioner for 20 years. Her research includes a book titled *Public Relations: Designing Effective Communication,* articles in the *Journal of Popular Culture* and *International Encyclopedia for Television,* and a chapter in a text titled *Advanced Interpersonal Communication.* She is working on a book titled *Public Relations: Creating Strategic Relationships.*

Cornelius B. Pratt is Carter G. Woodson Visiting Professor of Journalism and Mass Communica-

tions at Marshall University. He is a contributing editor of *Public Relations Quarterly.* In 1999, he served as Fulbright professor at the University of Zambia in Southern Africa. His more than 100 articles have been published in journals such as *Gazette, Howard Journal of Communications, Journal of Communication Management, Public Relations Quarterly, Journal of Health Communication,* and *Journalism Quarterly.*

Clark Robins is pursuing an M.A. in communication at the University of the Pacific.

Risë Jane Samra (Ph.D., University of Arizona) is Professor of Communication Studies at Barry University in Miami, Florida. She specializes in public relations and rhetorical criticism. She served on the 1998 public relations national task force to develop curriculum and pedagogy. She has been publishing and presenting public relations and rhetorical research focusing on image making in the Middle East and the physician in our changing health care system. She has taught and consulted for business/industry. She has been a strong advocate of Jewish-Christian-Muslim relations. In 1998, she was named Personality of the Year by the World Lebanese Cultural Union for her leadership in organizing and chairing international conferences aimed at finding a just and permanent solution for the Middle East conflict.

Philip Schlesinger is Professor of Film and Media Studies, Director of Stirling Media Research Institute at the University of Stirling, Visiting Professor of Media and Communication at the University of Oslo. An editor of the journal *Media, Culture, and Society,* his publications include *Putting "Reality" Together, Media, State, and Nation,* and *Reporting Crime.* He is researching political communication and national identity in the European Union, the United Kingdom, and Scotland.

Matthew W. Seeger (Ph.D., Indiana University) is Associate Professor of Communication and Assistant Dean of the Graduate School at Wayne State University. His research concerns organizational crisis and ethics and has appeared in *Com-*

munication Yearbook 21, Journal of Business Ethics, and *Communication Education.* His book, *"I Gotta Tell You:" Speeches of Lee Iacocca* (1994), examines 25 speeches. He also has authored *Organizational Communication Ethics* (1997) and edits the *Free Speech Yearbook.*

Timothy L. Sellnow (Ph.D., Wayne State University) is Associate Professor and Chair of the Department of Communication at North Dakota State University. He teaches organizational communication and research methods, and he serves as a consultant. His research has appeared in *Communication Education, Communication Quarterly, Communication Studies,* and *Communication Yearbook,* among others. His research focuses on ethical tensions created by the complexity of organizational audiences during crisis situations.

Valeria Shadrova is Associate Professor in the Department of Public Relations at the Electrotechnical University of St. Petersburg, Russia. She is co-author (with Lyudmila Azarova, Kira Ivanova, and Dmitry Shishkin) of *Public Relations: Theory and Practice* (1998).

Michael F. Smith (Ph.D., Purdue University) is Assistant Professor in the Department of Communication at La Salle University. He teaches courses in public relations, organizational communication, and conflict management. His research on the public relations activities of activist organizations and service learning pedagogy has been published in *Public Relations Inquiry as Rhetorical Criticism* and *Voices of a Strong Democracy.* He advises various activist and service organizations in the Philadelphia region.

Jeffrey K. Springston (Ph.D., Ohio State University), APR, is Associate Professor of Public Relations in the Henry W. Grady School of Journalism and Mass Communication at the University of Georgia. His research on public relations, health promotion, and organizational communication has appeared in *Public Relations Review, Journal of Public Relations Research, International Journal of Behavioral Medicine, International Journal of Intercultural Research, Bulletin*

of the Association for Business Communication, Small Group Research, and *Journalism Quarterly.* He is a co-principal investigator on a health promotion study funded by the National Institutes of Health, a principal investigator on a study funded by the Walther Cancer Institute, and a co-investigator on a study funded by the National Cancer Institute.

Kenneth Starck (Ph.D., Southern Illinois University; M.A., University of Missouri; B.A., Wartburg College) is Professor in the School of Journalism and Mass Communication at the University of Iowa, where he served 17 years as director. He has worked in public relations and as a journalist. He has held Fulbright professorships at the University of Bucharest and the Chinese Academy of Social Sciences and has taught in Finland. His research is on professionalism and responsibility in mass communication and cross-cultural communication. He is author of *The Dragon's Pupils: A China Odyssey;* co-author of *Backtalk: Press Councils in America;* and co-author of *Public Relations and Community: A Reconstructed Theory,* recognized for "outstanding developmental and educational research in public relations" by the Commission on Public Relations. He is past president of the Association for Education in Journalism and Mass Communication and of the Association of Schools of Journalism and Mass Communication.

Maureen Taylor (Ph.D., Purdue University) is Assistant Professor in the Department of Communication, School of Communication, Information, and Library Studies, Rutgers University. She researches international public relations and examines the role of communication in democracy building. She has traveled extensively throughout the world and has completed research projects in Malaysia and Bosnia.

John C. Tedesco (Ph.D., University of Oklahoma) is Assistant Professor in the Department of Communication Studies at Virginia Tech. His research interests include mass-mediated political communication content and effects, with particular emphasis on political advertising, political debates, and political public relations. His articles have appeared in the *Harvard International Journal of Press/Politics, Argumentation and Advocacy, Journal of Broadcasting and Electronic Media,* and *Journal of Communication Studies.* He is contributing author to *The Clinton Presidency, The Electronic Elections,* and *The Lynching of Language.*

Elizabeth L. Toth, Ph.D., is Associate Dean for Academic Affairs and Professor of Public Relations in the S. I. Newhouse School of Public Communications at Syracuse University. She co-authored *The Velvet Ghetto: The Increasing Numbers of Women in Public Relations; Beyond the Velvet Ghetto;* and the Public Relations Society of America "glass ceiling" studies. Her co-edited book, *Rhetorical and Critical Approaches to Public Relations,* won the National Communication Association PRIDE Award. She has published or presented more than 50 articles, book chapters, and papers. A co-edited book, *The Gender Challenge to Media: Diverse Voices From the Field,* and a co-authored book, *Women and Public Relations,* are forthcoming. She received the 1998 Institute for Public Relations Pathfinder Award for her research on gender issues and public relations.

Judy VanSlyke Turk, Ph.D., APR, Public Relations Society of America (PRSA) Fellow, is founding Dean, College of Communication at Zayed University in the United Arab Emirates. She was the PRSA's 1992 national "Outstanding Educator," is past president of the Association for Education in Journalism and Mass Communication, and is past chair of the PRSA's College of Fellows. She is co-editor of a new international journal, *Journalism Studies,* scheduled to debut in 2000.

Robert R. Ulmer (Ph.D., Wayne State University) is Assistant Professor of Communication at the University of Arkansas at Little Rock. His research interests include communication and organizational crisis, communication ethics, and pedagogy. His research has appeared in *Argumentation and Advocacy, North Dakota Journal of Speech & Theater, Communication Yearbook 21,* *Communication Studies,* and *Communication Quarterly.*

Dee Vandeventer is Managing Partner with Mathis, Earnest, & Vandeventer, an advertising, public relations, and fund-raising consulting firm. Her public relations career spans more than two decades and includes experiences in the financial industry, a university foundation, and television. She earned a B.S. from Iowa State University and an M.A. from the University of Northern Iowa.

Gabriel M. Vasquez is a member of the City Council of Houston, Texas.

Robert I. Wakefield (Ph.D., University of Maryland) is a consultant, author, and researcher emphasizing the cross-cultural aspects of reputation and issues in the multinational organization. He has coordinated communication or lectured on the topic of international public relations in 25 countries. Before forming Wakefield Communications, he was director of global public relations for Nu Skin International, a network marketing firm that generates more than $1 billion in annual revenues.

Ede Warner is Assistant Professor of Communication at the University of Louisville. He teaches argumentation, debate, and communication in the black community. His research interests include forensics and American public address.

Tom Watson is Managing Director of the U.K. public relations consultancy, Hallmark Public Relations Ltd. He is a graduate of the University of New South Wales and was a newspaper journalist before entering corporate public relations at the International Wool Secretariat in London. He earned a Ph.D. at the Southampton Institute for research on public relations evaluation models.

David E. Williams (Ph.D., Ohio University) is Associate Professor in the Department of Communication Studies at Texas Tech University. His research interests include crisis management and crisis communication.

Laurie J. Wilson is Chair of the Department of Communications at Brigham Young University, where she previously chaired the public relations emphasis. She is author of *Strategic Program Planning for Effective Public Relations Campaigns* and co-author of *Case Studies in Public Relations Program Management* and *The Passing of Modernity: Communication and the Transformation of Society.*

Diane F. Witmer (Ph.D., M.S., M.A., University of Southern California; B.S., University of La Verne), APR, is Associate Professor of Communications at California State University, Fullerton. Her practical experience includes corporate and not-for-profit public relations. Her research interests include computer-mediated communication and organizational communication. Her work has appeared in *Communication Monographs, Communication Education,* and the *Journal of Computer-Mediated Communication.*

Alan Wright (Ph.D., Michigan State University) is Managing Partner of Insight Consulting and Research, based in Huntington Beach, California. Before starting Insight, he worked as an organizational change consultant for Towers and Perrin. Insight's clients include Armor All, Clorox, Impact Training Associates, JLG Industries, Merchants HDS, RCI/RCIM, and Wells Fargo Bank.